CW01370191

International Construction Contract Law

International Construction Contract Law

Second Edition

Lukas Klee

Advisor, Lecturer
Arbitrator, Adjudicator
and Expert Witness
Owner at Klee Consulting
Prague, Czech Republic

WILEY Blackwell

This edition first published 2018
© 2018 John Wiley & Sons Ltd

Edition History
John Wiley & Sons (1e. 2015)

All rights reserved. No part of this publication may be reproduced, stored in a retrieval system, or transmitted, in any form or by any means, electronic, mechanical, photocopying, recording or otherwise, except as permitted by law. Advice on how to obtain permission to reuse material from this title is available at http://www.wiley.com/go/permissions.

The right of Lukas Klee to be identified as the author of this work has been asserted in accordance with law.

Registered Offices
John Wiley & Sons, Inc., 111 River Street, Hoboken, NJ 07030, USA
John Wiley & Sons Ltd, The Atrium, Southern Gate, Chichester, West Sussex, PO19 8SQ, UK

Editorial Office
9600 Garsington Road, Oxford, OX4 2DQ, UK

For details of our global editorial offices, customer services, and more information about Wiley products visit us at www.wiley.com.

Wiley also publishes its books in a variety of electronic formats and by print-on-demand. Some content that appears in standard print versions of this book may not be available in other formats.

Limit of Liability/Disclaimer of Warranty

While the publisher and authors have used their best efforts in preparing this work, they make no representations or warranties with respect to the accuracy or completeness of the contents of this work and specifically disclaim all warranties, including without limitation any implied warranties of merchantability or fitness for a particular purpose. No warranty may be created or extended by sales representatives, written sales materials or promotional statements for this work. The fact that an organization, website, or product is referred to in this work as a citation and/or potential source of further information does not mean that the publisher and authors endorse the information or services the organization, website, or product may provide or recommendations it may make. This work is sold with the understanding that the publisher is not engaged in rendering professional services. The advice and strategies contained herein may not be suitable for your situation. You should consult with a specialist where appropriate. Further, readers should be aware that websites listed in this work may have changed or disappeared between when this work was written and when it is read. Neither the publisher nor authors shall be liable for any loss of profit or any other commercial damages, including but not limited to special, incidental, consequential, or other damages.

Library of Congress Cataloging-in-Publication Data

Names: Klee, Lukas, author.
Title: International construction contract law / by Lukas Klee, Advisor, Lecturer, Arbitrator, Adjudicator and Expert Witness, Owner at Klee Consulting.
Description: 2nd edition. | Hoboken : Wiley, [2018] | Includes bibliographical references and index. |
Identifiers: LCCN 2018003980 (print) | LCCN 2018004778 (ebook) | ISBN 9781119430469 (pdf) | ISBN 9781119430520 (epub) | ISBN 9781119430384 (cloth)
Subjects: LCSH: Construction contracts.
Classification: LCC K891.B8 (ebook) | LCC K891.B8 K54 2018 (print) | DDC 343.07/8624–dc23
LC record available at https://lccn.loc.gov/2018003980

Cover Design: Wiley
Cover Image: © pixelparticle/Shutterstock

Set in 10/12.5pt MinionPro by SPi Global, Chennai, India

Printed in Singapore by C.O.S. Printers Pte Ltd

10 9 8 7 6 5 4 3 2 1

Contents

About the Author	xxiii
Foreword Svend Poulsen	xxv
Acknowledgments	xxvii
Introductory Remarks Shuibo Zhang	xxix
Introductory Remarks Robert Werth	xxxi
Introductory Remarks Ilya Nikiforov	xxxiii

1	**International Construction Projects**		**1**
	1.1	The unique nature of the construction industry	1
	1.2	Individuality of construction projects	1
	1.3	Roles and relationships	2
		1.3.1 Contractors	2
		1.3.2 Designers	3
		1.3.3 Regulators	3
		1.3.4 Employers	3
		1.3.5 Users	4
	1.4	Contract administration	4
		1.4.1 The Engineer	6
		1.4.2 The Engineer's certifications and fair determinations	7
		1.4.3 The Engineer's responsibilities and liabilities	9
		In-Text Vignette: Engineer's power to re-rate due to substantial increase in BoQ quantities by Albert Yeu (Hong Kong)	10
	1.5	Further important aspects of construction projects	11
		1.5.1 Overlap of construction project phases	12
		1.5.2 Admissibility of variations and the need for variation management	12
	1.6	Typical contractual relationships	12
		In-Text Vignette: Shipping and marine construction contracts in Asia by Knut Kirkhus (Oman)	12
	1.7	Motivation for international business	15
		In-Text Vignette: The Italian construction industry: Between past and future by SDG & Partners (Italy)	17
	1.8	Managerial analysis	20
	1.9	Hazards and risks	21
	1.10	Hazard identification	21

1.11	Risk analysis		22
1.12	Anti-risk measures		22
	1.12.1	Take	22
	1.12.2	Treat	22
	1.12.3	Transfer	23
	1.12.4	Terminate	23
1.13	Typical hazards in the international construction business		23
	In-Text Vignette: Corruption on Peruvian gas pipeline contract by Enrique Moncada Alcantara (Peru)		24
	In-Text Vignette: Anticorruption and construction contract law by Enrique Moncada Alcantara (Peru)		27
	In-Text Vignette: Indian law by C.K. Nandakumar and Rishabh Raheja (India)		33
1.14	Risk allocation in contracts		35
	In-Text Vignette: Wrong forms of contract by James Bremen (UK)		36
	In-Text Vignette: The importance of early analysis of risk, knowledge of efficient risk allocation and right choice of delivery method by Conor Mooney (France)		36
1.15	Form of Business Organization		42
	In-Text Vignette: To deal with subcontracts in international construction projects by Giuseppe Broccoli and Fabio Zanchi (Italy)		42
	In-Text Vignette: Interface agreements between subcontractors by Bernd Ehle and Sam Moss (Switzerland)		48
	1.15.1	Representative office and domestic or foreign subsidiary	50
	1.15.2	The consortium and the joint venture in construction	51
	1.15.3	The consortium	52
	1.15.4	The joint venture	53
	1.15.5	ARGE	53
	References		54
	Further reading		54
2	**Civil Law and Common Law**		**55**
2.1	Specifics of the governing law		55
2.2	Common law versus civil law: Differences and interconnections		55
	In-Text Vignette: The common law of Australia and the influence of statutory law by Donald Charrett (Australia)		57
2.3	Delay damages (liquidated damages) versus contractual penalty		59
	In-Text Vignette: The use of liquidated damages in construction projects by Rob Horne (UK)		60
	In-Text Vignette: Penalty clauses and liquidated damages under Brazilian law by Thiago Fernandes Moreira and Caio Gabra (Brazil)		72
2.4	Substantial completion versus performance		76
	2.4.1	Taking over of the works	77
2.5	Binding nature of adjudication awards		78
2.6	Limitation of liability		79

2.7	Lapse of claim due to its late notification (time bars)		79
2.8	Allocation of unforeseeable and uncontrollable risk to the contractor		80
	2.8.1	Principle of good faith (good manners) protection	80
	2.8.2	Imprévision	84
	2.8.3	Protection of the weaker party	85
	2.8.4	*Force majeure*	86
	2.8.5	Hardship	87
	2.8.6	Frustration of purpose	87
	2.8.7	Impossibility	88
	2.8.8	Impracticability	89
2.9	Contract administration (the Engineer's neutrality and duty to certify)		90
2.10	Termination in convenience		90
	In-Text Vignette: Is an employer in breach of contract prevented from terminating the contract for its convenience? by Cecilia Misu (Germany)		91
2.11	Time-related issues		93
	2.11.1	Delay	93
	2.11.2	Disruption	93
	2.11.3	Ownership of floats	93
	2.11.4	Time at large and extension of time	93
	2.11.5	Concurrent delay	94
	2.11.6	Constructive acceleration	94
2.12	Quantification of claims		94
	2.12.1	Headquarters overhead claims	94
	2.12.2	Global claims	94
2.13	Statutory defects liability		95
2.14	Performance responsibility: Reasonable skill and care versus fitness for purpose		95
2.15	Common law, civil law, and Sharia interconnections		96
	In-Text Vignette: Considerations for the construction of offshore oil and gas structures in the Middle East by Faisal Attia and Fernando Ortega (Qatar)		97
References			99
Further reading			100
Websites			101
3	**Common Delivery Methods**		**102**
3.1	Common delivery methods: Main features		102
	3.1.1	Design responsibility	103
	3.1.2	Contract price determination	103
	3.1.3	Contract administration	103
	3.1.4	Risk allocation and admission of claims	104
3.2	General contracting		104
3.3	Design-build		105
	3.3.1	Design-build procurement	106

		3.3.2	Employer's requirements in design-build projects	107
		In-Text Vignette: Dutch design and construct of infrastructural projects in complex environments by Joost Merema (the Netherlands)		109
		In-Text Vignette: Best value in the Netherlands by J.N. (Jaap) de Koning (the Netherlands)		126
		In-Text Vignette: Concern over increasing adoption of design build for infrastructure works—JICA funding projects by Takashi Okamoto (Japan)		128
	3.4	Construction management		131
		3.4.1	CM-at-risk	132
		In-Text Vignette: Interface management and interface agreements by Zachary Ferreira (the United States) and Alex Blomfield (UK)		132
	3.5	Multiple-prime contracts		138
	3.6	Partnering		138
		In-Text Vignette: Integrated project delivery—"Collaborate rather than litigate" by Edward J. ("Ned") Parrott (the United States)		139
	3.7	Alliancing		140
		In-Text Vignette: Target price and early risk identification/ management: London 2012 Olympics by Klaus Grewe (UK)		140
	3.8	Extended delivery methods (PPP, BOT, DBO)		143
		In-Text Vignette: Public-private partnerships by Steven Van Garsse (Belgium)		144
		In-Text Vignette: Infrastructure through public-private partnerships in the Philippines by Aris L. Gulapa and Dan Kevin C. Mandocdoc (the Phillipines)		146
	3.9	Further aspects of delivery methods		153
		3.9.1	Fast-track projects	153
		3.9.2	Target cost contracts	153
		3.9.3	Early contractor involvement and the pre-construction services agreement	154
		3.9.4	Building information management systems	155
		In-Text Vignette: BIM—The way forward? by Christopher Miers (UK)		156
		In-Text Vignette: Developments in BIM application: Legal aspects by Joost Merema (the Netherlands)		159
		In-Text Vignette: BIM: A superior approach for infrastructure construction by Josef Žák (the Czech Republic)		166
	References			170
	Further reading			170
4	**Specifics of EPC and EPCM**			**172**
	4.1	EPC and EPCM		172
	4.2	Engineer procure construct (EPC)		172
		4.2.1	Main advantages and disadvantages of EPC	174
		4.2.2	Key issues with the EPC delivery method	175

		In-Text Vignette: The employer's pitfall in the use of FIDIC conditions of contract for the EPC/turnkey projects (Silver book) in Indonesia by Sarwono Hardjomuljadi (Indonesia)	175
	4.3	Bespoke EPC contracts	177
		In-Text Vignette: Mitigating the risk of delays in power plant projects: An EPC contractor's view on different contractual concepts by Jacob C. Jørgensen (Denmark)	178
	4.4	Turnkey EPC contracts	185
		In-Text Vignette: Water treatment, wind farm, and road construction projects in Asian and African countries by Stéphane Giraud (France)	186
	4.5	Front end engineering design	188
		In-Text Vignette: Key issues in the procurement of international hydropower construction contracts by Alex Blomfield (UK)	189
	4.6	Engineer procure construction management (EPCM)	192
		4.6.1 Key competencies of the EPCM contractor	192
		4.6.2 Main advantages and disadvantages of EPCM	194
		4.6.3 Key issues of the EPCM delivery method	195
		In-Text Vignette: The use of the EPCM delivery method in the mining industry by Mark Berry (UK) and Matthew Hardwick (UK)	195
	4.7	EPC versus EPCM	200
		In-Text Vignette: Offshore construction by Fernando Ortega (Qatar)	202
	Bibliography		212
	References		213
	Further reading		214
5	**Unification and Standardization in International Construction**		**215**
	5.1	Unification of contracts	215
	5.2	Unification per law, principles, and sample documents	215
		5.2.1 Unification per law	215
		5.2.2 Unification per principles	216
		5.2.3 Unification per sample documents	217
		5.2.4 INCOTERMS	217
		In-Text Vignette: Resolving construction claims under investment treaty arbitration by Fernando Ortega (Qatar)	218
	5.3	Lenders and their influence on unification	220
		5.3.1 European union funds	220
		5.3.2 The European Investment Bank (EIB)	220
		5.3.3 The European Bank for Reconstruction and Development (EBRD)	221
		5.3.4 The World Bank (WB)	221
	5.4	Standard form of contract in a governing law context	222
	5.5	Purpose of sample documents in construction projects	222
	5.6	Standard sample forms as a source of law	224
	5.7	*Lex causae*	224

	5.8	Interpretation	225
		In-Text Vignette: Inconsistency in contract documents by Patrick Kain (South Africa)	226
	5.9	Trade usage and business custom	229
		In-Text Vignette: A common law of construction contracts—or Vive La différence? by Donald Charrett (Australia)	230
	5.10	*Lex constructionis* principles	232
		5.10.1 Proactivity and good faith protection related to time for completion	233
		5.10.2 Admissibility and necessity of variation procedures	234
		In-Text Vignette: Contractor's duty to mitigate delay and damages under FIDIC 1999 standard forms and in lex mercatoria by Vladimir Vencl (Serbia)	234
	5.11	The use of *lex constructionis*	240
		In-Text Vignette: Future-proofing construction contracts by Shy Jackson (UK)	240
	References		243
	Further reading		243
	Websites		243
6	**Price**		**244**
	6.1	Contract price	244
		6.1.1 Project finance	245
		In-Text Vignette: International construction measurement standards: Global consistency in cost analysis by Simon Collard (United Arab Emirates)	245
	6.2	Bid pricing methods	247
	6.3	Methods of contract price determination	248
		6.3.1 Economic influences on the contract price	249
		6.3.2 Formation of total contract price	249
	6.4	Re-measurement	249
		6.4.1 Methods of measurement	250
		6.4.2 Provisional sum	250
		6.4.3 Options	251
	6.5	The lump sum	252
	6.6	Cost plus	252
	6.7	Guaranteed maximum price	253
	6.8	Target price	253
	6.9	Payment	254
		6.9.1 Progress payments	254
		6.9.2 Milestone payments	255
		In-Text Vignette: Taxation in international construction contracts by Alex Blomfield (UK)	255
		In-Text Vignette: Managing the risk of non-payment by Sean Sullivan Gibbs (UK)	257
	6.10	Contract price under FIDIC forms	261
	6.11	Cost overruns	263

	6.12	Abnormally low tender (ALT)	264
		In-Text Vignette: Best value approach in the Netherlands by Wiebe Witteveen (the Netherlands)	265
	6.13	Claims as part of contract price	273
		6.13.1 Limitation and prescription periods for claims	273
	6.14	Public procurement law limitations	273
		In-Text Vignette: A concept of variation in a construction contract under Polish public procurement by Michał Skorupski (Poland)	275
	References		278
	Further reading		278
	Websites		279
7	**Time**		**280**
	7.1	Time in construction	280
	7.2	Delay	280
	7.3	The United Kingdom Society of construction law delay and disruption protocol	282
	7.4	Time program	283
		7.4.1 Critical path method	284
	7.5	Ownership of floats	285
		In-Text Vignette: Time extension and float ownership under the FIDIC Red and Yellow Books (1999) by Frank Thomas (France)	285
	7.6	Time at large and extension of time (EOT)	298
	7.7	Concurrent delay	300
		In-Text Vignette: Delay clauses in different jurisdictions by Jacob C. Jørgensen (Denmark)	301
	7.8	Disruption	302
	7.9	Time for completion under FIDIC forms	303
	7.10	Time program under FIDIC forms	304
		In-Text Vignette: A lack of realism in negotiations by James Bremen (UK)	306
	7.11	Delay and suspension under FIDIC forms	306
		7.11.1 Delay under FIDIC forms	306
		7.11.2 Practical recommendations for EOT claims	307
		7.11.3 Suspension of work under FIDIC forms	308
	7.12	Contract termination under FIDIC forms	309
		7.12.1 Employer termination	310
		7.12.2 Contractor termination	311
		7.12.3 Termination in convenience	311
		7.12.4 *Force majeure* termination	311
	References		312
	Further reading		312
8	**Variations**		**313**
	8.1	Variation clauses	313
	8.2	Variations under FIDIC forms	315
		In-Text Vignette: Sub-Clause 13.2 value engineering under the FIDIC forms by Manuel Conthe (Spain)	316

	8.3	Claims related to variations	319
		8.3.1 Directed variation	319
		8.3.2 Constructive variation	320
		8.3.3 Voluntary variation	321
		In-Text Vignette: The nightmare of valuing omissions by Aymen K. Masadeh and Remon Farag (UAE)	321
	8.4	Acceleration	329
		8.4.1 Directed acceleration	329
		8.4.2 Constructive acceleration	329
		In-Text Vignette: Drafting acceleration agreements by Alan Whaley (UK)	333
		In-Text Vignette: The U.S. approach to constructive acceleration by Robert A. Rubin and Sarah Biser (the United States)	336
		In-Text Vignette: Constructive acceleration claims: A common law perspective by Alan Whaley (UK)	339
		8.4.3 Voluntary acceleration	340
	8.5	Proving the acceleration claim	340
	8.6	Substantial change	342
		In-Text Vignette: Modification of contracts during their execution under EU law by Odysseas P. Michaelides (Cyprus)	343
		In-Text Vignette: ITER—An International project for the construction of a first-of-a-kind fusion nuclear installation under the FIDIC forms by Karoly Tamas Olajos (France)	347
	References		363
	Further reading		363
	Websites		363
9	**Claims**		**364**
	9.1	Claims	364
		In-Text Vignette: Claims caused by deficiencies in tender documents by James Bremen (UK)	368
	9.2	Contractor's claims under FIDIC forms	368
	9.3	Employer's claims under FIDIC forms	369
		In-Text Vignette: Employer's notices by Victoria Tyson (UK)	369
		In-Text Vignette: Claims in the St. Petersburg flood protection barrier construction by Aleksei Kuzmin (Russia)	373
	9.4	Lapse of claim	377
		9.4.1 Risk allocation and claims interconnections	377
	9.5	Cause of the claim	378
	9.6	Limits of the lapse of claim	379
		In-Text Vignette: Construction claims in the UK by Garry Kitt (UK)	381
		9.6.1 Evaluation of a particular lapse of claim	383
		In-Text Vignette: Condition precedent and time-barred claims under Polish law by Michał Skorupski (Poland)	383

		In-Text Vignette: Australian position on time bars by Andrew P. Downie (Australia)	385
		In-Text Vignette: Time bars under Kuwaiti law by Dina Al Ansary (Kuwait)	392
	References		393
	Further readings		393
10	**Claim Management**		**395**
	10.1	Claim management	395
	10.2	Claims for extension of time (EOT)	396
	10.3	Claims for additional payment	398
		10.3.1 Claims resulting from variations	399
	10.4	Claims resulting from delay and/or disruption under the provisions of the contract	399
		10.4.1 Delay claims	399
		10.4.2 Site overhead claims	400
		In-Text Vignette: Considerations related to site overhead claims by Gary Kitt (UK)	400
		10.4.3 Headquarters overhead claims	402
		10.4.4 Subcontractor claims	405
		10.4.5 Lost profit claims	406
		10.4.6 Prolongation costs and interest claims	406
		10.4.7 Increased cost of material, labor, and equipment	407
		10.4.8 Claim preparation costs	407
		10.4.9 Disruption claims	408
		In-Text Vignette: Head office overhead claims under FDIC contracts by Alan Whaley (UK)	410
		In-Text Vignette: Calculation and recovery of home/head office overhead in North America by James G. Zack (the United States)	412
	10.5	Claims resulting from governing law	424
	10.6	Global claims	425
		In-Text Vignette: All global claims are not negatively "global"! by Frank Thomas (France)	428
	10.7	Contractor's claim management under FIDIC forms	429
	10.8	Employer's claim management under FIDIC forms	431
	10.9	Intercultural aspects	432
		In-Text Vignette: "Claim" as perceived in the Polish civil law environment by Michał Skorupski (Poland)	434
	10.10	Claim management implementation	436
		In-Text Vignette: Claims in a tunnel construction in the Republic of Serbia by Radim Wrana (the Czech Republic)	437
		In-Text Vignette: The evolution of contractor's claims in Peru/South America by Jerry Pessah (Peru)	438
	References		440
	Further reading		440

11 Construction Dispute Boards — 442

11.1 Construction disputes — 442
In-Text Vignette: Construction dispute in sheet metal galvanizing line project by Patrick Kain (South Africa) — 442

11.2 Dispute boards — 444
    11.2.1 Dispute avoidance — 445
In-Text Vignette: Project dispute avoidance by Christopher J. Mather (the United States) — 445
In-Text Vignette: Dispute resolution boards: The long-term experience from the United States by Robert A. Rubin (the United States) — 451
    11.2.2 Dispute boards: Advantages and disadvantages — 453
    11.2.3 Dispute Adjudication Board (DAB) — 453
    11.2.4 Dispute Review Board (DRB) — 454

11.3 Contractual adjudication: The use of DAB in FIDIC forms — 454
    11.3.1 FIDIC policy statements to ADR — 457
    11.3.2 Independence and impartiality — 457
In-Text Vignette: Construction disputes in Ukraine by Roger Ribeiro and Yaryna Bakhovska (Ukraine) — 457

11.4 Enforcement of dispute board decisions — 464
    11.4.1 Non-binding recommendations — 465
    11.4.2 Interim-binding decisions — 465
    11.4.3 Contractual sanctions for non-compliance with dispute board decisions — 466
In-Text Vignette: The Persero proceedings and the issue of the enforcement of a non-final DAB decision under the FIDIC conditions by David Brown (UK) — 469

11.5 Statutory adjudication — 471
In-Text Vignette: Statutory adjudication by Nigel Grout (UK) — 471
    11.5.1 UK statutory adjudication regime — 472
    11.5.2 The scheme for construction projects in the UK — 472
    11.5.3 Some procedural aspects of statutory adjudication — 473
In-Text Vignette: Settling construction disputes in Hungary by Tamás Balázs (Hungary) — 474
In-Text Vignette: Statutory adjudication in Australia by Donald Charrett (Australia) — 475
In-Text Vignette: Statutory adjudication in Malaysia by Albert Yeu (Hong Kong) — 481

References — 483
Further reading — 483

12 FIDIC — 485

12.1 FIDIC expansion — 485
In-Text Vignette: Using translated texts in FIDIC contracts: The Spanish case by Ignacio de Almagro (Spain) — 485

12.2 FIDIC — 487

12.3 FIDIC's influence on the construction industry — 488

12.4	FIDIC membership	488
12.5	Networking activities	489
	12.5.1	Translations and local use of FIDIC forms	490
		In-Text Vignette: The use of FIDIC forms in Russia by Dmitry Nekrestyanov (Russia)	492
		In-Text Vignette: The use of FIDIC forms in Brazil by Rafael Marinangelo (Brazil)	493
		In-Text Vignette: The use of FIDIC Forms within the construction contract law of Turkey by Yasemin Çetinel (Turkey)	493
		In-Text Vignette: The use of FIDIC forms in Azerbaijan by Farid Nabili (Azerbaijan)	502
		In-Text Vignette: The use of FIDIC forms in Nigeria by Marc J. Enenkel (Germany)	505
		In-Text Vignette: The use of FIDIC forms in Ukraine by Svitlana Teush (Ukraine)	507
		In-Text Vignette: The use of FIDIC forms in Vietnam by David Lockwood (Vietnam)	513
		In-Text Vignette: The use of FIDIC forms in Kazakhstan by Artyushenko Andrey (Kazakhstan)	517
12.6	FIDIC forms of contract	522
		In-Text Vignette: Journey to the "kitchen" of FIDIC: How FIDIC publications are produced by Husni Madi (Jordan)	524
12.7	The structure of the contract under FIDIC forms	527
	12.7.1	Particular conditions	527
	12.7.2	Employer's requirements	528
	12.7.3	Contractor's proposal	528
	12.7.4	Drawings	529
	12.7.5	Bill of quantities and specifications	529
12.8	Conditions of contract for construction (CONS)—1999 Red Book	530
	12.8.1	Structure of CONS	530
		In-Text Vignette: Misapplications of FIDIC contracts in the United Arab Emirates by Kamal Adnan Malas (United Arab Emirates)	531
12.9	Conditions of contract for plant and design-build (P&DB)—1999 Yellow Book	535
	12.9.1	Structure of P&DB	535
12.10	Conditions of contract for EPC/Turnkey projects (EPC)—1999 Silver Book	536
	12.10.1	Structure of EPC	536
12.11	Short form of contract—Green Book	537
	12.11.1	Structure of short form of contract	537
12.12	Construction subcontract	537
	12.12.1	Structure of construction subcontract	538

	12.13	Conditions of contract for design, build, and operate (DBO)—Gold Book	538
		12.13.1 Structure of DBO	539
		In-Text Vignette: The 2017 updates of the 1999 FIDIC forms of contracts (Red, Yellow, and Silver Books) by Zoltán Záhonyi (Hungary)	541
	12.14	Other FIDIC standard forms	547
		In-Text Vignette: FIDIC suite of consultant agreements by Vincent Leloup (France)	547
		In-Text Vignette: The use of FIDIC contracts by the mining industry in Africa by Coenraad Snyman (South Africa)	551
	12.15	Risk allocation under FIDIC forms	553
		12.15.1 Risk allocation in CONS	553
		In-Text Vignette: China's standard form of construction contract in comparison with FIDIC forms by Shuibo Zhang (China)	556
		12.15.2 Risk allocation in P&DB	560
		12.15.3 Risk allocation in EPC	560
		In-Text Vignette: Explanation of FIDIC EPC risk allocation by FIDIC	561
		In-Text Vignette: The FIDIC golden principles—A new approach to discouraging inappropriate amendments to standard form contracts by Donald Charrett (Australia)	563
	12.16	Design responsibility under FIDIC forms	566
		In-Text Vignette: Design Liability: risk share, conflicts and a little bit of common sense? by Cecilia Misu (Germany)	568
	References		578
	Further reading		579
13	**Other Standard Forms of Construction Contracts: NEC, ICC, ENNA, IChemE, Orgalime, AIA, VOB**		**580**
	13.1	Common standard forms of construction contracts	580
	13.2	The NEC (New Engineering Contract)	580
		13.2.1 NEC forms of contract	583
		In-Text Vignette: The NEC form of contract—ready for the international market by Rob Horne (UK)	585
	13.3	FIDIC forms versus NEC3	594
	13.4	ICC forms of contract	597
	13.5	ENAA forms of contract	597
	13.6	IChemE forms of contract	598
	13.7	Orgalime forms of contract	599
	13.8	Standard forms of construction contracts in the Czech Republic	600
		In-Text Vignette: United States standard form contracts by Edward J. ("Ned") Parrott (the United States)	602
	13.9	VOB: German standard	607
		13.9.1 Content of VOB/B	609
		13.9.2 VOB limitations	611
	13.10	Invalid clauses in German case law	613

		In-Text Vignette: The standard forms of construction contract in Australia by John Sharkey (Australia)	614
		In-Text Vignette: Construction contracts in the Republic of Ireland by Arran Dowling-Hussey (Ireland)	617
	References		621
	Further reading		621
	Websites		622
14	**Risk and Insurance**		**623**
	14.1	Insurance in construction	623
	14.2	Commercial risk, risk of damage, and exceptional risk	624
		In-Text Vignette: Weather risk in offshore wind construction contracts by Alex Blomfield (UK)	627
	14.3	Risk management in the standard forms of contract	630
	14.4	Hazards and risks in construction projects	632
		14.4.1 Project preparation risks	633
		14.4.2 Design risks	633
		14.4.3 Site risks	634
		14.4.4 Execution risks of a technical nature	634
		14.4.5 Execution risks of an anthropogenic nature	634
		14.4.6 Post-construction risks	635
		In-Text Vignette: The difficulties connected to construction risk quantification by Dejan Makovšek (France)	635
	14.5	Insurance requirements in standard forms of contract	640
		14.5.1 Insurance requirements in FIDIC forms	640
		14.5.2 Design risk and insurance	640
		14.5.3 General insurance requirements	641
		14.5.4 Insurance for works and contractor's equipment	641
		14.5.5 Insurance against injury of persons and damage to property	641
		14.5.6 Insurance for contractor's personnel	642
		In-Text Vignette: Professional indemnity insurance under the FIDIC yellow book by Richard Krammer (Austria)	642
		In-Text Vignette: Insurance in hydropower projects by Alex Blomfield (UK)	651
	14.6	Practical aspects of insurance in construction projects	652
		14.6.1 Recommendations for negotiating insurance	652
		14.6.2 Compatibility of the construction contract with the insurance contract	654
		In-Text Vignette: Incompatibility of the construction contract with the insurance contract by Karel Fabich (the Czech Republic)	655
	14.7	International insurance law and insurance standards in the construction industry	655
		14.7.1 Standard insurance terms of ABN 2011 and ABU 2011	656
		14.7.2 Conditions of ABU—Section A	656
		14.7.3 Conditions of ABN—Section A	657
		14.7.4 Munich CAR and EAR insurance terms standards	657

		14.7.5	CAR terms	657
		14.7.6	EAR terms	658
		In-Text Vignette: Construction/erection all risk insurance in the offshore wind industry by Gregory Efthimiu (Germany)		658
	References			662
	Further reading			662
	Website			663
15	**Risk in Underground Construction**			**664**
	15.1	Underground construction hazards and risks		664
	15.2	Code of practice for risk management of tunnel works		665
	15.3	Alternatives of unforeseeable physical conditions risk allocation		667
		In-Text Vignette: Geotechnical baseline reports as a risk management tool by Randall J. Essex (the United States)		668
		In-Text Vignette: Geotechnical baseline used in contractor's bid by Michal Uhrin (the Czech Republic)		679
	15.4	Unforeseeability		684
	15.5	"Unforeseeability" according to FIDIC forms		684
	15.6	Site data		686
		In-Text Vignette: Water-related construction projects by Robert Werth (Germany)		689
	15.7	Sufficiency of the accepted contract amount		691
	15.8	Unforeseeable physical conditions		692
		In-Text Vignette: Ground conditions risk in an EPC contract for a gas treatment plant by Cristina Della Moretta (Italy)		693
	15.9	Unforeseeable operation of the forces of nature		697
		In-Text Vignette: Clairvoyance: A contractor's duty? by Gustavo Paredes and Katherine Waidhofer (Peru)		697
	15.10	Force majeure		700
	15.11	Release from performance under law		701
	References			701
	Further reading			701
	Website			702
16	**Securities**			**703**
	16.1	Securities in construction		703
	16.2	Bank guarantees		704
	16.3	Functions and parameters of bank guarantees		704
		16.3.1	Vadium/tender guarantee/bid bond	704
		16.3.2	Advance payment guarantee/down payment guarantee/advance payment bond	705
		16.3.3	Performance guarantee/final guarantee/performance bond	705
		16.3.4	Warranty guarantee/maintenance guarantee/maintenance bond	705
		16.3.5	Retention guarantee/retention bond	706
		16.3.6	Payment guarantee/payment bond	706

	16.4	Specifics of retention guarantee	706
		In-Text Vignette: Performance security and termination payment security in hydropower projects by Alex Blomfield (UK)	708
	16.5	Governing law	709
		In-Text Vignette: Common law specifics related to securities by Rupert Choat and Aidan Steensma (UK)	710
	16.6	ICC rules related to securities	712
	16.7	Suretyship	712
	16.8	Stand-by letter of credit	713
	16.9	Securities under FIDIC forms	714
	Further reading		715
17	**Civil Engineering Works: Infrastructure Construction Projects**		**716**
	17.1	Investments in developing countries	716
	17.2	The approach to the risk allocation in the United States	717
	17.3	The approach to the risk allocation in the United Kingdom	719
		In-Text Vignette: Construction of airports by Patrick Kain (South Africa)	720
	17.4	The approach to the risk allocation in Central and Eastern Europe	722
		17.4.1 Restricted competencies of the Engineer	723
		17.4.2 Inefficient risk allocation	724
		17.4.3 Limitation of contractors' claims	725
		17.4.4 Contractual determination of a maximum total contract price	725
		In-Text Vignette: The Romanian experience by Claudia Teodorescu (Romania)	725
	17.5	The Polish experience	731
		In-Text Vignette: FIDIC Forms and contractual relationships in Poland by Aleksandra Marzec (Poland)	731
		In-Text Vignette: Market environment prior to and after 2008: The need for change in procurement by Michał Skorupski (Poland)	734
		17.5.1 Abnormally low price	735
		17.5.2 Inefficient risk allocation	736
		17.5.3 Consortiums	738
		17.5.4 Contract administration: the Engineer	738
		In-Text Vignette: Claims considerations by Aleksandra Marzec (Poland)	740
		17.5.5 Specific legislation for subcontractors	742
		17.5.6 Courts and litigation	742
		In-Text Vignette: Contractor defense measures by Michał Skorupski (Poland)	745
		17.5.7 Consequences of inefficient risk allocation	746

	17.6	The Czech experience	748
		In-Text Vignette: Local limits for development: An interview with Shy Jackson (UK) by Lukas Klee (the Czech Republic)	750
	References		754
	Further reading		755
	Websites		755
18	**Building Construction: Health Care Facilities**		**756**
	18.1	Health care facility construction project	756
	18.2	Pre-design planning phase	756
	18.3	Design phase	757
	18.4	Basic structure of a hospital	758
	18.5	Efficiency and cost effectiveness	758
	18.6	Flexibility and expandability	759
	18.7	Therapeutic environment	759
	18.8	Cleaning and maintenance	759
	18.9	Controlled circulation and accessibility	760
	18.10	Aesthetics	760
	18.11	Health and safety	761
	18.12	Use of information technology	761
	18.13	Relevant regulations and standards	761
	18.14	Health care facility construction project: Suitable delivery method	762
		18.14.1 Extent of employer's involvement in the project	762
		18.14.2 Employer's right to instruct variations	763
		18.14.3 Employer's position in claiming design defects	763
		18.14.4 Speed	763
		18.14.5 Certainty of the bid price	764
		18.14.6 Final evaluation of the suitable delivery method	764
	Further reading		765
Appendix A: Interactive Exercises			**766**
	A.1	Interactive exercise 1: Delivery method selection	766
		A.1.1 Task	766
	A.2	Interactive exercise 2: Claim for delayed site handover	767
		A.2.1 Task	767
		A.2.2 Time schedule (program)	768
		A.2.3 Site handover procedure	768
		A.2.4 Mobilization	768
		A.2.5 Acceleration	768
		A.2.6 Claims	768
	A.3	Interactive exercise 3: Claim due to suspension of work	769
		A.3.1 Task	769
		A.3.2 Suspension	769
		A.3.3 Mobilization	769
		A.3.4 Claims	770

	A.4	Interactive exercise 4: Subcontractor claim for contractor delay (lack of cooperation, inadequate on-site coordination and improper, unclear, and delayed instructions)	770
		A.4.1 Task	770
		A.4.2 Fact 1—Lack of cooperation	771
		A.4.3 Fact 2—Inadequate on-site coordination	771
		A.4.4 Fact 3—Improper, unclear, and delayed instructions	771

Appendix B: Sample Letters (Examples of Formal Notices) — 772

B.1	Contractor's sample letters: Notice of probable future event	773
B.2	Contractor's sample letters: Notice of contractor's claims	774
B.3	Contractor's sample letters: Contractor's claim No._____ submission (quantification)	776
B.4	Contractor's sample letters: Request for evidences of financial arrangements	777
B.5	Contractor's sample letters: Written confirmation of oral instruction	778
B.6	Contractor's sample letters: Notice of dissatisfaction with a determination of the engineer	779
B.7	Contractor's sample letters: Notice of contractor's entitlement to suspend work	780
B.8	Contractor's sample letters: Notice of contractor's claim under the sub-clause 16.1	781
B.9	Contractor's sample letters: Application for taking over certificate	782
B.10	Employer's sample letters: Notice of employer's claim	783
B.11	Employer's sample letters: Answer to request for evidence of financial arrangements	784
B.12	Engineer's sample letters: Engineer's determination	785
B.13	Engineer's sample letters: Engineer's instruction	787
B.14	Engineer's sample letters: Engineer's notice to correct	788
B.15	Engineer's sample letters: Engineer's instruction to remove a person employed on the site	789
B.16	Engineer's sample letters: Engineer's instruction—lack of mobilization	790

Appendix C: Dictionary of Construction Terms: English, German, French, Hungarian, Czech, Russian, Polish, Spanish, Portuguese and Chinese — 791

C.1	Dictionary—General part	792
C.2	Dictionary—Contractor's claims	800
C.3	Dictionary—Employer's claims	804

Appendix D: Claim Management System Under FIDIC Forms — 807

D.1	Claim management team responsibilities		807
	D.1.1	E1—Project manager	807
	D.1.2	E2—Design and time schedule (program)	808

		D.1.3	E3—Site manager	808
		D.1.4	E4—Contract interpretation, monthly statements, invoicing, insurance, subcontractors, employer's claims, mutual claims in a joint venture	809
		D.1.5	E5—Administrative support	809
	D.2		Claim management processes	810
	D.3		Table of contractor's claims under FIDIC CONS	811
	D.4		Table of employer's claims under FIDIC CONS	811

Appendix E: FIDIC Forms Risk Allocation Charts — 813

	E.1	Chart No.1: Basic risk allocation alternatives in connection with unforeseeable physical conditions	813
	E.2	Chart No. 2: Basic comparison of risk allocation (claims options) in FIDIC CONS/1999 red book, P&DB/1999 yellow book, and EPC/1999 silver book	813

Index — 817

About the Author

Dr. Lukas Klee, LL.M., Ph.D., MBA, is an independent expert in international construction contracts, adjudicator, arbitrator, state-registered expert witness, and currently the owner at Klee Consulting. He lectures on international construction law and contract management, for example, at the Brno University of Technology, Charles University in Prague, and other universities. Lukas regularly gives lectures for many organizations including FIDIC, provides training and consultancy, publishes articles worldwide and is the author of several books related to international construction contracts.

Contact details: www.klee-consulting.com

Foreword

Svend Poulsen
Chief Project Manager, COWI Consulting Engineers, Chairman FIDIC Contracts Updates Task Group

We often hear the word "project" when work needs to be done. "I have a project at home" is a regular phrase in daily conversation. In general, we see more and more of our life as a series of projects. Going on holiday is a project; preparing a dinner with friends can be a project and training for a marathon can be a project. This mindset is likely to be something we have adopted from the construction industry.

One of the first things you notice when starting work in the construction industry is that the unknown has a major impact on any project. You can even divide the unknown into the "known unknown" and the "unknown unknown." The way to handle the unknowns is to use tools developed in the risk management field. These tools have been developed over many years and, when used correctly and continuously, can lead to more successful projects.

We do not know all the risk aspects when starting a project. For example, can we know and predict all the risks and problems associated with an industrial process for mass manufacturing? Designing a new car is a project. Once the design is agreed upon and all the details for manufacture are in place, the task is complete. The next step is industrial production with certainty of performance and quality of the car known—at least in principle.

Projects in the building and construction industry are unique and often only have a limited aspect of industrial process. For example, construction might use some well-defined processes such as the laying of sleepers and rail on a railway using a track-laying machine. However, uncertainty of the sub-soil conditions and other specific local conditions for the completed works will always sow the seed for risks and surprises. During execution of the works, the weather, the market situation, labor availability, and so on influence the progress and certainty of achieving the agreed quality, budgeted price, and finishing date.

An essential element of any project is the need for good agreements between the parties to a project. Since the 1950s, FIDIC has produced standard contracts for the construction industry. The principles of these contracts focus on fair risk sharing and the most effective mechanisms for administering the project. FIDIC contracts for construction and design-build make the engineer the responsible party for administering the contract and managing the project. Thus, FIDIC contracts are two-party agreements for a three-party process.

The role of the engineer is an issue that is often discussed. As an example, how can the engineer avoid actual or apparent bias toward/against the contractor when being paid by the employer? The engineer is an agent of the employer but their job is also to act fairly when making determinations under the contract. Contract conditions do state this obligation and it is paramount for the correct administration of contracts that the assigned engineer acts in accordance with this requirement. One of the advantages of having an engineer and not a project manager is that the engineer has the technical understanding of the project complexity and can manage the project so that questions and unforeseen events are handled properly. Therefore, it is very difficult to succeed with a complex project without the right understanding of the contractual arrangements and the nature of the project.

In the construction business, various kinds of standard contracts are available and set different priorities depending on where they are from. Some have a very strong focus on administrative procedures and are very prescriptive. Others set up a standard framework for the contract and are very dependent on a set of special or particular conditions. Thus, choosing the right form of contract from the outset is critical. The employer should think about how they want to monitor the project and handle risks. On one side of the spectrum are the works designed by the employer and, on the other, turnkey agreements. Some extreme versions of the latter place all risk on the contractor. Risk and influence, therefore, go hand in hand.

Transfer of all risks to the contractor under a turnkey form of contract gives the contractor full control of the processes to mitigate consequences of risks. The employer has to accept that by transferring risk, they also transfer control. Why is this form of contract so popular then? Answer: the industry has seen a growing need for certainty of price and time. Financial institutions focus on budgets and time more than ever. Under these circumstances, it is extremely important that the technical requirements for the project are well defined because changes at a later stage are, in principle, not possible.

The reader of this book will see that there are a lot of people in the industry striving to make projects successful and they put in a lot of effort into improving contracts, procedures, and tools to become even better at managing complex projects. Our industry has produced spectacular achievements throughout modern history. In particular, the world's need for efficient transport has been a huge driver for the engineering industry. When new and more efficient transport is introduced, society prospers. Today the focus on sustainability also influences the way we design and construct. New ways of working, new ways of cooperating, and new types of projects call for new types of agreements.

Whether you read this book from cover to cover or as reference guide, you should realize that because of this book your contribution to more successful projects will have a higher value. The book gives you access to a treasure chest of knowledge collected by experienced engineers and contract managers—experience you can use when faced with the challenges that projects bring—challenges that arise from the basic fundamental nature of projects themselves.

We who work with projects know that successful projects give out positive energy and a good feeling of developing our society. With this book in hand, it is now your turn to feel the power of this positive energy.

Acknowledgments

Many thanks to Andrea, Sam, Ben and the whole family.
 Special thanks to Martin Udall as English language editor for his tireless work and assistance.
 Many thanks to Paul Sayer and Viktoria Hartl-Vida.
 Many thanks to all my friends and colleagues who contributed with a vignette or helped with particular chapters. Your worldly insights have given this book a truly global perspective:

Dina Al Ansary, Andrey Artyushenko, Faisal Attia, Yaryna Bakhovska, Tamás Balázs, Mark Berry, Sarah Biser, Alex Blomfield, James Bremen, Giuseppe Broccoli, David Brown, Yasemin Cetinel, Donald Charrett, Rupert Choat, Simon Collard, Manuel Conthe, Alberto Croze, Ignacio De Almagro, Jaap De Koning, Cristina Della Moretta, Arran Dowling-Hussey, Andrew Downie, Gregory Efthimiu, Bernd Ehle, Marc Enenkel, Randall Essex, Karel Fabich, Remon Farag, Thiago Fernandes Moreira, Zachary Ferreira, Caio Lucas Gabra, Sean Gibbs, Stephane Giraud, Klaus Grewe, Nigel Grout, Aris Gulapa, Sarwono Hardjomuljadi, Matthew Hardwick, Khalil Tayab Hasan, Andy Hewitt, Rob Horne, Shy Jackson, Jacob Jørgensen, Patrick Kain, Knut Kirkhus, Gary Kitt, Richard Krammer, Aleksei Kuzmin, Vincent Leloup, David Lockwood, Husni Madi, Dejan Makovšek, Kamal Malas, Dan Kevin Mandocdoc, Rafael Marinangelo, Aleksandra Marzec, Aymen Masadeh, Christopher Mather, Joost Merema, Odysseus Michaelides, Christopher Miers, Cecilia Misu, Enrique Moncada, Conor Mooney, Samuel Moss, Farid Nabili, Chakravarthi Nandakumar, Dmitry Nekrestyanov, Takashi Okamoto, Karoly Tamas Olajos, Fernando Ortega, Gustavo Paredes, Edward Parrott, Jerry Pessah, Rishabh Raheja, Roger Ribeiro, Dario Rizzi, Robert Rubin, Patrizia Sangalli, John Sharkey, Michał Skorupski, Coenraad Snyman, Aidan Steensma, Claudia Adalgiza Teodorescu, Svitlana Teush, Frank Thomas, Victoria Tyson, Michal Uhrin, Steven Van Garsse, Vladimir Vencl, Katherine Waidhofer, Robert Werth, Alan Whaley, Wiebe Witteveen, Radim Wrana, Albert Yeu, James Zack, Fabio Zanchi, Zoltán Záhonyi, Shuibo Zhang, Josef Žák, Petr Dobiáš, David Hruška, Xavier Leynaud, Alicia Martin, Hana Nevřalová, Ilya Nikiforov, Daniel Nový, Svend Poulsen, Zuzana Rollová, Ondřej Ručka, Tomáš Staněk, Roman Turek and Andrea Wernicke.

Introductory Remarks

Shuibo Zhang
Professor of international construction contracts, Tianjin University, People's Republic of China

God says, "*If as one people speaking the same language they have begun to do this, then nothing they plan to do will be impossible for them.*" (Genesis 11:6)

The modern era has brought with it a never-before-seen demand for high-quality and high-quantity civil infrastructures and industrial facilities. Their importance cannot be underestimated in raising the living standards of human beings, particularly in developing countries. Estimates of global demand for infrastructure over the next decade is somewhere between US$10 to 20 trillion. Meanwhile, with the advances in productivity, construction projects are getting larger in scope and more complex in technology. They usually involve an input of vast resources, including human expertise, equipment, and various materials, among other things. This makes it very hard, if not impossible, for a single country or region to cope alone. In addition, comparative advantages make it more likely and efficient for construction-related firms from all over the world to work on the same project. As a matter of fact, large and global projects are ubiquitous on current international construction markets. Take China's World Bank-financed *Xiaolanglangdi* Multipurpose Hydro Project as an example. More than one hundred organizations participated in the construction, including contractors, subcontractors, suppliers, and consultants, from over 50 countries/regions. This project was thus nicknamed the "small United Nations." According to the *Engineering News Record*, the overseas turnover of the top international 225 contractors has been increasing for the past 10 consecutive years, reaching a total of US$511 billion in 2012 compared to US$116 billion in 2003. This indicates an annual average growth rate of more than 15%.

Indeed, the construction industry has been globalizing with the globalization of the whole world. However, globalized construction projects are temporary and inter-organizational activities and require intense communication and coordination efforts from many participants who possess different cultural and legal backgrounds. Such institutional differences tend to act as obstacles and pose problems in communication among project participants, resulting in poor coordination, misunderstandings, chaos, and even unfortunate project failures. The project of the A2 motorway in Poland undertaken by a Chinese contractor is a good illustration of the latter situation. The frequent occurrence of disputes in international construction is an ever-occurring phenomenon. Therefore, a good mechanism must be designed to alleviate such a situation—namely, the construction contract. This document, at its core, is designed to make all participants *speak the same language*.

Project contracts are legally enforceable and binding, and managerially instrumental, offering "the rules of play" to act as a guide for the parties to work together. To cooperate efficiently and effectively, it is a must for all parties involved in international projects to have a good understanding of the rules first. However, due to the very nature of construction contracts and the different legal systems governing each individual contract, confusion may arise in the understanding, interpretation, and execution of a given contract. For construction project professionals in general, this presents a challenge unless they are well informed with sound knowledge of construction-related contractual and legal issues. To the best of my knowledge, very few books on the market are available to explicitly deal with this topic.

I am pleased to learn that Dr. Lukas Klee, an experienced lawyer in international construction, has filled this gap with this new book that specifically targets international construction contracts in practical terms. This book covers the key legal and contractual knowledge areas for international construction, such as civil law/common law interrelationships, delivery methods, standard forms of contracts, risk allocation, variations, claims, dispute resolution, insurance, and securities. Accompanying these subjects, the lessons learnt from the industry and many vignettes collected from all continents make this book a real "international" and "practical" guide. The comprehensive knowledge conveyed in this book, in my personal judgement, will perfectly cater for the urgent needs of international construction professionals.

I am confident that this new book will be a great help to professionals allowing them to speak the same construction language in international projects and, in turn, will facilitate them in building a *stairway* to a better world in an efficient and harmonious way.

Introductory Remarks

Robert Werth
Owner of Werth-Consult Dispute Resolution Services, Essen, Germany

Construction law literature is usually written by lawyers for lawyers. This often means that texts are very technical and contain a lot of law-related jargon. To a large extent this is necessary, but may exclude or "scare off" the majority of construction project practitioners.

My daily business experience has shown me that the biggest issues in international contracts are managing communication and understanding of the behavior of people. We all know that international contracts are usually large, contain/demand complex documents and we could assume that the people involved have the proper skills to do the job. But do these people have the proper skills under the conditions agreed to under the terms of the contract? Many construction project participants (usually engineers) use their skills gained from working with domestic construction contracts and apply this knowledge internationally. Effectively, this often means that the job goes ahead, irrespective of what the contract says. This approach may be correct from a technical aspect, but riskier when considering the administrative requirements under international contracts.

For these reasons, the most important issues for management staff when dealing with international contracts is an understanding of (1) the contract itself; and (2) the legal system in which it operates.

The advantage of this book is that it covers all important international construction law aspects in a comprehensible, easily readable, and user-friendly manner. This enables finding a common understanding of an issue, before it can be discussed in terms of specific contract conditions in a particular case. It is an essential reference for all parties involved directly or indirectly in international construction projects.

This book is particularly helpful because it contains a number of practical examples from real "on-site" experience that can assist the practitioner to immerse themselves quickly into the specifics of construction projects. This also makes the book interesting and "readable."

I highly recommended this book to anyone involved in international construction contracts, wherever adequate. And there was something unique, I have noticed, when I made some recommendations about that book during lectures in many places of the world. People replied: "I have read that book," which is different to just saying "I have or own that piece of literature."

And that is what makes the book different. It is a book to be read, not owned, written by practitioners. And finally, I am really proud to be a member of that illustrious team behind Dr. Lukas Klee to support him and also making one of the best even better. Thank you, Lukas.

Introductory Remarks

Ilya Nikiforov
Managing Partner, Egorov, Puginsky, Afanasiev & Partners, Russia

My experience with international contracting in Eastern Europe, Russia, and the CIS spans some 25 years. I have learned that in spite of international prominence of commonly applicable construction practices (e.g., under FIDIC standard forms of contract) their use and implementation in construction projects are relatively unknown in Russia and the CIS. Domestic industries in the region work on the basis of traditional workflow documentation and contract writing dating back to the socialist era. These practices experience substantial turbulence when international construction projects "come to town." Typically, there is a conflict of expectations of accepted standards of contract and the rights and responsibilities of the parties.

In a fast-moving and globalized world, developers and constructors need a quick-reference guide to manage their expectations in an international construction project environment. As a professional in this field, I have many books in my legal library dealing with construction projects. However, these are mostly limited in their scope to a particular legal system or territory of implementation. First edition of this book has broken a new grand of omnibus coverage of construction topics at a global level.

Construction disputes are infamous for being costly, lengthy, and voluminous. In an industry where "time is money," participants in the field need knowledge, a calm head, and oversight to minimize delays and keep the project moving. This book is a vital tool for making this possible. Therefore, it is of great benefit to all private consultants involved in the industry, engineers in developing countries and emerging markets where international practices of implementation of infrastructure projects are just becoming known will find it particularly useful. The title also appeals to in-house counsel and private practitioners for whom construction law is not a mainstream practice area. It's also a "must read" for the wider audience of consultants, surveyors, architects, employers (public and private), and domestic construction industry specialists.

This book is praised for its practical approach, lucidity of text and clarity. The author's experience, know-how, and international prospective in major construction company make him perfectly positioned to write this text.

The book has the further advantage of being written by an author from a non common law country. He provides a unique, fresh, and unbiased look at the subject matters as they stand today, for example, the chapters on claims and claims management. These two chapters are literally "from the front lines" and convey the author's experiences in a practical way.

The majority of prominent publications are written by Anglo-American authors. Mr. Klee was trained and practices in a continental European law setting. The legal system is based on Roman and Napoleonic Law principles that operate not only in continental Europe, but also in South-East Asia, the Middle East, Africa, and South America. For this reason, readers in these jurisdictions will find this title an invaluable, relevant, and user-friendly tool to solve daily questions that arise in construction, for instance, how to apply the standard forms of contract developed in common law countries locally. Common law practitioners will benefit from knowing what to expect when dealing with colleagues and partners in non-common law countries.

A key feature of this book is the fact that the author is not a native English speaker. Most of the forms and precedents relating to the subject matter are in English. Thus, the author is in the best position to assess "translation difficulties"—in other words, managing the linguistic aspect. Readers will become familiar with technical terms used in the industry. Moreover, the reference material included in the appendices—charts/diagrams, a dictionary of construction terms, add great value, and facilitate learning. This treatise is an information source, which the reader will turn to time and time again as construction project demands unwind and develop.

Supranational construction law lives and develops primarily through arbitration. Arbitration awards are not systematically published and the counsel who practice in the field "learn by doing." Unfortunately, the benefits of experience of arbitration are seldom passed down to other participants of construction projects (including to those whom counsel represent). The book is generously enriched and illustrated by case studies and references to arbitration awards, decisions, and findings of arbitration tribunals. It is an entertaining and excellent supplement to the black letter law.

We have all been told to write in plain, easy-to-understand terms, to avoid legalese and to employ construction industry terms where possible while maintaining accuracy. This is not always an easy thing to do. The title successfully implements these principles and empowers its readers to steer the construction project.

1 International Construction Projects

1.1 The unique nature of the construction industry

The construction industry does not have clearly defined borders and its characteristics range from simple to complex. Construction supplies basic materials (such as aggregate, cement, steel reinforcement, and pre-packaged mixtures) right up to cutting-edge technology developed and used by experts. The industry has contributed to, and is a vital element of, almost everything we see around us. For example, the diversion of water courses, land reclamation, houses, shopping centers, offices, factories, health care facilities, and large infrastructure-related civil engineering works such as bridges, tunnels, highways, airports, and harbors. Others installations include water treatment plants, dams, nuclear power plants, wind power plants, and projects in the field of electricity generation. The contribution made by the construction of factories, warehouses, and production lines that serve other industries, (including mining and research centres) cannot be ignored. The particular activities relate not only to new construction works, but also repairs, extensions, reconstructions, and demolitions.

The diverse nature of the construction industry reflects the complexity of contemporary society as a whole, leading then to necessary specialization of particular activities in construction. A construction project is further composed of complex processes, services, and supplies reaching beyond the scope of this industry alone. For example, insurance, financing, bonds and guarantees, purchase of plant and equipment, security guards, operations, and maintenance of work processes.

1.2 Individuality of construction projects

A construction project is a specific process or, rather, a sum of many processes. Mostly, it is an individual process. There are variables relating to the positions of its participants, their assignments and relationships, external conditions (concerning the economy, the nature of the site, climatic conditions, project risk, and hazard levels in general), project management and delivery methods, procurement methods, and public support.

Construction projects face hazards of various kinds, caused either by humans or natural elements. Therefore, people, time and environmental elements play a major part here. The construction project itself tends to be a unique setup of processes with unpredictable impacts caused by individual hazards. For large construction projects, their duration will often exceed two years. These projects are realized over extensive areas and are often difficult to safeguard perfectly. Therefore, a construction project is not a production line you can just program to smoothly create a product, within a well-defined time, quality, and financial outlay.

Design errors, extremely adverse climatic conditions, unforeseeable on-site conditions in physical or social terms, site access-related issues, building permit problems, delays due to the requirements of environmentalists, and variations are just some examples of potential complications.

Effective risk management must be the aim of everyone involved in a construction project. In other words, to identify patterns and potential problems, variations, hazards, and risks in order to manage them effectively. This can only be achieved through the perfect preparation of each particular project. This is the theory.

However, in practice, the lowest bid price tends to be the most important criterion in public tender evaluations nowadays. This is also a reason why contracts (for works or for design) that determine particular project relations must anticipate and involve transparent, efficient, and reasonable solutions to potential problems and complications.

1.3 Roles and relationships

In the course of time, five main groups of construction project participants have emerged as major players in the construction industry. These groups are directly involved in construction projects or have an influence or a particular function within the industry. They are the contractors, designers, regulators, employers and users (Murdoch and Hughes, 2008). Lenders (banks), insurance, and reinsurance companies must also be mentioned as further (indirect) construction project participants because of their significant influence on construction projects. We will now discuss these important roles in the construction project.

1.3.1 Contractors

Most frequently, contractors can be encountered as either global or local construction companies. Construction companies differ in specialization and size—from small contractors for specialized activities up to supranational organizations that enjoy major industrial and political influence.

In the field of large construction projects, contractors often collaborate within joint ventures, setting up delivery chains at numerous levels. A general contractor enters into relationships with the subcontractors who further delegate parts of their obligations down to other specialized trade contractors, and so on down the chain. A particular delivery method will influence the positions of the individual contractors.

1.3.2 Designers

The role of a designer is to provide the employer with solutions, drawings, and specifications. Working on a construction project, the designer will often provide project management, contract administration and supervision services to the employer. When hearing the word "designer," one usually imagines an individual, but less often a company providing the services in support of construction project realization. Today, the latter prevails, as design works becomes ever more demanding and too large to be dealt with by an individual on their own.

1.3.3 Regulators

In the construction industry, regulators apply their professional expertise, for example, in the following areas:

- land planning and related processes;
- building permit applications;
- health and safety;
- environmental issues;
- quality assurance;
- to ensure fair business competition; and
- to ensure proper management of public resources.

1.3.4 Employers

Project realization by the contractor is a service to the employer. Someone about to build a house for their family may be an employer. A developer, who is funding a shopping center construction to sell to potential operators, may be an employer. The employer themselves may be a future owner or an operator.

A taxpayer, who is financing public projects via a public authority in the fields of transportation, infrastructure, construction of prisons, health care facilities, and so on, can also be considered an employer. An employer's characteristics depend, therefore, on whether the related funds are public or private. Significant differences between the private and public employers can be encountered. For example, in France, the contractor cannot suspend the works if the employer does not pay for the works performed in a public project. The so-called *"l'exception d'inexécution"* known in private projects in France cannot be used. According to Article 48-3 CCAG Travaux 1976, the contractor can suspend the works only after three unpaid monthly invoices (Wyckoff, 2010).

In contracts, the employer is often referred to as "the owner," "the buyer" or "the client," and so on. For the purposes of this book, we will mainly use the term "the employer."

1.3.5 Users

All of us are users of products that are the result of construction efforts—whether we like it or not. Our views on construction projects are often subjective and vary for many different reasons. Other vital aspects are how the public perceive the inconvenience and nuisance that can occur during the course of construction or if the public really think that there is a need for a particular building. Specific traditions and cultural influences of the relevant society are a significant factor as well.

As a field of activity, the construction industry is traditionally burdened by uncertainties that may cause distrust between the employer and the user.

1.4 Contract administration

Construction contracts are different from other commercial agreements because of the high degree of uncertainty. While the contract documents will provide a definition of the scope of works to be performed, a high degree of project complexity still leaves a lot of room for uncertainty along the way to the final result. This makes the task of administering the contract an important part of the larger process of "managing uncertainty."

Furthermore, the question of "moral hazard" is sometimes mentioned (Winch, 2010), that is, the difficulties the employer can face in ensuring that the contractor will perform the contract in good faith and bring it to its desired outcome. As a rule, the contractor possesses better technical and managerial skills than the employer. The absence of a proper contract that will provide clear terms and procedures regarding all relevant aspects and an efficient risk allocation may leave the less-informed employer exposed to the risks associated with moral hazard and suffering from a potentially severe compromise regarding the desired outcome.

On the other hand, large public procurement construction projects are often accompanied by political irresponsibility on the employer's side, mainly when problems are encountered. Nobody wants to be responsible for cost overruns and delays. To avoid responsibility, employers sometimes shift the risk of negative consequences of badly prepared projects onto contractors (e.g., delayed expropriation risk or bad ground conditions risk in underground works). Such "one-sided contracts" actually negatively affect the smooth implementation of projects and consequently are considered disadvantageous to the borrowers due, among other things, to the late completion of the project (JICA, 2011). If this is done systematically, it is also dangerous for society. From a socioeconomic point of view, it leads to frustration and a waste of resources in the short term and more expensive construction works and damage to the local economy over the long term.

Corruption is another "moral hazard," which is much more serious and can cause damages to the construction industry as a whole.

There are certain well-known rules of risk allocation. The ultimate rule is that risk allocation must be efficient and if there is a non-insurable risk that is hard to quantify, the risk should be borne by the one who bears the majority benefit. It is self-evident who bears the majority benefit if it is a public construction project. In this case, it is the employer and the users. Furthermore, the state as an employer is often the stronger party (applying a take it or leave it approach to contracts). Thus it seems to be appropriate to apply the principles of protection of the weaker party (the contractor) in such public construction projects.

Another principle that must be stressed is the principle of good faith protection. The governing law usually does not protect the one who is not fair, misuses their position and, as in the case of public employers, invites contractors to deliver projects where risks are speculatively shifted onto contractors and the terms of reference of the particular contract happens to be a sophisticated trap.

Another problem seems to be the fact that international contract forms are often "imported" to developing countries. Naturally they are less familiar to the local employers in both legal terms and working procedures (Banica, 2013). Employers in both the private and public sectors do not pay enough attention to the uneven knowledge asymmetry when facing and entering an agreement with a contractor, as well as to the need to manage this risk through contractual means and by employing a consultant as contract administrator or project manager. Employers tend to show an exaggerated optimism and focus extensively on establishing an initial contract price, without a clear understanding of the importance of setting clear rules regarding the management of change, regardless of the source of the change such as claims, variations, disputes, additional work, and so on (Banica, 2013).

Add to this the fact that the construction industry in developing countries (still in the first stages of modernization) has not yet formed a body of knowledge or produced a significant number of contract managers/consultants familiar with international contracting and procurement practice and the local specificities and working culture (Banica, 2013).

The position of the "contract administrator" is of key importance. A contract administrator hired by the employer on a professional service agreement basis deals with coordination, monitoring, supervision of compliance with standards, certifies the works done, testing, taking over, participates in variation, price and time management, claim evaluation, contract interpretation, and dispute avoidance. They should help to complete a successful project in a fair way and in accordance with the contract, achieving the demanded standard in the agreed time and for the agreed price.

The contract by itself is not enough to solve the problem of moral hazard and the asymmetry of knowledge between the employer and the contractor. The second key element required is the presence of a third contractual party—namely, the contract administrator (Banica, 2013).

In terms of contract administration, there are three usual arrangements in force:

- The "engineer" as an employer's agent, whose job is to monitor and supervise the work, whose duty is to make fair determinations on certain matters (e.g., on claims for extension of time and additional payments; see an example of such determination in Appendix B). The engineer issues certificates on payments, taking over, and performance.
- The employer's representative where the contract is administered directly by the employer or its representative. This is often the case in small projects or under EPC or PPP project with large shift of risk to the contractor.

- The construction manager as an employer's agent hired to coordinate all processes on a professional service agreement basis without direct responsibility for design and works (see Chapter 3).

1.4.1 The Engineer

The engineer's rights and duties consist simultaneously of two parts. The first is acting on the employer's behalf, where the contractor can take the engineer's conduct as the employer's conduct and misconduct (such as the engineer's instructions regarding variations). Acting in their second role, the engineer is an impartial third party who is professionally skilled to maintain an equitable balance between the contractor and the employer (such as in settling disputes). The independence of the engineer (an entity/person appointed and funded by the employer), often becomes the topic of numerous debates. It is in the interests of all construction project participants to ascertain and clarify the engineer's competencies to limit disputes about who will, in fact, act as the engineer on a particular project. The question, "What are the attributes of the engineer and when can a party be said to have tacitly accepted someone as the engineer?" (ICC, 2009) was answered, for example, in the ICC case no. 10892 (the tribunal found that the engineer was the employer itself in this case).

A competent engineer (allowed to do their work by the employer) is in many cases a mandatory prerequisite for a successful construction project. A company or a group of consulting engineers and designers are mostly acting in the role of "engineer." Their specific representatives have to be appointed for particular activities. An engineer can also be an employee of the employer, but this may be a problematic approach in practice. In respect of this, Jaeger and Hök (2010, p. 222) refer to a decision of the Arbitration Court of the International Chamber of Commerce. In this case, the arbitrators dealt with the replacement of the engineer with an employee of the employer (where the employer was a statutory body). According to the arbitrators, this replacement resulted in contract frustration. The authors support the view that it is unacceptable for the employer and the engineer to come from the same organization. However, in this case, the International Federation of Consulting Engineers (FIDIC) conditions included an express impartiality clause.

As a rule, the engineer's individual rights and duties are assigned by a particular agreement with the employer. The engineer is typically entitled to give the contractor instructions related to work executed (and to remedy any defects) and the contractor is obliged to follow their instructions. The engineer must usually, for example, clarify any ambiguities and discrepancies should they appear in the contract. But it is not within the engineer's powers to change the contract—they are not, therefore, empowered to relieve either of the parties of their duties, commitments, or responsibilities arising from the contract. Their assignment does not exempt the contractor from any liability they have under the contract.

The engineer should be a professional with all necessary skills and experience, and have a good knowledge of the contract and contractual procedures (e.g., methods of re-measurement, extension of time procedures, and so on). The engineer should be able to foresee all legal, commercial, and technical consequences of their instructions, particularly those that lead to variations. They should be able to fairly evaluate the adequacy of new rates or prices where it is necessary to create them. The engineer should also be able to fairly determine—in terms of claims—additional payment or extensions of time for completion (Jaeger and Hök, 2010).

According to the FIDIC CONS MDB/Red Book (2005 MDB Edition), the engineer has the following roles (JICA, 2011):

1. *Employer's agent*: the engineer provides the following services to conduct the contract management:
   - production of detailed design drawings under Sub-Clause 1.9;
   - issuance of instructions for variation of the works under Sub-Clause 13.1;
   - review of plans and drawings submitted by the contractor under Sub-Clause 4.1;
   - carrying out project management services including time and cost management, quality control, testing and inspection, safety and environmental management under various Sub-Clauses especially 8.3, 13, 7, 9, and 4.9.
2. *Certifier*: the engineer issues various certificates certifying the quality of the contractor's performance and payment is therefore at the engineer's discretion. The engineer's certificates have a strong binding effect on both the employer and the contractor. Examples of certificates follow:
   - taking over certificate under Sub-Clause 10.1;
   - certification of work completion date under Sub-Clause 11.9;
   - interim payment certificate under Sub-Clause 14.6;
   - defect liability certificate under Sub-Clause 4.9;
   - final payment certificate under Sub-Clause 14.13.
3. *Determiner in claim settlement*: The contractor and the employer have a right to claim settlement from the engineer. The engineer should consult with both parties on the matter in question based on Sub-Clause 3.5 in order to come to an agreement. If the consultation reaches an impasse, a fair determination should be made based on the contract.

1.4.2 The Engineer's certifications and fair determinations

Within the scope of their activities, the engineer can issue various types of certificates. The FIDIC forms, for example, presume numerous certificates. These include mentioned interim payment certificates, final payment certificates, taking over certificates, and performance certificates. Pursuant to the FIDIC forms, any approval, check, certificate, consent, examination, inspection, instruction, notice, proposal, request, test, or similar act by the engineer (including absence of disapproval) shall not relieve the contractor of any responsibility they have under the contract. This includes responsibility for errors, omissions, discrepancies and non-compliances. Pursuant to FIDIC forms, for example, it further applies that the engineer may, in either of the payment certificates, make any correction or modification that should have properly been made to any previous payment certificate. A payment certificate alone shall not be deemed to indicate the engineer's acceptance, approval, consent, or satisfaction.

Under FIDIC, whenever the employer or the contractor submits a claim, the engineer is required, in the first instance, to mediate between the parties to facilitate agreement. If the parties cannot agree, the engineer must make "a fair determination in accordance with the contract, taking due regard of all relevant circumstances." Accordingly, any determination must express the rights and obligations of the parties in accordance with the contract and applicable law, irrespective of any preference expressed, or pressure exerted by either party.

In terms of engineer certifications, it is very interesting to compare the opinions of lawyers from different countries (available at: http://globalarbitrationreview.com) who responded to the following questions:

1. When must a certifier under a construction contract act impartially, fairly, and honestly?
2. To what extent are the parties bound by certificates (where the contract does not expressly empower a court or arbitral tribunal to open up, review, and revise certificates)?
3. Can the contractor bring proceedings directly against the certifier?

- *England and Wales*: Where a person is employed by the employer under a construction contract to issue certificates or make decisions as part of the administration of the contract, he is required to act in accordance with the contract, fairly and impartially, and holds the balance between the employer and the contractor. Whether or not a certificate is binding and conclusive will depend upon the interpretation of the contract as a whole. If the contract, properly interpreted, provides that a certificate is to be binding and conclusive, the grounds for attacking such a certificate are much narrower. Inclusion of an express power for arbitrators to open up, review, and revise certificates is necessary if arbitrators are to have that power. By contrast, no express wording is required in order for the courts to have the power to open up, review and revise certificates, and so on. Nevertheless, the absence of the open-up review and revised wording does not necessarily mean that the certificate cannot be challenged in arbitration. Unless the contract provides that a certificate is to be binding and conclusive, it can be attacked on various grounds, including where the certifier acted outside his jurisdiction, dishonestly or partially in issuing the certificate or where the certificate is otherwise defective as a matter of form, substance or intent.

  Where the certificate can be opened up, reviewed, revised, or otherwise challenged, the contractor will, unlikely, have a cause of action directly against the certifier. Absent the ability to challenge certificates, it is possible that the contractor may be able to proceed directly against the certifier but the contractor would have to show that the certifier owed it a duty of care in issuing the certificate and that the certifier was in breach of that duty. This will depend upon the facts (Choat and Long at globalarbitrationreview.com).

- *France*: Architects or engineers who verify payment certificates as part of their supervision of the works must act with due care within the scope defined in their contract with the employer. The extent to which parties are bound by certificates will generally depend on contractual terms. Where there is an over-certification of payments, the certifier may be held jointly liable with the contractor. Administrative case law also shows that a contractor can bring proceedings against the certifier (Gillion and Rosher at globalarbitrationreview.com).

- *Germany*: A certifier under the construction contract is obligated to act impartially, fairly and honestly. Such obligation derives from its mandate/contract with the parties and—depending on the nature of the certifier—from its administrative duties deriving from his or her official role as (state-certified) certifier. The parties are generally not bound by certificates, but may have them reviewed under the construction contract's dispute resolution regime. Claims may be brought against the certifier him or herself outside of the contract by both the contractor and the employer as obligations and duties of care are created through the mandate to certify certain facts in connection with the construction contract (Kremer at http://globalarbitrationreview.com).
- *Ireland*: There is an implied contractual obligation for the certifier to act independently, fairly and impartially as between the contractor and the employer. It is not unusual in Ireland for the employer to appoint an employee within its organization as an employer's representative and certifier under the construction contract. The commonly held position in Ireland prior to 2007 was that a contractor was entitled to enforce an interim payment certificate by way of summary judgment as a debt due. Following the decision of the Irish High Court in *Moohan & Bradley Construction Limited v. S&R Motors Limited* (2007), contractors operating under the standard RIAI contract terms can no longer rely on being awarded summary judgment in court on interim certificates where a valid defence is raised. In such cases, even where judgment is granted, the execution of that judgment may be stayed pending the outcome of an arbitration hearing on all the issues between the parties (Killoran, O'Higgins, and Cooney at http://globalarbitrationreview.com).
- *Korea*: (1) A certifier or an engineer is administered under the *Construction Technology Management Act* ("the Act"), which categorizes the work scope of a certifier into three different areas: design, inspection and survey, and construction. The Act requires any certifier to act honestly, with dignity and in the interests of quality improvement. (2) The parties are bound by certificates to the extent required by the contract, but these are not mandatory requirements for the completion of the works under the contract. (3) The contractor may bring proceedings directly against a certifier based on wrongful conduct and is able to claim damages for tort liabilities, which is also stipulated in the Act (Oh and Park at http://globalarbitrationreview.com).

1.4.3 The Engineer's responsibilities and liabilities

Under the conditions of the contract with their employer, the engineer is responsible for the duties they undertake (designer, agent, supervisor, certifier, adjudicator). The engineer under FIDIC forms owes a duty of care also to the contractor in exercising their discretion in a neutral manner within the terms of the contract, and having regard to all circumstances. This duty of care exists alongside the other duties which may be imposed in tort under the governing law in order to avoid causing physical loss or damage or, in some cases, economic loss, with or without physical damage. The engineer may be responsible (and liable) for negligent design and supervision, negligent under-certification, negligent statements and instructions, lack of cooperation, lack of prevention of damage, and so on. The engineer is also responsible against third parties. The potential liability and the form and extent of liability depend on the governing law (Bunni, 2005).

Engineer's power to re-rate due to substantial increase in BoQ quantities by Albert Yeu (Hong Kong)

It has long been a debate in remeasurement contracts about the use of bills of quantities rates in valuation of variations, omitted BoQ items, and sometimes change of contract scope. In a standard government form for civil engineering works, a term provides that *"should the actual quantity of work executed in the contract be substantially greater or less than that stated in the bills of quantities and if in the opinion of the engineer such increase or decrease shall render the rate unreasonable or inapplicable, the engineer shall determine as appropriate increase or decrease of the rate of the item using the bills of quantities rate as the basis."*

What amounts to a substantial increase or decrease is not defined and sometimes elusive. In an appellate case *The Secretary for Justice v. Sun Fook Kong (Civil) Limited (HCCT 94/1997)*, the court supported the arbitrator's narrow interpretation of substantial increase or decrease in relation to the method of working or the economics of a working method. The arbitrator said that, in order to justify a re-rate, the engineer would have to be satisfied that, as a result of the change in quantities, there was a change in the method of working of which change itself led to a saving in costs. The court supported that if there had been no change in the method of working, it is difficult to see how there could be any change in the economics of a working method. The only legitimate basis for decreasing a BQ rate was that the increase in the quantity decreased the actual costs of the contractor. So the profit margin of the unit item shall not be altered.

The other contention was about one cubic meter BQ items against actually quantities at least 20 times higher. The arbitrator equally concluded the quantities were not substantially higher and no reason found to re-rate. The court disagreed with this finding but did not grant leave of the appeal unless the question of law concerned could substantially affect the rights of one or more of the parties. The court presupposed the same arbitral judgment if the arbitral award were to be remitted to the arbitrator to decide on the merits of change of method of working.

In another appellate case *Maeda Gorp v. Government of HKSAR (CACV 230/2011)*, the situation reversed. Here, the arbitrator ordered discovery of a rate buildup and concluded that the increase in quantity rendered the application of the original rate both unreasonable and inapplicable. He took the view that if there is an obvious increase in quantity, an obvious disproportion between the rate and the nature of the work covered by the rate, a composite nature of the item and an uncertainty as to what costs the rate included, then to apply such rate to a significantly increase or decrease in quantity of work will be unreasonable since the contractor will be over-reimbursed in the case of an increase in quantity or under-reimbursed in the case of a decrease in quantity. The court found for the arbitrator's inquiry as to the buildup of the rate was reasonable. It did not reconcile with the method of working or economics of working method as contributing factors toward the re-rate power.

To bridge the gap, it is the pro-arbitration nature of Hong Kong courts that reinforces Hong Kong's position as an attractive seat for commercial dispute resolution. The courts uphold the independence and finality of arbitration and the minimum court intervention objective of the arbitration law. When a tribunal takes an inquisitorial role to open up a composite rate to find the pricing intention, it is not easy for the court to find a serious doubt in this exercise or it is obviously wrong to do so, where the Arbitration Ordinance (Cap. 341) confers the court this power to interfere the arbitral proceedings on the ground of errors of law. The result was favored by the limiting courts interference rather than an analysis of a point of law and might have been different if the arbitrator did not order a discovery of the tender breakdown. However, it will jeopardize uncertainty of the law if the decision is reversed just because the tender breakdown is available in one case but not another. A persisting battle on varying a tender rate will continue between one of these cases with the tribunal's power to order discovery of documents conferred by the Arbitration Ordinance.

Albert Yeu
Chartered Civil Engineer, HKIAC Arbitrator
KLRCA Adjudicator, HKMAAC Mediator
Expert Witness

1.5 Further important aspects of construction projects

A construction project is a temporary configuration of processes—a temporary multi-organization. Every construction project will bring together large numbers of people in their joint efforts who are aware of the temporary nature of the project. Large numbers of professionals and specialists cooperate within every construction project.

Employers, designers, and contractors are the most frequent, direct participants in construction projects. Large construction projects also have large numbers of employed people representing these direct participants. Each of them is an employee of an organization and, frequently, a member of a professional association with different interests, roles and priorities. It is therefore important to set up an efficient method of management and organization within a particular project to help create a common synergy for construction project success. It is equally important to establish a certain positive social atmosphere to help overcome problems that accompany every construction project.

A typical yet important issue that often arises is a change in the function of the engineer, contractor, or employer's representatives over the course of the project. The removal or replacement of a vital project management position can cause confusion and lead to technical complications, contract price increases, and delays.

Representatives of construction project participants have various levels of knowledge, different specializations, and varying interests. As a result, the competency and authority of these parties may be unclear. When things go wrong, it is not unusual for some people to avoid responsibility completely and for others to unfairly get the blame. It is extremely difficult to harmonize the interests of all participants.

It must be remembered that the duty to deliver value for money, quality, and timeliness prevails over individual interests.

1.5.1 Overlap of construction project phases

Three phases of a construction project can be distinguished: preparation, design, and realization. The operating phase, if any, can be seen as a part of the realization of the project. Often intentionally or inevitably, these phases overlap with each other. The overlap of the design and realization phases may appear in cases of Design-Build Projects (see Chapter 3). This may speed up construction or make it more effective where a variation in, or clarification of, the design becomes necessary during realization. Variation management (or change management) is a key aspect of project management in construction and a contract must be the main instrument used to define respective procedures.

1.5.2 Admissibility of variations and the need for variation management

The emergence of unforeseen events in construction projects is inevitable. It can almost be guaranteed that a large construction project will deviate from the employer's, designer's, or contractor's original vision. The ability to foresee such modifications in the contract and provide respective solutions from the outset is critical to avoiding disputes. Good contracts envisage this and therefore contain variation clauses and procedures (see Chapter 8).

Obviously, variations administered on the basis of a variation clause cannot imply breach of contract, as it is the contract which enables variation. When used in a contract, the variation procedures include, for example, the way to propose the variation, a form of instruction to vary, periods, pricing method, and sample variation orders.

1.6 Typical contractual relationships

Typical contractual relationships among direct construction project participants are mainly expressed in contracts for works, contracts for purchases, and professional service agreements.

The fundamental risk allocation and delivery method must be stipulated in a contract between the employer and main contractor. This is the "main contract." Other contracts arise within the delivery chains. A joint venture agreement is also common and important in practice.

Further contractual relationships arise in connection with insurance (see Chapter 14) and securities (see Chapter 16).

Shipping and marine construction contracts in Asia by Knut Kirkhus (Oman)

Shipping and marine contracts are represented by various standard forms of contracts used in the offshore oil and gas industry, drilling and exploration and shipbuilding and marine constructions. There are several initiatives to standardize such contracts using assorted model form of agreement consisting of marine constructions, constructions, well services, design, mobile drilling rigs, supply of major items of plant of equipment, purchase order terms and conditions (short form), small/medium enterprises (SME) services and subcontract small/medium enterprises (SME) services.

In terms of standard forms of contract used, shipping and marine construction contracts appear in various forms, such as LOGIC former CRINE (cost reduction in new era; initiative with the objective of reducing costs by 30% and helping to simplify the industry's procedures; LOGIC currently supports a suite of 10 standard contracts that are available for use throughout the oil and gas industry) standard for the North Sea offshore oil and gas industry, IADC (International Association for Drilling Contractors) standard drilling contracts for contractors where the length of such contract usually is determined by the number of wells the operator wants to drill. It must be decided whether a term contract or a contract for a specific number of wells is best for the specific program. The use of a long-term contract is usually driven by market conditions, with a tight rig market usually resulting in term contracts. This is especially true if a new rig build is involved; the drilling contractor's financial institutions may require a reasonable payback on the loan before the contractor can sign a contract and build the unit. Others use FIDIC standards or tailor made EPC contracts, they all are negotiated to different degrees depending on the contract complexity, value of the contract, the level of risk involved, specifically the risk of overcapacity (as a site condition), with reference to for instance the shipbuilding yards in Korea and China, which has been flooded with many new construction orders, and the existence of country specific forms that may also dictate terms.

In South Korea, for example, the Standard contracts are published by the Ministry of Land, Infrastructure and Transport (MOLIT) and the Korean Fair Trade Commission (KFTC). For government projects, the General Terms and Conditions of Construction Contracts (GTCCC) are published by the Ministry of Strategy and Finance (MSF) and serve as the general terms and conditions, whereas special terms may be added based on the relevant project.

For private projects, there are no standardized forms of contract, and as the GTCCC are not mandatory they have however been widely used.

For large-scale shipping and marine construction projects, the parties separately negotiate and agree the terms of the contract. Usually, the terms agreed are tailor made close to FIDIC standard forms rather than the GTCCC. The terms usually discussed is about the concept of corresponding IFC (issued for construction) MTOs (material take off) dates from company, the accuracy of IFC MTO, re-measurement of quantity between FEED (front-end engineering design) MTO and the final MTO and the specific definition and agreement for the final MTO in the contract as the parties may have different view in their interpretations.

However, shipbuilding contracts, which have basis in Japanese standard shipbuilding contracts made by the SAJ (Shipbuilders' Association of Japan) standard from 1970 to 1980 are still being used. At that time there existed over 5,000 shipbuilding yards. It was published by SAJ in January 1974 and the framework of this form is still commonly used in South Korea, China, Singapore, and Taiwan. These contracts initially was drafted to protect more the ship owners and relayed most risk to the shipbuilder.

In the past, claims for upward adjustments of the contract price due to extensions of time were not common in practice because the contractors rarely raised them, in many cases it was culturally negative to discuss or admit to any form of delay caused by the client and this is why the issue was usually hidden and incorporated into other contractual issues for negotiation.

But as the courts in South Korea are given more supportive judgments the contractors are raising more claims, which consequently have resulted in a significant increase of extension of time claims.

Due to the volatile and high oil prices in the recent years the shipping and marine market became friendlier, which gave cause to higher rates and favorable terms. However, as the oil prices dramatically decreased, most oil companies had to consequently cut their budget for oil expenditures, and subsequently reduce cost on existing shipping and marine contracts and press to achieve better terms (such as lower ship rates) on their new contracts.

Oil companies will continue to be affected by the current volatile oil and gas market and with reduced prices on various levels. It will affect how they are tied in to long term shipping and marine construction contracts, and they will experience maybe further revenue funds, and be forced to cancel or renegotiate terms of these contracts. Inescapably, this will lead to an increase in contract disputes.

According to the Asia-Pacific Arbitration Review 2018 (Duncan Speller, Jane Rahman and Jonathan Lim): *"Given the importance of the oil and gas sector to the Asia-pacific economics, it is perhaps unsurprising that oil and gas arbitrations have increased in both prominence and frequency. … out of 72 LNG disputes observed globally since 2010, there has been no reports of arbitrations brought by Japanese, Chinese or Korean LNG Asian market participants. Not much information is publically available and there are suggestions that Asian market participants prefer to negotiate rather than arbitrate price adjustment issues."*

As for new shipping and marine construction contracts the oil companies, beyond their obvious desire to gain lower ship rates, still want increase flexibility in the contract terms, rebalance the risk/reward profile, and reduce the fixed cost elements of the contract.

Awareness and understanding of critical terms including international construction contract standards that may be integral part to a shipping and marine agreement is of paramount importance during the negotiation process to minimize the incidence of misunderstandings and conflict during and after execution.

A recent typical case I was engaged with was a ground conditions risk dispute between Songa Offshore, an offshore drilling contractor, and South Korea's shipbuilder Daewoo Shipbuilding and Marine Engineering Co. Ltd. (DSME) regarding a construction contract for the Songa Equinox drilling CAT D rigs (a series of four rigs) built by DSME. Songa received claim submissions from DSME in which DSME asserts a claim of $329 million, along with a request for repayment of liquidated damages in a total amount of $43.8 million, totaling $372.8 million. DSME alleges that the cost overrun is caused by inherent errors and omissions in the design documents (often referred to as the FEED package). According to Songa DSME was responsible for the delays and any attempt to recover cost overruns was of no merit due to the "turn-key" nature of the construction contract.

CAT D—are new tailor made mobile offshore drilling rigs—designed by the industry on behalf of Statoil (Norwegian international energy company and the world's largest offshore operator) for mature fields on the Norwegian continental shelf (NCS). These new drilling rigs can easily be converted for work in deep water, high-pressure high-temperature (HPHT) operations and the artic regions.

As a fair viewpoint from this case would be to continue to endeavor to be prepared for the complexity and the nature of future shipping and marine construction contracts, especially on risk allocation, awareness and understanding of the contractual terms. To continue striving

> to avoid poorly drafted or incomplete and unsubstantiated claims and to cleverly manage the utilization of highly skilled contracts and claims resources proportionate to the complexity of awarded contracts.
>
> Knut H. Kirkhus
Contract Manager
Sultanate of Oman

1.7 Motivation for international business

The construction industry and construction projects were, traditionally, local by nature. Construction contractors and their employers were typically limited to businesses/projects in their geographical area. These days, by contrast, the construction industry is witnessing globalization. Integrated processes, newly emerging supranational formations, government programs supporting investment, the expansion and development of means of communication, social networks, increased mobility of goods, capital, and labor, have all had a major impact on the construction industry.

The fall of socialism and the consequent liberalization in the 1980s in Eastern Europe and Russia led to a relaxation of the formerly protective policies in many countries. The end of central planning created new opportunities for construction companies from First World countries in the West where the infrastructure was already well developed.

Preconditions for international construction business expansion can include any of the following: implementation of clear and open international rules of commerce, foreign investment incentives, availability of credit, trade agreements, contract law modification, development of alternative dispute resolution, international treaties on investment protection, enforceability of arbitration awards, and protection of new technologies under intellectual property laws—particularly in terms of EPC contractors in oil, gas, and energy projects.

Global companies are using their know-how, synergy, and financial strength to expand their business. In numerous developing and Third World countries, foreign companies have acquired state-owned companies or entered into joint ventures with local private companies.

Contrasting examples of international projects in a globalized world can include a small warehouse for an international vendor, a complex strategic energy project with the involvement of several countries as employers or an international joint venture as a contractor under different applicable laws and rules of dispute resolution. The element of internationality can mainly be found in the place where the project is implemented, in the parties to the contract, in the procurement and contracting procedure, and in the technical and legal standards.

Cross-border projects foster competition, but also put pressure on employers to properly manage international tenders in terms of how to engineer, procure, construct, and supervise work. In the case of public tenders, an employer must, first of all, be able to ensure proper preparation of the project. In particular, to provide funding, obtain building permits and provide access to the site including archaeological surveys and settlements with utility owners and land owners. Local laws must be ready for international construction projects, mainly in terms of public procurement, construction law, environmental protection, technical and quality-related standards, commercial contractual relationships, dispute resolution, and competition law. The employer must provide appropriate design documentation and technical specifications. Most importantly, the employer must provide the people well qualified enough to act as their competent representatives/agents in the other country. Last but not least, the employer must select an appropriate delivery method (see Chapter 3). The risks that result from shortcomings in the mentioned domains complicate financing, tender procedures, and sometimes can even jeopardize the implementation of a particular construction project.

The above-mentioned risks will obviously prolong the realization and increase the cost of construction projects. Therefore, the international construction business is very demanding for construction companies that want to conduct their ventures abroad. By the same token, local companies are challenged by international competition. Ventures abroad increase demands on the employees of both local and international contractors. Recruiting and educating these employees form one of the most demanding missions of an international construction contractor.

The primary motivation of a contractor for an international venture is either "offensive" or "defensive." Here, the "attack" is to be perceived as a proactive, strategic decision ensuring another business opportunity to sustain growth and the "defense" is to be perceived as a response to a lack of work and opportunity in the country of origin.

An interesting case study of a unique international project was presented at the 2012 International Engineering and Infrastructure Congress (Scott, 2018). Fredric S. Berger, the chairman of the Louis Berger Group, Inc. shared with the attendees his firm's experience in carrying out a US$250 million project in 2003 to reconstruct 384 km of roadways and bridges in Afghanistan from Kabul to Kandahar. The firm was given an eight-month deadline and the work had to be carried out while military operations were proceeding. "We had a war going on," he explains in summarizing his remarks at the conference:

> We were working on a road that served 30% of the population but we could not enter because it was in the most heavily land-mined country in the world and had been destroyed by war for over thirty years. So there was no construction machinery, no construction industry, no construction workers, and no construction materials. We not only had to resolve the question of how to get equipment, workers, and materials into the country fast enough [to complete the project on time] but we all had to do that in the context of a threat-prone environment.

Berger says that, after the landmines had been removed from the roads and rock quarries, all of the contractors brought equipment in from outside the country. In some cases it was flown in, and in others it was brought in by road from Pakistan. Berger had to get a special waiver from President Bush for the contractors in Turkey to bring their equipment through Iran. "We had to modify the standard FIDIC contract," says Berger.

We were in a war environment, and we could not allow the contractors to exercise the *force majeure* clauses and shut down their projects. So we pre-negotiated stand-down daily rates so that if there was an incident in their area we could tell them to go inside the camp and lock the gate. So we paid them a fixed rate per day; it was pre-negotiated rather than let the project be shut down.

The Italian construction industry: Between past and future by SDG & Partners (Italy)

Introduction

The Italian construction industry approached foreign markets for the first time during the late first decade of the last century, as a direct consequence of the Italian colonial expansion in Africa.

On the contrary, it is necessary to wait until the second post-war period to note the first significant presence of foreign companies in the Italian market, especially those involved in noteworthy and strategic public tenders.

However, the Italian construction industry remained fundamentally isolated for a long time, since the Italian companies concentrated on operating in their local market and protecting their interests from the curiosity of foreign competitors.

Only with the recent recession (2009–2016) have things began to change.

In order to correctly understand the phenomenon, it is necessary to enlarge the view to the entire Italian industrial model as it evolved during the last half-century; while in Europe, it took root in a number of big corporations that were strongly competitive in both domestic and foreign markets, in Italy, they opted for an industrial-districts based economy.

According to the scholars, the industrial district is essentially defined "*as a socio-territorial entity characterized by the active co-presence, in a limited area, of a community of people and a population of industrial firms.*" And also: "*[...] the district is the concrete form, defined on two dimensions - the industry and the territory - of the principle of increasing returns to the widening of demand in a competitive environment*"(Giacomo Becattini, "Riflessioni sul distretto industriale marshalliano come concetto socio-economico", Stato e Mercato, pp. 111–128 (1989)).

In this context, also the construction field has been for a long time (and partially is still so) typified by a highly pulverized industry structure, with a great number of small companies acting in their own specific territory.

According to ANCE (the Italian national builders' association), in 2012, there were 142,182 enterprises in the construction industry, employing 1.5 million people. Many of these firms are midgets: 60% of them are one-man businesses, whereas 37% have less than 10 employees. Only 0.2% of Italian builders employ more than 50 people, and that's considered large (ANCE, "Osservatorio congiunturale sull'industria delle costruzioni" 2013).

In spite of their dimensions, Italian companies have historically been very efficient in defending their market from the competition of foreign companies. In fact, not only has the Italian legislation always supported and favored the cooperation between single entities, but the same nature of the industrial district model forces the enterprises to join the efforts and operate all together as a single organism.

The situation does not substantially change until the recent crisis of (not only) the construction market: in Italy, in the period 2008 to 2014, the construction industry has lost the 31.7%

of the investments (about 58.800 million Euros) and the current level of the investments is comparable to the level registered in 1967 (ANCE, "Osservatorio congiunturale sull'industria delle costruzioni" 2014).

In this scenario, the Italian construction companies have increased their overseas activities in order to balance the contraction of the domestic market. New international markets have been targeted with *"dynamism and determination"* (Italian Ministry of Foreign Affairs, Press room (10/05/2015): "2015 ANCE Report - Gentiloni, Farnesina and government help enterprise with foreign investment opportunities") the numbers of ANCE Report (ANCE, "Rapporto 2015 sulla presenza delle imprese di costruzione italiane nel mondo") confirm the tenth year of growth for construction firms abroad, with an increase of 10.2% in turnover: over 237% in ten years (from 3 to 10 billion euro).

Although only a small number of Italian companies has the dimension and the capacity to singularly compete on the global markets, as already observed with reference to the protection of the domestic market from the intrusion of foreign competitors, the key brick of such success has been always the same: the cooperation.

*

The Italian cooperation model

Construction projects are generally executed by general contractors who retain the services of special trade subcontractors. This form of organization is preferable to vertically integrating these trades because of the transaction cost implications of construction technology. The general contractor and special trade subcontractors can form a stable organizational unit when conditions permit. This organizational form, is called by the scholars (Robert Eccles, " The quasifirm in the construction industry" in *Journal of Economic Behavior & Organization*, December 1981, pp. 355-357) the "quasifirm" (The "quasifirm" model is analogous to the 'inside contracting system' discussed by Williamson (1975).).

Under the Italian law, the "quasifirm" can be incorporated in a plurality of legal forms.

In detail, the "quasifirm" is frequently incorporated in the form of the Consortium (*Consorzio*), in the form of the Temporary Association of Enterprises (*Associazione Temporanea di Imprese – ATI*) or simply in the form of the Company.

*

The new legislative decree No. 50/2016 in the name of the transparent cooperation

One recent trend in the public procurement sector, the aim of which is greater procedural transparency, is an increase in the range of activities the awarding body must carry out in public sessions (e.g., opening of envelopes that contain the administrative documentation, the technical offer, and the economic offer).

No statistics are available on the cases that ended up in court, nor is there any record of the number of cases involving an application for an ineffectiveness order.

To increase transparency in the public procurement sector, according to article 29 of the Legislative Decree 50/2016, any act of the public procurement procedure must be published on the website of the specific public authority.

We would like to underline how the recently introduced Legislative Decree No. 50/2016 strongly encourages the stable cooperation between single entities, (i) enlarging the number of the legal forms entitled to participate to public tenders and (ii) imposing them to formally undertake the commitment of a long-lasting partnership.

In this respect, please note that the previous art. 34 of Legislative Decree 163/2006 (replaced by the abovementioned provision) permitted to participate to public tender only to few specific entities, without any further requirement about the nature, the purpose, and the duration of such entities.

The new current regulation, therefore, is firstly aimed to strengthen the competitivity of the Italian—not only—construction industry, permitting an easier access to public tenders to cooperating small entities and, meanwhile, to guarantee the respect of the rules in a long-term perspective.

Once again, Italian legislator bets on the cooperation model that, during the decades, represented the Italian way to the economic success.

*

In any case, the new regulations does not change the nature of the legal forms provided for the "quasifirm" by the Italian Civil Code

As previously mentioned, in order to participate to public tender such particular entities are still frequently incorporated under the form of the Stable Consortium, of the Temporary Association of Enterprises (ATI) and of the Company.

The reason of the preference for these legal forms is mainly connected with their better regulation from a civil and fiscal point of view and the consequent lesser operative uncertainty in respect of newer legal forms.

***

Conclusions

The above gives an excellent view of the legal framework within which the construction industry can undertake and perform construction works in Italy.

However, one must not forget that in order to attain the final goal of any construction work under any of the above described contractual solutions, a swift and well-functioning conflict resolution system must exist.

Civil works in particular are historically most likely to give rise to conflicts between the main contractor and the subcontractors.

Unfortunately, the Italian civil judicial system is still (notwithstanding recent changes that go in the right direction) slow compared to international standards.

Therefore, arbitration clauses are a must in any construction contract; in particular the emergency arbitrator clause is very important to quickly decide any issue that could halt or delay the works.

*

SDG & Partners, Milan, Italy
Patrizia Sangalli, FCIArb, Partner
Dario Rizzi, Senior Associate
Alberto Croze, Of Counsel

1.8 Managerial analysis

In the international construction business, careful risk analysis is of the utmost importance. In general, there are two basic levels of risk analysis: (1) the analysis of a particular target market; and (2) the analysis of a particular construction project. Many various management techniques and formulas are used in conducting market analyses. To evaluate the external environment in terms of political, economic, social, technological, environmental, and legal factors and their influences, the PESTEL analysis is often used.

- Tax policy, labor legislation, environmental legislation, restrictions on trade, customs, and political stability reflect how and to what extent the government intervenes in the economy are among the political factors.
- Economic growth, interest rates, exchange rates, inflation rates, and GDP are ranked among the economic factors.
- Social factors comprise cultural aspects such as health care awareness, age structures, the demographics of an ageing population, the value of human life, and emphasis on safety.
- Technological factors include technological aspects such as research and development, automation, levels of innovation, technological stimuli, and the rate at which the technological changes occur.
- Environmental factors are the ecological and environmental aspects (weather, climate, climate change) that may have a major impact on industries such as tourism, agriculture, insurance, and, of course, the construction industry.
- Legal factors concern consumer rights, competition law, labor legislation, health and safety, and commercial law.

Strategic capacities are often explored by means of the SWOT analysis. They are, in particular, resources (i.e., what we have) the competencies (i.e., what we are good at). SWOT stands for *Strengths, Weaknesses, Opportunities* and *Threats*. The questions, therefore, are:

- What are our strengths?
- How can they be exploited?
- How can the impacts of our weaknesses be minimized?
- What are our opportunities?
- How they can be used?
- What are the threats preventing us from making use of these opportunities?
- How can these threats be overcome?

For these reasons, careful analysis and investigation of the internal and external environment are required.

Another popular analysis is the *Porter's Five Forces Analysis*. This can assist in setting up a business analysis framework. The Porter's Five Forces Model defines the forces that determine the level of competition in an industry and, therefore, its attractiveness.

Porter defined two vertical forces—the power of suppliers and employers, along with three horizontal forces—the threat of new competitors in the market, the threat of substitutes, and the threat of established competitors. Having analyzed the external and internal environments, one has to assess the influences on product or business plans and draw up a strategy.

1.9 Hazards and risks

Large construction projects are regularly exposed to numerous hazards. Construction project participants (mainly the employer and the bidding contractor) should identify potential hazards and carry out a systematic risk analysis to assess the respective risks of a particular project properly. Lenders (such as banks) and insurance and re-insurance companies often require a risk analysis before providing loans or insurance. Every contract must contain instruments to cope with foreseeable hazards and risks. A risk can be defined as the probable value of damage caused by the realization of a hazard.

Concerning risk, it is not the contractor's objective to avoid it completely, but to identify and be able to mitigate it in order to achieve a competitive advantage. Three main phases can be distinguished in respect of handling risk:

- hazard identification
- risk analysis
- anti-risk measures.

1.10 Hazard identification

Risk, in principle, is not a bad thing. Naturally, people tend to seek certainty by avoiding change and risk. One can even benefit from risk if one is not afraid of it. In construction, the aim must be to avoid risk and adverse consequences by systematically identifying, analyzing, and taking action.

Individual hazards and associated risks may have different levels of importance in particular projects and must be considered from the point of view of the employer's and the contractor's priorities. In some projects, price will be seen as a priority, in others the time for completion or the highest standard of performance.

A construction project—like any other industrial or non-industrial project—faces external hazards, internal hazards, and mixed hazards. A hazard of external origin can be defined as a hazard arising from the natural technical, economic and social environments in which the project takes place, for example, poor cash flows, religious unrest, floods, aircraft crashes, and unstable currency exchange rates.

A hazard of internal origin, on the other hand, arises from the project itself and includes hazards that threaten the project directly and indirectly. Examples of direct internal hazards include embezzlement, delays, as well as decision-making faults and errors. Indirect internal hazards are those that jeopardize the project in a secondary way and may involve external third parties, for example, disputes with authorities on matters of environmental pollution and activism by environmentalists. The latter may result in disruption through protests or even court-ordered injunctions.

A mixed hazard is one which arises when project management erroneously or inappropriately responds to an external hazard.

Hazards threatening a construction project can be further broken down into two broad groups:

- *anthropogenic hazards*—caused by people in various forms (individuals, groups of individuals, an organization, and the like);
- *natural hazards*—caused by natural elements (storms, earthquakes, black ice, and other natural disasters).

1.11 Risk analysis

Identification of hazards is followed by risk analysis in which the probability of adverse consequences (frequency of occurrences, implications, and the like) are evaluated and lead to a decision regarding the selection of appropriate risk management strategies.

1.12 Anti-risk measures

Measures to be taken to reduce or eliminate risk depend on the decision-maker's financial and human resources as well as on the feasibility and availability of respective measures. Some risks cannot be prevented at all.

In general, in risk analysis, four strategies can be distinguished, called the "4 Ts":

- Take
- Treat
- Transfer
- Terminate.

1.12.1 Take

A risk management strategy that relies on the wilful absence of any precautions and involves accepting the loss (or benefit of gain), from a risk when it occurs. This is a viable strategy where potential risks are small or where the cost of insuring against the risks would be greater over time than any potential losses sustained. The same can be said for risks that are so large that they are either uninsurable or the premiums are unfeasibly high. A solid budget contingency is the only possible way to secure against this kind of risk.

1.12.2 Treat

This risk management strategy is based on risk prevention and allocation. This strategy follows the principle of "prevention being better than cure" and adopts both proactive or reactive approaches. The first rule gives preference to proactive management, which is focused on avoiding hazards so that they are not realized. Complete prevention may not always be feasible so, in this case, hazards need to be effectively mitigated. The realization of a hazard or a risk will always adversely impact upon the project as it may increase prices, cause delay or disruption, and potentially affect output quality. A reactive approach can be taken where proactive management is impossible. In this case, it is necessary to adequately prepare for the realization of potential hazards to mitigate potential, adverse consequences.

Good contracts push the construction project participants toward proactive approaches. This can be implemented through contractual duties such as early warning obligations (i.e., timely notification of events that will have an effect on time or price) and obligations to prevent and mitigate damage.

The treatment of risk also involves an efficient allocation of risk between the project participants. Two principles can be distinguished here. This first is the centralization principle where risk is borne by a single party, and, second, the decentralization principle where risk is borne by the party most able to manage it efficiently.

1.12.3 Transfer

Risk is transferred to a third party against payment, usually in the form of insurance. In fact, the risk always stays with the project participant and the insurer provides an agreed indemnity. Risk may also be shared, such as with a partner in a consortium or joint venture.

1.12.4 Terminate

It is easy to refuse a project because of a potential pending hazard, but "he who doesn't risk never gets to drink champagne."

1.13 Typical hazards in the international construction business

When trying to expand its business abroad, a contractor mainly considers the following areas and issues:

- the political situation or stability of the country and related trend prognoses;
- business-related legislative conditions, opportunities in the market;
- international treaties (e.g., on investment protection), bilateral conventions, diplomatic missions, membership of FIDIC;
- employment of foreign labour (or sending the labor abroad), the taxation, social security, and health insurance payments and other accounting requirements that would follow;
- legislative conditions under which local labor can be employed, the wage and social conditions, protection of health and safety, and visas;
- labor union requirements;
- availability and cost of local lawyers and other counsels;
- public procurement procedures and qualification criteria;

- customs duties, taxes and fees;
- forms and conditions for doing business in a particular market in respect of foreign entities;
- standard forms of contracts and related restrictions, if any, imposed by mandatory law;
- the enforceability of laws, local litigation, local arbitration, and the enforceability of their awards;
- building permit proceedings, the functions of local building authorities, and their control;
- the specifics of the governing law;
- the level of endemic corruption;
- technical standards and their sources, certifications, and licenses;
- the largest private and public employers and the financial institutions and their particulars;
- delivery methods of choice;
- the relationships between employers and contractors;
- the availability of technologies, equipment, labor, and materials;
- the main players in the construction market and their strengths, contractors/suppliers and their references and strengths, a list of suppliers of key materials (steel, concrete, aggregate, sand, cement), power and other utility services;
- passing on of market experience, maturity of business relationships, reliability and availability of local business partners;
- reliability of internet browsers, and electronic sources of information;
- the currency in which the work, materials, plants, and equipment are to be paid;
- insurance availability and requirements;
- availability and requirements of securities (bank guarantees, bonds, suretyships);
- import restrictions, restrictions applicable to foreign companies and subsidies.

Corruption on Peruvian gas pipeline contract by Enrique Moncada Alcantara (Peru)

On June 14, 2014, the Peruvian government awarded consortium "Soth Peruvian Gas Pipeline" (or in Spanish called GSP) with the concession of project that had 1080 kilometers of pipeline and was valued in US$ 7 billion. The original partners of the consortium where Latin America's construction giant Odebrecht with 75% stake and Spanish national gas pipeline operator ENAGAS with 25% stake.

Such a consortium had a contract with the Peruvian government that had main obligations of designing and engineering, building, operating, and maintaining the gas infrastructure. The designing engineering and building obligations where transferred throughout mirror clauses of a EPC Contract with a second consortium called in Spanish "Consorcio Constructor Ductos del Sur" or CCDS, which had as partners the main companies of Odebrecht in Peru: Norberto Odebrecht and Odebrecht Peru Ingenieria y Construccion. Later by the end of the 2015 a new partner appeared, Peru's biggest engineering company Graña y Montero, would take up 20% of stake from Odebrecht, and would have around 29% stake in the construction consortium.

This second consortium made EPC contracts with three different companies, transferring all risks and construction responsibilities, but retaining control through management obligations on compliance of its programs: Environmental Protection, Community and Social affairs, Safety and Security, Pipe Welding, and Quality and Code of Conduct. The building activities started by September 2014, and went on uninterrupted until April 2016, when an important loan was denied to the GSP consortium by the 13 banks in charge of the financing a new loan for the project.

Lava Jato case arriving to Peru

Since the first semester of 2016 it was known in Peru of the urge of Odebrecht to find a buyer of its stake in the GSP consortium, since the banks that originally loaned the project the initial money found out of the Lava Jato case investigations. Back in Brazil the ongoing investigations against Odebrecht Ex-CEO Marcelo Odebrecht and dozens of employees, finally had 19-year sentence for Marcelo Odebrecht, finding him guilty of criminal charges. But no one on Peruvian soil at the time had evidence of a link between this and corruption activities at the highest levels of Peruvian government spheres.

The year 2016 was also a presidential and congress election year, so the election process gave Odebrecht something to avoid media and public scrutiny, but this was not the case when it was made public during the second auction process (September 2016 to January 2017), which occurred after the presidential June election of Pedro Pablo Kucinsky, that the main candidates for buying Odebrecht's stake in GSP were interested in changing the anticorruption clause of the concession contract. This turned the alarms on at the Peruvian Congress and specially because this happened during the last three months of 2016 when the GSP consortium was running out of time. According to the project planning of GSP they had a project finance milestone established for January 23, 2017, which if not accomplished would be a contract breach. As the year 2016 went by and Odebrecht wasn't able to sell its stake, after two failed auctions, it was inevitable to start thinking that something was really wrong with the project.

By December 21, 2016, a report from the U.S. Department of Justice indicates that Odebrecht admitted to having engaged in a massive and unparalleled bribery and bid rigging scheme since 2001. During for about 15 years Odebrecht paid approximately US$ 788 million in bribes to public officers, politicians, and political parties from various countries as to be awarded over 100 projects. The criminal conduct as we mentioned was directed by the highest levels of the company, with bribes paid through a complex network of shell companies, off-book transactions, and off-shore bank accounts.

Among those countries, Peru's officials and politicians had received 29 million dollars from bribes made by Odebrecht. By the time this news had made to Peru (December 22, 2016), the GSP project had been restarted twice and Odebrecht had already twice put on the market its total participation in the GSP consortium. There was no self-exclusion from the consortium, neither was it a declaration of guilt, Odebrecht only complied with the banks requirements to continue financing the projects. The new group of banks required Odebrecht to sell its total stake in GSP consortium as to reduce risk and approve a second project loan, but Odebrecht expected to be paid a part of US$ 2 billion for the works the GSP and CCDS consortiums had advanced, which was around 30% of project progress by April 2016. In order to do so, and according to the trust arrangements, the GSP consortium first had to pay off its loans with the banks, second with its partners (ENAGAS and Graña y Montero), third pay off its employees and fourth pay local government sanctions. After paying of its loans and debts, it could have income. What never was contemplated in those arrangements was paying the three main contractors.

The termination of GSP concession contract

By January 2017, the Odebrecht had pleaded guilty in the United States of the bribery and having a financial department dedicated to funding bribery acts, they had not been able to sell their stake in the GSP consortium, but worst they finally breach the concession contract, the only real blue chip they had on the GSP project. The termination of the GSP concession contract occurred because of:

(a) Breach of the project finance milestone.
(b) The Peruvian government's denial of changing the anticorruption clause of the concession contract.
(c) Odebrecht's plea agreement on corruption activities.

I particularly think that the inflection point for the GSP project was the government position on the anticorruption clause not being negotiable. According to Fernando Zavala—Peruvian Prime Minister—and Guillermo Thorne—Minister of Economy and Finance until July 2017—they had a very upfront and straight strategy with Odebrecht, they wanted no more corruption and they wanted them out of Peru. For this they worked on the Urgency Decree No. 003-2017 that prohibited money or assets transfers to other countries and obligated companies found guilty of corruption activities in Peru and abroad to pay fines. The problem with this anticorruption regulation was judges never had fine calculation guidelines approved, so Odebrecht has tried to sell four of its main projects in Latin America, which all are in Peru, but no transaction has been able to be successful since the Peruvian government has not implemented an adequate calculation system in order for district attorneys to retain any money or the Ministry of Justice approve the project transfer to buyers.

Risk allocation and corruption activities just cross one out of another. Effective risk allocations like influencing the risk magnitude, controlling the effects of risk or incentive of risk reduction does not have to do with corruption. Corruption activities are either black or white, they either qualify as such or they do not, they are not a risk which can be controlled; they are just not accepted by the parties. So this is a basic part of why potential buyers of Odebrechts stakes in the GSP consortium did not have clear. They all thought about being able of changing the contract rules about the anticorruption clause, by indicating that any responsibility corresponded to the previous owner would not affect the new partners in the consortium. Somehow Odebrecht had misguided the potential buyers into thinking that corruption activities are contract risks that can be acceptable by the parties if allocated to a previous stake partner. This risky way of contracting by Odebrecht fortunately was discovered by the Peruvian government, and was understood as clear indicator of Odebrecht's real intentions when later on the U.S. Department of Justice make its findings public.

Enrique Moncada
Responsible for Project Contract Management
Peru-Spain
Elecnor Perú S.A.C.

Anticorruption and construction contract law by Enrique Moncada Alcantara (Peru)

Corruption in its classic sense describes something that has become impure or perverted. In Aristotle's words, "The true forms of government … are those in which [rulers] govern with a view to the common interest; but governments which rule with a view to the private interest … are perversions". Aristotelian corruption as we know it, has served as the fundamental key for democratic systems to aim toward anticorruption measures. For example, U.S. courts since the nineteenth century have worked on different concepts around the terms of "corruption," "intend to influence," or describing bribery acts. To this day, over regulation is not the way U.S. courts and officers are fighting against corruption or looking for a better definition of intend to influence, instead jurors and scholars have proposed that *ex ante* regulation is worked onfor specific situations. These regulations include campaign-finance limitations of the sort today's Supreme Court strikes down, gratuity prohibitions, and ethical codes forbidding the creation of some conflicts of interest. Trying to block all functional equivalents of bribery even through specific, *ex ante* regulations, however, would do more harm than good.

Currently the Supreme Court has defined corruption acts: "[F]or bribery, there must be a *quid pro quo*—a specific intent to give or receive something *in exchange for* an official act," and campaign contributions may be treated as bribes only when "the payments are made in return for an explicit promise or undertaking … to perform or not to perform an official act." In *McCormick v. the United States,* however, the court held that campaign contributions may be treated as bribes only when "the payments are made in return for an explicit promise or undertaking by the official to perform or not to perform an official act." This does not go to extent of making contributions with the general hope of a universal well-being.

As so, general jurors and scholar positions understanding of corruption as a description of an emotional orientation, rather than a description of contract-like exchange a key result. Now following the idea of *ex ante* regulation, its more beneficial for public officers to be told what they can or can't do before they act, instead of waiting for courts to define corruption acts. Also, we can engage preventing private acts of corruption by improving compliance methods and third-party codes enforcement through contractual clauses.

Private compliance and anticorruption

In today's regulatory environment it is a constant challenge for anyone to achieve consistent legal compliance. This goes from governmental oversight and legal enforcement to companies having to face a variety of substantive and process oriented compliance obligations, which are imposed by trading partners and other private organizations, sometimes but not always promoted by government. Composed of contract clauses and codes of conduct for business partners, these obligations often go beyond mere compliance with law and recur to the methods by which compliance is assured. They do this by creating new compliance obligations and enforcement mechanisms and rely on the structure, design, priorities, functions and administration of corporate ethics and compliance programs. These obligations are increasingly accountable not only for their own compliance but also that of their supply chains, so therefore companies must seek corresponding contractual assurances upstream. Compliance is becoming privatized, and privatization along the supply chain and among employers and contractors is spreading.

Company compliance is covering up for government monitoring

Let's take for example in the United States, its state incentive privatization model of compliance has been enforced since the establishment of the Federal Sentencing Guidelines for Organizations. The government's limited regulatory and enforcement resources need some cover up, which is done by offering a strong incentive for companies to take on more of the state's monitoring activities (prevention, detection and enforcement). So corporate compliance programs allow state oversight to be increased by performing tasks that governments lack the resources for. But even though it is a privatization model it still reflects the traditional vertical relationship between government and the governed.

Private-to-private compliance

Major corporations are requiring their business associates to commit to them on their own codes or to third-party codes of conduct and related contract clauses. Complying to internal codes makes the employer-contractor relationship asymmetrical in terms of experience, know-how and process methods, which all make the contractor side carry such a burden that can affect supply terms and time requirements. Committing to third party codes signals a growing appreciation that enterprises across the value chain share one another's reputational and compliance risks, and that compliance processes play an important role in translating legal commands into lawful conduct. It reflects an awareness that if you are dependent on a business partner to keep you out of legal trouble, it might pay to take an interest in how they intend to accomplish that. Coming now from external business partners rather than just the internal ethics and compliance staff, this message has the potential to re-orient some attitudes and remove some ethical blinders. As more businesses are forced by their counterparties to examine their compliance processes and routinely accept business and legal consequences for them, we can expect increases in overall investment in compliance, in the scope and robustness of the average compliance program, and in ambient awareness of compliance issues outside the compliance, audit, and legal staffs.

Systems integration

The privatization of compliance is horizontal, networked, and qualitatively different, based upon the translating of legal commands into lawful conduct. We can trace the origins of this trend to three main protagonists:

(i) governments, both in their sovereign roles and as customers;
(ii) the human rights/corporate social responsibility movement; and,
(iii) companies themselves.

The sentencing guidelines model simply mitigates the risk of compliance failure. It does not expose companies to new forms of risk, liabilities, or forfeitures or to the possibility of multiple conflicting standards, but private-to-private compliance may do so. Program elements and ethical policies become contractual obligations, vulnerable to such contractual remedies as indemnities, damages, audits, default declarations, loan acceleration, and termination.

Private-to-private compliance is reshaping the compliance task portfolio and raising new questions about who is answerable to whom, both internally and across company boundaries.

Private compliance pressures may originate from any point in the value chain: suppliers, customers, capital markets, insurers. Compliance officers may find themselves caught in the middle between demanding customers and reluctant suppliers, or, in the other direction, between manufacturers vitally interested in how their products reach market and resellers seeking the shortest route to revenue. They may be simultaneously pitted against their own colleagues in charge of operations, procurement, business acquisition and contracting. And unlike the sentencing guidelines and most other government leniency programs, many of the privatized compliance requirements are truly mandatory—at least if you want to do business with the other party.

Government instigation in the enforcement and procurement spheres, blockbuster fines, civil penalties and disgorgements, monitor and burdensome settlement agreements are attention-getters. They provide not only object lessons about compliance risk—and lately, third-party risk especially—but also a bundle of examples from which officials can provide specific guidance to an increasingly attentive audience about compliance program features that will affect enforcement decisions.

For example, FCPA deferred/non-prosecution agreements today as its sending a message by routinely requiring settling defendants to institute appropriate compliance process controls over business associates, such as advance due diligence and ongoing oversight, "flowing down" codes of conduct, imposing training requirements, and securing contractual commitments covering recordkeeping, audit rights, vendor compliance undertakings, and associated termination rights—all principles that are echoed in more conventional Department of Justice guidance and in official guidance on the U.K. Bribery Act as well. The government's role as a customer may be even more influential. All the contractors of large federal contracts are now required to institute compliance programs that track the sentencing guidelines' (otherwise voluntary) criteria, and are specifically required to contractually flow down these obligations to large subcontractors.

Anti-corruption compliance

Governmental enforcement and procurement mandates, corporate social responsibility, and risk management across the global supply chain all converge upon the problem of official corruption, and anyone curious about the future of privatized compliance should consider the current state of anti-corruption compliance. Enforcement of anti-corruption laws has reached new heights and, encouraged by the OECD anti-bribery convention, national anticorruption laws continue to proliferate. Several prominent NGOs including the World Economic Forum, Transparency International, the ICC, the World Bank, and the OECD itself have published detailed guidance on third-party compliance management, guidance that universally includes:

(i) due diligence,
(ii) flow-down of anti-corruption policies,
(iii) training and communication,
(iv) documentation of business associates' compliance efforts, and imposition of audit rights,
(v) ongoing monitoring, and
(vi) contract remedies such as termination.

These recommendations have been implemented by a growing number of companies as a way of adaptation of accepted anti-corruption methodology to other risks. Third-party due diligence is commonplace and anti-bribery provisions appear frequently in international contracts and universally in private-to-private codes, quite often with domino-style flow-down requirements. With this pattern firmly established, code and contract language that was originally drafted only for the anti-corruption context is now being extended to cover other high-priority compliance domains such as export sanctions, money laundering, data privacy and conflict minerals.

1. **Anticorruption according to the FIDIC and ICC**

    The FIDIC standard on anticorruption matters is of having the contractors comply with applicable laws of the host country that relate to corruption. This is not a risk itself when FIDIC contracts and standards have OECD countries as one of the contract parties, since those countries have developed specific regulation on anticorruption, which is a crucial matter because it is not or barely regulated in various under developed countries that aren't even part of the OECD. OECD looks to change this by requiring such regulation to be issued in case the underdeveloped country has the interest of forming part of the OECD.

    On the other hand, lack of regulation is a situation that may be salvaged by applying FIDICs Multilateral Development Banks (MDB) general conditions of contract Sub-Clause 15.6. Now this clause only allows termination by the employer in case of determination of corrupt and fraudulent practices by the contractor. Some may see a danger in such provision as allowing the employer to abuse by threating the contractor, and that reciprocity for contractors should be an available tool. This would mean additional provisions on Clause 15.6 like a mirror clause in favor of the contractor or the possibility to involve a third party who determines the occurrence of an act of corruption. The anticorruption clause is set on

    Another type of tool we found was the ICC anticorruption rules for 2011, which are set of regulations that emphasizes the critical role of compliance by enterprises with self-imposed rules. This tool aims at fighting corruption, but form a double-post, which should be at the core of corporate responsibility and good corporate governance. These rules are intended as a method of self-regulation by business contrary to the applicable national laws and international instruments like FIDIC contracts. Such rules provide the enterprises to comply with their legal obligations and anti-corruption initiatives at the international level by:

    (i) Establishing anticorruption rules.
    (ii) Identifying the corporate policies required to support compliance with anticorruption rules.
    (iii) Determination of efficient corporate compliance programs.

    The ICC anticorruption clause aims at creating predictability and trust between parties by combating bribery and other corrupt practices. So not only before contract signing but also during its execution there is a need to ensure that corrupt practices do not achieve results and meanwhile maintaining trust in the *pacta sunt servanda*. Therefore, what is needed is a fine balance between the efforts to fight corruption and the treatment of corruption as a breach of contract, to have integrity prevail as the champion of the tender process, during contract execution and the life cycle of business transaction.

    The anticorruption rules set is very simple, it concentrates on prohibited acts and zero tolerance for employer's, contractor's, subcontractor's, and third parties acts of corruption or usage to conduct any act of corruption. This are the prohibited acts of corruption are bribery, extortion or solicitation, trading influence and laundering property that proceeds from crime.

Eventually, an anticorruption clause according to ICC rules, would take the wording from paragraph 1 used in the OECD Convention on Combating Bribery of Foreign Public Officials in International Business Transactions (1997) and the United Nations Convention against Corruption (2003). The corrupt practices covered by such paragraph include: i) extortion (active corruption) and solicitation (passive corruption), ii) bribery and trading influence, iii) corruption of officials, iv) private-to-private corruption, v) corruption in the national and international sphere, vi) corruption with or without the use of intermediaries, vii) bribery with money or through any form of undue advantage, and viii) bribery with or without laundered money.

Zero tolerance on corruption demands that the enterprises ensure that is central management has adequate control over the relationship with third parties, or that with respect to a consortium or join venture their partners anticorruption policies are consistent the enterprises standards. With respect to contractors and suppliers, the enterprise should take measures within its power and, as far as legally possible, to ensure that they comply with these rules in their dealings on behalf of, or with the enterprise, and avoid dealing with contractors and suppliers known or reasonably suspected to be paying bribes. The way out is to have provisions in which the enterprise can suspend or terminate the contract in case it has good faith concern that a business partner has acted in violation of the anticorruption rules or laws.

2. **Project risk allocation and corruption**

Risk can be defined from various perspectives, but I refer to it as a circumstance or an event that, if it occurs, it shall influence achieving the project's goal. As so, owner's goal can be best achieved by choosing that one contract that will motivate the contractor to achieve that same goal. Such a context is related to tender time, during which the amount of information put out for the bidders and the extent of risk the owner is willing to intake are set up front by the owner for the tenders to know and evaluate.

Construction projects due to their own "nature," involve quite many interacting activities that are full of risks, each of which has its own impacts, to some extent, on cost, time and quality. This whole scenario allows us to acknowledge that every contract allocates various types of risks, but not all contracts allocate risk equitably or the power/authority to manage each risk allocation.

In an ideal world, efficient risk allocation would mean a parallel risk reduction and project performance improvement. Unfortunately, we humans do not always choose efficiently and therefore owners have commonly aim for avoiding risk by allocating risk on the contractor's side.

Now on the tendering field and on the project execution, we engage risk with risk management systems, which usually comprises identification, analysis, and response, so that when they do eventually occur, they are overcome. A main task for employers, contractors, advisors, and subcontractors and all project participants should be risk source identification, communication and response, all as part of a risk management strategy and system. See construction Project Risk Categorization Framework in the Figure 1.1.

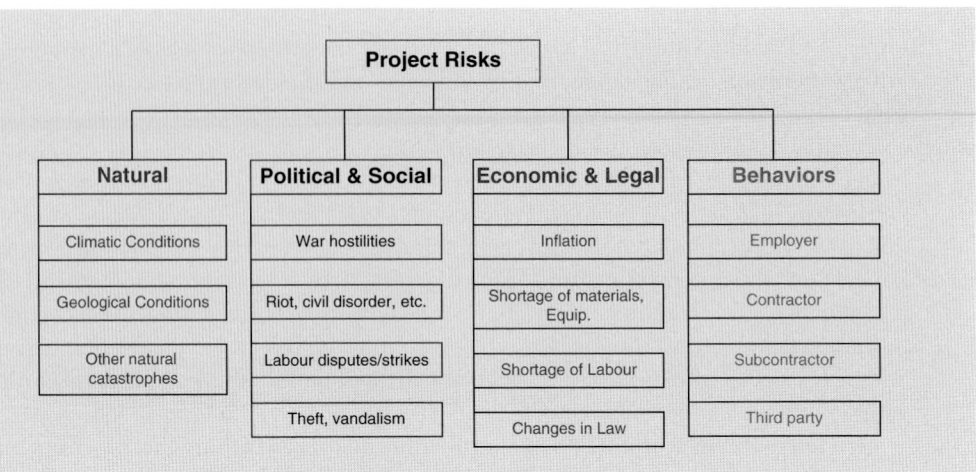

```
                         ┌──────────────┐
                         │ Project Risks│
                         └──────────────┘
        ┌───────────────┬─────┴──────┬──────────────┐
   ┌─────────┐  ┌───────────────┐ ┌───────────────┐ ┌──────────┐
   │ Natural │  │Political & Social│ │Economic & Legal│ │Behaviors │
   └─────────┘  └───────────────┘ └───────────────┘ └──────────┘
```

Figure 1.1 Construction Project Risk Categorization Framework

Natural: Climatic Conditions; Geological Conditions; Other natural catastrophes.
Political & Social: War hostilities; Riot, civil disorder, etc.; Labour disputes/strikes; Theft, vandalism.
Economic & Legal: Inflation; Shortage of materials, Equip.; Shortage of Labour; Changes in Law.
Behaviors: Employer; Contractor; Subcontractor; Third party.

From a contractual point of view risk management strategy is to allocate risk, through contract regulation, in such a way as to enable parties to manage risk efficiently and effectively throughout the construction process. The five theoretical principles proposed by Abrahamson recognized in construction projects are the following:

(i) If the risk is of loss due to his own willful misconduct or lack of reasonable efficiency or care;
(ii) If he can cover the risk by insurance and allow for the premium in settling his charges, and it is most convenient and practicable for the risk to dealt with in this way;
(iii) If the preponderant economic benefit of running the risk accrues him;
(iv) If it is in the interest of efficiency to place in the risk on him; and
(v) If, when the risk occurs, the loss happens all on him, and there is no reason under any of the above headings to transfer the loss to another or it is impracticable to do so.

Since corruption acts can be made by any party of a contract it should be first understood that any anticorruption program, compliance system or rules will need to have ways of discovering, identifying and responding to corruption acts as a risk category (behaviors) and in respect of the principle which makes the corrupted party assume the risk of its loss due to willful misconduct. As so, any contract breach which comes from a willful misconduct, should make the corrupted party assume the contract termination. Now to complete the idea, we must understand that such breach in contract execution not only affects the opposite party, but also can affect subcontractor's and third parties. So, anticorruption clauses should not only be designed about the termination are to assume the risk of corruption, since in a lot of cases when corruption acts are done by the contractor, this has cost impacts on its subcontractors, which may not know of the corruption acts. Main contract termination clauses upon corrupted conduct are the start of assigning behavioral risk, but termination procedures should allow subcontractors to recover costs assume in their contracts with corrupted contractors.

A very complex scenario for anticorruption measures occurs when a main contract between two parties has construction, design, built, operate and transfer clauses, which later are transferred through mirror clauses to an engineering contract or a management contract and later to an EPC contract. This will mean different levels of compliance systems for companies that if they are of the same corporate group, the contracts binding all parties should have specific measures of anticorruption compliance specially detailed in a way that they reassure subcontractors and third parties for any cost in case corruption acts occur cause of the contractor's misconduct.

Enrique Moncada
Responsible for Project Contract Management
Peru-Spain
Elecnor Perú S.A.C.

Indian law by C.K. Nandakumar and Rishabh Raheja (India)
Background

The growth and interest in the construction sector in India is reflective of the rapid strides that the Indian economy has been seeing in recent years. With among the fastest growing cities in the world, emphasis on housing and infrastructure have thrown several challenges to the legal system to respond to.

The construction industry has faced some challenges in gearing up to urban growth and the thrust on infrastructure. Infrastructure projects in India are often either sponsored, controlled or monitored by the government, increasingly in conjunction with the private sector. The level and nature of private participation has been increasing in this sector. So also, the "real estate" sector, focusing on development of land into apartment complexes, commercial buildings, has been a boom sector—mostly for private retail or commercial investment.

Some aspects from the Indian law relating to the construction industry are highlighted here—mostly on infrastructure and government construction contracts.

Pre-contractual stage

At the pre-contractual stage, letters of intent to and from government construction authorities are not uncommon in India. However, these are generally not considered binding. Notwithstanding that, preparatory works based on the letter of intent would be compensable under the principle of *quantum meruit*, even if a contract is not concluded. In fact, Indian courts have begun to refer parties to arbitration in pre-contractual disputes in cases where arbitration clauses are present in the letter of intent.

Standard forms

There is an increasing trend of Indian construction companies taking up projects outside India and for construction groups from outside India to participate in Indian projects. Various standards such as FIDIC are often prescribed in contracts. Indian government has a central standard prescribed by the Central Public Works Department (CPWD) and another by several State Public Works Department (SPWD). These standard form contracts are often made the norm in contracts where the government or a government body is the employer.

Force majeure at the performance and breach stage

Indian law is largely consistent with the defences provided to parties under several popular standard form construction contracts, particularly the FIDIC suite of contracts. Unlike many civil law countries, Indian law does not explicitly provide the defence of *force majeure*. However, this concept is either read in contractually or as a part of the common law principles of contract (both as a part of the Indian Contract Act and from judicial precedent).

While Indian law does not stipulate for *force majeure*, it does provide the parties with an escape from their obligations where the contract is "frustrated." However, the Indian Supreme Court has recently held that the doctrine of frustration will be inapplicable where the parties have included *force majeure* clauses in their contract. Since several of the standard form construction contracts popular in India contain *force majeure* clauses, parties do not have to worry about any interference or supplementation from Indian law in this respect as well.

Dispute resolution

At the dispute stage, there are various fora and mechanisms that parties resort to in Indian construction contracts. These include different combinations of non-binding processes such as dispute review boards, adjudication, conciliation, mediation, as well as binding processes such as arbitration and litigation. There has long been discontent in the construction community with arbitration and litigation in India for being lengthy, rigid, and unreliable. However, recent years have seen a revolution in both of these fora.

The 2015 Amendment to India's Arbitration and Conciliation Act has addressed the two greatest concerns of construction players—court intervention and duration. There was a tendency of Indian courts to interfere at all stages of a construction arbitration—most notably, at the setting aside stage by revisiting questions of fact and law addressed by the tribunal. Given the highly technical nature of construction disputes, an evaluation of these matters by courts despite there being qualified and specialist arbitrators was considered to be inappropriate. Further, detailed setting aside proceedings would also cause the project in question great harm, cost and delay, especially in projects involving horizontal or vertical multiplicity.

However, the amendment has gone a long way in eliminating this problem. It limits judicial review of the merits of an arbitral award, and provides that an award shall not be set aside merely on the ground of an erroneous application of the law or by re-appreciation of evidence. This ensures that the arbitrators in construction disputes do not have to worry about being second-guessed by Indian courts in setting aside proceedings. The amendment also restricts the duration for determination of a setting aside application to one year. This greatly minimizes the risk and harm that will be faced in construction projects that involve multiple players and strict timelines. Judicial intervention has been minimized in the other stages of the process as well—for instance, courts are now required to refer almost all pre-arbitral controversies to the tribunal.

The greatest game-changer in the arbitration of construction disputes is however, the introduction of a mandatory one-year time limit (extendable by six months with the consent of the parties, and extendable further with the permission of the court) for the completion of all India-seated arbitrations. While this time limit definitely addresses the problem of lengthy arbitrations that has plagued the construction industry in India, its mandatory nature fails to account for the often inherent complexity of construction disputes.

Meanwhile, the litigation regime for construction disputes has also been greatly improved. The creation of specialized "Commercial Courts" for all construction disputes *inter alia* above the sum of INR 1,00,000,000 (10 million Indian rupees) has brought with it expertise and expedition, through specialized judges, and short and strict timelines for the conduct of cases, submission of documents, and delivery of judgment.

At the relief stage

Indian courts only require the establishment of the fact of breach and not the quantum of breach in construction contracts providing for liquidated damages, as long as the quantum specified is a genuine pre-estimate of losses suffered, rather than a penalty. In the absence of a price escalation clause, the specification of liquidated damages in the contract would deny a party the right to claim price escalation upon breach beyond the liquidated damages. Whereas the presence of a mere price ceiling (and not liquidated damages) would not apply to a price escalation claimed upon breach.

C. K. Nandakumar
Advocate, Arbitrator
Member of the Chartered Institute of Arbitrators (U. K.)
Bangalore, India

Rishabh Raheja
IV Year Student
NALSAR University

1.14 Risk allocation in contracts

As previously mentioned, risk management may take the form of a contractual risk allocation between the project participants. In practice, an inefficient allocation (of an unclear risk or of a risk that the party is not able to control) will result in speculative claims, disputes, or even contractor bankruptcy. Furthermore, a contractor may allow for risk in their bid price via a "risk surcharge." The employer pays for the transfer of risk in such a situation.

Standard forms such as the FIDIC conditions of contract will guarantee a balanced and efficient risk allocation, provided they are not significantly altered. Such standard forms are commonly prepared by professional organizations or representatives of various interest groups such as contractors, lenders, employers, consulting engineers, and so on, to achieve well-balanced risk allocation.

It is worth mentioning here that common law practitioners seek to exhaustively list and describe all risks in the contract. Civil law practitioners rely on civil codes. Lawyers in the Anglo-Saxon jurisdictions may then be surprised by the fact that the governing law can influence contractual risk allocation. Similarly, judges in the common law world respect contractual risk allocation more so than their learned colleagues from continental Europe.

Wrong forms of contract by James Bremen (UK)

Many state entities either have their own (usually common law-based) historic form of bespoke construction document, or prepare their own set of amendments to a standard form (e.g., FIDIC or NEC). Whether or not a bespoke form (or amended standard) is used, there are a number of recurrent problems which plague projects in the emerging markets:

- Where the contract has not been adapted for the location and governing law of the project, many of its provisions will either not operate or provide a basis for claims and disputes into the build-phase.
- Often sponsors use the wrong form of contract (e.g., a lump-sum turnkey form, where the appropriate form may be construct-only or design and build).
- Insufficient analysis carried out of project-specific risks, with the result that risks are often inefficiently allocated to the contractor where the employer ought to carry them, as they are in the best position to manage them. This rarely addresses the risks, and ultimately results in a claim by the contractor.
- Because different departments often prepare the forms of contract and technical schedules, there are very often significant inconsistencies in these documents which are the basis of contractor claims.

James Bremen
Partner, Construction and Engineering
Herbert Smith Freehills
London
UK

The importance of early analysis of risk, knowledge of efficient risk allocation and right choice of delivery method by Conor Mooney (France)

Risk allocation

It is said that in construction, "the rewards should go to the efficient, not the lucky or the litigious" (Abrahamson, 1990). Much difficulty arises in construction projects through the inappropriate allocation of risk. Inappropriate allocation of risk is best explained by first outlining what is understood by appropriate allocation of risk. Leading thought on risk, in whatever form it manifests, is best borne by the party in the best position to manage it (Pickavance, 2010). To expand on this simplistic statement, the *Abrahamson Principles* on risk allocation are that a party should bear risk where:

- the risk is within that party's control;
- the party can transfer the risk (such as by insurance, for example), and it is most economically beneficial to deal with the risk in this fashion;
- the preponderant economic benefit of controlling the risk lies with the party in question;
- to place the risk upon the party in question is in the interests of efficiency;
- if the risk eventuates, the loss falls on that party in the first instance and is not practicable, or there is no reason under the above principles, to cause expense and uncertainty by attempting to transfer to another (Pickavance, 2010).

Inherent here is the concept of allocation of risk: that is, that risk must be allocated to one or other party to a construction contract. It may either happen by default, in that one party automatically and/or unknowingly retains or accepts a risk. Conversely, it may happen deliberately, whereby a conscious decision is made by one party (usually the employer, as the party who generally decides on the details of the tender and contract documents), to transfer a risk to the contractor or to accept a risk if it wishes to do so. Either way that this occurs, it is important to acknowledge that all risks in construction projects must be accounted for as being the responsibility of one or other party to the contract. The process by which the employer transfers some risks and retains others is the core subject of the *Abrahamson Principles,* which offer guidance as to which risks should be transferred and which should be retained. Since construction projects can only rarely determine all possible risks at the outset of a project, decisions must be made by the procuring body as to what risks are determinable, what risks are residual, and which party should bear those risks.

A simple and straightforward contract requires the parties to try to foresee all possible risks. Sometimes this is difficult to achieve in practice, when the complexity of the nature of the work covered by the contract is high. In construction project situations, where a feature of the work is its uniqueness, to whatever degree, there are almost invariably issues that arise during the project making it virtually impossible to allow for all eventualities in the contract. Construction projects can experience this situation to quite a profound level, due to the unforeseen and unforeseeable nature of some of the risks which manifest.

There are many categories of risk in projects in general; and construction projects encompass some specific types of risk. Each of these risk types, when considered at the outset of a project, can be contractually provided for to a greater or lesser degree. What is important to note is that regardless of the amount of pre-contract work conducted for the purposes of identifying and managing all risks, it is rarely the case where a construction project does not experience the eventuation of some risk which was not foreseen at the outset of the project.

Construction has been described as an industry where those involved in project delivery are "continually faced with a variety of situations involving many unknown, unexpected, frequently undesirable and often unpredictable factors" (Akintoye and MacLeod). These risks do not always disappear or reduce of their own accord; instead they must be dealt with in a satisfactory way to bring them to a tolerable level:

"No construction project is free of risk. Risk can be managed, minimised, shared, transferred or accepted. It cannot be ignored" (Latham, 1994).

In order to successfully manage risks on construction projects, a primary method of doing so is the allocation of risks between the parties (Binga et al., 2005). The web of risks: their interconnectivity and consequential effects, all require detailed consideration at the commencement of the project in order to allocate effectively and correctly. Failure to do so, together with the resultant eventuation of risks raise difficulties for their management because, if variations to the contract are required because of the risks occurring, the traditional rules of contract enforcement apply to construction (as with most other) contracts. The industry has adopted varying methods of project delivery in order to try to cope with differing degrees of residual risk. Most crucially, it should be accepted that changes will almost invariably occur on construction projects, but that the ability for all changes to be instructed under the contract is limited. Under such circumstances where the change cannot be instructed, then it becomes necessary to agree a variation to the contract. Agreeing such variations requires that all the formalities of contract formation are met once again, despite the fact that both parties may wish to continue their commercial arrangement, and, as far as the parties are concerned in practical terms, the change to be covered under a contract variation is little different to a change instructed under a variation order.

Note on terminology: variations, changes, and amendments

Construction contracts are somewhat unique in the world of contracts in that they have a mechanism to allow one party (the employer) to instruct (via the engineer) a unilateral change to that which was agreed originally in the contract, and the other party (the contractor) must follow that instruction, subject to certain limits. This mechanism **within the contract** is often referred to as *variations* or *changes*, but is sometimes confused with *variations* or *changes* **to the terms of the contract itself**. These are obviously two very different things. Given the risk of confusion between these two types of changes (i.e., inside the contract and outside of the contract), it is proposed here to refer to changes within the contract as "variations," and changes to the contract itself as "amendments." The engineer can order "variations," but "amendments" require the agreement of both parties to be enforceable.

Risk allocation and delivery methods

A choice of procurement route (such as where design responsibility lies, the sequencing of design and construction) depends on a number of factors, including the risk appetite of the employer, the level of involvement the employer wishes to have during implementation, the requirement for time to be a high project priority, the level of specialization and technical complexity involved in the works, the requirement for a high degree of cost certainty at the outset, and the ability for the employer to make changes to the project during design and construction. To a secondary degree, it will depend also on the industry norms and capacity within the country, and political influences on project implementation. Each of these aspects should be weighed in terms of their relative importance (which can vary among stakeholders— the financiers may have different priorities to the investor, for example), and an appropriate procurement route selected.

The contract choice is a consequence then of the procurement route choice. The procurement decision is strategic; the contract selection is more operational. In terms of contract choice, civil and common laws provide a very wide measure of freedom of contract so that parties are generally free to choose their own terms. Although this is the case, in practice parties to an agreement rarely have either the desire or the ability to work out all the terms which are required to govern their construction contract, and as a result, standard forms are most widely used. Studies carried out in the UK indicate that bespoke forms of construction contract are used as infrequently as on less than 10% of construction projects (RISC, 2010). The need for a standard form of building contract became apparent in the nineteenth century (Hibberd, 2006), in view of the complexity of rights and liabilities in building projects, and to avoid the expense and hazard of special, bespoke contracts (Furst and Ramsey, 2006).

In the construction industry therefore, contracts almost invariably contain a set of standard conditions, but in addition many other contractual provisions must be specifically formulated. A feature of a combination of standard conditions and specially prepared provisions then is that the resultant contract is rarely identical to that used on previous projects, and as a consequence, decisions based on a standard form may not have universal application to that form of contract. Furthermore, it should be noted that since many parts of the standard forms are interdependent, to alter a provision in one clause but not in another upon which it depends is likely to produce ambiguities and may defeat the objective of the alteration.

A major advantage of using a standard form of contract is that those who use it regularly become familiar with its contents, and a body of case law emerges around its practice. Practitioners thus become aware of its strengths and weaknesses and its suitability for specific purposes. The actual choice of a standard form of construction contract will depend upon a number of considerations, which include the following as key considerations:

Nature of Employer: If the employer is commissioning a publicly funded project, the choice of form may be limited, for example in Ireland, to the Public Works Contract suite of contracts (as part of the Capital Works Management Framework), whereas with a private employer the choice is much wider. Moreover, since the choice of form of contract in Irish public works limits to two procurement routes, public works projects do not have the same level of freedom of choice of procurement route as private projects.

Composition of the team: The agreed contract will confirm who is to undertake certain specific duties and accept certain obligations. For example, the extent to which construction and design responsibilities are allocated as between the professional consultants, the main contractor and specialist subcontractors should be evident from the terms of the contract. If a specialist contractor is to become involved in the design process, then contractual provision must be made for this to be effected.

Documents for pricing purposes: With traditional procurement, the appropriateness of fixed price lump sum contract will depend on tenders having been prepared on the basis of the fullest possible information. Where that information is unlikely to be available at tender stage, lump sum contracts are unlikely to be satisfactory and alternatives, such as re-measurable, will have to be considered.

It is noted that risks can only be assessed in as much as is practicable, and allocated in an agreed manner. It is highly unlikely that, in the majority of cases, the completed project will exactly resemble the initial, contracted project. In order to achieve the completed project, it is inevitable that all risks must have been somehow allocated, and some of these risks may have eventuated as the completed, varied project emerged. Consequently, how the variations are dealt with has a direct bearing on the successful completion of projects, or whether they result in lengthy and costly dispute proceedings. If construction contracts were a single standard construction contract the world over, it would still pose significant difficulty to determine and enforce each and every variation to the contract, but this matter is greatly compounded on the opposite dimension of often radically different conditions of construction contract themselves.

Construction projects can be complex undertakings, and the construction industry does have an undoubted degree of uniqueness: in the combination of characteristics evident in its nature; its risk profile; the magnitude of time, cost and effort expended in it; and the implications of ensuing difficulties. The complexity of construction projects stems from the type of project, the technology used, logistical issues, the scale of the project, the nature of the environment in which it is to be constructed, the personnel involved and the political issues associated with its delivery, and the changing needs of the end users. Such complexity cannot usually be fully understood at the outset of a project, save for the most trivial of projects.

Case study: when risk allocation goes wrong

As alluded to earlier, there is a risk of misunderstanding the differences between variations within a contract and amendment to the contract itself. The former is a vital and unique mechanism of construction contracts to facilitate the reality that projects will change as they progress through construction, and the variations facility of most construction contracts allow the engineer to make certain changes unilaterally in the interests of not having to renegotiate every change with a contractor. An example of this in practice, and where changes to the standard terms of contracts can have unintended effects during the construction phase, was on a building project in the former Yugoslavia. The FIDIC MDB contract had a comprehensive set of particular conditions to the standard version, as is normal. What was unusual about the particular conditions was a requirement, in Sub-Clause 8.4 [Extension of Time], that any "extension of time [be] approved by issuing an amendment to the contract signed by both parties." The intention of this particular condition was (presumably) to ensure that a) the financier would be aware of any changes to the completion date for financing/control purposes, since any amendments to the contract required its approval, and b) to prevent the engineer from agreeing to extensions of time without the employer's approval, since any amendments to the contract also required approval from the project's inter-ministerial supervisory board.

Consequently, in an attempt to mitigate the risks of uncontrolled project extensions, the particular conditions resulted in removing the authority of the engineer to change the time for completion within the contract. Instead, the particular conditions put in place a requirement that every change to the date for completion became an amendment to the contract itself. Naturally, an amendment to a contract requires the agreement of both parties, which in and of itself can be problematic, but what about a situation whereby the contractor does not agree with the engineer's determination over its request for an extension of time? A provision for extension of time is a usual feature of standard forms of construction contract which is intended to defer the date for the invocation of liquidated damages against the contractor in the event that the employer has experienced a risk for which he is responsible, or has instructed a variation. Essentially this is a provision for the benefit of the employer, since if the contractor causes the delay or experiences a risk for which he is responsible, no extension of time would be permitted and liquidated damages would be applied from the original date of practical or substantial completion. So the standard forms of contract therefore provide to allow the employer to make changes it wishes on projects, and enable it to move the completion date accordingly, and without penalty to him. In this case, the contractor sought 178 days' extension of time, but the engineer determined that the contractor was only entitled to 136 days, so the contractor refused subsequently to sign the amendment to the contract as required by the particular condition Sub-Clause 8.4, leading to a situation whereby time becomes at large once the agreed time for completion (which was actually agreed) had elapsed. Since the contractor had to agree to any change to the time for completion, the engineer had been stripped of its ability to grant extensions of time, and the balance of power shifted dramatically away from the employer's side and firmly to the contractor.

Risk allocation is not a neat affair. Allocating certain risks to one party can have unintended consequential effects on other risks, or create new risks in their own right. It is therefore important when allocating risk to reassess the risks holistically during the allocation process to understand if there may be new or altered risks, which were not considered previously.

Conor Mooney
Technical Advisor
Council of Europe Development Bank
Paris

Bibliography

Abrahamson, M. W. (1990). *Engineering Law and the ICE Contracts* (4th Edition). Thomas Telford, London.

Akintoye, A. S., and MacLeod, M. J. (1997). Risk analysis and management in construction. *International Journal of Project Management*, 15, 31–38, at 31.

Binga, L., Akintoyea, A., Edwards, P. J. and Hardcastle, C. (2005). The allocation of risk in PPP/PFI construction projects in the UK. *International Journal of Project Management*, 23, 25–35.

Furst, S. and Ramsey, V. (eds) (2006). *Keating on Construction Contracts*, (8th Edition), Sweet & Maxwell London, at Chapter 19.

Hibberd, P. (2006). Is single-point design responsibility under JCT 05 illusory? Society of Construction Law, London.

Latham, M. (1994). Constructing the Team, Joint Review of Procurement and Contractual Arrangements in the United Kingdom Construction Industry, Final Report The Latham Report, The Stationery Office, London.

Pickavance, K. (2010). *Delay and Disruption in Construction Contracts*. (4th Edition). Sweet & Maxwell, London, at Chapter 2.

RICS (2010). *Contracts in Use - A Survey of Building Contracts in Use during 2010*. (RICS).

1.15 Form of Business Organization

To deal with subcontracts in international construction projects by Giuseppe Broccoli and Fabio Zanchi (Italy)

In international construction projects, it is rather standard that the contractor will subcontract part of the scope of works. This may happen for different reasons such as, for instance, because the project is complex or because the contractor does not have the specific skills and expertise to carry out part of the works.

It happens often that the employer will request expressly that certain works (usually the supply and installation of highly technological items) or part of the design be carried out by a specialist subcontractor or supplier who has specific experience or track records. In such a case the employer could eventually award directly the execution of said works to the specialised contractor. This would certainly imply a substantial involvement of the employer, at least in terms of coordination between several contractors and risk of lack of cooperation between the contractors (see for instance Sub-Clause 4.6 [*Co-operation*] of the FIDIC books). This is the reason why in such a case the employer may prefer to award the entire execution of the scope of works to one main contractor who will be then under the obligation to subcontract part of the works to the specialist subcontractors designated by the employer.

In general terms, in many jurisdictions the subcontractor (even if designated by the employer) will have no direct recourse against the employer. As a direct consequence the liability for any fault of subcontractors will remain with the contractor (see for instance Sub-Clause 4.4 [*Subcontractors*] of the FIDIC books). The reason is quite obvious. The subcontractor is appointed by the contractor and the legal relation is between the contractor and the subcontractor. It goes without saying that, in the standard practice, the subcontractor is (or should) be selected directly by the contractor with no interference by the employer.

It is clear that the employer (and certainly the contractor) may suffer the consequences of a wrong selection of the subcontractor and this may have an impact on the timing for completion and/or on the quality of works executed.

In the present vignette two main issues are considered in relation to the subcontracting: (i) the selection process of subcontractors and, more importantly, (ii) the issue of risk allocation between the parties involved.

Selection of subcontractors

As mentioned above, the legal structure of the subcontracting is that the contractor will award part of its scope of works to a selected subcontractor. The legal structure of the entire project is, however, of such that the main contractor is in the middle, caught between its obligations toward the employer and the obligations of the subcontractor toward him.

In general terms (considering also that in certain jurisdiction the subcontract is not even legally feasible), the main contractor will be entitled to subcontract only "part" of the scope of works (see for example Sub-Clause 4.4 [*Subcontractors*] of the FIDIC books).

It is clear that, even in the phase of the bidding process, the tenderer shall consider very carefully the scope of works, its ability to subcontract and the skills and track record of potential subcontractors

When allowed, the selection of subcontractors is without any doubt a key moment of the project. Traditionally, the appointment of subcontractors can be finalized either before or after the signature of the construction contract. Obviously, the choice is left up to the employer and it entails different implications.

Appointment before the signature of the contract

If appointed before the signature of the contract, the selection may be made by the main contractor alone or with a certain involvement of the employer.

There are various possibilities: (i) the contractor can state directly the name of the subcontractor (or a list of subcontractors among which the contractor will chose one); (ii) the contractor can submit the name of the potential subcontractor (or a list of potential subcontractors for the evaluation of the employer; the contractor can submit the name of a potential subcontractors (or a list) for the consent or approval of the employer.

As mentioned above, however, there can be cases where the employer can select directly the subcontractor and might even agree directly with the subcontractor terms and price of the works/supplies to be provided and, as such, impose them on the main contractor. The reasons behind this choice may be, inter alia, because the works require to obtain components with a long delivery time or situations where design of a specific part of the works or the manufacturing of highly technological components cannot be put on hold until the main contractor has been appointed.

Certainly, such approach might avoid potential delays, but might increase the risk of some "discussions" between the employer and the main contractor in relation to the performance of the subcontractor.

Sub-Clause 5.1 [*Objection to Nomination*] of the FIDIC Red Book, despite providing certain requirements under which the main contractor can object to the employment of a nominated subcontractor makes clear the most frequent issues that might arise out of engaging a subcontractor.

It must be stressed that even when the subcontractor is actually selected or designated by the employer, any legal liability attributable to the performance of the subcontractor will remain with the main contractor.

In cases where the subcontractor is designated directly by the employer, the contractor will be prevented from engaging in the (sometimes) unethical practice of bid-shopping, bid-peddling, and bid-chiselling. It is not rare, in fact, that once awarded the contract, the main contractor reaches out some of the subcontractors listed with the intent to obtain lower offers.

It is clear that the main risk involved with such practices is that any reduction in the original proposal put forward by the subcontractor will have an almost immediate impact on the quality of the works (and unfortunately sometimes on the costs of safety at workplace).

An even more "dangerous" risk is that the subcontractor, by accepting for various reasons a loss-making contract, might sooner or later prejudice the completion of the works.

In an alternative scenario, the employer may include in the tender documents a short list of potential subcontractors. The main contractor then selects one of the listed companies. While this approach does not eliminate in its entirety the risk of the abovementioned practices, it is certainly more appealing for both the main contractor and employer due to the fact that it gives them more room to evaluate which subcontractor fits better for the works that have to be performed.

The employer must, however, keep in mind that under such approach the main contractor will incur extra expenses while selecting the subcontractor and this might be priced by the main contractor resulting in a higher price for the employer.

Unfortunately, in all those situations where the subcontractor is selected before the signature of the contract, it is not rare the main contract will not put the due attention to the skills and capabilities of the subcontractor. Rather often, in fact, the main contractor will look at the price offered by the subcontractor as the main important issue while neglecting to consider, for instance, the track records of the subcontractor, which certainly may affect the performance and execution of the entire scope of works.

Appointment after the signature of the contract

When the subcontractor is appointed after the signature of the contract, again the selection process may follow different routes.

In general terms, the employer, despite the fact it should have no direct power in the selection process, usually wants to maintain a certain control over the selection procedure. If on the one hand, the employer should fully rely on a proper evaluation of the main contractor on the most suitable subcontractor to perform the works (as for example in the EPC contract), on the other hand it is not unusual that the employer reserves the right to have the final word on the selected subcontractor (for instance with its consent and/or approval).

In particular it might happen that:

1. The subcontractor is appointed directly by the main contractor subject to the consent of the employer; or
2. The subcontractor is selected among a list of potential subcontractors agreed in advance with the employer.

In both cases, it is rather usual that the employer seeks to exclude expressly any responsibility in the selection process by inserting a specific provision which might read as follows:

> *"the engagement of any Subcontractor will not imply any direct relation between the employer and the Subcontractor and will not diminish in any manner the liability of the Contractor for any failure of the Subcontractor to perform its obligations".*

The approach of the FIDIC books is, as mentioned, in the same direction and, unless otherwise stated in the particular conditions, the main contractor shall be responsible for faults of *any* subcontractor engaged in the works (see Sub-Clause 4.4 [*Subcontractors*]).

The same situation will occur in all those cases when it is the employer who nominates directly a subcontractor. In such cases, however, the main contractor will be entitled to object to such nomination on the basis of reasonable grounds.

Sub-Clause 5.2 [*Objection to Nominate*] of the FIDIC Red Book mentions certain cases that would be considered as "reasonable objections" to the nomination of subcontractors made upon instructions of the engineer:

(i) the main contractor has a grounded belief that the subcontractor does not have enough competence, resources or financial strength to carry out its obligations;
(ii) the subcontract does not make clear that in case of negligence of the subcontractor, his agents or employees, the main contractor must be indemnified;
(iii) the subcontract does not make clear that the subcontractor will perform the works in such way to fulfil the obligations of the main contractor under the main contract;
(iv) the subcontract does not make clear that the subcontractor shall indemnify the main contractor in case of any failure to perform its obligations.

It is obvious that in all those circumstances in which a subcontractor is appointed after the signature of the contract a dispute might arise in connection with the selection process.

In such circumstances, it is desirable for parties to agree in the contract on a swift dispute resolution procedure concerning objections raised by the employer or the main contractor in order to downplay and prevent a potential suspension or delay of the works.

This can be achieved allowing either party to submit the dispute for settlement if the employer or the main contractor raise any objections within an agreed period of time from the notice of the intention to appoint a proposed subcontractor. The contract shall also provide that a final decision must be rendered within a short time so to avoid long and damaging discussions which will only delay the project.

In terms of effectiveness of one or the other option, it seems reasonable to suggest that the best approach would be to appoint or nominate a subcontractor before the contract is signed. This will certainly save time and avoid disputes and delays in the project completion.

Risk allocation

Regardless of when the subcontractor is designated and what selection approach parties select, the main contractor will, in any case, be liable toward the employer for any default of the subcontractor. As mentioned earlier, there is no direct legal relation between the employer and the subcontractor. This means that the main contractor, in the majority of the cases, will not be released from its liabilities for acts or omission even if attributable to the subcontractor.

As a consequence, one of the main relevant issues for the main contractor is to secure full "control" over the subcontractor last but not least by retaining a full right to terminate the subcontract (even in those cases where the employer has had an active role in the selection) by including in the main contract a provision such as the following:

> *"The Contractor shall reserve the right to replace at any time the Subcontractor in case of failure by the latter to properly and timely perform its obligations under the Subcontract".*

Having said the above, it is clear that the subcontractor will be in charge of some of the obligations that the main contractor has agreed to in the main contract. It will be therefore crucial to properly allocate the risk and find the right balance between the obligations that, on the one side, the main contractor has toward the employer and those that, on the other side, the subcontractor has toward the main contractor. In other words, the main contractor will need to be in the position to claim against the subcontractor any claim that comes from the employer and that can be actually attributable to the subcontractor.

It goes without saying that the subcontract (and its drafting) will have a crucial role in the risk allocation.

In terms of drafting, the aim of the main contractor will be to avoid any gaps and inconsistencies between the obligations assumed toward the employer and the obligations undertaken by the subcontractor.

In this respect there are different ways to achieve such result.

A. BESPOKE CONTRACTS

In particularly complex projects, it occurs rather often that the employer and the main contractor use bespoke contracts. In such case the best option for the main contractor when subcontracting part of the scope of work would be to go through every single clause of the main contract and carefully evaluate if (and how) the obligation of a specific clause should (and how) be passed down the chain to the subcontractor. Moreover, in such case the parties will have the opportunity to discuss relevant unique issues and, once executed, will only have to refer to the subcontract avoiding any cross-reference to the main contract, which can easily cause confusion. The main disadvantages are that a well-drafted bespoke subcontract requires a great deal of time and that in case of amendments to the main contract, the subcontract will have to be revised accordingly.

B. STANDARD FORMS

In other circumstances, parties might use standard forms of contract (for instance, FIDIC books). These forms are widely used since parties do not have to draft contracts from scratch and only have to amend the particular conditions.

In such case, the subcontract will be either governed by a specific standard subcontract (for instance, the FIDIC conditions of subcontract for construction) or will instead replicate mutatis mutandis the terms and conditions of the main contract.

Also in this hypothesis, however, the parties could pay not the right attention to the particular conditions, if any, and there might still be holes in the legal relation and in the risk allocation.

C. BACK-TO-BACK CONTRACTS

A third method (widely used and often the source of many disputes) is to use back-to-back agreements and clauses, also known as flow-down clauses. A flow-down clause is a contract provision by which the parties incorporate by reference into the subcontract agreement some or all of the terms and conditions of the main contract. Parties usually perceive this method as a short cut to make clear that the intention of the parties (main contractor and subcontractor) is for the subcontractor to bear toward the main contractor the same liabilities that the main contractor bears toward the employer.

However, parties are often not fully aware that, if poorly drafted (as it is often the case), a back-to-back agreement could lead to future disputes simply because inserted without a proper analysis of what clauses of the main contract can be actually applicable to the subcontractor. To have an efficient flow-down clause it would be sufficient a clear wording and that some of the relevant clauses of the main contract are expressly redrafted. A back-to-back agreement, despite the fact it saves a lot of time in terms of drafting, does not really avoid parties from digging into the contract.

In back-to-back scheme, particular attention should be paid to specific clauses such as:

(i) Conditional payment

In the attempt to produce a back-to-back effect, the main contractor will often request to include in the subcontract a provision pursuant to which payment to subcontractors shall be made only when the main contractor receives payment from the employer. Generally known as paid-when-paid clauses and despite any intent of the parties, this is a typical example where the parties should be very careful at drafting since it might be not enforceable under certain jurisdictions or in certain circumstances. Rather often the subcontractor would try to avoid any such clause especially because it might have a severe effect on its own cash flow.

(ii) Early completion bonuses

This clause is certainly one of those that should be redrafted with the utmost care. By way of example, if under the main contract the employer and the main contractor have agreed that for each day of early completion the main contractor will receive 100 Euro and the same concept applies to the subcontractor, it is pretty obvious that the subcontract should provide for a mechanism of fair apportionment of the early completion bonus that the main contractor will receive.

(iii) Liquidated damages

This is another clause that should be drafted with due care since a simple reference to the main contract liquidated damages clause may lead to consider the corresponding clause in the subcontract as a liability for indirect or consequential damages (and therefore unenforceable under certain jurisdictions). In addition, if the intent of the main contractor is to actually pass on to the subcontractor the liquidated damages eventually requested by the employer, it will be crucial to properly apportion the liquidated damages that can be claimed against the subcontractor.

(iv) Contractual dates

Reference here is made specifically to all those deadlines that are included in the main contract and that may refer to completion dates, submissions deadlines (for instance, in respect of document to be approved) and claims notification. All such contractual dates shall have to be included in the subcontract but shall be adequately adjusted so that they will be aligned with those included in the main contract.

(v) Dispute resolution

Another clause that should be examined carefully is the one on dispute resolutions such as the arbitration clause.

Parties often have a tendency to underestimate the implications of an arbitration clause embedded in the main contract. Referred to as boilerplate or midnight clauses, many contractors ignore that arbitration clauses incorporated by reference in the subcontract, in order to be enforced, might require to be expressly accepted by the parties. The first step for the parties is to check if, under the applicable law of the subcontract, the incorporation of an arbitration clause by reference meets the "in writing requirement" that, pursuant to the New York Convention on the Recognition and Enforcement of Foreign Arbitral Awards an arbitration clause must have.

The "in writing requirement," however, is not applied uniformly by national courts (e.g., in some jurisdictions "an oral agreement to arbitrate will be regarded as being 'in writing' if it is made 'by reference to terms which are in writing,' or if an oral agreement 'is recorded by one of the parties, or by a third party, with the authority of the parties to the agreement.'"

In addition, the law of the place of enforcement should be carefully considered when drafting the dispute resolution clause and this is another reason why a simple back-to-back clause might create additional disputes and require an ad hoc drafting.

(vi) Termination

The same applies to the termination clause. The main contract will usually contains provisions on termination for default or for convenience of the employer. It is clear that not only the subcontract should contain a clause, which will cause the automatic termination of the subcontract in case of termination of the main contract, but also the consequence of the termination of the main contract should be adjusted adequately to the termination of the subcontract (let's consider for instance the payment obligations in case of termination for convenience or the obligation to vacate the site and those concerning the safety and security of the work site).

Conclusion

In the reality, the subcontract is one of the most important part of any mid or big size project. On the one side there is the difficulty for the employer to have full control over the subcontractor and on the other side there is often an underestimation by the main contractor of the various aspect of the subcontract that might have a negative impact on the execution of the scope of works.

The main contractor should pay particular attention to the drafting of the subcontract because it might have not only a massive impact on the completion of the scope of work (any delay or fault of the subcontractor will have to be remedied in a way or in another) but also in terms of liabilities of the main contractor that, in frequent situations, which do not flow down properly to the subcontractor due to a poor drafting of the subcontract agreement.

Giuseppe Broccoli
Managing Partner, BDA Studio Legale

Fabio Zanchi
Associate, BDA Studio Legale

Interface agreements between subcontractors by Bernd Ehle and Sam Moss (Switzerland)

Interface issues arise in virtually all construction projects that require coordination between several actors. For instance, in projects involving multiple subcontractors, a subcontractor may be prevented from accessing the construction site or commencing or completing parts of its scope of work by the activities and/or delays of other subcontractors. If such interface issues are not managed adequately and expeditiously, they can have a considerable impact on the completion schedule and costs of a project.

One way of managing interfaces is for the subcontractors to conclude interface agreements addressing various issues such as duties of cooperation and reciprocal liability and indemnity between them. These agreements can provide a contractual framework for anticipating and resolving interface issues without having to involve the main contractor. For example, in the event that one subcontractor's actions cause another to incur additional costs, an interface agreement may permit the first subcontractor to bring a "horizontal" claim directly against the other, instead of having to bring a "vertical" claim against the main contractor, who would then have to seek to recover amounts from the subcontractor that caused the additional costs. An interface agreement can therefore reduce the main contractor's management obligations and costs, as it would not have to manage claims and act as an intermediary between subcontractors. They can also incentivize subcontractors to cooperate and coordinate their activities, as they cannot simply rely on the main contractor to resolve any issues arising from the activities of other subcontractors.

However, subcontractors will often be reluctant to conclude interface agreements, as such agreements can complicate the contractual framework for their involvement in a project by requiring them to undertake obligations both vertically to the main contractor, and horizontally to the other subcontractors. Indeed, such agreements can impose an additional source of liability, and require subcontractors to coordinate activities that the main contractor would otherwise be responsible for coordinating. Interface agreements therefore tend to be used in construction projects in which there is a particular reason to conclude them, due to the specific characteristics of the project.

For instance, interface agreements are frequently used in public-private partnerships (PPP) or private finance initiative (PFI) projects, in which private firms are contracted by public authorities to finance, build, and manage public projects. These projects often involve a thinly capitalized project company that acts as a main contractor, and several key subcontractors, including a construction subcontractor and a facilities management subcontractor, to which the project company steps down its obligations to build and operate the project. Interface agreements are used in this context to protect the project company from issues arising between the subcontractors. By way of example, the project company could be exposed to cashflow risks if any claims between the subcontractors had to go through it, as it might be liable to pay compensation to one subcontractor before it is able to recover the amounts from the other subcontractor. Interface agreements can also provide a framework for the reallocation between the subcontractors of liabilities passed down by the project company to one or several of the subcontractors.

Interface agreements are also often used in the context of complex construction projects in which the scope of works is split into several contractual packages, and in which there is no general or main contractor and the employer is not equipped to deal effectively with the significant interfaces of the project. Employers may adopt such a structure for various reasons, including to save costs. In such projects, interface agreements provide the contractors with a forum for addressing interface issues.

The content and structure of interface agreements can vary significantly from one project to another. However, issues that are commonly addressed in such agreements include the following:

- **Delays**: delays in the works of one subcontractor will often impact the work of other subcontractors, for instance, because aspects of their scope of works are interdependent, or because they are prevented from accessing the site. In PPP/PFI projects, the facilities management subcontractor may also lose revenues or incur additional costs if it is prevented from commencing its operation of the project due to a delay by the construction subcontractor.
- **Defects**: In PPP/PFI projects, the facilities management subcontractor is often liable under its subcontract with the project company for defects caused by the construction subcontractor. Interface agreements therefore often define the obligations of the construction subcontractor towards the facilities management subcontractor in respect of defects.
- **Coordination of works**: In addition to identifying who has the responsibility to coordinate the works, interface agreements may set up tools and structures to facilitate coordination, for example, a coordination committee that acts as bridge between the different subcontractors. Such committees may be assigned specific roles, such as managing claims, and/or preparing weekly risk reports.
- **Risk management**: Interface agreements will often establish tools to help the parties manage risks. One such common tool is the risk register (also referred to as a risk log), which seeks to identify common and project-specific risks, their potential cost and delay impacts, and which party is responsible for monitoring and mitigating each risk. The agreements may also set out arrangements to split the benefit of underspend and the cost of overspend on the project.
- **Dispute resolution**: Interface agreements will usually contain dispute resolution provisions that permit subcontractors to bring claims directly against other subcontractors.

Bernd Ehle
Partner, LALIVE SA

Sam Moss
Associate, LALIVE SA

1.15.1 Representative office and domestic or foreign subsidiary

In general, there are two ways of doing non-collaborative business abroad. This can be done through a representative office based abroad or via a domestic or foreign subsidiary. Selecting the appropriate business form for a particular country or for a particular construction project is one of the keys to success.

The right to do business will usually be granted on completion of an entry in the local business register. The cost and time demands in connection with setting up a representative office or a subsidiary will vary depending on the target market.

Both forms of doing business abroad have to be chosen with the social-political situation, tax considerations, financial planning, commercial objectives and priorities, risk management, and business-related legislative conditions in mind.

The major difference between both forms is in the legal status and responsibility. A representative office is not a separate legal entity—it is merely a tool to prolong the company's reach. As a result, any contract-related liabilities or even damages can still be borne by the company itself. A brand-new, independent legal entity, on the contrary, will arise if a subsidiary (sometimes also called a "daughter company") is founded. The reasons for creating a subsidiary to operate in a foreign country usually center on tax and liability concerns. However, subsidiaries with limited liability may experience difficulties in obtaining credit, insurance, securities, and so on.

1.15.2 The consortium and the joint venture in construction

Consortiums and joint ventures are collaborative forms of business organizations. In construction, it is not always clear what the factual and legal meanings of these particular terms are. Both of these business forms are commonly used in joint construction projects by contractors. In practice, the contractors usually unite for large construction projects because the nature and demands of such projects are beyond the capacity of an individual contractor. A single contractor is sometimes unable to meet the qualification criteria for the project or is lacking the resources as they are engaged in other projects. Take, for example, the construction of a railway corridor—such a project will require the cooperation of companies specializing in landscaping, traction power lines and design.

Another reason is the need for strategic partnerships in international business. A local partner is often indispensable whenever a new market is entered, as they already have established relationships with the employer, designer, or contract administrator, have experience with local subcontractors, suppliers, and unions, and are familiar with local business rules and practices. The formation of an association is also a way to deal with risk and to improve marketability and credibility. Risks are divided between the parties and the specialist skills on offer collectively strengthen the bid.

As in life, the biggest challenge is to find a reliable partner for a particular collaboration. Therefore, it is important that a contractor learns as much as possible about their potential partner. In particular, their financial status and good references. After such a "due diligence" check has been completed, a contract can be signed and a successful partnership developed.

Employers often require bidders to enter into collaborative forms of business organizations so that they are jointly and severally responsible for the fulfilment of their obligations under the contract with the employer. Having become part of such a venture, each of the participants must be prepared to deal with the issue of becoming solely liable for the other participants' obligations should the latter collapse (e.g., due to insolvency).

In practice, potential contractors join forces at the tender stage, though there is nothing to prevent such a joint venture from being created during the construction phase. In the latter case, such a joint venture is internal in its nature and therefore excludes any joint and several liability to the employer.

The governing law, its respective limitations and accepted forms of association should always be evaluated whenever a consortium or a joint venture is to be established. Contractors must take into consideration any statutory requirements and the mandatory provisions of a particular applicable law. For example, they must consider if it is necessary to conclude the respective contract in writing, how to determine the governing law in the absence of a selected jurisdiction, when exactly the consortium or joint venture is to be founded, etc.

It is the responsibility of the contractors and their actual priorities in particular projects to determine what kind of "form" of cooperation they choose. Consortiums are easier to create and require fewer resources and commitments than joint ventures.

1.15.3 The consortium

A consortium is the most widely used association by contractors to join their efforts in construction projects. A consortium consists of two or more contractors uniting to set up an association of independent contractors. A consortium is not a legal entity, bids are jointly submitted and the parties are jointly and severally liable for work performed under the contract. Commonly, consortium members perform the works separately as they distribute the particular parts of the work between themselves. Moreover, the consortium's losses and profits are borne separately by the particular members. Right from the bidding phase, the project is usually subdivided into a number of parts that are then priced and executed independently by the members of the consortium. Not being a legal entity, the consortium is represented in dealings with the employer and third parties by a leading participant who also, as rule, prepares invoices for the employer (being paid to the common account) and distributes the received payments to other participants afterward.

At the top management level, the consortium is usually managed by a board consisting mainly of the participants' executive directors. The board can resolve disputes and give instruction to the consortium's "on-site" administrative body, which coordinates design, construction, accounting, and engineering. The administrative body acts on the consortium's behalf, communicating on a daily basis with the employer's representatives or the contract administrator.

Relationships between the members of a consortium can take other forms. The works, for example, may be carried out separately with one shared profit and loss account, the balance of which is then distributed among the venture participants once the project is completed (perhaps on a pro rata basis), depending on the individual participants' share in the project.

A further example of a different kind of consortium is the "tacit association" or *Beihilfegemeinschaft* in Germany. Such a "silent association" comes into being where a contractor executes part of the works through a third party under the consortium contract but not via a subcontract. Despite being associated with the contractor, such a third party is not a party to the contract entered into with the employer (the main contract). This form is particularly useful where a part of the works necessitates the close cooperation of human resources, special equipment, technology, copyrights and know-how, and where the contract for works cannot adequately regulate such part of the project.

Consortium agreements may contain various rights and obligations ranging from loose to strict forms of contractual relationships. It is common for the consortium agreement to deal with matters such as the purpose of the consortium, mutual rights and responsibilities, joint and several responsibility to the employer, bid evaluation, representation, decision-making, management, duration, account and payments, profit and loss distribution, insurance, bonds and guarantees, insolvency, termination, and so on. Consortiums are often regulated by statute in civil law countries as they are recognized forms of business cooperation. This factor must be taken in consideration when negotiating or preparing a contract. In Poland, for example, a consortium can be created by a verbal agreement with the consequence of joint and several liability imposed by statute.

1.15.4 The joint venture

Joint ventures are more complex than consortiums. They exist as distinct legal entities—often with their own employees and objectives as well as financial, tax, and legal issues to deal with. Joint ventures differ among jurisdictions and the actual form will depend on the requirements of particular contractors.

There also exist associations known as equity joint ventures (EJVs). In this case, a joint venture or partnership of a domestic and foreign entity operates under the umbrella of a limited liability company. In China, an EJV is a limited liability entity established by a foreign investment entity and Chinese investors. Under Chinese law, all foreign business activity in China must be conducted in this way. In the UK, the principal types of joint ventures are contractual joint ventures, general partnerships, consortium companies, limited liability companies, and hybrid companies. A consortium company, where each partner takes an agreed percentage of the issued share capital, is probably the most common form of joint venture in the UK (Venoit, 2009).

If there is no mandatory regulation prescribing the use of the EJV there can be a strategic interest in creating an EJV where business priorities include long-term business relationships, risk and liability limitation, tax, and other practical issues.

1.15.5 ARGE

The *Arbeitsgemeinschaft* (ARGE) is a specific form of joint venture in Germany. Issued by the *Hauptverband der Deutschen Bauindustrie* (the German Construction Industry Association), it stands apart from other European jurisdictions by unifying sample forms of joint venture contracts in law.

Unlike the consortium, the ARGE is a legal entity (a *Gesellschaft des bürgerlichen Rechts* ("civil rights company")) whose characteristics are defined by the *German Civil Code* (BGB). The ARGE is independent from its shareholders, can sue or be sued and can act independently of its joint venture partners. In contrast to a common consortium whose participants perform the work separately, the ARGE participants execute the works as individual contractors, with the profits distributed and losses to be borne on a pro rata basis, depending on their shares in the ARGE. As an independent legal entity and a daughter company of its participants, the ARGE enters into the main contract with the employer.

At the bidding phase of a project, the future participants in the ARGE will first enter into the *Bietergemeinschaftsvertrag* ("contract on joint bid submission"). Sample forms of this contract are unified in law as well as in the wording of future ARGE contracts. The *Bietergemeinschaft* will turn into ARGE only when the contract is awarded. Otherwise, the *Bietergemeinschaft* lapses and does not give rise to ARGE.

An ARGE foundation agreement is valid when made orally but has to be concluded in writing for practical reasons. Partners may freely depart from the provisions of the BGB except in two specific cases. Case 1: no participant shall acquire a controlling stake in ARGE (be in control of it). Case 2: no participant shall be deprived of the option to leave ARGE.

References

Banica, S. (2013). Standard forms of construction contracts in Romania. *Urbanism. Arhitectură. Construcţii*, 4(4).
Bunni, N. G. (2005). *The FIDIC Forms of Contract* (3rd Edition). Blackwell Publishing, Oxford.
ICC (2009). *International Court of Arbitration Bulletin*, 19(2) – 2008.
Jaeger, A.V. and Hök, G.S. (2010). *FIDIC: A Guide for Practitioners*. Springer Verlag, Berlin.
JICA (2011). Check list for one-sided contracts for use with 'sample bidding documents under Japanese ODA loans : procurement of works'. Available at: http://www.jica.go.jp/activities/schemes/finance_co/procedure/guideline/pdf/check_e.pdf (accessed 1 March 2018).
Murdoch, J.R. and Hughes, W. (2008). *Construction Contracts : Law and Management*. Taylor & Francis, New York.
Scott, D. Panama Canal Congress focuses on risk management on large infrastructure projects. Online. Available at: http://www.asce.org/ascenews (accessed 12 Jan. 2018).
Venoit, W.K. (2009). *International Construction Law: A Guide for Cross-Border Transactions and Legal Disputes*. ABA Publishing, Chicago.
Winch, G. (2010). *Managing Construction Projects*. Wiley-Blackwell, Oxford.
Wyckoff, P.G. (2010). *Pratique du Droit de la Construction: Marchés Public et Privés*. Eyrolles, Paris.

Further reading

FIDIC (2000). *The FIDIC Contracts Guide* (1st Edition). FIDIC, Lausanne.
FIDIC (2011). *FIDIC Procurement Procedures Guide* (1st Edition). FIDIC, Lausanne.
Klee, L. (2012). *Smluvní vztahy výstavbových projektů*. Wolters Kluwer, Prague.
Knutson, R. (2005). *FIDIC: An Analysis of International Construction Contracts*. Kluwer Law International, London.
Kobayashi, K. and Khairuddin, A.R. (2012). *Joint Ventures in Construction 2*. ICE Publishing. London.
Miller, R.W. (n.d.). Joint ventures in construction. Online. Available at: http://suretyinfo.org/pdf/JointVentures.pdf (accessed 12 May 2018)
Mintzberg, H., Ahlstrand, B. and Lampel, J. (2004). *Strategy Safari*. Prentice Hall, London.
Perkins, S.J. (1997). *Globalization: The People Dimension*. Kogan Page Limited, London.

2 Civil Law and Common Law

2.1 Specifics of the governing law

International construction contracts address the most common problems and allocate most standard risks accordingly. However, no perfect contract exists because of the uniqueness and unforeseeable nature of this field. While governing laws contain mandatory clauses as a rule, adjustments in negotiating and drafting procedures increase the likelihood of ambiguities and may lead to invalid provisions. Therefore, the governing (applicable) law remains of great significance in international construction.

Governing (applicable) law is agreed upon by the parties as a general rule. Despite this, many international contracts do not contain a clause defining the choice of law. This may lead to conflict of law issues and, therefore, a different risk allocation than the one that the parties intended. A great deal of international construction takes place in less-developed countries with undeveloped or not fully adopted applicable law. Therefore, the characteristics of the applicable law are a key factor. These characteristics vary depending on their common or civil law origins.

2.2 Common law versus civil law: Differences and interconnections

When considering contract law in its widest sense, there are a number of key differences between the Anglo-American common law and European civil law systems. The Anglo-American system has its basis in precedents and builds on customs, pragmatic approaches, and emphasizes the principle of contractual freedom. The European system, on the other hand, is composed of civil codes and is based on Roman law and legal theory. The cornerstone of the civil law system is the importance of written law and mandatory provisions. This is of great significance as they can influence original agreements between parties.

International Construction Contract Law, Second Edition. Lukas Klee.
© 2018 John Wiley & Sons Ltd. Published 2018 by John Wiley & Sons Ltd.

At present, both systems seem to be moving closer to each other (a similar process is taking place in the other systems such the sharia, socialist and religious law). The main differences are still apparent but, without doubt, the similarities of both systems prevail over the differences. In the United States, for example, legislators create lengthy acts and large volumes of legislation that bind the courts. In the civil code countries, on the other hand, decisions of the superior courts often enjoy such respect that a new law is created on the basis of these decisions.

However, different approaches are especially visible in construction project management and dispute resolution. Let us consider the British example. In construction projects, the British invented some now "traditional" sample contract forms used internationally that are highly developed but formal in nature. These formalities may give rise to disputes in numerous countries that follow European law. For example, the requirement to strictly adhere to the contractual procedures when dealing with claims for additional payment and extensions of time for completion, notification of claims in short periods of time and a risk of lapse of claim in cases of late notice, can all easily be seen as offending the good faith protection principle typical in civil law jurisdictions.

The sample contracts used in the large-scale international projects are often based on the common law. However, the large and rapidly growing building markets in the Middle East, South America, the former states of the USSR, Central and Eastern Europe, and many African countries are heavily influenced by the civil law tradition. Therefore, tensions and uncertainty can arise when sample contracts based on the common law conflict with local governing laws and customs that are based on civil law.

A governing law can hardly be found that does not influence a particular contractual relationship. At least in cases where a contract fails to address an issue, there are the obligatory and mandatory provisions, precedents and rules of interpretation meeting the same purpose. The principles of freedom of contract and *pacta sunt servanda* (Latin for "agreements must be kept") form the basis of construction law around the world, and ensure that there is a thriving international construction industry (Charrett, 2012). The governing law sets limits of the traditional *pacta sunt servanda* tenet.

From a legal point of view, the differences tend to occur in the following areas:

- delay damages (liquidated damages) versus contractual penalty;
- substantial completion versus performance;
- binding nature of adjudication awards;
- limitation of liability;
- lapse of claim due to its late notification (time bars);
- allocation of unforeseeable and uncontrollable risk to the contractor;
- contract administration (the engineer's neutrality and duty to certify);
- termination in convenience;
- time-related issues;
- quantification of claims;
- statutory defects liability; and
- performance responsibility: reasonable skill and care versus fitness for purpose.

The above list is not exhaustive but serves as a summary of commonly encountered issues. Additional issues may include the right to interest, the approach to differing site conditions, changes in local laws, escalation of labor and materials, the impact of domicile in situations where some of the contractor's performance is executed in a different location than the project (e.g., fabrication of technological plant and design), local laws in respect to dispute resolution, the impact of implied terms and general aspects of commercial law, the right to suspend the works and the consequences of suspension, the rights of local subcontractors, limitation and prescription periods, liens, specifics of local public employers, etc.

There are other particularities and risks of local construction markets and international business. For example, the availability of skilled labor, labor law, local permits, necessary licences, government regulation, political instability, government expropriation of private property, and corrupt judicial systems. Some of these risks could, however, become a reason for contract renegotiation or termination entitlement with different legal consequences in particular legal systems. For example, Latin American labor laws (which tend to be more protective of workers' rights than those in the United States) may require use of local labor and usually require significant social welfare contributions as strikes can be considered a legitimate tactic for negotiation in certain regions (Venoit, 2009).

For every large international construction project, it is highly recommended that the influence of the governing law and the efficiency of respective contractual provisions in the mentioned areas are evaluated. In the following passages, some of the issues mentioned will be dealt with in more detail to provide better context for the remainder of the book.

More information can be also found at: http://globalarbitrationreview.com/know-how/topics/73/construction-arbitration/.

The common law of Australia and the influence of statutory law by Donald Charrett (Australia)

Much of Australia's common law is not substantially different from the common law of England where it originated. While Australia is a federation of six states and two territories, the High Court of Australia, the country's final court of appeal, has recently fostered the view that not only is there a "common law of Australia" but also that it is "a single and unified one." However, not uniquely, the legislators of the nine Australian legal jurisdictions (including the federal) have intervened to supplement or replace the common law in many areas.

As with other common law jurisdictions, the common law in Australia grew from its single English root. Applicable English common law was taken at a given point in time to the Australian Colonies established by England, and incorporated by the enactment of reception statutes. The received common law was subsequently and gradually changed by judgments in local courts, and increasingly, by local statutes.

In principle, judgments in other common law jurisdictions (particularly England, New Zealand, and Canada, but also other ex-English colonies such as the United States, South Africa, and Singapore) may be consistent with the common law in Australia, and relied upon by Australian judges if the factual circumstances are sufficiently similar: as Justice Paul Finn has put it, the High Court has viewed such foreign materials as being "persuasive to the extent they could persuade."

The major statutory departures from the common law relevant to construction law are:

1. "fair trading" legislation (primarily the Federal *Australian Consumer Law*, also incorporated into state and territory statutes);
2. proportionate liability in lieu of joint and several liability for a failure to take reasonable care (federal, state, and territory); and
3. "security of payment" reforms designed to enforce rights to payment across the contractual chain (state and territory).

It would be hard to overstate the impact of the *Australian Consumer Law* (*ACL*) on commercial arrangements in Australia. The shadow of this statute (previously the *Trade Practices Act*) falls on every commercial transaction in Australia, and it has had a significant influence on conditioning acceptable commercial behavior before and during the execution of construction contracts. Its effect is so pervasive that it can impact on the freedom of parties to contract, to an extent that is surprising to lawyers from other jurisdictions. Of the three types of statutory intervention listed above, it is the only one in which the various Governments of Australia have cooperated—albeit only recently—to produce uniform legislation that applies in all Australian jurisdictions.

Thus, conduct in the performance of a contract that might not amount to breach of contract can nevertheless be classified as misleading or deceptive conduct actionable under the *ACL*. For example, an architect who was retained to plan a residence to a price specified by the client, and represented that the house could be built for that price in accordance with the plans he drew up, was found to have engaged in misleading or deceptive conduct (*Coleman v. Gordon M Jenkins & Associates Pty Ltd* (1993) 9 BCL 292), when the price was exceeded.

Lawrence C. Mellon (2009) has recently observed: "[I]n the United States, construction law is most accurately characterized as a morass of inconsistent legal principles, each of narrow application, varying significantly from jurisdiction to jurisdiction." The same could be said of Australia where construction law consists of common law, except to the extent that the common law has been changed by statute law. Until recently there was little statute law that had an impact on construction law: the principle of freedom of contract prevailed, and tort law was almost exclusively common law.

That situation has now been overtaken by extensive (and generally different) legislation in each Australian jurisdiction in the areas referred to above. In particular, statutory adjudication of disputes over payment claims under many construction contracts has become the primary means of dispute resolution. This is considered in more detail in Chapter 11.

Donald Charrett
Barrister, Arbitrator & Mediator
Melbourne
Australia

2.3 Delay damages (liquidated damages) versus contractual penalty

Delay damages are a type of "liquidated damages." They are typically paid as lump sum compensation for damages. According to Anglo-Saxon tradition, liquidated damages are the sum agreed by the parties to the contract, authorizing the party suffering from the other party's default to receive a predetermined indemnity, following a particular breach. A court will decide on the validity or level of these damages unless such future compensation is specified in the contract (damages at large).

Pursuant to common law principles, liquidated damages will not be enforceable if they are designed to punish rather than compensate. Under the principles of equity, judges strive for fair solutions instead of enforcing the conditions that lead to unjust enrichment. Two conditions must be satisfied where liquidated damages are to be awarded. First, the sum must approximately match the actual or potential damage incurred. The purpose of damages is to return the plaintiff to their original position before the damage occurred. Damages are not an instrument of profit or unjust enrichment. Second, the damages must be a reasonably foreseeable consequence of the breach. If the liquidated damages are not recoverable, the employer will be left with the common law remedy for damages.

In construction disputes, the courts sometimes refuse to enforce liquidated damages because of the doctrine of concurrent delay in cases where contributory negligence can be proved.

Under English law, liquidated damages are generally regarded as the only remedy for the breach of contract to which the liquidated damages relate. In the absence of interim contractual milestone dates, liquidated damages for delay to completion will normally be the only damages recoverable for slow progress and then only if a delay to completion results. The employer may, however, have a right to terminate the contract. This depends upon the terms of the contract and the facts. Critical delay caused by the contractor's fraud, willful misconduct, recklessness, or gross negligence will not normally affect the position in regard to liquidated damages but may provide grounds for termination of the contract (Choat and Long at www.globalarbitrationreview.com).

In the civil law environment, liquidated damages may potentially be in conflict with the governing law in two instances. First, there is a liability limitation issue and, second, the issue of contractual penalty. Liability limitation will be discussed below in the Section 2.6.

As for the contractual penalty, this is a form of lump sum compensation for damages and, therefore, is similar to liquidated damages. However, unlike under common law, the contractual penalty acts as a sanction in addition to prevention and compensation. In civil law countries, the contractual penalty provision must be drafted in the contract precisely and in strict accordance with the governing law. Contractual penalties are often seen as invalid by judges if they are unreasonably high or not drafted in strict accordance with the governing law.

In Germany, for example, a contractual penalty (*Vertragsstrafe*) will not be enforceable if it is against good manners ("*Verstoss gegen die guten Sittten*" under §138 BGB) or against good faith ("*Verstoss gegen Treu und Glauben*" under §242 BGB). Furthermore, the judge can decrease the value of the contractual penalty if it is too high. The key aspects of an enforceable contractual penalty under German law are:

- It is efficient only if there is a default.
- Its daily value is not higher than 0.2 to 0.3% of the contract price.
- The maximum amount of the penalty is not higher than 5% of the contract price (Vygen and Joussen, 2013).

The use of liquidated damages in construction projects by Rob Horne (UK)

There has, following the recent English Supreme Court decision in *Cavendish Square v. Makdessi and Parking Eye v. Beavis*, been a lot of commentary on the perceived change in approach to assessing liquidated damages. I have explored, in a practical way, how liquidated damages can be utilized and what other options to their use are available.

I have set out step-by-step information on what liquidated damages provisions are and how they operate, together with the key legal and commercial issues which need to be addressed in either inserting a clause into your contract or in assessing the scope of such a clause inserted by someone else.

First, however, a high-level overview and introduction to the topic. While this is primarily a review of the law and practice of liquidated damages in England a section has been included highlighting important differences to that approach in other jurisdictions including Dubai, China, France, Hong Kong, Spain, and Australia.

Relevance of liquidated damages

Construction projects are inherently uncertain, based, as they are, on unique parameters for each project, be that design differences, construction method differences, differences in out-turn purpose or just differences in physical environment. Given the large amount of money spent on construction projects, and the impact on cost and value relatively small changes caused by these uncertainties can have, parties and their advisors have long looked for ways to eliminate these uncertainties or at least make them manageable.

This can essentially be down in one of two ways:

- the uncertainty can be eliminated through investigation; or
- the risk of the uncertainty arising can be managed through ascribing that risk to one party or the other.

Of course, in reality, it is usually a combination of some investigation and then an identification and application of risk. Where exactly that balance sits will depend on the nature of the contract and the appetite of the market to take on such risk.

One part of the uncertainty in a project that can make a significant difference to its commercial pricing is taking away the uncertainty of what happens if things don't go to plan. What if the project isn't finished on time, what if new work is instructed, what if the desired output is not met, what if the quality is not right, what if key performance indicators are not achieved? In the broad sense, the answer to all of these questions is relatively straight forward, you would be entitled to damages to recompense for any loss caused from these breaches. However, if you try to go behind that and say, yes but what cash sum might that amount to, the answer generally will be that nobody knows until after it has happened. Commercially, in terms of running a business, whether buying or selling construction services, only knowing the price after the event is not very attractive.

Where the parties can foresee a type of problem the uncertainty could be removed by agreeing a specific consequence for a breach. Then, rather than being unknown, the loss or damage is then identified or liquidated. While this doesn't remove the uncertainty entirely as the event may still occur, it does at least add some predictability to the consequence of the event.

The essential characteristic then of a liquidated damage is really to introduce predictability and foresight to the consequence of a breach of contract. The aim in doing so is to remove some risk and thereby reduce the overall contract price. That way everyone wins; the contractor limits his liability and makes the outcome of the project more predictable and the employer reduces the overall cost of the project by removing some risk but also achieves certainty of the consequences of a failure on the project.

Are there special rules for establishing liquidated damages?

In order for any provision for liquidated damages to be enforceable there are a number of requirements that need to be met. The key point for these requirements is explaining and understanding exactly what is meant by "liquidated." However, a better starting point is that liquidated damages are still damages for breach of contract.

The basic principle, in an English law sense, is that damages for breach of contract should put the party who has not breached the contract into the position he would have been in if the contract had been properly performed. While the mechanism around the recovery of liquidated damages may be different, this basic premise remains. Therefore, before one looks at the detailed rules surrounding the use of liquidated damages one must first identify and establish a breach.

To be liquidated, the damages being agreed need to deal with the following two points:

A. **Relate to a specific breach.** The breach must be clearly described and must, in fact, be a breach (without a breach there cannot be damages). A common example in a construction contract would be a failure to complete the works by a specified completion date. However, that is not quite enough, given how uncertain construction projects are. A better identification of the breach would be a failure to complete by the contractual completion date or any date that is moved to in accordance with the contract. We all know that things change on construction projects, new work is added, third parties get in the way, access cannot be achieved when it was expected and so on. If the liquidated damages clause does not deal with those eventualities then you could end up in a position where the party in breach can benefit from its own breach (e.g., by an employer delaying the completion and then charging the contractor the cost of that delay), a position the English courts will not support. If the contract then does not deal with identifying the breach precisely enough, the liquidated damages provision may fall away and general damages, with all their uncertainty, be the only remedy.

B. **Provide for a specific amount.** Once the breach is defined with sufficient clarity the consequence of the breach needs to be set out. The more complicated the project the more difficult this can be however. Taking a very simple example, a project for the construction of an industrial warehouse could provide for damages in the event that completion was not achieved by a certain date with the consequence being a specific amount of money being paid as damages each week it remains incomplete.

A more complicated scenario could arise in the construction of a hotel where delay damages are calculated by reference to completion of individual rooms. You now have a *"per day per room"* calculation, which is relatively straight forward but may raise queries around how general guest areas (such as restaurants and lobbies), service areas (kitchens, laundry) and external areas (gardens and access roads) fit into that calculation. Are they included or excluded? If excluded, are general damages available for any failure to complete them?

The complexity can be increased further, for example, where the project is a mixed use residential, commercial and retail development with the calculation of damages being based on the building type. In addition to the problems above in relation to the hotel further problems can arise if the mix of building types changes or different and new building designations are given. This could be further complicated if, rather than by building type, the damages were to be per zone of the development. If the zone sizes and mixes then change is the calculation of the liquidated damage still appropriate?

The above are not fanciful *"what ifs"* but real scenarios that the writer has been involved in. They raised serious issues in formal proceedings some with values into many millions of pounds.

The basic premise, for both breach and amount, is that the clause must be specific and certain either in absolute terms or by way of a specific calculation method set out in the contract.

Finally, the method of calculation must be capable of being carried out in advance of the breach actually happening. Therefore, the contractor must be in a position to be able to know (or ascertain) what liability he will incur if he fails to complete the works until seven days after the contractual completion date. A failure by one party, or a third party such as an Engineer, Project Manager or Architect, to assess the period of delay properly will not render the liquidated damages provision inoperable as long as it could have been done. It will only be unenforceable if, through operation of the contract, on the specific facts, the calculation was impossible and therefore the party in breach could not tell what risk he faced.

What can liquidated damages attach to?

In simple terms, liquidated damages can attach to any breach that can be defined with sufficient clarity and for which a specified amount can be assessed in advance. That is, of course, easy to say in the abstract. However, it can be much harder to identify the sorts of issues suitable for attaching liquidated damages to in practice.

Not only must the breach be capable of being clearly identified and defined but, to be commercially viable, the result of the breach must be capable of a fairly narrow band of damages. If the damages could vary greatly then an employer is unlikely to want to set them too low and increase his risk and the contractor is unlikely to accept them being too high and increasing his risk. The wider the starting band the harder it is, often, to find some acceptable common ground in the middle.

There are a number of areas, however, in which liquidated damages are more likely to be seen. These fall into the following three broad categories:

A. **Time-related damages.** This is probably the most common form of liquidated damage provision in a construction contract. Whether referred to as delay damages, liquidated and ascertained damages or even in some contexts delay penalties, the essence of this provision is to compensate for works not being completed on time. The key issues arising in this type of liquidated damage are:
   1. what area or part of the works does the clause relate to;
   2. when should that part be completed;
   3. what does complete mean;
   4. how can the time be extended; and
   5. what is the correct time factor to apply (that is do you assess the delay damages daily, weekly or, in some cases, hourly).

   The problem areas here are how to deal with early takeover of parts of the work and how that impacts the calculation as well as ensuring that the mechanism for extending time is robust. Without a robust mechanism the liquidated damages won't be enforceable. Particular care needs to be taken where there are interfaces between different contracts (whether or not there are different parties to each contract) such as shell and core to fit out where a delay in one package may impact the other.

B. **Quality related damages.** Identifying a liquidated damage to deal with quality is relatively unusual but not impossible. The easiest way to use this type of provision would be in conjunction with a robust series of KPIs where the performance being tracked is significant. As an example, a common KPI is response time in a term maintenance contract where a specified percentage of calls must be dealt with within a specified time period. Failure to achieve that KPI requirement would amount to a breach and therefore a properly calculated liquidated sum could be attached to it as damages. The major problem area here is:
   1. identifying the KPIs in a robust enough way to allow any failure to be readily identified at the time and to allow both parties to know and understand the risk.

   Particular care needs to be taken to ensure that the breach is objectively verifiable and not just a matter of opinion (statements like finishes shall be of good quality in this context are not going to be sufficient). As with delay related liquidated damages, some thought needs to be given to the impact of other changes in the contract and the impact they may have on the KPI or quality regime.

C. **Performance related damages.** Providing for liquidated damages attached to performance is most likely when the basis of the contract is the achievement of an output specification, at least in part. These are often found in utilities contracts, such as in the power or water sector, where there is a definite output to be achieved (e.g., the delivery of a certain volume of water per day or the generation of a certain amount of electricity or even the disposal of a certain tonnage of waste). Away from utilities it could, perhaps, be used where a particular BREEAM standard is required or a certain level of CO_2 emission stated. Quite often in England the performance risk will be taken by the employer and therefore a liquidated damages provision would not be necessary. However, there remain quite a lot of contracts where performance is relevant. It is obviously important, for this sort of provisions to work as intended, that the baseline performance is clear as a stated performance requirement, or is capable of calculation.

The method of calculating liquidated damages, as explained by the supreme court in *Cavendish Square v. Makdessi and Parking Eye v. Beavis*, has expanded the potential areas in which it is suitable to use liquidated damages provisions. A detailed explanation of that method follows in the next part. However, with the focus now much more clearly on the protection of legitimate business interests (rather than the rather narrower genuine pre-estimate of loss which had become the common benchmark) the scope and opportunity for imposition of liquidated damages provisions is much wider, and not necessarily in a positive way.

How are liquidated damages evaluated?

So far we have looked at when and how liquidated damages might be imposed and considered the elements necessary for a successful clause to be used. In essence, there needs to be certainty on breach and certainty on damage. How then does one go about assessing, in advance, the damage which might arise as a result of a certain breach?

The starting point, under English law, is that parties are free to contract in whatever way they see fit. So the starting point for working out what you can use as a sum for liquidated damages is that it could be absolutely anything, up to and including all the money in the world! There are, of course, some safeguards and caveats that then get applied to the basic proposition of freedom to contract. The one most relevant to liquidated damages provisions being that a liquidated damages provision cannot be a penalty. Essentially it must still be a clause that grants a sum of damages as a result of a breach, damages being a sum to put the party who has not breached in the same position as he would have been in had there been no breach.

That is, relatively, easy to do with the benefit of hindsight where one can see the breach and the consequences. However, the principle of a liquidated damages provision is that you are setting the rate in advance. So how do you do that without straying into creating a penalty? If you can show that the loss which was in fact suffered was less than that stated in the liquidated damages provision does that mean the liquidated damage cannot be enforced as it must be penal (being more than the actual loss)?

The court grappled with this question 100 years ago in *Dunlop Pneumatic Tyre Co v. New Garage and Motor Co*. In that case the court set out a four part test to establish whether a liquidated damage had strayed over the line into becoming a penalty and asked the following questions to determine that question:

A. Is the amount extravagant compared to the greatest loss that could be suffered as a consequence of the breach
B. If the breach is non-payment of money is the liquidated sum greater than that amount
C. Is the same amount used for different types and severity of breaches
D. The fact that the consequence of a breach is difficult to determine does not, of itself, make a sum estimated a penalty

Many commentators reduced this test to a short hand of "a genuine pre-estimate of loss is not a penalty." That phrase was then drawn into contract drafting with the parties agreeing that the amount stated was a genuine pre-estimate. This continued on until it was the general belief that the test set out in *Dunlop* was really just one of whether there had been a genuine pre-estimate.

Since 1916 there have been many cases where liquidated damages provision have been challenged for amounting to a penalty because, in the event, they were higher, even significantly higher than the actual loss. In general, however, the court was supportive of the underlying principle of the freedom to contract. If the parties agreed to a sum then, unless it was so obviously wrong as to be inconceivable (essentially the first test) then the liquidated damages provision was allowed. (It should be noted that this approach is not the same in many jurisdictions, particularly those with a civil code, where there is much more constraint around the freedom to contract and attempt to achieve a reasonable outcome.)

In 2016, the English Supreme Court, decided two related cases on the question of enforceability to liquidated damages. One related to the consequence of breach of a non-compete clause in the sale of a business amounting to many tens of millions of pound. The other related to a parking fine of £85 for overstaying a free parking period. While the amounts were vastly different the underlying principles of liquidated damages were the same.

The court found that the test from *Dunlop* was being applied too rigidly. They also made clear that the adoption of a "genuine pre-estimate of loss" test was not right. Instead the court provided an effective two-stage test:

A. Is a legitimate business interest being protected by the liquidated damages provision; and
B. Is the amount nevertheless extravagant, exorbitant, or unconscionable?

A further threshold test was stated, that the clause had to operate on a breach.

The court noted that in negotiated commercial contracts (such as the majority of construction contracts) the presumption will be that the parties are best placed to judge what is legitimate. In other words, the presumption will be for retaining the liquidated damages amount. The court further noted that whether the amount was a genuine pre-estimate, or even a deterrent, was irrelevant. The two stages noted above were simply to be applied.

What then does that mean in a practical sense?

To start with, the liquidated damage must attach to the protection of a legitimate business interest. That could be related to one particular project or it could be escalated up to the interests of a large corporate group. In the two cases before the Supreme Court the business interests were having a period of competition free trading in the non-compete provision and, in relation to the parking fine, the provision of parking services as the company operated only through the collection of these fines. These business interests are obviously quite different and very much focussed on the nature and subject matter of the contract they were found in.

Working out what legitimate business interests might be taken into account in assessing liquidated damages could be difficult. However, slightly more nebulous issues like future work, loss of reputation, and lost market opportunity would all seem to fall within the general definition. Equally, given the court's guidance, a deterrent can be used as long as it doesn't fall foul of the second limb of the test. More detail in relation to this point is provided later.

Turning to the second limb of the test, there could be argument about whether "extravagant, exorbitant, or unconscionable" amount to three different things with different levels applying to each. The more likely formulation will be that the court will read those words together to give a flavor against which the presumption that commercial parties can judge best for themselves can be tested. There is little doubt, therefore, that the bar has been set at a high level if you want to defeat a liquidated damages provision on the basis of the amount being too high.

How are liquidated damages approached in other jurisdictions around the world?

While England has wrestled with the issues around the proper formulation and assessment of liquidated damages for a long time that is not to say that nowhere else in the world has struggled with the same issues. In some countries, many of the principles will seem familiar, though often the detail is different. Whereas in others, the underlying principles themselves are quite different.

The differences in approach arise, to a large extent, from whether the system of law governing a particular country is based on case law, such as England, often referred to as a common law jurisdiction or whether it is based on a more developed code of law, such as France, often referred to as a civil law jurisdiction. Set out below are some examples of civil and common law jurisdictions and their essential approach to liquidated damages, highlighting the differences with the English approach set out so far.

Common law jurisdictions outside the UK

A. **Singapore** - The penalty rule in Singapore law is well established. (It was most recently reaffirmed by the Singapore Court of Appeal in *Xia Zhengyan v. Geng Changqing* [2015] 3 SLR 732; [2015] SGCA 22 citing Lord Dunedin's speech in *Dunlop Pneumatic Tyre Co Ltd v. New Garage and Motor Co Ltd* [1915] AC 79.) *Cavendish Square* has not been followed by the Singapore courts, but was referred to in a recent decision (*iTronic Holdings Pte Ltd v. Tan Swee Leon and another suit*, [2016] 3 SLR 663; [2016] SGHC 77). The High Court cited *Cavendish Square* not simply for the proposition that the penalty rule applied only to the consequences, which arose for breaches to primary obligations and not to the primary obligations themselves, but also for the proposition that *"in a negotiated contract between properly advised parties of comparable bargaining power, the strong initial presumption must be that the parties themselves are the best judges of what is legitimate in a provision dealing with the consequences of breach."*

In any event, notwithstanding its reliance on *Dunlop*, the Singapore position appears closer to the current English position than might be thought to be the case. Singapore case law already drew a distinction between primary obligations and secondary obligations in the applicability of the penalty rule. The Singapore courts have also recognised that a clause providing for a transfer of property upon a breach can constitute a penalty and that the penalty rule could apply to the forfeiture of a deposit.

One potential key difference between the Singapore and English position is that under Singapore law, it does not appear that "commercial justification" will save a clause if it is deemed to be a penalty. The Singapore High Court *(Pun Serge v. Joy Head Investments Ltd [2010] 4 SLR 478)* refused to adopt the English test of *"commercial justification."* The learned judge noted that the innocent party had simply conceded that the clause was an unenforceable penalty clause *"without offering any genuine or compelling reason for the court to prefer the alternative "commercial justification" test,* and that if it were to apply the proposed "commercial justification" test, the innocent party in that case was unable to show why the clauses were not a penalty.

However, it should be noted that an earlier Singapore Court of Appeal decision (*Hong Leong Finance Ltd v. Tan Gin Huay* [1999] 1 SLR(R) 755) had approvingly cited *Lordsvale*

Finance plc v. Bank of Zambia [1996] QB 752 and its use of "commercial justification" to uphold a clause.

B. **Australia** - The law on penalties in Australia has been developing differently to English law, but in relation to liquidated damages clauses the differences are minimal. In 2012 the High Court (*Andrews v. Australia and New Zealand Banking Group Ltd* (2012) 247 CLR 205 ("Andrews")) held that it was not necessary for the offending provision to operate on the breach of a primary provision in the contract for it to be a penalty. Rather a pre-stipulated sum that was payable upon the happening of an event could also amount to a penalty if the purpose of this sum was to secure performance. The High Court re-confirmed the application of the traditional test in Dunlop to determining if the pre-stipulated sum was a penalty, i.e. if the amount is extravagant or unconscionable in comparison to the maximum conceivable loss.

In July 2016 the High Court (*Paciocco v. Australia and New Zealand Banking Group*) gave judgment as to whether the actual fees in question (bank charges for the late payment of credit card bills) were penalties. In deciding that the bank charges were not penalties, the High Court held that in assessing whether a clause is a penalty the court is to look at whether the payment/remedy specified was exorbitant, out of all proportion or unconscionable to the legitimate interests of the innocent party. The legitimate interests of the innocent party could include other commercial interests beyond the damage directly caused by the breach. In doing so the judgments adopted the modern interpretation of the test in Dunlop given by the UK Supreme Court in Cavendish (although not adopting other aspects of the Cavendish decision that would be inconsistent with Andrews).

Practically what does this mean for construction contracts:
1. potentially a wider range of charges/fees could be considered penalties under Australian law; and
2. it will be more difficult to draft to avoid the penalty doctrine by structuring the clause to be a primary obligation;

Nevertheless in considering whether or not a charge/fee/liquidated damages clause is a penalty, an Australian court will look at the wider commercial justifications for such a clause.

C. **Hong Kong** - While English law is highly persuasive in Hong Kong, in a decision of the Hong Kong Court of Appeal (*Brio Electronic Commerce Limited v. Tradelink Electronic Commerce Limited* [2016] HKCA 164) concerning penalties handed down on May 5, 2016 no reference was made to Cavendish Square. In that decision, the Court reaffirmed the principal in Dunlop with Hon Barma JA delivering the leading judgment stating that "*there is much to be said for the first proposition stated by Lord Dunedin in Dunlop—that a clause will be held to be a penalty where the amount stipulated for is extravagant compared with the greatest loss that could be proved to flow from the breach.*"

Accordingly, Hong Kong law continues to follow the traditional pre-Cavendish Square position on the law of penalties. Whether the Hong Kong Courts will apply Cavendish Square if raised by the parties in the future remains to be seen.

The Court of First Instance has previously made reference to Cavendish Square (*Leung Wan Kee Shipyard Ltd v. Dragon Pearl Night Club Restaurant Ltd and Another* [2015] HKCFI 2225) however only for the purposes of answering a question on relief from forfeiture.

Civil law jurisdictions

A. **France** - Article 1152 of the French Civil code regulates liquidated damages under French law. Pursuant to article 1152, the party who has breached the contract must pay to the other party damages in the amount agreed in the contract. Like under English law, liquidated damages under French law must be commensurate with the loss suffered. Otherwise, article 1152 of the French Civil Code provides that a judge can, at the request of a party or even without such a request, either lower or increase the contractually stipulated damages if it is obviously excessively high or low.

Based on article 1152, articles 1226 to 1233 of the French Civil Code regulate penalty clauses (*clause pénale*) pursuant to which a party undertakes to do something—not only to pay damages—in the event of non-performance or delayed performance of its main obligation, in order to compensate the other party for the loss suffered. As mentioned above, the judge can intervene and lower or increase the penalty.

The declared purpose of the penalty clause is to ensure the performance of the contract. It is still debatable in French case law and doctrine whether the penalty clause may only compensate for the loss caused to the non-defaulting party or whether it can also have a punitive function.

The reform of the French Civil Code (October 1, 2016) sheds a light on this debate. Pursuant to the new article 1231-5 of the French civil code, the penalty clause becomes equivalent to the liquidated damages, under a unique regime. Thus, the amount of the liquidated damages should put the non-defaulting party in the same position as it would have been in, had there been no breach; should the stipulated indemnity be obviously excessive or ridiculously low, the judge can either lower or increase it.

B. **Spain** - There are two types of penalty clauses recognized in Spanish law:
1. The penalty can be a substitute for the damage compensation; or
2. The penalty can be cumulative to the damage compensation.

However, the parties shall not be exempted from fulfilling their obligations under the contract by paying the penalty, unless there has been an agreement to the contrary.

In any case, the courts are entitled to moderate the amount of the penalty in the following cases:
1. if the main obligation has been partially or irregularly fulfilled (art. 1154 Spanish Civil Code), or
2. if the amount is deemed to be unreasonably high, based on equity reasons. (Art. 1103 Spanish Civil Code)

Spanish and English law both allow the parties to pre-agree damages that will be payable automatically in certain circumstances. In Spanish and English law there are also restrictions—equity reasons (Spanish law)/genuine pre-estimate of loss (English law)—on the level at which the liquidated damages may be set. Under Spanish law, the parties also need to consider the impact of partial performance on the ability to recover liquidated damages.

C. **Peoples Republic of China** - Under PRC law, the right to apply liquidated damages is stipulated under Article 114 of the PRC Contract Law which provides that *"parties may agree on the amount based on the circumstances of breach of contract, or the method of calculating the amount."* This is subject to the following caveats:

1. if the agreed amount is lower than the actual losses incurred the court or arbitration institution may increase the agreed amount; and
2. if the agreed amount is excessively higher than the losses incurred the agreed amount may be appropriately reduced.

According to the 2nd Interpretation of Contract Law from the PRC Supreme People's Court and Supreme Court Case Gazette, the court may deem liquidated damages excessively high if they exceed the actual loss by 30%. Further, when considering "excessively high" liquidated damages, the court shall take the actual loss to both parties as the basis, and take the performance of the contract, the degree of each party's fault and expected profits into considerations, and then make a decision weighing the principles of equity and good faith. Importantly, even after paying the agreed damages, the party in breach will still be required to perform any outstanding obligations under the contract.

D. **UAE** - Liquidated damages are often applied in construction contracts in the UAE. However, pursuant to Article 390 of the Law of Civil Transactions of the State of the United Arab Emirates, Federal Law No. 5 of 1985, the courts retain the discretion to increase or decrease the damages awarded to ensure that the compensation is equal to the harm caused.

The courts, however, apply a considerable burden of proof on the challenging party in this regard. For example, the contractor seeking to reduce the liquidated damages will need to prove that the employer suffered no loss or a lower amount of loss than the contract provides. Equally, if an employer is seeking to increase the liquidated damages amount, it will need to prove that the loss suffered exceeds the contractual amount.

Any attempt to contract out of Article 390 will be treated as void.

E. **Netherlands** - Under Dutch law, there is no distinction between a liquidated damages clause and a penalty clause. Section 6:91 of the Dutch Civil Code ("DCC") states in this respect that any clause which provides that, *if a party should fail in the performance of its obligation, it must pay a sum of money or perform another obligation,* is considered to be a penalty clause, irrespective of whether this is to repair damage or only to encourage performance.

Whatever is due pursuant to a penalty clause takes the place of damages due by law, unless the parties explicitly agree otherwise (Section 6:92 sub 2 DCC). This means that, unlike under English law, under Dutch law there is no need to agree upon a reasonable sum in relation to the damages that it is supposed to cover.

Although a liquidated damages/penalty provision cannot be set aside due to the unreasonableness of the agreed sum, the court may reduce the sum upon the demand of the paying party if it is evident that fairness so requires. The court, however, may not award the receiving or innocent party less than the damages due by law for failure in the performance (Section 5:94 sub 1 DCC).

On the other hand, the court may award supplementary damages upon the demand of the innocent party if it is evident that fairness so requires; these are in addition to the stipulated penalty intended to take the place of damages due by law (Section 5:94 sub 2 DCC). These exceptions are, however, rarely applied. Normally, the contract is followed even if the actual damage is only a fraction of the sum due.

What should you do to make your liquidated damages provisions enforceable?

In light of the two stage test now set out for liquidated damages how, in practical terms, should one go about ascertaining the amount to include as a monetary value? Clearly a good starting point would be to take the wording of the first limb of the test and apply it. Set out what business interests you are seeking to protect through the liquidated damages provision. Depending on the nature of the clause and the novelty of the contract and project, that could require some reasonably detailed thought, or a fairly standard and simple list.

To try and put that into a real world context; a liquidated damages provision for late completion of a residential scheme of ten homes might have some or all of the following legitimate business interests to protect:

A. Recovering financing costs in the extended period;
B. Paying any compensation to new owners who cannot move in;
C. Paying extended and any additional site supervision costs;
D. Reputation damage;
E. Risk of residential market fluctuations; and
F. Deterrent from over-running

You could assign specific sums to each interest ending in the liquidated sum to be applied. Indeed, each line item may itself have a calculation attached to it. Alternatively, you could simply jump straight to the bottom line amount having considered the interests to be protected. In either case, the key point is being able to demonstrate that the protection of legitimate business interests has been considered in ascertaining the rate to be used.

It would be unusual to disclose this consideration at the outset of a project (though perhaps if there is a particularly good, transparent, and cooperative relationship it could add to that). This information is, rather, to be stored on file in case the rate used is ever challenged.

While the bar has been set high by the court in terms of what will fall over the line into being an unenforceable penalty, rather than a liquidated damage, there is a much more important factor to bear in mind. The legitimate business interest that could, for example, be taken into account in the late completion of an oil pipeline, would generate such a large amount of liquidated damages that the risk to any contractor would be prohibitive.

To try and reduce the scope for challenge, once you have been through the process of identifying and valuing the legitimate business interests to be protected by the liquidated damages provision a confirmation could be added to the contract. Such a confirmation could be along the following lines *"The parties hereby accept and understand that the liquidated sum protects the legitimate business interests of [ ] and that the sum is a reasonable one in all the circumstances."* While the end of that provision does not directly match the test set out by the court, the repetition of the sum not being extravagant, exorbitant or unconscionable, feels a little too much for normal circumstances.

What alternatives to liquidated damages are available?

In the previous part it was identified that one of the major controls on the amount of liquidated damages will be market forces. However, the premise of liquidated damages is still one with very negative tones, based as it is, on a breach occurring first. Is it possible, rather than penalizing for failure to incentivize success?

Incentivization

The answer is of course yes you can structure an incentivization program as easily as a liquidated damages program. Of course, you do have to consider whether you are genuinely creating an incentive or whether you are just painting your stick orange and calling it a carrot.

Incentivization, in its basic form, will be the flip side of a liquidated damages clause. For example, if the liquidated damage were £100/day for late completion then the incentive could be £100/day for early completion. Of course the numbers don't always match (sometimes the incentive can be even more than the damage … though I have not seen that actually appear in a contract myself) but have to be aimed at achieving one end, the successful completion of the project. That is, after all, why the parties signed the contract in the first place. The incentivization can apply equally well to other areas of the contract from exceeding KPI requirements to beating output specifications.

All that being said, incentivization remains rare in the UK construction market. What other options are available then other than a simple liquidated damages sum?

Sophistication

The first step might be to make your liquidated damages sum a little more sophisticated. For example, rather than having a flat daily rate for late completion why not have an escalating or de-escalating rate (depending the business model and the interests being protected). The liquidated damages could be capped to a total amount or by reference to some other amount in the contract (perhaps the total contract value). While capping the damages might seem to restrict recovery it should also have the effect of reducing risk, shifting focus away from demonstrating a right to finish late so more attention is given to actually finishing early. This approach is common in many other jurisdictions but relatively uncommon in the UK.

Some additional sophistication could be added to defining the breach to which the damages attach. For example, in relation to damages for late completion, are all of the works really needed or could you better define when completion is achieved so that the project can be put to user sooner rather than later. Do you really need all of the landscaping done before you open a road?

In construction contracts, by far the biggest use of liquidated damages is by reference to late completion. Perhaps a better approach would be to focus on achieving quality and value KPIs, attaching liquidated damages to those, rather than just to the time of completion.

Primary obligation—drafting to avoid penalties

There is always the question of whether you can "draft your way around" the penalty provisions. This has been addressed to an extent when looking at liquidated damages in other jurisdictions, but what about the UK?

There is a way to do that, in theory, but finding practical application is harder. As confirmed in *Cavendish* the penalty rule is only engaged in relation to a breach not a primary obligation. If therefore you can structure your clause to be a primary obligation rather than a consequence of a breach then the penalty test will not apply. This has been confirmed since *Cavendish* by the Court of Appeal (*Edgeworth Capital (Luxembourg) S.Á.R.L and Aabar Block S.Á.R.L v. Ramblas Investments B.V*). In that case, default under one contract created a payment obligation under a second contract. The court held that the payment under the second contract was not as a result of a breach and was a primary not a secondary obligation. Therefore the rules around penalties were not engaged.

Translating that across into a construction context, if there were one contractor appointed on multiple packages of work under separate contracts a failure to complete one, or a failure to achieve output or other KPIs in one, could lead to a direct consequence under the other package contracts. Those consequences would not be damages for a breach and therefore would not be subject to the penalty rules. Another example could be where you have an employer contracted to a developer, which then contracts with the building contractor. A failing in the building contract could create an obligation in the development agreement which again would not then be subject to penalty provisions. This is particularly important as many of these types of structures have the same entity as the developer and the contractor.

A similar structure could exist in a PFI or PPP with a failure of the construction or FM contactor giving rise to an obligation on the SPV to make a payment, not through a breach of the SPV contract with the authority and therefore outside the bounds of the penalty provisions. With the SPV being supported by guarantees back to the main contracting parties this could create more risk for those contractors considering entering into PFI/PPP structures. This is definitely an area to be cautious of as PPP is still struggling to find its feet again in the UK without more risk being added to it.

Non-cash protection

Lastly, rather than cash starving the contractor at the end of a project when it is tantalisingly close to completion, can the damages be bonded or insured against to give the receiving party appropriate protection without slowing down completion. Again, the key factor here is to ensure that the focus remains clearly on project delivery and does not get dragged into an overly rigid focus on perceived contractual rights.

The construction industry thrives on innovation and must innovate to compete in a global market place. That innovation must go beyond construction methods right down into the underlying contractual documents. Parties to construction contracts should expect and require that innovation of their advisers to ensure that the right balance of incentivization and protection is incorporated to enable the project to proceed in the most economical way possible.

Rob Horne
Partner
Osborne Clarke LLP

Penalty clauses and liquidated damages under Brazilian law
by Thiago Fernandes Moreira and Caio Gabra (Brazil)

Introduction

Although extensively debated by scholars and courts, the mechanisms of penalty clauses and liquidated damages do not cease to fuel debates throughout the globe. While in a local scale the topic is treated as a sensitive issue, in an international level, with the constant flow of international businesses across different jurisdictions and legal systems, it represents a sure meeting point for a clash of cultures.

The core questions related to the application (or not) of penalty clauses and liquidated damages concern more concrete and down-to-fact aspects, such as (i) the nature of the obligation; (ii) the proportionality of the amounts involved; and (iii) the degree of a party's liability for a specific conduct or effect. However, discussions on this topic always involve much more abstract and fundamental concepts, which, at times, trace back all the way to the foundation of a legal system, namely, the integration of principles of good faith, autonomy of the parties and the interference of the state.

Penalty clauses and liquidated damages in Brazil

Legal background concerning penalty clauses and liquidated damages

Following its widely known civil law and legalist approach, the Brazilian legal system has extensively regulated penalty clauses, dedicating a full chapter in the Brazilian Civil Code to this topic (Articles 408 to 416).

Brazilian law uses the terms "penalties" and "penalty clauses" to refer to liquidated damages as a whole, since, as we will further explain, Brazilian law does not repeal, but instead, embraces some deterring/coercive nature of penalty clauses.

The law distinguishes the types of penalty clauses to which we will further discuss in this paper: compensatory and delay penalties.

Article 410 of the Brazilian Civil Code contemplates compensatory penalties, which are permitted when a party fails to perform a contract entirely. It also establishes breaches of specific obligations, in which the innocent party may alternatively seek payment of the amount established in the penalty clause (especially when the performance of the relevant obligation is no longer possible and/or worthy) *or* demand the performance of the breached obligation.

Conversely, Article 411 establishes non-compensatory penalties, which are claimed in case of delays in the performance of an obligation or breach of a particular provision. Non-compensatory penalties are not an alternative to the obligation, but instead, the innocent party claims them along with the overdue obligation. This delay penalty, although understood as non-compensatory in its nature as the primary obligation remains enforceable and demandable, also serves to compensate the damages arising from the delay itself.

Another basic concept of penalty clauses and liquidated damages under Brazilian law lies on Article 412 of the Brazilian Civil Code, which establishes that the penalty may never exceed the value of the secured obligation. This statutory provision falls within the principle of full compensation for civil liability under Brazilian law, by which a party must be fully recovered for the losses suffered from the other party's breach whenever it is impossible or should have been impossible to revert to the status quo.

Similarly, unless otherwise stated in the contract, the contractual penalty represents the maximum indemnification due to the innocent party, even if the actual damages incurred were higher. However, one can typically carve out the penalty clause by contemplating in the contract the possibility that the innocent party seeks further damages in addition to the penalty amount. In this case, the contractual penalty works as a minimum indemnification amount and, if the innocent party manages to demonstrate that it has incurred in higher damages, it will be entitled to indemnification.

Reduction of excessive or disproportional penalties

As previously explained, although the law uses the terms "penalty clauses," penalties, under Brazilian law, are mainly established to indemnify the non-breaching party for damages it has incurred or is presumed to have incurred due to acts or omissions of the breaching party.

Pursuant to Article 413 of the Brazilian Civil Code, the court has the duty to equitably reduce a penalty established by the parties in a contract. Furthermore, with the increasing application of the social function of legal relationships and the influence of constitutional rights on private law, what was initially designed as a mere authority of the courts to calibrate a blatantly disproportional penalty under the former Brazilian Civil Code has gained status of statutory obligation to the court to act and repeal the application of penalties that are (at times subjectively) deemed disproportional and/or unfair.

In sum, to allow otherwise could cause not only the unjust enrichment of one contracting party over the other, but could also, in a larger scale, stimulate market practices grounded on penalty-based gains, which goes against the Brazilian modern principle of contractual good faith, as well as the principle of full compensation, consubstantiated in Article 944 of the Brazilian Civil Code.

In practice, however, reducing the penalty to a reasonable and proportional level remains a dish with no clear receipt and the application of the statutory command relies mostly on the courts assessment of the particularities of each case.

One of the main reasons for the wide range criteria for measuring the excessiveness of a penalty is the fact that Article 413 expressly allows the court to reduce penalties in an equitable manner. Although some courts will seek a more accurate solution from a mathematical perspective, many judges rely on a degree of discretion granted by the law.

Justice Sanseverino in the Brazilian Superior Court of Justice, in Special Appeal No. 1.212.159-SP, ruled over in June 2012, declared disproportional the application of a full termination penalty, which was claimed by a sports gear company that had terminated a sponsorship agreement with an Olympic medalist half way through the contract. The court decreased the penalty to exactly 50% of the penalty amount stipulated in the contract, applying, therefore, a perfect mathematical proportion between the completion of the contract and the application of the contract's termination penalty.

However, Justice Salomão, also in the Brazilian Superior Court of Justice, on Special Appeal No. 1.186.789-RJ, ruled over in March 2014, reasoned that the mere time and mathematical proportions may not suffice to: (i) repair the damages suffered by the non-breaching party; and (ii) encourage the performance of contracts. He highlighted specifically that the equitable character of the penalty reduction and that the law does not bind the courts to a mathematical analysis.

The justice then evaluated that, in that particular case, establishing an absolute proportionality between the remaining contract term and the penalty would not compensate the plaintiff for the damages suffered due to the untimely resignation of one of its professionals, who had earned his reputation while working in the company. He also noted that, applying absolute proportions to termination penalties would encourage parties to execute efficient breaches of contract, becoming economically rewarding to one of the parties with gains outweighing losses.

Punitive damages under Brazilian law

When it comes to penalty clauses, those in favor of the coercive nature of penalties under Brazilian law, and ultimately, in favor of the concept of punitive damages under Brazilian law, often raise Article 416 of the Brazilian Civil Code to support their arguments. Article 416 contemplates mandatory application of penalty clauses regardless of evidence of the losses and damages suffered by the non-breaching party. In other words, an argument can be made that, if the law disregards the existence of a damage to uphold a penalty clause, its main concern would be indeed to punish the breaching party and prevent breaches as a whole.

However, the wording of Article 416 should not be interpreted apart from other legal provisions, but instead it must be systemically interpreted with the Brazilian Civil Code as a whole. In this regard, it is clear that the Brazilian Civil Code has dedicated several provisions to connect contractual penalties to the actual damages that a non-breaching party might suffer, such as: (i) the limitation of the amount of penalties that must correspond to the amount of the obligation; (ii) the possibility of improving the amount of contractual penalty if demonstrated that the damages suffered are higher than such amount (provided that it is established in the contract); and (iii) the court's duty to reduce the amount of the penalty if excessive.

In truth, the teleological interpretation of the mechanisms described above, as well as applicable court decisions, lead us to the conclusion that Brazilian law has embraced that penalty clauses have a dual purpose. The first purpose, which is its most relevant, is to pre-estimate damages and compensate the non-breaching party. The second purpose of the penalty, reflected in Justice Salomão's view reported above, is the deterring function, which aims to protect the legitimate interest of a party, while discouraging the breach by the other.

Nonetheless, this deterring purpose should not be confused with punitive will, which is represented by excessive penalties with no nexus to the damage or interest it intends to secure.

Non-existence of the english law dichotomy of liquidated damages and penalty clauses

As it is possible to realize right from the start, the very famous English law dichotomy between liquidated damages and penalty clauses does not exist under Brazilian law. According to Brazilian law, while penalty clauses have a predominant compensatory nature, they also carry, to a reasonable extent, a deterring purpose/coercive character to protect a party's legitimate interest, either by securing the main object of the agreement, its right to a timely completion, or a particular obligation under the contract.

Nonetheless, the most important distinction between Brazilian and English laws is that while English law has always rejected the enforceability of remedies considered punitive in their essence, assigning to the non-breaching party the burden of demonstrating its actual loss to receive indemnification, Brazilian law preserves the effectiveness of the penalty clause.

Under no circumstance a Brazilian court would be authorized to set a penalty clause aside. Instead, as thoroughly explained in Section 2 above, it would exercise an equitable reduction of the penalty in order to make its application fair to the case at hand and base its decision on the nature of the transaction and the nature and commercial purpose of the breached provisions.

> In 2017, Justice Nancy Andrighi in the Brazilian Superior Court of Justice, on Special Appeal No. 1.641.131-SP, ruled over in February 2017, declared that the validity and effectiveness of even the most exorbitant of the penalties should not be disregarded. In that case, one of the parties delayed the payment of two installments of the contract price by respectively two and three days, during the course of performance of the contract. Due to the delay, the non-breaching party claimed the application of the contractual penalty, which was established in the contract as 30% of the full contract price.
>
> Justice Nancy Andrighi in her vote reasoned that, considering that the payment obligations were substantially completed, the delays claimed were kept to a minimum, and therefore, the penalty should be reduced, pursuant to Article 413 of the Brazilian Civil Code.
>
> The justice also followed the principles of good faith and the economic function of the contract and application of the penalty, to substantially decrease the penalty amount from 30% of the full contract price, as claimed, to a minimum of 0.5% of the amount of each overdue installment, without, however, barring or disregarding the validity of the penalty clause.
>
> Thiago Fernandes Moreira
> *Partner and Head of the Construction practice at Mattos Filho, Veiga Filho, Marrey Jr. e Quiroga Advogados*
> *Co-Vice Chair of the Projects Execution Sub-Committee of the International Bar Association and member of the Society of Construction Law*
>
> Caio Gabra
> *Associate of the Construction practice at Mattos Filho, Veiga Filho, Marrey Jr. e Quiroga*

2.4 Substantial completion versus performance

The common law distinguishes between such completion of work that allows the work to be used for an agreed purpose (substantial completion) and whole fulfilment of the contractual obligations (performance). Most sample forms of contracts used in international construction projects are therefore based on the substantial completion concept from the common law. This approach presumes the takeover of the work by the employer after substantial completion. Of note is that the contractor is not discharged of their contractual obligations until the performance certificate is issued. It often applies, however, in the civil law countries (pursuant to civil codes) that the "work is performed if completed and handed over." In some European jurisdictions, there may be disputes about when the statutory warranty for defects is triggered (see below the Section 2.13).

The principle of deemed acceptance exists, for example, under German law. If the employer refuses to accept the works even though they would be obliged to do so (if the works are in fact free of defects and materially completed), acceptance is deemed to have taken place. Deemed acceptance is also assumed where the employer takes possession of the works or starts using the works as per their intended purpose. The principle of deemed acceptance may be waived by the parties by explicit agreement (Kremer at www.globalarbitrationreview.com). French courts may consider that there is an implied acceptance of the works (*réception tacite*) in circumstances where the employer has taken possession of the works or paid nearly all of the contract price. However, this is subject to the terms of the contract not providing otherwise (Gillion and Rosher at www.globalarbitrationreview.com).

In South Africa, there is no provision in common law that determines whether or not the works are completed. It is therefore advisable for parties to have adequate procedures and organization to cope with the administrative matters in monitoring, updating and managing programs and assessing whether completion has been achieved. In practice, the contract will provide a procedure for certification of completion of the works; and the contracts generally contain a provision that where the employer takes occupation and possession of the works and starts to use them, the works will be deemed to have been completed. However, it is emphasized that this only arises as part of a contractual provision and not under governing law (Hoeben at www.globalarbitrationreview. com).

2.4.1 Taking over of the works

A common subject of disputes is whether the work was substantially completed and should therefore be taken over with the consequence that the employer cannot impose contractual penalties (or delay damages). In the ICC case no. 10847 (2003) (ICC, 2012), for example, the contractor claimed that the works met the requirements for the issuance of a taking over certificate at a particular date, in that they were capable of being used for the purpose for which they had been designed. The engineer had refused to issue the taking over certificate at that date on the basis that certain finishing works were outstanding and that certain items prevented some testing and commissioning operations. The tribunal declared that for the issuance of the taking over certificate, the works must be at a stage so as to allow for the beneficial use of the facility being constructed. In the tribunal's opinion, the items of work that can properly be undertaken after issue of the taking over certificate are items that do not interfere with the employer's beneficial use, such as architectural finishing works, repair work, fencing, landscaping, and demobilization. On this basis, the tribunal saw no reason to overturn the engineer's decision and dismissed the contractor's claim that the taking over certificate should have been issued on an earlier date.

Under the FIDIC forms (1999, 1st Edition and similarly also in the 2017, 2nd Edition) Sub-Clause 10.1:

> The contractor may apply by notice to the engineer for a taking-over certificate not earlier than 14 days before the works will, in the contractor's opinion, be complete and ready for taking over. If the works are divided into sections, the contractor may similarly apply for a taking-over certificate for each section. The engineer shall, within 28 days after receiving the contractor's application: (a) issue the taking-over certificate to the contractor, stating the date on which the works or section were completed in accordance with the contract, except for any minor outstanding work and defects which will not substantially affect the use of the works or section for their intended purpose (either until or whilst this work is completed and these defects

are remedied); or (b) reject the application, giving reasons and specifying the work required to be done by the contractor to enable the taking-over certificate to be issued. The contractor shall then complete this work before issuing a further notice under this Sub-Clause. If the engineer fails either to issue the taking-over certificate or to reject the contractor's application with the period of 28 days, and if the works or section (as the case may be) are substantially in accordance with the contract, the taking-over certificate shall be deemed to have been issued on the last day of that period.

However, according to Sub-Clause 11.9:

Performance of the contractor's obligations shall not be considered to have been completed until the engineer has issued the performance certificate to the contractor, stating the date on which the contractor completed his obligations under the contract. The engineer shall issue the performance certificate within 28 days after the latest of the expiry dates of the defects Notification Periods, or as soon thereafter as the contractor has supplied all the contractor's documents and completed and tested all the works, including remedying any defects. A copy of the performance certificate shall be issued to the employer. Only the performance certificate shall be deemed to constitute acceptance of the works.

Regularly, the governing law must be considered in terms of the taking-over procedures. How it was mentioned, in France, a so-called "*réception tacite*" will arise if the employer simply takes possession of the works under certain conditions both in civil and public tender (Wyckoff, 2010). In France, according to the Cour de Cassation in order to determine if any implied approval of the employer to take over the works occurred, the courts should see if the employer has demonstrated an intention to approve the works. There are three material conditions of such implied approval: (1) the works are nearing completion; (2) the employer has taken possession of the works and (3) nearly all the contract price has been paid. CCAG (the French standard form for public construction works) states for example that the employer shall not use the works without approving them first. This is to protect contractors against employers delaying the approval and the taking-over procedure (Teillard, 2014).

According to the New Czech Civil Code (§2628), the employer is not entitled to refuse to take over the works because of minor defects that by themselves or in connection with others do not prevent the works from being used for their purpose both functionally and aesthetically, nor do they constrain the use of the works in a significant manner.

2.5 Binding nature of adjudication awards

Settlement of disputes in construction projects requires speed, an informal approach and expertise. This is why adjudication is commonly used. In practice, we most frequently deal with dispute adjudication boards (DABs). The parties may submit their dispute to a DAB for its judgment. The DAB must decide in compliance with the process most clearly defined in the contract. Sometimes, it is also a statutory adjudication, as is the case in the United Kingdom, where either of the participants of a construction project can use the opportunity to resolve a dispute in statutory adjudication within 28 days.

In the civil law jurisdictions, the decisions handed down by DABs may be persuasive in nature but not binding or enforceable. In the common law jurisdictions, on the other hand, the decision is often final and binding if the parties do not appeal it within the contractually agreed period of time.

If the contracting parties (under a governing civil law) want to make a DAB's decision enforceable, they can, for example, modify the DAB's status to ad hoc arbitration. The parties can agree to use the arbitration clause for an institutional arbitration court (or for an additional ad hoc arbitration) so that this arbitration court (or the arbitrator or the arbitrators ad hoc) would become the authority to examine the DAB's award or resolution, should one of the contracting parties challenge the award or resolution via a lawsuit. For more details, see Chapter 11.

2.6 Limitation of liability

In common law, there is a tradition of highly esteeming the principle of contractual freedom and it is generally allowed to contractually limit liability, including liability for damages. In civil law countries, however, the governing law sometimes contains provisions that do not allow the imposition of such limits. For example, provisions may be encountered that stipulate that claims for damages may not be waived before an obligation is breached that gives rise to damage.

In the majority of legal systems, however, such limitations are acceptable. Under English law, such provisions can be effective but may be subject to the *Unfair Contract Terms Act* (1977).

Under French civil law, limitations and exclusions of contractual liability are normally effective. There are, however, two broad exceptions: (1) where the breach was caused by a *faute dolosive* (i.e., typically fraud or a particularly serious wilful misconduct) or *faute lourde* (i.e., a serious breach, which often corresponds to the common law concepts of recklessness or gross negligence), both defined on a case-by-case basis by the courts; and (2) where the contractual liability provided for is considered derisory or insignificant. Courts will consider the economic rationale for the clause. These principles apply even if the contract is silent as to such behavior and the parties cannot agree otherwise. Limitation and exclusion clauses are not valid where the contractor is liable by reason of a law that is a matter of a public policy (such as decennial liability). In principle, it is not possible to exclude or limit liability in tort (Gillion and Rosher at www.globalarbitrationreview.com).

2.7 Lapse of claim due to its late notification (time bars)

Construction contracts usually contain provisions that establish a duty to notify a claim for additional payment or extension of time in a certain period of time. If the claim is not notified, it is "time barred."

When considering time bars, it is very important to evaluate: (1) if it is possible to contractually agree on such a consequence within a particular jurisdiction; and (2) what exactly the consequence is of filing a claim notice out of time.

The precedents in respect of the admittance and status of contractually time-barred claims are generally ambiguous across different jurisdictions. Every particular time-barred claim must be evaluated individually in respect of the particular delivery method, related risk allocation, nature of the claim and the limits imposed by governing law. This issue is dealt with extensively in Chapter 9.

2.8 Allocation of unforeseeable and uncontrollable risk to the contractor

In some construction projects it can be efficient to allocate the majority of risk to the contractor. This is especially so where it is possible to transparently control and evaluate the risks and allow for risk contingencies in the contract price. The knowledge of the total contract price (no matter how high it is) may be an employer's priority in certain cases. In common law jurisdictions, the contract will be usually respected and even an extreme risk shift to the contractor will be protected by the governing law. More complications can be encountered in civil law jurisdictions and the parties to the contract must recognize the existence of the following principles of civil law:

- good faith (good manners) protection;
- imprévision;
- protection of the weaker party;
- *force majeure;*
- hardship.

Such risk allocation has its limits also in common law jurisdictions. Parties to the contract must also be aware of the potential effects of the following principles applicable to both in common law and civil law countries:

- frustration of purpose;
- impossibility;
- impracticability.

2.8.1 Principle of good faith (good manners) protection

In civil law countries, local civil codes usually contain a general provision protecting and requiring the parties to the commercial, contractual relationship to act in good faith, to be fair, and comply with good manners. Good faith lacks a universal definition but it is usually perceived as a sincere intention to deal fairly with others. Similar provisions may be encountered that protect the public order in general.

For example, §307 (1) of the *German Civil Code* (BGB) states that the terms and conditions are void if they unreasonably disadvantage the contracting party that accepted them. In practice, this provision is applied in cases of extremely onerous and ambiguous conditions. In Germany, this provision does not apply to consumer protection only, but also to contractual relationships between business people.

The provision reflecting *Inhaltskontrolle* (test of reasonableness of contents) states (English translation):

1. Provisions in standard business terms are ineffective if, contrary to the requirement of good faith, they unreasonably disadvantage the other party to the contract with the user. An unreasonable disadvantage may also arise from the provision not being clear and comprehensible.
2. An unreasonable disadvantage is, in case of doubt, to be assumed to exist if a provision:
    1. is not compatible with essential principles of the statutory provision from which it deviates, or
    2. limits essential rights or duties inherent in the nature of the contract to such an extent that attainment of the purpose of the contract is jeopardized.

A further example is §242 of BGB reflecting *Leistung nach Treu und Glauben* (performance in good faith), which states (English translation):

An obligor has a duty to perform according to the requirements of good faith, taking customary practice into consideration.

Any conduct must therefore comply with the principles of good manners and mutual honesty. In civil law jurisdictions the provisions can stipulate similar matters to the *New Czech Civil Code* which is based on traditional and modern civil codes from different civil law jurisdictions, for example:

- Agreements breaching good manners and public order are prohibited.
- Legal conduct must follow both good manners and law in content and purpose.
- Legal conduct that goes against good manners and law is invalid.
- The court, even ex officio, will take into account the invalid nature of the legal conduct that evidently goes against good manners or law or overtly violates public order.
- Everybody is obliged to act honestly in contractual relationships.
- Nobody is allowed to benefit from their own dishonest or unlawful act or illegal status they themselves have caused or are responsible for.

As a further example, Article 124 of the *Egyptian Civil Code* provides that:

A party who has committed a mistake cannot take advantage of the mistakes in a manner contrary to the principles of good faith. Such a party, moreover, remains bound by the contract, which he intended to conclude, if the other party shows that he is prepared to perform the contract.

Under French law, there is a general duty to perform contracts in good faith, for example:

1. The employer is under a duty to cooperate with the contractor. Courts have considered that this duty to cooperate includes an obligation not to unduly interfere

with the contractor's works. Any undue interference of the employer with the works (*immixtion caractérisée*) may excuse the contractor from liability.
2. Courts may prevent a party from relying on a termination clause if it is not invoked in good faith. Similarly, the general right to suspend performance if the other party fails to perform its own obligations (principle of *exception d'inexécution*) must be invoked in good faith.
3. While the employer is entitled to rely on a pre-agreed damages clause when a particular obligation has been breached, this would (in principle) be subject to the general requirement that contracts must be performed in good faith. Courts may modify the pre-agreed amount where this amount is "manifestly excessive or derisory" (Gillion and Rosher at www.globalarbitrationreview.com).

The purpose of such provisions is to provide the parties with ultimate protection against unfair behavior and extreme dishonesty and injustice. A similar approach is contained in the *Unidroit Principles of International Commercial Contracts (2010)*:

> ARTICLE 1.7 (Good faith and fair dealing)
> 1. Each party must act in accordance with good faith and fair dealing in international trade.
> 2. The parties may not exclude or limit this duty.

In common law jurisdictions, equity is a set of legal principles that supplement strict rules of law where the application of such rules would operate harshly. Equity has a similar purpose as the general provisions in civil codes and it is commonly said to "mitigate the rigour of common law" by allowing courts to use their discretion and apply justice in accordance with natural law. In practice, equity no longer applies in English law so there is no general duty of good faith as in civil law countries. Modern equity is limited to trusts and certain remedies such as injunctions.

In recent cases, certain developments have been encountered which seem to be aimed at establishing a good faith obligation as an implied term. Here are some examples.

In *Yam Seng PTE Ltd v. International Trade Corporation Ltd* (2013), the judge ruled that:

> I doubt that English law has reached the stage, however, where it is ready to recognize a requirement of good faith as a duty implied by law, even as a default rule, into all commercial contracts. Nevertheless, there seems to me to be no difficulty … in implying such a duty in any ordinary commercial contract based on the presumed intention of the parties.

The English Court of Appeal in *Mid Essex Hospital Services NHS Trust v. Compass Group UK and Ireland Ltd* took a stricter view, commenting that:

> [T]here is no general doctrine of 'good faith' in English contract law, although a duty of good faith is implied by law as an incident of certain categories of contract [i.e. such as in employment contracts and partnership deeds] … If the parties wish to impose such a duty they must do so expressly.

Another case is *TSG Building Services plc v. South Anglia Housing Ltd* [2013] EWHC 1151 (TCC) where the judge ruled that:

> I do not consider that there was as such an implied term of good faith in the contract. The parties had gone as far as they wanted in expressing terms in Clause 1.1 about how they were to work together in a spirit of 'trust, fairness and mutual cooperation' and to act reasonably. Even if there was some implied term of good faith, it would not and could not circumscribe or restrict what the parties had expressly agreed in Clause 13.3, which was in effect that either of them for no, good or bad reason could terminate at any time before the term of four years was completed.

In general, English law still has not accepted the good faith obligation as an implied term and relies on express terms of the contract. There has been an increase of good faith duties expressly stipulated in English contracts (e.g., in NEC forms: "the duty to act in a spirit of mutual trust and cooperation") in recent years. The trend of such express terms is positive and, without doubt, useful for all participants (mainly the employer, contractor, designer and contract administrator) of an international construction contract.

In the United States, the *Uniform Commercial Code* has enshrined in legislation the obligation of good faith in the performance of contracts. In *Metcalf Construction Co. v. the United States*, (U.S Ct. of Appeals for the Federal Circuit, Case No. 2013-5041, Feb. 11, 2014) the U.S. Court of Appeals for the Federal Circuit dealt with a breach of the implied duty of good faith and fair dealing (in case of Government misinterpretation of differing site conditions clause) and reversed a decision of the U.S. Court of Federal Claims. The Court of Appeals decided that the government is held to a higher standard with regard to the duty of good faith and fair dealing owed to the contractor than had been applied by the claims court (for more information see http://www.constructionrisk.com). In Australia, the High Court has not considered the issue, but there is case law which indicates that there may be a general duty of good faith in the performance of some contracts in Australia (Charrett, 2013).

Experience also shows that in many countries the participants of international construction projects tend to misuse their position and the contract. The general motivation is short-term gains being set as priorities—even in large public projects. A typical case is a situation where the contract administrator (the engineer) has, for example, 14 days to approve the contractor's design or time program and waits until the last day of this period, causing critical delay. This in turn allows the employer to impose contractual penalties/delay damages. Another example of conduct done "in bad faith" is where the employer creates artificial reasons to refuse taking over the works to impose contractual penalties/delay damages.

In both legal systems it is not universally accepted whether it is appropriate to disrupt commercial relationships with general good faith obligations. This can be perceived as restriction of contractual freedom that creates uncertainty. In both legal systems it is, however, accepted as necessary to evaluate the actual context and intention of the parties. There is no universal, international benchmark of "fairness"—much of which depends on contextual and cultural aspects.

General principles of good manners and good faith protection can lead to invalidity of a contractual provision or even the contract. A good example of a provision at risk of being held to be invalid is Sub-Clause 4.12 of the FIDIC EPC form/1999 Silver Book, under the heading "Unforeseeable Difficulties." This Sub-Clause reads:

> Except as otherwise stated in the contract, the contractor shall be deemed to have obtained all necessary information as to risks, contingencies and other circumstances which may influence or affect the work; by signing the contract, the contractor accepts total responsibility for having foreseen all difficulties and costs of successfully completing the works; and the contract price shall not be adjusted to take account of any unforeseen difficulties or costs.

Some authors speak about "legitimate interests of both parties" relate to the issue of efficient risk allocation. In terms of the choice of delivery method for example, the employer has in general two choices. Formulate the objectives of the delivery in global fashion, and turn over the detailed execution to the contractor (design-build) or provide the contractor with detailed description of the works (design-bid-build). It is not in "legitimate interests of both parties" to transfer a completeness risk to the contractor in the latter case. This is why the Sub-Clause 4.12 above or for example the Sub-Clause 5.1 of FIDIC EPC/1999 Silver Book is seen as invalid in Germany (Kus, Markus, and Steding, 1999).

2.8.2 Imprévision

Lawyers from the common law jurisdictions will often insist on the *pacta sunt servanda* principle, having its traditional limitations in the *rebus sic stantibus* tenet (Latin for "things thus standing"). The latter, however, should only be used in exceptional cases, as the contractor ought to be able to assess the foreseeable risks in their bid.

Obviously, some uncertainties may result in contract variations or termination. The *French Civil Code* traditionally makes reference to the so-called "*théorie de l'imprévision*," that is, the situation (obstacle), which was not foreseeable and is now complicating the realization and, therefore, is providing the contractor with the right to claim increased costs and/or to terminate the contract. This theory is typical of administrative law and imposes on the public authority the obligation to help the contractor if the equilibrium of the contract is shaken. The grounds for use of this theory can be extremely diverse, such the increase in cost and wages, interventions by public authorities, social unrest, forces of nature, and so on (Malinvaud, 2010).

An example of the price escalation clause is often quoted, leading to extreme impact on price. In this situation, the common law position, based on the *contra proferentem* (Latin for "against [the] offeror") principle, would likely be that the price escalation clause applies as it is written in the contract along with all the adverse impacts. The civil law position might be that the clause cannot be, as per the imprévision doctrine, construed in a manner which produces results the parties could not have reasonably intended.

Pursuant to the Article 147 (2) of the *Egyptian Civil Code* (1949), it applies that when contractual performance has resulted from an extraordinary or unforeseeable event that is general in nature, not impossible, extremely adverse, or just adverse to the extent to which it poses for the debtor a threat of tremendous loss, then the judge may, regarding the circumstances and having taken into account both parties' concerns, reasonably reduce the obligation of fulfilment which became excessive. Any agreement which stipulates otherwise is invalid.

Similar provisions can be found in the legal codes of the following states (Seppala, 2012):

- Algeria (Article 107 of the Civil Code);
- Bahrain (Article 130 of the Decree No. 19 of 2001);
- Iraq (Article 146 of the Civil Code);
- Jordan (Article 205 of the Civil Code);
- Kuwait (Article 198 of the Civil Code);
- Libya (Article 147 of the Civil Code);
- Qatar (Article 171 of the Civil Code);
- Sudan (Article 117 of the *Private Law Transaction Act*);
- Syria (Article 148 of the Civil Code);
- United Arab Emirates (Article 249 of the Civil Code); and
- Yemen (Article 211 of the Civil Code).

2.8.3 Protection of the weaker party

Provisions protecting the weaker party in contractual relationships are sometimes encountered in civil codes. For example, §1800 (2) of the *New Czech Civil Code* reads:

> [W]hen a 'take it or leave it' contract contains a clause, which is particularly disadvantageous for the weaker party, without reasonable cause for it, especially if it deviates seriously and without specific reason from the usual conditions agreed in similar cases, the clause is invalid.

A similar approach is also encountered in English law under the *Unfair Contract Terms Act* 1977 (UCTA). Broadly, this provides that: (1) a term of a contract that excludes or restricts liability for negligence must be reasonable in all the circumstances; and (2) where one party (A) deals upon the other party's (B's) standard terms of business, a clause that excludes or restricts B's liability for breach of contract must also be reasonable in all the circumstances. If these clauses are not reasonable, they will not be enforceable. A standard form of contract published by an industry body (e.g., FIDIC) does not constitute "standard terms of business" unless a party habitually uses a particular standard form for all its construction business undertakings (Choat and Long at www.globalarbitrationreview.com).

2.8.4 Force majeure

In most civil codes a definition of the *force majeure* or a similar principle can be found. This is contrary to the common law which is missing such a definition. In common law, it will be impossible to rely on a statutory definition where the contract fails to define the meaning of *force majeure*. Thus, it will not be possible to avoid the *force majeure* responsibility without specifying so in the contract.

The aim of the *force majeure* provision is to relieve a party of its performance under the contract upon the occurrence of an event where unforeseeable consequences cannot be predicted while being beyond the control of the contracting parties. In the French original (Malinvaud, 2010) "la force majeure se définit comme un événement imprévisible, irrésistible, extérieur aux parties contractantes." In most legal systems, *force majeure* events excuse contractual performance, but unless stated otherwise in the contract, do not create an entitlement for additional payment. However, according to its original meaning, *force majeure* entitles compensation in favor of the contractor. This right is, however, limited to prejudice directly attributable to the *force majeure* event. It is not extended either to lost profit due to the termination of the work following the occurrence of the event of *force majeure* or to the loss caused by the demobilization of the equipment and personnel. The events that constitute *force majeure* are diverse and include forces of nature, legal, social, or economic events, such as a strike, for example (Malinvaud, 2010).

Even the best-drafted *force majeure* clause in a contract can be in conflict with similar provisions of the governing law and this can cause confusion in realization and in settlement of disputes. It is therefore always necessary to formulate such a provision in respect of the governing law or to rearrange the wording of a *force majeure* clause where a sample form of contract is to be used. A full enumeration of the *force majeure* events may limit existing statutory definitions. For example, extreme weather conditions and severe industrial disputes have been identified as *force majeure* events in common law. In contrast, in many parts of developing world, these events would be considered reasonably foreseeable (Venoit, 2009).

Under Brazilian law, if the contract does not establish a limited list of events considered as *force majeure* which are all unavoidable, unforeseeable events and not caused by the actions of the parties, it may affect a party's right to relief. Nevertheless, such an event should have taken place after the execution of the agreement. Additionally, the legal principle of *force majeure* is not a matter of mandatory law and may be waived by the parties, should they opt to allocate all the risks to one or other singular party, or *force majeure* events and consequences can be adapted and/or excluded by the agreement (Marcondes, Salla, Nakagawa, and Diniz at www.globalarbitrationreview.com).

Under French law, for an event to constitute legal *force majeure*, it must:

1. make performance of the contract impossible, not merely impracticable;
2. have been unforeseeable at the time the contract was made;
3. have been "irresistible" in the sense that the event could not have been avoided or surmounted by the party affected; and
4. be external to the party invoking it.

The practical effect of "legal" *force majeure* is merely that each party is released from the obligations affected by the *force majeure* event, until the *force majeure* ceases to exist. Neither party can claim additional compensation directly on account of legal *force majeure*. The contract can define *force majeure* events and their consequences (Gillion and Rosher at www.globalarbitrationreview.com).

Under Spanish law, no person is liable for non-foreseeable events or, if foreseeable, inevitable (Article 1105 of the Civil Code that is not mandatory). The event must be unforeseeable or inevitable for the person to invoke their lack of liability (Iglesia and Fortún at www.globalarbitrationreview.com).

Organizations such as FIDIC have departed from using the *force majeure* term and have adopted clearer expressions such as "exceptional risks" with exact contractual definitions to avoid the above-mentioned problems and confusion in international projects.

Under FIDIC DBO:

> 'Exceptional Event' means an event or circumstance which is (a) beyond a party's control; (b) which the party could not reasonably have provided against before entering into the contract; (c) which having arisen, such party could not reasonably have avoided or overcome; and (d) which is not substantially attributable to the other party.

2.8.5 Hardship

Another similar principle known as "hardship" is perceived as a civil law tenet. As defined by UNIDROIT principles, where a party claims hardship, it is entitled to a renegotiation of terms and, in the absence of agreement, to rescind the contract or to amend it on "just terms" wherever possible. The hardship must be quite substantial, though not as severe as would be required for the application of the common law doctrines of impossibility or commercial impracticability.

In Brazil, Article 478 of the Civil Code establishes that the debtor may terminate the contract if the obligation becomes excessively expensive as a result of extraordinary and unforeseeable events, leading to an extreme and disproportionate advantage to the other party. The hardship hypothesis is regulated in Article 480, and allows the affected party to request the judge/arbitrator to modify the contract in order to make it feasible (Marcondes, Salla, Nakagawa, and Diniz at www.globalarbitrationreview.com).

Under Section 313 of the BGB in Germany, the contractor may seek adjustment of the contract price if unforeseen events that are not within the sphere of either party have affected the contract and its performance to such extent that either party could reasonably request a contract adjustment (Kremer at www.globalarbitrationreview.com).

2.8.6 Frustration of purpose

The common law principle of frustration of purpose (i.e., frustration of the purpose of the contract where the purpose was known to both parties when executing the contract) is the next example of a general principle that can influence contractual risk allocation.

Based on the English case of *Davis Contractors v. Fareham UDC*, 2 All ER 145, the common law's concept of frustration can be applied where fulfilment of a certain contractual obligation differs a lot from the original contract arrangement due to an external circumstance, but without any breach of either party's contractual obligations.

Under English law, where a supervening event or change in circumstances occurs which renders performance of the contract radically different from what the parties contemplated when they made their contract and for which the contract does not expressly allocate the risk or imply that, the contract is automatically "frustrated" and the parties are discharged from further performance of it. Payments are governed by the provisions of the *Law Reform (Frustrated Contracts) Act* (1943). In general, these provide for payments made for which no benefit has been received to be repaid and for benefits received for which no payment has been made to be paid for. Frustration is extremely rare. The fact that the contract has become more expensive to perform than had been anticipated does not on its own amount to frustration (Choat and Long at www.globalarbitrationreview.com).

2.8.7 Impossibility

To distinguish frustration of purpose from impossibility, it can be said that in frustration cases, the party seeking discharge is not claiming that it "cannot" perform, in the sense of inability. Rather, it is claiming that it makes no sense to perform, because what it will get in return does not have the value the party expected at the time they entered into the contract.

Generally speaking, if a court concludes that performance of the contract has been rendered "impossible" by events occurring after the contract was performed, the court will generally discharge both parties.

In the United States, since *Taylor v. Caldwell* (122 Eng. Rep. 309 (K.B.1863))—the case that gave rise to the modern doctrine of impossibility—it has been held, rather consistently, that impossibility is an excuse for non-performance where there has been a fortuitous destruction, material deterioration, or unavailability of the subject matter or tangible means of performance of the contract (Perillo, 2007).

A similar approach is encountered in civil law jurisdictions. Article 188(1) of the *Qatar Civil Code* provides, in the context of bilateral contracts, that if the performance by one of the contracting parties of his obligation(s) becomes impossible (that is, not merely difficult) due to an extraneous cause beyond his control, the contract shall be dissolved— automatically, by force of law. Article 188(2) confirms that in the event of partial impossibility (or where the event did not have a permanent effect), the creditor may, as his option, request performance of those obligations that remain possible to perform, or request the dissolution of the contract. Where no external events are at play, the contractor will be responsible for performing his obligations in full, even where to do so is burdensome (Al Naddaf and Kelly at www.globalarbitrationreview.com).

If it is impossible for the contractor to fulfil a certain obligation under the contract, the contractor is "freed" from performing such obligation. If such impossibility is accompanied by the default of the contractor, the employer may be entitled to damages. If performance of the obligation is impossible for reasons other than a fault of the contractor, the contractor is excused from its performance, as is the employer from the corresponding consideration, in general, payment of the respective contract price. The employer may also—depending on the nature of the obligation that has become impossible—withdraw from the contract (Kremer at www.globalarbitrationreview.com).

2.8.8 Impracticability

The doctrine of impracticability in the common law of contracts excuses performance of a duty, where that duty has become unfeasibly difficult or expensive for the party who was to perform it. Impracticability is similar in some respects to the doctrine of impossibility because it is triggered by the occurrence of a condition which prevents one party from fulfilling the contract. The major difference between the two doctrines is that while impossibility excuses performance where the contractual duty cannot physically be performed, the doctrine of impracticability comes into play where performance is still physically possible, but would be very burdensome for the party whose performance is due. Thus, impossibility is an objective issue, whereas impracticability is a subjective issue for a court to determine.

It is now recognized, for example, after the case *Transatlantic Financing v. U.S.*, 363 F.2d 312, 315 (D.C.Cir. 1966); 41 Tul.L.Rev. 709 (1967); 8 Wm. & Mary L. Rev. 679 (1967) that "A thing is impossible in legal contemplation when it is not practicable; and a thing is impracticable when it can only be done at an excessive and unreasonable cost." When the issue is raised, the court is asked to construct a condition of performance based on changed circumstances, a process which involves at least three reasonably definable steps. First, a contingency—something unexpected—must have occurred. Second, the risk of the unexpected occurrence must not have been allocated either by agreement or by custom. Finally, occurrence of the contingency must have rendered performance commercially impracticable.

An illustration of a contingency that alters the essential nature of the performance arose in *Mineral Park Land v. Howard* (172 Cal. 289, 156 P. 458 (1916), 4 Cal. L. Rev. 407 (1916). In this case, the defendant agreed to fill the requirements of gravel needed for a bridge-building project by removing it from the plaintiff's land and agreed to pay for it at a rate of 5 cents per yard. The defendant removed all of the gravel above water level but refused to take gravel below the water level on the grounds that the cost of removal would be ten to twelve times the usual cost, because of the need to use a steam dredge and to employ a drying process. The court held that the defendant was excused from performing the duty. It reasoned that though it was not impossible to remove the additional gravel, for practical purposes no additional gravel was available and therefore, performance was excused because of the non-existence, for practical purposes, of the subject matter of the contract. In exceptional cases such *ALCOA v. Essex Group*, 499 F. Supp. 53 (W.D.Pa.1980); *Florida Power and Light v. Westinghouse Elec.*, 826 F.2d 239 (4th Cir. 1987), impracticability was the foundation of a defence solely on the basis of increased cost (Perillo, 2007).

2.9 Contract administration (the Engineer's neutrality and duty to certify)

A construction project has two direct participants: the employer and the contractor. In addition to these parties, a construction project regularly sees the participation of the "engineer" hired by the employer, who conducts the "contract administration," the scope of which depends on the particular project and the authority delegated to the engineer by the employer. The involvement of the engineer is part of a long tradition from the Anglo-American system.

Within their duties, the engineer is a neutral third party (representing mainly the tradition and concept of an independent consulting engineer), who is professionally skilled to maintain a fair balance between the contractor and the employer.

The engineer should support the most convenient solutions within contractual limits. Therefore, they are key to any successful construction project. Appointed and provided by the employer, the engineer will work at the employer's expense. However, the engineer remains neutral to a certain extent. In European law, this presumption faces misunderstandings. The engineer tends to be placed in a difficult position when working on large international construction projects in the civil law countries. This is because employers from these countries often fail to understand or respect the engineer's mandatory impartiality. This can lead, sometimes, to a collapse of project management and contract administration, as well as damages and delay.

Bunni (2005) deals with the engineer under FIDIC forms and his role of a designer, employer's agent, supervisor, certifier, adjudicator, and quasi-arbitrator, recognizing his proactive, reactive, and passive duties and authority under the contract. In a traditional way, the consulting engineer is perceived to fulfill a broad scale of activities, starting with the preparation of the design for tender (including specifications and bill of quantities), the preparation of all documents to obtain a competitive price in finding a competent contractor and advising on the selection of the contractor. Once work starts, the engineer will supervise and inspect the work in order to ensure conformity with the design requirements and administer the contract, to deal with the situations as they arise, to certify and to act as an adjudicator of disputes. In almost all of the above-mentioned activities and roles, a conflict with the governing law may be encountered, mainly in the civil law countries.

2.10 Termination in convenience

Another widely used clause in international construction contracts is unilateral contract termination by the employer at their own discretion ("in convenience"). This provision is typically encountered within public contracts that are not subject to negotiation. The contractor who is allowed to negotiate over the contract should not accept such a provision without further indemnification (granted in cases of termination in convenience) as this kind of termination can easily be misused.

When insisting on the necessity of such a provision, the employer can put forward as an argument the wish to avoid indemnity payments to the contractor, which may arise due to unauthorized contract termination. The provision applies in most U.S.

jurisdictions. On the other hand, employers using FIDIC forms should not terminate the contract in order to execute the works themselves or to arrange for the works to be executed by another contractor (after a termination in convenience). The contractor will then receive payment for all already completed work plus all costs that would have been reasonably incurred by the contractor in the expectation of completing the works. The FIDIC contracts guide reminds us of the problematic nature of this provision, alleging that it can be in conflict with governing law. A similar provision is encountered in the German standard §8 (1) *Vergabe- und Vertragsordnung für Bauleistungen, Teil B* where it states that the employer may terminate the contract at any time before the work is finished. Termination in convenience cannot be considered a typical provision for any particular system but—in a civil law context—the provision (if wrongly drafted) will be subject to invalidity for going against good manners or being in conflict with mandatory provisions for contract termination. For example, under Brazilian civil law, the parties are bound by their contract; however, should the agreement be silent on that matter, the employer may impose early termination unilaterally, but must bear all the costs incurred up to that point by the contractor. The employer may also be liable to compensate the contractor for its potential direct and indirect damages caused by the termination (Marcondes, Salla, Nakagawa, Diniz at www.globalarbitrationreview.com).

In England, on the other hand, the employer cannot usually exercise the power to omit work in order to employ another contractor to do that work. If the employer does so, this will be a breach of contract entitling the contractor to damages (normally loss of profit on the work omitted).

The same principle may apply to clauses permitting the employer to terminate at will. In the event that the employer exercised its rights under such a clause in order to give the work to another contractor, then, unless the clause was clearly worded so as to enable the employer to do this, the contractor would be entitled to claim that the employer had repudiated the contract and could recover damages from the employer. Such damages would probably include loss of profit that the contractor would have made had it been permitted to complete the contract (Choat and Long at www.globalarbitrationreview.com). Termination in convenience clause under English law was considered in TSG Building Services Plc v. South Anglia Housing Limited [2013] EWHC 1151 (TCC).

Is an employer in breach of contract prevented from terminating the contract for its convenience? by Cecilia Misu (Germany)

Convenience termination clauses, originally used in public procurement as a tool to allocate risk to help prevent government waste, have spread to the private sector and can be found nowadays in all major standard contracts used in the international construction industry. Such clauses provide the employer with the option to terminate the remaining balance of the contractual work at any given time for reasons other than contractor's default, without having to establish any grounds, and/or (usually) pay lost profit to the contractor for the unperformed works.

Due to the ongoing financial recession and its effects on the global construction economy, employers may be tempted to use convenience clauses as additional bargaining power to lower construction costs or to benefit by abandoning a project partway through, if it is financially attractive to do so.

In view of the above and considering that at a particular point in time during the performance of a contract, each party may well be in breach of one of its multiple contractual obligations, and given that a termination for the employer's convenience involves a substantial financial risk for contractors, it is questionable whether an employer in breach of contract can be prevented from exercising its right under the convenience clause.

There is little authority available in this regard, but it appears that, unless expressly defined in the law applicable to the contract, there is no implied requirement for an employer not to be in breach of contract in order to exercise its right to termination under the convenience clause. Nevertheless, depending on the particular circumstances, the exercise of such a right by an employer in breach of contract may amount to that party's attempt to escape the obvious consequences of its breach.

Therefore, some limitations are set out where:

- The employer's default is a breach of the contractual obligation owed to the contractor (see *Cheall v. Association of Professional, Executive, Clerical and Computer Staff* [1983] 2 AC 180, per Lord Diplock at p. 189).
- The employer's convenience termination arises as a direct consequence of the employer's prior breach (see *Nina's Bar Bistro Pty. Ltd. v. MBE Corp. (Sydney) Pty. Ltd.* [1984] 3 NSWLR 613).

    Moreover, where these limitations do apply, the long-established legal principle that a party is not permitted to take advantage of his own wrong (see *Rede v. Farr* (1817) 6 M&S 121 per Lord Ellenborough CJ at 124, *New Zealand Shipping Co. Ltd. v. Société des Ateliers et Chantiers de France* <1919> A.C. 1 at p. 8) shall be given effect as:
    - a principle of law precluding the wrongdoer from taking advantage of his own wrong, whatever the contract may say and however clearly the contract may appear to confer on the wrongdoer an unqualified right to enjoy such advantages, or
    - a presumption of construction of the contractual convenience clause (see *Peregrine Systems Ltd. v. Steria Ltd.* [2004] EWHC 275 (TCC) per HHJ Seymour Q.C. at para. 106).

The dictum in the Australian case *Emhill Pty. Ltd. v. Bonsoc Pty. Ltd.* ([2003] V.S.C. 333) appears to confirm that, unless the employer's breach is clearly independent of the grounds to terminate for its convenience, it would require clear words to permit such a construction of a convenience clause. Otherwise, that clause would allow employers in breach of contract to ignore and take advantage of their own default. It can be concluded that the employer's contractual power to terminate the contract, at any given time he deems such a termination to be in its best interest and without regard to employer's defaults or omissions, is likely to be subject to judicially imposed restrictions, which, depending on the law applicable to the contract, are implemented by explicitly drawing on the concept of good faith and fair dealing.

Cecilia Misu
Contract and Dispute Manager
Germany

2.11 Time-related issues

2.11.1 Delay

Delays may be caused by the employer, the contractor, the contract administrator, third parties, or by reasons beyond the parties' control and they may lead to an extension of time for completion (EOT). Sometimes only some works (activities) are delayed and they do not require an extension of time for completion of the whole work. They may, however, cause a "disruption" (see Section 2.11.2), that is, more difficult working conditions. For details, see Chapter 7.

2.11.2 Disruption

Disruption can be defined as any change in the method of performance or planned work sequence contemplated by the contractor that prevents the contractor from actually performing in that manner. This material alteration results in increased difficulty and cost of performance (Cushman, 2011). Standard forms of contract and governing laws do not usually expressly deal with disruption. For details, see Chapter 7.

2.11.3 Ownership of floats

Comprehensive time schedules in large construction projects cover an enormous volume of activities that are interrelated, overlapping and running concurrently. Each of them can contain a time allowance at their beginning and/or end. In the case of delay or extension of time for completion, it often becomes difficult to determine who is the one entitled to make use of this allowance (the "float," i.e. the time for completion of the critical path). Commonly, these significant issues are neither solved by sample contracts (including those from FIDIC) nor via the governing law. For details, see Chapter 7.

2.11.4 Time at large and extension of time

"Time at large" is a common law principle, according to which the agreed time for completion (under delay damages) no longer applies if its fulfillment is prevented by the employer and when either the contract lacks any mechanism for extension of time for completion or when such a mechanism is non-functional. Under these circumstances, the contractor is excused from the duty to complete the work by the original contractual deadline, being instead obliged to do so within a reasonable period of time. The employer may not then claim delay damages.

It is without doubt that, in both legal systems, a party with a proactive approach (i.e., the one that flags events with potentially adverse impacts on quality, time, price, is timely in notifying and submitting their claims and is inclined to solve the complications in time), being in good faith, must always be protected in case of a dispute. For details, see Chapter 7.

2.11.5 Concurrent delay

The above tenet of time at large is based on the common law "prevention principle." In civil codes, similar provisions are regularly encountered. These provisions protect the contractor in delay who is prevented from performance by the employer in cases where the contractor was acting in good faith.

It is not uncommon for both parties to be in delay simultaneously. Frequently, the issues of concurrent delays are not covered in detail by governing law or in the contracts. For details, see Chapter 7.

2.11.6 Constructive acceleration

Constructive acceleration is encountered where there is a delay caused by the employer (after an employer risk event) and where the contractor has notified the employer of a claim for extension of time for completion. The employer may then refuse this claim, insisting via an instruction or request, that in fact no delay has occurred and the works should be finished on time. The contractor may express their disapproval and demonstrate an endeavor to accelerate. The acceleration will take place and additional costs will arise as a result of such acceleration. The particular governing law will strongly influence the success of a constructive acceleration claim. For details, see Chapter 8.

2.12 Quantification of claims

2.12.1 Headquarters overhead claims

In general, the contractor is entitled to be compensated for indirect costs in the form of increased, non-absorbed headquarters overhead expenses if, for example, the work completion date is extended on the employer's side. This is because extra payment for such a prolongation by the contractor would not have been factored into their bid price. In the Anglo-American world, various formulas are frequently used to quantify the cost because of the difficulty of exact assessment. The reason is the difficulty or impossibility of identifying the headquarters overhead for a particular contract in the bill of quantities as it consists of the expenses incurred by the contractor's administrative units (such as top management, office staff, and services). These administrative units concurrently handle a large number of projects and the related allocation of costs can be very complicated. The governing law and the method of dispute resolution may influence the outcome in dealing with headquarters overhead claims. For details, see Chapter 10.

2.12.2 Global claims

A global claim is one in which the contractor seeks compensation for a group of employer risk events but does not or cannot demonstrate a direct link between the loss incurred and the individual employer risk events (the SCL Protocol).

Recently, some courts have been accepting global claims or modified versions of them. This is due to the complexity of activities performed on a construction site that make the process of individual claims, precise documenting and quantifying (where each cause has a distinctive effect and a distinctive loss) almost impossible (Haidar, 2011). Also in this case the governing law and the method of dispute resolution may influence the outcome in dealing with global claims. For details, see Chapter 10.

2.13 Statutory defects liability

A "decennial liability" (*responsabilité décennale* in French) appears in some jurisdictions. Some civil codes (such as those of Kuwait, Iraq, Jordan, Egypt, and Lebanon) contain such provisions, thereby expanding the contractor's liability for the defective work, particularly in structural stability (i.e., an objective liability). Reduced liability can be claimed on the basis of *force majeure*, for example and will vary from jurisdiction to jurisdiction. In other words, it is in fact a specific warranty which runs in parallel to contractual defects liability, if any. In some countries, this liability is closely related to decennial insurance and is a typical example of a mandatory provision that may have major impacts on contractual relationships in an international project (Malinvaud, 2010).

2.14 Performance responsibility: Reasonable skill and care versus fitness for purpose

In construction projects, the contractors and designers are often responsible for the results of their works at a professional duty of care level (or reasonable skill and care) basis. In this case, they are not responsible for the result but only the correctness of the process leading to the result to be achieved. The governing law or contract frequently defines the details of the standard to be achieved. Where the contract and/or governing law is silent on the matter, this principle often manifests itself as an implied term.

In the case of design-build projects, for example, construction contractors and designers are typically responsible for the result of their works in more rigorous terms. The result must then meet the fitness-for-purpose criterion. In other words, the employer will define the dimensions and the main parameters of, for example, a power plant. The employer must specify the amounts of power to be generated in a given period of time and for what consumption of fuel (coal, gas, biomass, etc.), waste production and air pollution rates. The contractor frequently has to scrutinize an employer's requirements to remedy all discrepancies. The above-mentioned implied term is followed then.

Concerning the status of performance responsibility, the differences are also in the sample documents coming from diverse conveniences. In France, for example, the *Cahier des Clauses Administratives Générales* (CCAG) contract forms are used. The Institution of Civil Engineers (ICE), Joint Contracts Tribunal (JCT), and the New Engineering Contract (NEC3) sample documents are used in the United Kingdom.

The mentioned sample forms contain various significant differences but regulate the same or similar relationships. When, for example, a CCAG form is used, the designer must provide for the design and be responsible for the respective fitness for purpose. The terms will be looser where the British forms are used, as these are based on the "professional" standard of care.

2.15 Common law, civil law, and Sharia interconnections

The chosen dispute resolution procedure in a particular jurisdiction may be crucial when evaluating a specific contractual provision or circumstance in respect of the governing law in European or Anglo-American jurisdictions. Most frequently, such a dispute will be dealt with through adjudication, arbitration, or litigation.

An arbitrator or judge from a common law country may hand down different decisions to their counterparts from civil law jurisdictions. An experienced common law arbitrator may accept, for example, a lapse of claim ("resting on one's rights") in whatever context. Lawyers from these jurisdictions respect, almost absolutely, the agreed wording of the contract.

In contrast, a judge from a civil law jurisdiction may refuse the validity of such a clause (or forgive the lack of notice) considering the claim in view of general principles of the governing law and arguing that if damage is caused by the employer and the employer knew about the event causing the claim (e.g., delayed access to the site), then the contractor has the right to claim damages despite the lack of notice. For this reason, civil law lawyers will refer to good manners and good faith protection when preparing their submissions.

It is further worth mentioning that particular common law jurisdictions can find themselves in conflict regarding certain matters. For example, while the doctrine of constructive acceleration is recognized by U.S. law, it is not recognized in Ireland. The same applies to the lack of an "exact character and composition" doctrine of *force majeure* even between U.S. jurisdictions. Furthermore, in the United States, the employer's duty to make progress payment is a condition precedent to a contractor's obligation to continue work. In Commonwealth countries, however, progress payment is not a condition precedent (Venoit, 2009).

Despite some differences, both civil and common law systems are rather similar when compared to other legal systems. In Middle Eastern countries, for example, it is necessary to take into account the Sharia system of law. Currently, nearly all Arabic countries have modern civil codes based on the *Egyptian Civil Code* and Islamic law. There is no unified Arabic law, but the individual legal systems share numerous similarities. General rules of Sharia may then be used to fill gaps in jurisdictions ruled by national constitutions such as in Egypt, Syria, Kuwait, Bahrain, Qatar, the UAE, and Yemen. This can sometimes make contractual provisions void. Some void provisions may include inadequate interest rates or contractual penalties, establishing general legal principles for protection of good manners, and good faith as in the civil codes in Europe. Despite their relative similarity to the civil law system, the above countries predominantly use FIDIC forms, which are based on the common law. In some of these countries, FIDIC forms were made a part of their local public procurement legislation. This situation is reflected in Europe as well.

Evidently, the legal systems are now undergoing a natural convergence (rather than any artificially planned unification) in the field of large construction projects, influenced by the sample documents (mainly the FIDIC forms) used over long periods of time in particular regions. The use of sample forms leads to a degree of convergence, which can also be attributed to other factors such as international treaties, economic and political unions, model laws, standard terms and the business practice of international lenders, insurers, investors and contractors and the lack of clear construction law principles in many jurisdictions.

Considerations for the construction of offshore oil and gas structures in the Middle East by Faisal Attia and Fernando Ortega (Qatar)

Introduction

There are many issues that may impact the construction of offshore oil and gas structures in the Middle East. However, for the purposes of this book, we will only address two issues, namely the effect of decennial liability on an offshore oil and gas structure and the lack of regulatory framework for the decommissioning of these structures.

Decennial liability

Across the Middle East, many countries will contain within their civil code (and in some cases within their public procurement laws as well) decennial liability provisions. Decennial liability provides that a contractor and the supervising architect will be jointly liable to compensate the employer for a period of ten (10) years from the taking over of the project if the structure suffers a total or partial collapse, or there is a defect that threatens the stability of the structure. The period can be less than ten (10) years depending on the jurisdiction. Decennial liability is a strict liability matter and negligence does not need to be proved.

The decennial liability rules are mandatory and therefore a contractor and/or an architect cannot contract out of or limit their liability. However, they can deny liability on the basis of force majeure, or show that the cause of the failure of the structure was due to an external cause after handover (i.e., the employer or a third party caused the structure to collapse). Further, decennial liability does not apply to subcontractors. The burden of proof of this defence lies with the contractor and/or the architect. Main contractors will not benefit from the strict nature of decennial liability against its subcontractors.

The question of whether decennial liability would apply to offshore oil and gas structures (among other structures) was subject to great debate and division among Middle Eastern civil law jurists. However, some of leading jurists are of the view that decennial liability will apply to any structure as long as they are "*fixed to ground*" including if the structure is offshore.

Based on the latter opinions, it is likely that decennial liability would apply to the following offshore oil and gas structures in the Middle East:

(i)   Fixed platforms;
(ii) Complaint towers;
(iii) Gravity-based structures;
(iv) Offshore export and import terminals (LNG and LPG);

(v) Offshore wind-power foundations;
(vi) Pipelines; and
(vii) Underwater oil storage tanks.

Decommissioning

In the Middle East, the decommissioning of offshore oil and gas structures is not as common as compared to the Gulf of Mexico or in the North Sea. The principal reason behind this is that since offshore oil and gas fields in the Middle East will typically have a longer field life, older offshore oil and gas structures will be expected to operate for many years and therefore prolonging any abandonment or decommissioning of these structures. However, when the time comes for the abandonment or decommissioning of these structures, the regulatory framework for many of the countries in the Middle East will be an issue of concern and uncertainty.

At the moment many of the countries in the Middle East (with the exception of the United Arab Emirates) do not have a domestic regulatory framework in place to address abandonment or decommissioning of offshore oil and gas structures.

For many countries in the Middle East, the host government instrument (i.e., production sharing agreement (PSA), concession, service agreement) is the primary method to implement some decommissioning obligations on the contractor. For example, in Bahrain, there is no domestic regulatory framework that addresses the abandonment or decommissioning of an offshore oil and gas structure. Instead, Bahrain through its Oilfield Development and Production Sharing Agreement (DPSA), requires a contractor to maintain an abandonment fund and to ensure that any decommissioning works must be in compliance with international standards.

Many of the older host government instruments found in the Middle East contain no provisions and/or requirements for abandonment or decommissioning of the structures used in the production of oil field assets. Rather, the host government instrument would only require the contractor to comply with general requirements relating to the pollution and protection of the environment under the environmental law of the host government. For example, in Egypt, older model concession agreements issued by Egyptian General Petroleum Corporation (EGPC), Egyptian Natural Gas Holding Company (EGAS), and the Ganoub El Wadi Petroleum Holding Company (GANOPE), did not contain any obligations for the contractor to create and/or maintain a decommissioning fund, or develop a decommissioning plan. The contractor during the life of the concession would only be required to comply with the environmental law of Egypt (Environmental Law No 4 of 1994), which imposes criminal penalties for failing to abide by the rules aiming to prevent pollution from oil spills.

The Egyptian Model Concession Agreements would require ownership of the structure to be transferred gradually from the contractor to EGPC or EGAS as part of the contractor's cost recovery for the construction of the structure. Once the contractor has recovered its costs, the government entity will own the structure and will be left to decommission the offshore structure at its own cost. Recent changes were made to the Model Concession Agreements to contain abandonment provisions that require a contractor to submit an abandonment plan which will contain the abandonment procedures and estimated costs.

Further, the decommissioning of an offshore oil and gas structure in the Middle East is also govern by two (2) regional conventions:

(a) The Kuwait Regional Convention for Cooperation on the Protection of the Marine Environment from Pollution (the Kuwait Convention) and subsequent protocols—signatories: Bahrain, Iran, Iraq, Kuwait, Oman, Qatar, Saudi Arabia, and United Arab Emirates; and
(b) The Regional Convention for the Conservation of the Red Sea and Gulf of Aden (the Jeddah Convention) and subsequent Protocols—signatories: Djibouti, Egypt, Jordan, Saudi Arabia, Somalia, Sudan, and Yemen.

1. The regional conventions provide a legal framework to prevent, abate, and combat pollution of the marine environment caused by offshore operations, discharge (intentional or accidental) from ships, the dumping of waste from ships, and the exploration and exploitation of the sea.
2. The Jeddah Convention and its subsequent protocols do not specifically address the removal or decommissioning of oil and gas structures. However, the Kuwait Convention does provide a framework for the removal of offshore platforms and pipelines.
3. Article XIII of the Kuwait Convention's Protocol Concerning Marine Pollution Resulting from Exploration and Exploitation of the Continental Shelf requires platforms and other sea-bed structures to be removed in whole or in part to ensure the safety of navigation and lawful fishing. For pipelines, a contractor is required to 1) flush and remove any residual pollutants from the pipeline and 2) bury the pipeline, or remove part and bury the remaining parts of the pipeline, so to eliminate any foreseeable risk to navigation or fishing.

Faisal Attia
Director, DWF (Middle East) LLP

Fernando Ortega
Legal Consultant, DWF (Middle East) LLP

References

Bunni, N.G. (2005). *The FIDIC Forms of Contract* (3rd Edition). Blackwell, Oxford.
Charrett, D. (2012). A common law of construction contracts – or vive la différence? *International Construction Law Review*, 29(1).
Cushman, R.F. (2011). *Proving and Pricing Construction Claims*. Wolters Kluwer, New York.
Haidar, A.D. (2011). *Global Claims in Construction*. Springer Verlag, London.
ICC (2012). *International Court of Arbitration Bulletin*, 23(2).
Malinvaud, P. (2010). *Droit de la Construction*. Dalloz, Paris.
Mellon, L.C. (2009). What we teach when we teach construction law. *The Construction Lawyer*, 29(3), 8.
Perillo, M.J. (2007). *Calamari and Perillo on Contracts* (5th Edition). Thomson West, St. Paul, MN.
Seppala, C. (2012). Cost management in FIDIC Conditions of Contract. Paper presented at the 25th FIDIC International Contract Users' Conference, London.
Venoit, W.K. (2009). *International Construction Law: A Guide for Cross-Border Transactions and Legal Disputes*. ABA Publishing, Chicago.

Vygen, K. and Joussen, E. (2013). *Bauvertragsrecht nach VOB und BGB: Handbuch des privaten Baurechts* (5th Edition). Werner Verlag, Cologne.

Wyckoff, P.G. (2010). *Pratique du Droit de la Construction: Marchés Publics et Privés*. Eyrolles, Paris.

Further reading

Bailey, J. (2011). *Construction Law*. Vol. I. Routledge, London.

Baker, E. (2009). *FIDIC Contracts: Law and Practice*. Routledge, London.

Bellhouse, J. and Copan, P. (2007). Common law 'time at large' arguments in a civil law context. *Construction Law Journal*, 8.

Budin, R.P. (1998). *Guide pratique de l'exécution des contrats internationaux de construction*. Staempli Editions SA, Berne.

Burr, A. and Lane, N. (2003). The SCL delay and disruption protocol: hunting Snarks. *Construction Law Journal*, 3.

Charrett, D. (2013). The use of the Unidroit Principles in international construction contracts. *International Construction Law Review*, 20(4).

Charrett, D. and Bell, M. (2011). Statutory intervention into the Common Construction Law of Australia: progress or regress? *Australian Construction Law Newsletter*, 137(March/April).

FIDIC (2000). *The FIDIC Contracts Guide* (1st Edition). FIDIC, Lausanne.

FIDIC (2008). *Conditions of Contract for Design, Build and Operate Projects* (1st Edition). FIDIC, Lausanne.

FIDIC (2011a). *FIDIC Procurement Procedures Guide* (1st Edition). FIDIC, Lausanne.

FIDIC (2011b). *FIDIC DBO Contract Guide* (1st Edition). FIDIC, Lausanne.

Finn, P. (2010). Internationalization or isolation: the Australian cul de sac? The case of contract law. In: Bant, E. and Harding, M. (eds) *Exploring Private Law*. Cambridge University Press, Cambridge.

Glover, J. United Kingdom: Force Majeure under common law and the Civil Codes: the FIDIC Form and NEC Contract compared. Online. Available at: http://www.mondaq.com (accessed 3 May 2018).

Hermida. J. Convergence of civil law and common law in the space field. Online. Available at: http://www.julianhermida.com (accessed 3 May 2018).

Jørgensen, J.C. (2010). *Delay Clauses in International Construction Contracts*. Kluwer Law International, Alphen aan den Rijn.

Kus, A., Markus, J. and Steding R. (1999). FIDIC's New Silver Book under the German Standard Form Contract Act. International Construction Law Review, Informa, London.

Majid, S. Worldwide: Application of Islamic Law in the Middle East. Online. Available at: http://www.mondaq.com (accessed 3 May 2018).

Melis, W. (1984). *Force Majeure* and hardship clauses in international commercial contracts in view of the practices of the ICC Court of Arbitration, 1 *Journal of International Arbitration* 1984, at 213 et seq. Online. Available at: http://www.mondaq.com (accessed 3 May 2018).

Messitte, P. Common law v. civil law system. Available at: http://web.ntpu.edu.tw/~markliu/common_v_civil.pdf (accessed 3 May 2018).

Pinto-Ward, R. Construction contracts: common law v. civil law – de vrais faux amis! Online. Available at: http://www.ice.org.uk (accessed 3 May 2018).

Society of Construction Law (2002). Delay and disruption protocol 2002. Online. Available at: http://www.scl.org.uk (accessed 3 May 2018).

Society of Construction Law Users' Guide to Adjudication: A Guide for Participants in Adjudications Conducted under Part II of the Housing Grants, Construction and Regeneration Act 1996. Online. Available at: http://www.scl.org.uk (accessed 3 May 2018).

Sunna, E. and Al Saadoon, O. FIDIC in the Middle East. Online. Available at: http://www.fidic.org (accessed 3 May 2018).

Teillard, A. (2014). The Start Date for Post Contractual Liability in French Law in the FIDIC Red and Yellow Books. International Construction Law Review, Informa, London.

Websites

http://globalarbitrationreview.com/know-how/topics/73/construction-arbitration.
http://www.constructionrisk.com.

3 Common Delivery Methods

3.1 Common delivery methods: Main features

A construction project is a unique individual arrangement of processes that involves various participants with different tasks who are constrained by various factors, hazards and related risks. With that in mind, the right delivery method (form of construction project management and organization) should be selected—with the employer taking the lead role in this decision.

In general, three basic delivery methods are most frequently encountered. Their names may differ, depending on a particular author and country of use. They are most frequently called:

- *General contracting or design-bid-build* (often abbreviated as DBB). General contracting is a traditional form of project delivery where the employer is responsible for the design that includes drawings, specifications and bill of quantities with rates and prices quoted in the contractor's bid at their risk. It is a re-measured contract with the works measured on actual need and paid on the basis of monthly instalments for works done. Contract administration is done by the engineer.
- *Design-build* (often abbreviated as DB), including engineer-procure-construct (EPC). The design-build delivery method is typical of contractor design responsibility with the employer's requirements specifying only the purpose, standards, scope and performance criteria for the works. It is a lump sum price contract without a bill of quantities. Payments are made in accordance with a payments schedule. With the design-build delivery method, the employer should gain higher predictability of price and time for completion. The contractor assumes higher risk, so their bid price usually contains a risk surcharge.
- *Construction management* (often abbreviated as CM), including CM at-risk and engineer-procure-construction management (EPCM). The construction management delivery method assumes that the employer concludes direct contracts with particular contractors on a lump sum basis. For the sake of their

---

International Construction Contract Law, Second Edition. Lukas Klee.
© 2018 John Wiley & Sons Ltd. Published 2018 by John Wiley & Sons Ltd.

coordination, a construction manager is hired by the employer on a professional service agreement basis. The construction manager is paid on a cost plus basis, so the general contractor's surcharges are restricted. The construction manager is liable for bad management, planning and coordination but not for bad performance by particular contractors.

"Multiple-prime contracts," partnering and alliancing as separate delivery methods are sometimes found as well.

It is impossible to define the best method and, as a result, hybrid arrangements often tend to appear. Obviously, the most suitable delivery method has to be formulated for every particular project. Financing conditions, employer priorities, project difficulty, the socio-political situation, and many other factors are relevant variables which need to be considered.

Particular delivery methods differ mainly in respect of the following:

- design responsibility;
- contract price determination;
- contract administration approach; and
- risk allocation and admission of claims.

3.1.1 Design responsibility

In terms of design responsibility, we encounter main two options:

- The employer is responsible for preparing a detailed tender design (drawings, specifications, and bill of quantities). Under such an arrangement, the participants of a particular construction project will usually have to deal with a conflict among designers because the contractor usually adjusts the tender design to suit their own implementation design.
- Contractor's "single-point responsibility" for the design and works. The employer submits requirements with minimal detail at the tender stage, stating only purpose, scope and other technical criteria (such as performance criteria) often on a fitness-for-purpose basis.

3.1.2 Contract price determination

In terms of contract price determination, there are, in general, three main payment bases:

- lump sum;
- re-measurement;
- cost plus.

3.1.3 Contract administration

In terms of contract administration, there are three usual arrangements with the following people:

- the engineer: this is the employer's agent whose job is to monitor and supervise the work and make fair determinations on certain matters, for example, on claims for extensions of time and additional payment. The engineer issues certificates.
- the employer's representative: the contract is administered directly by the employer or their representative.
- the construction manager: the employer's agent hired to coordinate all processes on a professional service agreement basis without direct responsibility for design and works.

3.1.4 Risk allocation and admission of claims

In general, there are three basic rules of appropriate risk allocation:

1. allocate risks to the party best able to manage them;
2. allocate the risk in alignment with project goals; and
3. share risk when appropriate to accomplish the project goals.

In certain circumstances, the risk allocation does not need to be balanced but still needs to be efficient. Under such arrangements an efficient risk allocation can still exist even where the majority of risk is shifted to the contractor and almost no claims are allowed. For example, where it is possible to control the risk and where there is enough time to prepare the bid and an allowance is made for an appropriate risk surcharge in the bid price.

Inefficient risk allocation can therefore do the following:

- lead to project complications;
- have a negative influence on price, time and quality; and
- lead to speculative claims, disputes, potential contractor bankruptcy, and early project termination.

3.2 General contracting

General contracting, or design-bid-build presume a higher level of employer responsibility by implying that the employer will bear responsibility for its preparation and execution.

Tender documents include detailed designs that contain drawings, technical specifications, and a bill of quantities. The contractor will stipulate particular rates and prices in its tender quotations (which become binding during realization), with the risk of errors in estimation to be borne by the contractor. The amount of work to be carried out is measured to reflect the reality necessary for proper completion of the work. It is, therefore, a type of "re-measurement contract." The main advantage of general contracting is that it enables the use of competitive bidding to select the contractor. Many employers are pushed by public procurement law or simply prefer to select the contractor on the basis of lowest price. For this reason, general contracting is the most convenient method. This approach is traditional and well known, more user-friendly, familiar, and comprehensible to the participants in international construction projects. In many countries, it is in fact the only delivery method used in public procurement projects— even in cases where different delivery methods would be much more appropriate.

The following are often taken as given in general contracting:

- The main contractor will execute a part of the contract through their own capability.
- The employer will prepare the design and be responsible for it. A substantial part of the design will have to be completed before the contractor is selected and then finalized via a detailed design.
- Standards and quantities are defined in the contract and the contractor will perform the activities as scheduled in the bill of quantities.
- An engineer will be appointed.
- An independent quantity surveyor is appointed to supervise the re-measurement of works.
- The contractor executes the work, being responsible for compliance with the standard of workmanship and abiding by the engineer's instructions. The works carried out within a particular time (usually a month or 28 days), as surveyed and approved by the engineer in the contractor's statement are invoiced.
- It is not the top priority to execute the works as quickly as possible.
- Risk allocation is balanced and respective claims admitted.

3.3   Design-build

According to the design-build (DB) delivery method, the contractor is expected to be responsible for the design, execution and sequencing of works. The amount of design works depends on a particular project. Sometimes it is also up to the contractor to obtain the building (or other) permits and include this in their package of services.

As a part of the tender documents, there are the *employer's requirements* that specify the purpose, scope, design requirements, and/or additional technical criteria for the project. The employer's requirements will usually identify the parts of the works to be designed by the contractor and the criteria the design will reflect (such as the shape, dimensions, technical specifications, and standards). The employer's requirements must be clear and unambiguous. The contractor will submit a proposal within their bid based on the employer's requirements.

A bill of quantities is usually omitted in DB projects and there is no re-measurement of works actually carried out. As mentioned, invoicing will follow the payment schedule or can be contingent upon the completion of predefined parts of the work.

In the case of DB, price bears the characteristics of a lump sum. The bid price tends to be higher than in general contracting, as greater risk passes to the contractor. The employer, however, has an option to commence the works earlier because of the overlap of the design and construction phases. Furthermore, with DB, the probability is higher that the initial estimate of the bid price will be close to the actual final price. This is because the single point contractor's responsibility for work realization limits contractor claims. The employer also has the added advantage of making use of the contractor's expertise in design preparation. This can lead to a decrease in the total price. The contractor is responsible to produce a final work fit for required purpose. This may be based on express contractual clause or in some jurisdictions DB contracts may be subject to an implied term of fitness for purpose (for different opinions see the case Trebor Bassett Holdings Ltd v. ADT Fireand Security plc [2011] EWHC 1936 (TCC); [2011] BLR 661 (CA) [2012] EWCA Civ 1158).

The following are often taken as given under DB:

- Responsibility for design rests with the contractor.
- DB is not suitable for projects where numerous variations are expected and requested by the employer during realization.
- General contracting provides employers with more control over a construction project. Employer priority may be to waive such control if they decide to implement DB.
- More certainty that the quoted bid price will reflect the completion price. The DB method is not recommended for high-risk projects, as it is inefficient to allocate risks to the contractor where the contractor cannot control these risks.
- DB will allow quicker commencement of realization by making the overlap in the design and realization phases possible.
- Risk allocation is balanced, but some risks are shifted onto the contractor such as the risk of design errors and the risk of estimation errors in rates and prices in the contractor's bid. Claims are admitted but narrowed respectively.

3.3.1 Design-build procurement

The evaluation of bidders is an indisputable problem with the DB method when used in a public procurement context. The bill of quantities is most frequently priced under general contracting, with the lowest price being the only crucial criterion for succeeding in a tender ('competitive bidding'). This approach is popular because it is very easy and traditional. Also other technical parameters are used in the evaluation of tender participants using the DB method and the subjective nature of selecting individual proposals cannot be eliminated. The problem is how to ensure transparent and objective evaluation when the individual bids are matched against each other.

Procurement of a design-build contract is often a very complex process with plenty of potential pitfalls for inexperienced or unprepared employers. The following issues may be encountered (Clark, 2013):

- Lack of appreciation of the complexities involved in procuring a DB contract. It is not possible to procure a DB contract following a "tick-box" approach to procurement. If the employer does not have the full range of technical, commercial and legal expertise in-house, they should consider engaging a qualified consulting firm.

- An inflexible approach to procurement (i.e., use of single-stage tendering), which leads to protracted and, in some cases, distorted procurement exercises. The employer should consider the benefits of a prequalification phase, where appropriate. The employer should use an appropriate and flexible procurement strategy which provides for dialogue with tenderers prior to the submission of priced tenders. The first stage tender should be a technical proposal without price. Price evaluation is part of the second stage tender.
- The key aspects of the design should be given to the contractor. The employer should let the designer design.
- Inappropriate qualification criteria.
- Lack of understanding by foreign contractors of local design and licensing requirements that lead to delays in approval of the detailed design and contentious claims.
- Poor drafting of the employer's requirements and failure to address conflicts with national regulations through the particular conditions can lead to many problems during the procurement and contract implementation phase.
- Claims during the contract implementation phase (often as a result of an issue that could have been identified and addressed earlier in the process), which lead to cost and time overruns.
- The employer should ensure that the conditions of the contract are consistent with the applicable law and national procedures.
- The employer should avoid the temptation to introduce provisions from other contract forms (particularly those pertaining to allocation of risk, i.e., unforeseeable difficulties/costs as contained in the FIDIC EPC/1999 Silver Book).
- The employer should allow contractors a sufficient tender preparation period.
- The employer should not underestimate the importance and the role of the engineer in successful implementation.

Because the distinction between design services and construction work is not always clear on a design-build project, obtaining guarantees, and insurance can sometimes be difficult. Design services are generally not bondable. Similarly, the insurance carried by most contractors excludes any liability for design work (Kelley, 2013).

3.3.2 Employer's requirements in design-build projects

In design-build projects, the "employer's requirements" is an engineering document crucial to the success or failure of the project. Being a precise requirement for the completed works, it must cross-refer to the conditions of contract when being drafted. Therefore it is of utmost importance to maintain the consistent use of terminology (Poulsen and Záhonyi, 2013).

The document must include all the definitions and purposes of the work, a definition of the site, a definition of interfaces between disciplines and other contracts, quality and performance criteria (including testing) and special obligations such as training, spare parts and warranties.

The quality and performance specification should be prepared only to the extent necessary. Detailed specifications may lead to a reduction of contractor design responsibility. Furthermore, the specifications must be precise to enable enforceability and cannot be subjective (e.g., specified "according to the opinion of the engineer").

The employer's requirements should contain only a reference (illustrative) design with simple drawings and schematics as appropriate to the discipline. This must be done with caution to ensure that design responsibility is not transferred back from the contractor to the employer. Such a conceptual design is part of the employer's requirements to the extent necessary to define the works (e.g., 10% of total design input). In the instructions to tenderers, the requirements for a preliminary design (that will be a part of the contractor's proposal) are described. The final design is then part of the contractor's realization documents (Poulsen and Záhonyi, 2013).

In terms of accuracy, sufficiency, and completeness of employer's requirements (as established by FIDIC forms), there are substantial differences between the particular 1999/2017 forms (mainly the P&DB/Yellow Book and EPC/Silver Book).

In FIDIC P&DB/1999 Yellow Book (and DBO) the employer is responsible for the correctness of the employer's requirements. The employer's responsibility related to employer's requirements is subject to a three-tier procedure (Poulsen, Záhonyi, 2013):

1. Clarification questions (tender/pre-contract phase):
   The procedural aspect of tender clarification depends mainly on the particular governing law and the procurement rules that were used.
2. Under the Sub-Clause 5.1 (general design obligations):
   Upon receiving notice of the commencement of works, the contractor shall scrutinize the employer's requirements (including design criteria and calculations, if any) and the items of reference mentioned for the purpose of setting out the works. Within the period stated in the appendix to tender, (calculated from the commencement date), the contractor shall give notice to the engineer of any error, fault, or other defect found in the employer's requirements or items of reference.
   After receiving this notice, the engineer shall determine whether a variation procedure shall be applied, and shall give notice to the contractor accordingly. If and to the extent that (taking account of cost and time) an experienced contractor exercising due care would have discovered the error, fault, or other defect when examining the site and the employer's requirements before submitting the tender, the time for completion shall not be extended and the contract price shall not be adjusted.
3. Under the Sub-Clause 1.9 (errors in the employer's requirements):

   > If the contractor suffers delay and/or incurs cost as a result of an error in the employer's requirements, and an experienced contractor exercising due care would not have discovered the error when scrutinising the employer's requirements, the contractor shall give notice to the engineer and shall be entitled subject to (a) an extension of time for any such delay, if completion is or will be delayed and (b) payment of any such cost plus reasonable profit, which shall be included in the contract price.

In FIDIC EPC/1999 Silver Book it is the contractor who bears responsibility for any errors, inaccuracies or omissions in the Employer's Requirements.

1. Under the Sub-Clause 5.1 (general design obligations):

   The contractor shall be deemed to have scrutinised, prior to the base date, the employer's requirements (including design criteria and calculations, if any). The contractor shall be responsible for the design of the works and for the accuracy of such employer's requirements (including design criteria and calculations), except as stated below.

   The employer shall not be responsible for any error, inaccuracy or omission of any kind in the employer's requirements as originally included in the contract and shall not be deemed to have given any representation of accuracy or completeness of any data or information, except as stated below. Any data or information received by the contractor, from the employer or otherwise, shall not relieve the contractor from his responsibility for the design and execution of the works. However, the employer shall be responsible for the correctness of the following portions of the employer's requirements and of the following data and information provided by (or on behalf of) the employer:

   (a) portions, data and information which are stated in the contract as being immutable or the responsibility of the employer,
   (b) definitions of intended purposes of the works or any parts thereof,
   (c) criteria for the testing and performance of the completed works, and
   (d) portions, data and information which cannot be verified by the contractor, except as otherwise stated in the contract.

The specifics of EPC and EPCM are discussed in Chapter 4.

Dutch design and construct of infrastructural projects in complex environments by Joost Merema (the Netherlands)

General introduction

For every construction project the employer can choose which contract model should be applied. The employer has to answer some important questions, like: who should design and engineer the project? On which level of functionality should the employer's requirements be formulated? What is the level of involvement which employer would want to see for a contractor? One of the possible choices is to contract a party who should design and engineer the project, and also build it. The most common names for such a contract are: engineering, procurement, and construction (EPC), design and build (D-B or D/B), engineering and construct or design and construct (D&C). For this article, the term "design and construct" or D&C in short is used to describe all these forms of contracts. My purpose with addressing these issues is for the reader to reflect on them, and to start up a discussion on them within the legal practitioners within the construction community. They are not intended as a legal and academic evaluation of these issues.

The basic idea of any D&C contract is that an employer sets out his requirements (the employer's requirements or ER in short), and the contractor will use these requirements to manage all required phases to deliver the project. Whether from pure functional and top-level specifications or quite detailed engineering requirements and designs, it's the duty of the contractor to fulfill the need for further engineering and design. In most of the projects, that process of formulation of further requirements, the designing, engineering, and construction phases are managed by systems engineering. Depending on if you do that based on, for example, a Yellow Book or Silver Book contract will determine who is responsible for the integrity and correctness of the employer's design and/or specifications.

The main strength of a D&C contract is that designing and construction are done by one party. The employer has therefore one point of responsibility, and during the design phase (which can overlap with construction) the methods and planning of construction should be integral part of decision making. The contractor has his responsibility to deliver the project—regardless any mistakes in the design. With that responsibility comes the freedom of making choices (of course within the possibilities of the employer's requirements) and the possibility to use methods, solutions, and techniques, which are his strengths and for which he has the best experiences. In essence, that gives a contractor more opportunity to distinct himself from his competition during tendering.

This vignette is meant to share some experiences in infrastructural D&C projects. Globally, the population is growing. People are living more and more in dense urban areas. Challenges for a lot of projects globally lie not only purely in the technical area, but also increasingly environmental, esthetical, and political—and those areas combined. Also, the way we as professionals approach projects changes: we tend to look more for purposeful solutions where every party benefits in one way or the other instead of a "all for one" solution. The idea that it's logical to design a project fully in detail by one party years before the other one even starts constructing seems more and more obsolete. I hope some of our Dutch experiences can contribute to D&C approaches globally. Infrastructure projects are becoming more and more complex: there is less space left, and more wishes and demands to be fulfilled.

Dutch design and construct—less room and still beneficial?

In the Netherlands D&C contracts are based on the UAV-GC 2005 model. The model is developed in the late 1990s on a combination of FIDIC Yellow and Silver Book on one hand and existing Dutch traditional contract models. The UAV-GC (which in translation stands for "*Uniforme Adminstratieve Voorwaarden voor Geïntegreerde Contracten*"—Uniform General Conditions for Integrated Contracts) is developed to facilitate both projects where the employer already took on parts of the design, or a specific level of design (as used in FIDIC Yellow Book) and project where the employer only formulates top lever requirements without any designing (as aimed for in FIDIC Silver Book).

The Netherlands rank first in EU and sixth globally in population density of countries with populations more than 10.000.000. There's not much building in the so called "greenfield" left. Because of this, the spatial planning for infrastructural projects is subject to strict rules (environmental codes) and planning procedures. So, when leaving designing of infrastructure to a contractor, we have to do without the luxury of starting with a surplus of space in anticipation of design optimizations or different options for infrastructural works. This is most noticeable in projects for new infrastructure or significant upgrading of existing infrastructure.

A very important effect of having such extensive planning procedures and environmental codes is that in the years of planning procedure before there is a definitive "go" on an infrastructural project, there is a need for detailed information to base the spatial claims and political decisions on. Most of the time, these decisions are getting challenged in legal procedures, up to the "*Raad van State*": the highest court available for such cases. From the perspective of design and construct contracting, that means that the most important decisions about available space, available heights, depths, and trajectory are already made. There's literally and figuratively little room left to really design from scratch.

One would expect that in Dutch projects, there's not much interest in D&C contracts. But that's not the case: it's the opposite. All major infrastructure projects for main road network, the main waterway network and water systems are by default contracted by the Ministry of Infrastructure and the Environment based on the UAV-GC, thus design and construct. Only in specific conditions or for special projects other contract forms (primarily RAW—the most comparable with Red Book principles) are used. On a local level D&C are used just as often as traditional RAW contracts, however, the trend is that most of the larger (in terms of contract value) of these local projects are contracted based on UAV GC.

The experiences of D&C in the Netherlands at first sight seem to show a contradiction: in the planning procedures there is a need for more information and details. If a lot of details are already filled in during planning procedures, there is little room for improvements and not much designing left to do for the contractor. That leaves the contractor with the obligation to deliver a design within a lot and very strict specifications in terms of space or requirements. Why even bother? Well, the answer is pretty straight forward: even with strict requirements and only design choices on detailed level to be made, it still pays off to let a contractor do the designing. The integral approach, a single point of responsibility, and the combination of designing and constructing still delivers more innovations, takes less time and gives employers during tendering more options to choose from. Yes, most of the time in the infrastructural project is little room for large design choices; and yes—the use of D&C contract is still beneficial.

Some observations about the development and use of D&C in the Netherlands

D&C in recent Dutch infrastructure projects has been developed in the nineties of the last century. It is still in development, and the introduction and development of these contracts have become a major game changer in construction. I'd like to share the following observations, which were made during this time by me and other professionals.

1. *Design and construct contracting opens up more possibilities for procurement by MEAT (plus price fixing is less easy)*

    Recently, the European Public Procurement Directive is aimed to less procurement on the lowest bid, and more on "value for money," or the most economical advantageous tender (MEAT). When awarding based on MEAT, an employer (e.g., contracting authority, CA in short, in public procurement law terms) should define on forehand on which part of the scope he wishes to see bidders try to add more value. In other words: to procure successfully on decent MEAT criteria, the employer has to approach the scope more functionally and decide on which parts he will not define the solution, but just set a minimum in requirements or baseline. By not defining the solution, the employer has only one rational option: define his employer's requirements on a more functional or output level. Yes, a decent and functional design and contract on public infrastructure gets a lot better by contracting on MEAT criteria, which focus on added value of the different bids. It also works the other way around: if a contracting authority decides that his default modus of procuring is by awarding the MEAT, a fixed design with no design component for the bidders will have less potential in terms of added value.

And there is an attractive additional "plus" in the combination of using design and construct and MEAT criteria. When MEAT is used widespread and price-quality ratios are more focussed on quality and added value, the combination of D&C and MEAT puts a nail in the coffin of price fixing from a construction cartel. The UAV-GC was developed in the late nineties and the first model of the standards was published in 2000. After a few years of piloting and evaluating around 100 projects, the standards where updated to its definite shape in 2005 (hence UAV-GC 2005). The real push toward UAV-GC in terms of policy came in the years after the proven discovery of a widespread construction cartel in 2001 and 2002 in the Netherlands. With new procurement laws, adding more focus on making bids less comparable, came the deep conviction that till the moment contracting authorities would leave the race to the bottom in price-based tenders, the cartel would not easily cease to exist.

2. *Design and construct contracts give contractors more flexibility in planning, used methods and using innovative techniques—and it does not cost extra*

D&C contracts should ideally be clear of the "what" in terms of scope and desired scope output, and give the contractor room to figure out the "how" and "when." Expectations in the early days of UAV-GC were sky high about all the innovations and new techniques contractor's would use to "impress" the employer. The truth is that most of the time, skillful employers with enough capacity in the preparation phase are hard to beat in terms of innovations and creativity on infrastructure projects. Also, contractors show a tendency to choose the proven technology about state of the art in design and construct. Most of the time, the risk of failure outweighs the benefits of using an innovative solution.

It probably sounds like a cliché, but the area where contractors "beat" the employers in terms of choosing the better techniques, planning or additional risk management measures is almost always when the contractor has executed more projects in it and thus has gained more experience. That's where added value of a contractor is significant. And that's why in my opinion best value procurement in its core is pretty straightforward in identifying the best expert for a project: it's evidence based and references should be verifiable. Of course, it's the employer who has to start with defining the area's where he (as contracting authority) is not the expert in comparison with the knowledge level of "industry practice" (and be at peace with that—but that's beside the point of this vignette).

This trend of relying more on the experiences of the contractor is more an evolutionary process for a whole sector than one major change. During that process, contractors will make mistakes and misjudge the risks (and their ability of managing them) and will be confronted by claims and losses. The challenge should be for contracting authorities in a specific country or industry to look for tools in terms of policy to make sure the learning curve of both contractors and employers is as steep as possible, and that mistakes are evaluated and experiences about them shared. Only then will contractors be able to improve and innovate in the long run, and be able to cope with the occasional and unfortunately inevitable losses on projects.

One could argue with all this focus on quality, value, and freedom in terms of choices in techniques and so on, the prices of infrastructural projects based in D&C and MEAT should skyrocket: less focus on lower prices would lead to higher prices. The interesting thing is that it doesn't. Long-term research by the Dutch Ministry of Transport show that there is a significant correlation between a low price and a high score on added value of the bid (it goes without saying that during a procurement procedure, the quality of the bid is assessed first and separately from the prices of the bid). The conclusion of that research shows us that most of the time the bid which was assessed to add the most quality turns out to be the lowest or second to lowest price: it seems that if a contractor really knows his own skillset and understands the scope of the employer very well, he is able to submit a lean bid, at least without the burden of extra costs in his tender bid for unforeseeable events. Focus on quality and prices leads to more quality for lower range market prices!

Within certain conditions regarding the functional level of requirements, design and construct contracts together with a good application of procurement with MEAT show very good results in more quality for the same amount of money.

3. *Just changing the contracts is not enough to change the mind-set of the key players involved. Really changing the roles, traditions and rituals sector takes a decennium (or two).*

In the part above I shared the timeline involved with the general introduction of D&C and the impact it had on procurement procedures. The idea of a new and fresh contract model seems to imply that organizations and the people working on the projects will "fit" into the working processes of that new model. Like it's something like an automatic reflex for a full and complete change. Of course, everybody understands these kinds of structural changes take time. One of the observations of the last decennia in the Netherlands is that you can change the concept and the rules game, but if you don't address what that means to particular players they will end up playing the old game in a new setting. The cultural and behavioral customs people have, based on their experiences, are very hard to change. It's a factor to take in consideration when implementing new contract models. The projects and risk allocation will change, but getting the project members act accordingly is not a natural consequence: it is something you have to manage and provide people with training, coaching and tooling.

The effect of having played a lot of "old" games and how that reflects on a "new" setting is recognizable in how to deal with design changes. In the traditional allocation of tasks, the contractor has to comply with all the design choices that the employer made. If he does not comply, he will be fined or not payed at all. When a design is inconsistent or impossible, it has to be changed by the employer. Consequences of those kinds of design changes are fully compensable in terms of cost and time (of course within certain boundaries and general principle of reasonability). On infrastructure projects those claims are relevant and significant—and both the employer and the contractor are aware of that when they close the contract.

The following may sound generalizing; however, it is meant to be observational— and not in a judgmental way of "good" and "bad" behavior. One of the effects on the people involved in those traditional contracts, is that they generally focus on what changes in a design, and secure strategic position based on those changes. Experience in those contracts teaches them (and have awarded them over their careers) to over-estimate those consequences. There are several writers pointing out that in a low-price system with traditional contracts the people who play that game make a career and end up in higher management functions. However, the behavior that got them successful in the first place is contra-productive in D&C contracts.

D&C contracts ask for a more pro-active and solution driven modus, where designs must be able to change to adapt the project scope to lessons learnt or occurring risks allocated to the contractor. If (project) management overestimates consequences and because of that hesitates to make decisions, or if project management starts a lengthy claim procedure or uses an occurring risk on one item to do a full stand-still on the project—that is contra-productive when you're responsible for a functional output. And it is probably more difficult for project teams than one would expect to adapt to this way of working on a project if your management has been "seasoned" in experience in more traditional models.

So, in the end it's not enough to change contract models to change the way projects are executed. Special attention should also be given to training, coaching, and policy on behavior and cooperation in a broader evaluation when contract models with new ways of working and risk allocation are introduced. National knowledge institutes for infrastructure projects (like in the Netherlands the "CROW") or international organizations like EFCA/FIDIC can be of service in developing tools and exchanging that information in order not only produce new models, but also support on successfully implementation on a project and management level. In the Netherlands, there were national drivers to accelerate the use of D&C contracts. However, it took us more than 10 years of executing projects with that model to really learn how to do it effectively and without unacceptable risk taking—thus be successful in using them in a beneficial way for all parties involved.

4. *The contractors also started engineering departments. Engineering companies became more technical consultancy firms. But old habits die hard.*

The early years of D&C was quite a shock for classic Dutch engineering companies. After decades of making Red Book-like designs (RAW) with all that detail—contractors would take over the designing part of the project. Or at least, that was the expectation. The engineering companies responded by trying to position themselves as total engineers and construction managers, but the critical mass already had shifted toward D&C contracts. The contractors quickly established that they would need in-house engineering capacity to develop their long-term transition toward EPC Contractors. The contractors took strategic positions by taking over good engineering firms with decent quality track records. Local active small and middle enterprises (SMEs) would instead of taking over engineering companies, just build a small extension to their existing technical back office by hiring a few designers and CAD people.

Fast forward to 2017: every national active contractor, and most of the larger SMEs in the Netherlands are capable of successfully executing both RAW and UAV-GC contracts. For larger projects, the contractors and their engineering departments form joint ventures with the larger engineering companies. On a national level, there have not been "dedicated UAV-GC" contractors, in contrast with original expectations. The base of revenues in traditional RAW contracts is probably still needed for business survival and risk distribution, as UAV-GC contracts contain generally more risks.

Also, with the last decade of economic contraction and absence of growth, the price level of D&C projects is generally regarded as low and around cost price. Essentially, the contractors take on D&C projects for price levels which are comparable with RAW (e.g.,

Red Book-like) contracts. That means that every risk that actually occurs in a project, eats away profits pretty quick—leaving less and less financial space to deal with other risks later on in the project. In the long term, the current price level of large D&C contracts for infrastructural projects in the Netherlands is only sustainable with more focus on lowering (design) failure costs and better risk management, or by adding more risk mark-up on the cost price. The smaller and more regional markets show some similar trends, however, it seems that SMEs that thrive and grow also do more UAV-GC projects than the ones that are in decline. It is possible that for those projects, the risk allocation and risk management are better "manageable," or conflicts over occurring risks tend to end less in high costs for those contractors.

One trend (which is open for debate) is that the original engineering companies who wrote large RAW contracts, in the first years started to write bulky ERs for those UAV-GC contracts. That is contrary to what was intended with the introduction of UAV-GC in 2005: the "dream" of a lean ER with just a few functional requirements was never established in a broad sense. Possible explanations could be that employers were afraid contractors would take on too much risk by misusing the room in the ERs. It also may be a trust issue of employers, thinking that if something wasn't clearly specified, they would end up with something considered less of quality. It may be also possible that it's a rational effect of the continuation of the business model of the engineering companies, hourly billable on fixed tariffs. How wants to pay an engineer a high fee for "just" 20 requirements? It's better to understand it took 2,000 hours to produce a large ER with more than 1,500 requirements than that it took 1,000 hours to make one with 20. A definitive research on this topic isn't available, however it's generally assumed within the Dutch UAV-GC community that a mix of above resulted in old habits dying hard.

Requirements that are not in the contract, but are still part of the obligation

In most of the D&C contracts, there is an abstract approach on how to handle what could be called "obvious requirements." Every contract is considered by legal standards to be complete and binding, while we know in practice that a contract never fully is. When it comes to formulating requirements, an employer tries to be complete. But we see also that sometimes obvious requirements are not formulated precisely or not at all. Examples could be that a road bridge should have a barrier to stop cars from falling off, a waste incinerator should be closed during operation or that a roof should be fitted on top of a building. These kinds of obvious and reasonable requirements should be part of a D&C contract, even if an Employer didn't mention them in the requirements.

The FIDIC contract models handles this by adding obvious requirements to the Contractor's Obligations in Clause 4.1 (Yellow and Silver Book, 1999):

"The Contractor shall design, execute and complete the Works in accordance with the Contract and shall remedy any defects in the Works. When completed the Works shall be **fit for the purposes** for which the Works are intended as defined in the Contract. [...] The Works shall include any work which is necessary to satisfy the Employer's Requirement, Contractor's Proposal and Schedules, or is **implied** by the Contract, and all works (although not mentioned in the Contract) are **necessary for stability or for the completion, or safe and proper operation**, of the Works."

So, even when certain requirements about *what* the contractor should design and construct are not mentioned in the contract, they still are demanded because the works should be fit for purpose. The obligation for those requirements still exist if they follow out of the necessity of functionality, as long as that functionality is stated or implied by the contract.

In Clause 7.1 (again both Yellow and Silver Book) there is a similar clause but about *how* the contractor should design and construct:

> "The Contractor shall carry out the manufacture of Plant, the production and manufacture of Materials, and all other execution of the Works:
>
> (a) in the manner (if any) specified in the Contract,
> (b) in a **proper** workmanlike and **careful** manner, in accordance with **recognised good practice**. […]"

Again, if it's not in the contract, it is still part of the requirements as long as these requirements follow out of the principle of proper workmanship and are in accordance with recognized good practice.

In the Dutch UAV-GC 2005, some similar clauses are mentioned. The mechanism is that the UAV-GC introduces the principle of "ordinary use" and "specific purpose" in Article 2.3 of the Model Agreement ("Basisovereenkomst"):

> "With regard to the requirements referred to in clause 4 section 3 UAV-GC 2005, which are derived from the **specific purpose** for which the Works will be used, the parties conclude that they have discussed **these requirements** sufficiently prior to signing this Agreement and that **the said requirements** are stated in full in the **Employer's Requirements**."

The basic idea is that only the requirements of specific purpose are needed to be put into the employer's requirements. The other clause of the general conditions Clause 4 contain the following to add to Article 2.3:

> "4-1 The Contractor shall carry out Design Work and Construction Work in such a manner that, on the date of completion and acceptance stated in the Agreement, the Works will be in accordance with the requirements of the Contract. […]
>
> 4-3 The requirements referred to in sections 1 and 2 include requirements resulting from the **ordinary use** for which the Works are intended as well as the requirements resulting from the specific purpose for which the Works will be used, only in so far as the requirements resulting from the **specific purpose** are stated in the Employer's Requirements."

So by combining Article 2.3 of the model agreement and Clause 4-3 of the general conditions, a contractor is obligated to perform and deliver the Works in accordance to requirements, which are obvious and follow of the ordinary use for which the works are intended.

The similarity in approach between FIDIC Yellow or Silver Book model and a Dutch design and construct contract is that the purpose for which the works is used is key in determining what the exact scope is and which requirements are part of the contract. FIDIC adds that the purpose of the works must be defined in the contract, where the UAV-GC doesn't require an explicit mentioning of the purpose of the works. The model agreement mentions that both parties declare that these requirements are sufficiently discussed.

The difference with FIDIC Yellow and Silver Book with UAV-GC is about what's ordinary use and specific purpose. The UAV-GC makes a distinction between what is obvious and therefore an requirement which results from ordinary use of the works, and specific requirements which are stated in the employer's requirements.

This legal distinction has not led to major discussions in projects. The practice of how employer's requirements in the Netherlands are written is that they tend to be describing all requirements, leaving no implicit requirements. Most of the time, the method of systems engineering results in employer's requirements contain already a system breakdown structure (SBS) with requirements connected on corresponding system elements within the SBS. On a top level one should see requirements that will define functionality and therefore the purpose of the works. I recommend therefore for all design and construct to focus as soon as possible on determining the purpose of the works, and define explicitly those top level requirements. Either as an employer, so you won't have to use the "fit for purpose" clauses, or for a contractor, who could be surprised by unseen and implicit—but in the eyes of employer—requirements that follow from the ordinary use of the project.

Experiences in liability and risk allocation between employer and contractor on D&C infrastructure projects

The risk allocation to one party can be an earnings model for another. With D&C contracts that becomes very relevant. Because of D&C contracts have a single point of responsibility and the obligation to deliver, the way risks are allocated between employer and contractor and quantified by the contractor in the tendering phase is an essential ingredient for a successful delivery of the project.

1. *Beware of wishful risk allocation*

    The last observation to make from the period of introducing and implementing D&C contracts evolves around risk allocation and risk acceptance. There is always an information inequality between contractors and employers during a tender procedure. An employer initially has more time to investigate, research, and weighs different options for his requirements than a contractor. A contractor is assumed to have more insight in the real costs of not only his operation, but specifically certain risks management measures.

    It's quite understandable if an employer decides that the ultimate risk management measure is to make the management of a certain project risk the task of the contractor. It almost always ends up in disaster (project wise, not necessarily from the perspective of legal consultants of course) when an employer overestimates the effectiveness of the ability of the contractor to manage the risk, and/or when an employer underestimates the impact of an occurring risk in terms of time, cost and quality. In both scenarios, if the risk is allocated to the contractor, it's up to him to define management measures—and to take the costs (unforeseeable risks and risk management measures) for that in his bid. However, if he fails to do so, the allocation of the wrongfully assessed risk ends up with the contract party which is not the best one to manage it—or at least has not enough budget and measures in place to manage that risk.

    Why is that a specific problem of D&C contracts? Well, in preparation of these contracts for employers it's almost an irresistible temptation to say "oh, that's a complex risk to manage for me in this phase, let the contractor take care of that—it will be much easier for him once the project is in execution" or "the contractor should be able to manage that without too much costs." You could call this a way of wishful thinking about the abilities of a contractor for certain risks: a "wishful risk allocation" so to speak. That's a big gamble when contractors are opportunistic and start off with a lot of risks that were not taken in account. A lucky employer will have a contractor who will take big financial losses on a project, and survive those losses without a lot of claiming and fighting: I've yet to come across that employer.

The best remedy to prevent that scenario, is to try to get senior-level construction experience involved in the review process of the risk allocation during the preparations of the tender procedure. Not only will it helpful to define relevant risks, but also to advise the employer to define what is needed in terms of scope, requirements or information for a contractor to assess the risk correctly and take proper measures in account. From a contractual point of view, you can allocate every risk to a contractor—*"pacta sunt servanda"*: a contract is binding. However, when a case goes to court, at least in EU courts, an unreasonable and unfair risk allocation will not be fully enforceable. And it's also in the interests of the contract parties to work with a contract with reasonable and realistic risk allocations. Otherwise the project will easily end in endless claims and missed milestones during the project. Sadly, this is well-known trend within some countries. A professional employer should therefore resist the temptation of wishful allocation of risks in order to get in the end the most out of a D&C contract. It just makes more sense.

2. *Insurance and the cap of liability*

For national infrastructural projects in the Netherlands, employers accept the standard CAR insurances that contractors have with additional provisions for coverage for design errors. For public procurement procedures, the standard coverage as requested and offered doesn't lead to problems very often. Some large contracting authorities, like the municipal of Amsterdam, procure their own CAR insurances that also will cover the liability for damage caused by a D&C contractor, to file a case against that contractor later on. It's important to note that the Dutch UAV-GC caps for non-performance and penalties toward the employer liability to 10% of the original sum. That appears to be workable and also accepted in general by insurance companies. There have been projects where that cap was lifted, with disastrous impact on the contractor when problems did arise. These kinds of professional (mostly design) errors were generally not payed for by insurances and were payed "out of pocket" by the contractors. For example, in 2016, a large national contractor stood on the brink of bankruptcy, and until this day faces big challenges partly due to exposure to claims by the employer for non-performing in contracts with no, or a higher than standard, cap. A few contractors already went bankrupt in the period between 2015 to 2017, partly because of liability in some large projects. Such cases are—luckily—not the standard, but they trigger questions like how far contracting authorities are willing to go with regard to hold large contractors liable and how to keep up a healthy and competitive market with enough professional parties.

3. *Foreseeable mistakes—obligation for employers to warn a contractor*

In most of the contract models the employer bears responsibility for any conflicts between (or in) contract documents, for example, requirements. In FIDIC Yellow Book (1999), this is formulated in Clause 1.9:

> "If the Contractor suffers delay and/or incurs Costs as a result of an error in the Employer's Requirements and an experienced contractor exercising due care would not have discovered the error when scrutinising the Employer's Requirements under Clause 5.1, the Contractor shall give notice to the Engineer and shall be entitled subject to Sub-Clause 20.1 [...]"

So, there are two important parts of this clause. First, the employer should determine in preparation of the tender that there are no errors in the ER, and realize if there are any, he as the employer is responsible and liable for those errors. Secondly, this article is not a "carte blanche" for the contractor: only errors that were actually missed in the tender phase and after scrutinizing (after the Commence of Works, as obligated in 5.1 junction 8.1). To put it simple: an error in the employer's requirements is in essence the problem of the employer, unless the contractor should have seen the error earlier.

The interesting part of that (at least from a EU–continental point of view) is that it seems a bit odd for an employer to blame the contractor for missing an obvious error, which the employer made himself. That would mean that an employer with due care can make a mistake and "hide" behind the argument of incompetence and thus allocate the risk to a contractor. Ignorance would seem to be a bliss indeed—I doubt if a judge in the Netherlands would follow up on that argument.

This base of rule also fits the way the contract handles mistakes in design of any part of the works by employer, as stated in Yellow Book (1999) Clause 17.3 (g):

> "The risks referred to in Sub-Clause 17.4 (Consequences of Employer's Risks) below are:
> [...]
> (g) design of any part of the Works by the Employer's Personnel or by others for whom Employer is responsible, if any."

Interesting enough, the draft version of the new FIDIC Yellow Book (2016) contained a more explicit risk allocation in 17.1 sub (b) under (ii):

> "[...] the risks allocated to the Employer and for which the Employer is liable are divided into:
> [...] (b) the Employer's risk of damage, which are those that result in physical loss or damage to the Works [...] arising from:
> [...] (ii) fault, error, defect or omission in any element of the design of the Works by the Employer or which may be contained in the Employer's Requirement (and which an experienced contractor exercising due care would not have discovered when examining the Site and the Employer's Requirements before submitting the Tender)".

In both cases, the FIDIC Yellow Book instructs the contractor to rectify and the employer to pay the costs (plus reasonable profit). Of course, the exact formulation of the new FIDIC Yellow Book could defer, but there doesn't seem to be a fundamental change in how the risks regarding this omissions or errors are allocated.

In FIDIC Silver Book, the allocation of this risk regarding the design lie more with the contractor. In the Clause 17.3 employer's risks, the exact same text is found as in Yellow Book about employer's risks:

> "The risks referred to in Sub-Clause 17.4 (Consequences of Employer's Risks) below are:
> […]
> (g) design of any part of the Works by the Employer's Personnel or by others for whom Employer is responsible, if any."

However, Silver Book contains a very important Clause 5.1, which states:

> "The Contractor shall be deemed to have scrutinised, prior to the Base Date, the Employer's Requirements (including design criteria and calculations, if any). The Contractor shall be responsible for the design of the Works and for the accuracy of such Employer's Requirements (including design criteria and calculations), except as stated below. […]
>
> (a) portions, data and information which are stated in the Contract as being immutable or the responsibility of the Employer,
> (b) definitions of intended purposed of the Works or any parts thereof,
> (c) criteria for the testing and performance of the completed Works, and
> (d) portions, data and information which cannot be verified by the Contractor, except as otherwise stated in the Contract."

So, the contractor has an obligation to really check the complete employer's requirements on any omissions, errors, and so on prior to the base date (which is 28 days prior to the latest date for submission of the tender, so well before signing the actual contract!). After that moment, the risk of any error is allocated to the contractor, as Clause 5.1 defines:

> "The Employer shall not be responsible for any error, inaccuracy or omission of any kind in the Employer's Requirements as originally included in the Contract and shall not be deemed to have given any representation of accuracy or completeness of any data or information, except as stated below. Any data or information receive by the Contractor, from the Employer or otherwise, shall not relieve the Contractor from his responsibility for the design and execution of the Works."

So, a Silver Book should be very comfortable for employers regarding any errors in the employer's requirement: if a contractor doesn't notify about those in the tender process, their essentially not the employer's problem.

The Dutch UAV-GC looks more like Yellow Book in the perspective than on the Silver Book. The base clause is found in the agreement, where in Article 2 the following is defined:

> "2.4 The Employer shall bear the responsibility for any conflicts between requirements in the Employer's Requirements."

To fit the UAV-GC 2005 model to general contract law in the Netherlands regarding the duty of warning, the following article was added:

"2.5 The provisions of section 4 shall not affect the obligation of the Contractor to warn the Employer in the event of an apparent conflict as referred to in that section."

In the general conditions, the following is added about the duty to warn:

"4-7 The Contractor shall warn the Employer in writing without delay if:

(a) the Employer's Requirements; or
(b) information provided to the Contractor by the Employer pursuant to clause 3 section 1 subsection a; or
(c) the land and/or the water put at the Contractor's disposal by the Employer pursuant to clause 3 section 1 subsection b; or
(d) goods put at the Contractor's disposal by the Employer pursuant to clause 3 section 1 subsection c; or
(e) any measure taken by the Employer pursuant to clause 43 section 2; or
(f) any Variation ordered by the Employer to the Contractor pursuant to clause 14 section 1;

evidently contain or show such faults or defects that the Contractor would be in breach of the requirements of good faith if he were to continue Work without issuing any warning about such faults or defects."

In a first glance, this text may seem a different wording for more or less the same approach of the Yellow Book clauses. However, there are two important differences.

First, the UAV-GC doesn't define a phase of scrutinizing: the risk allocation is based on the text of the employer's requirements and the conflict or error or omission they contain. The way and the moment when the contractor read of assessed it is irrelevant, as long as the contractor notifies the employer as soon ("without delay") as the contractor discovers the error. Only a silent and passive contractor can be allocated the risk of errors in the ER, and that is to be proven by the employer.

Secondly, the bar of what an "apparent" conflict in the employer's requirement is lies pretty high. The conflict has to be recognizable and obvious for the contractor during the tender phase. However, it is recognized by judges and mediators that the period of tendering is shorter than an employer has in preparation of the ER. So, when the error is not obvious and thus apparent, the contractor can claim time delay and costs. Also, when the error is very obvious and very apparent, the employer will be judged as breaking due care in preparation of the ER—if it's apparent enough, the employer should have seen it himself.

Thirdly, the (probably universally) discussion is if there is a conflict at all. These kind of discussions are more drawn from project experience than analyzing the actual texts of the contract models themselves. For any of the clauses about conflicts and hierarchy to be activated in a discussion, there has to be of course an actual conflict. Because the structure of the Dutch D&C contract, if the tendency of an employer is to define in a lot of detail, it is more likely that a contractor claims a conflict situation. The employer can easily argue that from his perspective there is not a conflict, but a further articulation of a specific requirement. So for example, if all doors in a building should be painted yellow in the ER, and the requirement drawn from the safety regulations defines that all emergency exits should be painted red, a contractor could declare a conflict of the ER. In Dutch contracts an employer would probably argue that the ER show an hierarchy of the requirements itself: a "*Lex specialis derogat legi generali*" reasoning.

In the end for the UAV-GC it is the question what error lies between hidden and not apparent enough so it should be seen, and very obvious and thus preventable? Conclusion is that any omission, error, or conflict is the problem of the employer, regardless of the moment when the error was identified—as long it is communicated without any delay by the contractor.

Soil conditions: employer's obligation to inform and the design obligations of contractor to perform

1. *Soil conditions in the Netherlands*

    The conditions of the soil where an infrastructural project should be built form a special theme within the design obligation of a contractor with D&C contracts. Most of the theme, an infrastructural work requires a lot of soil preparation and sub-surface construction. Or to put it more bluntly: in civil engineering most of the works are covered with soil and below ground level after completion. It's therefore very important what soil conditions are to be expected. Especially in the Netherlands, soil conditions are challenging. In a way, for Dutch Engineers "weak" soil (meaning the low geotechnical support capacity of the soil) has been a part of life: about 55% of the Dutch land area lies below water level (26 below sea level and 29 below river levels). If you dig a hole in the ground in the Netherlands, most of the time it will have filled itself with groundwater before you excavated two meters deep. Also, the mixture of ground in the Netherlands consist typically of sea- or river clay, peat, and/or sand: bedrock or other stable underground with high support capacity are simple not there.

2. *FIDIC and UAV-GC 2005 comparison regarding soil conditions*

    In the traditional Dutch contracts, the risk of soil conditions is fully allocated with the employer. The employer is obligated to do inspection and research and to come up with a design and construction method based on these particular soil conditions. In the FIDIC Red, Yellow, and Silver Book (1999) something similar is found in Clause 4.10. That clause defines that the employer has the duty to hand over all relevant and available information, and that the contractor has an obligation to check on that data and verify them:

    > "4.10 The Employer shall have made available to the Contractor for his information, prior to the Base Date, all relevant data in the Employer's possession on sub-surface and hydrological conditions at the Site, including environmental aspects. […]"

    In Yellow Book and Red Book, the following is added to this Clause 4.10:

    > "To the extent which was practicable (taking account of cost and time), the Contractor shall be deemed to have obtained all necessary information as to risks, contingencies and other circumstances which may influence or affect the Tender or Works. To the same extent, the Contractor shall be deemed to have inspected

and examined the Site, its surroundings, the above data and other available information, and to have been satisfied before submitting the Tender as to all relevant matters."

In the Silver Book, the following is added instead of above:

"The Contractor shall be responsible for verifying and interpreting all such data. The Employer shall have no responsibility for the accuracy, sufficiency or completeness of such data [...]"

In the Yellow Book and Red Book, Clause 4.11, after acceptance of the contract amount, the risk of underground conditions is in principle allocated to the contractor, but with the restriction of Clause 4.10 (the research of contract to the extent that was practicable), and with addition of the risk of unforeseeable physical conditions, Clause 4.12:

"In this Sub-Clause, "physical conditions" means natural physical conditions and manmade and other physical obstructions and pollutants, which the Contractor encounters at the Site when executing the Works, including sub-surface and hydrological conditions but excluding climatic conditions.
If the Contractor encounters adverse physical conditions which he considers to have been Unforeseeable, the Contractor shall give notice to the Engineer as soon as practicable."
[...] the Contractor shall be entitled subject to [...]:

(a) an extension of time for any such delay, if completion is or will be delayed, under Sub-Clause 8.4 [Extension of Time for Completion], and
(b) payment of any such Cost, which shall be included in the Contract Price."

In the Silver Book, such a clause is absent. Instead, in Clause 4.12 the Silver Book determines that it's not an employer's issue if something regarding soil and soil conditions comes up during design or construction:

"Except as otherwise stated in the Contract:

(a) the Contractor shall be deemed to have obtained all necessary information as to risks, contingencies and other circumstances which may influence or affect the Works;
(b) by signing the Contract, the Contractor accepts total responsibility for having foreseen all difficulties and costs of successfully completing the Works;
(c) and the Contract Price shall not be adjusted to take account of any unforeseen difficulties or costs."

This Clause 4.12 to my opinion would never hold up in Dutch court, unless the employer really did his research well and fully, so according all scientific standards, by all possible means and without any errors at all.
The draft of the new Yellow Book (2016) shows changes in Clause 4.10 determining explicitly the process of assessment of a claim and clarifying some parts in terms of cause

and effect. The employer has the duty to inform the contractor about the soil conditions, and the contractor has to verify and scrutinize those— within the boundaries of what is practicable (taking in account cost and time).

In the UAV-GC 2005 there are more clauses in comparison with FIDIC models dedicated to soil conditions (Chapter 6, Soil and Site). That's understandable if you take the Dutch situation in account as described above—even in the order of naming the chapter, putting "soil" before "the site" itself makes sense.

Without having the desire to copy the complete chapter into this vignette, I'd like to point out some differences in approach between FIDIC contracts and the Dutch D&C contract. The main difference is that there is an explicit difference in what the contractor should do, and what he should have taken in account in terms of cost and time in his bid. That is because UAV-GC 2005 introduces the duty "to gear" the works to soil conditions, meaning that whatever these conditions are: the contractor is obligated to fit his design and construct to meet the actual soil conditions. In the first article, one could understand a Silver Book-like clause, where every delay or adjustment in costs is for the contractor (work in this manner is defined as all the activities necessary, including designing and construction):

> "13-1 The Contractor shall be responsible for gearing Work to the soil conditions. If the manner in which Work has been geared to the soil conditions causes delay in the execution of the Contract, damage to or defects in the Works or damage to other goods of the Employer or third parties, the Contractor shall be liable for such delay, damage or defects, subject to the provision of section 2."

In Dutch, there is a saying which says that a soup is never eaten as hot as it's being served, meaning sometimes things appear to be a certain way, but get "watered down" further in time. The same goes with this particular set of clauses. Let's see how the soup loses its heat:

> "13-2 The Contractor shall cease to be liable pursuant to section 1, if he proves that he has taken all precautions that may expected of a prudent Contractor in order to prevent delay, damage or defects, given the nature and the contents of the Contract, the nature of the Works, the nature of the Long-Term Maintenance and any other circumstances of the case."

So in Clause 13-2, the contractor can lose his liability if he can prove that he has taken reasonable and expectable precautions during construction the moment soil conditions showed different in such way that the contractor had to do something else (in design and/or construction method), in order to "gear" the works to the soil conditions. The necessary changes in design and/or construction are treated as Variations and triggers the according procedure based on Clause 14-3 because Clause 13-2 defines such an event as a necessary change for which the employer is responsible:

> "14-3 Any change or adjustment of Documents, Work or results of Work that has become necessary as a result of a circumstance for which the Employer is responsible by law, the Contract or opinions prevailing in society, shall be deemed to be a Variation ordered by the Employer as referred to in section 1.

Please note the additional "opinions prevailing in society" phrase, which is a codification of Dutch rulings of what in the German literature and rulings is called "*Verkehrsauffassung*" and in English translation is mentioned as "generally accepted views" by the EU High Court and in some literature as "common opinion."

All in all, comparing FIDIC models with the Dutch D&C model, one can draw that the conclusion that on all sorts of contracts the employer has a duty to inform contractors on forehand with all data about soil conditions he has in possession. In most of the cases the employer has to make sure he also delivers and thus does field research to gather all data which employer assess as relevant. Different is the way Dutch D&C contracts handle risk allocation. In most of the cases, if the contractor uses the data supplied and checks on forehand if there are obvious errors, he can trust the UAV-GC 2005 to allocate the impact of most of the differences in soil conditions to the employer. The FIDIC models have a more explicit task for contactors to scrutinize and depending if and how contractor fulfilled this task, the allocation of cost and time delays are possibly for employer. Within the Silver Book, it's very hard and probably impossible to claim any time delay or costs because of soil conditions being different than contractor took in consideration in his original bid. At least, by the letter of the contract, because by Dutch law, this Silver Book clause would probably be considered unfair and not according "common opinion."

3. *Early contractor involvement: a just and good habit for tendering D&C contracts*

After the first experiences with UAV-GC, more and larger projects were contracted by national authorities. With that came the realization that there should be enough time for tendering contractors to understand and fully develop a tender submission which could serve as a complete and fair start for the projects. It was of little discussion that contractor's should be able to reflect on the ER and have the time to interact with the contracting authorities. After introduction of the competitive dialogue procedure in the 2004/17 and 2004/18 Public Procurement Directives, Dutch authorities quickly started to widely use the CD procedure for large D&C (and also DBM(aintance), DBFM and DBFMOT) projects. Within Dutch way of the application of competitive dialogues, it is common to use a two-stage process (commonly starting with five contractors, with a second phase of three, which will finally submit their proposal). During that process, the requirements of the scope are developed further, resulting in the same goal as NEC ICE clauses intends; cooperation, more involvement, and better planning. Interacting by means of a dialogue before contracting, makes that that phases also works as a clarification.

It's therefore easy to understand why the practice of dialogue within CD and the positive experience of team interaction before contracting within the strict rules and principles of public procurement led to adopting and further developing best value procurement on those infrastructural projects. It should be noted that the original CD procedures were considered—besides their positive aspects in terms of interaction and preparation—both lengthy (more than 12 months was no exception) and very expensive. Early contractor involvement within public procurement procedures is also possible with the EU selective procedure. By organizing between three and five rounds of confidential dialogues, contractors are given the opportunity to talk freely about the set scope and ER. One important rule is that when the dialogue leads to changes in the ER, those changes are applied in general for *all* contractors, to preserve the level playing field during the procurement procedure.

One of the most important effects of these confidential sessions is that both parties can inform each other about the way they quantify certain risks—regardless the contractual allocation. In that way, both parties are able to prevent unpleasant and unnecessary surprises after contracting. One important principle is that these sessions are in no way used to anticipate on the MEAT assessment of the bid. It's okay to warn each other and to check on risk allocation and clarification—it's a no-go to qualify MEAT proposal before hand within the public procurement procedures.

Conclusion

The use of D&C contracts in the Netherlands for infrastructural projects is common and to general opinion with much success. The way these contracts handle information, design obligation and the validity of employer's requirements are in principle the same as FIDIC contract models, but adjusted for Dutch law, practice and the way construction project are managed. This adjustments in general take much of the risk allocated by FIDIC to the contractor more toward employer.

Although it may seem that by defining a lot of detail in the employer's requirement, and thus leaving contractor not very much room for making radical different design choices, the combination of D&C contracts and a procurement procedure based on MEAT still delivers a lot of added value. An important condition for that is that the ER itself is structured in a transparent hierarchy, and therefore contains no big errors or conflicts, and the price-quality ratio within the MEAT criteria leans more toward quality than price.

If D&C and MEAT are used consequently within the construction sector, the lessons learned are that contractors are able to add value to the minimum scope baseline of employers, with an extra plus for society that comparing bids to rig a procedure by forming a cartel is very difficult and thus unlikely. Using D&C and procuring based on quality instead of just price pays off, because the better contractors understand the initial scope of the employer, the better they are able to develop a design a construction method which keeps the risk for contractor low. Therefore, D&C with MEAT is not a more expensive way of procuring. Interaction between a contracting authority and tendering contractors in either ECI, CD, BVP, or by any other way within the procedure, is almost always productive and leads to better risk assessment and therefore a better start for D&C projects.

The most important aspect in changing from traditional contract toward more D&C projects is that all parties involved should be aware of the change in routines and the effect it has on the people involved. To change the way projects are executed, you should use different contract models but also help the professional involved to make that transition.

Joost Merema
Partner at PRO6 managers

Best value in the Netherlands by J.N. (Jaap) de Koning (the Netherlands)

In 2004, professor Dean Kashiwagi, from the Arizona State University, came to the Netherlands. He gave a lecture on the philosophy of best value PIPS (performance information procurement system). In the audience were the leading procurement managers from the largest employers in the Netherlands. They were very interested and curious about his approach and the results he claimed, but actually, nothing happened. Not until Rijkswaterstaat (the biggest employer on infrastructure in Holland), in 2009, decided to use the best value approach on a special project, called "Spoedaanpak wegverbreding." This project consisted of 16 projects, with the objective to increase road capacity on highways. The total project value was 800 million Euro. The project was a great success and best value was appreciated by the construction firms, in the procurement phase and in the execution. Since then, hundreds of projects have been carried out, using best value. Not only in the construction industry, and not only by Rijkswaterstaat, but—as an example—also in health care.

Best value consist of four phases, in which the procurement phase (number two) is the most prominent. This is how the philosophy became popular, as best value procurement. In this phase, the selection of the vendor is organized using several filters and some very specific criteria. The interview of key-personnel and a RAVA-plan are two new elements in this. RAVA stands for risk-assessed value added plan. Vendors are asked to describe how they will control risks, but also what opportunities they see, which can add value for the employer. All these elements are part of the total mix of award criteria on the basis of which the choice is made. Price is also part of the mix, but contributes only for 30%. The aim is not to select the vendor with the lowest price, but the vendor who can offer the best value, in other words, look for the expert. Vendors are therefore challenged on quality and price.

But best value is more than a specific procurement approach, it is a complete project management approach. It is based on the observation that the construction industry is inefficient, only price-based, ineffective as it comes to communication and exchange of information. If processes would be more efficient, they need less management, control and regulation. Best value is also about the relationship between vendors and employers. Vendors can perform much better if they are challenged on creating extra value, instead of being strictly controlled and managed on outcome, time, and money. Best value is also about risk management in a very open and balanced way. Risks for the employer should be managed by the employer, risks for the vendor are for the vendor. The vendor is asked to think about specific measures which might contribute to more control of the employer risks, but the management of these risks stay with the employer.

It is sometimes stated that best value is about trust between vendor and employer. That is a misunderstanding, best value is very much about accountability and transparency. Information should be dominant, which means that it is not only data, but it can also be used by non-experts. That is necessary, because in best value, the employer is aware that he is not the expert, but the real expertise is somewhere else (the vendor). And the employer should be able to understand the information, given by the vendor.

It is also questioned if best value complies with (European) rules about procurement, such as the Directive 2014/24/EU, about procurement of works, services and deliveries. Questions are raised about the use of award criteria that are subjective, like the interviews. In Holland, there is hardly any discussion about this legal issue. One can conclude that criteria like these are not forbidden. In article 66 of Directive 2014/24/EU, the use of MEAT (most economically advantageous tender) is strongly recommended. Best value procurement is nothing else than a form of MEAT. It is therefore not a legal discussion, but a discussion about the acceptance of this method by vendors and employers. Since vendors can show what they can, and have the possibility to procure a project using quality in combination with a reasonable price, they are in favor of best value as well. And as long as employers are transparent about the process and the rating of offers, vendors will accept the outcome.

In 2017, best value is an accepted and widely spread method in Holland. There is a Best Value Association, books are being written, there are education programs and once a year a National Best Value Congress. Elements of best value are more and more used in regular procurement procedures, which is discussed, but can also been seen as positive, since it proves that the message is coming through. In other (European) countries, best value is still controversial. The main reason for the success in Holland is perhaps the relationship between vendors and employers. This relationship can be described as normal and relatively open. There is discussion about contract conditions and procurement procedures and there are court cases, but usually, both parties are willing to work together and want to achieve a good project-result. And that is what best value is about, the ultimate goal is a good project.

J.N. (Jaap) de Koning MA MSc
Head Contract and Procurement Amsterdam, Witteveen+Bos

Concern over increasing adoption of design build for infrastructure works—JICA funding projects by Takashi Okamoto (Japan)

JICA is one of the world's largest bilateral aid agencies with some 90 overseas offices, carries out works in over 154 countries and regions, and implements Official Development Assistance (ODA) operations consisting of technical cooperation, loan, and grant aids. In the fiscal year of 2015, JICA provided 920 million US$ equivalent for the grants and 18,700 million US$ equivalent for loan aids. As for the loan aids in the same year, 65% of loans were provided for Asian countries, 9.5% for Middle East and then 7.5% for African countries. The vast majority of JICA finance is invested in the construction of infrastructure projects, by sector 44.0% in transportation, 18.4% in power generation and transmission, and 18.0% in public services like potable water or wastewater and communications.

In order to maintain implementing voluminous projects in satisfactory standards, JICA has published the following documents for the loan aid projects. They are available through JICA website (https://www.jica.go.jp/english/our_work/types_of_assistance/oda_loans/oda_op_info/guide/index.html).

Handbook for Procurement under Japanese ODA Loan (2012) (This handbook is based on the Guidelines for the Employment of Consultants under Japanese ODA Loans and the Guidelines for Procurement under Japanese ODA Loans.)

- Standard Prequalification Documents under Japanese ODA Loans
- Standard Request for Proposals under Japanese ODA Loans—Selection of Consultants (2012) [CONSULTANTS]
- Standard Bidding Documents under Japanese ODA Loans
    - Procurement of Works 2012 [WORKS]
    - Procurement of Plant Design, Supply and Installation 2013 [PLANT]
    - Procurement of Electrical and Mechanical Plant, and for Building and Engineering Works, Designed by the Contractor 2015 [DESIGN BUILD] (trail version)

- Procurement of Goods 2013 [GOODS]
- Procurement of Small Works 2013 [SMALL WORKS]
- Check List for One Sided Contracts (2011)
- Dispute Board Manual (2012)

Standard Bidding Documents (SBD) [WORKS], SBD [DESIGN BUILD] and SBD [PLANT] as above listed are based on FIDIC MDB Harmonized Edition (2010), FIDIC Yellow Book (1999), and ENAA (Engineering Advancement Association of Japan) Model Form [1992] respectively.

SBD[WORKS] is applied for construction only designed by the client type of projects, and both of SBD[DESIGN BUILD] and SBD[PLANT] are for design build projects.

JICA, having acknowledged that design build type of contracts are gradually increasing in the international infrastructure market, is cautious of imprudent applying design and build contracts to infrastructure projects.

Design and build contract benefits to the client:

1. Total project period including financial arrangement may be shorten due to unnecessity of separation of the design phase from the construction phase (not drastically though).
2. A design-build contractor takes whole responsibilities under a fit for purpose discipline, alternatively called "a single point of responsibilities by a contractor."
3. A fixed lump sum price may prevent cost overrun since a large part of the scope and specifications are the choice of the design-build contractor, and a limited changes are envisaged.

On the other hand, a client may encounter problems, for example:

1. Design services and constructions are often somewhat different from a client has initially intended.
2. Abnormally high bid prices may be offered due to obscure and mal-balanced risks allocation to a design-build contractor.

Satisfactory design build projects can be achieved by virtue of mutual trust and cooperation among the client, the design-build contractor and the consultant, and of carefully prepared contract documents. It is evident that all parties related to the project must establish a confident project management team through reliable and sufficient communications. Thoughtful and well-balanced project risk allocation to the parties is a crucial issue in order to establish such management team avoiding unnecessary suspicions among the parties. Sir Michael Latham wrote in the first page of "Constructing the Team, 1994," (in order to obtain High quality projects, it) "requires better performance, but with fairness to all involved. Above all it needs teamwork. Management jargon calls that 'seeking win-win solutions.'"

In reality, it is regrettable that majority of current bidding documents submitted to JICA for its concurrence have been found not being drafted based on such thoughtful and well-balanced risk allocations, for example:

1. No detailed site survey data is incorporated in bidding documents whereas bidders are required to make preliminary design for setting their bid prices.

    A client recklessly or carelessly thinks that a design-build contractor is to perform everything including detailed site surveys during the contract period under the single point of

responsibilities, but it never considers that bidders would not be able to analyze precise project cost through the bidding process.
2. A detailed design has been practically completed by a client, however, a subsequent requirement to bidders is to trace the client design, to take design responsibility and to offer a firm lump sum price, which is malicious consideration contrary to pursuing trustworthy and cooperative relationship among the contracting parties.
3. Although a contractor is requested carrying out only a part of design services of the project, bid documents explicitly requires the contractor to take entire turnkey like fit for purpose obligations. It is not justifiable to let the contractor be liable for the part where such part has not actually been performed.

Those written above are typical unbalanced risks allocated to bidding documents that JICA often encounters.

JICA is, however, receptive to use of design build contracts if the following conditions are met:

1. The nature of a project is suitable for the design build contract, for example, power plant and water plant constructions are in general suitable for design build contract, but underground works, road and railway constructions and marine port constructions are not suitable because they are highly influenced by unforeseeable risks.
2. A design build contract is more favorable than a construction only designed by the client contract in terms of timeline, cost, and/or quality. In certain type of projects, seeking innovative technologies owned by private companies are more beneficial for the project. However, major infrastructures such as bridge and road constructions have been traditionally designed by the client, and it is conceivable that most construction companies have less experience in designing of such structures.
3. Risks are fairly allocated between a client and a design build contractor. It is considered that risks are taken by a party who is more capable to handle such risks, for example, suitability of site for a project is a risk of the client. Fairly and precisely allocated risks must be achieved for a design build contract.
4. A detailed site survey has been made by the client and supplied to bidders. The bidders are dependent upon the project information provided by the client, therefore, unless such detailed information is provided, the bidder is unable to analyze its bid to his satisfaction. A careful minded bidder may inevitably add a large risk contingency, to the contrary an aggressive minded one may not consider any risk involvement in the project at all.
5. Client's requirements are precisely defined so that a client is able to attain a project what it exactly intends. Under a design build contract, once a contract has been entered, most of activities are performed by a design build contractor and little intervention by a client is occasioned. "Let the contractor be responsible for everything" type of attitude is obviously not appropriate, whilst giving too limited design liberty to a contractor is also not justifiable.

Takashi Okamoto
Senior advisor
Infrastructure Engineering Department,
JICA (Japan International Corporation Agency)

3.4 Construction management

Under construction management (CM), an employer has direct contracts with the individual prime contractors and hires a construction manager as their consultant for the purpose of coordination. The manager is paid on a cost-plus basis (i.e., a surcharge to the direct costs of the individual prime contractors' prices).

CM (sometimes called pure CM or agency CM) originated in the United States. CM was developed in the 1960s and early 1970s because of the need to realize complicated construction projects in a short time while meeting top standard requirements. This necessity led to the creation of a system within which the effectiveness of a construction manager's competencies is crucial. Among the construction project participants, priority position is therefore given to the employer's representative in the form of the "construction manager" in charge of management and coordination.

A further purpose of CM is to limit the main contractor's surcharges which burden the employer in general contracting. Payments to contractors are direct and without any intermediary. Individual contractors (including a designer or DB contractor) perform particular parts of the works on a lump sum contract basis. CM is typically used in building construction in projects with numerous subcontracts that have to be effectively coordinated.

The construction manager is not responsible for subcontractor performance but is responsible for negligent acts of management, for example, lack of skill and adequacy of management leading to maladministration, bad coordination and poor planning.

Performance risks—particularly the responsibility for on-time completion—rest with the contractor. Performance guarantees are required by the employer and include, for example, bank guarantees to ensure on-time project realization and remedying of any defects within the defects notification period. Even one problematic subcontractor may cause substantial damage and delay to the entire construction project.

The following are often taken as expected norms under CM:

- The CM concept assumes and expects the employer (often being a developer) to take an active role, have extensive experience and to cooperate closely with the construction manager. Ideally, the construction manager and the employer should know each other and have worked together on a long-term basis. For this reason, CM is often unsuitable for public contracts.
- Timely completion is often an employer's top priority. Using CM allows for faster decision making and can result in reduced cost. Similarly, the employer's expectation when using CM are quick startups and financial returns.
- From the employer's point of view, the priority is not lowest construction cost but "value for money." In other words, return on investment.
- The construction manager is paid on a cost plus basis. Total construction costs are difficult to foresee due to the fact that no one contractor guarantees overall price.
- Risk allocation, design responsibility, price determination, and claims admission depend on the contracts between the employer and particular prime contractors that are liable for bad performance. The construction manager is only liable for bad management, planning and coordination.

3.4.1 CM-at-risk

CM-at-risk is a delivery method derived from CM where the construction manager is responsible for delivering the project within the limits of the *guaranteed maximum price* (GMP).

The construction manager not only acts on the employer's behalf during the preparations and pre-award engineering, but also acts as a *de facto* main contractor in the construction phase. The CM undergoes a fundamental change with the manager being obliged to adhere to the GMP. To avoid exceeding the GMP, it is in the manager's own best interest to manage and control construction costs.

Such a system, however, must be perfectly devised in terms of risk allocation, insurance, securities and contingencies. Reserves must be properly established by the employer and construction manager. Such a setup is not appropriate for projects posing numerous pending hazards with major risks.

Interface management and interface agreements by Zachary Ferreira (the United States) and Alex Blomfield (UK)

A. *What Are Interfaces?*

Interfaces are points of contact or shared boundaries, interaction, and information exchanges between interdependent but independently managed systems within a complex project. These systems interfaces may be technical, virtual, physical, organizational, social, and even temporal (e.g., where the work schedules of two subcontractors come together in alignment at a job site). In project development and construction, the failure of interfaces to interact as intended is often a root cause of cost overruns, delays, warranty disputes, mechanical failures, project inefficiencies, and economic loss.

Taking the context of software engineering as an example to illustrate virtual and physical interfaces, the content displayed by software on a monitor may be considered a virtual interface between a user and software running on a computer, while the keyboard and mouse function as a physical point of contact between the user and the machine. From a mechanical engineering perspective, the interaction of two mechanical systems may occur over an interface, even though both mechanical systems might be integrated into a system made up of multiple systems that together perform as a unit, such as when the transmission system, the ignition system, the fuel injection system and the breaking system of a car all interact to allow a driver to start a car, move a car, stop a car, and turn a car off.

Most important for the construction or project lawyer, however, is that interfaces can be defined and understood much more broadly than as mere technical or design boundaries between software, electronic parts or machine components. Those points in contracts where one contractor's obligations in its scope of work scope cease and another contractor's obligations in its scope of work begin are also interfaces. The boundaries and points of contact between the scopes of work of two subcontractors on a construction job or two stakeholder groups in a project create interfaces between different groups or organizations. From a project contract perspective, these organizational interfaces often pose the most significant legal risks. For example, where two or more subcontractors must coordinate their work and cooperate on the same schedule in order to achieve a project milestone, the failure to coordinate their work and cooperate on the same schedule and timeline could mean the failure to achieve the project milestone as intended.

B. *Interface Management*

Interface management arises from the idea that deliberate, informed action with respect to such interfaces between systems—whether technical, organizational, or contractual—can reduce the risk that the project will fail to achieve a planned or desired result as a consequence of the failure of two or more systems to communicate or interact satisfactorily.

For the purpose of managing interfaces, it can be useful to distinguish between internal and external interfaces. There is nothing inherently "internal" or "external" about an interface, per se. From a systems engineering point of view, for example, all interfaces are by definition external, that is, points of external communication and contact between separate or distinct systems. Rather, this distinction is made in regard to the ability to control a given interface.

An interface that is entirely within the control of a single stakeholder—whether that be a subcontractor, a project design team, or a single engineer, for example—could be said to be "internal" with respect to that stakeholder's work. Under a turnkey EPC contract, where all responsibility for design and construction of a project rests with the general contractor, all of the project's interfaces are "internal" to the general contractor, from the project sponsor's point of view (even if the general contractor has the burden of managing such interfaces as external interfaces among the various project sub-systems being delivered by different sub-contractors). For quality control, inspection, or testing purposes, a project sponsor may be keenly interested in a contractor's internal interfaces, even where contractually the contractor is assuming full responsibility for the performance of a scope of work that includes that contractor's internal interfaces. A well-drafted construction contract will typically contain various provisions that provide a project sponsor with the oversight rights that can be exercised to verify that a contractor's internal interfaces are not significantly at risk of failing.

On the other hand, these risk allocation and work performance oversight provisions of a construction contract between a turnkey contractor and a project sponsor that ensure adequate management of interfaces internal to the contractor's scope of work are not adequate where a project depends on the performance of multiple contractors performing their work independent of one another, giving rise to external interfaces. Such external interfaces are the focus of concern for the project lawyer seeking to document the appropriate allocation of risks across multiple project contracts. In particular, a well-conceived and properly drafted interface management plan is an essential tool for project success with regard to those points where the physical, technical, or mechanical interfaces of the various systems of a project align or coincide with contractual scopes of work of separate contractors working on limited parts of the overall project.

(i) *Simple Projects*

Just because a project lacks complex, highly engineered technologically advanced systems does not mean that it is necessarily free of the risks created by interfaces. Projects do not have to be technologically complex to reap the benefits of careful interface management.

Whenever external interfaces exist that create risks to a project, interface management can become an effective project management tool for seeking to minimize that risk. Any time there are multiple independent project stakeholders whose coordination and cooperation are required for overall project success, these points of coordination and cooperation—these social or organizational interfaces—present specific challenges, justifying the incorporation of interface management provisions into project documents to provide project managers with the tools for effectively controlling these risks.

(ii) *The Interface Committee*

A core tool that is routinely built into the contractual documents of projects with external interface risks is the concept of an interface committee (coordination committee) with some degree of oversight over and control over the external interfaces of a project. Whether the interface management provisions of the project documents prescribe with considerable detail and precision, the composition, function, and authority of such a committee, or merely delegate such details to the resolutions of the committee itself once constituted during project execution, may depend on factors and considerations such as the scope and complexity of the known external interfaces, the need to ensure bankability of the project to the satisfaction of risk averse lenders, and even the relative negotiating leverage of contractors and the project sponsor. Typically a reasonable bankable interface committee clause of a project document might include provisions for defining (a) the number of members, (b) which stakeholders these members represent, (c) the basic decision-making mechanics of the committee (e.g., agenda definition process, quorum standards, and voting pass mark mechanisms), (d) methods for resolving impasses and disagreements among committee members, (e) the frequency of meetings, and (f) some basic rights of committee members with respect to interface management matters (e.g., whether representatives can invite technical specialists or experts to speak to specific interface issues). An interface committee might even be empowered to make changes to contracts, such as changes to specific designs and plans or to contract schedules or milestone dates, where such changes are critical to ensure successful integration of project works across external interfaces.

(iii) *Contractor Interface Covenants and Responsibilities Owed to Project Sponsor and Other Contractors*

By itself, an interface committee designed to deal with project external interface risks is only one tool for managing interfaces. To supplement the function of the interface committee, contractors may be required to commit in their contracts with a project sponsor to perform certain covenants and obligations to put the contractor on notice of, and encourage due attention to, the contractor's external interfaces with other contractors. Such provisions may begin with an acknowledgement by the contractor to establish knowledge of the risk and possibility of external interfaces. Contractors customarily are expected to agree to cooperate reasonably with other contractors with respect to external interface matters, typically agreeing to a standard of care with respect to performance of work along the boundaries of the interface with another contractor's work to prevent damages to the respective work scopes of the contractors. A contractual duty to coordinate in good faith and fairly, including with respect to the sharing of appropriate information to ensure interface success, is usually appropriate as well. Contractors are usually expected to keep other project stakeholders informed and promptly to give notice to appropriate stakeholders when they become aware of issues that could impact the satisfaction of specified interface requirements (such requirement is sometimes known as "early warning notification").

Some interface agreements or interface management plans require an owner's engineer to record early warning notifications in a risk register. Such an engineer may instruct a contractor or contractors to attend a risk reduction meeting, which may take place contemporaneously with a meeting of the interface committee. Each contractor may request other contractors or the project owner to attend such meeting but such other contractors and the project owner shall have no obligation to attend such meeting. Those who attend a risk reduction meeting may be obliged to (a) cooperate in making and considering proposals for the avoidance or reduction of the effect of the registered risks, (b) seek solutions that will bring advantage to all those affected, (c) decide on the actions to be taken and who, in accordance with any interface agreement or interface management system and other relevant contracts, will take them, and (d) decide which risks the owner's engineer can now remove from the risk register following their avoidance, mitigation or passing. The owner's engineer may be required to revise the risk register to record the decisions made at each risk reduction meeting and issue the revised risk register to each contractor. If a decision requires a variation, the owner's engineer may be obliged to instruct such variation at the same time as it issues the revised risk register.

(iv) *The Interface Matrix*

As part of the interface management plan, project managers will attempt to identify and document in a register each known or identified external interface for the execution of the project. The development of such a matrix or register is often a collaborative effort, with input from each contractor coming as part of the tender or bid submission process, as well as during project execution. At a minimum, such an interface matrix or register may serve to establish which contractor work scopes are implicated by the interface as well as some dates or project schedule points when key actions for the satisfaction of the interface are required. In some project industries, such a matrix may also identify for a given system element the party responsible for its design, its fabrication or supply, its transportation to and installation in the project site, and its integration and testing as part of the project.

Project lawyers may attempt to allocate responsibility to one of the contractors identified for a specific interface in the matrix. Where the performance of one contractor's work is a clear, unambiguous dependency for the performance of the other contractor's work, such unilateral contract responsibility allocations may be uncontroversial, both in negotiations and in project execution. But interface risk allocations are not often so clear or uncontroversial in real projects. For example, the contractor responsible for designing and fabricating the hydrocarbon processing system modules to be installed on the topside of a floating oil production unit may need to coordinate with the contractor responsible for fabricating and installing the flowlines that move well fluid from the well head to the point of introduction into the topside processing system so as to ensure that volume of well fluid arriving through the flowline into the processing system matches what the processing system is capable of handling. But if the interface between the flowlines and the hydrocarbon processing system fail to perform within the requirements, it may not be a satisfactory outcome for the project company to hold either the processing system contractor or the flowline contractor liable, since there might be a number of factors involved - many far outside the scope of either contractor's ability to control—that could lead to a failure of this interface, including factors caused by the project company itself, or other contractors whose work was not even captured in the interface matrix as impacting this interface.

(v) *Interface Agreements*

In terms of establishing these and other interface management provisions in project documents, project lawyers customarily take one of two approaches, although for reasons discussed below, different industries have clear preferences in favor of one approach or the other. The first approach is to create a stand-alone agreement as part of the suite of project contracts called the interface agreement (or interface deed or interface contract) that must be signed by all contractors as well as the project company. By requiring all project contractors to enter into a single, stand-alone contract with each other and the project company, a project sponsor is able to eliminate any issues with regard to lack of privity or third-party beneficiary standing between individual project contractors.

The alternative approach is to establish a uniform interface management plan and identical terms and conditions integrated into each project contract between the project sponsor and its individual project contractors, binding each contractor to a uniform set of contract terms, and possibly even giving certain contractors status as third-party beneficiaries under other contractors' contracts, but without creating any direct contractual privity between the various project contractors.

Whether one or the other approach is most appropriate for a given project depends on a number of factors, such as the number and nature of interfaces, the number of contractors involved, and the financing structure of the project. The interface agreement approach is particularly well suited for projects with a limited number of multi-variable, technology interface risks or in industries that tend to depend on project finance for funding, as the stand-alone interface contract facilitates the satisfaction of certain bankability requirements.

1. *Case Study 1: Hydropower*

A case on point, the stand-alone interface agreement is the dominant approach for hydropower projects that employ split-contract construction procurement as opposed to a single EPC turnkey construction contract, that is, separate contracts for civil and electro-mechanical works and sometimes also hydraulic steelworks and other works packages. The interface agreement for split-contract hydropower projects manages interface risk among the various construction tender packages, creates a forum for contractors to work through interface issues among themselves and provides for a common dispute resolution process for all contractors, the owner's engineer and the project owner. It can also contain a bonus scheme for early completion.

A stand-alone interface is feasible and valuable in this context for a number of reasons. First, where such projects are financed through project finance, the interface agreement is critical for the overall bankability of the construction contracts. Second, these projects often require multiple contractors to work in parallel with numerous schedule dependencies (such as between design and construction and between the civil and electro-mechanical contractors' scopes in the powerhouse) albeit that external interfaces are fewer where there are less contracts and contractors. Third, hydropower is generally regarded a 'tried and tested' technology without "first of a kind" technologies as project system elements.

2. *Case Study 2: Offshore Oil and Gas Production*

On the other hand, the second approach is very common in extremely complex, highly engineered deepwater oil and gas field development projects. Deepwater oil and gas field development and operations projects are extremely high cost, technologically complex, and involve extensive uncertainty and risk. Offshore oil operators routinely ask their contractors to push technology boundaries in their search for new oil in ever deeper and more remote and difficult subsea locations. The technological and other uncertainties that characterize deepwater oil field development projects create many very complex interface risks that demand management and mitigation. As a consequence, offshore field development and operations projects typically involve the integration of state-of-the-art technologies provided by many different specialty technical contractors often working independently of each other in separate locations with no privity of contract between them, only a shared employer, the operator of the field. And yet the success or failure of such a project depends on the ability of these advanced technologies when delivered and deployed to function effectively as an integrated whole both upon commissioning and through the economic life of the oil field. Successful integration and coordinated deployment and operation of these independently delivered, heavily engineered systems require careful management of interfaces. With all of these very elaborate engineered interface elements, which commonly deploy untested "first of its kind" technologies and the large number of specialty contractors involved in stages over a very long project delivery schedule and project life cycle that can sometimes take one or more decades to complete, it is potentially impractical or unrealistic for a project sponsor to implement a stand-alone agreement that binds all contractors to each other across time. Because deepwater oil field development projects are notoriously high risk, with many uncertainties beyond the control of any project participants, these projects are not particularly suited for project financing and tend to be funded with the capital of project sponsors. All of this makes the integration of interface management plans into each project contract the preferred approach for such projects.

C. *Conclusion*

Regardless of the approach chosen, the general methods tend to focus on (a) proper identification, documentation and definition of all interfaces and their attributes (internal and external) in the early design and engineering phase, (b) correct identification of the stakeholders for each interface, (c) proper definition and review of work scope of the project as an integrated whole, (d) division of the work scope assignments and roles among the stakeholders, and (e) regular, open, managed, and structured channels of communication between stakeholders regarding interfaces, project schedules, and execution.

Zachary Ferreira, Of Counsel
Alex Blomfield, Special Counsel
K&L Gates LLP

3.5 Multiple-prime contracts

Under the multiple-prime contracts delivery method, a large number of main contractors work under the employer or under an employer's representative on the basis of separate contracts. The employer will have under their direct control the particular prime contractors, thereby avoiding the main contractor's surcharges. However, the employer will assume the duties of coordination and surveillance which bring with them significant risk. Many American states (Pennsylvania, Ohio, New York, New Jersey, and North Carolina) have amended their public procurement legislation to include the mandatory use of this delivery method (Cushman, 2011). The employer must not assign the duty of coordination and management in such cases. Where the duty to use the multiple-prime contracts delivery method is not imposed by law, the duty of coordination, and management is most frequently delegated to one of the main contractors. The position of a coordinating contractor will then arise and does not differ from a traditional general contractor. In such cases, the particular rights and obligations must be defined in the contract, for example, the coordination and management duty and the way to execute the defined duties during realization.

3.6 Partnering

Partnering is not a clearly defined concept in construction. It is not a delivery method but rather a commitment of construction project participants to work together cooperatively, rather than competitively and adversarially. Partnering is a pre-realization measure that has an indirect, positive influence on project realization. Partnering is, more or less, the formal attempt of all participants to implement and use a common forum. This creates opportunities for regular, open communication between the parties and joint solutions to problems.

Partnering originated in the United States, though most of the processes adopted in partnering come from the Japanese construction industry. These are, in turn, the application of total quality management and lean manufacturing concepts from manufacturing industries.

An initiation meeting where the individual representatives (such as the employer, contractor, designer, and/or the contract administrator and important subcontractors) get acquainted is held right upon commencement of the project. To facilitate this meeting, an independent consultant can take part in the agenda and may include discussions and/or presentations that will clarify the steps to realization and the parties' obligations. The main purpose of partnering, therefore, is to strengthen the participants' commitment to strive for open and well-informed solutions to problems.

Partnering is a method that allows participants to minimize or avoid conflicts when they are engaged in a complex project. It is a way of unifying all parties as stakeholders to a project into a team. Experienced contract administrators use this process as a polite and routine form of mutual communication throughout construction project realization.

Partnering is in fact a code of conduct, a working agreement intended to create a non-adversarial culture and to promote a "win-win" relationship between the parties. The disadvantage of partnering is that it is based on a "gentleman's agreement." Despite being well intentioned, if a conflict arises, the parties almost always revert back to formal contractual procedures.

Integrated project delivery—"Collaborate rather than litigate" by Edward J. ("Ned") Parrott (the United States)

In the world of twenty-first-century construction, the cost of failing to collaborate with project partners is too often litigation. The fees, costs, administrative burdens, and lost opportunities associated with construction litigation are justly viewed as wasteful and non-productive. Under the traditional construction contract paradigm, there is a high potential for adversarial relationships. It is implied that the most the owner will receive is the minimum the contractor and designers can get away with. There is a high potential for adversarial relationships with each party acting to protect their own interests. The end result can be poorly functioning, unmaintainable designs, delays, cost surprises, numerous RFIs and changes orders, claims and disputes, unmet expectations, productivity losses in the field, no fun, and lawsuits.

For this reason, multi-party collaborative construction contract agreements (Integrated Project Delivery), such as the "ConsensusDocs" family, deserve serious consideration by innovative construction project participants. Collaborative agreements such as the ConsensusDocs require that all parties depart from traditional project delivery systems and assumptions. Decisions about budgets, equipment, schedule, scope, systems, and so on, must be made early in the process and made jointly. The collaborative agreement requires owner commitment as well as engineering, design, and contractor commitment and cooperation. All parties are contractually and financially incentivized to work together (e.g., "Pulling rope in same direction").

Selection of contractors is no longer based on competitive price bidding but rather on new selection criteria such as safety, experience, and relationships. The collaborative project delivery team members agree on the development and establishment of responsibilities and the establishment of collaborative principles such as collective sharing in project losses or profits. Key elements in the integrated project delivery system are the financial/incentive agreements that incentivize model behavior such as collaborating intensely, optimizing the whole, improving continuously, innovating, and building trust.

The results of integrated project delivery/collaborative contracting can be striking. One case study is based on the $46M, 120,000-square-foot expansion of a congested urban hospital campus. Employing the collaborative system rather than the traditional contract delivery vehicle, project planning and scheduling improved, coordination and communication improved, and the project team functioned as a unit. The project only had 63 RFIs and was completed at 2% under the original construction budget. The owner reinvested its portion of savings in added scope, there were no disputes or claims, and the project was completed 45 days early. Morale was very high at this preferred site with high-quality work and an excellent safety record.

The case for collaboration is strong.

Edward J. ("Ned") Parrott
Senior Partner
Watt, Tieder, Hoffar & Fitzgerald L.L.P.
Construction, Government Contract, Surety & Contract Law

3.7 Alliancing

In contrast to partnering, alliancing involves a formal contract under which the parties undertake to act in the best interests of the project. It seems that alliancing has been accepted as a specific delivery method but its use in international construction projects is not significant. When alliancing, the parties commit to work cooperatively and to share risk and reward, measured against performance indicators.

The birth of the alliancing concept, notably "Project Alliancing," originated in the UK where British Petroleum (BP) developed a new "painshare—gainshare" compensation program called Project Alliancing for the North Sea Andrew's Field Project. The alliance was established in the early 1990s and resulted in a reduction of capital costs by 21% and the production of oil six months earlier than originally scheduled. The emergence of alliancing received a great deal of attention from industry practitioners and researchers—particularly in the Australian construction industry (Rowlinson and Cheung, 2013).

The allied participants of a particular construction project work as a single integrated team and their commercial interests are aligned with actual project objectives. They are selected on capability approaches and systems and other soft criteria such as enthusiasm, commitment and chemistry. A commercial framework is created that drives "best for project" decisions that share the rewards of outstanding performance and the pain of poor performance. All risks are shared by all members of the alliance.

Alliancing is a valid option for the delivery of projects that have a relatively high level of uncertainty in their project definition, are complex in form or have very tight delivery timetables. Where it is difficult to allocate risks sensibly or where there are complex issues which are difficult to manage, alliance arrangements between competent parties have much to offer. When successfully implemented, the integrated project team focuses on project delivery and high performance, rather than their potential exposure and liability under contract. Typically having an "open book" price determination, (i.e., guaranteeing payment for all project costs), alliancing provides little incentive for keeping costs under control—particularly when relatively modest contractor margins are at stake.

During realization, alliance partners must share resources including professional expertise. To ensure success, this must be facilitated through a continuous flow of information and communication. In alliancing, "No Dispute" clauses are sometimes used. Under such clauses, the parties agree to waive rights of action against each other in arbitration and litigation.

Target price and early risk identification/management: London 2012 Olympics by Klaus Grewe (UK)

The London 2012 Olympics are one of the best games ever held, but a successful construction project too. The construction project with a budget of £9.3 billion was delivered four months before time and £1.1 billion under budget. The success was based on a consequent program, risk, and cost management. The project was divided in approximately 100 particular projects like the Olympic stadium, the utilities, an so on.

As for myself, I worked on this project as a senior program manager, coordinating over 100 projects and participated in development of mentioned project management tools.

The following text explains two of the specific methods that lead the project to be managed in cost and time, that is, by risk management and specifically the use of target price contacts.

Program management

Program management is a management tool that helps to coordinate several projects on a central level implementing the same structure and methods at each of the projects. Each project works under the same governance, escalating identified risks to the next level through a short but fixed meeting structure. Meetings are organized with the ability to decisions to be made in a very short time.

Baseline

Central document for any kind of efficient program management is the so-called baseline. The baseline describes the scope, technical descriptions, milestones, major risks, and the cost of each project. The London 2012 baseline was developed during the design phases and completed before tender. Each design stage was finalized with a report (preliminary baseline) comparing the developments (design, costs, time, risks) against the phase before. After the design phase completion and before tender the final design report was transformed into a frozen baseline containing scope, technical description, major risks, costs, and milestones.

From the tender phase on, the baseline is the foundation for the steering and controlling of the project. The content of the baseline was transferred into the time schedule, cost control, change control, and risk management mechanisms. Within a strict monthly governance each single project task was monitored against the baseline task and if necessary mitigation measures were introduced immediately.

Risk management

The London 2012 risk management experience has been an inspiration for current even much more detailed approaches to identify and mitigate risks. Not only major risks are to be managed. In large projects hundreds of unforeseen minor risks may result in major impacts for the project. A missing approval for a small variation could delay the entire completion of a project by months.

Current understanding of risk management is that each task described in the baseline (it could be 10,000) will be discussed and tracked within team workshops. If the task represents a risk, the risk must be identified and mitigation measures must be taken. The team risk workshops start already during the design phases in a three to four months' rhythm. The identified risks must be mitigated via design changes or reviews.

Tender

Before the tender, final risk workshop must identify all remaining construction, production, approval procedure, and similar risks. The major risks will be described in the baseline report and all other risks will be implemented in a baseline risk register. Baseline report and the identic task column in the risk register will be frozen.

In a large project a high number of tasks with a significant level of risk will be identified. The tasks must be listed in the tender document and for each task the bidder is asked to describe possible risks and his mitigation measures. The bidders answers and proposed measures to that identified risk tasks are the main evaluation criteria when looking for the most economically advantageous tender (MEAT). The bidder is obliged to split his bid price estimate into basic costs, project overhead, company overhead, margin, and risks.

The final bid price was a detailed estimate broke down in particular items as requested in the tender documents. The bidder was obliged to price all positions and split the price in basic direct and indirect cost including separate item related risks cost. The sums of all risks were reviewed via the Monte Carlo method and a final decision by each bidder was made to relocate and relate the sums of for particular risks to each item. Profit and overhead were allocated over all positions.

In terms of delivery methods, both integrated design-build contracts and traditional design-bid-build contracts were used as it was appropriate. For most of them the particular NEC3 standard form was used.

Procurement

In terms of particular criteria for bid evaluation, the weight of the final bid price counted only from 40% to 50%. Furthermore, based on a monitored point system, the bidders answered to a technical and organizational questionnaire that weighted up to 30% of the bid evaluation. The questionnaire was based on the client's own evaluation of contractors risks. Two reviewers and one overall reviewer per theme evaluated each answer within a point and rating system. The other 20% were allocated to the financial liability and the track record of former projects of the bidder.

The selection process was without any involvement or further meetings with the bidder. Before the tender the final bidders were invited to join a general information sessions.

Only in one case a bidder finally won a contract based on an abnormally low price answering the questionnaire only in a rudimentary but acceptable fashion. This resulted in one of the biggest program challenges.

Target price contract

At the London Olympics, we used a target price mechanism for 12 of 100 major contracts. After the successful tender the price of the winning tender is fixed as the target. Under a target price contract, if the project achieves a result under the target both client and contractor share the gain, if it goes over target both share the pain.

Within 10 days after the contract is signed the contractor is obliged to open his basis bid estimate, now developed to a target price. The basic estimate is divided into groups such as basic costs, project overhead, company overhead, margin, and risks. The basic costs estimate is undergoing a validity check and further monthly reviewed against scope and progress. The bidder was obliged to provide a detailed quantity survey of the monthly performance of each item (xy cbm concrete for column A). The survey was double-checked by a quantity surveyor on the client side. The development of the basic cost was monitored monthly. The bidder, now contractor project overhead, company overhead, and margin cannot be further monitored or touched. They are fixed items.

Central focus points during construction and key elements to achieve a gain and to avoid the pain are the identified and estimated risks in the contractors bid. In monthly joint detailed risk workshops the participants discuss the appearing risks foreseen within the next 3 to 6 months task by task. What are the hazards, how much risk they bring, what the mitigation could be. Often it is necessary that both parties jointly endeavor to avoid or reduce a specific risk.

As a result risk for some of the tasks could be reduced. At the end of the day, if all monitored risks result in the overall contract price under the target, the margin will be shared 50/50 between the client and the contractor, if overall contract price goes over the target, again the 50/50 of the pain is shared.

The development of possible gains or pains was monitored monthly within the risk workshops and actions agreed.

Klaus Grewe
Principal, Program Management, Advisor

3.8 Extended delivery methods (PPP, BOT, DBO)

The public and private partnership(PPP) method was developed to enable and make optimal use of private funding and expertise for public projects. In practice, it usually applies to a public investment or service performed, operated or provided directly by the private sector (a company other than one owned by the state or an association (consortium) of companies) instead of the public sector (such as the state, regional or local municipality). After an agreed operation and maintenance period, the work will pass into public ownership. In PPP projects, the public sector will then act as a manager and supervisor over the private contractors.

In the past few years, public employers have chosen this approach as it does not burden the budget or increase public debt directly. The long-term effects are hard to foresee, however. The main advantage is the opportunity to start new projects that could not have been financed without private resources. The negative aspects are higher overall transaction costs and loss of employer control.

PPP is, in practice, more of a brand name for different kinds of projects known as DBO, BOT, and so on. The exact meaning of these brands must be examined according to a particular project. The following abbreviations and their respective combinations express the delivery method most often encountered:

D – Design
B – Bid
B – Build
O – Operate
M – Maintain
O – Own
T – Transfer
F – Finance.

Public-private partnerships by Steven Van Garsse (Belgium)

Public-private partnerships (PPPs or P3s) have become a widespread phenomenon all over the world. There is no universal accepted definition of what a PPP is. In fact one can say that PPPs come in many forms and are still an evolving concept. PPPs involve private sector supply of infrastructure assets and services that have traditionally been provided by the government. The World Bank, for example, defines PPPs as "long-term contracts between a private party and a government agency, for providing a public asset or service, in which the private party bears significant risk and management responsibility." This definition makes clear what (most) PPPs have in common: projects are long-term, usually bundling design, construction, and maintenance and possibly operation and with the objective of providing a public service. It also involves performance-based elements with private capital at stake to such performance and associated risk allocation between the public and private sectors. Typical contractual arrangements involve BOT, BOOT, and concession contracts. Quite popular are also the so-called DBFM(O) type contracts.

A DBFM(O) contract is an integrated type of contract in which a range of activities are contracted out by the government to a private sector consortium that will form, after the award of the contract, a special company (a special purpose vehicle, SPV, see also Table 3.1). It is the SPV that signs the contract and implements the PPP project. Under a DBFM(O) agreement, the SPV in turn brings together the design, build, financing, maintenance and operation activities, usually through sub-contracting to a range of private sector parties.

It is for the private market players to submit, during the public tender procedure, an offer for the design, financing, construction, maintenance, and, as applicable, the operational running

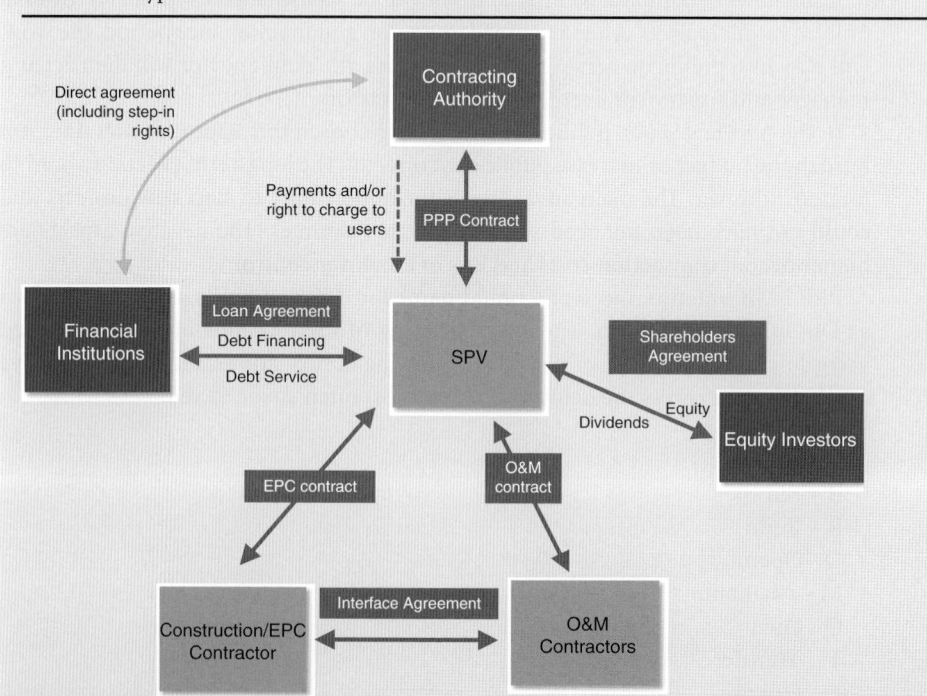

Table 3.1 Typical PPP Structure

of the project. It is also up to the private partner to assume the risks associated with the various aspects. The private partner is therefore responsible for designing the facility and building it in order to deliver the service outputs in accordance with the specifications set out in the tender documentation of the contracting authority. In order to be able to finance the design and construction of the facility, the private partner will need to ensure the financing is in place. It will do so by committing equity finance in the SPV and by attracting long-term debt (bank loans, sometimes bonds, etc.). Once the facility is constructed, the SPV will make it available and maintain it in return for payment by government of a performance related availability payment or a user charge paid by users. These performance-based payment mechanisms lie at the heart of the financial and risk structure of the contract and are driven by private capital being at risk to such performance.

The DBFM(O) contract may involve the renovation of an existing facility (brownfield), or it may involve construction of new facility (greenfield). As a rule, PPP contracts are signed for a relatively long period of time, which is proportionate to the life cycle of the relevant infrastructure. This is important so that life-cycle risks of the facility are properly transferred.

The rationale for doing PPPs and especially DBFMO is based on the claim that they have the potential to close the infrastructure gap by leveraging scarce public funding and introducing private sector technology, know-how and innovation to provide better-quality public services through improved operational efficiency and quality and, perhaps most importantly, long-term life-cycle maintenance of the facility. Value for money is usually put forward as the main rationale for PPP. The government will often carry out, and is usually even obliged to carry out, an ex-ante assessment as to whether or not the PPP project is expected to represent value for money. This value for money analysis often involves a process that compares the long-term present value cost of a PPP project against that for a traditional comparable public alternative. This usually involves the creation of a so-called public sector comparator, which estimates the whole-life hypothetical risk-adjusted cost of carrying out the project through a traditional approach. This is compared with the estimated or offered whole-life cost of the PPP option. Qualitative aspects of the two alternatives also figure in the assessment, especially those aspects that may be difficult to quantify (such as required flexibility). The quantitative approaches are only as good as the assumptions behind them and thus they are necessarily approximate.

In practice budgetary reasons often also have a major, if not overriding, impact on the political decisions in this regard (S. Van Garsse, K. Van Gestel, K. MC Kenzie (2017), PPP-Contracts: On or Off Government Balance Sheets?, EPPPL 4, 3-15). The very fact that DBFM(O) contracts can lead to an off-balance sheet treatment appears to be very attractive and influences decision making. Therefore, by using DBFM(O) contracts contracting authorities can sometimes defer spending on infrastructure without deferring its benefit. In other words, it can increase investment without potentially immediately adding to government borrowing and possibly even bypass spending controls. Of course this situation is not without risks as contingent and future liabilities are created and future fiscal space and flexibility is reduced.

PPPs usually require complex financial arrangements, presenting higher transaction costs at the start compared to traditional public procured government contracts, although this comparison is sometimes exaggerated: many of the disciplines required of a PPP, such as defining up-front the long-term costs of maintenance and clarity as to the long-term requirements and nature of the service, should also be carried out for traditional procurement, but in the absence of the PPP disciplines, are not (Table 3.1).

The main relationship is the PPP contract (e.g., DBFMO). It regulates the rights and obligations of the SPV and the contracting authority. It will also reflect the financial structure and payment mechanisms (how the private party will be compensated or paid for the works and services it delivers) and the risks transferred. The SPV will develop and manage the project and will "pass through" most of the rights and obligations though a structure of downstream contracts (EPC contracts, O&M contracts, insurance contracts) allocating responsibilities, obligations, risks, and cash flows from the SPV to the different private actors involved. However, it is to be noted that the construction/EPC and O&M contractors are often shareholders of the SPV.

Because PPP projects are long-term contracts and tend to be very complex disputes are always an area of concern. Potential disputes include the consequences of unexpected circumstances, discussions on unclear contract terms/provisions subject to interpretation, changes in specifications, lack of cooperation between parties, non-achievement or non-compliance of contractual criteria/with performance levels, and so on.

Most PPP contracts nowadays include dispute resolution mechanism. In recent years, the trend has been to include dispute resolution Boards, besides mediation and national or international arbitration.

Dr. Steven Van Garsse
Universities of Hasselt & Antwerp, Belgium, attorney-at-law, Brussels Bar
Former manager PPP Knowledge Centre & Taskforce, Flemish Government

Infrastructure through public-private partnerships in the Philippines by Aris L. Gulapa and Dan Kevin C. Mandocdoc (the Phillipines)

Overview

The Philippine government envisions bringing the country to its "golden age of infrastructure" in the near future. Other countries like China and Japan have extended financial support to the country's massive infrastructure plan. Aside from foreign governments, the country's private sector has also shown keen eagerness to support this endeavor—particularly through the public-private partnership (PPP) scheme.

The use of PPP in developing infrastructure projects is consistent with the constitutionally enshrined state policy to recognize the indispensable role of the private sector, encourage private enterprise, and provide incentives to needed investments (Article II, Section 20, *Philippine Constitution*). The primary law for this purpose is Republic Act No. 6957 (as amended) or the "Build-Operate-Transfer (BOT) Law." Together with its implementing rules and regulations (IRR), the BOT Law provides the procedure in the tender of PPP projects.

Contrary to its short title, the BOT Law—because of the amendment introduced by Republic Act No. 7718—enumerates different PPP contractual arrangement: build-transfer (BT), build–own–operate (BOO), build–lease–transfer (BLT), build–transfer–operate (BTO), contract–add–operate (CAO), develop–operate–transfer (DOT), rehabilitate–operate–transfer (ROT), and rehabilitate–own–operate (ROO). These contractual arrangements may be used in developing infrastructure projects. Infrastructure projects may also be undertaken through other contractual arrangements that are not listed under the law. The use of these other contractual arrangements, however, requires prior approval from the President of the Philippines.

In addition, PPP infrastructure projects have also been undertaken through the 2013 or 2008 Guidelines and Procedures for Entering into Joint Venture (JV) Agreements Between Government and Private Entities (NEDA JV Guidelines). For example, the 2013 NEDA JV Guidelines is now being used in the implementation of the Upgrade of the Lima Center High Security Printing Plant—a US$4 million brownfield project intended to upgrade and operate an existing printing facility into a world class high security printing plant for government documents, while the 2008 NEDA JV Guidelines is being used in the implementation of the Tamugan River Bulk Water Treatment Project—a US$267 million-worth infrastructure project involving the construction and operation of a bulk water supply facility in Southern Philippines. Compared with the BOT Law, the NEDA JV Guidelines has a more limited scope. It is only applicable when the government entity involved is a government-owned and/or controlled corporation, government corporate entity, government instrumentality with corporate powers, government financial institution, or state university or college.

Infrastructure projects may also be undertaken through Republic Act No. 9184 or the "Revised Government Procurement Act (GPRA)." Under this law, the construction, improvement, rehabilitation, demolition, repair, restoration, or maintenance of infrastructure projects may be conducted by the private sector. Unlike the BOT Law, however, the GPRA does not allow the private sector to finance the infrastructure projects. As a result, the participation of the private sector on projects undertaken under the GPRA is limited and is on a short-term basis.

Payment mechanism

Under the BOT Law, the private sector participant (PSP) "shall be repaid by authorizing it to charge and collect reasonable tolls, fees, and rentals for the use of the project facility." In practice, the payment mechanism for PPP projects is determined by the contractual arrangement between the government and the PSP:

Contractual Arrangement	Payment Mechanism under the BOT Law IRR
BOT, CAO, DOT, ROT, BOO, and ROO	PSP can collect reasonable tolls, fees, and charges for a term not exceeding fifty (50) years. PSPs for projects under BOO and ROO arrangement may still collect fees after fifty (50) years if payment is for the operation of the facility or the provision of service.
BTO	Two options: 1. the government may provide amortization as may be appropriate and reasonable. Under this payment scheme, the tolls that the PSP may collect while operating the facility or the management fee in the management contract may be applied to the amortization. 2. the PSP may also be allowed to directly collect tolls, fees, and charges for a fixed term.
BT and BLT	As may be appropriate and reasonable (*i.e.*, according to the scheme proposed in the bid and incorporated in the contract).

The PSP "may likewise be repaid in the form of a share in the revenue of the project or other non-monetary payments, such as, but not limited to, the grant of a portion or percentage of the reclaimed land."

148 International Construction Contract Law

Risk allocation

In terms of risk allocation, the Generic Preferred Risk Allocation Matrix (GPRAM) serves as guide for the government and private sector in determining the most suitable risk allocation for each PPP project. The GPRAM provides risk allocation preferences based on a study conducted under the Philippines-Australia Partnership for Economic Governance Reforms (PEGR) Facility. Below are some of the major risk allocation preferences under the GPRAM:

Risks to be Borne by the Government	• Regulatory risk • Availability of site risk *(except for unsolicited projects where PSPs have control in selecting the site)*
Risks to be Borne by the PSP	• Site conditions risk *(PSPs are expected to validate the geotechnical study undertaken by the government)* • Design risk in projects where the project involves the design and construction of an infrastructure *(unless government initiates change in design)* • Construction risk *(except for delay caused by the government)* • Sponsor and financial risk *(includes risks involving interest rates, exchange rate, inflation, unavailability of financing)* • Operating risk *(includes risks involving inputs/operating cost overrun, maintenance and refurbishment, operator failure/short fall in service quality, technical obsolescence, or innovation)* • Demand risk *(i.e., the risk that operating revenues fall below forecast because of a decrease in service volume due to an economic downturn or change in consumer habits)* • Network and interference risk *(i.e., the risk that an existing network is extended, changed, or re-priced so as to increase competition for the facility)* • Industrial relations risk *(e.g., risks of delays caused by employee strikes and other union actions)* • Approvals risk *(but the government is required to provide assistance in obtaining the approval and permits)* • Changes in law or policy risk *(but government bears the risk if change is discriminatory against the project)* • Asset ownership risk
Risks to be Borne by the Government and the PSP Jointly	• Force majeure risk

It must be noted that the GPRAM is merely recommendatory. Ultimately, the risk allocation will depend on the nature of project and the positions taken by the government and the PSP during the negotiations of the concession agreement prior to the bid submission date.

Further, during the negotiations, PSPs are also given the opportunity to request risk mitigating mechanisms from the government. For example, with respect to demand risk, in an integrated bus terminal PPP project, PSPs were skeptical of the government's ability to compel all provincial bus operators to abandon their private terminals within Metro Manila and use the integrated bus terminal. Given that the government was unwilling to take the demand risk, PSPs requested that they be allowed to submit a bid in the form of an annual grantor's payment (*i.e.*, government will pay the winning bidder an annual subsidy for undertaking the project). The government allowed this. Thus, while the PSP still maintained the demand risk, the annual grantor's payment served as an assurance that the PSP would still earn an amount from the project even if the private bus operators would not use the integrated bus terminal. In another example but relating to network and interface risk, during the negotiation stage for certain airports projects, PSPs requested the government to insert a non-compete clause in the concession agreements—the non-compete clause contains an assurance from the government that it will not allow the construction of an airport within a certain radius to ensure the project's commercial viability.

Thus, at bid submission date, the applicable risk allocation for the project would already be in place through the use of the GPRAM, the negotiation of the final draft of the concession (PPP) agreement, and the risk mitigating mechanisms agreed upon by the government and the PSPs. PSPs take this allocation into account in pricing and submitting their bid for the project.

Transportation-related PPP projects

In 2010, the Philippine government started the active use of the BOT Law to obtain private sector participation in transportation-related infrastructure projects. Below are some of the PPP projects approved to be tendered to the private sector:

	North-South Railway Project–South Line (NSRP)
Project Value	Approximately US$ 3,800,000,000.00
Project Description	The biggest PPP project in the Philippines to date, the NSRP involves the construction, finance, operation, and maintenance of a 653-km long railway linking Metro Manila with provinces in Southern Luzon, the biggest Philippine island.
	The project's tender has been on indefinite suspension since April 2016. Because of this, information relating to the project is limited to those available in the Project Information Memorandum.
Contractual Arrangement	Build-Transfer-Operate-Maintain (BTOM) or Build-Gradually Transfer-Operate-Maintain (BGTOM).
Risk Allocation	Construction risk–PSP
Payment Mechanism	After receiving partial payment for the construction costs, the PSP will receive the remaining balance (covering the constructions costs and costs for financing, constructing, and maintaining the facility) may be collected using the three forms:
	(a) Farebox Revenues – PSP will be authorized to charge and collect fares from end users;
	(b) Ancillary Revenues – PSP will be permitted to maximize revenue potential from other commercial revenue sources, and
	(c) Infrastructure Fees/Availability – additional support for the PSP will be given through infrastructure fees/availability payments for the first four (4) years of construction and the first eleven (11) years of operations.
	In addition to the payment of the constructions costs in the schemes mentioned above, the government undertook to pay certain (acquisition of right-of-way, resettlement costs, real property tax for the core facilities along the alignment, and provision of depot space at key locations).

	LRT 1 Extension and O&M Project
Project Value	Approximately US$ 1,292,000,000.00
Project Description	The project involves the (a) financing, design, and construction of an 11.7 kilometer extension of LRT Line 1 system from its last station to the adjacent province of Cavite, (b) the operations and maintenance of the current 20.7 kilometer existing system of LRT Line 1, and (c) the operations and maintenance of an integrated system upon the completion of the extension line.
Contractual Arrangement	Build-Transfer-Operate (BTO).
Risk Allocation	Availability of site risk – government Demand risk – PSP Construction risk – PSP Operating risk – PSP Sponsor and financial risk – PSP Industrial relations risk – PSP
Payment Mechanism	The Concession Agreement provides that the PSP would be entitled to collect and receive its revenue consisting of the farebox revenue, deficit payments (if any), compensation payments from the government (if any), and Commercial Revenue or those from the commercial assets.

	LRT 6 Project
Project Value	Approximately US$ 1,300,000,000.00
Project Description	The project involves the design, construction, operation, and maintenance of a 19-kilometer light rail line parts Cavite to the ongoing LRT 1 Cavite extension project. Based on initial studies, however, the ridership fg LRT 6 Project will be those traveling within the Cavite area. The project's tender has been in indefinite suspension since September 2016. Because of this, information relating to the project is limited to those available in the Project Information Memorandum.
Contractual Arrangement	Build-Transfer-Operate-Maintain (BT+O&M) or Build-Gradually Transfer-Operate-Maintain (BGTOM).
Risk Allocation	Exogenous, project environment desk – PSP and government Design risk – PSP Finance risk – PSP Construction risk – PSP Availability of site risk – government Demand risk – PSP Operating risk – PSP
Payment Mechanism	The LRT6 Project Information Memorandum provides that PSP shall be entitled to collect and receive: • Fare box revenue • Commercial revenue fee • Capacity/availability payments – if required, the government will pay the PSP a portion of the total infrastructure costs during the construction period; and (b) a constant amount (availability payments) during the operations period.

	Davao Sasa Port Modernization Project
Project Value	Approximately US$ 240,000,000.00
Project Description	The project involves the development of the most important container terminal in Southern Philippines into a modern, international-standard container terminal. A brownfield project, the modernization capitalizes on support that was already in place (customs, depots/warehouses, and shipping agents) while aiming to reduce shippers' logistics costs.
	The project was aborted in mid-2017. Because of this, information relating to the project is limited to those available in the Project Information Memorandum.
Contractual Arrangement	Build-Transfer-Operate (BTO) arrangement and structured a "landlord port" concession. Under this structure, the PSP will finance, design, construct, install, and acquire all necessary infrastructure to operate and maintain the port while the government will retain ownership of the entire port area and infrastructure performing both technical and economic regulatory functions.
Risk Allocation	Demand risk – PSP
Payment Mechanism	PSP would directly collect agreed fees or charges for cargo-handling and other ancillary services provided at the port over the duration of the concession for the recovery of investments and a reasonable rate of return.

	Mactan-Cebu International Airport Passenger Terminal Project
Project Value	Approximately US$ 350,400,000.00
Project Description	The Mactan-Cebu International Airport (MCIA) is the second largest airport in the Philippines in terms of domestic traffic. The project involves the construction of a new world-class passenger terminal building (with an annual capacity of about 8 million passengers), the renovation of the existing terminal, and the operation of both terminals of this gateway airport to various destinations in central Philippines.
Contractual Arrangement	Build-Operate-Transfer (BOT) arrangement.
Risk Allocation	Operating risk – PSP
	Sponsor and financial risk – PSP
	Design and technical risk – PSP
	Construction risk – PSP
	Availability of site risk – government
	Asset ownership risk – PSP
	Industrial relations risk – PSP
Payment Mechanism	The concession agreement provides that the PSP is entitled to collect and receive its revenue consisting of the passenger service charge, aircraft parking fees, and tacking fees; other apron charges; deficit payments (if any); compensation payments from the government (if any); and Commercial Revenue or those from the commercial assets.

Airport Development, Operations, and Maintenance for the Bacolod-Silay, Davao, Iloilo, Laguindingan, and New Bohol (Panglao) Airports PPP Project	
Project Value	Approximately US$ 2,300,000,000.00
Project Description	The project involves bidding for the financing and undertaking of the expansion and enhancement of landside and airside facilities, and the operation and maintenance of five key regional airports in the Philippines, namely: the Bacolod-Silay, Davao, Iloilo, Laguindingan, and New Bohol (Panglao) airports.
	The project, which was originally offered as a bundled package, was indefinitely suspended in June 2016. After six months, the project was unbundled (one bid per airport). In May 2017, the Philippine government announced that the project would be aborted. The information provided here are limited to the information obtained during the tender of this project.
Contractual Arrangement	Operate-Add-Transfer (OAT).
Risk Allocation	Sponsor and financial risk – PSP
	Operating risk – PSP
	Design and technical risk – PSP
	Construction risk – PSP
	Availability of site risk – government
	Industrial relations risk – PSP
	Approvals risk – PSP
	Risk of loss or deterioration – PSP
Payment Mechanism	The draft concession agreement provides that the PSP is entitled to collect and receive revenues on the passenger service charges from the departing passengers, aircraft parking fees, landing and take-off fees, cargo fees, lighting charges, fuel charges, and tacking fees. The PSP is also entitled to collect commercial charges.

Issues and challenges

The challenges that the Philippines face in developing its PPP regime are based primarily on the said regime being at its nascent stage. As a practical result, foreign participation in these projects is very limited—both in terms of numbers and of roles undertaken. In most projects, the primary bidders are local business enterprises that are unable to satisfy the technical qualification requirements for the project due to lack of previous experience. These local business enterprises often have a hard time looking for foreign entities that are willing to participate in the project either as a minority partner in the joint venture or as a subcontractor for the primary bidder.

The hesitation to participate is also attributable to the perceived inexperienced of the Philippine government in handling the bidding process. While the BOT Law has been in effect since the early 1990s, it was only in the year 2010 that the government started utilizing it actively to boost the country's infrastructure development. Because of this, there is still lack of expertise in the government side and it is often forced to rely on the experience of its technical advisors. This, in turn, results to nuances in the bid submission procedure and requirements on a per project basis. Best practices and lessons learned from previous projects have yet to be adopted across all projects despite the participation of the PPC Center, the government's central coordinating and monitoring agency for all PPP projects in the Philippines.

> More than these, however, the biggest issue relating to the Philippine PPP regime is the lack of assurance by the government to the PSPs that the former will complete the bidding of the PPP projects and award the projects to the winning PSP. The instructions to prospective bidders all contain a disclaimer that the government has the right to not accept any of the bids submitted and each PSP shall bear all costs and expenses related to the submission of the bid documents regardless of the conduct or outcome of the bidding process. Recently, upon the change of administration in the Philippines, projects initiated by the previous administration were suspended and some, despite being in the last stage of bid submission already, were re-evaluated and aborted. As a result, in several projects last year, these projects did not even reach bid submission (where the PSPs submitted their bids) despite the PSPs spending money for the due diligence exercise on the projects, feasibility study on the technical and financial aspects of the project, and preparing the bid proposal and voluminous supporting annexes. This issue must be addressed to prevent the PSP from being absolutely discouraged in participating in PPP projects.
>
> *Aris L. Gulapa*
> *Managing Partner, Gulapa Law Office*
> *Head, Projects and Infrastructure Department*
> *Professor, Law on Public-Private Partnerships, Ateneo de Manila University School of Law*
>
> *Dan Kevin C. Mandocdoc*
> *Senior Associate, Gulapa Law Office*
> *Member, Projects and Infrastructure Department*
> *Professor, Legal Writing, Ateneo de Manila University School of Law*

3.9 Further aspects of delivery methods

3.9.1 Fast-track projects

A construction project management system known as "fast track" is focused on cutting the duration of a construction project as much as possible. Its characteristics can be described as follows:

- Mutually independent processes run concurrently.
- Design work runs almost simultaneously with realization, being only a short time ahead of it.
- Many of the designer's decisions take place on site.

Fast-track contracts lead to price uncertainty. Shorter time for completion is balanced against uncertainty and higher costs.

3.9.2 Target cost contracts

One of the challenges of every project is achieving an environment where both parties collaborate together and have a common commercial interest. It is therefore necessary to design contractual mechanisms which provide a commercial incentive for the parties to communicate and collaborate to ensure that the project is a success.

One such mechanism is a "target cost contract." As part of the contractual negotiations, the parties agree on a target price based on their knowledge of the project conditions and their assessment of potential risks. The works then begin and during the works two things occur in parallel:

1. The contractor is generally paid their actual costs (less disallowed costs) plus a fee on a regular basis (usually every four weeks).
2. The initial target price is adjusted during the works in accordance with compensation events and their estimated cost.

On completion, these two elements are compared. If there is a saving or a cost overrun, then the parties share such savings or cost increases in the agreed proportions set out in the contract.

One of the ways of ensuring that the correct target is fixed is by engaging in early contractor involvement and, where appropriate, pre-construction services agreements.

3.9.3 Early contractor involvement and the pre-construction services agreement

A common reason for problems is that a contractor is often introduced to the project just before the work starts. Contractors typically have no involvement in the design phase and have no opportunity to contribute their expertise and insights to the design. In addition, the contractor's lack of familiarity with the project often leads to cost increases due to greater risk allowances. To avoid such issues, the practice of early contractor involvement has developed in the UK.

The basis for early contractor involvement relies on parties entering into a pre-construction services agreement (PCSA). Under such an agreement, the contractor is paid by the employer to develop the initial design. Once this has been done, the employer has the choice of either continuing with the same contractor and entering into a full construction contract or tendering the works again on the basis of the design produced by the first contractor.

This therefore allows the employer to benefit from the contractor's expertise and allows the contractor to familiarize themselves with the project. The contractor can then confidently offer a lower price by reducing the allowance for risks. The PCSA further allows the employer and the contractor to develop and improve their relationship and cooperation.

The UK government has identified a good example of this process in the contract negotiations for Bank Station in London, a part of the Crossrail project. In this project, the employer pre-qualified contactors who demonstrated an ability to innovate. The employer then undertook detailed, confidential discussions with three contractors in order to identify ways in which the works could be improved. Although only one contractor could win the tender, the contractors that were not successful in the bid were compensated for their time and would be paid if any of the methods they suggested were used by the employer.

3.9.4 Building information management systems

The use of building information management systems (BIMS) is becoming increasingly popular. In simple terms, BIMS are processes that use software to create a model of a completed project. The processes seek to enhance the design, construction, and post-occupancy of a building, road, bridge, or other structure. It does so by enabling the information to be used in a much more intelligent way than is the norm in the construction industry.

BIMS have been used for many years and are perhaps most established in the United States. Advanced computer modeling (e.g., 3D and CAD) have been used extensively in steel fabrication. For other designs, computer modeling has been deployed more discreetly with the traditional "siloed" method remaining popular. For BIMS to achieve their full potential requires an integrated and collaborative approach to construction so that many discipline-specific models can be integrated with one another to simulate a fully working building. In doing so, changes to one part of the model allow other parts of the model to alter.

BIMS also bring one-time information input and its transfer across the construction life cycle closer to reality. The end result of BIMS can be enhanced predictability in construction. For example, depending on the functionality of the software, the "build twice, once virtually" philosophy of modelling can achieve reduced risk on construction sites by identifying health and safety issues in a virtual environment. Designs can be improved by eliminating design clashes virtually. Applications can be further developed to improve cost and programming predictability. At completion, asset information can be handed over to the owners in a way that enables its use to achieve greater accuracy in thermal efficiency projections and asset life-cycle replacement.

At the heart of BIMS are designs through the use of "objects." These are separate representations of parts of a building (e.g., a door, window or wall) that are selected by designers from predeveloped object libraries. The fundamental design, therefore, does not involve drawing lines but arranging objects. Objects are advanced digital creations, each having a "parametric" relationship with other objects in the same family of compatible software. This allows changes to one object to be reflected in changes in related objects, for example, changing the size of a door may alter the size of a wall.

For these reasons, BIMS require a different way of thinking. It requires a move away from the traditional workflow, with all parties (including designers, surveyors, employers, and contractors) sharing, and effectively working on, a common information pool so that each can create models that are compatible. This is a substantial move away from more traditional conventions where the parties often work on separate information pools using several different (and usually incompatible) software packages or working methods. For example in the UK, the Construction Industry Council published a protocol for the use of BIMS, which provide a best practice guide and an outline scope of services for the role of information management. Nowadays also other standardisation institutions in many countries publish technical standards, which cover collaborative production of construction information.

BIMS are a particularly attractive proposition for the public sector in tough economic times. They promise greater whole-life asset efficiency as well as construction stage savings. BIMS are currently being promoted by governments around the globe for centrally procured construction.

BIM—The way forward? by Christopher Miers (UK)

We are accustomed to designing using 3D software. However building information modeling (BIM) is much more than this. We are also accustomed to designing, constructing, and handing over a project at the point of completion of construction. However, BIM creates the opportunity for us to consider the project over a longer term than this, through its entire lifecycle of operation.

There are many definitions of BIM. The definition, which I prefer is:

"building information modeling (BIM) is the management of information through the whole life cycle of a built asset, from initial design all the way through to construction, maintaining and finally de-commissioning, through the use of digital modelling.
BIM is all about collaboration – between engineers, owners architects and contractors in a three dimensional virtual construction environment (common data environment), and it shares information across these disciplines."

BIM is a developing field and there is a wide range of knowledge surrounding the BIM process. This range of knowledge varies with world regions and between consultants, contractors and employers.

The cycle of design, construction, operation, modification, and disposal

In response to user demand, the construction industry has had to move beyond the concept that a project is completed once construction is completed. For many projects our focus is changing, to the provision of a long-term, efficient operating environment. The BIM-related British standards PAS 1192-2 and 1192-3 highlight the hard asset management cycle of: create/acquire; operate/use/maintain; modify/replace/enhance; dispose/demolish/sell.

Our industry has therefore had to develop its focus towards the provision and maintenance of a required user environment—whether it refers to power generation (power plant), infrastructure transportation (tunnels, roads, bridges, rail networks), a working environment for manufacture or administration (factories, offices), healthcare (hospitals) or similar: we refer to a cycle of built asset management.

Alongside this, across many international regions there is a renewed interest in how to achieve effective foreign investment and create public-private partnership arrangements for design-construct-operate concessions. Such long-term concession projects also link the process of design and construction to the subsequent period of operation.

The comparison between the cost of design and construction and the cost of operation is often made, to assist in making capital expenditure decisions. The "Designing Buildings" Wiki knowledge base refers to a rough assessment of the typical costs of an office building over 30 years in the ratio:

- 0.1–0.15 for design costs (ref OGC Achieving Excellence Guide 7 - Whole-Life costing).
- 1 for construction costs.

- 5 for maintenance and building operating costs during the lifetime of the building.
- 200 for the cost of operating the business during the lifetime of the building.

Thus where a decision made during the stage of design and construction, even at increased capital cost, can have a benefit in reducing operating costs, the benefit is clear. The BIM processes can enable us to create a single model to incorporate construction costs through to anticipated life-cycle operation costs (see BIM level 7D below).

Misunderstood terminology

Misunderstandings are common regarding BIM terminology. Where such misunderstanding is embedded into employer's requirements specifications, for example, this can give rise to the potential for disagreements. Employers may find themselves requesting BIM requirements, which are not yet possible to deliver, or are not necessary for the project. Such requests may have an unexpected or unnecessary cost impact on bid prices.

For example, a project being required in the employer's requirements that the contractor was to "ensure a fully *integrated* [BIM] approach." Within BIM terminology, we differentiate between a *federated* model [BIM level 2] and an *integrated* model [BIM level 3], and at the time a federated model would have been possible and normal, and an integrated model was not generally available. In BIM terms, "a fully integrated approach" could not be delivered at the time.

NBS, which in the UK has developed BIM-related specifications, forms a useful source for a knowledge base as well as a BIM library.

BIM level 2

This is the BIM process, which is currently typically achievable today. It is distinguished by collaborative working—all parties use their own "federated" 3D CAD models, but not necessarily working on a single, shared model. The collaboration comes in the form of how the information is exchanged between different parties—and is the crucial aspect of this level. Design information is shared through a common file format, which enables any organization to be able to combine that data with their own in order to make a federated BIM model, and to carry out interrogative checks on it. Hence any CAD software that each party used must be capable of exporting to one of the common file formats such as IFC (industry foundation class) or COBie (construction operations building information exchange).

Typical current challenges are that there is a wide variation in industry take up on the use of BIM. Therefore, within a project team of designers, suppliers, and contractors, there is inconsistent use of BIM leading to incomplete models.

BIM level 3

This represents full collaboration between all disciplines by means of using a single, shared "integrated" project model, which is held in a centralized repository. All parties can access and modify that same model, and the benefit is that it removes the final layer of risk for conflicting information. This is known as "Open BIM."

Challenges yet to be resolved center around concerns for the intellectual property ownership of designs within an integrated model, and questions of potential liabilities, and the associated contractual frameworks. In the UK, "Integrated Project Insurance" is being investigated as a blame-free insurance.

BIM level 4D+

Adding to the BIM level 3 project model brings further opportunities: with construction sequencing (4D), cost (5D), energy, sustainability, and project life-cycle information for asset management from design to demolition (6D/7D).

Modifying our contracts for BIM

Effective BIM implementation bridges across the traditional divide between client and contractor obligations, and bridges across the traditional differentiation between design and construction.

Integrated BIM implementation also requires consistent adoption of procedures and protocols across multiple stakeholders in the design and construction process. Some industry observers question whether the traditional two-party contract is likely to disappear. A new role has also appeared, in respect of the BIM information manager.

It is clear, in my opinion, that contracts needs to be modified and developed to accommodate the effective use of BIM. Some of the widely used forms of contract such as the FIDIC 1999 edition suite, need project specific modification since the contract drafters have not yet published guidance or standard form modifications. NEC4, as published in 2017, introduces an Option X10, for "Information Modeling." JCT introduced its BIM-related amendments in its 2016 editions.

All of these primary contracts for design, supply, or construction will require the integration of additional standardized documents in the form of a BIM protocol. This in turn requires further, new project documents in the form of a BIM execution plan and model production and delivery table.

BIM—can we ignore it?

Pressure for change is coming from various sectors:

Governments in various parts of the world are encouraging or requiring the use of BIM. In Dubai, for example, the Dubai Municipality (see Circular 207, 23/07/2015) requires the use of BIM on larger projects "because of how much it lowers the cost of construction projects and the time taken to finish them; and increases the level of coordination between the engineers working on designing and implementing the project, and their counterparts in the management and funding and manufacturing the project." In the UK, from April 2016 the government mandated the use of Level 2 BIM on all centrally procured public sector projects. And in the United States, for example, the General Services Administration of the federal government established some years ago the National 3D-4D-BIM Program.

Clients in many sectors are requiring a BIM model to be delivered with the completion of the construction phase, for ongoing facilities management use during operation. In some instances clients are also requiring the use of BIM during construction, in order to facilitate their verification of design development and the achievement of key project milestones. In my experience, the client side of the construction industry does not yet have a consistent view of the value of BIM.

Designers and contractors report advantages gained from the adoption of BIM, through the facilitation of coordinated design information. There is clearly an initial investment hurdle to overcome in respect of equipment and training. Once this is overcome, for companies with established expertise in BIM they report improvements in productivity, reduced rework, reduced conflict and clashes during construction, and fewer late changes.

The UK government, for example, assesses that increased construction productivity will facilitate savings of £1.7 billion between 2016 to 2020, with the increased use of BIM level 2 as one of the key procurement gains. Such prospects are likely to continue to guide public and private sector clients to press for wider industry take up of the use of BIM.

Standard form construction contract drafting needs to respond across all sectors of the supply chain.

Christopher Miers, BA, DipArch, MSc(Constr.Law), DipICArb, RIBA, FCIArb, MAE
Founder and CEO
Probyn Miers, London and Dubai

Developments in BIM application: Legal aspects by Joost Merema (the Netherlands)

General introduction

BIM (building information modeling) is fairly new in construction projects. In the late 1970s the first digital drawing stations entered construction sites. From that moment, computer aided design (CAD) changed the way designs were made. However, designing was still based on digitizing the analogue way of drawing: designing with focus on 2D (x-y). 3D modeling (x,y,z) was only to enter designing processes in construction late 1990s/early 2000s on a large scale. The link with time scheduling software was introduced shortly after, called 4D. The way CAD empowered designers to optimize is already very impressive. And we've only just begun. Adding materialization information, cost details, and any other kind of information to objects brings us all kinds of extra dimensions.

The recent breakthroughs in technology and software functionality regarding BIM are very interesting from a legal point of view. Typical BIM-related legal issues and dilemmas arise on project level. For most of the projects where innovation with BIM is practiced, a pragmatic "can do" approach may lead to less focus on fundamental legal discussions about that innovation. But with a large group of innovation adaptors, the fastening pace of evolution of BIM these issues should be addressed: the carillon of new solutions and experiences may sound like one Big Ben, but BIM is just not a one-time "bang."

Before the specific legal issues are mentioned, it's good to have a basic understanding of what BIM exactly stands for, four levels of maturity can be distinguished: BIM level 0, 1, 2, and 3. Let's set up a baseline of definition.

- BIM level 0 describes the situation where separate files (drawing, calculations, models) are separately exchanged on between individual users in a team. Level 0 looks a lot like exchanging paper designs, but then with a lot of email and printing going on. It can be described as "unmanaged computer aided design."

- BIM level 1 is the step where information is connected to specific objects in the project, for example, doors, piles, or concrete walls. In a BIM level 1 situation the data-like requirements, verifications, and testing are all documented and registered by their connection to a specific object. When you add integration of that information, you reach BIM level 1. You are able to search for all requirements for a specific object, or search that objects change by a specific requirement. For every object designs are made, but most of the time these designs are separate from the requirements: you can manually link from a drawing file to the objects within a project, but changing a requirement still requires a designer to assess the impact on the design and change a drawing file.
- In BIM level 2 different databases are combined to one model of the project. So planning, calculation, and requirement management are all accessed in their own environment or application, but the data is connected to the total model. Make a wall in the design application two times higher, and it shows up in planning, calculation and verification of the design. Level 2 is available at the moment on projects, but a lot of software development is needed to implement this kind of designing on the majority of projects.
- The current highest BIM level is level 3. Projects that operate on level 3 not only access and combine several databases, but are developed in a common data environment (CDE, "shared database"). Those databases are prepared for future collaboration by working object based according open BIM standard protocols, for all the phases in the lifetime cycle of the project. The goal of that is that all involved parties work from existing datasets, so you have a complete integrated use of data during the complete lifecycle of the project. In other words, there should be minimal issue transferring the data of the as-built situation to asset management after final completion of building the project. The world biggest CAD software developers are now in the process to develop methods and tools to implement level 3 on projects. However, this way of working is still very demanding for the individual project members: it's all just very new, and a lot of aspects still have to be figured out.

Why is it relevant to know about these levels? There are two main reasons to mention them before addressing a few legal issues regarding BIM. The first being the aspect of evolution. With time, the "normal" will shift from level 0, to level 1 and higher up. Of course, that doesn't mean there won't be projects executed on level 0 within 15 years. But the way we define our standards and expectations will evolve. Knowing and understanding the levels will give you a rough map of developments.

The second reason of mentioning these levels is that in my assessment, the legal issues get more impact when you look at them on a higher level. The issues stay more or less the same, but they become more relevant and probably more complex.

What are those legal issues? To me, the most interesting and pressing legal issues regarding BIM at this moment are the following:

1. Intellectual property on BIM models
2. Data integrity of the BIM databases and defect liability caused by incorrect data

My purpose with addressing these issues is for the reader to reflect on them, and to start up a discussion on them within the legal practitioners within the construction community. They are not intended as a legal and academic evaluation of issues which should be complete and validated by peers.

Intellectual property on BIM models

Intellectual property (IP) is a legal concept that basically protects all kinds of creators for others to copy their different creations and thus infringe the creators' rights. IP is the international framework that includes trademarks, copyright, patents, and industrial design rights. IP is defined in international multilateral treaties like WIPO (Stockholm, 1967) and EPC (Munich, 1973), EU Law like the Orphan Works Directive (2012/28/EU) and directive on collective management of copyright (2014/26/EU) and of course national laws. The issue is addressed with three questions:

1. How does the employer acquire IP on the documents/design of the contractor that are formed in a BIM model/database?
2. Does contractor receive IP rights on information of employer, which contractor alters during design?
3. What is the impact on IP when several parties contribute to one BIM model?

FIDIC and NEC, and IP

So how does the employer acquire IP on the documents/design of the contractor? The basic concept of IP is not addressed explicitly in most standard contract models aimed at design and construct concepts. The FIDIC contracts mentioned in Sub-Clause 1.10 are the employer's use of contractor's documents. The basic principle is that the employer receives a complete license to copy, use, and communicate on every document the contractor makes. FIDIC 1999 standard contracts add the following to this license:

> "This licence shall […] (c) in the case of Contractor's Documents which are in the form of computer programs <u>and other software</u>, permit their use on any computer on the Site and other places as envisaged by the Contract, including replacements of any computers supplied by the Contractor."

FIDIC updated the so-called rainbow contract series in 2017 adding Advisory Notes for BIM at the end of respective books. On the topic of BIM, however, no significant changes have been met directly within the FIDIC Forms. It seems like FIDIC aims at following the fast pace of developments by leaving the topic to particular conditions or additional contract documents, updating only the necessary. Below is the Clause 1.10 of FIDIC Yellow Book (2017) with the additional parts emphasized in bold:

> "This licence shall […] (c) in the case of Contractor's Documents **and such other design documents** which are the form of **electronic or digital files**, computer programs and other software, permit their use on any computer on the Site and**/or at the locations of the Employer and the Engineer and/or at** other places as envisaged by the Contract; […]"

So, the FIDIC contracts speak of documents; and the design of the project being a set of documents. It's interesting to see that the current standard clauses won't explicitly address databases, digital workflows, or models. It is reasonable to assume databases and cloud services are part of the definition of documents.

Another well-known set of contract models is the NEC framework. Since 2005 when the third edition was launched there has been a significant rise in the use of, and interest in, early *contractor* involvement (ECI) and the use of electronic modeling of design through to construction, now commonly referred to as building information modeling (BIM). The basic NEC3 framework doesn't provide IP-related clauses. However, there are general so-called "X and Z-clauses," which are amended as optional clauses. Generally spoken, they follow the FIDIC principle of granting the employer/client an IP license of all designs and documents, just like FIDIC models.

Supplements to address both of ECI and electronic modeling had been released by NEC before the launch of the fourth edition but are now incorporated as secondary options X10 for BIM and X22 for ECI. Although there are standard provisions for the use of both of these they provide only a framework and further detail needs to be added in the contract in order to bring them to life.

In the fourth edition, BIM is referred to simply as "information modeling." This is, in reality, just a difference in the title—tying back the contracts engineering roots and to avoid an implications that the process is limited to building rather than a wider range of construction project. Two important terms to understand in relation to BIM in the fourth edition are the "information model" and "project information" both of which are defined at X10.1. The information model is the electronic integration of project information. The project information is information from the *contractor* used to build the information model. Liability for any failure in the provision of project information is on a reasonable skill and care basis.

So, the framework contract models of FIDIC and NEC provide a basic license model for employers. Why could that be an issue when working with BIM? Well, the first issue is of course the absence of definitions regarding BIM. This makes BIM as a topic not directly recognisable in the contracts. Legal practitioners and contract specialists are forced to transpose general clauses and definitions to the digital world of BIM and data handover. With that comes the problem of judicial interpretation of the clauses: every legal system handles interpretation different. With Anglo-Saxon legal systems leaning more to a literal and strict interpretation of clauses, one could argue that if databases are not in the contract, the data they hold fall out of the definition of document or software—and therefore outside the license of employer. With an interpretation with purpose, function, and context in mind, a broader interpretation would be reasonable and sensible for other legal systems, like the ones within the EU. But where would that license of employer stop? Would the employer also receive for example the full license of concepts (or iterations), which an EPC contractor develops during value engineering within one BIM level 2 model *even* if they are not implemented in the actual design? That could mean that without additional clauses, every design option or concept of a variation could be used by the employer in a different contract or project at anytime and anywhere. I can imagine that a mediator or judge would be sensitive for the clear argument that the designing of those concepts is being paid for by the employer, since the work is being done and payed for within the obligations of the existing contract. However, that could mean that after finishing a project, the contractor has learned a lot from all the different variations, options, and design changes and took the risks, but the employer receives the reward of a license for every single one of them. That seems to me like an undesirable outcome too.

My assessment based on the first question is that there is too much room for interpretation in current standard contract models. This in the long term leads to undesirable legal uncertainty. As a pragmatic approach, I'd like to suggest using current definitions within database rights laws, for example, as mentioned in European Directive 96/9/EC or UK Copyright and Rights in Databases Regulations 1997 and formulate standard amendments. By joining the general legal framework vocabulary, the room for interpretation should be minimized. The current ISO BIM standards ISO 12006-2:2015/3:2007 and ISO 16739:2013 provide in all kinds of technical classification, and little on legal aspects. The ISO/TS 12911:2012 delivers a framework, but—besides some general recommendations—doesn't specify legal consequences nor specific clauses that can be used in contracts.

A second aspect of the ownership of intellectual property with BIM is about the right or permission to change something in a model. The background of this issue is that the moment "a work" (being almost anything, from for example a poem to the design of a bridge) is being "freezed" or "fixed," copyright has been created and therefor ownership of the IP on that work in that particular state has been established. This concept is introduced by the Berne Convention (Berme, 1886), which includes 170 UN member states. The WIPO Copyright Treaty (Geneva, 1996) adds with regard to BIM database specific clauses for databases, including databases in the definition of "works." A basic rule of IP is that the definition of "work" (not to be confused with work as in construction contracts) is also applicable if the work is the result of the change of another "work," as long as the changes are significant and result in a "original and creative character." In normal IP scenarios the creation of a new "work" by copying and altering some details is not possible if the creator of the original "work" hasn't given his or her permission. In the scenario of a construction project based on EPC, it's the other way around. The contractor is contractually obliged to alter, change, and "mold" information, data, and designs of the employer in such a way that the scope is constructed. The contractor has therefore permission for changing any work (in terms of IP) of the employer. This could very well result in the contractor acquiring the IP of designs as output from his activities with BIM databases. That leaves the employer receiving only a license on those designs—even if the employer stood at the base of these designs with his own data. By altering information, the original work is changed and after a lot of changes by both contractor and employer the ownership of the new set of information gets a bit "blurry." My suggestion for this aspect is that it deserves more and thorough study in how construction contracts could address this aspect in a reasonable and sensible way. One could expect architects and engineers demanding a bit more legal certainty about the IP of the design with BIM. At least the situation with level 0 BIM projects should be more or less in line with projects where BIM will be used extensively.

The last aspect of IP when working with BIM I'd like to address sees on multi-party involvement in one model. The situation that both contractor and employer are working in one model is already discussed in the part above. For this new aspect, I'd like to show an example from the situation that there is only a BIM model on contractor's side. Contractor's side can consist of contract with several sub-contractors or a contractor formed with a project specific special purpose vehicle. In both possibilities, it of course all depends on what the sub-contract contracts or the consortium agreement define about IP. But what if those contracts define nothing or not enough detail? If a BIM model—whether it's one database or a combination of files and databases, depending on the BIM level—is formed by contributions of several parties, the IP generated is distributed (generally spoken) to all contributors. That means a situation of co-ownership where each party receives unrestricted use of the jointly owned IP. For a construction project, the actual IP of the BIM model is most of the time only relevant for the specific project. However, specific concepts or designs can be easily used by parties on other projects. When those concepts are part of a jointly owned IP of the original project, all owners of that IP probably have to give formal permission to one of the parties make use of the IP for a purpose outside the specific project. So, especially with IP management (protection, maintenance, and defense), the co-ownership can result in unpleasant surprises of one of the parties involved in the BIM model decides to exercise its IP rights and "veto-block" use of the IP of all the other parties.

In overview, there seems to be quite a solid case to review the way intellectual property is handled in a BIM environment. IP has definitely significance in construction contracts when regarded from a BIM perspective (and even more for industrial projects like plants compared to infrastructural projects). The links to existing IP laws and database rights cannot be neglected: clauses in the current contract models leave to much space for interpretation and therefore for unnecessary discussions. Also development of specific amendments to consortium agreements and sub-contractor agreements seem to be a justifiable effort. The current use of employer's information requirement (EIR), BIM protocols and BIM execution plans (BEP) are excellent to determine on what, where, and how information is created, named, and exchanged. The next step should be developing general clauses to determine different "what if" scenarios when it comes to IP ownership and licenses that are uniform and acceptable for all contract parties.

Data integrity of the BIM databases and defect liability caused by incorrect data

There is a whole subgenre of complex, plot-driven detective stories under the name "whodunit." Every legal practitioner on a construction project tasked with claim management will probably ask themselves at least once in their lifetime if they've ended up in one of those stories: "Who has done it?" For a lot of claims the research of the chain of cause and effect is relevant to establish the root error or mistake. All contracts involving concepts of design and construct (e.g., Silver/Yellow Book, NEC) have specific clauses for design errors. In FIDIC Silver and Yellow Book, Clause 5.8 reads:

> "If errors, omissions, ambiguities, inconsistencies, inadequacies or other defects are found in the Contractor's Documents, they and the Works shall be corrected at the Contractor's cost, notwithstanding any consent or approval under this Clause."

With a BIM model, the input of data generally comes from both employer and contractor. Here the Yellow and Silver Book differ when an error in the employer's data is the reason of a design error. According to Yellow Book Clause 1.9, the employer is liable for his incorrect data in the employer's requirements:

> "If the Contractor suffers delay and/or incurs Cost as a result of an error in the Employer's Requirements[..] the Contractor […] shall be entitled […]to:
>
> (a)   an extension of time for any such delay, if completion is or will be delayed […] and,
> (b)   payment of any such Cost plus reasonable profit […]."

The relevant clause of Silver Book is different, because in Silver Book EPC contracts, the main rule is that the contractor is responsible for mistakes or discrepancies in the employer's requirements. Clause 5.1, however, shows interesting exceptions from the perspective of BIM:

"[…] The Contractor shall be responsible for the design of the Works and for the accuracy of such Employer's Requirements (including design criteria and calculations), except as stated below.
[…] **Any data** or information received by the Contractor, from the Employer or otherwise, shall not relieve the Contractor from his responsibility for the design and execution of the Works.
However, the Employer shall be responsible for the correctness of the following portions of the Employer's Requirements and of the **following data** and **information** provided by (or on behalf of) the Employer:

(a) portions, data and information **which are stated in the Contract as being immutable** or the responsibility of the Employer,
(b) definitions of intended purposes of the Works or any parts thereof,
(c) criteria for the testing and performance of the completed Works, and
(d) **portions, data and information which cannot be verified by the Contractor**, except as otherwise stated in the Contract."

The defined exceptions of FIDIC Silver Book can very much contain data that is immutable. For example, if the employer already has done a 3D laser point scan of the project site—a so-called "point cloud"—that data set will be used as input by the contractor. If in that way the design contains errors that trace back to errors or wrong offsets in the point cloud, the employer could be easily held liable.

This also could lead to a reflex of employers not to share too much information which would be used as reference in a BIM model. For a significant amount of infrastructure projects in the Netherlands that was the case. Certain employers would share none or minimal amount of data, and contractors would (based on the Dutch design and construct contract) be obligated to investigate that data themselves—bearing fully the risks themselves. Especially in a country below sea level and with generally spoken poor soil conditions, a good set of geotechnical data is very important for every construction project. In the end the lack of information would end up in a high amount of claims and a lot of discussions about risk allocation. The last few years, employers and contractors agreed upon which data should be shared up front and therefore collected by employers, in such a way the risks for contractors would become manageable.

So the quality of the input of the data for the BIM model is very, very important. And in practice, tracing back the origins of input data for a BIM model can be very challenging—not to say practical impossible. Another example would be the lack of "forensic certainty" that the original input is not tampered with in the BIM model. People make mistakes, and it's sometime difficult to prove that the original data set was good, but the import of the data went wrong—or somebody changed some data in the model after importing. We are just at the pioneering phase of how we protect our building information data not only against hackers, but also against unwanted changes due to "molest" or mistakes. Securing data integrity of the BIM database (and therefore contract requirements integrity), and still be able to design and add data to the model is one of the key issues where legal framework, software developers, and end users have to find new ways of managing the consistency of the used data.

Conclusion

The rapid speed of availability of more computing power and the ability to connect all kinds of databases online "in the cloud" makes BIM an integral part of every construction project nowadays. Looking at publications and prospects of several developers BIM promises all kinds of wonderful developments: disappearance of paper drawings, 3D printing on the spot, seaming less integration of maintenance, and completion management into asset management.

The reality, however, is that changes and possibilities in technology are going faster than our working processes and design methods on construction projects can keep up with. New possibilities with BIM are forcing designers all over the world to rethink their approach to design. That maybe sounds worse than it probably is. But we don't have room for a lot of errors. Construction is always cost intensive and errors can cost people's lives. Developments in technology could stretch the way we approach design and construction, but not at any risk. Legal aspects are very relevant to establish fair, transparent and sensible agreements, addressing the most important issues regarding BIM. There is just not that much room for "trial and error" when it comes to construction projects. So, innovation is most of the time evolutionary, not revolutionary. When evolution with BIM is taking a faster pace—we don't want to stumble!

Joost Merema
Partner at PRO6 managers

BIM: A superior approach for infrastructure construction by Josef Žák (the Czech Republic)

Introduction

Building information modeling is a process involving the creation, use, and management of construction data throughout an asset's entire life cycle. Some of its principles have been known since 1975. The enhancement in information, communications technologies, and construction processes have become the catalyst for data utilization.

Processes commonly using paper-based documentation are changing, due to the use of electronic data in civil construction. The use of data comprises a set of strategies, processes, applications, construction technologies, and technical architectures that streamlines design and construction. Database-driven document management solutions allow the storage, management, visibility, exchange, and distribution of data in many formats. Most of that data is in ASCII, PDF, XML, SQL-based, and CAD system file formats.

These technologies provide historical, current, and predictive views of project preparation, permit processes, and construction operations. Such data can be used by public bodies and enterprises to support a wide range of decisions, ranging from operational to strategic.

When digitization and automation took place in the automotive industry it increased production efficiency by 75%. A parallel can be drawn in construction: The introduction of information modeling in the life cycle of construction increases both automation and prefabrication in the construction industry. Quantifying the savings in transportation construction by individual authors ranges between 8% and 35%.

This case study combines experiences from several projects where building information modeling (BIM) principles were used in the Czech Republic, United Kingdom, Sweden, and the Netherlands. The text focuses on recent projects constructed during the last four years (as of 2013) or have been currently under construction.

BIM is commonly used in the Netherlands, Norway, Finland, Sweden, and Singapore in civil engineering. France is the latest country planning to introduce BIM for procurement from 2017. In Germany this is expected to be the case from 2020. Unlike Europe, North American countries know BIM under the term virtual design and construction. It is an inseparable part of the preparation of project documentation, construction, and management of large highway projects.

BIM in the UK

One of the examples worth mentioning is the use of BIM in the United Kingdom (UK), where it is compulsory to use BIM principles for publicly funded civil projects.

BIM in the UK is governed by British Standard BS 1192:2007 Collaborative Production of Architectural Engineering and Construction Information—Code of Practice. It defines the process for using a common data environment and code conventions for document status and numbering. It is supported by the suite of publicly available specifications (PAS) 1192 documents, which give practical guidance for information management during the delivery of projects using building information modeling. It outlines the information flow throughout the asset life cycle, including the management documents that must be produced, as well as project delivery team roles and responsibilities.

In 2011, the British Government published a strategy for reducing the cost of publicly funded assets, which required the use of BIM level 2 (as defined by the Bew-Richards BIM Maturity model below) for all centrally procured government construction projects by 2016.

Current state of BIM implementation in the Czech Republic

A. *Public Procurement*

One of the bases for the drafting of the new Czech Law on public procurement was the Directive of the European Parliament and of the EP Council 2014/24/EU, which recommends using these principles of information modeling. According to the Law on Public Procurement, § 103, Paragraph 3, the "contracting authority may specify in tender conditions mandatory requirement to use special electronic formats, including the tools of information modeling." The law came into force on October 1, 2016, allowing governmental authorities to require the use of the information model for the construction and preparation of works.

The Czech State Fund for Transportation Infrastructure (SFDI) issued a press release at the end of 2016, expressing the intention to gradually introduce BIM principles into design and construction. Press releases followed Government Resolution, dated November 2, 2016, no. 958, on the importance of BIM for civil engineering practice and suggested the next steps for its introduction. In acknowledgment of the need to tackle the topic, the SFDI established an Expert Working Group dedicated to the topic of information modeling and its implementation within the transport sector.

SFDI declared that, in cooperation with the Road and Motorway Directorate of the Czech Republic and Railway Infrastructure Administration, they already plan the use of

BIM in several pilot projects in 2017. The goal is to broaden the use of digital methods in projects financed by SFDI.

The Expert Working Group began work on two basic parallel tasks:
- Preparation of the strategy for the introduction of BIM in construction of transport infrastructure and
- Support for the preparation of pilot projects, including their implementation.

The Road and Motorway Directorate of the Czech Republic and Railway Infrastructure Administration will begin their selected pilot projects in 2017.

B. *Associations*

The Czech BIM council (CZ BIM) elected a new Board of Directors on November 15, 2016. Following this, the Expert Working Group for Information Modeling in transportation was established. Currently, industry partners are actively represented in the Expert Working Group.

An internal working group, dedicated to the topic of information modeling is also based at the think-tank Association for Infrastructure Development (ARI). The first internal ARI member meeting was held on January 13, 2017.

C. *Standards*

The Czech office for Standards, Metrology, and Testing established "152 TNK": the Technical Normalization Committee (TNC) for BIM. The committee was named the Information Organization of Construction and Building Information Modeling.

Comments and revisions to the following standards are currently ongoing: ISO 12006-2 Building Construction—Organization of Information about Construction Works—Part 2; Framework for Classification and ISO 16757-1—Data Structures for Electronic Product Catalogues for Building Services—Part 1: Concepts, Architecture and Model.

Examples of BIM utilization

One of the contractors who finds significant advantages in the use of BIM is Skanska. The use of the data-driven processes and technologies is constantly evolving throughout Skanska's business operation units in countries where it operates (UK, United States, Sweden, Norway Finland, Poland, Czech Republic, and Slovakia).

Data is used to detect inaccuracies in project documentation and resolve potential issues before they happen onsite. Information on the construction works is taken from the information model in certain cases rather than project documentation. One very important use for this data has been for earthworks, pavement/trackbed construction and geodetic works. For such purposes, machines (dozers, graders, pavers, excavators) are equipped with GNSS or UTS machine control systems. Data are converted in machine-readable file formats and loaded in control boxes that control machine hydraulic systems.

Operators have a display in view where they can select automatic positioning or indicative modes. Machines equipped with these technologies are capable of achieving significantly higher production performance and improved precision. There are many other examples of projects that utilize data in this manner. Buitering Parkstad Limburg, the Netherlands, D4 Skalka—Crossroads II/118, D1 Prerov—Lipnik nad Becvou in the Czech Republic, and D1 Budimir-Bidovce in Slovakia are all examples of machine control technologies and data utilization becoming standard.

In practice, project data and asset information is electronic, with design in the form of one 3D coordinated model and accompanying documents that range from quality assurance plans to contract documents. The use of these BIM processes is currently widely adopted across projects, as the industry recognizes the benefits. Examples of the advancing the use of this information during the delivery phase include 4D planning by adding a time dimension to the 3D model and 5D modeling using the 3D model to produce a bill of quantities and a calculation of embodied carbon during the tender phase. The use of 3D information has also led to the use of survey techniques such as the use of 3D laser scanning and the production of digital terrain models for earthworks.

"4D planning" is typically referred to as 4D simulation and construction planning. Thus linking schedule and time as a fourth dimension to the 3D model. 4D planning supports construction planning and assesses the impact of proposed design features and construction technologies on both construction schedules and workflow. These simulations provide valuable information concerning which basis construction schemes are to be reconsidered or changed. Software used for such simulations is capable of detecting schedule-space anomalies and minimizes risk during construction. As an example, reconsidering reinforcement (steel bars shapes and positions) was used when the reinforcing workflow was been simulated on the Kungens Kurva project in Stockholm, Sweden.

5D modeling puts 3D models, schedules, and pricing together. As the model grows in complexity, it becomes the basis of project management. 5D modeling may be performed in two stages—as an estimate of future construction costs or to monitor performance of construction teams and machinery. When used as a forecast, such data-rich simulations allow necessary decisions to be made at an early stage of project preparation to influence the total project cost.

The performance of each individual worker or machine may be evaluated and linked to penalty/bonus systems on site when 5D modeling is continually applied during construction. The D4 Skalka—Interchange II/118 in the Czech Republic is a project where cost monitoring was piloted. The project manager utilized these techniques to monitor the ongoing project as well as enhance his forecast for the cost of future projects.

Mobile technology has also become a familiar sight on construction sites, with smartphones and tablets linked to the common data environment. This access to the coordinated model, drawings, and other project documentation improves the quality of work, reduces rework and time spent searching for information. The use of mobile technology has grown organically from its potential for data and technology access, as construction industries find ever more innovative uses for them.

Such devices are also currently used to produce paperless quality documentation, carry out site inspections, markup drawings, and keep site progress records. The move toward paperless documentation has created efficiencies in administrative processes, as well as created data that can be used to drive continuous improvement during the construction process. An example uses data from health and safety inspections and quality checks to analyze trends and address them accordingly.

Aside from the above-mentioned uses, BIM models are applied to traffic safety inspections and visualizations in the Netherlands. Construction and infrastructure projects benefit from the use and application of 3D visualization. Context is an integral aspect when developing and creating visualizations. An understanding of construction sequence, methods, manpower, and materials is required to enable effective representations of real-world construction processes.

Visualizations are used for traffic safety inspections and to create a link between client and contractor, as it is far easier to overcome obstacles and delays when both understand the project, how proceeds and what it looks like. Visualizations are also used when communicating project aspects to public presentations prior to project preparations and construction. A typical project using these techniques is "A4all" A4 Delft— Schiedam or "Avenue2," which is a double-layered traffic tunnel under Maastricht, the Netherlands.

The BIM model and project data is also used for many types of analyses necessary for construction permits and environmental impact assessments. Traffic flow analysis that evaluates the probability of congestion and suitable selected solutions, as well as flood risk analysis are both examples. These analyses were used in Leiden, the Netherlands, when modernization of one of the intercity cross-sections was modernized to an interchange.

The use of data ICT technologies and construction automation both enhances quality and lowers the cost of infrastructure design and construction.

Josef Žák
Head of VDC department & Lecturer
Skanska CZ/SK/RO/HU & CTU in Prague
Czech Republic

References

Clark, G. (2013). EBRD experience under design-build contracts. Paper presented at the 26th FIDIC International Contract Users' Conference, London.

Cushman, R.F. (2011). *Proving and Pricing Construction Claims*. Wolters Kluwer, New York.

Kelley, G.S. (2013). *Construction Law: An Introduction for Engineers, Architects, and Contractors*. John Wiley & Sons, Inc., Hoboken, NJ.

Poulsen, S. and Záhonyi, Z. (2013). Employer's requirements. Paper presented at the 26th FIDIC International Contract Users' Conference, London.

Rowlinson, S. and Cheung, Y.K. Success factors in an alliancing contract: a case study in Australia. Online. Available at: www.construction-innovation.info/images/pdfs/Research_library/ResearchLibraryA/Refereed_Conference_papers/Refereed_Conference_Paper_Success_Factors_in_an_Alliancing_Contract.pdf (accessed 20 May 2013).

Further reading

Barber, J. and Jackson, S. (2010). Pre-construction services agreements: early lessons from experience. *Construction Law Journal*, 8. Sweet and Maxwell.

Ibrahim, C.K.I., Costello, S.B. and Wilkinson, S. Overview of project alliancing-based studies in the construction management literature. Online. Available at: http://emnz.webs.com (accessed 20 May 2013).

Jackson, S. (2011). A target cost contract for High Speed Rail. *Civil Engineering Surveyor*, May, p. 32.

Jackson, S. (2012). The NEC contract: a new approach. *Construction Europe*, 23(2), 18.

Klee, L. (2012). *Smluvní vztahy výstavbových projektů*. Wolters Kluwer, Prague.

MacDonald, C.C. What are the important differences between partnering and alliance procurement models and why are the terms so seldom confused? Online. Available at: http://cms.3rdgen.info/3rdgen_sites/107/resource/MacDonald-AIPMOct05.pdf (accessed 20 May 2013).

Murdoch, J.R. and Hughes, W. (2008). *Construction Contracts : Law and Management*. Routledge, New York.

Tichý, M. (2008). *Projekty a zakázky ve výstavbě*. C. H. Beck, Prague.

Venoit, W.K. (2009). *International Construction Law: A Guide for Cross-Border Transactions and Legal Disputes*. ABA Publishing, Chicago.

Walton, J.G. Alliancing contracts: a panacea to all that ails construction and infrastructure development? Online. Available at: http://www.johnwalton.co.nz/bits/alliancing_agreements.pdf (accessed 20 May 2013).

4 Specifics of EPC and EPCM

4.1 EPC and EPCM

At present, the engineer procure construct (EPC) delivery method is used as a brand name for certain types of design-build (DB) projects and contractors. The abbreviation is used mainly to label a specific risk allocation. In EPC projects, the contractor is responsible for engineering including design (the engineer duty), organizing procurement of works, plants, materials, and services (the procurement duties), and executes the construction works (the construct duty). Compared to the standard delivery methods described in Chapter 3, EPC contracts exhibit some differences. Therefore, EPC deserves separate consideration and discussion.

The EPC delivery method was very popular in the construction industry because it allowed greater prediction of overall price and time for completion. The resulting popularity led to a growing demand for sample contract forms based on the EPC method. This encouraged organizations such as FIDIC to produce separate sample forms (FIDIC EPC/1999 Silver Book). Organizations such as Orgalime, the AIA, the ICC, the ENAA, the ICE (see Chapter 13), and others also issued their own sample contract forms in support of the EPC delivery methods.

An alternative to EPC is the engineer procure construction management (EPCM) delivery method. This approach can be found mainly in the mining, petrochemical, and power engineering sectors. EPCM appears similar to EPC in name, but in fact is different in many other aspects.

In EPC and EPCM projects, the plant contractor is in possession of the know-how and copyrights to manufacturing processes. Therefore, they are a key element of the contracting chain. This contractor is usually the lead participant in the contractors' joint venture or a representative of the main EPC contractor.

4.2 Engineer procure construct (EPC)

EPC projects come under the umbrella of the DB delivery method. EPC projects are characterized by the fact that they allocate the lion's share of risk to the contractor.

International Construction Contract Law, Second Edition. Lukas Klee.
© 2018 John Wiley & Sons Ltd. Published 2018 by John Wiley & Sons Ltd.

The expectation then is that the contractor will be able to control and assess risks in their bid price. This is especially so in construction projects for power plants, steel mills, factories, and manufacturing plants in the petrochemical and mining industry and in the field of environmental and water treatment projects. In these projects, in general, plant delivery prevails over construction works to be contracted. The significance attributed to plant delivery and uniqueness of product will no doubt affect the contractor's negotiating position. For example, when a nuclear power plant is to be constructed, delivery may account for 70% to 80% of the contract price with the plant contractor being a key player.

Typically in EPC projects, the contractor is responsible for whole-project realization and for fitness for purpose of the result. The contractor is obliged to scrutinize the employer's tender documents, including specifications, geological surveys, and design documents (if any). Barring exceptions, responsibility for related errors lie with the contractor. The contractor, for example, is usually obliged to verify the physical environment on site and bears the responsibility for complications caused by geological and hydrological conditions. The contractor only has limited options to claim for additional payments. Naturally, this approach can efficiently be used only in specific construction projects—particularly where there is enough time to scrutinize the employer's requirements, verify site conditions and where there are only limited risks foreseen. The contractor must assess the risks and include a risk surcharge in their bid price and the employer must expect this.

In EPC projects, the contractor has to deliver work fit for the intended purpose. Because of the lump sum price model, it is in the contractor's own economic interest to deliver at the lowest possible cost. Most probably the contractor will select and implement cost-reduction methods and technical solutions within realization. For this reason, an EPC employer will have to survey the work in progress and verify work performance through frequent testing. Tests in EPC projects are typically divided into three phases: individual, complex (on completion), and warranty tests (after completion). In their tender requirements, some of the employers extend the contractor's obligations to include operation and maintenance of the work for a certain time after completion. This motivates the contractor to deliver the work at the lowest operating cost and at the highest possible quality.

A DB contractor is responsible for ensuring that the completed work is fit for purpose. EPC contractors and designers are therefore responsible for the results of their work in the same way. In accordance with the employer's tender requirements, the employer will define the scope and key criteria. In the case of a thermal power plant, for instance, the employer would typically specify the amount of power to be generated over a given period of time, for what consumption of fuel (coal, gas, biomass), and the waste production and the air pollution limits. If an employer fails to include a vital item in their tender requirements, the EPC contractor must remedy such shortcomings in their bid in order to complete the predefined purpose of the work.

It is extremely important for an EPC employer to prepare their tender requirements as accurately as possible. In particular, the project must be feasible and the performance criteria achievable. These performance and functional criteria may also be simply defined as "categories" with particular values to be filled out by the contractor in its bid. These values often become subject to evaluation along with the price and other criteria quoted in the contractor's bid. It is vital for the contractor to have enough time to prepare the bid and to scrutinize the employer's requirements.

The specifics of EPC risk allocation are further confirmed, for example, in the following ICC case no. 12090 (2004) (ICC, 2012). In this case, an employer (a company) entered into an EPC contract under English common law with the contractor (also a company) for the supply, installation and commissioning of 80 wind turbine generators for a wind farm project. Within five years of installation, most of the wind turbine generators had ceased functioning due to high wind turbulence and a high rate of grid failures at the site (despite being designed to have a 20-year useful life). A damages claim followed. The contractor argued that based on its past dealings with the employer, it was only responsible for supplying standard turbines and that it was not responsible for investigating wind conditions at the site. The tribunal found that, according to the EPC contract, the contractor was responsible for supplying site-appropriate turbines as the contract referred specifically to the particular conditions at the site, including wind data in several places. The tribunal found that it was up to the contractor to design and supply the wind turbine generators that would suit the site and it was also up to the contractor to ensure that it had all the relevant data about the site (and to make appropriate use of the data), in order to ensure that the wind turbine generators supplied would fulfil the requirements of the contract. This applies to the wind conditions, the characteristics of the terrain, the electrical grid characteristics and everything else about the site that any wind turbine generators designer would need to take into account. The contractor sought to avoid liability for the failure of its wind turbine generators by further referring to an expert report that claimed the effect of high wind turbulence and the high rate of grid failures at the site were so extraordinary that the contractor could not have been expected to have provided for them. However, the sole arbitrator decided that the allocation of responsibility provided by the EPC contract prevailed over these conditions.

4.2.1 Main advantages and disadvantages of EPC

The following are often recognized as advantages of the EPC delivery method:

- single point contractor's responsibility for construction works and design;
- lump sum (foreseeable) price;
- simpler budget policy from the lender's perspective;
- faster project implementation and foreseeable completion date;
- enforcement of performance liabilities can be narrowed to one particular entity;
- contractor efficiency in searching for cheaper and quicker solutions.

The following are often recognized as disadvantages of the EPC delivery method:

- Limited employer control over the design in progress and over project realization. In conventional DB projects, the engineer—who is often also a designer as the author of the basic tender design documents—is in control of design

development. However, there is usually no engineer in an EPC project and the competence of the employer's representative and their capacity to supervise design and project realization depend on their abilities in these fields.
- The final contract price tends to be higher than in a conventional DB or where general contracting is used, mainly due to (1) higher bid preparation costs; and (2) delegation of more risk to the contractor. This in turn may lead to contractor profit when the risks are not realized. The level of competition and the particular phase of the economic cycle can impact on the contractor's prices and risk surcharges.

4.2.2 Key issues with the EPC delivery method

The key issues that must be dealt with whenever an EPC contract is being prepared are as follows:

- definition of the scope of works, its performance, and other technical criteria;
- a contract administration approach;
- allowance for claims for additional payments or extension of time for completion;
- risk allocation (mainly the responsibility for errors in the employer's requirements, errors in setting-out, errors in the employer's design, risk allocation of unforeseeable difficulties, exceptional events, or *force majeure*);
- responsibility for obtaining the respective permits and licences;
- variation procedures;
- tests and taking over procedures;
- performance and other guarantees provided by the contractor;
- defect notification and operation period;
- training of employer's employees;
- responsibility for delivery of spare parts and other necessary service materials;
- intellectual property rights and their protection, licenses, and know-how for plants;
- insurance and securities. See Loots and Henchie (2013) for more details.

The employer's pitfall in the use of FIDIC conditions of contract for the EPC/turnkey projects (Silver book) in Indonesia by Sarwono Hardjomuljadi (Indonesia)

The use of the Silver Book is the choice of the Indonesian Government Institution as well as private sector, but unfortunately with some so-called "modification," which is in my terminology could be classified as "mutilation." The employer deleted some clauses, which in their opinion, may put the employer in the difficult position in case of contractor's claims.

The main reason for using the Silver Book in Indonesia is that the design and drawings are not ready and the employer thinks the simplest way around it is to let the contractor prepare the detailed design, which will cause that the design is wholly at the responsibility of the contractor.

The contractor will be responsible for the design and construction until the completion of the work, and the employer will be safely protected because the project contract price will be fixed. This is a perception by the employer, the banks as well as the auditors from the anti-corruption commission. Such a wrong perception, in addition to the misinterpretation of the meaning of some clauses, may create inevitable disputes.

The employer point of view: Since they have to start the construction but design is not available yet, the time is strictly constraint and the budget is limited, the fastest way and the best model of contract that should be used is the FIDIC EPC standard form. The design and the detailed ground investigation are not available, and the way the Employer's approach to the Sub-Clause 4.12 (unforeseeable difficulties) is that the contractor will be responsible for all risks, contingencies, and other circumstances. The contract is a lump sum fixed price and no compensation as Sub-Clause 4.12 unforeseeable physical condition could be provided, there will be no payment for any variation as it is also stipulated in the government regulation, where a restriction of the additional contract price increases is established in case of lump sum contracts.

The employers overlook the FIDIC suggestion, however, on how to use or not to use the EPC/turnkey project model. This model should not be used:

- if there is insufficient time or information for tenderers to scrutinize and check the employer's requirements or for them to carry out their designs, risk assessment account of studies and estimating (taking particular account of Sub-Clause 4.12 and 5.1);
- if the employer intends to supervise closely or control the contractor's work, or to review most of the construction drawings;
- if the amount of each interim payment is intermediary to be determined by an official or other intermediary;
- if construction will involve substantial work underground or work in other areas which tenderer cannot inspect and also if there is part of the design is made by the employer and is binding on the contractor and the tender is in competitive bidding without negotiations.

Mentioned misperception of the employer and even some consultants is not correct, because the FIDIC EPC form contains a variation clause and there can be additional contract price increases and decreases in case there are some variations instructed and/or approved.

The FIDIC EPC form contains also sub-clauses that establish a potential additional contract price increases and decreases because of claims (for example, the Sub-Clauses 2.1, 4.24, 7.4, 10.3, 13.7, 16.1, 17.4, and 19.4).

Case

The construction of bridge above the sea in Indonesia, based on the ground investigation given by the employer during the pre-bid conference. The contractor should prepare the design and conduct the construction.

In the implementation of the project, it was found that the depth of the hard rock for foundation is 25 m instead of 16 m preposition stated in the data from the investigation given by the employer. The contractor did the job professionally by installing the pile with the understanding that the depth of hard rock is 25 meters. Furthermore, there was a clause in the contract that the contractor has to get a prior approval from the employer (most of the contract in Indonesia have this clause added within the particular conditions), if the contractor wants to execute any part of the work. With the understanding that without such prior approval the contractor is not allowed to start the works, it could be concluded that such approval could be classified as a "variation order," since the drawing proposed included the additional length of the pile.

This is a good warning against misperceptions related to the FIDIC EPC form and against dangerous adjustments of the general part via particular conditions.

Sarwono Hardjomuljadi
FIDIC Affiliate Member, FIDIC International Accredited Trainer
Arbitrator
Professor in Construction Contract Management
Mercu Buana University
Jakarta, Indonesia

4.3 Bespoke EPC contracts

Contractual relationships in EPC often take the form of a "bespoke contract." EPC employers, engaged in the fields of power engineering or manufacturing plants, often have their own employees to take care of procurement and management. These employers are usually well experienced in project management within their field, being competent to manage and efficiently cooperate with the contractors.

Take a worldwide active steel manufacturer as an example of such an experienced EPC employer. Every steel mill is a complex system of technologically diverse, but separable and independent assemblies. Such steel mills often have their own coke-oven batteries, blast furnaces, and/or electric furnaces and related power plants to power them. Closely related to such a steel mill tend to be manufacturing plants such as a rolling mill or a forge. Possible combinations of various independent technological units are numerous there. In the overwhelming majority of cases, such a business entity will have these technological units built by independent manufacturers within EPC projects for both greenfield constructions and reconstructions or extensions of existing manufacturing capacities.

Sometimes it can be the case, however, that an experienced EPC employer will naturally maintain, on a long-term basis, its own capacities for the procurement and management of the EPC contractors. This can lead to a partial cost saving on activities that need not necessarily be undertaken by the contractor because the employer will retain these activities. At the same time, an experienced employer's team will manage and supervise project costs so that they are incurred in a reasonable way. Last, but not least, the employer's EPC team must coordinate the technological compatibility of independently built (or existing) plants by formulating specifications and supervising the work while it is being carried out.

Mitigating the risk of delays in power plant projects: An EPC contractor's view on different contractual concepts
by Jacob C. Jørgensen (Denmark)

Introduction

The international power plant industry is a risky place—especially, if you are an EPC contractor. The financial risks associated with project delays are significant due to the elevated level of liquidated damages in the EPC contract.

The EPC contract, which is typically based on the FIDIC Silver Book conditions, offers only very limited extension of time possibilities and places most of the project risks on the EPC contractor, including notably the risk of delays resulting from unforeseeable, adverse site conditions.

An EPC contractor will usually have to furnish the owner with a 10% on demand guarantee from a top-rated bank and in some cases also with a parent company guarantee. Accordingly, the chances of escaping liability for delays are very limited in practice.

The risk of delays is amplified by the fact that the EPC contractor only has limited *direct* control of the multitude of design, procurement, and construction activities since the majority of the activities are carried out by third party sub-contractors and suppliers.

Thankfully, a large portion of the "hardware" that is needed to build a power plant comprises short lead items, but a certain portion of the power plant's key components are complex and tailored, and can therefore not be procured on short notice. In the following, I will refer to these components, which for example include the boiler in a biomass power plant, as "key components" and to the suppliers of such components as "sub-contractors" or "suppliers."

It is generally not possible to push the full economic risk of delays associated with key components downstream onto the responsible suppliers at commercially viable terms. Nor is it possible to effectively insure the EPC contractor against the risk of defaulting key component suppliers. Accordingly, the EPC contractor is largely stuck with the risk of project delays, and the problems and expenses resulting from this risk, which may for example include exposure to commercial duress from less honest suppliers seeking to exploit the EPC contractor's vulnerable position.

This article explores how the risk of project delays related to key component suppliers may be mitigated in practice by implementing clauses in the key sub-contracts aimed at leveraging the EPC contractor's chances of achieving specific performance, or quickly replacing a defaulting supplier where specific performance is not a viable option.

The traditional approach to risk mitigation

First of all, the EPC contractor should attempt to mitigate the above-described risk by subjecting its key component suppliers to a due diligence investigation prior to entering into any type of contracts with them.

In most cases, the EPC contractor will demand a performance bond at an amount, which typically corresponds to 10% to 15% of the value of the sub-contract.

If the due diligence reveals financial problems that could prevent the sub-contractor from fulfilling its contractual obligations and/or if the sub-contractor cannot provide a performance bond, the EPC contractor should probably consider an alternative sub-contractor candidate.

Assuming that the sub-contractor is not facing detrimental financial problems and is able to provide a performance bond from a bank with a reasonable ranking, the EPC contractor can engage the sub-contractor in two basic contractual ways:

Joint venture

In some situations, the EPC contractor may be interested in and able to engage the sub-contractor as a partner in a joint venture to thereby incentivize timely performance on the basis of the joint and severable liability, which a joint venture contract imposes on the venturing partners.

In its purest form, a joint venture agreement will presumably mitigate the EPC contractor's risk exposure to delays caused by a joint venture partner who is financially strong because the exposure to claims for liquidated damages by the owner under the EPC contract will be equally threatening to all of the partners in the joint venture.

However, in practice the joint venture agreement will usually contain caps limiting the partners' liability to a certain percentage of the value of their respective shares of the scope of work. Moreover, the joint venture agreement will rarely obligate the partners to furnish *each other* with performance bonds, since the partners will use their respective credit lines to furnish the owner with a joint performance bond or with separate bonds under the EPC contract.

In practice, the formation of a joint venture between an EPC contractor and a key component supplier may therefore not effectively mitigate the EPC contractor's exposure to the risk of project delays caused by the supplier. This is particular so, in situations where the supplier is financially weak.

Sub-contract

Where the formation of a joint venture is not commercially possible or desirable, for example because the key component supplier is unwilling to share technical know-how and design information with the EPC contractor or any other third party for that matter, the EPC contractor will usually choose to enter into a sub-contract with the supplier.

The sub-contract will usually contain conditions that are largely back to back with the EPC contract, and place an obligation on the supplier to furnish the EPC contractor with a performance bond at an amount matching the overall liability cap in the sub-contract.

Payments

Furthermore, if the key component supplier's financial strength is questionable, the EPC contractor may seek to mitigate the risk of its prepayments "going astray" by paying the supplier's sub-suppliers and sub-contractors directly. Where this is not possible, the EPC contractor could propose to pay the sub-contractor via an earmarked account owned by the EPC contractor. In such an arrangement, the sub-contractor will often be given a revocable power of attorney to operate the account up to certain transactional thresholds per day, week and/or month, whereas the EPC contractor will reserve the right to approve transactions above such thresholds. A simple clause to this effect could be drafted as follows:

> "*All payments made in accordance with this contract shall be in € as set out and specified in Schedule x (The Milestone Events and Payment Schedule) and shall be paid into an*

earmarked account owned by the EPC contractor. The EPC contractor shall grant the sub-contractor with a revocable power of attorney to make payments from the account up to an amount of € per transaction and a total aggregate amount of € per month. Payments from the account in excess of these thresholds shall require prior written approval from the EPC contractor. The Parties agree to sign an online banking agreement with the EPC contractor's bank so that payment instructions and approvals may be given via online access."

Delays

Regardless of whether the key component supplier is engaged on the basis of a joint venture agreement or a sub-contract, the EPC contractor's remedies in case of delays or non-performance are usually restricted to claiming liquidated damages up to the agreed liability cap. Once the cap is reached, the contract will usually allow the EPC contractor to terminate and replace the supplier.

In power plant projects, the sub-contract (or joint venture agreement) will normally identify a number of sections in the sub-contractor's scope, which must be completed according to a milestone program. The contract will allow the EPC contractor to claim liquidated damages in case the sections are not completed on time.

A clause allowing the EPC contractor to claim liquidated damages for *interim* delays motivates the sub-contractor to perform the sub-contract in a timely manner throughout the project. Most importantly, such a clause gives the EPC contractor a chance to react *before* a delay materialises into a failure to meet the final handover date.

Termination

To strengthen the EPC contractor's strategic position and ability to counter a key component supplier's anticipatory breach of contract, the contract should ideally stipulate that the cap on liquidated damages cannot be relied upon in case the contract is terminated.

Furthermore, the sub-contract should contain a clause exemplifying what constitutes gross negligence as this may improve the EPC contractor's chances of defeating the supplier's liability cap, for example in situations where the supplier seeks to exploit the EPC contractor's exposure to liquidated damages by suspending or slowing down its construction activities (or threatening to do so) if the EPC contractor refuses to accept the supplier's (contested) claims for extra payment and/or time extensions. In this author's experience, these tactics are unfortunately not at all uncommon in large scale, international construction projects. For example it could be considered stipulating that the following acts and omissions will be deemed to constitute gross negligence: (a) Suspending the works or threatening to suspend the works in connection with claims for an extension of time and/or additional payment; (b) Failing to pay sub-suppliers and sub-contractors in a timely manner; (c) Refusing to accelerate activities in case of delays or threatening delays; etc.

The sub-contract should also provide for termination in case the sub-contractor goes bankrupt, is wound up, liquidated or otherwise loses control of its business. Sometimes the sub-contract will also allow the EPC contractor to terminate in case the sub-contractor suspends performance or refuses to accelerate its activities to comply with the time schedule.

Replacing the supplier?

The existence of a performance bond and the threat of liquidated damages and ultimately termination will of course incentivize the supplier to comply with the contract, but a fundamental weakness of the above-described remedies is that they do not increase the EPC contractor's chances of quickly and successfully *replacing* for example a defaulting boiler builder. This is unfortunate, since a quick replacement may often be the only relevant remedy from the EPC contractor's point of view in case the boiler builder lacks the *ability* or *will* to perform the contract on time. This shortcoming in the traditional approach to mitigating the EPC contractor's exposure to the risk of project delay is especially problematic in situations where the default (or threatening default) of the boiler builder is rooted in financial problems.

Replacing a boiler builder is fundamentally problematic because the boiler is a highly complex and tailored component that cannot easily be finalized by a new sub-contractor. The EPC contractor can, however, as explained in the following, seek to contractually alleviate this basic challenge by facilitating access to or control of the three main elements, which the construction or manufacturing of most key components entail, namely:

(a) The "hardware," that is, the bolts, valves, steel, which the component is made of;
(b) The "design," that is, the software, blue prints, calculations, technical descriptions, and other intellectual property that is required to build, hand over, test and use the component; and
(c) The manpower, that is, the engineers, project managers, software experts, and one or more "workshops" where the key component is assembled.

In the following, I will describe and comment on some different contractual concepts that may be adopted by EPC contractors seeking to increase their control of these three main elements.

An alternative risk mitigation approach

The hardware

On the basis of collateral warranty agreements (sometimes also called "step in rights clauses") with the key component supplier's sub-suppliers and sub-contractors, the EPC contractor will usually have a fairly good legal chance of securing access to the *physical* elements of the key component in case the supplier defaults.

Clauses allowing the EPC contractor to step into the supplier's sub-contracts will usually be accepted by the sub-suppliers in that such clauses increase their chances of receiving payment for the materials sold to the key component supplier. A simple step in rights clause could be drafted as follows:

> "*The supplier undertakes to implement the following step in rights clause in its main sub-contracts and sub-supply agreements that are listed in schedule x: 'The Parties agree that the EPC contractor, after having given written notice to both of the Parties to this present Contract, shall have the right to immediately replace [name of key component supplier] and take over all of [name of key component supplier's] rights and obligations under this present Contract.'*"

The sub-contract between the key component supplier and the EPC contractor should then regulate under which circumstances the EPC contractor may exercise the step in right, for example as follows:

> "The EPC contractor shall have the right to step into the supplier's main sub-contracts and sub-supply agreements that are listed in schedule x in any of the following situations: (a) if the supplier becomes insolvent, files for bankruptcy, goes into liquidation, has a receiving or administration order made against it, compounds with its creditors, carries on business under a receiver, trustee or manager for the benefit of its creditors, or if any act is done or event occurs with under applicable laws has a similar effect to any of these acts of events; or (b) if there is a Change in Control of the supplier or its parent entity as defined in clause xx, or (c) if the EPC contractor has the right to suspend or terminate the this present Sub-Contract.

Finally, the EPC contractor should seek to contractually ensure that ownership to the hardware passes to the EPC contractor (or if required to the owner) as soon as possible. Ownership should preferably pass as soon as the key component supplier has entered into its sub-supply agreement, where this is possible under the applicable law. To this end, it will often be necessary to ensure and document that the hardware is kept duly labelled and individualized. In some situations, depending on the *lex rei situs*, it may alternatively be possible (or preferable) to establish a floating charge covering the hardware during the assembling of the key component in a workshop.

The design

Providing the EPC contractor with fast and smooth access to the blueprints, technical descriptions, software components and any other intellectual property relating to the design of the supplier's scope of work, in case the supplier defaults, is both commercially and legally problematic.

First of all, the design is typically the supplier's main asset, and an EPC contractor wishing to obtain any extended legal rights to the design, beyond a standard single user license, will inevitably be met with resistance in the contract negotiations.

Relying solely on the typical non-exclusive, single user IP license, which most standard contracts grant the EPC contractor, is not always sufficient in case the supplier defaults as a result of bankruptcy, in that the administrator of the bankruptcy will often, under the *lex concursus*, have a right to repudiate the license agreement as an executory contract, i.e., a contract on which performance remains due on both sides.

This appears to be the case under German law, where sec. 103 and sec. 112 of the German Bankruptcy Act ("*Insolvenzordnung*") grant insolvency administrators with broad discretion to assume or reject executory contracts such as IP license agreements.

A similar result seems to flow from sec. 61 of the Danish Bankruptcy Act, which allows the administrator to terminate executory contracts for an extended duration with a "usual notice" in spite of the fact that such contracts may stipulate that they cannot be terminated, or that they may only be terminated with a very long notice.

On the other hand, §365(n) of the U.S. Bankruptcy Code specifically exempts a wide range of IP license agreements from repudiation by a bankruptcy administrator.

In the absence of clear statutory rules in the jurisdiction of the company where the design rights of the supplier have been placed, protecting the rights of the EPC contractor to continue to use the IP license in a situation where the supplier becomes insolvent, the EPC contractor will in most cases have an interest in obtaining an IP pledge, which embraces the design and other IP related to the key component. Such a pledge should be established and duly registered as a supplement to the usual IP license to use the supplier's design. This will in most jurisdictions, increase the EPC contractor's chances of successfully completing the component on the basis of the supplier's design in case the supplier goes bankrupt before the sub-contract is performed.

Establishing a first priority IP pledge will, however, sometimes prove to be difficult because the IP portfolio of the supplier has already been securitized in favor of the supplier's bank or other major creditor under a floating charge or a similar multi-asset-embracing securitization arrangement.

However, as the bank may sometimes have an economic interest in a successful performance of the sub-contract by the supplier, the EPC contractor may be able to strike a deal with the bank aimed at ensuring a continued and unhindered access to use the design rights, which will fall into the hands of the bank following the supplier's bankruptcy. It may in particular be possible to reach such an agreement in situations where the bank has issued a performance bond for the supplier in favor of the EPC contractor and/or in situations where the supplier has assigned its right to receive payments under the sub-contract to the bank.

Under any circumstances, the EPC contractor should always consider pursuing an agreement according to which the supplier undertakes to copy all design data related to the key component from its own server onto an escrow server owned and operated by a third party. The main purpose of such a "design escrow agreement," which is a common feature in contracts related to solar and wind power projects, is to give the EPC contractor a right to access and take over the updated design data (blueprints, software components, calculations, technical descriptions, etc.) if the supplier defaults so that the sub-contract can be handed over to a new supplier and performed with as little delay as possible.

The core clauses of a "design escrow agreement" could be drafted as follows:

"The EPC contractor shall have a full and unrestricted right to access and freely use the Data in any of the following situations: (a) if the Supplier becomes insolvent, files for bankruptcy, goes into liquidation, has a receiving or administration order made against it, compounds with its creditors, carries on business under a receiver, trustee or manager for the benefit of its creditors, or if any act is done or event occurs with under applicable laws has a similar effect to any of these acts of events, or (b) if there is a Change in Control of the Supplier or its parent entity as defined in clause xx, or (c) if the EPC contractor has the right to suspend or terminate the Sub-Contract.

The EPC contractor or an IT consultant appointed by the EPC contractor shall have the right to access the Escrow Server and the Supplier's own Server to verify that the Data has been duly backed-up in the agreed format and is up to date.

In case the EPC contractor exercises its right to access the Data pursuant to clause xx, the Supplier shall as of the date of the notice given by the EPC contractor be deemed to have given a time-unlimited, royalty-free, irrevocable and unrestricted license to the EPC contractor to use all of the Data for the purposes of successfully constructing, testing, handing over and where applicable later operating and maintaining the Works".

If the escrow server is operated from and located in a jurisdiction that does not readily recognize and enforce rulings of the bankruptcy courts of the supplier's jurisdiction, a "design escrow agreement" may in practice largely alleviate the above-described problems facing an EPC contractor in case the administrator of a key component supplier's bankruptcy decides to repudiate the EPC contractor's license to use the design of the key component.

The manpower

Even if the EPC contractor manages to quickly gain access to a defaulting key component supplier's updated design data and to the hardware, the EPC contractor will often face serious project delays due to the absence the supplier's *key employees*.

Without the specific project know-how of the supplier's project managers, lead engineers, software developers, and others who have been involved in project, the EPC contractor will rarely be able to finalize the defaulting supplier's key component on time.

It is therefore of paramount importance for the EPC contractor to take measures to increase the chances of having the supplier's key employees continue their work on finalising the key component even in a situation where the supplier becomes insolvent.

For example, the EPC contractor may be able to incentivize the supplier's key employees to finalize the key component by offering a cash bonus upon successful completion. Such a bonus should be paid by the EPC contractor directly to the key employees in accordance with the terms of the sub-contract.

The sub-contract will often contain a standard non-solicitation clause. In some cases, it may be relevant to add wording to such a clause, allowing the EPC contractor to actively engage the sub-contractor's key employees in case the supplier becomes insolvent or seriously breaches the sub-contract.

Depending on the nature of the key component, the supplier will sometimes have entered into an agreement with a workshop where the component is assembled. The EPC contractor should ensure that step-in rights clauses are implemented into agreements with the supplier's workshop. The type of clause set out above under Section 3.1 may be used in this regard.

Conclusions

In general, standard construction contract forms do not effectively support the EPC contractor's chances of quickly and successfully *replacing* a key component supplier, which is often the only relevant remedy worth pursuing for an EPC contractor in case the supplier lacks the ability or will to perform the sub-contract on time.

Replacing, for example, a boiler builder in a power plant project is fundamentally problematic because the boiler is a highly complex and often tailored component. The EPC contractor can, however, seek to contractually alleviate the challenges of replacing a defaulting boiler builder by facilitating quick and unhindered access to the three main elements, which the construction of any key component entail, namely: The hardware, the design, and the manpower.

Whereas step in rights clauses, designed to secure access to the *hardware* in case of a defaulting supplier, have become more or less standard due to demands from the lenders involved in the non-recourse financing of thermal power plant projects, it is somewhat surprising that the need for contractual leverage in relation to securing a continuous exploitation of an insolvent key component supplier's *design rights* has apparently only attracted attention in relation to solar and wind power projects. In the opinion of this author, there is a need for design escrow arrangements in most types of contracts with key component suppliers in light of the fact that the laws of most European jurisdictions apparently allow bankruptcy administrators to freely repudiate IP licenses granted by suppliers with dire consequences for the EPC contractors.

Where a design escrow arrangement is not practical or possible, the problems arising in relation to the EPC contractor's continued use of a bankrupt key component supplier's design may in some situations be avoided if the design rights and related IP can be placed in an SPV incorporated in the United States or in another "IP license rights friendly" jurisdiction. An alternative solution could be for the supplier to transfer the design rights to a trustee to thereby safeguard the IP if the supplier becomes insolvent.

Jacob C. Jørgensen
Advokat (H), LL.M., FCIArb, TEP
Copenhagen, Denmark

Bibliography

Jørgensen, Jacob C., "International Construction Project Joint Ventures under Swiss Law", The International Construction Law Review, 2006/10, p. 394 ff.
Jørgensen, Jacob C., et al. in "Delay Clauses in International Construction Contracts", 1st edition, 2010.
"Konkursloven med Kommentarer", by Anders Ørgaard et al., 12th edition, 2013, at §61.
"Finding, Freezing and Attaching Assets – a Multi-Jurisdictional Handbook", by Jørgensen, Jacob C., et al, 1st edition, 2016.
Sjørslev, Henrik, and Højslet, Dennis, in "The International Insolvency Review", 2nd Edition, 2014, p. 114 ff.

4.4 Turnkey EPC contracts

EPC projects are sometimes called "turnkey projects." There is typically minimal employer intervention during realization and they assume takeover of a fully functional work that is fit for purpose. Even though the "turnkey projects" brand has many diverse uses and an unclear meaning, the approach is appreciated and used by employers in need of implementing a one-off or very specific EPC project. Turnkey projects are preferred where the employers lack the necessary experience or where such projects include extensive plant delivery or risks that cannot be assumed by the employer—particularly where the objective is to allocate maximum risk to the contractor. The FIDIC EPC sample form (the Silver Book) is a template for use intended for such employers.

Imagine, for example, an investor, a member of a traditional and large business holding in a developing country engaged in a variety of activities, ranging from industrial production to import and representing foreign contractors. In response to the newly liberalized local power market, this investor decides to extend their business activities in an attempt to penetrate the power market as well. This is why they, as one of the first applicants, have obtained the necessary energy producer's licence issued by the government of this country. However, due to a shortage of power plants and a growing need for energy by the country's rapidly growing economy, the licence is of limited duration. Due to this time limitation, the government motivates the investor to commence construction of a power-generating unit as quickly as possible. The investor must therefore commence construction without any undue delay, as they face the further risk of potentially losing the licence. Such a situation will hardly allow the investor to develop their capabilities and capacities within a reasonable timeframe. Therefore, they have to engage an experienced contractor with expertise in power engineering—someone who is able to supply such a new turnkey power-generating unit quickly and without undue delay. An EPC contract for a power-generating unit construction project will be the best option for this investor.

Take another example of an experienced local investor with long-term involvement in running power plants, including construction and overhaul. This investor decides to include a new nuclear power plant in their portfolio, following a long-term strategy of product diversification. More than 70% of such nuclear power plant construction rests with the technologies to be delivered. Despite the investor's extensive experience, the key role will belong to the contractor who will deliver the parts not available and known to the investor. The investor has neither the necessary know-how, nor the resources to allow them to complete the construction on their own. In such a case it will be advantageous for the investor to procure the nuclear power plant construction project as an EPC with a contractor or perhaps even with a joint venture of other contractors. The contractors will design, construct and put into operation a fit-for-purpose product and provide the necessary training of the investor's personnel for safe operation of the plant.

Water treatment, wind farm, and road construction projects in Asian and African countries by Stéphane Giraud (France)

I have participated directly in several construction projects in Asian and African countries, mainly in the position of project manager/project director and contract administrator (the engineer under FIDIC). Several lessons were learned in completing these projects and I make some useful recommendations with respect to each project.

The first project following the 1999 FIDIC Silver Book was to rehabilitate three wastewater treatment plants and to build a new wastewater treatment plant in an Asian country. The project was funded both by a multilateral bank and a local bank amounting to €50 million over the duration of 30 months.

The contractor was initially very reluctant to follow the Silver Book and required some adjustments in risk allocation. However, the project was completed on time and within the timescale.

Furthermore, the use of the contract administrator (the engineer, included as per the 1999 Yellow Book in place of the employer's representative) was advantageous, as the employer did not have the proper team/capacity to manage such an international project.

During the course of the project, two main disputes could have been successfully solved by a DAB (including a claim for a new pumping station caused by a level error in the initial setting out) but the DAB was not used.

In general, it is recommended to amend the Silver Book (or directly use the Yellow Book) to balance some responsibilities (mainly the onerous Sub-Clauses 4.10 and 4.12) and incorporate an engineer sub-clause similar to that in the Yellow Book (in Chapter 3), especially for the construction of wastewater treatment plants in a developing country. An ad hoc DAB (or better a "full-term DAB" in major projects) is recommended to avoid loss of time and money as a sound disputes resolution process.

The second project was to build a wind farm (250 MW) in an East African country. It was funded both by a multilateral bank and a local bank, amounting to €350 million over a duration of 36 months, also on the basis of the 1999 FIDIC Silver Book. The site was in a remote place, with access difficulties and at high altitude.

No major amendments were made during the contract negotiations (via the particular conditions) as both parties (the contractor and the employer) signed the contract without having a substantive knowledge or experience with the FIDIC forms.

The two first contractor claims were caused by errors in the site data (including errors in setting out) and lack of access to the site. The employer relied on a weak feasibility study at the tender stage. Those studies did not deal with two major issues: the local farmers and the actual site conditions. It is recommended that employers appoint high-level professional consultancy services in such circumstances (for both local and contractual issues), before launching the tender.

The parties signed the contract without a good knowledge of the FIDIC provisions and mechanisms. They did not read and apply the contract at site, preferring to apply their own knowledge based on their previous experience. My recommendation is that all participants must read and abide by the contract during realization (not only once at the beginning of the project) and should participate in a kick-off meeting that includes a "training" course on FIDIC principles.

The third project was to reconstruct an old, major road (120 km) in an East African country. It was funded both by a multilateral bank (80%) and local funding (20%) amounting to €48 million over a 24-month duration. The general conditions used were the 2005 FIDIC Multilateral Development Bank Red Book.

During the course of the project, a lot of issues that could have been dealt with by a DAB never were. This is because both parties considered it too expensive—particularly since no allowance was made for it in the original budget. In some developing countries, it seems that an ad hoc DAB (less expensive) or other dispute board (or DRB) should be recommended. It is recommended that lenders insert a DAB provision in the project budget forecast to avoid missing the opportunity to use a DAB.

The lack of FIDIC experience created a common misunderstanding about the defects notification period (DNP) mechanism shared by all parties, including the engineer. At the end of the DNP, it was believed that the performance certificate would be automatically issued even if the defects had not all been remedied. Practical training on FIDIC mechanisms would have been of great benefit to project management (and, for that matter, to all the other parties including the engineer).

In conclusion, I take this opportunity to point out some final recommendations. In particular, I would stress that:

- The engineer should be involved even where the Silver Book has been used (via an amendment in particular conditions).
- All parties must read and understand the contract. A "kick off meeting" should be organized for all parties together to make everybody acquainted with FIDIC principles.
- A provision for DAB or DRB should be made in the initial budget prepared by the lender/employer and with a further provision that a DAB be funded by multilateral banks.

Stéphane Giraud
Director, 'Dams & River Works'
FIDIC expert – Accredited Trainer & Adjudicator (French list)
Egis Group
France

4.5 Front end engineering design

Normally, an EPC employer prepares the initial design for the purpose of awarding the contract on a Front End Engineering Design (FEED) basis. With the employer's requirements to hand, the contractor will provide the detailed design and be supervised by a representative hired by the employer.

When formulating their requirements, the employer will further, as a rule, elaborate on a preliminary time schedule, contract price estimation and obtain some of the necessary permits from the public authorities. The amount of detail of the employer's tender documentation will depend on the particular project, the specific branch of industry, the country, the location of project implementation, and so on.

Within the limits of this preliminary phase—but preceding the commencement of the contractor selection stage—the employer must make a choice between EPC and EPCM for project implementation.

EPC projects often involve more plants to be delivered than the volume of pure construction activities. Therefore, EPC contractors often do not have the manufacturing capacity to construct the buildings or civil engineering works, despite having their own designers. For construction activities, EPC contractors usually hire subcontractors or enter into joint venture contracts with specialized contractors in possession of the manufacturing and assembling capacities at the construction stage of the contract. The same will apply when the role of EPC contractor is filled by a foreign technology provider with inadequate knowledge of local conditions. In such situations, the local partner is able to counter-balance such an inconsistency by being invited to become a member of a joint venture or to act as the main subcontractor. Key competencies of EPC contractors often comprise not only plant delivery, but also design and related engineering activities, procurement, and management of the realization itself.

The term "engineering" means, in practice, providing pre-design activities that include obtaining the necessary permits from the public authorities if the employer has not already done so. In general, it further means that the concept of "engineering" has to be understood as set out in its contractual definition and depends on particular clauses, governing law and customs.

Key issues in the procurement of international hydropower construction contracts by Alex Blomfield (UK)

Compared to thermal power projects, hydropower projects generally involve longer periods of construction, higher construction risk, and higher construction costs. Successfully reflecting these well-known characteristics of hydropower projects in construction contracts in a manner tailored to the unique nature of each hydropower project is not an easy task. It requires a careful and balanced approach that does not try to win every point in a negotiation but instead recognizes that a robust and workable contract will have a higher chance of delivering a project on time, on budget and to specification if it provides not only firm incentives and disincentives but also the necessary flexibility to accommodate the complexity and unpredictability of hydropower construction. Based on extensive experience acting as legal counsel to project sponsors and employers on hydropower construction projects in more than 15 countries across Africa, Latin America, Europe, and Asia, generally financed on a limited-recourse basis, this vignette will identify a number of trends in international hydropower construction contracts.

Employers and contractors generally choose FIDIC contracts as the standard construction contract for international hydropower projects. FIDIC contracts can save time and minimize transaction costs due to the fact that they are internationally known and recognized. FIDIC contracts also generally adopt a fair and balanced risk allocation and have a tried and tested track record. However, FIDIC contracts require extensive modification to work in a hydropower context, to reflect the unique site-specific characteristics of each particular hydropower project and to meet the requirements of non- or limited-recourse debt financing. Given the large number of changes to FIDIC's general conditions that are necessary, one can discern a clear trend among employers, and increasing acceptance among contractors, toward consolidation of the FIDIC general conditions and particular conditions into one conditions of contract document in order to avoid lengthy and highly complex particular conditions and facilitate easier contract administration. This approach requires a licence from FIDIC, which FIDIC generally grants on a project-specific basis.

International hydropower projects tend to use one of two key construction contract procurement approaches: (1) the engineering, procurement and construction contract (the EPC contract) approach, in which the contractor engineers, constructs, and procures equipment/materials on a lump-sum, fixed-price basis; or (2) the split-contract approach, in which the employer enters into separate contracts with different consultants and contractors to perform different scopes of work, such as civil works, electro-mechanical works, hydraulic steelworks, design, and contract administration. The approach an employer chooses should take into account not only the characteristics of the particular project but also the level of sophistication of the employer/sponsors and likely contractor(s)/consultant(s) in hydropower project execution.

The EPC approach offers the following advantages to an employer: a single point of responsibility, maximum allocation of construction risk to the contractor, a full wrap guarantee on all aspects of project, maximum budget control, comparatively low transaction costs, and minimum owner oversight. However, such advantages come with an expensive risk premium, which may even offer poor value to an employer if the contractor has not been able during the bidding process to properly price its risk due to inadequate opportunity to conduct due diligence, in particular, for tunneling and other projects particularly prone to unforeseen geological conditions. Furthermore, sophisticated hydropower sponsors will see it as a disadvantage that the EPC approach allows only limited sponsor involvement in the design phase and construction process. In addition, a limited (or sometimes even non-existent) EPC contractor market can often inhibit use of the EPC approach.

While lenders generally prefer fixed-price, single-package EPC contract models, the project finance market has more recently started to accept a split-contract model with between two and four main packages so long as the sponsors provide some level of completion-related support to mitigate the interface risks between the various construction packages. To the extent that a project encounters cost overruns or schedule delays that jeopardize the completion of the construction, such support allocates most of this residual completion risk to the sponsors and will likely take the form of a commitment by the sponsors to contribute funds to the employer (above their base-equity commitments) in the event that the employer suffers cost overruns, or cash shortfalls when remitting debt service, prior to project completion. The level of sponsor support typically increases as the number of contract packages increases and can become one of the most important points of discussion with lenders when arranging debt financing for a project. Employers need to keep the level of potential sponsor support in mind when designing and negotiating the construction contract packages.

The split-contract approach has the advantage of much lower cost compared to the EPC approach and also offers sponsor involvement in the design phase and construction process, which tends to suit sophisticated hydropower sponsors. The disadvantages of the split-contract approach include interface risk, coordination risk, low liability caps, less budget control, high transaction costs, non-uniform contract conditions, a greater need for sponsor oversight, an increased likelihood of warranty period disputes, and the possibility of parallel litigation risks. This seems like a long list but sponsors can employ various contractual techniques to mitigate these risks to some extent. One might also observe that only larger hydropower projects—say, perhaps larger than 50 MW in installed capacity—tend to justify the increased transaction costs and lower risk premium of the split-contract approach.

After deciding whether to follow an EPC or split-contract approach, the employer needs to decide whether to use bespoke drafting or a standard form. As noted above, the most widespread standard form is FIDIC. Employers following the EPC procurement approach commonly use the FIDIC Silver Book. Employers using the split-contract approach may use a variety of different contracts with varying scopes. Table 4.1 sets out one such approach with the typical FIDIC forms used.

A critical contract for the split-contract approach is the interface agreement. This agreement manages interface risk among the various tender packages, creates a forum for contractors to work through interface issues among themselves and provides for a common dispute resolution process for all contractors, the engineer and the employer. It can also contain a bonus scheme for early completion. No standard form exists for the interface agreement. Some contractors

Table 4.1 Typical FIDIC forms used for the split-contract approach in hydropower construction contracting.

Contract	FIDIC contract	Work covered
Civil works contract	Red Book 1999	Civil works (site development, construction, tunneling, earthworks, etc.)
Electro-mechanical contract	Yellow Book 1999	Electro-mechanical equipment (turbines, generators, transformers, etc.) design, supply, installation, commissioning and testing
Transmission works contract	Yellow Book 1999	Transmission line and facilities design, construction and installation
Hydraulic steelworks contract	Yellow Book 1999	Hydraulic steelworks (gates, penstock, etc.) design, construction and installation
Engineering agreement	White Book 2006	Engineering consultancy services including detailed design and contract administration
Interface agreement	Bespoke non-FIDIC contract	Coordination and interfaces among contractors, common dispute resolution, bonus scheme

welcome the interface agreement and see it as a constructive way to provide a regime to cooperate with the other contractors toward the common goal of delivering a project by its scheduled completion date. Other contractors tend to resist the whole concept of an interface agreement because they see it as a source of liability additional to their main contract.

Some utilities with a strong hydropower tradition have an in-house design function but most hydropower project sponsors/employers today contract out the detailed design of a hydropower project, whether as part of the EPC contract under an EPC contract approach or to an independent design engineer if following the split-contract approach. In a FIDIC context, the consultant carrying out the design pursuant to a FIDIC White Book contract will often also act as engineer under the other FIDIC contracts used (usually the FIDIC Red Book for the civil works and the FIDIC Yellow Book for electro-mechanical works, and hydraulic steelworks to the extent tendered separately). Under FIDIC, the engineer administers all claims, performs quality control functions, proposes/negotiates variation orders with the contractor and otherwise manages the construction process for and on behalf of the employer. The employer may modify this engineer role somewhat depending on the degree that it desires to directly involve its own or sponsor employees in the contract administration. Furthermore, some employers may wish to split the design and engineer functions so that they have someone to oversee the work of the designer, though the interfaces between those roles can make such a split challenging.

Under the FIDIC Red Book and the FIDIC Yellow Book, the contractor may claim time and cost for unforeseeable sub-surface conditions. FIDIC defines "unforeseeable" as 'not reasonably foreseeable by an experienced contractor by the date for submission of the tender." Under the FIDIC Silver Book, the contractor "accepts total responsibility for having foreseen all difficulties and costs of successfully completing the Works." In each of the Red, Yellow, and Silver Books, the contractor is discharged from further performance "if an event or circumstance outside the control of the parties arises which makes it impossible or unlawful for either or both Parties to fulfil its or their contractual obligations." Irrespective of the type of contract used, the risk of unforeseen geological (or subsurface) conditions represents one of the most challenging risks to manage during the construction of any hydropower project and particularly on any project that contains tunnels. To help mitigate this risk, employers should allocate significant resources for geological surveys of the project site and tunnel locations. The inclusion of a geological baseline report in any construction contract for a hydropower project which may suffer significant unforeseen geological conditions increasingly seems to represent best practice, and is also encouraged by the insurance industry.

Long construction periods, high construction risk and high construction costs do not have to mean high transaction costs and long negotiation periods for international hydropower construction contracts. However, choosing the wrong procurement method or allocating risk unfairly will certainly have an adverse result, and that is even before the groundbreaking ceremony. The above gives a brief overview of only a handful of the large number of issues that need to be overcome and details, which need mastering in order to close an international hydropower construction contract, a critical step toward the execution of a successful hydropower project.

The contributions of Alex Blomfield to this textbook have been adapted from a paper given by him at the HYDRO 2013 Conference, on October 7, 2013, in Innsbruck, Austria, organized by *The Journal of Hydropower and Dams*.

Alex Blomfield
Special Counsel
K&L Gates LLP
London
UK

4.6 Engineer procure construction management (EPCM)

From the contractor's point of view, the purpose of EPCM is to provide services over and above delivery of construction works or plants. A cursory examination is enough to reveal that EPCM projects fall under the category of CM delivery methods. The CM contract (being a professional service agreement) can be considered a variant of an agency agreement. The main difference between EPCM and the standard CM model is that an EPCM contractor will also provide design and other engineering activities in their own respective capacities.

4.6.1 Key competencies of the EPCM contractor

As such, the EPCM contractor is mainly responsible for the following:

- detailed design for realization—sometimes even the basic design (FEED), according to employer requirements;
- procurement of construction works, deliveries of material, equipment and plants; and
- contract management and administration.

An EPCM contractor acts as an intermediary between the employer and their contractors but is not responsible for the construction activities carried out, nor the material, equipment and plants delivered.

An EPCM employer must coordinate and supervise realization and have adequate human resources and suitably qualified and experienced employees. This is because all potential claims for damages arising during realization are part of the employer's allocated risk.

Liabilities for breach of EPCM contractor obligations typically relate to the following:

- delivery of design;
- budget preparation;
- time schedule preparation;
- management of procurement;
- coordination of the design and construction works.

Regarding the above points, it will likely be difficult to prove unambiguously the causality between breaches of EPCM contractor obligations and damage done.

Friction over liability may further arise in connection with the design of key plants themselves, or with the responsibility for fitness for purpose of the plants subject to expected performance and other technical criteria. Neither EPC nor EPCM contractors will be willing to assume this responsibility and both will want to considerably limit their liability—unless they themselves will be the contractors selected to deliver the respective plants.

Concerning the motivation of an EPCM contractor to keep to the anticipated budget, the following should be mentioned. The EPCM contractor is paid on a "cost plus basis," which means that actual costs plus profit margin and overhead expenses are reimbursed. A contract with a target price can motivate the EPCM contractor to keep to or reduce the budget. Projects with "target prices" are characterized by the fact that the employer and the contractor share not only the money saved below the level of the agreed target price, but also any losses, that is, price increases as against the agreed target price as per the pain/gain mechanism.

A situation where an EPCM contractor guarantees, with a high level of certainty, that the bid price will be kept to cannot be expected. The contract must therefore contain a detailed provision defining the cost control methods to avoid unnecessary increases.

A similar situation arises where responsibility for keeping to the time for completion schedule is important. The EPCM contractor is not responsible for individual construction and plant contractor performance, but is responsible for timely delivery of the design. EPCM contractors must also be responsible for delays caused by negligence in procurement, coordination and management. The EPCM contractor can be motivated to keep to the budget with an incentive, such as a timely completion bonus. Even under EPCM, the employer must engage employees capable of determining who caused a particular delay and to what extent. Therefore, the contract must also contain a clear and elaborate dispute resolution mechanism.

The following example can serve to illustrate the use of the EPCM model. An entrepreneur, with other participants, run an extensive network of petrol filling stations and decide to expand the business vertically by entering into fuel production. To meet this purpose, they further decide to build a brand-new refinery. An EPCM method was bilaterally selected during the negotiation process with the most promising potential contractor.

Both parties found the selected solution satisfactory. The contractor is willing to provide the employer with their know-how, experience, and construction management skills. The contractor understands that there is lower level of risk offered to them by this EPCM model. The employer, on the other hand, can recruit the necessary human resources that allows them to grow independently of the contractor. Using the "learning by doing" method, the EPCM contractor will then hand a considerable portion of necessary experience over to the newly set up employer's team during realization.

4.6.2 Main advantages and disadvantages of EPCM

The following are commonly observed advantages of EPCM projects:

- Reduced costs in cases of smooth realization of work, that is, no main contractor's surcharge has to be paid for project risks.
- Broader access to contractors' market—breaking down into works packages procured broadens the choice of contractors.
- Flexibility—all required variations, such as those relating to the scope of work can be easily and directly agreed upon by particular contractors.
- Lower risk of non-performance or contractor insolvency—risk is spread to facilitate fewer "sub-risks" allocated to more contractors.
- Single point responsibility for the design and coordination of the works.

The following are commonly observed disadvantages of EPCM projects:

- Difficulty in coordinating individual contractors (compatibility of plants, coordination of sequencing, and the like), the success of which largely depends on the EPCM contractor's experience.
- Difficulty in allocating and demonstrating responsibility where individual contractors should fail.
- Difficulty in coordinating liabilities between the EPCM contractor and the main plant contractor.
- Lower level of contractual penalties and liquidated damages in contracts with smaller contractors.
- High demands on employer capacities.
- Non-conventional delivery method limits available financing options; this delivery method might appear risky to lenders. See Loots and Henchie (2013) for more details.

4.6.3 Key issues of the EPCM delivery method

Key issues that must be dealt with whenever an EPCM contract is being prepared are as follows:

- Selection of competent EPCM contractor (mainly the set up of the criteria to meet this purpose).
- Setting up of a contractual and commercial relationship between the employer and the EPCM contractor (especially the EPCM contractor supervision method).
- Defining the algorithm to determine the level of the EPCM contractor's remuneration in respect of optional motivating bonuses and relationships with other contractors.
- Assessing the EPCM contractor's responsibility for keeping to budget and the time schedule.
- Sharing of liabilities between the EPCM contractor and the main plant contractor.
- Relationship between the EPCM contractor and other key construction contractors.

The use of the EPCM delivery method in the mining industry by Mark Berry (UK) and Matthew Hardwick (UK)

Most mining projects require the delivery of process plant infrastructure, whether relating to initial refinement and the sorting of raw materials at the mine site, for transport and secondary processing elsewhere, or full processing to final product at or near the mine site for sale direct to the relevant off-take market. Indeed, there is a trend for the governments of, for example, African countries to require a greater amount of in-country processing/refining in order to increase the economic benefit to the country of the natural resources.

The need, however, for good supporting infrastructure (e.g., road, rail and port facilities), particularly in Sub-Saharan Africa, to facilitate transportation of the raw materials as refined product, often means that there is a need for a number of separate infrastructure packages requiring delivery before the project can be realized and before the asset can be placed into full operation and production. The lack of supporting infrastructure in Sub-Saharan Africa often means that the realization of a mining project involves high levels of capital expenditure, with construction delivery costs running into billions of dollars.

The EPCM contract structure is used across a number of sectors, but has been particularly prevalent in the mining sector where its use has more recently become a market norm, particularly for projects in Africa. For such projects, the perceived "country risk," the size of the project in terms of initial capital requirements and the need for delivery of a number of separate works packages over a prolonged and often fragmented procurement period, has tended to mean that no single contractor has been willing or able to offer a single turnkey EPC solution. Even if this were to be achievable, the level of contingency included in the EPC price would be likely to impact on project economics and affordability for the employer.

While sometimes confused with the EPC contracting solution (simply because of the use of a similar acronym), the EPCM and EPC contracting solutions are very different in terms of the nature of the obligations undertaken and the risks assumed by the respective contractors. An important difference between the two contract structures is that an EPCM contractor will not usually accept time or cost overrun risks: these are the risks that are retained by the employer. The employer will therefore need to manage these risks with the professional assistance and support of the EPCM contractor through the construction and equipment/plant supply chain.

The quality of the EPCM contractor's performance will be determined by reference to the extent to which it has performed its services in accordance with the level of skill and care required by the EPCM contract, rather than by reference to the achievement of overall project budgetary or scheduling targets.

It is usual, however, for EPCM contracts to incorporate contractual "incentivization" provisions under which the EPCM contractor will achieve a profit 'uplift' should key contract targets (e.g., the achievement of key construction milestones by agreed milestone dates, project delivery for a capital cost equal to or less than that budgeted) be achieved or exceeded. In a hard market, EPCM contractors may additionally agree to place an element of their profit at risk should the key targets not be achieved. While the EPCM contractor will not be standing behind achievement of the key targets (in terms of liability), the incentivization provisions are seen as an important tool in encouraging and securing proper performance. Where there is significant cost and/or time overrun, these provisions may, however, lose their benefit and instead the employer's leverage tends then to be limited to restrictions on the EPCM contractor's right to recover profit on the increased levels of work required above that budgeted at the date of the EPCM contract.

EPCM contractors will expect to limit their liability under the terms of the EPCM contract. The liability accepted by the EPCM contractor must be appropriately sized but the ethos of EPCM contracting is that the EPCM contractor is providing consultancy services only and is not underwriting project delivery risk. The size of the liability caps under the EPCM contract will therefore be reflective of this and are usually in the order of the amount of "profit" that the EPCM contractor expects to make on the budgeted manhours it charges for the performance of the EPCM services.

An important negotiation point will typically be the extent to which the EPCM contractor is responsible for the consequential losses flowing from its failure to perform. Experience shows that EPCM contractors are extremely reluctant to accept such liabilities. This would leave, for instance, the cost risk with regard to any rework required as a result of defective design produced by the EPCM contractor with the employer. This risk may, however, be mitigated to the extent that professional indemnity insurance is available to cover these types of losses. If this is the case, the EPCM contractor may be prepared to accept these consequential liabilities on an unlimited basis, to the extent covered by the relevant insurance policies. There will then be a negotiation to be had around insurance recovery risk and the party responsible for the insurance deductible.

Many EPCM contractors look to limit their liability to "re-performance" of defective services only. This is a difficult concept for an employer to accept, particularly given the likely consequential losses flowing from the relevant defective services. It also ignores the purpose of any professional indemnity cover placed or available to cover project risk. Furthermore, it is important to remember that many liabilities that should be captured by the EPCM contract liability regime may not be remediable through re-performance of defective services alone, so this approach will not provide for an appropriate remedy in many circumstances. Ordinarily, re-performance of defective services should instead be considered a cost of performing the services for which the employer will have made payment, and not a liability.

Given the nature and extent of the liabilities assumed by an EPCM contractor, the EPCM contract will not contain the types of sanctions for breach and requirements as to security typically found in an EPC contract. The focus will instead be on the use of provisions concerned with the restriction on the right to payment, restriction on the right to profit recovery, and rights of the employer to step in and self-perform and/or terminate and permanently replace the EPCM contractor.

It is important to recognize that an EPCM contractor will not itself perform construction works. The EPCM contract is essentially a professional services appointment under which the EPCM contractor's services will usually be limited to the production of detailed design and the procurement, construction management, and coordination of the works and services necessary to deliver the project.

The EPCM contractor will be responsible for the development of detailed design, which may incorporate conceptual design produced by or on behalf of the employer during the project feasibility stage. The employer will look to the EPCM contractor to check any conceptual design to verify its accuracy, completeness, and fitness for purpose. The extent to which employers can expect the EPCM contractor to take full risk in conceptual design will, however, vary from one project to the next and will ultimately depend on the liability provisions agreed in the EPCM contract.

The detailed design responsibilities of the EPCM contractor will typically cover most aspects of project design. It would not be unusual, however, for specific aspects of the project to be packaged up into separate EPC packages (e.g., on site power production) or design and build packages (e.g., buildings housing the process plant). These packages will remain under the administration of the EPCM contractor but the EPCM contractor's design responsibility in relation to them will be limited to a checking and coordination role.

Where the EPCM contractor is responsible for detailed process design, it would be usual for the EPCM contractor to guarantee levels of plant performance/output. The EPCM contract should therefore document the performance testing regime, which should reflect the procedures for establishing actual plant output/performance and the extent to which the levels of plant performance/output guaranteed by the EPCM contractor have been achieved.

The EPCM contractor should be responsible for any shortfall in performance/output from that guaranteed, save where such shortfall arises due to risks retained by the employer. Retained employer risks in this context will usually include the occurrence of supervening events outside of the control of the parties, out-of-specification feedstock and poor operation of the process plant, in each case, insofar as the relevant circumstance impacts on testing or the achievement of the guarantees. The nature of employer-retained risks in this regard will tend to be more widely defined than those adopted under an EPC solution. This, among other things, is reflective of the fact that the EPCM contractor will have less day-to-day control over the construction and assembly of the plant and, of course, accepts a more limited liability position. This being said, it is not usually the case that the EPCM contractor is relieved of liability upon the occurrence of an employer risk event. Employers will instead look for the performance testing regime to be repeated when the relevant employer risk has subsided.

Where the guaranteed levels of output/performance are not achieved but output/performance is above a minimum required level, the EPCM contractor may, in lieu of a requirement to oversee further rectification works, be required to pay performance liquidated damages. The performance liquidated damages payable should reflect the costs, losses, and liabilities of the employer arising from underperformance of the plant. This liability will usually be subject to a limit beyond which the residual underperformance risk will rest with the employer.

The EPCM contractor will be allocated responsibility for the overall procurement strategy. He will be responsible for splitting the works and supply elements into appropriate packages with a view to minimising interface risk. Where interfaces are created, the EPCM contractor should be responsible for implementing a strategy to manage them. He will additionally source contractors, consultants, and the necessary plant and equipment in consultation with the employer and in accordance with employer's requirements and any assumptions established at feasibility stage.

Experienced EPCM contractors will normally hold a suite of standard form contracts (with appropriate employer-friendly amendments) that can be used for the procurement of the relevant packages. The FIDIC forms of contract remain the most common ones but given the provenance of many resource companies, it is also quite usual to see the Australian Standards form employed. Employers will want to take an intrusive role in the negotiation and approval of these terms, particularly for important and/or high-value packages that could materially impact on the achievement of the key project targets should problems arise.

The employer will ordinarily enter into all works and supply contracts. While we have seen the EPCM contractor assume the role of contract counterparty, we would suggest that the former position is more appropriate for the employer, since it will retain direct control of the supply chain arrangements, should relations with the EPCM contractor break down. Irrespective of the approach taken, the EPCM contractor will be responsible for the day-to-day administration of the works and supply contracts and the EPCM contract should describe the extent of the EPCM contractor's authority in this regard, with certain key rights being expressed as exercisable only with the consent of the employer.

The EPCM contractor will be allocated responsibility for overall management of the carrying out and completion of the works. This will include the coordination of the works and services being procured on the employer's behalf to achieve completion of the works in accordance with the project schedule, the project budget and to meet the required technical and performance specifications.

The construction management services will also typically include the management of health and safety at the site, program management and control, capital expenditure monitoring and control, the management of disputes between the employer, the works contractors and/or the suppliers, the establishment of quality assurance systems, the monitoring and certification of completion and handover of the relevant packages in accordance with the procedures agreed with the employer and the management of the remedying of defective works and/or services provided by other parties.

There is no international standard form template contract for the EPCM contracting solution, unlike for EPC turnkey or traditional build contracts.

EPCM contracting is essentially contracting for the delivery of professional services. There are numerous published standard forms of contract (e.g., the FIDIC White Book) that could be adopted for these purposes. A typical professional services appointment will, however, tend to lack the sophistication necessary to readily address many of the issues that arise or need to be considered in the context of EPCM infrastructure delivery (e.g., incentivization structures, performance guarantees, and performance liability regime). It is usual therefore that bespoke solutions are adopted by the parties.

The EPCM contract will provide for the EPCM contractor to be paid on a rates reimbursable basis. The rates should include a cost and overhead element only with the EPCM contractor's profit being recovered under a separate regime. Often employers will look for the EPCM contractor to warrant that the rates do not include any profit element and will retain rights of audit in respect of the same. Any profit disclosed or detected through audit will then be payable back to the employer on demand, or by means of contractual set-off.

Employers may require the EPCM contractor to guarantee that the aggregate level of the rates of the reimbursable element, which was estimated at the time of the contract signature for performance of the services necessary to achieve realization of the project, is correct. Where it can be established that the EPCM contractor failed to prepare the estimate in accordance with the level of skill and care required by the contract, the employer would have a breach of warranty claim against the EPCM contractor. The extent to which any such claim would provide the EPCM contractor with any real leverage in a material cost overrun scenario may, however, be open to question. It is usual that employers instead concentrate on detailed cost monitoring procedures aligned with early warning provisions, to identify cost overrun at a point at which the likely cause can be identified and mitigated.

Less usually, we have seen EPCM contractors in the mining sector accept a cap on the reimbursable element of their fee. While this looks attractive from an employer's point of view, the overrun may of course arise for reasons outside of the EPCM contractor's control. Employers may therefore be reluctant to restrict further payment at the point at which the EPCM contractor's assistance is needed the most.

The EPCM contractor's profit will usually be expressed as a fixed percentage of the estimated rates reimbursable element. This will not be subject to increase where the cost of the services increases beyond the estimated rates reimbursable element agreed at the contract signature. The availability of an increase in profit in these circumstances may act as a negative incentive to the control of cost overrun.

Most developing countries have tax regimes that seek to control, through taxation, the amount of investment in a development that does not become directly invested in the country (e.g., professional services fees). Withholding tax is the most common form of taxation that needs to be considered when structuring the construction development stage of any project.

It would be unusual for any EPCM contractor to bear the risk of withholding tax and, if it did, then it would simply become a "cost" to the project that would add to the overall project economics. It is important therefore for employers to give proper consideration to the structuring of construction contracting arrangements very early on in the procurement of an infrastructure project to obtain the early buy-in by the local tax authorities (either directly or through local advisers) to those arrangements.

One of the most common means of mitigating withholding tax exposure is to adopt a split "onshore" and "offshore" contract structure. This usually means that there will be two contracts, each entered into by a different EPCM contractor entity and each containing different scope of services. For example, there will usually be one contract for those services which may take place outside of the country in which the works are being delivered, payment for which may therefore be structured to avoid withholding tax. This contract will typically be entered into by a non-local EPCM contractor entity (the "offshore contract"). There will then be a further contract for those services that must be performed in the country in which the works are being delivered, such as the EPCM construction management services (because there must be personnel present on the ground in order to carry out the supervision), payment for which may be subject to the relevant local withholding tax regime. This contract will typically be entered into by a locally registered EPCM contractor entity (the "onshore contract").

The obvious risk to an employer with a split structure is that he is required to deal with two contractors, each with a separate scope of work and separate rights and obligations. It is important therefore that these contracts are well drafted and dovetail together.

The employer will usually look to limit its exposure to breach by the separate onshore and offshore contractors by putting in place further contractual arrangements that provide for the offshore EPCM contractor entity (or a suitable parent) providing a performance and financial guarantee (backed by indemnities and, possibly, suitable financial security) in respect of discharge by both the onshore and offshore entities of their respective and collective obligations. This guarantee (which could be wrapped into the offshore contract) is often referred to as an "umbrella agreement."

However, in jurisdictions where the tax authorities do not recognize this "split" due to the presence of the guarantee (or "wrap") provided by the umbrella agreement, then further careful consideration is required in the drafting of the onshore and offshore contracts in order to deal specifically with the above concerns.

Mark Berry
Partner
Norton Rose Fulbright LLP
London
UK

and

Matthew Hardwick
Partner
Norton Rose Fulbright LLP
London
UK

4.7 EPC versus EPCM

The EPC method is used most frequently where large, expensive projects are to be constructed within a sophisticated industrial environment where unique know-how, technologies and processes are typically used. Higher levels of risk, failures, and related damages appear where complicated systems are used.

The engineering, procurement, and installation or construction of the work are diverse activities that have to be managed and coordinated. Hence, high demands are placed on individual contractors. Only a contractor who is part of a large organization with adequate human and material resources can accomplish such a mission. It is appropriate to use the EPC method where the employer is not in possession of the know-how and resources (human and material) without which they could not do the work on their own.

An EPC contract may also be used where the work is not too demanding or unique but the employer is too inexperienced or lacks sufficient know-how to carry it out. They may be, for example, an investor using the EPC contract as a form of outsourcing or when working with vast public sector investments, such as the development of industrial capacities, power engineering, and the like.

By adopting EPC, the employer benefits from the fact that the resulting work passes into their ownership, say, as a turnkey item. This may lead to considerable savings of resources and capacities. Another substantial advantage on the employer's side is the employer's position in enforcing related contractual obligations. This allows claims arising from work (such as damage liability) to be made against one particular contractor rather than against a number of smaller individual contractors collectively.

Another argument in favour of EPC contracts is that the contractor has unique know-how and resources at their disposal which the employer does not have and cannot or does not want to acquire. This puts the contractor in a rather unique position versus the employer. The position is reflected in the intricate set-up of an EPC contract.

Despite being similar in name, the EPCM contract is different in concept from its EPC counterpart. The difference is that the EPCM contract delegates a substantial portion of the activities—and thus the related risks—to the employer. The contractor then enjoys a more "comfortable" position and reliable profit rate.

The EPCM contractor will provide the design and contractually agreed engineering. In matters of procurement (purchases) and construction/erection, however, the contractor will only provide their know-how in the form of management and coordination. They do not perform these activities themselves and let others be responsible for them, in contrast to EPC. Typically, the contractors and construction/installation companies enter into contracts directly with the employer. The EPCM contractor will manage and coordinate the procurement and construction/installation processes in full. They are then entitled to receive remuneration from the employer. This may include motivating bonuses, if any, generated, for example, by positive differences in terms of actual cost versus target price.

Such concepts imply a higher level of risk on the employer's side. The employer must manage contractual agendas and communicate with many different contractors responsible for individual parts of the work. In other words, the responsibility for various undertakings and misconduct and execution of (contractual and statutory) rights is shared by a variety of entities which makes the project even more demanding for the employer. It is further worth mentioning that a simple cost-plus principle may result in an increase in employer costs, such as contractor remuneration when determined on the basis of total costs for work completed. This may easily distract the contractor from taking efficient cost-minimising measures where the EPCM contractor remuneration system fails to be properly set up.

On the other hand, the EPCM model, if set up properly, may save time and money, mainly on behalf of a well-experienced employer. Costs may fall where the employer will directly carry out numerous activities that would otherwise be carried out by an

EPC contractor. As for reducing contractor risk, the EPCM may also help to avoid the contractor's risk surcharges, which are often seen in EPC projects.

Last but not least, the EPCM model may help to train the employer's own capacities when cooperating with a well-experienced contractor.

Offshore construction by Fernando Ortega (Qatar)

Introduction

The construction of offshore structures and pipelines present many issues that are not seen with the construction of structures onshore. Many of these issues the parties do not have control over. For example, the construction of an offshore facility will be highly dependent on the weather conditions. If there are strong weather conditions, the delivery of materials and personnel to the work front will be impacted and as result delays may incur.

Ground conditions where the intended site of the offshore structure will also provide issues that will not be in the parties' control. The seabed at the foot of the structure or where pipelines are to be laid may not be sufficiently clear from the geotechnical surveys. Additional data may be required in order to determine the existence of any cables, pipelines, shipwrecks, or any other hazard.

Further, if the offshore construction is delayed, this can have a greater impact in terms of time and money than the construction of a facility onshore. For example, many of the offshore projects require specialist vessels that are in short supply and have long lead times. If a project is in delay the vessel may not be available to compete the works when the vessel was originally required to perform since the vessel will more than likely be committed elsewhere.

In this chapter, we will provide a basic overview of the construction of offshore structures. We will also look at types of contracts involved and key issues within these contracts. Finally, we will consider other critical issues concerning the construction of offshore structures such as the transportation and installation of these structures, and their subsequent decommissioning.

Types of offshore structures

The following is a brief overview of some of the various types of offshore structures:

(a) Harbor structures – include quay or marginal wharves, finger piers, and trestle bridges. A quay or marginal wharf are used for the unloading and loading of containers. Finger piers are used for the transfer of petroleum products. Trestle bridges are built to provide access to loading platforms and wharves.
(b) River structures – include locks, low-level dams, overflow structures and flood walls. These structures are constructed "*in-the-wet*" using marine construction methods and equipment which allows key structural components to be fabricated in a yard and then transported and installed underwater.
(c) Coastal structures – include ocean outfalls and intakes (large-diameter reinforced concrete or steel pipelines that are laid in a trench out to the depth where the storm waves break (usually 10-20 m), breakwater structures, and offshore terminals (consist of a loading platform, two large breasting dolphins, and four mooring dolphins which are connected by catwalk structures).

(d) Offshore platforms (steel jackets) – installed in depths of water of 12 m to over 300 m. The structural components are the jacket (which is prefabricated onshore as a space frame, then transported to the site and seated on the seabed), piles (which are driven through the sleeves of the jacket and connected to the sleeves), and the deck.

(e) Concrete offshore platforms (gravity-based structures) – designed to be found at or just below the seafloor, and the gravity-based platform is usually constructed of reinforced and pre-stressed concrete.

(f) Permanent floating structures – intended to remaining floating during their service life and can be moored, relocated during service or they can self-propel. Examples of the floating structures include oil storage vessels, concrete vessels, floating bridges of concrete, floating piers, ferry slip docks, floating guide walls for navigation locks, semi-submersibles, barges, floating airfields, and large floating storage and production vessels.

(g) Structures for the development of offshore energy resources – these structures include single-point moorings, articulated columns or articulated loading platforms, subsea production templates, underwater oil storage vessels, cable arrays, moored buoys, offshore export and import terminals for LNG and LPG, offshore wind-power foundations, wave-power structures, tidal power stations, and barrier walls.

(h) Subsea pipelines – pipelines used for the transmission of petroleum products, gas, water, slurries, and effluents. The steel pipelines normally run from 75 mm up to 150 mm with occasional lines running 1800 mm, while the wall thickness will normally run from 10 to 75 mm.

(i) Subsea cables – communication cables laid across the seabed.

Environmental issues impacting offshore construction

The construction of offshore structures face unique environmental challenges not seen with the construction of onshore structures. The environmental conditions presented at the site offshore will dictate various issues. For example, the environment will impact:

(a) The terms the parties will entered into (i.e., force majeure, extension of time, allocation of risk, delivery);

(b) The type of the equipment used which will be dependent on the availability of certain vessels and pieces of equipment used for the construction of the structure;

(c) The time of the year to build the structure (i.e., construction in the Arctic Ocean can only facilitated certain times of the year);

(d) The transportation of the structure to intended site (i.e., the structure is prefabricated in a yard and then transported to site for installation);

(e) When the structure can be installed at the site; and

(f) Whether the structure can be installed at the site given to changes to the seabed floor.

The following are a few the environmental issues to consider when constructing a structure offshore:

(a) The distance of the construction site from the shore and the depth of water where the structure will be installed. Construction of an offshore structure could take place close to

the shore or a substantial distance away. If the construction site is considerable distance from the shore the installation of the structure will be required to be manned and operated with little to no dependency from resources based onshore. Further, the construction of an offshore structure could extend into the deep ocean (sometimes in depths of over 4,000 m) where the water will be dark, cold, and very unpleasant. This will require the use of specialized equipment such as a work submersible, remote-operated vehicles (ROVs), fiber optics, acoustic imaging, and special gases for divers.
(b) The amount of hydrostatic pressure exerted on structures submersed in water.
(c) The temperature of the water can change tremendously from the surface to a lower depth. Surface temperatures can vary around the world from a low of -2°C (28°F) to a high of 32°C (90°F), and can decrease rapidly with lower depths.
(d) The impact of seawater on steel and concrete. Seawater's dominate chemical characteristic is its dissolved salts that contains sodium, magnesium, chloride, and sulphate. These act to reduce the protective oxidized coatings that form on steel and produce corrosion. Magnesium and sulphates can also attack concrete, which will cause its disintegration.
(e) The impact of currents on construction operations. Currents influence the movement of vessels and floating structures. They also change the characteristics of waves and can exert horizontal pressure against structures. Currents can also create eddy patterns that will have an effect to the sea floor where the structure is standing (in many cases erode the sea floor around the base of the structure).
(f) Waves impact on floating vessels and/or structure. This is the most obvious concern for offshore construction. The impact of waves is the primary cause of downtime and lowered operating efficiency.
(g) Winds and storms also impact the working program of the construction of the offshore structure. Hurricanes, typhoons, cyclones, and severe storms force operations to stop and move equipment and personnel off site.
(h) The detection and impact of sea ice and icebergs in the Arctic Ocean and the Sub-Arctic oceans.
(i) The impact of earthquakes and tsunamis on structures installed. Earthquakes can change the conditions of the seabed and generate landslides where the structure is located.
(j) The impact of climate change (global warming) on sea level and ocean currents on the structure.

Overview of offshore construction contracts

There are number of standard forms of contract used in the construction of offshore structures and pipelines. It is not uncommon to find bespoke contracts drafted for specific projects.

Some contracts are straight forward in their purpose, such as the construction of a vessel to be used as part of an offshore structure. However, with other projects, a contractor will find itself doing more than building the structure onshore then installing it offshore. In this case, a standard form onshore contract (such as FIDIC) will be used and modified to complete the project.

Another example would be the use of vessels for offshore. In the case of a floating, production, storage and offloading (FPSO) vessel, or a jack-up vessel/rig, will sometimes be contracted using amended FIDIC or LOGIC forms.

Below, we provide a basic overview of standard forms of contract used in offshore construction:

(a) FIDIC forms of contract
    (i) The FIDIC forms of contract have been in use for the construction of offshore structures for more than 50 years. They are designed to be used for engineering projects, and commonly used for offshore power generation and other permanent offshore installations. They are also used for the construction and installation of plants on a vessel.
    (ii) The FIDIC form used most often in offshore construction is the FIDIC conditions of contract for EPC/turnkey projects (commonly known as the FIDIC Silver Book). The FIDIC Silver Book is normally amended for the specific project through particular conditions of contract that are negotiated and drafted by the parties.
    (iii) The FIDIC Silver Book, or in general EPC contracts, require a contractor to perform the engineering, procurement and construction of a project. Usually in offshore construction projects, a project will not be handed over until it is installed and/or commissioned. The contract will normally be referred to as EPIC (engineering, procurement, installation, and commissioning), EPCI (engineering, procurement, construction, and installation), or EPCIC (engineering, procurement, construction, installation, and commissioning). For each, the contractor will have the same obligations as a contractor would under a normal EPC contract. However, the difference is when the contractor will be discharged from its obligations. For an EPCI/EPIC/EPCIC, the contractor will be discharged once the project has been installed and/or commissioned. It is typical to see the FIDIC Silver Book be modified to spell out this arrangement.

(b) LOGIC form
    (i) The leading oil and gas industry competitiveness (LOGIC) suite of contracts are predominately used in the O&G industry.
    (ii) The LOGIC forms that apply to the offshore construction are as follows:
        (A) General conditions of contract for construction – intended for the construction of major projects and topside works;
        (B) Marine construction edition – intended for pipe-laying works, offshore installation, and subsea construction;
        (C) Mobile drilling rigs – intended for the hire of rigs on a day work basis;
        (D) Services (offshore) – intended to apply to offshore services;
        (E) Supply of major Items of plant and equipment – intended for the purchase of plant and equipment for offshore use;
        (F) Well service edition – intended for well engineering works.

(c) NEC 4 suite of contracts
    (i) The new engineering contract (NEC) suite of contracts are used for large, high-risk, and complicated projects such as the London 2012 Olympic and Paralympic Games. The NEC contracts are not commonly used in the construction of offshore structures. However, the recent introduction of the new suite of contracts which were developed for international use are suitable for a full array of works including the construction of offshore structures.

(d) SAJ form
   (i) The Shipbuilders' Association of Japan (SAJ) form of contract was published in 1974 and is the most commonly used contract form for shipbuilding. The SAJ form is consider to be favorable to the ship builder and is usually revised by the owner.
(e) NEWBUILDCON form
   (i) The NEWBUILDCON form is a ship-building contract that is published by the Baltic and International Maritime Council (BIMCO). It is used as a standard form by the shipping industry and provides the necessary legal framework while leaving the technical specifications separate from the main contract. If any technical issues that are dealt within the main contract, they are there for the purpose of their legal implications to the main contract.
(f) CMAC form
   (i) In 2011, the China Maritime Arbitration Commission (CMAC) published a standard form contract entitled as the "*CMAC Standard Newbuilding Contract (Shanghai Form),*" which was intended for ships that are built in China by Chinese companies for the purchase by international buyers.
(g) AWES form
   (i) The AWES Form is a shipbuilding standard contract adopted by the Association of European Shipbuilders and Shiprepairers. The latest version of the AWES form was published in 1999 and is considered to be shipbuilder friendly. It is often subject to heavy revision by the owner.
(h) The Norwegian 2000 form
   (i) In 2000, the Norwegian Shipowners' Association and the Norwegian Shipbuilders' Association adopted the Norwegian Shipbuilding Contract 2000 (commonly known as the Norwegian 2000 Form) as a shipbuilding contract to be used by the international community. It was drafted in English and considered user-friendly.

Key issues with offshore construction contracts

Offshore construction contracts vary considerably and in most cases are modified to fit the specific project. There is no industry standard. Below, we briefly discuss some key issues involving these offshore construction contracts.

FEED design risk

Typically in the construction of offshore structures, a preliminary design in the form of a FEED (front-end engineering design) will be submitted by the owner to the contractor, which the contractor will be obligated to complete. The owner does not guarantee the FEED will be accurate since it only contains estimates and speculations. It is the responsibility of the contractor to correct the FEED defects and provide for a final design that is fit for purpose.

If the contractor agrees to a lump sum price and a delivery schedule for performance of the final design, the contractor will be responsible for completing this work without additional time and/or compensation.

Variations

All standard forms contain provisions designed to deal with variations or changes. Normally, during the construction of an offshore project there will be numerous changes that occur. For example, the change to the data concerning the environmental conditions frequently occurs on a project. As a result, variations will be expected and made since environmental conditions are out of the parties control and will impact the work program and costs to the project.

Any change to the construction of offshore structures can be very complex. For example, a variation to the design can substantially rework the entire schedule. A contractor may refuse to make such change since the scale of the costs and disruption will exceed what is permitted under the contract.

What constitutes a variation or whether variation can be made will depend on the terms of the contract. Parties to the contract are not allowed to make unilateral changes to the contract and consent will be required from all parties.

Finally, in some offshore construction contracts will contain a variation clause that will allow an owner to insist that the change in the work be performed by the contractor without first agreeing to the changes to the contract price or considering the impact the changes will have on the contractor's liability.

Delivery

Many issues present themselves during the handover of an offshore facility that are not present with the handover of an onshore facility. One main issue is the subsequent final completion and rectification of defects.

With an offshore facility, the contractor and the structure are exposed to environmental conditions offshore while finalising and/or rectifying any defects. If handover is to take place at a shipyard, it may be necessary to complete or rectify any defects while in transit to the intended site, at the intended site, or at another shipyard. If the handover is to take place at the intended site, then any completion or rectification of defects will be done at the offshore site.

Depending on the location of the offshore structure, the contractor could potentially be exposed to harsh conditions in order to complete and/or rectify any defects. This may cause delays and increase the costs to the contractor.

Force majeure

Force majeure provisions in offshore construction contracts are essential for the contractor to have. It is not uncommon for a force majeure–related event occurring during the construction of an offshore facility. Contractors will fight to have such provision in the contract and defined as broadly as possible since the consequences will be to pay liquidated damages for each day of delay to complete the project.

Force majeure is a term derived from the French legal system. It is a concept that is understood as a major disruption due to natural events (act of God) or human interventions such as wars or embargoes.

Offshore construction contracts will normally identify and/or include a long list of force majeure events which the parties agree are force majeure events. If an event were to occur to be considered force majeure, a contractor would be justified in an extension of time for completion of the project.

The party (usually the contractor) who claims the extension of time as a result of a force majeure event, will have the burden of proof that the event meets the requirements under the force majeure provision. Normally that would include for the contractor to prove the following:

(a) The force majeure event caused the delay;
(b) The contractor complied with the notice provisions in the contract;
(c) The force majeure event was beyond the contractor's (or, in some cases, the subcontractor) control;
(d) The contractor could not have avoided or mitigated the force majeure event; and
(e) At the time of contracting, the parties could not have foreseen the Force Majeure event.

Termination

In all forms of offshore construction contracts there are express provisions to permit either party to terminate the contract. These contracts will also set out the consequences of terminating the contract.

The thing to note with termination under offshore construction contracts, termination does not bring an end to all contractual obligations for a contractor. A contractor may be required to carry out other obligations under the contract. For example, a contractor may still be obligated to deliver the structure to a specific location (i.e. another shipyard), or at the site of installation in order for the owner to gain possession of the structure. This obligation as well as others will be spelled out in the contract as intending to survive termination.

The offshore construction contract will survive after termination but in a modified form.

Dispute resolution

Contracts for offshore construction will normally contain dispute resolution provisions. Typically, the preferred method used to resolve offshore construction disputes is arbitration. The place of arbitration and the institution used to govern the arbitration is usually specific to the type of contract used. For example, the FIDIC form of contracts does not define the place of arbitration but provides for the institution to be the International Chamber of Commerce's International Court of Arbitration (ICC), while the NEWBUILDCON form provides for the place of arbitration to be London and the institution to be the London Maritime Arbitrators Association (LMAA). In practice, the parties will usually modify these provisions.

Further, some offshore construction contracts may provide for preconditions to arbitration which will include but not limited to expert determination, mediation and/or dispute adjudication board (DAB). In some cases, the parties will modify or delete these preconditions.

Transporation

Once a structure to be used offshore is constructed in a shipyard, the next step in the process is to transport the structure to the intended site. The risks involved with this process is usually set out in the underlining contract between the owner and the contractor.

The transportation of the structure will be either by wet or dry tow. This process can be a very hazardous activity depending on where the site is located. Whether the installation is a fixed or floating platform, the transportation of the installation will be performed by a transportation contractor employed by the contractor or the owner (i.e., the party who is responsible for the transportation and/or installation of the structure).

The risk of loss and damage during transportation will depend on which party is providing such services. For example, under the LOGIC form, if the contractor is responsible for such services it will be responsible for the removal of any wreckage if damage occurs. If the owner is providing such services then the risk of loss and damage will fall between the owner and its subcontractor.

The risk of delay to the completion of the works as a result of the failure to timely transport the installation may be due to the acts of the subcontractor or due to a force majeure event. If the cause is the former, the risk of loss will more than likely remain with the contractor.

Installation

Installation of a structure or pipeline can be a challenging undertaking. There are many operational risks and uncertainties that will have an impact as to whether a structure or pipeline will be properly installed and installed on time. For example, whether the structure or pipeline is suitable for the site in order to be properly installed, and whether the conditions at the site and/or the seabed are what they were previously expected.

Parties will agree to a work program that will attempt to identify when conditions will be possible for installation. Ideally, installation operations require good weather and calm seas. However, in some places this is not the case (e.g., the Arctic Ocean where temperatures can be too extreme for most of the year). Contingencies in the contract should be made to take into account of the potential delays stemming from possible delay in transportation and/or unexpected changes to conditions at the intended site. In most cases, the contractor will be responsible for the delay and liquidated damages may be imposed.

Ground conditions may have an impact on installation as well. When the time comes to install the structure, the conditions at the site could have changed from previously surveyed. When compared to the construction of a project onshore the difficulty is that the site is under water and not obvious to the naked eye (in some cases under significant depths of water). Further, the site may have changed due to natural occurrences (such as an earthquake) and/or works performed by other contractors.

In most cases, the contractor and its specialist subcontractor will remain liable to the owner if the installation does not occur in accordance with contractual requirements even though there has been a change in circumstances. The contractor and the subcontractor are responsible to make themselves acquainted of the site and/or perform investigations of the site for any conditions that may impact the installation of the structure or pipeline. A contractor (and its specialist subcontractor) may be entitled to a variation to its scope of work for unexpected site conditions if the changes were unforeseen. However, this may not indemnify the contractor (and its specialist subcontractor) if the changes could have been anticipated by a careful reading of the available data and/or the contractor undertaking such installation had previous experience of installing the structure or pipeline in similar circumstances.

Decommissioning

The decommissioning of offshore structures can take several years to complete. The costs for decommissioning can be extremely high. The key with decommissioning is planning ahead and selecting the best decommissioning option. This is done through a balance of the following factors:

(a) Environment (land, sea, and air)
(b) Technical feasibility
(c) Cost
(d) Health and safety
(e) Political sentiment

Regulatory framework for decommissioning

The regulatory framework for the decommissioning of an offshore structure or pipeline is more complex than the decommissioning of an onshore structure. The decommissioning of an onshore structure is normally governed by the national or domestic law where the structure is located, and by a host government instrument (when applicable).

For offshore structures and pipelines, there are various types of regulatory frameworks that will determine how the structure or pipeline will be decommissioned. To properly determine the legal obligations for the decommissioning of an offshore structure or pipeline in a particular jurisdiction, a party will have to review all of the following:

(a) Host government instrument (if applicable)
(b) International conventions
(c) Regional conventions
(d) National law

Host government instrument

A host government may regulate the decommissioning of an offshore structure by contract. This is usually done through a production sharing agreement (PSA) or in some circumstances by a service agreement.

PSAs are used in the oil and gas industry, and are their own source of law and govern the petroleum operations from beginning to end. Under earlier PSAs, the contractor would build and own the facilities and then ownership of the facilities would gradually shift to the government through the process of cost recovery from any oil produced. Normally, by the end of the PSA, the government would own the facilities and therefore would be responsible for the costs of decommissioning. More recent PSAs now include provisions requiring the contractor to submit a decommissioning plan and the setting aside of funds for the decommissioning of the structure.

International conventions

There are international conventions and guidelines that apply to the decommissioning of offshore structures and pipelines. Whether the international convention applies will depend on the jurisdiction where the structure or pipeline is located has ratified the convention.

The most notable of the international conventions and guidelines are:

(a) The 1958 Geneva Convention on the Continental Shelf – came into force long before deep-sea structures were ever installed and it calls for the complete removal of all marine-based structures.
(b) The UN Convention on the Law of the Seas 1982 (UNCLOS) – provides for the removal of any installation or structure in order to ensure safety of navigation.
(c) London (Dumping) Convention – the 1972 Convention on the Prevention of Marine Pollution by Dumping of Wastes and Other Matter (London Dumping Convention) and the subsequent 1996 protocol provide specific guidance for different classes of waste, which includes offshore platforms and other man-made waste. The London Dumping Convention does not provide whether the abandonment of pipelines falls under this convention.
(d) International Maritime Organization (IMO) guidelines – in 1989, the IMO issued the IMO Guidelines and Standards for the Removal of Offshore Installations and Structures on the Continental Shelf and in the Exclusive Economic Zone (IMO guidelines). The IMO guidelines sets the standard and guidelines for the removal of offshore installations. They are not binding on states and only serve as a recommendation. The IMO guidelines recommend:
   (i) The complete removal of all abandoned or disused installation or structures in waters less than 75 m and weighing less than 4,000 tons;
   (ii) Structures in deeper waters can be partially removed leaving 55 m of clear water column for safe navigation; and
   (iii) All abandoned or disused installations or structures installed on or after January 1, 1998 that are standing in less than 100 m of water and weighing less than 4,000 tons must be removed completely.

Regional conventions

There are a number of regional conventions that govern the decommissioning of offshore structures and pipelines. The following is a brief list of the regional conventions:

(a) The North Sea – OSPAR Convention;
(b) Mediterranean – Barcelona Convention;
(c) Persian Gulf – Kuwait Convention;
(d) Red Sea and Gulf of Aden – Jeddah Convention;
(e) Black Sea – Black Sea Convention; and
(f) West Africa – Abidjan Convention.

By way of an example of a regional convention, in 1998 the Convention for the Protection of the Marine Environment of the North-East Atlantic (OSPAR Convention) came into force covering the North Sea and replaced the 1972 Oslo Convention on dumping from ships and the 1974 Paris Convention on discharges from land to protect the marine environment of the Northeast Atlantic from pollution.

The work carried out under the OSPAR Convention is made up of 16 contracting states (the OSPAR Commission): Belgium, Denmark, the European Union, Finland, France, Germany, Iceland, Ireland, Luxembourg, the Netherlands, Norway, Portugal, Spain, Sweden, Switzerland, and the United Kingdom. In 1999, the OSPAR Commission issued Decision 98/3, which applies to the disposal of disused offshore installations but not pipelines.

The Decision 98/3 provides:

(a) A general prohibition of dumping, and the leaving wholly or partly in place, of disused offshore installations within the maritime area;
(b) Complete removal of all steel installations put in place after February 9, 1999;
(c) An assessment to be made whether exceptions be made for installations with footings of large steal jackets weighing over 10,000 tons and concrete gravity–based installations can be removed; and
(d) Exceptions can be considered for structures with structural damage or deterioration that would prevent the removal of the structure.

National law

Decommissioning offshore is usually govern at the national or federal government level since it will deal with the nation's territorial waters and exclusive economic zone, and international treaty obligations.

The United States and the United Kingdom have extensive national or domestic laws that govern decommissioning of offshore structures. This is mainly driven from the extensive demand for decommissioning of offshore oil and gas installations in the Gulf of Mexico and the North Sea, respectively.

Many other countries around the world do not have laws in place that govern decommissioning of offshore structures and pipelines. There are a few countries that do have national laws or guidelines for decommissioning offshore structures (e.g., United Arab Emirates and Nigeria), however, these laws have not been tested fully since the demand for decommissioning is very low.

Fernando Ortega
Legal Consultant, DWF (Middle East) LLP

Bibliography

Offshore Book Oil & Gas, 3rd edition May 2014, available at www.offshoreenergy.dk.

Tim Martin, *Decommissioning of International Petroleum Facilities: Evolving Standards & Key Issues*, International Energy Law Course, RMMLF Mineral Law Series, available at: http://timmartin.ca/wp-content/uploads/2016/02/Decommissioning-of-Int-Petroleum-Facilities-Martin2004.pdf (accessed December 12, 2017).

Mohamed A El-Reedy, Ph.D., *Offshore Structures: Design, Construction and Maintenance*, Gulf Professional Publishing, 2012.

Adam Constable, QC, *Keating on Offshore Construction and Marine Engineering Contracts*, Sweet & Maxwell, September 2015.

Peter Roberts, *Oil & Gas Contracts: Principles & Practice*, Sweet & Maxwell, July 2016.

Stuart Beadnall and Simon Moore, *Offshore Construction: Law and Practice*, Informa Law from Routledge, June 2016.

Ben C Gerwick, Jr, *Construction of Marine and Offshore Structures*, CRC Press, 3rd Edition, 2007.

Marc Hammerson, *Oil and Gas Decommissioning: Law, Policy and Comparative Practice*, Globe Law and Business, 2nd edition, July 2016.

Peter Cameron, *Decommissioning of Oil & Gas Installations: The Legal and Contractual Issues*, (Research Paper for Association of International Petroleum Negotiators (AIPN)), Dundee, Scotland 1998.

OSPAR Convention – Convention for the Protection of the Marine Environment of the North-East Atlantic, available at: https://www.ospar.org/convention (accessed December 12, 2017).

Geneva Convention on the Continental Shelf 1958, available at: https://treaties.un.org/pages/ViewDetails.aspx?src=TREATY&mtdsg_no=XXI-4&chapter=21&lang=en (accessed December 12, 2017).

London Convention on the Prevention of Marine Pollution by the Dumping of Wastes and Other Matter, available at: http://www.imo.org/en/About/Conventions/ListOfConventions/Pages/Convention-on-the-Prevention-of-Marine-Pollution-by-Dumping-of-Wastes-and-Other-Matter.aspx (accessed December 12, 2017).

UN Convention on the Law of the Sea 1982, available at: http://www.un.org/depts/los/convention_agreements/texts/unclos/unclos_e.pdf (accessed December 12, 2017).

IMO Guidelines and Standards for the Removal of Offshore Installations and Structures on the Continental Shelf and Exclusive Economic Zone, available at: https://cil.nus.edu.sg/rp/il/pdf/1989%20IMO%20Resolution%20A.%20672%20(16)-pdf.pdf (accessed December 12, 2017).

Abidjan Convention – Abidjan Convention for Co-Operation in the Protection and Development of the Marine and Coastal Environment of the West and Central African Region, available at: http://abidjanconvention.org/index.php?option=com_content&view=article&id=100&Itemid=200&lang=en (accessed December 12, 2017).

Barcelona Convention – Convention for the Protection of the Marine Environment and the Coastal Region of the Mediterranean, available at: http://www.ypeka.gr/LinkClick.aspx?fileticket=30r%2B7BeaSOo%3D&tabid=406&language=el-GR (accessed December 12, 2017).

Kuwait Convention – Kuwait Regional Convention for Cooperation on the Protection of the Marine Environment from Pollution, available at: http://www.ropme.org/1_KAP_LEGAL_EN.clx (accessed December 12, 2017).

Jeddah Convention – The Regional Convention for the Conservation of the Red Sea and Gulf of Aden Environment, available at: http://www.persga.org/Documents/Doc_62_20090211112825.pdf (accessed December 12, 2017).

Black Sea Convention – The Convention on the Protection of the Black Sea Against Pollution, available at: http://www.blacksea-commission.org/_convention.asp (accessed December 12,

References

ICC (2012). *International Court of Arbitration Bulletin*, 23(2).

Loots, P. and Henchie N. *Worlds Apart: EPC and EPCM Contracts: Risk issues and allocation*. Online. Available at: http://m.mayerbrown.com (accessed 15 May 2013).

Further reading

Cushman, R. F and Loulakis, M.C. (2001). *Design-Build Contracting Handbook*. Aspen Publisher, New York.

FIDIC (2000). *The FIDIC Contracts Guide* (1st Edition). FIDIC, Lausanne.

FIDIC (2011). *FIDIC Procurement Procedures Guide* (1st Edition). FIDIC, Lausanne.

Greenhalgh, B. (2013). *Introduction to Estimating for Construction*. Routledge, London.

Huse, J.A. (2002). *Understanding and Negotiating Turnkey and EPC Contracts*. Sweet and Maxwell, London.

Jaeger, A.V. and Hök, G.S. (2010). *FIDIC: A Guide for Practitioners*. Springer Verlag, Berlin.

Klee, L., Ručka, O., and Nevřalová, H. (2013). *Specifika výstavbových projektů EPC a EPCM. Obchodní právo (Commercial Law)* 9/2013.

Murdoch, J.R. and Hughes, W. (2008). *Construction Contracts: Law and Management*. Taylor & Francis, New York.

Venoit, W.K. (2009). *International Construction Law: A Guide for Cross-Border Transactions and Legal Disputes*. ABA Publishing, Chicago.

5 Unification and Standardization in International Construction

5.1 Unification of contracts

All fields of human activity undergo natural unification and harmonization over time. Following successful unification, business negotiations become easier and cheaper, communication and management are simpler and distrust vanishes. Complications and disputes can then be settled with less effort, especially in international transactions.

In business, in general (and in construction, in particular), this issue is more complicated than anywhere else. In the past, construction used to be local by nature as an industry with local contractors and employers devising and implementing habitual rules that were rigid and difficult to alter or unify.

5.2 Unification per law, principles, and sample documents

Contractual relationships are subject to unification at three levels:

- Law;
- Principles;
- Sample documents.

5.2.1 Unification per law

Parties intending to enter into cross-border contractual relationships have a general freedom to choose the law that will govern their contract. A mandatory provision of law (i.e., the governing law) will prevail over a private choice of law with which it is in conflict. In general, if there is no choice of law available to the parties to a particular contract and the contractual relationship contains an international element, the regulations of private international law will have to be considered in finding the

---

International Construction Contract Law, Second Edition. Lukas Klee.
© 2018 John Wiley & Sons Ltd. Published 2018 by John Wiley & Sons Ltd.

relevant governing law. Choice of law conflicts are complex and difficult to resolve. For this reason it is advisable to select the governing (applicable) law *before* entering into a contract. Failure to do so could lead to unexpected outcomes or unexpected shifts in risk allocation because of unforeseen mandatory provisions of substantive or procedural law.

There is no particular regulation in private international law applicable to international contracts for works. By way of comparison, contracts for sale of goods, for example, fall under the *United Nations Convention on Contracts for the International Sale of Goods* (CISG).

The Convention on the Law Applicable to Contractual Obligations of June 19, 1980 ("the Rome Convention") became crucial for contractual obligations with international elements by creating a common choice of law system for contracts within the European Union. The Rome Convention was replaced by Regulation (EC) No. 593/2008 of the European Parliament and Council by way of *The Convention on the Law Applicable to Contractual Obligations* of June 17, 2008 ("Rome I") and by the Regulation (EC) No. 864/2007 of the European Parliament and Council on July 11, 2007 by way of *The Convention on the Law Applicable to Non-Contractual Obligations* ("Rome II"). Rome I, Rome II, Rome Convention (Article 3/1) and international private law respect the choice of law principle.

If there is no choice of law or if the choice of law is invalid, the applicable law will usually be the law of the state where:

(a) the works are executed;
(b) the contract was concluded;
(c) the contractor's business is registered; or
(d) the litigation or arbitration takes place.

The most significant example of the unification of law is the above-mentioned CISG, which, unless expressly excluded by contract, is automatically applicable to contracts for cross-border sales of goods in EU member countries.

5.2.2 Unification per principles

As a rule, the governing law will be agreed upon by the contracting parties to an international construction project. A situation, dispute, or particular problem without any clearly defined solution either in the contract or in the governing law can further be encountered. Business usage and general principles of law will often have to be used where there is a gap in the contract and/or governing law.

In terms of unification of principles, the most significant are the *UNIDROIT Principles of International Commercial Contracts* and *The Principles of European Contract Law*. These principles are a set of model rules drawn up by leading contract law academics in Europe. *The Principles of European Contract Law* are based on the concept of a uniform European contract law system and were created by the Commission on European Contract Law (the Lando Commission). The latest attempts are *The Definitions and Model Rules of European Private Law* or the *Draft Common Frame of Reference* (DCFR) prepared by the Study Group on a European Civil Code and the Research Group on EC Private Law (Acquis Group) and based in part on a revised version of the *Principles of European Contract Law*.

The Unidroit Principles have been referred to in a significant number of publicly reported international arbitrations (Charrett, 2013).

It should further be mentioned that unification is also imposed by legislative and quasi-legislative activities, treaties, international conventions, economic, and political unions. Furthermore, individual usages and customs in the construction business that are generalized in principles deserve a separate subcategory within the scope of *lex mercatoria* called *lex constructionis*. The *lex constructionis* principles come from the general *lex mercatoria* principles with necessary modifications due to construction specifics, see Section 5.10.

5.2.3 Unification per sample documents

Unification in the field of sample documents is represented by rules of trade such as the International Commercial Terms ("INCOTERMS") and sample forms of contracts published by FIDIC and many others.

5.2.4 INCOTERMS

INCOTERMS are a set of international rules for modes of transport expressed by a series of three-letter trade terms related to common contractual sales practices. INCOTERMS came into being in Paris in 1936. They were issued by the International Chamber of Commerce to avoid problems in connection with the nature and differences between business codes in different countries. The eighth edition of the INCOTERMS (2010) was reduced to 11 rules and came into effect on January 1, 2011.

The INCOTERMS rules are intended to clearly communicate the duties, costs, and risks associated with the transportation and delivery of goods. They also define where and how the goods are to be transported, and allocate responsibility to the parties. For example, Who bears the loading costs? Who is in charge of transportation? Who is responsible for damage and how and when they are to be paid? Who is to insure? Who is to pay customs and other duties? Who is to unload the goods and pay for them?

The FIDIC forms of contract define the most significant terms to be used in international construction contracts. Attention will be paid to the FIDIC forms in respective sections of this book. Another sample form receiving increasing attention in recent years is known by its abbreviated name of the NEC (the New Engineering Contract). For further details of the NEC, see Chapter 13.

Resolving construction claims under investment treaty arbitration by Fernando Ortega (Qatar)

Many contractors are not aware that as a contractor operating in a foreign jurisdiction you may have the right to pursue a claim (such as wrongful termination or non-payment) under a bilateral investment treaty (BIT). This is regardless if the construction/engineering contract requires for any claims to be settled through the local court of the host state.

In many BITs, a provision will exist where a contractor can elevate a breach of contract claim to the international treaty level as a breach of the investment treaty. Contractors have been slow to consider using this option. However, in recent years, a number of investment treaty claims have been brought by contractors arising out of construction projects.

In this article, we will review what is a BIT and discuss how a contractor can elevate its claim to the international treaty level and bypass any contractual dispute resolution provisions to resolve the claim. We will also discuss additional considerations for bring such claim to the international treaty level.

What is a BIT?

A bilateral investment treaty, or BIT, is an investment treaty in which two states agree to grant certain protections to investments made by an investor of the other state. Normally, these protections will include:

- Protection from expropriation/nationalization;
- Compensation for losses as result of war, armed conflict, a state of national emergency, revolt, insurrection, riot, and other similar situations in the host state;
- Host state will treat investments made by investors in a manner that is fair and equitable compared to investors from other states or the host state's citizens/companies (also known as fair and equitable treatment (FET) and national treatment);
- Repatriation of investments and earnings;
- Full protection and security of investments;
- Host state's observance of contractual obligations entered into with the investor;
- Host state provides treatment to an investor at least favorable as the best treatment afforded to an investor from a third state; and
- Commencement of dispute resolution proceedings against the host state or its entity when a protection has been violated under the BIT.

This is not a complete list of protections afforded to an investor under a BIT. Each BIT is different, however, a majority of the protections identified above will be present in most BITs around the world.

Requirements to bring a claim

Under a BIT, there are three (3) main requirements for a contractor to meet in order to bring a claim, namely:

1. The contractor must qualify as an investor as defined under the relevant BIT. In a majority of BITs, in order to qualify as an investor the contractor must be constituted or incorporated under the laws of the contracting state to the BIT.

2. The contract entered into between the contractor and the host state or its entity must qualify as an investment as defined under the relevant BIT and/or international law. Construction/engineering contracts have been established by BIT arbitral tribunals to qualify as investments under international law. Examples of construction/engineering works that have been established as qualifying investments include renovation works; the construction of a mosque, public roads, bridges, airport terminals, hotels, and other infrastructure projects; and dredging operations.
3. The host state or its entity must have violated a protection as set out under the relevant BIT. Above we identified certain protections usually contained in a BIT. However, as we will discuss further below, one of the protections afforded to a contractor will be that a host state or its entity will be required to observe any obligation that it has entered into with a contractor. If a host state or its entity violate this protection, it may be possible for a contractor to have the breach of this obligation be settled under the dispute resolution mechanism of the BIT, which will include international arbitration.

Bring a contractual claim under a BIT

A BIT may permit a contractor the opportunity to elevate its claim under a construction/engineering contract to the international treaty level if the BIT contains a provision called an umbrella clause. An umbrella clause will provide that a host state will observe any obligation it enters into with respect to any investment made by an investor from the other contracting state. If a host state or its entity fails to observe and/or breaches the obligation, the investor may seek to settle the breach through the dispute resolution mechanism contained in the BIT. This is regardless if the contract between the investor and the host state or its entity contains a dispute resolution provision or a forum selection clause.

Recent ICSID (The International Centre for Settlement of Investment Disputes) decisions have established that an arbitral tribunal constituted under the relevant BIT will have jurisdiction to hear and decide such claims if the relevant BIT contains an umbrella clause. This is despite the construction/engineering contract containing a local court or arbitration provision.

A typical example of an umbrella clause can be found at Article 2(2) of the United Kingdom-Turkmenistan BIT, which states:

> "Either Contracting Party shall observe any obligation it, may have entered into with regard to investments of nationals or companies of the other Contracting Party."

Further, the use of the umbrella clause can also be beneficial to a contractor since it will allow the contractor access to the dispute resolution mechanism contained within a BIT. Typically, a BIT will provide a contractor options to submit the dispute for settlement including the local competent court of the host State, the ICSID, or an ad hoc arbitral tribunal.

Other considerations for elevating a contractual claim

In addition to the above, there are other considerations for bring a claim under a BIT. These include:

- The opportunity to bypass a contractual requirement for claims to be resolved by a local court in the host state. Whether if possible will depend on the language of the BIT.
- The opportunity to bring parallel proceedings (under the construction/engineering contract and the BIT), which can exert additional pressure on the host state or its entity to honor its obligations under the construction/engineering contract.
- Provide additional leverage over a host state or its entity in negotiations for settlement since the host state will want to avoid the potential negative public exposure BIT arbitration may bring. This may also impact the relationship the host state may be seeking to develop with financial institutions (such as the World Bank and Export Credit Agencies), which could possibly put any financing of future projects in danger.
- If a contractor decides to submit a dispute for settlement to ICSID, the contractor will have the benefit of enforcing the arbitral award under the enforcement regime of the ICSID convention. An ICSID award is directly enforceable with all Contracting States to the ICSID convention. The contracting state must recognized the award as if it were a final judgment from its own national courts.

Fernando Ortega
Legal Consultant, DWF (Middle East) LLP

5.3 Lenders and their influence on unification

5.3.1 European union funds

The drive of international developers to invest in international construction projects using domestic or international construction companies and the expansion of the European Union (the EU) are the main reasons why the FIDIC forms of contract continue to spread across Central and Eastern Europe. The EU requires the use of the well-established sample forms of contract as a pre-condition for potential financing of jointly financed projects. This condition first appeared within structural funds such as the Instrument for Structural Policies for Pre-Accession (ISPA). ISPA found its focal point in financing infrastructure projects in the fields of environment and transport. Its aim was to simplify the implementation of the *acquis communautaire* (a law of the EU) in the candidate countries during the period from 2000 up to their membership to the EU by making contributions to sustainable development in these countries.

5.3.2 The European Investment Bank (EIB)

Another impetus for the use of FIDIC forms was provided by the European Investment Bank's requirement to use these forms in the projects financed by it. Established in 1958 by the Treaty of Rome, the European Investment Bank (EIB) is an EU institution set up to provide credit to public and private entities. The money lent is intended for projects that will benefit Europe, keep EU regions in cohesion, support small- and medium-sized businesses, protect the environment, support research and development, improve transport, and assist the energy industry.

The EIB is a non-profit bank and its activities aim to achieve political objectives and provide long-term credits for capital investment projects (mainly to cover long-term activities). The EIB does not, however, provide subsidies. Owned by the EU member states, the EIB cannot lend more than 50% of the total project costs. The projects that are financed are meticulously selected and must meet strict criteria. The EIB also fosters sustainable development in potential candidate countries, in EU neighbor states and in other partner countries.

5.3.3 The European Bank for Reconstruction and Development (EBRD)

The European Bank for Reconstruction and Development ("EBRD") provides project financing for banks, industry and businesses, new ventures and investments in existing companies. The EBRD also works with publicly owned companies. The EBRD provides loan and equity finance, guarantees, leasing facilities, and trade finance. Typically the EBRD funds up to 35% of total project costs.

The bank invests only in projects that would not otherwise attract financing on similar terms. The EBRD is committed to undertaking operations throughout the region and has engaged in projects in each country where it has a presence. To coordinate local activities, the EBRD has established resident offices in all of these countries.

The EBRD is composed of multinational staff and an in-house Board of Directors representing the shareholders (64 countries plus the EU and the EIB).

The EBRD develops partnerships with local and international business and the investment community. The bank acts in close cooperation with all members, public and private entities, and all multilateral institutions concerned with the economic development of, and investment in, countries from central Europe to central Asia. These include the EU, the EIB, the World Bank Group, the International Monetary Fund, and the United Nations and its specialized agencies.

The EBRD entered into a license agreement with FIDIC, which gives entities involved in EBRD-financed projects free access to the FIDIC-MDB Harmonized General Conditions of Contract for Construction (http://www.ebrd.com/work-with-us/procurement/project-procurement/standard-procurement-documents.html). Although the EBRD supports the use of these general conditions, they are not mandatory and other internationally recognized forms of contracts may also be used.

5.3.4 The World Bank (WB)

The World Bank (WB) is managed by 188 member countries and is composed of two institutions: the International Bank for Reconstruction and Development (IBRD) and the International Development Association (IDA). The IBRD's objectives are to reduce poverty in middle-income nations and countries with bad credit ratings. The

IDA focuses exclusively on the world's poorest countries. These institutions are part of a larger body known as the World Bank Group.

Established in 1944, the WB is headquartered in Washington, D.C., and employs 9,000 people in more than 100 offices worldwide.

Six strategic themes drive the WB's work: (1) the world's poorest countries; (2) fragile and conflict-affected states; (3) the Arab world (4) middle-income countries; (5) global public goods issues; and (6) the delivery of knowledge and learning services.

The WB provides low-interest loans, interest-free credit, and grants to developing countries. These support a wide array of investments in areas such as education, health, public administration, infrastructure, financial and private sector development, agriculture, and the environment and natural resource management. Some projects are co-financed by governments, others by multilateral institutions, commercial banks, export credit agencies, and private sector investors.

The WB recommends FIDIC forms of contract for projects where they lend money.

5.4 Standard form of contract in a governing law context

National substantive laws and regulations rarely provide sufficient rules for large construction projects. On the contrary, local commercial laws tend to be inadequate in terms of dealing with contract administration, price, time, variation procedures, risk allocation, and claims issues. The use of extensive sample documents has assisted in filling these gaps and has led to greater certainty and foreseeability in large construction projects.

Governing law ordinarily states that general terms and conditions, as prepared by professional or other organizations, will be part of the contract merely by being referred to. The position these terms and conditions are to occupy within the hierarchy of the contractual documents has to be defined in the contract.

5.5 Purpose of sample documents in construction projects

The long-term use of sample documents in a certain industry sometimes leads to their incorporation in local public procurement legislation. In this way, the FIDIC forms have become part of public procurement law in, for example, Central and Eastern Europe and the Middle East. Developments in some Arabic countries are now so advanced that standardized conditions or their parts have become mandatory elements of local public procurement law.

Specific provisions are encountered in international construction contracts. For example, large construction contracts often foresee the participation not only of the employer and the contractor, but also of a neutral third party (the contract administrator) authorized to make decisions and certify various operations or activities performed by the contracting parties. The meaning and effect of those certificates will always depend on a particular contract and the governing law. Concerning their meaning, these certificates usually reflect the as-built state. Such a certificate is scrutinized at a point in time specified in the contract and is usually a pre-condition for invoicing and payment. Contracts tend to include provisions that define the conditions upon which a performance certificate (or related payment) can be refused. It is not then surprising that numerous disputes arise at this point if the engineer proceeds contrary to the contract while issuing such certificates. British courts have ruled that the engineer is considered as incompetent in such situation, giving the contractor the right to claim payment even when lacking the certificate.

Complications also appear where common law principles are used in connection with completion where a distinction is drawn between such completion, thereby allowing the resulting work to be used for the agreed purpose (substantial completion) and fulfilment of the contractual commitment (performance). Most sample forms used in international construction projects build, therefore, on the substantial completion concept, coming from the common law. This approach presumes that the work has been taken over by the engineer, but without relieving the contractor of any of its contractual responsibilities. Only the performance certificate will have such consequences, once issued.

Typical features of international construction projects are discussed in other chapters of this book where common issues such as price, time, claims, variations, and risk allocation are explained.

These and other common features of large international construction projects frequently dealt with in sample forms of contract have arguably become part of *lex mercatoria* (from the Latin for "merchant law," i.e., supranational customs and rules of international trade).

International debates have been ongoing in professional circles for decades, but these efforts have not yet provided any statutory regulation for international construction contracts. The central question is whether such regulation is necessary at all. Even *lex mercatoria* itself owes its existence to the inadequacy and "stubbornness" of written law. International traders very often conclude that they do not need any such national law in any case. Owing to customs and the inflexibility of commercial law, traders create their own habitual rules. This extends to resolving disputes in the least painful way by using their own agreed alternative methods which exist separately to those prescribed by the state.

These days, FIDIC forms (as a standardized law applicable to construction projects) are without doubt part of *lex mercatoria*. However, many questions remain as to whether they are anything more than general terms and conditions of contract prepared by a professional organization. For example, what is their relation to international principles of contract law, general principles of law or the principles that prevail in the construction industry or trade in general? Can they become an international business custom? Can the individual provisions of FIDIC conditions be used in disputes even when there is no reference to a FIDIC sample document in the contract (i.e., where such document is not a part of the contract)? Would the selection of *lex mercatoria* as the governing law of a contract be deemed applicable and can FIDIC be subsumed under this category as a suitable source of regulation? And, finally, can the FIDIC contractual conditions replace applicable law?

Another issue centers around the option to fill the gaps in a national law with supranational regulations and the possibility of using the FIDIC forms in this context (Mallmann, 2002).

5.6 Standard sample forms as a source of law

FIDIC conditions were not created with the intent of becoming a source of law. What is relevant, however, is how they are practically applied by contract drafters, parties to the contract and in dispute resolution.

FIDIC forms are sometimes used as a source of law in disputes resolved in arbitration where there is a gap between contractual provisions and the governing law. When there is doubt or uncertainty, adjudicators, arbitrators or judges fill these "gaps" with generally accepted FIDIC form provisions. Similarly, FIDIC forms can be used to find out what clauses would be generally accepted in construction contracts before the project begins. For instance, it may be possible to compare unclear or potentially invalid clauses of a bespoke contract to a particular FIDIC clause at the negotiation stage.

The forms can further be used, when necessary, as a tool and reference to interpret particular contract clauses by judges, arbitrators or adjudicators. For example, if the contracting parties select the *lex mercatoria* as a contract governing law, a situation may arise where an arbitrator is left to analyze a particular provision of a contract that has been taken straight from a FIDIC form. In such a case, the arbitrator is more likely to interpret this clause in the original meaning given to it by FIDIC. This is likely to result in more consistent and predictable decision making.

The FIDIC forms can therefore be categorized under the *dispositive law of international construction arbitration* (Mallmann, 2002).

In this way the FIDIC forms are used mainly where the *voie directe* (i.e., direct use of a suitable governing law at the sole discretion of an arbitrator) is used by an arbitrator considering a dispute as an *amiable compositeur* (i.e., they may refrain from applying the governing law with the consent of the contracting parties). A similar approach can also be chosen where arbitrators are authorized to resolve the dispute considering solely what they perceive to be fair and equitable (*ex aequo et bono*).

Finally, in the case of *SocUti Pabalk Ticaret Sirketi v. SocUti Norsolor,* the court ruled that *lex mercatoria* can be applied without being chosen as governing law and without any authorization to decide as an *amiable compositeur.*

5.7 *Lex causae*

If there is a conflict of laws, *lex causae* (Latin for "cause for the law") is the law chosen by the court from among the relevant legal systems to arrive at its judgment of an international case. Some academic circles admit that generally accepted sample forms of contract form part of such selectable law. However, a view is also held that such sample forms cannot satisfy the governing law criteria. A solution may be, where the parties decide, to combine sample forms with another body of law, such as a national law of a particular country. The statutes can also be combined within the limits of *dépeçage* (meaning that the individual parts of the contract will be governed by different codes of law).

With its forms containing a choice of law clause, FIDIC is actually anticipating the above. A law governing a particular contractual relationship is determined on a regular basis under particular conditions. As such, FIDIC does not foresee the use of its conditions as *contrat sans loi* (i.e., as contracts without any governing law).

The applicable governing law should be determined at the procurement stage and it is essential for the contractor to be made aware of the governing law while the bid is being prepared. The requirement that the contractor should prepare its bid competently— while not knowing the governing law, but only speculating on it—can hardly be deemed reasonable. If, at the time of bid preparation, the contractor does not know or cannot find out how governing law will protect or expose them in a dispute situation, this must surely influence the bid price.

Besides, the presence of public law aspects in connection with the realization of construction projects cannot be avoided. Contracts aside, other legal issues may arise in the areas of labor law, real estate law, environment protection, and investment protection, and so on.

Several examples that highlight how governing law may affect the rights and responsibilities of contract participants include, for example, risks such as unforeseeable physical conditions (they will be allocated to the employer in some jurisdictions and to the contractor in others, irrespective of whether in a mandatory or dispositive way) or termination of a contract by the employer without giving any reason (i.e., at the employer's convenience).

There are countries (such as France, Belgium, Egypt, Malta, Romania, and Tunisia) where there exists a special 10-year defects liability period that starts to run after the taking over of the works. Sometimes, the contractor is obliged to be insured against the risks for the duration of the defects liability period.

Further examples of areas influenced by governing law are mandatory direct employer payments to subcontractors (such as in Poland and France), specific consequences of situations that give rise to major changes in project realization, various consequences of defective performance (such as the entitlement to claim for removal of the defects or to a discount from the contract price), and so on.

In every individual case, it is necessary to evaluate how the governing law and the customs will affect the contract.

5.8 Interpretation

The contract alone may not always provide adequate interpretation provisions. This situation may occur where a comprehensive definitions section is lacking, the contract is poorly drafted, excessive technical language is used or the contract is silent on important matters. Using common interpretation rules can be of assistance but may not be adequate.

When considering the issue of interpretation, legal codes and related precedents need to be taken into account as well as published arbitration awards from across the globe. A selection of "precedents" is published on a regular basis by the International Chamber of Commerce (ICC) in the *Journal du Droit International*. The ICC also publishes the *ICC International Court of Arbitration Bulletin,* which sometimes focuses on construction disputes. It mentions in this regard (ICC, 2012) that there is a long time lag (10 to 20 years or more) between when a new edition of the FIDIC conditions is introduced and when it comes into general use internationally. As a result, for long there were no dispute outcomes or extracts of awards dealing with the latest suite of FIDIC construction contracts for major works which were published in 1999. Outcomes are also available in the *Commercial Arbitration Yearbook,* the *International Construction Law Review*, the *International Arbitration Report*, and other yearbooks and publications of the individual arbitration tribunals; however, the number of published awards is very low.

Trade usage cannot be omitted from interpretation if it comes into existence as a result of certain business collaborations. Its interpretation can also be based on principles either at the level of the *lex mercatoria* principles described above or at the level of international contracting principles drawn up in writing (such as UNIDROIT). Use of the *FIDIC Contracts Guide*, a helpful interpretation instrument published by FIDIC, is recommended, and it covers interpretation of the FIDIC CONS/1999 Red Book, P&DB/1999 Yellow Book, and EPC/1999 Silver Book provisions. A larger number of interpretations are available for the individual sample forms in the *FIDIC Contracts Guide*—the only authentic guide published exclusively by FIDIC.

The interpretation used by arbitrators in award ICC 7910/1996 seems to be controversial in this regard. The issue at hand was that neither the second nor the third edition of the FIDIC Red Book gave a clear description of the procedural sequence where one of the parties was unwilling to accept the engineer's decision despite the fact that the decision should have been "final and binding." It was unclear if the dispute could be reviewed at arbitration. The arbitration tribunal proceeded to hear the case despite seemingly lacking the necessary jurisdiction. This complicated any future enforcement and enforceability of the award.

The arbitrators acknowledged the arbitration tribunal's problem but agreed with the plaintiff's argument that the tribunal did indeed have jurisdiction. This is because the matter was expressly dealt with in the fourth edition of the FIDIC Red Book which stated that: "disobedience of an engineer's decision and resulting dispute may be referred to arbitration by a party." However, the fourth edition did not form a part of the disputable contract. Such an argument will raise questions if it is possible to respect (in fact) the influence of an uninvolved third party (FIDIC) on a bilateral contractual relationship. It also confirms the extensive influence of FIDIC on international construction.

The recent judgment of the Queensland Supreme Court in *Sedgman South Africa (Pty) Ltd & Others v. Discovery Copper Botswana (Pty) Ltd* demonstrates that FIDIC users should refrain from reading and/or construing FIDIC forms of contract in the same way they read/construe domestic contracts. FIDIC forms should be read together with the existing guidance provided by FIDIC, and against the genesis of the clauses (Hök, G.S., 2014).

Inconsistency in contract documents by Patrick Kain (South Africa)

Background

The construction contract contains several documents including the agreement and other documents that define what is to be built, how it is to be built, the standard to which the facility is to be built, and finally how and when the work is to be paid for. With so many documents involved in a single contract, it is often the case that one or more of the documents may contradict another document.

To resolve the issue of conflicting information in the contract, most contract conditions specify an order of priority of documents to reduce disputes.

Under a FIDIC type contract, the normal priority of documents specified in Sub clause 1.5 for the Red or Yellow Book contract is as follows:

FIDIC priority (Red and Yellow Books):

1. Contract agreement
2. Letter of acceptance
3. Letter of tender
4. The particular conditions
5. The general conditions
6. The specifications (Red Book) or the employer's requirements (Yellow Book)
7. The drawings (Red Book only)
8. The schedules and any of the documents forming part of the contract

The Silver Book only contains items 1, 4, 5, and 6 (employer's requirements—just as in the Yellow Book) and lastly, 8 modified to read the tender and other documents forming part of the contract in that order.

There is a consistency in all these documents in that the requirements of the employer (and drawings in the Red Book) are the first of the documents specific to the works themselves. This is followed any other documents including documents stipulating how the contractor gets paid for the work he does.

Sub-Clause 4.11 "Sufficiency of Contract Amount, clearly states that the contractor has 'satisfied himself of the correctness and sufficiency of the Accepted Contract Amount'" (contract price in the Silver Book). This implies that the contractor will do the work required according to the requirements of the employer for the amount stated in the contract. It is significant that the requirements of the contract (specifications and drawings in the Red Book or in the employer requirements in the Yellow and Silver Books) take priority over other technical and financial considerations. Therefore, according to Sub-Clause 4.11, anything included in the specifications and drawings or the employer requirements in deemed to be included in the contract amount (or contract price in the Silver Book).

There should be no issue with this in either the Yellow or Silver Book that are lump sum contracts except if there is a variation issued under Clause 13, which brings its own issues especially with the Silver Book. But that is not a subject for this discourse. The contractor is requested to price the works specified according to the contract requirements and he will be paid according to the schedules.

The Red Book can be either a re-measure contract or a lump sum contract. In the latter case the payments are made in similar manner to the Yellow and Silver Book contracts. In a re-measure contract, which is more common, the contractor is paid for the work done at the rates entered in the bill or bills of quantities. Each of the FIDIC forms places the schedules and any other documents forming part of the contract as the last in order of priority.

Notwithstanding this, designers are free to change the order of priority in the particular conditions and I have seen the priority changed on some projects to include an item labeled "bills of quantities" and giving it a higher priority than the specifications and the drawings while still leaving the "schedules" in last place in the order of priority. As already clarified, "schedules" in the FIDIC documents mean also the schedules of payment, which include the bills of quantities or other schedule of payment based on milestones, and so on. By including an item labeled bills of quantities, the engineer in the cases cited demonstrated that it did not understand what is meant by "the schedules." Referring to the example above, the following is a demonstration of what can occur:

(a) Since the bills of quantities and the schedules refer to the same thing. Which one is correct?
(b) How does the engineer resolve this since there is conflicting information within in the priority itself?

The problems that this situation gave rise to are best demonstrated by what occurred when a dispute was referred to the dispute board. The board determined that by changing the priority of documents in this manner, the schedules are now excluded from the list of documents and that the bill of quantities governed the payment regime.

Carrying this ruling to its logical conclusion, the DB ruled that the contractor must be compensated for anything that was not included in the bills since the bills had a higher priority than both the specifications and drawings. This is in direct contradiction to the provision of Sub-Clause 4.11 "Sufficiency of Accepted Contract Amount," which requires that the contractor agrees to have satisfied himself that the tender has considered and priced for all the works included in the contract. Clearly this in itself raises other issues.

In this case, the problem was further exacerbated by the fact that the contractor was later on requested to re-design certain of the works. It prepared a bill of quantities purported to include all items for which it required payment. However, several items were excluded. Again, the DB ruled that the contractor should be paid for the "missing" BQ items.

While we may well disagree with the DB's decisions in the case cited above, this demonstrates how changing the priority of documents can expose the employer to unnecessary costs. Engineers who prepare documents on behalf of the employer should think carefully of the possible adverse implications of changing the order of priority of documents.

Contradictions between the specification and the conditions of contract

While standard specification documents are frequently used in contracts, this becomes an issue if engineers fail to ensure that terminology, time frames, and procedures are compatible with the conditions of contract. Where such differences occur reference to the priority of documents may solve the issue. However, confusion and disputes can and do occur when contradictory terms and time frames or requirements incompatible with the conditions of contract are included in the specifications. One recent matter that I have encountered revolved around the "handing over" of the works, which required certain procedures to be carried out within a time frame incompatible with the requirements of Clause 10 "Taking over of the Works," which effectively meant that the works were "taken over" at a different time to when they were to be "handed over." In fact, the handing over issue with its separate time frame and conditions should in fact been termed and dealt with as "tests after completion."

There was widespread disagreement on the issue and eventually the engineer incorrectly in my view, accepted that the requirements of the specification must overrule the requirements of

Clause 10. This led to a dispute, which was referred to the dispute board that ruled that while adherence to the specification was required the payment and commencement procedure must be according to the conditions of contract and that the contractor was entitled to interest on late payment occasioned by adherence to the specifications.

The failure to co-ordinate the specifications and the conditions of contract has caused a serious problem in this instance. A problem that could have been avoided if only the design engineers took the time to ensure that the specifications and the conditions of contract were properly coordinated in the first place and considered what the intent of the procedures and the time frame were—which was to ensure that the facility worked properly under working conditions for a period of time AFTER the project was handed over to the employer. Such issues are best dealt with by the engineer during the design stage by ensuring that the specifications and the conditions of contract are compatible. Unfortunately, the practice of using package specifications continues and the problems so caused also continue.

Patrick Kain
International Construction Expert South Africa

5.9 Trade usage and business custom

It must be possible to define, with certainty, a community who use the particular rules (e.g., the FIDIC conditions), otherwise the particular rules cannot be accepted as a trade usage in construction, that is, as a business custom to the widest extent. The community can easily be identified in the form of lenders and employers (states, banks, and investment funds), contractors (international construction companies able to comply with the demanding qualification criteria applied in large construction projects), and consultants—all respecting and using the FIDIC forms.

Another attribute is the repeated and long-term use of the particular rules with a general awareness that those rules are binding. FIDIC conditions, for example, have been used for more than 60 years and are still used to secure foreseeable development of a construction project and a balanced risk allocation by being consciously agreed only *inter partes* (Latin for "between the parties"). The missing *opinio iuris* (Latin for "an opinion of law or necessity"), being also the result of necessary updating of the individual provisions within the new versions, is an obstacle for the necessary *usus longaevus* (Latin for "long-time use").

In connection with the FIDIC forms, it should be noted that in some countries the participants of construction projects use them only because they are forced to do so. Many lenders require use of a generally accepted forms of contract in the projects they support. FIDIC forms are often used for this purpose. It is common, however, that there is neither experience in using the FIDIC forms nor any adequate education of those involved in many countries. Often, the parties simply ignore the rules stated in FIDIC forms and do everything as they had in the past. Consequently, disputes and ambiguities may arise because FIDIC forms impose numerous, strict and formal requirements on the parties.

The FIDIC forms, having now been used for a prolonged period of time, have set an international benchmark that makes the international construction business easier. In many countries, however, employers have changed the general part per the particular conditions to such an extent that the original risk allocation and systematic of FIDIC forms have shifted to create a new bespoke contract that has nothing in common with FIDIC forms. This was caused mainly by a lack of experience and the desire to shift more risk to the contractor—effectively destroying the main advantage of a sample form of contract (i.e., the foreseeability of the contractual relationship) with the parties often ending in dispute because of inefficient, unfair risk allocation, and ambiguous contractual terms.

The original text of a particular FIDIC form is an elaborate document with many internal interconnections. It is easy to upset this system per particular conditions but hard to carry out a project to successful conclusion with such disruptions.

The argument that a particular trade usage or business custom was created between the parties or in general can often be encountered while disputes are being resolved. It is reasonable and natural.

Mainly as result of constant development in the individual segments of business, the law of international merchants is broken down into individual domains. As such, specialized categories can be encountered, such as *lex petrolia* (oil and gas), *lex informatica* (for information and communications technology) and, finally, *lex constructionis* (to cover the construction industry). Modified *lex mercatoria* principles are to become principles of such customary law.

There are opinions, according to which, it is necessary to modify *lex mercatoria* principles, because the construction industry has its specifics and the public interest often conflicts with business here. It is actually a *lex specialis* and *lex generalis* relationship. Some of the *lex constructionis* principles overlap with the legal systems and their equivalents tend to appear in both common law and European civil codes. Others come from customs that developed in the construction industry over extended periods of time. In other words, the standard forms of contract are based on these principles in the same way as these principles arise on the basis of the customs that are themselves coming into existence by virtue of using the standardized sample forms.

A common law of construction contracts—or Vive La différence? by Donald Charrett (Australia)

Contract law (and therefore construction law) around the world are founded on two fundamental doctrines, operating within legal systems complying with the rule of law. The first of these, freedom of contract, sets the "ground rules," which govern the parties' rights to enter into the contract of their choice. The second, the principle of *pacta sunt servanda*, governs the performance of a contract after it has been entered into.

A recent succinct statement of the principle of freedom of contract under the common law is: "Subject to public policy and statute law, parties to a contract can agree to do anything." For details, see *Abigroup Contractors Pty Ltd v. Transfield Pty Ltd & Obayashi Corporation* [1998] VSC 103 [86] (Gillard J).

Freedom of contract is also a fundamental principle under civil law systems, for example: Art 1306 of the *Civil Code of the Philippines* states: "The contracting parties may establish such stipulations, clauses, terms and conditions as they may deem convenient, provided they are not contrary to law, morals, good customs, public order or public policy."

It is submitted that the freedom of parties to contract, subject to any constraints imposed by applicable statute law or public policy, is universally applicable across both common law and civil law systems. Both of these constraints vary from jurisdiction to jurisdiction, and construction law is therefore inevitably conditioned by the relevant jurisdiction. While it is usually possible for contracting parties to select the proper law of their contract, they have no choice over the jurisdiction of the site where the construction takes place, and any relevant statute law in that jurisdiction applicable to, for example, property, the environment, or employment will apply. Further, the heads of public policy will vary from jurisdiction to jurisdiction.

The obverse of the principle of freedom of contract is the doctrine of *pacta sunt servanda*: a fundamental principle of both domestic and international law that requires the provisions of agreements concluded properly to be observed. This means that once parties have exercised their freedom to enter into a contract, they have the legal rights and obligations they have agreed and are entitled to, and a court or an arbitrator will enforce them.

The universal nature of this principle has been stated as: "All the world's legal systems focus on the sanctity of contracts, and damages as the remedy for breach of contract." The consequences are important for the practice of construction law internationally: "the vast majority of construction disputes are fought and won or lost primarily over the wording of the contract (and alleged facts)" (Knutson, 2005). The universality of this principle across legal families is clear from its application in Shari'a law: "O you who believe! Fulfill your obligations."

In recent years there has been significant convergence between the common law and civil law:

- The volume of legislation in common law countries has grown substantially: increasingly, more of the law is explicitly stated in legislation, which either codifies or amends the existing common law, or forms new "social legislation," which mandates desirable community outcomes not achieved by the common law.
- The courts in civil law countries are relying to a much greater extent than previously on the precedential value of court judgments on a similar issue, because the answer to a legal issue may not be found in the codes (Jaeger and Hök, 2010).
- Despite the differences between legal theories, form, procedure, and terminology, in many factual situations, the two systems will arrive at essentially the same substantive result.

Further, the influence of international arbitration in bridging common law and civil law should not be underestimated. In an international arbitration, one of the parties may be from a common law system while the other may be from a civil law jurisdiction. Different aspects of the contract and the project may be performed in a number of different jurisdictions. In a dispute determined by international arbitration, the arbitrators may not only be from different countries, but from different legal systems, and the arbitration may be held in a "neutral" country, whose laws will govern procedural aspects of the arbitration. Inevitably in such cases, common ground in relation to legal principles must be established and is found between the potentially conflicting requirements.

In all jurisdictions, statute law related to construction contracts provides a significant constraint on the parties' freedom of contract (in addition to the common law in relevant jurisdictions). That statute law varies from jurisdiction to jurisdiction in many and various ways. Not surprisingly, there are differences in terminology and in legal principle that make it difficult to discern even broad principles of a common construction law. Nevertheless, the principles of freedom of contract and *pacta sunt servanda* form the basis of construction law around the world, and ensure that there is a thriving international construction industry. Construction contracts can be executed in the knowledge that, notwithstanding local law differences, there are appropriate methods of dispute resolution, broad agreement on what constitutes a just outcome in most situations, and international norms that ensure remedies can be realized.

Contracting parties can use the principle of freedom of contract to move closer to a common construction law, particularly by the use of the *UNIDROIT Principles* as the governing law of the contract, in conjunction with construction contracts written for international use such as FIDIC. There is ample precedent for such an approach to be supported by international arbitration tribunals.

Perhaps the clearest pointer to what there is of a common construction law is the following statement on the fundamental importance of the words of the contract itself, vindicating the twin principles of freedom of contract and *pacta sunt servanda*: "Finally, deep in the night, with no one else around, most lawyers in their heart of hearts will admit – the Contract usually decides the issues, despite what the law is" (Knutson, 2005).

Donald Charrett
Barrister, Arbitrator & Mediator
Melbourne
Australia

5.10 Lex constructionis principles

Besides the traditional ones, such as *pacta sunt servanda*, *rebus sic stantibus*, and *good faith protection*, there are several other principles that are typical to international construction contracts (Molineaux, 2013):

- Admissibility of "directed variations" that do not constitute any breach of contract.
- The employer will bear a reasonable increase in the contract price when the employer provides the site and the contractor encounters, during the realization, worse conditions that those defined in the tender documents. The reverse is also true when better conditions than actually expected are encountered, therefore implying a reduced contract price.
- The risk of unforeseeable physical conditions being allocated to the employer in underground construction.
- Construction and related methods and processes will basically be up to the contractor who, as such, should be stimulated to choose effective solutions.

- Judge or arbitrator rights to moderate in matters of liquidated damages and the admissibility of limitation of liability. Only damage reasonably foreseeable by a reasonable person at the time of entering into the contract will be compensated.
- Damage compensation claims should be thoroughly scrutinized, but not refused because of the difficulty of documenting them. Often liability is clear, but quantum is difficult to prove as is the case in headquarters overhead claims quantification or global claims in the case of complex delay and disruption. In both common law and civil law countries, judges are usually allowed in such situations to decide the quantum at their sole discretion, considering alone what they perceive to be fair and equitable (*ex aequo et bono*).

Proactivity and good faith protection relate to time for completion and admissibility of (directed) variation principles. This will be dealt with in more detail in Section 5.10.1.

5.10.1 Proactivity and good faith protection related to time for completion

It is said that "time is money." Nowhere else is this more true than in construction projects. Delays result in losses on the employer's side as investment returns (or public benefits) become more distant, the contract price increases and other adverse implications such as cash flow problems appear. If found responsible, the contractor may be sanctioned with a contractual penalty, liquidated damages, lost performance bonuses, and an impaired reputation.

Some standard forms of contract force construction project participants to be proactive in their obligations to warn and notify any events that will affect time and price in advance, to notify claims under time bars, to submit updated time schedules (either on a regular basis or each time when a deviation from the last updated schedule appears).

When considering time for completion, variation instructions regarding extension of the scope of works, instructions to accelerate, or the negotiations and decisions in terms of extensions of time for completion, these issues should be resolved as soon as possible by the employer to avoid "constructive acceleration claims."

A situation may also arise where the employer fails to respond to a contractor's warning, notification, or updated schedule. Here, the principle is that if the employer does not respond to a contractor's notice of claim for an extension of time for completion and fails to decide about the claim, then the time for completion is no longer of the essence. Known as "time at large" in common law, the contract will be interpreted accordingly.

The contractor shall then be obliged to complete the work within such period of time that is reasonable in respect of all the circumstances. In such a case, the employer will often point out the contractor's general duty to prevent damages to push the contractor to optimize the methods and sequencing of realization (regarding personnel, subcontractors, plants, deliveries, equipment, and so on) to avoid damages in the form of contract price increases.

The contractor will frequently see this situation as very complicated in terms of organization, financing and avoiding additional costs. Every day by which the realization of a large construction project is extended will usually cost huge amounts of money (overhead expenses, extensions to bank guarantees and insurance, real property rentals, machinery leases, and so on). The same applies to disruptions that may be caused for similar reasons. Proving causation in case of multiple disruptions is almost impossible and global claims are potentially unavoidable.

Logically, the party that is proactive (i.e., the one actively warning, notifying adverse events and respective effects on quality, time, and price), being in good faith, has to be protected in a dispute. An "early warning duty" is a contractual obligation that is being increasingly used in modern contracts to support proactivity. A traditional *vigilantibus, et non dormientibus, jura subveniunt* (the one heeding his rights is to be favored) applies here, and *qui tacet consentir videtur* (silence or refusing to respond) should be considered in disfavor.

5.10.2 Admissibility and necessity of variation procedures

A construction project is a set of interrelated activities that may sometimes give the impression of "coordinated chaos." Complications and problems are encountered in every project, often in the form of adverse climatic conditions, problematic ground conditions, accessibility issues, and lack of foreseeability. A construction project is also dependent on human factors, unforeseeable conditions and phenomena, as well as other factors. Therefore, it is more than likely that a construction project will deviate from what the employer, designer or contractor planned before starting the works. Good contracts are prepared for such situations and contain, therefore, variation clauses with respective procedures devised to enable rapid resolution of problems encountered. Those variations are described as "directed variations." Such variations do not, of course, imply a breach of contract because the contract itself allows for them.

Contractual variation procedures should regulate how to propose, approve, and instruct variations (and within what periods of time) and how to calculate and document them including the respective forms of variation orders, and so on.

If the variation procedures are set functionally and reasonably in a contract, they cannot be in conflict with law as they are a necessity. Variations are an inherent part of large construction projects and the admissibility and necessity of variation procedures are no doubt one of the key principles of *lex constructionis*.

Contractor's duty to mitigate delay and damages under FIDIC 1999 standard forms and in lex mercatoria by Vladimir Vencl (Serbia)

When it comes to delay in construction projects due to events entitling the contractor for extension of time for completion, argument that often develops between the parties is that of mitigation of delay and damages. Most often, if not exclusively, raised by the employer (through the engineer as its agent) in defence against contractor's claims. The important question arises to what extent, if at all, the contractor is actually required to mitigate project adverse circumstances and resulting consequences, both in respect of time and financial losses, if these are attributable to the employer.

Under FIDIC 1999 standard forms these matters are not addressed in great details, which would allow for straightforward directions, but the following sub-clauses can be identifed as relevant:

- Sub-Clause 1.1.4.3 (definition of) "cost" as " ... expenditure reasonably incurred ... "; where the term cost is used in many other sub-clauses providing entitlement to the contractor to claim cost in case of employer's defaults or just risks, which employer took under the contract;
- Sub-Clause 4.21 h) where the contractor is obliged to present, within its progress reports "any events or circumstances which may jeopardise the completion in accordance with the Contract, and the measures being (or to be) adopted to overcome delays."
- Sub-Clause 8.3 "Program," which in its first paragraph stipulates: "..The Contractor shall also submit a revised program whenever the previous program is inconsistent with actual progress or with the Contractor's obligations ... "
- Sub-Clause 8.3 "Program," which in its penultimate paragraph stipulates: "The Contractor shall promptly give notice to the Engineer of specific probable future events or circumstances which may adversely affect the work, increase the Contract Price or delay the execution of the Works. The Engineer may require the Contractor to submit an estimate of the anticipated effect or the future event or circumstances, and/or a proposal under Sub-Clause 13.3 [Variation Procedure]."
- Sub-Clause 13.1 "Right to Vary," which in its third paragraph stipulates: "Each Variation may include: ... (f) changes to the sequence or timing of the execution of the Works. The Contractor shall not make any alteration and/or modification of the Permanent Works, unless and until the Engineer instructs or approves a Variation."
- Sub-Clause 19.3 "Duty to Minimize Delay," which obliges both the contractor and the employer to use "all reasonable endeavors to minimize any delay in performance of the contract as a result of force majeure."
- "First notice" sub-clauses where the contractor (sometimes also the employer—as noted further below) is obliged to issue "pre-claim" notices with purpose to notify the employer on events/circumstances, which may result in disruption, ultimately delay, and additional costs. Intention of these notices is to provide timely information and warn the other party on existence of adverse events/circumstances and activate the mitigation efforts of the parties. These "first notices" are (within the "Red Book"):
    - Sub-Clause 1.8 "Care and Supply of Documents," last paragraph (applies to either Party):
    " ... If a Party becomes aware of an error or defect of a technical nature in a document which was prepared for use in executing the Works, the Party shall promptly give notice to the other Party of such error or defect."
    - Sub-Clause 1.9 "Delayed Drawings or Instructions," first paragraph:
    " ... The Contractor shall give notice to the Engineer whenever the Works are likely to be delayed or disrupted if any necessary drawing or instruction is not issued to the Contractor within a particular time, which shall be reasonable. The notice shall include details of the necessary drawing or instruction, details of why and by when it should be issued, and details of the nature and amount of the delay or disruption likely to be suffered if it is late."

- Sub-Clause 4.12 "Unforeseeable Physical Conditions," second paragraph:
  "… If the Contractor encounters adverse physical conditions which he considers to have been Unforeseeable, the Contractor shall give notice to the Engineer as soon as practicable … The Contractor shall continue executing the Works, using such proper and reasonable measures as are appropriate for the physical conditions, and shall comply with any instructions which the Engineer may give. If an instruction constitutes a Variation, Clause 13 [Variations and Adjustments] shall apply … "
- Sub-Clause 4.24 "Fossils," second paragraph:
  "… The Contractor shall, upon discovery of any such finding, promptly give notice to the Engineer, who shall issue instructions for dealing with it."
- Sub-Clause 16.1 "Contractor's entitlement to Suspend Work," first paragraph:
  "… If the Engineer fails to certify in accordance with Sub-Clause 14.6 [Issue of Interim Payment Certificates] or the Employer fails to comply with Sub-Clause 2.4 [Employer's Financial Arrangements] or Sub-Clause 14.7 [Payment], the Contractor may, after giving not less than 21 days' notice to the Employer, suspend work (or reduce the rate of work) unless and until the Contractor has received the Payment Certificate, reasonable evidence or payment, as the case may be and as described in the notice."
- Sub-Clause 17.4 "Consequences of Employer's Risks":
  "… If and to the extent that any of the risks listed in Sub-Clause 17.3 above results in loss or damage to the Works, Goods or Contractor's Documents, the Contractor shall promptly give notice to the Engineer and shall rectify this loss or damage to the extent required by the Engineer."
- Sub-Clause 19.2 "Notice of Force Majeure," first paragraph (applies to either Party):
  "… If a Party is or will be prevented from performing its substantial obligations under the Contract by Force Majeure, then it shall give notice to the other Party of the event or circumstances constituting the Force Majeure and shall specify the obligations, the performance of which is or will be prevented. The notice shall be given within 14 days after the Party became aware, or should have become aware, of the relevant event or circumstance constituting Force Majeure."

On observation of the above, few arguments could be developed and conclusions made, namely:

- Contractor cannot be reimbursed, even with claims valid in principle, for unreasonably incurred expenditures as these are falling out of definition of cost. For example, we could observe the situation where the contractor could avoid/reduce damages by reasonable mitigation measures and it does not—instead it chooses not to act and in such way incurs and claims much higher costs resulting from adverse events for which the employer is liable. In such situation, employer could argue that difference in costs that would be incurred in reasonable mitigation efforts and claimed costs where no mitigation efforts are undertaken by the contractor are *"unreasonably incurred"* and therefore not reimbursable. On the other hand, reasonable mitigation measures, when undertaken, could result in additional costs and as such Contractor would certainly like to claim these against the employer;
- Although the contractor is obliged to register in its progress reports events or circumstances which may have adverse impact to the project and countermeasures adopted or

to be adopted, Sub-Clause 4.21 h) is not clear whether measures should be selfadopted or their adoption is dependant on, let's say, instructions of the engineer and progress reports are only to serve as a register;
- Above Sub-Clause 4.21 h) should be observed in relation to the contractor's obligation under penultimate paragraph of Sub-Clause 8.3 to notify the engineer on "..specific probable future events or circumstances which may adversely affect the work, increase the Contract Price or delay the execution of the Works." The engineer is then not obliged to, but "..may require the Contractor to submit an estimate of the anticipated effect or the future event or circumstances, and/or a proposal under Sub-Clause 13.3 [Variation Procedure]." This process definitely may result in mitigation of anticipated future harm but it is suggested that the engineer is the one to initiate the variation process, at its option, upon notification issued by the contractor. On the other hand, the contractor is obliged to issue such "early" notification and failure to do so could result in reduced entitlement under its later claim due to these events (when they eventually occur);
- The contractor who is already facing events causing delay is obliged to submit revised program under Sub-Clause 8.3 first paragraph as actual progress would be different to that previously programmed. Such revised program would have to be in compliance with its obligation to complete within the time for completion, which is being compromised. The conclusion would be that the contractor is obliged to adopt the mitigation measures through this revised program so to be able to fulfill its obligation to complete within the time for completion;
- Under Sub-Clause 13.1 it is stipulated that changes of sequence or timing in execution of works may be a variation—to be instructed or approved by the engineer (if it requests and receives from the contractor the variation proposal, which later it may approve). If the engineer does not initiate and formalize variation process, changes in sequence and timing in execution of works done by the contractor on its own would not grant the contractor with payment under variation process; also such self-initiated changes done by the contractor on its own may cause it to be in breach of its obligation under Sub-Clause 8.3 to proceed according to the program, which was contractually compliant;
- Various other sub-clauses, as listed above, foresee that the contractor (sometimes the employer also) issues early—first notices so the underlying issues could be managed in time and delay and additional costs are reduced—mitigated; failure to issue such notices may impact extent of the contractor's entitlement under later related claim, for example, if it is shown that such early notice could have led to adoption of measures that would result in reducing or avoiding delay and damage.
- Straightforward mitigation is required from the contractor, and the employer, in case of force majeure occurences.

Obviously, many issues may arise from above FIDIC 1999 standard forms provisions, some of which appear to be competing against each other.

In observing these provisions, or provisions of any other agreed contract form, one must consider and base its opinion on what is normal "good faith" and businesslike behavior of each party to each particular "situation." Extreme approaches to the problem can occur on both sides. Contractor could be forcing problems on the site just because they are on project's "critical path" in order to create "paper" claims although in reality consequences may be overcome by simple rearrangement of planned activities, at no or at minumum cost. On the other side, employer could be invoking mitigation obligation as defense against every problem encountered on the project for which it is liable and irrespective of the complexity and costs that would be required from the contractor to "mitigate" the delay and damages. Experienced and qualified engineer, acting as employer's agent, may by proper instructions, or requests for proposals prior issuing instructions, to the contractor assist and take lead in the process of mitigation of delay and damages through variations. In reality, an engineer would prefer to take no action being concerned about all the consequences resulting from its instructions and resulting liability.

It is worth noting that some of the mitigation-related issues are addressed in the new FIDIC Forms (2017). For example:

- Sub-Clause 4.20 "Progress Reports" still contains similar requirement under h) to that of FIDIC 1999 Sub-Clause 4.21 h) "Progress Reports"—for identification of events or circumstances which may adversely affect the completion of the works but now "in accordance with the program and time for completion" instead of previous "in accordance with the contract" and measures being (or to be) adopted to overcome delays. The new draft edition at its end now states that: "However, nothing stated in any progress report shall constitute a Notice under a Sub-Clause of these Conditions." So there are no more "hidden" notifications from the contractor under progress reports, often missed by the engineer and often causing the disagreements between the parties if progress reports may serve for issuing contractually required notifications to the employer;
- Sub-Clause 8.3 "Program" is significantly amended and the Program is required to include in its supporting report, inter alia, " ... the Contractor's proposals to overcome the effects of any delay(s)." On the other side it is not clear how these proposals are dealt with as the engineer is still obliged to review the program against the contract, actual progress, and contractor's obligations. Are these proposals already incorporated into the program, under which process they are accepted, can the contractor give more proposals for counteracting effect of a single delay (note the wording), will the contractor attach its conditions for following these proposals and how the engineer will react to the same.
- Sub-Clause 8.4 "Advance Warning" stipulates:

    "Each Party shall advise the other and the Engineer, and the Engineer shall advise the Parties, in advance of any known or probable future events or circumstances which may:
    (a) adversely affect the work of the Contractor's Personnel;
    (b) adversely affect the performance of the Works when completed;
    (c) increase the Contract Price; and/or
    (d) delay the execution of the Works or a Section (if any).
    The Engineer may request the Contractor to submit a proposal under Sub-Clause 13.3.2 [Variation by Request for Proposal] to avoid or minimise the effects of such event(s) or circumstance(s)."

    This sub-clause now replaces and enhances previous part of Sub-Clause 8.3 third paragraph and now both parties are required to "advise" each other and the engineer, and the engineer is obliged to "advise the Parties" in an effort to counteract probable future adverse events or circumstances. The engineer again may initiate variation process through request for a proposal so to "avoid or minimise the effects." Clear requirement for mitigation efforts is incorporated, but again, it appears—without proper closure.

In conclusion, the new FIDIC Forms (2017), and after observing all the other provisions, became much more complex and detailed, but this may well lead to difficulties in its interpretation and implementation. Will it suit demanding dynamics of construction projects remains a question.

Various provisions incorporated within the laws of the civil law systems, when these are governing the construction contracts, are relevant for the subject matter and are reflected in general principles of "good faith," "contributory negligence," "divided liability," "duty to warn" and so on. If we look into the "lex mercatoria" for the unified formulations of these general principles we could identify the following typical provisions:

PECL (The Principles of European Contract Law)

Article 9:504 "Loss Attributable to Aggrieved Party"

The non-performing party is not liable for loss suffered by the aggrieved party to the extent that the aggrieved party contributed to the non-performance or its effects.

Article 9:505 "Reduction of Loss"

1. The non-performing party is not liable for loss suffered by the aggrieved party to the extent that the aggrieved party could have reduced the loss by taking reasonable steps.
2. The aggrieved party is entitled to recover any expenses reasonably incurred in attempting to reduce the loss.

UNIDROIT Principles of International Commercial Contracts 2010

Article 7.4.7 "Harm Due in Part to Aggrieved Party"

Where the harm is due in part to an act or omission of the aggrieved party or to another event as to which that party bears the risk, the amount of damages shall be reduced to the extent that these factors have contributed to the harm, having regard to the conduct of the parties.

Article 7.4.8 "Mitigation of Harm"

1. The non-performing party is not liable for harm suffered by the aggrieved party to the extent that the harm could have been reduced by the latter party's taking reasonable steps.
2. The aggrieved party is entitled to recover any expenses reasonably incurred in attempting to reduce the harm.

Obviously there is great similarity between above two sets of principles and two key approaches to be observed are "contribution" and "mitigation."

Considering number of disputes (or disagreements at least) occuring on FIDIC contracts in relation to obligation to mitigate delays and damages by the aggrieved party, standard contract forms would certainly benefit from direct incorporation of provisions similar to above, instead parties searching for the same result wihin the interpretation of contract provisions under the umbrella of governing laws general provisions, resulting in loss of time in disputes and (further) disruption of relationship between the parties. Starting point for any third party observer, for example, dispute resolver, should be query if the parties approached to the particular situation in "good faith" and professional manner and solutions/decisions thereafter would be easily wrapped up in the concrete contractual/legal principles set out above.

Vladimir Vencl
MSc CE, MBE ICPL, MCIArb
Contract Manager at Belgrade Waterfront LLC
Belgrade, Serbia

5.11 The use of *lex constructionis*

There are views that the *lex mercatoria* (including its sub-groups, such as *lex constructionis*), are of no use in practice as a governing law for the purpose of choice of law. One of the main difficulties is a lack of consistency and completeness. However, it is usually clear from the international agreements and arbitration rules that the arbitrators, when finding a resolution, may apply the law they consider applicable. It is evident from published arbitration awards that the arbitrators make use of and apply *lex mercatoria* in practice. Given the use of *lex mercatoria*, it is of course always necessary to evaluate the risks concerning the enforceability of an arbitration award. The idea of international construction court is worth mentioning in connection with *lex constructionis*. Such a subject could be crucial in developing settled case law and interpretation of standard forms in construction. This can be critical in promoting commercial certainty. While there are differences in laws and practices across the globe, there is also notable commonality in the concepts and forms used by the construction industry (Menon, 2014).

The discussion of the principles of *lex mercatoria* in this chapter is demonstrative in its nature, and can serve as a guide, supporting both the decision making of the construction project participants and the resolution of any disputes that may arise.

Future-proofing construction contracts by Shy Jackson (UK)

Construction technology in the twenty-first century is very sophisticated, using computer models, advanced materials, and other techniques to construct bigger and taller buildings, bridges, and tunnels. But how often do we see the same old disputes, where parties spend years arguing about events that happened even further away in the past? With the benefit of hindsight and knowing how these disputes start and develop, can we modernize construction procurement and contracts to help avoid such problems or are such dispute a permanent feature of all construction projects?

Construction contracts are of course being reviewed and updated regularly and some may say that this is enough. This may well be right but it is still worth spending some time in thinking whether it is possible to develop procurement procedures and contractual arrangements so that they can help ensure projects are successful.

A simple example is the growing use of building information modeling (BIM). Such systems have the potential to make real changes to how projects are managed, but they need to be anchored in the contractual framework in order to ensure there is clarity on the process and how risks and liabilities are divided when using such systems.

But there are other more fundamental changes that can be made. At one extreme, a default position is that the lowest bid wins, on the assumption that there will be a negotiation and possibly a dispute once the works are completed in order to determine the final amount due. That model will be familiar and some use it as the basis for projects, despite some obvious drawbacks. People do not tend to buy the cheapest car or house, and construction should be no different.

If new models are being explored, there are some issues that need to be considered. To start with, though contractors often tend to get the blame, it must be recognized that it is employers who drive projects. That means that employers need to understand the construction processes, the contractual framework and, crucially, the construction risks and how they are managed. Employers who do not have the necessary skills and experience will fail to manage works properly and are more likely to cause delays and cost increases.

This is a real issue in parts of the world where substantial infrastructure projects are managed by local authorities who have not been trained to manage large construction projects built by international contractors. A program for educating and training the individuals who act as employers, to make them understand how a contract allocates risks and how time and money can change, will improve the overall performance in construction projects.

Another way to develop the understanding of employers is for them to work more closely with contractors at an early stage and discuss the proposed works before the contract is signed and the plans are fixed. There are of course issues in some countries regarding such pre-contract discussions due to procurement laws, but where it is possible to engage in such discussions, this is likely to result in a better understanding of the project, what risks there are and what can be done in advance to improve construction and limit risks. This will also help to reduce risk allowances which increase the price.

The employer drives the project but the contractor implements it. Both need to work together and anything which can help to create a better working relationship will ensure a successful project. One basic step is making sure that both the employer and the contractor's employees have copies of the contract and are familiar with its provisions and what it requires. Many disputes are the result of a party making a claim without first checking the position under the contract. Claims sometimes arise due to a simple failure to comply with notice or record-keeping provisions and disputes often are the result of failing to understand who has a specific risk under a contract.

A more fundamental question is whether the commercial interests of the employer and contractor can be aligned. All too often it is impossible to reconcile the employer's need to limit costs and delay (or create a landmark building) with the contractor's need to achieve an acceptable profit margin. This conflict is sometimes made worse by contract provisions that use financial penalties for poor performance but have no incentive for good performance. This approach is not always effective and a good example is liquidated damages clauses, which rarely compensate an employer in full for actual losses caused by delays. Bonuses for early completion are sometimes used and they can be much more effective in preventing delay than liquidated damages.

That principle can be used on a wider basis. In the UK, target cost contracts have become popular, where the employer and contractor share any savings if the final cost is below the agreed target but also share the cost overspend if the project ends above target. This means that there is a financial incentive for both parties to work together and find ways to reduce costs but also to manage risks. For example, if a contractor risk event occurs which will result in additional costs, the employer will share such cost (or have a reduced saving), which means the employer is interested in dealing with such issues instead of simply dismissing them as contractor risks. Similarly, a contractor is still keen to reduce the effects of employer risks rather than using them as a way to increase recovery.

Target cost contracts raise their own issues and the first challenge is agreeing a realistic target. Such contracts require parties to understand how the risk share mechanism works but when used correctly, there is a powerful incentive for parties to work together.

Another interesting question is whether parties should resolve disputes as they happen or resolve them once the works are completed. Disagreements as to the effect of a delaying cause, what is a defect or the cost of a variation, are part of a construction process and often there is genuine disagreement.

Dealing with all issues at the end of a project has the benefit of the participants being able to negotiate an overall and final settlement. Such an approach does mean that until the project is completed, there is uncertainty as to the final cost. This is of course an issue for both the employer, who needs to know if a budget will be exceeded, and a contractor, who needs to know if a project will result in a profit. Where banks fund projects, there is benefit in having a clear understanding of the ultimate project costs. In addition, leaving issues until completion often means that an opportunity to mitigate a loss is missed (since both parties deny liability) and relevant information is lost or forgotten, with both parties becoming entrenched in their position.

It is for that reason that the FIDIC form contains an adjudication provision and that the use of dispute resolution boards is being encouraged. This is not the place to discuss whether decisions should be binding or just recommendations, but any decision by respected and authoritative individuals who know and understand the project is a fairly reliable indication of what the ultimate outcome is likely to be. This provides a better understanding of the potential final cost for all parties. Regarding adjudication as a process aimed at achieving certainty instead of a hostile situation may increase its use and may help to avoid major post-completion disputes.

In conclusion, it is worth exploring what can be done to ensure that the parties involved in construction projects have a better understanding of the contracts they use and how contracts can be structured to encourage the parties to work together on the basis of aligned commercial interests. There are, however, no all-embracing solutions and the characteristics of each project, and the parties involved, will need to be considered. But if the construction industry is improving and modernizing, there is no reason why contracts should not develop in the same way. the parties involved, will need to be considered. But if the construction industry and modernizing, there is no reason why contracts should not develop in the same way.

Shy Jackson
Construction Lawyer
Pinsent Masons
London
UK

References

Charrett, D. (2013). The use of the Unidroit principles in international construction contracts. *International Construction Law Review*, 20(4).

Hök, G.S. (2014). Payments and Disputes under FIDIC, in Particular under the FIDIC Silver Book – The Sedgman Case. International Construction Law Review, Informa, London.

ICC (2012). *International Court of Arbitration Bulletin*, 23(2).

Knutson, R. (2005). *FIDIC: An Analysis of International Construction Contracts*. Kluwer Law International, London.

Mallmann, R. (2002). *Bau- und Anlagenbauverträge nach den FIDIC-Standardbedingungen*. Verlag C. H. Beck, Munich.

Menon, S. (2014). Origins and Aspirations: Developing an International Construction Court. International Construction Law Review, Informa, London.

Molineaux, C. Moving toward a construction *lex mercatoria*: a *lex constructionis*. Online. Available at: www.uni-koeln.de (accessed 3 May 2013).

Further reading

Charrett, D. (2012). A common law of construction contracts: or vive la différence? *International Construction Law Review*, 29(1).

Cushman, R.F. (2011). *Proving and Pricing Construction Claims*. Wolters Kluwer, New York.

Jaeger, A.V. and Hök, G.S. (2010). *FIDIC: A Guide for Practitioners*. Springer Verlag, Berlin.

Klee, L. (2012). *Smluvní vztahy výstavbových projektuů* . Wolters Kluwer, Prague.

Koran. Surah al Ma'idah (The dinner table) 1. Online. Available at: http://quod.lib.umich.edu/k/koran/browse.html (accessed 30 March 2013).

Websites

www.ebrd.com
www.eib.org
www.worldbank.org

6 Price

6.1 Contract price

The way that the contract price is established (especially in large construction projects) is problematic as adequate and clear guidelines are lacking in many countries. Undefined and ambiguous contractual terms tend to give rise to disputes.

Every construction contract should, above all, define sufficiently how the total contract price is to be created and what it should consist of. In many developing countries, the prices of products were formed artificially within a controlled economy. Prices were perceived as fixed and not influenced by market conditions, inflation, and so on. This allowed governments to use fixed prices as indicators for directive planning and as an instrument to regulate public consumption.

Construction projects are typically long-term processes. In the preparation phase or at the beginning of the design or construction works, the participants have only limited knowledge of the potential risk. These risks are typically allocated to the parties by contract, or moved to third parties through insurance policies or securities. Other risks will be dealt with by way of a contractor's risk surcharge or employer's financial reserve. If there is no financial reserve in a project and risks are hard to foresee and treat, or the contractor is not able to cope with a loss, the project can be negatively affected and, eventually, prematurely terminated.

Very often, the employer does not have sufficient financial resources and needs a loan or subsidy. The employer has to negotiate the conditions of the loan or subsidy with lenders (mainly banks) or an authority that provides such a subsidy. Lenders and such authorities are then closely engaged in the particular project and supervise if the employer and the contractor are complying with the agreed conditions. Some of the most sensitive issues involve the actual compliance with grant conditions, how the contract price is calculated and the handling of variations and claims.

6.1.1 Project finance

Sometimes what is called project finance is used as long-term financing of infrastructure and industrial projects. Project finance is based upon the projected cash flows of the project rather than the balance sheets of its sponsors. Usually, a project financing structure involves a number of equity investors known as sponsors as well as a syndicate of banks or other lending institutions that provide loans to the operation. These are most commonly non-recourse loans, which are secured by the project assets and paid entirely from the project cash flow, rather than from the general assets or creditworthiness of the project sponsors. Financing is typically secured by all the project assets, including revenue-producing contracts. Project lenders are given a lien on all of these assets and are able to assume control of a project if the project company has difficulties complying with the loan terms.

To satisfy the conditions established by the lenders (the subsidy providers) and to avoid disputes, the appropriate delivery method (including the method of total contract price determination and claim and variation management rules) must be chosen and described in full in the contract.

The contract price is usually one of the employer's priorities. The lowest price is often the only criterion in public procurement and, for this reason, the contract price frequently becomes a political issue. On the other hand, large construction projects are inherently prone to cost overruns.

International construction measurement standards: Global consistency in cost analysis by Simon Collard (United Arab Emirates)

The impact of globalisation continues to be felt throughout the built environment, with teams of professionals from different technical and cultural backgrounds working together to deliver projects of all sizes. Whilst international contractors and consultancies seek involvement in the pipeline of projects scheduled in the GCC (Gulf Cooperation Council), some of the region's largest developers are increasingly looking to invest in project opportunities away from their home markets. These factors, coupled with disruptive technologies such as BIM, present our industry with an opportunity to introduce standards that will become default practice for construction professionals across the world working to provide more clarity and certainty of outcome.

Take for example a claim for additional construction cost. The failure to apply consistent standards in recording and reporting additional cost can lead to misunderstandings and mistrust between the parties and potentially end up in an expensive, time consuming formal dispute resolution process. Equally, the absence of recognised standards may contribute to a lack of transparency, contrary to the ethics positions adopted by many international organisations and governmental bodies and prevent matters being resolved by the parties under the contract. Acknowledging the beneficial impact that international accounting standards have had in the financial sector, a group of over 40 construction and engineering bodies with a diverse multi-national membership (including AACE, ACostE, CIOB, ICE, RIBA and RICS amongst others) have committed to developing a consistent approach to measuring and recording construction cost: the International Construction Measurement Standards (ICMS).

Following on from the International Property Measurement Standards (IPMS) published in 2014, the ICMS Coalition held initial meetings at the International Monetary Fund in

Washington D.C. in June 2015 before a drafting process commenced. The consultation period for the draft standards ended in January 2017 and the first version of the ICMS was published in July 2017. If the bold vision projected by the ICMS Coalition is realised, the standards will influence the way costs are presented for a wide range of construction and engineering projects globally. The ICMS Coalition set out to develop standards that:

- Define what is included within construction costs for reporting and audit purposes;
- Facilitate the comparison of construction project costs between different countries;
- Assist governments and international bodies benchmark costs consistently and transparently;
- Aid in identifying the causes of cost differences between projects;
- Contribute to the decision making process when establishing a project location during the design phase; and
- Inform investment and financing decisions as well as the delivery strategy for the project.

The ICMS consultation paper states that it is envisaged that the standards will be used in dispute resolution work, as well as assisting in identifying capital construction and associated capital construction cost categories. In addition, the introduction of the ICMS should:

- Identify universal definitions of heads of construction costs;
- Recommend a standard reporting format;
- Codify terminology that will be familiar to professionals internationally; and
- Be adaptable to the changing needs of project stakeholders.

Publications compiled by the Royal Institution of Chartered Surveyors indicate that many project costs in the GCC are still prepared and recorded in accordance with the older Principles of Measurement International (POMI) standard, whereas current guidance by RICS suggests that the New Rules of Measurement (NRM) format is used. Any conversion between the two measurement and reporting standards is a laborious process and may lead to mistakes when calculating quantum at a later date in the event of a dispute. As the success of many common construction claims (such as those for disruption) will hinge on the adequacy and level of detail of records held by the claimant, it is noted that the ICMS offers guidance as to how records of costs can be prepared and recorded in a consistent manner. By following the ICMS, a claimant may present their substantiation from the outset in a recognised format familiar to the person(s) responsible for quantum evaluation.

An additional application of the ICMS will be the integration into Building Information Modeling (BIM) systems to allow a standard platform for digital cost management. It is noted that as de facto standards exist within the software used for technical drawing and delay analysis, a comparable standard for quantum analysis of construction claims could also be achieved.

It remains to be seen how long it will take for the ICMS Coalition to achieve international acceptance of the standards. However, as the standards have been developed with input from the professional bodies from which many technical arbitrators and expert witnesses are drawn, all parties responsible for cost planning and control in construction projects may wish to treat the guidance contained therein as the indicative level of detail required to help avoid disputes. Alternatively, should a claim situation arise, a clear categorisation of cost consistent with the

ICMS approach may contribute towards achieving an amicable settlement, particularly when working with international project teams.

The ICMS Standard is available for download at: https://icms-coalition.org/the-standard/.

Simon Collard
BSc (Hons) MSc (Const. Law)
MRICS MCIArb MCIOB
Managing Consultant
HKA
Dubai
United Arab Emirates

6.2 Bid pricing methods

To understand the limits of the foreseeability of the total contract price it is important to know how the bids are priced. Pricing methods may vary, depending on the practices used within a particular company. The pricing method that enjoys the widest use is based on a determined unit cost that is then increased by a percentage margin.

The bid price is usually the total sum of the direct costs of equipment, material and labor, site overheads, headquarters overheads, risk and profit surcharge. On the other hand, a claim for additional payment may rest only on the documented direct costs plus overheads and profit surcharge. Another method of claim quantification is to use a methodology for variation evaluation, that is, the rates and prices of a bill of quantities of a particular contract or a similar contract, industry standards or a new calculation for a particular rate or price. The common position on the relevance of tender allowances is that the tender allowances have limited relevance for the evaluation of the costs of prolongation and disruption caused by breach of contract or any other cause that requires the evaluation of additional costs.

To illustrate the pricing methods, let's take a particular product like a bridge. Once again, a problem appears in the uniqueness of such a bridge as a product because every construction project is unique in its own way. The designer, employer, on-site physical conditions, risks, and the like are always different. This is why there cannot be any all-embracing, unified bridge pricing methodology.

Having received and considered the tender documentation and bill of quantities, the contractor will determine what items of work (moving earth, bearing structures, and the like) they are able to construct by their own means and what other items of work (such as special foundations and formwork) the contractor will have to provide through subcontractors. With this decision made, the contractor will contact the subcontractors for their price quotations.

The items in the former group are subject to internal estimates. A budget is prepared for every individual item that covers the necessary materials complete with shipment, labor costs, and a time schedule. All items are then assigned a respective "weight" based on their nature, knowledge of the design, the manufacturing processes, and other methods used in general. Regardless of whether internally estimated or received from subcontractors, these costs are identified as direct costs.

Site and headquarters overheads constitute other components of the price. The wages of the project teams (the project manager and their team, the site manager, and their team), project team personnel expenses such as for transport, communication, training, and so on are included in the site overheads. The site overheads further cover flat, office and land rentals, cleaning, IT costs, power and water supply costs, and site facilities (including their setup, removal and maintenance, such as traffic ways, fences, traffic signs, and on-site security guards).

Headquarters overheads contain a percentage surcharge covering the cost of contractor headquarters.

The last component of the price consists of the risk surcharge and profit. Overhead items, risk surcharges, and profit are usually not subject to any separate item in the bill of quantities and the contractor must add them to the other items that are already defined.

Another major distinction to be drawn in connection with pricing and subsequent submission of claims may be the one between fixed and variable costs. Fixed costs are costs that are not directly dependent on production volumes and remain constant. Variable costs, on the other hand, rise and fall with production volumes.

Within a construction project, production volume depends on the time necessary for completion of the work. Variable costs grow with extensions of time, making it more expensive to run site facilities. However, the price of setting up and removing them remains the same (i.e., fixed) as they are one-time processes. As a part of variable costs, the price of works performance bank guarantees and any insurance must also be extended. Therefore, addendums to original contracts will also grow in response to an extension of time for completion.

The contractor may also submit what are called cover bids. The reasons behind submitting cover bids vary and can include motives such as not wanting to disappoint the employer, maintaining good relationships with other contractors, and so on.

A particular cycle in a market economy also plays a role in valuation. For instance, the risk surcharge is often left out in recessions with the priority being to maintain contractor turnover. Therefore, market economy cycles and project risks are important factors affecting valuation.

Cash flow can play a role as well. Many large construction projects last for a number of years so the contractor may charge higher prices for some items of work to be carried out in the later stages of the project, for example, to adjust for inflation or to incur a loss by the end of the first year of construction for accounting or tax reasons. Another factor may be the contractor speculating on the valuation of items in relation to known errors in the employer's basic design or foreseeable, necessary variations.

6.3 Methods of contract price determination

The following contract price determination criteria can be distinguished:

- economic influences (fixed or variable price);
- formation of the "total price," that is, mainly the content of total price and how the total price is calculated (lump price, re-measurement, and cost plus).

6.3.1 Economic influences on the contract price

Unlike variable price, the fixed price does not undergo any adjustments due to inflation, deflation, depreciation, changes in exchange rates, interest rates, economic cycle development trends, or to changes in costs in a particular market. Concerning the variable price, individual criteria have to be set out in the contract to allow for adjustments. For example, the FIDIC forms contain Sub-Clause 13.8, Adjustments for changes in cost, which reads:

> If this Sub-Clause applies, the amounts payable to the contractor shall be adjusted for rises or falls in the cost of labour, goods and other inputs to the Works, by the addition or deduction of the amounts determined by the formulae prescribed in this Sub-Clause. To the extent that full compensation for any rise or fall in costs is not covered by the provisions of this or other clauses, the accepted contract amount shall be deemed to have included amounts to cover the contingency of other rises and falls in costs.

6.3.2 Formation of total contract price

The total contract price is calculated on the basis of re-measurement, lump sum price, or the cost plus method. It should be emphasized that these terms are often used inconsistently. Therefore, it is always necessary to define and describe the contract price determination method as precisely as possible in the contract. The above-mentioned basic types of pricing methods can be used in various combinations and with different components to limit (maximum price) or motivate (target price). Larger projects may adopt a combination of the above-mentioned methods including different payment arrangements.

6.4 Re-measurement

Using the re-measurement method (the measured or unit price contract), the works actually done are measured based on the individual rates and prices offered by the contractor in their bid in the bill of quantities (prepared by the employer). The bill of quantities contains particular items and gives a description of the work and quantity. Every individual item and the respective rate or price must be properly contemplated and its content clearly understood to avoid disputes. The contractor will evaluate the rates and prices in the bill of quantities while keeping in mind prices for the materials, products, labor, equipment, plants, and so on (e.g., per cubic meter cost of the pit to be excavated). This process is called estimating and affords a means for the employer of comparing tenders received once they have been priced.

It was mentioned that sometimes estimates are not accurate and they may differ significantly from the actual price. This is especially true where prices have been taken over from past contracts. Works that are specific to the project such as pit excavation, for example, depend on things like subsoil, local hydrogeology and distance to temporary deposits which may be difficult to estimate accurately.

Next to the continuing re-measurement of the works, the contract price is also formed via claims, variations and adjustments based on the particular contractual risk allocation, claims options, and variation (and adjustments) procedure.

6.4.1 Methods of measurement

Methods of measurement are standardized processes that facilitate measurement and valuation. Standard methods of measurement specify how virtually all commonly encountered construction activities are to be measured. An example is the *Civil Engineering Standard Method of Measurement* (CESMM) developed by the Institution of Civil Engineers (ICE). The purpose of CESMM is to set out the procedure by which a bill of quantities should be prepared and priced and the quantities of work expressed and measured. The latest edition (fourth edition) was published in 2012. Another example is the *Standard Method of Measurement* (SMM) published by the Royal Institute of Chartered Surveyors (RICS) in 1988. The SMM is now in its seventh edition (SMM7) and was published in 1998. SMM7 provides detailed information, classification tables, and rules to create a uniform basis for measuring building works, in order to facilitate industry-wide consistency and benchmarking, to encourage the adoption of best practice and to help avoid disputes.

Re-measurement contracts without an agreed method of measurement are prone to disputes.

6.4.2 Provisional sum

Bill of quantities may contain various types of items and amounts serving different purposes. Their description and content depend mainly on the contract and the method of measurement used. One such item is the provisional sum. In construction contracts, a provisional sum may have various meanings, but usually it is the sum referred to as a provisional sum in the bill of quantities. The provisional sum is used for the payment of works or services for which the total price is difficult to foresee or there is some uncertainty as to whether the works or services will be performed at all. This is different from the contingency (the employer's financial reserve) used to cover the financial consequences of either known or unknown hazards or their respective risks that are not insured or secured. Contingency should be subject to confidentiality.

Under Sub-Clause 1.1.4.10 of the FIDIC CONS/1999 Red Book Provisional Sum means "a sum (if any) which is specified in the Contract as a provisional sum, for the execution of any part of the Works or for the supply of Plant, Materials or services under Sub-Clause 13.5 [Provisional Sums]."

Sub-Clause 13.5 further reads:

> Each Provisional Sum shall only be used, in whole or in part, in accordance with the Engineer's instructions, and the Contract Price shall be adjusted accordingly. The total sum paid to the Contractor shall include only such amounts, for the work, supplies or services to which the Provisional Sum

relates, as the Engineer shall have instructed. For each Provisional Sum, the Engineer may instruct: (a) work to be executed (including Plant, Materials or services to be supplied) by the Contractor and valued under Sub-Clause 13.3 [Variation Procedure]; and/or (b) Plant, Materials or services to be purchased by the Contractor, from a nominated Subcontractor (as defined in Clause 5 [Nominated Subcontractors]) or otherwise; and for which there shall be included in the Contract Price: (i) the actual amounts paid (or due to be paid) by the Contractor, and (ii) a sum for overhead charges and profit, calculated as a percentage of these actual amounts by applying the relevant percentage rate (if any) stated in the appropriate Schedule. If there is no such rate, the percentage rate stated in the Appendix to Tender shall be applied. The Contractor shall, when required by the Engineer, produce quotations, invoices, vouchers and accounts or receipts in substantiation.

Provisional sums under FIDIC forms are the amounts set out separately by the employer in the budget. These amounts are intended to cover particular works or services where the employer is unsure if they will be used or if the quantity or other attributes of them could not have been exactly known prior to commencement of construction. Such sums can be used for those particular items only.

These works or services are only performed after the instruction of the engineer. The quantity is to be measured and the employer will pay for the works actually done, either within a variation procedure as per Sub-Clause 13.3 or on the cost plus basis. As mentioned above, the provisional sum may have a different meaning in construction than under FIDIC.

A provisional lump sum may be encountered by project participants. This is a firm price for part of the works, with provisional rates to apply to a series of contingencies. For example, a range of potential ground conditions could be separately priced and the rates would simply be applied to match the conditions actually encountered. The employer then knows the "worst case scenario," but will benefit from paying the lower rates if the conditions encountered prove to be straightforward. A provisional lump sum also mitigates potential problems where the design is defined by reference to open-ended or general criteria by allowing alternative design solutions to be priced (Jenkins and Stebbings, 2006).

6.4.3 Options

In the context of procurement law, an option is a right of the employer to purchase products or services on terms and conditions determined in advance which the contractor is obliged to perform on the pre-agreed terms stipulated. Exercise of an option does not constitute a change of the contract but a change pursuant to the contract (directed variation), provided that: (1) the option is sufficiently clear in its description; (2) that the tender contains the price of the option so that the employer may take the option into account, directly or indirectly when awarding the contract; and (3) that the option may be exercised without prior negotiation between the parties. Options also have the commercial advantage of maintaining a fixed lump sum price in competition, that is, during the tender stage where the contractor fought to win the contract, as compared to changes agreed upon subsequently where the employer often has no alternative but to pay the price asked by the contractor (Hartlev and Liljenbøl, 2013).

6.5 The lump sum

Under the lump sum method, a pre-agreed sum (regardless of actual cost incurred) is paid by the employer and the works actually done are not measured but paid against the schedule of payments, mostly once the predetermined sections (or milestones) are finished or when the project is fully completed. The lump sum price is also influenced by claims, variations, and adjustments based on the particular contractual risk allocation, claims options and variation (and adjustments) procedure.

The lump sum should be sufficient to cover the anticipated costs, overhead, profit, and risk surcharge. The main advantage for the employer is cost certainty and simpler contract administration. This advantage is lost where the surcharge is too high and where the risks of a particular project are hard to quantify. Disputes arise in such circumstances where varied or additional works and claims in a lump sum contract are not solved by pre-defined rules or with a common-sense and fair approach of all participants involved.

An alternative called "detailed lump sum contract" is sometimes encountered for example in Germany. Some authors speak about a "system choice" that is to be made by the employer in this regard. If the employer has decided for the lump sum contract "system" with such detailed description of the contractual services, the contractor need only execute the services that are described in detail under the agreed lump sum. An employer attempt to evade this by adding a completeness clause to the "detailed lump sum contract" would be seen as invalid in Germany (Kus, Markus and Steding, 1999).

6.6 Cost plus

Under the cost plus method, the contractor receives from the employer not only the payment for reasonable and properly incurred cost, but also a fee for overhead and profit. This method is more appropriate for high-risk projects where a lump sum price (which takes all contingencies into account) would be too high. To encourage the contractor to perform the works for the lowest possible price, some additional mechanisms can be used, for example, the maximum guaranteed price or target price, described below.

Under this arrangement, contractors are usually obliged to maintain comprehensive and contemporary cost records and the employer usually reserves the right to audit the claimed cost to ensure they have been reasonably and properly incurred. The profit and overhead surcharge will be subject to competition in the tender period.

It was already mentioned that the cost plus method is often used for contractual claims quantification. Thus, if the contractor suffers delay or incurs cost under FIDIC forms in case of employer risk event, they are entitled to a payment of any such cost (including overhead) plus reasonable profit in some situations. Under Sub-Clause 1.1.4.3 "cost" means all expenditure reasonably incurred (or to be incurred) by the contractor, whether on- or off-site, including overhead and similar charges, but does not include profit. Profit is allowed only in specific claims, that is, usually those where there is an employer default.

The cost plus price is also influenced by adjustments based on the particular contractual risk allocation, and compensation events.

6.7 Guaranteed maximum price

Employers sometimes want to cap the total contract price using the guaranteed maximum price to allocate all risks of potential price increases to the contractor. This approach is used and accepted for example in the United States using the construction management at risk delivery method. The main drawback of such a system is that it must be perfectly thought out in respect of risk allocation, insurance, securities, and financial reserves (or risk surcharges). Such a setup is not appropriate for projects where numerous hazards with major risks are pending and it is not possible to price such risks transparently.

This method usually involves a two-stage procurement process. The first stage includes a preliminary investigation, a feasibility study, and outline design. The second stage is the development of the design and project construction. The first stage of the project is paid for on a cost plus basis. The contract then "converts" to a guaranteed maximum price once the scope and definition of the works become more certain. The employer retains the option not to continue with the project at all after the first stage if the guaranteed maximum price is prohibitively high or to discontinue cooperation with the contractor and tender the job anew on the basis of the completed preliminary design (Jenkins and Stebbings, 2006).

6.8 Target price

One of the biggest challenges in every project is achieving an environment where both parties collaborate together and have a common commercial interest. It is therefore efficient to design contractual mechanisms that provide a commercial incentive for the parties to communicate and collaborate in ensuring that the project is a success.

One such mechanism is a target cost contract. As part of the contract negotiations, the parties agree a target price based on their knowledge of the project conditions and their assessment of potential risks. The works then begin and during the works two things happen in parallel:

- The contractor is generally paid their actual costs (less disallowed costs if they are defined) plus a fee on a regular basis (usually every four weeks).
- The initial target price is adjusted during the works in accordance with claims and variations (compensation events) and their estimated cost.

On completion, these two elements are compared. If there is a saving or a cost increase as against the target, then the parties share such savings or cost increases in the agreed proportions set out when the contract was agreed. This is regarded as an incentive to efficient contract management because both parties share the risks (to varying degrees) and they both have an incentive to reduce the actual cost, so that a gain share is increased or a pain share is limited. Contractual mechanisms such as the early warning notices and the accepted program are designed to ensure that the contract operates on an open basis and both parties can take the initiative in seeking to reduce costs. For example, if there is a cost increase to specified materials, this is a contractor risk but it may result in the employer sharing a lower saving or sharing a cost increase. The employer is therefore motivated to discuss with the contractor how to reduce the impact of such an issue, for example, by looking to use other materials instead.

Target cost contracts can therefore be highly effective in motivating parties to cooperate and to increase their gain share or reduce a pain share. For that to happen, however, the parties must understand the key elements that form the basis of the contract.

It is crucial to agree on a target price at the appropriate level, so that it is a realistic and achievable target. If the target is set either too high or too low, the incentive mechanism is unlikely to operate as intended. By way of example, if the target is set too low, there will almost certainly be an automatic pain share which has the potential to disturb the commercial balance, especially where the pain share is not on a fixed 50% basis. One of the ways of ensuring that the correct target is fixed is by engaging early contractor involvement and, where appropriate, pre-construction services agreements.

6.9 Payment

It is often said that cash is the "blood" of the project. Without an appropriate cash flow, the contractor is not able to perform and construction projects end in trouble. This is the reason why some system of interval payment is required. On the other hand, the employer needs to ensure that they obtain value for their payments and the contractor remains motivated to finish the works in accordance with the contract. Various forms of interim payments are available in different combinations. The most common are progress or milestone payments.

6.9.1 Progress payments

The majority of construction contracts are based on progress payments payable on a monthly basis. The amount due to the contractor reflects the actual progress of the works recorded in an interim certificate issued by the certifier (usually the contract administrator).

With re-measurement contracts, the actual works done are usually measured by the engineer on a monthly basis against particular rates and prices in the bill of quantities.

With lump sum contracts, the schedule of payments is usually used for the payment of instalments of the lump sum. Sometimes, even with lump sum contracts, employers do not want to lose control in terms of the relation of instalments to works actually done and require the contractor to submit a breakdown of the lump sum to pay the lump sum instalments in an appropriate monthly proportion often also with connection to the time schedule (activity schedules). A situation may arise close to the end of the project when the lump sum has already been absorbed and the works are not finished. In such cases, it is the risk of the contractor to pay for the rest of the works to be completed. On the other hand, a situation may also arise when the works are finished and the lump sum is not paid out. In the latter, the unpaid portion of the lump sum becomes a profit to the contractor.

6.9.2 Milestone payments

Some construction contracts provide for payments to contractors upon achievement of milestones throughout the construction period. Milestones are set against the completion of certain activities or a section of work and, upon completing those works or that section, the contractor is paid for the works/section. Milestones are often incorporated into the time schedule (program). This type of payment gives the contractor an incentive to complete works on time and in accordance with the time schedule (Jenkins and Stebbings, 2006).

Taxation in international construction contracts by Alex Blomfield (UK)

Each international construction contract will require specialist taxation advice from tax advisers in the country of the project. For the sake of certainty, the employer and its lenders will prefer as much as possible for the contractor to include relevant taxes in its price and acknowledge that the contract price includes all taxes applicable under relevant laws to any payment related to the execution and completion of the works or the contract. If the contractor has difficulty conducting proper due diligence on such taxes or if there exists a compelling reason for the employer to take a certain tax risk, then in limited circumstances the employer may agree to retain responsibility for certain taxes such as value-added tax, import taxes, and duties and withholding tax.

While, for example, international hydropower construction contracts generally allocate most taxes to the contractor, the employer generally retains change in tax risk. This usually manifests itself through the change in law clause pursuant to which the contract price shall be adjusted to take account of any increase or decrease in cost resulting from a change in the laws or taxes of the country of the hydropower project (including the introduction of new laws and the repeal or modification of existing laws) or in the judicial or official governmental interpretation of such laws or taxes made after an agreed base date, which affects the contractor in the performance of obligations under the contract.

In an international hydropower context, the issue of withholding tax has most potential effect on the electro-mechanical contract. Offshore payments for services attract withholding taxes in many jurisdictions. This often drives a split of the electro-mechanical contract into offshore and onshore contracts, with a coordination wrap agreement, or at least separate onshore and offshore scopes. Under this approach an employer: (1) will pay no withholding tax on payments under the onshore electro-mechanical contract; and (2) will pay withholding tax only on the value of services provided under the offshore electro-mechanical contract. Structuring contracts in the most tax-efficient way always requires specialist tax advice from at least the jurisdiction in which the project is situated, if not also other jurisdictions as well.

Standard forms, such as FIDIC, contain no tax clause. An example bespoke-drafted tax clause for an international hydropower construction contract based on the FIDIC form follows.

Taxes

"*Taxes*" means any present or future taxes, levies, rates, duties, deductions, fees, withholding obligations, value added taxes, imposts (including importation of plant and materials), and other charges of a similar nature levied by any governmental authority, including authorities of the country, and all penalties, fines, surcharges, interest, or other payments on or in respect thereof, that may be imposed on or in connection with the contractor's obligations with respect to the performance of this contract, and "*tax*" shall be construed accordingly.

The contractor shall pay, and acknowledges that the contract price includes, all taxes applicable to any payment related to the works or the contract. In addition, the following conditions apply.

(a) If any withholding taxes apply, related to the payments to the contractor of amounts due under the contract, then the employer shall deduct such withholding taxes from such payment and remit the balance of such payment to the contractor without a gross-up; provided, however, that the employer shall promptly reimburse to the contractor, together with interest thereon at the default interest rate, any withholding tax wrongly deducted.

(b) If any laws require the contractor to make a deduction or withholding from any payment to a subcontractor or any other party, then the contractor shall have the sole responsibility before the tax authorities of the country for any withholding or deduction that such laws require it to make with respect to such payment, in accordance with tax laws of the country. The contractor shall have no right to any reimbursement or indemnification from the employer for any unpaid withholding tax, deduction or fine imposed on the contractor by such tax authorities of the country with respect to payments it has made to subcontractors or any other party, domiciled outside of the country.

(c) The contract price shall exclude import taxes and duties and value-added tax.

(d) The contractor shall bear all travel and lodging costs and expenses incurred by the contractor's employees.

(e) The contractor shall self-assess, and withhold, all taxes that may correspond to its employees, agents or representatives as a consequence of the subscription, fulfillment, and execution of their obligations under the contract. The contractor shall be solely responsible before the tax authorities of the country for any withholding or deduction applicable to the remuneration paid to its employees. The contractor shall not be entitled to any reimbursement or indemnification from the employer for any unpaid withholding tax, deduction or fine imposed on the contractor by the tax authorities of the country with respect to remuneration paid to its employees.

(f) The contractor shall provide supporting documentation and issue the corresponding invoice indicating the services provided, the applicable period, the determination of the compensation, as well as any other additional information requested by the employer.

(g) The contractor shall include in the determination of customs value of the imported goods, the value of engineering, development, artwork, design work, and plans and sketches undertaken elsewhere than in the country of importation and necessary for their production jointly with material, components, parts, tools, dies, molds, and similar items incorporated, used or consumed in the production of the imported goods.
(h) The contractor acknowledges that customs value shall not include charges for construction, erection, assembly, maintenance, or technical assistance, undertaken after importation on imported goods such as plant, machinery, or equipment, the cost of transport after importation and duties and taxes of the country of importation. To this effect, these items will be distinguished from the price actually paid or payable for the imported goods.
(i) The contractor acknowledges that the accepted contract amount includes any royalties or license fees related to the works, which the contractor shall pay, either directly or indirectly.

Alex Blomfield
Special Counsel
K&L Gates LLP
London
UK

Managing the risk of non-payment by Sean Sullivan Gibbs (UK)

Most international contractors will have experienced the problem of non-payment, whether for contracted works, variations, or claims. In jurisdictions where there are no equivalent provisions of the English Construction Act or as in the United States in the form of a lien, the contractor's only protection is found in the express terms of the contract.

While most employers and their advisers will not provide bonds to secure their payment obligation, they will often be prepared to accept standard form of contract provisions that help the contractor mitigate the risk of non-payment. The most common being the right to suspend performance, the right to terminate and tier dispute resolution clauses. Indeed, these terms are so widely encountered that they are increasingly being accepted in bespoke contracts such as those in EPC type arrangements.

The right to suspend performance in England

Prior to the Housing Grants Construction and Regeneration Act 1996, the contractor had no right under common law to suspend for non-payment as per the case of *Canterbury Pipelines ltd v. Christchurch Drainage Board* [1979] 16 BLR 76.

The Housing Grants Construction and Regeneration Act 1996 introduced that construction contracts to include the right to suspend performance for non-payment; this was later amended by Sections 138 to 145 of part 8 of the Local Democracy, Economic Development and Construction Act of 2009.

The writer has used this on numerous occasions in England, where specialist contractors were not paid by the main contractor, in order to stop work until payment was made. This is particularly useful if the activities being suspended are on a critical path, whereas if they are not, it was beneficial anyway to the extent it meant that expenditure could be decreased on the project and company cash flow maintained.

The revised right is stated at Section 112:

112 Right to suspend performance for non-payment
  (1) *Where the requirement in section 111(1) applies in relation to any sum but is not complied with, the person to whom the sum is due has the right (without prejudice to any other right or remedy) to suspend performance of any or all of his obligations under the contract to the party by whom payment ought to have been made ("the party in default").*
  (2) *The right may not be exercised without first giving to the party in default at least seven days' notice of intention to suspend performance, stating the ground or grounds on which it is intended to suspend performance.*
  (3) *The right to suspend performance ceases when the party in default makes payment in full of the amount referred to in subsection (1).*
  (3A) *Where the right conferred by this section is exercised, the party in default shall be liable to pay to the party exercising the right a reasonable amount in respect of costs and expenses reasonably incurred by that party as a result of the exercise of the right.*
  (4) *Any period during which performance is suspended in pursuance of or in consequence of the exercise of the right conferred by this section shall be disregarded in computing for the purposes of any contractual time limit the time taken, by the party exercising the right or by a third party, to complete any work directly or indirectly affected by the exercise of the right. Where the contractual time limit is set by reference to a date rather than a period, the date shall be adjusted accordingly.*

Parties using this must comply with the provisions strictly or risk not benefitting from the right to a reasonable amount in respect of costs and expenses reasonably incurred by that party as a result of the exercise of the right or an extension of time for the period of suspension.

Indeed, just suspending works without complying with the provisions could at least be a breach of contract or at worst a repuditory breach of contract.

The right to suspend performance under contract

The FIDIC forms of contract contain the right to suspend performance or reduce the rate of progress for non-payment. The contractual mechanism must be followed exactly, otherwise the contractor may be held to have repudiated the contract; and in particular, the notice provisions to the employer. When the contractor is subsequently paid they then are entitled to an extension of time and to payment of any reasonable costs plus a reasonable profit for the period of suspension, but they must resume work again as soon as is reasonably practicable.

The threat of suspension acts as pressure on the employer while allowing the contractor to reduce or completely suspend further expenditure.

Clause 16 of the FIDIC Red Book 1999 allows the contractor to suspend work or reduce the rate of work for one of three reasons:

1. The employer not complying with its obligation to disclose its financial arrangements under Sub-Clause 2.4

2. The engineer failing to certify an interim payment certificate under Sub-Clause 14.6
3. The employer failing to make payment under Sub-Clause 14.7

The first reason failure to disclose financial arrangements is the ongoing duty to supply financial information to demonstrate that the employer can pay the contractor for the work. If used throughout the project duration the contractor should be able to see if they are likely to be paid and if not can plan what action to take. It is best used early on before mobilizing to site.

The other reasons relate to interim certification and interim payment and are very much tied to the contractor's cash flow.

It has been the writer's experience that surprisingly many contractors in the Middle East do not enact these suspension provisions despite not being paid and pass this abuse along their supply chain rather than risk upsetting the employer.

The earlier versions of the Red Book do offer such protection but the heavily amended varieties commonly used in the Arabian Gulf region remove it. This omission means that the local civil code will apply. For example, in the United Arab Emirates, the contractor may have a right to suspend the works for non-payment as argument has been advanced that Article 247 could assist as it states that a party may refuse to continue its obligations if the other party is not performing its obligations.

The suspension provisions in FIDIC require 21 days' notice unlike the 7 days' notice period of Section 112 of the UK Construction Act but are still of real benefit.

The usual way that the general conditions in FIDIC are amended is by way of particular conditions; contractors must therefore be alert to any change to the standard terms during the tender period as employers advisers may try and change these areas.

The 2013 ICHEME Red Book for International Use is not as widely used as the 1999 FIDIC Red Book but it also offers protection to the contractor from his client the purchaser.

Where the purchaser does not pay in full by the final date for payment or an interim payment certificate is not issued then the contractor may give 7 days' notice of their intention to suspend performance and suspend seven days after giving the notice.

The usual way that the general conditions in the ICHEME suite is amended is by way of particular conditions; contractors must therefore be alert to any change to the standard terms during the tender period.

The NEC contracts are being increasingly seen internationally particularly in former British Common Law countries such as Hong Kong and South Africa. In international use, the right to suspend for non-payment is not the default choice as this is included by the secondary option Y (UK2) and this is only commonly used in the United Kingdom to comply with the Construction Act and suspension is compensated as a compensation event.

The right to terminate performance

The FIDIC forms of contract allow the suspension to become permanent by way of termination if payment is not received by the stipulated period provided that the notice requirements are complied with.

This more drastic action will focus the employers mind on the need to make payment if it wants the contractor to continue and is an effective tool where the employer has the funds but is not releasing them. Where the employer does not have funds it may allow for a negotiated form of security to be arranged.

The ICHEME and NEC include similar provisions as does the JCT.

Where the employer does not have funds it may allow for a negotiated form of security to be arranged but this is very much subject to the contractor being able to exert pressure by threat of complete withdrawal. This being particularly powerful where there is a specialist licensed process involved that no other replacement contractor can provide.

In looking to terminate, the contractor must ensure it follows the contract exactly otherwise it may be held to have not served a valid termination notice and if its act is held to be a repudiatory breach of contract and it will be liable for damages to the employer.

Turning to the United Arab Emirates Article 892 of the Civil Code applicable to Muqawala contracts (which covers construction agreements) stipulates termination may only occur in one of three ways:

- Completion of the agreed works/services
- Mutual consent
- Court order.

Termination by mutual consent would apply to terms of contracts where the provision was included, but otherwise a party would need a court order.

Once again the contractor must ensure that provisions to terminate are included in the contract and where a standard form has been used these have not been omitted in the particular conditions.

Tiered dispute resolution clauses

In conjunction with the rights to suspend and the right to terminate most contracts contain tiered dispute resolution clauses.

Their usefulness in getting paid though depends on the jurisdiction. For example, in the United Kingdom an adjudicator's decision on a FIDIC contract could be enforced immediately in the court using the summary judgement procedure the same could not be done in Saudi Arabia, where the local courts would not recognise the adjudicator's decision as being enforceable.

It is important that the type of dispute resolution is examined in detail before agreement. If the chosen tiered clauses cannot be enforced, the contractor must ask what benefit is there to agreeing to it, as a long process could lead to insolvency before payment.

Most contracts final tier of dispute resolution is arbitration but this cannot be invoked usually without exhausting the other steps in the process. You must ask yourself why waste time and resources on the other steps if a binding, enforceable decision is needed to ensure payment.

Governing law must also be a consideration linked to the three areas identified suspension, termination, and choice of dispute resolution.

Conclusion

The contractor must be pro-active in managing the risk of non-payment, this should of course involve the usual credit checks on the employer, identification of assets, and their location, choice of governing law but must also include the negotiation of favorable contract provisions that will assist the contractor recover payment in the shortest possible time.

The time to protect cash flow is during the negotiation stage before the contract is concluded. Tender documents must be inspected and amendments to general conditions by way of particular conditions checked against the contract.

Where non-standard forms of contract are proposed the contractor must not be hesitant to propose safeguards such as those highlighted above. The combined use of suspension termination and dispute resolution clauses in a thoughtful manner will ensure that payment is obtained or where loss is likely that is minimized.

However, the practical experience of the writer in various countries including Peru, United Arab Emirates, Qatar, Kuwait, Libya, South Africa, Saudi Arabia, and even England is that even where there are suspension and termination provisions available in the contract the contractor's team at project level does not want to antagonize the employer and will progress the works despite not being paid and unless head office management force the issue mentioned provisions are rarely used.

Sean Sullivan Gibbs
Director with Systech International
Fellow of the Royal Institution of Chartered Surveyors
Chartered Institute of Arbitrators
Chartered Institute of Building
UK

Bibliography

Bailey, J. (2016). *Construction Law*. Informa Law.
Baker, E. (2017). *FIDIC Contracts*. Taylor & Francis.
Burr, A. (2017). *Delay and Disruption in Construction Contracts*. Informa Law from Routledge.
Coulson, P. (2017). *Coulson on Construction Adjudication*. Oxford University Press.
Furst, S. (2017). *Keating on Construction Contracts*. Sweet & Maxwell.
Glover, J. (2017). *Understanding the FIDIC Red Book*. Sweet & Maxwell.
Thomas, D. (2017). *Keating on NEC3*. Sweet & Maxwell/Thomson Reuters.
Whelan, J. (2017). *UAE Civil Code and Ministry of Justice Commentary*. Sweet & Maxwell/Thomson Reuters.

6.10 Contract price under FIDIC forms

Concerning economic influences, FIDIC forms contain provision at Sub-Clause 13.7 (Adjustments for Changes in Legislation) and at Sub-Clause 13.8 (Adjustments for Changes in Cost). Sub-Clause 13.7 foresees adjustments to take account of any increase in cost resulting from a change in laws (including changes to interpretation). Sub-Clause 13.8 foresees adjustments for the rise or fall in costs of labor, goods, and other inputs, by the addition or deduction of the amounts determined by formulae that form a part of the contract.

In respect of the formation of the total contract price, FIDIC CONS/1999 Red Book are the conditions of contract suitable for the general contracting (design-bid-build) delivery method. Therefore, logically, it is a re-measurement contract that distinguishes between:

(a) The amount the employer has accepted in their letter of acceptance regarding the contractor's bid (Sub-Clause 1.1.4.1); being, therefore, an accepted tender price which is in fact a forecast of the contract price. According to Sub-Clause 1.1.4.1, the accepted contract amount means "the amount accepted in the letter of acceptance for the execution and completion of the Works and the remedying of any defects."

As stipulated in Sub-Clause 14.1: "Any quantities which may be set out in the Bill of Quantities or other Schedule are estimated quantities and are not to be taken as the actual and correct quantities: (i) of the Works which the Contractor is required to execute, or (ii) for the purposes of Clause 12 [Measurement and Evaluation]."

(b) Total contract price (Sub-Clause 1.1.4.2) defined in Sub-Clauses 14.1, 12.1, and 12.3 is to be determined by measuring works actually carried out and to be adjusted as stipulated in the contract, with all the amounts in the bill of quantities (part of tender documentation) being the estimated amounts. This is therefore an agreed price as after completion. The contractor shall base their invoices on the amounts of works carried out and certified by the engineer during a certain (such as monthly) period of time. According to Sub-Clause 1.1.4.2, contract price means "the price defined in Sub-Clause 14.1 [The contract price], and includes adjustments in accordance with the Contract."

Chapter 12 contains details of re-measurement in FIDIC CONS/1999 Red Book. Otherwise, P&DB/1999 Yellow Book and EPC/1999 Silver Book both lack Chapter 12 equivalents.

According to the P&DB, Sub-Clause 14.1:

> The Contract Price shall be the lump sum Accepted Contract Amount and be subject to adjustments in accordance with the Contract ... however, if any part of the Works is to be paid according to quantity supplied or work done, the provisions for measurement and evaluation shall be as stated in the Particular Conditions.

According to EPC Sub-Clause 14.1 "payment for the Works shall be made on the basis of the lump sum Contract Price, subject to adjustments in accordance with the Contract." Payments (being instalments of the lump sum) are based on a schedule of payments (agreed contractually) to reflect the costs foreseen over time. The employer bears no risk of changes in volumes of the individual items in the bill of quantities. In respect of the formation of the total price, it is therefore a lump sum price. Such an arrangement is typical for design-build (DB) contracts.

FIDIC also makes use of the cost plus method, for example, under "provisional sums – daywork" (Sub-Clause 13.6) and in contractual claim quantification. As per FIDIC CONS/1999 Red Book, P&DB/1999 Yellow Book, and EPC/1999 Silver Book, the claims are a form of foreseeable (but not yet clarified) component of the total contract price. The new 2017 edition does not bring anything new in terms of above mentioned concepts.

6.11 Cost overruns

Particularly large construction projects are prone to cost overruns. Sometimes it is difficult to foresee the overall cost because of the specifics of such projects. In some cases even the use of advanced technology can cause many complications. The influence of local politicians cannot be underestimated either. For example, cost forecasts can be deformed to get expensive projects started and many variations instructed that lead to time extensions and additional cost. Unrealistic terms may lead to work being done in haste that can cause further failures and additional cost.

A cost overrun is an unexpected cost incurred in excess of a budgeted amount due to an underestimation of the actual cost during budgeting. Cost overrun should be distinguished from cost escalation, which is used to express an anticipated increase in a budgeted cost due to factors such as inflation.

- The Suez Canal cost 20 times more than its earliest estimates. The Sydney Opera House cost 15 times more than was originally projected and the Concorde supersonic airplane cost 12 times more than predicted. Some more recent examples are as follows:
- The Channel Tunnel: a 50.5 kilometer-long (31.4 miles) undersea rail tunnel linking the United Kingdom with France. The tunnel was a build-own-operate-transfer (BOOT) project with a concession. Privately financed, the total investment costs at 1985 prices were £2.6 billion. At completion in 1994, actual costs were, in 1985 prices, £4.65 billion (i.e., an 80% cost overrun). The cost overrun was partly due to enhanced safety, security, and environmental demands. Financing costs were 140% higher than forecast.
- The Willy Brandt International Airport in Berlin; a project that has suffered significant extensions of time for completion and cost overruns. In 2006, costs were estimated at €2 billion. After four delays, this figure had increased to €4.4 billion. Many of those costs corresponded to the cost of maintenance of almost completed work. Thousands of failures were also encountered and technology was so advanced that the technicians could not figure out how to use it. Rumors also abound that politicians get these expensive projects started artificially by calculating down the real costs to get permission from parliament or other committees in charge. In addition to that, politicians at the city, state, and federal levels then often come with extra demands once construction is underway, which lead to expensive modifications. In the case of the Berlin Airport, it is said that approximately 300 ad hoc variation requests were ordered by politicians that created an explosion of costs and several delays. One of these was a last-minute wish to expand the terminal to include a shopping mall.
- Hamburg's concert hall should have been opened in 2010. The project started in 2006 and in 2005 estimated costs were €186 million. The project was finished in 2017, at a total cost of €800 million.
- Construction of Cologne's North–South subway line began in 2004. After cost overruns and a collapse that killed two people in 2009, officials say the entire

line may not be open until 2019. Costs have soared from €780 million to €1.08 billion.
- In Leipzig, the city tunnel for commuter trains was expected to open in 2009. Construction has still not finished, and costs have jumped from €572 million to €960 million.
- Another recent example is the Panama Canal expansion project that was intended to double the capacity of the Panama Canal. The plan was to create a new lane for traffic, thereby allowing more and larger ships to transit. In 2006, the estimated cost was US$5.25 billion. The largest cost associated with constructing the project are the two new locks on the Atlantic and Pacific sides. In 2013, the Spanish company Sacyr Vallehermoso, which leads the multinational consortium expanding the waterway, said it would halt work in 21 days if the Panama Canal Authority does not cover $1.6 billion in cost overruns.

Other projects prone to notorious cost overruns are the Olympics. From 1960 to 2012 the following cost overruns were encountered for the Olympic Games:

London 2012, UK	101%
Atlanta 1996, USA	147%
Lillehammer 1994, Norway	277%
Barcelona 1992, Spain	417%
Albertville 1992, France	135%
Sarajevo 1984, Yugoslavia	173%
Lake Placid 1980, USA	321%
Montreal 1976, Canada	796%
Grenoble 1968, France	201%

The Olympics stand out in two distinct ways compared to other megaprojects: (1) the Olympics overrun with 100% consistency. No other type of megaproject is this consistent regarding cost overrun. Other project types are typically on budget from time to time, but not the Olympics; (2) With an average cost overrun in real terms of 179%— and 324% in nominal terms—overruns in the Olympics have historically been significantly larger than for other types of megaprojects (Flyvbjerg and Stewart, 2012).

6.12 Abnormally low tender (ALT)

Seen mainly in public tenders, abnormally low tender (ALT) prices have caused enormous problems to the construction industry in many different countries. Clark (2013) explains that the issue of abnormally low tender prices has, in a number of cases, had a major impact on the successful implementation of bank-financed projects in the public sector and frequently result in:

- the creation of an adversarial relationship between the employer and the contractor (and its sub-contractors);

- a significant number of variations orders and contractor claims that can be very burdensome for employers, their consultants, and lenders to review and process;
- cost and time overruns (as a result of the above);
- slow disbursement of loan proceeds (increasing the cost of the loan to the borrower);
- costly referral of issues to the dispute adjudication board (DAB);
- termination of contracts sometimes resulting in costly and time-consuming arbitration;
- last but not least, delays in procurement process (particularly tender evaluation).

In the majority of cases, an abnormally low tender price is a significant risk in construction projects. If the tender documents are not well prepared, the risks of contractors gambling, claims arising and increased final project costs will definitely be higher than usual.

There may be a number of different reasons for abnormally low tenders being given by contractors. These may include errors in tender documents or bids (wrong assessment of costs and risks), survival strategy, expectation of compensation through future claims, entering a new market, keeping competitors apart, preventing resources becoming idle, a hidden agenda to modify the design, and so on.

To avoid construction projects being threatened by the consequences of abnormally low tender prices, the following measures should be taken:

- The project must be well prepared and the tender documentation must be as precise as possible.
- Contracts must contain precise review (variation) clauses corresponding to the delivery method used.
- There must be adequate time for preparation of tenders.
- Experts on evaluation committees must be impartial and independent.
- Proper qualitative selection criteria related to the financial situation of the contractor must be applied.
- The MEAT (most economically advantageous tender) criterion must be used.
- Specific independent administrative bodies may be established to expeditiously solve the questions and requests during the tender process.
- Performance securities to cover bid, performance, and payment may be used.
- Abnormally low tender prices must be evaluated and requested by the employer and, if the reason for their use is not justified, they must be excluded.

Best value approach in the Netherlands by Wiebe Witteveen (the Netherlands)

Since 2003, public infrastructural asset managers in the Netherlands such as ProRail (railways) and Rijkswaterstaat (main roads and waterways) have adopted contractual arrangements that have transferred tasks and responsibilities to suppliers. Procurement has consequently become more and more critical for project success. In line with the outsourcing in the Netherlands developments the best value approach (BV) has become very popular among practitioners in recent years (Witteveen and Van de Rijt, 2013; Van de Rijt and Santema, 2012). In the Netherlands estimated 1,000 projects have been initiated using the best value approach.

Studies identified the delivery system of services as the problem and not the lack of technically qualified personnel (Kashiwagi, 2017). Price-based awards, which do not recognize or give credit to differences in vendor quality, value, and performance will motivate contractors to be more reactive, offer lower quality, not preplan nor utilize expertise. The price based system is nontransparent, requires more decision making, which increases risk of deviations and expectations. To move from low performance to higher performance, efficiency must increase, and the following factors must be minimized: cost, management, direction, and control from the client. The level of vendor expertise must increase. An increase in performance will only come with increased vendor accountability, preplanning, measurement of performance, and quality and risk management.

The best value approach identifies the contractor as an expert, and assigns quality control and risk management to the contractor. In the best value approach, the client's representative has a nontechnical quality assurance role of ensuring that the contractor has a quality control/risk management system that is being used to minimize deviations.

The best value approach (Kashiwagi, 2017) is a process or structure to optimize the delivery of services by hiring experts. The best value approach changes the procurement agent's role from being the guardian over the award of a contract, to a facilitator of the delivery of expert services. The best value approach has four phases: preparation, evaluation, clarification phase, and execution phase (Figure 6.1).

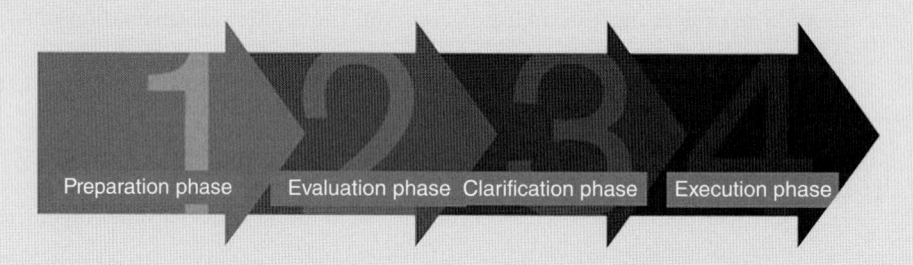

Figure 6.1 Four phases of the best value approach

The preparation phase should be shorter than traditional procurement, since the client is considered not to be an expert. This means that the client will outsource the problem instead of an often detailed specification.

The evaluation phase has the following filters: project capability, risk assessment plan, value added plan, interviewing key personnel, prioritizing the vendors, and performing a dominance check to ensure that the potential BV vendor truly is the best value. The client's representatives assume the vendors are experts throughout the evaluation process. The clarification phase is used to minimize the risk of the BV vendor not being an expert. The paradigm is to minimize the need for technical decision making in the evaluation process, and maximizing the need for the BV vendor to prove they are an expert in the clarification phase. The paradigm stimulates vendors to show dominant differential in performance that minimizes the need for any client technical decision making during selection. The risk is shifted to the vendors to show value through dominant expertise, knowing that experts minimize both risk and cost, thus providing the best value for the lowest cost.

After prioritization, only one vendor can move into the clarification phase. The clarification phase is the most important phase of the BV approach. If done correctly, the clarification phase should be used to clarify how the vendor will deliver what they have proposed. Once the client is convinced that the prioritized BV vendor is the best value, the best value vendor creates a risk management plan (RMP), weekly risk report (WRR), and performance measurements (PM).

In traditional procurement processes the clarification phase is usually the initiation of the execution phase. In the best value approach the clarification phase is still a part of the tendering process. The BV approach differs from more traditional procurement approaches on several other points.

According to Kashiwagi (Kashiwagi, 2013) the unique factors of the best value approach include:

- No-influence, no control, no management philosophy—BV gets the buyer to minimize direction and release control over the supplier, since the supplier is the expert. This system also focuses on making the supplier accountable for the project, due to the owner minimizing direction and decision making on the project.
- Seamless contract - Contract mitigates risk instead of being a legal/regulatory/control document.
- Supplier contract creation - The supplier creates the contract and the scope of the project.
- Pre-planning - BV places more importance on pre-planning before the contract is signed then after the contract is signed. The contract representing the start or implementation of the service, since usually the contract binds all parties to an identified project plan and set of activities.
- Problem contracting - BV does not require the buyer to identify the scope of the project. Allowing the buyer to only relay their intent and expectations.
- Communication minimization - System minimizes buyer/supplier communication.
- Expert supplier model - Supplier has no technical risk and focuses on mitigating risk the supplier does not control.
- Dominant information - Communication to be in simple, clear, and in non-technical terms.

Case study: fast track program

In the Netherlands the launching client for the best value approach was Rijkswaterstaat (Dutch highways and waterways agency). In 2008, Rijkswaterstaat decided to resolve 16 major road bottlenecks in the Netherlands using best value. The so-called fast track program (Programma Spoedaanpak Wegen) is the world's largest best value program with a combined worth of €600 million.

Rijkswaterstaat is the executive arm of the Dutch Ministry infrastructure and environment. To help solve the countries' congestion problems, the Dutch Ministry of Infrastructure and Environment has identified 30 major bottlenecks, which need to be (partly) resolved by May 1, 2011. The main reason for using the best value approach is that the procurement of design and build contracts usually leads to high transaction costs (efforts of all possible suppliers) and long tender procedures. In 2009 the tender capacity in the Dutch market was limited. Therefore, suppliers have asked Rijkswaterstaat to develop a procurement strategy heavily based on quality to lower the transaction costs and shorten the tender procedure. As a government agency

Rijkswaterstaat has to follow the European legislation on public works. The tender process needs to be transparent, nondiscriminatory and objective.

The projects were clustered in six clusters. The goals of the procurement strategy were to accelerate the delivery and the length of the tender procedure, to maintain the competition and to procure the best possible value. The first conclusion is that the procurement strategy has made the acceleration of the projects possible. All the tenders were executed within a period of five months, where a tender for this type of projects usually takes eight to ten months, approximately 50% faster. The transaction time is cut in half. The early involvement of the vendors has the potential to accelerate the delivery of the projects up to 18 months. The focuses on timely delivery of projects, lead to shortened proposals by the vendor during construction period. The number of vendors that participated in the six tenders was sufficient and comparable to the usual number for projects of this size. One of the most important findings of the market consultation was that there was a shortage in tender capacity in the infrastructure market in 2009. The risk for Rijkswaterstaat was that not enough vendors would want to bid for the projects of the fast track program. On average every tender has had five vendors bidding, with a minimum of three on one project and six on two projects. The vendors by their participation, keen interest in the best value approach.

The third goal of the procurement strategy was to achieve the best possible value for the projects. In 50% of the tenders the vendor with the highest quality is also the winner. In the three other tenders the winner had the second or third quality score. This suggests that the procurement process had a bias to vendors with high quality (as expected and intended). Both quality and a competitive price were obtained.

Bibliography

Kashiwagi, D. (2017). *How to Know Everything Without Knowing Anything.* Delft University, the Netherlands.
Kashiwagi, J. (2013). Dissertation. *Factors of Success in Performance Information Procurement System / Performance Information Risk Management System.* Delft University, the Netherlands.
Van de Rijt, J. and Santema, S.C. (2012). The best value approach in the Netherlands: a reflection on past, present and future. *Journal for the Advancement of Performance Information and Value,* 4 (2).
Witteveen, W. and Van de Rijt, J. (2013). Possible barriers to a successful further diffusion of the best value approach in the Netherlands: observations of major misunderstandings on the concept and theory, *Journal for the Advancement of Performance Information and Value,* 5 (2), 79–88.

What makes best value different from traditional MEAT systems?

The European legislation demands from public contracting authorities (PCAs) that tenders are transparent, objective, and non-discriminatory. Within the European framework PCAs have a certain degree of freedom to select suppliers. In the past, procurement strategies based on the award criterion lowest price and detailed technical specifications have often been used to tender public works contracts. In many cases the outcome of these tenders has not been satisfactory. Choosing to tender with detailed specifications made low contractors' performance possible. Using the lowest price as an award criterion even led to fraudulent behavior by contractors. That is why PCAs in the Netherlands have made a shift toward using most economically advantageous tender (MEAT) to award tenders in the last decade. Using the methodology of MEAT certainly gives a client more opportunities than solely awarding on price, but applying MEAT does not always lead to a successful project.

When contracting authorities choose to award the contract to the MEAT they should determine economic and quality criteria that determine the most value for money. The quality criteria require a form of performance measurement. A performance measurement is an ordered set of plausible performance levels set on a quantatitive or qualitative scale (Mateus et al., 2010). When using evaluation or MEAT criteria PCAs use both types of performance measurement:

- Quantative scale, such as traffic congestion in traffic loss hours or delivery time in days.
- Qualitative scale, such as scoring predefined points on a project management plans.

In defining evaluation criteria, the following rules can be identified:

1. Alignment with project goals.
2. Organized in a hierarchal structure.
3. If necessary desegregation: evaluation criteria should be desegregated into subcriteria to further clarify the meaning of the criteria.
4. Intrinsic coherence of the evaluation model, such as isolability, non-redundancy, and measurability.
5. The criteria should only represent project objectives over which tenderers have direct influence such as traffic congestion during building.

Based on these five rules the conclusion appears to be that the quantitative scales are preferred over qualitative scales and the qualitative scales should be desegregated and be transformed into a scoring function that exactly represents the preferences of the PCA.

If qualitative scales are used, a common way of using MEAT is to decompose all MEAT criteria in detail prior to the bids. This notion assumes that the scoring rules before the tender are known and that the tender evaluation model is consistent with the real preferences of a PCA (Dreschler, 2009; Mateus et al., 2009). This assumes that the PCA is aware of all his preferences (and the exact utility function) before knowing what the tenderers can offer. It has been argued that qualitative scales are subjective and ill defined, because a performance measure should be as clear and objective as possible. The performance measurement should be measurable and the contract documents should clearly and objectively define the aspects that are in competition (Mateus et al., 2010).

To be able to compare the performance levels with each other scoring functions will have to be created. Scoring functions allow the transformation of the performance levels set on each performance into partial scores set on an numeric scale representing attractiveness ("preference" or "value") between each performance level on a given criterion (Belton and Stewart, 2001). Scoring functions can be relative or absolute. Relative scoring functions define the score of a tender by comparing its performance with the ones of other tenders. This implies that it is impossible to score a tender without having knowledge of other tenders. The accountability for the relative attractiveness of a performance level is shifted from the PCA to the tenderer.

In the best value approach, the client's representatives assume the vendors are experts through the selection process, then assume the best value vendor is not an expert in the pre-award phase tominimize the risk of the vendor. The paradigm is to minimize the need for technical decision making in the selection process, and maximizing the need for the best value vendor to prove they are an expert in the clarification phase (Kashiwagi, 2017).

The philosophy of best value assumes that the suppliers are the experts and the client is the non-expert. This notion implicates that the client (in this case a PCA) cannot understand or grasp ex-ante all possible ways to solve its needs. The client is not fully aware of all its preferences, due to the fact that is has incomplete knowledge on what is possible in the market (and what is not possible). In the philosophy of the best value approach the suppliers each set their own performance level, without the client indicating which performance level it wants (the client does not know what is possible).

Having a client set all criteria, standards, norms, and specifications leads to getting more or less the same bids from the different vendors. The advantage of this is that all bids can be easily compared. The downside however is that there is (almost) no differentiation between the bids. Another major disadvantage is that, because of the fact that the vendor is the expert and the client the non-expert, some possible solutions that the client could have gotten are left out upfront (because the client did not see it).

The best value approach seems to ignore most of the rules and demands on evaluation criteria based on the literature; the major exception being the alignment of evaluation criteria to the project goals. In the philosophy of the best value approach the performance level is set by the contractor and the client is not aware of its preference. It is therefore impossible to evaluate a tender without having knowledge of all the other tenders. These scoring functions are known as relative scoring functions. The problem of relative scoring functions is that the overall ranking of tenderers can be dependent of another tenderer and that a phenomenon called rank-reversal can take place.

An example is shown below. The project Extra Discharge Capacity Afsluitdijk (EDCA) of Rijkswaterstaat in the Netherlands aims to enlarge the capacity of the discharge sluices by building new sluices, necessary because of the climate change. Rijkswaterstaat has decided to outsource the responsibility to write the environmental impact report to an engineering firm. The engineering firm was selected using a best value process (with monetizing the award criteria).

An example is shown below. The budget for the project was €2.000.000. Next to "price," there were four other award criteria. These are all qualitative criteria, which reflect the value of the supplier. The four criteria were RAVA plan, scope document, schedule, and interviews. Each criterium had a weighing factor, for example, RAVA is "worth" 30% of the budget, hence €600.000. The four criteria combined had a value of 75% of the budget; hence a maximum deduction of €1.500.000 could be gained. If a supplier scored a "10" (excellent) on all four criteria, he would get a "fictitious deduction" of €1.500.000 to his bidding price, leading to a low fictitious tender sum (which is good, the lower the better!).

For the EDCA project price weights for 25% and the quality weights for 75%. Award criteria were:

Budget Ceiling price		€ 2.000.000,00	
Risk Assessments & Value add Plan	30%	€ 600.000,00	maximum fictitious value
Schedule	5%	€ 100.000,00	maximum fictitious value
Scope document	5%	€ 100.000,00	maximum fictitious value
Interviews	35%	€ 700.000,00	maximum fictitious value

The scoring table and corresponding addition/deduction looked like this:

Model	Fictitious Deduction					Fictitious Addition			
	100%	75%	50%	25%	0%	25%	50%	75%	100%
Score	10	9	8	7	6	5	4	3	2
Criterium					Value of the score				
Risk Assessments & Value add Plan	€ −600.000,00	€ −450.000,00	€ −300.000,00	€ −150.000,00	€ −	€ 150.000,00	€ 300.000,00	€ 450.000,00	€ 600.000,00
Schedule	€ −100.000,00	€ −75.000,00	€ −50.000,00	€ −25.000,00	€ −	€ 25.000,00	€ 50.000,00	€ 75.000,00	€ 100.000,00
Interview	€ −700.000,00	€ −525.000,00	€ −350.000,00	€ −175.000,00	€ −	€ 175.000,00	€ 350.000,00	€ 525.000,00	€ 700.000,00

Model	% of deduction / addition	Score	Risk Assessment & Value add Plan	Schedule	Scope document	Interview
Fictitious Deduction	100%	10	€ −600.000	€ −100.000	€ −100.000	€ −700.000
	75%	9	€ −450.000	€ −75.000	€ −450.000	€ −525.000
	50%	8	€ −300.000	€ −50.000	€ −50.000	€ −350.000
	25%	7	€ −150.000	€ −25.000	€ −	€ −175.000
Neutral	0%	6	€ −	€ −	€ −	€ −
Fictitious Addition	25%	5	€ 150.000	€ 25.000	€ −	€ 175.000
	50%	4	€ 300.000	€ 50.000	€ 50.000	€ 350.000
	75%	3	€ 450.000	€ 75.000	€ 450.000	€ 525.000
	100%	2	€ 600.000	€ 100.000	€ 100.000	€ 700.000

If the committee thinks the RAVA plan of one of the suppliers is excellent ("10") the supplier gets a "deduction" of €600.000 to his bidding price. If the evaluation committee values the RAVA plan of supplier as very poorly ("2"), the supplier gets a (fictitious) addition of €600.000. You can see that supplier B has a "9" on RAVA (and therefore gets a fictitious deduction of €450.000. He also scores "9" on Schedule (hence a fictitious deduction of 75.000; this amount is lower than the "9" of RAVA, as the RAVA plan has a higher weighting.). Supplier C has a "3" on RAVA (which leads to an addition of €450.000 to his price). Supplier D scores a "4" on Schedule (and gets a "fine" (=addition) of 50.000 to its price.

All actual scores (and corresponding additions/deductions) to the price were as follows

Scoring by assessment Committee				
Score Phase 1	A	B	C	D
Risk Assessment & Value add Plan	4	9	3	4
Schedule	4	9	3	4
Scope document	2	8	4	6
Monetary Value				
Risk Assessments & Value add Plan	€ 300.000,00	€ −450.000,00	€ 450.000,00	€ 300.000,00
Schedule	€ 50.000,00	€ −75.000,00	€ 75.000,00	€ 50.000,00
Scope document	€ 100.000,00	€ −50.000,00	€ 50.000,00	€ −
Fictious Value of the documents	€ 450.000,00	€ −575.000,00	€ 575.000,00	€ 350.000,00
Score Phase 2	A	B	C	D
Interview 1	6	8	6	5
Monetary Value				
Interview 1	€ −	€ −350.000,00	€ −	€ 175.000,00
Fictitous Value of the interviews	€ −	€ −350.000,00	€ −	€ 175.000,00
Total fictitious value (documents & interviews)	**€ 450.000,00**	**€ −925.000,00**	**€ 575.000,00**	**€ 525.000,00**
Fictitious Tender sum	**€ 450.000,00**	**€ −925.000,00**	**€ 575.000,00**	**€ 525.000,00**

The table shows supplier B has (by far) the best quality. To calculate the ranking, vendor B gets a deduction of €925.000 of its price. On the other hand, vendor C gets an additional €575.000 to its price. We cannot disclose the individual prices of the vendors but all vendors offered between €900,000 to €1,600,000. The price of vendor B was the second lowest price. By deducting the fictitious value (€925.000) to its price, vendor B had the lowest fictitious tender sum and was the winner.

Wiebe Witteveen MSc
Partner at Best Value Group
Amersfoort
The Netherlands

Bibliography

Dreschler, M. (2009). Fair competition. How to apply the "Economically Most Advantageous Tender (EMAT) award mechanism in the Dutch construction industry.

Kashiwagi, D. (2017). *How to Know Everything Without Knowing Anything*. Delft University, the Netherlands.

Mateus, R., Ferriera, J.A. and Carreira, J. (2010). Full disclosure of tender evaluation models: background and application in Potuguese public procurement. *Journal of Purchasing & Supply Management*, 16, 206-215.

6.13 Claims as part of contract price

Contract price is (next to re-measurement, installments of lump sum, or payments of cost in cost plus method) formed via claims, variations, and adjustments based on the particular contractual risk allocation, claims options and variation (and adjustments) procedure.

In case of a dispute it may be important to analyze if a particular claim is a component of the contract price or a mutual compensation for damages. This may be important in the evaluation of a possible lapse of claim under governing law.

6.13.1 Limitation and prescription periods for claims

Governing law usually contains a limitation (prescription) period that does not allow the aggrieved party to claim damages after such period expires. So when does this period start to run? The answer will usually be found in the contract or governing law. However, there are differing options and legal opinions on this issue. For example, does the period start to run when the damage occurs or when the damage stopped accruing, in the case of an event with continuing effect? What about if the contract administrator (or the employer) does not allow the processing of payments (of works done or a claim)? If the particular claim or its component is not seen as compensation for damages but as a part of contract price determination, the period could start to run when it was first possible to invoice the amount or after the final statement (or discharge) was submitted.

6.14 Public procurement law limitations

Employers and contractors regularly wish to modify existing contracts awarded on the basis of a public tender. For public employers, however, the principle of freedom of contract is usually limited because they are subject to a competitive procurement procedure in compliance with the principles of transparency and equal treatment. This may lead to a need of a new tender procedure connected to the performance of a particular, already running project. Employers may be in doubt as to whether a modification requires a new tender procedure and, in such situations, they may choose not to modify the contract. From a socio-economic perspective, however, it is hardly desirable if the employer (for fear of breaching procurement rules) continues to perform a project that does not completely fulfill their requirements (Hartlev and Liljenbøl, 2013).

It follows from the settled case law of the Court of Justice of the European Union (CJEU) that procurement rules (including principles of equal treatment and transparency) apply even after the conclusion of the contract. These principles set boundaries to the modifications, which the contracting employer may make to an existing contract. If the modifications are substantial, a new contract award procedure is required. Modifications that are not substantial may be agreed upon without the requirement of a new contract award. It may be a difficult task in practice to evaluate if the modification is substantive or not. Public procurement law in the EU allows the use of negotiated procedure with respect to changes of existing public contracts and contains several exemption provisions, which, if the conditions for their application are met, allow the employer to avoid publication of a contract notice and make a new call for competition. Instead, if they can agree on the terms, the employer and the contractor may agree to modify an existing contract. In other words, the change can take place by way of direct negotiations between the parties. However, in practice, it is very difficult to fulfil the conditions of the negotiated procedure. Even then, the employer is not permitted to agree with a contractor to modify a contract subject to the procurement rules without proceeding with a new call for tenders, if the change is substantial (Hartlev and Liljenbøl, 2013).

In order to provide flexibility in the period from signature until the end of the contract, the employer is advised (in the tender documents at tender stage), to refer to the possibility of subsequent changes so that any changes can take place in pursuance of the contract (and not as a change of the contract) via "directed variations." Such variation clauses (sometimes called "review clauses") may, to a certain degree, ensure flexibility in the terms of the agreement (see Chapter 8). However, such clauses cannot be drafted broadly enough to cover all possible requirements of change, as the transparency principle of the procurement rules implies that all terms of the contract must be precise and unequivocal. A variation clause implying that the parties are to negotiate the change entails a risk of unequal treatment. The challenge is to draft variation clauses that are both foreseeable and provide for the necessary flexibility. If the tenderers, already at tender stage, can take into account the possibility of variations, any subsequent exploitation of these possibilities will not be modifications to the contract but modifications *pursuant* to the contract (directed variations). Further, where changes of the contract are governed by the regulations regarding substantial changes, directed variations may, as a general rule, take place without considering whether or not the change is substantial.

Price will almost always be included in the evaluation of the most economically advantageous tender, and will typically be given a higher weighting. A change in price will therefore often constitute a substantial change. If, on the other hand, the change in price is prompted by objective criteria set out in the contract in the invitation to tender, then changes in price in favor of the contractor may be expected to be allowed without a new call for tenders. The possibility of adjusting the price upward would, in this situation, have been clear to all tenderers and thus open to competition. Therefore, it must not be left to the discretion of the parties to negotiate the price adjustments or in any other way to make an arbitrary change in price. In this respect, it is especially important to fix the pricing of the variations in accordance with the tender documents and thereby avoid negotiations. Often, however, it will not be possible to price a variation on the basis of unit prices. To avoid negotiation, the employer may apply a variation clause, which provides for a pricing of variations to be based on the open book principle with a view to keeping the contractor in a state of effective competition (similar to when they initially won the contract). Stated differently, the contractor may not make additional profit on the works covered by the variations other than on the principal works (Hartlev and Liljenbøl, 2013).

A concept of variation in a construction contract under Polish public procurement by Michał Skorupski (Poland)

The Polish system of construction contracts does not fully appreciate the idea of self-adjusting a contract that would include variation clauses typical of FIDIC forms. Polish jurisdiction has been burdened by a resolution of the Supreme Court (a resolution of the Supreme Court answers a generic legal question arising in relation to a particular case, contrary to a verdict of a court in a specific case itself) of May 22, 1991 (III CZP 15/91), which stated that clauses that entitle one party of the contract to change the contract in its own consideration are in conflict with the general regulations of the Polish Civil Code (Article 353).

Parties are free to stipulate the contract provisions unless such provisions contradict the principles of "community life." The judges ruled that leaving the unlimited possibility of introducing changes to the contract by one party is against the principles of community life. The principles of "community life" (in Polish: *zasady współżycia społecznego*) is a concept in the Polish legal system (especially the civil code), according to which relations between individuals, parties to the contract, the state, and so on, should reflect the generally accepted rules of fairness, honesty, and justice. The principle refers a lot to habits and established practice so if one party proposes a change to a contract, the other has to have an opportunity to reject it. A similar decision was handed down by the Supreme Court on March 18, 1993 (I CRN 22/93). Since then we have debated whether a variation or adjustment of the contract price, the time for completion, the program or the specification can constitute a change in the contract itself and would require a separate mutually agreed annex to it.

FIDIC contract conditions at Sub-Clause 13.1 gives the right to the contractor to refrain from executing the change if "the contractor cannot readily obtain the Goods for the Variation." Furthermore, it is stated that each variation "shall not comprise the omission of any work which is to be carried out by others." It is clear to construction professionals that the right to vary is not unlimited. It is also clear that a complex procedure for variations is in place to limit the powers of the employer's personnel.

However, the governing law and its interpretations are not really created by construction professionals in Poland. In particular, public employers follow the advice of lawyers to stay on the "safe side" when spending public money. In 2004, after accession to the EU, Polish institutions and beneficiaries started to pay special attention to the avoidance of risk of returning EU subsidies. Strict implementation of EU public procurement directives led to an important problem: which expenses can be safely determined as eligible for a subsidy? In general, illegal expenses cannot. Staying on the safe side meant that local legislation and interpretations should enforce "strict," "clear," "unequivocal," and, importantly, "legal" conditions of a contract.

The Polish Public Procurement Act of 2004 at Articles 29 and 31 requires public employers to specify the scope of a public construction contract by using adequately precise and clear drawings (*dokumentacja projektowa*), specifications (*specyfikacje techniczne wykonania i odbioru robót*) or functional specifications for D&B projects. However, in conjunction with Article 5 of the Ordinance of the Minister of Infrastructure of September 2, 2004, the drawings and specifications have to provide sufficient information not only to prepare the tender, but also to execute the works. Similarly, the employer's functional requirements shall be sufficient to calculate the tender price as well as to design the works (and then build them in accordance with this design).

In Poland, it is the role of the public client to prepare the whole scope of works, the contract conditions, other terms, and requirements. These are all, in principle, non-negotiable. You either accept them and submit a tender or reject them and withdraw. There is only a very limited possibility of challenging a client's proposal through the public procurement arbitration board (*Krajowa Izba Odwoławcza*). As a norm, the system does not allow contract particulars to be negotiated at all.

Between 2004 and 2007, many legal and bureaucratic interpretations were presented in the public domain in respect of how public employers in reality must prepare the contracts. If the specification has to be perfect enough for tender procedure and works, then any variations, changes, or instructions issued in the execution phase can be perceived as failures made at the preparation phase. As a precaution, the Ministry of Regional Development issued a memorandum with instructions to the beneficiaries of EU funds that any such changes, variations, or instructions (even if technically justified), would be treated as ineligible. At the same time, implementation of the EU procurement directive demanded additional orders (*zamówienie dodatkowe, zamówienie uzupełniające*) (note that in Poland according to the public procurement law, there was a separate procedure for additional works of the same kind, for example, another kilometer of the same road (*zamówienie uzupełniające*) and another procedure for additional works that were not foreseen at all in the terms of reference but are indispensable for completion of the basic works (*zamówienie dodatkowe*), and for works that could not have been foreseen at the time of the tender. Effectively, under Polish legislation, such additional orders were separate public contracts. And such orders would not be treated as eligible for EU subsidies. Even if the engineer determined additional costs to be paid to the contractor under the FIDIC terms, there should be an additional ineligible contract for that cost (sometimes it is extremely difficult to define the scope for such an additional contract if the only thing required is to cover the unexpected additional costs of works which have been already described in the original contract). In order to improve the situation, one of the amendments to the Public Procurement Act was that annexes of already executed contracts (rather than additional orders) could be foreseen in the terms of reference. Since 2004, there have been more than 30 amendments to the Public Procurement Act (being direct amendments or amendments resulting from other Acts).

The result is that a typical public construction FIDIC-based contract claims to be perfectly prepared and designed. The original and measured remuneration is changed into a lump sum (not more than the accepted contract amount) and the majority of risks are transferred to the contractor directly through specific contract conditions or indirectly by provisions of the technical specifications. Even if the contract allows for claims, the given specification allocates full responsibility and risk to the contractor. For example, negotiations with service providers, negotiating rights of ways, permits, or even errors in the tender design are all deemed to be included in the accepted contract amount.

When the need for a variation/change order/instruction actually materializes, the system does not offer any simple solutions. Given the likely outcome discussed above, many lawyers have proclaimed FIDIC forms to be practically "illegal" in Poland. Their main argument is that engineers routinely make adjustments to the contract price, scope, and time for completion and this is against the law. Employers, in order to protect themselves, make all variations and accepted claims into a form of an additional order or annex. The wording and conditions of the annexes are negotiated on a take-it-or-leave-it basis by the employer.

A typical FIDIC-based contract used in Poland includes amendments that limit the responsibility of the employer for actions and determinations of the engineers. For example, the specific conditions erase the provisions of Sub-Clause 3.1, which states that "whenever the Engineer exercises a specified authority for which the Employer's approval is required, then (for the purpose of the Contract) the Employer shall be deemed to have given the approval." In respect of determinations related to claims, the employer may add that "written consent of the Employer is required." Or, finally, somewhere in amendments to Clause 13 you may find a sentence like: "any Variation increasing the Contract Price requires an annex to the Contract Agreement otherwise it will be deemed null and void" (note, this is not required when decreasing the contract value).

In every project, claims, and variations are encountered, but unless the employer signs an annex, a determination or variation can be deemed non-binding retrospectively. Thus, the engineer is often used as a tool to promise scope and price adjustments, but with little factual power to implement it. At the end of the day the contractor is rarely sure of their legal position. When the annex is finally prepared, it usually eliminates any chances for further claims of the contractor. Polish courts respect the rule of *volenti non fit iniuria* (in English: to a willing person, injury is not done, that is, if you do something willingly, you must not claim damages, a concept widely used in European legislation). In practice, if the contractor signs an annex, say, in the third year of the contract (in which he agrees to a new time for completion, but the contract price remains unchanged), then the contractor has willingly agreed to the price being satisfactory and all potential claims are lost.

Of course, one can imagine a contrary situation, when it is the employer who wants a change of scope. Then the contractor is in better negotiating position and can try to impose unreasonable rates and prices. Both situations contradict the principle of a self-adjusting contract, where parties have agreed how and based on what rates they will administer variations.

Instead of having one variation procedure, all variations and determinations require further validation in the form of additional orders or annexes to the contract. This generates a constant uncertainty and weakens the bargaining position of the party demanding the change. Rather than using pre-agreed rates, parties always get into difficult negotiations as to which rates shall really apply: contractual rates, market rates, adjusted contractual rates, adjusted market rates, and so on. This has happened continuously in Poland since 2004.

I believe all of this is a good example of the consequences of misunderstanding the concept of a variation within the contract, rather than the change of the contract itself.

Michał Skorupski
Contract manager
Member of SIDiR
Association of Consulting Engineers and Experts in Poland
Poland

References

Clark, G. (2013). Abnormally low tender (ALT) prices under works contracts. Online. Available at: www.efcanet.org (accessed 3 Jan. 2013).

Flyvbjerg, B. and Stewart, A. (2012). Olympic proportions: cost and cost overrun at the Olympics, 1960–2012. Online. Available at: http://papers.ssrn.com (accessed 3 Jan. 2014).

Hartlev, K. and Liljenbøl, M.W. (2013). Changes to existing contracts under the EU public procurement rules and the drafting of review clauses to avoid the need for a new tender. *Public Procurement Law Review*. 2 (2013). Sweet & Maxwell.

Jenkins, J. and Stebbings, S. (2006). *International Construction Arbitration Law*. Kluwer Law International BT, Dordrecht.

Further reading

FIDIC (2011). *FIDIC Procurement Procedures Guide* (1st Edition). FIDIC, Lausanne.

Hoffman, S.L. (2008). *The Law and Business of International Project Finance: A Resource for Governments, Sponsors, Lawyers, and Project Participants*. Cambridge University Press, Cambridge.

Jaeger, A.V. and Hök, G.S. (2010). *FIDIC: A Guide for Practitioners*. Springer Verlag, Berlin.

Klee, L. (2012). *Smluvní vztahy výstavbových projektů*. Wolters Kluwer, Prague.

Klee, L. and Jackson, S. (2013). Procurement and management in construction projects: British experience in the Czech context I. *Civil Engineering*, 6.

Klee, L., Marzec, A. and Skorupski, M. (2014). The Use an Misuse of FIDIC Forms in Poland, *International Construction Law Review*, Informa, London.

Kus, A., Markus, J. and Steding, R. (1999). FIDIC's New Silver Book under the German Standard Form Contract Act. *International Construction Law Review*, Informa, London.

Murdoch, J.R. and Hughes, W. (2008). *Construction Contracts : Law and Management*. Taylor & Francis, New York.

Venoit, W.K. (2009) *International Construction Law: A Guide for Cross-Border Transactions and Legal Disputes*. ABA Publishing, Chicago.

Websites

www.acp.gob.pa
www.berlin-airport.de
www.miamiherald.com
www.nst.com
www.thelocal.de

7 Time

7.1 Time in construction

The concept of time, particularly in terms of *time for completion*, is one of the most important legal and managerial aspects in a construction project and ranks among the top priorities of construction project participants. When discussing "time" in a construction context, we usually think of time for completion. However, contracts contain many other specific time-related provisions and issues, for example, reaction periods, periods for mutual notices, fulfilment of partial duties, and so on.

7.2 Delay

Delays may be caused by the employer, the contractor, the contract administrator, third parties, or by reasons beyond the parties' control. This may lead to an extension of time for completion (EOT). Sometimes only some works (activities) are delayed and do not require an extension of time for completion, but may result in disruption (see below), that is, more difficult working conditions.

Delay may lead to damages on the employer's side and are typically in the form of:

- delayed yield (or public benefit) from an investment;
- increase in the price of the work and respective complications in relation to lenders;
- defective cash flow;
- loss of employer's goodwill.

If found responsible, the contractor may be sanctioned or be ordered to pay damages, in the form of:

- contractual penalty/delay damages;
- damage compensation;

International Construction Contract Law, Second Edition. Lukas Klee.
© 2018 John Wiley & Sons Ltd. Published 2018 by John Wiley & Sons Ltd.

- loss of performance bonuses; or
- loss of contractor goodwill.

If it is necessary to speed up the construction process, acceleration becomes an issue of interest to construction project participants (see Chapter 8).

An excellent summary of the principles applicable to claims for delay was set forth in the ICC case no. 12654 (ICC, 2012). Two European companies (incorporated as a limited liability company in a Balkan country), as the contractor, had to build a two-lane road for the local Ministry of Transport (General Roads Directorate) as the employer from the same country. The contractor argued that it was not given possession of the site in due time because the employer was late in expropriating and evacuating the necessary plots of land. On the other hand, the employer argued that the contractor had not submitted the final design for the road on time which prevented the employer from expropriating the land necessary to give the contractor possession.

The ensuing tribunal held that if a contractor is delayed in completing the work, its cost of performance increases simply because those elements of its cost that are dependent on time require more time. For example, the contractor is likely to have "field" overheads cost for its field offices, telephones, and field supervision. These costs (being directly time-related) represent pure delay cost. In addition to the purely time-related delay cost, the contractor's cost of performance may increase because: (1) delayed work itself is completed in an unproductive manner; or (2) subsequent related work may be done out of sequence or on a piecemeal basis instead of as an uninterrupted sequence as planned. Labor productivity rates may suffer as a result, causing contractor costs to increase. Although these disruption costs may, in the proper circumstances, be compensable elements of delay damages in that they are incurred as the result of delay, they may also be caused by factors unrelated to delay.

In order to recover its additional costs, it is not enough for the contractor to show that work was completed later than planned and that the contractor experienced coincidental cost increases. To demonstrate its entitlement to compensation for delay damages, the contractor must demonstrate that under the governing contractual provisions the delay is excusable—that is, the delay was of a type for which the contractor is not contractually liable—and that the delay is also compensable—that is, the delay was of a type that entitles the contractor to compensation and not just an extension of time to perform the work. Having established its entitlement to damages, the contractor must then demonstrate the quantum of its resulting damages.

Stated simply, excusable delays are those delays from which the contractor is excused from liability. As a general rule, a contractor is excused from liability for delays that are the result of causes beyond the contractor's control and delays that are the result of causes that were not foreseeable.

The contractors are entitled to compensation if they can show that they did not concurrently cause the delay and they can quantify its damages with reasonable certainty. Once the contractors have established that the individual delay for which an extension of time sought is excusable and, if compensation is sought, compensable as well, it is necessary to determine whether or not the contractors were independently delaying the work. If the contractors would have been delayed in any event by causes within their control, that is, if there was a concurrent non-excusable delay, the general rule is that it would be inequitable to grant the contractors either an extension of time or additional compensation; unless the contractors can segregate the portion of the delay that is excusable and/or compensable from that which is not. The contractors bear the burden of proving the extent of the delays for which they seek compensation and, in addition, the burden of proving damages incurred as a result of such delays. For the purposes of determining whether the project was delayed and for the purposes of apportioning delay, only delay on the critical path of the project figure in the analysis as relevant because, by definition, delays not on the critical path will not delay the completion of the project.

The tribunal ultimately concluded that part of the delay in giving possession of the site was due to the employer and awarded the contractors part of their claimed cost.

7.3 The United Kingdom Society of construction law delay and disruption protocol

In general, the common, significant aspects of construction project time management such as delay, disruption, time program details, float, and concurrency are insufficiently dealt with by sample contracts (including those of FIDIC), local codes of best practice and governing law. The most widely known exception is the United Kingdom with the SCL Protocol (the Delay & Disruption Protocol, published by the United Kingdom Society of Construction Law; free downloads are available at http://www.scl.org.uk/resources) that can be made a part of the contract by reference.

The United Kingdom Society of Construction Law published the SCL Protocol in 2002 to help construction project participants deal with time management issues that arise within construction projects by offering well-established dispute prevention and resolution methods. The SCL Protocol provides the fundamental rules applicable to delays, disruptions and compensation.

The SCL Protocol proposes an approach to extension of time for completion claims and delay compensation at different phases, for example, before realization, during contract administration and in dispute resolution. The authors of the SCL Protocol clearly emphasize in the introduction that the issue of delay and disruption raises many questions that have no definitive answers and must be assessed on a case-by-case basis. Despite extensive and constant critique in the UK, the SCL Protocol remains a useful reference and unique guide for time management in construction projects. A new form of contract was published in the UK, which is the first to adopt the principles contained in the SCL Protocol (the *CIOB Complex Projects Contract 2013* form of contract). In February 2017, the 2nd edition of the Protocol was published. Some of the key changes introduced by the 2nd edition relate to record keeping, the contemporaneous submission and assessment of EOT claims and factors that ought to be taken into account in selecting the most appropriate delay analysis methodology. Furthermore, the approach to concurrent delay in the original Protocol has been amended, more lenient approach towards global claims has been accepted, more developed guidance on disruption and a broader list of different types of disruption analyses have been discussed (see it here https://www.scl.org.uk/sites/default/files/SCL_Delay_Protocol_2nd_Edition_Final.pdf).

According to the SCL Protocol, delay and disruption issues that ought to be managed and dealt with by contractual provisions all too often escalate into full-blown disputes that have to be decided by third parties such as adjudicators, dispute review boards, arbitrators, and judges. The number of such cases could be substantially reduced by the introduction of a transparent and unified approach to the understanding of programmed works, record-keeping methods, and identifying the consequence of delay and disruption. Users of the SCL Protocol should apply its recommendations with common sense. The SCL Protocol is also intended to be a balanced document, reflecting the interests of all parties to the construction process equally. Some of its main features and principles will be discussed below.

7.4 Time program

One of the main goals of a good contract is to reduce claims and variations that may occur within construction projects while respecting that claims and variations are inevitable. Even the best contracts need tools to enable efficient claim and variation management. Next to the respective provisions for variation and claim management (such as those contained in Chapters 13 and 20 of the FIDIC forms), an instrument to control time for completion is important in this regard. The time schedule (the "program" in the FIDIC forms) is one of the most important tools to be used by individual project participants for the purpose of successful project management.

According to the SCL Protocol, the contractor should prepare (and the contract administrator should accept), a properly prepared program showing the manner and sequence in which the contractor plans to carry out the works. The program should be updated to record actual progress and any extensions of time granted. If this is done, then the program can be used as a tool for managing change, determining extensions of time for completion and periods of time for which compensation may be due. Contracting parties should also reach a clear agreement on the type of records that should be kept.

According to the SCL Protocol, most standard forms of contract contain inadequate requirements for generating an accepted program and/or keeping it up to date. The SCL Protocol recommends that the parties reach a clear agreement on the program. The agreement should cover:

- the form the program should take (including critical path and key resources attributed to particular activities);
- interaction with the method statement describing in detail how the contractor intends to construct the works and the resources (including sub-contractors) and being fully cross-referenced with the program;
- the "reasonable" time within which the contractor should submit a draft program for acceptance. Reasonable time will depend on the complexity of the project and should, ideally, be determined before the works are started.
- a mechanism for obtaining the acceptance of the contract administrator of the draft program. The contractor and not the contract administrator controls the method and sequence of construction and bases the tender price on their ability to do so. Therefore, the contract may contain a provision to the effect

that if the contract administrator does not respond to the contractor regarding the program within a specified time, it should be deemed to be accepted. Disagreements over what constitutes the accepted program should be resolved immediately and not be allowed to continue throughout the project. The SCL Protocol recommends the use of incentives or penalties such as liquidated damages to "encourage" the contractor to prepare and up-date the program.
- requirements for updating and saving of the accepted program. Actual progress should be recorded on a monthly basis by means of actual start and actual finish dates for activities together with percentage completion of currently incomplete activities and/or extent of remaining activity duration.
- methods of keeping accurate and current records.

7.4.1 Critical path method

The critical path method (CPM) was developed to reduce time-related disputes and enable efficient time management. In practice, a contract may include the contractor's obligation to mark out a *critical path* in the program whenever it is submitted (updated). Under the SCL Protocol, the critical path is defined as the "sequence of activities through a project network from start to finish, the sum of whose durations determines the overall project duration." There may be more than one critical path depending on workflow logic. A delay to progress of any activity on the critical path will, without acceleration or re-sequencing, cause the overall project duration to be extended, causing a critical delay.

The critical path method is, therefore, the process of describing the critical activities in a program by tracing the logical sequence of tasks that directly affect the date of project completion. It is a methodology or management technique that determines a project's critical path. The resulting program may be depicted in a number of different forms, including a Gantt or bar chart, a line-of-balance diagram, a pure logic diagram, a time-scaled logic diagram or as a time-chain diagram, depending on the nature of the works represented in the program.

The position of the SCL Protocol is that the contractor should submit (and the contract administrator should accept) a program (using commercially available critical path method project planning software) showing the manner and sequence in which the contractor plans to carry out the works. This should be done as early into the project as possible. Both the contractor and contract administrator should have a copy of the software package used to prepare the project program. For the program to be suitable for use as a tool for the analysis and management of change, it must be properly prepared so that, when a change occurs, it can accurately predict the effects of that change. The program should be provided in electronic form to the contract administrator and the critical path should be identified by the contractor. Every project has at least one critical path consisting of a list of activities that should be under constant supervision to secure the timely completion of the project.

The continuous monitoring and evaluation of the critical path and the causes of delay and disruption are often the only way to manage the variations and claims (including the effect on cost). The CPM allows easier and more efficient coordination of mutually related activities within a project.

7.5 Ownership of floats

Comprehensive time schedules in large construction projects cover an enormous volume of activities that are interrelated, overlapping and running concurrently. Each of them can contain a time allowance at their beginning and end. In the case of delay and extension of time for completion, it often becomes difficult to determine who is entitled to make use of this allowance (the float, that is, the time for completion not described in the critical path). A time schedule is usually prepared for tender by the contractor who distributes floats in their own favor (to procure materials, subcontractors, plants, and so on) and to reduce realization risks on their side. SCL Protocol deals with ownership of float, concluding that:

> Unless there is express provision to the contrary in the contract, where there is remaining total float in the programme at the time of an Employer Risk Event, an EOT should only be granted to the extent that the Employer Delay is predicted to reduce to below zero the total float on the critical path affected by the Employer Delay to Completion.

The authors of the SCL Protocol themselves warn that the adequacy of this rule must be considered on a case-by-case basis. For example, a situation may appear when the contractor-scheduled float may need to be drawn down due to a delay caused to the contractor by the employer, for example, when the employer delays the contactor by late submission of design approval. The contractor then appears to be in default by reason of milestone delay. This means that if a contractual penalty is sought by the employer, it would almost certainly be in conflict with good manners.

SCL Protocol further advises the contractor to identify every such float for the related activity by demonstrating their "ownership" of it.

If the Contractor wants to make allowance for the possibility of Contractor Delays (sometimes referred to as 'Time Risk Allowance'), then it should include in the activity durations in its programme such additional time as the Contractor believes is necessary to reflect the risk of such delays to those activities. Alternatively, it may identify such allowances as separate activities in the programme entitled 'Contingency for … [e.g., groundwork]'.

Time extension and float ownership under the FIDIC Red and Yellow Books (1999) by Frank Thomas (France)

In the construction industry, delay claims have been the subject of many debates and disputes between employers and contractors. This is especially so in cases where construction contracts do not explicitly establish the quantum technology to be applied when determining time extensions and handling float ownership. Disputes then usually become unavoidable. Currently, the majority of planning of the design and construction works is performed by powerful critical path method (CPM) planning software on computers operated by program specialists. Today, more and more employers require contractors to prepare their programs with specific CPM planning software. The main advantage of CPM planning software is that it is capable of breaking down the works into multiple detailed activities. Each activity has a specific duration and is interlinked to a sequence of activities (networks) with specific relationships in accordance with the construction logic and other time constraints (key dates, resources, working time, etc.). A CPM program also enables the contractor to identify the critical path and to monitor the works progress in real time, thus enabling the preparation of program updates whenever required. In addition, the contractor is also able to more precisely forecast the cost expenditures and to achieve the project within the planned time and cost budget by allocating and uploading the resources in the program.

Programs prepared with CPM techniques also have another great advantage: they are "dynamic." This simply means that any program with a proper critical path is able to simulate a "what if" scenario. For example, if a delay occurs during the construction period and delays specific activities, then it is possible to insert such a delay into the program. The potential effect on the project completion date can then be simulated by using a specific delay analysis technique (e.g., impacted as planned, time impact analysis). It is then possible to predict the effect of such a delay on the project completion date in a prospective manner which should then enable the engineer to determine any time extension efficiently. The CPM planning software is therefore a "dynamic" tool capable of demonstrating the effect of delays on the completion date.

One major disadvantage of CPM planning software is that it is complicated to use. Prior to becoming a successful CPM planning software operator, a long training period will be necessary in order to become familiar with all its features. This long learning curve and the difficulties encountered with CPM algorithm planning technicalities often discourage many construction engineers and lawyers from learning even the basic principles of the CPM planning software language. Operating CPM scheduling software should, however, be distinguished from programming such software. To draw a comparison: many people today use smartphones without knowing how they are actually programmed. It is true that construction planning software is not as user-friendly as the millions of applications developed for smartphones. However, some fundamentals like the intrinsic critical path logic of the planning software can be relied upon in order to establish the effect of delays on the project completion. In other words, it is possible to understand the meaning of a critical path in the CPM planning software language without the need to become a specialized CPM operator.

In this vignette, I analyze the question of time extension determination and float ownership under the FIDIC Red and Yellow Books (1999). The aim is to demonstrate that the time extension mechanism provided under these contract forms is actually reasonably clear and understandable when the standardized critical path terminology of the CPM planning software language is well understood and applied by the FIDIC contract users. It is true that Sub-Clause 8.4 does not refer to any "critical path" or "float" terminology. It does not mean, however, that such terminology should be ignored when it comes to the evaluation and determination of delay claims under the FIDIC conditions of contract. "Critical path" and "float" terminology is sometimes used by construction engineers and lawyers without knowing its true meaning in the CPM scheduling software language. Its proper definition and understanding in the CPM algorithm planning language are, however, very useful for FIDIC practitioners because it should help them to anticipate or solve disputes on many delay claims issues.

At first glance, it seems that the FIDIC Red and Yellow Books do not regulate the manner in how time extensions should be actually presented, evaluated and determined. Is it really so?

By cross-referencing the relevant Sub-Clauses 8.2, 8.3, 8.4, and 10.1 of the general conditions of contract ("GCC") of the FIDIC Red and Yellow Books (together with the meaning of the critical path mechanics of the CPM planning software language), it is possible to determine appropriate time extension quantum methodologies and to resolve the float ownership question unambiguously. The aim of this vignette is to give some practical guidance on how time extensions can actually be evaluated and properly quantified and to resolve the float ownership question in accordance with Sub-Clause 8.4.

First, I will briefly analyze:

- FIDIC Red and Yellow Books provisions related to time extension determinations;
- the critical path and float terminology defined by the most common CPM planning software.
- The resulting float ownership under the FIDIC Red and Yellow Books.

In addition to the capitalized definitions in the general conditions of contract (CoC), the following definitions will be used:

- contract completion date (CCD): the date of the last day of the time for completion period stated in the appendix to tender;
- actual completion date (ACD): the date certified by the engineer in the taking over certificate on which the works or Section were completed in accordance with the contract.
- planned completion date (PCD): the completion date of the works as planned by the contractor in its program, which can be earlier than CCD but not later, that is, the contractor's planned date for the ACD as shown in its program.

FIDIC red and yellow books provisions related to time extension determinations

Before considering the issue of which date is determinative in any entitlement to an extension of time (the CCD or the PCD) under Sub-Clause 8.4, it is necessary to first look at whether Sub-Clause 10.1 of the GCC refers to the CCD, the PCD or the ACD. Sub-Clause 10.1 states:
Except as stated in Sub-Clause 9.4, the works shall be taken over by the employer when:

(i) the Works have been completed in accordance with the contract, including the matters described in Sub-Clause 8.2 and except as allowed in sub-paragraph (a) below, and
(ii) a taking over certificate has been issued, or is deemed to have been issued in accordance with this Sub-Clause. The contractor may apply by notice to the engineer for a taking over certificate not earlier than 14 days before the works will, in the contractor's opinion, be complete and ready for taking over ... The Engineer shall, within 28 days after receiving the contractor's application:
    (a) issue the taking over certificate stating the date on which the works or Section were completed in accordance with the contract, except for ...
    (b) reject the application, giving reasons.

The reading and understanding of Sub-Clause 10.1 of GCC are clear. The contractor is free to apply for a taking over certificate if, "in his opinion," the works are "complete and ready to be taken over." The contractor has total freedom to determine (at any time) that the works have been completed for the purpose of Sub-Clause 10.1. If this is the case and the engineer confirms that the works have in fact been completed for the purpose of Sub-Clause 10.1, then the engineer shall issue a taking over certificate and the employer shall take over the works.

Note that the GCC states that the employer shall take over the works at ACD and is not allowed to refuse to do so by arguing, for example, that he would rather prefer to wait until the CCD prior to taking over the completed works. Completion for the purpose of Sub-Clause 10.1 means that completion of the works shall occur at the time notified by the contractor. The contractor is also authorized to anticipate the ACD by indicating such date in its program as the PCD. If the PCD is prior to the CCD, there is an inherent terminal float existing between these two dates. The term "terminal float" means the time period between the PCD and the CCD appearing in the contractor's program. If the contractor will have substantially completed its works at the ACD, as confirmed by the engineer's taking over certificates, several scenarios may then occur:

- The ACD equates to the PCD: the original terminal float remains intact.
- The ACD is achieved prior to the PCD: the terminal float increases.
- The ACD is achieved between the PCD and the CCD: the terminal float decreases.
- The ACD is achieved exactly at the CCD: the terminal float is completely exhausted.
- The ACD is achieved beyond the CCD: the terminal float falls into negative.

Sub-Clause 8.2 stipulates that:

> the contractor shall complete the whole of the works, and each section (if any) within the time for completion for the works or section (as the case may be), including:
>
> (a) achieving the passing of the tests on completion, and
> (b) completing all works which is stated in the contract as being required for the works or section to be considered to be completed for the purpose of taking over under Sub-Clause 10.1.

Sub-Clause 8.2 makes it clear that the contractor may complete the works at any time "within the time for completion," that is, at any date occurring prior to the CCD. Just as the contractor may actually achieve the ACD before the CCD, so too he has total freedom in his program to plan to achieve completion for the purpose of Sub-Clause 10.1 at the PCD prior to the CCD.

Sub-Clause 8.3 stipulates:

> The contractor shall submit a detailed time program to the engineer within 28 days after receiving the notice under Sub-Clause 8.1 [commencement of works]. The contractor shall also submit a revised program whenever the previous program is inconsistent with actual progress or with the contractor's obligations. Each program shall include:

(a) the order in which the contractor intends to carry out the works, including the anticipated timing of each stage of design (if any), contractor's documents, procurement, manufacture, inspection, delivery to site, construction, erection and testing, commissioning and trial operation,
(b) ...
(c) the sequence and timing of inspections and tests specified in the contract, and a supporting report which includes:
 (i) a general description of the methods which the contractor intends to adopt, and of the major stages, in the execution of the works, and
 (ii) details showing the contractor's reasonable estimate of the number of each class of contractor's personnel and of each type of contractor's equipment, required on the site for each major stage.

Unless the engineer, within 21 days after receiving a program, gives notice to the contractor stating the extent to which it does not comply with the contract, the contractor shall proceed in accordance with the program, subject to his other obligations under the contract. The employer's personnel shall be entitled to rely upon the program when planning their activities.

The contractor shall promptly give notice to the engineer of specific probable future events or circumstances which may adversely affect the work, increase the contract price or delay the execution of the works. The engineer may require the contractor to submit an estimate of the anticipated effect of the future event or circumstances, and/or a proposal under Sub-Clause 13.3 [variation procedure].

If, at any time, the engineer gives notice to the contractor that a program fails (to the extent stated) to comply with the contract or to be consistent with actual progress and the contractor's stated intentions, "the contractor shall submit a revised program to the engineer in accordance with this Sub-Clause."

Under Sub-Clause 8.3, the function of the program:

- is to plan the stages of the works by showing the "order" of the contractor's activities during the design, construction and commissioning phases accompanied by a supporting report on the contractor's construction methods and reasonable estimate of resources;
- must be updated whenever actual progress falls beyond the current program as may be notified by the engineer.

Under Sub-Clause 8.3, the contractor also has an early warning obligation. They shall give prompt notice to the engineer if of the opinion that "probable future events or circumstances" may adversely affect/delay the progress of the works or increase the contract price. Sub-Clause 8.3 does not specify if a "delay to the execution of the works" caused by a "probable future event" is to be proven on the basis of the program produced under this Sub-Clause. Indeed, Sub-Clause 8.3 does not require the contractor to prepare its program with a critical path (even if it is wise to establish a critical path). A linked Gantt chart program showing work activities without CPM relationships fulfills the requirements of Sub-Clause 8.3 (a), (b) and (c), namely, to show "the order [in which] the contractor intends to carry out the Works." In other words, unless specified otherwise in the particular conditions, the contractor is not obliged to show the CPM interconnections between activities by using the CPM planning software. Of course all contractors seek to gain by establishing and showing links between activities, relevant constraints and resulting critical path in their program. Any program update usually requires CPM critical path analysis that can be facilitated by using the CPM planning software. It is thus in the contractor's best interests to demonstrate that their program or update is technically feasible and in compliance with the Contract by providing a clear critical path.

No guidance is actually given in Sub-Clause 8.3 on the manner in which delays in the execution of the works should be quantified. This is probably due to the fact that contractor's notification is to be given in anticipation of a "probable future event," which may or may not occur. The contractor shall, if required by the engineer, produce an estimate of the time and cost effect of such future event on the execution of the works.

Sub-Clause 8.4 refers to any delay or projected delay in completion of the works for the purpose of Sub-Clause 10.1 (i.e., a delay to the completion of the works beyond the PCD), as being a condition precedent to the contractor's entitlement to an extension of the time for completion:

The contractor shall be entitled subject to Sub-Clause 20.1 [contractor's claims] to an extension of the time for completion if and to the extent that completion for the purposes of Sub-Clause 10.1 [taking over of the works and sections] is or will be delayed by any of the following causes:

...

If the contractor considers himself to be entitled to an extension of the time for completion, the contractor shall give notice to the engineer in accordance with Sub-Clause 20.1 [contractor's claims]. When determining each extension of time under Sub-Clause 20.1, the engineer shall review previous determinations and may increase, but shall not decrease, the total extension of time.

The extension of time objectives of the Sub-Clause 8.4 provisions of the GCC are of benefit to both parties as follows:

- Contractor: First it relieves the contractor from the payment of delay damages in the case of delays for which the employer is responsible under the contract terms.
- Employer: Second it establishes new section completion deadlines under the contract (subject to the application of delay damages) and therefore prevents the CCD becoming unknown/uncertain. This is also known as "time at large" in common law countries, that is, it preserves the contractual validity of any new, extended Section deadlines.

Sub-Clause 8.4 clearly stipulates that the contractor is entitled to an extension of the time for completion each time that any PCD of a section as forecast by the contractor in its program (i.e., for the purpose of taking over in accordance with Sub-Clause 10.1) is delayed (even if the effect of such delay does not result in the PCD exceeding the CCD due to the existence of a terminal float between the PCD and the CCD).

Sub-Clause 8.4 therefore requires the contractor to demonstrate cause and effect between an employer's risk event (entitling the contractor to "claim" a time extension) and its effect on the PCD. A "technical" correlation must be somehow established between the occurrence of an employer's risk event and its effect on the "as planned" project completion (the PCD). Indeed it is not sufficient for the contractor to prove the existence of an employer's risk event and damage (i.e., delay on the PCD) in order to be entitled to a time extension. In accordance with Sub-Clause 8.4, the contractor must further prove causation ("if and to the extent the completion for the purpose of Sub-Clause 10.1 is or will be delayed by any of the following causes" ...), that is, to establish and demonstrate the link between the cause and the damage (i.e., delay to the "as planned" completion of the works or the PCD). Causality between an event and its effect can be best proven by using CPM delay techniques. A CPM-based program is a mathematical model that combines activity durations with activity relationships. If the relationships between activities are accurate, well inter-connected and dynamically reactive, then the CPM program becomes a "dynamic program." It is then possible to "add" delays into a specific sequence of activities of the CPM program and to evaluate and predict the effect of such additions on PCD, that is, to rationally predict the resulting time extension in accordance with Sub-Clause 8.4. Such simulation can be made either prospectively or retrospectively by using different delay analysis techniques (impacted as planned, time impact analysis, collapse as built, and so on). Naturally then, it is essential to first understand the basics of critical path terminology in the CPM language.

Critical path terminology in the CPM language

It is very difficult to find a proper, homogeneous definition of the "critical path" in delay analysis literature. The common terminology used to define a critical path usually ignores the CPM algorithm language of the planning software. Many practitioners have, for example, attempted to define the critical path as the longest path to PCD; thus allowing a terminal float to "exist" between the PCD and the CCD in such a definition. Is this accurate? Is the CPM planning software algorithm flexible enough to accommodate such a definition? The answer is "No" because the longest path to the PCD would have to be manipulated in order to make it critical in the CPM algorithm language. Manipulation in this case would mean imposing an algorithm constraint on the PCD by declaring that the Project must finish at the PCD (early and late finish of the last activity must be the same). This would lead to a nonsensical result because the CPM algorithm would understand this constraint as a contractor's obligation to complete the works at the PCD. The consequence would be that the CPM algorithm would then "forbid" the contractor from freely consuming the terminal float and further prevent them from completing the works between PCD and CCD. This is also the reason why confusion of the true meaning of "critical path" is so globally widespread. The first question is therefore to understand what "critical" means in the CPM planning software algorithm language. Critical to what? PCD or CDD deadlines? The Red and Yellow FIDIC Books (1999 Editions) do not provide any definition or guidance in this respect and no reference is made to it in any of the Sub-Clauses.

The critical path method is a network program which models the construction logic between the activities in accordance with the "as planned" construction methods, time constraints (e.g., access dates of the parts of the site, penalty milestones, non-working days) and the resources (limited availability of equipment, labor, and supply of materials). The Society of Construction Law Delay and Disruption Protocol (SCLDD Protocol) defines the critical path as follows:

> The sequence of activities through a project network from start to finish, the sum of whose durations determines the overall project duration. There may be more than one critical path depending on workflow logic. A delay to progress of any activity on

the critical path will, without acceleration or re-sequencing, cause the overall project duration to be extended and is therefore referred to as a "critical delay."

This definition of critical path is given in *Mirant Asia-Pacific(Hong Kong) Ltd v. (1) Ove Arup and Partners International Limited (2) Ove Arup and Partners Hong Kong Limited* [2007] EWHC 918 (TCC). The SCLDD Protocol implicitly assumes that the program includes a critical path determining the overall project duration without defining whether such duration ends with the PCD or the CCD. The SCLDD, however, distinguishes in its definitions, the date for completion (the PCD) from the contract completion date (the CCD). But what does it mean in relation to the above-mentioned definition of "the critical path?" First of all, in cases where critical activities are overlapping, the sum of their durations will definitely not determine the overall project execution time (overlapping time must be deducted and this should be taken into account as well). Thus the critical path definition in the SCL Protocol does not apply to all situations.

In the CPM planning software language, a critical activity is an activity with "zero day" total float. The total float is the number of days that the start or the duration of an activity can be delayed without delaying the CCD. The critical path can therefore be defined as the sequence of critical activities linked to each other through a project network with "zero day" total float until the achievement of the works exactly at the CCD. It is important to note that as long as the total float is strictly positive (>0 day), then such activity is not critical. For example, an activity with 2 days total float means that you may delay the start or the duration of such activity by 2 days and still achieve completion of the works at the CCD.

In the first simplified program presented in Figure 7.1, 10 days of total float exist for each activity A and B. Both activities are non-critical, that is, no critical path exists in such CPM program despite the fact that activity A and activity B and the CCD (finish milestone) are all linked together as shown.

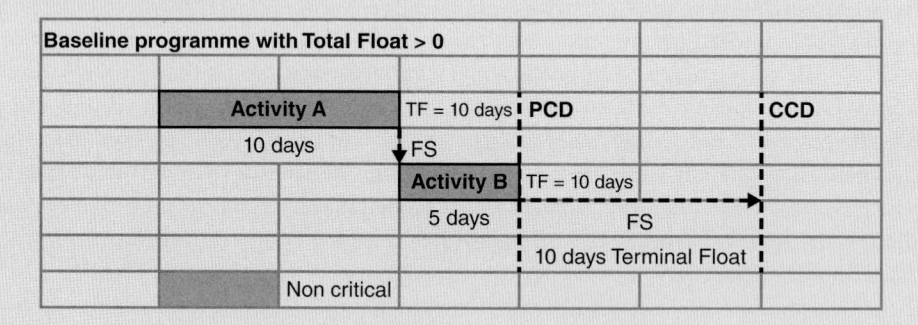

Baseline programme with Total Float > 0							
		Activity A	TF = 10 days	PCD		CCD	
		10 days	FS				
			Activity B	TF = 10 days			
			5 days	FS			
				10 days Terminal Float			
		Non critical					

Figure 7.1

In order to incorporate a critical path in the above-mentioned simplified program, it is necessary to eliminate the terminal float between the PCD and the CCD by introducing an activity bar called the "contractor's time risk allowance" (CTRA). The CTRA represents a time contingency available to the contractor for completing its works until the CCD. By introducing a CTRA between the end of activity B and the CCD, the critical path until the CCD is then clearly created and identified by reducing the total float of activity A and B to "0 day" (Figure 7.2).

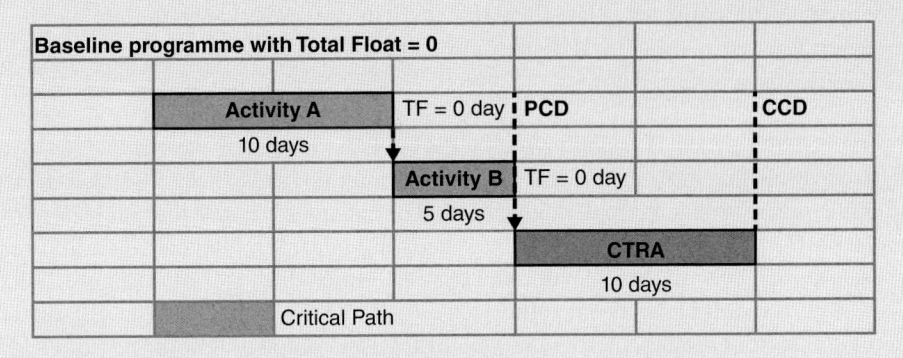

Baseline programme with Total Float = 0			
Activity A 10 days	TF = 0 day ¦ PCD		¦ CCD
	Activity B 5 days	TF = 0 day	
		CTRA 10 days	
Critical Path			

Figure 7.2

Without the CTRA activity bar, there would be no critical path existing under such program (i.e., activities A and B would have 10 days total float). The addition of a CTRA activity in a contractor's program provides a much better visualization of contractor ownership of the terminal float. (Note: The insertion of CTRA activities is not a tool intended to defend contractor ownership of the terminal float under the FIDIC Red and Yellow Books. This is discussed in more detail below).

It is further important to note that under the FIDIC Red and Yellow Books, the creation of a critical path in a program is a contractor right but not an obligation. Sub-Clause 8.3 of GCC does not require the contractor to produce a program with a CPM critical path even if recommended to do so. Sub-Clause 8.4 entitles the contractor to an extension of the time for completion to the extent that the completion date of the works is delayed beyond the PCD as a result of an employer's delay. In practical terms, however, it will be very difficult for a contractor to demonstrate to the engineer's satisfaction the extent to which the PCD is or will be delayed by an event for which the employer is contractually responsible if the contractor has not created a "dynamic" program showing how the PCD is affected.

Who then "owns" the float under FIDIC Red and Yellow Books 1999 editions? In order to understand this very important point, let us refer to a simplified program example. The simplified program in Figure 7.3 shows that the contractor will complete the works consisting of activities A and B in a "finish to start" scenario 10 days prior to the CCD. In other words, there is 10 days of terminal float in the contractor's simplified program between the PCD and the CCD.

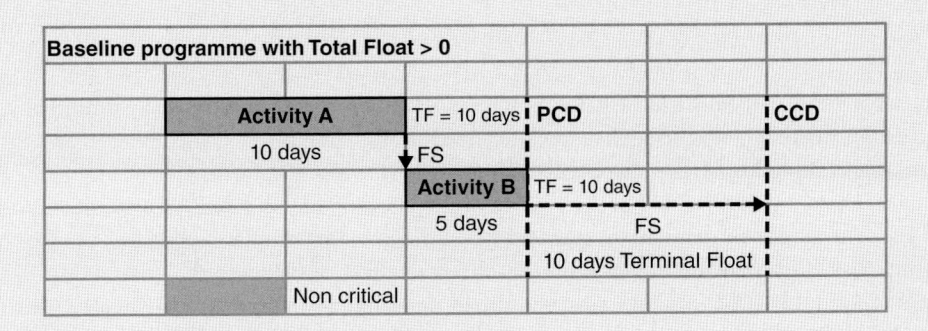

Baseline programme with Total Float > 0			
Activity A 10 days	TF = 10 days ¦ PCD ↓ FS		¦ CCD
	Activity B 5 days	TF = 10 days FS 10 days Terminal Float	
Non critical			

Figure 7.3

If, for example, the employer delays the start of activity A by 5 days, then the completion date of the Project forecast by the contractor to occur at the PCD will also be delayed by 5 days. Two possible scenarios may then follow:

- *Scenario 1*: The employer is authorized by the GCC to consume 5 days of the 10 days terminal float existing in the contractor's simplified program between the PCD and the CCD. In this case, the time for completion would not be extended because the completion of the project can still occur within the original time for completion (activity B is still finishing prior to the CCD) with the effect of reducing the terminal float to 5 days (Figure 7.4); or
- *Scenario 2*: If the employer is not authorized under the GCC to consume the terminal float in the contractor's simplified program then the time for completion would be extended by 5 days because the original forecast completion date (the PCD) is also delayed by 5 days. This has the effect of maintaining the contractor's 10-day terminal float, that is, the contractor "owns" the terminal float (Figure 7.5).

Baseline programme with Total Float > 0 and Employer's Delay (ED): Scenario 1						
			PCD	PCD'	CCD	
	ED	Activity A	TF = 5 days			
	5 days	10 days	↓FS			
			Activity B	TF = 5 days	No Time Extension	
			5 days			
		Employer's Delay (ED)				
		Non critical				

Figure 7.4

Baseline programme with Total Float > 0 and Employer's Delay (ED): Scenario 2						
			PCD	PCD'	CCD	CCD'
	ED	Activity A	TF = 10 days			
	5 days	10 days	↓FS		5 days EOT	
			Activity B	TF = 10 days		
			5 days		FS	
		Employer's Delay (ED)		10 days Terminal Float		
		Non critical				

Figure 7.5

In accordance with Sub-Clause 8.4, the effect of any potential employer's delay should be first of all evaluated and measured against the PCD deadline and not the CCD deadline: "if and to the extent that completion for the purposes of Sub-Clause 10.1 is or will be delayed by any of the following causes …." If this was not the case, then the wording of Sub-Clause 8.4 would stipulate that the contractor's entitlement to an extension of the time for completion is subject to demonstrating that a delay to the works is or will have the effect of delaying the completion of the works beyond the CCD. In such a case, the above-mentioned wording of Sub-Clause 8.4 would be amended as follows: "if and to the extent that completion for the purposes of Sub-Clause 10.1 is or will be delayed beyond the time for completion by any of the following causes …"

It is therefore important to adhere to Sub-Clause 8.4 of the GCC as it stands without distorting its meaning. In our simplified program example above, a 5-day delay in completion of works (i.e., PCD) entitles the contractor to an extension of the time for completion by 5 days as well (i.e., CCD) thus maintaining the 10-day terminal float in the contractor's ownership. If a contractor was not entitled to the terminal float, then they would need to provide a program to the engineer that had a terminal float = 0, even if the "real" program used to plan the project had contingency (TF). It is in the interests of good project management that the contractor provides the "real" program to the engineer so that everybody "is singing from the same hymn sheet."

The implicit correlation between the CCD and the PCD as delineated under Sub-Clause 8.4 in conjunction with Sub-Clauses 8.2 and 10.1 establishes, unambiguously, the contractor's ownership of the terminal float between the PCD and the CDD. If the contractor is not the owner of the terminal float between the PCD and the CCD, then the employer would, in effect, be allowed to take time away from the original time for completion. Thus the contractor would then be obliged to insert a constraint on the PCD in order to render the path to the PCD critical. Sub-Clause 8.4 concludes by confirming that the total of all extensions of time, either for the works or for a particular section, cannot be subsequently decreased. This is so even if a number of omissions are instructed as variations and the contractor is able to achieve completion sooner than is required under Sub-Clause 8.2. The employer or engineer is not then empowered to reduce the time for completion in this respect. The terminal float therefore legitimately belongs to the contractor. There is no mechanism in the contract which would enable the employer to take this time contingency away from the contractor. In other words, cross-referencing and literal interpretation of Sub-Clauses 8.2, 8.4, and 10.1 clearly establish the fact that the contractor owns any float existing between its "originally as planned completion date of the Project" (the PCD) and the "date of time for completion" agreed in the contract (the CCD).

The question remains as to whether there is any other float which could be jointly (as opposed to exclusively) owned by both parties under the FIDIC Red and Yellow Books? The answer is yes, that is, the "free float." The free float is the number of days that the start of an activity can be delayed without delaying the activity following it. By definition, the activities on the critical path have no free float. In such cases, any employer's delay having the effect of consuming the free float of any activities will have no effect on the completion of the works that can still be achieved at the PCD. The free float has to be, therefore, differentiated from the terminal float. The terminal float is a time contingency between the last activity of a sequence leading to the PCD and the CCD, while the free float is a time contingency between two activities. Usually all scheduling software is able to display the total float and free float in two separate columns, thus enabling establishment of party ownership of these time contingencies in an undisputed manner.

Findings resulting from the combination of CPM scheduling terminology with the FIDIC red and yellow books planning and time extension requirements

With the help of the CPM scheduling terminology, we have now determined that under the FIDIC Red and Yellow Books:

- A critical path is a sequence of a critical activities with "0 day" total float linked to the CCD (and not to the PCD).

- The terminal float between the PCD and the CCD is owned by the contractor and can be replaced by an activity bar called the contractor's time risk allowance.
- As long as consumption of the free float has no impact on the PCD, it can be consumed by either the employer or the contractor.

Analysis of Sub-Clauses 8.3 and 8.4 further reveals that:

- The Sub-Clause 8.3 program is aimed at planning the order of activities with supporting reports on resources and construction technology, to measure achieved progress and to produce updates when actual progress falls behind the current program. Sub-Clause 8.3 does not require the contractor to produce a program using CPM techniques even if advisable and recommended.
- The granting of an extension of the CCD under Sub-Clause 8.4 is subject to the contractor's capability to demonstrate that there is direct causation between an employer's risk event and its impact on the PCD (and not the CCD). This demonstration is best achieved by using the CPM program. This can be performed prospectively/retrospectively by predicting the effect of a delay on the critical path.

Even if common sense suggests using the Sub-Clause 8.3 baseline program for the purposes of evaluating and determining a time extension under Sub-Clause 8.4, such a program may not be suitable, especially if no critical path exists. As Sub-Clauses 8.3 and 8.4 are not cross-referenced, nothing prevents the contractor from creating a CPM baseline specifically for the purpose of Sub-Clause 8.4, that is, a CPM baseline program capable of demonstrating cause and effect "dynamically" (a "what if" program). Such a program can of course be prepared on the basis of a Sub-Clause 8.3 program, provided all relationships between activities are fully accurate, well inter-connected, and dynamically reactive. The best way to check this is to "add/insert" delays into a specific sequence of activities in order to see how the baseline program "reacts," that is, to observe how the PCD (if a terminal float exists) or the CCD are moving to the right. Engineers are usually keen to accept program in their "static" form (i.e., paper, pdf, Excel) without testing them for delays. Even if the baseline program is submitted in the usual CPM scheduling software format, engineers are usually reluctant to perform such a dynamic test because it is not required under Sub-Clause 8.3. The critical path of a program can, however, only be checked properly if typical "test" delays are "added/inserted" into the program in order to observe how the PCD and the CCD will react to them. This is a dynamic test setting the critical path in motion with the result of simulating the effect of delays on PCD and CCD.

This leads to the conclusion that, in almost all cases, it is recommended for the contractor to adjust its Sub-Clause 8.3 baseline program to create a critical path to the CCD for the purpose of quantifying time extensions under Sub-Clause 8.4. It means that in practice the contractor will develop a baseline program with a clear relationship in order to create a "host schedule" baseline capable of simulating the effect of parties' delays directly on the CCD. The first adjustment consists of eliminating the terminal float. This is replaced by a contractor's time risk allowance activity that properly links it to all other activities. Leaving the terminal float open would only complicate the delay and time extension analysis because the CPM critical path would only appear after its consumption. This is also consistent with the definition of the critical path discussed earlier. It is therefore wise to create the critical path to the CCD as soon as possible (e.g., in the first Sub-Clause 8.3 program to be submitted to the engineer). Of course, the "addition" of delays in this new host schedule baseline (created for the purpose of quantifying the time extension) will have to be performed according to specific delays analysis techniques. These are discussed further below.

In order to simulate/predict the effect of a delay event on CCD at the time of its occurrence, it is necessary to impact the relevant activities of the host schedule baseline with such a delay event (after quantification) in a chronological order. This simulation/prediction of the net compounded effect of several delays is made under the assumption that the original works sequence/logic and resource capacity will remain unchanged. The first step is to quantify the duration of each delay event from start to end. This can be estimated by using working ratios based on (1) the contractor's/engineer's own experience or (2) the time difference between the 'as planned' execution time of an activity in the contractor's baseline program and (3) the experienced "as built" execution time of such activity if no working ratio can be reasonably applied. For example, a permit/design resulting from the employer's delay can usually only be quantified in an "as built" manner, that is, after the delay event has ceased. Each individual delay is to be added into the host schedule baseline in chronological order in order to simulate and predict its critical effect on the CCD (prospective approach). The effect of such an addition is either to delay/shift the start of an activity or to prolong its overall duration. Prolonging the duration of an activity simply means linking the original activity duration to the relevant delay event, thus delaying the "as planned" activity (the original duration remains unchanged). Any CCD movement resulting from such a delay testing enables the analyst to predict the new time for completion date. The delay testing process is then repeated until all the delays have been added. The addition of delays is processed incrementally in a chronological order to determine the overall contractor's entitlement to an extension of the CCD resulting from the net compounded effect of delays.

This method is also known as the "impacted as planned" if the delays are added event by event. In "time impact analysis" (TIA) the delays are added window by window or in "slices" (e.g., month by month). If such an analysis is performed after completion of the works, the "as built" program should also be incorporated in the delay analysis for re-scheduling purposes.

Conclusion

Provided that the "total float" (TF) and the "free float" (FF) are always clearly identified in the contractor's program by appropriate CPM scheduling software and the wording of Sub-Clauses 8.3 and 8.4 of the FIDIC Red and Yellow Books:

- This fully supports the fact that the contractor "owns" any terminal float existing in his program, that is, when the total float is positive and the free float is zero days.
- This does not support the fact that the contractor "owns" any positive free float, which is then, at the disposal of the project. However, when such a free float is entirely consumed by the project (either by the employer or the contractor), then any remaining terminal float (when TF > 0 and FF = 0) remains in the ownership of the contractor.

As the definition of "critical path" in the CPM software language is linked to "zero" days total float, I would therefore suggest defining the critical path, total float and free float as follows:

- *Critical path*: The critical path is a series of activities linked to each other through a project network that determines the overall project's completion time. The duration of the activities on the critical path controls the duration of the entire project. Without acceleration or re-sequencing, a delay to any of these critical activities will delay the finish date of the entire project. A critical activity is an activity with "zero days" free/total float. The critical path is defined by the sequence of critical activities linked to the contract completion date (CCD).
- *Total float*: The total float is the number of days the start of an activity can be delayed without delaying the planned completion date (PCD).
- *Free float*: The free float is the number of days the start of an activity can be delayed without delaying the activity following it.

Frank Thomas
Claim Quantum Specialist
TK-Consulting
France

7.6 Time at large and extension of time (EOT)

Time at large is a common law principle. Under this doctrine, the agreed time for completion (under delay damages) no longer applies because its fulfillment is prevented by the employer risk event and the contract lacks any mechanism for extension of time for completion or when such a mechanism is non-functional. Under these circumstances, the contractor is excused from the duty of completing the work by the original contractual deadline, instead being obliged to do so within a reasonable period of time. The employer may not then claim delay damages.

According to the SCL Protocol an EOT (extension of time) is additional time granted to the contractor to provide an extended contractual time period or date by which work is to be (or should be) completed and to relieve it from liability for damages for delay. The benefit to the contractor of an extension of time for completion is to relieve them of liability for damages for delay for any period prior to the extended contract completion date. The benefit of an extension of time for the employer is that it establishes a new contract completion date and prevents time for completion of the works becoming "at large."

Good contracts contain a mechanism for an extension of time for completion. However, situations may arise when, for example, the employer fails to respond to the contractor's warnings, claim notifications, and updated time schedule submissions. Facing this, common law lawyers take the attitude that if the employer fails to respond to the contractor's notification and fails to make a decision about a claim, then the time for completion is not determined (time is at large). The contractor is then obliged to complete the work within a "reasonable period" in respect of all the circumstances.

There is no equivalent to the common law concept of "time at large" in civil codes. In such circumstances, various provisions of civil law may be used. Time at large is based on the common law "prevention principle," by which it would be inequitable for the employer to enforce the contractor's failure to meet the completion date when this was reasons for which the employer was responsible (an "act of prevention") and where the contract either has no mechanism for extending the completion date, or that mechanism has become inoperable.

In civil codes, similar provisions are regularly encountered. These provisions protect the contractor in delay who is prevented from performance by the employer in cases where the contractor was acting in good faith.

The related principle is contained in Article 5.1.3 of the UNIDROIT Principles (Co-operation Between the Parties), which states that: "Each party shall cooperate with the other party when such co-operation may reasonably be expected for the performance of that party's obligation." A further related provision is Article 7.1.3 of the UNIDROIT Principles (Withholding Performance):

> (1) Where the parties are to perform simultaneously, either party may withhold performance until the other party tenders its performance. (2) Where the parties are to perform consecutively, the party that is to perform later may withhold its performance until the first party has performed.

An interesting example of the admission of the time at large principle in the civil law environment is case no. 310/2002 Ad Hoc (final award dated 8.8.2005) decided in international construction arbitration at the *Cairo Regional Centre for International Commercial Arbitration*. This case involved a dispute between an European construction company and an Afro-Asian tourism company. The matter was resolved under Egyptian civil law before a British Chairman and two Egyptian members.

The arbitrators held that:

> [W]here a contract provides for a date for completion of the works, but the employer through its acts or omissions prevents the contractor from achieving that date and there is no entitlement to extension of time under the contract in such event, the time for completion in the contract is nullified. This in turn means that the employer loses his right to levy liquidated damages and, whilst the contractor's obligation to complete the works remains, he must do so only within a reasonably time.
>
> (Alam-Eldin, 2010)

In both legal systems, the party with the pro-active approach (i.e., the one that flags events with potentially adverse impacts on quality, time, price, is timely in notifying and submitting their claims and being inclined to solve complications timely), being in good faith, must always be protected in case of a dispute.

It is rare for sample forms of contract to deal with time-related issues sufficiently. On the other hand, it seems not to be appropriate to impose too complicated requirements for time management on international construction contracts where, sometimes, the participants are not prepared to fulfill such requirements and the practical effect would be that nobody would use the contractual procedures in practice. It would no doubt be welcomed by international construction practitioners to have detailed guidance on time-related issues (time program, time at large, concurrency, float, and so on) in materials such as the *FIDIC Guidance for the Preparation of Particular Conditions* or *FIDIC Contracts Guide* to establish international best practice in this area.

7.7 Concurrent delay

It is not uncommon for both parties to be in delay simultaneously. Frequently, the issues of concurrent delays are not covered in detail by governing law or in the contracts.

The mentioned "prevention principle" typical of common law is mirrored in the civil law as "concurrent delay." For example, *The Czech Commercial Code* established rules for the default by a debtor in Section 365. The same rule is contained in the *New Czech Civil Code* at § 1969. Under this body of law: "the debtor is not in default if he is unable to perform his obligation due to default by the creditor." Default by a debtor and a creditor are fully regulated by the provisions of *The Czech Commercial Code*. The provisions at Section 365, which define default by the debtor, are mandatory. Similar provisions are contained in the majority of civil codes around the world.

The same principle can be found in Polish law. A practical example is the recent case (I CSK 748/12) where the Polish High Court (last instance court in Poland) confirmed that contractual penalties imposed on the contractor after a delay caused by the employer are not acceptable for being in conflict with the principle that a debtor cannot be in delay if the creditor is in delay.

The purpose of the prevention principle is similar. If the employer caused a delay, it would be inequitable to enforce delay damages where the contract either has no mechanism for extending the completion date, or that mechanism has become inoperable.

In the above-mentioned case no. 310/202 Ad Hoc, the arbitrators stated:

> It is accepted in all international construction contracts that: (a) whereas it is the duty of the contractor to do what the contract requires to be done (as designed and specified by the employer), the employer shall allow the contractor to do that which is to be done without hindrance; and (b) a party cannot benefit of its breach to the detriment of the injured party.

In no way can the above-mentioned general regulation in both the common law and the civil law be seen as sufficient guidance for all the numerous time-related issues encountered in the daily practice of construction projects.

Research by Jacob C. Jorgensen (2010) in cooperation with construction law experts in 12 different jurisdictions around the world (both common and civil law countries were represented) produced interesting outcomes. The authors analyzed and responded to the same ten questions regarding the interpretation and application of delay clauses under the laws of their respective countries. It is, for instance, interesting to see that the important issues of concurrent delays and ownership of float have seemingly not been regulated in any of the countries.

England is apparently the only jurisdiction where an attempt has been made to regulate these issues in the mentioned SCL Protocol. Similar efforts have been lately made in the Czech Republic, see it here: http://www.sfdi.cz/soubory/obrazky-clanky/metodiky/2018_metodika_casove_rizeni_fidic.pdf.

Delay clauses in different jurisdictions by Jacob C. Jørgensen (Denmark)

In 2010, I finished a research project in cooperation with construction law experts in 12 different jurisdictions across the world. Both common and civil law countries were represented. The respondents analyzed and responded to the same ten questions regarding the interpretation and application of delay clauses under the laws of their respective countries. In addition, the respondents highlighted the pitfalls and advantages one should be aware of when dealing with a standard construction contract, such as the 1999 FIDIC Red Book, governed by the law of their respective countries. It is, for instance, interesting to see that the important issues of concurrent delays and ownership to float have seemingly not been regulated in any of the standard contracts used in the 12 jurisdictions examined. England is apparently the only jurisdiction where an attempt has been made to regulate these issues contractually in the Delay & Disruption Protocol published by the Society of Construction Law. In my view, further legal research in respect to these particular issues would be welcomed. It is also interesting to observe how the laws of virtually all of the jurisdictions (though they all claim to protect the parties' right to contractual freedom), levy a remarkable amount of restraint on the employer's right to claim liquidated damages even though the contract in most cases clearly provides for this. Under Danish law, for example, the employer is not allowed to claim liquidated damages for interim delays and liquidated damages cannot be claimed if the employer fails to give notice, even though the contract does not impose any notice requirement. The well-known common law "genuine pre-estimate rule" has been adopted by a number of civil law jurisdictions including Germany, China and Switzerland, where it exists in the form of rules limiting the amount of liquidated damages to a percentage of the contract sum.

Jacob C. Jørgensen
Advokat (H), LL.M.
FCIArb, TEP
Copenhagen, Denmark

The SCL Protocol also defines several key rules for concurrent delay stating that a true concurrent delay is "the occurrence of two or more delay events at the same time." One is an employer risk event, the other a contractor risk event—the effects of which are felt at the same time. Such a "true" concurrent delay will occur only rarely. For example, at the beginning of the project where lack of site access is caused by the employer and lack of mobilization is caused by the contractor.

Where contractor delay to completion occurs concurrently with employer delay to completion, the contractor's concurrent delay should not reduce any extension of time due. Furthermore, if the contractor incurs additional costs that are caused both by employer delay and contractor delay, then the contractor should only recover compensation if they are able to separate the additional costs caused by employer delay from those caused by contractor delay.

Concurrency is a cause of problems for both the contractor (who must prove and calculate a difficult claim) and the employer (whose liquidated damages entitlement may be challenged by a claim for an extension of time). It is also a complex situation for the contract administrator because deciding on responsibility remains a grey area.

A different approach was encountered in ICC case no. 10847 (2003) (ICC, 2012) where the contractor claimed an extension of time and additional costs due to alleged late issue of design drawings for a power station. While the contractor admitted that it was responsible for overlapping delay (in excavating the power station complex), it claimed that such concurrency should not affect the contractor's entitlement to an extension of time arising from delays attributable to the employer. The tribunal dismissed the contractor's claim on the basis of the contractor's pre-existing delay in the power station excavation works which were on the critical path. The tribunal did not subscribe to the view that an event that caused no delay to an activity on the critical path to the date for completion of the works can form the basis for an extension of time.

The principal problem with concurrency is that it leads to logical difficulties in applying simple concepts of causation. Very often, the underlying factual position will eliminate competing causes. However, causative events of the same potency (but with different parties being responsible for each one) will still remain. One particular problem is the absence of a consensus on the method of analysis. This applies both to the method of delay analysis and to the legal analysis of the consequences. The SCL Protocol sets out the following types of analysis that can be used: as-planned versus as-built, impacted as-planned, collapsed as-built or time impact analysis, time slice windows analysis or retrospective longest path analysis. While a method can be found that will support a case either for the contractor or the employer, the difficulty will be in predicting, objectively, the likely outcome of the case, since there is no single approach that the tribunal will follow. Self-evidently, this represents a problem for the tribunal as well as a risk for the parties (Ramsey, 2006).

7.8 Disruption

Disruption can be defined as any change in the method of performance or planned work sequence contemplated by the contractor at the time the bid was submitted that prevents the contractor from actually performing in that manner. This material alteration results in increased difficulty and cost of performance (Cushman, 2011).

According to the SCL Protocol, disruption (as distinct from delay) is a disturbance, hindrance or interruption to a contractor's normal working methods resulting in lower efficiency. If caused by the employer, it may give rise to a right to compensation either under the contract or as a breach of contract. Disruption *may* lead to late completion, but not always. It is possible for work to be disrupted and for the contractor to perform the contract on time. In this situation, the contractor will not have a claim for an extension of time, but it may have a claim for the cost of the reduced efficiency of its workforce.

Standard forms of contract and governing laws do not usually deal expressly with disruption. If they do not, then disruption may be claimed as being a breach of the term generally implied into construction contracts (via the governing law), namely, that the employer will not prevent or hinder the contractor in the execution of its work. In the majority of disruption evaluation cases, global and concurrent claims are unavoidable. Disruption evaluation is difficult as is the establishment of some universal rules for disruption evaluation. Case law in the common law systems has led to the establishment of best practice. Such best practice guidance helps to find fair solutions.

There seems to be no universally accepted method of disruption analysis (see Chapter 10 for details). In civil law countries, there is usually no best practice guidance at all and the parties and judges rely on expert and auditor reports. In civil law countries it is usually better to build up the disruption claim using direct cost evidence and contemporary records. SCL Protocol distinguish Productivity-based methods: 1. Project-specific studies such as (a) Measured mile analysis, (b) Earned value analysis, (c) Programme analysis, (d) Work or trade sampling, (e) System dynamics modelling, 2. Project-comparison studies and 3. Industry studies and Cost-based methods: 1. Estimated v. incurred labour and 2. Estimated v. used cost.

7.9 Time for completion under FIDIC forms

In terms of time-related issues, FIDIC forms are based on the Anglo-Saxon tradition. Parties usually agree on the time for completion in the appendix to tender or particular conditions. According to Sub-Clause 8.1 (of FIDIC forms in 1999 first edition), the time for completion shall start running when the engineer gives the contractor not less than seven (7) days' notice of the commencement date. Unless otherwise stated in the particular conditions, the commencement date shall be deemed to be 42 days after the contractor receives the letter of acceptance. The contractor shall commence the execution of the works as soon as reasonably practicable after the commencement date and shall then proceed with the works with due expedition and without delay.

As per Sub-Clause 1.1.3.3, time for completion means the time for completing the works or a "section" (as the case may be) under Sub-Clause 8.2 and as stated in the appendix to tender. If the contractor fails to comply with the time for completion, the employer shall have the right to claim delay damages under Sub-Clause 8.7. Should the failure to comply with the time for completion be compromised for a reason on the employer's side, the contractor shall have the right to claim an extension of time for completion, see Chapter 10.

This approach originates in English law, that is, when the employer's delay influences time, it triggers a contractor option (by contract) to claim an extension of time for completion. Time is therefore "of the essence." If the contract does not contain these options to claim, then time is not of the essence, implying that the employer shall not have any option to claim delay damages.

The very core of claims for an extension of time for completion is to allow the contractor to be relieved of their liability for delay damages and also to make it possible for the employer to have the time for completion (including the final date and/or milestones) retained with the option to claim delay damages if the claim for an extension of time for completion is notified and then accepted. In the event that the employer (the engineer under FIDIC forms) fails to proceed in compliance with the contract (i.e., not responding to the contractor's claims and so on), time is not deemed as being of the essence and is perceived as being "at large." Delay damages must be perceived, in principle, as a limitation of delay liability, and never as any kind of contractual penalty. FIDIC forms (1999) do not allow for milestone provisions and/or milestone damages, if not agreed so in the particular conditions. The 2017 edition contains additional options for Milestones clauses in the Notes for preparation of special provisions. According to FIDIC, it is up to the contractor on how to plan and execute their works. Sanctions for delay extending beyond milestones shall be applied even when the time for completion is kept. Such practice contains limitations as to the contractor's possibility to execute the works in compliance with the contract. Evidence of complexity and uncertainty in enforcing such contractual penalties can be seen, for example, in German courts that have acknowledged contractual penalty provisions as valid if they do not exceed 0.2% to 0.3 % of the contract price per day (Jaeger and Hök, 2010).

7.10 Time program under FIDIC forms

According to the Sub-Clause 8.3 (FIDIC CONS/1999 Red Book and P&DB/1999 Yellow Book), the contractor shall submit a detailed time program to the engineer within 28 days of receiving the notice of commencement of works. The contractor shall also submit a revised program whenever the previous program is inconsistent with actual progress or with the contractor's obligations. Sub-Clause 8.3 defines what information the program should include. Apart from defining the methods the contractor intends to adopt in the execution of the works—including the anticipated timing of each stage of design, the contractor's documents, the procurement, the manufacture, the delivery to site, the construction, the erection and the testing, the description of the nominated subcontractors' assignments, sequence and the timing of inspections and tests—the program should also include a supporting report with a general description of the methods (processes) which the contractor intends to use, the major stages (in the execution of the works) and details showing the contractor's reasonable estimate of the number of each class of contractor personnel and each type of contractor equipment required on site at each major stage.

The time schedule should also give a description of methods of construction and allocation of resources, and include a form highlighting links between individual activities.

The SCL Protocol recommends that the program should clearly identify all relevant activities, including those that relate to design, manufacturing, procurement, and on-site construction. It should also record the information the contractor reasonably requires from the employer or contract administrator, what that information is, when it is required and all employer and contract administrator activities and constraints (such as approvals and employer-supplied services or materials). One of the main features of the FIDIC Forms 2017 edition are more detailed program requirements that focus also on mentioned priorities and also add the requirement for critical path and float description.

The purpose of the program is to monitor progress and, therefore, to facilitate the comparison of the submitted program against the reality on site to enable it to be updated accordingly. According to Sub-Clause 8.3 unless the engineer (within 21 days of receiving a program) gives notice to the contractor stating the extent to which they do not comply with the contract, the contractor shall proceed in accordance with the program, subject to their other obligations under the contract. The engineer also has the right to prompt the contractor to revise the program if they fail to comply with the contract or if actual progress is inconsistent with the contractor's stated intentions.

This obligation, however, is closely tied with other contractor's obligations—particularly those under Sub-Clauses 8.3, 4.21 (h), and 8.6. It is primarily (according to Sub-Clause 8.3) the obligation of the contractor to promptly give notice to the engineer of specific, probable future events or circumstances that may adversely affect the work, increase the contract price or delay the execution of the works. The engineer may require the contractor to submit an estimate of the anticipated effect of the future event or circumstance, and/or acceleration proposal under Sub-Clause 13.3.

As per Sub-Clause 4.21 (h), the contractor should submit to the engineer in their progress report the comparisons of actual and planned progress, with details of any events or circumstances which may jeopardize the completion in accordance with the contract and the measures being (or to be) adopted to overcome delays.

In this context, Sub-Clause 8.6 rules that if actual progress is too slow to complete within the time for completion, and/or progress has fallen (or will fall) behind the current program (other than as a result of a cause listed in Sub-Clause 8.4, that is, the events upon which the contractor may claim an extension of time for completion), then the engineer may instruct the contractor to submit a revised program and supporting report describing the revised methods that the contractor proposes to adopt in order to expedite progress and comply with the contract.

Sub-Clause 8.6 further states that unless the engineer notifies otherwise, the contractor shall adopt these revised methods, which may require increases in the working hours or in numbers of contractor personnel or goods, at the risk and cost of the contractor. Unless the time for completion is extended based on events where risk is allocated to the contractor, the engineer may proceed per Chapter 13 and instruct the contractor to expedite (accelerate) under Sub-Clause 13.1 f), or request a proposal under Sub-Clause 13.3 that states that:

> If the engineer requests a proposal, prior to instructing a variation, the contractor shall respond as soon as practicable, either by giving reasons why they cannot comply or by submitting a description of the proposed work to be performed and a programme for its execution, a proposal for any necessary modifications to the programme as per Sub-Clause 8.3 (and to the time for completion) and a proposal for evaluation of the variation.

The engineer shall, as soon as practicable (after receiving such proposal), respond with an approval, disapproval or comments, provided that a variation is to be evaluated in compliance with Clause 12 (Measurement and Evaluation) unless the engineer instructs otherwise. Any additional instruction to accelerate may imply a variation. However, if the contractor decides to accelerate in order to comply with their obligations in accordance with the contract (mainly to proceed in line with the current program), the contractor shall also bear all related additional cost.

A lack of realism in negotiations by James Bremen (UK)

Often employers will put extremely challenging programs out to bid. Contractors bid for these programs and the employers assume that this is proof that the programs are achievable. That is usually an incorrect assumption. Instead, bidders do not wish to be disqualified and as a result will bid for work in a compliant manner, betting on the prospect that they can rely on the employer's actions, and inadequacies in the scope and the specification to escape the program. Beginning without a common understanding of the program is a relatively common feature of emerging markets projects, and one that can be easily overcome by better preparation on the employer side of realistic programs, and having a strong employer-side planning team.

Employers often operate under very onerous internal decision-making protocols, which result in delayed decision making, payment times, and approvals for contractors. Negotiators are aware of these impediments, but often fail to address them in the contracts, instead adopting market-norm positions. When these issues are then encountered during the contract execution phase, contractors will use them as a strong basis for claims and an increase in the contract sum.

These few examples are ones that can (and should) be addressed by emerging market governments in improving their approach to procurement. Often their projects are very significant and represent large capital expenditures. Thus it makes sense to really focus on structuring the procurement and the contract in a manner to ensure project success.

James Bremen
Partner, Construction and Engineering
Herbert Smith Freehills
London
UK

7.11 Delay and suspension under FIDIC forms

Contracts for works in large construction projects usually deal with delays, suspensions and termination of contract and related consequences. Details of mentioned issues and how they are dealt with under FIDIC forms are discussed below.

7.11.1 Delay under FIDIC forms

FIDIC forms distinguish between delays caused by employer risks events (i.e., the delays that authorize the contractor to claim an extension of time for construction according to the individual Sub-Clauses) and delays caused by contractor risks events authorizing the employer to claim delay damages.

Delay damages are one of the types of liquidated damages. In the Anglo-Saxon tradition of law, liquidated damages consist of the sum identified as such by the contracting parties in the contract. The purpose of this sum is to ensure that the party suffering damage due to the other party's breach of contract receives pre-determined compensation. If this compensation issue is not dealt with in the contract, a court will determine if these damages (damages at large) are justified or their quantum. According to common law principles, liquidated damages shall not be enforceable if their purpose is to punish rather than compensate. In equity, judges strive for a fair resolution and avoid enforcing conditions that lead to unjust enrichment. However, compliance with two conditions will allow the use of liquidated damages: (1) The sum must at least (approximately) correspond to potential damage; and (2) the probability that damage will ensue must be sufficiently low. When dealing with construction projects, the courts will sometimes refuse enforcement of such compensation, referring to the *Doctrine of Concurrent Delay* if there is evidence of shared responsibility for such a delay.

7.11.2 Practical recommendations for EOT claims

When dealing with delay under the FIDIC forms (and with every claim in general) it is recommended to notify the event within 28 days as required by Sub-Clause 20.1 to avoid the claim being time-barred. It is further recommended to do the following:

- Link the event to a Sub-Clause that entitles the contractor to an extension of time.
- Immediate collection of contemporary records (Sub-Clauses 6.10, 4.21, 8.3) and weekly program review meetings with the engineers to explain the event notification (this may be before the notice is sent).
- Afterward, the initial claim submission (quantification) must be submitted to the engineer within 42 days of becoming aware and updated monthly.
- An adequate number of experienced staff must be employed to manage claim submissions. Therefore, it is useful to "walk" the engineer through the initial submission with a short presentation and arrange a meeting with the engineer's program manager. Mitigation solutions should be prepared in mutual cooperation.
- Communication helps to find solutions so it is efficient to schedule review meetings with the engineer during their 42-day reply period. If there are some "no blame" events causing the claim, it is good to agree on them (e.g., unforeseen ground conditions). If the engineer's response is positive, it may be useful to request a meeting with the employer to reach an overall agreement. To control the impact on cost, it is worthwhile to prepare a monthly updated schedule to show the running cost of prolongation.
- If the engineer's response is negative, it is recommended to meet immediately with the engineer and find out if the difficulty lies in the facts, principle, liability, cost, and so on. Afterward it is good to continue dialogue with the engineer with a focus on alternative no blame events.
- If the engineer is directed by the employer, it is necessary to meet with the employer immediately to find out what is the cause of this difference (i.e., facts, principle, liability, cost, or political reasons). In this phase it is still worth continuing dialogue with presentations to the employer including alternative proposals for 'no blame' events and mitigation solutions.

- If resistance continues, it is necessary to start putting pressure on the engineer and employer to update claims in monthly applications for payment plus finance charges. If there is no agreement at this stage, it is necessary to commence correspondence referring to the engineer/employer's failure to fulfill obligations under the contract (lack of decision, instruction, cooperation and obstructive practice causing further damages).
- A request by the contractor under Sub-Clause 3.5 asking for the engineer's determination may follow. This could help as a precursor to a referral to the dispute adjudication board (Sub-Clause 20.2).
- If there is consistent non-acceptance of all time claims for political reasons it may be necessary to issue a 14-day notice under Sub-Clauses 16.1 and 16.2(d) because the employer substantially is failing to perform their obligations under the contract as a precursor to a termination notice by the contractor (or a similar instrument based on the governing law).

7.11.3 Suspension of work under FIDIC forms

Employer suspension

FIDIC forms also establish rules for suspension of realization. In general, as defined in Sub-Clause 8.8, the engineer may, at any time, instruct the contractor to suspend progress of part or all of the works. If the suspension is for a reason other than on the contractor's side, then:

- the contractor may notify a claim under Sub-Clause 8.9;
- if the suspension continues for more than 84 days, the contractor may request permission to proceed;
- if the engineer does not give permission to re-start within 28 days, the contractor may terminate the contract.

Contractor suspension

The contractor may suspend (or slow down) work as per Sub-Clause 16.1 until the situation is remedied if the employer fails to properly and timely meet their payment obligations or fails to prove that they are able to provide sufficient funding for the work. As per Sub-Clause 14.8, the contractor is entitled to payment of the financing charges in this case. Under Sub-Clause 16.1 the contractor (after giving not less than 21 days' notice) may suspend or reduce the rate of work unless and until the employer's breach of contract is eliminated. The contractor shall resume normal working activities as soon as is then reasonably possible.

If the contractor suffers delay or incurs costs as a result of suspending work or reducing the rate of work, the contractor shall give notice to the engineer and shall be entitled to compensation (subject to an extension of time) for any such delay if completion is or will be delayed, and payment of any such cost plus reasonable profit, which shall be included in the contract price.

Suspension (especially in cases of fully mobilized construction works) will lead to damages and claims and parties should do all they can to avoid it. It is common that claims are followed by counterclaims and concurrent delay is encountered.

Contractor claims are typically for additional payment because of demobilization (or standby labor and equipment), costs connected with their duty to protect, store, and secure the works against any deterioration, loss or damage, remobilization expenses, prolongation (or acceleration) disruption, and so on. The employer may then claim damages pointing out contractor concurrent delay.

A suspension may be a part of a complex delay and disruption claim. An interesting example is case no. 469/2006 Ad Hoc (final award dated 26.2.2007) decided in international construction arbitration at the *Cairo Regional Centre for International Commercial Arbitration*. This case involved a dispute between a Swedish and an African company in consortium (the contractor) and an African gas company (the employer) resolved under Egyptian civil law (using the FIDIC forms) before a Jordanian Chairman with two members from the UK and Egypt.

A contractor claimed an additional payment and extension of time on the basis of late site possession and because some employer risks (such as debris) had materialized and disrupted the dredging works. The employer argued that the site was handed over on time.

Another contractor's EOT claim was on the basis of adverse climatic conditions encountered as a consequence of the previous delay caused by the employer (shift to a less favorable season). The contractor also claimed *force majeure* events (one of them being the death of a member of its crew that delayed the works). All claims were refused by the employer, which then counterclaimed extensive damages and liquidated damages and "called" the performance guarantee.

Furthermore, during realization, the engineer instructed the contractor to mobilize an alternative dredger to complete the suspended dredging works. The contractor considered the engineer's instruction a variation arising as a result of the employer's various breaches of contract.

The tribunal held that the contractor was entitled to an extension of time and dismissed the employer's claim for damages and liquidated damages. The tribunal further held that the contractor was entitled to the reasonable costs of mobilizing the alternative dredger. In order to prove such costs, the contractor submitted, as evidence, a document containing details of the costs. After reviewing the evidence, the tribunal calculated the sum of costs but expressly excluded the following items as irrelevant: petty cash, accommodation, taxi expenses, flights, hotels (being internal costs) as well as time on site, charges for survey staff, gasoil, agency fees, and flight costs for an expert (being external costs).

The tribunal finally allowed the contractor's EOT and additional payment claim (with some deductions as described above), rejected the employer's claims for damages and liquidated damages and ordered the return of the performance guarantee (Alam-Eldin, 2010).

7.12 Contract termination under FIDIC forms

FIDIC forms foresee termination of the contract:

- by the employer (based on contractually given reasons at Sub-Clause 15.2);
- by the contractor (based on contractually given reasons at Sub-Clause 16.2);

- for the employer's convenience (Sub-Clause 15.5); and
- by termination by one of the contracting parties after a *force majeure* event (Sub-Clause 19.6).

7.12.1 Employer termination

As per Sub-Clause 15.2, the employer shall be entitled to terminate the contract upon giving 14 days' notice if the contractor does any of the following:

- fails to provide performance security or to comply with the notice to correct (under Sub-Clause 15.1 if the contractor fails to carry out any obligation under the contract, the engineer may, by notice, require the contractor to make good the failure and to remedy it within a specified reasonable time);
- abandons the works or otherwise plainly demonstrates an intention not to continue performance of their obligations under the contract;
- without reasonable excuse fails to proceed with the works in accordance with Clause 8 (Commencement, Delays and Suspension) or to comply with a notice issued under Sub-Clause 7.5 (Rejection) or Sub-Clause 7.6 (Remedial Work), within 28 days of receiving it;
- subcontracts the whole of the works or assigns the whole contract without required agreement/consent;
- becomes bankrupt or insolvent;
- gives or offers to give (directly or indirectly) to any person any bribe in connection with the contract.

The employer may then notify their claim under Sub-Clause 2.5 and withhold payments until full indemnification and clarification of consequences are received. In the case (under FIDIC P&DB/1999 Yellow Book) *Obrascon Huarte Lain SA v. Her Majesty's Attorney General for Gibraltar* [2014] EWHC 1028 (TCC) the judge dealt with many aspects of employer termination under the Sub-Clause 15.2 (including the notice to correct under the Sub-Clause 15.1). The judge said for example that Sub-Clause 15.1 relates only to more than insignificant contractual failures by the contractor (such as a health and safety failure, bad work, or serious delay on aspects of the work), which he said must be an actual failure to comply with the contract rather than something that may have not yet become a failure. Furthermore, the judge said that the time specified for compliance in the Sub-Clause 15.1 notice must be reasonable in all the circumstances at the time of the notice. The judge gave the example that if 90% of the workforce had gone down with cholera at that time, the period given for compliance would need to take that into account, even if that problem was the contractor's risk. He said that whether the notice came of the blue or if the subject matter had been raised before and the contractor had chosen to ignore what it has been told might also be relevant. To understand the difficulties of an employer contract termination in case of lack of contractor due diligence see *Sabic UK Petrochemicals Ltd v. Punj Lloyd Ltd* [2013] EWHC 2916 (TCC).

7.12.2 Contractor termination

As per Sub-Clause 16.2, the contractor shall be entitled to terminate the contract on 14 days' notice if:

- the contractor does not receive evidence within 42 days of giving notice under Sub-Clause 16.1 (contractor's entitlement to suspend work) in respect of a failure to comply with Sub-Clause 2.4 (to give evidence about the employer's financial arrangements);
- the engineer fails, within 56 days after receiving a statement and supporting documents, to issue the relevant payment certificate (within 28 days in general as per Sub-Clause 14.6);
- the contractor does not receive the amount due under the interim payment certificate within 42 days of the expiry of the time stated in Sub-Clause 14.7 (payment) within which the payment is to be made [except for deductions in accordance with Sub-Clause 2.5 (employer's claims)];
- the employer substantially fails to perform their obligations under the contract;
- the employer fails to comply with Sub-Clause 1.6 (i.e., fails to enter into the contract within 28 days after receiving the letter of acceptance) or with Sub-Clause 1.7 (assignment);
- a prolonged suspension affects the whole of the works as described in Sub-Clause 8.11 (prolonged suspension);
- the employer becomes bankrupt or insolvent.

The contractor will then receive payment mainly for what has been performed, and, moreover, for lost profit or damage suffered as a result of termination.

7.12.3 Termination in convenience

As per Sub-Clause 15.5, the employer shall be entitled to terminate the contract at any time for their own convenience by giving notice of such termination to the contractor. Termination shall take effect 28 days after the later of (1) the dates on which the contractor receives this notice or (2) the employer returns the performance security. The employer shall not terminate the contract under this Sub-Clause in order to execute the works themselves or to arrange for the works to be executed by another contractor.

The contractor will then receive payment mainly for what has already been performed and, moreover, for all costs incurred in expectation of works to be completed. The FIDIC Contracts Guide's position on this provision is that it can be problematic and contrary to governing law.

7.12.4 *Force majeure* termination

If, as under Sub-Clause 19.6, the execution of substantially all the works in progress is prevented for a continuous period of 84 days by reason of *force majeure*, or for multiple periods which total more than 140 days, then either of the parties (the employer or the contractor) may give a notice of termination to the other one. In this case, termination shall take effect seven (7) days after notice is given.

References

Alam-Eldin, M.E.I. (2010). *Arbitral Awards Rendered under the Auspices of CRCICA*. Lap Lambert Academic Publishing, Saarbrücken.
Cushman, R.F. (2011). *Proving and Pricing Construction Claims*. Wolters Kluwer, NewYork.
ICC (2012). *International Court of Arbitration Bulletin*, 23(2) – 2012.
Jaeger, A.V. and Hök, G.S. (2010). *FIDIC: A Guide for Practitioners*. Springer Verlag: Berlin.
Jorgensen, J.C. (2010). *Delay Clauses in International Construction Contracts*. Kluwer Law International, Alphen aan den Rijn.
Ramsey, V. (2006). *Problems of Delay and Disruption Damages in International Construction Arbitration in Evaluation of Damages in International Arbitration*. ICC Publication No. 668, ICC.

Further reading

Bellhouse, J. and Copan, P. (2007). Common law 'time at large' arguments in a civil law context. *Construction Law Journal*, 8. LexisNexis.
Burr, A. and Lane, N. (2003). The SCL Delay and Disruption Protocol: hunting Snarks. *Construction Law Journal*, 3. Sweet and Maxwell.
Dennys, N., Raeside, M. and Clay, R. (2010). *Hudson's Building and Engineering Contracts* (12th Edition). Sweet & Maxwell Ltd, London.
FIDIC (2000). *The FIDIC Contracts Guide* (1st Edition). FIDIC, Lausanne.
FIDIC (2011). *FIDIC Procurement Procedures Guide* (1st Edition). FIDIC, Lausanne.
Furst, S. and Ramsey, V. (2001). *Keating on Building Contracts* (7th Edition). Sweet and Maxwell, London.
Kitt, G. and Fletcher, M. (2013). Management of claims under FIDIC Forms of Contract. Paper presented at the conference, Practical Solution of Problems Related to the Realisation of Construction Projects: FIDIC Contracts and Claim Management, Prague.
Klee, L. (2012). *Smluvní vztahy výstavbových projektů*. Wolters Kluwer, Prague.
Ramsey, V. (2013). The evaluation of damages in international construction arbitration. Paper presented at the International Construction Contracts and the Resolution of Disputes ICC/FIDIC Conference, Paris.
Seppala, C. (2012). Cost management in FIDIC conditions of contract. Paper presented at the 25th FIDIC International Contract Users' Conference, London.
The Society of Construction Law Delay and Disruption Protocol (2002). Online. Available at: http://www.scl.org.uk (accessed 3 May 2018).
Venoit, W.K. (2009). *International Construction Law: A Guide for Cross-Border Transactions and Legal Disputes*. ABA Publishing, Chicago.

8 Variations

8.1 Variation clauses

Large construction projects are full of change, this is why they need due project management, clear responsibility allocation and change management processes to be implemented. There are different types of change. It is common to distinguish changes that are necessary for completion and changes that just improve the works. A variation is usually perceived as something that is necessary for completion of the works. On the other hand there may be improvements such as value engineering and extra works that are accepted by both parties because they simply like to proceed with the works differently than it was originally contemplated. Well-drafted variation clauses that describe necessary processes of variation management and respective knowledge of these processes by construction project participants are key factors to a successful project.

Variations can have major impacts on costs and time. Construction project participants must therefore know their respective rights and duties regarding variation management. Sample contract forms for large construction projects regularly contain clauses that allow the employer to vary, unilaterally, the scope, quality, sequencing, methods or design of the works. In the same way, the contractor can propose such variations or improvements, if there is a need for such variation or if a variation can improve the works.

Various reasons are quoted for initiating changes. These include for example:

1. External grounds for variations (outside the influence of the parties) such as:
    - Changed conditions and circumstances (weather, floods, earthquakes, legislative terms, and so on).
    - Uninformed or unrealistic expectations or conditions that differ from those actually encountered—such as unforeseeable ground conditions (of geological/hydrological nature or utilities). The physical on-site conditions in general may differ in material terms from those "foreseen" in the contract.

International Construction Contract Law, Second Edition. Lukas Klee.
© 2018 John Wiley & Sons Ltd. Published 2018 by John Wiley & Sons Ltd.

Physical conditions encountered on site may also differ from those normally encountered on similar sites within a particular region.
- Archaeological findings.
- Interference by state authorities.

2. Interest in improvement of the work during realization such as:
   - Technical innovations (and related time and cost savings), acceleration and so on.
3. Employer's default such as:
   - Errors of a technical nature in contractual documents. Defective and inadequate documents are the primary source of variations; drawings and specifications are often found to be defective and inadequately describe the nature and scope of the work.
   - Inefficient cooperation of particular contractors and employer's representatives (bad on-site coordination).
   - Lacking instructions, site access and permissions, insufficient funds leading to suspension and so on.
4. Contractor's default such as:
   - Lack of due performance caused by the ignorance of on-site conditions, ignorance of local specifics, ignorance of contract, and so on.

Variations are sometimes perceived as negative because of corresponding cost overruns; however, changes in projects are to be solved by the project participants and the use of variation provisions in good contracts confirms the inevitable nature of variations in every construction project.

Variation procedures cannot run smoothly without properly formulated contractual provisions to regulate them. In general, these provisions define the procedures the contracting parties must follow to implement a variation in compliance with the contract.

The following issues are usually addressed:

- Options and scope of variations to be mandatorily executed by the contractor as instructed by the employer, including the formal procedure for giving instructions and potential contractor responses.
- Process to be followed in preparing the design and method statements for new or different works.
- Impact on cost and time.
- Requirements and deadlines for notifications that must be sent to the employer by the contractor for proper and timely realization of the variation.
- Timeframe within which the contractor must submit the variation proposal.
- Timeframe within which the employer must evaluate the contractor's proposal and give instructions.
- Clear identification of persons authorized to instruct and execute variations.
- Sample variation sheets and forms (variation orders).

Variation procedures are often accompanied by requirements for formal early warnings and notices of pending hazards with impact on time for completion and additional cost. Delay, disruption, suspension, and acceleration of works may be caused by the employer's ill-considered instruction. Likewise, the employer must also be timely notified by the contractor of the consequences of the employer's defective activity or inactivity or negligence to be able to remedy such a situation in the most efficient and timely way. Therefore, employers and contractors need to effectively cooperate and communicate to mitigate the likelihood of any adverse variations and their impacts.

8.2 Variations under FIDIC forms

According to the FIDIC CONS/1999 Red Book and P&DB/1999 Yellow Book (see Chapter 12), the authorization to give variation instructions belongs to the engineer while it applies that "Variations may be initiated by the engineer at any time prior to issuing the taking-over certificate for the works, either by an instruction or by request for the contractor to submit a proposal."

The engineer's competences regarding variations tend to be limited in the engineer's contract with the employer. In the event of variations that affect the price or time for completion, for example, a limitation is that the engineer must first obtain the employer's prior consent before proceeding.

In general, the contractor does not need to verify if prior consent of the employer has been issued to the engineer. Whenever the engineer gives instruction beyond the scope of its authorization, the engineer is deemed to have received such consent.

The employer must consider thoroughly if, and to what extent, they really want to intervene and limit the engineer's responsibilities. If the employer needs to control and substantially supervise the engineer by requiring prior consent for the engineer's numerous decisions, the employer must have the human resources available to make quick and competent decisions and to assume a broad scope of responsibility. A delay on the part of the employer (the engineer) may occur where the review and approval procedures used (e.g., to approve the detailed design, method statements) are inflexible and unreasonable. In cases of delayed instruction, the contractor may claim an extension of time for completion and additional payment in the form of cost, overhead, and profit (subject to Sub-Clause 1.9 of the FIDIC CONS/1999 Red Book). If the engineer is unable to duly perform their duties because of limitations on the employer's side, then such an engineer is a great hazard to a construction project.

Variations are primarily carried out as instructed by the engineer. Variations can for example fall into any of the following categories (in accordance with the FIDIC CONS/1999 Red Book):

- changes to the quantities of any item of work included in the contract (however, such changes do not necessarily constitute a variation);
- changes to the quality and other characteristics of any item of work;
- changes to the levels, positions and/or dimensions of any part of the works;
- omission of any work unless it is to be carried out by others;
- any additional work, plant, materials, or services necessary for the permanent works, including any associated tests on completion, boreholes, and other testing and exploratory work, or
- changes to the sequence or timing of the execution of the works.

Concerning the variation procedure, it is stipulated that the engineer may (before giving an instruction to execute a variation) ask: (1) the contractor to give a description of the proposed work to be performed and a program for its execution; (2) for the contractor's proposal for any necessary modifications to the program and expected time for completion; and (3) the contractor's proposal for evaluation of the variation.

Such a procedure is appropriate as it can minimize future potential disputes where the effects of a variation on cost and time are not pre-agreed. The engineer must determine *ex officio* (by virtue of their position) the cost impacts caused by a variation instruction—without any other steps necessarily being taken by the contractor (such as to notify the claim).

According to the Sub-Clause 13.2 (FIDIC Forms), the contractor may, at any time, submit to the engineer a written value engineering proposal which will (in the contractor's opinion) and, if adopted, accelerate completion, reduce the cost to the employer of executing, maintaining, or operating the works, improve the efficiency or value to the employer of the completed works or otherwise be of benefit to the employer. The contractor will gain 50% in costs savings as a bonus should the realization be successful (under FIDIC CONS/1999 Red Book).

Sub-Clause 13.2 value engineering under the FIDIC forms
by Manuel Conthe (Spain)

The great pole vaulter Sergei Bubka became famous in 1983 when, still under 20 years of age, he got the gold medal in the World Championship in Helsinki with a mark of 5.7 meters (18.7 feet). After this early victory, he went on to win the six following championships, remained the leading male pole vaulter in the world for more than two decades, and broke his own world record as many as 35 times. In July 1985, he broke through the 6-meter (19.7 feet) barrier. His best indoor mark ever was in 1993, at 6.15 (20.2 feet). The following year, already 30, he jumped 6.14 meters (20.1 feet) outdoors. These remained unassailable world records for more than two decades, until February 2014, when a French pole vaulter jumped 6.16 meters (19.7 feet).

The remarkable thing was that, when achieving each new world record, Bubka seemed to fly well above the bar and left people with the impression that he could have easily improved that mark. Had he tried, he might have improved on his 1993 to 1994 records and achieved heights, which might probably remain still unsurpassed. It was the same with his female compatriot pole vaulter Yelena Isinbayeva, who in 2005 was the first woman to jump 5 meters (16.4 feet) and four years later jumped 5.06 (16.6 feet), still the world record today.

Why did Bubka and Isinbayeva not exhaust their full potential while at their prime?

Such behavior can be easily explained by the economic incentives they faced: both pole vaulters were paid a cash bonus every time they broke the world record and, so, were interested in breaking gradually their marks, step by step, so as to leave some slack for new records and maximize their cumulative income. When age dented their vigor and the decline in their performance set in, they were no longer physically able to improve the records set at their peak.

Drawing on that experience professor Justin Lewis described as the *Bubka principle*, the deliberate process of gradual limited improvements that some incentive systems bring about, a principle, which he sees at work in many innovation-intensive industries—like telecommunications or automobiles—where technological progress is gradual and innovations follow a pattern of "planned obsolescence," so that firms are able to sustain consumers' interest in their products over the long haul (Lewis, 2013 and Harford, 2008).

Thus, the incentive system offered to Bubka and Isinbayeva was probably the best to enhance people's interest in sports events and make sure that they resulted in new world records, but not the optimal one to induce the two pole vaulters to try their very best every single time.

That incentives influence behavior, so that they achieve their goal and do not backfire, was also nicely illustrated in soccer in September 2017's penaltygate, when during a match in the French league between Paris Saint German (PSG) and Lyon, a public spat broke out on the field between PSG forwards Cavani and Neymar as to who was to kick a penalty against Lyon. The problem was that, as in previous seasons, Cavani had been offered a $1 million bonus if he achieved again the title of top goal-scorer in the French league. Hence, he had a big incentive to preserve his traditional right to take the penalties. But a few weeks before the match, during the summer of 2017, Neymar had just signed for PSG, in the most expensive deal ever, and felt consequently entitled to become the club's penalty-taker. Unconfirmed rumors have it that in a bid to settle the dispute and avoid a looming crisis, PSG president Nasser Al-Khelaifi approached Cavani with an $1 million offer if he allowed Neymar to kick the penalties.

In construction projects, the Employer's objective is not to get the Contractor to achieve world records or score goals, but to find potential improvements that result in cost reductions while maintaining, or even improving, the quality of the works, as envisaged in Sub-Clause 13.2 of the FIDIC model contract on "value engineering." Here the right precedent is the incentive system set up by President Lincoln during the American Civil War to prevent price gouging by unscrupulous army suppliers who were in the habit of selling to to the Army decrepit horses and mules in ill health, faulty rifles, and ammunition.

The remedy was found in the 1863 *False Claims Act*, inspired in the *qui tam* private suits of medieval England (so called because of the Latin motto *qui tam pro domino rege quam pro se ipso in hac parte sequitur*, i.e., "he who brings a case on behalf of our lord the King, as well as for himself"). The Law granted significant bounties to those private citizens who could demonstrate that the Army had been overcharged by one supplier, with the resulting cost savings for the Army being shared with the private claimant. The law was softened during the Second World War, but tightened up again in 1986, during Ronald Reagan's presidency, when a public scandal broke out about the outrageous prices charged by some defense contractors (most notably for the infamous $700 toilet cover).

Under the current version of the law, suits lodged by private individuals (so called *relators*) against public suppliers are communicated to the Department of Justice. If the U.S. government endorses the suit and it is successful, the relator gets between 15% to 25% of the government's gain. If the Department of Justice does not support the claim but the relator continues with the case and eventually prevails, he or she is entitled to somewhere between 25% to 30% of the government's win.

In recent years the *qui tam* approach has been extended beyond public procurement. So, for instance, the 2010 Dodd-Frank Law authorized the Securities and Exchange Commission (SEC) to pay bounties—normally between 10% and 30% of the fine—to anyone providing critical information leading to the imposition of sanctions in excess of $ 1 million.

In the case of construction contracts the point is not so much to prevent fraud in suppliers, but to reward the discovery of potential design "variations" which, while maintaining quality, reduce the works' cost. The difficulty is that if the Contractor comes up with a potential improvement but cost reductions benefit only the Employer, the former will lack any incentive to look for improvements and communicate them to the latter.

Hence the wisdom of Sub-Clause 13.2 of the FIDIC contract, which grants the Contractor the right to submit proposals for variations that may accelerate the works, reduce the cost of their completion, maintenance or operation, improve their efficiency or value, or otherwise benefit the Employer.

If the engineer approves the proposed variation, the Contractor is entitled to 50% of the net savings of the Employer, a percentage, which is more generous than the 30% envisaged for the Contractor in the UNOPS model contract and higher also than the typical incentives in the *qui tam* mechanisms described before.

In my view, there is logic in the 50% percentage in the FIDIC contract, as this is the most common standard of fairness, as borne out by the results of experiments with the so-called *ultimatum game*, in which a *proposer* offers a *respondent* how to split a certain sum, with the respondent being only able to accept or reject the offer and both parties getting nothing if the offer is rejected (Henridh and Camerer, 2004).

A purely rational analysis of the game would indicate that proposers should suggest very favorable terms for themselves, as the alternative for respondents is to get nothing if they reject the offer. Experience shows, however, that respondents systematically reject unbalanced offers out of a sense of grievance and lack of fairness. As a consequence, to avoid such risk of rejection, or maybe as a result of their own sense of fairness, proposers typically offer respondents somewhere between 40% and 50% of the amount to be split.

The same may apply to the variations of a project, which are conceived by Contractor but benefit the Employer. The cost reduction may be seen as the equivalent to the amount to be split in the ultimatum game, with Employer playing the role of proposer and Contractor of respondent. If the latter does not consider fair how the prize is to be split, he or she will refuse to cooperate and, in our case, will not communicate to the Employer the cost-saving design variation.

To conclude, Sub-Clause 13.2 of the FIDIC contract reflects well human psychology and common standards of fairness when it foresee that the benefits resulting from the Contractor's suggested variation are equally shared between Contractor and Employer.

Manuel Conthe
International Arbitrator
Spain

Bibliography

Harford, T. (2008). *The Logic of Life: Uncovering the New Economies of Everything* (New York: Little, Brown).

Henridh, J., and Camerer, C, et al. (2004). *Foundations of Human Sociality: Economic Experiments and Ethnographic Evidence from Fifteen Small-Scale Societies* (Oxford: Oxford University Press).

Lewis, J. (2013). *Beyond Consumer Capitalism: Media and the Limits to Imagination* (New York: Polity Press).

8.3 Claims related to variations

The employer usually has the right to order the contractually defined and allowed variations. The contractor, in contrast, has the right to compensation in terms of time and price.

In most cases, variations are managed via the agreed variation orders.

The position of the SCL Protocol (the Delay and Disruption Protocol published by the United Kingdom Society of Construction Law) on valuation of variations is that (where practicable), the total likely effect of variations should be pre-agreed between the employer/contract administrator and the contractor: (1) to arrive, if possible, at a fixed price of a variation; (2) to include not only the direct costs (labor, plant, and materials) but also (3) the time-related costs, an agreed extension of time and the necessary revisions to the program. A complication often appears where one of the parties is breaching the contract or where contractual interpretation is unclear. In such a case, a routine variation procedure may become a claim for an additional payment and/or extension of time for completion.

In France, for example, the contractor is entitled to an extension of time for completion (*prolongation du délai d'exécution*), and financial compensation (*indemnization*) if there is a modification in the quantity of works or new works are instructed to be performed both in private and public procurement projects (Wyckoff, 2010).

To distinguish the contractor's individual claims for additional payment or for an extension of time for completion as a result of a variation, the following situations can be defined:

- directed variation;
- constructive variation;
- voluntary variation.

8.3.1 Directed variation

A variation instruction given by the employer (or on their behalf in compliance with the contract) is a directed variation usually taking the form of a written instruction negotiated in a variation order. It may also take the form of an express instruction given orally or implied by conduct. Directed variations are usually issued in compliance with a particular provision in the contract.

These contractual provisions define allowed variations, the period of time within which the contractor should respond to an instruction, the variation design, and the approval procedures, the range of additional costs that can be compensated, the pricing method, the specifications of the impact on time, and/or other formal procedures. An agreement on price and the time impact of a particular variation will be the key aspects of a successful variation.

If there is enough time, the employer will often proceed by asking the contractor for a variation proposal. The contractor will evaluate the required variation's influence on the time for completion and price of work. The contractor will then respond within the period of time determined in the contract by providing the proposal, with an evaluation of the feasibility of the variation, including design, impact on the time for completion, and price of work.

This will typically be achieved in a formal manner through a variation order which is usually in a form of a sample sheet that serves as a record of a change according and within the contract.

8.3.2 Constructive variation

Constructive variations are defined as any employer conduct that will not result in any directed variation (a formal variation order) but, as a result of which, the employer will require the contractor to carry out different work to that defined in the original contract.

For example, testing and surveillance, implementing higher standards or better workmanship, unjustified refusal to take over the works, performance obstacles, and the like. Constructive variations need not influence the technical solution, design, or amount of work. They may, for example, include a variation to methods of realization which is then, subsequently, reflected in price or time program changes. A change in sequencing of operations as instructed by the employer is a classic example. This is discussed in further detail in Section 8.4.2, Constructive Acceleration.

Constructive variations tend to appear during realization of large construction projects. Such variations may be instructed orally but a contractor must be able to document and prove any potential claims for additional payments and extensions of time for completion. Therefore, the practice of confirming oral instructions in writing is appropriate in such a case. 1999 FIDIC forms state (Sub-Clause 3.3), for example, that when the engineer:

(a) gives an oral instruction;
(b) receives a written confirmation of the instruction, from (or on behalf of) the contractor, within two working days after giving the instruction; and
(c) does not reply by issuing a written rejection and/or instruction within two working days after receiving the confirmation, then the confirmation shall constitute the written instruction of the engineer.

Whenever the contractor's claims are in dispute, the judge, arbitrator, or adjudicator may investigate whether: (1) the variation was outside the scope of a contractual obligation; (2) the variation was instructed by the employer; (3) if the employer agreed with the compensation; (4) if the necessity of the variation was not caused by a contractor's mistake; or (5) if the price increase and time impact claimed are adequate and reasonable. In this regard, it is very important to evaluate the potential impact of the governing law in every particular case.

The contract has to be taken as the basis from which variations are valued. It applies in general that either the bill of quantities of a given project, historical data from similar projects, new calculations of rates and prices or industry benchmarks will be used for appropriate valuation. An agreement on how to value a particular variation is then usually reached. Otherwise, retrospective evaluation approaches must be applied to the variation (often after a claim for additional payment is notified), based on actual documented direct costs and agreed surcharges (if any). Different approaches that compare the "as-planned" and "as-built" works need to be considered also. It is further possible to have the price determined by expert opinion, an expert witness or to use a method based on the rules of the unjust enrichment/*quantum meruit* (Latin for "what one has earned") as per the governing law. If the right method is not found and/or agreed upon, the parties have to treat the variation as a dispute to be resolved in adjudication, litigation or arbitration.

8.3.3 Voluntary variation

A voluntary variation is a variation that is fully under the control and convenience of the contractor. A voluntary variation may be used to re-allocate capacities, make an impression on the employer, manage contractor delay, and so on. Furthermore, if carried out without proper records and without following the procedures under the contract on the contractor's side, a constructive variation may easily be deemed a voluntary variation.

The nightmare of valuing omissions by Aymen K. Masadeh and Remon Farag (UAE)

Introduction

Disputes arising out of disagreements on how to value omissions in construction contracts have been lately increasing. The main reason behind such disagreements is usually about the valuation of such omissions. Prima facie, the issue may sound simple and easy; the omitted scope is to be first properly ascertained and then the contract provisions regarding valuation of variations to be applied and there you go; you have valued the omission. In fact; valuation of omissions can be that easy in some cases, however, it can be very tricky in others.

Lump sum contracts are considered to be a fertile medium for such disputes to arise especially when no detailed breakdown of the lump sum contract price is provided at the inception of the contract. It can be very challenging for quantity surveyors to value an omission during the course of such contract. The purpose of this article is to observe and give thought to the following illustration, which is not at all a straightforward example but unfortunately is a problem experienced in reality.

In a lump sum based tender, a tenderer conducted a quantity take-off exercise from the tender drawings. For a part of the works, the contractor, in the schedule of rates, recorded (by mistake) the inclusion of 2,000 square meters of ceramic tiles and priced them at a rate of AED 150/- per square meter so that this line item's amount is AED 300,000/-. This contractor won the tender and signed off with the employer a lump sum contract. At the time of actually carrying out that part of the works, the contractor found out that the relevant drawing (which had a higher contractual hierarchy over the schedule of rates in this example as it is usually the case) actually shows 6,000 square meters of ceramic tiles and not 2,000, of which the difference is the contractor's mistake. The contractor understands it is obliged to carry out the work for 6,000 square meters of ceramic tiles at a total amount of AED 300,000/- only, considering the associated risks of a lump sum contract that it accepted to assume. If, before carrying out this specific part of the works, the engineer instructs the omission of all of these ceramic tiles, that is, 6,000 square meters of ceramic tiles (for reasons not of relevance to the subject herein) and applies the valuation of variations clause (that directs to use the schedule of rates' rate as it is usually the case) that is, at AED 150/-, the omission would be AED 900,000/- and the contractor would be entitled to an amount of (300,000 (original item price) – 900,000 (omission amount) = - AED 600,000/-), that is, the contractor, within the contract's final settlement, would be obliged to pay the employer an amount of AED 600,000/- namely for *not* carrying out 6,000 square meters of ceramic tiles.

Many would label the valuation above mentioned as illogical and some would even bring arguments of unjust enrichment. Many others would accept this valuation considering the freedom of contract principle. The questions posed in this article re this valuation are: How does this valuation go with the parties' intentions in entering into a lump sum contract? Considering that the lump sum contract price is deemed to include a sum of money to do the 4,000 square meters of ceramic resulting from the difference between the 2,000 the contractor priced and the 6,000 he is forced to do, should the omission include such amount whatever it is?

Lump sum contract

Before jumping into valuation principles, it is important to first understand or perhaps confirm what is meant by entering into a lump sum contract from a price perspective. One of the definitions of a lump sum contract is: "a contract to complete a whole work for a lump sum, for example to build a house for 60,000/- pounds. If the house is completed in every detail required by the contract, the contractor is entitled to the 60,000/- pounds … If the contractor does not complete the house, detailed clauses may provide what amount, if any, he is to receive" [Keating on Construction Contracts, Seventh Edition, 4-02].

From a quantities perspective, Hudson explains the meaning of lump sum in this regard by saying: "differences between 'as built' quantities and those stated in bills or other contractual estimates in unit-price (measured) contracts, frequently come about … either because of errors in taking off quantities from the drawings in the first place or because of the inherently unpredictable or provisional extent of the particular work in question. The difference between a lump sum contract and measured contract in this situation lies in the fact that, in the former case, both parties carry the risk of both of these types of difference and the price will not alter, whereas in the latter the contract sum will be adjusted, up or down, to take account of these differences" [Hudson's, Eleventh Edition, 7-015].

Originally, the term "lump sum" is more of a legal term than a technical one. It stems from the term "entire contract," which simply means a contract under which the performance must be completed in its entirety before the entitlement for consideration arises [Keating on Construction Contracts, 4-04]. It is contrasted with the term "severable contract," which means that there are mutual obligations on either party of the contract that must be fulfilled simultaneously [Hudson's Eleventh Edition, 4-004].

In UAE, construction contracts are legally considered as entire contracts. Article 885 of the UAE civil code states that "The employer shall be obliged to pay the consideration **upon delivery** of the property contracted for, unless there is an agreement or a custom to the contrary." Evidently this article is supplementary, that is, not mandatory and this explains why almost every construction contract in UAE is actually severable (however "arguably" except for the last payment) but it generally gives an idea on how the legal system in UAE recognizes construction contracts.

Article 887 of the UAE civil code states that "(1) If a muqawala contract is made on the basis of an agreed plan in consideration of a lump sum payment, the contractor may not demand any increase over the lump sum as may arise out of the execution of such plan." According to this article, being in a lump sum contract means that a contractor will carry out the whole of the works as described in the contract documents, only against the contract price, no matter how much the contractor actually spends in carrying out the whole of the works.

This also means that, under a lump sum contract, the contractor is not liable for any error in the quantities that may be recorded in the schedule of rates considering that such is already considered as part of the contractor's risks.

For the purposes of the illustration herein, what is required for valuing the omission is, in fact, opening up what has been agreed to be closed and locked. In order to properly value an omission, the value of the item subject to omission contributes to the contract price should be ascertained. In case of lump sum, if the initial intention of the parties was to agree on a single figure consideration with no regard to how it has been arrived at, such mission could be, sometimes challenging. However, sophisticated contracts always provide a breakdown of how the lump sum has been arrived at in the schedule of rates (without giving such breakdown an overwhelming contractual priority), nevertheless, even if such breakdown is provided, the mechanism set out in the conditions of contract—if not properly drafted to consider a lump sum contract—may drive the parties into problematic results.

The contract price

In order to answer the question in the illustration above, we need to consider the contract price at two stages; stage one is the unvaried works, and stage two is when the works became varied.

Stage one: When the works are unvaried, the contract price (for a lump sum contract) does not change for any reason. In the illustration above, the AED 300,000/- is inclusive of all what is required for the contractor to fulfill its obligations under the entire contract documents, in respect to the subject item. In lump sum contracts, quantities recorded in the schedule of rates have no relevance at all. Therefore, any error therein (as described in the illustration) should not be addressed in certifying the works.

Stage two: When a variation is instructed, which is the case in the illustration herein, the valuation clause in the contract will dictate on the engineer how to value them. These valuation clauses (regardless how those are drafted) should not allow the engineer/employer to seek remedies agreed to be waived in disguise of valuing variations.

In a lump sum contract, the valuation of variations clause should be tested (at the drafting stage) to make sure its application would not lead to altering the parties' intentions in respect to quantities. If, however, the contract did not specify that errors in quantities shall not be addressed as variations, the application of the valuation of variations clause (in such case) can lead to the same without any threat of contradiction.

The valuation clause

As we are speaking of a lump sum contract, it would be useful to look at FIDIC's approach in valuation of variation clauses in lump sum contracts. The Red Book (the fourth edition and the 1999 edition) is basically a re-measured contract. However, it is almost common practice that it is being converted to be a lump sum contract. FIDIC issued a supplement [Supplement to the Fourth Edition 1987 of Conditions of Contract For Civil Works Engineering Construction Reprinted 1992 with Further Amendments] to its fourth edition in 1996, in which it has addressed this conversion and advised—specifically—what needs to be done to do this conversion in a correct manner.

Sub-clause 52.1 of the of the fourth edition's Red Book [Valuation of Variations] is styled in the manner called by Hudson as the "shopping list valuation clause" [Hudson's Eleventh Edition, 7-105]. The shopping list valuation clause is one in which a list of options is set out for the engineer to pick the appropriate one by which a variation can best be valued.

In converting the fourth edition's Red Book to a lump sum contract, the said FIDIC supplement advised to amend sub-clause 52.1 to read as follows "All variations referred to in Clause 51 … shall be valued at *suitable rates or prices,* which, after due consultation by the Engineer with the Employer and the Contractor, shall be agreed upon between the Engineer and the Contractor. In the event of disagreement the Engineer shall fix such rates or prices as are, in his opinion, appropriate … " It is clear that FIDIC advised abandoning the shopping list styled clause if the contract is lump sum.

Similarly, the shopping list principle has been maintained in the 1999 FIDIC Red Book in its Sub-Clause 12.3 [Evaluation]. If the 1999 Red Book is required to be converted to a lump sum, the FIDIC's guidance [Guidance for the Preparation of Particular Conditions, FIDIC Conditions of Contract for Construction for Building and Engineering Works designed by the Employer, Page 12] advised to delete the entire Clause 12 including Sub-Clause 12.3 which had the shopping list styled valuation of variation clause. It also advised to amend Sub-Clause 13.3 [Variation Procedure] to state that "upon instructing or approving a Variation, the Engineer shall proceed in accordance with Sub-Clause 3.5 to agree or determine adjustments to the Contract Price and to the schedule of payments under Sub-Clause 14.4 … ".

Similar to the advice given in the 1996 supplement, the shopping list principle is advised to be abandoned if a lump sum contract is considered.

In practice, it is noted that contract drafters, in converting the Red Book (either the fourth edition or the 1999 edition) from re-measured to lump sum, do not abide to the supplement's or the guidance's advice and leave the valuation of variation clauses as it is and just call their contracts as "lump sum".

But why has FIDIC so advised, and where is the problem in applying the shopping list styled valuation of variations clauses in lump sum contracts? Hudson makes a comment in this regard that "valuation clauses of these kinds (based on the shopping list principle) … may or may not distinguish between omitted and additional work, they pay little or no regard to the economics and pricing realities of construction contracts …. For example, large increases in quantities notified in good time may often be extremely profitable to the contractor, thus logically justifying a reduction of the unit price involved … while substantial omissions, on the contrary may justify an increase in the unit prices" [Hudson's Eleventh Edition, 7-103].

The commonly used construction contracts in UAE (usually FIDIC-based) do not include any provision to alter the unit rate (used to value a variation) depending on the cases described by Hudson herein.

A closer look on this type of valuation clauses, one would easily see they are designed mostly for additions rather than for omissions. For example, Sub-Clause 12.3 of the 1999 FIDIC Red Book; the question this clause raise whether the varied work is of a "similar character" to that in the contract (in order to decide on the "rate applicability" to value a variation) cannot possibly apply to omissions. In omission, the engineer would be instructing the omission of the work previously agreed to be carried out itself and the question of whether such is "similar" to that of the contract is evidently illogical. Although both additions and omissions have the same origin; "variation," both are in fact fundamentally different; as additions are foreign to the original scope of work, and do not form part of the estimates and calculations made by the contractor prior award, they are— therefore—considerably uncomplicated in their valuation. On the other hand, omissions are work that used to form part of the original scope of work, and perhaps also connected/related to other work that may not be subject to omission [Rachel Chaplin, The value of work not carried out, Construction Law, 2014].

The above being said, and considering the illustration above, there are cases where the engineer is actually forced to implement certain procedures that albeit may seem wrong if scaled on doctrinal textbooks as well as common sense, they already acquire the power of contract and are binding on the parties. In the illustration above, the engineer picked the option that says "use the contract rate" to value the variation, and considering that the items subject to omission are already part of the contract and not just of a "similar character," the engineer had no reason to disregard the contract rate and use another valuation procedure. It is not the subject here to discuss the obligations of the engineer to act reasonably and the engineer, in fact, should act reasonably, but it is the subject here to discuss how problematic a "badly drafted" contract can get.

But why the engineer's valuation above mentioned is criticized? What is so odd about valuing this variation at negative AED 600,000/-? The way the engineer has arrived at this valuation is as follows:

Varied works (omissions): 6,000 square meters of ceramic tiles.
Unit rate for valuation (contract rate is applicable): AED 150/-
Omission amount: AED 900,000/-
Variation amount: -900,000/- (omission amount) + 300,000/- (original item price) = -AED 600,000/-

In fact, every factor of this valuation is correct. The varied quantity is correctly gathered from the drawings (that has higher contractual priority in this illustration, which is usually the case), the rate used is correct and in line with the valuation clause as the varied works is of a "similar character" to the item linked to the selected rate. The omission of AED 600,000/- is correct in sense of following what the book says.

The shopping list principle's deadlock

Looking again on the above mentioned valuation, one would notice that although every step in the same has correctly followed the relevant condition of contract, this valuation has fallen in the prohibition of correcting the errors that the parties have agreed (as discussed above) not to address as variations unless if the parties have agreed otherwise (in such case, the parties cannot call their contract as lump sum).

It is not the aim of this article to establish that contractors do not owe any duty of care toward employers in respect to technical precision of any document they produce, however, the parties should not cherry pick and seek remedy for something already agreed to be disregarded.

If we arguably agree that the valuation mentioned in the illustration above mentioned is incorrect, and considering the bar on correcting any errors in the quantities, so the 4,000 square meters difference between the schedule of rates and the drawings cannot be addressed as a variation, therefore, we are left only with the unit price to change.

Some quantity surveyors may be tempted to get out of this dilemma by bringing the argument of rate inapplicability. This approach can be summarized as follows: if correcting the mistaken quantity is prohibited, and the omission must be applied on the quantity so recorded on the drawings (due to its higher hierarchy), then why can't we say that rate of that item so mentioned in the bills is not applicable for the purposes of valuation? If the argument of enforcing the intentions of the parties contracting in a lump sum contract is introduced, we can say that the parties actually did not mean that the rate of this item should be AED 150 considering that the quantities should not to be taken as correct and that the more likely practice is that the contract price prevails rather than a price revised to account of the error [Chandana Jayalath, Understanding the Generality of Variation Clauses and the Variety of Broad Interpretation that Exists under FIDIC based Contract Modalities in Gulf, Construction Management Guide, November 2012]. The principle of prevailing the contract price is undoubtedly correct, however, the practice introduced has been proven wrong as will be seen later herein.

If variations instructed by the engineer are to be valued at contract rates where applicable and reasonable, then failing that (supposedly and according to the shopping list clause in FIDIC both editions as explained above), rates agreed upon between the employer's engineer and the contractor are to be used for valuation. In the event of disagreement, the engineer fixes new rates. The engineer may determine that—considering the irregular result of using the rate in the contract—there is no applicable rate to value the omission herein. The engineer instead may use the available contract rate to derive the applicable rate for this valuation as follows.

If the quantity—for the purposes of the contract and this valuation—is agreed to be 6,000 square meters of ceramic tiles and the price agreed for carrying out those is no more or less than AED 300,000/- then the parties are deemed to have agreed—at least for the purpose of this valuation—that the unit price is AED 20/-.

Based on this approach, the valuation would be as follows:

Omission: 6,000 square meters x AED 20 (determined unit price) = - AED 120,000/-
Valuation: -120,000/- (amount of omission) + 300,000/- (original item price) = AED 180,000/-

Although this tempting solution may satisfy a contractor struggling with his own mistakes and a confused employer lost between securing his own rights and not being arbitrary on the contractor, it would be interesting to note the decision in the case of Henry Boot Construction v. Alston Combined Cycles [Henry Boot Construction v. Alstom Combined Cycles [1999]]: "Held: the basis for valuation under [Clause 52 of the ICE form of contract] could not be displaced on the ground that the rates or prices in a bill of quantities have been inserted by mistake. If, however, work carried out pursuant to a variation to a contract differed significantly from the work covered by the bill of quantities, it would be open to the engineer to carry out a valuation of his own. The words "so far as may be reasonable" had been inserted in [Clause 52 of the ICE form of contract] to cater for that eventuality. The exceptions set out in cl.52(2) and cl.56(2) of the conditions supported the conclusion that the rates or prices contained in a bill of quantities were not subject to rectification. To hold otherwise would lead to uncertainty and disturb the basis of competitive tendering. In the instant case, the arbitrator should have disregarded the contractor's mistake and carried out a valuation on the basis of the price which the contractor had quoted."

From the above decision, it can be concluded that the engineer should not misuse the authority given to him under the contract to determine that a rate is inapplicable for the purpose of valuing a variation for any other reason than those namely provided in the contract, that is, the item of work is not of similar character, or is not executed under similar conditions, as any item in the contract. Although questions may arise to what exactly may or may not amount to "similar character / similar conditions," this decision urges engineers to be very conservative in using that discretion.

The above being said, introducing the argument of rate inapplicability to reach to a "peaceful" valuation for the subject omission is categorically incorrect.

Taking 20 pounds out of 10

The real problem with the valuation illustrated herein is omitting from the contract more than what already is in the contract. The amount of the item subject to omission as recorded in the bills was AED 300,000/-. The meaning of this amount is; the price of carrying out the item so described in the bill description in full accordance with the provisions of all the contract documents with no regard to the correctness of the associated quantity in the bills is AED 300,000/-. The valuation shown in the illustration means that the contractor would be obliged to pay the employer an amount of AED 600,000/- namely for *not* carrying out 6,000 square meters of ceramic tiles and not for carrying out any work at all. This is categorically an illogical outcome. Although most contracts would direct using the rates of the contract to value any variation whether addition or omission (although FIDIC advised not to follow this procedure in case of lump sum), the parties' agreement on such rates was actually a promise to pay if the corresponding works are carried out and not if they are not carried out [Lord Justice Christopher Clarke, in the Appeal Decision of the case of Mt Højgaard A/S v. E.ON Climate & Renewables UK Robin Rigg East Limited[2013] EWHC 967 (TCC)].

The case of MT Hojgaard v. E. On

The case of MT Hojgaard v. E. On [Mt Højgaard A/S v. E.ON Climate & Renewables UK Robin Rigg East Limited[2013] EWHC 967 (TCC)] is a recent and very relevant case to the subject of this article. The dispute subject to this case was about valuing an omission for which no rates were available in the contract but the engineer's valuation of such omission adjusted the contract price by reference to the time it would have taken the contractor to carry out the omitted works should that omission had not been instructed. The logic of this engineer's valuation was rejected by the court because it ignored the fact that the sums that the contractor would be entitled to be paid for executing parts of the works would be the same, regardless how long it took to execute them and whether the contractor had overpriced or underpriced them. The court described such approach to be at best hypothetical and at worst fictitious. The employer was attempting to achieve additional contractual remedies for breach of contract under the guise of adjustment of the contract price.

Applying the decision above mentioned to the illustration herein, we would arrive at the same result. The parties agreed to enter into a lump sum contract under which no correction to errors in quantities is permissible, however, the engineer actually addressed such errors in disguise of valuing an omission regardless the fact that the contractor would have not been paid more money if the omission instructed in the illustration was not actually instructed.

Notwithstanding the court's decision in the above mentioned case, we still have to stress that the engineer's valuation in the illustration above mentioned is procedurally correct. This is where the purpose of this article reveals. The problem is bad contract drafting. We cannot include the shopping list valuation clause in a lump sum contract at all; otherwise, we will end up valuing wrong yet in accordance with the contract.

The correct valuation

Based on the above, if we consider the engineer's valuation in the illustration herein as incorrect, and we set aside the shopping list valuation clause, what would be the correct valuation in a lump sum contract?

In order to value an omission in a lump sum contract, the exact contribution of the omitted work to the contract price should be the value of the omission. Therefore, the valuation shall be as follows:

The original quantity of work against which the lump sum is payable = 6,000 square meters

- The omission required to be valued = 6,000 square meters
- The contribution of the omitted work to the contract price of the subject item = 100%
- The value of the omission = the amount of this item, that is, -AED 300,000/- x 1 = - AED 300,000/-
- The valuation = - AED 300,000/(amount of omission) + 300,000/- (original item price) = 0 (i.e. the contractor would not be receiving any amount against this item).

This valuation is logic. If the employer does not wish this item to be carried out, then the corresponding amount associated with such item (only) is to be omitted. This very basic and simple idea is unfortunately a subject of debate in numerous cases around in the world in arbitration and litigation. Thanks to bad practice of contract drafting.

Conclusion

In using the standard forms of contract, the relevant supplements and guidance are to be strictly followed by contract drafters in case they intend to deviate from the general conditions. Parties can agree to anything they wish, however, the basic principles of contract should be given regard in drafting the contract because, when a dispute arises, the parties, their attorneys, the judge/tribunal would only refer to what the contract say. Freedom of contract should not be abused to agree on incorrect/problematic terms. It is important to stick to the lump sum principles explained in Section 2 of this article if the intention is to enter into a lump sum contract and it is equally important not to call a non-lump sum contract a "lump sum contract."

Prof. Aymen K. Masadeh
Dean – Faculty of Law, Yarmouk University
Board Member of the ICLA

Remon Farag
Assistant Manager – Contracts, 'Damac Properties'
MSc. CLDR
Dubai, UAE

8.4 Acceleration

It is often necessary, for various reasons, to speed up the construction process by increasing efficiency of related realization processes. Delay may result in significant damages for all participants of a particular construction project. Faster construction leads to increased use of material, labor, and equipment or optimization of methods and processes. In other words, "acceleration." This specific variation deserves special attention.

The contractor and the employer (including the contract administrator) are generally obliged to mitigate delay and loss under the contract and the governing law. The position of the SCL Protocol is that the contractor has a general duty to mitigate the effect of employer risk events on its works. Unless expressly included in contract wording or by agreement to the contrary, the duty to mitigate does not extend to requiring the contractor to add extra resources or to work outside its planned working hours. The contractor's duty to mitigate its loss has two aspects: first, the contractor must take reasonable steps to minimize their loss; and, second, the contractor must not take unreasonable steps that increase their loss.

Acceleration is encountered mainly in the following form:

- Changes to sequence and timing of works in progress.
- Increases in labor (e.g., more workgroups, overtime additional shifts, or a combination of both).
- Use of additional equipment and machinery.
- Acceleration of deliveries of materials, products, plants, and the like.

Acceleration can take one of three forms:

- directed;
- constructive;
- voluntary.

8.4.1 Directed acceleration

Directed acceleration takes place where the contractor is instructed directly, indirectly or even requested by the employer to speed up works according to the contract provisions for variation. The price of acceleration should be agreed upon before an instruction of directed acceleration is given. In case of a subsequent claim for additional payment, the contractor must show their endeavor to accelerate, the acceleration must really take place, and additional costs arise as a result of such acceleration.

8.4.2 Constructive acceleration

Constructive acceleration is encountered where there is a delay caused by the employer (after an employer risk event) and where the contractor has notified the employer of a claim for an extension of time for completion. The employer may then refuse this claim, insisting via an instruction or request, that in fact no delay has occurred and the works should be finished on time. The contractor may express disapproval and will show its endeavor to accelerate. The acceleration will take place and additional costs will arise as a result of such acceleration. Constructive acceleration is therefore a good procedural defense strategy against delay damages and contractual penalties.

The SCL Protocol defines constructive acceleration as:

> an acceleration following failure by the employer to recognize that the contractor encountered employer delay for which it is entitled to an extension of time for completion and which failure required the contractor to accelerate its progress in order to complete the works by the prevailing contract completion date.

This situation may be brought about by the employer's denial of a valid request for an extension of time for completion or by the employer's late granting of an extension of time for completion.

The SCL Protocol further states that where a contract provides for acceleration, payment for the acceleration should be based on the terms of the contract. Where the contract does not provide for acceleration but the contractor and the employer agree that acceleration measures should be undertaken, the basis of payment should be agreed upon before acceleration commences. The SCL Protocol does not recommend a claim for constructive acceleration to be made. Instead, prior to any acceleration measures, steps should be taken by either party to have the dispute or difference in entitlement to an extension of time resolved in accordance with the dispute resolution procedures stipulated in the contract.

The particular governing law will strongly influence the success of a constructive acceleration claim. It is therefore very interesting to compare the opinions of lawyers from different countries at http://globalarbitrationreview.com. They responded to the following questions:

- How does the law view "constructive acceleration" in situations where the contractor incurs the costs of accelerating its works because an extension of time has not been granted that should have been?
- What must the contractor show for such a claim to succeed?
- Would your answer differ if the employer had acted unreasonably or in bad faith?

The following answers were given in particular jurisdictions.

- *Brazil*: In general, constructive acceleration increases contractor costs that should be borne by the employer if the contractor was somehow forced to comply with the original time frame, when a time extension should have been granted. In order to have a successful claim, the contractor must show that the works will be delayed unless acceleration occurs and that such delay would not be deemed a fault of the contractor. As for the employer's motivation, it does not matter if the act or omission was made on an unreasonable basis; however, if bad faith is proven, other costs derived from parallel damages, such as loss of profits, may also be claimed (Marcondes, Salla, Nakagawa, and Diniz at http://globalarbitrationreview.com).

- *England and Wales*: There is no objection (in principle) to a claim for constructive acceleration. Such claims are more easily made where there is no third-party certifier to administer extension of time claims. In such circumstances, the failure to allow a valid extension of time claim will usually be a breach of contract by the employer entitling the contractor to claim damages, which may include the reasonable costs of acceleration. Claims involving a third-party certifier are, however, rarely successful. The fact that the contractor was entitled to extensions of time that was not granted to them does not on its own mean that the contractor can make a claim for constructive acceleration. It would be necessary to show that the employer or the certifier had acted in bad faith in that, knowing that the contractor was in fact entitled to an extension of time, they refused to grant one, with the intention of putting the contractor under pressure to accelerate (Choat and Long at http://globalarbitrationreview.com).
- *France*: There is no established set of rules dealing with the concept of "constructive acceleration." In order to succeed in its claim for additional costs resulting from acceleration measures, the contractor will need to argue that they had been forced to take those measures so as to avoid liquidated damages claims being made against them in the face of what potentially might have become an unachievable contract time for completion. Their claim is more likely to succeed if an instruction to accelerate can be implied from the employer's conduct (e.g., the threat of liquidated damages because the contractor was behind schedule) (Gillion and Rosher at http://globalarbitrationreview.com).
- *Germany*: Generally, the contractor has a stark choice to make between (1) whether to hope that they can prove the extension of time or (2) whether they should accept the (temporary) default and take steps to mitigate the damages. The contractor must show the general prerequisites of an extension of time claim (i.e., an event not caused by the contractor that caused a delay to the works schedule of the contractor). If the contractor has "accepted" the fault temporarily, the contractor must also show that the steps it took to mitigate the delay were necessary and reasonable and how those costs incurred in connection are to be specified and quantified. If the employer acted unreasonably, a court or arbitral tribunal could ease the burden of proof on the contractor or even shift the burden of proof (in the event of bad faith) to the employer. Generally, though, a construction acceleration claim presents significant legal difficulties, because of which a disruption claim for the same facts may be more probable (Kremer at http://globalarbitrationreview.com).
- *Ireland*: The Irish courts have not yet had cause to determine whether a doctrine of "constructive acceleration" exists in Ireland, nor do standard form contracts in Ireland expressly recognize the concept. However, where an Irish court is called upon to consider the issue, it is more than likely to follow the position in England and Wales, in which no definitive authority exists for constructive acceleration. However, under Irish law, should a contractor be forced to accelerate their works due to the fault of the employer, a contractor may be able to recover the costs of acceleration by:

(i) a claim for loss and expense due to disruption (as distinct from delay costs), where the construction contract allows for recoverability of disruption costs;
(ii) a claim for damages for breach of contract by the employer in failing to grant an extension of time to which the contractor was otherwise entitled to, including the contractor's costs of mitigation (the contractor must make reasonable attempts to mitigate their loss; where they do so, the costs of such mitigation are recoverable).

A contractor may also be entitled to relief (as distinct from damages), under the prevention principle, in cases where some act of prevention by the employer puts time at large and the contractor's ability to complete by a specified date impossible (Killoran, O'Higgins, and Cooney at http://globalarbitrationreview.com).

- *Korea*: A claim based on "constructive acceleration" may be possible under general Korean law principles. However, there are no relevant court precedents to date. If the Korean courts were to accept a claim based on "constructive acceleration," elements of proof would be similar to general principles of damages (Oh and Park at http://globalarbitrationreview.com).
- *South Africa*: Where a contractor experiences a delay, they generally have two options: (1) either to claim an extension of time or (2) to accelerate the works. In certain instances, the construction agreement may make provision for a process to agree to an acceleration instead of an extension of time and to calculate the costs that the contractor may claim in those circumstances. An acceleration and an extension of time claim are generally mutually exclusive. The contractor should therefore choose which remedy they prefer to exercise. Where a claim for an extension of time is chosen, that ought to be granted but is not, the contractor is required in those circumstances either to accept the determination and to bear the consequences or to place the determination in dispute and to seek a revision of the determination through the dispute resolution mechanisms of the contract. If the contractor chooses not to apply for an extension or to dispute a claim for an extension that has been refused but instead to accelerate the works, the contractor does so on their own account (Hoeben at http://globalarbitrationreview.com).

Constructive acceleration was considered in the ICC case no. 10847 (2003) (ICC, 2012) under the governing law of an African state. The contractor, a joint venture of two European construction firms was claiming costs of constructive acceleration against an African company (the employer) in a project that comprised civil engineering works for the construction of a hydroelectric plant. In general, the tribunal recognized the doctrine of constructive acceleration. However, for the tribunal to entertain a claim for constructive acceleration (notwithstanding the fact that the contractor was due a greater extension of time than awarded by the engineer), the tribunal had to be convinced that the contractor did, *de facto*, accelerate because they were denied a contractual right to an extension of time and that the contractor did incur real additional costs by reason of the acceleration. The fact that additional resources were brought to the site does not, in itself, prove acceleration. Accordingly, the tribunal dismissed this head of claim.

Drafting acceleration agreements by Alan Whaley (UK)

Project delays are a common and often unavoidable risk in construction projects. Overrunning the planned completion date can increase outturn costs and reduce profits for both contractor and employer. This means the prospect of "acceleration," or speeding up the remaining work to reduce delays, may be an attractive option to the party with most to lose.

When an employer is responsible for some or all of the delay, an agreement must be made with the contractor to compensate the costs of acceleration if earlier completion is to be achieved. However, reaching agreement to accelerate is fraught with difficulties, because acceleration agreements introduce additional risk and uncertainty into the contract, and acceleration costs are notoriously difficult to estimate or ascertain.

For parties looking to negotiate acceleration agreements to recover employer delays, three principle challenges must be addressed:

1. Dealing pre-existing delays
2. Payment for acceleration
3. Dealing with subsequent delays

Dealing with pre-existing delays

The need to accelerate is normally triggered by forecast delays to completion. Where the delay is accepted as wholly the employer's responsibility, the entirety of the acceleration cost would normally be recoverable from the employer. However, things become more complicated where the parties share responsibility for the delay, as is often the case.

In order to form the basis for apportionment of acceleration costs, the certifier must determine any extension of time and additional payment for delay otherwise entitled under the contract. The objective is to break down the delay at the effective date of the acceleration agreement, and reach a conclusion on overall responsibility for the delay, expressed in a number of days. Only with this information available can the parties negotiate the amount of payment for acceleration on an objective basis.

The risks associated with failing to properly apportion responsibility for delay before proceeding with acceleration were demonstrated in *Mirant Asia-Pacific Construction Ltd v. Ove Arup and Partners International Ltd* ([2007] EWHC 918 (TCC)). In this case, the claimant contractor was unable to establish a right to payment for acceleration costs caused by an engineer's defaults, due to the lack of any assessment of delay at the time of entering into the agreement. The failure to link the acceleration to the delay claimed led to a substantial dispute, which could have otherwise been avoided.

Payment for acceleration

There are several potential ways by which a contractor can be compensated for acceleration. There may be a fixed lump sum payment agreed for the acceleration alongside a revised completion date. This payment may be conditional on completing all or part of the work by the prescribed dates. Alternatively, the parties might agree the right to compensation for acceleration in principle, to enable acceleration to commence, but the terms of valuing the acceleration effort may be left undetermined. These approaches are each associated with particular risks that warrant some further examination.

Lump sum payments

An acceleration agreement that fixes a new completion period (which is less than what would otherwise be available under the contract), and provides the contractor a lump sum payment (e.g., *Mirant Asia-Pacific Construction (Hong Kong) Ltd v. Ove Arup and Partners International Ltd & Anor* (n 14)), is arguably the most *balanced* approach in terms of risk between the parties. The employer retains the right to deduct late completion damages should the contractor fail to achieve the revised completion date, but the contractor receives the benefit of an unconditional payment for the acceleration effort.

However, the terms of this kind of agreement must be carefully negotiated. Except in the simplest of cases, the extent of acceleration that might be achieved could be difficult to determine in the face of pressure from ongoing delays. The contractor therefore risks incurring liquidated damages that might offset the payment obtained for acceleration if the acceleration fails. Equally, the benefit that the employer would otherwise obtain by might also be lost if the acceleration is unsuccessful.

In practice, the employer can offset some of the potential losses by setting a revised rate of liquidated damages. This may include some of the cost of the lump sum payment, or the value of the benefit that would have been gained had the acceleration been implemented. Considering an adjustment to the rate of liquidated damages is important, because liquidated damages are recognised as an exhaustive remedy for delay, and would therefore limit the employer's entitlement to further damages for the contractor's failure to meet the revised completion dates (*Temloc Ltd v. Errill Properties Ltd* (1987) 39 BLR 30 (QB)).

Conditional payments

More favorable to the *employer* are acceleration agreements that fix a new completion period, but make a lump sum payment conditional on the contractor meeting the revised completion date.

On these terms, the contractor faces a double-edged sword, with risk of liquidated damages for failing to complete by the revised date, coupled with the loss of the conditional payment. A contractor entering into this kind of agreement would be wise to negotiate a generous allowance for the additional risk.

However, if the contractor is prevented from meeting the revised completion date and obtaining the additional payment due to circumstances under the employer's responsibility, a contractor may be entitled to payment for some of the additional amounts that would have been paid had the acceleration measures succeeded. In *John Barker Construction Ltd v. London Portman Hotel Ltd* ((1996) 83 BLR3 (QB)), the High Court found that an agreement to accelerate that included for payments conditional on achieving the original completion date despite prior delays was payable at 50% of the agreed amount, on the basis that the contractor lost its chance to recover the additional payment.

Payment of reasonable costs

The approach presenting the least risk from the *contractor's* perspective might occur when the acceleration agreement anticipates payment based on a reasonable sum for costs incurred. This may be applicable where the revised completion date is not fixed, but the acceleration agreement places an obligation for the contractor to use reasonable endeavors to reach an earlier completion date.

If the parties agree that the acceleration should be undertaken but fail to stipulate the method of valuation, then the contractor would normally be entitled to a *quantum meruit* for the work performed (*Clarke & Sons v. ACT Construction* Court of Appeal ([2002] EWCA Civ 972) (CA)). However, there are difficulties in relying on a retrospective approach to value acceleration costs.

While the basis of such a claim is conceptually simple, an extensive examination of the contract cost records will be necessary to establish the costs associated with the acceleration measures. Even where records are available, some subjectivity is inevitable in determining what the situation would have been but-for the acceleration, which may act as a catalyst for disputes. It is always preferable, therefore, to express the method of valuation within the agreement *before* acceleration measures are begun.

To provide a degree of certainty, the parties may elect to agree fixed rates for valuing the acceleration. That was the approach taken by the Court of Appeal in *Cleveland Bridge UK Ltd v. Severfield Rowen Structures Ltd (Cleveland Bridge UK Ltd v. Severfield Rowenv Structures Ltd* [2012] EWHC 3652 (TCC)), where part of an award for acceleration measures was calculated based on a cost per additional shift introduced to mitigate the delay.

Alternatively, a formulae approach could be adopted as in *Amec Civil Engineering Ltd v. Cheshire County Council (*[1999] BLR 303 (QB)). The acceleration agreement required the contractor to use best endeavors to achieve completion by the date of October 25, 1995, on the understanding that the employer would make fair and reasonable recompense for the costs incurred (Ibid, 303). The court endorsed the parties' approach to valuing the acceleration based on the amount that the accelerated work actually cost ("X") less the amount that the works should have cost without acceleration ("Y"). Further deductions were then made for contractor culpable issues ("A") and the cost of variations undertaken during the acceleration ("B"). Thus, the method of valuation was expressed simply as X-Y-(A+B).

Dealing with subsequent delays

Perhaps the most important aspect to consider in the agreement of acceleration are mechanisms to manage situations in which the acceleration measures are only partially successful due to employer delays after the acceleration agreement.

Where the agreement is based on reaching a specific completion date, these could be mechanisms that simply duplicate the existing extension of time machinery in the contract. Continuing to operate the contractual machinery may be the simplest solution, where both parties remain clear on the circumstances that entitle extension of time but preclude recovery of additional payment. If the parties attached an amount of liquidated damages to the revised completion date, then dealing with contractor liability for intervening delays may be simply a matter of applying the liquidated damages to each day of the delay.

However, the contractor's acceleration efforts may need to be factored into any assessment of extension of time or additional payment arising from the excusable or compensable event. The agreement may therefore require provisions to follow in the event that the revised completion date is rendered unachievable by post agreement delays. For instance, should the contractor abandon the acceleration, or continue at the accelerated pace?

While establishing a properly drafted agreement at the outset of acceleration might be challenging, the parties do at least obtain commercial certainty of their entitlement to additional payment, and the consequences of failing to meet the intended completion date, significantly reducing the likelihood of a dispute.

Alan Whaley MCIOB MRICS FCIArb
Director
Arcadis
London, UK

The U.S. approach to constructive acceleration by Robert A. Rubin and Sarah Biser (the United States)

Constructive acceleration occurs when an employer orders a contractor to complete the work by the contract completion date—despite the existence of excusable delay or the addition of extra work that entitles the contractor to an extension of time. When an employer fails to recognize that the contractor is entitled to an extension of time, it forces the contractor to perform the work in a shorter period of time than would have been available had an extension been given. U.S. law readily recognizes this type of claim. U.S. courts require the following five requisite elements of a constructive acceleration claim:

1. The contractor encountered excusable delay or was ordered to perform extra work affecting the critical path.
2. The employer had knowledge of the excusable delay or extra work and that it affected the critical path.
3. The employer failed or refused to grant the contractor's request for an extension of time.
4. There was some act or statement by the employer that could be construed as an acceleration order, such as reference to liquidated damages or termination.
   (a) In some U.S. jurisdictions there is the additional requirement that the contractor must have notified the employer that the contractor deemed the employer's act or statement to be a constructive order to accelerate; that the contractor will accelerate; and that the contractor will claim additional compensation for any cost incurred.
5. In fact, the contractor did accelerate performance and incurred additional cost as a result.

An employer can order acceleration directly or indirectly. A direct order is usually obvious. What is less obvious is whether an employer intends the contractor to accelerate a job when it asks the contractor to adhere to the original schedule despite extra work or excusable delay, stresses the urgency of the project, or threatens the contractor with termination or liquidated damages. Therefore, an employer has to choose their words very carefully when they use such language, lest it be deemed a constructive acceleration directive.

Acceleration damages (whether ordered or constructive) can include the following:

1. increased labor costs due to increased numbers of crafts persons working on the job, or the same crafts persons working more hours per day or more days per week at overtime wage rates;
2. loss of craft labor productivity resulting from more laborers than can efficiently work together being required to work in a limited area so the job can be completed sooner,

or from fatigue working more hours per day or more days per week than usual for a prolonged period of time, or from working in climatic conditions under which they would not otherwise have worked;
3. increased procurement costs because a contractor had to pay extra for early delivery of materials, or had to procure materials locally on short notice, rather than from the usual sources with normal lead time; and
4. extra supervision costs incurred because of the need for more foremen to supervise the extra laborers.

The following two case examples illustrate how U.S. courts deal with constructive acceleration claims, one case granting the relief claimed and the other denying relief.

The first case *SNC-Savalin America, Inc.* ("SNC") *v. Alliant Techsystems, Inc.* ("ATK"), 858 F.Supp. 620 (U.S.D.C.,Va. 2012), involved a contract for the design and construction of a new nitric acid and sulfuric acid concentration plant at the Radford, Virginia, arsenal owned by the United States Army and operated by ATK. ATK and SNC entered into a multi-million dollar design-build contract pursuant to which SNC agreed to provide engineering, procurement, and construction services.

Unfortunately, the path to completion was fraught with delays, disputes, and plan alterations. In the end, SNC did not meet the deadline set out in the contract. Not surprisingly, the parties disputed where to place the blame for the delays. SNC contended that delays resulted from unusually severe winter weather. SNC asserted a constructive acceleration claim arising from ATK's denial of its weather-related time extension request. The parties' contract expressly permitted time extensions for "unusually severe weather," and it was undisputed that the winter during which the construction took place was the sixth coldest and second snowiest on record.

It was also undisputed that:

- SNC notified ATK that severe winter weather was impacting its performance.
- SNC formally requested a 30-day time extension, which was promptly denied by ATK.
- ATK threatened to impose liquidated damages if the work was not completed by the date established in the contract; and
- SNC actually accelerated its performance, incurring documented additional costs.

ATK's principal defense to SNC's constructive acceleration claim was that SNC failed to provide "post-denial" notice that it deemed ATK's actions as ordering acceleration for which ATK intended to assert a claim. The court, in rejecting ATK's defense, noted that while many construction contracts do, in fact, mandate such notice be given as a prerequisite to claims' assertion, the contract between the parties to this project did not impose such a requirement. Therefore, the court concluded that the time extension denial was wrongful and that SNC was entitled to recover additional compensation for its constructive acceleration claim.

The second case, *Fraser Construction Company v. the United States*, 384 F.3d 1354 (Fed. Cir. 2004), involved the claim of an excavation contractor on a U.S. government flood-control project on the South Fork Zumbro River in Rochester, Minnesota, alleging that they had been constructively accelerated by the Army Corps of Engineers' refusal to grant sufficient time extensions for high water flows, requiring it to perform work throughout the summer months of continued high water flows, whereas if the time extensions had been granted, it would have shut down its operations until the waters receded to levels that were more nearly normal.

The contract work entailed excavating material from the bottom of Silver Lake, a shallow reservoir located along the Zumbro River. Before the project began, the water level in the lake was to be lowered by approximately 8 feet to facilitate excavation of the lake bottom. At that water elevation, most of the lake would normally be dry, except for a small stream running through the lake bed.

The contractor, Fraser, submitted to the Corps a proposed plan of operations to divert the stream into a trench along the edge of the dry lake bed and to construct an earthen dike to confine the water to the trench. The dike was originally designed to withstand a water flow rate of 800 c.f.s. Government records, however, showed that water flow in excess of the flow the dike was designed to handle could destroy the dike and flood the lake bed. The records also showed that water flow of significantly more than 800 c.f.s. could be expected to occur, on average, approximately 2.4 times per year during the summer months.

In comments accompanying the Corps' acceptance of Fraser's plan of operations, the Corps pointed out that the diversion system Fraser had selected "will be susceptible to damage by flow amounts which are anticipated to occur during the May to August time frame. *Delays due to such flows are not justification for weather-related extension of the contract completion date*" (emphasis added).

The Corps' concerns turned out to be well founded. Because of wet weather in the region, Silver Lake began to experience high water flows shortly after the project started, damaging the dike, flooding the work site, and delaying the work. The Corps denied Fraser's time extension requests and sent Fraser a letter demanding that the company improve its progress and threatening to terminate the contract due to delays in the project. Fraser continued work without notifying the Corps that it deemed the Corps' action a constructive acceleration order for which it would claim additional compensation. After completion of the project, Fraser asserted numerous claims against the Corps, including a claim for constructive acceleration, which the Corps denied.

The Court upheld the Corps' denial of the constructive acceleration claim on the grounds that Fraser was not entitled to the time extension it sought, and, in any event, that Fraser had failed to provide the Corps with the requisite post-denial notice.

Generally speaking, U.S. law recognizes constructive acceleration claims, provided that the prerequisites for such claims have been satisfied.

Robert A. Rubin, Esq.
Construction Consultant
New York
USA

Sarah Biser
Partner
Fox Rothschild LLP
New York
USA

Constructive acceleration claims: A common law perspective by Alan Whaley (UK)

Constructive acceleration is an American law doctrine founded in contract Appeal Boards' decisions. The doctrine allows contractors to recover acceleration costs when an employer or certifier refuses a genuine time extension requests, and pressures for acceleration regardless. However, due to the doctrine's origins in U.S. government law, common law courts outside the United States are unlikely to accept claims for constructive acceleration unless formulated on more conventional common law grounds.

The basic argument advanced by contractors outside the United States is that an employer or certifier delay in awarding time extensions amounts to a breach of contract from which damages (in the form of acceleration costs) are recoverable. However, this argument is subject to significant challenges, and must be carefully approached in view of the facts of each case to have any chance to succeed. As with any claim for breach of contract, the contractor's principle challenge lies in demonstrating that the other contracting party has failed to comply with an express or implied term in the contract, and a loss has been incurred as a result.

In contracts that do not include for third-party certifier, for instance, subcontracts or EPC contracts, a breach of contract might be demonstrated with reference to the express terms dealing with extension of time, because the employer (or main contractor) would be directly responsible for any breach. One example is Clause 20.1 of the FIDIC 1999 EPCT contract, which requires the *employer* to respond to time extension requests within 42 days. However, common law courts are sometimes reluctant to enforce contractual time limits for issuing decisions on extensions of time—the English Court of Appeal concluded that such provisions were only "directory" in *Temloc Ltd v. Errill Properties Ltd* ((1987) 39 BLR 30 (CA)). Consequently, only a substantial delay in dealing with extensions of time by the employer (or main contractor under a subcontract) might amount to a breach material enough to justify recovery of any costs.

In contracts that include for a third-party certifier, attributing a breach to the employer for the certifier's acts or omissions may be more difficult. Any breach would require the implication of a term obligating the employer to step in and correct the certifier's failure in dealing with valid requests for extension of time. Such a term may be implied if the contractor has no access to fast-track dispute resolution, and faces a lengthy litigation to address the certifier's defaults. However, English courts have refused to imply such a term where a contractor does have access to fast-track dispute resolution. When the English Court of Appeal examined whether an employer was liable for the accuracy of the certifier's interim payment certificates in *Lubenham Fidelities v. South Pembrokeshire DC* ((1986) 33 BLR 39 (CA).0), the court rejected that the employer had an obligation to correct its certifier's defaults, even when requested to do so by the contractor. Instead, the court suggested that the contractor's proper recourse under the contract was to seek a declaration of its entitlement in arbitration, and therefore, no term rendering the employer liable for the certifier's failure could necessarily be implied.

Nevertheless, common law courts have demonstrated that there are circumstances in which a constructive acceleration claim might be justified, irrespective of a contractor's access to fast track dispute resolution. One situation is where there is an outright refusal to issue time extension requests driven by a *policy decision* of the employer. For instance, in *Perini Corporation v. Commonwealth of Australia* ((1969) 12 BLR 82 (SCNSW)) the Supreme Court of New South Wales found that the employer's refusal to allow the certifier to grant time extensions otherwise entitled under the contract amounted to a repudiatory breach of the contract. Similarly, the Canadian case of *Morrison-Knudsen Company v. B.C. Hydro & Power Authority* ((1978) 85 DLR (3d) 186 (BCCA)) followed in *W.A. Stephenson Construction (Western) Ltd. v. Metro Canada Ltd.* ((1987) 27 CLR 113 (BCSC)) also found that the employer's decision to refuse any time extension requests amounted to a contractual breach. In all of these cases, acceleration damages were deemed a foreseeable consequence of the breach, and recovered by the contractor.

A contractor might also justify recovery where there is a real and impending threat of liquidated damages. In *Carillion Construction Limited v. Felix (UK) Limited,* ([2001] BLR 1 (QB)) the court set aside a settlement agreement between a contractor and subcontractor made following the subcontractor's threat to suspend performance in the face of substantial liquidated damages under the main contract. The availability of an adjudication decision to the contactor was found not to be a practical alternative submitting to the subcontractor's threat. When applying this principle to constructive acceleration, a contractor may obtain a relaxation to the normal contractual rules governing recovery of costs if there is no reasonable alternative but to accelerate, although this exception may only apply towards the end of the contractual completion period.

Consequently, contractors operating under common law jurisdictions (outside the United States) who are faced with the prospect of acceleration where genuine time extension requests are withheld must consider their situation carefully. Where there is merely a delay in awarding time extensions, particularly in cases where there is a third party certifier, or where complex facts might justify such a delay, the most appropriate course of action may be to seek a declaration on entitlement under the dispute resolution mechanism in the contract. However, if the contractor can establish that the employer (or main contractor under a subcontract) has no intention to issue any time extension requests, however valid, or where the is a real impending threat of liquidated damages, then a constructive acceleration claim might conceivably be supportable.

Alan Whaley MCIOB MRICS FCIArb
Director
Arcadis
London, UK

8.4.3 Voluntary acceleration

A contractor that accelerates without being instructed to do so by the employer or fails to notify a claim for additional payment and extension of time for completion (because of a delay caused by the employer) is deemed a "volunteer." In other words, this situation is recognized as voluntary acceleration and claims by the contractor for additional payment are without legal standing.

8.5 Proving the acceleration claim

In the ICC case no. 10847 (2003) (ICC, 2012), the tribunal found that the mere presence of additional resources did not evidence acceleration. This should have been demonstrated by specific records of how the resources were used and permitted acceleration of the progress of the works. When acceleration claims are being proved and quantified, critical paths in as-planned (or last updated) and as-built time schedules are usually matched against each other to reflect, retrospectively, additional cost caused by acceleration and to prove that the acceleration has actually taken place. When providing such evidence, it is vital that contemporary records and documents be kept. For example:

- minutes and records of meetings;
- correspondence between employer/contract administrator and contractor;
- monthly bank statements;
- invoices;
- variation orders;
- changes in design;
- site logbooks, diaries, and daily records;
- photographs and videos;
- progress reports;
- construction organization plans;
- records of contractor's personnel and equipment;
- plans of work;
- attendance control sheets;
- time schedules with supporting reports including: (1) a general description of the methods which the contractor intends to adopt; (2) major stages in the execution of the works; and (3) details showing the contractor's reasonable estimate of the number of each class of contractor's personnel and of each type of contractor's equipment required on site at each major stage (as specified in the FIDIC forms).

Extra costs incurred by acceleration are similar to disruption costs. Take, for example, loss of efficiency (productivity) of coordinated and well-trained teams that are available for the planned works. A certain number of workers are on site and maximally efficient at certain time shifts. If there is acceleration, the workers may need to be re-trained, their job description altered and overtime work performed.

Increasing the number of workers on small building construction project sites (where a large number of workers are cooperating in the same time) creates a greater risk environment for processes. Furthermore, the price of materials may increase because of the necessity to accelerate deliveries, more machinery or equipment is required and surveillance processes are disrupted due to more difficult coordination. Higher subcontracting costs constitute another critical aspect. Given that the contractor requires greater capacity, it is often difficult to obtain this extra capacity quickly and at a reasonable price. Site and headquarters overheads may also increase and management must pay more attention to the project because the work is riskier and performed under time pressures (stress). Where acceleration is required by the employer, the above-mentioned costs and inefficiencies will pass onto them from the contractor.

Specialists in delay analysis are usually hired to deal with these specific issues.

8.6 Substantial change

Public procurement law aspects must be mentioned in connection with variation procedures and variation provisions in public contracts for construction works. What is called "substantial change" and its definition will be explained further here. Public procurement law allows for variations but traditionally defines limits applicable to variation procedures. It is therefore very important to set these limits reasonably as variations can potentially affect any construction project. Moreover, their consequences are often hard to foresee.

According to the case *Pressetext Nachrichtenagentur GmbH v. Republik Österreich and others* (Case C-454/06) ("Pressetext"), substantial changes are either not permitted altogether, or not permitted without first executing a new procurement procedure. This decision of the European Court of Justice arose from a claim brought by *Pressetext*, a news agency that unsuccessfully tendered its services to the Austrian government. *Pressetext* alleged that various amendments made to the contract between the Austrian government and its incumbent provider of news services, the Austria Presse Agentur, constituted an unlawful award of contract contrary to EU procurement rules.

In this case, the European Court of Justice has provided guidance on what constitutes a material amendment and when a proposed contract "variation" ought to be, in fact, dealt with by way of a new contractual procurement process. The key part of the European Court of Justice ruling is that a change to an existing contract would constitute a "material difference" where:

- the change to be introduced into the contract conditions, had it been part of the initial tender, "would have allowed for the admission of tenderers other than those initially admitted or would have allowed for the acceptance of a tender other than the one initially accepted"; or
- the change would result in the scope of the original contract being extended "considerably to encompass services not initially covered"; or
- the change would result in a shift in "the economic balance of the contract in favor of the contractor in a manner which was not provided for in the terms of the initial contract."

Other limitations prescribed by public law also need to be considered when dealing with variations—particularly in terms of additional works and their respective regulation; however, if there is a variation procedure contractually defined, and risks are allocated in an efficient way, and reasonable claims options are reserved, then the rules are the same for everybody—with free and transparent competition allowed in an appropriate way for such a specific process as the construction project is. The number of claims and variations depends then on how well the project is prepared and on the nature and foreseeability of risks in a particular project. The competence and common sense of the employer, the engineer and the contractor in variation and claim evaluation are the key to success and dispute avoidance. This requires that it is not left to the discretion of the parties to negotiate the price adjustments or in any other way to make an arbitrary change in price (Hartlev and Liljenbøl, 2013). The problem in many countries is ambiguous public procurement law. Public employers are often reluctant to approve even necessary variations and claims because of political pressure and fear of criminal responsibility. In terms of the projects subject to subsidies, the employers are often under pressure to follow strict rules. In cases of violations, they may also lose important grants. Particular variations are seen as risky in this regard and this leads employers to refuse to instruct and/or pay for variations and claims. Furthermore, even necessary variations may be paid from the employer's own resources without the opportunity to have it paid from subsidies.

Modification of contracts during their execution under EU law by Odysseas P. Michaelides (Cyprus)

Standard forms of work contracts, like FIDIC, generally provide for cases of variations of the works, usually initiated by the employer, the engineer (if applicable) or even the contractor. Such variations usually include changes to the quantities, the quality, or other characteristics of any item of the works included in the contract, additional work to be delivered, changes to the sequence or timing of the execution of the works, changes to the dimensions of the works, and so on.

The need for variations usually arises because, generally, contract documents cannot always foresee all the future events that may occur and the changes are required to deal with such unforeseen circumstances. Thus, quite often, variations are absolutely necessary for the completion of the works. For example, there could be the need for a change of the foundation of a bridge from a pad foundation to piles due to unforeseen ground conditions.

In other cases, variations are decided by the employer due to changed requirements or needs. For instance, the owner of an office building (the employer) could decide during construction that the meeting room is not big enough and that it should be enlarged into the neighboring open space. The contractor is bound by such variations instructed by the employer (or the engineer, as the case may be) unless otherwise provided in the contract. Moreover, some contracts provide for a mechanism that allows the contractor to propose variations. If the employer rejects these proposals, the contractor has no right to compensation.

In any case, the variation clause usually provides that when a variation takes place, then the contractor is compensated for any additional cost and, where appropriate, is given an extension of time.

Usually, variations may not (without the contractor's consent):

- Change the fundamental nature or the scope of the works.
- Be of a different character or extent than the one contemplated by, and capable of being carried out, under the provisions of the contract.
- Omit work if the omitted work will be carried out by another contractor.
- Be instructed after practical completion.

In most common law jurisdictions, no power to order variation is implied and hence, in the absence of express terms in the contract allowing variations, the contractor may reject instructions for variations without any legal consequences. That is why standard forms of contract generally include express provisions giving the employer (or the engineer) the power to instruct variations.

As explained above, a contract usually includes a mechanism that regulates the variation of the works to be executed. However, a need to change the terms of the contract (conditions of contract) sometimes occurs. This kind of change is referred to as an amendment to the contract. For example, the contract could provide that the works should be completed within 24 months but during the execution of the works a need for acceleration of the works reduces that time to 18 months. This constitutes a change to the contract terms that the parties had agreed and accepted when the contract was signed. Therefore, this kind of change cannot take the form of an instruction by the employer (nor by the engineer) and can be implemented only if mutually agreed to between the employer and the contractor in a new (supplementary) agreement.

The two parties are generally free to agree, either as part of their original contract or through a subsequent agreement, to change the contract terms or to vary the works to be executed. Such a decision to change the original contract is valid if the conditions (depending on the applicable law) necessary for a valid contract are fulfilled (e.g. parties capable of contracting, consent of the parties, a lawful object and consideration). However, this is not always true in the case of a public works contract within the European Union (EU). In accordance with EU law (which, until now has been mainly developed by case law), the implementation of a public works contract must not:

- substantially modify the provisions of the signed contract. A modification is considered "Substantial," if it substantially changes the contract compared to the original signed contract.
- Substantially alter the nature and financial scope of the contract during implementation.

If there is a need for such material changes to the initial contract—in particular to the scope and content of the mutual rights and obligations of the parties—then a new procurement procedure under EU law is required, since such changes demonstrate the parties' intention to renegotiate essential terms or conditions of that contract. This is particularly the case if the amended conditions would have had an influence on the outcome of the initial procurement procedure, had they been part of that procedure.

EU case law recognizes that contracting parties can be faced with external circumstances that they could not foresee when they entered into the contract. Therefore, a certain degree of flexibility is accepted as necessary to adapt the contract to these circumstances without a new procurement procedure. The notion of unforeseeable circumstances generally refers to circumstances that could not have been predicted despite reasonably diligent preparation of the initial award by the contracting authority, taking into account the available means, the nature and characteristics of the specific project, good practice in the field in question and the need to ensure an appropriate relationship between the resources spent in preparing the award and its foreseeable value. However, EU case law was never willing to accept that this approach could apply in cases where a modification of the outcome of the overall procurement was due to an alteration. For instance, by replacing the works to be delivered by something different or by fundamentally changing the type of procurement since, in such a situation, a hypothetical influence on the outcome may be assumed.

In line with the principles of equal treatment and transparency, the contractor cannot be replaced by another, cheaper operator without offering the contract to competition. However, the contractor may undergo certain structural changes during the performance of the contract, such as internal restructuring, mergers and acquisitions, or insolvency. Such structural changes should not automatically require new procurement procedures for all public contracts performed on that undertaking.

Based on the above, EU lawmakers seem to recognize that contracting authorities should have the possibility to provide for modifications to a contract by way of review clauses, but such clauses should not give them unlimited discretion. To this end, appropriate provisions have been included in a new EU Public Procurement Directive in order to set the extent to which modifications may be provided for in the initial contract.

In the Directive of the European Parliament and of the Council on public procurement published in 2014, the following article have been included to cover the modification of contracts during their term and to regulate the case of forced termination of a signed contract:

Article 72 modification of contracts during their term

1. Contracts and framework agreements may be modified without a new procurement procedure in accordance with this directive in any of the following cases:
    (a) where the modifications, irrespective of their monetary value, have been provided for in the initial procurement documents in clear, precise, and unequivocal review clauses, which may include price revision clauses, or options. Such clauses shall state the scope and nature of possible modifications or options as well as the conditions under which they may be used. They shall not provide for modifications or options that would alter the overall nature of the contract or the framework agreement;
    (b) for additional works, services, or supplies by the original contractor that have become necessary and that were not included in the initial procurement where a change of contractor:
       (i) cannot be made for economic or technical reasons such as requirements of inter-changeability or interoperability with existing equipment, services or installations procured under the initial procurement; and
       (ii) would cause significant inconvenience or substantial duplication of costs for the contracting authority.
       However, any increase in price shall not exceed 50 % of the value of the original contract. Where several successive modifications are made, that limitation shall apply to the value of each modification. Such consecutive modifications shall not be aimed at circumventing this directive;
    (c) where all of the following conditions are fulfilled:
       (i) the need for modification has been brought about by circumstances that a diligent contracting authority could not foresee;
       (ii) the modification does not alter the overall nature of the contract;
       (iii) any increase in price is not higher than 50% of the value of the original contract or framework agreement. Where several successive modifications are made, that limitation shall apply to the value of each modification. Such consecutive modifications shall not be aimed at circumventing this directive;
    (d) where a new contractor replaces the one to which the contracting authority had initially awarded the contract as a consequence of either:
       (i) an unequivocal review clause or option in conformity with point (a);
       (ii) universal or partial succession into the position of the initial contractor, following corporate restructuring, including takeover, merger, acquisition, or

insolvency, of another economic operator that fulfils the criteria for qualitative selection initially established provided that this does not entail other substantial modifications to the contract and is not aimed at circumventing the application of this directive; or

(iii) in the event that the contracting authority itself assumes the main contractor's obligations toward its subcontractors where this possibility is provided for under national legislation pursuant to Article 71;

(e) where the modifications, irrespective of their value, are not substantial within the meaning of paragraph 4.

Contracting authorities having modified a contract in the cases set out under points (b) and (c) of this paragraph shall publish a notice to that effect in the *Official Journal of the European Union*. Such notice shall contain the information set out in Annex V part G and shall be published in accordance with Article 51.

2. Furthermore, and without any need to verify whether the conditions set out under points (a) to (d) of paragraph 4 are met, contracts may equally be modified without a new procurement procedure in accordance with this directive being necessary where the value of the modification is below both of the following values:

(i) the thresholds set out in Article 4; and
(ii) 10% of the initial contract value for service and supply contracts and below 15 % of the initial contract value for works contracts.

However, the modification may not alter the overall nature of the contract or framework agreement. Where several successive modifications are made, the value shall be assessed on the basis of the net cumulative value of the successive modifications.

3. For the purpose of the calculation of the price mentioned in paragraph 2 and points (b) and (c) of paragraph 1, the updated price shall be the reference value when the contract includes an indexation clause.

4. A modification of a contract or a framework agreement during its term shall be considered to be substantial within the meaning of point (e) of paragraph 1, where it renders the contract or the framework agreement materially different in character from the one initially concluded. In any event, without prejudice to paragraphs 1 and 2, a modification shall be considered to be substantial where one or more of the following conditions is met:

(a) the modification introduces conditions, which, had they been part of the initial procurement procedure, would have allowed for the admission of other candidates than those initially selected or for the acceptance of a tender other than that originally accepted or would have attracted additional participants in the procurement procedure;

(b) the modification changes the economic balance of the contract or the framework agreement in favor of the contractor in a manner, which was not provided for in the initial contract or framework agreement;

(c) the modification extends the scope of the contract or framework agreement considerably;

(d) where a new contractor replaces the one to which the contracting authority had initially awarded the contract in other cases than those provided for under point (d) of paragraph 1.

5. A new procurement procedure in accordance with this directive shall be required for other modifications of the provisions of a public contract or a framework agreement during its term than those provided for under paragraphs 1 and 2.

It is anticipated that the new directive will dispel some ambiguities existing today on this issue due to the lack of concrete legal provisions. However, the myriad of different cases to be considered under the new regime will probably lead to some further debate on the correct interpretation of these provisions.

Odysseas Ph. Michaelides
Director of Control
Department of Control
Ministry of Communications and Works
Cyprus

ITER—An International project for the construction of a first-of-a-kind fusion nuclear installation under the FIDIC forms by Karoly Tamas Olajos (France)

Fusion

Fusion, which is the process powering the sun and the stars and which makes all life on earth possible, has a potential to become a long-term, environmentally friendly and material-efficient energy option that could at the same time address global climate change and gain public acceptance. Fusion offers the possibility of an energy source cleaner than fossil, safer than fission, with a system that, unlike renewables, could be deployed anywhere and work continuously. Fusion's fuel supply is indigenous to all nations and is essentially inexhaustible. Its fuel is so abundant that fusion would become a very sustainable energy source that would readily available to all mankind as long as there is life on earth.

International Thermonuclear Experimental Reactor (ITER)

ITER is a first-of-a-kind project from various perspectives, including science, technology, engineering, size, extent of international cooperation, project funding, and organization. An international collaboration of seven partners—Euratom, China, India, Japan, Korea, Russia, and the United States—was formed to build and operate ITER, which is the cornerstone of international fusion research and development efforts transiting it from laboratory to industrial scale. The example of ITER validates that the scale, scientific, and technological complexity of fusion research and development, its dimensions and cost render necessary joint international efforts in the form of an international organization maintaining public-interest character. ITER, which aims to demonstrate the scientific and technical feasibility of fusion energy, builds on six decades of worldwide magnetic confinement Tokamak research. It is not only at the frontier of technology but it is also the world's largest and most complex energy research and development project, driving forward technology on many fronts from superconducting magnets to remote robotic maintenance.

Nuclear

ITER in France is the first fusion installation for which a complete safety case had to be prepared under the scrutiny of a nuclear regulatory body in formal licensing. Besides, ITER is the first basic nuclear installation in France, operated by an international organization, the ITER International Fusion Energy Organization (ITER Organization), which, however, agreed to "observe" French nuclear and environmental regulations and to cooperate with the French regulatory bodies. Unless and until fusion installations continue to be fuelled by deuterium-tritium, ITER-like installations will remain subject to nuclear regulation due to the emission of ionising radiation. In this respect the licensing of ITER provides valuable input as it successfully demonstrated that ITER was inherently safe.

Fusion for energy (F4E)

According to the Agreement on the Establishment of the ITER International Fusion Energy Organization for the Joint Implementation of the ITER Project, the ITER Organization is responsible to design, assemble, operate, and decommission ITER. However, instead of pooling the majority of the resources required for the project under the authority of the ITER Organization, as would be typical for this type of project, the ITER partners decided that about 80% of the resources would be provided in kind through their domestic agencies established for this purpose, procuring from industry in their own territories. ITER is a flagship project for Europe to demonstrate its leadership in fusion research and development; therefore, Euratom, the host partner of the ITER project, agreed to provide approximately one-half of the components that make up ITER, out of which the ITER buildings represent around one-third. The Euratom contribution is exclusively managed by its procurement agency, the European Joint Undertaking for ITER and the Development of Fusion Energy (Fusion for Energy or F4E), acting as the Euratom Domestic Agency for ITER.

Procurement strategy

F4E's procurement strategy for the ITER buildings envisaged that three support contracts (respectively the Architect Engineer, Support to the Owner and Health and Safety Protection Coordinator) were needed to enable F4E to manage the buildings work while the construction works, which were let in tender batches for civil engineering; heating, ventilation and air-conditioning and electrical services; cranes and bridges; infrastructure works; and finishing works, were to be regulated by a large number of contracts, based on FIDIC forms, stipulated with consortia of large number of contractors. Most of these contracts had at least two main suppliers, one for the design and one for the construction. In addition, F4E deployed its own interface agreement to manage its contractors. Work coordination and supervision were carried out by a single entity which functioned as the resident engineer as envisaged under FIDIC forms.

Choice of FIDIC forms

In order to (i) attract European construction and engineering industry; (ii) increase competition; (iii) combine multi-package and split package procurement methods in the supply chain; and (iv) emphasize the international character of the project, F4E (and later the ITER organization) deliberately chose to use FIDIC forms during the construction of ITER as we believed that FIDIC provided for standard forms of contract, which were well-known in international infrastructure projects; they were considered international best practice due to their balanced risk allocation; they operated with clearly defined procedures, which were administered by a fair engineer; and more importantly, they were tested by the courts.

The F4E amended FIDIC forms of contract, which were customized to ITER although they preserved the basic characteristics of FIDIC forms, comprised one consolidated set of conditions of contract under licence from FIDIC, based on provisions from (i) FIDIC Red Book including some significant design obligations and a lump sum component; (ii) FIDIC Yellow Book including a re-measurable component; and (iii) FIDIC Gold Book for operation and maintenance obligations.

FIDIC and NEC3

As the ITER experience demonstrates, FIDIC forms of contract have considerable advantages for multiparty international construction projects; however, the author believes that it may be sensible to implement some of the NEC3 principles into the FIDIC forms by using the traditional language of FIDIC in relation to which the F4E contracts made an attempt. Such principles include among others an early warning mechanism, an enhanced good-faith cooperation obligation on the employer, the engineer, the contractor and other contractors interfering with the work of the contractor, an obligation to mitigate the cost and schedule impacts of events or circumstances giving rise to a claim. However, under an EU or equivalent public procurement regime it is the author's view that it remains crucial to maintain the differentiation between FIDIC variations and claims (and not to merge them into the concept of NEC3 compensation events).

Relevance of ITER

The ITER experience is a showcase to demonstrate that FIDIC forms of contract could be used as key project administration tool in nuclear new build projects while ensuring compliance, without modifying the basic characteristics of FIDIC forms, with mandatory provisions arising from (i) the employer's public body status; (ii) the public funding of the project; (iii) applicable public procurement rules; and (iv) nuclear regulations. F4E as a Euratom joint undertaking forms part of the EU-body family and is therefore subject to EU regulations. Due to such public body status and an income-determined budget, we had to ensure enhanced employer's involvement in the contract administration, which was on the other side a basic characteristic of nuclear construction projects. Similarly, as nuclear projects like ITER are prone to modifications, flexibility provisions needed to be introduced. Modifications during the contract implementation were a key issue for us in order to ensure compliance with mandatory public procurement rules. On the same ground, contrary to the industry practice, we had to unilaterally appoint a permanent dispute adjudication board for the construction of ITER. In addition, the choice of FIDIC forms brought the necessary flexibility to include robust quality assurance and control procedures tailored to the needs of ITER, allowing that requirements arising from nuclear regulations could be easily complied without unnecessarily overburdening standard FIDIC procedures. At last, the ITER experience was presented as a case study on the

2014 and 2015 FIDIC International Contract Users' Conference in London, which demonstrated our success in conciliating FIDIC forms with the distinctive requirements of the ITER project.

Prior approval versus authorization to proceed

Both F4E (funded by the general budget of the EU) and the ITER organization operate with income-determined budgets, which means that expenditure must equal to income. Before spending is made, it must be verified that income will cover it. In practical terms this requires that (i) budget commitment must precede a legal commitment; (ii) implementation of a legal commitment may not be commenced before the legal commitment enters into force; (iii) only the authorizing officer of the relevant public body may financially commit that public body; and (iv) financial delegation by the authorizing officer may only be given to the employees of that public body. Indeed, these rules aim at ensuring effective independence of international organizations such as Euratom and the ITER organization. However, these rules have fundamental effects on the engineer's powers requiring them to be subject, in general, to the prior approval of the employer. In order to overcome this constraint, F4E decided to have recourse to an "authorization to proceed" procedure rather than to a "prior approval" procedure when the engineer acted in his role as independent certifier. This way we believed we could preserve the continuing liability of the engineer for the contract administration and ensure that a fair decision was made also in the perception of our contractors, with special respect to their claims. The engineer was required to submit the employer a draft decision with supporting particulars. Grounds for refusal by the employer were exhaustively enumerated and agreed with the engineer in advance, which were subsequently communicated to our contractors. These were among others (i) material lack of substantiation by the engineer; (ii) manifest error of assessment on the substantiation provided by the engineer (which was at the same time defined as an indisputable error of judgement of the engineer, which completely disregarded the facts of the case); (iii) temporary unavailability of the employer's funds; and (iv) noncompliance with the employer's international obligations or nuclear regulations. Therefore, by no means, review of the merits contemplated in the engineer's draft decision was intended to be carried out by the employer.

Contract modifications in a nutshell

Contract modifications are a natural aspect of the life of a contract and there are many legitimate reasons for a contracting authority, such as F4E, which require it to instruct or agree to contract modifications. However, in contrast to private contracts where the principle of contractual freedom of the parties applies to contract modifications, EU public procurement rules impose restrictions on when and to what extent a public contract concluded between a contracting authority and an economic operator can be modified. F4E is bound by EU public procurement rules (although it is not directly subject to Directive 2014/24/EU) which restrict its flexibility to manage contract modifications without undertaking new competitive procedures or contract awards. Managing those modifications and their impacts on the contract value in a compliant way has been proven very challenging.

The general principle is that there must be some degree of control over possible modifications in order not to prejudice the principles of transparency, fair competition and non-discrimination that applied during the initial competitive procedure: the tenderer who was awarded the contract won because his tender was considered the best under the conditions of the competition that were known to all of his competitors. If, later, the conditions of that competition were substantially altered, it could put into question whether the award to that particular tenderer was justified. If, however, the possibility to deviate from the contractual provisions were known by all the competitors from the outset, then they all could make their offers in the light of that possibility. These are the considerations that have to be balanced with the practical requirements of changing circumstances that necessarily involve a modification during the contract implementation.

New EU Public Procurement Directive (Directive 2014/24/EU)

For the first time, public procurement rules on contract modification have been codified by Directive 2014/24/EU, providing for a clearer legal framework than before, which inspired also the public procurement rules applicable to the F4E contracts. These new public procurement rules are partly based on the settled case-law of the Court of Justice of the European Union (CJEU), partly they are completely new. While in the past contracting authorities had to justify that their contract modifications were non-substantial by verifying that the conditions triggering the need of a new competitive procedure as defined in Case C-454/06, Pressetext, and Case C-91/08, Wall AG, were not met (negative list), now their justification will rather focus on the fulfilment of the conditions required for a modification to be permissible under one of the legal bases provided for in Directive 2014/24/EU (positive list). Yet, this is—in the author's view—a significant shift in the underlying approach pursued by the new regime as it allows that previously non-permitted substantial modifications may become permissible if the legitimate interest of the contracting authorities defined in Directive 2014/24/EU to proceed with such modifications so justifies. Nevertheless, under both regimes the role of legal justifications seems crucial. Under the new regime however any justification for a legal basis will need to be published which may increase the risk of being challenged by unsuccessful tenderers of the initial competitive procedure or by others. To this end, the old test that required demonstration that the contemplated modification had it been known in the initial competitive procedure could have modified the outcome of that procedure seems no longer appropriate, and any such challenge to be successful will likely require that the conditions for a permissible modification under the legal basis chosen by the contracting authority are proven incorrect.

Flexibility provisions

The first thing to be assessed is whether the change that will require modification to the contract is foreseen by the initial contract itself. If the initial contract contains a review clause that regulates the relevant contract modification in sufficiently clear, precise and explicit terms, that modification could be considered by all tenderers at the time of making their offer. Hence, such a modification—irrespective of its monetary value—will be considered as the implementation of the commitments made and agreed upon by the parties in the initial contract which therefore has already been subject to competition. With a view to this, the most efficient way of dealing with modifications during the contract implementation is to include the required flexibility in the contract that is put out for a tender. This means that the contract notice and the initial call for tender documentation should already contemplate and provide for all foreseeable modifications in order to ensure that all potential and actual tenderers are informed upfront of the initial scope of the contract and of the foreseeable modifications during the contract implementation.

Standard FIDIC forms offer flexibility provisions which in the author's view meet the requirements of the public procurement exemptions such as: (i) re-measurement and evaluation of re-measurement component; (ii) omission; (iii) variation procedure provided that unit rates are obtained in the initial competitive procedure for pricing variations (including (1) percentage of (reasonable) profit; (2) exhaustive list of recoverable overheads and similar charges as well as risk items; (3) overheads, similar charges, and risk premiums in the unit rates; and (4) detailed breakdown of unit rates with special respect to direct cost items the granularity of which is a key for the employer to successfully manage contract modifications) and that a contingency pot is appropriated by the employer to such variations; (iv) value engineering; (v) price adjustment; (vi) delay damages; (vii) claim procedure; (viii) extension of time for completion being a necessary consequence of foreseen and unforeseen (but permissible) contract modifications (however, permissibility of an extension of time for completion would need to be separately assessed if the sole purpose of the modification was to extend the duration of the initial contract).

In addition to these, other flexibility provisions may be required to introduce in the initial contract such as: (i) predefined additions to and/or omissions from the initial scope and/or duration of the contract: (1) positive options providing for additional scope; (2) negative options providing for omissions; (3) options to use an alternative technology; (4) framework arrangement, which would contain template terms and conditions, a "call-off" mechanism, a mechanism for pricing each stage of work; (5) renewals and/or extension of the duration of the contract; (ii) predefined conditions for outstanding or poor performance: (1) conditional stages; (2) options providing for an extension of the contract following satisfactory performance or successful tests; (3) early completion bonuses; (4) key performance indicators and related incentives and penalties; (5) pain and gain sharing mechanisms; (6) termination fees in the case of termination for convenience; (iii) predefined conditions for unspecified changes resulting in modifications to the initial contract: (1) notice to proceed (NtP) mechanisms anticipating an earliest NtP date and a latest NtP date with appropriate early and late mobilization costs; (2) delivery notice mechanisms and prolonged storage of long-lead items; (3) known interfaces of which consequences to the extent unforeseeable could be channeled into the claim procedure rather than into the variation procedure; (iv) new works or services consisting in the repetition of similar works or services provided that the possibility to use a negotiated procedure without prior publication during the contract implementation was published in the contract notice of the initial competitive procedure.

Permissible modifications

Yet, modifications that are not regulated in the contract by a review clause have to undergo further assessment and they can be executed only provided that the public procurement rules specifically allow for them either as (i) permissible modifications for additional works, services or supplies; (ii) permissible modifications due to unforeseen circumstances; (iii) permissible modifications below the de minimis threshold; or as (iv) non-substantial modifications, which may be defined as modifications that meet all the following conditions: (1) modification would not allow for the admission of other tenders or a different award; (2) the initial scope would not be considerably extended by the modification; and (3) the economic balance of the contract would not be disrupted in favor of the contractor in a manner that was not provided for in the initial contract. Consequently, if the contemplated modification is neither governed by a precise review clause nor it fits into one of the legal bases for permissible modifications outside the contract provisions, including non-substantial modifications, then the contract may need to be terminated and its remaining scope or the modification alone has to be retendered through a new competitive procedure.

The absolute limit for the use of any of the above legal bases for permissible modifications is that the modification, individually or cumulatively with all other permissible modifications to date, may not alter the overall nature of the initial contract, which is to be interpreted as referring to the scope and content of the mutual rights and obligations of the parties arising from the initial contract, the alteration of which would change the essential or fundamental characteristics of the contract. This may include cases where, among others, pursuant to the envisaged modification the contract would no longer fall within the perimeter of the same public procurement regime (e.g., it would have to be considered as a service contract instead of a works contract), or, where the conditions for the choice of the type of procedure leading to the award of the initial contract would not have been met in the light of the modified contract (e.g., the legal basis for a negotiated procedure, competitive dialogue, or competitive procedure with negotiation would not have stood for the modified contract), where the initial risk allocation would be fundamentally altered, or where the modified scope would encompass scope clearly different from and unrelated to the initial scope. In addition, if the cumulative impact of all permissible modifications implied a change to the market segment in which the initial competitive procedure took place had such a modified contract been retendered, the overall nature of the initial contract could arguably be seen altered (e.g., while the initial contract could only be performed by economic operators operating in the specialized nuclear construction market, the modified contract could also be performed by others economic operators operating in the less specialized conventional construction market, which would in turn likely to attract increased competition). Therefore, the implications of a modified contract in the underlying market segment will have to be carefully assessed in order to determine whether such an absolute limit would be reached or not.

Choice of legal basis

If a modification is capable of fulfilling the conditions of more than one legal bases at the same time (e.g., the event or circumstance leading to the modification is unforeseen but interconnectivity is also an issue, or the modification is non-substantial and is also below the de minimis threshold), given that the legal bases are independent from one another, the contracting authority has discretion on the legal basis or legal bases it relies on for entering into a modification. For practical reasons, F4E decided to apply the following order of preference: (i) if both interconnectivity issues and unforeseen circumstances were present, either or both of such legal bases could be relied on; (ii) if neither of the conditions for these legal bases were present but the modification could be deemed non-substantial, then the legal basis for non-substantial modifications could be used; (iii) finally, if neither of the foregoing were adequate or time were an issue, only then should the de minimis rule be applied. As this legal basis needs practically no justification, but the 10% and 15% "pot" is filled up with each modification using the de minimis rule as legal basis, it should remain a last resort for cases where the use of no other legal basis could be justified, subject always to the absolute limit framed by the overall nature of the initial contract.

Initial contract value

The legal bases for permissible modifications concerning additional works, services or supplies and unforeseeable circumstances as well as the de minimis rule operate with the term of "initial contract value" the actual value of which needs to be recalculated before each modification is effectuated and will—by definition—fall between the minimum value corresponding to the accepted contract amount (which includes all the sums legally committed by the employer at the contract signature such as the baseline contract value, the value of each option exercised at the contract signature but which excludes the initial contingency pot) and the maximum value corresponding to the award value of the initial competition (which includes the accepted contract amount and the maximum cumulative value of all modifications foreseen and priced in the initial contract, including the value of the initial contingency pot to the extent it has been expended). Therefore, the initial contract value when calculated will necessarily include the value of the options and other foreseen modifications effectuated, including the value of the instructed variations covered by the initial contingency pot, the value of the re-measurement component of works exceeding the accepted contract amount and the price adjustment applied before the modification takes effect. If however a modification foreseen in the initial contract were not to be effectuated, its value could not be taken into account when the initial contract value would be established.

Price modifications

As price is an essential term of any contract, and modifications post-contract signature may easily violate the principles of transparency and equal treatment of tenderers, the underlying reason behind an increase of the contract price will need to be carefully assessed. Any such price increase may generally be the result of (i) increased quantities (re-measurement); (ii) additional scope (variations), (iii) changes to the conditions in which contract performance has to take place (claims); or (iv) price adjustment. Price increases in contracts for fixed quantities with a lump-sum are acceptable provided the overall nature of the contract remains the same, however, each such increase, necessarily arising from variations, remains on a cumulative basis subject to the public procurement constraints while measurement or cost plus fee contracts where the accepted contract amount and the target price are effectively notional amounts based on an estimation of quantities that will be re-measured according to actual requirements, or where the final price is difficult to measure and therefore to put into competition in the initial competitive procedure fall under the public procurement exemptions (unless price increases arise from variations) as they—being pricing mechanisms of the initial contract —essentially define the nature of such contracts.

EU and FIDIC approaches to contract modification

Considering the foregoing, we conciliated the different approaches to contract modification arising from our income-determined budget and FIDIC. The EU approach could be illustrated with an "onion." If we consider the core project contemplated in the initial contract as an "onion," new layers—the modifications—to such an "onion" could only be added if and when the impacts of each such modification were agreed by the parties. This is because the budget commitment had to cover all impacts of any modification by matching the legal commitment (i.e., a precise and final number had to be agreed). Consequently, no payment could be made until all impacts of any modification were agreed and the legal commitment was in place. It follows therefore that each variation was in fact an amendment to the contract. In contrast, under the FIDIC approach, modifications could be instructed and implemented provided that their cumulative impacts remained under the financial ceiling appropriated by the employer to a given project, which the author usually illustrates with an "umbrella." This "umbrella" allowed that no change impact had to be agreed before modifications could be implemented by the contractor ("requirements for recording of costs") and payment could be made as works progressed. In theory, there would have been only one condition to this: the employer should have had sufficient financial cover to pay for the modifications instructed (Sub-Clause 2.4 [Employer's Financial Arrangements]).

Amending and variation instruments

These differences required us to implement various forms of amending and variation instruments that operated in the frame provided by change management review meetings, having the purpose to discuss with the contractors in advance the modifications to come and agree if amending or variation instruments ought to be used. Contract modifications were managed against the employer's contingency pot, which he could unilaterally increase by notice. In addition, we found it practical to specify the method and form how all the contract documents could be modified during the contract implementation. The standard variation definition of FIDIC we were required to extend to modifications to our management specifications, including the ITER quality assurance and control procedures, which we had to introduce in our contracts.

While the engineer's right to unilaterally change the scope of the works on behalf of the employer is customary provision in FIDIC forms, due to our public procurement constraints, variations under F4E contracts had to become the employer's unilateral right to "amend" such contracts. Variations could not be effectuated alone by the engineer as originally foreseen under FIDIC forms; therefore, even if acting as the employer's agent, he could not determine any matters arising from change management review meetings. This view as we felt was supported by Sub-Clause 3.1 [Engineer's Duties and Authority] stating that the engineer had no authority to "amend" the contract.

Deviation notice, deviation request, and service order

Deviation notices and deviation requests (the instrument for value engineering), initiated respectively by the engineer or the contractor resembled the EU approach, which the author calls simplified amendments to the contract. They always required approval by the employer (either in the form of a deviation order or an approved deviation request) before they could be implemented. Consequently, deviation notices and deviation requests, jointly termed as amending instruments, could not only capture variations but also other modifications to the contract (i.e., modifications to the contract annexes and other contract documents): (i) consent of the contractor had to be obtained in each case; (ii) agreement between the parties had to be reached on the contractor's valuation of the variation in the form of an impact assessment report before the variation took effect and the corresponding works could be executed; and (iii) the amending instrument, once approved by the employer, had to be initiated also by the contractor.

On the other hand, service orders which resembled the FIDIC approach were used in the case of urgency where there would be no time to negotiate and agree on the impacts of such variations by the parties before their implementation had to commence. They were mainly associated with the nuclear operator's notifications to implement, with no delay, nuclear requirements in the supply chain. Unlike in the case of amending instruments, service orders were the instrument to instruct variations (i.e., modifications falling within the definition of variation). Notwithstanding, as to variations, deviation notices and service orders remained interchangeable. In order to enhance the contractor's cash flow, service orders included a fair and reasonable valuation of the variation by the engineer acting in his role as independent certifier based on the information available at the time of issuing the respective service order to which the employer agreed when issuing it. Among others, this valuation of the engineer allowed that the contractor could receive payment as work progressed under the service order, which was to be implemented immediately. In addition, such valuation effectively substituted the contractor's impact assessment report and served to identify the value of the legal commitment, that is, of the service order, which needed to be booked in the employer's contingency pot and had to be covered by the remaining balance of such pot appropriated by the employer to variations. If the contractor disagreed with the initial valuation included in the service order, he could, in accordance with Sub-Clause 20.1 [Contractor's Claims], submit a notice of claim to demonstrate the actual cost incurred arising from the implementation of the respective service order, while the employer might have agreed to issue an updated service order should the initial valuation of the engineer have been required to undergo adjustment due to the availability of further information to quantify the final impacts of the relevant variation. Therefore, the service order procedure successfully channelled the variation procedure into the claim procedure, requiring the contractor to demonstrate incurred cost in accordance with the requirements of the claim procedure, including keeping of contemporary records, where no unit rates of the contract could be relied on, should he have challenged the initial valuation provided by the engineer, which was by contrast based on an estimation using the unit rates of the contract. This had the positive effect that the contractors were incentivized to cooperate with the engineer to provide timely input in the change management review meetings as they ran the risk of not being able to demonstrate incurred cost beyond the impacts that were estimated by the engineer in his initial valuation.

Engineer's instructions

While in FIDIC forms of contract every variation literally takes the form of an engineer's instruction, in the F4E contracts variations and engineer's instructions were different instruments serving different purposes. Engineer's instructions were available to "implement" (and not to "amend") the contract. Consequently, engineer's instructions could not carry any cost or schedule impact other than what was foreseen (and therefore authorized by the employer) in the initial contract, or in amending or variation instruments. They could not either be considered modifications from a public procurement point of view. Yet, if the engineer's instruction constituted a variation in the contractor's opinion, he was required to promptly refer the matter to the employer for confirmation. Until he received a response from the employer, either in the form of a confirmation of the engineer's instruction or in the form of an amending or variation instrument, he was not obliged to comply with, and implement, the respective engineer's instruction. In order to protect the contractor from the misuse of engineer's instructions to instruct contract modifications this way, his right to submit a notice of claim under Sub-Clause 20.1 [Contractor's Claims] was preserved in respect of the contractor's entitlement to a variation arising from such compliance and implementation. If it was demonstrated by the contractor in the corresponding claim procedure that the engineer's instruction did constitute a variation, the engineer was obliged to exceptionally proceed in the claim procedure with the quantification of the impacts of the engineer's instruction according to the rules applicable to pricing variations, therefore, being subject to the public procurement constraints.

Deviation notice procedure AKA negotiated procedure

An initial contingency pot was included by the employer in our initial contracts, which served the purpose of covering foreseen but yet unspecified contract modifications during the contract implementation by offsetting additional works, services, or supplies that could be priced with sufficient precision through the application of the variation procedure of the initial contract. This was the reason why we could consider the corresponding increase of the contract price from such a contingency pot forming part of the initial contract as permissible modification. It was, however, the case that the initial amount of the employer's contingency pot had to be increased due to the fact that more additional works, services, or supplies had to be ordered than what we could reasonably foresee at the outset, which could not thus form part of the initial contract and which required therefore additional funding. To this end, we conciliated the deviation notice procedure with a negotiated procedure under the contract. We considered that the variation procedure served effectively the same purpose as a negotiated procedure. Indeed, in the case of a variation procedure—similarly to the negotiated procedure —the employer maintained full discretion as to agreeing on the impacts of a modification and instructing it as a variation. Therefore, we concluded that the variation procedure was best placed to accommodate such a negotiated procedure resulting in a new contract award. However, this we could only apply where the possibility to use a negotiated procedure with the incumbent contractor without prior publication was advertised in the contract notice of the initial public procurement procedure resulting in the award of the initial contract, or such use was otherwise justified.

In fact, there was a clear, precise, and explicit mechanism in the initial contract for instructing and pricing variations (including determining new unit rates where, as last resort, an incurred cost plus reasonable profit mechanism was applicable); a schedule of rates for variations were obtained in the initial competitive procedure to give effect to such a mechanism and the contractor was obliged to respond with an impact assessment report (financial offer) using the unit rates of the initial contract. In order to reinforce this, we even removed the FIDIC provision that would have allowed the contractor to refuse implementing a variation under certain circumstances as we felt this could have interfered with the use of discretionary powers of judgments, which had to be retained for the contracting authority in a public procurement procedure. This way we all agreed that the resulting outcome could not modify the overall nature of the initial contract. Moreover, we considered that there would have been no guarantee that in the case of a negotiated procedure with the incumbent contractor outside the contract, the contractor, being in fact in a monopoly position, would have offered lower unit rates than in the initial contract.

Variations versus claims

As the contractor enjoys some freedom under FIDIC forms of contract, interfering with this freedom is likely to have a cost and schedule impact; FIDIC contracts therefore do not only manage modifications in the form of variations but also in the form of claims. Consequently, we needed to adopt a methodology for differentiating the impacts of both in terms of public procurement rules, which the author recommends publishing for the sake of transparency as part of the initial call for tender documentation.

Variations generally concern future activities that are still to be performed. They are subject to the employer's prior approval and therefore discretion. Variations comprise changes and additions to the scope of the initial contract; they are therefore forward-looking. They presume prior agreement on cost and schedule based on the contractor's financial offer using unit rates obtained in the initial competitive procedure. Variations remain therefore being subject to public procurement constraints and may require a formal amendment to the contract unless they were foreseen in the initial contract and are covered by the initial contingency pot appropriated by the employer to variations.

On the other hand, claims fall under the category of public procurement exemptions due to the fact that they are generally related to past or current events or circumstances. The corresponding activities are being or have already been performed; therefore, they are retrospective. The employer has no discretion as to the consequences of the events or circumstances giving rise to a claim and therefore there is no presumption for a prior agreement on cost and schedule; claims are rather channeled into an incurred cost plus reasonable profit mechanism. Claims moreover do not change the scope of the initial contract and therefore never require a formal amendment to the contract, but may require the instruction of variations to overcome their consequences.

Claims as public procurement exemptions

Claims can be exempted from the application of public procurement constraints as FIDIC forms provide for a clear, precise, and explicit review clause foreseen in the initial contract. In addition, claims could also be characterized as non-substantial contract modifications as they meet the relevant conditions codified by Directive 2014/24/EU. Claims can be described as a predefined procedure for events or circumstances where the contractor becomes entitled to compensation in accordance with the initial contract: claims are the result of the risk allocation foreseen in the initial contract; therefore, they cannot modify the overall nature of the initial contract either. Moreover, the employer has no discretion as to determining or quantifying the contractor's entitlement as the eligibility and reasonableness of the cost incurred by the contractor and the corresponding evidence provided by the contractor are determined by the engineer in his role as certifier. Accordingly, modifications arising from the claim procedure are neither subject to monetary value limits imposed by Directive 2014/24/EU for certain types of permissible modifications.

Borderline cases

Notwithstanding the above, as the CJEU case law does not establish any special regime for modifications negotiated and agreed with a contractor as a result of a claim procedure, certain parts of the amounts awarded as a result of a claim procedure may still need to be considered as modifications subject to the public procurement constraints. Therefore, we had to adjust the claim procedure and follow the practice that: (i) each contractor's claim accepted for assessment by the engineer would necessarily result in an engineer's determination either as the engineer's decision or as a record of the parties' amicable agreement confirming the engineer's position; (ii) no settlement agreement could be entered into by the employer and the contractor within the claim procedure administered by the engineer (including as a result of the parties' consultation under Sub-Clause 3.5 [Determinations]); (iii) before such consultation would take place, either party would receive the engineer's draft determination, including his quantified assessment, which the parties could comment and endeavor to convince the engineer by referring to the requirements of the contract and the facts of the case to reconsider his position and/or adjust his assessment; and (iv) only if the contractor disputed the engineer's determination, the employer would be called upon to undertake a commercial review of the claim in an attempt to settle the corresponding dispute before it would be moved onto the dispute adjudication board. Any such commercial review would however be subject to the public procurement constraints.

Equally, claims under the public procurement exemptions could only be used in the narrow sense. As a general rule, no claims should have the purpose to cover up variations. For this reason, in our practice we found appropriate to pay special attention to the following cases: (1) if a notice of claim under Sub-Clause 20.1 [Contractor's Claims] were submitted by the contractor in relation to events or circumstances giving rise to a claim the effects of which would however only materialise in the future, the engineer would be required to proceed with an approval of the contractor's claim on the principle without waiting for a detailed claim to be received. If such an approval could confirm the modified technical requirements and the existence of the corresponding entitlement to additional cost and/or an extension of time for completion, the employer would be required to initiate a deviation notice procedure. Likewise, (2) if the employer (or the engineer) were aware of future events or circumstances giving rise to a claim, the employer (or the engineer on his behalf) could proceed with a variation, instead of waiting for a claim to arise (e.g., foreseen delay in the delivery of input data by, or on behalf of, the employer), provided that all information necessary to proceed with a variation would be timely available and the circumstances on which the corresponding variation instrument would be based would not likely to change (e.g., new, modified delivery date of input data).

Cost plus fee versus FIDIC

We consider introducing cost plus fee contracts with a target price as the standard FIDIC setup may not always be suitable for a first-of-a-kind research and development project that experiences, mainly due to the immaturity of the ITER systems design, a number of modifications the extent of which could not be foreseen at the outset. With respect to our existing contracts, however, we feel that any change to the pricing mechanism at this stage would be generally seen as substantial and non-permissible modification since the overall nature of the contract concerns the scope and content of the mutual rights and obligations of the parties, which are most prominently characterised by arrangements governing contract price, payments and the corresponding risk allocation. Therefore, introduction of a cost plus fee mechanism in existing contracts could only be permissible if such a mechanism was to apply to future unforeseen changes that could be instructed as variations. Due to the fact that FIDIC claims operate by default on an incurred cost plus reasonable profit basis, it is the author's view that any contract procedure channeled into the claims procedure, including the service order procedure in the

F4E contracts, could be replaced by a cost-reimbursable formula without modifying the overall nature of the initial contract. To this end, the cost definition provided by FIDIC should be substituted by provisions specifying the reimbursable type of costs and the method of determining it. Such a modification could then be seen permissible under the EU public procurement rules even if one may argue that with such a mechanism in place the FIDIC contract provisions (as to future claims and variations) would no longer be operable.

Dispute adjudication board

Our public procurement rules imposed on us one more constraint that we needed to overcome. As our contractors did not qualify as contracting authorities for the purposes of our public procurement rules, they could not enter into a dispute adjudication board service contract on the same side as the contracting authority employer, which on the other hand was required to let such contracts following public procurement rules. This was the reason why we needed to become alone responsible for establishing a single, permanent dispute adjudication board for the ITER construction, operating under all our contracts and the interface agreement. Accordingly, we entered into two-party contracts with the members of the dispute adjudication board. This had the consequence that the members of the dispute adjudication board, who were selected as a result of an EU-wide competition subject to our public procurement rules, had to be imposed on our contractors. In the absence of a contractual link between the members of the dispute adjudication board and the contractors, a recovery mechanism had to be introduced for the benefit of the employer in the case that the contractors would have failed to honour their obligations under any award of cost of the dispute adjudication board. This was a measure that warranted effective functioning of the dispute adjudication board all along the project.

In order to ensure the independence, fairness, and objectivity of the members of the dispute adjudication board: (i) objective quantitative criteria were defined and advertised by the employer based on EU law and industry best practice; (ii) compliance with which was verified at the dispute adjudication board service contract signature and was to be verified at each referral by either party of a dispute to the dispute adjudication board; (iii) each member of the dispute adjudication board was subject to a continuing liability to disclose, inform, and bring to the attention of the employer, the contractors and the other members of the dispute adjudication board any events or circumstances that might have called into question his independence, fairness, or objectivity; and (iv) only the dispute adjudication board had competence to decide on any such matters. In order to ensure effective independence of the dispute adjudication board from the employer, it was the chairman of the dispute adjudication board alone who was entitled (and obliged) to nominate one or three members of the dispute adjudication board to act as adjudicators in a dispute considering the parties' non-binding proposals. Yet, upon request of the contractor, members of the dispute adjudication board would have been required to provide a recommendation as to whether any member in the dispute adjudication board had been or would be brought into conflict with any of his undertakings or obligations, and whether such member should be recused temporarily or permanently from any adjudication.

In addition to the regular dispute-resolution function, the employer entrusted the dispute adjudication board also with a dispute-prevention function. Therefore, the members of the dispute adjudication board were invited to regularly visit the project site in order to become familiar and remain up-to-date with the progress of the works, and to encourage resolution of issues between the parties in meetings dedicated to each of the contractors and endeavor to prevent problems becoming disputes. One of such problems identified and successfully resolved concerned the effectiveness of communication channels and decision-making procedures among project stakeholders, including the employer, the engineer, the ITER organization and the contractors and the importance of their conciliation within the ITER building information modeling procedures, which facilitated to reinforce the collaborative management of interfaces among all these stakeholders.

Amicable settlement of disputes

Contrary to FIDIC forms of contract, in our contracts the amicable settlement procedure was placed before (and not after) adjudication. It was designed to provide a meaningful measure to the parties to resolve their dispute amicably. If dispute was constituted by either party, their high-level management representatives had to meet in person under the obligation to negotiate in good faith. The scope of the dispute, the legal arguments, the factual evidence and the remedy sought were fixed by the referring party at this stage for the purposes of the whole dispute resolution procedure. This procedure provided for a cooling-off period before the expiry of which no adjudication could be commenced. Discussions were held on a confidential and "without prejudice" basis.

Arbitration

Instead of an ad-hoc ICC arbitration, F4E, being an EU body, chose to have recourse to an Article 272 TFEU arbitration in its contracts. Therefore, the decisions of the dispute adjudication board could only be opened up by the CJEU unless they became final and binding. Although the CJEU's jurisdiction was based on an "arbitration clause," the CJEU's decision would take the form of a judgement rather than an award. Enforcement of those judgements would take place according to the same procedure that applies in the case of other judgements of the CJEU. The CJEU would follow its own rules of procedure and therefore the CJEU proceedings would be open proceedings (confidentiality would not apply in the sense as provided for in arbitration, for example, the judgment would be published). Moreover, as the CJEU could only interpret authentically EU law and it would not have the same prerogative as regards to national laws, assessment of the merits of a dispute by it would likely to be carried out in the light of the contractual provisions alone, which in turn strengthened the importance of the quality and the coherence of the contract documents, and recourse could be made to the applicable national law only if those provisions had not enabled the dispute to be resolved. Contrary to national laws, the CJEU arbitration would be a two-tier system as the Court of Justice would have the jurisdiction to review appeals limited to points of law in rulings of the General Court; appeals would not have however suspensory effect. Yet, there would be no possibility for the national courts of the Member States to review a CJEU judgment (neither from its merits nor from the procedural aspects) as it would neither fall under the scope of the 1958 New York Convention nor under the Brussels I Regulation. Therefore, national courts of the Member States could not refuse to give effect to a CJEU judgement on ground that the CJEU's jurisdiction was based on an arbitration clause that would be invalid under national law. On the contrary, such a judgment would be directly enforceable according to Articles 280 and 299 TFEU. As suspension of a CJEU judgment could only be granted by the CJEU itself, and non-compliance with a CJEU judgment would directly lead to national civil court enforcement proceedings, the choice of the final dispute resolution forum seemed to have effectively incentivized the parties to find amicable resolution of their disputes.

FIDIC for nuclear

Due to the major role played by the international supply chain in the nuclear field, FIDIC can provide them legal certainty abroad. FIDIC can also standardize multi-package and split-package projects as we can already see such a positive effect in the case of the UK new build projects. Since national climate mitigation efforts, for which nuclear remains a candidate, require significant amount of financing, it is expected that sustainable infrastructure will soon become a new asset class that will allow that clean technology projects be pooled and securitized. All of these will require standardization both at the level of financing and realising such projects. Consequently, it may become necessary that nuclear be represented in the global working-out of sustainable development efforts, for example, through the FIDIC Sustainable Development Committee as investors and funders are most familiar with FIDIC forms of contract: (i) a special form exists for Multilateral Development Bank–funded projects; (ii) Development Banks and other Climate Finance Institutions promote FIDIC forms; (iii) EU funding program and the European Investment Bank require FIDIC forms; and (iv) they are also popular in the emerging markets such as the Middle East where the nuclear new build boom is expected to happen. Nuclear new build projects may therefore need a standard form of contract, and as FIDIC is widely used in clean technology development projects, perhaps on the basis of FIDIC. However, such standard form customized for nuclear ought to, as a minimum, (i) incorporate proper project management and quality assurance and control tools and procedures, including promoting building information modeling to collaboratively manage interfaces in highly complex megaprojects; and (ii) consider cost-reimbursable type of options and alliancing models, which may be of great relevance in research and development and nuclear decommissioning and radioactive waste management projects. Yet, if nuclear received public funding and the project was subject to EU or equivalent public procurement rules, FIDIC could provide adequate tools and procedures to overcome the public procurement constraints through effectively differentiated variation and claim procedures combined with an "authorization to proceed" procedure and the negotiated procedure without prior publication with the incumbent contractor. Considering this, it is the view of the author that the ITER experience could become the Trojan horse for nuclear to FIDIC.

Karoly Tamas OLAJOS
Legal coordinator – ITER construction
Fusion for Energy
ITER worksite – Cadarache (France)

The views expressed herein are entirely those of the author and may not be regarded as those of Fusion for Energy.

References

Hartlev, K. and Liljenbøl, M.W. (2013). Changes to existing contracts under the EU public procurement rules and the drafting of review clauses to avoid the need for a new tender. *Public Procurement Law Review*. 2 (2013). Sweet & Maxwell.
ICC (2012). *International Court of Arbitration Bulletin*, 23(2) (2012).
Wyckoff, P.G. (2010). *Pratique du Droit de la Construction: Marchés Public et Privés*. Eyrolles, Paris.

Further reading

Cushman, R.F. (2011). *Proving and Pricing Construction Claims*. Wolters Kluwer, New York.
FIDIC (2000). *The FIDIC Contracts Guide* (1st Edition). FIDIC, Lausanne.
FIDIC (2011). *FIDIC Procurement Procedures Guide* (1st Edition). FIDIC, Lausanne.
Murdoch, J.R. and Hughes, W. (2008). *Construction Contracts : Law and Management*. Taylor & Francis, New York.

Websites

http://eur-lex.europa.eu
http://globalarbitrationreview.com
The Society of Construction Law, Delay and Disruption Protocol 2002. *Online*. Available at: http://www.scl.org.uk (accessed 3 May 2018).

9 Claims

9.1 Claims

Good contracts for construction works predefine mutual liability claims for the compensation of both parties, in particular, those that may arise from a delay or disruption in performance under the contract. Sound contracts also include a procedure that describes how to make and enforce a claim. Common examples of potential "claim" situations may include the project site being handed over later than foreseen at the tender stage, the tender documentation containing errors, and unforeseeable physical conditions leading to prolongation of construction. To avoid potential disputes, a contractual process of "mutual claiming" should be set up and observed.

An additional cost or delay (if any) caused by the employer, can become an additional payment to the contractor for performance under the contract (if claimed by the contractor). Examples include an extension of the insurance and the performance bank guarantee and unabsorbed time-related site and headquarters overhead cost (such as rentals for the project team offices). On the other hand, lack of standard or contractor's delay can lead to damage compensation or delay damages claimed by the employer.

The bases of claims are as various as construction projects are. For example, in developing countries, claims that are not common in more developed countries may be encountered. In the ICC case no. 10847 (2003) (ICC, 2012), the contractor argued that the employer breached its obligation to provide a telephone connection in time and that, when it did provide one, the telephone system gave a poor quality and unreliable service. The contractor claimed additional costs and an extension of time on these accounts. While the tribunal agreed that the employer was late in supplying a telephone system and that this would have caused disruption to the contractor, the tribunal held that the contractor could not expect service on a par with that in Western Europe or the United States. Consequently, the tribunal denied the contractor an extension of time and costs on account of the quality of the telephone service.

International Construction Contract Law, Second Edition. Lukas Klee.
© 2018 John Wiley & Sons Ltd. Published 2018 by John Wiley & Sons Ltd.

In the same case, the contractor further claimed that throughout the period of the works it suffered power outages which caused disruption and delayed completion. The contractor claimed that the employer was responsible for the same. The tribunal found that the power outages that occurred were worse than could have reasonably been expected and that, while the contractor had not shown the actual effect of such outages on the progress of the works, they adversely affected the contractor's progress and awarded the contractor an extension of time.

Mutual claiming is, in fact, a way to resolve mutual damages compensations while the project is still ongoing. A contractually prescribed assessment is used to estimate the costs; the contractor and the employer notify the claims to the contract administrator (to the engineer as per FIDIC) or to each other for further handling of them. Ideally, these claims should be quantified, submitted and invoiced on an ongoing (monthly) basis. The method of quantification should be described in the contract or agreed to by the parties.

To demonstrate that construction damages are a difficult area of the law, His Honor Ramsey (2006) commented on this subject as following:

> Burden of proof in any claim for damages usually rests with the party making the claim, the problems of establishing delay and disruption damages in international construction arbitration are felt most acutely by the contractor or, in the case of a sub-contract, by the sub-contractor. They may have suffered loss and expense, or may feel that they have, as a result of occurrences outside of their control or contractual responsibility. They may even consider that the employer is responsible for the delay. Nevertheless unless they can satisfy the applicable requirements of procedural and substantive law, they cannot recover compensation. So far as this goes, this may seem like a statement of the obvious; unless the claim can be established, it cannot succeed. But making out a claim for delay and disruption damages under a construction contract can be problematic.

According to the FIDIC forms, a claim implies a specific requirement raised by either of the contracting parties. Based on predefined situations in a particular clause or otherwise in connection with the contract, such a requirement must be notified to the engineer. The contract sets out a procedure for making a claim that must be followed for successful enforcement of the claim. On the contractor's side, the requirement is usually to extend the time for completion or to increase the price of work via an additional payment from the employer. The employer, on the other hand, usually requires an extension of the defects notification period or to decrease the price of the work via an additional payment from the contractor. A "claim" is a specific contractual procedure, distinct from a purely legal definition. However, entitlements to payment or damage compensation do inevitably overlap with the principles of the governing law. The actual legal status of a claim has to be evaluated on a case-by-case basis and stage of enforcement. This, however, does not relieve the contracting parties of the duty to follow contractual procedures whenever making a claim.

In the narrow sense, the word "claim" in the context of a common law construction contract is the assertion made by a party to a contract of an entitlement pursuant to the express provisions of the contract in question. However, in many countries, the word "claim" is interpreted to mean a civil action brought before a court of law.

In a construction project, it is important for the contractor to make the contract administrator and the employer familiar with a problem or with subsequent requirements to extend time for completion or increase in the price of the work as soon as possible to allow a fair and quick decision to be made. This helps to protect the employer, which then has more control over project costs and is able to make necessary adjustments to budget and use contingencies. The agenda as a whole comes from the contractual risk allocation to construction project participants. The ability to distinguish between the risks borne by the contractor and the employer further helps to avoid disputes.

It is also argued that the purpose of a claim is to provide the contractor with defensive mechanisms against arbitrary employer behavior, should the contractor's legitimate demands be refused. The employer is usually protected by time limits (and by related particular processes described below) within which the claim must be notified. An unwritten, traditional rule was that the contractor is subject to stricter and more formal claim procedures because the contractor is usually the best equipped (particularly in terms of human resources) for more aggressive enforcement of its requirements. Recent trends demonstrate the need to establish the same contractual rules and conditions of claim management for both the employers and the contractors. This trend is confirmed by the establishment of time bars for employer claims in the newest FIDIC forms 2017 edition, NEC4 contracts, and further forms to deal with "on-site realities." It seems there is no sound reason to distinguish employer and contractor compensation procedures within the contract. Contractual unification of claim procedures seems to be the only logical solution.

A claim is not a dispute. In fact, it is a method of avoiding disputes. Notice of a claim or of any requirement in general (whether by the employer or the contractor) cannot be perceived as an attack that must inevitably evoke a defense. It is an obligatory contractual requirement to be negotiated by the construction project participants. It is usually the employer who chooses this system as a part of the project management conditions by way of contract. If the contractor accepts this system, they are obliged to use it. In other words, the aim is to ensure that the significant issues that often lead to a price increase or extension of time are addressed and solved immediately (during the realization) and not after project completion.

Contractors frequently perceive claim procedures as unfair and unnecessary. The reason is that the contractor carries the burden of notifying, quantifying, documenting and proving the claims even if the claims arise out of events beyond their control. However, based on common law tradition, a notice of claim is a condition precedent for an additional payment or extension of time.

A notice of claim is ideally done via a letter signed by an empowered representative and delivered to the contract administrator (the engineer) in the form and by the period stated in the contract. In the recent case (under FIDIC P&DB/1999 Yellow Book) *Obrascon Huarte Lain SA v. Her Majesty's Attorney General for Gibraltar*

[2014] EWHC 1028 (TCC) the judge dealt with the form of a claim notice and established minimal requirements for a valid claim in the following way. The claim is (i) made by notice in writing to the engineer, (ii) the notice describes the event or circumstance relied on, (iii) the notice is intended to notify a claim for extension of time (or for additional payment or both) under the contract or in connection with it, and (iv) it is recognizable as a "claim." If the relevant information is transmitted from the empowered representative to the contract administrator (the engineer) and this can be proved, a notice of claim can be part of a record made at a meeting, if signed by the empowered representative and the contract administrator (the engineer). In some situations, a formal notice is not necessary as was held in the ICC case no. 10847 (2003) (ICC, 2012). In this case, the contractor claimed an extension of time and additional costs arising from a significant general increase in quantities that resulted from the contractor's purported acceleration of works. The tribunal considered that, while no formal notice of claim had been given, the notice provision to have been satisfied because the contract administrator (the engineer) would have been aware of the increase in quantities at the time they were incurred and had contemporary records of them.

Claim management is an integral part of project management in large construction projects worldwide. Contractors must understand that timely notices of claims are a necessary aspect of their routine work whenever FIDIC and similar forms are used. A situation may arise where the claims are not resolved "in time" according to the contract and may become time-barred. Late notice can lead to refusal to deal with claims by the contract administrator (or the employer) who can advise the contractor to initiate adjudication, litigation or arbitration for failure to follow formal procedures.

Compliance with claim management procedures will help to ensure that project participants cooperate. This will reduce the adverse impacts of all project-related risks (of the realized hazards) on the participants, as much as possible, and allow the project to be considered "successful" once completed. Claims are not positive things, but they can be efficiently avoided—particularly at the project preparation phase. In cases of ill-prepared projects, claims will become an unfortunate, daily routine. Most claims can be avoided by preparing clearly understandable and precise contractual documents.

The term "anti-claim management" is sometimes encountered. Following on from previous paragraphs, the primary "phase" allowing the use of anti-claim management is the tender preparation phase. Some countries have legal regulations dealing with claim management. For example, Germany uses the *DIN 69905 Standard* and the United States has *The False Claims Act* (31 U.S.C. §§ 3729–3733). The latter is also referred to as the "Lincoln Law." This is an American federal law that imposes liability upon persons and companies (typically federal contractors) who defraud government programs.

The listing of potential claims in the contract will facilitate claim management to reflect the original risk allocation. It is a general rule that if a risk of a specific hazard is allocated to one party, the other party can usually claim additional payment and/or an extension of time after risk realization.

Claims caused by deficiencies in tender documents
by James Bremen (UK)

Many major construction projects in the emerging markets are driven by the public sector. Those procurement processes are governed by procurement rules which very often have a two-stage process— technical qualification followed by commercial (i.e., price) evaluation. Far too often, the technical qualification phase is set at a low level, with the result that tenders are awarded to the lowest priced bidders whose technical qualifications are questionable. Bidding contractors are well aware of this "game" and accordingly approach pricing a job with the knowledge that very often the profitability of the contract will depend upon their ability to bring claims under it as they will have priced their bids as leanly as possible. Where contracts are often rushed to market (with the resulting inadequacies/deficiencies in the technical documentation that the contractor must price), the successful contractors often start to position their claims from day one. The poor quality of the specification and scope (and sometimes commercial documents) will often entitle the contractor to bring claims due to these deficiencies, as well as make it necessary for the employer to make any number of costly variations itself. In an environment where most state developers wish to avoid formal dispute resolution as much as possible, the result is protracted settlement negotiations at the end of projects. This approach is both highly inefficient and does not represent best value for money for developers and could be addressed through investing more time and effort in the preparation and execution of individual procurements.

James Bremen
Partner, Construction and Engineering
Herbert Smith Freehills
London
UK

9.2 Contractor's claims under FIDIC forms

The general definition of "claim procedure" is provided in Sub-Clause 20.1 of the 1999 FIDIC forms (the 2017 edition unified all claims procedures under the precisely structured Clause 20 - see also the chapter 12 for more detail). Procedures for claims for extensions of time for completion and/or for additional payment are laid down there. In general, contractor claims can be subdivided into two categories:

- those listed in the contract (*ex contractu*)—foreseeable events with corresponding article(s) in the contract; and
- others connected with the contract.

Claims for extensions of time for completion are defined specifically at Sub-Clauses 8.4 and 8.5. The option to raise a time claim is anticipated (under FIDIC CONS/1999 Red Book) where there is a variation to or other substantial change in the quantity, a cause of delay giving an entitlement to extension of time for completion under a particular Sub-Clause, exceptionally adverse climatic conditions, unforeseeable shortages of personnel or goods caused by an epidemic or governmental actions or any delay caused by the employer or authorities (meaning public administration authorities).

9.3 Employer's claims under FIDIC forms

The general definition of "claim procedure" is provided at Sub-Clause 2.5. The 2017 edition unified all claims procedures under the Clause 20. The claim is foreseen in the form of payment and/or an extension of the defects notification period. The employer's claims can also be subdivided into two categories:

- those listed in the contract (*ex contractu*)—foreseeable events with corresponding article(s) in the contract; and
- others in connection with the contract.

Employer's notices by Victoria Tyson (UK)

How important is it for an employer to give a Sub-Clause 2.5 notice under the FIDIC Red Book 1999 forewarning the contractor of a claim? Case law suggests that it is very important, unless the standard form has been amended.

Sub-Clause 2.5 details the steps an employer must take to bring a claim. The wording in Sub-Clause 2.5 is wide and applies to any claims the employer wishes to make. The employer must make such claims promptly and in a particularized form. Where the employer fails to raise a claim as required, the back door of set-off or cross-claims is firmly shut. These are the findings of the Privy Council in *NH International (Caribbean) Limited v. National Insurance Property Development Company Limited* ([2015] UKPC 37).

But, where specific reference to Sub-Clause 2.5 in a sub-clause has been omitted the employer may be excused from giving notice under Sub-Clause 2.5 despite its wide wording and the obvious desirability of such notice. Essentially, the Sub-Clause 2.5 notice provisions do not survive independently. These are the findings of the High Court in *J Murphy & Sons Ltd v. Beckton Energy Limited* ([2016] EWHC 607 (TCC)).

NH International (Caribbean) Limited v. National Insurance Property Development Company Limited

The case concerned two appeals from the Court of Appeal of the Republic of Trinidad and Tobago.

On March 6, 2003 a contract based on the FIDIC Red Book 1999 for the construction of a hospital in Tobago was entered into by National Insurance Property Development Company Limited (the "employer") and NH International (Caribbean) Limited (the "contractor") for an original Contract Price of TT$118 million.

The works commenced in March 2003 with an original completion date of March 2005. The contractor first suspended work in September 2005 and then terminated the contract in November 2006.

The disputes were referred to arbitration. Dr Robert Gaitskell QC was appointed as sole arbitrator in October 2005 and made five awards.

Two issues were challenged (i) the contractor's entitlement to terminate for the employer's failure to provide evidence of its financial arrangement under Sub-Clause 2.4 (which was decided in his second award), and (ii) the contractor's claim for financial losses arising out of the termination (which was decided in his third award).

In response to the contractor's claim for financial losses arising out of the termination, the employer submitted various counterclaims. The contractor argued that the employer's counterclaims were barred for a lack of notice under Sub-Clause 2.5. In fact, the first the contractor had heard of the counterclaims was during the arbitration proceedings!

Sub-Clause 2.5 is widely drafted. It states (with emphasis added):

> "*If the Employer considers itself to be entitled to any payment under any Clause of these Conditions or otherwise in connection with the Contract* ... the Employer or Engineer shall give notice and particulars to the Contractor ...
>
> The notice shall be given as soon as practicable after the Employer became aware of the event or circumstances giving rise to the claim ...
>
> The particulars shall specify the Clause or other basis of the claim, and shall include substantiation of the amount ... to which the Employer considers himself to be entitled. The Engineer shall then proceed in accordance with Sub-Clause 3.5 [Determinations] to agree or determine (i) the amount (if any) which the Employer is entitled to be paid by the Contractor ...
>
> This amount may be included as a deduction in the Contract Price and Payment Certificates. *The Employer shall only be entitled to set off against or make any deduction from an amount certified in a Payment Certificate, or to otherwise claim against the Contractor, in accordance with this Sub-Clause.*"

In November 2008 the arbitrator (Dr. Gaitskell) found that notice was not required for the employer's counterclaims because "*clear words are required to exclude common law rights of set-off and/or abatement of legitimate cross-claims ...*" and (by implication) the words of Sub-Clause 2.5 were not clear enough. The High Court (Claim No. CV2008-04998) and the Court of Appeal (Civil Appeal No. 246 of 2009) agreed.

This approach followed an established line of authorities including the *Interim Award in ICC Case 11813 (2002)* (ICC International Court of Arbitration Bulletin Vol. 24 No. 2), which noted that it is a well-established principle of English law that rights of common law and equitable set-off are not excluded in the absence of a clear contractual intention otherwise, and found that although the employer was in breach of Sub-Clause 2.5 there was no express language within the contract that excluded the employer's right to raise set-off. The employer was therefore permitted to raise by way of set-off its alleged entitlement to delay damages for delay.

The Privy Council took a different view. It said that the words of Sub-Clause 2.5 could not be clearer.

- Sub-Clause 2.5 applies to any claims the employer wishes to make (whether or not they are intended to be relied on as set-offs or cross-claims).
- The employer must make such claims "*as soon as practicable*" and in a particularized form. If the employer can rely on claims that were first notified well after that, there would be no point to the first two parts of Sub-Clause 2.5. Further, if the employer's claim is allowed to be made late, there is no method by which it could be determined, as the engineer's function

is linked to the particulars, which in turn must be contained in a notice, which in turn has to be served "*as soon as practicable.*"
- Where the employer fails to raise a claim as required, the back door of set-off or cross-claims is firmly shut in accordance with the final words of the Sub-Clause, which read "*The Employer shall only be entitled to set off against or make any deduction from an amount certified in a Payment Certificate, or to otherwise claim against the Contractor, in accordance with this Sub-Clause.*"

However, with reference to Hobhouse LJ in *Mellowes Archital Ltd v. Bell Products Ltd.* ([1997] 58 Con LR 22, 25-30) the Privy Council did concede that Sub-Clause 2.5 does not preclude the employer from raising an abatement—for example, that the work for which the contractor is seeking a payment was so poorly carried out that it does not justify any payment, or that it was defectively carried out so that it is worth significantly less than the contractor is claiming.

The third award was therefore remitted to the arbitrator (Dr. Gaitskell) with a recommendation that any sums, which (i) were not the subject of appropriate notification complying with the first two parts of Sub-Clause 2.5, and (ii) cannot be characterized as abatement claims as opposed to set-offs or cross-claims, must be disallowed.

The decision of the Privy Council came as a surprise to many and may not be followed in all jurisdictions. However, it was followed in the *Final Award in ICC Case 16765 (2013)* (ICC Dispute Resolution Bulletin 2015 No. 1). In that Eastern European arbitration, the employer had failed to comply with Sub-Clauses 2.5, 3.5, and 20.4 in respect of a counterclaim for delay damages under the FIDIC Yellow Book 1999. The tribunal considered these clauses to be "*mandatory and exclusive provisions of the Contract*" regarding its claim for delay damages. The employer was therefore contractually barred from bringing its counterclaim for delay damages in the arbitration.

J Murphy & Sons Limited v. Beckton Energy Limited

This case concerned an amended FIDIC Yellow Book 1999.

The works were delayed. The contractor (J Murphy & Sons Limited.) failed to reach a milestone and no extension of time was granted by the engineer (Capita Symonds). The employer (Beckton Energy Limited.) notified the contractor of its entitlement to delay damages with express reference to Sub-Clause 2.5. The employer, who was in financial difficulties at the time, then gave 23 days' notice of his intention to call on the bond for the contractor's failure to pay the delay damages within 30 days as required by a heavily amended Sub-Clause 8.7.

The contractor sought a declaration from the court that (i) the employer was not entitled to delay damages under the amended Sub-Clause 8.7 without agreement or determination by the engineer under Sub-Clauses 2.5 and 3.5, and that (ii) any call on the bond by the employer would be fraudulent (for which injunctive relief would then be sought).

The main distinguishing point in this case was that the FIDIC Yellow Book 1999 had been very heavily amended and reference to Sub-Clause 2.5 in Sub-Clause 8.7 had been deleted. The court therefore had to construe the effect of the deletion on Sub-Clause 2.5.

Mrs. Justice Carr found that while, on its face, Sub-Clause 2.5 was drafted in the widest possible terms (e.g., *NH International (Caribbean) Ltd v. National Insurance Property Development Company Ltd* [2015] KPC 37), in this case the right to delay damages under Sub-Clause 8.7

(as amended) was not subject to the engineer's determination under Sub-Clauses 2.5 and 3.5 for *(inter alia)* the following reasons:

- The wording *"subject to Sub-Clause 2.5"* had been deleted from the amended Sub-Clause 8.7. Objectively assessed on the facts, this selected deviation from the standard form was consistent with the parties' intention being not to make the employer's right to delay damages subject to Sub-Clauses 2.5 and 3.5.
- The amended Sub-Clause 8.7 set out a self-contained regime for the trigger and payment of delay damages.
- There were important and substantive differences between Sub-Clause 2.5 and the amended Sub-Clause 8.7, which were resolved if the amended clause was not subject to Sub-Clause 2.5. For example, amended Sub-Clause 8.7 referred to payment by way of deduction from the notified sum, whereas Sub-Clause 2.5 referred to payment by way of deduction from payment certificates.

As a result of this decision, where reference to Sub-Clause 2.5 in a sub-clause has been omitted and the employer believes he is entitled to payment or an extension of the defects notification period, the employer may now be excused from giving notice under Sub-Clause 2.5 despite the wide wording of Sub-Clause 2.5 and the obvious desirability of such notice.

Mrs. Justice Carr's decision is consistent with the normal principles of freedom to contract where there are commercial parties of roughly equal bargaining strength. The English courts will not rewrite a contract.

The FIDIC Second Edition 2017

Is the FIDIC Second Edition 2017 likely to change any of this?

In it the employer's claims are dealt with in Clause 20 alongside the contractor's claims. Sub-Clause 2.5 deals instead with site data and items of reference.

Sub-Clause 20.2 states (with emphasis added):

> "*If either Party considers that he/she is entitled to any additional payment by the other Party* (or, in the case of the Employer, a reduction in the Contract Price) and/or to EOT (in the case of the Contractor) or an extension of the DNP (in the case of the Employer) <u>under any Clause of these Conditions or otherwise in connection with the Contract</u>, the following Claim procedure shall apply:
>
> 20.2.1 *The claiming Party shall give a Notice to the Engineer* ....
> <u>If the claiming Party fails to give a Notice of Claim within this period of 28 days, the claiming Party shall not be entitled to any additional payment</u>, the Contract Price shall not be reduced (in the case of Employer as the claiming Party), the Time for Completion (in the case of the Contractor as the claiming Party) or the DNP (in the case of the Employer as the claiming Party) shall not be extended, <u>and the other Party shall be discharged from any liability in connection with the event or circumstance giving rise to the Claim</u>".

The wide wording referring to a party's entitlement to payment "*under any Clause of these Conditions or otherwise in connection with the Contract*" has not changed. If an employer does not give notice under Sub-Clause 20.2.1 of his entitlement to say, delay damages under Sub-Clause 8.8 of an un-amended FIDIC Second Edition 2017, (in the absence of fraud, deliberate default or reckless misconduct as expressly provided for in Sub-Clause 8.8) the contractor "*shall be discharged from any liability in connection with the event or circumstance giving rise to the Claim.*" This seems clear.

The philosophy behind the FIDIC Second Edition 2017 appears to have changed from 1999 edition, with the result that significantly greater importance is placed on the issuing of notices throughout the standard form contract to ensure certainty. The courts will have a choice: to hold employers to their notice obligations where FIDIC has so obviously presupposed a strict notice procedure as a matter of policy; or to liberate employers from such obligations where cause (for example, an insignificant oversight in the provision of notice) and effect (the other party being "*discharged from any liability in connection with the event or circumstance giving rise to the Claim*") are out of all proportion. In some jurisdictions the local law may provide for situations where the loss of an entitlement to claim is disproportionate to the loss suffered by the party to whom correct notice ought to have been given.

Conclusion

In summary, there is no excuse for poor contract administration. Employers should ensure that notices are given on time. It is obviously desirable for everyone to be kept fully informed and for problems to be avoided or mitigated where possible. However, where the standard form FIDIC Yellow Book 1999 has been amended by commercial parties of roughly equal bargaining strength so that it is not clear whether or not those parties intended for a notice regime to apply, such a regime is unlikely to be imposed given the very serious effect it may have on what could otherwise be good claims. It remains to be seen how the courts will interpret the new 2017 FIDIC forms edition.

Victoria Tyson
Director of Corbett & Co. International Construction Lawyers Ltd
UK

Claims in the St. Petersburg flood protection barrier construction by Aleksei Kuzmin (Russia)

Before I move on to my brief presentation of the use or rather misuse of the FIDIC conditions in Russia, I should make a small introduction into the history of the project that I will be referring to in my case summaries.

St Petersburg is a relatively young city. It was founded in 1703 by the Russian Tsar Peter the First, who was very intent on creating an Amsterdam of his own. However, just as the Netherlands, the landscape of the new capital turned out to be a low land prone to floods. Various ideas were used to protect the new city from this plague, starting from Peter the First's order to raise the ground level in the lowest parts of the new capital and including such useless endeavours as digging additional channels to duct the Neva river flow away from the centre of the city. Nonetheless, most of those projects failed, and only after the devastating flood of 1824, a prototype of the current barrier was devised and received proper consideration.

Unfortunately, due to the historical turbulence, lack of technical means, financial resources and political will for the implementation of this complex project, it had to wait until the 1960s to be approved by the Soviet government for detailed elaboration. It took another 20 years for the project to come to the pre-construction stage.

Between 1980 and 1990, the construction works on the barrier went at full swing. So when they were suspended because of various political and economic reasons in 1990, the northern half of the barrier had almost been finished. The four northern water sluices connecting the eight earth and rock dams were already operational by that time and the two construction pits for the future navigation channels had been fully ready for further construction works.

During the 1990s, the half-finished barrier was only maintained in stand-by mode and practically no construction activities were carried out. In 2002, after Mr Putin moved his career from St Petersburg to Moscow and came into office as President, the barrier finally got the chance of being completed in not such a distant future. The Russian government signed a loan agreement with the EBRD, which was later joined by the EIB and the NIB, and the project received the necessary financial support for the works to be resumed.

It took another decade to complete the barrier although initially the goal was to have it fully operational in 2008. Delays were mainly caused by the lack of as-built documents for the works carried out in the Soviet period, since some of them had been lost in the turmoil of the political changes in Russia, and by the need to replace a big volume of weak soils found in the construction area of one of the dams.

The completed barrier is 25 km long. It consists of eleven dams connected by bridges. There are six water sluices between the dams and two navigation channels. The sluices ensure continuous water flow from the delta of the Neva River into the Gulf of Finland and close when there is a forecast for the storm surge. Their structure and function resemble the Oosterscheldekering (Eastern Scheldt storm surge barrier) in the Netherlands.

The two navigation channels serve as the sea gates to the Port of St Petersburg. The bigger navigation channel is equipped with two large floating gates similar to those of the Maeslantkering storm surge barrier in the Netherlands and has a motorway tunnel under it which connects the two parts of the barrier. The smaller navigation channel is more of an emergency exit and a waterway for smaller vessels. It is not as deep as the first one and is only 110 meters wide. In case of a storm surge warning, it is closed with a flat steel gate.

All three cases summarised below were related to the completion of this smaller navigation channel. The contractor's task included finishing the concrete works on the aprons and the central part of the channel and the viaducts of the bridge over it, welding together the steelworks for the gate body, and completing the installation of the necessary mechanical equipment and the bridge steel span. The tender for the works was awarded to a large construction corporation, Transstroy, which originated from the former Ministry of Transport Infrastructure Construction of the USSR.

The Employer for the completion of all outstanding works on the barrier was the Russian government, represented by its specialised ministries. At the beginning of the barrier completion project, the functions of the Employer were delegated to the State Committee for Construction, which was later replaced by the Ministry of Regional Development. The loan agreements with the European banks required the Employer to draft all tender documents and contracts for the works to be completed on the basis of the FIDIC books.

The contracts mentioned below were all based on the Red FIDIC book. However, the Yellow book was also used by the Employer for one other contract.

Case 1

This case was initiated by the Contractor's claim for an extension of time which was rejected by the Employer. The Contractor became entitled for an extension of time on several grounds. To begin with, the Contractor encountered unforeseeable ground conditions at the stage of opening the channel to the sea. The cofferdams of the construction pit turned out to contain heavier and larger rocks than the Contractor expected, and the Employer had not been able to include that information in the tender documents for the lack of as-built documentation lost during the 1990s.

Although the Contractor had followed all necessary procedures required by Sub-Clauses 8.4 and 20.1 of the Red Book, the Engineer did not go further than informing the Contractor that he would send a request to the Employer about this problem. The Contractor tried to solve the problem by buying and importing special equipment. However, this process took almost half a yeardue to the specificity of the equipment required.

The works were further delayed by the time limits of the navigation period since the extraction of the rocks had to be performed from water. The size and weight of the rocks contributed to an additional delay of over four months. As a result, the Contractor's entitlement to an extension of time amounted to over ten months, which could be prolonged by an additional period of almost half a year due to several delays in payments by the Employer.

From the facts of the case one can infer that the relationship between the employer and the contractor was not idyllic as 10 days after the original completion date of the works under the contract the employer held a meeting and ordered the suspension of works for an "inventory check" of the works completed. The contractor received corresponding instructions with a letter from the engineer and suspended the works in accordance with Sub-Clauses 8.8 and 8.9. As a result, the contractor became entitled to another extension of the time for completion, amounting to 236 days. However, these extra days were not included in the claim brought to the attention of the court.

Further evidence of complicated relations between the parties to the contract is that they failed to appoint the DAB under Chapter 20 of the contract which is why the dispute ended up in court. The court of appeal ruled in favor of the contractor and extended the time for completion by 505 days as the contractor had pleaded. One could say that the contractor had tried to mitigate the problem, judging from the chronicles of the first two cases. Having lost Case 1 in the court of first instance on June 22, 2009, the contractor only submitted his appeal on August 12, 2009, received positive resolution on

September 8, 2009 and claimed additional payment on October 8, 2009. The Case 2 summary is below.

Case 2

Case 2 is in fact the continuation of Case 1. The employer refused to pay for the works completed by the contractor claiming that there were defects and the completion of the works had been delayed by the contractor. The employer also considered itself entitled to damages. However, the court decided in favor of the contractor, taking into account the resolution in Case 1 and noting that under Russian law, damages must be proven with substantial evidence. The liquidated damages referred to by the employer (or "pre-estimated damages" as they were put in the Russian translation of the FIDIC contract conditions used during the drafting of this particular contract) are not recognized as such under Russian law, but are rather closer to the concept of a "penalty" in the Russian legal system.

Case 3

Case 3 is especially interesting as here we find the contractor mentioned above as the defendant. Case 3 arose from a dispute between the contractor and its subcontractor. The subcontractor pleaded that he was entitled to the payment of works (about US $650,000) accepted by the contractor under the forms KS-2 and KS-3—these are in fact old, Soviet-style accounting documents, dating back to 1972, but revised in 1999 and still used in construction in Russia, stating which works have been completed under the contract during a certain period and their costs. They can be used under a contract based on FIDIC conditions, but should not be confused with taking over certificates. In Russian, their title is "Act of Delivery and Acceptance of Works/Services," which usually means that, by signing them, the employer accepts the quality and amount of works delivered and must therefore pay for the works in full as stated in the form. If the employer has objections, he should refuse to sign the form and state, in writing, the reason of his refusal. The courts interpret the forms as evidence of the delivery of the works by the contractor and their acceptance by the employer. Since the works mentioned above and other works had been accepted by the contractor, the subcontractor also considered himself entitled to the retention money withheld (about US$4.5 million) and to the use-of-money interest (about US$0.5 million).

The contractor contested those claims by a reduction of the subcontractor's remuneration for the additional works done by the subcontractor (about US$2 million), claiming that the additional works had not been agreed to by the contractor, and by LDs of about US$2 million due to delays in the completion of the works.

The court, as is often the case in Russia, started by considering the essential conditions of the contract and ruled that the contract had not been concluded since the time for completion was not stated properly in the contract (according to the *Russian Civil Code*, it must be expressed either with calendar dates or through an inevitable event). Therefore, the Contractor was obliged to pay for the works delivered by the subcontractor as, "according to the *Russian Civil Code*, Art. 711, the only grounds for the payment of completed works is the delivery of their result to the employer," and to release the retention money in full. However, since the contract had not been concluded, the court found no grounds under Russian law for the use-of-money interest calculated in foreign currency. The court further decided that the interest as a penalty did not correspond to the consequences of the breach of contract and decreased it by half.

Aleksei Kuzmin
PhD researcher
EUI
Russia

9.4 Lapse of claim

Contracts often contain a provision stipulating time limits within which the claims must be notified. These claims are subject to a sanction should they be notified late. A claim that is notified late is referred to as being lapsed ("time-barred"). For example, the 1999 FIDIC forms stipulate as follows:

> If the contractor considers himself to be entitled to any extension of the time for completion and/or any additional payment, under any Clause of these Conditions or otherwise in connection with the contract, the contractor shall give notice to the engineer, describing the event or circumstance giving rise to the claim. The notice shall be given as soon as practicable, and not later than 28 days after the contractor became aware, or should have become aware, of the event or circumstance. If the contractor fails to give notice of a claim within such period of 28 days, the time for completion shall not be extended, the contractor shall not be entitled to additional payment, and the employer shall be discharged from all liability in connection with the claim. Otherwise, the following provisions of this Sub-Clause shall apply.

Precedents in respect of the admittance and status of contractually time-barred claims are ambiguous across different jurisdictions. Despite this, the common opinion prevails that the aim of such provisions is to solve claims in a timely and transparent manner. The failure to follow formal procedures may lead to a situation in which the defendant may refuse to deal with the claims and refer the other party to litigation or arbitration. Every particular time-barred claim must be evaluated individually and in respect of the particular delivery method adopted, the related risk allocation, the nature of the claim and the relevant governing law.

9.4.1 Risk allocation and claims interconnections

Where a risk is allocated to one party, the other party may, once the risk is realized, claim an additional payment or extension of time for completion (or extension of the defects notification period on the employer's side). In general, four basic risk allocation "modes" with related claiming options can be distinguished, depending on the individual delivery methods:

- *General contracting mode*: Used when public infrastructure projects are implemented, in underground projects, or—in general—where there are very few foreseeable and controllable risks. Design risks are borne by the employer. The risks must be allocated reasonably and it is recommended to allocate the risk to the party which can best manage it. Therefore, it is necessary to allow "claiming upon realization" of the other party's particular risk.
- *Design-build mode*: Used in the realization of all projects—regardless of type. The contractor is responsible for design and construction and the risks must be allocated reasonably—particularly in respect of the project and its respective risk analysis. Even in DB projects, the priority must be to allocate the risk to the party which can best manage it. Claims must be allowed upon realization against the other party's particular risk.
- *EPC mode*: In EPC projects the lion's share of risk is typically allocated to the contractor. The contractor is therefore obliged to scrutinize the tender documents (including layout, design, and the like) and is responsible for almost all related errors. The contractor must also verify all on-site conditions and is responsible for any complications caused by adverse hydrological and geological conditions. The contractor usually has limited claim options and, therefore, the use of this approach is only appropriate for certain construction projects. In particular, those that allow enough time to appropriately scrutinize the tender documents and inspect on-site conditions. The contractor must price such projects with a substantial risk surcharge and the employer must understand and accept this surcharge.
- *CM mode*: The nature of a particular contract and employer priorities are key factors in terms of risk allocation and claims options under the CM mode. The CM mode can be applied to projects of all types including building, civil engineering, and EPC projects (the EPCM delivery method in such case). Direct contracts between the employer and individual prime contractors must allocate risk in an appropriate way and include the related claiming admission. By having no contractual responsibility for contractor performance, the construction manager may also act on the employer's behalf while dealing with the claims. The method the construction manager will apply to deal with these claims and the way the risks are allocated between the construction manager and the employer (including the mutual claiming options) must be appropriate for a particular construction project. The contract between the construction manager and the employer is usually in the form of a professional service agreement. However, it is still recommended to arrange the risk allocation and claiming options in line with standard construction contract forms (even where the CM-At-Risk approach is used).

9.5 Cause of the claim

It is essential to identify the material substance of a claim (the cause) whenever analyzing a lapse of this claim. The following are typical causes of contractor claims for additional payment or extensions of time for completion within large construction projects:

- *Employer delay.* For example, when providing a design, in approving a necessary document, in giving a necessary instruction, in handing over the site or obtaining required permission.
- *Errors in tender documents* such as defective setting out, design errors, errors in site data.
- *Employer obstructions.* For example, during tests, during the taking over of work
- *Unforeseeable conditions* such as unforeseeable physical conditions on site, unforeseeable forces of nature.
- *Consequences of employer risks.* Exceptional events (*force majeure*), such as a war, terrorism, unrest, strike, radiation and contamination, natural disasters.
- *Shared risks* such as extremely adverse climatic conditions and delay caused by third parties (authorities).
- *Other delays or disruptions* of the construction process with an employer's risk, such as archaeological findings, suspension instructed by the employer, site handed over not free of third parties rights (public and service utilities and the like), project termination consequences.

9.6 Limits of the lapse of claim

Due to differences in particular legal systems, it is important to analyze the limits for a potential lapse of claim in case of a failure to notify within the period prescribed in the contract. Whether the claim becomes time-barred or not depends mainly on the contract itself and governing contract law. In civil law countries, codified provisions may define:

- *Limitation of damages.* The governing law will sometimes include a provision, which excludes to cap the damages. Time bars applicable to claims could be interpreted as damages limitation (or as unfair penalty clauses or waivers) and may be deemed invalid.
- *Employer delay.* Another limit is the employer's delay. If damage (or late notice of claim) is caused by an employer's delay, this could imply a claim lapse limit because, as a general rule, nobody can profit from something caused through fault of their own. This is a relevant civil and common law doctrine. Under common law, the "prevention principle" is a long established rule whereby a party may not enforce a contractual obligation against the other party where it has prevented the other party from performing that obligation. The prevention principle is similar to the principle that no party may benefit from its own breach of contract (civil law).
- *Compliance with good manners and good faith protection.* In civil law countries, any conduct must be in compliance with good manners and honesty. Therefore, the claim lapse provision and consequences of late notification of a particular claim must be honest and in compliance with good manners and the principle of good faith.
- *Other mandatory, general provisions* prescribed by governing law.

In common law jurisdictions: (1) time bars are enforceable on the basis of contractual agreement—under FIDIC Sub-Clause 20.1 notice is a condition precedent to the right to recover either time or money; and (2) a party should not benefit from its own breach of contract (prevention principle).

In civil law countries, one has to evaluate what the following provisions (FIDIC Sub-Clause 20.1) really mean in law: "the Time for Completion shall not be extended, the Contractor shall not be entitled to additional payment, and the Employer shall be discharged from all liability in connection with the claim … "

There are three general interpretations available. First, time bars could be seen as a so-called "contractual preclusion." Preclusion cannot usually be agreed to contractually in civil law countries. Second, a time bar could be seen as a contractually agreed modification of limitation (prescription) period. In some jurisdictions this is valid and in others it is not. The third approach is that a time bar is simply a specific provision that has a different purpose and has nothing in common with the *Statute of Limitations*.

For example, according to Article 119 of the *Polish Civil Code*; "Periods of limitation may not be shortened or prolonged by a legal act." Since the *Statute of Limitations* cannot be contractually modified, the same principle should apply to a time bar. This can result in a Sub-Clause 20.1 time bar being deemed null and void.

Some recent civil law jurisprudence presents good examples:

- *Case 1*: The Appellate Court in Warsaw held that a FIDIC notice requirement is a contractual time bar and does not modify or offend *Statute of Limitations* rules. The court further stated that FIDIC forms are commonly used in the industry and constitute an integral part of the parties' freedom of contract. In terms of the notice of claim requirement, it is merely a precondition to arbitration and it is not contrary to Polish public policy.
- *Case 2*: The Regional Court in Warsaw ruled that the 28-day time bar contradicts *Polish Civil Code* provisions on the statute of limitations and is null and void in this respect; however, a contractor, despite lack of notice, does not lose their claims. The contractor is contractually liable for breach of contract (breach of a Sub-Clause 20.1 condition). Similar outcomes and court commentary have been encountered across a number of other jurisdictions.

Precedents from the common law domains are also inconsistent on the claim lapse issue; see, for example, *Turner Corporation Ltd (Receiver and Manager Appointed) v. Austotel Pty Ltd* (2 June 1994); (1997) 13 BCL 378 at 12 by Cole J., *Gaymark Investments Pty Ltd v. Walter Construction Group Ltd*[1999] NTSC 143; (2005) 21 Const LJ 71, *Multiplex Construction (UK) Ltd v. Honeywell Control Systems Ltd* [2007] EWHC 447 (TCC) and *Nat Harrison Associates, Inc v. Gulf States Utilities Company* 491 F.2d 578 (5th Cir. 1974).

The tribunal in the ICC case no. 10847 (2003) (as commented on in ICC, 2012) held that under Sub-Clause 53.4, a failure to notify a claim for additional payment does not bar the claim for additional costs but limits the amount that can be decided or awarded by the engineer or an arbitral tribunal, respectively, to sums, if any, which can be verified by contemporary records.

Sub-Clause 53.4 (FIDIC Red Book, 4th Edition, 1987) reads:

> If the contractor fails to comply with any of the provisions of this Clause in respect of any claim which he seeks to make, his entitlement to payment in respect thereof shall not exceed such amount as the engineer or any arbitrator or arbitrators appointed pursuant to Sub-Clause 67.3 assessing the claim considers to be verified by contemporary records.

Contemporary records have been held to mean records produced or prepared at the time of the event giving rise to the claim, whether by or for the contractor or the employer. As a practical matter this means that, in such a case, a party cannot rely on witness testimony alone to substantiate such a claim but must be able to justify it by means of contemporary records.

In one of the most significant common law cases, *Multiplex Construction (UK) Ltd v. Honeywell Systems* [2007] EWHC 447 (TCC), the court held that:

> Contractual terms requiring a contractor to give prompt notice of delay serve a valuable purpose; such notice enables matters to be investigated while they are still current. Furthermore, such notice sometimes gives the employer the opportunity to withdraw instructions when the financial consequences become apparent.

In England the trend still confirms that courts are prepared to enforce time bar clauses. See, for example, *WW Gear Construction Ltd v. McGee Group Ltd*. [2010] EWHC 1460 TCC and *Steria Ltd v. Sigma Wireless Communications Ltd*. [2007] EWHC 3454 (TCC). In Germany, the Sub-Clause 20.1 time-bar is seen as ineffective according to §9 AGBG (German Standard Form Contract Act) because it is inappropriately prejudicial to the contractor (Kus, Markus, and Steding, 1999).

Construction claims in the UK by Garry Kitt (UK)

In the UK, the courts (albeit with some reluctance) continue to support the doctrine of condition precedent. In *Bremer v. Handelsgesellschaft mbH v. Vanden Avenne Izegem* P.V.B.A [1978] 2 LLR 109, the House of Lords stated that a notice provision was unlikely to be a condition precedent unless "it prescribed a specific time for delivery of the notice and clearly stated that the rights would be lost in the event that notice was not given." Separately, in *City Inn v. Shepherd Construction* (2003) CILL 2009, the Inner House of the Court in Session confirmed that a properly drafted condition precedent clause would be enforceable.

The concept of "prevention" is based on the universally accepted proposition that a party to a contract is not entitled to benefit from its own breach. Accordingly it operates to defeat the employer's claims for, say, delay damages if, by its own acts or omissions, the employer has prevented the contractor from completing its work by the date for completion, and, as a consequence time becomes "at large".

To protect the employer's right to claim delay damages and to avoid the time for completion to be declared "at large," the contract makes provision for the contractor to seek an extension of the time for completion if the employer is responsible for the delay incurred by the contractor (see FIDIC Sub-Clause 8.4(e)).

The issue with the (FIDIC Sub-Clause 20.1) condition precedent to the contractor's right to claim for an extension of time, is that if the contractor fails to comply with the stated time bar, then their right to claim for additional time will be forfeit, and the question therefore arises as to whether the employer will then still be able to claim delay damages (and arguably rely on its own default).

The above matter was considered in 1999 in the case of *Gaymark Investments Pty Ltd v. Walter Construction Group* [1999] in the Northern Territory of Australia, where the court held that the "prevention principle" took precedence over the notification provisions, notwithstanding the fact that such provisions had clearly been drafted as a condition precedent. The employer was accordingly not allowed to claim for (delay) damages and the contractor was not deprived of their right to claim for an extension of time in spite of their failure to serve a valid notice.

This judgment has prompted a divided opinion as to whether the same principles should be applied in England and Wales and other common law jurisdictions. It has been argued that a similar approach might be adopted, whereas others have rejected the reasoning of the court in *Gaymark*.

In a number of jurisdictions, public policy, and/or mandatory provisions of the law place weighted emphasis on the concept and practice of "good faith" within commercial contracts. Good faith is difficult to define, though in the UK it is settled law that a party to a contract cannot benefit from its own breach. English courts have said (*CIA Borcad & Panona SA v. George Wimpey & Co* [1980] 1 Lloyd Rep 598) that

> it is a principle of Fundamentals justice that if a promisor is himself the cause of the failure of performance, either of an obligation due to him or of a condition upon which his own liability depends, he cannot take advantage of that failure.

At first glance, the above proposition may not be helpful in the context of mere failure by the contractor to satisfy the 28-day time bar for notification as required by Sub-Clause 20.1. However, circumstances where the claim would otherwise be patently admissible and derived from default by the Employer are clearly another matter. In the United Arab Emirates, Article 246 of the Civil Code provides: "a contract must be performed in accordance with its contents and in compliance with the requirements of good faith." Elsewhere the same code states: "the exercise of a right is considered unlawful in the following cases":

- If the sole aim thereof is to harm another person.
- If the benefit it is desired to realize is out of proportion to the harm caused thereby to another person.
- If the benefit it is desired to realize is unlawful.

Although the contractual obligation to comply with the Sub-Clause 20.1 time bar is likely to be enforced by the engineer (who is obliged to administer the contract on its terms), the conduct of the employer is of fundamental importance when such enforcement by the engineer could circumstantially amount to a breach of the employer's good faith obligations.

If the employer is aware in advance (of the expiry of the time bar) of the event giving rise to the contractor's claim, then having regard to its good faith obligations, the employer may not be able to rely on the contractor's failure to give notice as required by Sub-Clause 20.1.

Gary Kitt
Regional Head of Contract Solutions, Europe
Arcadis
London
UK

9.6.1 Evaluation of a particular lapse of claim

Every individual lapse of claim must be evaluated as a separate case in respect of the delivery method and related risk allocation, material substance of the claim and the limits imposed by governing law.

It should also be noted that it may be difficult to determine the point in time at which the claim lapse period starts running. Some events are difficult to identify as they occur during the course of a construction project and their onset will therefore remain unknown. Furthermore, under FIDIC, the notice shall be given as soon as practicable, and not later than 28 days after the party became aware, or should have become aware, of the event or circumstance, in respect of the possibility and ability to consider and evaluate the right to claim. In the recent case (under FIDIC P&DB/1999 Yellow Book) *Obrascon Huarte Lain SA v. Her Majesty's Attorney General for Gibraltar* [2014] EWHC 1028 (TCC) the judge answered the question when the 28 days do (under Sub-Clause 20.1) start to run. The judge concluded that the entitlement to an extension of time arises if, and to the extent that, the completion "is or will be delayed" by the various events. He mentioned that the extension of time can be claimed either when it is clear that there will be delay (a prospective delay) or when the delay has at least started to be incurred (a retrospective delay). He added that the wording in clause 8.4 is not "is or will be delayed whichever is the earliest" so that notice does not have to be given for the purpose of Sub-Clause 20.1 until there is actually delay although the contractor may give notice with impunity when it reasonably believes that it will be delayed.

Many times, even a time-barred claim can be pursued through litigation or arbitration. However, the failure to make use of contractual claiming procedures may mean embarking upon the hazardous, complex, and potentially costly road of litigation or arbitration. The one who does not follow the contractual procedures may be further liable for damages due to a breach of contractual obligations.

Condition precedent and time-barred claims under Polish law by Michał Skorupski (Poland)

There is a notable debate nowadays in Poland concerning conditions precedent for claiming. A recent decision of the Court of Appeals in Warsaw of March 14, 2013 (VI ACa 1151/2012) ruled, that the 28-day notification period in relation to Sub-Clause 1.9 of the FIDIC contract conditions shall be calculated not from the date of the event or circumstance but from the date when the contractor had become aware of the fact of suffering additional cost from late delivery of a drawing or instruction. The court seems to have favored the line of reasoning of the contractor, that it was not the lack of information itself (wrong drawings in the first place), but lack of proper cooperation of the employer and the engineer in solving the problem which ultimately had led to additional cost and delay.

Unfortunately, employers consequently try to escape their contractual responsibility of providing proper designs of the works and typically their engineers determine that the contractor had to analyze the documentation with due care soon after notice of commencement. Thus, the 28 days are counted from the commencement date. Furthermore, a typical EU-subsidized contract contains stipulations that "the contractor has acquainted himself with the drawings and specifications, is satisfied with their quality and will not claim in this regard"—or similar. Fortunately, in several decisions, such clauses have been ruled to have no effect, as the contractor in an employer's design contract cannot be deemed to perform the role of a design verifier. This is the sole responsibility of the employer—according to the courts so far (see the award of March 6, 2013 of the National Appeal Chamber for Public Procurement, file: KIO 411/13, or the award of the Court of Appeals in Katowice of October 18, 2013, file: ACa 272/13). Unfortunately, the practice of using such provisions as quoted above still exists.

Nevertheless, the debate on condition precedent is far from over. There are many construction lawyers who argue that Article 118 of the Polish Civil Code determines the limitation period for construction claims to be three years from the event or circumstance, and the freedom of contracts cannot take priority over this statutory rule because of Article 119 of the Polish Civil Code that reads "limitation periods cannot be shortened or extended by legal action." Usually, the more the given lawyer's client forgets to notify the engineer about the circumstances in due time, the more entitled they feel to quote the Polish Civil Code afterwards.

Time limits for claims under Sub-Clause 20.1 can be seen as shortening the limitation period. This opinion was confirmed in the judgment of the District Court in Warsaw on July 13, 2011 (file: XXV C-701/10) and also on June 11, 2012 (file: XXV C-567/11) including the confirmation by the Court of Appeals (on March 20, 2013; file No. VI ACa-1315/12), where it was ruled, that the respective part of Sub-Clause 20.1 is invalid under Polish law. The argument being that: "There is no reason to assume that the scope of freedom of contract goes so far as to allow for free creation of contractual deadlines causing the extinction of claims related to property, in particular, where such claims are subject to statutory regulation on limitation."

On the other hand, there are several awards of the same court stating the opposite. For example, in the judgments of June 6, 2012 (file: XXV C-1215/10), of March 7, 2012 (file: XXV C-249/11) and of April 30, 2013 (file: XXV C-355/10). In the latter case it was argued that:

> In accordance with the general principle of freedom of contract stated in the Article 353 [1] of the Polish Civil Code it is possible to contractually agree a period of time after which the creditor's claim expires. This is not contrary to the Article 119 of the Polish Civil Code. The effects and functions of time bars and periods of limitation are different.

In conclusion, until some firm, Supreme Court precedent is in place, there remains great uncertainty in this area of the law. Therefore, it is highly recommended to strictly observe the notification periods provided in the given contract.

Michał Skorupski
Contract Manager
Member of SIDiR
Association of Consulting Engineers and Experts in Poland
Poland

Australian position on time bars by Andrew P. Downie (Australia)

Time bars are commonly used in construction contracts. Generally speaking, time bars stipulate the giving of notice of a claim, or a foreshadowed claim, by a certain time: in default of the stipulation, the person making the claim, which ought to have been the subject of the notice, loses the right to do so. In this vignette, the person obliged to give the notice is referred to as the claimant, and the person to receive the notice is referred to as the recipient.

In Australia, the courts consider time bars to have important purposes, including:

1. to enable a claim to be investigated promptly and perhaps before any work comprised in it is rebuilt or built over; and
2. to enable the recipient to monitor its exposure to the claimant, and if the recipient is a head contractor, to enable it to assess its own position with respect to the principal (*John Goss Projects v. Leighton Contractors* (2006) 66 NSWLR 707).

A contractual provision will only be effective as a time bar where the provision makes it clear that if a claim for relief is not made or notified within a particular period or by a particular time, no claim may be made thereafter.

Construing time bars

The courts must be cautious in construing time bars in construction contracts because no case is decisive on the meaning of a particular clause in a contract: it is the words used in the relevant clause or clauses that are decisive (*Opat Decorating Service (Aust) Pty Ltd v. Hansen Yuncken (SA) Pty Ltd* (1995) 11 BCL 360 at 363). However, there are many examples of standard form contracts in the construction industry, and in construing particular terms of a standard form contract a court should generally follow a construction established in previous cases unless that construction is plainly wrong or the context requires a different meaning (*Dunlop & Sons v. Balfour, Williamson & Co* [1892] 1 QB 507; *Toyota Motor Corp Australia Ltd v. Automotive, Food, Metals, Engineering, Printing & Kindred Industries Union* (1999) 93 IR 95 at [60]). It is therefore reasonable to expect that where a court construes a particular time bar to have one meaning, when that time bar arises for reconsideration, the same meaning will be given to it unless the context requires otherwise.

Examples of common time bars

Four prominent examples of time bars considered by the courts are set out below. The first is NPWC Edition 3 "residual" Clause 47:

> The Contractor shall not be liable upon any claim by the Sub-Contractor in respect of any matter arising out of this contract unless the claim, together with full particulars thereof, is lodged in writing with the Contractor not later than fourteen (14) days after the date of the occurrence of events or circumstances on which the claim is based or written notice of intention to make the claim specifying the nature of the claim is lodged with the Contractor within that time and the claim, together with full particulars thereof, is lodged in writing with the Contractor not later than fourteen (14) days before the issue of the Final Certificate under the Head Contract.

The New South Wales Supreme Court considered this clause in *Jennings Construction Ltd v. QH&M Birt Pty Ltd* [1986] 8 NSWLR 18. There, the appellant was a builder and the respondent an earthworks subcontractor. An arbitrator decided that the respondent was entitled to payment for work in creating materials for the particular level of compaction required under the contract, and the work involved in creating the materials was not specified in the contract. On appeal, Smart J held that claims for this work ought to have been notified, and the decision was remitted to the arbitrator for reconsideration.

This clause, together with a specific extension of time clause, were considered by the Full Court of the Supreme Court of South Australia in an appeal on a preliminary issue in *Opat Decorating Service (Aust) Pty Ltd v. Hansen Yuncken (SA) Pty Ltd* (1995) 11 BCL 360. There, the court held that compliance with the clause was mandatory, and it was a condition precedent.

Second, the bespoke clause in *John Goss Projects v. Leighton Contractors* (2006) 66 NSWLR 707:

> 45.1 Notwithstanding any other provision of the Works contract to the contrary, [the Principal] will not be liable upon any claim by the Contractor in respect of any matter arising out of the Works Contract or otherwise but not limited to variations to the work under the Works Contract and claims for damages unless: (a) the claim together with full particulars thereof is lodged in writing with [the Principal] not later than ten (10) Business Days after the date the Contractor became aware or should have reasonably become aware of the occurrence of the events or circumstances on which the claim is based; or (b) written notice of intention to make the claim specifying the nature of the claim is lodged with [the Principal] within that time and the claim, together with all particulars thereof, is lodged in writing with [the Principal] before the Date of Substantial Completion.

In *John Goss*, a subcontractor served a payment claim on the contractor inclusive of $2 million of delay and disruption costs. The contractor responded with a payment schedule denying liability for the delay and disruption costs. The dispute was referred to adjudication (twice) and the subcontractor alleged that Clause 45 was void because it was inconsistent with the rights in the New South Wales security for payment legislation, the Building and Construction Industry Security of Payment Act 1999 (NSW). McDougall J held that compliance with Clause 45.1 is a condition precedent of any claim over and above the contract amount, and acts as a bar to claims if the notice provisions are not followed.

Third, the bespoke contract in *City Inn Ltd v. Shepherd Construction Ltd* [2003] BLR 468:

> 13.8.1. Where, in the opinion of the contractor, any instruction, or other item which, in the opinion of the contractor, constitutes an instruction issued by the architect, will require an adjustment to the contract sum and/or delay the completion date, the contractor shall not execute such instruction (subject to Clause 13.8.4 [dispensation with requirement to give notice]) unless he shall have first submitted to the architect, in writing, within ten working days (or within such other period as may be agreed between the contractor and the architect of receipt of the instruction, details of [estimates of the adjustment, additional resources, length of extension of time, and loss or expense].
>
> 13.8.5. If the contractor fails to comply with any one or more of the provisions of Clause 13.8.1, where the architect has not dispensed with such compliance under Clause 13.8.4, the contractor shall not be entitled to any extension of time under Clause 25.3.

In *City Inn*, the contractor claimed to have been delayed and sought an extension of time. The architect allowed an extension of four weeks, and the question of entitlement was referred to an adjudicator who decided that the contractor was entitled to an additional five weeks. The principal claimed that the contractor did not comply with the notice provisions in Clause 13.8.1 and therefore they were barred from any entitlement as a result of Clause 13.8.5. The contractor argued that Clause 13.8.5 was a penalty because it caused the imposition of liquidated damages on failure of the contractor to give notice. The Scottish Court of Session held that the failure to comply with the notice provision did not amount to a breach of contract, but the clause gave the contractor an option to take certain action if they seek the protection of an extension of time in the circumstances in which the clause applies. Further, the requirement in Clause 13.8 was a condition precedent to it gaining an entitlement to claim an extension of time, and the contractor was barred from a claim.

Fourth, the standard form AS 2124-1978, Clause 40.2:

> If, in the opinion of the Contractor, compliance with the Superintendent's [variation] order, pursuant to this Sub-Clause, is likely to prevent him from or prejudice him in fulfilling any of his obligations (including guarantees) under the Contract, he shall forthwith notify the Superintendent thereof in writing, and the Superintendent shall as speedily as is practicable determine whether or not his order shall be complied with. If the Superintendent determines that his order shall be complied with, he shall also determine the extent to which the Contractor is to be relieved of his obligations under the contract and thereafter confirm his order in writing to the Contractor and such confirmation shall contain particulars as to the extent to which the Contractor is to be relieved of his obligations under the Contract.

This clause arose for consideration in *Wormald Engineering Pty Ltd v. Resources Conservations Co Internationals* (1989) 8 BCL 158 in which the superintendent made a number of variation orders and the appellant carried out these works and was paid the cost of the actual work done. However, the payments did not take into account the effect that the additional work would have on the contract, nor the costs of the cumulative effect of the dislocated work. The contractor did not make a written claim for these amounts pursuant to Clause 40.2. However, during arbitration, the appellant claimed around $400,000 in respect of additional costs resulting from the variations. The arbitrator held that Clause 40.2 was a condition precedent and rejected the claim. On appeal, Rogers CJ noted that the purpose of the clause was to give the respondent the opportunity to make an informed assessment about whether to require the variation to proceed, and that an action for breach of the requirement for notice would not be a satisfactory solution. Rogers CJ therefore confirmed the arbitrator's decision.

In respect of the time bar clauses discussed above, in each instance of judicial consideration, the particular court has held that the relevant clause imposes a condition precedent to a claim that ought to have been (but was not) the subject of the notice.

Consequences of failure to give notice

There are two potential consequences of non-compliance with the above time bars depending on their terms:

- loss of an extension of time for delay caused by the relevant event; and/or
- loss of the right to claim costs incurred for additional work or loss caused by the relevant event.

The failure to give notice pursuant to a time bar that otherwise enables the contractor to claim an extension of time will usually cause the claimant to be exposed to liquidated damages for the delay caused by the event that ought to have been the subject of that notice. Although a consideration of the "prevention principle" is beyond the scope of this vignette, it is sufficient to say that the modern position of Australian courts is that the failure of a claimant to issue a notice claiming an extension of time in respect of the recipient's preventing conduct is usually fatal to the claimant's argument that time is set "at large" by that preventing conduct (*Turner Corporation Ltd v. Austotel Pty Ltd* (1994) 13 BCL 378 and *Turner Corporation Ltd v. Co-ordinated Industries Pty Ltd* (1995) 11 BCL 202). Because of this, the failure to issue a notice could have a catastrophic financial impact upon a claimant.

Australian penalty doctrine and time bars

The High Court of Australia's decision of *Andrews v. Australia and New Zealand Banking Group Ltd* (2012) 247 CLR 205 has been regarded by some commentators as supporting an argument that time bars are unenforceable as penalties, thereby giving relief to a contractor who has not given the appropriate notice so as to avoid the time bar.

The High Court in *Andrews* reviewed the history of the penalty doctrine, clarified the Australian position on the penalty doctrine and expressed that it is not restricted to instances of breach of contract. The High Court arrived at a formula for the penalty doctrine as follows:

> In general terms, a stipulation prima facie imposes a penalty on a party ("the first party") if, as a matter of substance, it is collateral (or accessory) to a primary stipulation

in favour of a second party and this collateral stipulation, upon the failure of the primary stipulation, imposes upon the first party an additional detriment, the penalty, to the benefit of the second party. In that sense, the collateral or accessory stipulation is described as being in the nature of a security for and *in terrorem* of the satisfaction of the primary stipulation. If compensation can be made to the second party for the prejudice suffered by failure of the primary stipulation, the collateral stipulation and the penalty are enforced only to the extent of that compensation. The first party is relieved to that degree from liability to satisfy the collateral stipulation.

This decision was an appeal from a class action brought by bank customers over fees charged by a bank on the happening of certain events. The fees included "honor fees," "dishonor fees," "overlimit fees," and "late payment fees." The customers claimed that these fees were penalties and therefore unenforceable. The primary judge held that only the fees that arose from breach of contract, being the late payment fees, were capable of being characterized as penal, because the penalty doctrine is restricted to instances of breach of contract. On appeal, the High Court clarified that the penalty doctrine was not so restricted because of its foundations in equity in relieving from penal bonds.

The decision in *Andrews* appears to have caused the Australian position on the penalty doctrine to differ from the English position. The latter requires a breach of contract as a prerequisite to the doctrine applying (*ECGD v. Universal Oil Products Co and Ors* [1983] 2 All ER 205; *Cavendish Square Holding BV v. Makdessi* [2016] AC 1172).

As noted in *City Inn* above, the failure to give notice required by a time bar may not amount to a breach of contract, which was the primary reason why the relevant clause in *City Inn* was not considered to be a penalty. It has been suggested that the *Andrews* decision could cause many time bars to be held unenforceable because they appear to fit within the *Andrews* formula, above. That is, a time bar usually contains a requirement to give notice of a claim (said to be the primary stipulation), and usually provides for the loss of entitlement to claim if the notice is not given (said to be the collateral stipulation and additional detriment). This view has not received universal support. Also, given the decision in *City Inn*, and a number of Australian and English decisions that are to the effect that the penalty doctrine is not engaged where the entitlement that is lost is not yet accrued (e.g., *Bysouth v. Shire of Blackburn and Mitcham (No 2)* [1928] VLR 562 and *SCI (Sales Curve Interactive) Limited v. Titus Sarl* [2001] 2 All ER (Comm) 416), it is unclear to what extent this reformulation of the penalty doctrine could apply to a time bar that is drafted as a condition precedent.

Andrew P. Downie
Barrister
Melbourne TEC Chambers
Melbourne
Australia

The particular governing law will strongly influence time-bar–related issues. It is therefore very interesting to compare the opinions of lawyers from different countries at http://globalarbitrationreview.com. They were asked the following questions:

- How do contractual provisions that bar claims (if not validly notified) within a certain period operate (including limitation or prescription laws that cannot be contracted out of, interpretation rules, any good faith principles, and laws on unfair contractual terms)?
- What is the scope for bringing claims outside the written terms of the contract under provisions such as Sub-Clause 20.1 of the FIDIC CONS/1999 Red Book ("otherwise in connection with the contract")?
- Is there any difference in approach to claims based on matters that the employer caused and matters it did not, such as weather or ground conditions?
- Is there any difference in approach to claims for (a) extensions of time and relief from liquidated damages for delay and (b) monetary sums?

They responded thus:

- *Brazil*: Claims based on circumstances not validly notified are unlikely to be accepted by courts and arbitral tribunals. Contractual provisions containing such limitations do nothing more than set a time limit for those claims. Claims outside the written terms of the contract may be brought as long as the object of the claim has nexus with the main contractual relationship. A case-by-case analysis is therefore required. When it comes to weather and ground conditions, it depends on the terms of other clauses of contracts dealing with *force majeure* events. As for the last question, there may be an impact on liquidated damages for delay because the time bar may limit the chance of gaining relief. Monetary sums, if they have been agreed to previously, should not be affected, unless such claim is based on the fact that it took place after the period designated in the contract (Marcondes, Salla, Nakagawa, and Diniz at http://globalarbitrationreview.com).
- *England and Wales*: Normally such provisions are operated in accordance with their terms. However, they do constitute exclusion/limitation clauses and may therefore be subject to the *Unfair Contract Terms Act* 1977. As exclusion clauses, time bar provisions may be used against the party seeking to rely upon them (the authorities conflict on this) subject to the conditions that: (a) they can bar claims based upon causes of action outside the contract; and (b) there is no difference in approach depending upon whether the claims are based upon matters that the employer caused as opposed to matters that they did not or upon which the claim was made for an extension of time or payment of money. However, a strict approach to the interpretation of the clause could produce different results in different circumstances (e.g., the adequacy of a notice where the employer was the cause as opposed to where a third party was the cause) (Choat and Long at http://globalarbitrationreview.com).
- *France*: The effect of time-bar provisions will depend on the wording of the contract and the intention of the parties. Such clauses should, however, be exercised in good faith. In practice, French courts tend to give effect to contractual provisions that bar claims if they are not validly notified within a prescribed period. Courts have not drawn specific distinctions between claims based on matters that the employer caused and on matters it did not or between claims

for extensions of time and claims for additional payment (Gillion and Rosher at http://globalarbitrationreview.com).
- *Germany*: The parties are free to raise claims outside the express terms of the construction contract unless the contract explicitly limits recourse and claims to those explicitly listed in the construction contract. If the contract provides for a notification regime, failure to notify a claim within such regime will—as a general rule—preclude the claim from being pursued. Nevertheless, the notification requirements, their formalities and the extent of failing to comply with them may be dealt with by the "good faith" principles. For example, a party materially in default may be barred from relying on the objection that a default was notified too late or "technically" incorrect (Kremer at http://globalarbitrationreview.com).
- *Ireland*: Time bar provisions are effective and upheld under Irish law. Thus they are commonly found in Irish construction contracts. The standard Irish forms do not make express reference to the notification of a claim being a condition precedent to the contractor's right to recovery but they are commonly amended by the parties to include such a provision. The Irish Public Works contracts have very prescriptive time bar provisions and can extend to notification of "any other entitlement the contractor has under or in connection with the contract." Generally, the notification of both employer-caused events and natural events are dealt with in the same manner under Irish standard forms of construction contracts. Under the Irish public works contracts, a claim based on weather or ground conditions generally gives rise to an entitlement to an extension of time but not to monetary compensation. The Irish public works contracts provisions regarding notifications of claims and time bars are more prescriptive and stringent on claims for monetary sums as opposed to claims for extensions of time. Certain bespoke forms have equally stringent time bar provisions both in respect of claims for time and money—with both having been upheld by the courts (Killoran, O'Higgins, and Cooney at http://globalarbitrationreview.com).
- *Korea*: (1) Right to a claim can only be waived if such intent is clearly stated in writing under Korean law. However, notification provisions that bar claims if such claims are not validly notified within a certain period are generally enforceable. An exception may be if a court finds the existence of unavoidable circumstances based on the principle of good faith. (2) In order to bring claims from outside the scope of the contract, such claims need to be based on applicable laws and satisfy any statutory limitation provided under such laws. (3) Approach may be different based on a court's interpretation of the principle of good faith. (4) Claims for an extension of time can only be used as a defense against other claims and cannot be used as an affirmative claim for relief in Korea (Oh and Park at http://globalarbitrationreview.com).
- *Qatar*: Article 418(1) of the *Civil Code* stipulates that contracting parties may not agree upon a prescription period different to that prescribed by law. Denial of access to justice is also prohibited, under general principles of Qatari law. As such, one could argue that brief claims notification periods in construction contracts contravene the mandatory provisions of Article 418 and are therefore unenforceable as a matter of Qatari law. However, it could also be said that by agreeing to include such notice periods in a contract, the parties are waiving their

underlying rights, rather than waiving their entitlement to claim those rights (i.e., their right of access to court, which cannot be prescribed other than in accordance with the law). Much would depend here on the wording of the contractual provision in question. No claims may be brought under the contract other than those arising from the performance by the parties of their respective obligations as set out in the contract. A contractor has no right to claim against an employer for matters not caused by the latter, or for which the employer did not contractually assume the risk. Qatari law does not recognize the concept of an extension of time *per se*. Claims for EOT are not pursued to vindicate a stand-alone substantive right, rather they aim to achieve one or both of two principal objectives: (1) to defeat or minimize a demand for payment of compensation in the form of liquidated damages; or (2) to claim for prolongation costs. In principle, the right to claim an EOT—which, in essence, concerns compensation—can validly be prescribed by contract. Insofar as they relate to variations, claims for money (for additional work performed) cannot be so prescribed (Al Naddaf, Kelly at http://globalarbitrationreview.com).

Time bars under Kuwaiti law by Dina Al Ansary (Kuwait)

Construction contracts in Kuwait are governed by the Kuwait's Commercial Law No. 68 and Civil Code Law No. 67 of 1980. While these codes cover the general aspects of "muqawala" (works undertaken in return for a consideration), there are many aspects of construction contracts that remain uncovered and vague in relation to the legal codes.

The standard contract for public works (MPW standard form) in Kuwait is based on the 1969 version of the FIDIC Conditions of Contract and is commonly used for projects in both the public and private sector. Similarly, the FIDIC 1999 Red Book is commonly used in major scale private sector projects. Both standard forms contain a range of provisions that are not addressed by the legal codes, causing construction and legal professionals in Kuwait to have varying and conflicting opinions about how certain provisions would be regarded by the courts in Kuwait.

Among the most significant of these is the time bar, which is stipulated in claim provisions. The FIDIC 1999 Red Book imposes a time limit of 28 days for the contractor to submit a notice to claim in line with the conditions of the contract. More strictly, the MPW standard form imposes a time limit of 28 days for the contractor to submit a complete and detailed claim.

Non-adherence with these durations is not uncommon in Kuwait. Contractors often argue that the contractual time bar would not be upheld by the court. Many engineers are left at a lost between time barring the claim, facing accusations of acting in "bad faith" and between their obligation to apply the conditions of the contract as agreed by the parties. The allegation that the time bar would not be upheld by the courts is not supported by a specific legal reference, and there is no published case law in Kuwait to determine the exact legal position of courts based on previous cases.

The principle of good faith, unjust enrichment, and prescription periods are among the most commonly referenced principles in civil code jurisdictions to suggest possible rejection of time bars from a legal perspective. However, they may be refuted by arguing that a contractor who does not submit timely claims may be conceived to be acting in bad faith. Similarly, significant harm may be faced by an employer who is not informed of project delays or additional costs in a timely manner to make decisions to reduce impact, hereby negating the argument of unjust enrichment. Further, contractual time bars do not restrict the contractor's right to seek legal action under the governing law and hence does not seek to alter the prescription period.

Perhaps the most difficult principle to refute within Kuwait is that related to Islamic law, "shariah," which is specified as a main source of legislation under Article 2 of Kuwait's Constitution of 1962 (reinstated in 1992). Under "shariah" the right to claim does not expire and is considered absolute. While legal action to recover the right may be limited after a defined duration, namely the prescription period, the right itself will be acknowledged by the courts. It would be difficult for an employer to convince the courts that the contractor's right has been forfeited for failure to submit within 28 days.

There is a fundamental difference between a clause that extinguishes a right and one that places an obligation to give notice to preserve a right. In other words, the principles of "shariah" would not be offended if the wording of the clause is such that the existence of the right depends on the notice being served within a specified duration, rather than extinguished due to a failure to submit. A clause that expressly conditions the establishment of the right to timely submission may, therefore, be more legally applicable under Kuwaiti law. To further increase this likelihood, the clause may place the burden of acting in good faith on the contractor, so that failure to submit on time is expressly perceived as acting in bad faith for the harm it may cause the employer.

In light of the practical benefits of time bar provisions that are established by contract drafting panels, it may be worthwhile to consider a rewording claim provisions for more widespread implementation. Construction professionals in Kuwait and in the Middle East should seek legal advice to modify clauses which may offend local legal principles. The required effect may be difficult to achieve, but it is an important task to reduce the risks undertaken by parties who do not know whether they are sufficiently protected by the contractual provisions and whether there are any limitations to the recovery of their rights. Meanwhile, the legal position of courts in Kuwait towards time bars remains debatable among project parties, and their implementation within projects a common cause of dispute.

Dina Al Ansary
MCIArb, PMP, PMI-RMP
LLM in Construction Law and Arbitration
Kuwait

References

ICC (2012). *International Court of Arbitration Bulletin,* 23(2) – 2012.
Ramsey, V. (2006). Problems of delay and disruption damages in international construction arbitration in ICC, *Evaluation of Damages in International Arbitration.* ICC Publication No. 668.

Further readings

Cushman, R.F. (2011). *Proving and Pricing Construction Claims.* Wolters Kluwer, New York.
FIDIC (2000). *The FIDIC Contracts Guide* (1st Edition). FIDIC, Lausanne.
FIDIC (2011). *FIDIC Procurement Procedures Guide* (1st Edition). Lausanne.

Jamka, M. and Morek, R. (2013). Dispute avoidance and resolution under FIDIC Rules and procedure: Polish experience. Paper presented at the seminar Making a Success out of a Construction Project: International FIDIC Standards and their Implementation in Ukraine, Kiev.

Kitt, G. and Fletcher, M. (2013). Management of claims under FIDIC forms of contract. Paper presented at the conference Practical Solution of Problems Related to the Realisation of Construction Projects: FIDIC Contracts and Claim Management, Prague.

Klee, L. (2012). *Smluvní vztahy výstavbových projektů*. Wolters Kluwer, Prague.

Kus, A., Markus, J. and Steding, R. (1999). FIDIC's New Silver Book under the German Standard Form Contract Act. International Construction Law Review, Informa, London.

10 Claim Management

10.1 Claim management

In construction projects, it is very important to solve problems that can influence price or time for completion as soon as they are encountered (or even earlier to avoid or mitigate the consequences) while all equipment, human resources, and witnesses are still on site. Negative consequences of specific hazards are allocated in the form of a risk to the parties by contract. If a risk is allocated to one party, the other party may usually claim additional payment or extensions of time after such risk is realized.

It is common in international construction contracts for parties who consider themselves to be entitled to a claim to be under a duty to notify it. This notice can draw attention to the problem. The duty to notify creates a natural responsibility to keep contemporary records. This brings with it a higher probability that faster solutions will be implemented (to mitigate consequences) and problems resolved in a timely manner. Claim management is next to variation management a specific part of change management within the general project management duties related to contractual aspects of the project also called as contract management.

A structured claim management system also prompts the contract administrator (the engineer), the employer, the contractor, and others involved in a construction project to respect and take claims seriously. They must follow the contractual claim procedure, document events, report, and quantify the consequences by paying more attention to the claims and related site inspections and investigations.

The claim management is, in the most general sense, created by being able to identify, document, and quantify a claim. It is strongly recommended to commence claim preparation and administration from day one, that is, from receipt of the tender invitation by the contractor. Well-experienced contractors, engineers, and employers prepare themselves for every individual project prior to its commencement by using a set of checklists, organizational charts and sample forms of letters that facilitate future claim management.

The principles of claim management are also discussed in case law. For example in *Attorney General for the Falkland Islands v. Gordon Forbes Construction Limited* and

National Insurance Property Development Co Ltd v. NH International (Caribbean) Ltd. Particular claims usually correspond to damages caused by the employer, the contractor, or external grounds. When proving damages, one has to deal with difficulties based mainly on the three following problems: causation, concurrency, and calculation. The subject of causation will be dealt with in connection with *global claims* (discussed below in Section 10.6), the subject of concurrency will be touched on in connection with *concurrent delay* (Chapter 7) and the difficulties with calculation will be dealt with in *headquarters overhead claims* (also discussed below in Section 10.4.1). Causation, concurrency, and calculation issues lead to uncertainty in the way the tribunals decide about claims for damages.

While there is no easy solution that can overcome these difficulties, if the parties are aware of the uncertainty, they can take steps at an early stage to assess the best way to establish the claim before a particular tribunal. This means that the party can carry out the necessary analysis to formulate a robust position and assess the risks that will increase the likelihood of successfully establishing the claim (Ramsey, 2013). The best place to prepare a strong claim is at the construction site itself provided that contemporary records of delay, disruption and their respective effect on costs is updated in the time program and progress reports.

An application for damages (whether in a court or via a claim submission), can be both confusing and tedious. Since the purpose of a claim is the recovery of damages, making the application clear, simple, and easily understandable is extremely important. The damages claimed should, whenever possible, reference and tie to the contractor's accounting documents and records. This provides evidence that can be verified and accessed. Damages that cannot be traced to accounting records are immediately suspect, no matter how reasonable the amount claimed may seem. There is a tendency for damages to be overstated in a claim submission, with the idea that it can later be negotiated down to a more realistic but still acceptable amount. However, this approach is not advisable, as the claimant will lose credibility and will eventually have to explain the discrepancy between the claim amount and the amount sought at trial (Schwartzkopf and McNamara, 2001).

There are three types of contractor claims in general, i.e. claims for:

- extension of time (EOT);
- additional payment;
- extension of time and additional payment.

10.2 Claims for extension of time (EOT)

In some situations, the contractor can claim extensions of time for completion. It is in fact a defense against contractual penalty/delay damages filed by the employer and a form of risk sharing in some of situations such as extremely adverse weather. The position of the SCL Protocol on the purpose of extension of time is that the benefit to the contractor is only to relieve them of liability for damages for delay for any period prior to the extended contract completion date. The benefit of an EOT for the employer is that it establishes a new contract completion date and prevents time for completion of the works becoming "at large." Entitlement to an

EOT does not automatically lead to an entitlement to compensation. The parties should attempt—as far as possible—to deal with the impact of employer risk events as the work proceeds in terms of EOT and compensation. Where the full effect of an employer risk event cannot be predicted with certainty at the time of the initial assessment by the contract administrator, the contract administrator should grant an EOT for the then predictable effect.

The employer usually claims an extension of the defects notification period in terms of time (under Sub-Clause 2.5 in the FIDIC forms). Under the FIDIC forms (CONS/1999 Red Book), the contractor may claim an extension of time for completion under Sub-Clause 8.4. The contractor is entitled (subject to Sub-Clause 20.1) to an extension of the time for completion if and to the extent that completion is or will be delayed by any of the following causes:

1. Variation (unless an adjustment to the time for completion has been agreed in the variation procedure) or other substantial change in the quantity of an item of work.
2. Cause of delay giving an entitlement to an extension of time under another Sub-Clause (mainly Sub-Clauses 1.9 (late information, instruction, delayed drawings), 2.1 (denied or late access or possession to site), 4.7 (errors in setting out information), 4.12 (unforeseeable physical conditions), 4.24 (fossils), 7.4 (testing), 8.5 (delays caused by authorities), 8.9 (engineer's instructions to suspend work), 10.3 (interference with tests on completion),16.4 (termination by contractor), 17.4 (employer's risks), 19.4 (*force majeure*), or 19.6 (optional termination)).
3. Exceptionally adverse climatic conditions.
4. Unforeseeable shortages in the availability of personnel or goods caused by an epidemic or governmental actions.
5. Any delay, impediment, or prevention caused by or attributable to the employer, the employer's personnel (including the engineer who is listed as employer's personnel under Sub-Clause 1.1.2.6.), or the employer's other contractors on site.

If the contractor considers themselves to be entitled to an extension of time for completion, the contractor shall give notice to the engineer in accordance with Sub-Clause 20.1. When determining each extension of time under Sub-Clause 20.1, the engineer shall review previous determinations and may increase, but shall not decrease, the total extension of time.

If the contractor obtains an extension of time, they may be in a position to recover costs associated with the delay. However, there is no link (obligation) between Sub-Clause 8.4 and additional payment.

The contractor must keep proper records of the consequences of the event causing the claim in order to prove it. Documentation and reporting must follow the particular contractual provisions. For example, the contractor must keep records of labor, materials, equipment, progress reports, photographic, and video documentation.

The importance of a maintained, detailed, and up-to-date time schedule should be noted here. A claim for extension of time for completion is often submitted along with the updated time schedule detailing how and to what extent the claim events have influenced the individual construction works and relationship between activities. Critical paths in the time schedule are then explored together with floats, if any.

In the event of extremely adverse climatic conditions, for example, the contractor shall submit records of the weather encountered that can then be checked against the official statistics of the local bureau of meteorology.

10.3 Claims for additional payment

Related to claims for additional payment, it is important to explain how the bids are priced (see Chapter 6). Pricing methods may vary, depending on the practices used within a particular company. The pricing method which enjoys widest use is based on a calculated unit cost which is then increased by a percent surcharge.

The bid price is usually a total sum of the direct costs of equipment, material, and labor, indirect costs of site overhead, headquarters overhead, risk and profit surcharge. Most frequently, a claim for additional payment rests on the documented direct costs plus overhead and profit surcharge.

Under FIDIC forms (Sub-Clause 1.1.4.3, for example), "cost" means all expenditure reasonably incurred (or to be incurred) by the contractor, whether on or off site, including overheads and similar charges, but does not include profit. Profit is allowed only in specific claims, that is, usually those where there is an employer default.

These surcharges should be defined or agreed for the purposes of claims quantification. It should further be noted that the terms "cost," "expenditure," and "overhead" could be interpreted differently in particular jurisdictions. For example, these terms may be interpreted in the common case law sense (see *Hadley v. Baxendale* (1854) 9 Ex. 341) or in the civil law sense (see *Compagnie Interafricaine de Travaux v. South African Transport Services and Others* (680/89) [1991] ZASCA 16; 1991 (4) SA 217 (AD); (21 March 1991).

With every claim, the first test to be done is the test of liability, that is, does the other party bear the risk of the particular hazard subject to claim? If so, it must be examined and potentially compensated.

The contract defines what claims the aggrieved party is entitled to and if there is also an entitlement for an additional payment. The claims for additional payment must be further subdivided into claims for:

- direct cost;
- direct cost and overhead;
- direct cost, overhead, and profit.

The structure of a particular claim for additional payment depends on the wording of the contract and/or the governing law.

In its most general form, the heads of contractor's claim for additional payment would include:

- claims resulting from variations;
- claims resulting from delay and/or disruption under the particular provisions of the contract;
- claims resulting from governing law.

The employer usually claims delay damages, liquidated damages (or contractual penalties), and an additional payment caused by a lack of quality (price reduction) because the works are not performed to the agreed standard.

10.3.1 Claims resulting from variations

The employer usually has the right to order the contractually defined and allowed variations. The contractor, in contrast, has the right to compensation in terms of time and price. In some cases, variations are managed smoothly via the agreed variation orders. A complication often appears where one of the parties is breaching the contract or where contractual interpretation is unclear. In such cases, a routine variation procedure may become a claim for an additional payment and/or extension of time for completion.

To distinguish the contractor's individual claims for additional payment or for an extension of time for completion as a result of a variation, the following situations can be defined:

- directed variation;
- constructive variation;
- voluntary variation.

For more details, see Chapter 8 (including acceleration claims).

Acceleration is an example of a claim for additional payment (but not additional time).

10.4 Claims resulting from delay and/or disruption under the provisions of the contract

The question of particular claims under the contract and time bars was discussed in Chapter 9. In the following part, the specific heads of claims will be discussed. See also the *Table of Contractor's and Employer's Claims* under FIDIC CONS/1999 Red Book in Appendix D. Many of those claims are typically both for an extension of time and additional payment.

10.4.1 Delay claims

If stipulated in the contract, an extension makes it possible for the contractor to claim an additional payment—particularly in the following circumstances:

- increased variable costs for site overhead expenses;
- increased variable costs for headquarters overhead expenses;
- pass through claims where a subcontractor usually claims disruption (if working under worse conditions) or when working overtime and wants to be compensated for increased variable costs;

- lost profit;
- financial costs and interest claims;
- increased cost of material, labor, and equipment;
- claim preparation costs.

10.4.2 Site overhead claims

It was mentioned above that the contractor prices the bid to include site overhead expenses. These expenses are often aggregated within the individual items in the price schedules and tend to cover operation of the site facilities, the wages of the project team management and other personnel costs, the rentals for offices and the like. Higher site overhead expenses on the contractor's side typically occur due to the delay. However, the contractor does not include these expenses in the bid price as the above items are time-dependent. Whenever submitting a claim, the contractor must, if it is possible, identify these expenses in the price schedules and document the actual direct costs as they arise.

Examples of costs of running the site for an extended duration include:

- site staff (including personnel costs and accommodation)
- site facility and accommodation
- attendant labor
- utilities
- plant and small tools
- communications
- reprographics
- insurance
- catering
- temporary electrics
- skips/rubbish removal
- scaffolding
- stationery/postage.

Considerations related to site overhead claims by Gary Kitt (UK)

Before compiling a site overhead claim it is necessary to consider the following:

- cost or value;
- period for which claim is to be made;
- allocation of resources.

Cost or value

If a delay is likely to be caused (under the FIDIC forms) by a variation and the engineer requests a variation proposal (under Sub-Clause 13.3), then this arguably opens the door for a contractor to value prolongation other than by applying cost, seeing as it is left to the contractor to propose an evaluation.

The simplest way to frame a claim for prolongation is to apply a simple percentage addition to the cost of the variation based upon the allowance for time-related items within the contract price. While this might seem an attractive proposition, there is the real risk that it would not represent the true cost of delay.

Alternatively, in a situation where the contract price does not include specific identifiable sums for site overheads, that is to say site overheads are allowed within the rates within the bill of quantities (BoQ), a contractor could calculate a daily rate for prolongation that would encompass all time-related items.

FIDIC Sub-Clause 20.1 refers to the contractor seeking additional payment under any clause of the conditions or otherwise.

For claims made under any of the clauses of the conditions the contract defines "cost" as "all expenditure reasonably incurred (or to be incurred) by the contractor, whether on or off the site, including overhead and similar charges, but does not include profit." In these instances a contractor would generally expect to recover additional payment for the above based on its actual incurred cost.

Compilation of prolongation claims can be time-consuming as it is necessary to identify specific time-related resources over the course of the project.

Period of claim

Another important point to address is when the delay actually incurred as the contractor's claim ought to be for those resources affected at the time that the delay was incurred rather than, as we have seen many times, claiming for the resources on site during the period of overrun beyond the stated time for completion.

Allocation of resources

A further complicating factor is allocation of resources to specific activities or locations in the situation where not all supervisory resources can be said to have been delayed as a result of the event leading to the claim.

By way of example, a new highway might consist of roadworks and construction of structures. In such a case it is necessary to ensure that, if the works to the roadworks are critically delayed, the claim consists of only those overhead resources that are project-wide, such as the Project Director or site secretary and those specifically working on the affected section of the road. The significance of this is that the contractor needs to maintain good records of its management and supervision allocated to the individual elements of the project. "Core" overhead, that is, project-wide management and supervisory resource and "task" and "work" related resources must be distinguished. Having established the total time-related resources, it is necessary to separate these into the categories of core- or task-related. It is only the core plus—the relevant portion of the task overhead that should be claimed as part of the claim for prolongation costs. The work-related resources are those whose cost is recovered through the BoQ rates.

Gary Kitt
Regional Head of Contract Solutions, Europe
Arcadis
London
UK

In terms of the above-mentioned period for evaluation of compensation, the position of the SCL Protocol is that once it is established that compensation for prolongation is due, the evaluation of the sum due is made by reference to the period when the effect of the employer risk event was felt, not by reference to the extended period at the end of the contract.

Where a delay in a large construction project occurs, it is often the case that a contractor and engineer (contract administrators) and the employer will hire additional supervisory and management staff to deal with the issues that have arisen. When this happens, claims will often be made for additional payment in respect of those resources that are in addition to that anticipated to be required.

10.4.3 Headquarters overhead claims

It was already stated that the contractor (and in certain situations also the employer) is entitled to be compensated for indirect costs in the form of increased, unabsorbed headquarters overhead expenses if, for example, the work completion date is extended or disrupted because of reasons on the employer's side. This is because extra payment has not been included in their bid price. This form of recovery received judicial approval in the case *Alfred McAlpine Homes North Ltd v. Property and Land Contractors Ltd 1995 76BLR59*. At paragraph 70G of the judgment, HHJ Humphrey Lloyd QC explains:

> The theory is that because the period of delay is uncertain and thus the contractor can take no steps to reduce its head office expenditure and other overhead costs and cannot obtain additional work, there are no means whereby the contractor can avoid incurring the continuing head office expenditure, notwithstanding the reduction in turnover as a result of the suspension or delay to the progress of the work. The reduced activity no longer therefore pays its share towards the overhead costs.

In order for such a claim to succeed, it is necessary for a contractor to prove the following:

> The loss in question must be proved to have occurred. The delay in question must be shown to have caused the contractor to decline to take on other work which was available and which would have contributed to its overhead recovery. Alternatively, it must have caused a reduction in the overhead recovery in the relevant financial year or years which would have been earned but for that delay. The delay must not have had associated with it a commensurate increase in turnover and recovery towards overheads. The overheads must not have been ones which would have been incurred in any event without the contractor achieving turnover to pay for them. There must have been no change in the market affecting the possibility of earning profit elsewhere and an alternative market must have been available. Furthermore, there must have been no means for the contractor to deploy its

resources elsewhere despite the delay. In other words, there must not have been a constraint in recovery of overheads elsewhere.

Where the parties have not agreed in advance on a definitive percentage or other amount for the head office overheads, the amount for overheads can usually (but not always) be evidenced by reference to pricing information supporting the tender or by using the contractor's audited accounts. If the accounts used are for prior years (i.e., other than the period during which the works were carried out), care should be taken to ensure that the attribution of overheads to the project is appropriate and not inflated. In practice, the hardest of the tests to satisfy when valuing head office overheads is the "but for" test (that is to say; "but for this delay, would the contractor have been able to recover additional monies in respect of the (claimed) overhead costs by taking on other work?"). Put another way, was the contractor deprived of the opportunity to mitigate these costs by, say, making staff redundant sooner? Proof that the contractor was turning workaway because of the delay to a particular project may be found by reference to the contractor's order books, invitations to tender and general market conditions (Kitt and Fletcher, 2013).

Various formulas are also used to quantify the head office overhead because of the difficulty of exact assessment. The reason is the difficulty or impossibility of identifying the headquarters overhead for a particular contract in the bill of quantities as it consists of the expenses incurred by the contractor's administrative units (such as top management, office staff, and services). These administrative units concurrently handle a large number of projects and the related allocation of costs can be very complicated, and, in many cases, impossible.

Ideally, a contractor would keep records of all activities carried out by head office personnel but this seldom happens in reality. To help solve this problem, UK courts appear reasonably happy to assess loss based upon industry-recognized formulas (Kitt and Fletcher, 2013).

The best-known and most widely used formulas for determining claims for costs incurred in connection with overhead increases are the *Hudson Formula* and the *Emden Formula*. The Hudson Formula comes from the *Hudson's Building and Engineering Contracts* publication. This publication is traditionally used as a source of information by lawyers and civil engineers worldwide (Dennys et al., 2010).

The Hudson Formula, for example, won recognition in the case *J F Finnegan v. Sheffield City Council (1988) 43 BLR*. Sir William Stabb QC sitting as Official Referee stated:

> It is generally accepted that, on principle, a contractor who is delayed in completing a contract due to the default of his employer, may properly have a claim for head office or offsite overheads during the period of delay, on the basis that the work-force, but for the delay, might have had the opportunity of being employed on another contract which would have had the effect of funding the overheads during the overrun period.

There are other formulas, such as the Ernstrom, Manshul, Carteret and Allegheny formulas—all derived from the cases where they have been used. They are mostly variations of the Hudson Formula. The Eichleay Formula is the most widely used in public contracts in the United States.

The subject of formulas is connected to the certainty of damages that was discussed in a more general sense in the cases *Canadian case of Wood v. Grand Valley Railway Company* (1915) 51 SCR 283 and *Chaplin v. Hicks* [1911] 2 KB 786 where the English Court of Appeal held:

> I do not agree with the contention that, if certainty is impossible of attainment, the damages for a breach of contract are unassessable … I only wish to deny with emphasis that, because precision cannot be arrived at, the jury has no function in the assessment of damages … In such a case the jury must do the best they can, and it may be that the amount of their verdict will really be a matter of guesswork. But the fact that damages cannot be assessed with certainty does not relieve the wrongdoer of the necessity of paying damages for his breach of contract.

Often imprecise documentation evidencing damages lead to the need for an "assessment" by the judge based on the particular submissions of the parties to the dispute. The main issue is the uncertainty of the outcome caused by the different approaches of judges, arbitrators, and adjudicators in particular jurisdictions and by the lack of universally accepted methods of delay and disruption analysis. Because of this, the use of expert evidence to support a quantum claim is widespread in international arbitration. Very often, the engagement of the expert is used as a means of presenting the case on quantum rather than limiting the expert's involvement to purely expert accounting issues or matters which require expertise in assessing the sum to be claimed (Ramsey, 2006).

As with global claims, this approach to damages calculation (use of formulas) may be viable in litigation, DAB or arbitration but it can be difficult to prove the claim and convince the decision maker.

It must be pointed out however that in the majority of civil law jurisdictions and under UNIDROIT principles, however, if the amount of the claim can only be determined with difficulty or cannot be determined at all, the court shall determine it at its sole discretion and where the amount of damages cannot be established with a sufficient degree of certainty, the assessment is at the discretion of the court.

The SCL Protocol also proposes some best practice guidance in terms of head office overhead. It divides head office overhead into: *dedicated overheads* through which administrative costs are assigned on the basis of good record keeping, and *unabsorbed overheads* (such as rent and some salaries) which are incurred by the contractor regardless of their work volume. Unless the terms of the contract make unabsorbed overheads irrecoverable, they are generally recoverable as a foreseeable cost resulting from prolongation. The contractor must then be able to demonstrate that because of employer risk events they were prevented from taking on other overhead-earning work.

The authors of the SCL Protocol recommend the Emden and Eichleay formulas. The authors further recommend that when the formulas produce an inaccurate or unsuitable result, verification is required by using another formula. At http://www.eotprotocol.com are guidelines for determining unabsorbed overhead claims. The guidelines are a useful tool because they take into account a number of variables.

In its original form, the Hudson formula appears as follows:

$$\frac{\text{Headquaters overhead \& profit \%}}{100} \times \frac{\text{Project price}}{\text{Construction time}} \times \text{Delay}$$

The Emden formula is as follows:

$$\frac{\text{Total overhead \& constractor's profit}}{\text{Total constractor's turnover}} \times \frac{\text{Project price}}{\text{Construction time}} \times \text{Delay}$$

In the United States, the Eichleay formula is used to recover unabsorbed home office overhead expense. In *Mech-Con Corp. v. West,* 61 F.3d 883, 14 FPD 65, 19 C.C. 395 (Fed. Cir. 1995), this formula was also used to evaluate damages arising from a suspension of work. The contractor established a *prima facie* case for Eichleay damages by showing: (1) the existence of a government-imposed delay; and (2) that the delay was for an uncertain period during which the contractor had to stand ready to complete the work. Because the delay was of an uncertain duration, the contractor did not have to prove that it was unable to take on other work during the period, or that it was unable to reduce its overhead. When the contractor can show that it was required to remain on standby during a period of uncertain government-imposed delay, the burden shifts to the government to show that the contractor could have reduced its overhead or taken on other work.

10.4.4 Subcontractor claims

A large part of a contractor's claim can be made up of subcontractors' claims. Contractors will often reach commercial settlements with their subcontractors because of the difficulty in identifying precisely what part of the settlement figure relates to the delay event in respect of which the contractor makes their claim.

According to Justice Akenhead in *Walter Lilly &Company Ltd v. Mackay &Anor* [2012] EWHC 1773

> The first step in this process is to consider whether or not the settlement was a reasonable one, having regard to cases such as *Biggin v. Permanite* [1951] 2 KB 314 and, more recently, *Axa Insurance UK Plc v. Cunningham Lindsey United Kingdom* [2007] EWHC 2023, *Siemens Building Technologies FE Limited v. Supershield Limited* [2010] BLR 145.

Having established that the settlement sum was reasonable, it is then necessary to establish what, if any, part of the sum paid to a subcontractor in settlement of its claims was attributable to a claim for delay or disruption arising out of a matter for which the employer was responsible.

10.4.5 Lost profit claims

The contractor can usually claim lost profit on the basis of the contract or governing law. The relation (including potential limitation) of contractual claims for profit surcharge/lost profit and statutory lost profit claims depends on the wording of contract and governing law. Contractual claims for profit surcharges (in addition to cost) are admissible, for example, under the following FIDIC CONS/1999 Red Book Sub-Clauses:

- Sub-Clause 1.9 Delayed Drawings
- Sub-Clause 2.1 Right of Access
- Sub-Clause 4.7 Setting Out
- Sub-Clause 4.24 Fossils
- Sub-Clause 7.4 Testing
- Sub-Clause 10.3 Interference with Tests
- Sub-Clause 16.1 Suspension by Contractor
- Sub-Clause 17.4 Employer's Risks.

The contractor can often claim lost profit in cases of delay or disruption caused by the employer. The significance of the above is that certain elements of a contractor's claim for recovery of prolongation costs attract the addition for lost profit where others such as delay caused by unforeseen physical conditions do not. This can lead to contractors effectively shopping for delay events to attract the lost profit addition—particularly in "mega" infrastructure projects. The amount of lost profit should be comparable to that in the tender, which can be proved by reference to tender pricing information. Alternatively, it is usual to state the addition for such profit within the particular conditions or appendix to tender as a percentage of cost.

Under particular governing law, lost profit is often part of a statutory compensation scheme in cases of breach of contract or law. In common law countries, it can further be based on tortious actions.

In U.S. jurisdictions, for example, the legal requirements necessary to establish lost profit claims are generally threefold. It must be shown that:

- The lost profits were reasonably foreseeable at the formation of the contract stage.
- The defendant's actions were the proximate cause of the lost profits.
- The lost profits can be proven with reasonably certainty.

10.4.6 Prolongation costs and interest claims

Further costs are encountered when there is a prolongation of performance guarantees and insurance. Such prolongation usually needs to be approved by the employer. Each respective claim is then quite easy to prove via contract addendums with the bank and insurance company. The same is relevant with site facilities used for more time than originally foreseen.

Another typical claim relates to payment of interest. In the UK, financing charges have become a valid head of claim as a result of the decision in *F G Minter v.*

Welsh Health Technical Services Organisation (1980). This case established that there are two types of financing charge. The first is the loss of interest on capital, which the contractor has not been paid and is therefore not able to put into their interest-bearing bank account. The second type is the interest incurred by the contractor on overdraft charges arising from the use of the contractor's own money to finance work. Normally they would expect to use the money paid to them under the contract for that purpose.

Financing charges are a secondary cost. If a contractor's claim for primary costs fails, then it follows that their claim for financing will likely fail with it. On the other hand, if the primary cost claim succeeds, it is possible to infer that financing charges have been incurred.

10.4.7 Increased cost of material, labor, and equipment

Contractors often claim increases in the costs of buying materials, labor, and equipment due to inflation over the period of delay. This head of claim needs to be supported by evidence providing details of the difference in cost between the price upon which the contractor's tendered rate was based and the actual cost paid as a result of the delay. Alternatively, such claims can be supported by the use of published indices. The success of such claims is highly dependent upon the governing law and local methods of dispute resolution. For details see also Sections 2.8 and 5.10.

10.4.8 Claim preparation costs

Construction claims are complex and sometimes great effort must be invested in putting together a precise claim, which has good prospects of success. It can be said that the preparation of claims has developed into a specific discipline, which is often extremely time-consuming and expensive because, almost always, this requires the participation of specialist consultants and lawyers. Contractors may have the right to recover the cost of claims preparation if it is proved that the additional payment or extension of time has been caused by the employer.

In this regard, ICC case no. 10951 (ICC, 2012) is worth a mention. In this case the tribunal accepted that claims preparation costs could include, in principle, the costs of in-house staff of the subcontractor tasked with dealing with the claim. The tribunal held that although the ICC Rules (the 1998 Rules) do not contain a definition of the "other costs incurred" by the parties, it has become more and more accepted over the years that "other costs" may also include the costs which a party incurred for in-house staff specifically appointed to prepare and support proceedings before an arbitration tribunal. In the case at hand, however, the evidence on record did not enable the tribunal to accept the full amount of salaries claimed.

> The arbitral tribunal is neither in a position to find out how much time the above-mentioned persons effectively dedicated to the preparation and support of the proceedings, nor to review whether the salaries claimed correspond to their employment agreements. On the other hand, the arbitral tribunal is aware that those persons in fact played a considerable role on

the subcontractor's side. All in all, the arbitral tribunal finds it appropriate to cut the total amount down to 50% … In view of the total amount in dispute …, the complexity of the case and the time spent, the arbitral tribunal finds that the aforementioned amount … represents reasonable legal and other costs incurred by the subcontractor.

According to Seppälä (ICC, 2012), the tribunal's finding that a subcontractor could claim adjusted costs representing approximately 4% of the amount in dispute to be fair and reasonable. But, in order to recover its full in-house staff costs, the subcontractor must provide the appropriate evidence, which in this instance the tribunal found to be: (1) evidence of the time effectively spent by in-house staff on the preparation and support of the arbitration; and (2) evidence of salaries claimed (such as employment agreements). Thus, this case provides support for the proposition that in order to permit the full recovery of the costs of in-house staff working on arbitration, such staff should (like lawyers in external law firms) keep time sheets and record their time on a daily basis. These should then be submitted, if necessary, to support any claim for the recovery of in-house staff costs.

10.4.9 Disruption claims

Disruption can be defined as any change in the method of performance or planned work sequence contemplated by the contractor at the time the bid was submitted that prevents the contractor from actually performing in that manner. This material alteration results in increased difficulty and cost of performance. Claims for disruption are prevalent on most major infrastructure projects. While permitted by contract, they are notoriously difficult to evidence and prove and tribunals remain skeptical of these types of claims (Cushman, 2011).

Events that cause disruption may include, for example, the employer stopping and starting the project, late design information, differing site conditions, delayed or uncoordinated instructions for variations, employer-instructed out-of-sequence work, overzealous inspections or testing, the presence of other contractors, damage caused to the works by other contractors, delayed or hindered access and late issue of or inaccurate drawings (Bunni, 2005).

Disruption claims are in themselves divided into two further types of claims. First, if the disruption caused is to a non-critical activity and the result is that the activity itself takes longer by using up the float time either before or after the date that the activity was to be performed. It will cost more because of the inefficiency in carrying out the activity but, because time is not critical, there is no delay in the time for completion and it will not entitle the contractor to an extension of time.

Second, where continuous, extensive and cumulative disruption is such that the flexibility in time allowed to the relevant activity is exceeded, then this non-critical activity becomes a critical one and further disruption ends in critical delay and prolongation of the time for completion. In such a case the contractor is entitled not only to the monetary cost of that disruption but also to an extension of time and the prolongation costs, if any, associated with such an extension (Bunni, 2005).

The impact of disruption is often a loss of efficiency in performance and increased costs. Time for performance alone may not necessarily be extended as a result of the disruption. Such loss of momentum leads to more labor and equipment hours required to do the same work (slower learning curve, overcrowding, and so on).

There are several methods for calculating loss of efficiency. According to Cushman, (2011), the following methods are typically used in the United States:

- total cost;
- modified total cost;
- measured mile;
- should cost estimates;
- industry standards and handbooks;
- time and motions studies;
- expert opinion;
- jury verdict.

Typical damages associated with disruption claims involve increased labor costs for additional employees used to perform extra work, increased costs for inefficiency caused by altered work conditions or overtime and increased equipment and material costs. It is extremely important for a contractor whose performance has been disrupted to keep accurate records of increased costs or time of performance.

There may be hidden disruption costs such as those associated with shutting down operations (demobilization) and starting up again (remobilization). The more current the records and the greater the accuracy, the higher the probability of recovery without lengthy dispute resolution (Kitt and Fletcher, 2013).

The starting point according to the SCL Protocol for any disruption analysis is to understand what work was carried out, when it was carried out and what resources were used. For this reason, record keeping is just as important for disruption analysis as it is for delay analysis.

In terms of "after the event" analysis, the SCL Protocol recommends that, in deciding entitlement, the adjudicator, judge or arbitrator should (so far as is practicable) put him/herself in the position of the contract administrator at the time the employer risk event occurred.

The most appropriate way to establish disruption according to the SCL Protocol is to apply a technique known as the *Measured Mile*. This method compares the productivity achieved in an unaffected part of the contract with that achieved in the affected part. The comparison can be made on the man-hours expended or the units of work performed. However, care must be exercised to compare like with like. For example, it would not be correct to compare work carried out in the learning curve part of an operation with work executed after the period.

It is worth examining the SCL Protocol further because it contains one of the few coherent opinions on disruption evaluation. If it is difficult to find unaffected parts in the contract, comparison of productivity with other contracts executed by the contractor may be an acceptable alternative, provided that sufficient records from the other contracts are available to ensure that the comparison is on a like-with-like basis. Failing that, it might be acceptable to use model productivity curves and factors developed by a number of organizations from data collected on a range of projects (e.g., by the U.S. Army Corps of Engineers, the International Labor Organization, the Mechanical Contractors' Association of America Inc., the Chartered Institute of Building, and so on). These curves provide general guidance and they should be used only if they are relevant to the working conditions and type of construction and are supported by evidence from the party seeking to prove disruption.

According to Bunni (2005), a proper evaluation of a claim for disruption requires the following prerequisites:

- Identification and an analysis of each of the operations claimed to have been disrupted. It is not sufficient to simply state that the execution of the works has been disrupted.
- The cause and the manner in which disruption has occurred should be established.
- The figures for the anticipated output, the resources planned, and the time required to achieve the completion of the disrupted operations as calculated in the tender have to be shown to be achievable.
- The effects of any inefficiency on the part of the disrupted party in carrying out the works should be properly calculated and its effect included in the calculations of disruption suffered.
- The number of hours actually logged in the time sheets for the disrupted operation has to be shown to be accurate.

Head office overhead claims under FDIC contracts by Alan Whaley (UK)

Recovering unabsorbed head office overheads based on lost commercial opportunity in the event of Employer delay is generally acceptable to the English courts. Akenhead J set down clear principles in *Walter Lilly & Company Ltd v. Mackay & Anor* ([2012] EWHC 1773) for recovery of head office overheads and profit:

1. The contract must entitle the contractor to claim for overhead and profit lost as a result of an employer responsible delay.
2. The contractor must prove, on the balance of probabilities, that it would have secured new work capable of producing a return if the delay had not occurred.
3. The contractor must prove, on the balance of probabilities, that it incurred a loss from the delay. The use of formulae for quantifying loss is acceptable.

However, *Walter Lilly* dealt specifically with a JCT SBC 1998 contract, which did not include a broad limitation of liability clause. Specifically, there was no express exclusion of liability for loss of profit or lost commercial opportunity, nor was there express definition of the kinds of cost that the contractor could and could not recover. The principles set down in *Walter Lilly* cannot therefore be applied universally.

The position under FIDIC contracts

Clause 17.6 of the FIDIC Red Book 1999 is typical of international forms in restricting liability between Parties for a range of costs and losses:

> "*Neither Party shall be liable to the other Party for loss of use of any Works, loss of profit, loss of any contract or for any indirect or consequential loss or damage which may be suffered by the other Party in connection with the Contract.*"

Sub-Clause 17.6 expressly excludes liability for "loss of profit" and "loss of any contract." These exclusions effectively restrict liability between parties for lost commercial opportunity, and are in addition to exclusions for "consequential loss or damage" of the kind envisaged under the second limb of *Hadley v. Baxendale* ((1854) 156 ER 145). *In Transocean Drilling UK Ltd v. Providence Resources Plc* ([2016] EWHC 2611 (Comm) (20 October 2016)), the Court of Appeal construed a similar limitation clause widely, including within its scope the cost of non-productive management resources arising from a delay.

Because the rules set down in *Walter Lilly* relate to claims based on lost commercial opportunity, contractors intending to recover head office overheads under FIDIC contracts may need to present their claim on terms different than those accepted in *Walter Lilley*.

Recovering overheads as "cost"

While the FIDIC Red Book 1999 precludes claims for loss of profit, it does not preclude recovery of head office overheads. Unlike the JCT forms, the FIDIC Red Book 1999 expressly allows for recovery of overheads by its definition of "Cost" under Sub-Clause 1.1.4.3:

> "*All expenditure properly incurred (or to be incurred) by the Contractor, whether on or off the Site, including overhead and similar charges, but does not include profit.*"

Sub-Clause 1.1.4.3 encompasses costs properly incurred (or to be incurred) "off the Site" (including, for example, head office costs), and these costs expressly include "overhead and similar charges," but exclude profit. The FIDIC Contracts Guide gives no explanation for the term "overhead and similar charges," save for clarifying that it may include finance costs. Therefore, the meaning of "overhead … charges" appears sufficiently wide to cover head office overhead costs "charged" (or distributed) to projects by a contractor's head office.

This interpretation would effectively reduce the burden placed on contractors to show that an opportunity to undertake further contracts was lost as a result of employer delay. Read together, Clause 1.1.4.3 and Clause 17.6 appear only to require evidence that (i) the contractor's company incurred (or will incur) business operation and overhead costs in amounts foreseeable at the date of the contract, and (ii) a fair proportion of these costs was (or will be) allocable to the project during the time of the delay.

A contractor may however recover less overhead costs on this basis than would be the case in a lost opportunity claim. Whereas a lost opportunity claim would (theoretically) restore the contractor the position it would have been but for the delay (including lost profit), recovering only the overheads chargeable to the project means that any reduction in overhead contribution would be shared between ongoing projects.

Alan Whaley MCIOB MRICS FCIArb
Director
Arcadis
London, UK

Calculation and recovery of home/head office overhead in North America by James G. Zack (the United States)

Introduction

Owner-caused delay or delay brought about by owner-assumed entitlement issues is common on construction projects. Delay may have many sources, including directed or constructive changes, delays in furnishing owner provided equipment or materials, differing site conditions, slow responses to shop drawing submittals or requests for information, and so on. Despite the numerous causes of owner caused delay, the result is almost always the same. Contractors typically request an equitable adjustment to the contract to compensate them for both time and cost resulting from the delay. It is often difficult for owners and contractors to reach agreement on the cause(s) of delay. Contractors tend to view most delays as the responsibility of the owner. Owners, on the other hand, often try to label such delays as either third party caused or concurrent delay, either of which results in excusable, non-compensable delay. Proper delay analysis usually sorts out this argument.

Most standard form contracts in both the public and the private sector deal with at least three types of delay in their terms and conditions, as follows.

- **Inexcusable Delay** – This is delay caused by the contractor or one their subcontractors or suppliers at any tier. Typically, most contracts deny any time or cost recovery to the contractor in the event of inexcusable delay and require the contractor to recover the lost time or pay actual or liquidated damages for late completion.
- **Excusable Delay** – This is delay brought about by a third party (i.e., neither the owner nor the contractor) or some outside force such as weather, acts of God, acts of war or terrorism, labor actions, and so on. Private contracts frequently deal with this situation in the force majeure clause while many public contracts include this type of delay in the termination for default clause. (See FAR 249-10(b) for a list of excusable delay clauses on typical U.S. government construction contracts.) Most standard form contracts allow the recovery of the delayed time but award no time related costs for the period of the excusable delay. Thus, the contractor receives time but no time related costs while the owner grants the time and cannot assess late completion damages for the delayed time.
- **Compensable Delay** – This is delay caused by the owner or someone for whom the owner is responsible (such as delayed return of drawings which impact the project schedule) or by an event for which the owner has assumed contractual liability (e.g., differing site conditions). Most standard form contracts allow the contractor to recover both the lost time as well as time related damages from the owner. Contractors are most often allowed to recover extended field office, storage, and equipment costs, idled labor and equipment costs; impact costs; lost productivity costs, and such other costs that can be shown to have been incurred as a result of the delay. Additionally, contractors may be allowed to recover extended or unabsorbed home office overhead costs.

Once agreement is reached concerning the cause of the delay, the argument turns more technical. What is the extent of the delay? Due to the complexity of modern day scheduling and multiple ways to perform delay analysis, negotiations over the extent of a delay are often difficult. Delay analyses performed by two different parties, on the same incident, can yield results substantially at odds with one another. (See AACE Recommended Practice RP29R03 – Forensic Schedule Analysis, 2011.) Generally, however, if both the owner and the contractor stay focused on resolution of the claim, agreement can be reached on both the extent and quantification of the delay (i.e., non-excusable, excusable, and compensable) and there is no concurrent delay. (See John Livengood, "Comparison of English and U.S. Law on Concurrent Delay," *The Construction Lawyer*, ABA Forum on Construction Law, Vol. 37, No. 2, Spring, 2017.)

The issue is now settled, right? Wrong! The argument now turns to financial impact. That is, what is the cost of a day of compensable delay? Provided that the contractor maintains reasonably good job cost records, determining daily field office overhead (FOOH) costs is not terribly difficult. However, in owner caused delay situations, contractors frequently seek recovery of extended or unabsorbed home/head office overhead (HOOH). This is where negotiations often deadlock. Why? There is no **standard** accepted way of calculating HOOH. Most contractors want to use formulas to calculate their damage. Most owners, on the other hand, want to see "real damage" based on some sort of audit—"Prove that your overhead increased as a result of my delay!"

This paper discusses the HOOH issue. What is HOOH? What are typical cost elements of HOOH? How is HOOH generated or recaptured under normal circumstances? The paper identifies nine different formulas that have been used in construction litigation in the United States and Canada and applies all nine formulas to the same delay situation to demonstrate the wide variance in resulting cost recovery. The paper also discusses some relatively new rules developed by the U.S. federal courts for use on government contracts concerning the recovery of unabsorbed HOOH.

Home/Head office overhead—what is it?

HOOH is generally described as company costs incurred by the contractor for the benefit of all projects in progress. This is the actual cost, which is an essential part of the cost of doing business (Schwartzkopf, William, John J. McNamara and Julian F. Hoffar. 1992. *Calculating Construction Damages*. New York, NY: John Wiley & Sons, Inc.). These are costs that cannot be directly allocated to a project. This definition excludes those costs incurred by the contractor solely in support of a single project or group of projects. Typical examples of HOOH discussed in the industry include

Executive and administrative salaries	Legal and accounting expenses
Home / Head office rent and expenses	Advertising
Company insurance	Recruiting costs
Utilities, telephone, fax and computers for the home office	Human relations costs
	Interest on company borrowings
Travel for home / head office staff	Bad debt
Depreciation of company assets	Entertainment
Professional fees	Contributions
Bid costs	

There are few government regulations concerning accounting for HOOH costs. Contractors are reasonably free to account for such costs in whatever manner they choose. They must, however, in the United States use the same system at all times and on all contracts. While the U.S. government's Federal Acquisition Regulations ("FAR") limit the recoverability of some types of HOOH costs these limitations apply only to direct contracts with agencies of the U.S. federal government (48 C.F.R. §§31.205-1 to 31.205-23 (1990)).

> Based on this discussion, in analyzing delay costs, one must distinguish between HOOH costs (those that support all projects) and FOOH costs (those that support a single project or group of projects). In performing such cost analysis, one also has to guard against the possibility of "double dipping." An example is a home/head office estimator who is assigned to a project for a few weeks to resolve a series of changes. If the estimator is typically accounted for in home/head office costs, they should not be charged to the project. If the estimator is charged to the project, over recovery will occur if the normal HOOH rate is applied since the estimator's cost will be included twice.

Inclusion and recovery of home office overhead

HOOH costs are generally added during the bid/tender process to the contractor's estimate of direct costs and field overhead costs. The markup cost, that includes HOOH, is typically added as a single percentage number—that is, "Let's use 7.5%!" Of course, this single multiplier actually includes home office costs, contingency, management reserve, and profit, unless another line item is added to the bid takeoff to account for these other numbers. That is how HOOH enters the budget.

How is HOOH typically recovered on the normal job? Few contracts have a pay item for overhead and profit. Most contracts tell contractor to spread or allocate their overhead and profit costs across all pay items in the Schedule of Values. Setting aside the issue of unbalanced bid breakdowns the contractor is expected to spread their overhead and profit cost uniformly across all pay items in the contract. Thus, when a contractor accomplishes pay item work, they recapture both the cost of the work as well as the overhead and profit associated with that work.

That gets the overhead and profit into the contractor's job cost accounts. But, one step in this financial transaction remains. The contractor must move part of the money received from the project job cost records to the corporate accounts in order to pay for HOOH costs. This is typically accomplished by cost adjustments moving funds from project costs to corporate overhead. This completes the financial transaction.

A summary graphic (in oversimplified form) is set forth below to illustrate how HOOH is collected from each ongoing project in the company in order to support the home/head office expenses.

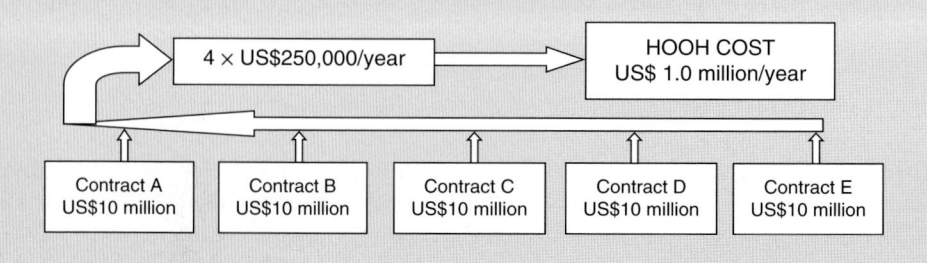

History of home/head office overhead recovery in delay situations

The recovery of HOOH, as a result of compensable delay, is <u>not</u> new law in the United States. As far back as 1941, U.S. federal courts awarded recovery of HOOH to a contractor for a government caused delay in *Herbert M. Baruch v. the United States* (93 Ct. Cl. 1078 (1941)). This court did not, however, discuss how the HOOH costs were calculated in this case. In 1945, a federal court again addressed the issue of HOOH in *Fred R. Comb Co. v. the United States* (103 Ct. Cl. 174 (1945)). Here, because of a government caused delay the court awarded " ... increased office overhead ... " as part of the damages due to site unavailability. Again, the decision did not include a formula for calculating HOOH.

The landmark case concerning HOOH in the U.S. is the *Eichleay Corporation* case decided in 1960 (ASBCA No. 5183, 60-2 BCA (CCH) ¶2688 (1960)). In this case, the Armed Services Board of Contract Appeals ("ASBCA") concluded that there were multiple work stoppages for which the government was responsible. The ASBCA concluded also that HOOH costs continued during the suspension periods; that the Eichleay Corporation was unable to take on new work during these periods to replace lost project revenue; and thus, had to absorb the unrecovered HOOH costs. The keys to the *Eichleay* decision appear to be as follows.

- A contractor is entitled to compensation for unabsorbed HOOH resulting from owner caused delay, if the contractor can meet certain criteria.
- There is no exact accounting method for calculating unabsorbed HOOH.
- Therefore, a fair, realistic cost estimating formula is necessary to determine the compensation owed.

Thus, the *Eichleay* Formula was born, a creature of the Boards of Contract appeals. There has been continuous controversy concerning this formula almost from the outset. Some courts have accepted it at face value—Virginia, for example (*Fairfax County Development and Housing Authority v. Worcester Brothers Company,* 257 Va. 382 (1999)). Other state courts have adamantly refused to use *Eichleay*—New York, for example (*Berley Industries v. City of New York,* 45 N.Y.2d 683 (1978)). And, many have tried to substitute other formulas in place of *Eichleay*.

Does it matter?

As a result, there are at least nine formulas that have been used, with varying degrees of success, in litigation in the United States and Canada. Now, if these formulas are all "fair, realistic methods" of estimating damages then it should <u>not</u> matter which formula is used, should it? To get an answer this question, let's look at the same case using all eight formulas. For the purposes of this paper, we will use the case set forth below.

ABC Construction, Inc. – Contract and Financial Data	
Total Firm Revenue: Original Period	$247,711,967
Total Firm Revenue: Actual Period	$381,095,333
Total Labor Cost: Actual Period	$137,194,333
Original Contract Value	$ 68,500,000

ABC Construction, Inc. – Contract and Financial Data	
Total Contract Value (before claim)	$76,866,128
Billings: Original Period	$69,753,854
Billings: Actual Period	$76,866,128
Billings: Delay Period	$7,112,274
Labor Costs: Delay Period	$2,560,419
Company Overhead: Original Period	$16,265,000
Company Overhead: Actual Period	$28,918,417
Total Overhead & Profit: Actual Period	$37,156,795
Planned Contract Duration	365 days
Actual Duration	655 days
Extended Duration	290 days
Owner caused Delay	235 days
Planned Overhead & Profit % at Bid / Tender	7.0%
Normal Home Office Overhead %	4.5%
Actual Home Office Overhead %	5.3%
Actual Home Office Overhead %: Delay Period	6.1%

Let's look at the same case using all nine formulas to see if the results are reasonably close.

Eichleay Formula (Eichleay Corporation, *ASBCA No. 5183, 60-2 BCA (CCH)* ¶2688 (1960))

The original *Eichleay Formula* enunciated in 1960 follows.

$$\frac{\text{Contract Billings}}{\text{Total Billings for Actual Contract Period}} \times \text{Total Company Overhead During Actual Contract Period} = \text{Overhead Allocable to Contract}$$

$$\frac{\text{Allocable Overhead}}{\text{Actual Days of Contact Performance}} = \text{Overhead Allocable to Contract/Day}$$

$$\text{Daily Overhead} \times \frac{\text{Days of Owner Caused Delay}}{} = \text{Home Office Overhead Owed}$$

This formula attempts to allocate HOOH for the entire contract period first to the project and then recalculate it for a specific project on a daily basis to determine the compensation owed. Using the numbers from the above tables, here are the results.

$$\frac{\$76,866,128}{\$381,095,333} \times \$28,918,417 = \$5,832,784$$

$$\frac{\$5,832,784}{655 \text{ cd's}} = \$8,905/\text{days}$$

$$\$8,905 \times 235 \text{ days} = \underline{\$2,092,675}$$

Modified Eichleay Formula—Variation 1 (*Capital Electric Co. v. the United States*, 729 F.2d 743 (Fed. Cir., 1984) and *Gregory Construction, Inc.*, ASBCA No. 35,960, 88-3 BCA(CCH) ¶20,934 (1988))

The first modification to the *Eichleay Formula* is set forth below.

$$\frac{\text{Contract Billings}}{\text{Total Billings for Original Contract Period}} \times \begin{array}{c}\text{Total Company Overhead}\\ \text{During Original Contract}\\ \text{Period}\end{array} = \begin{array}{c}\text{Overhead}\\ \text{Allocable}\\ \text{to Contract}\end{array}$$

$$\frac{\text{Allocable Overhead}}{\text{Original Days of Contact Performance}} = \text{Overhead Allocable to Contract/Day}$$

$$\text{Daily Overhead} \times \frac{\text{Days of Owner Caused}}{\text{Delay}} = \frac{\text{Home Office Overhead}}{\text{Owed}}$$

This formula attempts to allocate HOOH for the **original** contract period first to the project and then break it down on a daily basis to the impacted project to determine the compensation owed. But, it assumes that the HOOH rate from the original contract period should hold the same throughout the project, even during the delayed period. Using the numbers referenced above, here are the results.

$$\frac{\$76,866,128}{\$247,711,967} \times \$16,265,000 = \$5,407,102$$

$$\frac{\$5,047,102}{365 \text{ cd's}} = \$13,828/\text{days}$$

$$\$13,828 \times 235 \text{ days} = \underline{\$3,249,580}$$

Modified Eichleay Formula—Variation 2 (*G.S. & L. Mechanical & Construction, Inc.*, DOT CAB No. 1640, 86-3 BCA (CCH) ¶19,026 (1986) and *Schindler Haughton Elevator Corp.*, GSBCA No. 5390, 80-2 BCA (CCH) ¶14,871 (1980))

A later variation of the *Eichleay Formula* follows.

$$\frac{\text{Contract Billings}}{\text{Total Billings for Original Contract Period}} \times \begin{array}{c}\text{Total Company Overhead}\\ \text{During Original Contract}\\ \text{Period}\end{array} = \begin{array}{c}\text{Overhead}\\ \text{Allocable}\\ \text{to Contract}\end{array}$$

$$\frac{\text{Allocable Overhead}}{\text{Original Days of Contact Performance}} = \text{Overhead Allocable to Contract/Day}$$

$$\text{Daily Overhead} \times \frac{\text{Days of Owner Caused}}{\text{Delay}} = \frac{\text{Home Office Overhead}}{\text{Owed}}$$

Like the first variation to *Eichleay* this formula attempts to allocate HOOH for the **original** contract period first to the project and then on a daily basis to determine the compensation owed. It adds into the calculation the value of contract billings during the extended period in an attempt to compensate for overhead costs spread over a longer period of time. With the real numbers from the above referenced case, here are the results.

$$\frac{\$76{,}866{,}128}{\$254{,}824{,}241} \times \$16{,}265{,}000 = \$4{,}906{,}235$$

$$\frac{\$4{,}906{,}235}{365\,cd's} = \$13{,}442/\text{days}$$

$$\$13{,}442 \times 235 \text{ days} = \underline{\$3{,}158{,}870}$$

Hudson Formula (*J.F. Finnegan, Ltd. v. Sheffield City Council*, 43 Build. L.R. 124 (Q.B. 1989))

The *Hudson Formula* is set forth below.

$$\frac{\text{Planned Home Office}}{\text{Overhead \& Profit \%}} \times \frac{\text{Original Contact Sum}}{\text{Original Contract Period}} =$$

$$\frac{\text{Allocable Overhead}}{\text{Per Day}} \times \frac{\text{Period of Owner-Caused}}{\text{Delay}} = \frac{\text{Home Office}}{\text{Overhead}}\ \text{Owed}$$

This formula was created by the courts in the United Kingdom and later exported to Canada. It derives its daily HOOH rate on the basis of the as-bid calculations and assumes that the bid rate should hold constant throughout the life of the project. Some along the United States–Canadian border have started seeing this in claims. Using the information above, we have the following.

$$7.0\% \times \frac{\$68{,}500{,}000}{365 \text{ days}} = \$13{,}137/cd$$

$$\$13{,}137 \times 235 \text{ days} = \underline{\$3{,}087{,}195}$$

Ernstrom Formula (*The Construction Lawyer*, 3, 1, Winter, 1982)

The *Ernstrom Formula* can best be explained with the following formula.

$$\frac{\text{Total Overhead for Contract Period (All Projects)}}{\text{Total Labor Costs for Contract Period (All Projects)}} = \text{General Labor/Overhead Ratio}$$

Labor/Overhead Ratio × Labor Costs During Delay

= Overhead Allocable to Delay

This formula rests on the theory that there is a direct relationship between overhead costs and labor costs that can be calculated and applied to a delay situation. That is, as labor costs grow so do the corresponding home office costs. Thus, by calculating this ratio and applying it to the amount of labor expenses incurred during a delay period, the amount of damages due to the delay can also be calculated. Since this is a ratio formula, it does **not** develop a daily HOOH cost but rather calculates a lump sum cost. In discussing this formula with the attorney author, J. William Ernstrom, he advises that while there are **no** citations in New York case law, he has had some success in getting juries to accept this approach in jury trials.

Utilizing the number from the case set forth above, the Ernstrom Formula develops the following calculation.

$$\frac{\$28{,}918{,}417}{\$137{,}194{,}333} = 21.08\%$$

$$21.08\% \times \$2{,}560{,}419 = \underline{\$539{,}736}$$

Manshul Formula (Manshul Construction Corp. v. Dormitory Authority, 436 N.Y.S.2d 724 (App. Div.) (1981))

The *Manshul Formula* is shown below.

$$\frac{\text{Cost of Work Performed}}{\text{During Delay Period}} \times \frac{\text{Contract Cost \%}}{\text{Cost + Mark Up \%}} = \text{Direct Cost}$$

$$\frac{\text{Direct Cost Incurred}}{\text{During Delay Period}} \times \frac{\text{Home Office}}{\text{Overhead \%*}} = \text{Home Office Overhead Owed}$$

* Estimated or known HOOH % portion of bid markup.

This formula has also been referred to as the **Direct Cost Allocation Method**. It is a creature of the courts in the state of New York. When New York courts rejected *Eichleay* they were challenged to pose a substitute method of calculating overhead and created this formula. It does **not** arrive at a daily overhead rate. Rather, it uses the as-bid HOOH rate times the cost of work performed during the delay period to determine the overhead used. Using the information above, we have the following.

$$\$7{,}112{,}274 \times \frac{100\%}{107\%} = \$6{,}646{,}985$$

$$\$6{,}646{,}985 \times 4.5\% = \underline{\$299{,}114}$$

Carteret Formula (Carteret Work Uniforms, Inc., ASBCA No. 1647, 6 CCF §61,651-1951 (1954))

The *Carteret Formula* is displayed below.

$$\frac{\text{Actual Overhead Rate During}}{\text{Delay Period}} - \text{Normal Overhead Rate} = \frac{\text{Excess}}{\text{Overhead Rate}}$$

$$\text{Excess Overhead Rate} \times \frac{\text{Total Cost of Work During}}{\text{Delay Period}} = \frac{\text{Home Office}}{\text{Overhead Owed}}$$

Carteret is a formula that comes out of the manufacturing sector but some have attempted to apply the formula to construction delay cases. It assumes that there is a differential in overhead rates during a delay period when compared to a company's "normal" HOOH and calculates this difference. The formula then multiplies this rate differential times the cost of work performed during the delay period. Since this is a cost based formula, like *Manshul*, it does **not** derive a daily rate. The problem with this approach is that if **no** rate differential can be shown, then **no** HOOH is owed. Let's take a look at the hypothetical case numbers.

$$6.1\% - 4.5\% = 1.6\%$$

$$1.6\% \times \$7,112,274 = \underline{\$113,796}$$

Allegheny Formula (*Allegheny Sportswear Co.*, ASBCA No. 4163, 58-1 BCA (CCVH) ¶1684 (1958))

The *Allegheny Formula* is set forth below.

$$\text{Actual Overhead Rate During Delay Period} - \text{Actual Overhead Rate During Entire Project Performance Period} = \text{Excess Overhead Rate}$$

$$\text{Excess Overhead Rate} \times \text{Contract Base Cost} = \text{Home Office Overhead Rate Owed}$$

Like *Carteret* this formula comes to the construction industry from the manufacturing sector. And, like *Carteret* and *Manshul* it is cost-based, **not** time-based. Thus, it does not derive a daily overhead rate but calculates overhead from the rate differential times the base bid cost. Again, if **no** rate differential can be demonstrated, then **no** HOOH is owed even if owner caused delay is proven. Let's see how the numbers work out.

$$6.1\% - 5.3\% = 0.8\%$$

$$0.8\% \times \$68,500,000 = \underline{\$548,000}$$

Emden Formula (*Alfred McAlpine Homes North, Ltd. v. Property & Land Contractors, Ltd.* 76 BLR 59 (1995))

Finally, the *Emden Formula* is displayed as follows.

$$\frac{\text{Total Overhead \& Profit* / Total Company Turnover**}}{100} \times$$

$$\frac{\text{Gross Contract Sum}}{\text{Planned Contract Period}} \times$$

$$\text{Owner-Caused Delay Period} = \text{Home Office Overhead Owed}$$

* Total company overhead and profit during contract period
** Total company revenue for contract period

This formula is a creature of the Canadian courts. Its approach is similar to the *Eichleay* and *Hudson* formulas in that it attempts to allocate total company overhead to a project on first a proportionate basis and then a daily basis. It utilizes both overhead and profit costs as a part of the calculation and then multiplies the result times the amount of owner-caused delay incurred. Looking at our hypothetical case we find the following.

$$\frac{\$37{,}156{,}795/\$381{,}095{,}333}{100} \times \frac{\$68{,}500{,}000}{365\,\text{cd's}} = \$18{,}298/\text{cd}$$

$$\$18{,}298 \times 235\,\text{cd's} = \$4{,}300{,}030$$

Overhead formulas—results

To determine whether these nine formulas deliver approximately the same results, the final outcome of each is shown below.

Formula	Daily Rate	HOOH Recovery
Eichleay Formula	$ 8,905	$2,092,675
Modified Eichleay Formula – Var. 1	$13,828	$3,249,580
Modified Eichleay Formula – Var. 2	$13,442	$3,158,870
Hudson Formula	$13,137	$3,087,195
Ernstrom Formula	N/A	$ 539,736
Manshul Formula	N/A	$ 299,114
Carteret Formula	N/A	$ 113,796
Allegheny Formula	N/A	$ 548,000
Emden Formula	$18,298	$4,300,030

Based on the above analysis, it would appear that the answer to the original question of whether an owner should care which formula is used is clearly "Yes!" What is generally presented as an accounting technique is obviously an estimating approach which yields wildly different results, even when applied to the same case.

New definitions

In some recent court cases (cited herein below) U.S. federal courts have started using familiar terms but giving them different meanings. This obviously adds to the confusion surrounding the issue of HOOH. Three terms that need to be understood to participate in today's debate on HOOH are the following.

Unabsorbed Overhead: When a project's cash flow is substantially diminished due to an owner caused delay, the contractor's fixed HOOH costs are **not** absorbed by the project and must, therefore, be absorbed by other projects. This is the amount of overhead that occurs during this period.

Delay Period: Although a term long used in construction, the **new** use of this term in the context of the HOOH issue is the period of time that the project's cash flow has been substantially diminished.

Extended Period: This is the period of time beyond the original contract date due solely to owner caused delays—the compensable delay period.

Extended versus unabsorbed home office overhead

Based on current U.S. court rulings at the federal level, there is now a clear distinction between extended and unabsorbed HOOH, as follows. Extended HOOH stands for the proposition that for every day of owner caused delay, the owner owes the contractor HOOH based on a rate derived from one of the formulas outlined above. In contrast to this approach, unabsorbed overhead arises when a contractor's cash flow on a project is substantially diminished as a direct and sole result of an owner caused delay of unknown duration at the outset. The unknown duration at the start of the delay prevents the contractor from replacing the stopped work with other work, which could help support the overhead costs.

The keys to the recent unabsorbed HOOH cases at the U.S. federal court level can be summarized as follows.

- A contractor is entitled to recover unabsorbed HOOH **if** it arises due to owner caused delay, and provided that, the contractor can meet certain other criteria.
- There is **no** exact method of accounting for unabsorbed HOOH costs.
- Therefore, a reasonable "estimating formula" is necessary.

Prerequisites for recovering unabsorbed home office overhead

The prerequisites for recovering unabsorbed HOOH can be derived from reading a number of U.S. federal court decisions. The requirements, as they now stand, appear to be the following. The *Capital Electric Company* (GSBCA Nos. 5316 & 5317, 83-2 BCA (CCH) ¶16,458 (1983)) and the *Savoy Construction Company v. U.S.* (2 Cl. Ct, 338 (1983)) cases established the following.

- Compensable delay (owner caused delay) must be proven.
- The contractor must show a "reduction in the stream of income from payments for direct costs" resulting in a reduction of income available to offset HOOH costs. For example, a suspension of work order or a differing site condition resulting in stopped work.
- The contractor must show that they could not mitigate damages by taking on new work during the delay period (thus, the "unknown duration" rule) denying them the opportunity to replace the lost income.

Compensable delay

Other cases (**not** cited in this paper due to space limitations) have addressed the issue of unabsorbed HOOH and the following situations seem to meet the above tests.

- Work stoppages caused by design defects.
- Work suspension caused by resolution of bid protests.
- Work suspension due to owner failure to respond to contractor submittals or inquiries.

It appears clear that the contractor is only entitled to recover when there is pure owner caused delay. And, it is also clear that **no** recovery can be had when concurrent delay can be shown.

Reduction in stream of income

The contractor must demonstrate a clear cause and effect relationship between the owner caused delay or disruption and the reduction in the stream of income from the project. That is, if a delay occurs but project cash flow is **not** substantially reduced, then **no** unabsorbed HOOH is recoverable. The problem, at the time of this writing, is that there is **no** court decision defining the term "substantial reduction" in project cash flow—that is **no** court has decided that substantial reduction in cash flow must exceed 50% or some other percentage. Everyone, presumably, would agree that a complete stop work order, which stops all project payments, meets the test. But, what if the owner directs work stopped on only one half or two thirds of the project, is this "substantial reduction"?

Inability to mitigate damages

The contractor must demonstrate that it was impractical to take on new work during the period of the owner caused delay. The classic argument is that if the contractor does **not** know the duration of the delay at the outset, they are in **no** position to contract for new work. Additionally, some courts (cases uncited) have concluded that owner directives to "remain on standby" or "be ready to resume work on short notice" also preclude the contractor from seeking new work to replace lost income. Some examples of a contractor's inability to mitigate damages are the following.

- Numerous sporadic disruptions of the work,
- Exhaustion of a contractor's bonding capacity,
- Uncertainty of the duration of the delay,
- Size and capability of the contractor, and,
- All available equipment committed to this project.

Additionally, under a more recent U.S. federal court case, should the government's suspension of work order **not** contain the words "… remain on standby …" then the contractor **cannot** recover HOOH (*The Redlands Company, Inc. v. U.S.*, 2011 Ct. Fed. Cl. No. 08-606C (Apr. 7, 2011)) regardless of how long the suspension remains in place.

Corollary cases on HOOH recovery

In *Wickham Contracting Co. v. Fischer* (12 F.3d 1574 (Fed. Cir. 1994)) the court determined that the original *Eichleay* Formula is " … the exclusive means available for calculating unabsorbed home office overhead … " costs. This ruling applies only to contracts with the U.S. Federal government and is **not**, as yet, applicable to any state—except, perhaps, Virginia (*Fairfax County Redevelopment and Housing Authority v. Worcester Brothers Company*, 257 VA 382 (1999)). However, it comes after the court reviewed various formulas and the basis for each. In *Community Heating & Plumbing Co. v. Kelso* (87 F.2d 1575 (Fed. Cir. 1993)) the court decided that if the delay to the project grows solely out of change orders (contract modifications) rather than a work suspension, then the contractor is **not** entitled to recover unabsorbed HOOH. This court took the position that delay caused by changes to the work is properly compensated through application of the contract's overhead and profit rates and no unabsorbed overhead is owed.

General rules of recovery for unabsorbed HOOH

Based on the above, the general rules for recovering unabsorbed HOOH on U.S. federal contracts are the following.

- Owner caused delay must be proven
- The owner caused delay must result in a substantial reduction in project cash flow
- The contractor must show they were unable to take on new work due to the unknown duration of the delay and were unable to perform other work on this project to support their HOOH costs
- The contractor must show the owner required them to remain on standby, ready to resume work quickly once the problem was resolved
- The contractor must show that the project delay did **not** result from directed changes or modifications, and
- The contractor must calculate their unabsorbed HOOH cost using the original *Eichleay* Formula.

While most state courts have **not**, as yet, adopted these rules, it is reasonable to assume that owners will urge adoption when litigation arises which contains a claim for HOOH costs.

Conclusion

HOOH is recoverable in certain delay situations and has been so for more than half a century. HOOH costs are hard to calculate. While numerous formulas have been put forth over the years, they give wildly varying results even when applied to the same fact setting. The issue is still unsettled, especially in state, local, and private contracts. Owners seeking predictability with regard to HOOH damages in the event of owner-caused delay have a few choices.

- Contract language can be included which sets forth the rules outlined above, or something substantially similar, and specifies which formula is to be used if such delay arises.
- In the alternative, the owner may seek to limit recovery of such costs through use of a No Damage for Delay Clause if the project is located in a State where such clauses are still enforced.
- Or, the owner may insert the new American Institute of Architects (AIA) clause concerning Mutual Waiver of Consequential Damages (American Institute of Architects, Contract Document Form A201-1997, Clause 4.3.10) and preclude this claim all together.

James G. Zack, Jr., CCM, CFCC, FAACE, FFA, FPC, FRICS, PMP
James Zack Consulting, LLC and Senior Advisor
Navigant Construction Forum™
The United States

10.5 Claims resulting from governing law

Claims resulting from the governing law are included, for example, in FIDIC forms under claims made "otherwise in connection with the contract" (see Sub-Clauses 2.5

and 20.1). There is no reason to prevent either the contractor or the employer from making a claim for breach of either a contractual or tortious duty, if the contract does not stipulate otherwise. If the engineer receives such a claim, they should treat it in the same way as any other claim using similar principles mentioned above and take into account the options and restrictions given by the governing law.

The governing law will significantly influence, for example, claims connected to termination, proving differing site conditions and professional liability claims aimed at designers, engineers, construction managers, and so on.

10.6 Global claims

To prove that something caused an effect can be challenging in construction disputes. As discussed in *Keating on Building Contracts*:

> Contractors often have claims dependent on a number of separate causes, each of which has contributed to delay and extra cost. In principle, the loss attributable to each cause should be separately identified and particularised but separation may be difficult.

Such complexity leads to the development of "global claims." A global claim is one in which the contractor seeks compensation for a group of employer risk events but does not or cannot demonstrate a direct link between the loss incurred and the individual employer risk events (SCL Protocol).

Recently, some courts have been accepting global claims or modified versions of them. This is due to the complexity of activities performed on a construction site that makes the process of individual claims, precise documenting, and quantifying (where each cause has a distinctive effect and a distinctive loss) almost impossible (Haidar, 2011).

A global claim is one whereby an aggregated loss or period of time is based on a group of individual breaches or events without attempting to prove the individual impact of each breach or event. Where the claim is one for money rather than time, such claims are often referred to as *total cost claims* reflecting the fact that they often appear simply from the contractor's total cost for the project, less the amount paid to date by the employer (Choat and Peckett, 2012).

Even if the process of identifying individual causes and their effects and establishing the specific damages can be achieved, the time it can take to present individual claims is prohibitive—especially if the task could be repeated hundreds of times on very large projects. The courts are also showing reluctance to sift through and review thousands of documents just to prove liability or to decide on variation issues (Ramsey, 2013).

Critics of the global approach to claims often refer to the decision of the Privy Council in the Hong Kong case of *Wharf Properties v. Eric Cumine Associates (No. 2)*. In Australia, on the other hand, the courts have developed a more practical approach to the problems of global claims, as seen in *John Holland Construction & Engineering Pty Ltd v. Kvaerner R J Brown Pty Ltd*. This approach was accepted in England in *Bernhards Rugby Landscapes Ltd v. Stockley Park*.

One of the key precedents in this area is the UK case of *Walter Lilly v. Mackay*. The facts and outcome are as follows: in 2004, Walter Lilly & Company entered into a contract with an employer for the construction of three large houses on the site of what was previously the Earls Court Telephone Exchange. A dispute arose and it was argued that Walter Lilly & Company's claim should fail on the grounds that it was a "global" claim.

Ruling: Justice Akenhead (the head of the Technology and Construction Court) explained that such claims are usually formulated on the basis of

> numerous potential or actual causes of delay and/or disruption, a total cost on the job, a net payment from the employer and a claim for the balance between costs and payment, which is attributed without more and by inference to the causes of delay and disruption relied on.

Before *Walter Lilly*, certain cases suggested that a global claim would only be permitted where a contractor could show that it was impossible to separate individual losses caused by individual breaches. Justice Akenhead's judgment continued:

> Obviously, there is no need for the Court to go down the global or total cost route if the actual cost attributable to individual loss causing events can be readily or practicably determined … In principle, unless the contract dictates that a global cost claim is not permissible if certain hurdles are not overcome, such a claim may be permissible on the facto and subject to proof.

One of the most forceful ways in which a global claim can be undermined is to show that there are other causes for the loss claimed by the contractor for which there is no entitlement to recover under the contract. The approach preferred by Justice Akenhead was for any established counter-examples to be deducted from the global loss, insofar as they can be quantified "either precisely or at least by way of assessment." Such an approach was thought by His Honor to be:

> not inconsistent with the judge's reasoning in the Merton case that "a rolled up award can only be made in the case where the loss or expense attributable to each head of claim cannot in reality be separated," because, where the tribunal can take out of the "rolled up award" or "total" or "global" loss elements for which the contractor cannot recover loss in the proceedings, it will generally be left with the loss attributable to the events which [sic] the contractor is entitled to recover loss.

Before this case, a defendant could rely on a number of counter-examples in an attempt to show the claim was fundamentally unsound. A claimant might now simply respond that whatever counter-examples are proved can be deducted from the global loss and the remainder will "generally be … attributable to … events [for] which the contractor is entitled to recover loss." If pressed too far, this approach has the potential (in practical terms) to shift part of the burden of proof to the defendant (Choat and Peckett, 2012).

In January 2013, the Court of Appeal confirmed the decision in *Walter Lilly*. In doing so it remarked that it was "not reasonably arguable that the judge erred in his analysis of the law as to what is required in respect of a global claim." The decision in *Walter Lilly* does not change the fact that it is still very difficult to prove a global claim. It is worth mentioning here that standard forms usually do not deal with the admissibility of global claims. *Walter Lilly* may lead some employers to write into their contracts the terms prescribing when (if at all) global claims can be made (Choat and Peckett, 2012).

A completely global claim that piles up allegations and evidence in the hope that the tribunal will be overwhelmed by the complexity and will accede to a large claim is likely to fail outright. The claim should be divided up into discrete parts. This may be a division based on particular areas of a project, particular activities or trades or particular time periods. It may also be a combination of these. This allows the case to be presented to the tribunal in a logical manner and assists the tribunal to understand the factual position more easily (Ramsey, 2013).

Such a "global" approach to damage evaluation may be viable in common law litigation, DAB or arbitration but can be difficult in civil law litigation where judges strictly require precise evidence of damage via detailed documentation including causation and calculation of particular damages. On the other hand, it is common knowledge in civil law countries that it is sometimes difficult (or even impossible) to prove damages for breach of contract, even where there is no doubt that damages have in fact occurred. In its judgment 32 Cdo 4762/2010 dated 20 March 2010, the Supreme Court of the Czech Republic ruled that:

> If the claim to sue is legitimate in terms of its basis, the court cannot dismiss the lawsuit for the failure to satisfy the burden of proof requirements even if the burden of proof requirement is only in respect of the amount of the claim that the court considers.

The obstacle was in § 136 of the *Czech Civil Procedure Code*, which stipulates that "[if] the amount of the claim can only be determined with difficulties or cannot be determined at all, the court shall determine it at its sole discretion." Such provisions are common in the majority of civil law countries.

A similar provision is can be found in UNIDROIT principle 7.4.3, which refers to *Certainty of Harm* and provides: "(3) Where the amount of damages cannot be established with a sufficient degree of certainty, the assessment is at the discretion of the court."

In the daily practice of international construction projects, participants often have to deal with the issue of defining "cost" and "overhead" (under Sub-Clause 1.1.4.3 in the FIDIC forms 1999, First Edition) in relation to delay and disruption claims. Greater guidance on this issue would no doubt be welcomed by international construction practitioners, for example, in the *FIDIC Guidance for the Preparation of Particular Conditions* or *The FIDIC Contracts Guide* to establish international best practice in this area. The Czech State Fund for Transportation Infrastructure (SFDI) issued recently a methodology for claim quantification - see it here: http://www.sfdi.cz/soubory/obrazky-clanky/metodiky/2018_metodika_naroku.pdf.

All global claims are not negatively "global"! by Frank Thomas (France)

There is a continuous debate in the construction industry on the effectiveness and validity of global claims, which are presented during court and arbitration proceedings. On one hand, a global claim is very often associated with the claimant's incapacity to demonstrate how a group of delay events have actually affected the time for completion or claimant's working efficiency. On the other hand, a global claim may also mean something completely different such as the usage of a specific Forensic Delay Analysis (FDA) technique for proving causation between liability and damage of either party. For these reasons, the word "global" tends to bring with it negative connotations. Global claims can be categorized into two groups:

- *The global claim as a bag claim*: Under a bag claim all the events are collected in a non-structured manner and described as having a "global" effect without showing causality and effect on the critical path and/or resources. Under a bag claim, concurrency of events will usually be neglected or ignored and no proper FDA technique is actually used. Under a bag claim, the claimant is often relying upon the "magic" of the effect of grouping delay events together without proving any causation between liability and damage.
- *The global claim as a net compounded effect claim*: Under a net compounded effect (NCE) claim, all the events are evaluated/quantified separately on merit and quantum and their net compounded effect is then analyzed by using a specific FDA technique such as "impacted as planned," "time impact analysis in slices," "collapsed as built," and so on.

The NCE claim truly and correctly analyses and quantifies the effect of all delay events in a baseline program by taking into account their concurrency by using appropriate FDA techniques. There are different FDA techniques and the selection of one specific technique is usually dependent on contractual requirements. The FDA must prove three fundamental elements:

1. *Liability*: Parties' liability for a delay must be demonstrated under the contract terms and/or in accordance with applicable law.
2. *Causation*: The causal link between one party's delay and the delayed completion of the project must be demonstrated unambiguously and by taking into account the concurrency of delays of both parties.
3. *Damage*: The alleged damage suffered by one party due to the delay caused by the other party should be clearly established (i.e., extent of the delays and additional costs suffered by each respective party).

For example, when delays are evaluated retrospectively after project completion, it becomes almost unavoidable to apportion the delays between the parties in an objective manner. A critical path method (CPM) analysis, which includes a comparison of the "as built" with the "as planned" program on a month-by-month basis, usually constitutes a credible means of apportioning parties' delays and determines their impact on the project completion date. For example, a NCE claim can be prepared by using a detailed FDA taking into account all the delays encountered on the project such as the "time impact analysis in slices" technique. This FDA technique consists of the addition of delays in a relevant program at the beginning of a time slice (e.g., a month) and the comparison of the impacted program with the "as built" program at the end of the relevant time slice by establishing the gains and delays caused by each party and in the reiteration of such evaluation slice by slice. This FDA technique enables the delay analyst to exactly apportion delays between the parties. FDA techniques are usually found to be an acceptable means of proving, causation between liability and damage during court and/or arbitration proceedings.

A global claim becomes "positively" global when its aim is to demonstrate rationally (and not by magic) the link between causation and damage by using sound FDA techniques.

Frank Thomas
Claim Quantum Specialist
T-K Consulting
France

10.7 Contractor's claim management under FIDIC forms

Under 1999 FIDIC forms, contractor claim management must be supported by proper record keeping (see Sub-Clauses 6.10, 8.3(d), 14.5, and 20.1 of the FIDIC forms). The contractor also has an "early warning duty" Sub-Clause 8.3 and further Sub-Clauses that foresee the so called "first notices" about a risk (namely 1.8, 1.9, 4.12, 4.24, 16.1, 17.4, 19.2), the duty to notify the claim (not later than 28 days after the contractor became aware, or should have become aware, of the event or circumstance) and the duty to submit a fully detailed claim that includes full supporting particulars (not later than 42 days after the contractor became aware, or should have become aware, of the event or circumstance). Further, there is the duty to keep a summary of claims in a progress report as per Sub-Clause 4.21 (f) and reporting in the monthly statement as per 14.3 (f). See Appendix D Claim Management System under FIDIC forms, in this volume. The 2017 edition brings more detailed and structured claim procedures based on the exactly same principles however.

According to FIDIC, the basic procedure for a contractor's claim is described in Sub-Clause 20.1, according to which:

> If the contractor considers himself to be entitled to any extension of the time for completion and/or any additional payment, under any Clause of these conditions or otherwise in connection with the contract, the contractor shall give notice to the engineer, describing the event or circumstance giving rise to the claim. The notice shall be given as soon as practicable, and not later than 28 days after the contractor became aware, or should have become aware, of the event or circumstance. If the contractor fails to give notice of a claim within such period of 28 days, the time for completion shall not be extended, the contractor shall not be entitled to additional payment, and the employer shall be discharged from all liability in connection with the claim. Otherwise, the following provisions of this Sub-Clause shall apply.

The contractor shall also submit any other notices which are required by the contract, and supporting particulars for the claim, all as relevant to such event or circumstance.

The contractor shall keep such contemporary records as may be necessary to substantiate any claim, either on the site or at another location acceptable to the engineer. Without admitting the employer's liability, the engineer may, after receiving any notice under this Sub-Clause, monitor the record-keeping and/or instruct the contractor to keep further contemporary records. The contractor shall permit the engineer to inspect all these records, and shall (if instructed) submit copies to the engineer.

A claim quantification follows the notice of claim.
Pursuant to Sub-Clause 20.1, the following applies:

Within 42 days after the contractor became aware (or should have become aware) of the event or circumstance giving rise to the claim, or within such other period as may be proposed by the contractor and approved by the engineer, the contractor shall send to the engineer a fully detailed claim which includes full supporting particulars of the basis of the claim and of the extension of time and/or additional payment claimed. If the event or circumstance giving rise to the claim has a continuing effect:

(a) this fully detailed claim shall be considered as interim;
(b) the contractor shall send further interim claims at monthly intervals, giving the accumulated delay and/or amount claimed, and such further particulars as the engineer may reasonably require; and
(c) the contractor shall send a final claim within 28 days after the end of the effects resulting from the event or circumstance, or within such other period as may be proposed by the contractor and approved by the engineer.

After the claim is submitted, the following procedure by the engineer is foreseen:

Within 42 days after receiving a claim or any further particulars supporting a previous claim, or within such other period as may be proposed by the engineer and approved by the contractor, the engineer shall respond with approval, or with disapproval and detailed comments. He may also request any necessary further particulars, but shall nevertheless give his response on the principles of the claim within such time.

The following will further apply:

Each payment certificate shall include such amounts for any claim as have been reasonably substantiated as due under the relevant provision of the contract. Unless and until the particulars supplied are sufficient to substantiate the whole of the claim, the contractor shall only be entitled to payment for such part of the claim as he has been able to substantiate.

According to Sub-Clause 3.5, the engineer will decide about the contractor's claim to agree or determine (i) the extension (if any) of the time for completion (before or after its expiry) in accordance with Sub-Clause 8.4 [extension of time for completion], and/or (ii) the additional payment (if any) to which the contractor is entitled under the contract.

Provided on a monthly basis, the statements under 14.3 (f) shall then include as an item: "any other additions or deductions which may have become due under the contract or otherwise, including those under Clause 20 [Claims, Disputes and Arbitration]"

In addition to the above, the progress report under Sub-Clause 4.21 (f) shall include a list of notices given under Sub-Clause 2.5 [Employer's Claims] and notices given under Sub-Clause 20.1 [Contractor's Claims].

Sub-Clauses 6.10 and 8.3 are important for the management of contemporary records. Sub-Clause 6.10 further states that

> The contractor shall submit, to the Engineer, details showing the number of each class of Contractor's Personnel and of each type of contractor's equipment on the Site. Details shall be submitted each calendar month, in a form approved by the engineer, until the contractor has completed all work which is known to be outstanding at the completion date stated in the taking-over certificate for the works.

Sub-Clause 8.3 deals with the time program:

> The contractor shall submit a detailed time program to the engineer within 28 days after receiving the notice under Sub-Clause 8.1 [Commencement of Works]. The *contractor* shall also submit a revised program whenever the previous program is inconsistent with actual progress or with the contractor's obligations. Each program shall include ... (d) a supporting report which includes:
>
> (i) a general description of the methods which the contractor intends to adopt, and of the major stages, in the execution of the works, and
> (ii) details showing the contractor's reasonable estimate of the number of each class of contractor's personnel and of each type of contractor's equipment, required on the site for each major stage.

In the broader sense, contractor claim management also includes protection against the employer's claims and claims related to subcontractors and others.

10.8 Employer's claim management under FIDIC forms

Under 1999 FIDIC forms, employer claim management mainly requires proper record keeping, the duty to notify in accordance with Sub-Clause 2.5 (the notice shall be given as soon as practicable after the employer became aware of the event or circumstances giving rise to the claim) and proper quantification and documentation of the claim. More generally, the employer's claim management also provides protection against contractor claims or against the claims that other construction project participants may lodge.

According to Sub-Clause 2.5:

> If the employer considers himself to be entitled to any payment under any Clause of these conditions or otherwise in connection with the Contract, and/or to any extension of the defects notification period, the employer or the Engineer shall give notice and particulars to the contractor ... The notice shall be given as soon as practicable after the Employer became aware of the event or circumstances giving rise to the claim. A notice relating to any extension of the defects notification period shall be given before the expiry of such period. The particulars shall specify the Clause or other basis of the claim, and shall include substantiation of the amount and/or extension to which the employer considers himself to be entitled in connection with the contract.

Concerning the employer's claim quantification, it applies (pursuant to Sub-Clause 2.5) that the engineer must first decide about the notified employer's claim using Sub-Clause 3.5,

> to agree or determine (i) the amount (if any) which the employer is entitled to be paid by the contractor, and/or (ii) the extension (if any) of the defects notification period in accordance with Sub-Clause 11.3 [extension of defects notification period].

The following will apply after the engineer's decision:

> this amount may be included as a deduction in the contract price and payment certificates. The employer shall only be entitled to set off against or make any deduction from an amount certified in a payment certificate, or to otherwise claim against the contractor, in accordance with this Sub-Clause.

10.9 Intercultural aspects

Claim management (particularly in an international project management context) cannot exist in isolation of intercultural aspects. As the claims process is quite a strict system, it can create problems in some cultural backgrounds if the proper tactics and diplomacy are not employed. In developed countries, such formalized procedures have been used for a prolonged period of time and construction project participants are used to them. In less developed countries where claims management is a new concept, they may be problematic to implement.

For example, the contemporary Czech character is known for its attempts to avoid conflicts. Czech people prefer calm and a friendly social climate and may read a rigorous, formal advance as a personal attack. Among the Czechs, skepticism surrounds written communications, with oral communication and reporting being preferred as more reliable. This approach may be unacceptable or even dangerous in an international construction project setting.

Claim management is based on British traditions. Official correspondence is something natural for the Britons. On the contrary, they do not like talking about money, preferring to discuss it formally and in writing (Fox, 2010).

Another aspect, typical of many nations is that people consider a small delay to be normal, with no consequences and sanctions and often with problems often sorted out at the last minute. This is a very risky approach due to the fact that claim notifications are subject to certain dates (deadlines) and failure to keep them may threaten the enforceability of a relevant claim.

Southeast Asia is a sub-region of Asia, consisting of the countries that are members of the Association of Southeast Asian Nations (ASEAN) and East Timor. The members of the ASEAN are:

1. Brunei Darussalam
2. Cambodia
3. Indonesia
4. Laos
5. Malaysia
6. Myanmar
7. the Philippines
8. Singapore
9. Thailand
10. Vietnam.

Southeast Asia is a diverse mix of countries, people, cultures, religions, laws, and politics. The ASEAN mix of countries offer a stable political, legal, and business environment to a much less developed and much less certain legal, political, and business environment. There are also members of ASEAN that are currently in the process of transitioning to a more democratic form of government.

The culture in ASEAN is diverse: a mixture of Chinese, Indian, Spanish, Arabic, and the indigenous Malay cultures, including a number of other nationalities and ethnic groups. The Philippines, as an example, is influenced by Spanish and Western cultures derived from when the period the country was under Spanish and American rule.

Although English is the common language in the ASEAN countries, the level of speaking and understanding the English language varies among the members. According to the Department of Languages and Cultures of Southeast Asia, ASEAN is a region of enormous linguistic diversity where hundreds, or perhaps thousands of languages are spoken.

English is not the ASEAN's mother tongue, but rather is considered the language for business. While a number of countries view English as their second language, there are also several in ASEAN that are still in the process of learning and understanding English, see Table 10.1.

One of the main considerations is that countries in Southeast Asia are traditionally "high-context cultures," whereas Australia, Germany, England, Canada,

Table 10.1 Languages spoken in Southeast Asia

Country	Language spoken
Singapore	Malay, Mandarin, Tamil, English (national language is Malay with English as the language for business)
Brunei Darussalam	Malay (Behasa Melayu)
Cambodia	Khmer
Indonesia	Indonesian (Bahasa Indonesia)
Laos	Lao
Malaysia	Malay
Myanmar	Burmese
The Philippines	Filipino (English as language for business)
Thailand	Thai
Vietnam	Vietnamese

Switzerland, and the United States are typically low-context culture countries. High-context culture uses high-context communications. Communications are indirect and the message is delivered implicitly rather than explicitly and directly (Harris and Moran, 2004).

Within the ASEAN countries:

- Relationships are always more important in business than the contract.
- "Face saving" is regarded as one of the most important dimensions of context in business in the ASEAN countries, in order to preserve one's prestige, dignity, or reputation.
- High priority on keeping harmony, preventing anyone from losing face and nurturing relationships during the life of the contract.

For example, Filipinos are somewhat emotional people and very sensitive. "HIYA" in Filipino (meaning "shame") is an important social force for Filipinos that applies in business, to people, and society generally. People from all levels need to "save face" at all cost. This culture of "losing face" is also found among Thais and other members of the ASEAN. Indonesians are extremely indirect in business contexts. Therefore, it is very important to circumvent the subject before the critical issues are mentioned. Indonesians and other Malay countries in the ASEAN, in their business context try their best to avoid someone feeling "MALU" (in Indonesian, meaning ashamed, insulted or embarrassed). Presented by Salvador P. Castro, Jr. during the FIDIC Asia-Pacific Contract Users' Conference on 11 and 12 June 2013, Malaysia.

"Claim" as perceived in the Polish civil law environment by Michał Skorupski (Poland)

It seems there is a difference in the meaning of the word "claim" in particular cultures and legal systems. Take, for example, common law jurisdictions versus the Polish civil law jurisdiction. The Polish equivalent of "claim" ("*roszczenie*" in Polish) has a strong, negative connotation. Let me put it into context. In England, a worker claims his holiday entitlement, his expenses from his employer and his tax return from the Treasury. It seems that claiming is a natural feature of life and the public as well as the institutions and the state itself are quite used to it. In Poland, if someone has a claim—"*ma roszczenie*"—it means that other person has done something wrong to them. It is perceived as an act of self-defence or aggression related to some failure rather than a request for a normal entitlement.

A typical person dealing with "*roszczenia*" in the construction industry in Poland will be a lawyer rather than commercial manager or a quantity surveyor. Instead of concentrating on the subject matter of the event, lawyers will normally prepare a long essay presenting the legal standpoint and exaggerating the consequences.

Typical terms of reference for the role of an engineer of a public project, for example, issued by the Road Authority in Poland, will contain a sentence and obligation to 'predict and counteract Contractor's claims' ("*przewidywać i przeciwdziałać roszczeniom*"). The role of the FIDIC engineer is openly and blatantly altered to resist and oppose claims rather than analysing them and trying to reach agreement between the parties or making a fair determination in accordance to Sub-Clause 3.5.

Such a defense of claims often results in unfair actions, legal deliberations, and looking for loopholes in documents. Engineers have become more lawyers and essayists rather than professionals duly trained and experienced to perform the role according to the contract.

However, more and more contractors are progressively demanding the engineers (companies performing this role as well as individuals) perform their duties under the contract with due diligence, that is, take due regard of all relevant circumstances, including those circumstances that are advantageous to the contractor. It is quite typical (as a consequence) to prepare claims based purely on inadequate performance of the role of the engineer.

The negligence of the engineer is the contractual responsibility of the employer (Article 474, *Polish Civil Code*). However, the engineer may be personally liable for their actions if they exceed their proxy (Articles 103 and 104, *Polish Civil Code*). In all cases the engineer can be held responsible for the contractor's loss occurring as result of contravening the law (Articles 361, 415, and 430, *Polish Civil Code*). Reminding the engineers of their duties and potential individual responsibility has been highly recommended also. Since 2004, the employers who have an absolute monopoly on constructing the terms and conditions of the public works contracts have started to abandon the idea of using dispute adjudication boards or arbitration tribunals. In fact, the dispute is now limited only to the determination of the engineer which is subject to pressure from the employer before proceeding directly to a public court. This was meant to limit the influx of claims. Of course the actual result is the opposite with more and more cases left to the courts. The response of the contractors was to strengthen the claims policy in order to gain a better bargaining position in court.

This is a great example of lack of motivation to resolve naturally encountered problems on site with common sense. Despite the negative meaning of the word "claim" in Polish culture, more and more claims are being sought. Courts are now flooded with these cases—many of which could have been resolved on site in due time.

Michał Skorupski
Contract Manager
Member of SIDiR
Association of Consulting Engineers and Experts in Poland
Poland

10.10 Claim management implementation

Many countries in Central and Eastern Europe (CEE) went through significant changes after 1990. Democracy brought changes in economic systems and with these came new laws. These changes created a lot of opportunities and threats that had not been encountered before. After 1990, the construction market increased both within building construction and civil engineering. Market share, turnover, and profit of construction companies had been steadily increasing without major disruption. Then came the economic recession, reduced public spending on infrastructure projects, and new competitors. This caused upheavals in the CEE construction markets.

In an economic recession, construction companies face rapid change in the external environment. Their strategies must be changed respectively because of budget restrictions. Further, new and very competitive global markets are being established. Competing contractors often bid without profit, risk, and overhead surcharges. Sometimes their bid prices are so low that they make a loss on the project.

It is quite common that large, public construction projects are not properly prepared by the employer. One of the main reasons is that the employer is pushed by the lenders or sponsors to meet unrealistic deadlines. In such a project environment, claim management is crucial. In public procurement projects, the governing laws may affect the variation and claim procedures and cause many difficulties to the participants of construction projects. Whether a contractor is able to claim in compliance with the contract may become a question of survival for them.

Recent experience (1990–2018) from CEE countries shows that local construction practitioners and employers have not been prepared for the current environment that includes tough international competition and new global rules (such as FIDIC contracts). In many countries, formal contractual procedures have not been used even if they were anticipated by the parties as being contractually binding. A "peaceful and financially buoyant situation" on some markets has created complacency and caused formal procedures to be ignored in some cases. Parties were always able to find agreements because of sufficient budget contingencies.

An economic recession is a cause of stress. Budget contingencies are not sufficient and the authorities are required to strictly follow public procurement law. This pushes the contractors to adhere to contracts in the same strict way as with claim management procedures. After the need to claim formally is discovered, construction companies are in haste to implement their respective internal systems for claim management. Claim management is quite a formal process that is not natural for people in many countries. People, for example, in CEE countries are often heard saying "Why should I write a notice to a person sitting in an office next to me? I can simply tell them that something is wrong." Every construction practitioner should know that this premise is completely wrong. The "paperwork" is an important part of project management and claims have to be solved in a formal way. This common knowledge is based on experience and tradition spanning decades. In many countries, the participants of construction projects must develop their own traditions in the new global construction environment.

Claims in a tunnel construction in the Republic of Serbia by Radim Wrana (the Czech Republic)

A tunnel construction in the Republic of Serbia consisted of two double-lane tubes of speedway type. A Czech company came out as the tender winner. The conditions of contract are the FIDIC CONS/1999 Red Book. A state-controlled company is the employer. The role of the engineer is provided by a Joint Venture of companies from Italy, France, and Spain. The European Investment Bank acts as a funding agency.

It became obvious in the early phases of realization that cooperation with the contract administrator (engineer) would be very difficult. Despite official requests by the contractor, neither the land underneath the access route nor any exact location where the excavated material could be disposed of has been provided for the contractor. Moreover, the foundation pit for the cut-and-cover section was found to cross the boundary and extend outside of the expropriated land. The contractor has shown their willingness to resolve these serious problems by renting the neighboring land from the local owners and has succeeded in these efforts. However, no financial compensation for the relevant claim has yet been received from the employer.

Different ground conditions from those foreseen in the tender design have been encountered at the start of excavations. The contractor had insistently notified these findings and proposed counter-measures. The engineer ignored these, responding only when fissures appeared by giving instructions on how to secure the affected slopes. The work techniques used did not allow the already naked slopes to be treated and backfills and ramping therefore had to be used. The contractor further required reworking of the design to reflect the new geology and define the structural analysis of the slopes for their stability. For three months the employer's representatives have been promising this reworked design. With nothing coming, the contractor had to suspend the works in the cut-and-cover section of the tunnel in response to warnings by its geologists.

A month after this suspension, the employer provided a new design, but its engineering quality was appalling. Despite this, the contractor decided to resume work, following the new documentation. Currently, additional re-securing of the slopes is underway using fork trucks and climbers. These measures will cost much more than originally estimated.

Collaboration with the engineer's representatives was troublesome from the very beginning of the project. The engineer was ignoring written requests and was otherwise impossible to reach—even for discussion. Contacting the employer's designer was also difficult and, sometimes, impossible. According to the latest information, the designer believes their design to be without error and it is therefore unwilling to make any design amendments or extensions to them. The conduct of the engineer was very arrogant— stubbornly refusing all the contractor's suggestions to modify the design documents. In general, the basic tender design is of a very low standard.

Disrespecting the guidelines officially issued, the engineer still has not prepared a single variation. Concerning the forms for variation orders, the contractor should use when putting forward variations, the engineer handed them over one year after project commencement.

Another reason behind the mismanagement of the project was the lack of experience with this type of cooperation with the contract administrator (i.e., the engineer) as well as trilingual communications (contract and official communication in English), implying a significant hindrance for most of those involved in construction. Currently, a "paper war" is raging between the contractor and the engineer. An official letter must be sent in response to every request and then one has to wait for a reply. Mutual trust and cooperation became weaker and project fluency became paralyzed.

All these aspects resulted in a long-term dispute solved by a DAB and in huge financial losses for the contractor as well as enormous frustration for all the members of staff involved in the realization and administration of this project.

Radim Wrana
Project manager
Czech Republic

The evolution of contractor's claims in Peru/South America by Jerry Pessah (Peru)

The Republic of Peru is one of the countries located in South America bordering the Pacific Ocean on the West, Ecuador and Colombia on the North, Brazil and Bolivia on the East and Chile on the South. The official language is Spanish but multiple dialects are spoken by the indigenous population. The Peruvian law is based on "civil law." Peru's population is 31 million (2015) and is the fifth most populated in South America. Peru is a mining country by excellence, where gold, copper, and silver are the main mineral resources.

After working for different international investors on various multi-billion dollar projects in Peru and being very familiar with the Peruvian contractors, to achieve business with Peruvian contractors is proving to be difficult compared to North America, Europe, Asia, and other Latin America countries due to Peru's small economy, their culture, currency volatility, and a numerous amount of competitive contractors. These are just a sample of the difficulties one would encounter.

Multi-billion-dollar projects have been developed by international investors in the mining industry intensively in Peru during the last 20 years. The majority of the contracts were based on "unit prices with lump sum components," however, it is also common to find "time and material" contracts depending on the project's engineering development and risk assessments.

The main difficulties working with Peruvian contractors in multi-billion-dollar mining/oil and gas projects are limited amount of equipment, qualified labor, social factors, environmental issues, and language barriers. These are just a few to mention. International companies (hereinafter "investors" or "owners") must consider those and many other factors in their risk analysis during their pre-feasibility and feasibility studies. The contingency factor for these items are higher than working with American or European contractors.

It is interesting to understand how knowledge was transferred from investors to "local contractors." Local people participating in multi-billion-dollar projects gained experience and knowledge through the years, especially in contracts and claims management, knowledge that was not present 15 to 20 years ago. Now we have online information, training, claims management, and procedures adapted from global engineering, procurement and construction companies (EPC) that are available for local contractors.

The transfer of knowledge has raised a number of issues for Investors to manage contractor's variations and/or claims, which resulted in Investors making rigid contracts terms and conditions. These contract terms and conditions have benefited the investors to the detriment of the contractor, to mention two, schedule delays/cost increases. As an example, it was not common for contractors to document their requests for compensations with the proper backup information and on time. Contractors used to claim without proper backup and months after the events, bringing problems to clients. As a result, most clients incorporated into their contract terms and conditions specific requirements for communications, changes, among others. The non-compliance by contractors to the client's requests could be interpreted that contractors have waived their rights for further compensations.

Part of the contractual conflict starts by imposing investor's common law general terms and conditions rather than civil law regulation. Being the case, it is not uncommon that local Peruvian courts and arbitrators will determine contract clauses to be non-enforceable in detriment of Investors. In case of local courts, the civil law principles will aim to protect contract balance principles. In the case of arbitrators, depending on the type of arbitration (procedure and substantive law) the decision could aim to principles of fairness and equity (ex aequo et bono). Nevertheless, certain statutes of limitation exist for arbitrators with regard to specific contract provisions, for example, the arbitrator may not recalculate the amount of liquidated damages agreed to by the parties.

In Peru there are only a few local contractors big and formal enough who know how to deal with this problematic situation. These few contractors have learned how to manage such rigid clauses, increase their contingencies (remaining competitive), and negotiate such terms during the bidding phase. Local contractors have sophisticated their approaches and bidding strategies; they carefully evaluate the percentage of the engineering completed, and include overheads and profits whether on the indirect—lump sum portion or in the direct—unit price portion, resulting in contractor's overhead and profits increase depending on the number of changes and contract growth. On the other side, some investors have regulated the way and how contractors must present their pricing details in order to avoid such situations.

Another example occurs with the facilities and obligations to be provided by investors (power, main equipment, cranes, and material among others). Some contractors reduce their proposals to get the contract awarded with the further idea of recovering monies at a later stage by presenting claims (disruptions, loss of productivity, extension of time, financial costs, and others) in case that investors have breached their contractual obligations by not providing such facilities on time.

Also, despite of the onerous dispute resolution processes, local contractors have become more claim oriented and the majority of them have increased legal advice or created their own legal departments in order to reduce expensive external legal fees.

Additional sources of problems rise where mutatis mutandis conditions are enforced by Investors to EPC companies on a back-to-back basis. Being the case, the lump sum terms and conditions are transferred to subcontractors. Subcontractors who agreed to unit price contracts with the main contractor in some cases have gone bankrupt and disappeared from the market due to excessive conditions such as protracted payment conditions, excessive liabilities, warranties, guarantees, among others. In other cases, subcontractors have refused to accept the enforcement of those terms and conditions, and the lack of negotiation led to arbitration or litigation processes.

A particular note, some local contractors are not well structured when presenting their request for compensations (later claims) as they lack backup, they express themselves poorly, have a lack of contractual basis, knowledge or entitlement, not presenting on time, not following procedures, and making invalid requests all may result in millions of dollars of lose and or bankruptcy unless they endeavor on dispute resolution processes where recovery may occur or not.

Some investors have improved their dispute resolution clauses detailing the process, amounts, languages, venues and/or law to abide in arbitration. Others have not defined at all their procedures, which is a disadvantage for contractor to deal with if occasion arises.

In summary, investors and international EPC companies whether in mining or oil and gas projects have developed a more rigid and "shielded" clauses to prevent claims by local contractors. Proficient local contractors have become more claims oriented to survive in an extremely competitive market without losing margins and profits or being those ones significantly reduced.

In my experience, one of the most successful tools to avoid frictions between both parties and reduce potential problems, as well as to mitigate potential dispute resolution cases is to continue promoting a good contract management practice on a fair and reasonable basis and firm when necessary. Apply all procedures (or define them), present and provide support and backup to prove the case, read the contract specimen entirely (including all their exhibits, attachments, and appendices) and promote the most efficient action between both parties; communication and coordination for amicable resolutions.

Jerry Pessah
Contracts and Claims Management leader

References

Bunni, N.G. (2005). *The FIDIC Forms of Contract* (3rd Edition). Blackwell, Oxford.
Choat, R. and Peckett, V. (2012). *English construction law developments 2012*. CMS Cameron McKenna's Free Online Information Service, London.
Cushman, R.F. (2011). *Proving and Pricing Construction Claims*. Wolters Kluwer, New York.
Dennys, N., Raeside, M., and Clay, R. (2010). *Hudson's Building and Engineering Contracts*. (12th Edition). Sweet & Maxwell Ltd, London.
Fox, K. (2010). *Watching the English: The Hidden Rules of English Behaviour*. Hodder: London.
Haidar, A.D. (2011). *Global Claims in Construction*. Springer Verlag: London.
Harris, P.R. and Moran, R.T. (2004). Managing Cultural Differences: Leadership Strategies for a New World of Business (4th Edition). Elsevier, Oxford.
ICC (2012). *International Court of Arbitration Bulletin*, 23(2), 2012.

Further reading

Alam-Eldin, M.E.I. (2010). *Arbitral Awards Rendered under the Auspices of CRCICA*. Lap Lambert Academic Publishing. Saarbrücken.
Burr, A. and Lane, N. (2003). The SCL delay and disruption protocol: hunting Snarks. *Construction Law Journal*, 3. Sweet and Maxwell.

Chappell, D. (2005). *Building Contract Claims*. Blackwell Publishing, Oxford.
FIDIC (2000). *The FIDIC Contracts Guide* (1st Edition). Lausanne.
FIDIC (2011). *FIDIC Procurement Procedures Guide*. (1st Edition). Lausanne.
Furst, S. and Ramsey, V. (2001). *Keating on Building Contracts* (7th Edition). Sweet and Maxwell, London.
Jaeger, A.V. and Hök, G.S. (2010). *FIDIC: A Guide for Practitioners*. Springer Verlag: Berlin.
The Society of Construction Law Delay and Disruption Protocol (2002). Online. Available at: http://www.scl.org.uk (accessed 3 May 2018).

11 Construction Dispute Boards

11.1 Construction disputes

Construction projects are naturally prone to disputes. Even if contracting parties allocate risk to the party best able to control it. However, there is sometimes uncertainty about who is to bear a particular risk and to what extent. The reason may lie in a poorly drafted contract or ignorance of it. Sometimes the risks are allocated inefficiently in the contract. Other factors may include a lack of experience or to gain a short-term advantage. In other cases, the parties are not willing to bear the consequences of the risks allocated to them. These and many other situations often give rise to disputes. Settlement of disputes in construction requires speed, an informal approach and expertise. This is why every good contract includes a dispute resolution system.

Construction dispute in sheet metal galvanizing line project by Patrick Kain (South Africa)

The choice of an appropriate delivery method, including the form of contract, design specifications, and good contract administration, is essential for any project. It is also essential that employers rely on professional advice when implementing their projects. Inappropriate documentation, contract selection, and contract administration lead to project disasters.

Project background

The construction of a new sheet metal galvanizing line was awarded after direct negotiation by the developer. The employer discounted tenders on the basis of time considerations. The designer was excluded from the negotiations, which were conducted directly by the employer who had no experience in construction and contract administration.

During the negotiations, the contractor offered a significant reduction in price. The negotiations did not deal with technical issues. They only dealt with price and time. The final decision was made purely on the basis of price.

Project complexity

The project included an excavation to 6.0 meters. This was attempted by the selected contractor on the basis of a geotechnical investigation which only extended to 4.5 meters. Despite the obvious shortfall in the geotechnical investigation, the contractor did not question the investigation and proceeded on the basis of what was provided and even attempted the excavation without shoring up the sides against collapse. The excavation collapsed at a depth of 3.0 meters. In an attempt to mitigate the situation, the employer engaged a specialist contractor to install sheet piling so that there was no further collapse of the excavation. However, this led to a dispute over who should pay the cost involved in engaging the specialist.

The designer chose to manage the project alone without the benefit of a consulting engineer and, except for the geotechnical investigation, there was a marked absence of technical expertise on deep excavations.

Form of contract

The architect based the contract on a rather basic local form of contract that is only suitable for simple house construction. There was no requirement for the contractor to provide computations for shoring or approval of temporary works.

The contractor

The fact that the employer engaged the specialist contractor without first agreeing to the costs with the main contractor and without clarifying who should pay the costs opened the door for a major dispute.

The contractor claimed that since the employer engaged the specialist contractor, the cost should be borne by the employer. The employer claimed that the failure was attributable to the contractor's method of operation and therefore the contractor should bear the specialist contractor's costs.

Arbitration

The records of events were very sketchy. This made it difficult to understand the sequence of events that led up to the eventual impasse and arbitration. Although both parties produced long submissions to the arbitration, they were largely unsupported by evidence and contradicted one another. This made it an almost impossible task for the arbitrator.

Outcome

The final decision at arbitration was that the employer was responsible for the cost of the specialist contractor. The dispute further highlights a number of contractual errors that developers and consultants must be wary of:

- The form of contract is central to the success of any project and it is incumbent on construction professionals to use a form of contract that is fit for purpose and which has been tried and tested on similar projects.

- An employer should engage professionals in construction as the employer does not have the technical capability and qualifications to undertake the design and supervision of the works themselves and, therefore, should be prepared to seek advice on all contractual issues.
- Construction professionals must understand the limitations of their competence and seek specialist expertise where such expertise is required.

Patrick Kain
International construction expert
South Africa

11.2 Dispute boards

Every construction project is unique and perhaps this is why there is a general absence of "corporate memory" in the construction industry (Chern, 2010). Regrettably, similar types of disputes arise on many construction projects and it is naïve to think we can eradicate disputes by clever contract drafting alone. What parties want is a dispute review device that is considered fair, economic, and causes the least disruption to the due performance of the contract. The concept of dispute boards has been lately popular also in the United States, where they have been in use for over 30 years. Their earliest reported use was in the Boundary Dam project in Washington in the 1960s. Following successful use of dispute boards on large projects, implementation of dispute adjudication boards by the World Bank and FIDIC in their guides and sample forms were the further key aspects of their expansion (Chern, 2010). Similar alternative dispute resolution mechanisms were used in continental Europe already in the 19th and 20th century in some countries as it is obvious from sample forms of contracts that were used for example in the Czech Republic at the time of Austro-Hungarian Empire and the first Czechoslovak Republic.

A dispute board is a body set up to resolve disputes (prior to arbitration or litigation) that have arisen within a construction project. In general, there are two kinds of dispute boards: (1) the dispute review board (which makes recommendations); and (2) the dispute adjudication board (which makes resolutions).

In practice, there are not many alternatives to dispute boards. Courts often lack expertise with the exception of countries where specialized courts are established, such as in the UK or Germany. Some countries, for example, the Netherlands, have arbitration systems with tribunals that specialize in construction disputes (Lloyd, 2009). Furthermore, both litigation and arbitration are costly and time-consuming.

The arbitration process has become increasingly inefficient; however, construction disputes still represent a large share of the arbitration market. According to the ICC, construction and engineering disputes accounted for almost 17% of the total caseload in 2010. In 2011, the Chartered Institute of Arbitrators held a conference in London entitled "Costs in International Arbitration." It found that the typical amount spent by a party going through the arbitration process from pre-commencement to post-hearing (excluding enforcement) was in the region of £1.5m, where the median claim was just under £10m. In 25% of the cases of between £10m to £50m, the costs exceeded £5m. In over 50% of the cases where the dispute exceeded £100m, costs exceeded £5m. Nearly 75% of costs were for external legal representation.

(Chern, 2010) stated in an article on the role of dispute boards in construction that:

> The statistics show that if there is an operational Dispute Board in existence on a project, close to 99% of all disputes referred to it will be successfully resolved within less than 90 days and at a cost of about 2% of the amount of the dispute.

In Poland, for example, construction disputes in large transport infrastructure construction projects are dealt with by the High Court in Warsaw (XXV Civil Division) because the General Directorate of National Roads and Motorways (the GDDKiA) has its registered office in the court's district. Because of the large number of disputes in Poland in recent years, a natural process of specialization of the court's judges has followed.

Judges themselves admit that alternative dispute resolution (ADR) is a better model for hearing construction disputes. However, it is the employer who selects the method of dispute resolution and it is common for public authorities in the CEE (such as GDDKiA in Poland) to consistently delete DAB and arbitration clauses from the FIDIC forms in favor of domestic litigation.

11.2.1 Dispute avoidance

The construction industry has a reputation for disputes and conflict. Chern (2010) gives evidence from Australia where 50% of all legal costs associated with construction is expended in connection with disputes. In almost 10% of projects, between 8% and 10% of the total project cost was legal cost. Disputes are naturally connected to construction projects because of the amount of risk involved. Disputes are not completely avoidable but the participants of construction projects should do as much as possible to eliminate them. The situation is aggravated by the increased use of joint ventures both in consulting and in contracting. Such organizations are less autonomous and perhaps less able to negotiate settlements of their contractual problems. Dispute avoidance is, however, possible in the preparation phase via an appropriate procurement plan including the choice of delivery method, consultants, and designers. Other key aspects of dispute avoidance are: (1) the ability to procure the work by an experienced contractor for a realistic bid price; (2) efficient risk allocation; and (3) how time, variation, and claim management procedures are established and how disputes are resolved. Simply naming a dispute board in a project contract can be one of the strongest tools to avoid the dispute.

Project dispute avoidance by Christopher J. Mather (the United States)

I have been an advocate for over 25 years for the early negotiation of project disputes when they are first identified. This concept has not been actively endorsed, nor acted upon by all parties involved in the construction industry, nor readily accepted, until the past decade when parties began to realize that to arbitrate or litigate a dispute was not only a slow and cumbersome process, but also an expensive process, which, ultimately, did not necessarily reflect the merits of the case itself.

Many parties involved in the dispute process have walked away dissatisfied, feeling that only the lawyers and consultants involved in the dispute process are the winners. Additionally, many parties involved in disputes have concluded that the current process distracts its key personnel from their core tasks for which they were hired, namely, to complete the project on time and within budget.

In a webinar presentation I presented on the topic "Alternate Dispute Resolution: Taking Control of Your Disputes to Save Time and Money," over 80% of the respondents polled identified they preferred private (In-House) negotiations or a Mediation forum as the two most effective ways to expeditiously settle their disputes, instead of going to litigation or arbitration. These U.S. participants were clearly signaling their dissatisfaction at the litigation and arbitration processes currently available to them as other options they could elect to use to settle their disputes.

Factors that impact the project's planned and financial success

In a recent survey by Marc Howell of Paradigm Strategic Partners, Inc., dysfunctional project execution problems and issues were attributed to the following causes:

1. Some 9% indicated enforcement of government regulations as a contributing factor.
2. Some 10% indicated an over-zealous owner (employer) contract, statement of work (SOW), along with demanding terms and conditions with unrealistic "risk/reward" consideration as major contributing factors.
3. Some 13% indicated GCs and subcontractors deliberately "low bid" work, which leads to financial weakness.
4. Some 16% indicated a lack of trust, integrity, honesty, and lack of responsibility as contributing factors.
5. Some 21% of construction industry participants noted that there is an inadequate supply of trained, qualified, and experienced personnel.
6. Some 31% of the current project execution weaknesses noted by industry professionals were attributed to a lack of adequate integration and coordination between all parties and, specifically, a lack of teamwork.

What events cause construction claims and disputes?

To mitigate disputes and claims on a project you must learn to objectively investigate the "causation" (perform a root cause analysis) of the matter at hand. Once you have identified the issue and understand the causative events, you can take steps to mitigate possible future problems that may arise on the balance of the contract work to be performed.

Some characteristics and practices of parties involved in the construction process have elicited the following traits:

- Owner (employer)-caused problems:
  - Owner (employer) provided inadequate bid information.
  - Owner (employer) did not allow adequate time for bid/proposal preparation.

- Restrictive specifications.
- Owner (employer) changes to plans and specifications during construction.
- Owner (employer) understated design completion at time of contract negotiations.
- Contractor-caused problems:
  - Contractor fails to perform an adequate pre-bid site investigation.
  - Contractor submits an unbalanced bid; bid below costs.
  - Contractor's bid incorporates poor resource planning.
  - Contractor utilizes and applies improper "means and methods".
  - Contractor's philosophy is to "make it up on change orders".
- Contract document issues:
  - Contractor developed an unrealistic "as-planned" schedule baseline.
  - Mandatory advance notice of changes/disputes/claims.
  - Conflicting "changed conditions" clauses.
  - Engineer's final decision.
- Contract/commercial administration issues:
  - Contractor fails to follow contract/commercial procedures.
  - Poor coordination of owner (employer)'s responsibilities with contractor.
  - Contract Administrator's style and attitude.
  - Poor documentation of field performance records (e.g., daily reports).
  - Poor or inadequate document control procedures.
- Themes associated with "early" problem (dispute) resolution:
  - Encourage early on-site mitigation and settlement of disputes.
  - Delegate settlement authority to field supervisors (but stipulate their level of authority).
  - Have an effective POC in place between the home office and the site.
  - Identify and delegate an authorized company executive, who is specifically tasked as the company's representative on the project to resolve disputes if unresolved on a timely basis at the project level.
  - Communicate at all times with the party that has either a dispute with you, or you with them. The better each party understands the other side's position, the higher the likelihood and achievement of an early settlement via negotiation.

Does the "make-up" of a mediation or arbitration panel matter?

I am a strong believer that the make-up of a mediation or arbitration panel is essential in whether or not the disputed matter is expeditiously implemented and resolved cost effectively.

In the United States, when looking at the make-up of arbitration panel members available, there are about two attorneys to every industry professional available to be selected to sit on an arbitration panel that specializes specifically on construction dispute matters. However, when actually looking at who is selected as the arbitrator by the parties' attorneys, lawyers are primarily selected to act as the arbitrator(s) in the majority of cases; despite sometimes complex technical issues being at the core of the disputes being arbitrated.

If more industry professionals were selected by the parties' attorneys as arbitrators instead of attorneys, disputes would be more quickly resolved and it would be more economical for the disputing parties to achieve a final resolution to their disputes. In large, complex cases where there are three arbitration panel members, I would also advocate the inclusion of an experienced construction attorney to ensure that the legal interests of both parties are protected in a dispute of such magnitude.

This process can be addressed by the contracting parties stipulating that an industry professional is to be the preferred dispute resolution provider when they draft this section of the contract with the American Arbitration Association's "Clause Builder" tool that assists you to incorporate such a provision when delineating this as part of the contract's stated dispute resolution process (see below).

When looking at the make-up of mediation panel members available, there are about three attorneys to every industry professional available to be selected to sit on an mediation panel that specializes specifically in construction dispute matters. However, when looking at who is selected as the mediator by the parties' attorneys, lawyers are again primarily selected to act as the mediator despite sometimes complex technical issues being at the core of the disputes.

Introduction of "clause builder" by AAA to mitigate disputes

Last year, the American Arbitration Association (AAA) introduced to interested parties a software tool that it named "Clause Builder." It developed this tool, which is available on its website at www.clausebuilder.org. The AAA notes on its website:

> The American Arbitration Association's® Clause Builder tool is designed to assist individuals and organizations in developing clear and effective arbitration and mediation agreements.
> An effective dispute resolution process starts with a well-constructed dispute resolution clause.
> At this time, the Clause Builder is limited to providing assistance with commercial and construction arbitration and mediation clauses.

On its web site, the AAA asks "Why include an ADR (Alternate Dispute Resolution) clause?" It responds with the following points:

> ADR allows parties the ability to design their own dispute resolution process, and provides them with the flexibility to customize the process to their particular circumstances.

> The most frequently cited advantages of arbitration are:

- The speed with which disputes are resolved as compared to court litigation.
- Cost savings.
- Input and control in selecting an arbitrator with a background and expertise relevant to the dispute.
- Informal procedures.

Under the AAA's Rules, the procedure is relatively simple:

- Courtroom rules of evidence are not strictly applicable.
- There is no requirement for transcripts of the proceedings or for written opinions of the arbitrators.

Though there may be no formal discovery, the AAA's various commercial rules allow the arbitrator to require the production of relevant information and documents. The AAA's rules are also flexible and may be varied by mutual agreement of the parties. Finally, arbitration awards are final and binding and are enforceable in court. Court intervention in the arbitration process is very limited by state and federal laws, and enforcement is facilitated by those same laws.

It allows the user to propose ground rules to be incorporated into its contract based upon the interests and components that the two prime contracting parties (owner (employer) and contractor) wish to incorporate into the proposed contract language to be executed by the parties. This approach allows both parties to attempt to reduce their commercial and contractual risks before ever executing the contract. The lack of these risk-averse steps that could be applied to EPC contracts might explain and account for why approximately 25% of this type of contract is completed without dispute because they invariably come in late and over budget and the risk balance is disproportionate to one party's interests.

There has been much interest expressed in how to apply the Clause Builder tool during the contract negotiation phase of each project prior to contract execution. This tool: (1) allows you to create a customized ADR clause; (2) provides a simple self-guided process; and (3) allows you to preview, save, review and edit your proposed ADR clause for mediation and arbitration.

Other dispute avoidance "means and methods" that could be applied

Contract language can be developed by an owner (employer), to reflect an approach that mitigates its downstream risks. It can also incorporate and mitigate risks that the parties want to cover and incorporate into the Dispute Resolution section of their contract before the contract is executed by the parties.

One way to mitigate project disputes as they develop is to incorporate a "tiered-approach" language in one's proposed contract to mitigate contract disputes at project completion. This language, when incorporated into the contract, mandates the parties' attempt to resolve their disputes as the project proceeds following steps that are clearly delineated in the dispute resolution section of the contract. Although this process may require one additional commercial/contract manager be incorporated onto the on-site project team, that additional cost to both parties is significantly less than that expended by them at the project's completion if the dispute is not resolved. Attorneys play a crucial role during this stage.

Clients should be encouraged to include and involve their attorneys during the early phases of a dispute, and to be involved on an ongoing transactional basis, in conjunction with the parties trying to settle the project dispute when it arises. They could then be used to easily incorporate their legal expertise and personal knowledge of the dispute in question and help their clients to develop a contract addendum that incorporates time, additional compensation and risk mitigation factors up to the date of the proposed addendum (variation/change order). This is the role I had my company's attorneys fulfill when the tiered-approach process was incorporated into a project contract that was executed.

An example of "tiered-approach" language that could be used is as follows:

Sample "tiered-approach" language

16.5. Disputes. If there is a dispute between the Parties about a request for a Change by either party under this Article 16, such dispute shall be resolved in accordance with Article 34. Notwithstanding any provision of this Article 16 to the contrary, the Parties will execute a Change Order to reflect the resolution of such dispute.

34. Disputes

34.1. Negotiations. Any disputes arising pursuant to this Contract that cannot be resolved between the Project Owner (employer)'s Representative and the Contractors Project Manager within fourteen (14) calendar days or, in the case of Payment disputes, three (3) calendar days after receipt by each of Notice of such dispute (specifically referencing this Section 34.1) shall be referred, by Notice signed by the Owner (employer)'s Project Representative and the Contractor's Project Manager, to the Executive level officers of each entity comprising Owner (employer) and Contractor as their designated representatives (which shall not be the Owner (employer)'s Project Representative nor the Contractor's Project Manager) for resolution. If the parties fail to reach an agreement within a reasonable period of time, not exceeding thirty (30) calendar days or, in the case of payment disputes, ten (10) calendar days after such referral, then the Owner (employer) or the Contractor, may institute proceedings as set forth in Section 34.2.

34.2. Dispute Resolution. If each entity comprising Owner (employer) and Contractor, negotiating in good faith, fails to reach an agreement within the period of time set forth above in Section 34.1, then Owner (employer) and Contractor agree that any and all disputes arising from, relating to or in connection with this Contract, tort or otherwise shall be submitted to the jurisdiction of the federal or state courts located in _____, PA, to the exclusion of any and all other courts, forums, venues, and the Parties waive any and all rights to contest the exclusivity of such forum, including any rights based upon the doctrine of forum non conveniens. The court shall award to the substantially prevailing Party all of its costs, expenses, attorneys' fees, filing fees and court costs.

34.3. Work to Continue. Unless otherwise agreed in writing, the Contractor shall diligently carry on the Work and shall not interfere with, restrict or discourage the prompt completion of any portion of the Work, the correction of any Defects or the provision of any warranty service during the pendency of any dispute or arbitration proceedings.

In conclusion

If the major parties to a contract are willing to be collaborative and incorporate some of the suggestions discussed in this vignette, and are willing to share the project risk between the parties from the project's inception, then fewer disputes will arise.

When disputes do arise, if the following dispute resolution procedures are followed, then the dispute should be able to be resolved in a relatively short time frame (90–120 days after the disputed issue has first been identified). By following some or all of the suggested dispute resolution procedures now incorporated in the executed contract, all parties should be able to complete many more projects on time and within budget.

Lastly, if there are project disputes at project completion, they will have been significantly reduced in number at the time of project completion by following the dispute avoidance steps that have been applied throughout the project's execution. This will save all parties a lot of time at the completion of their projects when trying to settle any outstanding disputes. It will also save them a lot of money.

Christopher J. Mather
Managing Director
Construction Solutions International, LLC
Philadelphia,
PA
USA

Dispute resolution boards: The long-term experience from the United States by Robert A. Rubin (the United States)

In typical traditional construction cases conducted in the United States under court rules, roughly 75% of the cost and time is consumed in the discovery phase, at a time and place far removed from the construction, itself—all in an effort to sort out the facts and circumstances underlying the dispute. In contrast, the DRB process is "real time" disputes resolution. The DRB members are available virtually on the spot to more readily sort out the facts and circumstances underlying the dispute, at considerably less cost and time. DRBs have had the potential of revolutionizing the construction process.

Having spent the better part of my 50-year career as a litigator of construction disputes, DRBs now give me an opportunity to play a more constructive role in the construction process, as opposed to the after-the-fact role of just cleaning up messes created by problematic projects. DRBs have been, and continue to be, the most satisfying part of my career. My work with DRBs has enabled me to play a part in improving the overall construction process, instead of merely profiting from a distressed process.

"DRB" means different things to different people. This often creates problems and frustrations.

Because court litigation and arbitration have been around a long time, there is a relatively well-established understanding of what these processes are and how they work. This understanding is supported and reinforced by laws and rules. By contrast, the DRB process is relatively new; it is not supported by laws and rules; it is purely a creature of contract—and contracts most often differ from one to the next. For example, in current practice DRB decisions can be final and binding; or non-binding and serving only as recommendations; or something in between. DRBs can be established at the start of the project; or only after a dispute has arisen; or at some time in between. Lawyers can be permitted to fully participate in DRB hearings; or not permitted to participate at all; or something in between.

In the relatively short history of DRBs, the vast majority have been highly successful; some have been abysmal failures; others have been somewhere in between. But experience has shown that there is a strong positive correlation between DRB success and the extent to which the Dispute Resolution Board Foundation ("DRBF") model rules and procedures have been followed. In most instances of failed DRBs, the DRBF model rules and procedures have been significantly altered.

DRBs have been utilized in U.S. construction with increasing frequency. But I believe one reason that DRBs have not enjoyed even wider utilization is the adverse publicity given the relatively few failed DRBs. In an ideal world I believe it should be mandated that the name "DRB" may only be applied to those entities that operate under the DRBF model rules and procedures. By doing so, I believe the incidence of failed DRBs would be materially reduced, leading to an even greater utilization of the DRB process. Realistically, though, this is not an ideal world, and the possibility of such a mandate being adopted is highly unlikely.

The most difficult situation I have dealt with is one in which the relationship between the parties deteriorated to such an extent that I was unable to get the parties' respective project managers even to meet informally over breakfast. Let me explain.

I was appointed the Chair of a DRB that was first impaneled over a year after the project had started. By that time there was a backlog of some $50 million in unresolved disputes. As I walked into the room at the first DRB meeting, I sensed a peculiar atmosphere; something was not right. The meeting turned out to be the most contentious DRB meeting I have ever attended. The relationship between the parties had so soured to such a point under the weight of the long-standing unresolved disputes, that the parties were unable to agree on anything. Their arguments were endless.

Over lunch that day, the other two DRB members and I shared the observation that we had never experienced so much disharmony and ill will at a DRB meeting. Following the formal DRB meeting we decided to meet privately with the two project managers to formulate a plan of action to improve the situation. We strongly recommended that the two project managers meet periodically on an informal basis, perhaps weekly over breakfast, in an effort to forge a more cordial working relationship.

Our DRB functioned with the project for another year. We heard and issued recommendations on several disputes, somewhat reducing the backlog of unresolved disputes. However, the acrimony between the parties continued unabated. At one point, the parties each terminated its appointee to the DRB, without nominating a successor. Whereupon, I resigned as the chair. As of the date of my resignation, the two project managers still had not yet met informally with one another.

I see a bright future for DRBs, but there are several factors at play which I am afraid will continue to hamper the DRB process from realizing its full potential:

Some owners, out of fear and/or insecurity, will not be able to abide the creation of a "level playing field." They will insist on a DRB process that to some extent preserves their "home court advantage." That will result in contractors' lack of confidence, distrust, questioning fairness of the process and disinclination to support or participate in the DRB process.

Some owners will never even agree to the establishment of any form of DRB, out of concern that the mere presence of a DRB would somehow diminish their traditional control over ongoing projects, and create the risk of embarrassment if an impartial third party were to judge their action to be incorrect.

> Some attorneys representing owners, whether through hubris, ignorance, or inexperience, will not be able to resist the temptation to tinker with the tried and tested DRBF Model Rules and Procedures and thereby increase the risk of creating an unsuccessful DRB.
>
> Robert A. Rubin, Esq.
> *Construction Consultant*
> *New York, USA*

11.2.2 Dispute boards: Advantages and disadvantages

Due to the enormous volume of correspondence and occasional "friction" between participants, it is usual to see minor disputes accompany large construction projects on a daily basis. A certain, intermediate dispute resolution level is, therefore, widely appreciated. It can make people (such as the top management of the interested parties) sit together at a joint table to try to find a compromise approach and thus avoid costly arbitration or litigation proceedings. At these meetings, opinions can get vented, tensions released and personal antagonisms extinguished in the presence of impartial, well-informed experts. Experienced pundits provide the parties with a solution that will likely result in a required compromise. Active on these boards are experts who need not be lawyers (or if lawyers, lawyers with extensive practical backgrounds in the field of construction projects), which is why they are spoken of as being "user-friendly." The boards can also be made up of suitable combinations of personalities with varied experience and specializations.

A dispute board becomes part of the project administration and can thereby influence (during the contract period), the performance of contracting parties. It has "real-time" value. Many disputes concern "non-absolute" matters and, in such cases, the dispute board can devise solutions, which avoid "win-lose" situations while keeping within contractual limitations. Working relationships are less affected and site-level partnering can continue (Chern, 2010).

The use of dispute boards is the best method of dispute avoidance because it leads the participants to find agreement. For example, the Ertan Hydroelectric Dam in China, valued at US$2 billion, had 40 disputes referred to its dispute board for decision, with no decision of this board continuing on to arbitration or litigation. The Hong Kong International Airport, valued at US$15 billion, had six disputes referred to its dispute board and, of those, only one went on to arbitration (in which case the board's decision was upheld). The Katse Dam in South Africa, valued at US$2.5 billion, had 12 disputes referred to its dispute board. Again, only one decision went on to arbitration and was also upheld.

One disadvantage of these boards is that they tend not pay off in terms of cost in smaller projects (Chern, 2010).

11.2.3 Dispute Adjudication Board (DAB)

The DAB—that is, one or three adjudicators selected by the parties—must decide in compliance with the dispute resolution process described in the contract (see the procedure under FIDIC forms below). Alongside this contractual adjudication, there is also statutory adjudication available in some countries (see the procedure under UK and Australian statutory adjudication below).

In civil law jurisdictions, decisions handed down by DABs are persuasive in nature only and are usually not binding or enforceable. In common law jurisdictions, on the other hand, the decision is often final and binding if the parties do not appeal it within the contractually agreed period of time.

If the contracting parties want to make a DAB's decision enforceable, they can modify the DAB's status to ad hoc arbitration. The arbitration clause for an institutional arbitration court (or for an additional ad hoc arbitration) may be reworded so that this arbitration court (or the arbitrator or the arbitrators ad hoc) would become the authority to examine the DAB's award or resolution, should one of the contracting parties challenge the award or resolution via a lawsuit.

11.2.4 Dispute Review Board (DRB)

As with DAB, the DRB usually consists of three reviewers who must be impartial, experienced, and respected. The employer and the contractor select one member each. The chosen member must be approved by the other party. The two appointed DRB members then choose the third member who, in turn, also needs to be approved by both parties. All members select a chair of the DRB who, again, is subject to the parties' approval. Organization and setup of the DRB takes place before the commencement of the construction project.

The DRB familiarizes itself with the contractual documents, with the project procedures, with the participants themselves and closely follows the progress of the works. The members of the DRB conduct site visits periodically.

The system aims to resolve differences early on at the job level. Where formal disputes cannot be avoided, the DRB holds a hearing and issues a written recommendation. While not binding upon the parties, recommendations are, in practice, usually accepted by the parties to the dispute. By doing so, they help themselves and maintain the credibility, reputation and expertise of the DRB and its members. The contract may also provide that DRB recommendations be admissible in any potential future litigation or arbitration (DRBF, 2013).

11.3 Contractual adjudication: The use of DAB in FIDIC forms

Dispute boards first appeared in FIDIC forms in 1995 at Clause 20 and are now a common part of most FIDIC forms and many other contracts. FIDIC forms currently "presume" four levels of dispute resolution, which can be thought of as kind of dispute resolution "hierarchy." Level one is the engineer themselves making a determination about a claim (which is in fact an act of dispute avoidance rather than a dispute) and level two is adjudication through a DAB (DAAB/Dispute Avoidance and Adjudication Board in the 2017 edition). Following an unsuccessful, obligatory attempt to achieve an amicable settlement, a dispute can end up at an arbitration senate (level four).

An older version of the FIDIC Red Book (1957) dealt with dispute resolution in two phases. Dispute resolution was up to the engineer and their decision was deemed final and binding in relation to the employer and the contractor. Within 90 days, either of the parties could question the decision and file an arbitration suit. Barring minor modifications in arbitration clauses in the Red Book versions of 1969 (2nd edition) and 1977 (3rd edition), this dispute resolution concept has been retained. The above two-phase concept remained even in the Red Book of 1987 (1988), but dispute resolution had, in the meantime, undergone substantial change. For example, a formal obligation had been formulated to refer any dispute to Clause 67 to make it clear that a dispute had officially commenced. Another formal innovation was that the period of time within which the engineer's decision could be questioned was reduced to 84 days. A third fundamental change was the incorporation of amicable settlements as a compulsory item at Sub-Clause 67.2 with its wording as follows:

> Where the notice of intention to commence arbitration as to a dispute has been given in accordance with Sub-Clause 67.1, the parties shall attempt to settle such dispute amicably before the commencement of arbitration. Provided that, unless the parties otherwise agreed, arbitration may be commenced on or after the fifty-sixth day after the day on which notice of intention to commence arbitration of such dispute was given, even if no attempt at amicable settlement thereof has been made.

Therefore, a period of 56 days was newly established within which arbitration could be commenced regardless of any attempt to settle the dispute amicably. These changes, however, were not applied uniformly or in a systematic way across all FIDIC forms.

It was mentioned that FIDIC forms (in the 1999 edition) established four levels of dispute resolution, that is, the engineer (contract administrator), a DAB, amicable settlement and arbitration. The engineer will often make determination (after notification and quantification) about a claim submitted by one of the contracting parties. Prior to this determination the engineer is obliged to help the parties come to an agreement. This is, in fact, a form of mediation. The engineer's determination (as per Sub-Clause 3.5) must be given within 42 days after the engineer has received a claim quantification. If not satisfied with the engineer's decision, a party may forward the dispute to a DAB under Sub-Clause 20.4. The DAB must hand down its award within 84 days. The 2017 edition established a more structured but very similar procedure with an obligatory consultation to reach agreement within 42 days and a subsequent determination (if no agreement was achieved) within next 42 days (Sub-Clause 3.7).

It must be stressed that a determination about a particular claim made by the engineer is not by itself a dispute. It is the contractual method by which the participants deal with claims. However, the situation is often perceived as a dispute when, in reality, it is in fact a tool for dispute avoidance.

FIDIC DBO contains a Sub-Clause 20.5 that points out the potential mediation function of DABs stating:

> If at any time the parties so agree, they may jointly refer a matter to the DAB in writing with a request to provide assistance and/or informally discuss

and attempt to resolve any disagreement that may have arisen between the parties during the performance of the contract. Such informal assistance may take place during any meeting, Site visit or otherwise. However, unless the parties agree otherwise, both parties must be present at such discussions. The parties are not bound to act upon any advice given during such informal meetings, and the DAB shall not be bound in any future Dispute resolution process and decision by any views given during the informal assistance process, whether provided orally or in writing.

In a similar fashion the new 2017 edition introduced a new DAAB Sub-Clause with almost the same wording (21.3 Avoidance of Disputes). At this point it should be mentioned that a hazard may appear where the contract describes the obligatory dispute resolution instruments. Take, for example, the case of *The Channel Tunnel Group v. Balfour Beatty* (1992) 56 BLR 1 Court of Appeal in which the court did not grant leave for arbitration to commence because "time for arbitration had not yet come" due to the fact that the dispute had not been resolved in compliance with Sub-Clause 67 (1) (FIDIC Red Book, 4th edition, 1987). This was confirmed in the same case on appeal in 1993 (*BLR 22 House of Lords*) when Lord Mustill ruled:

> Those who stipulated a dispute resolution method by their mutual agreement must give significant reasons why not to use this method … if they had undertaken to submit their complaints to experts or, if necessary, to arbitrators, ought to take the steps like this. The fact that the plaintiffs now regard the method they selected as too slow to follow their intention is, in my opinion, groundless.

In the ICC case no. 12048 (2003) (ICC, 2012) the tribunal considered whether it had jurisdiction over counterclaims of the employer, which had not previously been submitted to the engineer under Sub-Clause Sub 67. The tribunal concluded that it did not. In later commentary, the ICC (2012) affirmed this as being correct explaining that under Sub-Clause 67 of the Red Book (4th edition) an arbitral tribunal only has jurisdiction over disputes resulting from claims that had previously been submitted to the engineer for a decision under that clause. The same is true of Clause 20 of the 1999 FIDIC books (which corresponds to Clause 67 of the Red Book, 4th edition) except that the DAB has replaced the engineer as the decision maker. In this case the tribunal also confirmed that the engineer's decisions become final and binding upon the parties if they are not contested within the appeal period stipulated in the contract.

Under FIDIC forms in the third instance, an obligatory attempt to settle a dispute amicably must be included as a rule. This applies to cases where there is a dissatisfaction with the DAB award and must be made within 28 days as per Sub-Clause 20.4. Amicable settlement is discussed in Clause 20.5. A particular form is not stipulated, but an expert examination or mediation will frequently be used. Arbitration Clause 20.6 requires arbitration to be finally settled under the Rules of Arbitration of the International Chamber of Commerce.

11.3.1 FIDIC policy statements to ADR

According to FIDIC, the adversarial model (involving litigation or arbitration), has serious limitations and drawbacks in the area of construction disputes resolution. The issues involved are usually very complex and hard attitudes of the parties involved in adversarial proceedings seldom lead to quick, effective and inexpensive resolutions. As FIDIC has noted:

> [Such a system] delays the execution of remedial measures, increases legal costs, creates adversaries and thus wastes resources unnecessarily. It also saps the energies of the parties in dispute, diminishing their ability to function effectively in the future. Both outcomes are detrimental to the parties, in particular, and to society, in general.

ADR models, on the other hand (such as negotiation, DRB, mini-trials, adjudications, conciliation, or mediation), are consensual as opposed to adversarial. While these consensual methods may not, unlike litigation or arbitration, lead to binding and final decisions, their outcome in the form of settlement agreements may be more compelling and more certain and, in any event, enforceable by courts in cases of default. For these reasons, FIDIC has asked its member associations to support ADR procedures.

11.3.2 Independence and impartiality

The independence of adjudication can be affected by the level of funding and remuneration received by its members. Another important aspect supported by FIDIC is the establishment of a national list of independent, key experts. One of the qualification criteria for listing on the FIDIC President's List of Approved Dispute Adjudicators, which are assessed by FIDIC and by its Assessment Panel, is the ability of the applicant "to be impartial [and] objective."

Complementing the FIDIC President's List of Approved Dispute Adjudicators, FIDIC also supports the development of national listings. Such national lists (based upon the FIDIC guidelines) have been created for example in Japan and France. Standards of adjudication on projects using FIDIC-based contracts are being monitored.

Construction disputes in Ukraine by Roger Ribeiro and Yaryna Bakhovska (Ukraine)

War conflict

In November 2013, Ukraine was expected to sign an association agreement with the European Union. When ex-President Viktor Yanukovych stopped preparations for signing, it caused mass protests, known as the "Euromaidan," which later turned into the "revolution of dignity" demanding the resignation of the president, crucial reforms, and signing of the association agreement. After four months of protests, which ended in the shooting of protesters, Yanukovych fled to Russia.

When the capital, Kiev, was still recovering, the epicenter of tension transferred to Crimea, where fully armed Russian soldiers took over the Supreme Council of Crimea and captured strategic sites across the peninsula.

Following the annexation of Crimea, demonstrations by pro-Russian groups began in the Donetsk and Luhansk regions of Ukraine escalating into an armed conflict between the Russian-backed separatist forces and the Ukrainian forces. Secretary General of Amnesty International Salil Shetty said that "satellite images, coupled with reports of Russian troops captured inside Ukraine and eyewitness accounts of Russian troops and military vehicles rolling across the border leave no doubt that this is now an international armed conflict". The conflict has also been classified as a "hybrid war" waged by Russia against Ukraine. Two years of armed conflict took more than 5,800 lives, according to the United Nations.

Banks

Since the beginning of 2014, 45 banks in Ukraine have gone bankrupt, according to the Deposit Guarantee Fund of Ukraine. The annexation of Crimea was the first painful blow. Ukraine's regulator has forbidden the country's banks to operate on the peninsula and they were forced to remove some of its Crimean assets and sell the rest.

The Deposit Guarantee Fund argues that a massive insolvency of banks during 2014 to 2015 provoked light-fingered owners and managers of financial institutions, the lack of exports, falling domestic consumption, and higher productions cost in Ukraine.

Economists see other causes of mass "bank fall." Independent expert Anatoly Drobiazko believes that one of the reasons is a ban for banks to create reserves in foreign currency against foreign exchange assets. "That means that the loans are in foreign currency and reserves—in UAH, contrary to all international rules of accounting," he writes in his blog for *Forbes* magazine.

Currency

Protecting the currency after the global crisis of 2008 drained the central bank of Ukraine's reserves, which tumbled from a high of $40 billion in 2011 to about $12 billion.

Beginning in 2014, the devaluation of Ukrainian Hryvnia was dramatic. On February 7, 2014, following political instability in Ukraine, the National Bank of Ukraine changed the hryvnia into a fluctuating/floating currency in an attempt to meet IMF requirements and to try to enforce a stable price for the currency in the Forex market.

Taking into account very difficult negotiations on the external debt restructuring, commitments to the Internatonal Monetary Fund (IMF), and hard economic conditions, the private equity firm Sigmableyzer forecasts the exchange rate to be around UAH 25/$1 in the second half of the year unchanged.

Inflation

The inflation rate in Ukraine was recorded at 58.40% in May 2015. The inflation rate in Ukraine previously averaged 36.37% from 1995 until 2015, reaching an all-time high of 530.30% in September 1995 and a record low of -1.20% in June 2012 as reported by the State Statistics Service of Ukraine. This increase in inflation was caused principally by a large increase in natural gas tariffs for households as agreed with the IMF.

Forms of construction contracts

The Euro 2012 football championships offered a great opportunity for Ukraine to improve roads, stadiums, hotels, airports, and related infrastructure. Of particular interest is how construction contracts are moving forward despite the current situation in Ukraine described previously.

FIDIC forms of contracts (Red, Yellow, and Pink Books) are already in place for several construction projects. However, some concepts such as lump sums, the role of the engineer, and the dispute adjudication board (DAB) are not well-understood by some employers and project implementation units (PIU). It is an opportune time to implement training sessions for all construction projects financed by the development banks prior to the start of the works.

European Bank for Reconstruction and Development (EBRD) contracts for works projects and for supply and installation projects also have their place in Ukraine. Their consultants defined a strategy during the procurement process based on the Ukrainian procurement rules and the procurement policies and rules for projects financed by the EBRD. Obviously, there is not a fundamental contradiction between the two procurement systems.

The very first output- and performance-based road contract (OPRC) was signed in 2013 and terminated in 2014. Due to the ongoing arbitration procedure, it is impossible to give more details as the parties chose this resolution forum for confidentiality reasons. A new contractor has been selected and the works were ongoing.

World Bank works contracts have been signed in roads, water supply and sewage treatment of solid waste, and district heating. The choice of the different contracts that is given to the employers is definitely very large. However, this choice may be done by asking a few basic questions such as: What is the allocation of functions? Allocation of risks? Evaluation and payment structure? Dispute resolution mechanism?

It may happen that employers use the standard tender documents and form of contract decided by the funding institution. However, the banks are not a party to the contract, and generally they do not accept legal responsibility for the adequacy of the contract forms.

Independent of the contract form, I have advised Ukrainian employers during tendering stage on the following:

> to ensure that the contract conditions are suitable and complete in respect of any particular contract and in accordance with the applicable law not to shift abusively their risks to the contractors nor to delete contractor's protection.

Construction disputes

The author is involved in the following five projects in Ukraine, explained here to give insight on construction claims and disputes in the country.

1. **Modernization of traction substations**

    The EBRD supply and installation contract has been concluded between the employer and the contractor to perform the modernization of 19 traction substations for the power supply of the electrical transport network as prescribed by the contract. The contract agreement was signed in September 2011, with the completion of the facilities to be attained within 18 months.

    The advance payment, according to the contract agreement "Appendix 1 - Terms and Procedures of Payment," is for 20% of the contract price for equipment and 20% of the contract price for installation works. For reasons related to the non-fulfillment of some conditions of the loan agreement by the employer and financing from the city budget, the employer could not receive the necessary funds to pay the advance payment.

    Due to the financial situation, the beginning of contract implementation was delayed and pending until the advance payment was finally paid to the contractor in mid-2013, with the delay of 21 months (from October 2011 when advance payment guarantee was presented by the contractor). Despite this delay and normal increase in costs over almost two years, the contractor has agreed without delay to extend the validity of the advance payment security and start the execution of contract in good faith.

    During the execution of the contract, due to the general situation in the country, the economic conditions of the contract significantly deteriorated, with rapid inflation and major economic and financial crisis in the country. The situation worsened when the Ukrainian bank, where the EBRD funds for the very contract were located, announced bankruptcy.

    In October 2014, an increase of the contract price by more than 10% was discussed by both parties, but a few months later it was no longer within the time frame allowed for when the parties have to agree upon the conditions for an addendum to the contract.

    In March 2015, the contractor proposed to introduce the price adjustment clause in the contract that would foresee the regular revision of the contract price based on currency exchange rate. The employer did not agree with this proposal and suggested agreeing upon a single adjustment of the contract price considering the significant and unforeseen change in economic conditions of the contract that happened mainly due to the delayed payments by the employer.

    In April 2015, the contractor claimed for an increase of the contract of around 35%. After long discussions, the parties succeeded to reach an agreement. In the beginning of July 2015, the dispute was resolved by intensive negotiation and the parties agreed to one increase of the contract of around 30%.

    It is worth noting that the EBRD staff has been providing support and advice to me during all the processes regarding increases of the contract price.

2. **Rehabilitation of a tram depot**

    A FIDIC Red Book contract has been concluded between the employer and the contractor to perform the execution and completion of works related to rehabilitation of the tram depot. The works on site have commenced, but the contractor has not substantially performed all the works. The nature of the case is delays, change to the scope of the works, payment issues, and termination of the contract.

    Pursuant to Clause 20 of the particular conditions, the mechanism for disputes resolution is through a DAB and arbitration. Mediation has been undertaken by the parties' own initiative, to terminate the contract. Both parties (employer and contractor) decided that the disputes should not be settled by a DAB or an international arbitration. It is worth noting that only the FIDIC White Book form of contract has mediation provisions.

    Pursuant to my recommendation as mediator, the parties agreed to amicably terminate the contract and sign one addendum which modified all the terms of the contract, including Clause 20.6 (arbitration). In the presence of the parties' respective lawyers, I fulfilled my tasks in line with the parties' requests to act neutrally and impartially.

    The contractor and the employer do not have to carry out their contractual obligations and duties under the contract anymore. The contractor has ceased to be liable for the care of the works performed and not performed from the date of the signature of the addendum. As of this date, the responsibility passed to the employer who has to launch a new tender based on existing site conditions.

    The bank did not object to the termination of this contract and recognized that the parties found agreement in just a few days.

3. **Construction of three tram lines**

    A FIDIC Red Book contract has been concluded between the employer and the contractor to perform the execution and completion of works related to the construction of a tram line. The works on site are going almost as per the latest revised contractor's program. However, delays have been recorded due to differing site conditions, a change to the sequence of works, payment issues, and design issues.

    Several addendums to the contract and variations orders have been agreed and signed by both parties.

    The delays on the design are more than ever the most worrying ones, especially since the designer is lacking reactivity. The contractor has submitted its claims but the parties would negotiate and try to find agreement.

    If the parties will not settle the disputes, those disputes will be presented to a DAB, which is a good mechanism to resolve the case.

    However, Clause 20.1 of the contract clearly states that the claims are submitted first to the engineer and he has 42 days to uphold or reject the claim, providing a full detailed justification for his decision.

    If the claim is rejected by the engineer and the contractor insists to have a determination, it becomes a dispute and therefore it should be submitted to the DAB.

    In Ukraine, there was a reluctance to use this form of dispute resolution, but the mechanism is simple and presents some advantages. The first step is the formation of the board according to Clauses 20.2 and 20.3. The parties have to enter in a contract called

"DAA (Dispute Adjudication Agreement)" in order to fix the warranties, obligations, form and payment of DAB members.

Under Clause 20.4, the DAB has 84 days to rule on a dispute, but it may propose a different deadline for the parties' approval if the referral or case is complex to analyze. The decision of the board is binding and the parties (employer and contractor) are required to comply with it promptly, unless it is modified through a conciliation procedure or by an arbitration award. A party has 28 days to reject the decision by notifying the other party. If the parties agreed on the decision, it becomes final. The engineer may have to include the sums agreed on the interim payment certificate or final payment certificate as per Clause 14.

If a party does not accept the DAB's decision, the parties should attempt to resolve the issue amicably under Clause 20.6. If that fails, the dispute should then be resolved by arbitration which is conducted under the rules of arbitration of the International Chamber of Commerce (ICC) by a panel of one or three arbitrators in the language determined by the parties.

4. **Construction of a metro tunnel**

The FIDIC design build Yellow Book form of contract was in use on two Ukrainian major projects, the Beskyd tunnel and the Chernobyl new safe confinement. In addition, there was a two-stage tender for a large-scale contract with works scheduled to start in 2016.

First, the lump sum approach has not been clearly understood by the employer and the PIU. The main point of the discussion was that the measurement of quantities performed by the contractor will be done according to bill of quantities (BOQ), which are quantities and unit rates provided by the contractor further to his design.

If the quantities performed by the contractor increase or decrease for any item of BOQ, he should be paid within the limit of the total amount of the BOQ for such items (unless there are exceptions such as variations, conditions that could not have been foreseen at the stage of working drawings, etc.)

Secondly, the employer flatly refused the use of a DAB arguing the costs and for reasons that show a misunderstanding of the role and obligations of a DAB.

The author spent hours explaining the following:
- The nature, rights and obligations of a DAB.
- The limitations of a DAB's power and jurisdiction.
- The method of initiating and processing a DAB.

The employer found it opportune to give power to the engineer to have the role and obligations of the DAB. For obvious reasons of independence and impartiality, this could not be accepted.

A "solution" was finally found to include the name of a DAB in the Appendix to Tender and Particular Conditions of Contract, and insert his CV in the tender document. The bank supports this idea to include the name of one independent expert and partially finance the DAB's costs. Lately a provision has been included giving rights for the tenderer to propose another candidate to act as a sole member DAB, should he reject the candidate proposed by the employer.

5. **Replacement of transmission lines in a district heating project**

The FIDIC Pink Book form of contract 2010 with particular conditions has been used for this project, and works were planned to start in September 2015.

As stated on the EBRD web page, clients should use the standard tender documents (STD) and form of contract appropriate to the objectives and circumstances of the project. The bank is not a party to the contract and does not accept legal responsibility for the adequacy of the contract forms contained in these documents. Clients are therefore advised to ensure that the contract conditions are suitable and complete in respect of any particular contract.

Also, the EBRD supports the use of the general conditions of the MDB Pink Book 2010. They are not mandatory and other internationally recognized forms of contracts may also be used.

Clause 20.6, which is related to arbitration of general conditions of MDB Pink Book 2010 can be the subject of misunderstanding and needs revision. It is not clear why the clause of the FIDIC Gold Book published two years earlier has not been used during the elaboration of this form of contract.

Under this clause, arbitration shall be conducted as follows:
(a) if the contract is with foreign contractors,
(b) if the contract is with domestic contractors, arbitration with proceedings conducted in accordance with the laws of the employer's country.

In Ukraine, there is a need for foreign companies doing business to be registered. The statutory time limits for registration of the representative office in Ukraine is 60 working days from the date of submission of required documents (Regulations: Law of Ukraine 959-12 "On foreign economic activity Ministry of Economy" "Instruction on registration of representative offices of the foreign economic activity agents in Ukraine"). Moreover, statutory time limits for license from the State Architectural Construction Inspection is 27 working days from the date of submission of required documents. The procedures must follow one another and the overall time can be of at least 88 working days (or at least 124 calendar days).

Once companies are able to present the evidence of the registered representation and obtained license together with the signed contract agreement within the time specified, it is unclear if the companies have to be considered as "Foreign" or "Domestic" regarding Clause 20.6 (Arbitration).

Future challenges

First, future confidence will be improved if strong reforms are introduced in Ukraine. War conflict in the east can both be seen as a tremendous obstacle or simply "tough conditions, " in any case it cannot be an excuse for postponing reforms. "Exogenous shocks undermined the efforts of authorities to stabilize the economy and jumpstart growth in 2014," said Qimiao Fan, World Bank Country Director for Belarus, Moldova and Ukraine. "Faster and deeper reforms are the best antidote to these exogenous shocks confronting Ukraine".

Ukrainian laws are under revision and talks with the European Union are ongoing. Ukrainians definitely expect a positive impact on currency, inflation and the stability of banks.

Construction projects are affected by the current situation and a few large European contractors have already declined to participate in tenders, while Chinese companies are still interested in the Ukrainian construction market.

Conclusion

Ukrainians and politicians have a challenge to reform their country in order to stabilize the economy and reassure investors, foreign companies and financial institutions. There is a special need to improve infrastructure (roads, motorways, railway, tram lines, and ports), and water supply, sewage treatment of solid waste, and district heating in numerous cities. Despite the situation in Greece, financial institutions and banks are not reluctant to support this Eastern European country.

In light of the above five projects, it is my opinion that various forms for dispute resolution can be used. The DAB is a good mechanism, and mediation presents a great future worldwide. DAB practitioners and mediators should play a better role in training and informing institutions, employers and PIU on their respective duties, obligations and authority.

In my opinion, the banks should not finance projects if the employer and contractor fails to appoint the DAB. The DAB in an ad hoc form as per the design and build FIDIC Yellow Book form of contract should definitely be part of the past and replaced with the standing DAB.

Moreover, it has become obvious that the arbitration clause of the FIDIC Pink Book 2010 should be amended, in particular the conditions in order to avoid misleading problems with foreign and domestic contractors.

In conclusion, the financial support from the European Union, EBRD, EIB, and World Bank for all these works has been important, and without them it would be difficult to achieve actual results to such important challenges.

> *Author's Note:* There is a special need to improve the infrastructure throughout Ukraine. Based on recent experiences on five projects in the country, the Ukrainian construction industry is suffering and improvements in the understanding of contractual issues should be emphasized. The purpose of this article is to provide an insight into the current situation and the different types of claims and disputes in Ukraine.
>
> Due to the sensitive situation in the Eastern part of Ukraine, political matters will not be discussed in this article. However, an overview is included in order to show where most of the construction claims and disputes found their origin. Due to confidentiality, project information cannot be disclosed.

Roger Ribeiro
Contracts Manager
Currie & Brown

Yaryna Bakhovska
Ukraine

11.4 Enforcement of dispute board decisions

A dispute board is a creature of contract: the parties establish and empower a dispute board with jurisdiction to hear and advise on the resolution of disputes. Benefits and shortfalls of non-binding recommendations and interim-binding decisions are being dealt with in practice. As such, there is no clear answer whether to use recommendations or adjudication and the success of a particular dispute resolution procedure will depend on the circumstances, jurisdiction, skills and credit of board members, the needs and priorities of the parties and their cultural backgrounds (Chern, 2010).

11.4.1 Non-binding recommendations

Even if the dispute board recommendation is contractually non-binding, this does not appear to impair the practical impact of the decision. This is because the recommendation is admissible in later proceedings and it is highly likely the judge will be persuaded by an opinion from experts familiar with the project during its realization. As strengths of non-binding recommendations, the following are mentioned:

- persuasiveness of the opinion—particularly if the experts are respected individuals;
- tendency to adopt recommendations by the parties to avoid further conflicts in some cultures (conciliation in China);
- non-threatening process;
- the preparation time for hearings is less than in other forums;
- shorter hearings;
- reduced hearing costs; and
- pragmatic decisions which avoid arbitration and, potentially, litigation.

The weaknesses of non-binding recommendations are as follows:

- They enable the losing party to postpone the day of reckoning by proceeding to arbitration;
- The effect of the recommendation may be nil (Chern, 2012).

11.4.2 Interim-binding decisions

A DAB decision is contractually binding with immediate effect. Thus the "losing party" will be in breach of contract if it were not to pay/grant time in accordance with the DAB decision.

The strengths of an interim-binding decision are as follows:

- If necessary, a decision may be enforced by legal processes (this may not be without difficulty depending on the jurisdiction);
- The binding nature of the decision can lead to early settlement;
- Disrespecting the decision will lead to breach of contract.

The weaknesses of an interim binding decision are as follows:

- There is more at stake, so the parties fight harder;
- The hearing preparation costs, hearing time and other related costs are higher;
- More chance of legal representation;

- The final decision is removed from the parties;
- Some matters are complex and the time limits can be tested when much turns on the decision (Chern, 2012).

11.4.3 Contractual sanctions for non-compliance with dispute board decisions

Extensive discussion is under way relating to DAB decisions (under FIDIC forms) in respect of which a notice of dissatisfaction has been given within 28 days, that is, a "binding but non-final DAB decision." The courts seem to interpret the respective FIDIC sub-clauses in a different way than their drafters intended (Seppälä, 2012).

A decision of the Court of Appeal of Singapore in *CRW Joint Operation v. Perusahaan Gas Negara (Persero) TBK* [2011] SGCA 33 is often quoted in this regard. In this case the court dismissed an appeal against the judgment of the High Court of Singapore setting aside an ICC arbitration award. The ICC Arbitral Tribunal, on the one hand, and two Singapore courts, on the other, arrived at widely different interpretations of Sub-Clauses 20.4–20.7 of the FIDIC CONS/1999 Red Book.

In some jurisdictions it is possible that a "binding but non-final DAB decision" might be enforced by the local courts despite the presence of an arbitration clause (Butera, 2014).

The UK courts view such DAB decisions the same way as a decision in statutory adjudication which was developed for speedy dispute resolution on a provisional interim basis, and require the decisions of adjudicators to be enforced pending the final determination of the dispute in litigation or arbitration. The decision in adjudication is binding and to be complied with until the dispute is finally resolved. It does not matter if this duty is implied or agreed. As a result, the court is not permitted to investigate whether the decision was right or wrong. All that matters is whether the adjudicator had the jurisdiction to reach the decision that they did, and that they reached it by a fair process (See *AMEC Group Ltd v. Thames Water Utilities Ltd.* [2010] EWHC 419 (TCC)).

When considering enforcement of interim binding dispute board decisions it is interesting to compare the opinions of lawyers from different countries (at http://globalarbitrationreview.com) who responded to the following questions:

- For a DAB decision awarding a sum to a contractor under, say, Sub-Clause 20.4 of the FIDIC CONS/1999 Red Book for which the employer has given a timely notice of dissatisfaction, in an arbitration in your jurisdiction, might the contractor obtain: (a) a partial or interim award requiring payment of the sum awarded by the DAB pending any final award that would be enforceable in your jurisdiction (assuming the arbitral rules are silent); or (b) interim relief from a court in your jurisdiction requiring payment of the sum awarded by the DAB pending any award?

They replied, as follows:

- *France*: Before the constitution of the arbitral tribunal, courts have wide powers to order interim measures, including a *référé* provision, which allows a court provisionally to order payment of an undisputed amount. This would not be possible in the event of a DAB decision that has been the subject of a notice of dissatisfaction. Once the arbitral tribunal has been constituted, the courts' powers to order interim measures will then be restricted by the terms of the arbitration agreement. Given the wording of Sub-Clause 20.6 [Arbitration] of the FIDIC CONS/1999 Red Book, it is unlikely that a French court would accept jurisdiction in connection with a party's application for interim relief requiring payment of the sum awarded by the DAB. However, that party may apply for an interim or partial award (in respect of the other party's failure to comply with the DAB decision in breach of Sub-Clause 20.4) and, if successful, may seek to enforce that award in France (Gillion and Rosher at http://globalarbitrationreview.com).

- *Germany*: If not finally binding, a DAB decision for payment will not be enforced by the arbitration tribunal nor may enforcement be sought by interim relief from a court. Interim decisions are not subject to enforcement. A party's failure to satisfy a binding DAB decision may constitute a new breach of contract entitling the other party to additional damages, which are typically of higher interest on amounts due. Nonetheless, such a breach of contract would have to be determined by means of the arbitration proceedings. Interim relief is not available as the grant of payment under an interim order would constitute a preliminary decision on the merits which may not be rendered through interim relief (Kremer at http://globalarbitrationreview.com).
- *South Africa*: Where a construction agreement makes provision for an award to be made by the principal agent or DAB—which may be disputed in arbitration by timely delivery of a notice of dissatisfaction—the agreement will generally either stipulate expressly or tacitly whether the disputed award is capable of enforcement pending the determination of arbitration. Where the agreement is silent on the enforceability of such an award, the party disputing the award would in all likelihood be able to resist enforcement as it is contractually entitled to have the dispute determined in arbitration and should therefore not be required to suffer the prejudice of payment before determination of the dispute (Hoeben at http://globalarbitrationreview.com).

The approach of UK courts does not necessarily have to be universal. Butera (2014) proposes the best procedure is to treat the failure to comply with the DAB decision as giving rise to another dispute (second dispute) that will be again referred to in the same DAB for its decision under Sub-Clause 20.4. The subject of this second dispute will be whether the DAB decision in the first dispute gave rise to an obligation to pay the amount of the decision and, if so, whether there was any legal justification for the respondent to withhold payment—and as to the relief to which the claimant is entitled. Once the DAB has made its decision in the second dispute, the same second dispute may then be referred to arbitration, the scope of which should be limited to the same issues. This approach was confirmed in ICC cases no. 15751 and no. 16948.

The merits of the first decision may nevertheless still be challenged by commencement of (separate) arbitration proceedings in relation to the first dispute.

As to the relief that may be granted, three options are discussed: (1) a claim for damages; (2) specific performance; or (3) to accept an opinion that a binding decision requiring payment of money creates a debt which may be enforceable as such.

In terms of a claim for damages, it would appear that the damages recoverable would be limited to a claim for interest and not the amount of the DAB's decision itself. Regarding specific performance, there are likely to be doubts whether the tribunal has the power to make such an order. Convincing the arbitral tribunal to exercise any such power will be difficult. The third option is that a contractual obligation to pay a sum of money is generally considered in common law jurisprudence to give rise to a debt.

Lloyd & Jones (2014) comment on Butera's conclusions and agree that the status of a "binding but non-final DAB decision" is the same as the status of a certificate that had been issued and not paid and on that basis it should be possible to allow for sanctions of suspension and termination to be available to a contractor.

Accordingly, where English law applies, the appropriate remedy in respect of failure to comply with a "binding but non-final DAB decision," which required payment of a sum of money is an order for payment of that sum as a debt (Butera, 2014). Because of this uncertainty, FIDIC published a Guidance Memorandum to Users of the 1999 Conditions of Contract, dated April 1, 2013.

It is explained in this document that a substantial number of arbitral tribunals have found Clause 20 to be unclear on the issue of whether a party may refer the failure of the other party to comply with a DAB decision that is "binding" but not "final" to arbitration as is explicitly the case of a "final and binding" decision under Sub-Clause 20.7. A DAB decision is "binding" and not "final" when either party, within 28 days after receiving the DAB decision, gives notice to the other party of its dissatisfaction with the DAB decision. International arbitral tribunals have been divided over whether, in the event of a failure to comply with a DAB decision issued under Clause 20 of the FIDIC CONS/1999 Red Book, which is "binding" but not "final," the failure itself may be referred to arbitration, without Sub-Clause 20.4 (Obtaining Dispute Adjudication Board's Decision) and Sub-Clause 20.5 (Amicable Settlement) being applicable to the reference.

The *FIDIC Guidance Memorandum* is designed to make explicit the intentions of FIDIC in relation to the enforcement of the DAB decisions that are binding and not yet final. Where there is a failure to comply with these decisions, the failure itself should be capable of being referred to arbitration under Sub-Clause 20.6 (Arbitration), without Sub-Clause 20.4 (Obtaining Dispute Adjudication Board's Decision), and Sub-Clause 20.5 (Amicable Settlement) being applicable to the reference. This intention has been made manifest in the *FIDIC Conditions of Contract for Design, Build and Operate Projects*, 2008 (the Gold Book) through Sub-Clause 20.9:

> In the event that a party fails to comply with any decision of the DAB, whether binding or final and binding, then the other Party may, without prejudice to any other rights it may have, refer the failure itself to arbitration under Sub-Clause 20.8 [Arbitration] for summary or other expedited relief, as may be appropriate. Sub-Clause 20.6 [Obtaining Dispute Adjudication Board's Decision] and Sub-Clause 20.7 [Amicable Settlement] shall not apply to this reference.

To make FIDIC's intention explicit, this Guidance Memorandum provides for changes to be made to the FIDIC dispute resolution Clause 20 (particularly Sub-Clause 20.7) and, as a consequence, to 14.6 and 14.8 of *the FIDIC Conditions of Contract for Construction*, 1999 (the Red Book), the *FIDIC Conditions of Contract for Plant and Design-Build*, 1999 (the Yellow Book), and the *EPC/Turnkey Projects*, 1999 (the Silver Book). Compliance with the guidance provided in this Memorandum is highly recommended when using the 1999 FIDIC Red, Yellow, or Silver Books. The new 2017 edition established for this purpose a new Sub-Clause 21.7 Failure to Comply with DAAB's Decision with a broader but similar wording as the DBO version above.

The Persero proceedings and the issue of the enforcement of a non-final DAB decision under the FIDIC conditions
by David Brown (UK)

Much ink has been spilled in professional journals over the vexed issue of the enforcement of non-final DAB decisions under the 1999 FIDIC conditions.

The issue, stated simply, is as follows:

- DAB decisions are contractually binding, but only become final if a notice of dissatisfaction is not served within 28 days.
- The FIDIC conditions only provide for referral to arbitration of a final and binding DAB decision in the event of non-compliance with the decision.
- How, therefore, should a party proceed if the other party has filed a notice of dissatisfaction but failed to comply with the DAB decision? In particular, should the party refer the failure to comply back to the DAB as a dispute requiring a further decision?

In the now notorious proceedings between PT Perusahaan Gas Negara (Persero) TBK and CRW Joint Operation (Indonesia), often referred to as the Persero saga, the party in question chose to refer directly to arbitration the failure to comply with the DAB decision. The majority decision of the ICC tribunal was a final award on the matters in the DAB decision on grounds of non-compliance. In other words, no consideration of the underlying merits of the disputes was needed.

This view was contested in the Singapore courts—first the High Court then the Court of Appeal—with the latter deciding that the FIDIC conditions do "not allow an arbitral tribunal to make final and binding DAB decision without hearing the merits of that DAB decision."

As an aside, it was the fear of such an outcome that prompted the author, when faced with a similar case of non-compliance, to seek a further DAB, although solely in relation to the question of non-compliance, before referring the matter to arbitration. In the subsequent arbitration proceedings (ICC case 16948, reports in various journals), the sole arbitrator had no difficulty in issuing a final award on the matter of non-compliance, and awarding the claimant the full amount decided by the DAB, since he was able to consider the merits of the DAB decision in question, as they related solely to the matter of non-compliance with earlier DAB decisions. There was no final award on the merits, since the other party could always attack the DAB decisions on the merits if it chose to do so.

Returning to the Persero saga, there was something of an outcry in the FIDIC world following the Court of Appeals decision mentioned above. Surely, it made no commercial sense to incur the time and cost of a further DAB proceeding in such circumstances! Further, doubts as to the efficacy of the wording of the FIDIC conditions were addressed by the publication on April 1, 2013 of a Guidance Memorandum setting out the intentions of FIDIC with respect to the matter as well as recommended revised wording for the provisions in question.

Last but not least, the issue of the enforcement of the original DAB decision in the Persero case was the subject of a second set of proceedings in the Singapore courts. This time round, the Court of Appeals overturned its earlier judgment, finding that:

- Sub-Clause 20.4 imposes a distinct contractual obligation on a party to comply promptly with a DAB decision regardless of whether the decision is final and binding or merely binding but not final,
- This obligation is capable of being directly enforced by arbitration without the parties having first to go through the preliminary steps set out in 20.4 and 20.5,
- A tribunal would be entitled to make a final determination on the issue of prompt compliance alone if that is all it has been asked to rule on.

In other words, the draftsman's intention to set up a security for payment regime — "pay now, argue later"—should be recognized and upheld.

The Persero saga, involving lengthy and expensive court proceedings over six years, is understood to be the last time the issue has been debated by state courts. And some might say that the matter is of little more than historical interest at present, since the problematic wording in the 1999 FIDIC editions was revised in the 2008 Gold Book to allow for direct referral to arbitration of non-compliance with both final and non-final DAB decisions, with a similar solution taken in the next edition of the major FIDC forms.

However, the issue cannot be said to have gone away. Parties continue to enter into contracts incorporating the 1999 FIDIC forms, and it is unlikely that many take into account the guidance memorandum mentioned above, with the result that our enforcement issue could still arise. And it must not be forgotten that the outcome in the Persero proceedings could have limited impact outside Singapore!

In fact, the matter has been the subject of a number of ICC cases since the Persero saga came to an end. The resulting arbitral awards have not yet been reported, and it is to be hoped that this state of affairs will be rectified shortly. What can be stated is that arbitrators have not always agreed with the majority view of the Court of Appeals in the second set of Persero proceedings ("Persero 2"). Thus, for example:

- In ICC case 19858, the tribunal was not prepared to support an "untenable explanation" of Sub-Clauses 20.4 to 20.7 of the FIDIC conditions simply to give effect to 'pay first, argue later' policy considerations. In other words, Persero 2 was considered to be unpersuasive given the clear wording of the FIDIC conditions.
- In ICC case 21004, the sole arbitrator found that the correct approach was to file a second DAB reference with respect to the failure to comply with the contractual obligation to give effect to the DAB decision.

Therefore, there still seems to be a strong case for inciting parties using the 1999 FIDIC forms to amend their contracts along the lines proposed by FIDIC in its 2013 guidance memorandum, in the hope of avoiding another Persero saga.

David Brown
Partner
Clyde & Co
UK

11.5 Statutory adjudication

Statutory adjudication by Nigel Grout (UK)

Statutory adjudication in the UK was established in 1998 when the Housing Grants, Construction and Regeneration Act 1996 (commonly referred to as the "Construction Act") came into force. This act gave parties to a construction contract a statutory right, save for a few exceptions, to unilaterally refer any dispute to adjudication at any time.

Prior to the provision of adjudication, the main means of resolving disputes in the construction industry was either by arbitration or court litigation. However, both of these methods were proving unsatisfactory due to their prohibitive costs, the length of time it took to get a decision, and the considerable cross-examination of witnesses. From the late 1970s and through the 1980s there were a high number of construction disputes in the UK, and the courts were experiencing rapid expansion in their workload for the construction sector. Consequently, it often took between 18 and 24 months for a case to be heard. Similar timescales were common in arbitrations.

The construction industry was also notorious for its bad payment culture, and this was made worse by the economic recession of the early 1990s. Against this background, and with litigation and arbitration still proving ineffective ways of enforcing payment, the Government and the UK construction industry jointly commissioned Sir Michael Latham to report on the industry. The publication of the Latham Report in 1994 recommended, *inter alia*, the introduction of statutory adjudication.

The main objectives of adjudication were to promote better cash flow, and to provide an interim binding, relatively cheap and quick means of deciding disputes until they were finally determined by arbitration or the courts. The ethos was "pay first, argue later."

In the early days of adjudication, one of the main concerns was that weaker contracting parties (generally subcontractors) would be reluctant to use the process as they might suffer the consequence of being denied future opportunities to tender for work. This concern proved unfounded, and adjudication quickly became the most popular process used in the UK to settle construction disputes arising under the contract.

Today, it is widely accepted that adjudication has been a success, and it continues to be by far the most preferred method for resolving construction disputes in the UK. The speed and cost effectiveness of the process are in contrast to the problems still associated with arbitration and litigation. Its popularity has had the consequential benefit of freeing up more court time, as the number of new proceedings in the Technology and Construction Court has decreased considerably from the pre-adjudication period. There has also been a substantial reduction in the number of construction arbitrations.

Another reason for the success is the willingness of the UK courts to enforce the decision of the adjudicator. Other than for reasons of jurisdiction and natural justice, there is very little scope for a losing party to escape interim compliance pending any final determination of the dispute. This robust enforcement policy has endorsed the objective of improving cash flow within the industry.

Nigel Grout
www.nigelgrout.com
Adjudicator, Arbitrator, Expert Witness
UK

11.5.1 UK statutory adjudication regime

In the UK, Section 108 of Part II of the *Housing Grants, Construction and Regeneration Act 1996* ("the Act"), provides for a statutory right and prescribes procedural rules of adjudication (the *Users "Guide To Adjudication, Construction Umbrella Bodies Adjudication Task Group,"* April 2003 ("Users' Guide") available at http://www.scl.org.uk/files/CUB_ Users_Guide_May_2003.pdf). Pursuant to the Act, "a dispute between parties to, and arising under, a construction contract, effective as of May 1, 1998 or later, may be referred for adjudication." Disputes encapsulate "any difference."

The act prescribes what provisions a construction contract shall contain in order to avail itself of the statutory regime. The contract shall thus provide for notices of a party's intention to adjudicate, set a timetable for an adjudicator's appointments and referrals, set time limits within which a decision must be reached and the adjudicator's powers. The act also prescribes that the parties' contract shall "impose a duty on the adjudicator to act impartially." The act further requires the parties' contract to provide that the adjudicator's decision be "binding until the dispute is finally determined by legal proceedings, by arbitration … or by agreement." The parties may also agree upon the acceptance of the adjudicator's decision "as finally determining the dispute."

Where the statutory requirements have not been complied with, the statutory regime of the act will not apply and the act itself falls back upon a default regime contained in the *Scheme for Construction Contracts (England and Wales) Regulations 1998* ("the Scheme").

11.5.2 The scheme for construction projects in the UK

Impartiality and independence are required of the adjudicator in the course of adjudication proceedings conducted pursuant to the Scheme. Paragraph 12(1) of the Scheme (which concerns the adjudicator's powers) imposes a duty upon the adjudicator to act impartially and in accordance with the law and the applicable contract. The duty of impartiality and independence also forms part of the requirement that the adjudicator must neither be biased (actual bias) nor must he or she be perceived to be biased (apparent bias), which is an aspect of the requirement of natural justice or procedural fairness. The second prong of natural justice is the duty to conduct a fair hearing.

The test for bias is objective: whether a reasonable observer would conclude that there is a *real possibility* of bias. Personal relations with a party to the contract and the proceedings, favouring or apparent favoring or supporting one party or interest in the adjudication are examples of bias.

The hearing shall be conducted fairly, that is, the parties shall have knowledge of the case and be given a reasonable opportunity to present their own case. Oral hearings do not seem to be a requisite part of the adjudication process and the adjudicator has the full discretion—within the limits and constraints of the law regarding procedural fairness—to decide whether or not to order an oral hearing or a meeting of the parties.

Lack of fairness during the adjudication process may be grounds for setting aside the adjudicator's decision by a court.

11.5.3 Some procedural aspects of statutory adjudication

Under the scheme, adjudication may be initiated by serving a written notice of adjudication to the other party. The notice specifies the matters which the party seeks the adjudicator to decide. An adjudicator must be appointed within seven (7) days of the submission of the notice. The adjudicator may be named in the construction contract in question, the contract may specify a panel of adjudicators or an adjudicator nominating body or, if the contract is silent on this issue, any adjudicator nominating body may be approached. After an adjudicator has been appointed, a referral notice with information that the adjudicator ought to consider is sent to him or her and to the other party. Generally, a decision must be rendered within 28 days of the receipt of the referral notice by the adjudicator.

A party may challenge the adjudicator's jurisdiction, for instance, on the grounds of an alleged conflict of interest or that the underlying contract is not a construction contract within the meaning of the act. While adjudicators generally (unless given such authority by the parties) lack the power to decide upon such jurisdictional challenges (i.e., they are left to the court), the adjudicators are advised to conduct an investigation into their jurisdiction and also in order to comply with their obligation to be, and appear, impartial.

In their decisions, adjudicators may issue an order to a party to pay money or may decide a fact or a matter of a technical nature that the parties failed to agree upon. The scheme requires that reasons for the decision be provided to the parties if and where requested.

The adjudicator also decides which party pays the adjudicator's costs. However, under existing law, each party is responsible for bearing their own costs and the adjudicator lacks the power to award costs orders.

The party against whom the adjudicator's decision was given will either comply with the decision or the decision may be enforced in court (which, in most cases, will uphold it in a matter of days), unless a party succeeds with a jurisdictional challenge or attacks the adjudicator's decision on natural justice grounds, that is, where the adjudicator had failed to act impartially or had not provided both parties with an opportunity to present their case. A party cannot appeal the adjudicator's decision but the matter may be heard as a new case, either in court or in arbitration proceedings.

Settling construction disputes in Hungary by Tamás Balázs (Hungary)

Two special Hungarian dispute resolution bodies need to be mentioned concerning the settlement of disputes in connection with construction contracts entered into on the basis of FIDIC terms and conditions of contracts. The power and procedures of these bodies to decide legal issues overshadow the triple hierarchy of FIDIC dispute resolution (Dispute Adjudication Board—Amicable Settlement—Arbitration) in Hungary. Legislation enacted into force on July 1, 2013 (Act XXXIV of 2013 on the Expert Body for Performance Certification, hereinafter: the "Act") set up the Expert Body for Performance Certification (EBPC) and regulated its functions and powers. The reason for enacting new legislation and establishing this body was in reaction to legal disputes having increased greatly in connection with the performance of construction contracts in recent years. Disputes were mainly between the employer and contractor and, to a lesser extent, between the contractor and their sub-contractors. Generally, these legal disputes took years to decide before a binding judgment was eventually handed down by the courts. The scope of the legislation covers all construction projects in Hungary. The act states that contractual clauses that exclude or restrict the powers or procedures of the EBPC or which attach any negative, legal consequence to initiating EBPC procedures are null and void. Therefore, if the construction project is implemented in the territory of Hungary, we are faced with a mandatory provision of Hungarian law that cannot be bypassed even if choosing the law of another country. However, the EBPC does not have jurisdiction over all legal disputes in the construction sector. Its jurisdiction only applies:

(a) to those cases in connection with the performance of construction contracts when no performance certificate is issued;
(b) where the issuance of a performance certificate is disputed;
(c) payment is not made despite being due; as well as
(d) to those cases when the ancillary obligations to guarantee the contract (bank guarantee, lien, surety) and their enforcement are disputed by the parties.

It is to be emphasized that the *ex officio* procedure of the EBPC is not mandatory and can be initiated upon request of one of the parties. The act grants priority and summary procedure to the parties involved in court litigation where they have attempted to use the EBPC. Presumably, this will motivate the parties concerned to avail themselves of the possibility granted by the new act instead of opting for the much longer 'normal' court procedure. The EBPC is composed of independent court experts and must deliver its expert opinion in 30 days from the date of receipt of the application. The party that disagrees with the expert opinion can enter into litigation within 60 days from the date of its receipt and the court is obliged to handle all such cases with priority in a summary procedure. The amended *Code of Civil Procedure* provides a number of guarantee provisions and preferential treatment to the party which sustained injury according to the expert opinion (e.g., judicial protective measures and prior enforceability).

This procedure is particularly advantageous to the contractor if the employer disputes performance or certain aspects of performance stated in the contract. Provided that an EBCP review is allowed, the contractor will probably decide against using arbitration. The other special bodies created to decide legal disputes are the conciliation boards attached to the regional Chambers of Industry and Trade. This institution enforces consumer protection regulation in Hungary and its functions are accessible to the consumer. The definition of "consumer" was broadened considerably as a consequence of an amendment to the *Consumer Protection Act* (2013), which came into effect in July 2013. The new definition covers not only natural persons acting to promote objectives outside the scope of their independent professions and activities but, among other things, micro, small, and medium-sized enterprises in the European sense. The conciliation board can give a binding decision with regard to the enterprise, which is subject to the complaint but *only* if it made a statement of submission before the adoption of the decision. It is further possible—even in this case—for the entity subject to the complaint to start litigation (i.e., appeal) against the conciliation body's decision within 15 days of the decision. Where the terms and conditions of the FIDIC contract are used in Hungary, the contract must contain the rules for deciding legal disputes in accordance with the relevant contract templates. Failing that—and if the competent court and the applicable law are not specified—the registered office of the Hungarian company subject to litigation in Hungary or the site of the construction project in Hungary may lay the foundation for determining the jurisdiction of the Hungarian court (see also Chapter 20 of the 1999 FIDIC Red and Yellow Books). The functions of the EBPC overlap those of a dispute adjudication board (DAB) under FIDIC if initiated by a party. Given the advantages of the EPBC mentioned above, the parties are likely to choose it over the DAB. The EPBC still remains somewhat of an "unknown" in Hungary because Act XXXIV of 2013 providing for the rules of EBPC procedure only came into effect on July 1, 2013. It is important to note that Act XXXIV of 2013 states that contractual clauses that exclude or restrict the applicability of the procedure of EPBC are null and void.

Tamás Balázs
Managing partner, attorney-at-law, professor of law
Balázs & Kovátsits Legal Partnership
Hungary

Statutory adjudication in Australia by Donald Charrett (Australia)

Cash flow is the lifeblood of the construction industry. The Australian construction industry includes many small organizations that rely on the cash flow from regular progress payments in order to pay their employees and creditors. Such companies are financially vulnerable to their employers withholding payment for any reason, whether valid or not.

The final report of the Cole Royal Commission into the Australian building and construction industry in 2003 (The Hon. T. R. H. Cole QC, *Final Report of the Royal Commission into the*

Building and Construction Industry: Vol. 8 (2003), Appendix 1) made recommendations on "one of the most significant and controversial issues impacting the success or failure of any party working in the construction industry." The report highlighted the rationale for security of payment as follows:

> Commission investigators were repeatedly told of the suffering and hardship caused to subcontractors by builders who are unable or unwilling to pay for work from which they have benefited. The subcontractors who experience payment problems are often small companies or partnerships. Frequently they do not have the expertise or resources to enforce their legal rights, because enforcement would require protracted litigation against much better resourced and more sophisticated companies. Consequently, subcontractors that have operated profitably and well for many years can be forced into liquidation through no fault of their own, often with devastating consequences for the owners of these businesses, their families, their employees and their creditors.

Prior to the Royal Commission's recommendations, the States of New South Wales and Victoria had each passed a Building and Construction Industry Security of Payment Act that addressed the issue of prompt payment. The Royal Commission's recommendations included the enactment of a Building and Construction Industry Security of Payment Act by the Commonwealth of Australia, along the lines of a draft Bill in the Royal Commission Report. The aim of this recommendation was to achieve uniform legislation across all states and territories. Unfortunately, the Commonwealth has never enacted legislation, with the inevitable consequence that Australia now has eight different acts for security of payment, each of them different.

The various Security of Payment Acts all set up a system of progress payments, rapid adjudication of payment disputes and contract reform. The first act (NSW) included similar adjudication provisions to the Housing Grants, Construction and Regeneration Act 1996 (UK), and formed the model upon which other Australian jurisdictions, to varying degrees, based their legislation. Unlike the UK act, however, statutory adjudication in Australia is confined to disputes over payment. Not only are there significant differences in detail between the individual Australian acts, there are conceptual differences between the Western Australia and Northern Territory acts ("west coast model") and the acts in the other jurisdictions ("east coast model"). The west coast model is similar to the construction industry payments legislation proposed by the Cole Royal Commission Report, and is more in harmony with the legislation passed in the UK and NZ.

> Whilst both models allow for a statutory adjudication scheme to determine, in the interim, disputed payment claims, they differ with respect to adjudicator appointment, submissions which may be considered by an adjudicator, and the approach which an adjudicator is to adopt in order to arrive at his or her determination. In all of these respects the East Coast Acts are more restrictive, disallowing mutual agreement of an adjudicator, consideration of reasons for withholding payment which have not been

duly submitted in accordance with the statutory payment scheme, and discouraging an evaluative approach to adjudicators' determinations.

(Coggins et al., 2003)

The significant differences between the acts and between the east coast and west coast models means that there is no "Australian adjudication" as such. As space here does not permit further comparison of the differences between the various acts, the following description refers to the operation of the Building and Construction Industry Security of Payment Act 1999 (NSW) ("the Act").

Main features of the act

The act provides various statutory entitlements that operate in addition to (or in substitution for inconsistent) contractual provisions. Operation of the act is mandatory for any "construction contract," covering both "construction work" and "related goods and services" as broadly defined. However, there are significant carve-outs for, for example, extraction of oil and gas or minerals and residential construction, with the consequence that it does not apply to a substantial part of construction work in NSW. The act provides an entitlement to progress payments, either in accordance with the provisions of the contract, or at monthly intervals if the interval is not specified in the contract.

The act fetters freedom of contract in several ways. Thus, "pay when paid," or "pay if paid" provisions in a contract are of no effect. Further, in the event that the agreed amount of a progress claim or the adjudicated amount is not paid, the claimant may stop working under the contract after giving two business days' notice. These provisions may not be contracted out of.

The act specifies a formal procedure that must be followed to recover progress payments, and details the consequences if payment is not made. In the event of a dispute over payment, the claimant can initiate an adjudication process that is intended to be speedy and cost-effective. Adjudication is carried out by an adjudicator who is formally accredited by an "authorized nominating authority." There is an expedited process for a claimant to obtain a debt judgment in court of a progress payment or the adjudicated amount of a progress payment.

It is important to note that the act is directed to maintaining cash flow in relation to progress payments, and does not override other legal rights that either party has under the contract or the law. An adjudication determines the amount of a progress payment on account only, and does not provide a final determination of the parties' legal rights. A respondent that is required to pay an adjudicated amount may therefore seek to recover that amount in subsequent court or arbitration proceedings, if the respondent can prove its legal entitlement pursuant to, for example, defect rectification or liquidated damages for late performance. Nevertheless, in practice, the adjudicated amount frequently becomes a final payment, as few payment disputes proceed to an ultimate determination of legal rights in arbitration or litigation.

Progress payments and adjudication

As the statutory entitlements under the act are additional to the provisions of the relevant construction contract, certain formalities must be complied with to invoke its operation. Thus, a "payment claim" must identify the construction work carried out or the relevant goods and services supplied and the amount of the claim. A payment claim must be made within the time provided for in the contract, but no more than 12 months after the relevant work was carried out or the goods and services supplied. Only one payment claim may be made in respect of each "reference date."

The person from whom payment is claimed ("the respondent") may respond by providing a "payment schedule" detailing the amount the respondent proposes to pay, and must specify the reasons for any difference between that amount and the amount claimed. If the respondent does not serve a payment schedule within the time provided by the contract, or a maximum of 10 business days, it becomes liable to pay the amount of the payment claim in full. In that event, the claimant may either recover the amount claimed as a debt in court, or make application for adjudication.

Similarly, if the respondent does not pay the full amount in its payment schedule by the due date, the claimant may either recover the amount claimed as a debt in court, or make application for adjudication. If the claimant seeks to recover the amount claimed in court, the respondent may not bring any cross-claim or raise any defence in relation to matters arising under the construction contract. Amendments made to the act in 2013 mandate payment periods for progress payments, irrespective of the provisions of the contract.

The claimant initiates an adjudication of its claim for a progress payment by submitting an application to an authorized nominating authority of its choice. If the respondent has not provided a payment schedule, the claimant must provide notice before submitting an adjudication application, and give the respondent five business days to provide a payment schedule. There are strict time limits for submission of an adjudication application: within 10 business days after a payment schedule has been received, within 20 business days after the due date if payment was not made in accordance with the payment schedule, and within 10 business days after the five-day period to provide a payment schedule if it was not originally provided.

The adjudication application may contain any relevant submissions that the claimant chooses to provide. An adjudication application must be served on the respondent. The authorized nominating authority must refer the application to an authorized adjudicator as soon as possible. The adjudicator accepts such nomination by serving a notice on the claimant and the respondent.

If, and only if, the respondent has provided a payment schedule, it may submit an "adjudication response" within five business days of receiving the adjudication application, or within two business days of receiving the adjudicator's acceptance of nomination. The adjudication response may contain such information as the respondent chooses to include, but may not include any reasons for withholding payment unless those reasons were already included in the payment schedule provided to the claimant.

The adjudicator may not determine the matter until after the period for submission of the adjudication response, and may not consider an adjudication response submitted outside the prescribed time. The adjudicator must determine the matter as expeditiously as possible, but within 10 business days after having notified the parties of acceptance of the nomination, unless the claimant agrees to an extension of time for the adjudication.

The adjudicator may call for further submissions, call an informal conference of the parties (without legal representation) or make an inspection of the subject matter of the claim. Failure of a party to make a submission or comment does not affect the adjudicator's obligation to make a timely determination. The adjudicator must determine the amount of the progress payment to be paid (if any), the date on which it is to be paid, and the rate of interest on any outstanding amount.

The adjudicator's determination must be in writing, and must include reasons, unless both parties agree otherwise. In making his/her determination, the adjudicator must only consider the provisions of the Act, the contract, the payment claim and payment schedule, submissions made to the adjudicator, and the results of any inspection. The adjudicator may make a correction to the determination arising from a clerical mistake, an error arising from an accidental slip or omission or material miscalculation or a defect of form.

The respondent is liable to pay the adjudicated amount within five business days of service of the determination, or by such other date as the adjudicator determines. If the respondent does not pay the adjudicated amount in full within the prescribed time, the claimant may request the authorized nominating authority to provide an "adjudication certificate." That certificate may be filed in any court of competent jurisdiction as a judgment debt and enforced accordingly. If the respondent files proceedings to set aside such judgment, it may not raise any cross-claim or any defence in relation to matters arising under the construction contract, or challenge the adjudicator's determination. Further, it is required to pay into court the unpaid amount of the adjudicator's determination pending the outcome of its claim to set aside the judgment debt.

Main advantages of adjudication

The "quick and dirty" adjudication process provided for in the act provides an affordable and speedy process for claimants to be paid progress payment amounts they are entitled to. Time of payment is fundamental to maintaining cash flow, and in many cases to the financial viability of contractors and subcontractors. Recourse to adjudication under the act levels the playing field by ensuring that large organizations with substantial assets cannot use long delays in the legal system to negotiate unfair or unwarranted financial concessions from their contractors or subcontractors. Even where the act is not invoked, its existence discourages bad behavior up the contracting chain.

Although conducted within a very tight timeframe, the parties are arguably afforded some measure of procedural fairness (but see Coggins et al. above), and determination of the adjudicated amount is made in accordance with the law and the contract, and the available evidence. In theory, there is some quality control on the process by virtue of authorized nominating authorities that maintain lists of qualified adjudicators. However, the significant number of adjudication determinations quashed in court proceedings (see below) indicates that in practice there is a problem of quality control in the appointment and registration of adjudicators.

The process is designed to promote a "pay now and argue later" mentality, by facilitating payment of progress claims that are *prime facie* genuine, without compromising the parties' ultimate legal rights. A respondent can still initiate legal proceedings to enforce its ultimate legal rights, irrespective of any payments that have been made in response to adjudication determinations, although this rarely occurs in practice.

Issues arising from operation of the act

The act applies to all work and goods and services carried out under a "construction contract" (subject to the defined carve outs of specific types of construction work), irrespective of the magnitude or complexity of a progress claim. A claimant may have many months to prepare a large and complex claim (that may subsequently form the basis of an adjudication application), comprising many lever arch folders of material, which may be served at a time chosen by the claimant. The respondent then has a very limited time to digest this material and respond—no more than 10 business days for a progress claim and five business days for an adjudication response. This is clearly inadequate for complex multi-million dollar claims (the largest adjudicated amount in Australia is in excess of $50 million). Similarly, the prescribed period of 10 business days for the adjudicator's determination is inadequate for large and complex claims. Any extension to such time is subject to agreement by the claimant who has every reason to require the adjudication determination in the shortest time possible, and veto any request for a time extension.

The claimant's sole choice of authorized nominating authority has proved to be problematic, as there is evidence that some authorities are much more "claimant friendly" than others. Further, the amount of fees charged by some "for-profit" authorized nominating authorities appears to be disproportionate to the services they render, adding further unwarranted expense to the process.

The objects of the act are fulfilled by payment of progress payments pursuant to adjudication determinations. Such payments are inevitably used in the claimant's cash flow in running its business. In a situation where the respondent has a legitimate claim against the claimant, it will only recover the amount it is legally entitled to after lengthy (separate) court or arbitration proceedings. Such vindication is of little value, if, in the intervening period since payment was made pursuant to the adjudication determination, the claimant has become bankrupt or gone into liquidation.

This issue is a consequence of the 'pay now and argue later' principle, and is probably the reason why there have been so many court cases over virtually every aspect of the act—where the respondent is required to pay a large sum pursuant to an adjudication determination, it is unsurprising if it pursues every legal challenge to that determination if there is any doubt about its ultimate recoverability pursuant to the respondent's legal rights.

Are the legislative objects being achieved?

Arguably, the east coast model (including the Act) is achieving its aims of providing "a fast, cheap, non-legalistic way of resolving payment for work done or material or services supplied" (Victorian Building Commission, Introduction to the *Building and Construction Industry Security of Payment Act 2002* (Victoria), at www.buildingcommission.com.au) to improve timely cash flow in the construction industry. There are a significant number of adjudications under the Acts in NSW and Queensland: by 2008/2009, the number of annual adjudication applications in each jurisdiction had reached approximately 1000, and the total value of payment claims in adjudication approximately $200 million.

However, many aspects of the act have been problematic. There has been, and still is, considerable litigation over the act—over 320 cases in the Supreme Court or Court of Appeal, the majority being cases where a respondent has attempted to have at least a part of an adjudicator's determination set aside (for an analysis of the case law in NSW and Victoria, see (Wilson, 2014)). After 14 years of operation of the act, there were still 23 cases in 2012 seeking to challenge an adjudication, and some 80% of these resulted in overturning of the adjudicator's determination on jurisdictional grounds, taint of bias, and so on. A recent thorough investigation of the operation of the various *Security of Payment Acts* in Australia resulted in a number of recommendations for significant reform of the east coast model to address its identified shortcomings (Australian Legislation Reform Sub-Committee of the Society of Construction Law Australia, 2014).

Notwithstanding over 13 years operation of the act, there were still problems of insolvency in the construction industry. A (2013) report made a number of recommendations to alleviate this problem, including the implementation of a statutory construction trust. In response to this report, the act was amended with respect to the timing of, and other requirements for, payments under construction contracts. These amendments simplify the procedure a subcontractor must undertake to obtain payment of an adjudicated amount (*Building and Construction Industry Security of Payment Amendment Act 2013* (NSW)). Details of the amendments were outlined in the Second Reading Speech of the *Building and Construction Industry Security of Payment Amendment Bill 2010* (NSW) by the Honorable Michael Veitch. However, there is controversy in relation to the unintended consequences of these amendments and as to whether they will achieve their aims. In the words of one author:

> Bizarrely, the bill [to amend the act] is anathematic to the central recommendation of the construction trust, and seems set, if passed, not only to reduce the effectiveness of the existing security of payment legislation, but also to itself be the cause of increased insolvency and to cause a mass criminalization of the NSW construction market.
> (Fenwick Elliott, 2013)

Donald Charrett
Barrister, arbitrator and mediator
Melbourne
Australia

Statutory adjudication in Malaysia by Albert Yeu (Hong Kong)

Delay payment in the construction industry has been a common problem in many countries that causes delay in completion of projects, jeopardizes the quality of works, increase risk of site safety and sustainability compliance. Projects are abandoned in some occasions where innocent third-party purchasers become the victims of delay payment.

Security of Payment Legislation (SOPL), or Construction Act, is enacted in the UK, Australia, New Zealand, Singapore, Malaysia, and Ireland to alleviate cash flow problems in the construction industry. In Malaysia, the Construction Industry Payment and Adjudication Act (CIPAA) 2012 came into force on April 15, 2014. The following four key features are provided in CIPAA to alleviate payment problems:

Statutory timetable for resolution of construction dispute

Once the payment due date has expired and the unpaid party does not receive the amount due in full, it has the right to serve a payment claim to the non-paying party stating the amount due and remedy sought. Within ten working days of the receipt of the payment claim, the non-paying party shall serve a payment response with the admitted amount in full or partially. Without submitting the payment response, the entire amount claimed is deemed to be disputed.

A claimant, either party, may initiate adjudication proceedings by serving a written notice of adjudication on the respondent. An adjudicator will then by appointed by the parties or by the Kuala Lumpur Regional Centre for Arbitration. Within 10 working days from the receipt of the acceptance of appointment by the adjudicator, the claimant shall serve an adjudication claim on the respondent and the adjudicator. Within 10 working days from the receipt of the adjudication claim, the respondent shall serve an adjudication response on the claimant and the adjudicator. Within five working days from the receipt of the adjudication response, the claimant may serve an adjudication reply on the respondent. The adjudicator shall then decide the dispute and deliver the adjudication decision within 45 working days from the service of adjudication response or adjudication reply, whichever is the later. The whole adjudication process takes approximately four months depending on the appointment and responses efficiency.

Prohibition of conditional payment

Pay-when-paid clauses have been a huge problem to sub-contractors and have led to unacceptable practices in positional bargaining. CIPAA expressly prohibits conditional payment that has the "effect of making payment" dependent on a third party such as the employer's certification or financing facilities' funding.

Remedies for non-payment

With 14 calendar-days prior notice, a contractor party may suspend performance or reduce the rate of progress of performance of any construction work if the adjudicated amount has not been paid wholly or partly after receipt of the adjudicated decision. Furthermore, the contractor who exercises the right of suspension is not in breach of contract and is entitled to a fair and reasonable extension of time and recovery of loss and expenses incurred as a result of the suspension or reduction in the rate of progress of performance.

Direct payment from principal

If a party against whom an adjudication decision is made fails to make payment of the adjudicated amount, the party who obtained the adjudication decision in his favor may make a written request for payment of the adjudicated amount direct from the principal of the party against whom the adjudication decision is made. Without the proof of payment provided by the party against whom the adjudication decision is made, the principal shall pay the adjudicated amount to the party who obtained the adjudicated decision in his favor, and subsequently recover the amount paid as a debt or set off against the party against whom the adjudication decision is made.

Albert Yeu
Chartered Civil Engineer, HKIAC Arbitrator
KLRCA Adjudicator, HKMAAC Mediator, Expert Witness
Hong Kong

References

Australian Legislation Reform Sub-Committee of the Society of Construction Law Australia (2014). *Report on Security of Payment and Adjudication in the Australian Construction Industry*. Canberra.

Butera, G. (2014). Untangling the enforcement of DAB decisions. ICLR *036*. Volume 31, 2014 – Part 1.

Chern, C. (2010). *The Law of Construction Disputes*. Routledge, London.

Chern, C. (2012). *Chern on Dispute Boards*, (2nd Edition) Wiley-Blackwell, Chichester.

Coggins, J., Fenwick Elliott, R. and Bell, M. (2010). 'Towards harmonisation of construction industry payment legislation: a consideration of the success afforded by the east and west coast models in Australia. *Australasian Journal of Construction Economics and Building*, 10(3).

DRBF (2013). Dispute Resolution Board Concept. Online. Available at: http://www.drb.org/concepts.htm (accessed 20 August 2013).

Fenwick Elliott, R. (2013). The road to hell. *Australian Construction Law Bulletin*, 25(9), 151.

Lloyd, H. (2009) Some thoughts on NEC3. *International Construction Law Review*. Online. Available at: www.neccontract.com (accessed 12 April 2013).

Lloyd, H. and Jones, D.S. (2014). Introduction. ICLR 001. Volume 31, 2014 – Part 1.

Seppälä, S.R. (2012). How not to interpret the FIDIC Disputes Clause: The Singapore Court of Appeal judgment in the Persero case. Online. Available at: http://www.whitecase.com/files/Publication (accessed 3 Feb. 2014).

Construction Umbrella Bodies Adjudication Task Group. (2003). Users' Guide to Adjudication, April 2003. ('Users' Guide'). Online. Available at: http://www.scl.org.uk/files/CUB_Users_Guide_May_2003.pdf (accessed 20 Aug. 2017).

Wilson, J. (2014). *Security of Payment in New South Wales and Victoria*. LexisNexis Australia, Butterworths, NSW.

Further reading

Balazs, T., Klee, L. and Gulyas, T. (2014). FIDIC contracts and Hungarian law: important aspects of using FIDIC contracts in Hungary [2014] *ICLR* 138.

Chern, C. (2010). The Dispute Board Federation and the role of Dispute Boards in construction: benefits without burden, *Revista del Club Español del Arbitraje*, 9.

Cole, T.R.H. (2003). *Final Report of the Royal Commission into the Building and Construction Industry*. Volume 8. Royal Commission, Canberra. Available at: http://en.wikipedia.org/wiki/Royal_Commission_into_the_Building_and_Construction_ Industry.

Construction Umbrella Bodies Adjudication Task Group. Users' Guide to Guidance for Adjudicators. Available at: http://www.scl.org.uk/files/GfA_0207.pdf (accessed 20 Aug. 2013).

FIDIC. Adjudicators. Online. Available at: http://fidic.org/node/802 (accessed 20 Aug. 2013).

FIDIC: 2011/2012 Annual Report. Online. Available at: http://fidic.org/node/813 (accessed 20 Aug. 2013).

FIDIC: Alternative Dispute Resolution. Online. Available at: http://fidic.org/node/761 (accessed 20 Aug. 2013).

FIDIC: Committees. Online. Available at: http://fidic.org/node/771 (accessed 20 Aug. 2013).

FIDIC Guidance Memorandum to Users of the 1999 Conditions of Contract dated 1 April 2013. Online. Available at: http://fidic.org/node/1615 (accessed 20 Aug. 2013).

FIDIC: International and National Lists of Adjudicators. Online. Available at: http://fidic.org/node/2555 (accessed 20 Aug. 2013).
FIDIC: Statutes and by-laws (October 2011). Online. Available at : http://fidic.org/node/769 (accessed 20 Aug. 2013).
FIDIC: FIDIC Guidance Memorandum to Users of the 1999 Conditions of Contract dated 1st April 201. Online. Available at: http://fidic.org/node/1615 (accessed 20 Aug. 2013).
FIDIC (2000). *The FIDIC Contracts Guide* (1st Edition). FIDIC, Lausanne.
FIDIC (2011). *FIDIC Procurement Procedures Guide* (1st Edition). FIDIC, Lausanne.
Guidance for Adjudicators, Construction Umbrella Bodies Adjudication Tasks Group Online. Available at: http://www.scl.org.uk/files/GfA_0207.pdf (accessed 20 Aug. 2013).
Housing Grants, Construction and Regeneration Act (1996). Online. Available at: http://www.legislation.gov.uk/ukpga/1996/53 (accessed 20 Aug. 2013).
ICC (2012). *International Court of Arbitration Bulletin*, 23(2) –2012.
Jaeger, A.V. and Hök, G S. (2010). *FIDIC: A Guide for Practitioners*. Springer Verlag, Berlin.
Jamka, M. and Morek,R. (2013). Dispute Avoidance and Resolution under FIDIC Rules and Procedure: Polish Experience. Paper presented at the seminar Making a Success out of a Construction Project: International FIDIC Standards and their Implementation in Ukraine. Kiev.
Klee, L. (2012). *Smluvní vztahy výstavbových projektuů*. Wolters Kluwer, Prague.
Klee, L. and Nový, D. (2014). *Construction Dispute Boards*. Czech and Central European Yearbook of Arbitration.
Scheme for Construction Contracts (England and Wales) Regulations 1998. Online. Available at: http://www.legislation.gov.uk/uksi/1998/649/made (accessed 20 Aug. 2013).
Venoit, W.K. (2009) *International Construction Law: A Guide for Cross-Border Transactions and Legal Disputes*. ABA Publishing, Chicago

12 FIDIC

12.1 FIDIC expansion

The conditions of contract prepared by the *Fédération Internationale des Ingénieurs-Conseils* (International Federation of Consulting Engineers, FIDIC) are nowadays the most widely used sample forms of contracts for construction projects. These sample documents are known as the "International Best Practice Documents" and are enjoying ever growing popularity. This is mainly thanks to significant international lenders who demand generally accepted and proven "rules of the game" in their construction projects. One of the advantages of FIDIC forms is that the user is presented with a complete toolbox of documents. Without these, successful realization of a project would be practically impossible. The documents include a variety of samples and templates ranging from tender forms right up to dispute adjudication issues. Commentary, explanations and user instructions can also be found in individual FIDIC forms.

Using translated texts in FIDIC contracts: The Spanish case by Ignacio de Almagro (Spain)

One of the many achievements of the FIDIC models is the standardization of the terms used throughout the text of its recent model contracts. All recent editions (from 1999) and models use the same terms, generally speaking. All terms have the same meaning across the different contracts independently of where in the world they are used, Australia, Barbados, or the United States of America; independently of the publisher or the model or the contract version. For example, the version of the Red Book published by the World Bank, and the one published by the Inter-American Development Bank use the same terms and definitions than the Red Book directly published by FIDIC, in English.

This is not the case in Spanish. Different institutions have translated the same text independently, in an uncoordinated way. This situation causes confusion and uncertainty, resulting in an added disadvantage for the users of FIDIC whose first language is Spanish. On occasions, the original balance of risk is shaken and even deadlines are changed.

In other words, there is no standardization of terms in FIDIC contracts in Spanish.

Until the time there is a coordination of the translations, which no doubt FIDIC and the institutions concerned are trying to achieve, FIDIC users of translated texts have to be aware of the existing differences and make up for the imbalances through the particular conditions.

We will give a few examples of the importance of translation and afterwards provide a list of the terms that have been translated differently into Spanish so users can take action and future translators of FIDIC contracts can be aware of them and take them into account if they think is relevant.

The importance of translation in general: The Florida case

A Latino teenager is admitted to hospital in a comatose state. His family is with him and try to explain what they believe has happened to the hospital staff. They don't speak English. The staff don't understand Spanish. A bilingual staff is called to translate. The bilingual staff is not a professional translator and translates "intoxicado" as "intoxicated." In fact, the family thought the teenager was suffering from food poisoning; in Spanish: "intoxicación por alimentos." Although the cause of the comatose state turned out to be a different one, the initial treatment was based on the assumption that the teenager was "intoxicated," implying the voluntary alcohol intake and/or the use of other drugs.

The delay in the right treatment was later found to be a major cause for the quadriplegic state in which the teenager was left. The hospital had to indemnify for malpractice in the amount of 71 million dollars.

The risks of translation in FIDIC contracts

"As soon as practicable" not the same as "as soon as possible."

Several cases in common law jurisdictions, for a value of millions of dollars, have clarified that "as soon as practicable" is not the same as "as soon as possible."

Courts in Hong Kong, New York, Texas, and London have decided that "as soon as practicable" doesn't always mean "as soon as feasible" and definitely not "as soon as possible"; it is necessary to take the facts and circumstances into account, including the state of mind of the parties.

In the cases studied, and in relation to the FIDIC standards, which use "as soon as practicable" throughout the contract and not a single time "as soon as possible," notifications that had to be submitted "as soon as practicable" were considered valid by the courts even when they were issued weeks after it was possible or feasible to issue them, having into account the circumstances, the facts and the state of mind of the parties. As an example: A contractual notification was not issued after the fulfillment of the condition precedent that gave right to one of the parties to issue it, triggering an obligation of the other party, because both parties were jointly trying to achieve the same result through other ways.

Two questions interest us within the FIDIC world: the first one is that "as soon as practicable" is more flexible than "as soon as possible" and common law jurisdictions will apply this flexibility; the second question is the issue of translations of the original FIDIC standards to other languages and particularly into Spanish. The translations I know (to French, Portuguese, and Spanish) eliminate the flexibility of "as soon as practicable" to the rigidity of "aussitôt que possible" in French, "logo que possível" in Portuguese and "tan pronto como sea posible" in Spanish. It is an unwanted consequence of the translations. The texts in French, Portuguese, and Spanish don't mean the same as the original English. Users have to bear in mind this fact when dealing with contracts written in these languages.

How to avoid this unwanted consequence?

Until current translations are updated, the parties should change the translated texts through the particular conditions. Also, users should recommend the institutions that translate FIDIC to address this issue in their future translations or updates.

We still need to solve the problem: how to translate "as soon as practicable" to Spanish and other languages without missing the flexibility of the term. French and Portuguese are the work of others. Of course, it is not an easy task to achieve a good and short translation, that's the reason why the current translations have missed the point. We propose: "tan pronto como sea prácticamente posible atendiendo a las circunstancias." If we choose "tan pronto como sea prácticamente posible" it may seem redundant in Spanish, but it is indeed a better translation than the current one, and shorter than the one proposed here, which is always welcome. Here is the challenge for users of FIDIC contracts in languages other than English. The Czech translation, by Lukas Klee addressed the issue by translating: "*co nejdříve, jak je to prakticky možné*" in which one can understand, even not knowing Czech, that the word "*prakticky*" means "practicable." Suggestions are, of course, welcome.

Ignacio de Almagro
Lawyer, FIDIC Consultant, Arbitrator, Mediator, Trainer
Spain

12.2 FIDIC

The International Federation of Consulting Engineers was founded in France in 1913 and is based in Geneva, Switzerland. Following its initial establishment, the organization expanded rapidly thanks to new membership from around the world. FIDIC is a non-government organization recognized by the United Nations, by major global banks, the European Commission and other international institutions. FIDIC was set up to support and promote the overall interests of its member associations. The organization's growth peaked in the post-WWII era when it started expanding at such a rate that it now unites associations from more than 100 countries on all continents.

The first sample, *Conditions of Contract for Works of Civil Engineering Construction* were released in 1957. This sample gave rise to the tradition of the "FIDIC Red Book." Due to ever-advancing technological developments in the construction industry, it became clear that contractual conditions would become redundant over time and would need to be revised. In 1999 the most used volume entitled the "First Edition" came into existence with its Red, Yellow, and Silver Books. These are the terms most often used by construction practitioners though the official abbreviations are CONS, P&DB, and EPC. To distinguish the 1999 forms from the older versions they are sometimes referred to as the "New Red, Yellow, and Silver Books." In 2017, the latest so called second edition of mentioned books was published which is a longer and more prescriptive version but still rather a refinement of the first edition than significant change.

According to FIDIC statutes and bylaws (October 2011), the federation's objectives are:

1. to represent the consulting engineering industry globally;
2. to enhance the image of consulting engineers;
3. to be the leading authority on issues relating to business practice;
4. to promote the development of a global and viable consulting engineering industry;
5. to promote quality;
6. to actively promote conformance to a code of ethics and to business integrity;
7. to promote commitment to sustainable development.

12.3 FIDIC's influence on the construction industry

In recent years, FIDIC has experienced growth in its influence on the construction industry worldwide. With the spread of globalization, international organizations are looking for a uniform set of construction project standards independent of countries and governments. Such organizations include the World Bank, the European Bank for Reconstruction and Development, the Inter-American Development Bank, the African Development Bank, and the Islamic Development Bank. Various other organizations are cooperating with FIDIC to develop broad, worldwide standards of business practice, ranging from the International Standards Organization, the International Labor Organization and others such as Transparency International or the United Nations Environment Program. Close cooperation with the above-mentioned organizations (and others) is helping the development of widely used best practice standards, not only for consulting engineers, but for the wider construction industry and business in general. Clearly defined, well-known, and globally recognized standards are helping to reduce various costs and to develop a predictable legal and business environment. This applies not only to countries in the developing world, but to countries of the developed world as well. FIDIC promotes its objectives through annual meetings and conferences. The first was held in London in 1988 with cities in South-East Asia, the Middle America, and North America added to the FIDIC annual program in recent years. Moreover, about 100 training events are held annually worldwide.

12.4 FIDIC membership

The nature and type of organizations who are FIDIC members are diverse. They range from individual members from independent countries to regional federations and broader member associations. For example, the African members of FIDIC associate themselves with the Group of Africa Member Associations (GAMA) with its FIDIC Regional Office in Dar-es-Salaam, Tanzania. Members from the Asia Pacific region are associated with the Asia-Pacific Group (ASPAC). The most important and influential members of FIDIC are regional federations, such the Pan American Federation of Consultants (FEPAC) and the European Federation of Engineering Consultancy Associations (EFCA). The latter closely cooperates with FIDIC in various areas and with international governmental and non-governmental organizations and individual states.

Aware of the growing popularity and support for its activities, FIDIC organizes a number of training events to help local businesses expand globally and to spread FIDIC values. These activities have culminated in the development of the *Business Practice Training Manual,* which is applicable in both the developed and developing world. Moreover, the organization of International Training Programs (in cooperation with member associations) is ongoing. FIDIC also accredits trainers and training suppliers through its *Accredited Trainer and Development Program*. Online training courses are available directly from FIDIC.

FIDIC training is focused on hard skills (such as the mastering of contract conditions and their use) and soft skills (such as the development of managerial skills) required for successful project implementation. The former includes courses on professional services agreements, practical use of FIDIC contracts, claims and dispute resolution, dispute adjudication boards and contract management. The latter comprises courses such as business development, business administration, risk management, quality management, business integrity management, and project sustainability management.

12.5 Networking activities

FIDIC influence goes beyond the formalities of international best business practice and commercial relationships. FIDIC's informal (but significant) influence on the opinions of global leaders and decision-makers is, arguably, even more important. Numerous meetings and events help FIDIC participants from across the globe to build specific professional communities, spread ideas and exchange valuable contacts. Networking and gatherings of consulting engineers, clients, contractors, and other professionals are crucial to promoting FIDIC values. Therefore, these events are strongly supported by the organization.

FIDIC currently presents the most common form of contract in large construction projects. These include monumental nation-building efforts such as the rebuilding of Libya after the Arab Spring revolution, the development of an independent Timor-Leste and the building of infrastructure for the FIFA World Cup in Qatar in 2022.

FIDIC is currently involved in a vast field of global activity. Such worldwide presence and influence also bring with it substantial responsibility and related commitments. Therefore, FIDIC representatives and members decided to use their organizational capabilities to promote values of sustainable development. Consultants participating in development and infrastructure projects can (and are encouraged to) use their experience and knowledge directly in cooperation with project investors and clients. Using valuable know-how from the beginning of every project to realization helps make it more effective and sustainable in every aspect.

12.5.1 Translations and local use of FIDIC forms

The FIDIC official position on copyright, modifications, and translations is that FIDIC discourages modification of the information and services it supplies, and only in exceptional circumstances will authorize modification, reproduction, or incorporation elsewhere. Permission to quote from, incorporate, reproduce, or copy all or part of a FIDIC publication, including documents, conditions of contract, web pages, and similar supports for information, should be addressed to the FIDIC Secretariat, which will decide upon appropriate terms. A license to prepare a modified publication will be agreed to under certain conditions. Specifically, the modified publication must be for internal purposes only, and not be published or distributed commercially. Under conditions that it will determine at its own discretion in each case and for a suitable consideration (usually, in the form of a license fee), FIDIC may agree to let other parties (normally, a member association) to make translations and publish the translated publication. Conversely, translating FIDIC publications or publishing such translations without FIDIC's duly obtained agreement is unlawful and may be sanctioned. The general principles under which FIDIC may grant such agreements and which should be used when interpreting any license given, are set out in guidance notes and a sample form of contract that are available from the FIDIC Secretariat. FIDIC will not authorize translations; in particular, FIDIC will not make any engagement or assume any liability concerning their completeness or correctness or adequacy for any purpose. Any such engagement or liability lies with the translator or the publisher of the translated document.

There are official translations of CONS available, for example, in Arabic, Bahasa, Bosnian, Chinese, Estonian, French, Japanese, Latvian, Polish, Portuguese, Romanian, Russian, Slovak, Spanish, and Vietnamese. P&DB is also available in Hungarian.

CONS and P&DB are extensively used for domestic projects, for example, in Poland, Slovakia, the Czech Republic, Hungary, Bulgaria, Romania, Croatia, and Serbia. There are several translations of FIDIC forms in Poland, one of them prepared by SIDIR (Stowarzyszenie Inżynierów Doradców i Rzeczoznawców, in English: Consulting Engineers and Experts Association).

To meet the public procurement needs in Estonia, the EAACEC (the Estonian Association of Architectural and Consulting Engineering Companies) have translated, among others, CONS and P&DB, both frequently used there.

According to HELLASCO (the Hellenic Association of Consulting Firms), there are no Greek translations. The same applies to Sweden, as reported by STD (the Swedish Federation of Consulting Engineers and Architects), Holland according to ONRI (the Dutch Association of Consulting Engineers), and Denmark as per FRI (Foreningen af Rådgivende Ingeniører). FIDIC forms are used in those countries only on international projects. Local forms of contracts have long been used there to meet the needs of local construction projects. Also according to ACE (the Association of Consulting Engineers), the FIDIC forms are not used in the UK, except on international projects. In the United Kingdom, the NEC is used (the New Engineering Contract) and JCT (Joint Contracts Tribunal), like VOB (*Vergabe- und Vertragsordnung für Bauleistungen*) in Germany.

According to USIC (*Union Suisse des Sociétés d'Ingénieurs-Conseils*), there are no local Swiss translations and the FIDIC forms do not enjoy much popularity in Switzerland, with the contracting processes varying from canton to canton. However, the ASINCE (*Asociación Española de Empresas de Ingeniería, Consultoría y Servicios Tecnológicos*) of Spain has its own translation.

As advised by ACEA (the Association of Consulting Engineers of Australia), the FIDIC forms are used in Australia in public projects financed by banks.

As reported by SAACE (the South African Association of Consulting Engineers), English-language FIDIC documents are extensively used in South Africa, having a long tradition there.

As per ACEZ (the Association of Consulting Engineers of Zambia), the FIDIC forms are not used to any great extent in Zambia, nor are any standard conditions. But there is, at the moment, a drive to extend and draw up some local versions of them.

FIDIC forms are widely used even in China, mainly in support of the projects funded by the World Bank, the Asian Development Bank, and by other international agencies.

It was presented (by Salvador P. Castro, Jr. during the FIDIC Asia-Pacific Contract Users' Conference on 11 and 12 June 2013, Malaysia) that it appears there are constraints or barriers in the use of the FIDIC contracts in Southeast Asia. These barriers are raised by employers, both in government and in the private sectors, by local contractors, and even by local consulting engineers despite the fact that FIDIC contracts were developed by consulting engineers and experienced lawyers, and in spite of the recognition that their conditions are widely applicable to the civil law and common law jurisdictions.

It was only in the past 10 years, and more so in the past five years, that a rise has been observed in the use of FIDIC contracts probably as a result of the introduction of the MDB harmonized editions by the multilateral banks, such as the World Bank, the Asian Development Bank and, recently, by the Japan International Cooperation Agency (JICA), in their foreign-funded, local, and foreign joint venture infrastructure projects in the region.

However, a number of the construction contracts used in the region are rather "modified FIDIC" or "patterned after FIDIC," some of which are not based on FIDIC at all.

There was an informal survey being conducted among participants who attended the JICA Practical Project Management Program, a JICA-grant project conducted in Manila since 2009. One of the questions we asked was: "Why is FIDIC not widely used in the infrastructure projects in your country?"

The 1000 or so participants comprised contract users (government and a few contractors and local engineers) from Bangladesh, Bhutan, Cambodia, Laos, Myanmar, Indonesia, the Philippines, Thailand, Sri Lanka, Vietnam, and as far away as Mongolia and Jordan. These are countries where the JICA has a presence.

Another survey was informally conducted among the participants of an in-house FIDIC contract training program in a Philippine construction firm with local and international operations. The key answers common to the majority of participants were:

FIDIC contracts in government projects are not used because they contradict our laws and government standard contracts.

Cultural differences in our country. We are too sensitive in so many aspects.

DAB is expensive and deleted in our contracts. There is no accredited DAB in the region.

FIDIC is strict and our government and other disciplines have an impression that FIDIC is a straitjacket contract and does not allow owners' flexibility.

Due to lack of knowledge of FIDIC, it is seen as an adversarial contract due to a lot of notices and time limits (more education of the engineers and lawyers is needed).

The use of FIDIC forms in Russia by Dmitry Nekrestyanov (Russia)

We are still not able to say that FIDIC contracts are well known and widely used in the Russian construction market. One reason for that is the current official translation of the FIDIC books into Russian. As the translation is quite bad, the popularity and confidence in this form tend toward zero for any contracts with Russian-speaking parties.

However, the trend in using FIDIC contracts in major construction projects is very clear. As an example of a project realized under FIDIC, the construction of the new terminal in Pulkovo Airport, St. Petersburg, comes to mind. Some of the enormous construction work carried out in preparation for the Winter Olympic Games was also realized under FIDIC (e.g. the new Park Inn hotel in Sochi).

What you should know when applying FIDIC principles in Russia:

1. The most popular forms of FIDIC contracts are contained in the 1999 Silver and Red Books.
2. Once the contract is signed in Russian, parties need to be very careful about the translation. There is no official translation of FIDIC contracts in Russian and most of the existing, unofficial translations are rather inaccurate.
3. There are a number of imperative provisions of Russian construction law that are different to those in FIDIC contracts. Thus, FIDIC contracts suffer because quite lengthy amendments need to be made to make them compliant under Russian law. First of all these amendments refer to: (1) the dispute resolution procedure; (2) how amendments in scope and price of works are dealt with; and (3) the status and the role of the engineer. As a result, the applicable law of a FIDIC contract is not usually compatible with Russian law.
4. Using FIDIC contracts is still considered like a kind of "high-class pilotage for the parties," so to make it work in reality, Russian parties are better off involving experienced consultants.

Dmitry Nekrestyanov
Partner
Head of Real Estate and Investment Practice
Kachkin and Partners LLC
St. Petersburg
Russia

The use of FIDIC forms in Brazil by Rafael Marinangelo (Brazil)

The importance of the FIDIC forms of contract in the Brazilian construction market is obvious. FIDIC forms, as an instrument widely used by international funding agencies, are gradually being implemented in infrastructure construction project negotiations in Brazil.

Contracts entered into by *Companhia de Saneamento Básico do Estado de São Paulo*—SABESP (Brazil's São Paulo state water utility, the country's largest water company, providing water and sewerage services in 363 municipalities and serving more than 27.1 million residential, commercial, and industrial clients or 60% of the state's urban population) and by *Companhia Paulista de Trens Metropolitanos*—CPTM (São Paulo Metropolitan Train Company, a commuter rail company owned by the São Paulo State Secretariat for Metropolitan Transport, and part of the Greater São Paulo rail network. CPTM has 89 stations in six lines, with a total length of 260.8 kilometers), to name just two examples, involve the use of FIDIC forms—thanks partly to foreign funding of these projects.

When not used in a complete form, the FIDIC patterns and principles appear in many contracts partially, denoting an inevitable trend of civil engineering and large building construction projects to approach contractual practices with the professionalism required worldwide.

Rafael Marinangelo
Construction lawyer
Marinangelo & Aoki Advogados
Brazil

The use of FIDIC forms within the construction contract law of Turkey by Yasemin Çetinel (Turkey)

Given its geographical location and regional alliances, Turkey boasts having a very competitive and energetic market for the construction sector as well as successful contractors providing materials and services and strategic partnerships within the country and also abroad. This competitive sector and strategic partnerships have increasing impacts on Turkey's economy since the modernization of the legislation starting from the 1990s.

As the international trade took a ground-breaking turn with the establishment of the World Trade Organization (WTO) in 1995, the modernization and approximation of the relevant legislation, especially related to public procurement for goods and services took place in Turkey parallel to the approximation that took place in the national laws of the European Union (EU) Member States and Switzerland. Turkey has adopted the Public Procurement Code No. 4734 of 2002 (PPC) and Public Procurement Contracts Code No. 4735 of 2002 (PPCC) in line with such approximation of the relevant regulations of the EU states and Switzerland. The PPC is the national legislation of Turkey enacted according to the rules prescribed by the Plurilateral Agreement on Government Procurement at the Annex 4(b) of the WTO Multilateral Trade Agreements signed in Marrakech on April 14, 1994 (Kaplan, 2013).

Main specifics of Turkish construction contract law

In principle, a construction contract is subject to private law provisions; however, if the contract was offered by a public entity or institution in a tender, it may also be subject to public law provisions for the tender stage. Contracts between the private law real and legal persons and contractors are subject to the provisions contract between them and its general specifications and the mandatory provisions of the Turkish Code of Obligations No. 6098 of 2011 (TCO), which is the *lex generalis*. General construction contracts are a sub-category of work contracts (*Eser Sözleşmesi*) regulated in the Articles 470-486 of the TCO and the fact that the owner/employer in such contract may be a public entity or institution subject to the public procurement legislations does not affect the main feature of such contract to be subject to the provisions of the TCO.

Under the TCO, the primary obligation of the contractor is to complete the works it undertook without any delays and defects. The TCO also requires the contractor to realize its duty with loyalty and care (Article 471(1) of the TCO). If the contractor does not deliver on time, default provisions of the TCO (Article 119, et al.) becomes applicable. As per Article 473(1) of the TCO, if the contractor does not start the works on time or falls in default in breach of the contract, or it becomes clear that due to the reasons not attributable to the owner the works would not be completed within the agreed time frame, the owner may terminate the contract.

As per Article 5 of the Turkish Commercial Code No. 6102 of 2011, Turkish Civil Courts of First Instance has jurisdiction over the construction contracts provided that no provisions exist in the contract regarding the arbitration, governing law or jurisdiction. It is practical to note that domestic and international arbitration clauses are frequently used in private construction contracts in Turkey.

Public procurement law and public procurement contracts under Turkish law

Turkey's legal system is based on the continental law or the civil law system. Furthermore, due to its candidate status aspiring to become a member state of the EU, Turkey is obliged to align its national laws, rules and procedures—in the EU terms, approximation of the law—in order to give effect to the *acquis communautaire*. For this reason, Turkey's public procurement legislation, has been reformed upon the latest international developments.

Currently, two types of procurement codes are in force in Turkey: the PPC and the State Procurement Code no. 2886 of 1983 (SPC). The difference between these two codes is that while the PPC regulates the expense procurements of the state bodies and entities; the SPC regulates both their expense and income procurements. Provisions of the PPC are be applicable to the public procurement for the goods, services, consultancy services, construction works for the tenders of public bodies and entities regarding their expenses providing that their threshold value, scales, and limits are above the thresholds stated therein (Article 8 of the PPC). As for the income generating tenders of public bodies and entities such as sale of goods and services, rent, exchange and the works regarding the creation of a right *in rem* and for the building and repairing works under the threshold stated in the PPC; the SPC continues to be applicable. This means that the PPC may not have abrogated the SPC, however, it has significantly narrowed its scope of application (Kaplan, 2013). Since the PPC is the most widely used code for the major construction works, we will briefly present its specific features in this section.

The PPC established a public legal entity, the administratively and financially autonomous Public Procurement Authority (Authority) whose is in charge for the evaluation of the tender bids and the preparation of standard contracts for construction works (*Yapım İşlerine Ait Tip Sözleşme*).

The PPC was amended various times in order to allow the law to be more contemporaneous. One of these amendments made the registration through an online platform for Electronic Notification and Electronic Public Procurements (*Elektronik Kamu Alımları Platformu* or EKAP) compulsory as of 01.01.2015. Electronic Tender Implementation Regulation published in the Official Gazette No: 27857 dated 25.02.2017 regulates rules and procedures of electronic tender process via EKAP entirely or partially.

Public procurement contracts in Turkey are based on the Public Procurement Contracts Code No. 4735 of 2002 (PPCC) and the General Specifications on the Construction Works (*Yapım İşleri Genel Şartnamesi* or General Specifications); which is basically consisting of the standard form of procurement contract provisions. As per its Article 1, the General Specifications have been prepared for the purpose of determining the general conditions to be applied in construction works and as per Article 2, the General Specifications comprise the construction works contracted in accordance with the PPCC.

Some of the major features of Turkey's public procurement legislation for construction works describing the typical contract structure and introducing the actors involved are as follows:

Contractor's obligations:

- *Design Duty:* As per Article 11(1), (2), (4) and (6) of the General Specifications establishes that in case the contract is a lump sum contract, the design projects as well as the implementation drawings shall be delivered to the Contractor by the tendering public bodies and entities and contracting authority (Administration); however, if the contract is a unit price based contract, the design projects are delivered to the Contractor and the Contractor shall provide the implementation drawings. However, the Administration may require the Contractor to provide the design projects as well. In such case, the Contractor has the full and aggravated responsibility over the design projects and the related drawings. The Administration is on the other hand obliged to review and approve the design and/or the drawings within one month unless otherwise agreed by the specific contract. If there is a delay in the approval phase, the Contractor is entitled for a time extension. The Contractor remains responsible for projects and/or drawings even if such projects and/or drawings are approved by the Administration. In case it is specifically set forth by the contract, the Contractor may be paid on unit price basis for the engineering services that the Administration requires to be provided by the Contractor (i.e., geotechnical surveys, drilling works).
- *Commencement:* As per Article 12(2) of the General Specifications, in unit price based contracts, the Contractor may not commence works until the drawings are approved by the Administration. In such commencement without approval, the Contractor is fully responsible for the compliance with the drawings and any outcomes thereof.
- *Variations:* Primary resource of the variations under the public procurement contracts is Article 24 of the PPCL on the additional works made in the scope of the contract, decrease of works and liquidation (as amended on 30.07.2003). The said article provides for separate regulations for the lump sum and unit price basis contracts. According to this article, the variation may be made in the ratio up to 10% for construction works tendered with turnkey lump sum base and to 20% for works with respect to purchase of product or service and construction works all tendered on a unit price basis provided that a) such additional works remain within the scope of the project which is the basis of the contract and b) separation from the main work [of such additional works] is technically or economically impossible

without putting a burden over the Administration. In construction works based on unit price contracts, the Council of Ministers is authorized to increase this ratio up to 40% to be determined in accordance with each specific contract. In line with the PPCL, as per Article 21 of the General Specifications, the Administration is entitled to make variations. In case the contract is a lump sum contract, the Administration may request additional works up to the 10% of the works under the contract. If the contract is a unit price based contract, the Administration may request additional works up to 40% of the works under the contract.
- *Errors, defaults or omissions by the Contractor:* As per Article 25 of the General Specifications, the Contractor is fully responsible for any errors defaults or omissions in the works and/or materials provided until the date of final acceptance. The Contractor is responsible for 15 years as of the final acceptance of the works for any defective works and/or materials provided by his side. It should be noted that the 15 years long responsibility provision is almost never referred to in practice.
- *Staff and Equipment:* As per Article 19 of the General Specifications, the Contractor is responsible of providing the required number of staff and equipment at the site. In practice, the contracts include specific liquidated damages in case the Contractor fails to provide the required number of staff and/or equipment at the site.

Administration's obligations:

As stated in the Article 45, the Administration is obliged to carry out its duties regarding the conclusion of the contract within the prescribed time period. If it fails to do so, the tenderer may renounce its commitments within maximum five days following the end of the period via a notice sent through a public notary with a period of 10 days—in order to claim the return of its tender security. Once the contract is concluded, the Administration is responsible for handing over the site to the Contractor in accordance with the contract and its addenda as per Article 7 of the General Specifications. In case there is a delay regarding such hand over and it reaches to the level of delaying the completion of a part or the entirety of the works, the Administration provides the Contractor with a proportionate time extension for the relevant part of the works. However, the Contractor cannot ask for additional costs associated with the time extension.

Engineer:

Article 5 (Definitions) of the General Specifications provide us with the third limb of the construction works, which is the Building Inspector (*Yapı Denetim Görevlisi* or Engineer) who can be a real person, a board and/or a legal person appointed by the Administration to inspect the works. As per Article 15 of the General Specifications, the Building Inspector (a) supervises the works performed by the Contractor, (b) supervises the materials provided by the Contractor and (c) carries out the required approval for the performed works and provided materials or (d) requests for the rectification and/or correction of any defaulted material and/or works performed or provided by the Contractor. In this way, the Building Inspector may be deemed as corresponding to the role of the Engineer in FIDIC contracts.

Subcontractors:

Article 20(3) of the General Specifications prohibits the works to be subcontracted in its entirety. As per Article 20, the contract shall include the specific clause as to whether the

Administration allows the subcontracting or not; if yes, with the conditions thereof. The subcontractors shall be approved by the Administration and the Administration may at any time require their dismissal. The Contractor is fully responsible for the works and acts of the subcontractor even if such subcontractor is approved by the Administration.

Payment structure:

As per Article 39(4)(a)-(g) of the General Specifications, unless otherwise agreed under each specific contract, the interim payment requests are issued monthly, shall be reviewed and approved by the Administration within 1 month as of the date of issuance and the payment shall be carried out within 15 days as of the date of the approval. The final payment certificate requires the determination by the Engineer. As per Article 40(4) of the General Specifications, should the Contractor have any objections, it shall do so within 60 days as of the Engineer's determination. The Administration shall review and approve the final payment certificate within 6 months.

Taking over:

As per Article 42 of the General Specifications, the period between the Provisional Acceptance and the Final Acceptance of the Works may not be less than 12 months unless otherwise is agreed in each specific contract. Article 45(3) establishes that the Contractor should submit a letter from the Social Security Institution stating that there are not any outstanding payments vis-a-vis the institution to be carried out in relation with the Contractor's employees. In case there are outstanding payments, such amounts may be set off from the retention amount that should be transferred to the Contractor under normal circumstances with the Final Acceptance Certificate.

Termination in case of force majeure:

Article 47(9) of the General Specifications enlists the force majeure events as natural disasters, strikes, epidemics, mobilization and any other events defined as a force majeure event by the Public Procurement Institution. In order for the contract to be terminated on grounds of a force majeure event, the occurrence of such event shall not stem from the Contractor's fault, the Contractor shall notify the Administration within 20 days as of the date of the occurrence of such event which shall be unpredictable and unavoidable.

Compensation:

Found in various provisions of the General Specifications (such as Article 29, 41, 44), liquidated damages are applied for the delayed works indicated in each specific contract. Delay-liquidated damages are very common in practice in two separate ways: (a) Delay in complying with the Schedule of the Works and (b) Delay in complying with the term of the contract. There are also liquidated damages related to the non-compliance with providing the required number of personnel and equipment at the site.

Method and principles of this application is provided in the General Communiqué on Public Procurement (Communiqué) published in the Official Gazette No: 27327 on 22.08.2009. The Communiqué aims to clarify uncertainty on the practice between the PPC and PPCC for the purpose of designating the relevant principles and subjects which are binding.

In public procurement contracts, in principle, the parties may agree upon resolution of the disputes via international arbitration due to the private law nature of these contracts. However, due to the mandatory wording of Article 51 of the General Specifications, the disputes between the Engineer and the Contractor would be resolved by the Administration, which requires the contract to include a specific dispute resolution clause for the disputes between the Administration and the Contractor.

Public private partnership scheme in Turkish legal system

Public Private Partnership (PPP) projects in transportation (airports, bridges, high-speed railways, metros) healthcare (hospitals) and energy sectors (dams, wind tribunes, solar energy plants, and nuclear power plants) are encouraged in Turkey by the laws and regulations such as the Law on Construction and Renovation of Premises and Obtaining Service through Public Private Partnership Model by the Ministry of Health and Amendment of Various Laws and Statutory Decrees No: 6428 of 2013; Law on Establishment and operation of Generating Plant and Regulation of the Electricity Distribution, No: 4283 of 1997 amended by the Law No: 5539 of 2006. Residential housing areas are also being re-constructed within the scope of the Law on Transforming Areas under the Risk of Disaster No. 6306 of 2012 under the Urban Transformation (*Kentsel Dönüşüm*) scheme.

Article 2 of the Law No: 6428 establishes the structures anticipated for PPP projects. The Ministry of Health should have the approval and authorization of High Commission of Planning (*Yüksek Planlama Kurulu*) to issue a tender. There exists three different types of PPP projects under this scheme: a) construction projects, b) refurbishment projects, c) research, consulting, developing and project services. As per Article 3 of the Law No: 6428, three methods may be used for PPP contracts: a) open tender procedure, b) restricted tender procedure or c) negotiated tender procedure. According to Article 5 of the Law No: 6428, the contractor is not entitled to any remuneration before the termination of the construction with the exception of partial termination and partial service offer with the administration's approval. One of the key features of the Law No: 6428 is that, in case the contract is terminated on grounds attributable to contractor, performance bond of the contractor is registered as revenue to the Treasury and such performance bond is not deducted from the liability of contractor. Contractor may not claim any rights, remuneration, or indemnification for such performance bond.

In PPP legislation–related contracts, it is observed that local arbitration is included and therefore, a positive step is taken for PPP-related disputes to be able to be referred to arbitration.

According to the data obtained from the PPP Report of the Confederation of International Contractors' Association (CICA), Turkey's economy appears to be amongst the five big economies along with Brazil, China, India, and Mexico, in terms of total investment commitments in infrastructure PPPs and having contributed to the global PPP investment during the 2005-2012 period (World Bank, 2016).

The use of FIDIC forms

FIDIC standard form of contracts are at times preferred by both local and international contractors operating within the Turkish construction sector due to their high-level standards providing a common understanding thereof, allowing the practitioners to overcome the contractual difficulties. But perhaps one of the most important reasons for this preference is financial. Usually, public projects are financed through the national budget, funds or external indebtedness—which can result in suspension or slowing down in such projects in times of crisis or economic recession. That is why, private sector methods of funding and funding from the international and regional creditors are preferred for the investments to be completed in a timely manner with the desired quality (FIDIC, 2017). Article 3(b) of the PPC allows the use of FIDIC forms for projects funded by the international credit institutions. International and regional credit institutions like the World Bank, International Monetary Fund, Asian Development Bank, European Investment Bank, and European Bank for Reconstruction and Development generally have strict requirements for funding major construction and infrastructure projects in order to secure an internationally recognized standard for the works and ensure minimum interference, risks, and surprises. Most preferred way to ensure the stability of these projects is make sure the contract between the employer and the contractor is a contract based on FIDIC standard form of contracts. Most commonly used forms are FIDIC Conditions of Contract for Construction (Red Book), FIDIC Conditions of Contract for EPC-Turnkey Projects (Silver Book), and FIDIC Contract Conditions for Plant and Design-Build (Yellow Book).

Some of the major construction projects in Turkey based on FIDIC contracts include:

- Baku-Tbilisi-Ceyhan Pipeline Project, a 1,768-kilometres-long crude oil pipeline, which connects capital of Azerbaijan and Turkish port in Ceyhan via capital of Georgia.
- Marmaray Rail Tube Tunnel and Commuter Rail Mass Transit System Project Contract CR3, a major transportation project, which includes construction of a rail tunnel under the Bosphorus Strait, and the modernization of existing suburban railway lines between the European side and the Asian side of the Istanbul Strait Istanbul. The works under the contract was implemented as per FIDIC Silver Book (http://www.ytmk.org.tr/files/publications/49/2bff0e55530a5f042b71b7245b9310a5_original.pdf).
- Reconstruction Works of Kartal Training and Research Hospital in Istanbul. The works under the contract was implemented as per FIDIC Red Book.
- In some lots of the third Bosphorus Bridge and the Northern Marmara Motorway Project boasts having built the world's broadest suspension bridge at 58.4 metres (192 feet) featuring 10 lanes, including two rail lines (ICA, 2017).
- In some lots of the Eurasia Tunnel, being the first two-layered/double-decked road tunnel crossing underneath the sea was officially put into service on December 22, 2016. The 5-km tunnel connects Kumkapi on the European part and Kosuyolu on the Asian part of Istanbul with a 14.6-km (9.1 miles) route (Eurasia Tunnel Project, 2017).

Turkey, being one of the candidate countries to join the EU, can benefit from the Instrument for Pre-accession Assistance (IPA) in its regional development projects. Pre-accession Financial Assistance for Turkey was adopted by the EU Council Regulation No. 2500/2001 of December 17, 2001. Between the years 2007 and 2013 (IPA I), Turkey has received approximately 4.8 mil. EUR within the framework of IPA and total allocation for Turkey for the years 2014-2020 (IPA II) amounts to 4.453,9 mil. EUR (http://www.ab.gov.tr/5.html). Central Finance and Contracts Unit (CFCU) under the Prime Ministry Undersecretariat of Treasury is in charge of budgeting, tendering, contracting, payments accounting, and financial reporting aspects of the procurement of the services, supplies, works, and grants for the EU funded programs in Turkey and finally management of financial assistance to Turkey (http://www.cfcu.gov.tr/about).

Some of the construction projects funded by the EU within the framework of IPA where the CFCU is the contracting authority are as follows:

- "Rehabilitation and Signalization of Irmak-Karabük-Zonguldak Railway Line" which comprises the reconstruction of the existing 415-km single track railway line with unchanged alignment and optimization of the track layout with installation of a new signalling system on the railway line. The works under the contract was implemented as per FIDIC Yellow Book.
- "Rehabilitation and Reconstruction of Köseköy-Gebze Section of the Ankara-İstanbul High Speed Train Project," which covers the rehabilitation and reconstruction of an approximately 56-km double-track railway line, which is one of the busiest sections from Köseköy to Gebze on the Ankara-İstanbul high-speed rail line corridor. The works include construction of infrastructure for railways including soil works, agricultural subways, and vents, various structures, drainage works, engirdling constructions, and the construction of superstructure of railway including ballast and track laying and the electromechanical works including electrification, signalization, and telecommunication of the railway line having maximum design speed of 160 km/hr (Works Procurement Notice, 2017). The works under the contract was implemented as per the FIDIC Red Book.

Turkish companies outside Turkey

While there are over 200,000 contractors undertaking business within Turkey; about 90% of the construction works undertaken abroad by Turkish contractors have been granted to the members of Turkish Contractors Association (TCA) and/or Turkey Construction Industry Employers' Syndicate (INTES), which amount to approximately 250 companies only (Köksal, 2011). As of the 1990s, Turkish contractors have been active in the Middle Eastern countries, Russia, Ukraine, Azerbaijan, Kazakhstan, Kyrgyzstan, Turkmenistan, and Northern African countries due to Turkey's geographical advantage, reasonable prices, and high-quality work, familiarity with the local culture and business environment, and a greater risk taking than their competitors.

According to TCA's data of March 2017, Turkish contractors first service abroad took place in Libya in the year 1972, which led the path for the Turkish contractors to heavily operate in the Middle Eastern countries such as Saudi Arabia, Iraq, Kuwait, and Iran between the years 1970 and 1979. The services mainly focused on the housing, port, industrial facilities, roads, bridges, tunnels, and urban infrastructure projects. The trend had expanded between the years 1980 to1989 for Turkish contractors toward the newly established countries along with Russian Federation in transition, which would cover almost 60% of the projects in 1990s. In this period, along with Russia, Kazakhstan, and Turkmenistan; Pakistan, Uzbekistan, Azerbaijan, Bulgaria, the United States of America, and Croatia have appeared as the new markets for Turkish contractors. Between the years 2000 and 2009, the majority of the Turkish contractors' operations abroad took place in Russian Federation followed by Libya, Kazakhstan, and Iraq. Although 30% of the contracting services were rendered in the housing sector; projects such as road/bridge/tunnel construction, business centers, industrial facilities, and pipeline projects have considerably increased. As for the period between 2010 and 2016, Turkmenistan, Russian Federation, and Iraq appear as the markets, Turkish contractors operate the most within the fields of road/bridge/tunnel (16.1%), housing (11.4%), airport (8.3%), business centers (8.1%), and power plants (7.2%) in ratio.

In summary, it can be inferred from the data that most of the projects Turkish contractors undertake take place in geographically close and strategically located countries, most of the time proportionate with the level of development and transition of the target country by taking into account of the country-specific risks.

According to a survey by KPMG, Turkish contractors defined the primary reason for their choice of country as being able to reach a new clientele and the second most important factor being the tax regime followed by the legal system of the country, transportation, infrastructure, and the stability of the political system. The survey concluded that perhaps Turkish contractors do not see the political stability as a problem because they themselves are not immune from the political instability.

Engineering News Report lists 46 Turkish companies in its list of top 250 contractors around the world. Turkish companies in the first 100 of this list are as follows: Renaissance Construction (38), Polimeks Insaat Taahhut ve San. Tic. AS. (42), ENKA Insaat ve Sanayi A.S. (72), TAV Construction (76), Yapi Merkezi Insaat ve Sanayi A.S. (78), Alarko Contracting Group (79), Limak Insaat Sanayi ve Ticaret A.S. (85), ANT Yapi ve Sanayi ve Ticaret CJSC (86), GAP Insaat Yatirim ve Dis Ticaret A.S. (92), Universal Acarsan Healthcare 6 Hospital Constr. (98) (ENR's 2017 Top 250 International Contractors, 2017).

Yasemin Çetinel
Partner, Çetinel Law Firm
Attorney at Law at Istanbul Bar Association
DRBF Representative of Turkey

Bibliography

Books:

Köksal, T. (2011). *Uluslararası İnşaat Hukuku [International Construction Law]*. Adalet Yayınları.

Kaplan, I. (2013). *Insaat Sozlesmeleri Hukuku ve Endustri Yatirim Sözlesmeleri [The Law of Construction Contracts and Industry Investment Contracts]*. Yetkin Yayinlari, p. 350; *Also see*: Revised Agreement on Government Procurement. Available at: https://www.wto.org/english/docs_e/legal_e/rev-gpr-94_01_e.htm (accessed 12 Sept. 2017).

Websites:

Brief History of the CFCU in the context of EU-Turkey Financial Cooperation. Available at: http://www.cfcu.gov.tr/about (accessed 20 Sept. 2017).

Cem Aktemur. *FIDIC Sözleşme Esasları ve Türkiye Uygulamaları [FIDIC Conditions of Contract and its Implementation in Turkey]*. Available at: http://anahtar.sanayi.gov.tr/tr/news/fidic-sozlesme-esaslari-ve-turkiye-uygulamalari/311 (accessed 20 Sept. 2017).

Aydın, D. *Süre Uzatımı ve Ek Ödemelerin KİK ve FIDIC Anahtar Teslimi Sözleşmeleri Çerçevesinde İncelenmesi [Examination of Extension of Time and Additional Payments within the scope of PPC and FIDIC Turnkey Contracts]*, pp. 62–63. Available at: https://polen.itu.edu.tr/bitstream/11527/14028/1/10077735.pdf (accessed 21 Sept. 2017).

ENR's 2017 Top 250 International Contractors. Available at: http://www.enr.com/toplists/2017-Top-250-International-Contractors-1 (accessed 11 Sept. 2017).

Eurasia Tunnel Project, Turkey. Available at: https://www.avrasyatuneli.com/kurumsal/ne/hakkinda (accessed 28 July 2017).
http://www.tmb.org.tr/arastirma_yayinlar/2009_2014_turk_firmalari_yurtdisi_yatirim_planlari.pdf (accessed 5 Sept. 2017).
ICA 3rd Bosphorus Bridge and Northern Marmara Motorway. Available at: http://www.3kopru.com/eng/project/ABOUT-PROJECT/1 (accessed 26 July 2017).
Revised Agreement on Government Procurement. Available at: https://www.wto.org/english/docs_e/legal_e/rev-gpr-94_01_e.htm (accessed 12 Sept. 2017).
The State of PPPs Infrastructure Public-Private Partnerships in Emerging Markets & Developing Economies 1991-2015, June 2016, World Bank Group – PPIAF, p. 2, 10. Available at: http://www.cica.net/wp-content/uploads/2016/09/160921_PPIAFState_of_PPPs__Report-FINAL_July16.pdf (accessed 11 Sept. 2017).
TR-AB Mali İşbirliği [TR-EU Financial Cooperation]. Available at: http://www.ab.gov.tr/5.html (accessed 20 Sept. 2017).
Türk Yurtdışı Müteahhit Hizmetleri, TMB – Yurtdışı Müteahhitlik Hizmetleri – 2017/Mart [Turkish Construction Services Abroad, TCA – Contracting Services Abroad – 2017/March]. Online. Available at: http://www.tmb.org.tr/doc/file/YDMH_mart_2017.pdf (accessed 5 Sept. 2017).
Turkish State Railways, High Speed Railway Projects. Available at: http://www.tcdd.gov.tr/content/57# (accessed 26 July 2017).
Uzun Soluklu Bir Plan - Türk şirketlerinin 2009 ve 2014 yıllarn kapsayan yurtdş yatrm planlarnn ele alndğ bir çalşma [A Lasting Plan - a study handling Turkish contractors' investment plans abroad covering the years 2009–2014] Online available at:
Works Contract Forecast for the Rehabilitation and Signalization of Irmak-Karabük-Zonguldak Railway Line. Available at: http://www.cfcu.gov.tr/sites/default/files/tenderfiles/forecastworks.HTM (accessed 20 Sept. 2017).
Works Procurement Notice for the Rehabilitation and Reconstruction of Köseköy-Gebze Section of the Ankara-İstanbul High Speed Train Project. Available at: http://www.cfcu.gov.tr/sites/default/files/tenderfiles/tender_notice.HTM (accessed 20 Sept. 2017).

The use of FIDIC forms in Azerbaijan by Farid Nabili (Azerbaijan)

The legal system of Azerbaijan Republic is based on the continental law system. This means that most of the principles and concepts of the continental law system are effective in Azerbaijani legal system as well.

The Civil Code of Azerbaijan Republic (hereafter, Civil Code) is the main law regulating the status of physical and legal persons, obligations, general provisions on contracts, and specific provisions on various types of contracts, inheritance, and so on. And under the Constitutional Law on Normative Legal Acts, the Civil Code shall prevail over other laws and regulations that regulate civil matters, including those that have been adopted after the Civil Code or those constitute special law.

International construction contract forms, particularly FIDIC construction contract forms are relatively new in Azerbaijan. Although not endorsed or approved by any legal instrument, it is used in construction industry mainly by government-funded large public projects or projects with involvement of a foreign party, such as international contractor, engineer, or construction management service provider.

FIDIC contract forms are used in multi-million-dollar public projects mainly due to the advice of international construction management consultants, but with special caution and considerations. Such special caution and considerations are maintained by stakeholders in private construction projects as well.

The reasons of special caution in application of FIDIC contracts are not only the lack of practice or experience of domestic stakeholders, but also interpretational questions and lack of clear guide regarding applicable or sometimes conflicting local rules.

As it is the case in other civil law based states, common-law elements of FIDIC contracts and domestic imperative rules of the statutes, particularly the Civil Code are part of the considerations of the lawyers and consultants involved in the projects. Moreover, in public projects funded by the government, public procurement legislation adds more of such considerations.

Civil code dimension

FIDIC contract forms are standard contract terms adjustable by the parties to their specific needs via particular conditions. Generally, this meets the criteria for standard contract terms defined under the Civil Code. Therefore, the party offering the use of FIDIC contract forms runs the risk that it might be nullified if the accepting party is not able to get acquainted with these terms. To avoid such risk, in practice both parties sign and seal general terms of FIDIC contract forms, as well. It is usually further advised to clarify and confirm the status of general terms of FIDIC contract form in the contract agreement to avoid this and further associated risks stemming from the unreasonable ("extra-ordinary") or vague terms.

The Civil Code specifies provisions and rights for parties related to amendment and termination of the contract. It shall be noted that these are applicable in addition to the conditions and cases specified in the construction contracts. For example, where circumstances have significantly changed after the conclusion of the contract, any of the parties are allowed to amend the contract to meet the concerns of the changed circumstances or terminate the contract in totality, unless otherwise provided for by the contract. A circumstance is considered as significantly changed if parties reasonable predicting such change would not have entered into the agreement at inception or would have agreed on significantly different terms. In practice, these provisions are "neutralized" by waiving such rights and clearly excluding such opportunities for parties in particular conditions.

Another interesting example of statutory provisions might be contractor's mortgage right over the land where the building is being constructed against the obligations of the employer.

Construction law dimension

Many other provisions that need to be considered and addresses while construction projects and drafting of contracts are not only present in the Civil Code, but other legislative acts related to construction, such as Urban Planning and Construction Code of Azerbaijan, Regulations of the Cabinet of Ministers.

Under the Urban Planning and Construction Code, the contractor shall provide a two-year warranty period starting from the date of occupation permit, which is issued after the completion and inspection of the constructed building. In practice, it is not easy to obtain occupation permit with the approval of all relevant state bodies due to strict inspection and documentation. It is, therefore, advised to consider these in line with the release of retention money clauses.

Moreover, the Code specifies general and specific obligations for the designer, contractor, employer, and technical consultants that need to be considered while engaging in contractual negotiations and drafting contracts. For example, designing of a construction project that requires issuance of construction permit is a licensed activity. Commercial construction projects and majority of constructions require such permit (with exception of smaller houses for personal use). Designer, by law, has duty to prepare design documentation in accordance with local standards and shall review and update design documentation during the construction period upon the instruction of state authorities. Furthermore, designer shall provide design review (authorship control) over the construction and monitor that the construction is conducted in accordance with the design documentation. Where designer finds breach of local rules or non-compliance of the ongoing construction works with the approved design documentation, it shall notify employer and contractor of such deficiencies and request reasonable steps to be taken. If neither employer, nor contractor takes reasonable steps to address such deficiencies, then designer has duty to duly inform relevant regulatory authorities of such concerns.

Public procurement dimension

As noted above, other dimension of considerations are associated with the public procurement legislation in government-funded public project. The Public Procurement Law is strict and at the same time "old fashioned." For example, the law specifies that the relations between the parties to procurement contract shall be governed by the law of the Republic of Azerbaijan. This leads to conclude and warn that applicable law to disputes shall be Azerbaijani law under the contracts, including FIDIC construction contracts. This implies that even the parties have chosen a different law for disputes, Azerbaijani law shall still be applicable.

The Public Procurement Law requires local individuals and companies to quote during the bidding process at public procurements only in local currency (New Azerbaijani Manat). Therefore, no subsidiary local company of a foreign company may quote and specify price in currency other than manat. But foreign entities (that includes local branches of foreign companies) may quote and specify price in other currencies, where the official rate of the Central Bank of Azerbaijan for the last day of tender submission shall be used for any calculations. Since bidding currency and contract currency (and value) are inter-related, these clauses would make great impact on the pricing of the quotes. It shall be noted that there has been two waves of devaluation of manat more than 200%, therefore, such clauses of law shall be considered while making a bid at public tenders.

Under the said law, variations and omissions are only acceptable up to 15% of the price, provided that such clause has been specified in tender documentation. Therefore, the first concern is that whether such clause has been specified in the tender documentation or not. If no such clause is specified, then variation and omission clauses of FIDIC contracts would not be enforceable. Second issue is the limit on variation and omission percentage at 15%. It would not be allowed to instruct variation or omission under FIDIC contracts exceeding 15% of the contract price. All these and more provisions shall be considered at the outset and reflected in particular where possible and necessary.

This Short Note serves only to give idea about the law and practice related to FIDIC construction forms in Azerbaijani experience. Therefore, naturally, there are much more issues of equal or higher concern for the involved parties both in private and public projects.

Farid Nabili
Partner
Caspian Legal Center
Azerbaijan

The use of FIDIC forms in Nigeria by Marc J. Enenkel (Germany)

As Nigeria became the biggest economy on the African continent, it developed to a highly interesting country for investments for foreign/international companies from several industrial sectors. Furthermore, the country requires considerable development of its infrastructure such as roads and bridges, power plants, and connected thereto power supply lines and accommodation facilities to cover the demands of the growing population. Another industrial sector, which, at the moment, reserves investments in plants and industrial facilities is the oil and gas sector due to the delay in passing the Nigerian Petroleum Industry Bill.

The lion's share of above-mentioned investments, except of roads and bridges, which will be financed by federal or state government, are or will be financed by international and non-Nigerian investors. As such foreign investors are not aware of Nigerian (contract) law most of them require their investments to be executed under a known and (internationally) well-established contract form—the FIDIC contract forms.

A peculiarity of Nigerian law is that the law indeed consists of four distinct legal systems: English law (due to Nigeria's colonial past with Britain), Common law (newly formed during past colonial time), Customary law and Sharia law (predominantly used in the Muslim north of the country). Foreign investment contracts are in most of the cases based on Nigerian Common law. Therefore the FIDIC contract forms are—in terms of governing law—suitable contract forms for usage in Nigeria.

As the FIDIC contract forms are in general well-balanced contract forms, it becomes apparent that when drafting the FIDIC contract forms not all the specifics of building in developing countries have been covered. However, as Nigeria has been through some non-negligible (positive) movements during the past century, it still is not that stable as other African developing countries, for example, in terms of legal certainty and public safety. This requires certain considerations which would not be necessary when drafting a construction contract for a project located in developed countries. Those considerations can be summarized, but are not limited to the following:

- Commencement date:
    Because of Nigeria's bureaucracy, negotiations with surrounding communities or the compilation of an environmental impact assessment report can be really time-consuming it is preferable for any contractor to amend Sub-Clause 8.1—Commencement of Work and make sure that the time for completion starts running not until certain pre-conditions have been fulfilled by the employer (such as procuring a building permit, concluding a memorandum of understanding with surrounding communities, receipt of an advance payment, etc.). Such an amendment brings the advantage for the contractor, not to claim for extension of time right in the beginning of the project and not to be obliged to commence the execution of the works without having received any payment to cover site setup mobilizing costs. Furthermore, it is advantageous to amend this sub-clause from the (governmental) employer's view, because for most of the governmental projects the project budgets are tight and they get determined anew for every year, and therefore, in most cases, there would not even be funds available to cover and pay contractor's EoT claim due to a differed project start.
- Clarification and agreement with surrounding communities:
    Many of the construction projects within Nigeria are located in remote areas where smaller communities are resided in the vicinity of the site. Such surrounding communities

often want to profit from the construction project and claim certain number of people which live in the community to be employed to work on the construction site—whether such workers are skilled or not or that certain material (such as sand or steel) shall be procured from (the small) companies of the community. This makes it necessary—before signature of the contract—to consider who will be responsible for dealing with the surrounding communities (i.e., concluding a memorandum of understanding with the community's chief) and what to do if the employed workers do not perform properly or if the supplied material is not of adequate quality. For sake of clarity, employment of such community workers as nominated subcontractors is, in most cases, a risk which contractors are not willing to accept. An adequate provision thereto has therefore to be included in the particular conditions to the contract.

- Foreign exchange risk:

  Within the last years, Nigeria pursued a stringent line to protect its local currency—the Nigerian Naira (NGN). Sections 15 and 20(1) of the Central Bank of Nigeria Act 2007 defines that the local currency of Nigeria is the Nigerian Naira and that such currency shall be obligatory in tenders for every products and services offered and/or consummated in Nigeria. This leads to the fact, that (governmental financed) construction projects are remunerated in NGN only.

  The Central Bank of Nigeria (CBN) on June 23, 2015 issued an official circular, which declares 41 listed items (it also lists certain materials required for construction projects, like steel sheets, steel pipes, etc.) to be not valid for foreign exchange (FOREX), when imported into the country. In particular that means, that the listed items can still be imported, but the importing party is not entitled to exchange NGN against hard currencies (such as Euro and U.S. dollar) for payment of such imported goods.

  Most of the construction projects require the procurement and importation of certain materials from abroad (e.g., Europe). Therefore, the contractors have to have an appropriate amount of hard currency available to buy materials from outside of Nigeria.

  Due to the above-mentioned currency protectionism of the CBN it is difficult for contractors to receive hard currency payments under the construction contracts. Also it is not possible to exchange NGN into hard currency for importation of materials listed in the circular of the CBN dated June 23, 2015.

  Furthermore, the Nigerian government tried to avoid an inflation of the NGN until the middle of June 2016. This position could not be maintained by the Nigerian government and thus, since the June 21, 2016 the NGN is subject to a flexible exchange rate regime and suffered further inflation of about 30% in comparison to the hard currencies. As a result of this the access to the official FOREX market (Nigerian Central Bank Rate and Nigerian Interbank Market Rate) is nearly impossible for private companies (such as engineering and construction companies), due to many restrictions in the allocation of available FOREX in Nigeria.

  Therefore, it is highly advisable or even obligatory for contractors to include a proper currency fluctuation clause in the particular conditions, which covers the risk of fluctuation of the NGN against hard currencies.

- Alternative dispute resolution:

  In their Clause 20 (Claims, Disputes and Arbitration), the main FIDIC contract forms foresee an extensive "Alternative Dispute Resolution (ADR) Clause," which covers the ADR methods of adjudication, amicable settlement, and as a last resort, arbitration. The Nigerian law does not explicitly regulate the ADR methods of amicable settlement and adjudication, but does also not prevent parties to a contract to use such.

When it comes to arbitration the Nigerian Arbitration and Conciliation Act (Cap A18, Laws of the Federation of Nigeria 2004)—the ACA—applies to such arbitral proceedings. As the ACA is mostly based on the UNCITRAL Model Arbitration law, it can be said, that the ADR clauses of the FIDIC contract forms are compatible with the statutory laws of Nigeria. And also the Nigerian courts tend to recognize the use of arbitration as a proper and valid dispute resolution method (e.g., *C.N. Onuselogu Ent. Ltd. v. Afribank (Nig.) Ltd. (2005) 1 NWLR Part 940, 577*). The standard wording of FIDIC in terms of arbitration states that the arbitration rules of the International Chamber of Commerce, Paris (ICC) shall apply to the arbitral proceedings. The Nigerian statutory laws and the case law do not prohibit the use of institutional arbitration rules, such as the ICC arbitration eules. Furthermore, according to Section 6 the Nigerian ACA, the parties are free to decide on the number of arbitrators, and therefore, the FIDIC's default arbitral tribunal setup of three arbitrators is also fine in Nigeria. Last but not least, one should note that Nigeria is a signatory of the New York Convention, which enormously enlightens the recognition and the enforcement of arbitration awards outside of Nigeria in several other states all over the world.

When one considers the above, it can be said that the FIDIC contract forms, after making some necessary changes and/or additions thereto, provide a well-balanced contractual basis which enables the parties to successfully execute construction projects in Nigeria.

Marc J. Enenkel, LL.M.
Contract- and Claim Manager
M+W Central Europe GmbH
Germany

The use of FIDIC forms in Ukraine by Svitlana Teush (Ukraine)

Over the last several years, Ukraine has made a significant progress in reforming the construction industry. Historically, this was the realm of state monopoly, overregulation, and centralization, with practically no room left for independent non-governmental expertise and competition. During the evolving construction reform, new market instruments and practices have begun to be introduced in Ukraine. These include certification of professionals by industry associations, liberalization of mandatory rules, facilitation of permit and licensing procedures; reallocation of powers from centralized governmental agencies to local self-governing authorities, and sharing state control functions with non-governmental self-governance associations. The industry is digitized, and becomes ever more transparent with the gradual introduction of electronic services and online public registers (such as the register of property rights to real estate, construction permits, construction licenses, land zoning documents, public procurement portal, etc.). A major landmark in the construction reform process has been the adoption of the Law of Ukraine "On the Regulation of City Planning Activities" No. 3038 in 2011. This contributed to a significant improvement in the regulatory framework, evidenced by Ukraine's rocketing score in World Bank's "Ease of Doing Business" over the past years. The full enactment of the EU-Ukraine Association Agreement is expected to give another strong impetus for Ukraine to intensify this reform and align its regulatory and operational environment with international standards.

In Ukraine, there is no codified legislative act that regulates on a comprehensive basis all of the principal aspects of construction, such as a city planning code. There are also numerous laws and by-laws governing licensing, construction permits, commissioning (putting into operation) of finished property, responsibility in construction, and so on. To name but a few: laws of Ukraine "On Architectural Activities," On Fundamentals of City-Building," "On Construction Rules," "On the Protection of Cultural Heritage," "On the Licensing of Types of Economic Activity," regulations of the Cabinet of Ministers of Ukraine "On Certain Issues of Preparatory and Construction Works," "Issues of Putting into Operation Completed Objects," and so on. Construction standards and norms are embraced by the so-called "DBNs" (the state construction norms). This is an odd conglomeration of the old-fashioned regulations inherited from Soviet times and modern, progressive regulations. Contract-wise, particular regard should be given to Regulation of the Cabinet of Ministers of Ukraine No. 668 approving "The General Conditions for Conclusion and Performance of Capital Construction Contacts" (the Regulation No. 668), adopted in 2005, which is described as binding for consideration in construction contracts. An exemption is made for the international treaties of Ukraine, which override the provisions of Regulation No. 668. For example, this carve-out works where FIDIC contracts are concluded by the international finance institutions (the IFIs) under the international agreements of Ukraine.

FIDIC's heritage is not well-known in Ukraine, except for the 1999 Conditions of Contract for Construction for Building and Engineering Works designed by the Employer (the Red Book) and the Conditions of Contract for Plant and Design-Build for Electrical and Mechanical Works Designed by the Contractor (the Yellow Book), which are typically used in the IFI-funded projects in Ukraine. Greater use of FIDIC contracts in Ukraine is hampered by the fact that there are no official translations of FIDIC forms of contract into the Ukrainian language.

The FIDIC contracts are used in Ukraine based on the fundamental principle of the freedom of contract, subject to restrictions imposed by mandatory provisions or prohibitions set by law. Mandatory provisions are usually understood to include, among other things, licensing, certification and permit procedures, technical regulations and standards, immigration and labor requirements, environmental and safety issues, and taxation.

Apart from regulatory and other mandatory requirements and the Ukrainian public order issues, it is necessary to account for the differences between FIDIC contracts and the law of contract rooted in the historical background of Ukraine and the peculiarities of the civil law system to which Ukraine adheres. Hence, there are difficulties with the interpretation and implementation of many terms, notions and principles of common law underlying FIDIC contracts (such as "time is of the essence," "dispute adjudication board," "variations," "value engineering," "early warning," "substantial completion," "constructive acceleration," "time at large," "experienced contractor," or "determinations").

The concept of a self-adjusting contract with the involvement of a third party (such as a consulting engineer) is not well-known in Ukraine. In FIDIC contracts with public employers it is often seen that powers of a consulting engineer are limited by the need to obtain pre-approval from an employer and formalize the outcome of the engineer's determinations (including variations) in additional agreements to be signed by both parties.

Ukrainian law does not classify, or allocate, risks in a manner similar to that of FIDIC contracts, and provides very limited guidance on the consequences of risk occurrence in terms of parties' entitlement to time extension or additional costs and/or profit or other practical consequences.

In contracts with public employers, there is usually a strong bias in shifting most of the risks to a contractor; this is hard to renegotiate after a contract has been awarded, due to the constraints of public procurement procedures. In international contracts concluded through the IFIs' procurement procedures, the core balance of risks is usually maintained as set in the General Conditions.

The allocation of risks is largely dependent on the type of the contract pricing (whether fixed or approximate). A fixed-contract price should remain unchanged for the entire volume of construction, and does not allow for adjustments other than by the agreement of parties in the instances provided by law or contract. An approximate (or "dynamic") contract price can be modified whenever there is a need to account for adjusted volumes of works, costs of resources, or other factors as may be set out and defined in contract.

The Ukrainian approach to cost and price formation in construction is based on a somewhat different philosophy than that of the FIDIC contracts. A contract is deemed to be based on a fixed price and fixed-cost estimates, unless the parties expressly agree otherwise.

The law expressly provides that, if there is a need to exceed a fixed contract price, it is the contractor who should bear all related costs; the contractor cannot claim an increase in costs, if, at the date of signing of a contract the parties could not forecast any changes in the full volume of works or necessary costs. However, in the event of a substantial increase in the value of materials, plant, or services provided by third parties to a contractor, the contractor can claim an increase in price, and if the employer does not accept it, the contractor can claim the dissolution of a contract. It is, therefore, important that parties determine, under a fixed price contract, the grounds for a price increase as well as the procedure for price adjustments. Where a contract is based on an approximate price, parties should state in a contract the procedure of cost adjustments that will apply during the performance of works.

The Ukrainian courts do not always strictly adhere to the contractual provisions on the admissibility of changes in the contact price and allocation of the associated risks among parties depending on the type of the contract price. The courts can take into consideration other factors such as a substantial change in circumstances, public interest, the potential costs in the event of retendering a project to another contract, and even shift the risk from one party to the other, as is exemplified by below case. The Commercial Court of the Zaporizhia Region considered Case No. 7/92/07 upon the claim of LLC "Trust "Zaporizhbud" (the Contractor) to Municipal Enterprise "Vodokanal" (the Employer) regarding the amendment of the contract for the procurement of works for the reconstruction of the Dnipro Water Supply Station (DVS-1) in the city of Zaporizhia (the Contract) based on the FIDIC's Red Book. The contract price was indicated as fixed and not be subject to any adjustment for labor costs, equipment materials, taxes, and so on, except as stated in sub-clause 13.7 (Adjustments for Changes in Legislation) of the General Conditions of Red Book. The Contractor requested the amendment of the Contract, and increasing the Contract price due to the alleged changes in legislation regarding the increase in minimal wages. The Contractor also referred to a material change in circumstances resulting from an increase in the average wages in the construction industry, the customer basket value, costs of construction materials, plant, fuel, or other associated commodities due to the growing inflation rate.

The Contractor claimed that, because of the increased wages and construction costs, continuation of the works on the initial terms and conditions of the Contract would have substantially violated the balance of the parties' interests, placed the Contractor at a significant loss, and deprived the Contractor of the profits that it had expected to receive when entering into the Contract. The Employer dismissed the arguments that the risks should be borne by the Contractor under the Contact. In the opinion of the court, the Contractor did not undertake the risk of receiving inadequate remuneration for the works due to the changes in legislation relating to an increase in wages or construction costs. According to the court, from the substance of the Contract and the custom, it did not follow that the risk of a material change in circumstances should be borne by the Contractor. Based on this reasoning, the court fully satisfied the claim of the Contractor, and ruled on the amendment of the Contract to reflect the increase in the Contract price. This decision was further upheld by both the Commercial Court of Appeal and the Superior Commercial Court of Ukraine.

When contracting with a public employer, it should be remembered that payment by a public employer under a contract can be subject to different restrictions and procedures. Price formation is generally over-regulated, and is not indicative of market values and practice. Contractors have often faced delays in payments due to bureaucracy and lengthy approval processes, even where a prompt response is required in the interest of the efficiency of a construction process.

The FIDIC contracts in Ukraine are usually modified through the Particular Conditions in order to take into account local peculiarities. One of the most examples of such modifications are the incorporation of mandatory procedures of acceptance and commissioning (putting into operation) of property into the Particular Conditions.

As other civil law jurisdictions, Ukraine supports the concept of "acceptance" of works by an employer, which is key to the construction process. The date of completion of works (construction of an object) is deemed to be the date of acceptance of works by an employer. Acceptance entails important legal consequences such as shifting the risk of accidental loss or damage to works to an employer as well as the transfer of title ownership to finished works (a constructed object) to an employer, where a contractor is deemed to be the owner before such acceptance. Acceptance also marks the time when the contract price becomes due for payment, unless parties agree otherwise, and when the statute of limitations and the statutory guarantee (defects liability) terms commence. Acceptance is formalized by the signing of a transfer and acceptance act (protocol) by an employer and a contractor. The commissioning procedures are within the domain or public (mandatory) law, and, as such, they cannot be changed by agreement of the parties.

The concepts of "partial acceptance," "provisional acceptance," or "substantial acceptance" are not well-known in Ukraine. There is also no provision in Ukrainian law for a two-stage process—as set out under the Red Book or Yellow Book—which involves the issuance by an engineer of a taking-over certificate and then of a performance certificate.

Notably, modifications to FIDIC contracts (via the Particular Conditions) aimed at integrating the above elements of "acceptance" and commissioning concepts usually relate to the taking-over of works, and not the performance phase. It can be argued that the reason is that taking-over of works entails major legal consequences that can be compared to those of acceptance in Ukrainian law.

Claim management practices under FIDIC contracts are often not properly or efficiently applied; delays or other breaches of claim management procedures by parties are common. A common pitfall in claim management procedures observed in practice has been a failure by a party to duly submit either a notice of the claim—or the full details of the claim—in due time; and/or inconsistencies between the notice and the details, either in form or substance.

The prevailing approach in construction projects has been to litigate in the local Ukrainian courts rather than referring disputes to arbitration, although both litigation and arbitration are deemed legal and viable options for dispute resolution in construction disputes. Recent years have seen a growing number of contracts include an arbitration clause rather than a reference to local Ukrainian courts. Dispute adjudication boards (DABs) or equivalent institutes are not common in Ukraine. The provisions of the General Conditions of FIDIC contracts on the appointment of DABs (or dispute review boards (DRBs) are often deleted by operation of the overriding Particular Conditions. The procedures involving DABs or DRBs are viewed by local market players as causing unnecessary delays and adding no practical value, since they are not enforceable under Ukrainian law.

The Ukrainian court practice on the use of FIDIC contracts is very limited and not well-established.

For the proper application of FIDIC contracts, pivotal is the role of consulting engineers, and of the consulting engineering profession in general. Until recently, there has practically been no dedicated regulatory framework defining the notion or role of consulting engineers in Ukraine. In 2017, a landmark Regulation No. 1065 of the Cabinet of Ministers (the Ukrainian government) was adopted entitled "On the Approval of Requirements to Quality Control of Construction, Reconstruction, Repairs and Maintenance of Motor Roads of General Use" (the Regulation No. 1065). This Regulation, for the first time in Ukraine, introduced the definition of a consulting engineer with reference to FIDIC contracts, defined the scope of the functions of consulting engineers, and set the general framework for interaction amongst employers, engineers and contactors. An express reference was made to FIDIC conditions of contract, which engineers should take into consideration. Thus, FIDIC contracts became expressly associated with the institute of consulting engineers, for the very first time in Ukrainian law. With the enactment of Regulation No. 1065, it will be easier for public employers to engage independent consulting engineers on international construction projects. Although in need of further improvements, the new independent quality control requirements introduced by Regulation No. 1065 mark a significant step forward in the evolving reform of the construction industry in Ukraine. Further to this, in August 2017, the Ministry of Regional Development, Construction, Housing and Communal Services of Ukraine approved qualification requirements to the profession of a consulting engineer. It is expected that the regulatory framework governing the activities of consulting engineers will continue to evolve.

The absence of a well-developed legal framework does not preclude consulting engineers, both local and international, from operating in Ukraine based on the general legal grounds and requirements relating to works and services. In practice, the powers of a consulting engineer are often limited by contract (e.g., through the Particular Conditions and/or a consultancy contract with an engineer), and engineers should obtain pre-approval from the employer in many instances; under some contracts, such pre-approval was required for all actions of an engineer.

This far-reaching extension of employer's powers is usually preferred by public employers who are concerned about the increase in budget expenditures, liability, or other exposure as a result of engineer's decisions.

Typically, employers appoint the consulting engineers for large infrastructure projects from amongst international companies or their subsidiaries. Local consulting engineers, although present in the market, are not sufficiently represented in large construction projects, including those based on FIDIC contracts. Local players are striving to foster their market position by organizing themselves into professional industry associations and promoting their activities both in the domestic Ukrainian market and abroad, including through cooperation with FIDIC as well as regional and peer associations of consulting engineers from other countries. As a general observation, recent years have seen an unprecedented growth in the role of self-governed industry associations, and some of them are even assigned authority to carry out certification of experts, which had traditionally been the exclusive remit of state authorities.

As mentioned, in Ukraine, FIDIC contracts are most frequently used in construction projects funded by IFIs and procured under such IFIs' procurement rules and procedures. The local public procurement framework is not quite compatible with the FIDIC contracts, but it assigns priority to the IFIs' procurement rules and procedures. Even then, parties to the FIDIC contracts procured under the IFIs' rules and procedures may encounter practical difficulties (especially where public employers are involved), as they need to take account of the mandatory provisions of Ukrainian law and reconcile them with the provisions of the FIDIC contracts.

The Ukrainian Public Procurement Law recognizes the concept of the most economically advantageous tender. Formally, the price should have a weighting (the share) of not less than 70% in the total mix of evaluation criteria. In practice, even where a mixture of the evaluation criteria should be used, the price component often determines the outcome of a bid. The Public Procurement Law does not expressly embrace the concepts of quality-based selection or the best-value procurement, nor does it make any reference to the abnormally low price, except that certain remedies can be invoked within the competition protection framework where there is evidence of anti-competitive actions.

Notably, there is a growing trend of engaging international suppliers and contractors by public employers, which pay their works or services from public budget. An important precedent has been set by State Enterprise "Ukrainian Sea Ports Authority"—and an innovative development—to invite bidders at an early procurement stage with the aim to develop an acceptable form of contract for incorporation into the tender documents, which international contractors could live with. Thus, the principle "take it or leave it," which had traditionally dominated public tenders appears to be giving way to a more open and communicative approach among stakeholders. State Enterprise "Ukrainian Sea Ports Authority" announced plans to carry out a number of tenders in 2018 and the years to follow for the performance of design, construction, and reconstruction works, including dredging and reclamation works, in several ports across the Southern Ukraine (Odesa, Mykolayiv, Berdyansk, Mariupol, etc.), as well as for ship-building works. A number of international companies expressed their interest, and this is expected to further contribute to streamlining the contract framework and adjustment of procurement practices in line with international standards.

The Public Procurement Law does not provide a crystal-clear regulation as to the contract modification post-award and the criteria triggering the need for retendering. As a general rule, the concluded procurement contract should not derogate from the essential terms of the tender specification until the obligations of the parties have been fully performed, except a very limited number of cases, which do not always meet the needs of complex construction and engineering projects. The Public Procurement Law does not tackle, to a sufficient extent, the diversity of situations which may call for contract modifications, such as, for example, the contractor's replacement or succession, substantial changes related to unforeseeable circumstances (other than the time extension) or other causes, situations when additional works should not require retendering, and so on.

The work on reforming the Ukrainian public procurement system and its alignment with the EU public procurement has been ongoing for several years now. An important landmark has been the enactment of a new Public Procurement Law and introduction of a public electronic procurement platform in 2016, "Prozorro." At the end of 2016, Prozorro was honoured by the Open Governments Award 2016 at the Open Government Partnership Summit in Paris. There are plans to further integrate the electronic procurement platform with e-data on the annual procurement plans and public funds' spending as well as various public registers in Ukraine. It is also contemplated that notices of public procurement in Ukraine should also be published in the EU, subject to the implementation of the common procurement vocabulary. The local law would obviously need to be amended also to better account for the needs of international construction projects.

***

Ukraine has been significantly progressing with construction sector reform toward deregulation and demonopolization of the market, opening up to inward investment, and integration in European and global markets. Recent legislative developments have raised the outlook for both growing the institute of consulting engineers and a broader use of FIDIC contracts and other best practices. The Civil Code of Ukraine has many dispositive rules, which translate the principle of freedom of contract, and are supportive of the use of the FIDIC contract in Ukraine. In addition, reform of the system of public procurement has begun. Yet, the law of contracts and public procurement law in Ukraine should be further liberalized and adapted to meet the needs of international construction projects and to improve the efficiency of project and cost management.

Svitlana Teush, PhD
Counsel for Construction, Energy and Infrastructure Matters
Redcliffe Partners Law Firm
Ukraine

The use of FIDIC forms in Vietnam by David Lockwood (Vietnam)

The Vietnamese construction industry is rather unique in many respects in that the country as a whole has undergone seismic changes in the last 30 years commencing from the implementation of the so called "Doi Moi policy," translated literally as "open-door" policy in 1986.

The government decided in the aftermath of the American war that Vietnam was now ready once again to engage with the international community, albeit in a controlled and progressive manner and actively invited and encouraged foreign direct investment

This was followed by lifting of the U.S. trade embargo in 1995, accession to the World Trade Organization in 2007 and the introduction of numerous laws and decrees including the legalization of private business for the first time by the promulgation of the Law on Enterprises in 2000 resulting in reduced state control and less reliance on a centrally planned economy.

This backdrop is extremely important in understanding the Vietnamese construction industry as it means that the private sector including the construction related supply chain comprising main contractors, sub-contractors, suppliers, and consulting firms such as architects, engineers, project mangers, and quantity surveyors have been in existence for less than two decades.

The last 20 years have witnessed a steep but steadily climbed learning curve for all firms and individuals engaged in construction and today the Vietnam construction industry now resembles that of other countries albeit with an arguably less sophisticated and integrated supply chain found in developed economies.

Gradually a number of international practices and procedures have been adopted progressively but often cautiously as there are a number of different cultural, political, legal, and economic factors that continue to have an impact on how the construction industry operates and engages between the various entities.

Despite the transition of Vietnam from a centrally planned economy to a market-based economy, Vietnam is still classified as developing country with a lower-middle income population. Project finance raised from local bank lending is a relatively new concept and improved access to finance has created a burgeoning demand for construction expertise and resources in order to keep pace with development needs.

Importantly, Vietnam Law is based on a civil law (codified law, which is a unique blend of both French and Chinese law). This means many of the precepts of common law are not understood or even applicable in Vietnam.

Vietnam has a significant infrastructure "lag" meaning the availability of paved roads, bridges, international standard container sea ports, modern air, and rail hubs and networks and water sanitation and power generation is not sufficient to sustain Vietnam's economic growth measured by year on year gross domestic product.

This places huge pressure on the public sector resources to procure and develop projects of national importance in order to reduce the infrastructure lag and to meet Vietnam's goal for developed country status by 2020 and beyond.

Given the limited availability of finance by the central government, finance for these projects is predominantly provided by Official Development Aid (ODA) from donors such as World Bank, Asia Development Bank, KfW, and the European Investment Bank.

ODA funders have their own procurement guidelines and require a high degree of accountability as well as transparency with fair and equitable procurement practices with significant consequences for any bribery and corruption discovered throughout the procurement and construction phase.

FIDIC being the preferred if not mandatory contract for ODA funders is widely used for all public sector projects and has therefore led to a proliferation of its use through to the private sector and is predominantly used on all projects in Vietnam.

The most common form of procurement for the public sector is a preference for lump sum open tendering based on weighted key selection criteria. Development aid will often by tied to the donor country as a mandatory condition of the soft loan and normally specifies a percentage of construction value, which must be awarded to companies from the donor country.

Where a lump sum contract is required the FIDIC Red Book will almost exclusively be utilized with amendments of the general conditions of contract contained in the particular conditions of contracts to convert the general conditions from a measure and value contract (as the default contract version) to the intended lump sum format.

These amendments are not always performed properly leaving behind some clauses that are no longer relevant and thereby creating inconsistencies and problems of interpretation for both the parties to the contract and other users such as engineers and quantity surveyors resulting in claims and sometimes disputes.

Another challenging feature when using the FIDIC Red Book in Vietnam and perhaps other civil law countries is concept of the independent engineer procured and contracted by one party and who acts for that party but is required to act fairly to both parties.

This concept originates from English common law and has been widely criticized by bodies such as the European Contractors Association as being outdated and not entirely relevant in today's commercially aware world with inevitable questions on how this arrangement actually works in practice.

In Vietnam the employer's roles and functions under the contract are usually performed by project management units (PMUs) under the relevant governmental body and they are often formed specifically for the project and early on in the procurement phase. The PMUs are often involved in procuring (in conjunction with a constituted panel) the engineering design and supervision consultants and the various contractors for the project.

Usually an independent tender agent is also engaged to provide transparency and accountability to the procurement process by preparing and adopting key selection criteria that are weighted and scored by the constituted panel for technical, contractual, and commercial attributes and competencies.

The clear separation of powers of the employer and engineer contemplated by the FIDIC drafters and more readily accepted in common law countries also poses some challenges during the construction phase.

The PMU acting as the employer have their own administration and reporting functions required under Vietnam Law, which means they still need to retain control and approval over some important project matters such as extensions of time and the approval of variations which under usual circumstances when using FIDIC would fall under the ambit of the engineer's role and responsibility.

Often it is simply not possible under Vietnam law for the PMU (or the engineer) to make decisions or give approvals without reference to higher authority within the relevant ministries of government. For this reason, employer bodies (PMU) in Vietnam do not tend to be "agile" in that they cannot always make unilateral decisions on contract administration matters and particularly on projects of national significance which encompasses virtually all infrastructure projects.

This results in a slow claims agreement and approval process, which may impact project progress as important commercial and contractual matters are set aside pending resolution at higher government level.

The use of design and build (D&B) or engineer procure and construct (EPC) contracts using the Yellow Book or Silver Book is still relatively uncommon in Vietnam and many of the contractors based in-country do not have the technical capability to execute a D&B or EPC effectively. This form of procurement and contract is perceived as high risk for contractors sometimes leading to tender offers that are not commercially viable or competitive.

One of the key contractor design risks perceived by potential bidders is the lack of relevant local codes and standards. To address this gap, local codes and standards are almost always supplemented with international codes and standards from a myriad of different sources, the most common being British standards, American, Australian, and Japanese standards.

The overall result is that there are probably no two projects in Vietnam procured using exactly the same combination of Vietnamese and international standards, which means documentation requires careful scrutiny and checking by bidding contractors.

As the Vietnam construction industry develops, the use of design and build contracts is likely to increase. This trend follows countries like Singapore and Malaysia that have previously taken the path from developing to developed nation status and experiencing a concurrent maturing of the construction industry. This has been evidenced by the use of both the Yellow and Silver Book for selected packages for the forthcoming Ho Chi Minh City metro project for specialist systems.

The use of FIDIC in Vietnam poses a number of important challenges and issues that need to be addressed in order for the FIDIC forms to be used effectively and efficiently as a tool for delivering construction projects to time, quality and cost objectives.

Firstly, the FIDIC Red Book not actually being drafted as a lump sum contract. The use of lump sum contracts and indeed the term *lump sum* is often widely misconstrued between both the legal profession and lay parties users of the contract. In order to successfully use a lump sum approach, drafters need to pay close attention to the intended definition and application of the lump sum. There is no internationally accepted lump sum definition and often the contract wording inaccurately conveys the drafter's intent possibly leading to claims and disputes. Local laws also differ between countries on the definition and application of lump sum contracts adding to the challenges surrounding understanding and usage.

Another difference in approach is that penalties are allowable but capped under the commercial law of Vietnam and need to be inserted into the contract in order to be enforced. This is contrary to the common law notion that penalties are not admissible in a contract. Contractors therefore need to be aware of the Employer's remedies both under the terms of the contract and at law.

Given the occurrence of global and local price spikes and shortages and other factors impacting cost increases, cost reimbursement clauses are an important issue on all construction projects in Vietnam. The FIDIC forms (like many contracts) rely on the use of indices to settle claims for cost reimbursement for increases in the price of labor, materials, and plant. In reality, the construction indices in Vietnam are not always robust or reliable enough to be used as a contractual mechanism to provide an appropriate level of compensation. This has resulted in a number of claims for inadequacy of indices in providing compensation and claims being based on the use of proxy indices instead of the indices stated in the contract on the basis that they provide "fairer" relief to the claimant.

Against this backdrop and the very nature of the construction industry claims and disputes are not uncommon in Vietnam.

Vietnam's policy makers have recognized the need for a high level of investor confidence in order to attract foreign direct investment and have among other initiatives ratified the New

York Convention in 1995, which recognizes the enforcement of arbitral awards given outside of Vietnam's territory limits but falling under Vietnam's legal jurisdiction.

The Vietnam government also first passed the Arbitration Ordinance in 2003 and was later replaced by the Law on Commercial Arbitration in 2010 aimed at encouraging dispute resolution by arbitration. The law recognizes that foreign parties may require arbitrations to be held in another country with foreign arbitrators. It is not uncommon for Hong Kong International Arbitration Center or Singapore International Arbitration Center or International Chamber of Commerce rules and facilities to be used for arbitrations especially when one party is a foreign entity.

Disputes between the involved parties may be settled by arbitral tribunal organized by a local arbitration center such as the Financial and Commercial Center for Arbitration (FCCA), Vietnam International Arbitration Center (VIAC), or through ad hoc arbitration set up by the parties involved.

A local arbitral tribunal will usually be composed of one or more arbitrators as agreed by the disputing parties. If the parties cannot agree on the number of arbitrators, the arbitral tribunal will be composed of three arbitrators.

Foreign arbitral awards will usually be upheld in Vietnam but incapacity or invalidity of the arbitration agreement and contravention of the mandatory laws of Vietnam are grounds for not upholding awards.

In summary, the FIDIC drafters objectives when drafting the 1999 "rainbow suite" envisioned its widespread use across common and civil law jurisdictions and that the suite would be the preferred contract of choice especially where no local standard form of contract exists. To an extent this has been achieved but certainly parties and users need to be aware of the common pitfalls when using the FIDIC forms in Vietnam.

David A.R. Lockwood FRICS, MCIArb, LLM (Dist) BSc (Hons) PGDip Arb
Contracts Advisor
C7 Consultant Services Co. Ltd
Vietnam

The use of FIDIC forms in Kazakhstan by Artyushenko Andrey (Kazakhstan)

FIDIC contracts are used in Kazakhstan in the construction of facilities on a "turnkey" basis, for example, social projects like sport, education, health care, in general for infrastructure projects and production facilities, and so on. Especially when it is important for the employer to achieve a certain result, control financial issues and ensure the subsequent effective operation of the constructed facility for years. The government, when acting as employer, often faces the situation when a facility constructed by local one-day contractors loses quality in operation after a short period of time. It is almost impossible to make the contractor fix failures, because of the fly-by-night nature of such companies. Or they simply do not have enough skills to do this work.

To address these issues, in particular, the Kazakhstan's Ministry of Transport and Communications as from 2006 has repeatedly recommended hiring contractors and engineers under the FIDIC forms when tendering for road and infrastructure construction. This has resulted in large international construction firms with adequate qualification and experience taking part in the bids. One important point for them to note is that construction contracts procured under FIDIC forms could be governed by the laws of the Republic of Kazakhstan if the parties wish so.

Here I will try to outline some features of the Kazakhstan national laws related to the construction, directly set forth in the legislation, which are often mandatory. If a construction contract is signed based on the FIDIC and it is governed by the laws of the Republic of Kazakhstan, the lawyers from other jurisdictions should pay special attention to imperative and dispositive national legislation norms. If it is mandatory norm of law then whatever you will put in the contract such mandatory norm prevails.

Terminology

The term "construction on a turnkey basis" is established in the Civil Code of the Republic of Kazakhstan. It differs from what Russian Federation has in its civil code. There is no "turnkey" legal terminology in Russia.

In the Republic of Kazakhstan in turnkey construction contracts, the contractor takes all obligations of the construction and maintenance of a facility and delivers it to the employer in a condition ready for operation, according to the contractual terms and provisions.

This means that the contractor undertakes within the time for completion, by order of the employer, a certain facility or perform other construction operations. The employer undertakes to create the necessary conditions for the contractor to do the work, deliver its result and pay the lump sum for it.

Structure of FIDIC forms

The structure of FIDIC forms of construction contracts suggests that the contract represents the text on one page (named the contract agreement), indicating a project name, the names of the parties, and the agreement in principle of the parties on implementation of some work. The scope of work, the name of the facility, term, total cost, and payment procedure are specified in annexes to *the contract* and other documentation. This approach is contrary to the imperative norms of the Republic of Kazakhstan, since it is mandatory to specify *essential conditions* of the contract in the contract itself. In this regard, it is mandatory to cover all these essential conditions in the contract itself, not only in annexes, means in contract agreement.

The second issue with the FIDIC structure is that we do not recommend binding the contract with the tendering documentation. All *essential conditions* should be strictly written in the contract, without referring to the tendering documentation.

Risk

The risk of accidental appreciation of the works rests with the contractor. It is imperative with some exclusions. The contractor is entitled to demand a revision of the estimates if, due to circumstances beyond its control, the cost of works exceeds the estimate by at least 10%. In other words, if such excess is say 3% or 9%, and the need to increase the cost of works was caused by business risks of the contractor, then the contractor is not entitled to demand any revision of the cost of works under the contract.

The contract may contain a clause allocating all possible construction risks to the contractor. These construction risks include, for example, the cost of restoration work caused by *force majeure*. To avoid the application under Kazakhstan law of such broad interpretation, it is necessary to know it when drafting the particular conditions of the FIDIC contract.

Once the employer accepts the interim stages (parts) of works, it shall bear the risk of any loss or damage caused not through the fault of the contractor. This includes cases where the contract places the risk of performance of the works on the contractor.

Transfer of a construction site to the contractor

As a mandatory provision (Sub-Clause 2.1): *The Employer shall give the Contractor right of access to and possession of, all parts of the Site within the time (or times) stated in the "Particular Conditions." The right and possession may not be exclusive to the Contractor.* With this, the mechanism of transferring the construction site is limited to the simple signing of the acceptance certificate. However, in practice, the availability of such an acceptance certificate is not enough, and by virtue of Kazakh legislation, we recommend that the transfer of the construction site is under a separate contract (e.g., the Trust Deed). The text of such a "Trust Deed" shall be part of the binding documents and the part of the FIDIC contract documents as annex.

Additional work

If, during the course of construction, the contractor finds out there is a need for additional work not covered by the design and estimate documentation, and that this would increase the estimated cost, then it has to inform the employer. There are terms in the FIDIC forms that already cover such issues, but you will have to correct them by particular conditions taking into account the following Republic of Kazakhstan imperative norms.

If the contractor fails to get a response to its request from the employer within 10 days (another term can be provided by the FIDIC particular conditions), it may suspend the relevant work, with the allocation of losses caused by downtime at the expense of the employer.

If the contractor fails to perform its obligation to inform the employer of the need for additional work and resultant increase in estimated cost, it shall not be entitled to demand that the employer pay for additional work and compensation. However, the stipulation does not apply if the contractor has proved the need for immediate action done in the employer's interest where suspension of work could lead to the destruction or damage of the facility under construction.

If the employer agrees the additional work to be executed by the contractor and agrees to pay for it, the contractor is entitled to refuse to perform these works, but only in cases when the work is beyond the scope of its professional activities or cannot be performed due to reasons beyond its control.

Control and oversight by the employer

The employer is entitled under the Kazakhstan law to exercise control and oversight of the progress and quality of work performed; the compliance with the deadlines and schedules; the quality of materials provided by the contractor, as well as the correct use by the contractor of the employer's materials; while not interfering with the contractor's activities. In recent changes of Kazakh legislation, there are some obligatory terms for parties and the engineer. Thus I would recommend specifying such control in detail in the FIDIC particular conditions. It is important that the control exercised by the employer does not hinder the contractors work.

If, while exercising its right to control and oversight of the works, the employer reveals any deviations from the terms and conditions of the contract which may impair the quality of works, or other shortcomings, it shall immediately inform the contractor. If employer fails to inform the contractor, it will lose its right in the future to refer to the shortcomings. Such limitations contradict some fundamental points when using, for example, the FIDIC Red Book or Silver Book. Proper work with FIDIC particular conditions will help you to solve this issue.

The employer is obligated to provide the technical supervision and author supervision companies with proper conditions for work execution. It is not specified what exactly conditions should be provided as a minimum. We recommend to frame it by particular conditions.

The employer is obliged to ensure the execution of the prescriptions issued by the state architectural and construction control and supervision bodies during the construction. Need to add the particular conditions with the mechanisms for that or equal some existing obligations in FIDIC as a performing of such mandatory Kazakh law terms.

Permits and approvals

As a mandatory provision (imperative in Kazakhstan), the employer must arrange all necessary permits and approvals, thus all risks with this are on the employer. It is impossible to refer it to contractor in full. In the FIDIC particular conditions or in general construction contracts usually employer links the obligation to get all necessary permits and approvals to the contractor. We recommend that the employer shall provide assistance to the contractor (upon request) in the obtaining of local permits and approvals, also in the delivery of a notice to the authorized body as to the start of the construction, among others. Under Kazakh law, the obligations for obtaining construction permits and approvals, and sending notifications are the employer's obligations.

Time frames for receiving necessary design documentation approvals from the authorities

Bear in mind here that such procedures in Kazakhstan could take longer than usually required. In particular for parties that are working in Kazakhstan for the first time.

Consultancy fees under the white book

As a mandatory provision of the FIDIC forms of contract, consultancy fees tend not to be fixed or paid in one lump sum. However, for state-run companies and quite often many other companies in Kazakhstan this approach is not always acceptable (for state-run companies it is prohibited). In this regard, consultancy fees should be the lump sum, or at least should have the maximum possible amount.

Employer's personnel terminology

The term "employer's personnel" (in the Red Book): *means the Engineer, the assistants referred to in Sub-Clause 3.2 and all other staff, labour and employees of the Engineer and of the Employer; and any other personnel notified to the Contractor, by the Employer or the Engineer, as Employer's Personnel.*

This term should be translated carefully into Russian because an incorrect translation could mean that it is unlikely to meet the Labor Code of Kazakhstan. Employer is applicable only within the labor legislation. In construction, it is the "client" or the "customer," based on the Kazakh Civil Code.

FIDIC's concept is that the term **"employer's personnel"** does not only refer to those employed on a permanent basis (not the services but the employment contract) by the employer, but also those engaged by the employer as subcontractors.

Common law clauses

Such terms like **"reasonable efforts", "applicable", "acceptable"**, are common clauses used in English law contracts that are often not commonly used or recognised terms in Kazakh law. Thus, we recommend that particular attention is made on explaining these terms to your partner in Kazakhstan to clarify in the FIDIC particular conditions what is meant by this phraseology, as in some cases, it is better to determine these common terms in a more detailed way.

Language

Sub-Clause 5.2 ("Silver Book") states: *Unless otherwise stated in the Employer's Requirements, the Contractor's Documents shall be written in the language for communications defined in Sub-Clause 1.4.*

It is mandatory (imperative in Kazakhstan) to identify the need of the *technical, as-built,* and other *documentation* to be in the Russian language. In some regions of Kazakhstan, it should be in Kazakh language as well. Otherwise, there could be suspensions and delays for passing some obligatory state construction procedures and control stages. If parties have decided that documents should be submitted in two or more languages then we recommend parties identify the language of priority.

Building registration in authorities as a real estate

The contractor is liable for the construction and its results to comply with local Kazakhstan construction requirements.

The contractor is liable for any failure to reach performance indicators specified in the design and estimate documentation, including indicators such as production capacity.

It is very important that international contractors know how to comply with the building codes, construction rules, and regulations in Kazakhstan. These codes and regulations govern both common approaches to construction and individual aspects, depending on the particular type and place of work.

Recent changes in Kazakh law

As from the end of 2014, the construction legislation in Kazakhstan is changing a lot. We will point some major items, which are already changing the construction market in Kazakhstan:

- As from 2015 it is possible to apply Eurocodes in construction (instead of Soviet Union SNIPs, construction rules established in Soviet Union). It is a part of construction regulation reform that includes: 2011 to 2014 Eurocodes adaptation period, 2015 to 2020 Eurocodes and Kazakhstan construction terms and rules jointly application period, 2021 to 2025 the

generalization of application and adjustment of the new regulatory framework. It means that Kazakhstan is planning to construct under Eurocodes rules only, approximately after 2025 (all Soviet Union construction rules will not be applicable).
- The role of the engineer in the construction has increased as from 2015. Previously there was no project management, financial control rights and other things already existing in FIDIC.
- Now almost all construction specialists, including engineers, design developers, technical control specialists, are obligated to pass a local (Kazakhstan based) attestation (to prove their qualification) to work on construction projects in Kazakhstan. There is an online available database where it is possible to check the list of people passed the attestation.
- As from 2016 there is no state commissioning of the constructed objects. The commissioning procedure becomes easier and faster.
- As from 2016 the state is not responsible for the construction quality. Previously, the commission for building commissioning consist of local city administration (in charge), the employer, the contractor, local construction control authority, other related state authorities, and public utilities suppliers. In case of building collapse, the first responsible person going to prison was the city administration chief who has signed the final commissioning act, then head of local construction control authority. Now it is the employer, project design developers and then the contractor who will be responsible for such building collapse or any other damages.
- Before 2015, around 80% of all projects constructed in Kazakhstan was under the obligation to pass the state construction expertise. As from the 2015, the state is planning to decrease the quantity of projects that are obligatory for state construction expertise. This should be done in several steps. And at this moment les projects are obligatory for state construction expertise.

Andrey Artyushenko, Managing Partner
Artyushenko & Partners
Republic of Kazakhstan

12.6 FIDIC forms of contract

At present, the most popular FIDIC sample conditions of contract are those published in the 1999 first edition. In particular:

(a) *Conditions of Contract for Construction* (abbreviated as "CONS" or the "Red Book"), being the conditions with well-balanced risk allocation and intended for projects where the risks associated with the design are to be borne mainly by the employer. CONS are the contractual conditions for the design-bid-build (DBB) delivery method. It is common in such arrangements that the employer (their designer) prepares a detailed design including the bill of quantities, specifications, and drawings for the purpose of the tender (terms of reference). The contractor evaluates the rates and prices of the tender bill of quantities. Works are measured on the basis of actually completed works, using the fixed rates and prices. Contract administration is done by the Engineer.

(b) *Conditions of Contract for Plant and Design-Build* (abbreviated as P&DB or the "Yellow Book"), being the conditions with well-balanced risk allocation and intended for use in design-build (DB) projects where risks associated with design are to be borne mainly by the contractor. Unlike CONS, P&DB does not use the employer's detailed design for the purpose of the tender (terms of reference). These come from the "employer's requirements," which define, above all, the purpose, scope, standard, performance and other criteria, depending on the employer's expectations and priorities. The employer's requirements are not assumed to contain exhaustive details. The contractor shall prepare their proposal based on the employer's requirements to become part of the contract. Even though the contract price is taken as a lump sum price, it may be subject to modifications through variations and claims raised for additional payments and extensions of time. Contract administration is done by the engineer.

(c) *Conditions of Contract for EPC/Turnkey Projects* (Engineer, Procure, and Construct, abbreviated as EPC or EPCT or the "Silver Book") are intended for DB projects where most of the risks are allocated to the contractor. These risks are typically associated with design, site conditions, and complications affecting time and price. This form is recommended where entire investment sets (such as nuclear power plants) are to be contracted out and where the requirement is to secure, more reliably, total price and completion time. It also applies to EPC that the price is taken as a lump sum. Works are not measured, but they can become subject to modification through variations and a limited number of claims raised for additional payment and extensions of time. Contract administration is done by the employer or their representative.

It is necessary to be able to distinguish between P&DB and EPC conditions. FIDIC discusses cases and circumstances when it is recommended applying P&DB conditions in practice. These are as follows:

- Insufficient time or information for bidders to scrutinize and check the employer's requirements or for them to carry out their own designs, risk assessment studies, and estimations.
- If construction will involve substantial underground work or will take place in other areas that bidders cannot inspect.
- If the employer intends to closely supervise or control the contractor's work, or to review most of the design.
- If the amount of each interim payment is to be certified by a contract administrator or other intermediary.

FIDIC has published many other forms of contract and documents including the Short form of Contract or the "Green Book." These are contractual conditions intended for construction works which are of small value or straightforward. Furthermore, there are the "*Conditions of Subcontract for Construction*," that is, a construction subcontract, issued by FIDIC in 2009 for use in combination with CONS.

For DB projects where an operation period is needed, FIDIC prepared *Conditions of Contract for Design, Build and Operate Projects* (abbreviated as DBO or the "Gold Book") in 2008 (first edition). This form reflects the trend that contractors not only construct but also maintain and operate the facility for some time.

FIDIC has also published a client/consultant *model services agreement* in the fourth edition in 2006 (the "White Book") and the model representative agreement in the first edition in 2013 (the "Purple Book").

The terms of the model representative agreement are intended for consultants wishing to enter into a contract with a representative to provide representative services.

Journey to the "kitchen" of FIDIC: How FIDIC publications are produced by Husni Madi (Jordan)

Introduction

The Fédération International des Ingénieurs-Conseils (FIDIC) is world-renowned for its excellently crafted General Conditions of Contract, in addition to its other publications.

FIDIC drafts its General Conditions of Contract based on fair and balanced risk/reward allocation between the Employer and the Contractor, bearing in mind the wide applicability in all legal jurisdictions around the world.

As such, the FIDIC General Conditions of Contract has become the hallmark of standard forms of contract, so much so that Employers often opt to use FIDIC General Conditions of Contract to attract more bidders and reduce the tender prices. This is because FIDIC Conditions of Contract are familiar to contractors, whom in turn need not to include high contract risk contingencies into their bids.

Nevertheless, little is known about the huge efforts and the intricate processes behind the production of the publications of the FIDIC Contracts Committee (typically General Conditions of Contract, and the various Contract/Agreement Forms). In the following paragraphs, an attempt has been made to unfold what takes place behind the scenes, and the unknown soldiers responsible for the drafting of the said several FIDIC publications; from its inception until it reaches the hands of the users.

Procedure

The people

The FIDIC Contracts Committee (CC) is responsible for the drafting of all of the FIDIC General Conditions of Contract and the various Contract/Agreement Forms, by mandating several Task Groups (TG) to draft the different FIDIC CC's publications. TGs can be thought of as sub-committees of the CC assigned a certain task.

The CC and the TGs are composed of volunteers operating on a voluntary basis for FIDIC. The TGs are required to report back to the CC, which in turn reports to the FIDIC Executive Committee (EC).

The TG members are nominated by the CC. Usually, TGs choose from among its own members the TG leader, and the principal drafter. The establishment of the TGs and its membership are subject to the approval of the EC.

The TG leader is mainly responsible for the administrative matters including communication with the CC's Liaison Person. An important role of the TG leader is to ensure that the time program, and deadlines are met by the TG. The principal drafter's main responsibility is the drafting of the vast majority of the prospective form of contract for onward review by the other TG members, the CC, and others.

The inception phase

After the appointment of the TG members, they are presented with the Terms of Reference (TOR) from the CC. The TOR is simply a document prepared by the CC, which identifies in full detail the TG's objectives, and mandate, together with the procedures, time program, and deadlines to be followed by the TG in order to achieve its task.

Generally, the TG kicks off with a face-to-face meeting for its members and the CC's Liaison Person, to make sure that the TG members perfectly understand their task, and to brainstorm on how the TG intends to tackle its mandate.

The Inception Phase is concluded with an Inception Report containing the TG's view on the methodology it intends to follow in order for it to achieve its mandate and objectives. Basically, the skeleton of the TG's work from now onward is established in this report. The Inception Report is submitted to the CC for its review.

The drafting phase

After the receipt of the CC's comments on the Inception Report, the TG starts with the drafting process after taking the said comments and directives into consideration.

This is preceded by compiling all of the comments, observations, suggestions, and current best practices from across the construction industry around the world, and deciding on its relevance to the prospective publication. This is essential in making sure that the prospective publication would provide the users with the most up to date best practices.

Naturally, further enhancements on the contents of the Inception Report are introduced, in addition to the CC's said comments. It is in this stage that the bulk of the drafting work takes place, and the TG's mandated deliverable starts to take its final shape.

The Drafting Phase ends with the submission of the A-Draft by the TG to the CC within the stipulated deadline, for the CC's review. The A-Draft is in essence the first draft of the TG's deliverable as mandated by the TOR.

The review phase

The Review Phase starts with the CC's review of the A-Draft. After concluding its review, the CC relays its comments on the A-Draft to the TG, for the latter's examination and consideration.

The TG in turn takes the CC's comments on the A-Draft into consideration, and possibly some enhancements by the TG, to produce the B-Draft.

Now the B-Draft is not reviewed by the CC, rather it shall be reviewed by the Special Advisors. The Special Advisors are highly respected senior experts and permanent FIDIC contributors such as CC ex-members, or other persons of the same caliber.

The C-Draft is produced after the receipt of the Special Advisors' comments on the B-Draft, and the TG's attendance to such comments. The C-Draft is then transmitted to Friendly Reviewers for their comments and feedback.

Friendly Reviewers are expert professionals from within the FIDIC family whom are not involved in the drafting of the reviewed document, where their views and opinions are well-heard and respected. Friendly Reviewers are considered as peer reviewers performing an internal review of the draft publication in question.

The TG compiles the comments received from the Friendly Reviewers for examination, and caters to those appropriate comments it decides to take on-board. This process will yield the D-Draft.

Thereafter, the D-Draft is transmitted to the Legal Advisors for their legal review. Similar to the EC, the CC, the TG, Special Advisors, and Friendly Reviewers the Legal Advisors conduct their legal review on a volunteering basis. Those legal advisors are internationally recognized lawyers who frequently contribute to FIDIC's publications.

The purpose of this legal review is to make sure that the end FIDIC CC's publications are legally sound, and are in compliance with most of the legal jurisdictions most of the time, as it is nearly impossible to take into account all of the legal jurisdictions around the world.

Finally, the TG updates Draft-D in light of the Legal Advisors' comments to produce the Final Draft for onward submission to the EC via the CC. The final approval of the TG deliverables, and whether or not to publish such deliverables rests with the EC. The EC will of course take the CC's recommendations into consideration during the EC's review to arrive at its final decision.

The publishing phase

After the EC's approval has been secured, it is the FIDIC Secretariat that assumes the responsibility of publishing the approved FIDIC CC's publication. The FIDIC Secretariat will perform the processes of the graphic design, pre-printing, printing, and binding of the hard copies. Afterward, the Secretariat will handle the sale of the soft and hard copies of the approved FIDIC CC's publication to the public.

Thereafter, the publication takes a life of its own where FIDIC starts collecting feedback from users across the construction industry worldwide. These feedback, comments, observations, and suggestions are taken very seriously by FIDIC, for it shall provide an invaluable input for the future update of this publication after being in use for a number of years.

This is an important aspect of FIDIC CC's publications, where these publications are progressively evolving to reflect actual experience and state of the art best practices.

In conclusion, from the forgoing brief description of the processes behind the production of the various FIDIC CC's publications, one can immediately recognize the tremendous efforts and care that are put into each single FIDIC publication. Therefore, the usual critical acclaim with which FIDIC CC's publications are received, should come to no surprise to anyone.

Husni Madi, PMP, PMI-SP
Chairman of FIDIC Task Group TG15
FIDIC International Accredited Trainer
FIDIC Affiliate Member
Friendly Reviewer of FIDIC Updates

Founder, Chief Executive Officer
Shura Construction Management
Amman, Jordan

12.7 The structure of the contract under FIDIC forms

The main structure of the contract is defined in Sub-Clause 1.5 (1999 edition). Documents forming part of the contract are to be taken as mutually explanatory of one another. For the purposes of interpretation, the weights of the individual documents are determined in this sub-clause. If any ambiguity or discrepancy is found in the documents, the engineer shall issue any necessary clarification or instruction. The specific parts and details as found in particular forms are described below.

12.7.1 Particular conditions

FIDIC recommends that their forms be subdivided into general and particular sections. In the "particular section," there should be provisions in respect of the specifics of a particular project, employer, lender or of a given governing law. The general section should be left unchanged. This approach (i.e., the use of two separate sections) is practical and purposeful because it is quite obvious how the general part within a particular tender may have been changed. As an annex to individual forms, FIDIC forms include elaborated guidelines for preparing these particular conditions, giving comments and instructions (including alternative wordings) on how to modify the individual articles of the general part.

Supplementing CONS and P&DB, other practical information appears in a specific document called the "appendix to tender," namely:

- Name and address of the employer
- Name and address of the contractor
- Name and address of the engineer
- Time for completion
- Defects notification period
- Systems of electronic transmission
- Governing law
- Official language
- Language for communications
- Time for access to the site
- Amount of performance security
- Normal working hours
- Lump sum for delay damages
- Provisional sums
- Adjustment for changes in costs
- Total advance payment
- Number and timing of instalments
- Currencies and their fluctuation
- Percentages of retention
- Currency of payment
- Insurance policy submission dates
- Dispute adjudication board

Some other items are facultative. There is no appendix to tender under EPC. The 2017 edition distinguish two parts of particular conditions. Part A is newly called

"Contract data" and Part B "Special provisions". Part A is in fact an extended version of the appendix to tender as known in the 1999 edition.

12.7.2 Employer's requirements

As per P&DB and EPC, the contractor is, in principle, responsible for the design, workmanship and sequencing of the works. When completed, the work must meet its intended purpose as required by contract—namely, the employer's requirements and the contractor's proposal. Under EPC, the contractor's position is more complicated, as the employer's requirements are considered to have been "scrutinized" in detail by the contractor prior to base date (Sub-Clause 5.1). Exceptions to this rule are described in the same sub-clause. With P&DB, the contractor is under less pressure, being allowed to notify the engineer of an error in the employer's requirements, with potential claims for an additional payment or extensions of time for completion.

According to Sub-Clause 1.1.1.5, "Employer's Requirements" means the document entitled "employer's requirements," as included in the contract. Any additions and/or modifications to such a document must be in accordance with the contract. The contract must specify the purpose, scope and/or design and technical criteria for the works. The employer's requirements shall specify the parts of the works to be designed by the contractor, and the criteria its design must meet (e.g., the dimensions, shape, technical specifications, and standards). Particular methods of construction should not form a part of the employer's requirements. They should remain within the responsibilities of the contractor who shall then submit them, in compliance with Sub-Clause 8.3, as a part of its time schedule. The purpose of this procedure is to allow the engineer to have oversight of the construction processes and to minimize the possibility of their actions adversely affecting the intended purpose of the works.

Employers often use excessively detailed designs as part of the terms of reference, thus restricting the contractor's options to propose alternative solutions and sometimes better methods of realization, even though the design-build concept works best with less detailed employer's requirements. Nevertheless, it is vital for the employer's requirements to clearly define the standards of material, workmanship, aesthetic/functional requirements, performance, and other criteria.

The employer's requirements constitute one of the most important documents to form part of the contract, and it is the responsibility of the employer to make sure the document is complete in all respects when the tender documents are sent out to bidders. In this document the employer gives their precise requirements for the completed works, including all matters in the various clauses of the contract which makes reference to the employer's requirements, and all matters which they wishes to include, even if not covered in the general conditions. In particular, the employer must clearly state the purpose of the works so that the contractor can ensure the works are "fit for the purposes for which the works are intended" (FIDIC, 2011a).

12.7.3 Contractor's proposal

"*Contractor's proposal*" means the document entitled "Proposal," which the contractor submits with the letter of tender, as included in the contract (Sub-Clause 1.1.1.7 P&DB). Such a document may include the contractor's preliminary design.

With EPC, the contractor's design is an expected part of the contractor's letter of tender. Stipulating the priority of the documents, Sub-Clause 1.5 requires the contractor's proposal be located behind the employer's requirements.

The purpose of the contractor's proposal is to provide the employer with a detailed description of how the contractor intends to perform the works in compliance with the contract and employer's requirements.

12.7.4 Drawings

Drawings constitute a fundamental part of the contract whenever CONS is used. According to Sub-Clause 1.1.1.6, "*Drawings*" mean the drawings of the works, as included in the contract and any additional and modified drawings issued or approved by (or on behalf of) the employer in accordance with the contract. As per Sub-Clause 1.9 of CONS, if the contractor suffers delay and/or incurs costs as a result of a failure of the engineer to issue the notified drawing or instruction within a reasonable time, the contractor may notify its claim for additional payment and/or extension of time for completion.

12.7.5 Bill of quantities and specifications

According to Sub-Clause 1.1.1.10, "*Bill of Quantities*" is the document so named (if any) located in the schedules. According to the *Dictionary of Construction Terms* (Tolson, 2012), the bill of quantities is:

> [A] written document which provides a detailed description of the quantity and quality of the works to be carried out on a project broken down into sections. They are typically prepared in accordance with an agreed standard method of measurement, and their principal purpose is to enable the contractor to prepare his tender sum. The contractor provides either a specific price for each item listed, or alternatively a rate for a quantity of work or materials.

The specifications are defined in Sub-Clause 1.1.1.5 of CONS as the document entitled "*Specifications*," as included in the contract, and any additions and modifications to the specification in accordance with the contract. Such a document specifies the works.

As per Sub-Clause 12.2 (b), the method of measurement shall be in accordance with the bill of quantities or other applicable schedules. To avoid disputes between the parties, it is recommended that the method used to prepare the bill of quantities is published. In the case of CONS, it is vital that the employer prepares the basic design for the tender. The specifications and bill of quantities should, therefore, allow the contractor to confidently offer a price covering the full scope of necessary works to be done.

When using CONS, the employer should be aware of the fact that the bid price (the accepted contract amount) will be modified to match changes in the amount of works necessary to be done (as under individual items of the bill of quantities) based on the certification and re-measurement made by the engineer. The 2017 edition uses also a more general term schedule of rates and prices for price breakdowns mainly in connection with lump sum price.

12.8 Conditions of contract for construction (CONS)—1999 Red Book

The conditions of contract for construction for building and engineering works designed by the employer ("CONS"), or the "Red Book" are the most frequently used of all the FIDIC forms. The abbreviation is a derivative of the word "construction."

Even today, previous versions of this book are still used in practice, for example, the fourth edition (1987) Red Book. This book is significantly out of date and its use is no longer recommended. The CONS were revised and republished in 2005, 2006, and 2010. Practitioners may come across the "CONS MDB" often referred to as the "Pink Book." In 2017 a new second edition was published with almost the same structure and philosophy.

12.8.1 Structure of CONS

A contract agreement on its own is a very simple document and usually only deals with the price and content of the contractual relationship. Much of the detail is contained in attachments referred to in the contract agreement. The hierarchy in respect of the legal weight and priority of these attachments are interpreted in accordance with Sub-Clause 1.5.

The documents forming the contract are to be taken as mutually explanatory of one another. For the purposes of interpretation, the priority of the documents shall be in accordance with the following sequence:

1. the Contract Agreement (if any)
2. the Letter of Acceptance
3. the Letter of Tender
4. the Particular Conditions
5. the General Conditions
6. the Specifications
7. the Drawings
8. the Schedules and any other documents forming part of the contract.

If an ambiguity or discrepancy is found in the documents, the engineer shall issue any necessary clarifications or instructions.

In their general section, the CONS (the same as P&DB and EPC) make use of a clearly structured compilation of 20 chapters. These chapters are further broken down into sub-clauses. The first chapter contains general provisions and definitions. Chapters 2 to 5 define the participants and explain the status of the employer, the engineer, the contractor, and the nominated subcontractors. Chapter 6 deals with the working conditions of the staff and labor in general (including labor law), health, and safety. Chapter 7 addresses performance in respect of the plants and materials (including quality control); in Chapters 8 to 11, solutions for realization aspects are discussed, in particular those dealing with commencement, delays, suspensions of work, tests on completion, taking over of the works, and defects liability issues. Contract price, variations, and payment conditions are dealt with in Chapters 12 to 14. Chapters 15 and 16 deal with termination of the contract and suspension of works. Chapters 17 to 19 include key provisions regarding risk allocation in connection with insurance and *force majeure*. The last chapters deal with claims, disputes, and arbitration when CONS include all necessary documents for the appointment of the dispute adjudication board, including procedural rules.

The particular conditions contain guidance for their preparation, followed by sample documents such as a letter of tender, an appendix to tender, contract agreement, performance security, and guarantees for advance payment and to remedy defects and an ADR clause (dispute adjudication agreement).

The contract agreement includes specifications and drawings where CONS is used.

Misapplications of FIDIC contracts in the United Arab Emirates by Kamal Adnan Malas (United Arab Emirates)

Over the past 10 years, the United Arab Emirates have proven themselves internationally to be one of the most rapidly developing countries in the construction field. Large infrastructure projects and high-rise buildings together with thousands of villas have been constructed to a high standard in a very short period.

In 2013, Dubai won its bid to host EXPO 2020, which will provide fresh fuel to the construction industry "fire" in the UAE.

As there is not a unique, typical form of construction contract in the UAE, the engineers (i.e., consulting engineering offices who have a license and accreditation from the municipality to perform engineering works) use various types of construction contracts (around 100 forms); including the FIDIC forms of contracts.

We have noticed in the past 10 years that the FIDIC Red Book (1987 edition) is the most used FIDIC form for construction works in the UAE. Some engineers use the FIDIC 1999 suit of contracts but the FIDIC 1987 Red Book still prevails.

Through our expertise in the state courts as court-appointed experts and arbitrators, we noticed that the engineers were not applying FIDIC forms of contracts properly. There are misapplications of FIDIC contracts initiated by the engineer who prepares the tender and the contract conditions in a way to suit their needs, wants and control of the project. This minimizes contractor bargaining power and increases control by the engineer and the employer. For legal reasons, this is sometimes to their detriment. We will explain in the following text some major misapplications of the FIDIC 1987 Red Book that were encountered in the UAE. As a result we conclude that these kinds of biased contracts which are departing from the original form of FIDIC are not useful for all parties.

The engineer cancelled the priority of documents (clause 5.2)

- The Engineer cancelled the Priority of Documents (Clause 5.2): The FIDIC 1987 Red Book Clause 5.2 states that the priority of documents is as follows:
  1. The Contract Agreement (if completed)
  2. The Letter of Acceptance
  3. The Tender
  4. Part II of these Conditions
  5. Part I of these Conditions and
  6. Any other document forming part of the Contract.

The engineer deleted Clause 5.2 from the contract so that the priority of documents was not known. In case of discrepancies between the documents (which is common), disputes arise because of the different views of the engineer and the contractor. This ultimately leads to arbitration or litigation.

The decision and positions of the arbitrators are hard to predict and may be contrary to the engineer's and the employer's because the arbitrators have the freedom to choose the priority of documents. This situation was created originally by the engineer's misunderstanding of the importance of stating the priority of documents and how this clause is applied under the law of the country where the construction is taking place. In the UAE, arbitrators are free to apply such priority of documents if they think it fits the case they are handling. They may use the original priority stated in the FIDIC general conditions or they may apply their own priority if they, for example, consider the period which was granted to the tenderers to be too short to verify all tender documents and discover all discrepancies.

The engineer cancelled the maximum variation cap (clause 51.1)

In another example, the engineer cancelled the maximum variation cap (Clause no. 51.1). In the FIDIC Red Book, the variation cap is 15% (positive or negative). The engineer deleted this cap provision, presuming that by cancelling the variation cap, he could order as much variation as he wants.

The consequences are often the opposite to his intention because, as per UAE law, the scope of work is fixed to what is agreed in the contract and the variation needs now to be negotiated with the contractor and the price has to be mutually agreed. This of course will delay the construction process especially if the engineer and the employer are slow in coming to an agreement.

The lack of a variation cap may also affect the employer contract termination. If the employer decides to terminate the contract at his convenience, he will pay the loss of profit to the contractor. The compensation for loss of profit in the UAE is 10% of the non-executed works. In the absence of a variation cap, the employer cannot deduct the totals of compensation for the negative variations from lost profit compensation. If there is a cap percentage for the variations, then the employer and the engineer will first of all order these negative variations (which are usually not more than 25% of the contract price), then they will terminate the contract. In this way they exercise their rights in ordering negative variations and by doing so, they save 2.5% of total contract price.

The taking over certificate (clause 48.3)

The contractor applied for a taking over certificate, the engineer examined the works and issued the list of deficiencies to be corrected. After removing the deficiencies, the contractor applied for a municipality completion certificate. The employer, the engineer, the contractor and the municipality's engineers signed the municipality completion certificate, which included a confirmation that construction works had been completed according to the specifications. The municipality engineers checked the project and determined that the works were acceptable for handing over and they issued the municipality completion certificate.

The works were substantially completed; however, the engineer refused to sign the taking over certificate (as required by the FIDIC contract) on the grounds that there were still some works to be finalized and issued another list of deficiencies.

After finalizing the requested works, the contractor activated the arbitration clause claiming prolongations costs due to engineer's obstructions which are in conflict with the contract.

The fact ignored by the engineer was that the refusal to issue the taking over certificate did not grant the engineer the right to issue another list of deficiencies especially when he had already signed the municipality completion certificate after the deficiencies in the first list had been corrected by the contractor. The engineer's presumption that the municipality completion certificate had no value (because it was not mentioned in the FIDIC contract) was wrong. Moreover, it is usually accepted in arbitration or litigation that the contractor is entitled to be paid the prolongation costs after such obstructions caused by the engineer.

Another negative consequence for the employer is that equipment guarantees last only for a period of 18 months from the date of purchase so that prolongation may lead to expiry of these guarantees before the equipment is even used.

Partial taking over certificate (clause 48.3)

Clause 48.3 of FIDIC Red Book (1987 edition) states:

> If any part of the permanent works has been substantially completed and has satisfactorily passed any tests on completion prescribed by the contract, the engineer may issue a taking-over certificate in respect of that part of the permanent works before completion of the whole of the Works and, upon the issue of such certificate, the contractor shall be deemed to have undertaken to complete with due expedition any outstanding work in that part of the permanent works during the defects liability period.

To explain the misapplication of this clause, let us assume that we have a project consisting of an 80-floor building. At the contractor's request, the engineer issued a taking over certificate for the first 40 floors, which included 400 apartments, without taking over the lifts because the lifts were not completed and they were to be used by the inhabitants of the whole building not only by those living on the first 40 floors. This is a misapplication of Clause 48.3 because the employer cannot benefit from the use of the first 40 floors due to non-operating lifts. The engineer actually put the employer and the contractor in a dilemma when the delay penalties were calculated. The contractor argued that the 40 floors be handed over in time so that the respective delay penalty might be deducted from the total amount of delay penalties on a pro-rata basis. The employer claimed that he could not benefit from the use of the first 40 floors because the lifts were not completed and the tenants could not use their apartments. In the end, because no beneficial use was provided, penalties were imposed without any deductions.

Termination of the contract (clauses 63.1–63.4)

If a project is performed in the UAE and it is governed by UAE Law (Article 267 of UAE Civil Law no. 5/1985 and its amendments), it cannot be terminated by the unilateral will of any party, except if it is expressly allowed by law.

Furthermore, the Dubai Supreme Court issued a ruling allowing unilateral termination of the construction contract by the employer on the basis that the employer will pay the contractor for costs of work done and also compensate the contractor for all loss of profit for the non-executed works.

In practice, however, we are seeing that many engineers are applying the related Clause of FIDIC contracts with the presumption that they (employer and engineer) have the right to terminate the contract without any consequences. They simply send a termination letter to the contractor requesting handing over of the work to the employer and order the contractor to leave all equipment on site until completion of the project by the employer to make the exact, final statement of account between the employer and contractor.

This mere misapplication and misunderstanding of a FIDIC contract will lead to damages claims against the employer. Under UAE Law (Article 879 of the UAE Civil Law no. 5/1985 and its amendments), the contractor is entitled to refuse to hand over the works to the employer if the employer has not paid the contractor's dues. In practice, the contractor will (after receiving the termination letter) conserve the suspended works, "close the entrance" and request the employer to pay the dues. This is of course not mentioned in the original FIDIC contract and the inexperienced employer will circulate the termination letter through his inexperienced engineer without knowing the real consequences which will take place.

Delayed decisions about contractor claims

The engineer refused to decide about the contractor's claims in reasonable time during the construction period by leaving the decisions to the end of the project. The results are: the contractor is entitled to an extension of time due to non-payment of the contractor's claims in reasonable time. This is because of the specific regulation of UAE governing law (Article 247 of UAE Civil Law no. 5/1985 and its amendments). The contractor is also entitled to compensation for the engineer's delay in replying to contractor claims.

Modification of the arbitration clause

The engineer, in an attempt to gain more control, drafted the arbitration clause to read as follows:
   The engineer is the arbitrator and its decisions are binding on both parties.
   The above-mentioned clause shows the misapplication of Clause 67 of the FIDIC Red Book (1987 edition). The engineer is not eligible to be the arbitrator as per UAE law because he is the employer's representative on site (in the UAE the engineer is considered to be the employer's representative on site and, at the same time, (as per UAE law) the arbitrator must be impartial and independent, that is, the engineer cannot be an arbitrator). The above provision is not an arbitration clause and is in fact a specific adjudication point regarding the engineer's determination. However, as per UAE law, the dispute must still be submitted to the engineer in such an arrangement before starting any arbitration proceedings because the above-mentioned engineer's determination is considered as a condition precedent (this step is considered a mandatory condition which must be applied before recourse to arbitration, similarly to the mandatory amicable settlement attempt under the FIDIC forms).
   Two examples of badly drafted arbitration clauses follow:
   In the case of any dispute arising in application of this construction contract, the parties will revert to arbitration and then to the state courts to resolve their disputes.
   All Disputes shall be resolved through arbitration or state courts.
   The above-mentioned clauses are not only a misapplication but are also misleading because one of the parties may revert to state courts, and the other to arbitration to resolve the dispute. This will significantly complicate the dispute resolution procedure.

> **Deleting the DAB section from FIDIC 1999 suite of contracts**
>
> In many cases we noticed that the engineer deleted the DAB section from the wording of FIDIC Red Book (1999 Edition) in order to keep more power during the construction period. The implementation of DAB in the 1999 First Edition of FIDIC forms proved to be effective in reducing disputes and the above-described modification of FIDIC principles is considered a significant misapplication of the FIDIC Red Book (1999 Edition).
>
> Kamal Adnan Malas
> *International Arbitrator*
> *United Arab Emirates*

12.9 Conditions of contract for plant and design-build (P&DB)—1999 Yellow Book

The full name of these conditions is *Conditions of Contract for Construction Plant and Design-Build for Electrical and Mechanical Works and for Building and Engineering Works Designed by the Contractor* (P&DB).

Like CONS, the use of previous versions of the P&DB form, such as the third edition (1987), can still be found. As the third edition is out of date, its use is not recommended. In 2017 a new second edition was published with almost the same structure and philosophy.

12.9.1 Structure of P&DB

As with the CONS, the contract agreement only confirms the price and content of the contractual relationship. Being a simple document in itself, much of the detail is contained in attachments referred to in the contract. The hierarchy in respect of the legal weight and priority of these attachments is interpreted in accordance with Sub-Clause 1.5 as follows:

(a) the Contract Agreement (if any)
(b) the Letter of Acceptance
(c) the Letter of Tender
(d) the Particular Conditions
(e) the General Conditions
(f) the Employer's Requirements
(g) the Schedules
(h) the Contractor's Proposal and any other documents forming part of the Contract.

The structure of the general part of P&DB is identical to CONS but differs in two chapters. The main difference is that the contractor provides the design and the total price of the work is not measured but structured as a lump sum. As such, Chapter 5 does not deal with nominated subcontractors as in the case of CONS, but with the design issues. In other words, with the contractor's obligations in respect of the design, including the design errors which shall be at the contractor's expense as per Sub-Clause 5.8 of P&DB. Chapter 12, which deals with measurement and evaluation in CONS, is omitted and replaced with a chapter which describes the tests after completion.

P&DB also contain all the necessary documents for appointment of the dispute adjudication board and include the procedural rules.

The particular conditions give guidance for their preparation. In the final section, there are sample forms of the letter of tender, contract agreement, performance security, guarantee for advance payment, and guarantee for remedying of defects.

Whenever P&DB is used (because the design is provided by the contractor), the contract agreement will, therefore, include the employer's requirements and contractor's proposal in its attachments.

12.10 Conditions of contract for EPC/Turnkey projects (EPC)—1999 Silver Book

EPC is recommended for all-inclusive delivery, for example, power plants, factories, or other similar facilities where a higher degree of certainty is required for final price and time for completion. The contractor takes full responsibility for the design and performance of the works.

A common feature of contracts of this type is that the contractor provides all designing and engineering, procurement of subcontractors and deliveries, performance of the works and handing over of a complete and ready to operate facility. Unlike other FIDIC books, the EPC form allocates more risk to the contractor. Hence, some problems may be encountered from a legal standpoint if this form is used in countries with European systems of law. In 2017 a new second edition was published with almost the same structure and philosophy.

12.10.1 Structure of EPC

As with CONS and P&DB, the contract agreement alone only specifies the price and content of the contractual relationship. Being a simple document in itself, much of the detail is contained in attachments referred to in the contract. The hierarchy in respect of the legal weight and priority of these attachments is interpreted in accordance with Sub-Clause 1.5 as follows:

(a) the Contract Agreement
(b) the Particular Conditions
(c) the General Conditions
(d) the Employer's Requirements
(e) the Tender and any other documents forming part of the contract.

The structure of the general part of EPC is again identical to CONS (P&DB), but differs from CONS in three chapters. Like P&DB, the contractor provides the design and the contract price is determined as a lump sum. As with P&DB, Chapter 5 does not deal with nominated subcontractors but does deal with design issues. Chapter 12

(Measurement and Evaluation) is again replaced with a chapter which outlines "after completion tests."

The differences between CONS and P&DB can also be found also in Chapter 3. In particular, EPC no longer refers to the role of engineer but to an "employer's representative" as contract administrator.

EPC also includes all the necessary documents for the appointment of the dispute adjudication board as well as the procedural rules.

As with CONS and P&DB, the particular conditions include guidance for their preparation. In the last section, there are sample forms of a letter of tender, the contract agreement, performance security, guarantees for advance payments, and guarantees for remedying defects.

An EPC contract agreement will include the employer's requirements and the contractor's proposal as its attachments.

12.11 Short form of contract—Green Book

The use of a *short form of contract* (the "Green Book") is anticipated in construction works with a relatively small capital value. Depending on the type of work and circumstances, this form may also be appropriate for relatively simple or repeated work of a short duration.

12.11.1 Structure of short form of contract

This form came from CONS, but establishes a much shorter document. Considerably simplified chapters constitute only a basic contract framework for less demanding projects.

12.12 Construction subcontract

In 2010, FIDIC published its *Conditions of Subcontract for Construction* (the "Construction Subcontract"). The use of a construction subcontract can usually be expected where the relationship between the main contractor and employer (the main contract) is based on CONS. This form of construction subcontract works on the principle of transferring most contractor risk to the subcontractor (back to back). Some contract provisions typically encountered in subcontracts originate from civil law jurisdictions. These provisions, however, are not widely used in the common law countries. Take, for example, Sub-Clause 14.6. According to this sub-clause, a contractor may withhold payment from a subcontractor if they (the contractor) have not been duly paid by the employer (pay when paid). Many rights and obligations of sub-contracting parties are copied from the main contract, such as the contractor's right to terminate the contract. Others undergo a natural adaptation, such as the subcontractor's obligation to notify its claim for additional payment or extensions of time for completion. In accordance with Chapter 20, this is a shortened period of 21 days. Submission of claim quantifications must be made within 35 days.

12.12.1 Structure of construction subcontract

A subcontract agreement typically only confirms the price and content of the contractual relationship as expressed in the *main contract*, referring to the documents that constitute the contract with a structure as follows:

(a) Contractor's letter of acceptance
(b) Letter of subcontractor's offer
(c) Particular conditions of subcontract
(d) General conditions of subcontract
(e) Subcontract specification
(f) Subcontract drawings
(g) Subcontract bill of quantities and other schedules of rates and prices in the Subcontract
(h) Other annexes to subcontract.

In its general part, the construction subcontract follows the pattern of 20 chapters broken down into sub-clauses. The first chapter contains general definitions and explanations. Chapter 2 describes the main contract. Chapters 3 to 5 define the parties, that is, the roles of the contractor and of the subcontractor. As in CONS, Chapter 6 deals with the working conditions of technical staff and labor in general; including labor law aspects, health, and safety. Chapter 7 addresses the details in relation to plants and materials (including quality control). In Chapters 8 to 11, problems and suggested solutions involving realization aspects are covered, for example, commencement, delay and suspension of works, tests on completion, taking over of the subcontract works and defects liability. Chapters 12 to 14 deal with subcontract price, variation of subcontract works, and payment conditions. Chapters 15 and 16 specify termination of subcontract and suspension of works. Chapters 17 to 19 contain base provisions concerning risk allocation in connection with insurance and *force majeure*. The last section deals with claims and subcontract dispute resolution.

The particular conditions also contain guidance for their preparation, followed by the related annexes, that is, the documents called particulars of the main contract; scope of subcontract work and schedule of subcontract documents; incentive(s) for early completion, taking over by the contractor and subcontract bill of quantities. Further, there are the documents; "Equipment," "Temporary Works, Facilities and Free-Issue Materials to Be Provided by the Contractor," "Insurances," and the document "Subcontract Program." Further, there are sample forms of the letter of subcontractor's offer, appendices to subcontractor's offer, contractor's letter of acceptance and subcontract agreement.

12.13 Conditions of contract for design, build, and operate (DBO)—Gold Book

The ever-growing need for a document was identified where the contractor would be: (1) responsible not only for the design and realization of the works itself; but also (2) bound to operate the resulting works for a certain period of time after the above-described edition of FIDIC forms (1999) had been published. FIDIC realized that there were various alternatives, but determined in favor of the so-called "greenfield scenario," that is, where there is a brand new construction to be performed. FIDIC have, therefore, prepared the *Conditions of Contract for Design, Build and Operate* projects. This form it not suitable for "brownfield scenario" projects, that is, reconstruction of an existing works (facility) known as *Operate-Design-Build* (ODB).

According to FIDIC, the DBO is typically intended for construction projects in the field of transport and engineering infrastructures where the resulting works will bring a turnover and profit to the employer and where the employer has neither the human resources nor the experience to be able to operate the works on its own and would have to look to hire an external operator.

Feasibility studies in respect of environmental impacts and economic benefits shall be provided by the employer, as well as land, financing, planning permission, and construction permits.

As foreseen by DBO, the contract should be awarded to one contractor only, as one coordinator can then ideally coordinate preparation of the design, realization of the works, quality control, and innovation within the operation period. The contractor shall therefore be responsible for:

1. Design (i.e., for providing the design documents).
2. Build (i.e., realization of construction works).
3. Operate and maintain (i.e., operation service and maintenance of the works).

The DBO sample form presumes that the contractor will operate the works for 20 years. Ownership to the works shall pass to the employer at the start of commissioning. During the operation period, the contractor will operate and maintain the works on the basis of a license. The main advantage of this approach is that the contractor is more motivated to design and build the works in accordance with short-term and long-term goals.

This particular part is of extraordinary significance whenever the FIDIC DBO form is used. Specifics of the works operation period cannot be unified too much, and the individual requirements of those involved in a respective project (such as a PPP project) can always be encountered.

In 2011, FIDIC prepared the *DBO Contract Guide*, which must be consulted whenever the particular conditions are put together. The particular conditions newly include two sections which provide enough space for defining the specifics for the works operation service period.

12.13.1 Structure of DBO

A DBO contract agreement confirms only the price and content of the contractual relationship. It is, as usual, a very simple document that refers to the attachments which constitute the contract in the hierarchy with respect to their legal weight in accordance with Sub-Clause 1.5:

(a) the Contract Agreement (if any)
(b) the Letter of Acceptance
(c) the Letter of Tender
(d) the Particular Conditions Part A—Contract Data
(e) the Particular Conditions Part B—Special Provisions
(f) the General Conditions
(g) the Employer's Requirements
(h) the Schedules
(i) the Contractor's Proposal and any other documents forming part of the contract.

FIDIC DBO is based on FIDIC P&DB, being in fact its updated wording (FIDIC P&DB is nine years older than FIDIC DBO), with the operation service period added and necessary modifications made to accommodate the specifics of a long-term relationship. Many useful adjustments were incorporated and this form was also the base for the further 2017 updates of FIDIC forms.

The DBO form uses employer's representative instead of the engineer. In the part describing time for completion, Chapter 8 underwent natural modifications to allow for the operation period. Chapter 9 deals with designs coming from P&DB. Chapter 10 newly handles the operation service period. In its part on payment conditions, Chapter 14 is set to reflect both the payments for performance of design and construction works and financing within the operation period. The same applies concerning the issues of contract termination in Chapters 15 and 16. Risks are described in Chapter 17 as allocated not only to the employer in particular, but to the contractor as well. Newly described in Chapter 18 are the "exceptional risks" (instead of *force majeure*). In the period of operation service, the dispute adjudication board is foreseen as an ad hoc committee.

The main structural difference between FIDIC DBO and the forms in the 1999 first edition is the fact that FIDIC DBO contains, at its beginning, illustrative charts that describe important procedures to be applied within this type of contract. Their purpose is to facilitate working with the contract and accelerate understanding of the basic principles, such as:

- The overall contract period;
- The design-build period;
- Commencement of design-build commissioning;
- Operation service period;
- Payment during the design-build period;
- Payment during the operation service period;
- Determination by employer's representative;
- Contractor's claims—submission;
- Contractor's claims—determination;
- Settlement of disputes.

Other differences in form include an alphabetically ordered list of definitions, updated provisions regarding risk allocation, insurance, claims, as well as a greater number of sample documents in the annexes. This clearer designation of risks and claims will facilitate the avoidance of disputes.

Key material differences between FIDIC P&DB and DBO are that DBO include a 20-year operation service period and further, for example, a facility refurbishment fund to cover the costs for replacement of worn parts of the facility while it is operated. Surplus funds, if any, will be equally distributed to the parties. Lack of funds is a contractor risk.

Other necessary extensions beyond the scope of FIDIC P&DB are that the employer may retain 5% of payments if the contractor fails to uphold its obligation to maintain the works. Furthermore, an independent supervisor is nominated to monitor how the contractual obligations are performed. The parties are then obliged to obey the supervisor's opinions. In addition, the dispute adjudication board is appointed and replaced every five years.

The 2017 updates of the 1999 FIDIC forms of contracts (Red, Yellow, and Silver Books) by Zoltán Záhonyi (Hungary)

After publishing the fourth edition of the FIDIC Red Book (Conditions of Contract for Works of Civil Engineering Construction) and the third edition of the Yellow Book (Conditions of Contract for Electrical and Mechanical Works) both in 1987, actual trends identified by FIDIC proved increasing demand for updating these 1987 editions. A number of significant changes were implemented as a result of the update process in the new editions published in 1999.

It was recognized that despite these forms intended to cover different types of construction projects, these were common to a great extent. Therefore, uniform drafting (wherever was found reasonable) was one of the main goals when the 1999 Forms were produced.

Another significant change in the approach was to distinguish the different contract types by one of the most significant risk factors: which party is responsible to provide the designs for the project.

From legal perspective, the universal application of FIDIC forms urged for more neutral legal approach to make these contract conditions more suitable for their use under different legal systems.

All the above-mentioned core principles (among many others) resulted in an all-new suite of FIDIC Conditions of Contract published in 1999. It is not an exaggeration to state that they became the etalons for best practice construction contract conditions worldwide over the years.

What happened after 1999 become part of the FIDIC history. The new FIDIC Forms conquered the construction contracts market all over the world—with all good reason. This success was not spoiled by some features of these forms, which were found not fully and perfectly functioning in real practice on site. Maybe the best proof of the quality was the adoption of these forms by multilateral development banks (MDBs). FIDIC provided MDBs with a specific license to draft their own customized form of the 1999 Red Book (the so-called MDB Form, or Pink Book).

After having FIDIC's well-known 1999 Red, Yellow, and Silver Book in circulation for about ten years, FIDIC decided to launch a new specific task group to update these forms. The terms of reference for this update task group were provided with special care by FIDIC's Contracts Committee. The core aims for the update included:

- to keep existing features of the 1999 versions, which had been proven to be successful;
- changes to be made only where found necessary and resulting in improvement;

- update the documents by all those new features that have been introduced since the launch of the 1999 forms (especially, the 2008 DBO form and the recent forms of the MDB Conditions of Contract for Construction); and
- the basic principle: "Wording shall be same as 'Gold Book' where intended to be for the same purpose."

The main sources that had to be considered for the updates (beyond the more recent forms of contracts as referred above):

- the Terms of Reference provided by FIDIC's Contracts Committee (including the core requirements and expectations regarding the updated Forms);
- proposed update items by the FIDIC Contracts Committee's Special Advisors (who are FIDIC contributors serving in the previous Contracts Committee, many of them being among the authors of the 1999 documents);
- contract users' feedbacks gathered over the years of using the 1999 forms for thousands of construction projects worldwide.

The underlying philosophies for the update included:

- the updated forms are to be drafted by engineers for engineers, but as a legal document, with the support of experienced international construction lawyers;
- project management features and tools are to be enhanced for clarity and certainty;
- the role of the engineer had to be reinforced;
- more equality was aimed between the parties through balanced risk allocation,
- current international best practice had to be reflected;
- issues, comments raised by users/practitioners to be addressed and
- most recent developments with latest FIDIC forms adopted.

The update process was divided into two major stages: first, the update of the Yellow Book was envisaged and after concluding this process, the Red, and the Silver Book to be completed. This idea was based on the fact, that among the three books it is the Yellow Book, which represents the middle ground as far as risk sharing (e.g., design risks and quantity risks are on the contractor's side) and core mechanisms (see administration of the contract by an engineer) of the contract forms are considered.

For both major stages the documents had to go through several levels of systematic reviews and controls: first review by the Contracts Committee then special advisors' review, after that friendly review (over 50 eminent and experienced professionals, specially chosen and invited by FIDIC from across the spectrum of interested users including employers, contractors engineers, lawyers, and MDBs, from around the world), then as the final major revision stage, the legal review. After completing each review stage, the actually prevailing draft wording was reviewed and revised.

As being the pioneer from among the three books, the initial processing and drafting of the Yellow Book update took considerable time. The drafting of the updates was carried out by not just one, but two task groups (the first engaged with the Yellow Book update, the second task group in charge with producing the Red and Silver Book updates, based on the Yellow Book). The work of these two groups were complemented and finalized by the Contracts

Committee Update Special Group (all names contributing are acknowledged at the end of this vignette).

The total amount of time (about eight years) spent on the update process finally is attributable to this several-stage iterative document development process and also, that all contributors provided their inputs on a voluntary basis.

At first sight, the final products of the update process appear to be longer, than their 1999 predecessors. For example, the updated General Conditions parts became nearly 1.5 times longer than before. When looking at the details of the differences, it is not difficult to find the reasons for such increase in volume. The updates became more prescriptive because the clearer and the more certain the wording of a contract, the higher the chance of no difficulties in understanding or interpretation and so the higher the chance of successful project.

What is most important, the initial expectations regarding these updates are fulfilled: there are no substantial changes to the basic principles and the risk sharing as they were introduced in 1999. The only identifiable apparent change is that the main clause structure of 20 increased to 21 in the updates—the reason for that is that one of the most important aims was to separate claims and disputes, each included in an individual major chapter in order to reinforce the original intentions, whereas these were never meant to be the same, not even similar. In the current form, claims are dealt with under Clause 20, meanwhile disputes are dealt with in Clause 21.

Having a closer look at inside the updates, it is easy to establish, that certain clauses became significantly longer than they used to be—mainly, as a result of their more detailed structure, providing detailed, step-by-step procedures for the contract users' convenience.

In summary, the following main features and procedures became updated in the 2017 suite of contracts:

- The definitions part lists the terms in alphabetical order. Furthermore, there are a number of new defined terms—all with the aim to make the conditions easier to interpret and supporting the contract users.
- In general, project management procedures were significantly improved, by giving details of expected actions by the stakeholders, wherever it was possible, in a well identifiable sequential (itemized) order of actions. This may be referred to as the conditions became more prescriptive, but on the other hand, such approach may be highly appreciated by all those, having less experience in managing complex construction contracts.
- The procedures in the updates offer solution and definite consequences in many cases, where there was no explicit way forward under the 1999 forms (e.g., what action to be taken if the contractor does not submit the fully detailed claim within 42 days of becoming aware of it, or if the engineer does not give a notice of agreement or determination within the time limit set).
- Management of time was a focus area of the update process in at least three ways. Some procedures received explicit time limits (but NOT time bars)—if these are not met (or exempted), then there is a specific outcome (= no stoppage, deemed procedures to follow). The obligation to serve an early warning now became more exposed, having it placed in an individual sub-clause. Also, the expected content of a program is included and once reviewed (or deemed to be reviewed) by the Engineer, the program submitted by the contractor will become the program.
- Clauses 17 to 19 were subject to complete revision regarding "Care of the Works and Indemnities," "Exceptional Events" (previously: "Force Majeure"), and "Insurance." After careful

considerations, these parts were returning back to the basic principles regarding these areas, as they were included in the 1977 FIDIC Red Book.
- The 2008 FIDIC Gold Book included the dispute avoidance feature of the DAB in the General Conditions of Contract (previously referred to only in the General Conditions of Dispute Adjudication Rules in the Red Book). Some critics thought that this was an action against the role and powers of the Engineer. By maintaining this important new feature for the DABs, the updates made it absolutely clear, that such additional feature does not decrease the engineer's power, what is more, the engineer now especially enjoys much greater freedom in dealing with agreements and/or determinations.
- As mentioned, the DAB now got its new role (dispute avoidance) as a standard service for the parties as it was proven to be successful in the 2008 Gold Book and now, enhanced further in the Updates. This includes more explicit authority and duty for the DAB (including avoidance and not just adjudication of disputes). In order to emphasize the new function, the Contracts Committee decided to re-name this important body: from now on, it is called dispute avoidance/adjudication board (DAAB). Also, the new forms include an updated set of dispute avoidance/adjudication rules, together with a refreshed general conditions of dispute avoidance/adjudication agreement as well as a new form for the tripartite DAAB Agreement.

It is not possible to provide a full comprehensive comparison of all the changes for the purposes of this short chapter, but a few examples of the changes are introduced hereunder:

Among others, the following newly defined terms help the parties to interpret the provisions better: claim (to make it entirely clear, what this term is expected to cover, so it is just a request for entitlement, not a declaration of war and certainly not a dispute); cost plus profit (now this way, in a combined form); date of completion (enabling shorter, more specific references made to this important point in time throughout the whole conditions); dispute (to establish exactly, when the DAAB should move from assisting the parties in its dispute avoidance role, to the process of getting to a decision on the dispute within 84 days); exceptional event (to cater for the new provisions under Clauses 17, 18, and 19); no-objection and notice (to help management procedures); notice of dissatisfaction (NOD) (to make obligations clear after engineer's determination and/or DAAB decision); QM system (to help improving the quality control procedures), and many more.

Regarding the engineer's roles and strengthened functions it should be mentioned, that it got clarified, who the engineer is expected to be. The engineer's representative got declared to be part of the normal course of actions (to infuse real-life practice" in the conditions, so the engineer has the option to delegate authority to this representative, within specified limits). In the updated Red and Yellow Book, "the engineer" is expected to be a professional engineer having suitable qualifications, experience and competence to act as the engineer and also, shall be fluent in the ruling language of the contract.

The contract users may find Sub-Clause 3.7 (agreement or determination) (previously Sub-Clause 3.5 determinations) much more structured as having a step-by-step procedure been introduced. What is different in comparison with the 1999 version is that these procedures are given specific time limits and deemed consequences, if not met. It shall be mentioned, that these are NOT meant to be time bars as users are invited to change any of these periods (in the special provisions), and the stakeholder subject to the given time limit may always request extension of the time for these procedures. Deemed consequences apply only if action is not taken and the original limit expired. Another important improvement to this part of the conditions is, that the engineer operating under Sub-Clause 3.7 is expected to be "neutral" and shall not be deemed to act for the employer! The procedures under this sub-clause are to apply not just in cases of claims, but also in a number of other processes (e.g., variations, issue of interim payment certificates, etc.).

The engineer's actions as far as quality of the works and safety is concerned are supported by a number of new provisions (e.g., Sub-Clause 4.8—Health and Safety plan; Sub-Clause 4.9—Quality Management and Compliance Verification Systems).

For the Yellow (and Silver) Books conditions related to contractor's obligation to design the works became more explicit, by providing requirements concerning the designers. In case of the Yellow Book, the engineer's review process is more structured, step-by-step procedures are included.

Similar changes can be observed for the variation procedures. It has become clearer what are the types of variations and what are the procedures to follow. Also, in the case of a number of sub-clauses it is explicit, that variation procedures should be followed. Some examples: in case of Sub-Clause 1.9—Correction of Errors in the Employer's Requirements, and Sub-Clause 4.12—Unforeseeable Physical Conditions where the engineer's instructions given will result in variations.

As just in many other cases, the payment procedures became more structured, step-by-step procedures can be followed easily. For convenience of the contract users, the employer may include the percentage of profit in the contract data, which profit could be used for the purposes of the contract. If this is not included, than following a fall-back scenario the profit shall be 5% of the cost.

Regarding termination of the contract, users may find some new (refined) features. For example, in case of employer's termination for contractor's default, now clear, that the employer becomes entitled to recover delay damages. In case of termination for employer's convenience, the contractor becomes entitled to recover loss of profit, in case the employer intends to complete the works.

Claims became balanced between the parties: the claims procedures that apply under the updates are now the same for the contractor's claims and employer's claims. Hence, Clause 20 now covers all claims with no distinction between contractor's claims and employer's claims. As just in many other cases, this clause was changed to follow a logical sequence of activities step-by-step: Notice of Claim ->> Engineer's initial response (e.g., time bar met or not) ->> Contemporary records ->> Fully detailed claim ->> Agreement or Determination. Similar procedures apply to claims of continuing effect as in the previous edition.

The time bar may be applicable in two cases: notice of claim and providing statement of contractual/legal basis of claim. In both cases the party, whose claim was declared to be time barred may have the right to express disagreement with the engineer that the notice of claim was indeed given out-of-time. In this case such disagreement shall be subject to engineer's reconsideration as carrying out the procedures under Sub-Clause 3.7 facilitating the parties agreement and if not agreed, then to determine the issue of the time bar. Should either party be dissatisfied with the engineer's determination, then the question of waiver can be referred to the DAAB for a decision. These procedures in the updates represent an enhancement what was included in the 2008 Gold Book.

The proven success in practice of standing DABs in the past 18 years (made standard for dispute resolution procedures in case of the Red Book of the 1999 forms) has lead to FIDIC's decision to provide for standing DAABs under all the three books. The major reason for this is as mentioned earlier: the DAAB's new function: providing support and assistance for the parties in avoiding disputes. This cannot be achieved unless the DAAB is standby on the project, appointed at the beginning. For convenience of those users, who might still favor ad hoc DABs, alternative wording is provided in the Guidance for the Preparation of Particular Conditions.

It goes without saying that the above brief introduction of the updated suite of FIDIC Conditions of Contracts (2017) cannot include all changes and new features, therefore, all FIDIC contract users are warmly welcome to get acquainted with these updates, which were made available by FIDIC in a hope, that the future projects run under these updated provisions will become even more successful, implemented with less disputes, to the best satisfaction for each of the stakeholders! Time will tell, to what extent these aims were possible to achieve.

Finally the list of all those volunteers, who contributed directly to the production of the updated Forms:

FIDIC Contracts Committee's Updates Special Group:

Siobhan Fahey, Consulting Engineer, Ireland (Principal Drafter); Zoltán Záhonyi, Z&Partners Consulting Engineers, Hungary; Christoph Theune, GKW Consult GmbH, Germany; and William Howard, CDM Smith, USA (Executive Committee liaison).

Initial Update Task Group:

Svend Poulsen, Atkins / COWI, Denmark (Group Leader); Aisha Nadar, Runeland Law, Sweden (task group principal drafter); Robin Schonfeld, SMEC, Australia (task group principal drafter); Darko Plamenac, Consulting Engineer, Serbia; Jan Ziepke, Consulting Engineer, Germany; and Zoltán Záhonyi, Z&Partners Consulting Engineers, Hungary (Contracts Committee liaison).

Second Stage Update Task Group:

Simon Worley, EIA Ltd., UK (Group Leader); John Greenhalgh, Greenhalgh Associates, UK; Leo Grutters, Consulting Engineer, the Netherlands; Aisha Nadar, Runeland Law, Sweden; and William Godwin, Queens Counsel, UK.

Special Advisors to the Contracts Committee:

Christopher Seppälä, White & Case, France (legal advisor); Nael G Bunni, Ireland (risk and insurance advisor); Axel Volkmar Jäger, Germany; Michael Mortimer-Hawkins, UK / Sweden; Christopher Wade, UK.

Also, all those further contributors, who participated the update process in any way, such as "Friendly Reviewers" are acknowledged hereby.

Zoltán Záhonyi

Chair, FIDIC Contracts Committee, leading partner, Z & Partners Consulting Engineers, Hungary

12.14 Other FIDIC standard forms

For completeness, a brief overview of some previous versions of FIDIC forms (the "old series," that is, the versions preceding the first edition, 1999) is included:

(a) *Conditions of Contract for Works of Civil Engineering Construction with forms of Tender and Agreement*—"The Red Book," fourth edition, 1987, reprint 1992.
(b) *Supplement to the Fourth Edition 1987 of the FIDIC Conditions of Contract for Works of Civil Engineering Construction*—"The Red Book," first edition, 1996.
(c) *Conditions of Contract for Electrical & Mechanical Works/including erection on site/with forms of Tender and Agreement*—"The Yellow Book," third edition, 1987, reprint 1988.
(d) *Supplement to the third edition 1987 of the Conditions of Contract for Electrical &Mechanical Works*—"The Yellow Book," first edition, 1997.
(e) *Conditions of Subcontract for Works of Civil Engineering Construction*, first edition, 1994.
(f) *Conditions of Contract for Design-Build and Turnkey*—"The Orange Book," first edition, 1995.

The following are from the "New Series" (besides CONS, P&DB, EPC, short form, and DBO):

(a) *Client/Consultant Model Services Agreement*, third edition, 1998—"The White Book." A sample form of a professional service agreement, such as for the preparation of a design or to provide other services (technical assistance, supervision, and so on). This document is supplemented by two other documents: (1) a consultant/sub-consultant model contract; and (2) a joint venture sample contract for design works or provision of services.
(b) *Client/Consultant Model Services Agreement,* fourth edition, 2006, as an updated version with partial modifications.

Worth mentioning is also a standard form of contract intended for the use in the mining industry, the so called "Blue Book." The most recent form is the model representative agreement in the first edition, 2013 (the "Purple Book").

Even the oldest versions of the FIDIC forms provide solid guidance but FIDIC does not recommend their use as they have been superseded by newer editions. The federation cannot forbid or restrict their use but it is self-evident that the development of the individual books must reflect development in the economy, the construction industry in general, law and management, dispute resolution, and all other related aspects.

FIDIC suite of consultant agreements by Vincent Leloup (France)

FIDIC embarked over the recent years into a full update process of its suite of agreements, namely:

- The FIDIC Client/Consultant Model Services Agreement, aka the White Book, whose former edition (fourth) was dating back to 2006,

- The FIDIC Sub-Consultancy Agreement, whose former edition was dating back to 1992, and
- The FIDIC Model Joint-Venture (Consortium) Agreement, whose former edition was also dating back to 1992

The Suite of Agreement was recently released by FIDIC in February 2017, and provides to the market a valuable update at once of key agreements that a consulting engineering firm is meant to use in connection with its regular business dealings, either being toward a client, a sub-consultant, or a partner in a JV or Consortium.

The FIDIC White Book ("WB"), which covers the delivery of services from a consultant to a client, is of particular interest to the market and, as member of the task group, which was in charge of drafting the 2017 Suite of Agreements, I present below the main changes users will identify against the former 2006 edition.

First of all, and as a basis for this update work, we within the task group considered the latest developments in the construction industry worldwide with due regard to consultancy services, and reviewed over 20 standard forms of services contracts used in different jurisdictions (both civil and common law) across the globe. We also took into consideration critics formulated over the years against the White Book fourth edition. For example, it was found by some practitioners that the White Book was somehow unreasonably in the favor of the consultant (as illustrated by Sub-Clause 6.1.1 on the consultant's liability), or to be rather unclear in some instances (such as when dealing with suspension and termination situations under Clause 4.6). Through this 2017 fifth edition, we accordingly aimed at providing better clarity in the agreement provisions, and at upholding the FIDIC principles of a fair and balanced risk allocation. Future, and feedback from the industry, will tell us whether we achieved such goals.

Under **Clause 1 – General Provisions** - all the definitions applicable across the WB have now been sorted in alphabetical order, as it is the regular practice of FIDIC since the release of the Gold Book back in 2008. Still following the Gold Book approach, any communication in between the parties shall now be identified as such (i.e., as being a notice, a variation notice, or otherwise) and state to what clause or sub-clause it refers. We also found useful to introduce, under Clause 1, some additional general administration provisions (often referred to as "boiler plate clauses") covering, *inter alia*, the severability of the agreement provisions, or the non-waiver of rights.

The priority order of the documents forming the agreement was found to be confusing under the WB 2006: this is now corrected through the introduction of a Clause 1.15, which provides that the order found under the form of agreement shall be the one prevailing for interpretation purposes.

Parties to the agreement are to act in good faith—a provision that is specifically meant for some common law jurisdictions, which do not expressly accommodate for such obligation in their contract law. Civil law practitioners will only find there a provision which is generally already enshrined in their respective civil code.

Consultants are regularly required to perform their services on the basis of information provided by clients—geotechnical surveys, existing infrastructure maps, and water quality data are typical examples of such kind of supporting information that consultants may have to rely upon when delivering their services, and in particular when designing building or infrastructure. It was felt required under **Clause 2** of the agreement to better stress the allocation of responsibility for such information. This is expressly stated as resting with the client, but the consultant, using reasonable skill and care, is to review such information and advise the client of any adverse finding. Any error, omission or ambiguity accordingly spotted shall be rectified by the client but this may also lead in some circumstances to a variation to the consultant's services. The above means that there would also be a possible client's defense in case the consultant fails to spot errors, omissions, or ambiguities that a consultant, acting under such standard of care, would have been expected to find.

Such standard of care expected from the consultant remains, under **Clause 3.3**, the *"reasonable skill, care and diligence to be expected from a consultant experienced in the provision of such services for projects of similar size, nature and complexity."* We however now stipulated that the consultant is, under Sub-Clause 3.3.2, to *"perform the Services with a view to satisfying any function and purpose that may be described in Appendix 1 [Scope of Services],"* but this is valid only *"to the extent achievable using the standard of care in Sub-Clause 3.3.1."*

We took good note of certain client's inclination (including contractors who wish to subcontract design services to a consultant under a design-build contract), as well as the view of some civil law jurisdictions practitioners, who strongly advocated for the consultant under the WB to be given a higher standard of performance, namely to provide a warranty that his services would be fit for the purposes intended under the agreement. However, such practice is clearly not to date the international practice, and such standard of performance would generally be uninsurable by the consultant under reasonable commercial terms. Some countries like France make consultants strictly liable at law within 10 years from completion of the works (the so-called "decennial liability," enshrined under Article 1792 of the French civil code), together with the rest of the construction team, for any defect making the works unfit-for-purpose, but they also provide an insurance relief to such onerous obligation by giving a legal obligation to the insurance market to provide insurance cover for it (as laid down under the 1978 "Spinetta law" in France). Those examples remain marginal at the international level, and despite the merits the task group could see in the eyes of a client for such a mechanism, it was felt inappropriate to make it an international standard. The wording developed under Clause 3.3 is consequently as far as we felt reasonable to go to uphold the client's legitimate interests in the function and purpose of the services, while at the same time not bringing the consultants to unreasonable and uninsurable, hence adverse, business grounds.

Current practices show that the market is probably not ready to accommodate for such radical change yet. Consultants have so far managed to limit their liability in this respect to a standard of performance, which is insurable, while design-build contractors do provide such fitness for purpose warranty and bear such liability despite its general lack of insurability. Of course the contractor's contract values provide for larger financial cover, hence risk absorption capacity, than those of consultants, but future will tell whether this gap will be bridged at some point, or will persist. The position of clients in drafting agreements, the position of consultants in negotiating those, and the position of the insurance market in providing fitness-for-purpose cover or not, will be instrumental in defining the trends of the industry in this respect over the years to come. Undoubtedly this shall form another vivid matter of discussion when the next WB update publication is considered in future.

Still under **Clause 3** a new provision has been included allowing the consultant to suspend the services if an exceptional event occurs. Also a new provision has been added to expressly address the situation where the consultant may be asked to carry out the function of engineer under a works contract—this is the so-called "Construction Administration" Sub-Clause 3.9.

Users will note the following important provision, which harmonizes the consultant's obligations toward the client under the White Book with the engineer's obligations to the parties under a FIDIC works contract (see for example under SC 3.5 or 14.6 of the 1999 Red FIDIC Book and Yellow FIDIC Book):

> "If the Consultant is authorised under the Works Contract to certify, determine or exercise discretion in the discharge of its duties then the Consultant shall act fairly as go between the Client and the contractor, exercising independent professional judgement and using reasonable skill, care and diligence."

Under **Clause 4** detailed provisions have been included covering program requirements (included under Appendix 4 to the agreement) with the anticipation that such program will be consented to by the client. Delays will be measured against the program, which itself shall be kept under constant review by the consultant. As with the FIDIC suite of works contracts express reasons for granting any extension to the time for completion have now been provided. Services are often subject to causes of delay such as variations, and it was accordingly found beneficial to provide a contractual machinery for handling those instances. Financial compensation is also available when those excusable delay events make the consultant suffer from exceptional costs, which is made a defined term.

Exceptional events have been introduced, in similar but not identical terms to the ones found under recent FIDIC works contracts since it not only looks at the effect of an exceptional event on whether services can still be performed or not, but also on the scope of services and a possible variation this may generate.

Under **Clause 5** new provisions have been included, bringing the variation of services provisions up to date with modern agreement practice. Variations to the agreement and additional services were little expanded upon under the WB 2006 fourth edition—a full clause now covers such matter. Provisions are broadly similar to those found in FIDIC works contracts. As a difference though, they anticipate that the parties will endeavour to agree the full effect of a variation to the services in advance of the implementation of the variation. Failure to do so would, however, give possibility to the client to instruct the consultant to nevertheless commence work, in which case he will be paid on a time-spent basis until such time an agreement is reached as to the effects of the variation.

However, importantly for consultants, variations are expressly required not to substantially change the extent or nature of the services. The WB fifth edition provides for possible objections from the consultant in that respect: he would not be bound to execute a variation instruction to which he objected along those grounds. Similarly, he can object to, and be bound by, a variation for which he does not possess the relevant skills or resources.

We took the opportunity, under **Clause 6**, to clarify the delicate matter of suspension of the services and termination of the agreement. Indeed in the 2006 WB fourth edition the provisions found under Clause 4.6 were said to cause uncertainty to users, in particular for the mechanism of agreement termination by the consultant. We felt important to clearly and expressly lay down the:

- Causes for suspension and termination,
- Procedural steps to be followed by the parties in such instances, and
- Effects of suspension and termination

The above now runs over a full new clause, which hopefully will be seen as providing sufficient certainty as to how handling such sensitive issues.

Under **Clause 8** the consultant is liable to the client for any breach of the agreement, while under the 2006 WB fourth edition he was only liable for a breach of its standard of performance to act with reasonable skill, care, and diligence. This was rightfully considered as an excessive limitation of the consultant's liability toward the client, and, despite the fact that governing and applicable laws would anyhow in some instances defeat such contractual limitation of liability (on the basis of reasonableness tests as to such limitation, as provided for at law), we felt necessary to expressly provide fair and reasonable contract terms for that important and sensitive matter.

Finally, under **Clause 10** the dispute resolution provisions have been amended so as to remove the mediation foreseen under the 2006 WB fourth edition and replace it with a dispute adjudication provision for which rules are inserted under Appendix 5 to the agreement. Despite its merits within the range of alternative dispute resolution options available in the industry, mediation was not further considered as an effective mean to increase the chances to avoid the cost and duration of a full arbitration, since its efficiency is (too) highly depending on the joint will of the parties. Reaching agreement while parties are in dispute can prove to be an insurmountable challenge, hence an adjudicator being given the power to issue binding decisions was found a preferable option in that respect.

Owing to the financial magnitude of consultancy services agreement, and of any related dispute, it was found preferable to provide for a single adjudicator who would only provide dispute resolution services. In other words, he is not required to be mobilized from the outset of the agreement implementation and is not required to deliver routine duties toward the parties in the absence of any dispute.

Arbitration remains the final instance for dispute resolution, and no arbitration can commence unless and until a notice of dissatisfaction as to the adjudicator decision has been issued. In effect, this does make adjudication a mandatory first step of dispute resolution—a similar principle as the one developed under FIDIC forms of works contracts. As for other recent FIDIC forms of contracts, it is expressly made possible to refer the failure to comply with an adjudicator's decision (whether binding or final and binding) directly to arbitration. Those familiar with the *Persero* judicial (and arbitral) saga in Singapore will there recognize the new language introduced by FIDIC since 2013 following the developments of that case.

Vincent Leloup
Member of the FIDIC Contracts Committee
Member of the FIDIC Task Group 4, in charge of drafting the FIDIC 2017 Suite of Agreements

The use of FIDIC contracts by the mining industry in Africa by Coenraad Snyman (South Africa)

Many gold, copper, coal, platinum, and diamond mines are situated on the African continent. Invariably, these mines are often located in isolated regions and often, also, in developing countries. This poses unique challenges, ranging from very poor infrastructure (hindering the delivery of goods and materials to the site— including the ability of employers to deliver free-issue materials in time), delays at borders and by authorities (ranging from custom officials who have to clear goods to be imported into the country, environmental agencies who have to issue permits, etc.), corrupt practices, illiteracy, uneducated and inexperienced contractors, and sub-contractors. Not only is the mining industry inherently a risky one, it is exceptionally so in Africa.

Using form contracts, such as FIDIC, has many advantages since it increases the odds of mining houses and contractors being familiar with the contractual terms and hence also with the manner in which risk and responsibilities are allocated, shared or distributed. FIDIC contracts are, however, often being amended substantially and this has proven to be problematic. Typical changes and amendments that have been made to FIDIC contracts include changing the 1999 "Yellow Book" into a re-measurable contract and changing the 1999 "Red Book" into a lump-sum contract.

The contract entered into by a major gold producer for the refurbishment of their gold processing plant situated in Ghana, was let on such a basis. The contractor, in that case, not only determined its own scope (by deciding what parts or components of the plant needed replacement) but also took responsibility for any designs that might be required in order for them to do the work. Because the volume of the work was largely unknown at the tender stage, a "Yellow Book" contract was entered into but on a re-measurable basis. The employer assumed the role of engineer himself.

Mining houses typically employ engineering houses to carry out the design of processing and water treatment plants or tailing dams, for example, and this is often done during the feasibility study phase of the project. Tenders for the construction of the works are thus being sought based on the employer's design. The 1999 FIDIC Red Book, which is drafted for works designed by the employer, would be the logical choice of contract. Many employers, however, prefer to obtain a lump-sum offer and price for doing such work, hence the need to amend the Red Book's payment provisions. This is, however, not just a simple and straightforward matter, which can be accomplished by merely swopping the payment provisions found in the Yellow Book with those found in the Red Book.

In the case of major plant upgrades, EPCM contracts, using the FIDIC White Book, are often entered into in order to appoint a contractor to carry out the pre-feasibility, feasibility studies, and designs. This happened, for example, in connection with the project involving the upgrade of a gold processing plant situated in Mali. A redesign and upgrade of the plant became necessary due to the fact that the nature of ore changed tremendously (in hardness, etc.) once it was extracted from deeper levels and from different pits. The intention was that the contractor would, in that case, also manage the project's execution once the construction phase started.

A US$60 million contract for the construction of a greenfield copper processing plant situated in the DRC (Democratic Republic of Congo) was let on the basis of a 1999 FIDIC Silver Book. Interestingly, although the Silver Book was used in that instance, the contractor did not carry out nor was it responsible for the design of the work.

An important part of mining activities do, by their very nature, happen underground. Such work typically involves and includes "building" or sinking ventilation and access shafts, stopes, underground workshops, facilities for working crews, backfilling, and so on. In the case of open-pit mines, "contract mining" contracts are generally entered into with third parties since few mining houses have the capacity (on interest, perhaps) to so such work themselves. These contracts are normally bespoke.

Any important part of the contractor's obligation (both in the case of underground as well as open pit mining operations) is to extract, to haul to the surface and/or to the "run of mine" or ROM pad sufficient ore so that employer's mineral processing activities can continue uninterrupted and at a predetermined and steady rate. This obligation to extract sufficient quantities of ore is an important and cardinal one, which is far removed from the type of obligations encountered in traditional or typical building and engineering contracts.

Where (and to some extent also "when") the work will happen depend upon a succession of mining plans produced by the employer. The ability and extent to which contractors involved with mining work can, therefore, program, schedule, and plan their work are subject to constant and frequent change.

Unlike the case which may exist in the case of "pure" building contracts these changes are not treated as variations entitling the contract to submit a claim for addition costs or for additional time within which to complete the work. Changes such as these are the "norm" rather than the "exception." Standard FIDIC provisions dealing with variations and the consequence thereof will simply not do or suffice.

Due to the ongoing and constant changing nature of this work, it is also difficult (if not near impossible) to set and to specify specific completion dates by when the work (or a section thereof) must be complete and hence it is equally difficult to apply delay damages.

Although FIDIC contracts are frequently used by the mining industry, their use is often limited to building work that must be carried out "above ground," whereas what happens below-ground or in the mining pit is invariably the subject matter of bespoke contracts, which bears little or no resemblance to FIDIC contract forms.

Coenraad Snyman
Independent construction law and claims consultant, trainer and facilitator
South Africa

12.15 Risk allocation under FIDIC forms

FIDIC forms build on sophisticated inter-connections between the individual sub-clauses—particularly in risk allocation, claims and dispute resolution. In the following text, attention will be paid to risk allocation according to the 1999 first edition FIDIC forms and differences between these particular sample forms, that is, CONS, P&DB, and EPC. There is no substantial change in the 2017 edition in this regard.

12.15.1 Risk allocation in CONS

Employer's and shared risks

General provisions for risk allocation are contained in Chapter 17 of CONS, P&DB, and EPC. However, a risk allocation systematic has to be perceived in the context of a contract as a whole. Sub-Clause 17.6 provides an important provision concerning the limitation of liability. As a general rule, total mutual liability of the contractor shall not exceed the accepted contract amount as per Sub-Clause 1.1.4.1.

Contractual risk allocation has to be viewed in respect to the limits stated by the governing law in conjunction with Chapter 19 (provides a contractual definition of *force majeure*), and together with Chapter 18 (defines insurance-risk transfer). Risk allocation is interconnected with claims (as per Sub-Clauses 2.5 and 20.1 in general) and with the system of employer and contractor rights and obligations: Chapters 2 and 4.

According to CONS, the employer shall bear mainly the risks from the hazards under Sub-Clause 17.3:

(a) war, hostilities (whether a war be declared or not), invasion, acts of foreign enemies;
(b) rebellion, terrorism, revolution, insurrection, military or usurped power, or civil war within the country;
(c) riots, commotion or disorder within the country by persons other than the contractor's personnel and other employees of the contractor and subcontractors;
(d) munitions of war, explosive materials, ionizing radiation or contamination by radioactivity, (within the country), except as may be attributable to the contractor's use of such munitions, explosives or radioactive material.

Further risks referred to in Sub-Clause 17.3 are:

(e) pressure waves caused by aircraft or other aerial devices travelling at sonic or supersonic speeds;
(f) use or occupation by the employer of any part of the Permanent Works, except as may be specified in the contract;
(g) design of any part of the works by the employer's personnel or by others for whom the employer is responsible; and
(h) any operation of the forces of nature which is unforeseeable or against which an experienced contractor could not reasonably have been expected to have taken adequate preventative precautions.

The employer shall bear further risks in connection with its obligation to obtain permission from public authorities, that is, as per Sub-Clause 1.13, permission in connection with public-law zoning and planning processes and construction permissions for the permanent works. The employer is further to provide the contractor with site access rights as per Sub-Clause 2.1. A separate category of employer's risks consist of unforeseeable physical conditions as per Sub-Clause 4.12 (in respect of Sub-Clause 4.10). The definition of "unforeseeable" is available in Sub-Clause 1.1.6.8 and states that "unforeseeable" means not reasonably foreseeable by an experienced contractor at the date for submission of the tender. Evaluation of unforeseeable natural events in a particular situation must be done in respect of the contract time for completion and frequency of occurrences of this particular situation according to historical records. The following example is published in the FIDIC contracts guide

(2000, p. 274): If time for completion is three years, an experienced contractor should reasonably foresee an event occurring once in every six years but not an event occurring once in 10 years, which would be considered unforeseeable.

Employer's risk may also be costs incurred in connection with archaeological findings (as per Sub-Clause 4.24). Due to the inter-connections with contractual claims, the shared risks from Sub-Clause 8.4 are also worth mentioning. They are, in fact, the time-related impacts of variations to the works, of contractual claims, of exceptionally adverse climatic conditions, of shortages in availability of personnel (such as epidemics) and time-related impacts of any delay, impediment or prevention caused by, or attributable to, the employer (including the engineer).

As per Sub-Clause 8.5, the parties shall share the risks of delays caused by public authorities, bearing also, pursuant to Sub-Clause 13.7, the risks of adjustments for changes in legislation and, pursuant to Sub-Clause 19, also the risks of *"force majeure."* Where a contract contains a provision about cost adjustments, the related risks shall be borne by both parties, depending on the particular setting. According to the standard setting, total price of the works can either increase or decrease.

Furthermore, according to Sub-Clause 17.1, the employer shall indemnify the contractor against all claims, damages, losses, and expenses in respect of bodily injury, sickness, disease, or death attributable to any negligence, willful act or breach of contract by the employer—including liabilities excluded from insurance cover.

Other employer risks mainly arise from contractual or other claims of the contractor. The employer shall regularly bear some of the risks that arise from their contractual obligations and the governing law. For example, risks from the employer's obligation to pay the contract price, general duty of prevention, the duty to cooperate, and so on.

Contractor's risks

The general Sub-Clause 17.1 further describes (as contractor risks) those risks that relate to a potential bodily injury, sickness, disease, or death arising out of the contractor's works (or by reason of the contractor's design) and the risks from breaching of the contractor's contractual obligations in general. According to Sub-Clause 17.2, the contractor shall take full responsibility for the care of the works and goods until the taking over certificate is issued. At this point, responsibility for the care of the works shall pass to the employer. If any loss or damage happens to the works, during the period when the contractor is responsible for their care (from any cause not being employer's risks), the contractor shall rectify the loss or damage at the contractor's risk and expense.

According to Sub-Clause 4.1, the contractor shall mainly bear the risks of executing and completing the works in accordance with the contract. This implies the duty of due (including timely performance), see Sub-Clauses 1.13 (b), 4.9, 7.1, 8.2, 8.7, 9.1; remedying defects during realization and defects notification period (see Sub-Clauses 7.6, 11.1), for adequacy, stability and safety of all the site operations and of all methods of construction (see mainly Sub-Clauses 4.6, 4.7, 4.8, 4.18, 6.7, 6.9, 6.11). Where the contractor is designing a part of the works, the contractor shall bear the related risks (see also Sub-Clauses 4.1 and 17.5).

Sub-Clause 4.10 states that, to the extent practicable (and taking into account cost and time), the contractor shall be deemed to have obtained all necessary information as to risks, contingencies, and other circumstances, which may influence or affect the tender or works. To the same extent, the contractor shall be deemed to have: (1) inspected and examined the site and its surroundings; (2) inspected and examined the site data; (3) considered other available information; and (4) to have been satisfied before submitting the tender as to all relevant matters, including (but without limitation to):

(a) site characteristics including sub-surface conditions
(b) hydrological and climatic conditions
(c) extent and nature of the work and goods necessary for the execution and completion of the works and remedying of any defects
(d) laws, procedures, and labor practices of the country; and
(e) contractor requirements for access (as per Sub-Clauses 4.13 and 4.15), accommodation, facilities, personnel, power, transport, water, and other services.

As per Sub-Clause 4.11, the contractor shall bear the risk of insufficiency of the accepted bid price; in accordance with Sub-Clause 4.19 it is the risk of failure to provide all power, water, and other required services; and, in accordance with Sub-Clause 4.22, the risk of security of the site (see Sub-Clause 4.23).

Other risks come mainly from contractual or other claims of the employer. The contractor will also bear some other risks that come from the governing law and general duties of prevention, the obligation to cooperate, statutory liabilities and warranties and so on.

For the latest developments of FIDIC risk allocation, see Chapter 14.

China's standard form of construction contract in comparison with FIDIC forms by Shuibo Zhang (China)

Global construction is and will be the trend. Although the FIDIC New Red Book (CONS/1999 Red Book) is a contract for an international setting and the *China's standard form* is meant for a domestic setting, they are basically similar in nature. Both (1) are prepared by a somewhat neutral contract committee; (2) have the role of "engineer" who acts fairly for contract administration; and (3) are intended for "construction" with only little or no design responsibility on the part of the contractor. As a matter of fact, the New Red Book is not a "pure" international form because, with some or even minor modifications, it can also be used in domestic contracts. Thus, such similarities merit a comparison between these two forms, particularly in terms of risk allocation.

The first edition of *China's Standard Form of Construction Contract* (GF-91-0201), ("China's Standard Contract") was published in 1991 and is used for construction projects nationwide.

In the past 10 years, the Chinese construction industry has been developing very quickly. Some fundamental construction laws, such as the building law, the tendering law, and the contract law, have been laid down to regulate the construction industry in recent years. The change and development of the Chinese construction industry made it necessary to modify the first edition of the model contract. In 1999, the second edition of China's standard contract was prepared by a contract committee, which consisted mostly of consultants and government officials who held a neutral position among employers, contractors, consultants, and scholars. It was published jointly by the Ministry of Construction of China, in conjunction with the China State Administration for Industry and Commerce, to supersede the first edition with reference to standard contract forms, including the FIDIC forms. Similar to the new Red Book, China's standard contract consists of three parts: contract agreement, general conditions, and particular conditions.

Compared with the FIDIC form, China's standard contract is rather short and concise. This characteristic is also reflected in its risk allocation clauses. Some risks dealt with in the FIDIC form are even left unmentioned. The following is a brief summary of risk allocation in China's standard contract.

- *Natural risks*: Climatic risk events are not dealt with explicitly in China's standard contract; however, under Sub-Clause 13.1 and Clause 39 (*force majeure*), the contractor shall be granted an EOT if some natural catastrophes such as avalanches, floods, and typhoons occur that impact project progress.
- *Force majeure* events may also include strong wind, heavy rain, and snow if agreed by both parties in the particular conditions of contract under some circumstances. Sub-Clause 39.1 expressly states the definition of *force majeure* for construction contracts under the Chinese legal system. Other catastrophes are also covered under Sub-Clause 13.1, such as earthquakes and volcanic activities. Regarding geological conditions, the employer shall provide geological data and existing sub-surface piping systems data of the construction site and shall be responsible for the accuracy of such data. If, due to the inaccuracy of such data, the contractor incurs additional costs and/or suffers delay, the employer shall compensate and grant an EOT accordingly (Sub-Clauses 8.1 and 8.3).
- *Political and social risks*: These risks are dealt with very much less directly. In the case of occurrence, several clauses can be applied. Sub-Clause 1.22 definition of *force majeure* and Clause 13 (schedule delay) covers some political risk events, such as war, riots, and so on, in which case the contractor shall be allowed an appropriate EOT and share the relevant costs with the employer. Social risk events are covered under Clause 9, which requires the contractor to be responsible for site security by providing lighting and fencing to prevent possible theft and vandalism (Sub-Clause 9.1).
- *Economic and legal risks*: Sub-Clause 23.2 specifically deals with these risks. It is provided that the contract price can be adjusted when it is impacted by the following circumstances:
    - changes in law;
    - changes in administrative regulation;
    - changes in government policies;
    - changes in price indices published by construction cost authorities.

It can be seen from such a provision that the employer shall, in general, bear the risk of price fluctuation. No mention is made of the shortage of equipment, materials, and labor in China's standard contract. This may be due to the thinking style of the Chinese construction culture, that in the domestic market, such a shortage is unlikely to occur. All these should be available in the current Chinese construction market. It is just a matter of price fluctuation to procure these

558   International Construction Contract Law

supplies. Introduction of such a "shortage" concept into the contract may lead to complications and confusion.

Behavioral risks

1. *Employer Behavioral Risks (including the engineer's)* are mainly the following:
   - late or incorrect instructions from the engineer on behalf of employer (Sub-Clauses 6.2, 6.3, 16.4);
   - employer-or third party-caused emergent remedy (Sub-Clause 7.3);
   - land requisition (Sub-Clause 8.1);
   - late (or failure to provide) drawings or meet commencement requirements as agreed (Sub-Clause 13.1);
   - late payment (Sub-Clauses 13.1, 24, 26.4);
   - failure to provide instruction or approval (Sub-Clause 13.1);
   - disturbance of contractor's normal working on site (16.3);
   - interference with inspection for acceptance or taking over (Sub-Clauses 17.2, 32).
2. *Contractor behavioral risks* are mainly the following:
   - contractor-caused accidents and casualties (Sub-Clause 22.1); Improper interference of the public (Sub-Clause 9.1);
   - acts or defaults by subcontractors (Sub-Clause 38.3);
   - environmental protection (Sub-Clause 9.1);
   - quality defects (Sub-Clause 15.1).
3. *Risks caused by third party's behavior* are mainly the following:
   - suspension of delivery of water, electric power, and gas by utilities authorities (Sub-Clause 8.5);
   - under China's standard contract, the employer is responsible for both his and the third party's risks as listed above, while the contractor is responsible for his own.

Although the risk allocations are not totally the same under the two construction contracts, they are, for the most part, consistent with the best practice risk allocation principle concerning the behavioral risks. For example, the employer and the contractor are responsible for their respective behavioral risks. This echoes the principle that each party shall be responsible for their misconduct or lack of care; however, under both the FIDIC form and China's standard contract, the employer is responsible for a risk caused by authorities. This may be due to the fact that it is impracticable, if not impossible, for the contractor to insure against such an 'unforeseen' event. In an international setting where the FIDIC form is intended for use, the employer (which in some cases, is the local government or related entity), is more efficient in coordinating with such third party's interfering behavior. As for China's standard contract, which is for domestic use, the purpose of the provision may be due to the "Chinese construction culture." This means that the employer, as a traditional practice, provides water, power, and access road for the contractor to commence the site work as part of the employer's contractual obligation as stated by Clause 8—work of the employer—in China's standard contract. Thus, it seems logical for the employer to be responsible for the shut-off of water and power supply for a continuous period of time. Concerning natural risks, both the FIDIC form and China's standard contract advocate the sharing of the risk but the specific division principle is different to some extent. For example, under the FIDIC form, occurrences of exceptional adverse climatic conditions allow the contractor to extend the completion time implicitly. The contractor is, however, responsible for the incidental costs. China's standard contract is silent on this issue. In extreme *force majeure* cases, the contractor is entitled to both an EOT and financial compensation under both the FIDIC form and China's standard contract (Clause 19 of the FIDIC form and Clause 39 of China's standard contract); however, under the latter, such compensation is only limited to the repair of the damaged permanent work while the contractor is responsible for the injury and damage of his own personnel and construction equipment (Clause 39 of China's standard contract), implying that the employer and the contractor share the risks under *force majeure*. China's standard contract is very clear in allocating the geological risk by stating that the employer is responsible for providing the geological data and for its accuracy (Clause 8). This clear-cut contractual language helps reduce disputes between the two parties. However, the FIDIC form uses very vague language in allocating such geological risk. It might be argued that, if the geological risk is completely allocated to the employer as is the case under China's standard contract, the contractor, who directly undertakes the construction work may lose motivation to take active and positive measures and precautions to deal with the geological conditions, thus reducing its work efficiency; however, at the tendering stage, the employer (or the engineer on his behalf) should be more knowledgeable of the site conditions than the contractor as it is the party who has the most information to forecast risk. The FIDIC form, however, attempts to strike a balance by stating that, on the one hand, the employer is not responsible for the accuracy of the site data provided by him and the contractor is responsible for its interpretation (Sub-Clause 4.10); and that, on the other hand, the employer is only responsible for such geological risk if such risk event is reasonably unforeseeable by the contractor at the tendering stage (Sub-Clause 4.12). While this may, theoretically, make the contractor take the initiative in dealing with the geological problem encountered, the intention to prove such a risk event was unforeseeable by him at the tendering stage. By relying on such contractual language to potentially make a claim against the employer, the contractor's initiative may be reduced and even result in his inaction. This is contrary to FIDIC's original intention as such ambiguous language is more likely to lead to frequent disputes that consume a lot of unnecessary stress and effort by both parties. Further, such a provision might discourage the employer from providing the best possible accurate data, or can even result in the employer concealing negative site conditions to elicit low bids (Sub-Clause 4.10). The fact that disputes in international contracting occur rather frequently suggests the inefficiency of such ambiguous contractual language. Language clarity may be a more specific and practical principle in risk allocation and may outweigh the seemingly reasonable but ambiguous language that may result in frequent disputes. Social risks, such as theft and vandalism, are borne by the contractor under both the contracts. Such losses happen to the contractor in the first instance and it seems to be more efficient for the contractor to take care of site security, as specified in the two contracts. For political risks, such as war, riot and strike, the FIDIC form is seen as pro-contractor, in that the contractor is entitled to an EOT and compensation caused by the occurrence of such external events (Sub-Clause 19.4). China's standard contract stands somewhat neutral in dealing with the political risks. The contractor is entitled to an EOT for such risks but shares the costs with the employer, that is, the contractor shall bear the costs for injuries and damage of his site personnel and construction equipment. The employer shall bear other costs, such as repairing the permanent works and clearance of site debris (Sub-Clause 39.3), as the employer is in a better position to "control" their own properties in such events. Sharing political risks is conducive to motivating both parties to make efforts to mitigate losses caused by such risks.

Under both the FIDIC form and China's standard contract, economic and legal risks are mostly retained by the employer, by means of clear contractual language. Such clear language helps reduce disputes in dealing with price adjustment regarding legal changes and price fluctuations. Lastly, *force majeure*, as one of the important topics in risk management, merits special attention. Both contracts adhere to the principle of sharing the risks of *force majeure* events between the employer and contractor (FIDIC Sub-Clauses 19.4 and 19.6; China standard model contract 39.3).

Shuibo Zhang
Professor of Construction Law
China

12.15.2 Risk allocation in P&DB

Risk allocation in P&DB comes from CONS. The differences mainly relate to the fact that the contract price is not measured (being a lump sum) and that the contractor bears greater risk in connection with the design, its own technical concepts and sequencing of works. The contractor is further exposed to higher demands whenever discrepancies come to light in tender documentation. See also the Chapters 3 and 15 for more details.

12.15.3 Risk allocation in EPC

EPC allocates some of the above-described employer's risks to the contractor (beyond the limits of P&DB), mainly in connection with errors in tender documentation and with examination of the on-site physical conditions. Only limited possibilities to claim are then available to the contractor. Primarily, the contractor's claims under Sub-Clauses 1.9— delayed drawings or instructions, 4.7—setting out and 4.12—unforeseeable physical conditions are not permitted.

Under EPC, the contractor is not entitled to an extension of time for extremely adverse climatic conditions, unless they constitute *force majeure* under Clause 19. On the other hand, EPC limits the extent of the employer's instructions to: (1) those necessary for the contractor's obligation; and (2) which must be clearly identified and communicated. The employer is not empowered to instruct the contractor to complete prior to the time for completion and the contractor is not obliged to comply with any such instruction.

Design risks lie fully with the contractor being, in EPC, deleted from the enumeration under Sub-Clause 17.3 (g) of CONS and P&DB. The same applies to risks of unforeseeable natural forces except for those that are so adverse and exceptional that they will become *force majeure* events as per Sub-Clause 19.1 (v) of EPC, where (within a demonstrative enumeration) natural catastrophes such as earthquakes, hurricanes, typhoons, or volcanic activity are specified as being subject to contactor claims for an extension of time for completion only. Exclusively man-made *force majeure* events are subject to contractor's claims for additional payments.

A substantial risk shift is encountered in Sub-Clause 4.12 of the FIDIC EPC/1999 Silver Book, which has an updated title "*Unforeseeable Difficulties.*" Sub-Clause 4.12 stipulates that "except as otherwise stated in the contract, the contractor shall be deemed to have obtained all necessary information as to risks, contingencies and other circumstances which may influence or affect the works." It is further stipulated that the contractor—by signing the contract—accepts total responsibility for having foreseen all difficulties and costs of successfully completing the works and the contract price shall not be adjusted to take account of any unforeseen difficulties or costs.

Such a contract is appropriate only for specific projects. The FIDIC position is as explained in the following foreword to the FIDIC EPC/1999 Silver Book.

Explanation of FIDIC EPC risk allocation by FIDIC

FIDIC's Red and Yellow Books have been in widespread use for several decades, and have been recognized, among other things, for their principles of balanced risk sharing between the employer and the contractor. These risk-sharing principles have been beneficial for both parties, the employer signing a contract at a lower price and only having further costs when particular unusual risks actually eventuate, and the contractor avoiding pricing such risks that are not easy to evaluate. The principles of balanced risk-sharing are continued in the new "construction" and "plant and design-build" books. In recent years it has been noticed that much of the construction market requires a form of contract where certainty of the final price, and often of the completion date, is of extreme importance. Employers on such turnkey projects are willing to pay more—sometimes considerably more—for their project if they can be certain that the agreed final price will not be exceeded. Among such projects can be found many projects financed by private funds, where the lenders require greater certainty about a project's costs to the employer than is allowed for under the allocation of risks provided for by FIDIC's traditional forms of contracts. Often the construction project (the EPC—engineer, procure, construct—contract) is only one part of a complicated commercial venture, and financial or other failure of this construction project will jeopardize the whole venture. For such projects it is necessary for the contractor to assume responsibility for a wider range of risks than under the traditional Red and Yellow Books. To obtain increased certainty of the final price, the contractor is often asked to cover such risks as the occurrence of poor or unexpected ground conditions, and that what is set out in the requirements prepared by the employer actually will result in the desired objective. If the contractor is to carry such risks, the employer obviously must give him the time and opportunity to obtain and consider all relevant information before the contractor is asked to sign on a fixed contract price. The employer must also realize that asking responsible contractors to price such risks will increase the construction cost and result in some projects not being commercially viable. Even under such contracts the employer does carry certain risks such as the risks of war, terrorism and the like and the other risks of *force majeure*, and it is always possible, and sometimes advisable, for the parties to discuss other risk-sharing arrangements before entering into the contract. In the case of BOT (build-operate-transfer) projects, which are normally negotiated as a package, the allocation of risk provided for in the turnkey construction contract negotiated initially between the sponsors and the EPC contractor may need to be adjusted in order to take into account the final allocation of all risks between the various contracts forming the total package.

Apart from the more recent and rapid development of privately financed projects demanding contract terms ensuring increased certainty of price, time, and performance, it has long been apparent that many employers, particularly in the public sector, in a wide range of countries have demanded similar contract terms, at least for turnkey contracts. They have often irreverently taken the FIDIC Red or Yellow Books and altered the terms so that risks placed on the employer in the FIDIC books have been transferred to the contractor, thus effectively removing FIDIC's traditional principles of balanced risk sharing. This need of many employers has not gone unnoticed, and FIDIC has considered it better for all parties for this need to be openly recognized and regularized. By providing a standard FIDIC form for use in such contracts, the Employer does not have to attempt to alter a standard form intended for another risk arrangement, and the contractor is fully aware of the increased risks he must bear. Clearly the contractor will rightly increase his tender price to account for such extra risks. This form for EPC/turnkey projects is thus intended to be suitable, not only for EPC contracts within a BOT or similar type venture, but also for all the many projects, both large and smaller, particularly E&M (electrical and mechanical) and other process plant projects, being carried out around the world by all types of employers, often in a civil law environment, where the government departments or private developers wish to implement their project on a fixed-price turnkey basis and with a strictly two-party approach. Employers using this form must realize that the "employer's requirements," which they prepare should describe the principle and basic design of the plant on a functional basis. The tenderer should then be permitted and required to verify all relevant information and data and make any necessary investigations. He shall also carry out any necessary design and detailing of the specific equipment and plant he is offering, allowing him to offer solutions best suited to his equipment and experience. Therefore, the tendering procedure has to permit discussions between the tenderer and the employer about technical matters and commercial conditions. All such matters, when agreed, shall then form part of the signed contract. Thereafter the contractor should be given freedom to carry out the work in his chosen manner, provided the end result meets the performance criteria specified by the employer. Consequently, the employer should only exercise limited control over and should in general not interfere with the contractor's work. Clearly, the employer will wish to know and follow progress of the work and be assured that the time program is being followed. He will also wish to know that the work quality is as specified, that third parties are not being disturbed, that performance tests are met, and otherwise that the "employer's requirements" are being complied with. A feature of this type of contract is that the contractor has to prove the reliability and performance of his plant and equipment. Therefore special attention is given to the "tests on completion," which often take place over a considerable time period, and taking over shall take place only after successful completion of these tests. FIDIC recognizes that privately financed projects are usually subject to more negotiation than publicly-financed ones and that therefore changes are likely to have to be made in any standard form of contract proposed for projects within a BOT or similar type venture. Among other things, such form may need to be adapted to take account of the special, if not unique, characteristics of each project, as well as the requirements of lenders and others providing financing. Nevertheless, such changes do not do away with the need for a standard form by FIDIC.

The FIDIC golden principles—A new approach to discouraging inappropriate amendments to standard form contracts by Donald Charrett (Australia)

Introduction

The Fédération International des Ingénieurs-Conseils (FIDIC) publishes general conditions of contract that are used for international construction contracts in all legal jurisdictions.

FIDIC general conditions are drafted by FIDIC to be based on fair and balanced risk/reward allocation between employer and contractor, and are widely recognized as striking an appropriate balance between the reasonable expectations of the contracting Parties.

General conditions prepared for use in a wide range of projects and jurisdictions inevitably require supplementing with particular conditions that address the particular requirements of the site location and the unique features of the specific project. It is also often necessary for such particular conditions to amend the general conditions to comply with mandatory law that applies to the site or the legal jurisdiction.

The FIDIC golden principles

In an endeavor to promote the use of its contracts as fair and balanced, FIDIC has articulated those essential characteristics of FIDIC general conditions that should not be amended if it is to be recognized as a FIDIC contract. These are referred to as the **FIDIC Golden Principles (GPs)**.

To promote understanding, the GPs have been formulated at a conceptual level to encapsulate the essence of a FIDIC contract. Each GP expresses a single, readily understood and generally accepted concept. The GPs have been limited to the minimum number necessary for completeness.

The following key considerations underpin the GPs:

- The terms of the contract are comprehensive and fair to both contracting parties.
- The legitimate interests of both contracting parties are appropriately considered and balanced. The legitimate interests of each party include the right to enjoy the benefits of the contractual relationship generally recognized as implicit in the general conditions.
- Best practice principles of fair and balanced risk/reward allocation between the employer and contractor are put into effect in accordance with the provisions of the general conditions.
- No party shall take undue advantage of its bargaining power.
- The contractor/subcontractor is paid adequately in accordance with the contract to maintain its cash flow.
- The employer obtains the best value for money.
- To the extent possible, cooperation and trust between the contracting parties is promoted, and adversarial attitudes are to be discouraged and should be avoided.
- The contract provisions are not unnecessarily onerous on either party.
- The contract provisions can be practically put into effect.
- Disputes are avoided to the extent achievable, minimized when they do arise, and resolved efficiently.

The golden principles

GP1: The duties, rights, obligations, roles, and responsibilities of all the contract participants must be generally as implied in the general conditions, and appropriate to the requirements of the project.

As with most construction contracts, FIDIC contracts refer to several other persons (such as the engineer, subcontractors and dispute avoidance board), in addition to the contracting parties (employer and contractor). All the persons referred to in a FIDIC contract (contract participants) have clearly defined roles, duties, and obligations important to the efficient administration and proper functioning of the contract. Concomitant with those roles, and so on, are rights defined in the contract.

The allocation of specific roles, duties, and obligations to the various contract participants in FIDIC contracts has evolved over a long period, and has stood the test of time. Experience has shown that this allocation is consistent with widely accepted and understood international usage.

The delivery of a large construction project involves a complex interaction between all the contract participants. Each has his/her own roles, duties, and obligations, which interface with the roles, duties, and obligations of the other contract participants. The roles, duties, and obligations defined in a FIDIC contract are considered by FIDIC to be those most appropriate to the efficient delivery of the contractual objectives, and best suited to the skills and expertise normally expected of and exercised by the different contract participants.

A FIDIC contract is based on the employer and the contractor undertaking their roles, duties, and obligations and having the rights generally as defined in the general conditions. For the employer this involves, for example, providing access to the site at the time contracted for, and paying the contractor. For the contractor it involves, for example, executing and completing the works in accordance with the contract, and rectifying defects during the defects notification period.

The roles, duties, and obligations of other contract participants as defined in the general conditions are equally important for efficiently delivering the contractual objectives (notwithstanding that, not being parties, they are not bound by the terms of the contract). Thus, for the Red, Pink, and Yellow Books, this requires that an engineer be appointed with appropriate authority, competence and resources to carry out his/her role, and that s/he fulfils their duties and obligations as defined in the contract. Further, the engineer must exercise his/her contractual authority and make fair determinations in accordance with the contract, taking due regard of all relevant circumstances. This means that s/he must not make determinations that only suit the employer's interests, without having due regard to the contractor's rights and entitlements under the contract.

Similarly, for the Silver Book, the employer's representative (if appointed) must have appropriate authority to carry out his/her role, and must carry out that role to enable the Contractor to enjoy its contractual rights.

GP2: The contract conditions must be drafted clearly and unambiguously.

FIDIC general conditions undergo a comprehensive drafting and independent review process to ensure that they are clear and unambiguous. Clear and unambiguous drafting is fundamental to all contract participants understanding their roles and duties, in order that they can fulfil their obligations and exercise their rights.

The conditions of a FIDIC contract comprise the general conditions and the particular conditions, which incorporate any additions or changes to the general conditions. A FIDIC contract will only be clearly and unambiguously drafted if the particular conditions are clearly and unambiguously drafted, and interface harmoniously with the general conditions.

GP3: The particular conditions must not change the balance of risk/reward allocation provided for in the general conditions.

Fair and balanced risk/reward allocation is widely accepted as the most appropriate basis for drafting of construction contracts to minimize the prospects of disputes and enhance the likelihood of achieving successful project outcomes. It is a fundamental principle on which FIDIC contracts are based.

GP4: All time periods specified in the contract for contract participants to perform their obligations must be of reasonable duration.

Time periods specified in the general conditions have evolved as a consensus among the international construction community as an appropriate balance between the interests of a contract participant required to perform a duty, and the interests of the party whose rights are dependent on the execution of that duty. FIDIC considers they are reasonable time periods for the particular matters to which they refer, but without undue delay.

The consequences of reducing the time periods provided for in the general conditions may result in a contract participant having insufficient time to properly perform their required duties or to exercise their rights. An earlier trigger of a time bar than is contemplated in the general conditions is one potential consequence of reducing time periods.

Conversely, significantly extending those time periods may adversely affect the rights of the party for whose benefit the duties are being performed. For example, a much longer period for a contractor to suspend work may substantially increase the likelihood of not recovering amounts due under the contract.

In many provisions of the general conditions the parties are invited to amend the default time periods by agreement, using words such as unless otherwise agreed. Such time periods are recognized as being fixed by negotiation if appropriate, while providing a default option considered to be a reasonable time period.

GP5: All formal disputes must be referred to a dispute adjudication board for a provisionally binding decision as a condition precedent to arbitration.

The dispute adjudication board (DAB) (termed the dispute board in the Pink Book) has evolved as an important mechanism to provide the parties with a procedure for resolving disputes (at least provisionally) at much lower cost and in much less time than required for arbitration. It resolves the conflicts of interest that can occur, where the engineer (engaged and paid by the employer) not only certifies the contractor's entitlements under the contract, but also has the authority to resolve disputes.

The DAB procedure provides an independent third party that promotes early resolution of disputes to enable the project to proceed without unnecessary disruption, and assists in maintaining appropriate communication between the contracting parties. Additionally, a full-term (standing) DAB (as provided for in the Red and Pink Books, and as will be provided in the second editions of the Yellow and Silver Books) may contribute to dispute avoidance.

If one of the parties is not satisfied with a DAB decision, it can issue a notice of dissatisfaction and trigger the arbitration process. However, arbitration can be delayed until the project is complete, avoiding project personnel from becoming distracted. In the meantime, the parties have a decision that provides a provisional resolution of the dispute.

FIDIC considers the availability of an independent and impartial standing DAB to (provisionally) resolve disputes is fundamental to a fair and balanced contract. A standing DAB can resolve disputes in real time, and thereby enable the Parties to plan their future activities based on the reasoned decision of experienced, independent and impartial persons who are familiar with the execution of projects and administration of construction contracts.

Donald Charrett
Barrister, Arbitrator & Mediator Melbourne TEC Chambers Melbourne Australia

12.16 Design responsibility under FIDIC forms

In general, responsibility for design is governed by Sub-Clause 4.1, stipulating that the contractor shall design, execute, and complete the works as specified in the contract and with the engineer's instructions and shall remedy any defects in the works. The scope of design may be defined in the *particular conditions* (and/or in other contractual documents, such as the *specifications*) including details of design approval procedures and so on. In the general part of the FIDIC forms, it is mainly the contractor's obligation under Sub-Clause 7.1 to manufacture or acquire the *plant and materials* and further execute the works with care, in a proper workmanlike and careful manner, in accordance with recognized good practice and to properly use equipped facilities and non-hazardous materials. It is further stated in Sub-Clause 8.3 (d) that the contractor shall submit a detailed schedule to the engineer (including a general description of the methods, which the contractor intends to adopt) and the major stages, in the execution of the works.

Moreover, in P&DB and EPC, there is a whole new chapter dealing with design (Chapter 5), which has been added. When completed, the works shall be fit for the purposes for which the works are intended as defined in the contract. The contractor is responsible the design under both mentioned design-build forms. However, it is worth emphasizing that under Sub-Clause 1.13 the employer must obtain (or shall obtain) the planning, zoning or similar permission for the permanent works. According to Sub-Clause 4.1 of CONS, if the contract specifies that the contractor shall design any part of the permanent works, then, unless otherwise stated in the *particular conditions*, the contractor shall be responsible for this part and the works shall, when completed, be fit for the purposes for which they are intended as specified in the contract.

With the traditional form of design-bid-build (i.e., CONS), a major portion of responsibility for the design is borne by the employer. The tender specifications contain a more detailed design. Under the design-build delivery method, the employer's requirements specify only the purpose, scope, and/or design and/or other technical criteria for the works. The contractor will then prepare their proposal (usually complete with the basic design). The financial investment the contractor is willing to commit to tender will always depend on a particular project, priorities, time for bid preparation, and economic cycle. The contractor will certainly oppose excessive expenses involved in bid preparation—especially in cases where these expenses can only be recovered, if the bid is successful.

The approach to design preparation is different in particular countries and under different public law related to individual stages of the design. The practice of employers who, for example, refund the cost of bid preparation to applicants may also be of importance.

Concerning the procedures for preparing and approving the design during the execution of the works, P&DB and EPC provide further details in Sub-Clause 5.2. As stipulated here, if the *employer's requirements* specify that the *contractor's documents* are to be submitted to the engineer for review and/or for approval, they shall be subject to the "review period." Unless otherwise stated in the *Employer's Requirements*, each review period shall not exceed 21 days—calculated from the date on which the engineer receives the contractor's document and the contractor's notice. The notice shall also state that the contractor's document is deemed as ready for both review (and, if specified, for approval) and use. Sub-Clause 5.2 further deals with the conduct of the engineer. The engineer may return the documents to the contractor during the review period if they do not comply with the conditions of contract. The engineer may also approve the documents with or without comments. However, execution of works shall never commence until the engineer has approved the *contractor's document*. Apart from the above, the engineer shall be (within a P&DB) deemed to have approved the *contractor's document* upon the expiry of the review periods for all the *contractor's documents* which are relevant to the design and execution of such part. The above described procedure was criticised as inefficient and changed in the 2017 edition to a clearly structured review process based on comments and no objection statements to avoid the problematic need for design approvals.

Another significant provision of P&DB's Clause 5 are Sub-Clauses 5.2 (d) [5.2 (c) in EPC]. These instruct that if the contractor wishes to modify any design that has previously been submitted for review, the contractor shall immediately give notice to the engineer and submit the revised documents to the engineer. It is stipulated in general that any approval, consent, or review by the engineer shall not relieve the contractor of their responsibilities. It applies under Sub-Clause 5.8 of P&DB and EPC that if errors, ambiguities, inconsistencies, drawbacks, or other defects are found in the *contractor's documents*, they and the works shall be remedied at the contractor's expense notwithstanding any consent or approval under Chapter 5.

The requirements for as-built documents and/or for various partial shop drawings shall regularly be provided by the contract (specifications, particular conditions, and so on) and/or by the governing law of contract. The contractor is obliged to update their documents in response to changes in legislative requirements, technical standards, and so on. The consequences shall be dealt with as a variation in compliance with Clause 13 or as a claim under Sub-Clause 20.1.

Under P&DB, upon receiving notice of commencement of works:

> The contractor shall scrutinise the employer's requirements (including design criteria and calculations, if any) and the items of reference mentioned in Sub-Clause 4.7 [Setting Out]. Within the period stated in the appendix to tender, calculated from the commencement date, the contractor shall give notice to the engineer of any error, fault or other defect found in the employer's requirements or these items of reference. After receiving this notice, the engineer shall determine whether Clause 13 [Variations and Adjustments] shall be applied, and shall give notice to the contractor accordingly. If and to the extent that (taking account of cost and time) an experienced contractor exercising due care would have discovered the error, fault or other defect when examining the Site and the Employer's Requirements before submitting the Tender, the Time for Completion shall not be extended and the Contract Price shall not be adjusted.

EPC Sub-Clause 5.1 deems the contractor to have scrutinized (prior to the base date), the employer's requirements (including design criteria and calculations if any). The contractor shall be responsible for the design of the works and for the accuracy of such employer's requirements (including design criteria and calculations) except as stated below. The employer shall not be responsible for any error, inaccuracy, or omission of any kind in the employer's requirements as originally included in the contract and shall not be deemed to have given any representation of accuracy or completeness of any data or information, except as stated below. Any data or information received by the contractor (from the employer or otherwise), shall not relieve the contractor of their responsibility for the design and execution of works. Therefore, this represents an almost complete design risk shift.

The exclusive limits for the above-described risk shift are stated in the last part of this sub-clause that stipulates that the employer shall be responsible for the correctness of the following portions of the employer's requirements and of the following data and information provided by (or on behalf of) the employer:

(a) portions, data, and information that are stated in the contract as being immutable or the responsibility of the employer;
(b) definitions of intended purposes of the works or any parts thereof;
(c) criteria for the testing and performance of the completed works; and
(d) portions, data and information which cannot be verified by the contractor;
(e) except as otherwise stated in the contract.

Design Liability: risk share, conflicts and a little bit of common sense? by Cecilia Misu (Germany)

Introduction

The law and the construction industry have had a narrow, if not always fortunate, relation.
Traditionally, the roles in construction projects were clear: design professionals provided the plans and drawings and the builder built following these designs. However, back then as well

as today, problems arose when the parties crossed the line: either builders providing design works and in consequence assuming responsibility for design deficiencies, or designers performing traditional builder activities or supervision of the works and thus losing any limitation of liability traditionally enjoyed by design professionals.

While contractors are usually familiar with the standard terms found in international construction contracts, they are less familiar with the issue of design liability and risk, so that they may underestimate its impact and consequences.

The purpose of this article is to examine basic liability matters that affect employers, designers and construction contractors in international infrastructure projects. It does not intend to assess merits and shortcomings of the liability framework in international construction, but rather to highlight some aspects of the design liability in the context of commonly used procurement methods.

To illustrate the contract language used on the topics in discussion, this article cites provisions taken from specific contracts.

Design liability

The design of complex infrastructure assets is a challenging undertaking and, despite the best efforts in the provision of professional design services, real or perceived design problems inevitably occur.

The standard forms of contract commonly used in international infrastructure projects provide for contractor's obligation to deliver construction work of good quality, free from defects, and in strict conformance with the contract documents. The question is, what exactly does this mean in terms of the contractor's design liability?

In order to provide an answer to this question, the procurement methods used in international infrastructure projects will be briefly discussed.

Key procurement methods

Traditional Procurement Route

This method, also called design-bid-build ("DBB"), is one of the most commonly used procurement methods in infrastructure projects. It requires multiple points of responsibility for delivery of the project, i.e. the employer designs the works in detail either with their own personnel or through a professional designer team, and then employs a contractor, selected on the basis of a competitive tender, to undertake the whole of the construction works.

When using this procurement route, the employer needs to conclude two separate contracts: one with the design consultant, to design the project and prepare tender documentation including drawings, work schedules and bills of quantities, and the other with the construction contractor.

The contractor is obliged to provide materials and equipment that are new and of good quality, the works have to be

1. performed in accordance with the plans and specifications, and
2. free of defects in materials and workmanship.

The Contractor may bear no responsibility for any design other than the temporary works or the sections of the works for which the construction contract expressly delegates design responsibility upon him.

Liability issues under this procurement method are affected by the liability gaps between the mentioned contracting arrangements. This may entail considerable risks for the employer, for instance in cases where it is difficult to determine conclusively whether defective design or defective construction is the root cause of a problem that impacts construction. The same risks are in cases where the construction contractor fully complies with the employer's plans and specifications, but the project fails to meet the employer's intended purposes, or where the employer is obligated to pay the contractor for the implementation of design omissions.

The design professionals' liability for errors and omissions such as those mentioned above, and in consequence employer's entitlements in case of designers' mistakes, will be determined by whether the design consultants have performed their services with the prevailing standard of care consistent with other design professionals in their community (if the contracts were silent on standard of care) or with the standard agreed upon in the underlying contract between the employer and the design consultant.

Although construction contractors have no responsibility for design under DBB, they should be mindful of some implied obligations that might lead to them becoming liable for design defects. For example, this would be the case, if the contractor fails to bring an obvious design error to the designer's attention or proceed with works to a design, which the contractor knew, or ought to have known, was defective.

The incorporation of contractor-designed sections is becoming increasingly common in DBB projects as shown in the provisions below that allocate full design and build liability to the contractor for a discrete portion of the works:

Sub-Clause 4.1 [*Contractor's General Obligations*] Pink Book 1999

"*(c) The Contractor shall be responsible for this part and it shall, when the Works are completed, be fit for such purposes for which the part is intended as are specified in the Contract; …*"

Sub-Clause 4.1 [*Contractor's General Obligations*] Red Book 2017

"*(e) The Contractor shall be responsible for this part and it shall, when the Works are completed, be fit for such purpose(s) for which the part is intended as are specified in the Contract (or, where no purpose(s) are so defined and described, fit for their ordinary purpose(s)).*"

Even under this traditional method, an employer can shift design responsibility to the contractor, for instance when there are no plans or specifications for a particular work to be done and the contract merely describes the results to be accomplished without requiring the construction contractor to use a certain method to accomplish that result. In both cases, the contractor warrants that the work will be fit for its intended use as to both workmanship and materials so that its risk in case of defective design is extremely high. This requires contractor's assessment of the added cost and risk exposure related to assumption and professional performance of the design works as well as of risk-mitigation measures through insurance or otherwise.

Design and build

This method allows the employer to contract on a "single point of responsibility" basis for the project, i.e. the employer enters into a contract with a single entity (D&B contractor / design-builder), which assumes the responsibility to design as well as to construct and perform all services required to deliver and complete the works in accordance with the requirements of the contract, as well as all applicable codes and regulations.

This amalgamation of functions (design development, approval and construction) within the construction process blurs the traditional responsibilities of the design professionals and the construction contractors. In consequence, the design-builder voluntarily assumes the obligation to comply with building codes, statutes, as well as all regulations governing the responsibility of design professionals.

Due to D&B contractor's hybrid responsibilities it is irrelevant for the employer whether a problem is caused by errors or omissions in design or by a defective workmanship: a D&B contractor is liable for both. This situation that significantly impacts the treatment of the contractor's design liability does not create, however, a risk-free project for the employer.

Design-builders commonly fulfil their design obligations either by using the services of an in-house design team or by sub-contracting out that function to independent design consultants. The latter case requires the design-builders to carefully assess the extent to which design obligations from their D&B contractual relationship with the employer may be flow-down to the parties actually carrying out the design. In absence of contractually agreed risk transfer mechanisms and even where the contract with the design professional contains all the appropriate risk transfer provisions, the design-builder, who remains liable towards the employer for the acts of its design professional subcontractor, still bears a significant degree of risk for the consequences of deficiencies in the design documents. This often leads to the fact that in the event of a serious design defect the D&B contractor and the design professionals start pointing fingers at each other and are likely to end up in litigation.

The D&B forms commonly require that the finished project comply with the employer's expectations of performance. This results in the design-builder assuming not only the obligation to provide labour, materials, plant and the working methods selected to perform the works, but also assuming the risk in respect of fitness for purpose of the design. Such an obligation exists from the moment that the design-builder becomes aware of a particular requirement that the design has to fulfil.

Some Areas of Concern

Defective specifications at tender stage

In traditional contracting, the contractor is obliged to comply with the detailed plan and specifications furnished by the employer. A non-compliance with these contract documents trigger specific remedies for the benefit of the employer, such as the right to reject the works and instruct the contractor to make good the defect(s) at their own cost or may even give ground for terminating the contractor for default. A construction contractor is, however, not responsible for errors in the design that the contractor could not have reasonably foreseen. In consequence, if the contractor fully complies with the detailed plans and specifications furnished by the employer, and the project fails to meet the employer's intended purposes, the employer has no recourse against the contractor.

From employer's perspective, his design consultant is liable for the defective specifications. However, unless the employer and the design consultant expressly agreed to a particular standard of care for the performance of the design services, it can be difficult for an employer to obtain compensation for sums paid to the contractor for the performance of additional works related to design deficiencies. Only in the case that the agreed standard of care of the design professional was not met, i.e. that the design deficiencies amount to a level of professional negligence, the employer is entitled to obtain compensation for:

- the additional cost resulting from having the work performed by the contractor in a non-competitive environment;
- the additional costs of demolition work required to erect the omitted work; and
- the additional costs resulting from schedule disruptions.

It is needless to say that if the deficiencies in the design are detected early enough, i.e. before the contractor actually performed any work that had to be removed, the financial consequences of the design errors or omissions can be relatively low.

Notwithstanding the above, a contractor who becomes aware of an obvious design defect during the tendering process has the duty to warn the employer; his failure to warn of the design insufficiency will be deemed as the contractor having assumed the related risk. However, if the design documents contain errors that a contractor could not reasonably determine from the review of the tender documents (i.e. latent errors), then the contractor does not assume the related risk.

It has to be mentioned that in a number of cases where an employer provided a detailed specification during the tender phase that was reasonably relied upon by the tenderers, the courts in different jurisdictions have decided that the principles mentioned above apply irrespective of the procurement method. In this regard refer, for example, to the cases cited in Legal Aspects of performance-based specifications for Highway Construction and Maintenance Contracts, (Nat'l Cooperative Highway Research Program, Legal Research Digest No. 61, Transportation Research Board, 2013).

The application of the above concepts can be slightly – but not totally – different in D&B contracting.

The fact that in a D&B project, the contractor will ultimately provide the final design for the works does not appear to alter these principles, given that it cannot be required that tenderers during the tender phase go through an extensive engineering effort to establish the adequacy or correctness of the substantial amount of information, among others preliminary design data and performance specifications, furnished by the employer during the design–build procurement process.

As shown below, employers often attempt to absolve themselves and shed all design responsibility for the information provided to the tenderers and transfer the risk of errors or omissions in it to the D&B contractor by means of disclaimer language in the contract forms. However, if the risk of defective employer-furnished data is shifted to the D&B contractor, proposal pricing may increase given that contractors would have to provide for contingencies to cover this risk.

Sub-Clause 5.1 [*General Design Obligations*] paragraph 4 of the FIDIC Silver Book 2017 states:

"The Employer shall not be responsible for any error inaccuracy or omission of any kind in the Employer's Requirements as originally included in the Contract and shall not be deemed to have given any representation of accuracy or completeness of any data or information except as stated in this Sub-Clause below. Any data or information received by the Contractor, from the Employer or otherwise, shall not relieve the Contractor from his responsibility for the design and execution of the Works."

This sub-clause also contains a list of the limited exceptions that may entitle contractors to claim for damages caused by defective employer-furnished data and information.

" ... the Employer shall be responsible for the correctness of the following portions of the Employer's Requirements and of the following data and information provided by (or on behalf of) the Employer:

(a) *portions, data and information which are stated in the Contract as being immutable or the responsibility of the Employer,*
(b) *definitions of intended purposes of the Works or any parts thereof,*
(c) *criteria for the testing and performance of the completed Works, and*
(d) *portions, data and information which cannot be verified by the Contractor, except as otherwise stated in the Contract."*

Some forms of contract commonly used, establish a period of time during the design development process, where the contractor is entitled to submit claims in respect of deficiencies in employer-furnished information at tender stage. After the end of that period, D&B contractor's claim rights are waived for all matters not previously raised.

Employer's involvement in approval process of Design Submittals

Employer's involvement in the review and approval of design submittals on D&B projects may have greater implications on employer's liability than under other procurement systems.

In the absence of express provisions addressing the design development process in a D&B contract, questions may arise as to whether an employer, is potentially taking on design liability in performing a review function.

Disputes occur as to whether an employer waived his rights in respect of certain design deficiencies in cases where the design submitted by the D&B contractor contained errors or clearly showed contractor's interpretation of certain design aspects and the employer did not object during the design review.

Under the circumstances, the D&B contractor has the chance to succeed with an allegation that employer's approval of a defective design may shift design-builder's liability for design defects and/or absolve him from fulfilling the performance criteria agreed upon in the contract, if the contractor demonstrates that:

(i) the employer was aware during the design process that the mentioned component/section of the works was unsuited or only suitable for considerably limited use, but none the less approved it,
(ii) the employer knew that a component/section of the works unfit for the proper fulfilment of his expectations of performance had been erected in the project,
(iii) based on employer's approval, the contractor completed the project with the defective design, which would be expensive to be made good at that point.

Possible solutions of such a dispute demand a thorough evaluation of the design and construction functions in the context of the particular D&B project.

In order to avoid this kind of problems and disputes, most design–build contracts used in infrastructure projects include a clause similar to SC 5.8 [*Design Error*] of the FIDIC Yellow and Silver books 2017 stating that:

> "*If errors, omissions, ambiguities, inconsistencies, inadequacies or other defects are found in the Contractor's design and/or the Contractor's Documents, they and the Works shall be corrected in accordance with Sub-Clause 7.5 [Defects and Rejection]. If such the Contractor's Documents were previously the subject of a Notice of No-Objection given (or deemed to be given) by the Engineer under Sub-Clause 5.2.2 [Review by Engineer], the provisions of Sub-Clause 5.2.2 shall apply as if the Engineer had given a Notice in respect of the Contractor's Documents under sub-paragraph (b) of Sub-Clause 5.2.2.*
>
> *All corrections and resubmissions under this Sub-Clause should be at the Contractor's risk and cost.*"

In addition to liability matters, issues can arise as to whether the employer's actions during the design review and approval process make it liable for causing delay to the contractor.

D&B contractors often complain that the employer:

- was dilatory in performing the design reviews,
- incremented contractor's scope of work, and
- took a formalistic approach, nit-picking the submittal

thus, preventing the contractor from moving efficiently from the design to construction phase.

Should the employer interfere during the review and approval process of the D&B contractor's design documents, the employer may be liable for the design-builder's resulting delay, provided that the design-builder's claim proves that:

(i) employer breached its contractual obligations (e.g., unreasonable response times or added scope of work);
(ii) contractor gave notice, within a defined period of time after employer's breach, that the progress of the works was being negatively impacted; and
(iii) employer's breach actually affected the completion date.

It has to be noted that the mentioned claims often fail because the design-builders either never objected to the employers' actions throughout the period that the employer was allegedly dilatory or were unable to prove the impact of employer's interference on the critical path of the project, or contributed to the project delay (for instance, the submission in issue was incomplete).

In order to prevent this kind of allegations, most D&B contracts expressly specify the level of design submittals expected from the contractor and the response time required by the employer. For instance, Sub-Clause 5.2.2 [*Review by Engineer*] of the FIDIC Yellow and Silver books 2017 defines Review Period as:

> "*the period not exceeding 21 days, or as otherwise stated in the Employer's Requirements, calculated from the date on which the Engineer [Employer in the Silver book] receives a Contractor's Document and a Contractor's Notice.*"

Protection Mechanisms

Whether reliance is placed on a standard contract form, a bespoke contract, or some combination of the two, realistic and practical contract provisions are a necessary and critical element in the risk-management process for design-builders and other parties to a design-build project.

In this context, D&B contractors often seek to limit their liability for defects or design deficiencies through contractual terms.

Limitations of Liability

The purpose of this type of clauses in DBB and D&B contracts is not to release the design-builder from any liability towards the employer, but to apportion, avoid or manage contractor's risk exposure to loss or damages as a result of its performance of the contract. At the very end, limitation clauses allow contractors to accurately assess their 'worst-case' scenario under the contract and provide employers with precise information on their 'best-case' recovery if things go wrong.

There are numerous forms of limiting liability in a contract. These include:

- establishing a cap on the total amount of damages a party will be liable for,
- excluding liability for consequential damages,
- limiting recovery for certain events,
- establishing liquidated damages for certain breaches of contract, …

It has to be noted that these clauses' drafting will be primarily influenced by the availability of insurance at economic levels against the risks to be limited. In addition, particular care should be taken to avoid unnecessary complexities that could undermine the enforceability of a successfully negotiated limitation clause when claims arise.

In this regard, to ensure that the "limitation of liability" clause withstands scrutiny in the courts of the relevant jurisdiction if and when a dispute arises, it needs to be incorporated into the project contract using clear and unambiguous language that identifies:

(i) the party benefiting from the limitation of its liability;
(ii) the party agreeing to limit its own rights and remedies by placing a cap of damages for losses suffered due to the benefitting party's (e.g. D&B contractor, design professional) defective design or negligence;

(iii) the type of claims to which the limitation applies; and
(iv) the amount of the limitation.

By way of example, Sub-Clause 1.14 [*Limitation of Liability*] of the FIDIC Silver Book 2017 provides for a default aggregate cap of 100% of the contract price as follows:

"The total liability of the Contractor to the Employer, under or in connection with the Contract ... shall not exceed the sum stated in the Contract Data or (if a sum is not so stated) the Contract Price stated in the Contract Agreement."

The Sub-Clause also provides for:

- general exclusions from this cap

  "This Sub-Clause shall not limit liability in any case of fraud, gross negligence, deliberate default or reckless misconduct by the defaulting Party."

- mutual exclusion of liability for what is commonly referred to as "indirect or consequential loss or damage"

  "Neither Party shall be liable to the other Party for loss of use of any Works, loss of profit, loss of any contract or for any indirect or consequential loss or damage which may be suffered by the other Party in connection with the Contract ..."

Carve-outs from the exclusion of liability for loss of profit/indirect and consequential loss include Delay Damages, Variations, claims under the IP indemnities, losses incurred following termination for convenience under Sub-Clause 15.7, and also losses incurred in respect of omissions of work to give it to third parties.

Indemnification

The principle of indemnification is a three-party concept, which involves a party providing indemnity ("indemnitor"), the indemnified party ("indemnitee"), and a "claimant".

Indemnity clauses are liability-related provisions that transfer risk for certain types of losses - resulting from a claim or claims brought by a third-party - from the claimed party to the other contractual party.

This type of provisions, which retain their validity and legal effects even if the contract is set aside, generally require the indemnitor to:

(i) defend the indemnified party from third party claims that bear a sufficient connection to the indemnitor's activities, and
(ii) pay the indemnified party's legal fees.

The precise consequences of an indemnity provision, particularly in the case of defective design, will depend on the wording in the context of the contract. By way of example, refer to

SC 17.4 [*Indemnities by Contractor*] of the FIDIC 2017 books, which requires the Contractor to indemnify the Employer for failures of the Works or any Section or any major item of Plant not being Fit for the Purpose. This requirement is tempered to some extent by the exclusion of liability for indirect and consequential losses and the fact that any liability under this indemnity will fall within the cap on the Contractor's liability.

Particular aspects that can have a major financial impact on contractors are whether the clause:

- requires an indemnity only against losses of the indemnitee arising out of the indemnitor's conduct,

  for instance, Sub-Clause 17.4 [*Indemnities by Contractor*] of the FIDIC 2017 books states that:

  "*The Contractor shall indemnify and hold harmless the Employer, the Employer's Personnel, and their respective agents,* **against and from all claims, damages, losses and expenses (including legal fees and expenses)** *in respect of:*

  (a) *bodily injury, sickness, disease or death, of any person whatsoever* **arising out of or in the course of or by reason of the Contractor's execution of the Works** …
  (b) *damage to or loss of any property, real or personal (other than the Works), to the extent that such damage or loss:*
      (i) **arises out of or in the course of or by reason of the Contractor's execution of the Works***, and*
      (ii) *is attributable to any negligence, wilful act or breach of the Contract by the Contractor* … " [emphasis added]

- excludes negligence on the part of the indemnitee,

  Sub-Clause 17.4 [*Indemnities by Contractor*] of the FIDIC 2017 books paragraph 1 lit. (a) provides that:

  " … *unless attributable to any negligence, wilful act or breach of the Contract by the Employer, the Employer's Personnel, or any of their respective agents* … "

- covers all losses no matter how they were caused.

In most contract forms used in international construction projects, indemnification interacts with insurance clauses requiring the indemnitor to carry insurance coverage - as appropriated to the works performed under the contract - in order to transfer the risk from the indemnitee's insurance carrier to the indemnitor's insurance carrier.

It has to be noted that the Fit for Purpose obligation and the related indemnity in the FIDIC books 2017 are backed up by an express requirement in Sub-Clause 19.2.3 [*Liability for breach of professional duty*] that, if so stated in the Contract Data, the Contractor's professional indemnity insurance must indemnify it against its liabilities for failure to achieve the fit for the purpose(s) requirements under Sub-Clause 4.1 [*Contractor's General Obligations*].

During the review of this vignette, Lukas submitted for consideration following short, but very interesting comment from a colleague:

> "It is always repeated as a mantra that no insurance policy is available for Contractors for a design based on "fitness for purpose". When I was running the legal and insurance activities of a large company all around the world, I have faced a majority of contracts binding the Contractor to deliver the plant fit for the purpose. The practice in terms of insurance was to deliver a local insurance Policy backed on the French insurance Policy covering the company. No difficulty! Moreover, the Civil law countries are divided into two categories in terms of decennial warranty: those that only include safety when the Works are undermined and those that include also fitness for purpose. For these countries, the insurance market has adapted its practices and deliver fit for the purpose insurance policies."

Therefore, it appears to be in the best interest of contractors to gain a thorough understanding of the different forms of indemnification, the possible statutory restrictions placed on these forms as well as a thorough knowledge regarding the insurability of contractor's indemnification risk through liability coverage and possible statutory restrictions placed on such coverage.

Conclusion

The merger of design and construction obligations into a new super-entity "design-builder" impacts contractor's standard of care as well as its liability in infrastructure projects.

In D&B projects the contractor / design-builder assumes liability for the "sum of all the parts" and therefore owes the employer fitness for purpose duties in respect of the works.

The issues of design liability are far more complex in D&B than in DBB projects. However, employers trying to shield themselves from liability under the "single point of responsibility" concept of the D&B procurement method need to notice that the courts in different jurisdictions have up to this day protected D&B contractors. The courts consider that design–builders should not be held financially responsible for the consequences of defective employer-furnished information that they reasonably relied upon during the tender.

The design approval process may become a major administrative challenge for D&B contractors, as they can significantly be impacted by late and disorganized employers' actions upon submittals. In such a case the design–builder may have a remedy against the employer if he can prove that the notice requirements in the contract were met and can demonstrate the cause-and-effect that the employer's actions had on the project's overall schedule.

References

FIDIC (2000). *The FIDIC Contracts Guide* (1st Edition). FIDIC, Lausanne.
FIDIC (2011a). *FIDIC DBO Contract Guide*. (1st Edition). FIDIC, Lausanne.
FIDIC (2011). *Statutes and By-Laws (October 2011)*, Online. Available at: http://www.fidic.org (accessed 12 July 2018).
Tolson, S. (2012). *Dictionary of Construction Terms*. Routledge, London.

Further reading

Baillon, F. (2013). The Use of FIDIC Contracts Worldwide: FIDIC. Paper presented at ICC Conference, Paris.
FIDIC (1999a). *Conditions of Contract for Construction* (1st Edition). FIDIC, Lausanne.
FIDIC (1999b). *Conditions of Contract for Plant and Design-Build.* (1st Edition). FIDIC, Lausanne.
FIDIC (1999c). *Conditions of Contract for EPC/Turnkey Projects.* (1st Edition). FIDIC, Lausanne.
FIDIC (2008). *Conditions of Contract for Design, Build and Operate Projects.* (1st Edition). FIDIC, Lausanne.
FIDIC (2009). *Conditions of Subcontract for Construction.* Test Edition. FIDIC, Lausanne.
FIDIC (2010). *Conditions of Contract for Construction.* MDB Harmonised Edition. FIDIC, Lausanne.
FIDIC (2011b). *FIDIC DBO Contract Guide.* (1st Edition). FIDIC, Lausanne.
FIDIC (2011c). *FIDIC Procurement Procedures Guide.* (1st Edition). FIDIC, Lausanne.
FIDIC *Annual Report 2011–2012*. Online. Available at: http://www.fidic.org (accessed 12 July 2013).
Jaeger, A.V. and Hök, G.S. (2010). *FIDIC: A Guide for Practitioners.* Springer Verlag, Berlin.
Klee, L. (2011). *Smluvní podmínky FIDIC.* Wolters Kluwer, Prague.
Knutson, R. (2005). *FIDIC: An Analysis of International Construction Contracts.* Kluwer Law International, London.

13

Other Standard Forms of Construction Contracts: NEC, ICC, ENAA, IChemE, Orgalime, AIA, VOB

13.1 Common standard forms of construction contracts

The most frequently used international standard forms of construction contracts are the FIDIC forms, the NEC3 and the ICC Model Turnkey Contract for Major Projects. Other respected forms include ENAA, IChemE, and Orgalime (Grutters and Fahey, 2013). The German standard VOB and the American standard prepared by the AIA are both worth mentioning because of their long tradition and established use in their home jurisdictions.

FIDIC forms are used almost universally. They have the widest geographical acceptance because of their strong tradition, support of lenders, well-known familiar principles, and greatest flexibility of use (for a discussion of FIDIC forms, see Chapter 12).

While NEC forms are gaining increasing popularity, they bring a new, but unfamiliar style and most users face a significant learning curve. Moreover, precise NEC project management tools are hard to implement universally.

13.2 The NEC (New Engineering Contract)

The New Engineering Contract (NEC) was published in 1993 for the first time with the second edition of the box set (launched in 1995), adding several new documents to the family, including a professional services and adjudicator's contract. This led to 10 years of extensive and successful usage with significant feedback from the industry on the contract in practice. This feedback was integrated into the development process and culminated in the launch of NEC3 in 2005 (reissued in April 2013 with minor changes).

With an estimated total cost of £14.5 billion and a peak workforce of 14,000 people by 2013, Crossrail in London is Europe's largest construction project and the biggest ever to be procured by NEC3 contracts.

International Construction Contract Law, Second Edition. Lukas Klee.
© 2018 John Wiley & Sons Ltd. Published 2018 by John Wiley & Sons Ltd.

The London 2012 Olympic Park is also one of the most successful projects where NEC3 contracts were used. With risk to the Olympic Delivery Authority very high and enormous pressure to deliver under public scrutiny, a solid procurement strategy was fundamental. However, after handling in excess of 50,000 compensation events over the life of the project, only one issue went to adjudication.

The NEC was created by the Institute of Civil Engineers as an attempt to move away from traditional forms of contract, which were only about legal rights and obligations and to create a contract that would encourage good project management as well as being easy to use. It is the UK government's contract of choice at present.

The NEC form of contract was referred to in the report published by Sir Michael Latham in 1994, entitled *Constructing the Team*. That report reviewed the construction industry in detail and called for greater collaboration and for parties to align their commercial interests to avoid disputes. This report also led to the government introducing legislation that regulated construction contracts by requiring certainty on payment and giving each party a right to refer disputes to adjudication with an enforceable decision on payment within 28 days (*The Housing Grants, Construction and Regeneration Act* 1996b as amended by the *Local Democracy, Economic Development and Construction Act* 2009).

The Latham Report was followed by *Rethinking Construction*, a report produced by Sir John Egan in 1998. That report also called for greater collaboration and a move from the traditional ways of managing construction projects. It identified the key drivers for change as committed leadership, a focus on the customer, integrated processes and teams, a quality-driven agenda and commitment to people.

It was the recent financial crisis, however, that provided a real driver for change because it was necessary to find ways of reducing the costs of infrastructure projects. These issues were covered in two reports produced by Constructing Excellence: *Never Waste a Good Crisis*, and *Infrastructure in the New Era*.

On the basis of these developments, the UK government has also looked at the UK's spending on infrastructure. In 2011, it published a National Infrastructure Plan to provide a full and coherent strategy for infrastructure in the UK (updated in 2012). In March 2013, the UK government published for consultation its infrastructure route map where it sets out how it will provide cost savings and improve infrastructure projects. In 2014, the UK government had trialed three new methods of procurement: cost-led procurement, integrated project insurance, and two-stage open book to achieve the most cost-effective and value for money solutions by integrated project teams working collaboratively.

The use of the NEC form of contract has been endorsed as a contract that also promotes collaborative working. NEC is designed as an international contract and the first clause of the NEC sets out an overarching obligation on the parties to act in accordance with the terms of the contract and in a spirit of mutual trust and cooperation. This is intended to emphasize the collaborative nature of the contract and the expectation that parties will cooperate to help each other. In that respect, it should be noted that under English law there is no general duty of good faith and such obligations may not be enforceable.

Unlike other forms of contract, the NEC is short, written in simple language and meant to be used by people on site. It is intended as a tool for good project management and is more than a mere contractual document.

An important feature of the NEC contract is the concept of "early warnings." The principle is simple and means that whenever a party (whether employer or contractor) identifies an issue that could affect cost, time, or performance in general, it should notify the other party. The parties would then meet to discuss how that risk can be avoided or limited. This is a step away from the traditional "who has the liability?" approach and recognizes that it is in both the employer's and the contractor's interest to avoid risk, regardless of whose risk it is.

The program plays a key role in the NEC contract. It is intended as a joint tool that sets out the obligations of both parties. There is a detailed list of what the program must include. For example the order and timing of works by other parties, float and time allowed for risk, dates where information from other parties is needed and, for each operation, a statement of how the contractor plans to do the work and identifying the equipment and resources.

The program is therefore used by the project manager to monitor and manage the works and to assess the entitlement to an extension of time in the event of changes or other employer risks (known as compensation events). The program has to be updated on a regular basis (usually every four weeks) and submitted for approval. When this is done, both parties will have a comprehensive updated program that helps to manage the works efficiently and to determine any potential entitlement more accurately.

Under the NEC, change and other employer risks lead to *compensation events* and they provide one single process for assessing additional costs and extensions to the completion date. A contractor must submit a quotation within three weeks and the project manager must make an assessment within two weeks. The intention is to deal with payment and delay as they happen and on the basis of forecasts so that price and the period for completion can be updated within a very short period. As a result, there should be no need for a final account process as issues should be decided as the works progress.

The NEC has six main options that set out different bases for payment. The most popular form appears to be Option C, which is a target cost contract.

If there is a dispute, it must be referred to adjudication in the first instance before court proceedings or arbitration. The NEC provides for a decision to be made within a four-week period, which will be binding unless a party serves a notice within four weeks.

Adjudication has proved very popular in the UK because it allows a quick resolution of disputes in a short period at a much lower cost than arbitration or court proceedings. In many cases, the outcome is acceptable to both parties and they can move on instead of having to direct resources to a lengthy arbitration process. This is especially the case where the identity of the potential adjudicator can be agreed to in advance in the contract. Adjudication may not, however, be suitable for all types of disputes.

It is important to appreciate that using the NEC form or its principles will require a change in culture and thinking, as well as an effort to manage change and risks as they happen. Nonetheless, if used as intended, such an approach can benefit both parties.

13.2.1 NEC forms of contract

Based on the information at http://www.neccontract.com, NEC sample forms of contracts for works encompass purchases such as the construction of buildings, highways, and major process plant and equipment. The contracts for services include purchases of both professional services such as engineering, architectural, and consultancy works along with more composite maintenance or management services such as soft/hard facilities management, cleaning, catering, security services, maintenance of a specific plant/building, data processing, and ambulance services.

A contract for supply includes the supply of high-value goods and associated services such as transformers, turbine rotors, rolling stock, loading bridges, transmission plants, and cables and process plants together with lower risk goods and associated services such as building materials, simple plant and equipment, stationery, PPE, manufacturing parts, components, and store items.

The NEC contracts for works are namely:

1. NEC3 engineering and construction contract (ECC). This contract should be used for the appointment of a contractor for engineering and construction work, including any level of design responsibility.
2. NEC3 engineering and construction short contract (ECs). This contract is an alternative to ECC and is for use with contracts that do not require sophisticated management techniques, comprise straightforward work, and impose only low risks on both client and contractor.
3. NEC3 engineering and construction subcontract (ECs). This contract should be used for the appointment of a subcontractor for engineering and construction work where the contractor has been appointed under the ECC and is written as a back-to-back set of terms and conditions.
4. NEC3 engineering and construction short subcontract (ECss). This contract can be used as a subcontract to ECC or ECsC. it should be used with contracts that do not require sophisticated management techniques, comprise straightforward work, and impose only low risks on both the contractor and subcontractor.

The NEC contracts for services are namely:

1. NEC3 term service contract (TsC). This contract should be used for the appointment of a supplier to maintain a service or manage and provide a service. These services may include elements of design and relate to physical works or soft services such as facilities management. They may have discrete packages of project works, though where the bulk of the scope is about delivering a physical end product it may be appropriate to use the ECC/ECsC as an alternative. The TsC contains a *call off* facility.
2. NEC3 term service short contract (TssC). This contract is an alternative to TsC and is for use with contracts that do not require sophisticated management techniques, comprise straightforward services, and impose only low risks on both client and a contractor.

3. NEC3 professional services contract (psC). This contract should be used for the appointment of a supplier to provide professional services such as engineering, design or consultancy. Unlike the TsC, which is about maintaining an asset, this contract concerns the provision of professional advice. This contract, like the TsC, contains a *call off* facility.

The NEC contracts for supply are namely:

1. NEC3 supply contract (sC). This contract should be used for local and international procurement of high-value goods and related services including design.
2. NEC3 supply short contract (ssC). This contract should be used for local and international procurement of goods under a single order or on a batch order basis, and is for use with contracts that do not require sophisticated management techniques and impose only low risks on both the purchaser and the supplier.

Other NEC sample forms include:

1. NEC3 adjudicator's contract (aC). This contract should be used for the appointment of an adjudicator to decide disputes under the NEC3 family of contracts. It may also be used for the appointment of an adjudicator under other forms of contract.
2. NEC3 framework contract (FC). This contract should be used for the appointment of one or more suppliers to carry out construction work or to provide design or advisory services on an "as instructed" basis over a set term. This umbrella contract must be used in conjunction with one or more of the other NEC3 contracts and comes with a sophisticated *call off* mechanism.

The ECC, ECS, PSC, and TSC offer a range of options to select from that builds up the contract terms to suit the works or services. At the heart of the contract conditions are the core clauses which contain the essential common terms. To this must be added a main option, which will determine the particular payment mechanism. Finally, the selected secondary options are combined with the core and main option clauses to provide a complete contract.

Based on the information at http://www.neccontract.com, this approach gives even greater choice to contracting parties to assemble the appropriate contract conditions to suit. The ECC, ECS, PSC, and TSC offer different basic allocations of financial risk between the parties through the main options. The ECC main options are as follows:

1. Options A and B: these are priced contracts with the risk of carrying out the work at the agreed prices being largely borne by the contractor.
2. Options C and D: these are target cost contracts in which the out-turn financial risks are shared between the client and the contractor in an agreed proportion.
3. Options E and F: these are cost-reimbursable types of contract with the financial risk being largely borne by the client.

The particular options lead to the following basic forms of contracts:

A. Priced contract with activity schedule
B. Priced contract with bill of quantities

C. Target contract with activity schedule
D. Target contract with bill of quantities
E. Cost-reimbursable contract
F. Management contract
G. Term contract

Key to the successful use of NEC is users adopting the desired cultural transition. The main aspect of this transition is moving away from a reactive and hindsight-based decision-making and management approach to one that is foresight-based and encourages a creative environment with proactive and collaborative relationships.

Based on the information at http://www.neccontract.com, NEC offers a range of measures from which the parties can select some to give best value for any particular project or program of work. These are present at a bi-party level and there can be common incentives across a number of partners when *Option X12 Partnering* is used. The range of NEC incentives includes matters that affect time, cost and quality. The following list gives some examples:

- Bonus for early completion – in ECC there is provision for introducing a bonus for each day the contractor completes the works ahead of the contractual completion date.
- Target cost – in ECC, TSC, and PSC, the client can utilize target cost arrangements if the supplier delivers the out-turn cost below the level of the final target. Savings are then shared according to a pre-agreed formula. A similar sharing arrangement of over-run reciprocates this arrangement.
- Key performance indicators (KPIs) – KPIs can be introduced through *Option X12 Partnering* and *Option X20* for any matter the parties care to agree upon. Examples include the number of defects, whole project costs to the client, rate of progress of certain works, whether client satisfaction levels were reached, whether the asset is cheaper to operate and maintain than expected, and so on.

The NEC form of contract—ready for the international market by Rob Horne (UK)

The NEC is now an established form of standard contract in the UK, particularly for public sector works. While its origins may have been in the civil engineering sector, it has grown beyond that to now, arguably, be the dominant standard form of construction contract in use in the UK (only really challenged by the JCT contracts). Despite the enormous success of the NEC within the UK market, its ability to travel and be adopted on major international projects has been limited. It is used in multiple jurisdictions around the world (South Africa, Hong Kong, New Zealand, and others) but these project have never come close to challenging the dominance of the FIDIC forms.

The latest revision to the NEC suite, the fourth edition, was launched at the end of June 2017 under a banner of "evolution not revolution" but with much of the change clearly aimed and enabling NEC4 to be more easily adopted on the international stage. The key question is has NEC4 done enough to break the dominance of FIDIC?

In the following pages there are some specific examples of changes to the NEC4 form of contract (focussing mainly on the main contract form, the engineering construction contract) but first an overview of the key features of the NEC generally to give some context to the changes. The NEC states that it has three principles: clarity and simplicity, flexibility, and good project management. I have added to these the idea of collaboration, which again runs throughout the NEC, as a means of giving that overview.

Collaboration

Unusually for a contract emanating from the UK, where the enforceability of collaboration or good faith clauses remains at best in doubt and more likely unenforceable, the NEC is based around this idea. Indeed the first clause of the NEC (10.1 in NEC3 and below now 10.2 in NEC4) identifies that the parties (and indeed those otherwise involved such as the project manager) shall act both as stated in the contract and in a spirit of mutual trust and cooperation. While in the UK that particular provision has given rise to much commentary on what exactly it means and how it should be interpreted, in the international context, particularly in civil law jurisdictions, the idea of trust and co-operation sits much more comfortably within the legal framework. In every sense, the ideology the NEC is to promote collaboration, albeit within a contractual framework.

Project management

The NEC strives to provide a framework not only for collaborative working but also to enable, and act as a stimulus for, good project management. The idea of good project management really being to focus on the project and look ahead to the challenges still to come adapting and refining the approach of the project team to meet those challenges. That is in contrast to most other contract forms that are more backward looking in assigning rights and responsibilities after problems have occurred. The project management aspects of the NEC really come through in three major areas:

1. **The program**. The NEC requires a program to be submitted at regular intervals (usually monthly) showing a wide range of information including progress and sequence changes to deal with any problems.
2. **Early warning**. To deal with challenges a project may face the NEC requires both the *contractor* and the *project manager* to gives notices if something is identified, which may impact time, cost, or quality of the works. It is intended within the NEC that this is an opportunity creation tool; an opportunity to avoid or minimize the impact of an event while you have time to do something about it, rather than just assigning responsibility for it and requiring mitigation (whatever that might amount to) after the event.
3. **Change management**. Perhaps most controversially and most unusually among contracts of its type, the NEC bases change management (whether that be arising from delay and disruption, variation, or any number of other possible causes) on a prospective view of the likely impact of that event. The intent is that the parties identify events early and then agree the consequences, in both time and money, ahead of the event impacting on the project. Once agreed, the amount is not then changed if actual cost or time is different, thus intending to incentivise both parties to mitigate. This compensation event process should build on and support the program and early warning mechanisms described above. However, from experience, it really does need a collaborative approach in order to succeed and is relatively easy to derail if either party really wants to.

Flexibility

Again unlike its major rivals, the NEC goes out of its way to try and retain standardized drafting. It does that by adopting main options, which allow for different price and risk structures (Option A Fixed Price with an Activity Schedule to Option E Cost Reimbursable) then adding a number of secondary options (W, X, and Y clauses) to tailor those main option contracts. Only as a last resort does the NEC envisage bespoke drafting (Z clauses). The approach, terminology, and general layout is then common across the suite of contracts from the professional services contract, through the engineering construction contract to the supply contract achieving, it is intended, flexibility and commonality at the same time. While this array of options can be off-putting to the novice or new user of the NEC it does allow, once one is familiar with it, a very quick understanding to be gained of the intent and risk profile of the contract. Much more so than the often heavily amended standard forms, which bear little resemblance to the starting contract. Of course, while that may have been the intent of the NEC the contracts are still heavily amended on a regular basis and often those amendments are poor or unnecessary and based on an incomplete understanding of how the NEC works.

Clarity and simplicity

The intention is that the NEC should be an everyday read for the project delivery teams, not a rule book, which only the lawyers really understand. That is a laudable goal and the terminology and structure of the NEC certainly seem to lend themselves to that approach. However, it would be wrong to think of the NEC itself as a simple contract. The language may be simple but the concepts and obligations created by it are anything but. There is, for example, little cross referencing between the clauses but, more so than many other contracts, the clauses interact with each other to support the idea of good project management. This is a form of contract where reading a clause in isolation can be very dangerous indeed.

NEC4

The latest edition has retained all of the basic and underlying principles as described above, along with their inherent benefits and problems. The introduction of NEC4 as evolution rather than revolution is therefore probably fair. However, to make a mark on the international stage something a little more radical to address some of the underlying uncertainty and reliance on just doing what the contract says (as once you are off the path it can be hard to find your way back) may have been needed.

While the changes and adaptations now described for NEC4 go some way to internationalizing the contract, it will likely remain in the shadows unless and until the international construction market makes a real and concerted move towards collaboration, or mutual trust and cooperation.

New terminology

The main theme of NEC4 is that it represents an evolution rather than a revolution in thinking. Many of the changes are therefore updating and adjusting to approach and terminology of the NEC from 2005, when the third edition was published, to 2017. There are four key changes that become apparent early on in reviewing NEC4:

- **Employer → Client**. This is a change really in form rather than substance. It brings the suite of contracts in line with a single term being used. It also adds to the ease of international understanding of the NEC.
- **Works Information → Scope**. This is again mostly form rather than substance. The term scope becomes common through the suite of contracts and is a more widely recognized industry term. The use of scope rather than works information makes the contract easier to adopt internationally where most of those involved readily understand what is intended by the scope.
- **Risk → Early Warning**. The risk register has now become the early warning register. This should help with the confusion between an NEC risk register managed by the *project manager* and a more general project risk register, which most parties maintain separately.
- **Gender neutral**. This is a small change, again in form more than substance, but is to be greatly welcomed nonetheless. References to project participants as "him" and "his actions" are now stated in a neutral voice.

New contracts

The "design, build, operate" or DBO contract is intended to focus first on the operation of an asset, with the design and build being the enabling phase to the operation. Where the operational phase may be 10 to 20 years, using that as the focal point for the contract is appropriate. While it is possible to achieve a similar outcome by "bolting together" a construction form and a term service contract from the NEC suite, it does not work as well as bringing all rights and obligations together in one contract. There does however remain a question mark over why, having reached DBO, a financing option was not also provided, even if by way of secondary option.

The alliance contract is intended to be a more fully formed multi-party partnering contract than the standard NEC form, even with the use of X12 (now called multiparty collaboration). The alliance contract should bring together, under a single contract, all of the key stakeholders for the project.

This can carry many advantages from allowing more direct access through the delivery team to an enhanced ability for the parties to the alliance to resolve problems themselves.

The DBO contract may fall a little behind where other more established forms of the type (FIDIC Gold for example) sit and the alliance contract is only in consultation. However, the response to market demand is encouraging.

Program

The program has always been a central feature of the NEC suite and a key distinguishing feature between the NEC and other standard forms. Despite the very significant management and project controls feature the accepted program has proven to be, there have been a small number of criticisms over how it operates in practice.

The first, and smaller, point was that in the third edition there was specific reference to implemented compensation events being shown on the accepted program. Some had taken this to mean that notified but unimplemented compensation events did not need to be shown. There is now no specific requirement relating to compensation events in Clause 32, which defines what must be shown in updating the accepted program. There remains a concern that some will take that change to suggest that no compensation events should be shown.

The larger change is at Clause 31.3. This now provides that if the *project manager* does not answer a program submission, the program can be accepted by default. As with the default mechanisms in the compensation event clauses there is a requirement to notify the *project manager* of his failure first.

While many commentators have been calling for this for change a number of years (particularly following the deemed notification and quotation for compensation events) two issues arise. Possibly you will see a rise in poorly reasoned rejections (and there is a question mark over whether a poor non-acceptance is effective) or you will see poorly constructed programs accepted by default and issues arising as and when compensation events come to be impacted on it. An interesting change, but it will need to be approached with caution.

Contractor proposals

In the third edition there was no explicit wording allowing for a *contractor* to propose a change and take any share of the savings such a change generated. Clause 16, now titled *contractor's proposals* creates just that opportunity. There are a number of features of this clause to focus on and understand before use:

1. The proposal can only be given for a proposed change that reduces the amount payable to the *contractor*. While this is a good starting point it does not cover changes in other costs, perhaps relating to Others or even the *employer's* own costs through whole life maintenance or even in design and project management. The breadth of the opportunity therefore appears somewhat hampered.
2. It does not deal with potential time or key date reductions. While it could be argued that the acceleration process already exists for this the feel is not quite the same. More likely, the benefit of time saving is always shared in any event and is predictable based on an up to date and accurate accepted program (see Clause 36 now either the *contractor project manager* may propose acceleration).
3. Clause 16 proposals lead to a compensation event for changed scope. Clause 16 does not, however, provide guidance on how that cost saving is to be shared, a key ingredient in incentivising the proposal process. When turning to the core clauses, in Section 6, there is no further specific guidance. However, if you keep hunting, you will find 63.12 for options A&B, which takes you to the *value engineering percentage*, and 63.13 for options C&D, which repeats 63.3 and leaves the proposal saving to the incentive share.

Compensation events

An important change is the introduction of 60.1(20) as a compensation event. This allows for a change to the prices and completion date where the *project manager* asks for a quotation for a proposed instruction, which is not then instructed.

While there has been an addition to the NEC for *contractor's* proposals, there remains the exclusion at 60.1(1) for a change to the scope provided by the *contractor*. This seems to create some tension and may cause significant problems where the contract data, scope, or a Z clause makes all scope *contractor* scope.

Clause 63.1 has been adjusted slightly to clarify the dividing date for when one uses a forecast and when one uses actual costs incurred. The definition and application is straightforward and relatively simple, applied now to both time and money. The simplicity is helpful but gives rise to issues relating to the assessment of delay.

It is important to note that there has been no clarification around the use of an out of date accepted program, whether it should be updated, and if so how, before impacting a compensation event. This seems like a missed opportunity for the fourth edition. Expect to see some industry guidance published on this in the near future.

Dividing date

A challenging feature of a contract, such as the NEC, which uses the same program for project management, project controls, and change management through compensation events is how to identify the right program update to use.

Under the NEC there will, generally, be a new program issued for acceptance every month. There is capacity in the contract for intermediate updates in addition. That provides very useful data and information for proactive management of the project. However, as there can then only be one accepted program (being the latest programme accepted) how does one utilize it for assessing the impact on the program of compensation events? Outside the question of updating, where the accepted program may not properly reflect the status of the project immediately before the compensation event (an issue not addressed in the fourth edition), the question of what happens when the accepted program is updated between occurrence of the event and assessment of the same event arises.

In the fourth edition it is quite clear that you use the accepted program current at the dividing date (Clause 63.5). However, that can lead to some significant problems. For *contractor* notifiable events, for example weather, the *contractor* can (and for weather most likely will) take some time to notify the compensation event as it may not be apparent early on. If the *contractor* notifies 8 weeks after the event (as it is entitled to under Clause 61.3) the accepted program could have been updated twice between the event and the dividing date (being the date of notification). The updated programmes should contain the effects of the compensation event so, when it is assessed, there will be no delay entitlement.

ECI and BIM

Since 2005 when the third edition was launched there has been a significant rise in the use of, and interest in, *early contractor involvement* (ECI) and the use of electronic modeling of design through to construction, now commonly referred to as building information modeling (BIM).

Supplements to address both of these issues had been released by NEC before the launch of the fourth edition but are now incorporated as secondary options X10 for BIM and X22 for ECI. Although there are standard provisions for the use of both of these they provide only a framework and further detail needs to be added to bring them to life.

In the fourth edition BIM is referred to simply as information modeling. This is, in reality, just a difference in title tying back the contracts engineering roots and to avoid an implications that the process is limited to building rather than a wider range of construction project. Two important terms to understand in relation to BIM in the fourth edition are the information model and project information, both of which are defined at X10.1. The information model is the electronic integration of project information. The project information is information from the *contractor* used to build the information model. Liability for any failure in the provision of project information is on a reasonable skill and care basis.

ECI under the fourth edition is restricted to being with option C and E contracts. As ECI will be used to build a Price, a cost based approach, such as option C or E, is needed. The underlying contract is for the whole of the works with acceptance of detailed proposals allowing the project to continue, rather than separate contracts.

Dispute resolution

Under the third edition there were no real options around dispute resolution save for a choice of tribunal, effectively between arbitration and litigation. While there were options W1 and W2 the choice didn't arise as one was compulsory where the Housing Grants, Construction and Regeneration Act (HGCRA) applied.

Under the fourth edition W1 and W2 remain as the primary options dealing with the HGCRA. However, added to both W1 and W2 is now an escalation provision. This allows (where the HGCRA applies) or requires that the parties refer any dispute first to senior representatives to meet and discuss as many times as they consider necessary.

In addition to the escalation provision a new optional provision has been added, W3. This secondary option provides for the establishment and use of a dispute avoidance board to help the parties resolve any disputes prior to submission to the tribunal. While W3 is stated to be applicable only where the HGCRA does not apply, primarily because it requires all disputes to be first sent to the dispute avoidance board, which is inconsistent with the requirements of the HGCRA, it could be used as long as consensual words, such as those for escalation under W2, are added.

W3 establishes a standing dispute avoidance board. That means that a three-person board is established at the outset of the project and meets regularly (standing rather than ad hoc) and does not decide any dispute referred to it by the parties. It simply offers guidance (avoidance rather than adjudication). That said, if a recommendation is made it becomes binding if no dissatisfaction notice is issued in four weeks.

Liabilities and insurance

Section 8 of the NEC, under the third edition, was titled "risk and insurance" and dealt with what was then referred to as risk events. This has been reworked to title Section 8 in the fourth edition "liabilities and insurance" with commensurate changes in the language throughout. The use of the term "risk" in the third edition was somewhat softer than describing and defining liabilities. However, in turn that perhaps led to some misunderstanding about the distinction between risks in the context of section 8 (really meaning liabilities) and risks in the context of early warning (really meaning chance of a future event occurring).

Section 8 had in fact generated more case law under the third edition than any other section of the contract. Much of that case law and guidance has now somewhat fallen away with the changes in this part of the fourth edition. The references to cross party undertaking and their impact on insurance and liability have been removed making the whole section much simpler and easier to operate.

Clause 80.1 makes clear that liabilities or payments to others are to be met by the *client* where they relate to occupation of the site for the works. This however needs to be read in conjunction with the linked *contractor* liability to others where the claim or cost arises in connection with the *contractor* providing the works. Understanding the interplay between these two provisions will be important.

Section 8 also, in the third edition, made clear that anything that wasn't an *employer* risk was a *contractor* risk. Under the fourth edition 80.1 provides a list of *client* liabilities while 81.1 provides the equivalent for *contractor* liabilities. There is no longer a catch all statement for any liability not appearing on either list.

Third party issues

The Third Edition was a contract suite focused very much on bi-lateral relationships, that is, the contractual relationship between the two relevant parties. The Fourth Edition has done more to address this shortfall by core clause 28 regarding assignment, secondary option X4 as an improved parent company guarantee (now called ultimate holding company guarantee) and X8 as a form of collateral warranty (now called undertaking to *Client* or Others).

These changes bring the Fourth Edition very much more in line with usual practice in the market at present, both internationally and domestically in the UK. This should reduce one area of need to include Z clause provisions in order to meet the needs of funders in particular, which is vital if NEC is to spread beyond being just a UK public sector focussed contract.

It is perhaps slightly surprising that assignment has made it to the core clauses where the other third party provisions are retained as secondary options. Another unusual feature, which seems more intent than enforceable, is the requirement in clause 28.1 that the *Client* will not assign if the party receiving the benefit of that assignment does not intend to act in a spirit of mutual trust and cooperation. This not only seems difficult to apply but also appears a tacit acceptance that a *Contractor* can make such an assignment.

While X8 provides a mechanism for introducing an obligation to procure and provide undertakings to the *Client* and Others it is a bare mechanism. The form and content of the assignment still has to be agreed and it is not clear yet whether the NEC intends to publish a standard for undertaking for use with this secondary option.

Payment

In the third edition there were two anomalies that were often referred to and which often ended in the addition of Z-clauses. Those anomalies were that the starting point for an interim payment was assessment by the *project manager* and that there was no definitive final account process. These issues have both been addressed in the fourth edition.

Clause 50.2 now provides that the *contractor* submits an application before each assessment date setting out the amount it considers is due. This brings the payment mechanism in line with the rest of the industry and reflects what, in reality, was happening in any event. Clauses 50.3 and 50.4 then go on to distinguish the amount due depending on whether the *contractor* has made an application or not. Essentially 50.3 provides the standard calculation of price for work done to date, plus any amount to be paid, less any amount to be retained. 50.4 then goes on to say that if the *contractor* does not make an application then the *project manager* assesses as if the *contractor* did make an application. However, there is a sting in 50.4. If the *contractor* does not make an application then the amount due is the lesser of the previous assessment and the current one. The best case therefore for the *contractor* who fails to submit an application is a nil valuation, with the possibility of a negative valuation remaining.

Clause 53 now provides for a final payment mechanism. The starting point for the final assessment, unlike interim assessments, is with *project manager* and it is only in default of the *project manager* assessing in time that the *contractor* then makes an application to the *client*, not the *project manager*. The assessment, whether *project manager* or *contractor* driven, is conclusive evidence of the final amount due and can only be challenged through W1 (senior representatives), W2 (adjudication) or W3 (dispute board) subject to essentially a four week time period. Reference to the tribunal direct does not prevent conculsivity.

Cost components

The NEC suite has always adopted the use of the schedule of cost components (SCC) for pricing compensation events and assessing interim payment under some of the main options. It is of such central importance to payment that even relatively small problems tend to generate significant comment (very much like the compensation event provisions is Section 6 of the contract).

The fourth edition has certainly looked to evolve, rather than revolutionize the SCC through a number of small tweaks and improvements. There are five key changes to note:

Subcontractor cost. In the third edition payments to subcontractors had been cost based so the *contractor* had to remove any subcontractor fee. That has been simplified so the *contractor* now recovers whatever it pays to subcontractors.

Working area overhead. This was intended to be a simple mechanism in the third edition and before to recover sundry items. As it became very complex and controversial to apply in practice it has been removed. Now everything must be claimed separately as cost items.

Amounts payable tied to contract. Under the third edition people costs were based on time worked in the working area. This caused problems for people working outside the working area and in defining some costs, such as bonuses. The fourth edition simplified this to costs incurred for time worked on the contract, though perhaps it should have been in providing the works.

Single fee percentage. In the third edition there were two fee percentages; one for the *contractor* and the other for subcontractors. As the recovery of cost from subcontractors has been simplified so this fee percentage, which was often misunderstood and misapplied, has fallen away.

Short and full SCC. In the third edition the shorter SCC could be used under all the main options for assessing the value of compensation events, whereas the full SCC was used in options C, D, and E for assessing the amount due at interim payments. The fourth edition has simplified this so that Options A and B use the shorter SCC and C, D, and E use the full SCC for all purposes.

Other notable changes

In the process of evolution rather than revolution there are numerous small changes throughout the fourth edition that add to or alter the approach from the third edition. A few of those other issues are identified below:

Termination. Section 9 of the NEC remains relatively unchanged. However, Option X11 has been added to allow for the *client* to terminate the obligation to provide the works for any reason. The process and amount due as a result are essentially the same as where the *contractor* terminates for default or insolvency of the *client*. Therefore, if the *client* terminates at will, the *contractor* is paid its fee on the outstanding balance of the work.

Quality Management. A new Clause 40 has been added to the fourth edition requiring the *contractor* to produce a quality policy statement and a quality plan both to be issued to the *project manager* for acceptance. While it is perhaps a little strange that the quality plan and statement go to the *project manager* rather than the Supervisor the contractualization of this requirement and focus on quality is a good step forward.

Corrupt Acts. Provision against the *contractor* undertaking any such acts and requiring the *contractor* to take steps against any subcontractor undertaking corrupt acts which the *contractors* knows or should know about is now at core Clause 18. It is not clear why the *contractor* is referenced rather than the parties.

Publicity. Core Clause 29 has been added to the fourth edition to restrict how project information is used other than to provide the works.

Rob Horne
Partner
for Osborne Clarke LLP
UK

13.3 FIDIC forms versus NEC3

NEC is intended for global application and has been adopted in many multi-disciplinary projects worldwide. However, the NEC's common law pedigree continues to cause problems in an international construction law context. To quote Lloyd (2009):

> [S]ince NEC3 is written in plain and simple English, it ought to be capable of being used throughout the world without the possibility of its meaning varying with whatever law governs it. That may not always be true, if only because whoever is to decide what the contract means may not have the requisite background or experience or simply because some of the assumptions upon which the NEC has been constructed are implicit or not sufficiently explicit.

In terms of risk allocation, NEC3 is based on similar principles to FIDIC, that is, a balanced risk allocation.

Both FIDIC forms and the NEC3 include re-measurement and a lump sum form. The NEC3 has a special form for construction management (management contracting) and cost plus price determination (cost-reimbursable). The FIDIC Blue Book also uses the cost plus approach and the White Book can be used for construction management delivery method. The most popular, however, is the target price option for which is no equivalent under FIDIC forms. There is not a contract with EPC risk allocation (e.g., such as the FIDIC EPC/1999 Silver Book) under the NEC forms.

In terms of the interim payments, the NEC3 requires works to be paid on the basis of forecasts (of payments to subcontractors) plus a fee. FIDIC is based on retrospective valuations.

The approach to risk allocation and claims are similar. Both forms enumerate employer risks and contain *ex contractu* claims (compensation events in the NEC3).

The NEC3 supports best practice project management by using early warning notices, risk reduction meetings, time bars, deemed acceptances, prompt resolution of problems and assessment of financial implications of claims. In comparison to the 1999 FIDIC forms, those instruments represent a positive development but the question of whether they can be used successfully outside the UK remains.

If the contractor claims a compensation event under the NEC but fails to give an early warning, Sub-Clause 63.5 states that its entitlement to an extension of time and financial compensation will be assessed "as if the contractor had been given an early warning" (Downing, et al., 2013). Such events must be entered into a risk register for their influence to be decreased in risk reduction meetings.

The NEC3 contains an eight-week time bar in Sub-Clause 61.3 in contrast to 28 days in FIDIC forms. According to Lloyd (2009), employers are usually concerned about the effectiveness of contractual sanctions. From this aspect, Sub-Clause 61.3 is a key provision for notifying compensation events stating that:

The contractor notifies the project manager of an event that has happened or which he expects to happen as a compensation event if:

- the contractor believes that the event is a compensation event; and
- the project manager has not notified the event to the Contractor.

If the contractor does not notify a compensation event within eight weeks of becoming aware of the event, he is not entitled to a change in the prices, the completion date or a key date unless the project manager should have notified the event to the contractor but did not.

If the project manager does not respond to a claim for a compensation event or a quote, the contractor can warn them of this. If no response is received within two weeks, their acceptance is deemed (see minor changes in Sub-Clauses 61.1, 61.3, 61.4 and 63.1 in the NEC3 2013 edition).

A significant difference arises in claim quantification. Under FIDIC, claims by the contractor are evaluated retrospectively. Under the NEC, the project manager is required to assess the impact of a compensation event on the program and budget by forecasting its time and cost effects. This is done based on the information available at the time. Once assessed, the compensation event cannot be revisited and reassessed if the forecasted effects turn out to be inaccurate or are overtaken by later events. Where the effects are too uncertain to predict, it can state the assumptions on which the assessment is based. If any of these assumptions are found later to be wrong, a correction can be made. From the contractor's perspective, it must ensure that its quotations are comprehensive. Quotes cannot be revised once submitted, even if the contractor discovers that they have failed to allow for all additional costs or delays. The basic principle is that claims should be dealt with and finally resolved on an ongoing basis even if this means accepting an imprecise, "rough and ready" approach. The underlying philosophy is that it is better to dispose of claims promptly, rather than allowing them to remain unresolved and potentially sour the relationship between the employer and the contractor (Downing et al., 2013).

FIDIC does not contain an express good faith obligation such as the NEC duty to act in "the spirit of mutual trust and cooperation." The phrase "mutual trust and co-operation" implies not only honesty and reasonableness but an obligation to do more than the contract calls for if it is truly to be performed co-operatively (Lloyd, 2009).

On the other hand there is an obligation of the project manager to act fairly and impartially. This fact was established in the case *Costain Ltd. v. Bechtel Ltd* [2005] EWHC 1018 (TCC) where the court held that the project manager does, under the NEC3, have a duty to act impartially where they act as a certifier or assessor of claims.

Under the NEC3, the employer must be fully engaged in the project's daily routine in contrast to the FIDIC EPC/1999 Silver Book approach, for example. Instead of an engineer, the employer appoints a supervisor to monitor the quality of the work to identify defects. The key administrative role is then undertaken by the project manager. The project manager (either an independent consultant or an employee of the employer) and supervisor can be one person. In practice, this means that further project management resources must be hired on behalf of the employer.

The importance of the project manager is defined by their extended responsibility. For example, when both the employer and the contractor want to terminate the contract, they must notify the project manager and receive a certificate to that effect from the project manager.

Contract administration is done by the project manager who has a key role under NEC according to Lloyd (2009). There are numerous references to what is expected of the project manager. For example, the employer has to appoint someone who will discharge a wide range of duties as required by the contract. The employer is free to replace the project manager on the giving notice of the name of a replacement (see core Clause 14.4), though the employer's freedom must not infringe core Clause 10. The core clauses on payment (Section 5) and compensation events (Section 6) envisage that the project manager will make assessments as to money (Section 5) and of compensation events (Section 6). According to Lloyd (2009), the NEC3 appears to provide no mechanism whereby the project manager can revise a decision, for example, where there has been an over-estimate of additional time required (and, with it, cost).

The time schedule (program) is a key instrument under the NEC. The requirements of the time schedule are much broader under the NEC than under FIDIC, for example, the project manager can withhold 25% from interim payments until the first program is submitted by the contractor (Downing et al., 2013).

The NEC3 provides for a dispute to be referred to an adjudicator under option W1 (W2 in the UK). According to Lloyd (2009), whatever reservations there may be about some aspects of adjudication, there is now no doubt that decisions made by adjudicators are generally either accepted by the parties or are used by them as the basis for an agreement to finally settle the dispute. Sir Michael Latham in recommending adjudication as part of his proposals drew on its success under the

NEC, especially when employed as it should be, to resolve disputes as they arise—as opposed to leaving them to the end of the contract and thus converting (or "perverting" as some might say) adjudication into a mini-arbitration. Option W1 therefore ought to be adopted. A party that is dissatisfied has the right to take the resulting dispute to the tribunal, arbitrator or court as stipulated in the contract. That tribunal decides the dispute referred to it. It does not act as an appellate tribunal but as a tribunal of first (and possibly last) instance with the obligation to reach its own decision. Lloyd's (2009) view is that this is especially important for the NEC that has been written on the assumption that those using it will have been trained in and will understand its concepts and philosophies. Whoever decides disputes arising under any construction contract must have the ability to stand in the shoes, as it were, of those who were there at the time and see things as they were then perceived.

13.4 ICC forms of contract

Based on the information at http://www.iccwbo.org, the International Chamber of Commerce (ICC) is the largest business organization in the world comprising hundreds of thousands of member companies in over 130 countries with interests spanning every sector of private enterprise.

The ICC Commission on Commercial Law and Practice (CLP) develops ICC model contracts and ICC model clauses, which give parties a neutral framework for their contractual relationships. These contracts and clauses are carefully drafted by CLP commission experts without expressing a bias for any one particular legal system. They are constructed to protect the interests of all the parties by combining a single framework of rules with flexible provisions allowing participants to insert their own requirements.

The most popular form is the ICC model turnkey contract, which provides a balanced contract specifically for the EPC delivery method with the main priority being price and scope certainty. In terms of style and content, this contract sets out its purpose at the beginning, followed by a description of the obligations of good faith (together with a description of what that means in practice) as well as detailed clauses on software issues, bribery and corruption. ICC forms are drafted along well-established legal and contractual principles and are easy to interpret, apply, and implement.

The acceptance of ICC documents is increasing, but these forms are perceived as limited in their use in large engineering and plant projects (Grutters and Fahey, 2013).

13.5 ENAA forms of contract

Based on the information at http://www.enaa.or.jp, the Engineering Advancement Association of Japan (ENAA) is a non-profit organization established in 1978. Its aim is to develop diversified activities such as advancement of technological capabilities and promotion of technical development.

The third edition of the ENAA Model form for International Contracts for Process Plant Construction (turnkey lump-sum basis) was published in March 2010. Both the first (1986) and second (1992) editions have been well received by the engineering and construction industries and were widely used in many plant projects throughout the world.

In addition, the ENAA Model form—International Contract for Power Plant Construction (turnkey lump-sum basis) (ENAA model form) was published in 1996 to meet the growing needs for an international contract model form for construction of power plants. A new, updated power plant model form is currently being prepared by the ENAA.

In preparing the ENAA model form, its committee extensively referred to, and took into consideration the comments, recommendations, advice, and suggestions of various sources such as the World Bank, other major financing institutions, potential customers and contractors and other relevant organizations in the United States and Europe.

The model form was designed to provide a flexible, fair, and reasonable balance between the employer and the contractor in terms of the various risks involved in international projects. The ENAA model form is intended for a wide range of users including in-house legal and sales personnel and those who are involved in the various phases of actual project implementation.

13.6　IChemE forms of contract

Based on the information at http://www.icheme.org, the Institution of Chemical Engineers ("IChemE") is the global professional membership organization for people with relevant experience or interest in chemical engineering. The IChemE forms of contract are developed specifically for performance-based plant and process industries.

IChemE has published forms of contract for over 40 years. There are two contract suites available: forms for use in the UK and forms for international use. Both suites are used across a wide range of process industries and are suitable for the provision of any performance-based plant or project. The contract forms have been formulated to reflect best practice and relationships within the process plant sector.

Each form of contract contains a sample agreement and a set of general conditions. Guidance is provided on compiling the *Specification and Schedules* that are referenced in the agreement. Extensive explanatory notes give users a fuller understanding of the contracts.

The international forms were only recently added to the traditional forms for use in the UK (2007). They recognize the need for greater cooperation rather than claims in the process industry by including:

- clauses drafted with cooperation in mind;
- precise procedures for disputes;
- the aim for parties to achieve their individual objectives without confrontation;

- encouragement of each party to optimally contribute their specialist expertise essential to the process industry.

In terms of international contracts, the following forms are presented:

- *Lump Sum, The International Red Book, First edition, 2007*. An international version of the lump sum contract with additional clauses to meet the special requirements of international projects. Written in user-friendly English, it removes specific references to UK law while maintaining the tradition of extensive guidance to the schedules and clauses.
- *Reimbursable, The International Green Book, First edition, 2007*. An international version of the reimbursable contract with additional clauses to meet the special requirements of international projects.
- *Target Cost, The International Burgundy Book, First edition, 2007*. An international version of the target cost contract, this contract maintains the tradition of extensive guidance notes to both the schedules and the clauses.
- *Subcontracts, The International Yellow Book, First edition, 2007*. An international version of the subcontract with additional clauses to meet the special requirements of international projects.

IchemE forms are accepted by the process and plant industry. Drafted along well-established legal and contractual principles, they are easy to interpret, apply and implement but remain limited to plant and process projects (Grutters and Fahey, 2013).

13.7 Orgalime forms of contract

Based on the information at http://www.orgalime.org, Orgalime is the European federation representing the interests of European mechanical, electrical, electronic and metal articles industries as a whole at an EU level. Orgalime further represents the interests of both buyers and sellers, licensors and licensees and is the peak body for the European engineering industry.

Orgalime publications aim to provide European engineering industries with documents that can help them to draw up adequate business contracts and give practical advice on frequently occurring legal questions. The publications are, for the most part, drafted by Orgalime member association lawyers.

The first Orgalime legal publication was issued in the 1950s and the current listing now includes 27 titles, some of which have been revised several times in order to reflect new or changing legislation. The publications are divided into four different categories: model forms, guides, general conditions of contract, and other publications. The model forms, general conditions, and some of the guides are written to provide practical assistance to companies when they draw up different types of contracts commonly used in international trade. The guides also cover other contractual and legal issues of particular importance to the engineering industry.

All general conditions and model forms have been designed to reflect normal contract practice in industry. These are as follows:

- *S2012 : General Conditions for the Supply of Mechanical, Electrical and Electronic Products (ex-S2000)*. These are an updated version of the S 2000 conditions (originally the S 92 conditions). They are primarily intended for use in international contracts for delivery of engineering industry products in general. They can also be used for national contracts but are unsuitable for use in consumer contracts.
- The *Turnkey Contract* issued by Orgalime is for use in industrial works as a new standard contract covering the delivery of complete industrial installations or plants. These are often complex installations and works that need flexible and complete contracts.

The following contract forms have also been made available by Orgalime:

- R02: General Conditions for the Repair of Machinery and Equipment.
- SE 01: General Conditions for the Supply and Erection of Mechanical, Electrical and Electronic Products.
- SW 01: General Conditions for Computer Software, supplement to Orgalime S2000 & Orgalime SE01 (ex-SE94).
- M2000: General Conditions for Maintenance.
- S2000S: Supplementary Conditions for the Supervision of Erection of Mechanical, Electrical and Electronic Products, delivered in accordance with S2000.
- SP 99: General Conditions for Series Processing.
- SC 96/06: General Conditions for the Supply of Specially Designed and Manufactured Components.

13.8 Standard forms of construction contracts in the Czech Republic

Despite the fact that the tradition of construction standard forms in the Czech Republic was hardly disrupted because of the political consequences of the Second World War, historically, the level of standardization in this geographical area was obviously significant, especially in the context of public construction projects.

Already at the time when the country was part of the Austro-Hungarian Empire the General Technical and Administrative Conditions for Construction - 1893 (Všeobecné technické a administrativní stavební podmínky) were used in Czech language. These and also the below mentioned standard forms of contracts for public construction projects surprise with their clear pragmatic language and high quality using the concepts of time bars, alternative dispute resolution, re-measured or lump sum contracts under the surveillance of a contract administrator.

At the time of the first Czechoslovak Republic a standard form of contract was used in Czech language, for example in case of the General conditions for the construction of the Agricultural Museum in Bratislava - 1925 (Všeobecné podmínky pro stavbu Zemědělského Musea v Bratislavě) that was an equivalent of the German standard form that is still used in Germany today after many updates (the VOB/B described below). The wording of both contracts in Czech and in German is almost the same. The Czech version being more detailed. The German VOB has not been established until 1926 however.

Later after the 1948 the obviously highly developed tradition was destroyed. Even at the communist time, the Decree No. 104/1973 Coll. on the State Arbitration of the Czechoslovak Socialist Republic, which sets out basic conditions for the delivery of construction works (Vyhláška č. 104/1973 Sb. státní arbitráže Československé socialistické republiky, kterou se vydávají základní podmínky dodávky stavebních prací) created a surprisingly developed standard distorted by the centrally planned nature of the regime however.

After 1989 political changes, the FIDIC forms found their new home also in the Czech Republic. The FIDIC Forms are in use here mainly at infrastructure projects for more than 20 years. In 2015, new translations of 1999 FIDIC forms were introduced and implemented step by step in large construction projects financed by the Czech Infrastructure Funding Agency as a part of a broader strategy of the Ministry of Transport that should bring more efficiency and attractiveness for the infrastructure construction.

New balanced particular conditions for highway projects were prepared within a broad industry stakeholders discussion and FIDIC Rainbow Suite experience a "re-implementation". Further public clients such Railway Agency, Waterways Agency, City of Prague, Universities and Ministries now follow this path. Examples are to be seen for example here:

- http://www.pjpk.cz/obchodni-podminky
- http://www.rvccr.cz/informacni-servis/ke-stazeni/smluvni-dokumenty-fidic
- http://www.szdc.cz/modernizace-drahy/podminky-fidic.html

This strategy is accompanied by implementation of particular sector methodologies such as the:

- Methodology for Public Procurement of Design and Build Projects under FIDIC Forms (see it here http://www.sfdi.cz/soubory/obrazky-clanky/metodiky/2015_metodika_db_zaverecna_prezentace.pdf),
- Methodology for Variations Administration under FIDIC Forms for Public Procurement Projects under Czech/EU Public Procurement Law (see it here http://www.sfdi.cz/soubory/obrazky-clanky/metodiky/2018_metodika_variaci_1_vydani.pdf),
- Methodology for Construction Projects Time Management under FIDIC Forms (see it here http://www.sfdi.cz/soubory/obrazky-clanky/metodiky/2018_metodika_casove_rizeni_fidic.pdf),

- Methodology for Quantification of Financial Claims under FIDIC Forms (see it here http://www.sfdi.cz/soubory/obrazky-clanky/metodiky/2018_metodika_naroku.pdf),
- Methodology for Re-measurement under FIDIC Forms (see it here http://www.sfdi.cz/pravidla-metodiky-a-ceniky/metodiky/),
- Methodology for Most Economically Advantageous Tenders Procurement (see it here http://www.sfdi.cz/pravidla-metodiky-a-ceniky/metodiky/),
- Methodology for Abnormally Low Tenders Treatment (see it here http://www.sfdi.cz/pravidla-metodiky-a-ceniky/metodiky/),
- Methodology for Value Engineering under FIDIC Forms (see it here http://www.sfdi.cz/pravidla-metodiky-a-ceniky/metodiky/).

Next to the above mentioned standardization effort another initiative has been established to implement the so called "Czech Standard Form of Contract for Construction" and "Czech Standard Form of Contract for Services" to be available here https://www.stavebni-smluvni-standardy.cz and here http://www.agentura-cas.cz/node/100, with a vision to create a neutral Czech Standard for firstly the local and later also international projects.

United States standard form contracts by Edward J. ("Ned") Parrott (the United States)

Introduction

As a general proposition, there are three types of construction projects in the United States: 1) private, 2) public, and 3) public private partnership (PPP). In 2016, the U.S. construction industry spent roughly $876 billion, $286 billion, and $11 billion, respectively, on each of these three types of projects. Industry experts, however, expect the PPP to become an increasingly larger share of the U.S. market as public entities turn from government funding (taxpayers) to the PPP model as a way of improving infrastructure without use of increasingly scarce taxpayer funds.

In the United States, there are nearly as many standard form contract documents as there are types of projects. Below we will provide an overview of the most prevalent contract forms in the United States private and public markets, as well as practice tips particular to each form. Forms at this time are not generally available governing the PPP market, due to its infancy and complexity.

American Institute of Architects (AIA) Forms (Private Projects)

In existence for over a century, the American Institute of Architects documents arguably form an industry standard in U.S. contract documentation. The AIA publishes over 180 industry standard construction contracts and forms at https://www.aiacontracts.org. Prepared by the AIA with input from owners, contractors, lawyers, architects, engineers, and subcontractors, the AIA documents have been fine-tuned by thousands of court decisions and represent near industry consensus for allocating risk. While any contract form will need project specific information (schedule, liquidated damages, payment, etc.) it is recommended that modifications to the AIA form language be minimized. Substantial alterations of the AIA often lead to unnecessarily protracted negotiations and an inefficient allocation of risk.

Many of the AIA documents were modified in 2017, and all reflect the current state of the construction industry. AIA documents are best suited for private projects, and do not include standard forms for public or PPP projects. AIA forms are grouped into "families" on the basis of delivery method, size and participants involved. The most popular AIA forms are discussed below:

- *Conventional A201 Design-Bid-Build.* The A201 is for use when the owner's project is divided into separate contracts for design (architect) and construction (contractor). The A201 family is used in the traditional design-bid-build format where the owner initially contracts with the architect (A201 and B101) to provide a complete 100% design and thereafter enters into a separate construction contract with the general or prime contractor (A201 and A101) to construct the project. This is the most widely used family suitable for conventional project delivery (design-bid-build) on small, medium, and large Projects. The A201 general conditions set the rights, responsibilities, and relationships of the owner, architect, and contractor. The owner retains the architect. The architect prepares the drawings and specifications. The contractor builds the work. Perceived drawbacks to the traditional A201 design-bid-build arrangement include protracted schedule (construction cannot begin until after 100% completion of project design and subsequent bidding and award to construction contractor) and a lack of single source responsibility for successful project completion.
- *The Design-Build family A141* addresses a more modern project delivery system intended to allow expedited project delivery, as well as single source responsibility for both the design and construction of a project. In design-build project delivery, the owner enters into a single contract (A141) with a design-builder who is obligated to both design and construct the project. Single source responsibility allows for faster project delivery because the design-builder can release early construction work (excavations/foundation/site work) while the mechanical/electrical/finish designs are being finalized. The use of this form is intended for small, medium, and large public and private sector projects. Experience with the design-build model, however, has proved it is not precisely the panacea called for. The very fact that the design is not 100% complete at award can lead to disputes over scope, therefore, it is vital that the owner express its program requirements as explicitly as possible in the solicitation.
- *Construction Manager as Advisor (CMa) family C132.* Under the AIA construction manager as advisor family, the owner's project incorporates a fourth prime player (the construction manager) on the construction team (in addition to the owner, architect and contractor). The CMa acts as an independent advisor on construction management matters over the course of both design and construction. The prime contractor retains responsibility for construction, labor and materials. It is believed that the CMa approach enhances the level of expertise applied to managing a project from start to finish. This approach preserves the CMa's independent judgment by keeping that individual from being influenced by any monetary interest related to actual labor and materials incorporated in the construction

work. The use of this form is intended for small, medium and large public and private sector projects.
- *Construction Manager as Constructor (CMc) family A133/A134*. Under the AIA construction manager as constructor family, the owner's project again incorporates a fourth prime player (construction manager) on the construction team (in addition to the owner, architect, and contractor). The CMc, however, will complete the construction and also provide construction management services. The single party (construction manager) provides construction management services in pre-construction phase and then completes construction (constructor). Under the CMc approach, the functions of contractor and construction manager are merged and assigned to one entity. The CMc typically assumes control over the construction work by direct contracts with subcontractors. The use of this form is intended for small, medium and large public and private sector projects.
- *Integrated Project Delivery (IPD) family A295*. Problems inhering to contemporary construction include buildings that are behind schedule and over-budget as well as adverse relations among the owner, general contractor, and architect. The integrated project delivery system is a direct response to these problems. IPD is a collaborative project delivery approach that uses the talents and insights of all project participants across all phases of design and construction. Every member of the design build team (owner, contractor, and architect) completely shares responsibility, as well as the financial risks and rewards, for the entire project. The AIA IPD family provides agreements for three levels of integrated project delivery:
    1. Transitional forms: modeled on existing construction manager agreements, which offer a comfortable first step into integrated project delivery.
    2. The *Multi-Party Agreement*: a single agreement that the parties can use to design and construct a project using integrated project delivery.
    3. The *Single Purpose Entity* (SPE) creates a limited liability company for the purpose of planning, designing and constructing the project. The SPE allows for complete sharing of risk and reward in a fully integrated collaborative process. The use of this form is intended for large private sector commercial projects.
- *AIA Interiors family*. These documents are intended for use as the contract between an owner and vendor for furniture, furnishings, and equipment (FF&E) on small to large tenant projects and for FF&E procurement combined with architectural interior design and construction services. These documents anticipate procurement of FF&E under a contract separate from design services. The *Interiors* documents procure FF&E under a contract separate from design services and preserve the architect's independence from any monetary interest in the sale of those goods. AIA Document B152 may be used as the employer/architect agreement for the design of both FF&E and architectural interiors. AIA Document B153 is not suitable for construction work (such as major tenant improvements) but is suitable for design services related solely to FF&E. The use of this form is intended for small, medium and large tenant projects.
- *International Family AIA B161/162*. The international family is intended to assist U.S. architects involved in projects based in foreign countries. Because U.S. architects usually are not licensed in the foreign country where a project is located, these agreements identify the U.S. architect as a consultant, rather than an architect. The document is intended to clarify

the assumptions, roles, responsibilities, and obligations of the parties; to provide a clear, narrative description of services, and to facilitate, strengthen, and maintain the working and contractual relationship between the parties. Because of foreign practices, the term owner has been replaced with client throughout the document. Also, since it is assumed that the U.S. architect is not licensed to practice architecture in the foreign country where the project is located, the term consultant is used throughout the document to refer to the U.S. architect. The use of this form is intended for small to large projects.

- *Small Projects Family AIA 105.* Appropriate for projects which are straightforward in design, of short duration (less than one year from start of design to completion of construction), without delivery complications (such as competitive bidding) and when project team members already have working relationships. A105-2007 is a stand-alone agreement with its own general conditions; it replaces A105-1993 and A205-1993. A105-2007 is for use on a project that is modest in size and brief in duration, and where payment to the contractor is based on a stipulated sum (fixed price). For larger and more complex projects, other AIA agreements are more suitable, such as 107™-2007, Agreement between Owner and Contractor for a Project of Limited Scope. A105-2007 and B105™2007, Standard Form of Agreement between Owner and Architect for a Residential or Small Commercial Project, comprise the Small Projects family of documents. Although A105-2007 and B105-2007 share some similarities with other agreements, the small projects family should not be used in tandem with agreements in other document families without careful side-by-side comparison of contents. This family is suitable for residential projects, small commercial projects or other projects of relatively low cost and brief duration.
- *AIA Contract Administration & Project Management Forms* are quite useful for all project delivery methods. The variety of forms in this group includes qualification statements, bonds, requests for information, change orders, construction change directives, payment applications, certificates of substantial completion, contractor's affidavit of payments of debts and claims, contractor's affidavit of release of liens, and consent of surety to final payment. The use of these forms is intended for small, medium and large projects. The AIA forms are very helpful in establishing basic contract form documents.

One major advantage of the AIA documents is that they have been tested in the courts countless times and there is a wealth of literature devoted to each clause. See, for example, Sweet, Jonathan J., *Sweet on Construction Industry Contracts: Major AIA Documents*, Fifth Edition, Volumes 1 and 2, Wolters Kluwer, 2009; Sink, Charles M., A. Holt Gwyn, James Duffy O'Connor and Dean B. Thompson, *The 2007 A201 Deskbook*, ABA Publishing, 2008; and The American Institute of Architects, *The Architect's Handbook of Professional Practice*, Fourteenth Edition, John Wiley & Sons, Inc., 2008. The AIA documents, particularly the A201, reflect a consensus as to how a typical construction project is run in the United States, who does what, and what the standards in the construction industry are at this time. The A201 represents what a construction project in the United States looks like in the early twenty-first century.

ConsensusDOCS (private projects)

Like the AIA documents, the ConsensusDOCS family pertains exclusively to private contracting, not public. The ConsensusDOCs offer a form of integrated project delivery. In September 2007, a broad-based consortium of construction industry trade and other organizations jointly released this new family of model contract documents—as competitors to the AIA documents—called ConsensusDOCS. Approximately 20 construction associations, including the Associated General Contractors of America (AGC), Associated Builders and Contractors, The American Subcontractors Association, The Construction Users Roundtable, The National Roofing Contractors Association, The Mechanical Contractors Association of America, and the National Plumbing, Heating-Cooling Contractors Association participated in developing the ConsensusDOCS and endorsed them.

According to the website, http://www.consensusdocs.org., the ConsensusDOCS offer 80 forms designed to avoid favoring one party over another, and set forth a balanced approach to the rights and obligations—as well as to risk allocation—imposed on participants in the construction process. The ConsensusDOCS emphasize communication and collaboration among all project participants from the time of contract negotiation through project completion. The stated goal of the ConsensusDOCS participants and endorsers was to reduce transaction costs and the time required for negotiation of contracts and to reduce the frequency and severity of disputes during the construction process. The ConsensusDOCs emphasis in resolving disputes can be seen in the range and number of steps established in the dispute resolution sections.

1. ConsensusDocs contract document series include:
   - 200 Series – General Contracting
   - 300 Series – Collaborative
   - 400 Series – Design-Build
   - 500 Series – CM At-Risk
   - 700 Series – Subcontracting
   - 800 Series – Program Management

Design Build Institute of America (DBIA) Form Documents (Private Projects)

Like the AIA and ConsensusDOCS forms above, the DBIA family is exclusively for use on private projects. The DBIA documents, as the name suggests, are drafted exclusively for use on projects employing the design-build project delivery vehicle. The standard design build contracts include #525—Standard Form of Agreement between Owner and Design-Builder—Lump Sum; #530—Standard Form of Agreement between Owner and Design-Builder—Cost Plus Fee with an Option for a Guaranteed Maximum Price; #535—Standard Form of General Conditions of Contract between Owner and Design-Builder; #545—Progressive Design-Build Agreement for Water and Wastewater Projects.

Federal acquisition regulations (public projects)

The AIA, ConsensusDOCS, and DBIA form documents described above can govern all aspects of contracting on private projects. On public or government contracts with the United States, however, an entirely different set of forms and rules apply. The Federal Acquisition Regulations (FAR) set forth the principal set of rules and forms that govern the formation of construction contracts between private contractors and the U.S. government. The purpose of the FAR is to provide uniform policies and procedures for contracting with the government.

The largest single part of the FAR is Part 52, "Solicitation Provisions and Contract Clauses," containing standard solicitation provisions and contract clauses. There are hundreds of clauses that pertain to different types of contracts such as construction, supply, or architecture/engineering. An exhaustive study of the FAR is beyond the scope of this chapter, but it is instructive to understand the types of clauses required in federal government contracts by the FAR. Typical of the clauses required in Federal government contract forms are:

1. FAR §52.249-14 Excusable Delays
2. FAR §52.249-10 Default
3. FAR §42.249-1 Termination for Convenience of the Government
4. FAR §52.248-1 Value Engineering
5. FAR §52.246-12 Inspection of Construction
6. FAR §52.243-7 Notification of Changes
7. FAR §52.236-4 Physical Data
8. FAR §52.236-5 Material and Workmanship
9. FAR §52.232-25 Prompt Payment
10. FAR §52.247-4 Patent Indemnity Construction Contracts
11. FAR §52.225-9 Buy American – Construction Materials
12. FAR §52.211-12 Liquidated Damages
13. FAR §52.233-1 Disputes
14. FAR §52.236-2 Differing Site Conditions

Edward J. ("Ned") Parrott
Senior Partner
Watt Tieder Hoffar & Fitzgerald LLP
The United States

13.9 VOB: German standard

VOB, *Vergabe und Vertragsordnung für Bauleistungen*; in English: *Procurement and Contracting Rules for Construction Procedures* (VOB) is divided into three sections: (1) VOB/A (DIN 1960: 2012–2009) determines general provisions relating to the award of construction contracts mandatory for public entities in the procurement process; (2) VOB/B (DIN 1961: 2012–2009) sets general conditions of contract relating to the execution of construction works; and (3) VOB/C comprises extensive general technical specifications for building works (so-called DINs from the *Deutsches Institut für Normung*, that is, the German Institute for Standardization) which form part of the technical state of the art. At the same time, VOB itself is neither an act nor any other legislative regulation but part of a construction contract complementing the general provisions of the *German Civil Code* (BGB). VOB is issued and updated regularly by an autonomous body consisting of those acting on behalf of leading German construction employers and contractors from *Deutscher Vergabe- und Vertragsausschuss für Bauleistungen* (the German Procurement and Contracts Committee). The first edition of VOB dates back to 1926, having seen

15 (Part A) and 18 (Part B) amendments since then. The latest version of VOB was released in 2016.

Public employers in Germany must use the VOB/B conditions of contract by law. Private employers do not have to use VOB but appreciate their tradition and well-balanced nature and often use them in practice as general terms of conditions due to the incomplete BGB rules for construction contracts. Public employers are further required to use the newest edition of VOB/B, whereas private employers are allowed to use any earlier version. It is therefore important to know what version of VOB/B is, in fact, incorporated in the contract, especially in the case of private employers.

VOB is issued in the "DIN" form. DIN recommends general standards for various fields of human activities and behavior, which are not binding by virtue of law. They become legally binding and enforceable only when referred to by law or incorporated in a contract. Only then do the DINs lose their "persuasive" nature and become binding as part of the VOB/B as general terms and conditions.

The main conceptual differences between the conditions of contract in Germany and many other countries should also be noted. The parties may, as part of the contract, agree upon preformulated conditions introduced by one party, very often as standard conditions of contract and normally attached to the contract. But such standard conditions of contract may be subject to a rigorous control of content by the courts. By way of example, a provision in the standard conditions of contract is invalid according to §§307 BGB if it unreasonably puts the contractual partner of the party who introduced the clause at a disadvantage. The courts only apply control of content if the provisions to be assessed are contained in *Standard Terms and Conditions* under §305 BGB which state that such form of contract must be namely, (1) meant for use on more than one occasion; and (2) imposed by one party on the other. The question of whether a clause creates an "unfair disadvantage" for the other party depends mainly on whether it "contradicts" the essential, fundamental principles of law. The question asked by the court when determining whether a "contradiction" of principles exists is whether the content reflects justness/fairness.

There is an exemption from this control-of-content rule under §310 Sub-Clause 1 sentence 3 BGB being the *privilege of VOB/B*. According to this section, should VOB/B be incorporated in the original wording, the clauses are not subject to control of content and the court will regard them as fairly balanced. Where the parties deviate from the standardized version on only one single point—be it expressly or by agreement upon additional conditions (which often happens)—all clauses are separately subject to control of content and individually assessed. In practice, many such VOB/B provisions are seen as unbalanced and therefore considered invalid by the German judges if disputes arise. VOB/B clauses can be changed through direct negotiation between the parties (see Kus, A., Jochen, M. and Stering, R., 1999).

As mentioned above, the VOB system of standards is divided into three parts: A (procurement), B (execution of the works), and C (technical standards). A summary of these standards is as follows.

Section A of VOB (DIN 1960) includes all the general rules of construction procurement. VOB/A is harmonized with the relevant EU directives regulating the stages of construction project from a tender announcement by an employer up to the point of awarding the contract to a contractor. §6 of the German *Vergabeverordnung* (public procurement regulation) prescribes that (mainly) public entities must apply VOB/A during the procurement of construction works.

General Conditions of Contract for Execution of Construction Work constitute the scope of Part B of VOB (DIN 1961). This document regulates the stages of a construction project from the signing date of the contract for construction up to the end of the *Defects Liability Period*.

As under §1, Sub-Clause 1 of VOB/B, Part C of VOB is also a part of a (VOB/B) contract for construction works, regulating the technical conditions of contract, standard, and scope of the works if not otherwise agreed upon. As per §1 Section 2, Point 5 of VOB/B, the VOB/Cs prevail over VOB/B in case of conflict between VOB/B and VOB/C clauses.

According to VOB/A §8 Sub-Clause 3, public entities must use VOB/B and VOB/C in construction contracts.

13.9.1 Content of VOB/B

Allgemeine Vertragsbedingungen für die Ausführung von Bauleistungen; in English: *General Conditions of Contract for Execution of Construction Work* (VOB/B) contain, for example, the following.

§1 stipulates the nature and scope of performance. This includes the legal force of particular documents forming the contract.

§2 details how contract price is determined. Measurement is the primary approach (on the basis of unit prices and work actually done) unless another way to determine the contract price (e.g., based on the lump price, hourly wage rates, cost plus) is agreed to. §2 sets out which works are part of the agreed contract price and which works have to be paid additionally, especially when changes to the scope of works are made.

§§3 to 6 generally address execution of works. §3 specifically deals with the employer's and/or contractor's documents necessary for execution of works.

§4 determines the details for the execution of works. In particular, that the contractor shall carry out the works at their own risk as stipulated in the contract while observing the law and standards. The contractor, for example, is also obliged to notify the employer about their (the employer's) improper instructions.

§5 deals with time for completion,

§6 specifically deals with an extension of time for completion and/or additional payments because of obstacles and suspensions in work, stipulating that if the contractor is, in their own opinion, restricted in properly executing contractual performance, the contractor must promptly notify the employer in writing. If the contractor fails to do so, the contractor is entitled to require that the above obstacles are taken into account only when this situation and its effects became "known" to the employer. If either of the parties is responsible for the obstacle, the other party is entitled to claim damages. Claims for lost profit may only be made on the basis of intention or gross negligence of the other party.

Under VOB/B, time for completion can only be extended provided that the obstacles hindering the execution of the works emerge. §6 also covers situations where additional time is required because of increased amounts of work, variations, and necessary additional performances instructed by the employer but unforeseen by the employer when concluding the contract. Such additional works (e.g., ordered according to §No. 3 VOB/B or necessary according to §1 No. 4 VOB/B) are considered to fall under §6 No. 2 VOB/B, that is, the contractor has to give notice that they are impeded. The lack of such notice would mean a lapse of claims for an extension of time and damages (except where the obstruction is obvious to the employer).

§7 deals with risk allocation issues. Should, for example, the fully or partially completed works before the employer's acceptance be damaged or destroyed due to a *force majeure* event, war, unrest or under any other circumstances beyond the control of the contractor that could not objectively be avoided, the works already performed shall be charged for in accordance with the contract. Other damages are excluded from any mutual compensation duty. It is worth mentioning that the taking-over procedure under FIDIC forms is not the same as the *Abnahme* under German law which is in fact an acceptance (i.e., performance). There is no defects notification period under German law. After acceptance, the defects liability period begins to run (*inter alia*).

§8 deals with the employer's right to termination, their pre-conditions (grounds and written form) and consequences. The employer may terminate the contract at their own discretion and any time before completion of performance (equivalent to §649 BGB) but, in principle, has to pay the contract price to the contractor. Standard "reasons" for termination are prescribed for the notice of termination, namely, contractor default, insolvency, and so on, including the employer's right to complete the works themselves or through a third party and to claim the related damages from the contractor after the contract is terminated in this way.

§9 Notice of termination given by the contractor is permissible when the employer fails to act in compliance with the contract, making it thus impossible for the contractor to carry out their performance. For example, if the employer fails to pay on time but only after granting the employer a reasonable extension of time to pay.

§10 deals with the contracting parties' liability for damages incurred by themselves or their vicarious agents against each other and to third parties.

§11 and §12 deal with the validity and rules of contractual penalties regarding acceptance of the works, that is, the end of the execution/performance stage and the beginning of the liability for defects. The main legal consequence of the acceptance is that the burden of proof of the existence of defects shifts to the employer, that is, the contractor needs no longer show that the works are free of defects. Instead, it is up to the employer to prove that the works contain defects at the time of the acceptance, but not known by the employer. If the employer knew of the defects, they may reserve their right of acceptance (§640 para 2 BGB). The risk of loss and damage to works thus passes over to the employer.

§13 specifies the definition of a "defect," the contractor's obligation to perform the works free of defects, the procedures to be kept by the employer and how claims resulting from defects are regulated. This includes different defect liability periods for different types of work (e.g., construction four years, plant two years). Liability periods start running from acceptance of the works.

§14 deals with invoicing and accounting of the executed works. The items invoiced must be verifiable and supported by relevant documents giving evidence of the type and scope of performance carried out.

§15 determines the rules for billing, acceptance, and settlement of work performed on an hourly wages basis if so agreed. Before work on an hourly wages basis can begin, the employer must be notified of it. The contractor shall then submit time sheets for each working day or week as the case may be.

§16 specifies *inter alia* that the payment of interim invoices shall be due within 18 working days. It is further set out that unconditional acceptance of the final payment shall preclude subsequent contractor claims. Furthermore, if the employer fails to pay in time, the contractor may allow reasonable, additional time for the employer. If the employer fails to pay within this additional time either, the contractor shall have a claim (calculated from the expiration of the additional time) for statutory delay interest unless the contractor can prove higher damage due to such delay.

§17 prescribes, in detail, how the employer may secure execution of the works pursuant to the contract and any defect claims.

§18 deals with the disputes to be resolved by a court in the employer's jurisdiction (usually established by the employer's registered address). The parties are free to agree to alternative dispute resolution. No disputes shall authorize the contractor to suspend the works.

VOB/B is prepared for construction contracts where the employer usually engages a designer to deliver the design for the works and to supervise the works. The rules for design works are stipulated only partially in the VOB. The issues of who is to submit the detail design or design variation proposals, when, in what way and to whom as well as the rules for approving/rejecting this documentation are also not dealt with. This problem can be rectified by adjustments, addendums or attachments to the contract.

In terms of time management, the approach of German law is similar to the majority of civil codes. The common attitude is that contracts contain binding interim payments based on milestones. German law also provides rules for penalties. §11 No. 1 VOB/B refers to the respective §§339–345 of the BGB, which deal with contractual penalties. Penalties for delay are widely used in practice.

13.9.2 VOB limitations

Although VOB/B conditions are widely regarded as fairly balanced, they should only be used in their unchanged form in small or medium construction projects. Large and complex works where the contractor coordinates their subcontractors and is responsible for the design as well as specific activities (such as construction projects under traffic, underground works, and so on) presume significant modifications and adjustments to VOB/B. In doing so, all VOB/B clauses are exposed to significant risk of strict control of content by the courts.

VOB/B also has some limitations. For example, VOB/B is not clear about who is to bear the risks of unforeseeable ground conditions. At the moment, the majority view seems to be that the ground itself is a "material delivered by the employer" as per §645 BGB. Thus, if such material causes deterioration, destruction, or collapse of the works the risk lies with the employer. §644 BGB, on the other hand, imposes the general risk of deterioration, destruction, or collapse of the works on the contractor until acceptance except when otherwise agreed upon.

The question, however, remains: What does the contract say about the ground conditions and who bears the risk of unforeseeable ground conditions? The answer to this question depends on the contractually agreed terms and their interpretation (see, e.g., BGH, 20.08.2009 VII ZR 205/07, Rz 77).

If, for example, VOB/B is agreed upon, VOB/C applies and the national standard called DIN 18299–18325 is to be used. DIN 18300 obliges the employer to give information in the tender documents about *inter alia* the ground conditions, e.g. to rank the ground in the given classification scheme: 1–7, 1 is humus, 2 is a fluid/mushy and very difficult to dredge soil, soil of the classes 3–5 normally causes no special problems, 6 and 7 are rock, where 7 may even need blasting. The contractor can rely on the given information and, therefore, the risk of additional costs due to unforeseen soil conditions lies with the employer, for example, when the tender documents state ground classes 3–6 and 2 have been found.

Take, for example, the case *OLG Hamm, 17.02.1993 26 U 40/92*. This case dealt with *Bodenklassenfall* (Ground Classification Fall) where ground classes 3–5 were stated and "more difficult ground conditions" were found. In this case, the ground conditions classification provided by the employer indicated classes 3–5. This soil classification was not given by a soil expert and no additional questions were raised either by the employer or contractor. The contractor relied on data given by the employer in the terms of reference. Worse conditions than those indicated were encountered and the contractor claimed additional payment. The employer refused to pay but the judge confirmed the contractor's entitlement stating that the contractor could rely on the data in the tender which gave them the basis for the price calculation. Therefore, the contractor was not under a duty to make further inquiry and could price the risk on the basis of the ground classification provided by the employer.

Very often in practice, tender documents provide a soil "waiver," which in itself expressly states that no guarantee is made for findings outside the exact boreholes done and, thus, the risk is shifted to the contractor who can control such risk (i.e., has the opportunity and duty to calculate such risk in their bid price). On the other hand, if the soil conditions found are outside the range to be expected from the soil "waiver" and involve much higher effort and cost for the contractor, courts may hold this exceptional risk was not assumed by the contractor in the contract and that §645 BGB applies, that is, additional costs have to be borne by the employer.

Generally speaking, every particular situation must be evaluated taking into account the context and circumstances—especially the tender and contract documents.

Just as within the scope of control of content, the courts have also held that if the contractor (in a re-measured contract) is to bear the risk of different ground conditions (without being allowed to claim additional payment), such a clause is invalid. Not only does it unreasonably disadvantage the other party but such a clause shifts not-transparent risk. According to the duty of contract clauses, transparency (*Transparenzgebot*) at §307 BGB or, more specifically, lack of transparency, may also arise from the provision not being clear and comprehensible (Kleine-Möller and Merl, 2009).

13.10 Invalid clauses in German case law

German judges regularly publish lists of invalid clauses. The following are some examples:

1. "Specifications and drawings were handed over to the contractor only for his information as non-binding propositions; in this respect the contractor takes over the responsibility for the usability and correctness of those documents." In other words, this clause rolls over errors in the employer's specifications and drawings to the contractor through the contract and is invalid (Vygen, K. and Joussen, E., 2013).
2. "With the submission of the bid the contractor gives a guarantee that the bid contains everything what is necessary for the completion of the works." The clause is invalid because such a bid would not be considered transparent (*05.06.1997 – VII ZR 54/96 BauR 1997, 1036, 1038 = NJW-RR 1997, 1513, 1514*).
3. "The agreed price is fixed and cannot be increased because of any claims" and "The employer can require additional works from the contractor without additional remuneration if such works are necessary for the completion." These clauses also lack transparency (*OLG Hamburg, Urt. v. 06.12.1995 – 5 U 215/94, Beschl. v. 05.06.1997 – VII ZR 54/96, ZfBR 1998, 35. 36 f.*).
4. "The contractor informed himself about the geological and hydrological site conditions and therefore cannot claim additional payment on those grounds." It is employer's duty to provide information about geological and hydrological site conditions to allow for transparent bid evaluation (Vygen, K. and Joussen, E., 2013).
5. In a re-measurement contract where "The contract price cannot be higher than the accepted contract amount (bid price)." Such a clause makes no sense. The employer does not know at the time of bid acceptance what works will need to be paid for under the re-measurement contract. Such limitation of price unreasonably disadvantages the other party (*BGH, Urt. v. 14.10.2004 – VII ZR 190/03, BauR 2005, 94, 95 = NJW-RR 2005, 246 f*).
6. A lump sum contract clause stating that "If the changes in quantity of the works arise, they will be re-measured and invoiced based on rates and prices." This clause goes against the basic principles of lump sum contracts (Vygen and Joussen, 2013).

7. Unreasonable time-related clauses such as: "The contractor will start with the performance immediately after having been instructed by the employer; the time for completion is 5 months." Such clause is invalid due to vagueness. The contractor does not know when performance will start. A clause like this would be valid only if it allows for contractor claims for additional payment which relate to unforeseeable costs associated with the lack of knowledge about the commencement of performance (minimally the adjustments for changes in cost; see BGH, Urt. v. 10.09.2009 – VII ZR 152/08. BauR 2009, 1901, 1904 = NJW 2010, 522, 524).
8. "The contractor gives guarantee for meeting the deadline. The contractor is responsible for all legal and administrative requirements and cost." The contractor could potentially be responsible for delays caused by third parties such as state authorities. This is an unreasonable disadvantage (Vygen, K. and Joussen, E., 2013).
9. A clause is invalid for the same reason as (8) above if states that: "A suspension for more than three months does not entitle the contractor to terminate the contract or submit claims nor compensate damages."
10. "The taking-over through employer's use of the works is excluded (the employer reserves the date of taking-over the works to be announced by his site manager without foreseeing a period of time for it)." It is impossible to be sure when taking over will take place and therefore this clause gives an unreasonable advantage to the employer (Vygen, K. and Joussen, E., 2013).

The standard forms of construction contract in Australia by John Sharkey (Australia)

The history of Australian standard forms of construction contract is best understood by reference to the English standard forms. For most of the twentieth century the majority of the forms in use in Australia were direct descendants of well-known English forms and two streams were discernible: a building stream derived from the RIBA forms and a civil stream derived from the ICE forms.

In what was known as the edition series the Master Builders Association of Australia and the then Royal Australian Institute of Architects published forms for use on building construction projects where an architect performed the functions of superintendent. The forms were derivatives of the RIBA forms and employed a similar risk profile and similar language.

Publication of the edition series came to an end in the early 1980s when the Building Owners and Managers Association of Australia Ltd (BOMA) joined with the builders and architects to commence publication of the JCC series of forms. In 1998, BOMA, as the Property Council of Australia, went its own way with the publication of the PC 1 form. The most significant change that PC 1 introduced to the industry was the concept of the superintendent, or as the form called him/her, the contract administrator, performing all functions under the contract as the agent of the owner, and not as an independent certifier, assessor, or valuer.

In competition with PC 1, the builders and architects commenced publication in 2003 of the Australian Building Industry Contract, or ABIC, form retaining the traditional function of the superintending architect as independent agent, and not the agent of the owner, where he/she acted as assessor, valuer, or certifier.

Current usage of Australian standard forms

While PC 1 and the ABIC forms continue in use, the forms published by Standards Australia (SA) now dominate the market for all types of construction works. The SA forms were originally intended for projects of an engineering nature and for several decades ran as a series in parallel with the above-mentioned building forms. However, and despite being somewhat dated, the SA forms and particularly AS 2124 and AS 4000 (construct only) and AS 4300 and AS 4902 (design and construct), remain the preferred starting point for the majority of those charged with drafting a suitable construction and engineering contract.

AS 2124 and its earlier iterations were based on the ICE forms, even employing the same clause numbering. Clause 12 of AS 2124, for example, is the latent conditions clause. However, Australian courts often developed their own responses to problems that were identified when the forms came before them for judicial consideration.

Some Australian solutions

Thus when the High Court of Australia in *Carr v. J A Berriman Pty Ltd* (1952) 89 CLR 327 characterized as repudiatory an owner's conduct that included failing to give possession of the site by the date agreed in the contract, the drafters amended the standard forms to have parties expressly agree that delay in giving possession of the site would not constitute a breach of contract (See, e.g., Clause 24.1 of AS 4000).

When the superintendent's tardiness in determining upon the contractor's extension of time claims in *MacMahon Constructions Pty Ltd v. Crestwood Estates* [1971] WAR 162 resulted in the loss of any claim by the owner for liquidated damages for delay, the drafters amended the CA 24.1 form in 1964 so as to empower the superintendent to grant the contractor an extension of time at any time up to the issue of the final certificate (See, e.g., Clause 34.5 of AS 4000). That step has led to considerable litigation and debates about the ambit of the power and whether, considered in the context of other contractual provisions and taking the contract as a whole, the power can effectively amount to an obligation to extend time in an appropriate case (See *Peninsula Balmain Pty Ltd v. Abigroup Contractors Pty Ltd* [2002] NSWCA 211; *620 Collins Street Pty Ltd v. Abigroup Contractors Pty Ltd (No.2)* [2006] VSC 491.).

Extensions of time in the SA forms

Over the years SA has attempted, not entirely successfully, to wean users off the AS 2124/AS 4300 forms and onto the later AS 4000/AS 4902 series and the experience has said something about the simple importance to users of familiarity in the choice of standard form.

By far, the most controversial aspect of the AS 4000/AS4902 series is its discarding of the traditional approach to extensions of time where ordinarily a form will list the events, which qualify for an extension. Rather, the approach taken by AS 4000/AS 4902 is to allow the contractor extensions of time for any event except the contractor's breach or omission, industrial conditions or inclement weather occurring after the date for practical completion and such events as the parties expressly agree are excluded. (See definition of "qualifying cause of delay" in Clause 1). The approach demands particular care from lawyers and contract administrators and poses difficulties for the lazy and the careless.

The approach to dispute resolution

The approach to dispute resolution by the Australian standard forms is, generally speaking, a traditional one with little or no embrace of such modern techniques as professional or non-binding determinations, expert determination, early neutral evaluation or dispute boards. The model adopted by the SA forms can generally be described as a process of notice followed by executive meeting with litigation or arbitration to follow if a final determination is needed.

Perhaps more in tune with contemporary thinking about dispute resolution are the PC 1 and ABIC forms. Before any final determination by arbitration PC 1 allows for expert determination of disputes concerning directions of the contract administrator (*Cl.15*). The ABIC forms invite the parties to have a conversation about such matters as mediation, expert determination and arbitration.

Amendment

The use of the Australian standard forms in their unamended state is rare to the point of non-existent. The afore-mentioned SA forms, while enjoying the largest share of the Australian market for standard forms, predate major legislative changes in the country such as, proportionate liability, security of payment and occupational health and safety. So significant drafting amendment is inevitable, irrespective of one's views about the suitability of a particular form's risk profile.

Amendment to alter the risk profile of the forms, invariably by shifting risk to the services provider, is commonplace. An SA form is the product of work by an SA committee whose members are drawn from a broad range of industry interests. The inevitable, while understandable, compromises within the committees produce a risk profile in the forms that is invariably viewed by an owner as unsatisfactory when the context is project-specific. One accordingly sees risk regularly shifted to the contractor by amendment to the forms, especially in connection with such matters as extensions of time, latent conditions and time bars.

It is thus timely that SA should presently be undertaking a review with the objective of producing a new set of forms that will, at the least, address some of the issues flowing from the legislative changes the twenty-first century has brought. It is another question entirely whether as a result of the review we shall see much change to the risk profiles of the SA forms that practitioners and industry players have become accustomed to.

International forms in Australia

It is fair to say that the forms European lawyers are more familiar with have received little acceptance in Australia. The NEC form is practically unknown in the country. FIDIC has received more sightings, largely as a result of European contractors bringing their expertise and practices to the energy sector in areas such as Western Australia, but remains a form of rare take-up in the country.

John Sharkey
Professorial Fellow of the University of Melbourne
Australia

Construction contracts in the Republic of Ireland by Arran Dowling-Hussey (Ireland)

The Republic of Ireland is an English-speaking common law jurisdiction of just under 5 million people that is proximate to two other common law jurisdictions: Northern Ireland and England and Wales. While a neutral country it is a member of the European Union and the United Nations and a signatory to various international legal treaties such as the New York Convention. As is well known the effect of the latter, and other treaties, is to make the enforcement of arbitral awards in a jurisdiction other than where the award was made normally very straightforward. The system of precedent prevalent in any common law jurisdiction operates, in the Republic of Ireland, such that decisions from countries such as England and Wales do not bind an Irish Court but have persuasive value. The instant author cannot find any empirical evidence on the issue but would be personally of the view that judgments from the courts of England and Wales are very often, but not always, followed by the courts of the Republic of Ireland. The two jurisdictions share a number of similarities albeit one is about 14 times larger than the other. Normally legal issues of controversy are considered in the courts of England and Wales earlier than in the Republic of Ireland and more often than in the smaller jurisdiction. During what was described as the *Celtic Tiger* construction related activity came to total a huge part of the Irish economy and there were often construction related disputes. Just before the economic crisis of 2008/9 construction made up 25% of Irish GNP, which reduced to 6% a couple of years after the start of the crisis. There is now a significant uplift in construction activity again—on a basic level the volume of construction disputes depends on the level of overall construction activity.

The construction market in the Republic of Ireland is heavily standardized and there is wide use of standard form contracts. As would be expected such frequently used contracts are reviewed and revised from time to time. The Government Contracts Committee for Construction (GCCC) Public Works Contracts hold wide currency. Representations on the form of contracts like this, for government construction projects/public bodies contracts, are made via the (Irish) Construction Industry Council. The Construction Industry Council is a representative body made up of professional bodies such as the Royal Institute of Architects in Ireland (RIAI), Engineers Ireland, Association of Consulting Engineers of Ireland (ACEI), and the Construction Industry Federation (CIF). Outside of the sphere of public works contracts the standard form contracts offered by the RIAI are well known and popular. RIAI "yellow" form contracts are used where quantities form part of the contract. Where quantities do not form part of the contract the RIAI "blue" form contracts are used. The Institute of Engineers in Ireland (IEI), albeit the IEI is normally referred to as "Engineers Ireland," engineering contracts are the most popular form of contracts in relation to engineering contract. It should be noted that substantial building projects that are based in the Republic of Ireland but may have an international element to them may make use of the well-known suite of FIDIC or JCT standard form contracts that are seen around the world.

Construction-related disputes are, it is thought, often determined by the use of alternative dispute resolution (ADR) in the Republic of Ireland. The instant author practices in this area as a lawyer and has discussed this issue with colleagues at the time of writing no other source for this contention is available to the author. The distinction between alternative dispute resolution/appropriate dispute resolution and amicable dispute resolution is one that falls outside the scope of this chapter and the term ADR is used hereafter in its traditional meaning such that it should be taken to refer to alternative dispute resolution.

Until very recently the processes used were arbitration, conciliation, and mediation with the second of these three methods being very popular indeed. Statutory construction adjudication has now become part of the Irish landscape and the first couple of adjudications under the 2013 Construction Contracts Act, (notwithstanding that the legislation is referred to as the 2013 Act it did not in fact commence until July 25, 2016 and was not retrospective in terms of its operation so it took time for relevant contracts entered in to after the commencement date in the summer of 2016 to lead to adjudications) have at the time of writing been heard—albeit no applications have yet arisen to the Irish High Court on foot of the 2013 Act. Irish statutory adjudication is arguably narrower in scope than some of its common law cousins and the different constitutional framework that exists in the Republic of Ireland compared to countries such as England and Wales means that it is not fully clear to what degree jurisprudence from outside the Republic of Ireland will be followed on questions related to a statutory construction adjudication.

Construction disputes that are not resolved by ADR methods may be heard by the fast track commercial division of the Irish High Court.

Disputes that are heard neither by way of ADR or via the fast-track Commercial Court proceed through the ordinary courts and might take up to 6 to 7 years to be concluded. For more details of the Irish court system see *inter alia*: http://www.courts.ie/courts.ie/library3.nsf/pagecurrent/96153C6B3484308480257FBC0043CFA4?opendocument&l=en (accessed on May 30, 2017). The delay of 5 to 7 years with a case that is heard neither by way of an ADR process or via the fast track Commercial Court can be seen to arise as there are often significant delays in getting a date for trial due to pretrial motions and a time lag after the decision of the first instance court such as say the High Court and before the Court of Appeal hears the matter on appeal. At the time of writing the 2017 Mediation Bill is thought likely to increase the use of ADR once this legislation is passed and commenced as it will compel lawyers to explain to their clients that they can rather than litigating a dispute through the courts also utilise mediation. For a full discussion of the Irish Commercial Court see inter alia Dowling, S., Commercial Court, (2nd edition), (Round Hall, Dublin 2012).

Notwithstanding the forum in which a case is heard a legal dispute in Ireland will be prepared for in the same way as would occur in many other jurisdictions in the common law world. There is normally no prohibition on parties representing themselves but where the construction dispute is over a medium to large value this is probably uncommon. As is seen in other countries an order can be made against a litigant who has been held to be vexatious so as to restrict the ability of that person to institute legal proceedings without the leave of the court.

In the Republic of Ireland a litigant in this position is made subject to what is known as an Issac Wunder order, whereas in England and Wales someone held to be a vexatious litigant is made subject to a civil restraint order, whereas in other common law jurisdictions, states within Australia, such as New South Wales, the Register of the Supreme Court maintains a vexatious litigants register. There are 10,000 solicitors in the Republic of Ireland, on that point see: https://www.rte.ie/news/business/2017/0203/849782-10-000-irish-solicitors-registered-to-practice/ (accessed on May 30, 2017) (It might be noted that a large number of lawyers from England and Wales have been registering with the Law Society of Ireland subsequent to the referendum result in 2016, which will see the United Kingdom leave the European Union in a couple of years albeit at the time of writing most of these English solicitors who have registered, with the Law Society of Ireland, have not yet gone on to apply for Irish practising certificates), and around 2,100 barristers. Details on the Bar of Ireland and the number of practising barristers can be found at www.lawlibrary.ie (accessed on May 30, 2017).

Parties in a small- to medium-value construction dispute will usually engage a solicitor to advise them through the currency of the dispute and the solicitor will not advise using a barrister. In a medium- to high-value construction dispute it is far more normal for the solicitor to advise the client that the nature of the dispute means they would be best served, in making their case, if they also instructed junior and/or senior counsel. A Barrister in the Republic of Ireland who has been in practice for at least 10 years can apply for what are known as "letters patent" and take silk and become a Senior Counsel. S.Cs are known in other common law jurisdictions as Queen's Counsel or Senior Advocates. There is no rule or practice as may have been followed in the past that a senior counsel needs to appear at a hearing with a junior counsel also in attendance. Irish arbitrators who were questioned on the issue in May 2017 advised that they often had S.Cs appear before them in arbitrations with no junior barrister also in attendance.

Recent changes in legislation in the Republic of Ireland allow that solicitors can take silk but as of May 30, 2017 this is yet to occur. The lawyers in a construction dispute, however, many of them there are will advise as to the necessity to obtain expert reports from architects or engineers as the case may be.

Legal costs in the Republic of Ireland are normally described by commentators as high by international standards albeit the fees that some top rank lawyers in the city of London would charge are not thought to be replicated in Dublin. Media reports in London suggest that whilst it may not be common for lawyers there to charge more than £1,000 it is not unusual. See inter alia: https://www.theguardian.com/law/2016/feb/05/city-law-firms-charging-up-to-1100-an-hour (accessed on May 30, 2017). Legal fees of £1,100 an hour are at the time of writing approximately €1,350 an hour. No public reports can be found of Dublin-based lawyers charging more than €500 an hour. No doubt higher fees than that rate are charged but it is doubtful that they approach €1,350 an hour. Usually at the conclusion of the dispute a judge or arbitrator will follow the approach, in terms of awarding costs, which is frequently expressed as "costs follow the event."

In other words the party who lose the case will expect to pay not only their own legal costs but the costs of the victorious party. Lawyers may take a case on, what is often still described as a "no foal no fee" basis where the client is impecunious and they hold a professional belief that there is a high chance that they will recover a fee on foot of their client being awarded their legal costs. Conditional fee arrangements (CFAs) are not part of the framework of the Irish legal system. Contingent fees or conditional fee arrangements differ from the Irish idea of "no foal no fee" legal funding in that the former models of funding unlike the Irish model allow for "success fees."

The party who has engaged their lawyer to act under a conditional fee arrangement will not have any financial obligations if they lose their case but if they win than the lawyers can charge an uplift or "success fee," which usually may not be more than 100% greater than the fee that would have accrued had a conditional fee arrangement not been in place.

Nor is it possible to seek third party funding. The Irish Supreme Court has very recently considered the issue of third-party funding, which is allowed in a number of other jurisdictions around the world. For more details on that recent decision see *inter alia* Andrew Mizner's report "Irish Supreme Court rejects litigation funding" in http://www.cdr-news.com on May 24, 2017 (accessed on May 31, 2017). The court reiterated that the common law offence of maintenance and champerty precluded the plaintiff from obtaining funding from a third-party funder. While the decision triggered calls, among some observers, for the Irish parliament to introduce legislation to allow for companies get funding from third parties it does not seem that there is any basis to suggest that the government will follow this suggestion any time soon if at all.

Some construction disputes in the Republic of Ireland will fall outside the scope of the legislation that allows for statutory adjudication. Disputes falling outside the remit of statutory adjudication may be resolved by litigation, arbitration, conciliation, or mediation. Those disputes that are admitted to the Commercial Court are often resolved within very short periods of in and around 6 months of their admission to that court's lists. As to the length of Commercial Court lists see *inter alia* Mary Carolan's report "The Commercial Court: where dark corners of economy dominated the dock." In the *Irish Times*, October 8, 2014 (accessed on the newspaper's website on May 30, 2017). Arbitration is thought likely to suffer in popularity as a result of the introduction of statutory adjudication.

As of the time of writing there is no specific empirical evidence to signal that there has been that change that was seen in other similar jurisdictions once they started using statutory adjudication. Users of dispute processes will avail of the suite of resolution methods that can be followed in the Republic of Ireland having regard to the advice that their lawyers offer and consequent to their personal experience as to which methods best suit certain disputes. Suffice to say as has already been made clear in some instances the particular nature of the dispute will mean that no choice presents and the dispute will fall within the ambit of the 2013 Construction Contracts Act. Statutory adjudication is too new for any significant hostages to fortune to be offered at this time as to what might be the Irish experience.

Practitioners from other jurisdictions have suggested when speaking, in Dublin, on the topic of statutory adjudication that it is likely that Irish adjudicators will, as elsewhere in the common law world, fall into error but the party on the wrong end of the decision will, as often as not, be advised that to look to then proceed to litigation or arbitration will be throwing good money after bad. David Brynmor Thomas, a barrister from 39 Essex Chambers in London, spoke at a Chartered Institute of Arbitrators event held in the offices of McCann Fitzgerald in 2013 and made remarks in the terms just set out.

Arran Dowling-Hussey
B.A., M.Econ.Sc, LL.M, Dip. Construction Law, Dip. Arb., Dip. Int. Com. Arb.
F.C.I.Arb, Barrister-at-Law (King's Inns & Middle Temple)
London

References

Downing, N., Ramphul, M. and Healey, T. (2013). Is NE3 a realistic alternative to FIDIC for major international projects? *International Construction Law Review*.

Eggleston, B. (2006). *The NEC3 Engineering and Construction Contract: A Commentary*. Wiley-Blackwell, Chichester.

Grutters, L. and Fahey, S. (2013). Presentation and analysis of FIDIC contracts. Paper presented at the International Construction Contracts and the Resolution of Disputes ICC/FIDIC Conference, Paris.

Infrastructure Routemap. Available at: http://www.hm-treasury.gov.uk/iuk_cost_review_index.htm (accessed 25 Dec. 2013).

Kleine-Möller, N. and Merl, H. (2009). *Handbuch des privaten Baurechts*. Verlag C.H. Beck. München.

Lloyd, H. (2009). Some thoughts on NEC3. *International Construction Law Review*. Online. Available at: www.neccontract.com (accessed 12 April 2013).

National Infrastructure Plan. Online. Available at: https://www.gov.uk/government/organisations/hm-treasury (accessed 25 Dec. 2013).

Sabo, W. (2013). *The Definitive Guide to the American Institute of Architects (AIA) Construction Contract Documents: Legal Guide to AIA Documents* (5th Edition). Aspen Publisher, Chicago.

Vygen, K. and Joussen, E. (2013) *Bauvertragsrecht nach VOB und BGB Handbuch des privaten Baurechts* (5th Edition). Werner Verlag, Köln.

Ward D. 'Never Waste a Good Crisis': a challenge to the UK construction industry. Online. Available at: http://www.constructingexcellence.org.uk (accessed 25 Dec. 2013).

Further reading

Infrastructure in the New Era. Online. Available at: http://www.constructingexcellence.org.uk (accessed 25 Dec. 2013).

Kus, A., Jochen, M. and Stering, R. (1999). FIDIC's New "Silver Book" under the German Standard From Contracts Act, International Construction Law Review, Informa, London.

Zimmermann, J. and Hamann, M, (2009). *Vergleich bauvertraglicher Regelungsmechanismen im Hinblick auf eine optimierte Abwicklung und zur Senkung von Konfliktpotential am Beispiel von VOB, NEC und FIDIC*. Fraunhofer IRB Verlag, Stuttgart.

Websites

http://www.aia.org
http://www.enaa.or.jp
http://www.iccwbo.org
http://www.icheme.org
http://www.neccontract.com
http://www.orgalime.org

14 Risk and Insurance

14.1 Insurance in construction

One of the first, clear definitions of insurance principles was formulated by the *English Insurance Act* (1601). According to its drafters, insurance was intended to meet the following primary functions:

- to distribute individual loss across many;
- to encourage individuals to take a risk by promising them compensation in case of loss; and
- to motivate young people to become entrepreneurial.

The large number of restoration programs that followed the devastation of the world wars (going hand in hand with the rapid development of manufacturing processes) resulted in a consolidation of the risk management principles of responsibility, liability and indemnity. Consequently, it was at this point in history that insurance became recognized as an important need in the construction industry.

Construction insurance covers all indemnity agreements within the limits of individual construction activities where insurance is selected as a risk (liability) assignment instrument. The following are the main types of insurances relevant to construction projects:

- political risk insurance;
- exchange risk insurance;
- bank guarantee insurance (guarantee for bid, performance, advance payment);
- lost profit insurance;
- construction all risk insurance;
- erection all risk insurance;
- professional liability insurance;
- employer's liability insurance;
- public liability insurance.

International Construction Contract Law, Second Edition. Lukas Klee.
© 2018 John Wiley & Sons Ltd. Published 2018 by John Wiley & Sons Ltd.

Within construction projects, risks are usually allocated by the two most important contracts—the contract between the employer and the service provider (contract administrator, designer, and so on), and the contract between the employer and the contractor.

Insurance costs have escalated so much in recent years that they have become one of the most important cost items of a construction project. Construction project participants must, therefore, understand risk management issues, in particular, risk allocation and insurance. Insurance is widely recommended to protect the contracting parties against the financial implications of unexpected losses, damage, or liability. The primary participant (i.e., the employer) usually requires of the secondary party (parties) (i.e., the contractor, designer, consulting engineer as a contract administrator, and so on) to be insured against risks in connection with their role and activities. Therefore, a primary party is not then necessarily a direct party to the insurance contract.

The level of the insured amount shall be determined on an estimate of the potential damage the other participants can cause to this party by their activity or inactivity. Potential damage also depends on the nature and duration of the contract, the place where realization takes place and on other circumstances (risks).

14.2 Commercial risk, risk of damage, and exceptional risk

When analyzing individual construction project risks and their likely nature, we can distinguish between two main categories. The first contains the hazards and risks leading to injuries, death and physical damage, such as defective materials, floods, and work-related accidents. The second comprises hazards and risks giving rise to financial losses and delay, such as late site handover, delayed instructions, and variations.

The above categories further differ because the former (i.e., physical risks) are insurable risks and the latter (i.e., non-physical risks) are not insurable. These categories are handled in different ways even within the standard forms of contract that normally regulate the issues of insurance. The first category is typically dealt with by a separate, specific chapter in the contract. The second category is usually "spread across" the entire contract with basic risks typically specified in one section.

The question still remains: who is to bear the risk, which is not expressly allocated to one of the parties? The answer is that the party bearing such risk depends on the particular wording of the contract and/or on the governing law.

FIDIC forms in the 1999 First Edition did not solve this problem. FIDIC DBO, published in 2008, contains a significant update of mentioned risk and insurance provisions. The clauses have been restructured in a more logical sequence matching the natural flow from risk allocation to responsibility to liability to insurance. Furthermore, the risks carried by both the employer and the contractor have been identified and allocated and different types of risks have been identified as the commercial risk (risk that results in financial loss and/or time loss for either party where insurance is not generally or commercially available) and risk of damage (risk that results in physical loss or damage to the works or other property belonging to either party, other than a commercial risk).

"Exceptional risks" were established to replace the *force majeure* that is preserved under the term "exceptional event" (FIDIC, 2011a).

Other risks such as *The Employer's Risks during the Design-Build Period* are found at Sub-Clause 17.1 and read as follows:

> Subject to the provisions of Sub-Clause 17.8 [Limitation of Liability], the risks allocated to the employer and for which the employer is liable during the design-build period are divided into:
>
> (a) The employer's commercial risks, which are:
>   (i) the financial loss, delay, or damage allocated to the employer under the contract or for which the employer is liable by law, unless otherwise modified under the contract;
>   (ii) the right of the employer to construct the works or any part thereof on, over, under, in, or through the site;
>   (iii) the use or occupation of the site by the works or any part thereof, or for the purpose of design, construction, or completion of the Works other than the abusive or wrongful use by the contractor; and the use or occupation by the employer of any part of the permanent works, except as may be specified in the contract; and
> (b) The employer's risks of damage, which are:
>   (i) damage due to any interference, whether temporary or permanent, with any right of way, light, air, water, or other easement (other than that resulting from the contractor's method of construction), which is the unavoidable result of the construction of the works in accordance with the contract;
>   (ii) fault, error, defect, or omission in any element of the design of the works by the employer or which may be contained in the employer's requirements, other than design carried out by the contractor pursuant to his obligations under the contract;
>   (iii) any operation of the forces of nature (other than those allocated to the contractor in the contract data) against which an experienced contractor could not reasonably have been expected to have taken adequate preventative precautions; and
> (c) The exceptional risks under Clause 18 [Exceptional Risks].

The biggest difference is in the new wording of Sub-Clause 17.2, where "The Contractor's Risks during the Design-Build Period" are stated as follows:

> Subject to the provisions of Sub-Clause 17.8 [Limitation of Liability], the risks allocated to the contractor and for which the contractor is liable during the design-build period are all the risks other than those listed under Sub-Clause 17.1 [The Employer's Risks during the Design-Build Period], including the care of both the works and the goods.

Exceptional risks are defined in Sub-Clause 18.1, which reads:

> An exceptional risk is a risk arising from an Exceptional Event, which includes, but is not limited to:
>
> (a) war, hostilities (whether war be declared or not), invasion, act of foreign enemies;
> (b) rebellion, terrorism, revolution, insurrection, military, or usurped power, or civil war, within the country;
> (c) riot, commotion, or disorder within the country by persons other than the contractor's personnel and other employees of the contractor and subcontractors;
> (d) strike or lockout not solely involving the contractor's personnel and other employees of the contractor and subcontractors;
> (e) munitions of war, explosive materials, ionizing radiation or contamination by radioactivity, within the country, except as may be attributable to the contractor's use of such munitions, explosives, radiation, or radio-activity; and
> (f) natural catastrophes such as earthquake, hurricane, typhoon, or volcanic activity that are unforeseeable or against which an experienced contractor could not reasonably have been expected to have taken adequate preventative precautions.

The list is not exhaustive and the contractor may claim that an event gave rise to an exceptional risk allocated to the employer under Sub-Clause 18.1 if the contractor considers that an event has occurred, which falls within following definition (Sub-Clause 1.1.37):

> "Exceptional Event" means an event or circumstance which is (a) beyond a party's control; (b) which the party could not reasonably have provided against before entering into the contract; (c) which having arisen, such party could not reasonably have avoided or overcome; and (d) which is not substantially attributable to the other party.

The reasons that these exceptional risks are allocated to the employer include the fact that they are the initiator, ultimate user, and beneficiary of the project. Furthermore, it would be extremely difficult for the contractor to price such a risk if they were required to bear it. Moreover, the likelihood of such risks arising is small and it is better for the employer to absorb the costs of such risks if and when they occur, rather than ask the contractor to include it in the contract price and be responsible for them (FIDIC, 2011a). It must be stressed that the above mentioned wording was changed in the 2017 FIDIC second edition. Clauses 17 to 19 were subject to complete revision regarding "Care of the Works and Indemnities," "Exceptional Events", and "Insurance." These parts were returning back to the basic principles regarding these areas, as they were included in the 1977 FIDIC Red Book.

The following risks can be categorized as belonging to the first category. That is, hazards and risks that lead to injury, death, and/or physical damage:

- insurable risks that are required to be insured on the basis of a contractual agreement;
- insurable risks that are not required to be insured on the basis of a contractual agreement; and
- non-insurable risks.

The insurable risks that are required to be insured on the basis of a contractual agreement are most frequently covered by the contractor's comprehensive insurance policy, construction all-risk insurance, public liability insurance, professional liability insurance, or contractor's and employer's liability insurance (for employee workplace-related accidents).

Insurable risks that are not required to be insured on the basis of a contractual agreement are most frequently the subject of a contractor's, consulting engineer's, and designer's professional liability insurance and employer's liability insurance.

Non-insurable risks are the contractor's or employer's responsibility, depending on their allocation.

Weather risk in offshore wind construction contracts by Alex Blomfield (UK)

Adverse weather constitutes one of the main risks in any construction project. This risk comes to the fore even more in offshore wind projects, particularly as such projects are built increasingly further from shore and in increasingly deeper waters. Severe weather conditions, including high waves, strong and turbulent sea currents and tides, and strong variable winds have the potential to significantly disrupt the construction and installation of offshore wind components, particularly given the limited weather window often available to deploy massive components to site, and install, test, and commission them. Managing such weather conditions and dealing with the difficulties they cause for transportation, installation, testing, commissioning, and the logistics of offshore wind project construction in general constitute one of the greatest challenges involved in delivering offshore wind projects on time and on budget.

The difficulty of managing adverse weather risk in offshore wind construction is exacerbated by the industry preference to deliver projects using a multi-contract rather than an EPC-wrap approach. The multiple contracts in place with the various stakeholders, such as vessel operators and suppliers and installers of foundations, wind turbines, cables, and other electrical parts and substations, often make it the case that one party's delay will cause serious delay to other parties. For example, if a vessel has been reserved for a particular time slot, and bad weather prevents work from being carried out during that period, it may be some time before another slot for that vessel can be reserved. Furthermore, variations in the weather tolerances of different vessels and the windows of good weather required for different scopes of work can create major challenges for the scheduling of installation that requires multiple vessels.

Weather risks need to be quantified at the time when the contract is negotiated and the risk allocated to the appropriate project participants at the various stages of the project. This requires careful due diligence, planning, and legal drafting tailored to the particular weather risks and remuneration mechanism of each contract. Contractors who have not adequately protected themselves contractually may suffer the consequences of adverse weather through a reduction in their profit margin or, worse still, through the payment of liquidated damages and/or increased labor and other costs arising from the disruption to the works. Project finance lenders will also require a higher level of contingency funding and sponsor support in projects where their technical advisors assess a higher adverse weather risk.

No single standard form construction contract exists for the offshore wind sector. To date, BIMCO, LOGIC and FIDIC construction contract forms have proved popular in the European offshore wind market.

Under the BIMCO Supplytime 2005 form, payment for vessel hire continues irrespective of delays or stoppages caused by adverse weather conditions. However, if weather conditions are unexpected and exceptionally bad, then a party may be able to claim relief under the *force majeure* provisions. Under the Supplytime form, neither party is liable for any loss, damage or delay if the party invoking *force majeure* is hindered from performing any of its obligations under the charter. However, the party relying on an event of *force majeure* is expected to make all reasonable efforts to minimize or avoid the effect of a *force majeure* event. Furthermore, a *force majeure* event may result in termination, if it prevents the performance of the charter for an extended period.

The FIDIC conditions of contract (the Red and Yellow Books) deal with adverse weather risk differently and allow the contractors an extension of time for completion of construction if they suffer a delay caused by "exceptionally adverse climatic conditions." However, the contractor has no entitlement to compensation for such conditions, and may even suffer the cost of any acceleration methods designed to mitigate the effects of such delay.

The FIDIC conditions do not define what weather events fall within "exceptionally adverse climatic conditions" nor is there a universally accepted definition of this term. When negotiating a contract based on the FIDIC conditions parties are therefore advised to define what constitutes adverse weather conditions as well as the location where the applicable weather measurements are to be taken.

One approach could be to compare actual weather conditions experienced during construction with historical weather data for the site in question. Whether or not this is feasible depends on the availability of historical data. Given that the first offshore wind project in Europe dates back to the early 1990s, the data available to permit a meaningful comparison of current and historical weather information are limited and may not be conclusive. For instance, metmasts, which are used to collect wind data, have only been installed in recent years, thereby limiting the empirical value of such data.

The FIDIC conditions also contain *force majeure* provisions, the definition of which includes natural catastrophes such as earthquakes, hurricanes, typhoons and volcanic activity. Although *force majeure* events do not affect the obligation to make payments to the contractor, the challenge lies in establishing that the adverse weather conditions being experienced are sufficiently serious to constitute natural catastrophes.

The LOGIC general conditions of contract 2003 also deal with adverse weather as part of the *force majeure* clause. However, in these conditions, *force majeure* only extends to physical disasters and excludes all other weather conditions regardless of severity. In contrast to the FIDIC conditions, the LOGIC form does not have a general extension of time clause. Instead, the contractor will be held responsible for the timely completion of all work done and will have to notify the company of any proposed or actual stoppages of work and any other matter likely to affect its completion. The LOGIC contract does favor the contractor in so far as it gives the contractor the unilateral right to suspend works "in the event that suspension is necessary for the proper execution or safety of the work, or persons."

Unless work is suspended due to contractor default, the LOGIC contract stipulates that the contract shall be adjusted in accordance with the relevant provisions relating to remuneration. Parties will need to take this into consideration and allow for appropriate rates in the event of suspension due to weather-related conditions.

None of the three standard form construction contracts discussed above provides a satisfactory solution as to how to deal with the risk of delay and disruption caused by adverse weather. This means that parties who use these forms as the basis for their agreements will need to negotiate specific provisions to deal with adverse weather risk and with the impact that adverse weather may have on time and cost incurred during a project. These provisions will need to be tailored to the specific project and the parties may need to be quite creative to mitigate the potential impact of adverse weather to the project as a whole.

Before entering into negotiations, due diligence should be carried out as to the weather conditions at the relevant site so that the parties can negotiate an approach tailored to those conditions. This would facilitate a better understanding of the potential impact of adverse weather risk at the outset of the project and reduce the risk of significant schedule and/or cost adjustments during the execution of the contract.

An allowance for adverse weather conditions can be built into a construction schedule. However, calculating a realistic allowance can be extremely challenging. Weather data may provide predictions of likely conditions over the course of a fixed period of time. However, each operation may require specific windows of "good" weather, such as, for example, a specified number of hours to relocate from one location to another, or to install one or more blades on a turbine. At times or locations where weather is particularly changeable, such weather windows may take substantially longer to appear than can be deduced from the mean weather readings.

The potential margins of error in building contingency into a project schedule are huge. Where there are multiple vessels working on an integrated schedule, errors in these calculations are likely to prove costly. Where a contractor contracts on the basis of a lump-sum, fixed schedule contract, it would be prudent to include significant contingency in terms of time and cost to reflect this risk. However, this means that if the weather is favorable, the contractor may receive a considerable windfall and the employer may face substantial wasted costs in terms of the rest of the spread. Employers, therefore, may attempt to carve out adverse weather in general, or some excess of adverse weather, from the lump-sum contract price and include it as a reimbursable element. This enables the project schedule to be calculated against the most realistic projected weather patterns, thereby minimizing the risk of wasted spread costs where the weather follows the projections. However, this will not cut out all of the fat, the employer will still need to ensure the availability of the spread in case the projections are wrong.

Another consideration is how adverse weather delay should be reflected in the remuneration of a contractor, in particular, in cases where the contractor does not assume the weather risk. This issue is straightforward in the case of day-rate contracts, such as the Supplytime, where each day of adverse weather is compensated at the day rate (or perhaps a reduced rate), as a further day of hire. For lump sum contract where instalments of a lump sum are paid against specified milestones, the picture is more complicated. In such cases, the contractor may risk liquidity issues where completion of the relevant milestones is delayed due to adverse weather. It is possible to solve this issue by including an "adverse weather day" payment milestone. Another way might be to maintain a minimum monthly payment under the contract in addition to the milestone payments. In the former case, if the period of adverse weather exceeds the stipulated allowance, the contractor will be reimbursed on the basis of the additional "adverse weather day" milestone.

Contractors will need to be careful to observe any notice or other formal requirements relating to claiming an extension of time due to adverse weather. Daily weather logs should be kept as well as records of the work, which has been affected by weather, the nature and cost of the delay and the steps taken to minimize such delay. These records should be as detailed as possible so as to ensure there is sufficient evidence of the severity of the weather conditions.

Developing a market standard approach to the issue of adverse weather risk in the construction of offshore wind projects should be a priority for the offshore wind sector. However, it is likely that some degree of tailoring would remain necessary to reflect the peculiarities of the individual projects. Nevertheless, all parties would benefit from the reduced negotiation time and increased certainty that this would bring, not least given the complexity of multi-contracting structures for offshore wind projects. However, no amount of clever contractual drafting will eliminate the dramatic impact that adverse weather can have on the timely and on-budget completion of offshore wind projects.

Alex Blomfield
Special Counsel
K&L Gates LLP
London
UK

14.3 Risk management in the standard forms of contract

Associations of professional organizations have created standardized sample forms of contract in order to ensure well-balanced and fair contractual relationships. This form of unification reflects the preferred tendering method based on comparisons of individual contractors' bids to employer unified requirements. A side effect of this is that the provisions of such sample forms of construction contracts concerning risk and insurance are becoming increasingly complex.

The British tradition has had the biggest influence on such sample conditions of international construction contracts. Based on Anglo-Saxon principles, the purpose of the contract is not only to define the scope of work, price and time for completion, but also to allocate the risks the project is exposed to and to establish the way the risks will be treated and managed. The need to insure various aspects of a construction project is tied to the above trend and to the use of the standard forms of contract.

Within most sample conditions of contract, certain risks are usually allocated to one of the parties and the remaining risks belong to the other party. The risks are normally allocated to the party most capable of managing them efficiently. Some of the risks are non-insurable and must be allocated to one of the parties, based on a prevailing benefit from participation in the project.

With the risks identified, they should then be allocated to the individual construction project participants. This allocation should be based on sound evaluation of the participants' interactions and the risks themselves. The most fitting method may be allocation based on the mentioned ability to manage and control an adverse situation and its consequences. However, this may not always work in practice. For example, one of the parties may be optimally equipped to carry out a particular task but may not be prepared to accept a particular risk.

Should there be no risk allocation (or if the allocation is incorrect) and adverse events arise causing loss and damage, disputes are sure to occur. The risks should, therefore, be conveniently allocated to the party, which has the expertise to control them or to reduce the probability of their occurrence or to mitigate adverse implications of such an event.

If a risk is allocated to one of the parties, this party shall bear the adverse consequences of the respective realized risk. Such party, however, may assign these risks to the other party by means of an *indemnity provision*. This other party must then fully trust the indemnified party or stipulate the conditions and requirements the indemnified party must observe.

Take, for example, *construction all-risk insurance* where the insured party (contractor): (1) assigns the adverse liability implications to the insurer (insurance company), which then (2) stipulates the conditions and requirements for the contractor, concerning diligent work practices and mitigation of the potential occurrences and consequences of an adverse event (risk management requirements).

Poor risk management will result in bad risk allocation, damage, losses, and disputes. Whenever a proper risk allocation is sought, the allocation must be reasonable, fair (balanced), and efficient. In practice, there is rarely any consensus on what is "reasonable and fair." Further criteria should therefore be specified to ensure optimum risk allocation so that best value for invested money can be found.

The following questions need to be raised (Bunni, 2011):

- Which of the parties can best control the events leading to a risk occurrence?
- Which of the parties can best control a risk once it appears?
- What if the employer wants to get engaged in risk control?
- Which of the parties is prepared to bear a risk beyond their control?
- Is the payment for risk transfer reasonable and acceptable?
- Is the party bearing the risk able to bear the consequences of risk realization?
- Can a particular risk transfer from the employer (to another party) lead to a potential transfer of another risk back to the employer (from another party)?

Answers to the above questions will help formulate unambiguous and realistic conditions. These requirements will also assist the contractor to transparently evaluate the bid.

To determine which party ought to bear a particular risk, these further summarized sets of criteria are available (Bunni, 2011):

- Is the party able to control the risk?
- Is a party able to transfer the risk and have the related transfer costs refunded by the other party? (Such an approach is economical and most advantageous to keep the given risk under control).
- Which party has the highest economical benefit from particular risk acceptance?

- Is risk allocation to a particular party beneficial for the construction industry's long-term prosperity?

As such, there are in fact three risk allocation scenarios:

- All the risks to be borne by one of the parties.
- Risk allocation is well balanced.
- Risk allocation is based on specific criteria to be efficient.

The specific criteria of efficient risk allocation are as follows:

- the ability to control a realized risk (to avoid its realization, reduce the probability of its occurrence, and to mitigate its consequences);
- the ability to perform a particular activity the risk relates to;
- inability to accept a risk.

14.4 Hazards and risks in construction projects

A construction project is exposed to a large number of hazards and respective risks (Bunni, 2011), related to:

- The time necessary for planning, site inspection, design, and construction. Completion of projects often extends across a long time horizon and some phenomena and related hazards can occur repeatedly or on a regular basis within a single project. There are also climatic conditions to contend with such as severe winters, monsoons, and so on.
- The number of people who participate in the project, that is, those who initiate, prepare, finance, design, provide the supplies of materials and plants, construct, supervise, administer, operate, secure, and repair can be enormous. These people usually come from various social classes and from many different countries and cultures in cases of international projects.
- Numerous engineering works are executed in isolated locations with complicated surfaces, often extending across large areas and being exposed to natural hazards with an unforeseeable intensity and frequency.
- New materials and products—not yet proved over time—might be used. Advanced technologies also tend to appear which are necessary for some projects.
- An extensive interaction involving large numbers of companies and individuals with different goals and commitments.

Due to the above, risk management (including insurance risk management) is of great importance in construction projects. The importance of risk management increases two-fold when dealing with large construction projects. Individual risks multiply with the growing size of a project and, frequently, new significant risks appear.

Risks include but are not limited to (Bunni, 2011):

- Lack of experience by construction project participants as a result of a limited number of large projects realized. Moreover, it is complicated to gain and transfer experience and information because the parties may be against

its publication. For example, litigation often takes the form of confidential arbitration as do alternative dispute resolution methods. Insurance and reinsurance companies are not actively communicating or willing to communicate information and experience.
- More institutions will often take part in financing due to the need for extensive funding. It is sometimes impossible to employ private resources as they may be unavailable or insufficient and public resources must therefore be used. Incorporation of public financing will, however, bring additional new risks.
- The impact of even one unsuccessful, large construction project on the contractor's financial position may be devastating. There may also be adverse consequences for other participants and the project as a whole.
- Time for completion of a large project may take several years. Thus, risk occurrence is more likely. Shortening of this time will then bring other, new risks. Once complete, the entire project may become redundant and inefficient due to the availability of new technologies and user requirements.
- A number of specialists are often involved in a large construction project. Their efforts are difficult to unify but they must cooperate on matters such as planning, preparations, engineering, execution, financing, operation, maintenance, securing insurance, and so on.
- Managers must be willing to give their time, sacrifice privacy/personal life, and dedicate a significant part of their career to a single, particular project.
- Projects frequently take place in complicated geological and climatic conditions and can extend across vast areas of land.
- Complicated delivery methods are used to execute projects involving a number of contractors, subcontractors, service and material providers, their subcontractors, and so on.
- New technologies appear. These may have to be implemented in practice by thousands of people with inadequate experience in these new technologies.

Individual hazards then give rise to risks that can be divided into the following categories of hazards and risks (see Bunni (2011) as an excellent source of details in this regard).

14.4.1 Project preparation risks

- Employer's selection of the contract administrator and consultants.
- Employer's requirements for the contract administrator and consultants.
- Selection of the site.
- Adequacy of site surveys and inspections (including underground sections).
- Adequacy of financial funds and accuracy of necessary cost estimations.

14.4.2 Design risks

- Improperly selected design documentation in respect of its intended users and society.
- Negligence.
- Technical standards.
- Lack of knowledge, lack of supervision, and hasty work.
- Lack of communication.

- Inability to foresee problems.
- Use of unproven technologies.
- Improper use of, and reliance on, software, automatic processes, and mechanical and electronic equipment.
- Lack of safety measures.
- Selection of contractor and subcontractor.

14.4.3 Site risks

- Excessive rain.
- Floods and inundations.
- Winds and storms.
- Hurricanes and tornados.
- Subsidence, landslides, rockslides, and avalanches.
- Extreme temperatures.
- Cyclones.
- Earthquakes.
- Political, economic, legislative, tax, transport, and other risks in connection with the country where project execution takes place.
- *Force majeure.*
- Adverse sub-surface and geological conditions.
- Anthropogenic underground obstacles (power and service utility lines).
- Lack of project acceptance by local population and neighbors.

14.4.4 Execution risks of a technical nature

- Extended duration of the project.
- Technical complexity and innovation in design requiring new methods of construction and/or erection.
- Removal of temporary structures.
- Defective temporary structures and their poor design.
- Dangerous substances and materials.
- Defective design.
- Defective workmanship and materials.
- Lack of supervision.
- Failures and collapse of mechanical and electrical systems.
- Inadequate site management.
- Ground movement.
- Explosions and fire.
- Vibrations and oscillations.
- Corrosion.
- Collapse.
- Collapse of a temporary structure.

14.4.5 Execution risks of an anthropogenic nature

- Human failure.
- Negligence.

- Fraud and other criminal acts.
- Programming of work.
- Lack of communication.
- Failure to ensure compatibility with insurance conditions.
- Riot and commotion.
- Strikes.
- Incompetence.
- Malicious acts.
- Inefficiency and delays.
- Insufficient site supervision.
- Variations in technical specifications.
- Dispute resolution risks.

14.4.6 Post-construction risks

- Security/safety.
- Serviceability.
- Material fatigue.
- Fire and arson.
- *Force majeure*.
- Natural hazards including inefficient remedies.
- Human errors and anthropogenic risks (including vandalism).
- Risk in connection with making the work fit for intended purpose.
- Project operation risks.
- Wear and tear risks.

The difficulties connected to construction risk quantification by Dejan Makovšek (France)

Every day we make decisions based on imperfect information. We make bets. Our bets are based on past experiences and our behavioral traits. For example, we choose our daily train to work not based on the time table only but based on our experience how late that train on average is. We build our train delay contingency on past experience. If we travel somewhere else, where we have no way of knowing how late the train can be our contingency will be higher. The more information we have, the more accurate our "risk pricing."

An abundant volume of empirical literature on risk pricing exists in finance, where it is possible to study vast sets of data on the performance of past investment decisions. The more information investors have the more accurate their risk pricing, resulting in a lower cost of financing they provide assuming there is competition.

The principles of risk pricing are generic, that is, relevant for every domain, where decisions need to be made based on imperfect information and that includes construction. A particularly challenging field is the construction risk involved in the delivery of major schemes—for example roads, bridges, tunnels, dams, and so on.

For the construction company the relevant measure of risk exposure is a risk contingency, an amount added to a central estimate of cost to cover future cost overruns that are realized. A range of techniques for quantifying construction risk have been propounded in academic construction literature, including deterministic methods, probabilistic methods, and fuzzy-logic (Baccarini, 2006). There is, however, inherent complexity and a lack of historical information that restrain construction companies from applying these methods to major infrastructure construction projects. Accordingly, construction risk (and the resulting contingency amount) is normally estimated subjectively through risk workshops: that is, experts scrutinize the design and assign probabilities and impacts of various events (Infrastructure Risk Group, 2013). Though such exercises are invaluable in terms of due diligence, there is no empirical research available on their ex post accuracy, making it difficult to form a view on the accuracy of contractors' perceptions of risk.

In the introduction above we illustrated the importance of information about risk to risk pricing. Very few examples exist how additional available information can affect construction risk pricing (e.g., De Silva et al., 2008) in for example traditional highway procurement. Oklahoma's Department of Transportation changed its procurement policy to publicize the state's internal cost estimates during tendering. After this information was released, winning bids were reduced by an average of 11% for more risky and complex projects (e.g., a bridge construction), but were unaffected for low-risk projects (e.g., asphalt pouring). The authors applied a difference-in-difference approach, observing thousands of bids over multiple years. In summary, the particular market was competitive, but the availability of the state's estimates still improved bidders' willingness to reduce their contingencies.

What should matter aside from competition for the contract and information about risk is also the power of the construction contract. Low-powered contracts transfer less risk to the contractors (e.g., DBB/Red Book FIDIC), whereas high-powered contracts transfer most of the construction risk at a fixed end cost and also involve high penalties for delays (e.g., Silver Book FIDIC). The latter are typically used in PPPs, where the lenders in the project company prefer to be as insulated as possible from construction risk. Sparse existing evidence below does indicate contract power matters.

In traditionally procured road projects (=low powered contracts) the state absorbs significant cost overruns. These cost overruns (measured against the detailed design or contract value) reach, on average, 9% at most over large samples in different studies.

If we were to use a higher powered contract it is not the 9% of cost variability above that would be transferred to the construction contractor. Whether the project is delivered using traditional procurement or a PPP, the primary cause of cost overruns is scope creep, at least in the case of transport infrastructure (Makovšek, 2013). Under the terms of either contract, it is the responsibility of the procuring authority to define what it wants to build. Thus, in either case, the cost overrun is not necessarily a risk to the construction company or the project company, as the additional cost can be passed back to the procuring authority. To the extent that much of the 9% mentioned above would reflect the responsibility of the procurement authority in defining the scope, the actual risk to be managed in a PPP would be smaller.

Using a high-powered contract to deliver infrastructure greatly reduces end cost variability. In the single available study of construction contract performance for 75 major PPP projects the median and average cost overruns were zero and 2.3%, respectively (Blanc-Brude & Makovšek, 2013). Construction risk in infrastructure project finance (EDHEC-Risk Institute Working Paper, EDHEC Business School). This result was indifferent to the sector (not only roads were in the sample) and geography (project location).

Table 14.1 Presents a summary of existing studies of construction cost overruns in traditional procurement.

Source	Reference estimate	Project type	Time period	Observ.	Average Cost overrun (%)	Area
Cantarelli et al., 2012b; Flyvbjerg et al., 2003	Decision to build	Roads	1927–2009	278	21.2	NW Europe
		Bridges, tunnels		39	25.3	
Cantarelli et al., 2012a	Decision to build	Roads	1980–2009	37	18.9	Netherlands
		Bridges, tunnels		15	21.7	
Makovšek et al., 2012	Decision to build	Roads	1995–2007	36	19.19	Slovenia
Lundberg et al., 2011	Decision to build	Roads	1997–2009	102	21.2	Sweden
Lee et al., 2008	Decision to build	Roads	1985–2005	138	11.0	South Korea
Ellis et al., 2007	Detailed design	Roads & bridges	1998–2006	1847	−13.40	USA
Odeck, 2004	Detailed design	Roads	1992–1995	620	7.88	Norway
Cantarelli et al., 2012c	Detailed design	Roads	1980–2009	23	−2.9	Netherlands
Ellis et al., 2007	Contract value	Roads & bridges	1998–2006	1908	9.36	USA
Bordat et al., 2004	Contract value	Roads	1996–2001	599	5.6	USA
Hintze and Selstead, 1991	Contract value	Roads	1985–1989	110	9.2	USA

Despite the relatively small amount of risk transferred to PPPs, there is clear evidence that the cost of infrastructure is higher when built via a PPP than when it is built traditionally via the state. Blanc-Brude, Goldsmith, and Välilä (2009) observed ex ante construction cost (contract prices) in 162 traditionally procured and 65 PPP road projects in western Europe: PPPs were found to be 24% more costly on average than the equivalent traditionally procured projects. Daito and Gifford (2014) found an even greater cost premium of 64% for PPP over traditionally procured road projects. Due to the limited PPP experience in the United States and data issue encountered this study is less robust but nevertheless points in the same direction.

Since the Blanc-Brude, Goldsmith, and Välilä (2009) study used ex-ante cost (at contract close) we could correct these by adding average cost overruns for traditional procurement (i.e., 9%) and PPPs (2%), which would make the PPP 17% more expensive than traditional procurement. While such a correction is speculative (as the averages have been derived from different samples) and the exact percentage can be argued about it is nevertheless clear that already the ex-ante difference is of an order of magnitude.

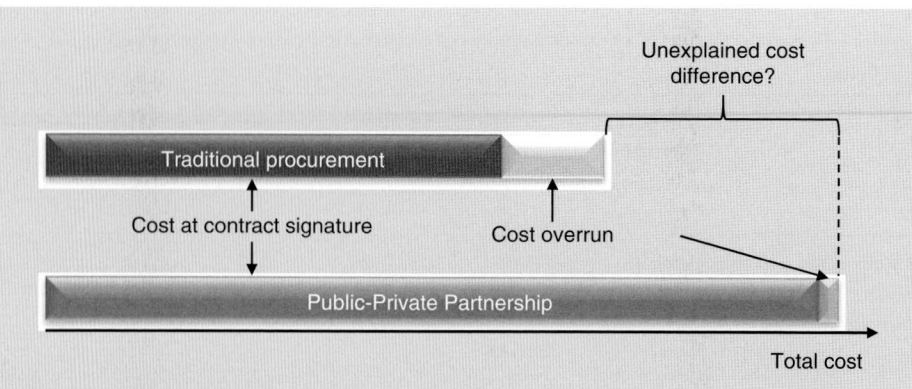

Figure 14.1 conceptually illustrates construction cost at contract signature and cost overrun for traditional procurement compared to PPP.

Taken together, these strands of evidence suggest that the cost to governments of transferring risk to the private party in a PPP is significantly above the efficient price (i.e., the unexplained cost difference in Figure 14.1).

Two further arguments may compound this finding. First, lenders and investors may avoid the riskiest of projects, suggesting the portfolio of projects delivered as PPPs is actually lower risk than the traditionally procured one. Second, traditional procurement mainly relies on lower powered contracts, which provide fewer incentives to efficiently manage risk, whereas the PPP model relies on fixed-price turnkey contracts. Effectively better management of risks is expected, which reduces their impact and/or probability. Interestingly, practitioners report that the use of a lump-sum turn-key construction contract generally involves a premium of 20% against a less-restrictive contract types, such as DBB, regardless of whether it is part of a PPP or not (Yescombe, 2014).

An argument against the conclusion that these outcomes are a source of inefficient risk pricing or extraordinary profits in PPP projects is that higher quality infrastructure is built to optimize the LCC of infrastructure management (Soliño and Gago de Santos, 2010).

This should be true for capital-intensive PPPs in any sector. There is, however, little evidence that this is the case or that in all traditionally procured projects the opposite is true. On a declarative level, there is a widespread embrace of LCC optimization principles in PPPs in the UK, but there are practical obstacles to its execution (Meng and Harshaw 2013).

There is evidence to support this proposition. An available study on social infrastructure by NAO (NAO, 2007)—a construction review of PPP hospitals in the UK—found that these were not built to a higher standard of quality than traditionally procured hospitals. A report by the Bundesrechnungshof (German Court of Audit, 2014) in review of seven German PPP motorways comes to the same conclusion, albeit in the context of investigating innovation. PPP motorways were built to the same standard as traditionally procured ones.

The German example cited two reasons: first, even though contracts were output-based, building to a different standard is difficult due to strict technical rules and regulations. Second, as lenders are risk averse, they may prefer tried and tested methods rather than experimentation.

In summary, there is reason to suspect that high-powered contracts are disproportionately more expensive than low-powered ones. If that is the case there are major questions that need answering. How much risk should we transfer for what type of product? What can the procuring side do to better inform the bidders so as to improve the competition for the contract outcomes?

The overview above suggests that there is much to learn about how different construction contracts perform and how the broader settings (product complexity, competition and so on) affect their outcome. In fact it is surprising how little we do know given that the practice and common sense recommendations captured in the rest of this book have been evolving for decades.

The immediate reason for this is clearly that the researchers do not have sufficient data to investigate this area in greater detail.

Contract outcomes are in many cases market sensitive and private information. Some would call this a market failure, but it should come as no surprise that contractors do not share such information between themselves or with others.

On the other hand, governments spend billions of different currencies around the world on procuring major assets from construction contractors. Not having a good understanding how the contracts that they use work could mean they spend many more billions than they should. Hence, it is the governments that should have the foremost interest to collect and enable access to data on contract characteristics and historical performance.

The first step toward more data and progress though is to make them aware, where is there room for improvement. This text is a contribution in that direction and is based on the previous work of Makovsek and Moszoro also published in *Transport Reviews*.

Dejan Makovšek, PhD
Economist
International Transport Forum at the OECD
Paris

Bibliography

Baccarini, M. (2006). The maturing concept of estimating project cost contingency: a review. Proceedings of the Australasian University Building Educators Association Annual Conference, Sidney, July 2006.

Daito, N., and Gifford, J. L. (2014). U.S. highway public private partnerships: are they more expensive or efficient than the traditional model? *Managerial Finance*, 40, 1131–1151.

De Silva, D.G., Dunne, T., Kankanamge, A. and Kosmopoulou, G. (2008). The impact of public information on bidding in highway procurement auctions. *European Economic Review*, 52(1), 150–181.

Infrastructure Risk Group (2013). Leading practice and improvement: Report from the infrastructure risk group. Technical report. Infrastructure Risk Group/Institute of Risk Management.

Makovšek, D. (2013). Public–private partnerships, traditionally financed projects, and their price. *Journal of Transport Economics and Policy*, 47(1), 143–155.

Meng, X. and Harshaw, F. (2013). The application of whole-life costing in PFI/PPP projects. In: Smith, S.D. and Ahiaga-Dagbui, D.D. (eds) *Proceedings 29th Annual ARCOM Conference*. Association of Researchers in Construction Management, Reading, UK, pp. 769–778.

NAO (2007). Improving the PFI tendering process (Report by the Comptroller and Auditor General HC 149: 2006–2007). Author, London.

Soliño, A. S. and Gago de Santos, P. (2010). Transaction costs in transport public–private partnerships: comparing procurement procedures. *Transport Reviews*, 30(3), 389–406.

Yescombe, E. R. (2014). *Principles of Project Finance* (2nd Edition). Academic Press, London.

14.5 Insurance requirements in standard forms of contract

14.5.1 Insurance requirements in FIDIC forms

The conditions of contract of the *Fédération Internationale des Ingénieurs Conseils* (FIDIC; International Federation of Consulting Engineers) are the most widely used sample conditions of contract in international construction projects. These sample forms are now perceived as international best practice documents and their popularity is ever growing. This is thanks to international employers and lenders wanting reliable and proven "rules of game" for their construction projects. Three basic forms (1999 version) are now most frequently used for delivery of construction works (including the design and plant). In particular:

- Conditions of Contract for Construction (CONS/1999 Red Book);
- Conditions of Contract for Plant and Design-Build (P&DB/1999 Yellow Book);
- Conditions of Contract for EPC/Turnkey Projects (EPC/1999 Silver Book).

As foreseen by FIDIC, there is risk inherent in every construction project. Therefore, the risk should be insured to the greatest extent possible.

In the case of CONS, they follow similar general insurance conditions as applicable to P&DB and EPC. With P&DB and EPC (and/or CONS), the employer or the governing law will often require that the contractors themselves or their subcontractors have professional liability insurance cover as a precondition to the contractor designing a part of the work. These requirements should be described in the tender documentation for the contract. The scope of the contractor's compulsory insurance will cover the design risks where P&DB and EPC are to be used. As already mentioned, the 1999 wording was changed in the 2017 FIDIC second edition. Clauses 17 to 19 were subject to complete revision. These parts were returning back to the basic principles regarding these areas, as they were included in the 1977 FIDIC Red Book.

14.5.2 Design risk and insurance

Liability and insurance problems that relate to designer responsibilities and defective design appear worldwide. It is widely assumed that if a product or material is selected as built in, then the party responsible for its selection is, to an extent, protected by the manufacturer's warranty or insurance. Concerning design documentation, the designer will not provide such a warranty and the designer's professional liability insurance is not based on the fitness-for-purpose liability principle. Even when not covered by any designer warranty or by indemnification promise given by an insurance company *per se*, the contractors are responsible for such defects where the preparation of the design is one of their contractual obligations.

Designers, in general, lack the resources to be able to underwrite the risks a design error may cause to a large construction project, to other participants and to society at large. Professional liability insurance providers will then refuse to insure the designer's fitness-for-purpose liability, arguing non-insurability on the basis that they go against insurance principles. The contractors will then, naturally, argue that their liability should only be of the due-skill-and-care type. Actual contractor and designer liabilities will then depend on a particular contract and governing law.

FIDIC DBO Sub-Clause 17.9 reads that:

> The contractor shall also indemnify the employer against all errors in the contractor's design of the works and other professional services which result in the works not being fit for purpose or result in any loss and/or damage for the employer.

14.5.3 General insurance requirements

General requirements for insurance are defined in Clause 18 of the above forms. At Clause 18, "insuring party" means, for each type of insurance, the party responsible for effecting and maintaining the insurance specified in the relevant sub-clause. Sub-Clause 18.1 reads that whenever the contractor is the insuring party, each insurance policy shall be effected with insurers on terms approved by the employer.

Furthermore, whenever the employer is the insuring party, each insurance policy shall be entered into with insurers on terms consistent with the details as stated in the particular conditions.

14.5.4 Insurance for works and contractor's equipment

As required by FIDIC forms, the insuring party shall insure the works, plant, materials, and contractor's documents for not less than the full replacement cost (including costs of demolition), removal of debris, professional fees, and lost profit. The insuring party shall maintain this insurance until the date of the taking over certificate. This insurance is to be effected and maintained by the contractor as an insuring party.

14.5.5 Insurance against injury of persons and damage to property

Concerning the definition of "insurance against injury of persons and damage to property":

> The insuring party shall insure against each party's liability for any loss, damage, death or bodily injury which may occur to any physical property (except things insured under Sub-Clause 18.2 [Insurance for Works and Contractor's Equipment]) or to any person (except persons insured under Sub-Clause 18.4 [Insurance for Contractor's Personnel]), which may arise out of the contractor's performance of the contract and occurring before the issue of the performance certificate.

This insurance can have a minimum guaranteed amount per occurrence with no limit on the number of occurrences.

The insurance shall also be effected and maintained by the contractor as the insuring party. Even here, however, an optional liability limit may sometimes be determined.

14.5.6 Insurance for contractor's personnel

Under Sub-Clause 18.4:

> The contractor shall effect and maintain insurance against liability for claims, damages, losses and expenses (including legal fees and expenses) arising from injury, sickness, disease or death of any person employed by the contractor or any other of the contractor's personnel.

The employer and the engineer shall also be indemnified under the policy of insurance, except that this insurance may exclude losses and claims to the extent that they arise from any act or neglect of the employer or of the employer's personnel.

As such, the FIDIC forms require the contracting parties to have three insurance policies:

- *Property insurance* to cover damage to works and on-site property, being realized in practice as the contractor's construction all risk insurance (CAR).
- *Liability insurance* that protects the employer and the contractor against statutory liability for injury, disease and death of contractor personnel occurring in the scope of their performance in a construction project. This insurance is executed via *employer's liability insurance*.
- *Liability insurance* that protects the employer and the contractor against statutory liability for injuries, disease and death of third parties and against damage to third party property in connection with the contractor's activities in a construction project. This insurance is executed via *public liability insurance*.

Such insurances are negotiated on a project-by-project or yearly basis in cases of projects with long time horizons for completion. Coverage can be broken down into three individual insurance contracts or take the form of one composite contract.

Professional indemnity insurance under the FIDIC yellow book by Richard Krammer (Austria)

Although under the Yellow Book (or P&DB) conditions of contract risks associated with design are predominantly to be borne by the contractor, the requirements regarding insurance are very much like the Red Book. The differences relate to the necessity of insurance cover to explicitly also having to comprise damage caused by the contractor during tests after completion (Clause 18.2 with reference to Clause 12). The insurance requirements fall in the following categories:

- 18.1 General Requirements for Insurance
- 18.2 Insurance for Work and Contractor's Equipment
- 18.3 Insurance against Injury to Persons and Damage to Property
- 18.4 Insurance for Contractors Personnel

The fact that substantial design risks are transferred between the parties compared to the CONS edition is not immediately reflected in the general contract conditions dealing with insurance. This may surprise since design is generally acknowledged as being a possibly very complex part of every project with far reaching consequences while representing a comparably low share of the total expenditure.

In a regular design-bid-build setup, the owner would contract with separate entities for the design and construction of a project. As such, the contractor could claim or counter a claim by the owner with the argument that the design was insufficient and he still did not violate a duty to warn. Under a design-build system as the Yellow Book, a more comprehensive set of works and services are contracted from a single entity whereby a reduction of risk for the project owner is achieved. Typical examples of categories of claims under this type of contract hence comprise clarification of the brief, responsibility for estimates, knowledge of current standards and codes, specification of materials, duty to warn of further investigations (e.g., regarding ground conditions), and inspection/supervision of the works.

The only reason given in the FIDIC Contracts Guide for a requirement for professional indemnity insurance not already being dealt with under Clause 18 Insurances is that the employer should consider whether he requires this insurance, in consideration of the solvency and apparent ability of the contractor to bear losses and liabilities himself. After all, insurance fulfills several functions, a very important one being relief of own risk capital and procurement of external capital in the case of damage. For an insured, this may mean the difference between economic survival and insolvency. For a principal it means achieving increased stability and security. If the risk is deemed to be low or the financial standing of a company deemed adequate to meet all conceivable future obligations, omitting the insurance may be an option. The question may of course be raised why the current form of contract permits this flexibility for design related insurances while following a stricter regime for the general third party liability insurance (Clause 18.3), damage to the works (Clause 18.4) and even risks, which, generally speaking, can have less detrimental effect on the successful completion of a project, such as the insurance of the contractor's equipment.

However, there is an example for an additional sub-clause titled "Insurance for Design" in the Guidance for the Preparation of Particular Conditions (GPPC). The intention is to give the employer additional protection:

"The Contractor shall effect professional indemnity insurance, which shall cover the risk of professional negligence in the design of the Works. This insurance shall be for a limit of not less than [...]. The Contractor shall use his best endeavours to maintain the professional indemnity insurance in full force and effect until [...]. The Contractor undertakes to notify the Employer promptly of any difficulty in extending, renewing or reinstating this insurance."

Given current market conditions and the fact that a new edition of FIDIC forms was published with changed insurance clauses it is to be expected that this will have an influence on the topic of professional indemnity insurance.

New conditions of contract for plant and design-build

Current new edition foresee as fundamental change especially in respect of design insurance, effectively underlining the relevance of the topic that, for many practitioners, has been obvious from a claims side for some time.

The most recent 2017 version available is already different in terms of structure when it regulates under Clause 19. Insurances along the following headlines:

19.1   General Requirements
19.2   Insurance to be provided by the Contractor
19.2.1 The Works
19.2.2 Goods
19.2.3 Liability for breach of professional duty
19.2.4 Injury to persons and damage to property
19.2.5 Injury to employees
19.2.6 Other insurances required by Law and local practice

It is notable that actually all insurances are to be concluded by the contractor. This makes redrafting necessary should a principal decide to procure some insurances (such as insurance for the works and an excess third-party liability insurance) himself and leave other requirements or also some freedom to the contractor. Additional control can always be added by loss payee provisions or contractual regulations detailing the process for claims collection in excess of attritional losses.

An eminent change with respect to insurances is to be seen under the heading of "Liability for breach of professional duty" under Sub-Clause 19.2.3. The contractor would now by standard be required to insure for this risk. It is actually not foreseen that this insurance is contingent on an amount to be set forth in the schedule but if there is no amount agreed on in the contract data (a part of the particular conditions) it shall still be procured, albeit with a limit agreed with the employer. Though there is no explicit mention within the paragraph of how to proceed of no agreement with the employer can be reached the change in significance with regard to this topic is quite palpable.

A considerable debate has evolved around the new Sub-Clause 14 dealing with the indemnities and limitations on liability. It maintains that "The Contractor shall also indemnify and hold harmless the Employer against all acts, errors or omissions by the Contractor in carrying out the Contractor's design obligations that result in the Works (or Section or Part or major item of Plant, if any), when completed, not being fit for the purpose(s) for which they are intended under Sub-Clause 4.1 (Contractor's general obligations)." However, the Sub-Clause 1.15 (Limitation of liability) limits liability in terms of loss of use of any Works, loss of profit, loss of any contract of for any indirect or consequential loss or damage to the sum stated in the Contract Data or (if a sum is not so stated) the Accepted Contract Amount.

It may well be that the new requirements—as suitable as they may be with respect to the underlying risk—push the envelope of what is achievable on the commercial insurance market for some buyers or in some regions. Since the FIDIC contract conditions are applied on an international level it is understandable that many local specifics cannot be foreseen. With respect to insurances discussions often revolved around the scope of insurances during the maintenance period (extended maintenance versus guarantee maintenance cover) and availability of sums insured in general third party liability (aggregated sums insured versus unlimited occurrences). The appropriate sum as a limitation of liability becomes a key aspect of a design-build contract under the FIDIC Forms.

The difficulty in drafting a standard which is internationally applicable and practicable is certainly to address the relevant topics such as risk allocation while providing for sufficient freedom, in order to be usable in various jurisdictions.

Users across the globe tried to adapt and merged the intentions of the contract conditions—which highlight the important aspects and provide a suggestion of how to draft them—with the preferences of the actual parties and commercial realities, such as availabilities of insurance covers.

The new 2017 edition in the Sub-Clause 19.2.3 imposes an insurance requirement for the mentioned Sub-Clause 17.4 design liability, which may exceed what is feasible on insurance markets. At the same time, it highlights one of the central aspects of design and build contracts in connection with insurance and as such also serves as a basis for discussion of what the risk is, which party bears it and whether it can effectively be transferred.

It could be maintained that the current wording will push the parties to analyse and negotiate the issue of design liability carefully. Almost coincidentally it seems that the new requirement is quiet on the number of occurrences to be insured which may be seen as beneficial for many global insurance markets, which want to calculate aggregate sums insured.

The quite extensive requirement on the fit for purpose aspect, however, is apt to be grounds for considerable future discussion evolving around the very term, its distinction to a mere guarantee and its insurability as will be laid out in greater detail below.

It is to be expected that the term "fit for purpose" will be scrutinized in much greater detail and on a comparative basis across jurisdictions or at least be critically discussed between the parties which in itself may be seen as progress.

Current requirements

Coming back to the 1999 edition, confusion sometimes arises as to why a professional indemnity insurance would make sense or be required in addition to the insurances already outlined in the standard wording.

The design risk itself can indeed be subject of the cover obtained under the Sub-Clause 18.2. Damage consequential upon faulty design, material or workmanship can be covered under readily available construction all-risk covers. Standard market clauses have been established which adjust the insurance ranging from outright exclusion over covering consequential damage to parts of the works free of any defect to clauses also covering the damaged defective part or item itself.

Relevant endorsements comprise particularly Munich Re Contractor's All Risk and Erection All Risk Endorsements 115 and 200 as well as the regime of London Engineering Group (LEG) under the 1996 and 2006 clauses as well as the design improvement exclusions (DE). There is a line of case law pertinent to this aspect of loss or damage under construction policies following from design errors (e.g., *Promet Engineering (Singapore)PTE Ltd v. Sturge & Others*; *Hutchins v. Royal Exchange*; *Pilkington v. CGU*; *Graham Evans & Co (Qld) Pty Ltd v. Vanguard*; *Walker Civil Engineering v. Sun Alliance*; *Seele Austria Gmbh & KG v. Tokio marine*; *CA Blackwell v. Gerling All gemeine Versicherungs AG*; *Cementation Piling v. Aegon*; *New South Wales v. AXA Insurance Australia Ltd (Australia)*; *Manufacturers' Mutual Insurance Ltd v. Queensland Government Railways (Australia)*; *Railway Co. v. Royal and Sun Alliance Insurance Co. of Canada*).

It should also be noted that the term design has been the subject of debate. Even under Red Book arrangements, execution designs will be the responsibilities of the contractor and project management itself is a form of professional service. As such, the following should not be read with a restriction in mind to the particular type of contract but always rather the risk of the underlying activity and its potential to cause unforeseen deviations from expected or desired results.

The relevant passage in this respect is found under Sub-Clause 18.2 (e) (i) where there is set forth that, unless stated otherwise in the particular conditions, loss of, damage to, and reinstatement of a part of the works, which is in a defective condition due to a defect in its design, materials, or workmanship may be excluded from the insurance cover. It shall, however, include any other parts, which are lost or damaged as a direct result of this defective condition.

The important aspect here is that the insurance cover in question will always only relate to property damage to the works. There is a substantial body of literature and also rulings to the question of when a property damage is established in distinction to a mere defect, which shall not be the subject of the insurance regularly understood under Sub-Clause 18.2. Moreover, the design cover under contractors all risk insurances varies over the life cycle, quite often in a very reduced manner in the phase following practical completion. It is in this phase where the difference between the so called extended maintenance cover (generally excluding damage consequential upon design) and guarantee maintenance cover (including the same) becomes relevant and obvious.

It is the additional costs and expenses a claimant incurs due to a design error as opposed to only the damage to already executed works, which is the main scope of application of a professional indemnity insurance for design.

The second area of discussion, is whether a third-party liability insurance is actually the right product. After all, the Yellow Book is a contract for design and construction. The very fact that both activities are bundled in one legal entity makes it difficult to imagine how there could be a legal liability claim before works have actually been handed over.

After completion of the works the employer will have his rights under the maintenance provision and will not revert to claiming under legal liability regimes without reason. In addition, it is a basic principle in third-party liability insurance in that the insurer tries to avoid stepping in in lieu of the contractor and fulfill the contract in his stead.

So, in this case it may be the same legal entity finding itself having made and error in design and being the contractor and therefore not be insured under regular insurance solutions. Were the design part subcontracted to another company, legal liability between two legal entities could be established and the essentially same risk be insurable on conventional markets. The reluctance of insurance carriers to write this risk emanates from a certain moral hazard on the side of the insured and difficulties in assessing organizational responsibilities and conflicts of interest.

This goes in hand with something not uncommonly observed: checking the existence of insurance on the basis of just a headline or designation instead of its contents. Concluding just any professional indemnity insurance often suffers the severe flaw that common wordings exclude claims if the insured also participates in the execution of the works. Design and construction policies feature additional covers effectively providing insurance coverage just as laid out above, when design and execution are the responsibility of the same legal entity. The policy wording is different in that it addresses defects caused by a design fault that can arise at any time following the commencement of the construction.

An important aspect is loss, cost, or expenses incurred prior to final contract completion to mitigate a loss or potential loss. Essentially, this extends the cover into the period of execution of the works. Quite often it is already during the execution of the works that the design error is encountered and when insurance coverage is needed, when there could impossibly already be an employer claiming.

Fitness for purpose

Finally, a central point of discussion evolves around reasonable skill and care versus fitness for purpose.

To some extent, the discussion on this topic may also have been shaped by the high relevance of the London insurance market in international construction insurance as well as the influence of UK law and jurisdiction in countries following common law. Under common law, the pre-eminent concept for establishing the grounds for liability for designers is the exercise of reasonable skill and care (exception for instance the Defective Premises Act 1972, which sets the requirement of the works having to be fit for habitation).

It is essential to see that for traditional general contracting (contractor executing a design provided by the principal) does not automatically imply a requirement for the works to be suitable for some purpose. Specifically, for a construction contractor, under the Supply of Goods and Services Act 1982, there exists a requirement to use material fit for the purpose, but no such requirement actually exists for the finished works.

This changes in the case where a contractor designs and executes the works (Smith and Snipes: *Hall Farm Ltd v. River Douglas Catchment Board* [1949] 2 K.B. 500, 513; *Lynch v. Thorne* [1956] 1 W.L.R. 303, CA; *Greaves v. Baynham v. Baynham Meikle* [1975] 1 W.L.R. 1095, 1098, CA; National Coal Board *v.* Neill [1985] Q.B. 300, 317. *Independent Broadcasting Authority v. EMI Electronics Limited and BICC Construction Limited*; *Viking Grain Storage Limited v. T H White Installations Limited*). Here, implied terms or express warranties become pertinent.

The issue of design liability under a FIDIC form of contract may be more relevant than under other standardized forms of contract. The matter was to some extent defused when, for example, under Clause 2.17.1—JCT Design and Build Contract and Option X15 of NEC3—a liability regime is being imposed with reasonable skill and care.

Overall, it is important to assess the contract in its entirety as a more recent case (MT Højgaard A/S *v.* E.ON Climate & Renewables UK) shows, where the contractor had to design, construct, and install the foundations for sixty offshore wind turbines. The contract foresaw a requirement for exercising due care and diligence so that each item of plant and the works as a whole "shall be fit for its purpose as determined in accordance with the specification using good Industry practice"; and when completed comply with and "be wholly in accordance with this agreement and any performance specifications or requirements of the employer as set out in this agreement."

The employer's requirements set out a minimum design life of 20 years and demanded that "The design of the foundations shall ensure a lifetime of 20 years in every aspect without planned replacement."

The foundations were found to be defective and it turned out that the universally accepted industry standard applicable to the design of such foundations was incorrect. A dispute arose around whether the contractor would, within its fitness for purpose obligation, be able to effectively discharge of its duties by adhering to the prevailing standard or not.

Under reference of two Canadian cases (*The Steel Company of Canada Ltd v. Willand Management Ltd* [1966] SCR 746 and *Greater Vancouver Water District v. North American Pipe and Steel Ltd* [2012] BCCA 337) it was found that "the existence of an express warranty of fitness for purpose by the contractor can trump the obligation to comply with the specification even though that specification may contain an error." As a consequence, it was established that the contractor had assumed full design responsibility and warranted a service life of 20 years, irrespective of its obligation to design in accordance with the standard.

In the United States, there appears to be a nationwide trend of states moving away from broad indemnity provisions from designers and architects. As a result of a 2010 California Court of Appeal ruling, a design professional who contracts to defend and indemnify its client for negligence is responsible for that defense, regardless of whether he or she is found liable for the underlying claims involving private contracts. Furthermore, a decision by the California Supreme Court in the *Crawford v. Weather Shield Manufacturing* has created problems for subcontractors, suppliers, consultants, or anyone else who assumes the obligation to defend an upstream party. A recent California Appellate Court decision in the *UDC v. CH2M Hill* case reinforced this decision, which leads to a situation in which a party has to indemnify another irrespective of any negligence.

Under the amended California Civil Code Section 2782.8, the professional's indemnity obligations will be enforceable only "to the extent that the claims against the indemnitee arise out of, pertain to, or relate to the negligence, recklessness or willful misconduct of the design professional." Moreover, the design professional's defense obligation may not exceed "the design professional's proportionate percentage of fault." An interesting aspect with this legislation is that it will not apply in cases where there is a project policy insuring all project participants on a primary basis, if the design professional is a party to a written design-build agreement or the contract is with a state agency. Design professionals will no longer have unlimited liability with respect to indemnity and the duty and cost to defend. Design professionals will not have to indemnify their clients for claims that are not tied to their negligence, recklessness, or misconduct. Although not immediately connected to the topic of fitness for purpose is shows that also here and also under the amended legislation, design-build contracts lead to particular challenges.

Despite this influence from common law it is of course imperative to also look at how the outlined requirements would be perceived in other jurisdictions. A general fitness for purpose requirement is by no means unknown and could, among others, be ascribed to Bulgaria, France, Greece, Luxembourg, and the Netherlands where an actual requirement of habitability, usability, or fitness may be applicable in addition to warranty periods stretching over several years.

Mandatory insurance covers within the European Union may be seen in Denmark, Finland, France, Italy, Spain, and Sweden while it is worth noting that corresponding insurance cover comprise structural defects and sometimes also major other defects such as water ingress. Mandatory latent defect covers may be further divided into property damage covers and liability covers with Denmark, Italy, and Sweden showing mandatory insurances responding in the event of existing defects regardless liability of any party to construction operation. On the other hand, in Finland and Spain the mandatory cover is a liability cover, that is, it covers liability of the insured parties for construction defects. In France, there are actually two mandatory covers existing in parallel: property damage insurance covering latent construction defects regardless of liability (dommage ouvrage insurance) and decennial liability insurance. An overview that may be recommended in this context is the "Liability and insurance regimes in the construction sector" procured by the Elios project. The project has been realized by CEA (Centre d'Etudes d'Assurances) and CSTB (Centre Scientifique Technique de Bâtiment) at the request of the European Commission and studied the building insurance systems of the 27 EU member states. Its works can be found under www.elios-ec.eu.

Quite recently, the international commercial insurance market has picked up this topic and now more proactively offers stand-alone insurance products for latent defects in many territories worldwide. They are based on the concept of a property damage cover and as such are more readily usable across jurisdictions while insurance solutions tailored to a certain liability regime will be merely impossible to transfer abroad since the legal framework in the corresponding country will be missing.

Countries such as Germany know the term of "Beschaffenheitsvereinbarung," which translates as agreement on the legal and factual nature of an object and follows, contrary to the regime outlined for common law countries, which focuses on an activity driven aspect skill and care, on an actual success or result (Erfolgshaftung). The pertinent legal regulation found in § 633 Par 2 Sentence 1 of the BGB sets forth that the work rendered has to suffice the actually agreed requirements or, in absence of such, that it has to be usable according to general standards, which can be customarily be expected with regard to the nature of the work or service. It depends on the respective circumstances to differentiate between an actual guarantee and an agreement on the legal and factual nature. What they have in common is that they trigger a liability of the supplier to rectify the defect, which is not reflected under insurance covers. Only in case of negligence a claim in tort will be feasible and also be dealt with under a professional indemnity insurance.

Professional indemnity policies generally cover liability according to the requirement of reasonable skill and care, which is a negligence standard. Fitness for purpose is a more entailing concept by which the contractor essentially agrees to deliver so that the product will be suitable for the requirements communicated and will perform to the level required by the client. Fitness for purpose warranties may either be found expressly or implied, which sometimes makes it difficult to assess at first glance whether a fitness for purpose warranty exists.

From a risk and insurance perspective there are several possibilities to approach this.

The first is contractual risk management and the effort to reduce this exposure from the outset by trying to avoid express and implied warranties as far as legally permissible. The common law position regarding fitness for purpose can, and often is, modified by the terms of a contract. It could expressly be agreed that the contractor will only be expected to exercise the level of skill and care that would reasonably be expected from a separately engaged designer. Since this may not hold before court other, more intricate forms were conceived, all aiming at making it clear that the will of the parties is to establish a skill and care regime and to clarify to what extent the principal specifically relied on the contractor.

The second is the quite onerous fitness for purpose exclusion that will exclude liabilities incurred under fitness for purpose conditions that may lead to the undesirable situation of insurance cover also not being given if the insured has actually been negligent. A more reasonable approach may be seen in the exclusion of liabilities in excess of reasonable skill and care, which will still cover negligence, even though if it was incurred in connection with a fitness for purpose warranty.

The next wider coverage comprises the implied fitness for purpose coverage, which essentially relieves the insured of the uncertainty of implied warranties found later in a contract by court. If there is no express standard of care defined a fitness for purpose obligation could easily be construed. A case cited quite often is that of *Viking Grain Storage v. TH White Installations*. White had to design and construct a grain silo from materials that were of good quality and reasonably fit for purpose, that the completed works should be reasonably fit for their intended purpose. The defendant accepted that there was an obligation to use good-quality materials but disputed the requirement of fitness for purpose. The court held that this fitness for purpose obligation could be implied to apply with respect to the design of the works as well. The corresponding insurance coverage here would be available if a court decided that there is an implied fitness for purpose obligation in a contract, which was otherwise entered into in good faith.

The limited express fitness for purpose coverage goes still some further and will cover express fitness for purpose agreements. In exchange for that it will bring additional requirements such as a clear definition of the intended purpose of the works, since quite often it is tacitly assumed or implied purposes that as a gray zone pose substantial problems. In addition, a state of the art defense clause restricts the cover quite substantially. Essentially it states that a cover is limited to that which would have existed if the insurance contract had entitled it to defend the claim on the basis that the design was "in accordance with practice conventionally accepted as appropriate at the time having regard to the size, scope and complexity of the project." While understandable that the insurance cover would be even more far-reaching without this regulation, it should be understood that the rationale for this is to prevent having contractors speculate on untried materials or techniques at their insurer's risk.

Depending on the experience, track record of the insured as well as commercial factors there also is an extended fitness for purpose coverage available on insurance markets though availability is somewhat restricted due to the sensitive nature to larger portfolios or PPP projects.

Professional indemnity insurance may be concluded based on different triggers, meaning the definition of the insured event and its allocation within the insurance period. The concept most commonly used is the claims made policy, which sets the actual reception of a claim as relevant event. Another form is the occurrence or infringement policy, which focuses on the actual activity (the execution of the design) as relevant for the policy being applicable. Also mixtures of the two are widely used practice, where the design activities under a claims made policy may not lie longer in the past than a defined period. All this is important when understanding that design errors can take a long time to become fully obvious. Having the timing parameters set too tight may lead to a situation where there technically is a professional indemnity insurance in place, but insurance coverage is very limited or even negligible because of the time constraints.

As laid out above the design risk has relevance in connection with Sub-Clause 18.2 Insurance of the Work as well as in addition from a liability perspective. As such, those insurances should be dovetailed to the specific projects. Caution has to be exercised when works are to be built for some defined purpose. Finally, under the envisaged new Yellow Book Contract conditions a clarification on limitation of liability should be openly discussed.

Richard Krammer
Group Practice Leader Construction and Real Estate
GrECo JLT

Bibliography

Centre d'Etudes d'Assurances (CEA) and Centre Scientifique et Technique du Bâtiment (CSTB) (2010). "Liability and insurance regimes in the construction sector: national schemes and guidelines to stimulate innovation and sustainability".

Hillig, J.-B. (2010). *Die Maengelhaftung im deutschen und englischen Recht*. Liability for Defects under German and English law.

The Insurance Institute of London. Professional Indemnity Insurance, Advanced Study Group Report 228.

Insurance in hydropower projects by Alex Blomfield (UK)

International hydropower construction contracts usually require one or both of the parties to take out at least the following three types of insurance:

1. property insurance, covering transport, and equipment while on site;
2. liability insurance, covering damage to third party's property, or death or injury caused by the insuring party; and
3. workmen's compensation and/or employer's liability insurance, at a level customary or statutorily required for the country of the project or in accordance with the employer's minimum requirements.

The conditions of contract (Clause 18 in a FIDIC contract) will specify general requirements for such insurances, and an insurance annex will specify more detail with respect to such requirements, including minimum ratings (e.g., Standard & Poors "A-") and insured parties, coverage/conditions, period, sum insured, and deductibles for each category of insurance. The insured parties will include the contractor, the employer, the engineer (if applicable) and subcontractors at any tier and, in a project-financed deal, the lenders. The cover shall apply separately to each insured as though a separate policy had been issued which, in relation to liability policies, shall include the ability to make cross-suites with no exclusions. The employer, together with its insurance adviser/broker, will initially decide the coverage and conditions, period of insurance, sum insured and deductibles for each insurance and assist in placing in the insurances. However, the lenders' insurance adviser will review all insurance requirements, in particular, the insurance requirements for the employer. As part of the dialogue on appropriate levels of insurance, the employer may also need to correct a common misconception in the construction industry that simply referring to a required quantum of insurance in a contract does not cap liability at that level.

Contractors may need to take out project-specific insurances to meet the project-finance requirements such as insured parties, cross-liability and waiver of subrogation, which can delay the occurrence of the commencement date on a construction contract if that contractor had previously assumed it could rely on its group company insurance policies, which often do not meet such requirements. A lack of familiarity with local fronting requirements, considered together with minimum rating requirements for the insurers, may also cause a delay to the occurrence of the commencement date as the employer may need to enter into a waiver with the contractor and a separate waiver with its lenders to deviate from such minimum rating requirements. An employer can mitigate against this potential delay by properly conducting due diligence on the local insurance market and requesting draft insurance certificates from the contractor at the tender stage. This allows the employer to enter into a dialogue with the contractor's insurance adviser to ensure that it has compliant insurances before the delivery of insurance policies required as a condition precedent to commencement date.

Alex Blomfield
Special Counsel
K&L Gates LLP
London
UK

14.6 Practical aspects of insurance in construction projects

Insurance of large construction projects is an integral part of the project itself or of its execution. The employer and the contractor are capable and willing to bear the financial risks in connection with unexpected damage during construction, but only to a certain extent. The admissible sum (called the excess) tends to be set just at this "limit" and the parties then may assign their risks for extra payment if such risks exceed this "limit."

Troubles and "incompatibility" tend to appear in practice because two quite different industries and practices meet here. The first is the purely technical field of construction projects, and the other is the field of law (finance and civil law), represented by insurance. This can give rise to a communication barrier where the insurance experts do not fully understand the technical aspects of the works and its execution, and where the construction specialists, on the other hand, tend to underestimate the insurance aspects (or allow for such aspects, burdened by technical and managerial duties).

14.6.1 Recommendations for negotiating insurance

An insurance contract is, in principle, based on the Anglo-Saxon doctrine of *utmost good faith*. It is a principle of utmost good faith that an insured will provide the insurer with complete and true information of the risk and the insurer will then sell the promise of the circumstances under which they shall indemnify. As such, the contractual relationship is based on mutual trust between the contracting parties.

Two basic conditions must be stressed and detailed:

- the duty to inform the insurer of what is relevant in terms of the insurance; and
- the duty to adhere to the conditions under which the contract has been entered into.

The employer's intention must be defined at the beginning. For example, defining their purpose, location, design, financial amounts, time for completion, and other parameters shapes the initial skeleton of the insurance policy. The insurance issue must be considered at the design preparation phase at the very latest.

An insurance specialist, whether an in-house employee (of the employer) or, more frequently, an insurance broker ("broker"), plays an indispensable role here. Experience shows that it is always better when a well-experienced and assertive broker takes over this role in cases of large construction projects. The broker ought to be a dignified, competent, and respectful partner to the insurers at the local or, better yet, international insurance and reinsurance market level. The requirements (on the basis of which an optimum insurance contract can be compiled) have to be put together for this specialist. Of course, these requirements will include all the relevant, underlying documents to be provided, as they relate to the intended works. Moreover, they must include partial documentation such as that in support of geological surveying and the report prepared by a hydrologist, for example. Finding an external broker may be done through a tender process.

The first output of the broker's efforts will be a risk report he/she submits to the insurers along with a request for preparation of the respective insurance bids. The employer (and also the contractor if known at this stage) must, prior to submission of the report to the insurers, make themselves familiar with this report and find out if their requirements are met and if the information contained in it is correct and current.

With bids from potential insurers obtained, the broker must prepare a written, detailed analysis of the bids submitted by the insurers. This analysis will contain detailed comparisons regarding the level of premiums, insurance cover ranges and various limitations imposed by the insurer on the constructed work. Limitations and additional conditions that are not normally included in the insurance conditions are included in various special clauses.

For example, the standard practice of the Munich Reinsurance Company is to include tens of such additional clauses in its construction all risk insurance policies. These clauses deal with, for example, limitations and exclusions in tunneling and underground works, reservoirs, dams, and damage to existing underground pipelines and cable lines. Routine checking and revision of the insured sum and its correctness are essential.

Due to various limitations and conditions, analysis of insurance bids should be made subject to the objections and suggestions given by the employer and respective contractors. This should include an estimation of any risks and costs of the measures to be taken at the insurer's request. All these underlying documents must identify the person who has prepared them and to whom they have been handed over.

The broker must have professional liability insurance in the event of a mistake or negligent conduct on their part. This obligation is usually assigned to the broker by operation of law.

14.6.2 Compatibility of the construction contract with the insurance contract

At the conclusion of the tender, the broker must ensure compatibility of the insurance contract with the work being constructed. A contingency plan (with insurance as its integral part) should be prepared for large construction projects. This plan must address the protocols to be followed in case of potential damage.

All managers must be made fully aware of the actual cover of the insurance contract. This includes top management of the employer and contractors right down to the level of site managers.

A list of the insurance contract parameters extracted from the insurance contract should also be prepared. This will allow the parties to quickly and accurately identify any works/activities, which may breach, deviate from, or be incompatible with what is actually insured. This is of critical importance because, in any construction project, there will almost certainly be deviations in terms of the time horizon of the work, changes in technology employed, and so on. All of this can be incorporated into a single manual tailored for a respective insured project. All levels of management (including site managers) should be made familiar with this manual.

A particular procedure has to be defined, should a deviation appear. It is mainly up to the broker to evaluate the deviation and determine (and then notify) whether it is enough to inform the insurer about new circumstances or to resolve the matter via an addendum to the insurance contract. The principle of utmost good faith applies when informing the insurer about new, relevant facts. Usually these facts relate to information upon which the insurance has been effected.

As a matter of good practice, site documents such as daily logs, time programs, progress reports and taking over protocols have to be properly kept.

The broker should, ideally, be present at the on-site progress meetings and regularly review relevant documents, for example, reviewing and checking design documentation of the project to ensure that it respects the requirements of the insurance contract. This may include issues dealing with the installation and operable condition of pumps used to drain water from a foundation pit in the capacity as prescribed, or the adequacy and operability of anti-flood barriers required by the insurer.

The procedure to be performed in response to potential damage subject to insurance must be clearly spelt out and communicated as well. The broker is best able to determine which situations and/or damage should be reported to the insurer. However, the contractor must set up the system of communication so that the broker is made aware of such situations on a timely basis and has the opportunity to respond accordingly. A raised claim may also include expenses incurred in avoiding damage.

Construction all risk insurance ranks among the most complicated kind and the role of an insurance specialist is critical here. Cooperation does not end at the signing of the insurance policy—the specialist should provide their client with relevant after-sales support throughout the execution of the works and over duration of the insurance contract.

Incompatibility of the construction contract with the insurance contract by Karel Fabich (the Czech Republic)

Unfortunately, not even simple things are actually simple in practice. I am now involved in liquidating two cases of damages in a construction project before it is handed over to the employer, that is, while the contractor is still responsible for them. Being a medium to large enterprise, the contractor has an insurance contract in place for the works under construction. The works are automatically included in the comprehensive insurance contract when they meet certain conditions. A premium is then paid to complete a straightforward insurance process.

Working according to schedule, the contractor is building conscientiously on a river bank and the river bed. In my opinion, the contractor cannot be making much of a profit in these times of strong competition and price-cutting. The contractor does seem to care much about the compatibility of its insurance contract with the works under construction. It is written in the insurance contract that any construction works taking place close to rivers (as predefined) have to be made known to the insurer in advance. But the insured contractor fails to announce anything and the insurance broker is oblivious to the situation. It is the height of the construction season and there are other things to worry about after all.

A rain shower and what a pity! Flooding damages reach between 3%–5% of the total contract value. I assume the contractor to be without profit and remuneration—or even suffering a loss if the insurer refuses to pay on the basis of breach of contract conditions. Two simple emails might have been enough to save the day—one to the broker and the other to the insurer.

Karel Fabich
Insurance liquidator
Czech Republic

14.7 International insurance law and insurance standards in the construction industry

Currently, there is no insurance standard in the construction industry applicable worldwide. International insurance is fragmented but some uniformity is reflected in the terms and conditions used by the biggest and most renowned insurance companies and/or their associations. The following paragraphs will turn attention to two groups of general insurance terms used by German insurance companies. The first set of terms are the provisions of the General Terms for Construction Insurance of the Association of the German Insurance Industry. In particular, the *General Terms for Construction Insurance Agreed with Employer* and the relevant interpretation clauses (TK ABN 2011) (ABN) and the *General Terms for Construction Insurance Agreed with Contractor*, including the relevant interpretation clauses (TK ABU 2011) (ABU) will be analyzed.

Second, the chapter will deal with the standard forms, terms, and clauses prepared by the International Association of Engineering Insurers (IAEI). The IAEI currently has a membership of 20 countries. The IAEI has created two sets of insurance terms, both used in construction; see: http://imia.com/munichre_examples.php#220. The terms include *Construction All Risk Standard Insurance*

(CAR) and the *Erection All Risk Standard Insurance* (EAR). To avoid confusion, the abbreviations of CAR and EAR mean conditions prepared by IAEI unless otherwise stated.

14.7.1 Standard insurance terms of ABN 2011 and ABU 2011

The most recent editions of the ABN and ABU conditions are dated January 1, 2011. Both ABN and ABU are consistently interlinked with the *Verdingungsordnung für Bauleistungen* (VOB) construction contract procurement regulations. Construction risks insurance mainly includes the insurance of construction works and building materials. The purpose of ABU insurance is to protect the contractor from the necessity to rebuild works at their own expense, should they suffer destruction or damage in the course of construction. Under ABN terms, insurance will provide the employer with protection against the necessity to pay the costs of the rebuild of a building that has been destroyed or damaged by an incident. The first notable difference between ABU and ABN terms is the party insured against risk (ABU—contractor, ABN—employer). There is also another major difference in the scope of insurance. In compliance with § 1 of ABU, all building materials, construction elements and construction works intended to fulfil the purpose of a construction project as defined in the insurance contract (including the temporary works and materials) must be insured. As such, the ABU conditions apply to both construction (reconstruction) of the buildings and construction of civil engineering works (roads, railways, bridges, tunnels, and so on). Paragraph 1 of the ABN conditions only applies to insurance of a newly erected or reconstructed building. Nevertheless, the scope of the subject of insurance can be modified (extended) via insurance clauses by agreement (for example, Clauses TK 5862, 6364, and 6365). If these clauses are agreed upon, the differences between ABN and ABU will actually vanish in respect of defining the scope of the subject of insurance.

The ABU and ABN terms can be subdivided into two parts. The first regulates the issues typical of construction risk insurances only (Section A), and the second defines the general insurance terms (Section B). A brief explanation will be given of both Section A conditions.

14.7.2 Conditions of ABU—Section A

Following the exhaustive list of insured and uninsured items at § 1, Section A of the ABU terms further consists of insured and uninsured risks and damage (§ 2), insurable interests (§ 3), insurance location, (§ 4), insured value, sub-insurance (§ 5), insured and uninsured costs (§ 6), scope of insurance indemnities (§ 7), payment of insurance indemnities and interest on insurance indemnities (§ 8), and expert proceedings (§ 9).

As per § 1 of ABU, the term "work" means "any building work at any phase of construction. All the preparatory and temporary works are insured." ABU falls under the category of all risk insurance, covering nearly all risks except those listed in § 2, sub-sections 2–4. The provisions of § 2 of ABU defines damage, subsuming damage or destruction of an insured item under them. This definition, however, does not cover damage caused by a defective method of construction or error in design. Other basic preconditions upon which indemnity can be paid out is unforeseeability of damage occurrence. Damage is unforeseeable if the insured or their representatives (who are professionally skilled in the particular construction process) could not have foreseen it or when caused by gross negligence.

The work can be extra-insured against fire and floods. This leads to the necessity to specify respective terms in the insurance contract. For example, the absence of a definition of "uncommon and extraordinary levels of water" in § 2, sub-section 2 (b) of ABU is widely criticized by the German literature on the topic. Damage to glass, metal, or plastic materials while they are processed during construction are fully excluded from insurance cover. This does not mean that the exemption applies to damage caused to parts of the building already completed or under the construction. Damage caused by abnormal levels of water in watercourses, strikes, and political turmoil are also exempted from insurance cover.

14.7.3 Conditions of ABN—Section A

The main difference between the ABN and ABU conditions is that the employer is the insuring party in the case of ABN. Civil engineering works are widely exempted from insurance cover under ABN. Another difference between ABN and ABU is in the definition of "insurable interest." In principle, ABU terms relate to contractor insurable interest. According to § 3 Section 1, the ABN terms—even though applying primarily to an insurable interest of the employer as the insured—cover the insurable interests of all contractors with an insurable interest in execution of the employer's works (including their subcontractors). They are also secondarily covered in accordance with § 3, Section 2 of ABN. As such, additional contractors become co-insured with the employer.

14.7.4 Munich CAR and EAR insurance terms standards

The ABN and ABU insurance terms are rather regional in their nature because they are primarily used to insure construction risks in Germany. The standards of CAR and EAR are also used in international construction projects. The concepts of CAR and EAR come from the Anglo-American insurance model. Prepared by IAEI, CAR, and EAR constitute a combination of a contract sample form with insurance terms.

The CARs and EARs consist of a preamble, general conditions, tangible damage cover conditions (Section 1), conditions upon which indemnity can be provided for injury and damage caused to a third party (Section 2) and the conditions upon which indemnity can be provided for lost profit (Section 3). The forms where particular policy-related data can be filled in are attached to the CAR and EAR terms. Like the ABN and ABU: (1) the CAR and EAR standard insurance terms can be modified by means of clauses which allow policy tailoring for a particular insured; and (2) the CAR and EAR terms contain a variety of identical provisions.

14.7.5 CAR terms

The CAR insurance terms are designed for policies entered into between construction contractors and insurers in large (often international) construction projects.

The preamble of CAR insurance terms outlines general exemptions from insurance cover (such as war and civil unrest, nuclear events, deliberate acts of the insured, and their representatives and suspension of works). The preamble also defines the start and end points of insurance cover. In general, insurance cover starts with the commencement of construction works or with placing the insured things on the construction site and ends by acceptance of the works or their commissioning.

The general terms outline the insured's notification duties, specification of the official inspection by the insurer and the insured's obligation to promptly repair damaged things should an insurance event appear. An arbitration clause appears at Paragraph 7 of the general terms to facilitate quicker settlement of disputes.

Tangible damage is included in comprehensive insurance cover, except for cases specified in Section 1. These exemptions are more extensive than those set out in the EAR terms. Compared to EAR terms, items such as costs for repairing defective materials, wear and tear, corrosion, repair of on-site damage arising from blackouts (including to machinery and plants) and damage to vehicles and watercraft are exempted from insurance cover under CAR terms.

The condition upon which insurance cover can be provided for injury, death or damage caused to a third party is that the event has occurred directly in connection with construction or during the installation of insured things. Here CARs offer identical provisions to EARs.

Concerning the conditions upon which the insurance cover provides for lost profit, CARs are identical to EARs. In the third Section, there is a list of definitions (such as turnover, yearly gross profit) for the purposes of insurance indemnity. This section also contains a series of exemptions and provisions (such as periods of time and their calculation).

14.7.6 EAR terms

The EAR terms have been put together for erection all risk insurance. Deviations are reflected in their CAR counterparts. In addition to the discussion above, the definition of when insurance cover actually ends is critical. Insurance cover will end either after taking-over or after the field tests or load tests are commenced, depending on which comes first. In general, insurance cover will not end later than four weeks after commencement of the first test. Every other agreement must be made, according to EARs, in writing—despite being an excessive provision as the insurance terms can be modified by the parties without the necessity to have such an option expressly stated in them. The end of the insurance cover will be determined as separate for every particular facility or part of the work as gradually commissioned.

Construction/erection all risk insurance in the offshore wind industry by Gregory Efthimiu (Germany)

Introduction

In large construction projects, it is common that project assets are insured against physical damage to protect the interest of the employer during the construction phase. This applies especially in offshore construction projects like the erection of a windfarm, where the project assets are highly expensive long-lead items and are exposed to higher risk compared to an onshore construction site. The common vehicle to do so is the construction or erection all risk insurance (EAR/CAR insurance).

In general, it needs to be clarified that a CAR insurance is an asset insurance covering the physical assets of the project. When a complete offshore windfarm is built likely all components (e.g., foundations, transition pieces, wind turbine generator including tower, blades, and cables) are insured. The usual constellation is that the employer provides the CAR insurance.

When talking about the coverage reference is often made to the term of "all contract works." It is important to understand that this is a description of the asset to be installed under the project and not the activities performed under the contract by the contractor, since activities cannot be insured under an asset insurance. In other cases when the CAR policy refers to "covered activities," this must be understood as a limitation, meaning that the assets are only insured when performing certain covered activities. However, at the end the actual scope of coverage of the insurance is always subject to the specific wording of the insurance policy.

The first mentioned distinction is mainly relevant in cases where a substation (transformer station) or a converter station is already installed and the contractor performs works close by. Such preexisting assets are likely not or only limited insured under the CAR insurance.

Another major part of a standard offshore construction insurance is a third party liability (TPL) insurance, which covers damage to third-party assets when performing construction activities. It must be emphasised that damages caused by a vessel are in the majority of the cases excluded from the coverage of the TPL insurance. Therefore, employers do often require contractors to obtain a so-called "hull and machinery insurance," as well as a "protect and indemnity (P&I) specialist operations insurance," which cover damages occurred to and by the installation vessels.

Exclusions

As in every insurance, the exclusions are the interesting part. When talking about CAR policies a focus should in any case be on defect related damages. As already mentioned above, the insurance only covers physical damage of the project asset. Therefore, a defect itself is not insured under such insurance, which is traceable, since the defect-free delivery of the works is a major obligation under the main contract of the respective contractor.

However, how is dealt with a physical damage to the asset caused by a defect in design, workmanship, or material?

The London Engineering Group, a consultative body for insurers in the engineering business, developed standard clauses to define the limits of the insurance cover for damages arising from a defect in the works. Although, there is no obligation to use such clauses for an insurance company, the so-called "LEG clauses" are often implemented in CAR insurance policies, to determine whether damages arising from defects are covered or not.

Overview—LEG 1 to 3

It has to be noted beforehand that the below stated clauses are left without any commas by the London Engineering Group, which partially increases the incomprehensibility and ambiguity of the wording.

1. LEG 1/96

    The LEG 1/96 clause is short and easy to understand, but it is also the most limiting one of the three LEG clauses, since damages arising from defects of workmanship or material, design or specification are simply not covered.

LEG 1/96	Model **"outright"** Defects Exclusion "The Insurer(s) shall not be liable for Loss or damage due to defects of material workmanship design plan or specification."

2. LEG 2/96

    The LEG 2/96 clause covers the cost for remedying the damage arising from a defect, minus the cost, which would have been accrued if the defect would have been remedied immediately before the damage occurred.

    The idea is to give an incentive to the contractor not to install defective works, therewith gain coverage, and claim money under the CAR insurance, if the defect results into a physical damage.

LEG 2/96	Model **"Consequences"** Defects Wording "The Insurer(s) shall not be liable for All costs rendered necessary by defects of material workmanship design plan specification and should damage occur to any portion of the Insured Property containing any of the said defects the cost of replacement or rectification which is hereby excluded is that cost which would have been incurred if replacement or rectification of the Insured Property had been put in hand immediately prior to the said damage. For the purpose of this policy and not merely this exclusion it is understood and agreed that any portion of the Insured Property shall not be regarded as damaged solely by virtue of the existence of any defect of material workmanship design plan or specification."

3. LEG 3/06

    The LEG 3/06 clause excludes any cost incurred to improve the original contract works, with an explicit exclusion of defective but not damaged property.

LEG 3/06	Model **"Improvement"** Defects Wording "The Insurer(s) shall not be liable for All costs rendered necessary by defects of material workmanship design plan or specification and should damage (which for the purposes of this exclusion shall include any patent detrimental change in the physical condition of the Insured Property) occur to any portion of the Insured Property containing any of the said defects the cost of replacement or rectification which is hereby excluded is that cost incurred to improve the original material workmanship design plan or specification. For the purpose of the policy and not merely this exclusion it is understood and agreed that any portion of the Insured Property shall not be regarded as damaged solely by virtue of the existence of any defect of material workmanship design plan or specification".

Practical application

Example case

A is an offshore cable installation company and installs a high voltage cable from a supplier.

Due to defective workmanship during cable manufacturing, the cable insulation is too thin and therefore not in accordance with the contractual specifications, which constitutes a defect of the asset and is hence not covered under the CAR insurance.

The defect is not discovered and the cable is installed. When the cable is energized, the defective insulation within the cable causes a short circuit, which damages the (1) cable and a (2) transformer to which the cable is connected.

The question if the damage to cable and/or the transformer is covered depends on which LEG clause is used in the insurance policy.

LEG 1

The damage to cable and transformer was caused by a defect in workmanship during manufacturing. Therefore, both damages are not covered.

LEG 2

LEG 2/96 states that damages due to defect in the works are covered, however minus the cost for remedying the defect one moment before the damage occurs.

The cost of replacing the damaged cable can be split roughly into (1) cost for the new cable (2) cost for removal/ installation of the cable. Since the cable was already installed offshore the moment before the damage occurred, the cost to remedy only the defect at that point of time are similar to the cost to remedy the damage. Therefore, the cable is covered under the CAR insurance, since it is a physical damage to the insured property, but the majority of the cost will be excluded due to the LEG 2 clause wording.

Example calculation

Cost for rectification <u>after the damage</u> occurred:	
1. New cable	100
2. Installation of new cable	100
3. Transformer repair	100
(−) Cost for (hypothetical) rectification <u>before the damage</u> occurred:	
1. New cable	−100
2. Installation of new cable	−100
= Covered amount	**100**

Regarding the damaged transformer, it is clear that when the defect in the cable would have been remedied before the damage occurred, there would be no need to replace said transformer. Therefore, the costs for replacing the transformer are not deducted from the rectification cost and hence covered by LEG 2 wording.

LEG 3

Following the logic from LEG 1 to LEG 2, LEG 3 must provide the widest coverage for damage to the work caused by defect and indeed the LEG 3 only excludes cost for improvement of the work. In this case, this would exclude the additional cost for installing an advanced cable or using alternative materials with a higher level of quality for installation. Such scenario is not very likely since the employer will not vary the product specifications during installation phase.

A scenario like this could be relevant if acceleration measures must be performed due to a delay caused by the damaged work, which of course would result in higher costs for advanced installation technology and/ or workmanship.

Summary

As one can see, the coverage provided by a CAR insurance in the offshore construction industry can vary and requires special attention when it comes to the explicit wording of the policy. The CAR insurance is a tool to allocate risk and protect against defective products or defective workmanship—and therewith from enormously high costs—during the offshore installation process. All this depends on the respective wording of the defect coverage clause included in the CAR insurance policy. In most of the cases, the employer has the last word regarding the contents and therewith the coverage-scope of the insurance clauses, but with correct awareness, it is possible and advisable to consider such topics during the contract negotiations phase.

Gregory Efthimiu
Contract Manager
Siem Offshore Contractors GmbH

References

Bunni, N. (2011). *Risk and Insurance in Construction*. Spon Press, London.
FIDIC (2011a). *FIDIC DBO Contract Guide*. (First Edition). FIDIC, Lausanne.

Further reading

Baumann, H., Beckmann, R.M., Johannsen, K., Johannsen, R., and Koch, R. (2012). *Bruck/Möller Versicherungsvertragsgesetz – Großkommentar*. De Gruyter, Berlin.
Englert, K., Grauvogl, J., and Maurer, M. (2011). *Handbuch des Baugrund- und Tiefbaurechts*, Werner Verlag, Düsseldorf.
Englert, K., Motzke, G. and Wirth, A. (2009). *Baukommentar*. Werner Verlag, Köln am Rhein.
FIDIC (1999a). Conditions of Contract for Construction (*First Edition*). FIDIC, Lausanne.
FIDIC (1999b). Conditions of Contract for Plant and Design-Build. (First Edition). FIDIC, Lausanne.
FIDIC (1999c). *Conditions of Contract for EPC/Turnkey Projects (First Edition)*. FIDIC, Lausanne.
FIDIC (2011b). *FIDIC Procurement Procedures Guide* (First Edition). FIDIC, Lausanne.
FIDIC (2000). *The FIDIC Contracts Guide* (First Edition). FIDIC, Lausanne.

Halm, E., Engelbrecht, A., and Krahe, F. (2011). Handbuch des Fachanwalts Versicherungsrecht, *Luchterhand*, Köln am Rhein.

Klee, L. (2012). Smluvní vztahy výstavbových projektů. Wolters Kluwer. Prague.

Klee, L., Dobiáš, P. and Fabich, K. (2013). Pojištění velkých výstavbových projektů, *Stavebnictví* [Civil Engineering], 10/13.

Levine, M. and Ter Haar, R. (2008). *Construction Insurance and UK Construction Contracts*, Routledge, London.

Murdoch, J.R. and Hughes, W. (2008). *Construction Contracts: Law and Management*. Taylor & Francis. NewYork.

Palmer, W.J., Maloney, J., and Heffron, J. (1996). *Construction Insurance, Bonding, and Risk Management*, McGraw-Hill Professional, London.

Tichý, M. (2008). *Projekty a zakázky ve výstavbě*. C. H. Beck, Prague.

Venoit, W.K. (2009). *International Construction Law: A Guide for Cross-Border Transactions and Legal Disputes*. ABA Publishing, Chicago.

Website

http://imia.com

15 Risk in Underground Construction

15.1 Underground construction hazards and risks

Underground construction projects differ from other construction types and are project-specific due to the environments in which the construction takes place. The underground environment is diverse and fewer risks are foreseeable prior to project implementation. The structure of such an underground work is influenced significantly by nature. Rugged geology co-exists with structures built through human efforts. Therefore, a successful outcome can only exist where there is a mutual symbiosis between natural and human factors.

Underground construction contracts must, therefore, anticipate a higher level of risk, which can never be fully eliminated. As the work takes place in natural surroundings, the characteristics and behavior of these surroundings are not always foreseeable. A final prognosis can only be defined during the realization phase.

Geology-related anomalies are ranked among the major hazards, for example, excavation instability. Should the necessary measures not be taken correctly and in time, these instabilities can spread and reach breaking point. Depending on the particular conditions and size of the rock cover, breaking point can result in cave-in phenomena that pose a threat to surface structures above the underground works.

The largest underground construction works are usually tunnels. The following problems are ranked among the main tunnel construction hazards:

- loss of tunnel face stability;
- portal collapse;
- collapse of tunnel ceiling (ground arch) at the heading, resulting potentially in:
  - excessive overbreak;
  - ceiling collapse up to the surface.
- face fall-out on tunnel;
- low stability of tunnel face;

International Construction Contract Law, Second Edition. Lukas Klee.
© 2018 John Wiley & Sons Ltd. Published 2018 by John Wiley & Sons Ltd.

- tunnel bottom growth, lining pervasion into soft subsoil;
- excessive growth of convergences—tunnel profile squeezing, primary lining deformations;
- excessive ground water inflow into the tunnel;
- sudden water/mud/runny sand breakthrough into the tunnel;
- dangerous gas or radiation bursts into the tunnel from:
  - methane;
  - natural gas from ruptured piping;
  - CO_2.
- occurrence of stray currents;
- excessive surface sinking above the tunnel and related impacts on surface structures, power and service utility lines;
- drawdown, destruction of water wells around the tunnel;
- damage and destruction of water courses near the tunnel by mine water discharges that may have substantially changed their chemistry (for example, concrete extracts);
- damage due to pressure grouting compacting the rock massif or due to anchor grouting (damages to power and service utility lines, surface swelling);
- improperly selected and implemented tunnel insulation and water infiltration into the tunnel.

15.2 Code of practice for risk management of tunnel works

The first national document that deals integrally with how to assess, analyze, and control the above risks is *The Joint Code of Practice for Risk Management of Tunnel Works in the UK* issued by the British Tunneling Society (BTS) in September 2003. A closely related document striving to become internationally renowned is *A Code of Practice for Risk Management of Tunnel Works*, prepared by the International Tunneling Insurance Group in January 2006 (the codes). These codes are not enforceable or legally binding. However, they do contain some important principles, which endeavor to make all parties involved take the right approach to risk identification, control and elimination.

The codes came into being through the cooperation of the Association of British Insurers, Assurance Companies, BTS, the International Tunneling Association (ITA), and the International Association of Engineering Insurers (IMIA) also in reaction to some of the larger insured accidents that include (in US$): the Great Belt Link Fire (Denmark, 1994, damage $33 million), Munich Metro Collapse (Germany, 1994, damage $4 million), Metro Taipei Collapses (Taiwan, 1994 and 1995, combined total damage $24 million), Metro Los Angeles Collapse (USA, 1995, $9 million), Hull Yorkshire Collapse (UK, 1999, $55 million), TAV Bologna-Florence Collapse (Italy, 1999, damage $9 million), Anatolia Motorway Earthquake (Turkey, 1999, damage $115 million), Metro Taegu Collapse (South Korea, 2000, damage $24 million), TAV Bologna-Florence Collapse (Italy, 2000, damage $12 million), Taiwan High Speed Railway Collapse (Taiwan, 2002, damage $30 million), SOCATOP

Paris Collapse (France, 2002, damage $8 million) and the Shanghai Metro Collapse (China, 2003, damage $60 million).

Particular mention will be made of the collapse, which took place during the construction of the Heathrow Express Rail Link. On October 21, 1994, the tunnel at Heathrow Airport in London caved in and became one of the most extraordinary construction events of the last quarter century. The collapse caused the cancellation of hundreds of flights, a six-month delay of track commissioning and caused damage totalling more than $141 million. The court ordered a record fine of £1.2 million against the contractor Balfour Beatty plc for endangering the safety of the public and for gross violation of occupational safety. On the supplier of geo-monitoring (the Austrian company, Geoconsult GmbH), the court imposed a fine of £500,000. In addition, the court ordered each company to pay a further £100,000 in legal costs.

Large, insured accidents make tunnel construction more expensive. The codes, therefore, aim to unify and determine a minimum standard of risk control methodology. The codes cover all phases of underground construction efforts, that is, the preparations, engineering, project allocation, and implementation. The codes emphasize the insurers' involvement in the contract. An insurance company is authorized to perform site inspections and require a remedy should discrepancies be found.

The following are among the main principles of the codes:

- The requirement to submit the register of risks. The register of risks is an open document (it is possible and desirable to extend it during the course of construction), which clearly defines to whom a risk belongs, how it is to be controlled and how it is to be mitigated. The register of risks is a part of a quality control system, being, as such, subject to independent audits.
- Use of the "standard forms of contract" and technical standards.
- The contract should include a risk allocation and sharing clause, concerning geology or unforeseeable physical conditions.
- The contract should include a provision regulating the geo-monitoring process.
- The contract should include a provision allowing variations and implementing value engineering.
- The employer must have sufficient knowledge of geological risk control. If lacking this knowledge on the side of its own staff, they are obliged to hire a consultant or a contractor able to meet this requirement.
- The employer is obliged to invest sufficient funds in geological and hydrogeological surveying. This allows bidders to prepare and price the offer in respect of the known ground conditions and related risks in connection with tunnelling.
- The employer is also obliged to have sufficient funds and time for project preparation.

A project may be deemed "uninsurable" where the above requirements are not met. This, in itself, is a project commencement obstacle.

15.3 Alternatives of unforeseeable physical conditions risk allocation

Underground construction risk tends to be allocated to contracting parties through standard forms of contract. The risks in connection with unforeseeable ground conditions are usually borne by the employer and the technology-related risks by the contractor. It is nevertheless important to know the exact wording of the specific conditions or modifications of the standard form within every individual project.

Mere use of any standard contractual conditions will not eliminate unforeseeable risks and lack of proper project preparation. In general, three approaches to unforeseeable (physical conditions) ground conditions cost risk allocation can be distinguished and are discussed below:

1. *Full risk of ground conditions is borne by the employer.* Given such a risk allocation, the actual costs incurred in connection with the work completion under the encountered ground conditions, agreed headquarters, site overhead costs, and lost profits are paid to the contractor regardless of total expenses.
2. *Sharing of ground conditions risks.* Given such a risk allocation, the contractor is compensated for all actual costs incurred (regardless of the total) in connection with work completion and agreed headquarters and site overhead costs. The contractor is not, however, compensated for lost profit in connection with adverse ground conditions encountered if they differ from the expectations spelt out in the terms of reference.
3. *Full risk of ground conditions is borne by the contractor.* Given such a risk allocation, the contractor is not compensated for the actual costs incurred in connection with the work completion, agreed headquarters and site overhead costs and lost profit. This approach is not recommended for underground construction projects.

Where the employer does not invest any funds into geological surveying and risk analyses, the bidders must do so at their own expense, resulting in increased costs in connection with submitting the offer and, inherently, restricting the number of bidders. Bidders must be provided with enough time and space to carry out a site inspection and investigation. In the case of underground projects, only a part of the site is available for inspection. The technology employed in construction may prove unsuitable, should the employer assign all the responsibility to the contractor who, in turn, comes across unforeseeable ground conditions during underground works. In such cases, the economic sustainability of the bid may collapse as a whole.

A contractor bearing the risk of unforeseeable ground conditions is forced to adapt the project and method of construction in line with expected economic returns. In the event of a high level of losses, the contractor will almost certainly look for all possible ways to terminate the contract prematurely. This can impact on the total costs, quality, safety and service life of the entire tunnel. As an example see the recent case of a tunnel construction early termination in *Obrascon Huarte Lain SA v. Her Majesty's Attorney General for Gibraltar* [2014] EWHC 1028 (TCC).

Geotechnical baseline reports as a risk management tool
by Randall J. Essex (the United States)
Where the Saga Began

In the early days of underground construction projects, owners retained engineering consultants to carry out subsurface investigation programs to support the project design. In some cases, separate geotechnical consultants were retained to complete the exploration programs, and the other firms were retained to carry out the project designs based on the results of those investigation programs. Whether as a stand-alone project or a component of a larger program, the results of the investigation program were assembled in one or more geotechnical reports that were referenced in the bid package. Often the reports themselves were provided "for information only" and were not to be relied upon in developing the contractor's bid. Similarly, the details in the boring logs were to be considered representative, at most, of the cylinders of coverage themselves, and were not to be considered indicative of conditions in between the borings. The contractor was advised to make its own investigation of the site, and that the contractor was solely responsible for the conditions encountered on the project. The phrase often used to describe this contractual condition was "You bid it, you build it."

As time progressed, construction became more complex, project depth below ground surface increased, and projects were undertaken with newly developed equipment and in increasingly difficult ground conditions. A cornerstone program that helped confront many of these issues and challenges was the 106-mile long subway system in Washington, DC, owned by the Washington Metropolitan Area Transit Authority (WMATA). Begun in the late 1960s, the polarizing dynamics became more and more apparent. The owner provided an investigation database that indicated a broad array of physical ground and groundwater conditions, and allocated the risk of interpreting those conditions to the contractor. Because of the competitive bid basis, bidders were compelled to make optimistic interpretations or risk not winning the bid. The two parties were at opposite ends of a difficult dynamic from the start—the owner expected the contractor to be responsible for all of the data provided, while the low bidder's interpretations were at the optimistic end of the spectrum. When the contractor encountered less than optimum conditions, unanticipated costs were incurred and claims were filed.

WMATA's disputes procedures followed the U.S. Army Corps of Engineers Board of Contract Appeals process. One administrative judge heard testimony from both parties, including personnel and expert witnesses, the transcript and admitted documents were shared with two other administrative judges, the three conferred, and a majority, non-binding recommendation was presented to WMATA's Contracting Officer. If either party chose to contest the recommendation, the next step was court.

The process for any individual contract took years to resolve, sometimes extending 5 years or more after the construction was completed. The only entities who "won" in these instances were the lawyers. Even when the contractors were paid money they were due, it was not until years later. The consequences of having the contractor under-capitalized resulted in shortcuts in the field, construction problems, ground instabilities, surface settlement, and third-party impacts that delayed contract completion. The owner and contractors both suffered.

The need for change

Based on adverse outcomes on the WMATA system and elsewhere, the U.S. tunneling industry recognized that if they did not do something to improve the situation, the public would look to other technologies than tunneling to address their infrastructure needs.

This led to the creation of a number of organizations that helped to communicate the need for change, and developed improved contracting practices to help avoid and resolve disputes. These organizations included the U.S. National Committee on Tunneling Technology (USNCTT), within the National Academy of Sciences, and the Underground Technology Research Council (UTRC), under the auspices of the Construction Division of the American Society of Civil Engineers (ASCE). One of the first documents to be issued was the 1974 USNCTT publication "Better Contracting for Underground Construction." The document summarized existing contracting practices in the United States and in Europe, and presented a number of recommendations to improve contracting methods for underground construction. Items included the disclosure of all data gathered during exploration, lack of exculpatory clauses disavowing the accuracy of such data, the need to have provisions that addressed extraordinary problems associated with groundwater inflow, and the advantages and disadvantages of different types of construction contracts. A subsequent study by the USNCTT in 1984 entitled "Geotechnical Site Investigations for Underground Projects," summarized the results of an analysis of more than 200 underground construction contracts, about 80 of which were complete records from design through construction close-out. A key finding of this report was a causative relationship between the amount of exploration carried out prior to construction and the potential for claims on the project. The results were reported in a number of ways, including: the money invested in geotech exploration as a percentage of the construction cost; and the total length of borings drilled as a percentage of the length of the tunnels driven. These presentations clearly showed that projects that skimped on site exploration had a higher likelihood of justifiable claims, and that the claim-driven change orders dwarfed the exploration cost differentials. One of the "fathers" of the U.S. tunneling industry, Al Matthews, expressed the opinion that within the critical range of investment, within about 1% to 2% of the project value, $1 of exploration saved $10 in potential impact cost. The analyses also demonstrated that investments in exploration had a point of diminishing return beyond which additional investment had no bearing on the incidence for claims. Perhaps there are other studies in other countries of similar effect, but not to the author's knowledge. In addition to the exploration/claim relationships, the report strongly asserted that the owner needed to prepare an interpretive report of the indicated subsurface conditions, and include that report in the Construction Contract. This would require a fundamental shift in thinking on behalf of project owners.

Underground technology research council publications

Building on the findings and recommendations of the USNCTT reports, the UTRC produced a series of guideline publications that expanded the discussion. One document entitled "Avoiding and Resolving Disputes in Underground Construction" was published in 1989, followed by a second edition in 1991. Its most compelling recommendation was for the incorporation of four key contract provisions to help avoid and resolve disputes:

- Differing Site Conditions Clause
- Geotechnical Design Summary Report (now called a GBR)
- Escrow Bid Documents
- Disputes Review Board

Each of these provisions is described briefly below.

Differing site conditions clause

The U.S. federal government first instituted a "changed conditions" clause in 1921 to provide a contractual basis for relief to the contractor for encountered site conditions that were more adverse than indicated in the contract. By providing a form of contractual relief, it was hoped that bidders would exclude contingencies for such conditions, a practice that was increasing the cost of government contracts. In 1968, the term "Changed Conditions" was changed to "Differing Site Conditions."

The function of the Differing Site Condition (DSC) clause is twofold. First, it relieves the contractor of assuming the risk of encountering conditions differing materially (i.e., in a significant, meaningful way) from those indicated or ordinarily encountered. Second, it provides a remedy under the construction contract that addresses the matter as an item of contract administration.

Geotechnical baseline report

As explained above, owners previously gave all the data to the bidders and said "you decide, but you are responsible." The inclusion of a geotechnical interpretive report in the contract provides bidders with a clear understanding of anticipated ground conditions in a concise manner. All bidders have the same interpretations as a starting point—a "leveling of the contractual playing field." Finally, if conditions are encountered that are markedly different from those expressed in the report, and the contractor suffers financial impact related to that difference, the contractor is entitled to reimbursement of the additional costs. Expressed in another manner, the contractual role of the interpretive geotechnical report is to assist in the administration of the DSC clause in the contract. The interpretive report took on different names as the practice evolved—first "Geotechnical Report for Construction," then "Geotechnical Design Summary Report," and finally "Geotechnical Baseline Report." The focus of the document adjusted through this development as well.

Escrow bid documents

The Escrow Bid Documents (EBDs) contain the contractor's assumptions, calculations, and information used in preparing its bid, assembled in a format that can be accessed during the project if a dispute arises. The EBDs would also include any reports prepared by outside consultants in support of the contractor's bid. The documents are typically submitted by the low bidder and possibly the second or third low bidder, within several days following bid receipt. Prior to award of the contract, selected owner representatives review the documents of the low bidder for completeness, in the presence of the contractor. The documents are then escrowed with a third party, and are maintained unopened and confidential until and unless either party requests a review to help resolve a dispute. The EBDs are always reviewed in the presence of both parties. In this manner, the proprietary nature of the contractor's ideas and estimates comprising or supporting the bid is preserved.

The EBDs benefit both parties. The basis of the contractor's bid is documented at the time that the bid is submitted, rather than at some future point in time when the quantum of a claim is presented. If a claim is judged to have merit, the EBDs offer clear evidence of what the cost basis was, and therefore the degree to which its assumed costs have increased. This streamlines the determination of the additional compensation due the contractor.

Dispute review board

A Dispute Review Board (DRB), also referred to as a Dispute Resolution Board or Dispute Board (see www.drb.org), is an expedient means for resolving disputes during the construction phase of the project, rather than experiencing protracted litigation in court. A DRB is generally created by contractual agreement, and typically comprises three members. The members are not lawyers, but rather experts in one or more aspects of the proposed construction, and cannot be employees or associates of the parties. There are several approaches by which the members are identified and selected, and a chairman appointed.

The DRB is established at the beginning of the project, and is kept apprised as the work proceeds, by means of progress reports and periodic site visits, whether there is a dispute or not. In this manner, the DRB has an opportunity to hear from all parties how the project is proceeding, and can view the site conditions in a "non-dispute" environment. This experience provides the DRB with an excellent basis for assessing the merits of a claim if one arises. In the event that a disagreement cannot be resolved at the field level between the parties, a joint hearing is held. The DRB hears the perspectives of both parties relative to the dispute, asks questions of both parties, and then prepares and presents to the parties a written summary of its findings and recommendations. The recommendations are generally non-binding, and most often limited to merit-related arguments. If a claim is found to have merit, the DRB generally recommends that the parties attempt to resolve the financial portion themselves. If necessary, the parties can ask the DRB to address quantum as well, either in concert with or subsequent to the merit evaluation.

There are significant benefits that the DRB process offers that are not available through other means such as arbitration or mediation: (1) the DRB is composed of experts respected by both parties for their relevant expertise; (2) the DRB is engaged at the beginning of the project and therefore has the benefit of "contemporaneous knowledge" of the job conditions; and (3) the early existence of the board serves to encourage cooperation between the parties, which serves as a deterrent, rather than an incentive, to pursue claims.

In response to positive industry feedback following the 1991 publication, the UTRC decided that additional publications were warranted to provide further guidance with regard to the Interpretive Geotechnical Report and Dispute Review Boards. In 1995, the "Construction Disputes Review Board Manual" was published. In 1996, the Dispute Resolution Board Foundation was created, and an online version of the manual was updated in 2007. In 1997, "Geotechnical Baseline Reports in Underground Construction—Guidelines and Practices" was published. The author led the development of the 1997 publication, as well as a second edition published in 2007 (known as the Gold Book). The 1997 publication was written in consideration of traditional design-bid-build contracting. One of several new chapters in the 2007 edition addressed the application of GBRs within a design-build (also known as design and construct) context. These aspects are described below.

The first geotechnical interpretive report was prepared for a WMATA tunnel contract in 1972. In the late 1970s and 1980s, more of these documents were written for tunneling projects, known and "Geotechnical Design Summary Reports." However, claims still occurred at an unacceptable rate. It was recognized that while the intent was good, the focus was not on the right issues. What matters most to a contractor is how the ground is anticipated to behave *during construction*, not what the ground conditions were expected to be for *design* purposes. Over time, practitioners changed the focus of the report as well as the title, from "Geotechnical Design Summary Report" to "Geotechnical Baseline Report." The 1997 and 2007 GBR publications make this distinction in the recommendations.

Fundamentals of a GBR

Risk-sharing philosophy

A fundamental assumption in the use of a GBR as well as the other improved contracting practices noted above is that the owner "owns the ground" through which the facility is to be constructed. The business proposition is that since the owner wants a functioning facility to extend from Point A to Point B, it should be expected to pay a fair price for constructing the facility between those two points. Given the variability that subsurface conditions can exhibit along a tunnel alignment, and the impact on cost and schedule that such variability can have, sharing the ground risks between the owner and contractor is judged to be the best approach to successfully constructing challenging projects in increasingly difficult ground conditions. This perspective applies irrespective of the form of contract delivery, be it traditional DBB, DB, or PPP (which is discussed later in this chapter).

Primary purpose of a GBR

The primary purpose of a GBR is to establish a single source document where contractual statements describe the geotechnical conditions anticipated (or to be assumed) to be encountered during underground construction. The contractual statement(s) are referred to as baselines. Risks associated with conditions consistent with or less adverse than the baselines are allocated to the Contractor, and those materially more adverse than the baselines are accepted by the Owner. Other important objectives of the GBR are to discuss the geotechnical and site conditions related to the anticipated means and methods of constructing the underground elements of the project. The GBR needs to be binding between the parties, and therefore should be a Contract Document.

Roles of other geotechnical documents

The factual information gathered during the project investigations should be summarized in a Geotechnical Data Report (GDR). The GDR should also be included as a Contract Document also, however, the GBR should be ranked higher than the GDR within the Contract Documents hierarchy. The importance of including the GDR as a Contract Document points to two areas.

One is if the Contractor proposes a design or construction innovation, and the information presented in the GBR does not fully address the circumstances. In this instance, the information in the GDR is available for the Contractor to rely upon. A second item is that it is impossible for an author of the GBR to be able to describe all possible ground behaviors "under the sun." If the GBR is silent on a specific matter, the information in the GDR can and should be sought to help clarify what was known at time of bid.

Other interpretive reports may be prepared by the design team that address a broad range of design issues for the team's internal consideration. It is recommended that such reports be referred to as Geotechnical Design Memoranda, and should be clearly differentiated from the GBR. In order to avoid ambiguity in the Contract, the GBR should be the only interpretive report prepared for use in bidding and constructing the project. Preparation of other interpretive "Reports" in the course of design development should be avoided.

Types of baseline statements

With the change in focus came an appreciation for two fundamental types of baselines, physical and behavioral. These parallel clauses in the Federal Differing Site Conditions Clause that addressed a "Type 1 DSC," which pertains to physical conditions that are different from those indicated in the Contract, and a "Type 2 DSC," which pertains to a condition such as adverse behavior, that could not have been gleaned from the Contract indications at time of bid. Thus, physical baselines address the relevant physical conditions that are expected to be encountered at the site, irrespective of the methods of excavation and ground support utilized. In contrast, behavioral baselines relate to the ground behavior when the contractor's means and methods engage the ground during excavation. An example will help clarify the differences. In the instance of a large-diameter tunnel required for a highway tunnel project, two possible methods of construction could be used: a tunnel-boring machine with a one-pass precast concrete liner; or a sequential excavation method (SEM) with a one or two-pass lining of shotcrete or cast concrete. While the physical baselines are identical for the two approaches, the ground and groundwater behaviors will be different in the two cases, as will key aspects that will influence items such as over-excavation, ground loss, ground displacements, seepage, excavation equipment usage and wear, and muck handling and disposal. It becomes apparent that one must start with the design and construction approach and then address the ground behaviors critical to the success of that approach. Section 5 discusses how GBR development must be altered to accommodate differences in contracting method, so that the party most in control of the design and construction approach can have input to the behavioral baselines contained in the GBR.

Setting the baselines

There should be a logical linkage between the risk register prepared during design development and baseline statements in the GBR. One might reason that the baseline statements or warnings are mitigation measures to specific risks identified in the risk register that are allocated to the contractor. By providing estimates of the quantities of the extent of the risk (number of boulders, length of abrasive ground, the number of faults to be encountered on hard rock projects, etc.) the risks can be managed in a quantitative manner. The contractor is responsible for the quantified conditions as indicated in the GBR, and the owner is responsible for conditions that exceed those indicated quantities.

The question will always arise—"what should be baselined?" In the author's experience, one must ask the question "What will the consequence (to the project) be if the baseline parameter or condition or quantity is wrong?" If the potential impacts are significant, those aspects should be baselined. However, if the risk of being wrong is insignificant or non-existent, it may be that that parameter or condition does not warrant a baseline statement or portrayal. The key is to focus on the anticipated subsurface conditions that will impact the cost of construction in a significant way. Providing overly excessive or detailed baselines about parameters that will have no influence on the project should be avoided.

The baselines are the means by which risks for certain conditions are transferred to the contractor. An owner wanting to transfer all of its risks to the contractor might conclude that an overly conservative baseline is a good way to accomplish this. This is not recommended. The baseline portrayals should be a realistic assessment based on the results of the site exploration program and experience from relevant projects. If a baseline condition is more austere than might otherwise be gleaned from the supporting data, the GBR should provide an explanation for the difference. In the case where overly adverse baselines are used, the owner carries the risk that that unreasonable baselines could be put aside or overturned by the DRB or other adjudication process as being unreasonable.

Use of GBRs beyond the United States

The use of the GBR originated in the United States, perhaps out of sheer need as there are probably more attorneys per capita in the US than elsewhere on the planet. At its inception, bidders would ask "Why is a GBR a part of the contract?" As GBR usage increased and beneficial outcomes were realized, the question transformed to "Why isn't there a GBR in the contract?" In several instances, due to the outcry from bidders, owners decided to "change their ways" and reissued their bid documents with a contractually binding GBR in concert with a DRB provision. Fundamentally, contractors see the use of a GBR as a commitment on behalf of the owner to provide a fair basis for contracting. The converse is also true.

Over the years, the use of a GBR as a risk identification/risk-allocation tool within the construction contract has gained increasing acceptance by designers, contractors, owners, and dispute adjudicators. The use of a GBR was cited in the "Joint Code of Practice for Management of Tunnel Works in the UK" (September 2003), by the Association of British Insurers and the British Tunneling Society, as an example of how the owner should represent anticipated subsurface conditions in the contract. Different versions of the Joint Code have subsequently been prepared, including the International Tunnel Insurance Group (ITIG, 2006) and a version for application in the United States (2015).

With time, the benefit and use of GBRs has extended to other countries, including Canada, New Zealand, Australia, Singapore, HK, the UK, UAE, South Africa, Chile, and India. Other countries have reportedly worked with contract elements that mirror the GBR principles, including Switzerland.

FIDIC provides a respected, widely used international set of contract forms that have been applied around the world. A collaborative effort is currently underway between FIDIC representatives and members of the Contractual Practices Working Group within the International Tunneling Association, to provide alternative contract language that calls for the use of a GBR and an adjudication process such as a DRB, for projects involving underground construction.

Further efforts of the ITA Working Group are ongoing to prepare guidelines that will help users adapt the use of GBRs to other forms of contract around the world, including NEC in the UK, and the Swiss forms of contract.

Design-bid-build versus design-build and PPP

As discussed in Section 4, how the GBR is prepared and by whom needs to reflect the form of contract delivery. For traditional design-bid-build (DBB) contracts, the owner retains a designer to prepare a 100% design with a 100% GBR. The GBR addresses the baselines as reflected in the site exploration and the anticipated construction means and methods consistent with the engineer's design. In this instance, the ability for bidders to influence what is said in the GBR is limited to asking questions in the form of Requests for Information (RFIs) during the bid period. Owners may or may not make appropriate changes to the document through the addendum process, and any requested changes will necessarily be shared with all the bidders.

In the instance of a design-build (DB) contract, the owner retains a designer to prepare a reference design that is somewhere between 60% and 90% complete. In this instance, each contractor retain its own designer to carry out a final design consistent with the contractor's proposed construction approach. Hopefully, the owner has carried out as close to a 100% site exploration program (and has prepared GDR) as possible (see Robinson et al., 2015). The owner should prepare an initial GBR that addresses the relevant physical conditions. However, the contractor/designer teams are in the best position to describe the behavioral baselines consistent with their individual design and construction approaches. To address DB situations, a three-step process for GBR development is proposed:

- A GBR for Advertisement (GBR-A) is issued by the owner that includes a description of the project and key constraints, the site geology, and the physical baselines consistent with the known site conditions. The GBR-A contains gaps where the owner solicits responses to specific issues and risks associated with each bidder's design and construction approaches, as well as the anticipated behaviors associated with the proposed approaches.
- Each bidder submits their responses in a GBR for Bidding (GBR-B). The owner then reviews the responses and may seek clarification of certain entries that may warrant revisions and a resubmittal of the GBR-B. This "cure" process is carried out prior to submittal of financial proposals.
- Upon successful completion of the cure process, financial proposals are received and a preferred contractor/designer team is selected. The team's GBR-B becomes the GBR to the Contract.

In many respects, the above process represents a bilateral approach to creating the GBR, where there is opportunity for extended discussions of means, methods, anticipated behaviors, and risks between the owner and the bidders. The outcome is likely a better risk sharing tool than one written primarily by the owner for acceptance by the contractor or contractor team.

As infrastructure demands are confronted with dwindling public funds, Public-Private-Partnership (PPP) schemes are emerging as a last resort alternative. In this instance, a financier and concessionaire arrangement incorporates a DB contractor-designer relationship for the constructed facilities. From a risk management standpoint, the stakes are raised and the need for risk management increases. With publicly funded DBB or DB delivery, schedule-driven liquidated damage levels are typically limited to the owner's ongoing construction management services. However, under PPP, if liquidated damages for delayed completion are compounded by an interest-bearing financing penalty at the front end and a revenue or availability loss on the back end. These phenomena can trigger a four-fold increase in delay-related costs. Given the higher cost-based risks, the need to share ground-related production losses that contribute to schedule delay is paramount.

The conundrum is that some advisors for PPP delivery espouse a single point responsibility for cost and schedule. For a hospital or a library, or some other above ground project, this may be appropriate and manageable. However, given the extraordinary impact that ground conditions can have on the completion of a tunnel project, the sharing of subsurface risk needs to be incorporated into the mix. As such, the use of a GBR and some form of dispute resolution should be seen as essential components of a risk allocation process. Attempting to "push all of the risk across the table" to the contractor is not a desirable approach and is likely to result in additional costs to the owner despite the legalize to the contrary. Section 7 discusses one possible solution for risk sharing on a PPP tunnel project.

Payment mechanisms

Risk sharing is driven by the fundamental principle that the Contractor is entitled to be paid a fair price for the work actually performed. How the contract payment provisions are set up can simplify the ability to adjust quantities as the ground conditions dictate. Perhaps the best example of this is in the application of the sequential excavation method (SEM). In this instance, a base design can be augmented with additional ground support measures, with each ground support increment assigned its own payment provision. This is often referred to as a "tool box" approach—the ground dictates what additional support is required, and the contractor is paid according to the unit price(s) for the additional support elements. Examples include vacuum lances, spilling, additional shotcrete, and pocket excavation. By building delay-related costs into the payment terms, the contractor is fully compensated on a "pay-as-you-go" basis for the direct and indirect costs of the supplemental work. This approach has been used successfully on many projects, including the challenging Beacon Hill Station and Tunnels in Seattle.

In areas where high-quality rock mass conditions are anticipated, "baselines" may combine a ground classification, required ground support, and advance rate, with payment terms assigned to each ground class baseline. As the excavation advances, and the rock mass is mapped and classified, payment items can be confirmed and approved as the basis for payment. Again, a "pay-as-you-go" mechanism can be established. In this case, if, in the aggregate, more adverse ground was encountered than anticipated, the Contractor may have a justifiable basis for additional compensation due to the extended length of time required to complete the work. Building indirect cost bases into the payment provisions, such as explained above, will address the indirect costs of delay, in addition to the direct costs of the additional work.

Other contracts may contain a more simplified payment provision that consists of a single price per linear foot or meter for all excavation and support work, with no reference to ground class or ground condition. This approach would be more typical where a closed face or pressurized face TBM is used in conjunction with a precast bolted and gasketed concrete lining. In this instance, the GBR should provide an estimate of the lengths of different ground types to be encountered, and the characteristics of each ground type that will impact, among other items, advance rate and downtime to replace cutter tools. Considerations might include abrasive vs non-abrasive ground, cohesive or granular soils, whether fat or sticky clays are anticipated, cobbles or boulders, faults with potential for increased water pressures, potential for high cutter wear and more frequent interventions to facilitate cutter tool replacement, etc. There should be sufficient detail in the Contractor's Escrow Bid Documents to indicate how the Contractor accounted for the different characteristics described in the GBR, and the bases for advance rate estimates for the different ground types. Again, if evidence shows that more adverse conditions were encountered in aggregate or within each tunnel reach than was indicated in the GBR, and the contractor can demonstrate financial impact as a result, the contractor may be entitled to a change order for the increased cost.

Paying for conditions beyond the baselines

How the contractor will be paid for the cost of constructing the project should be clear in the documents, and should address payment for conditions encountered that fall within and beyond the baselines. There are many ways to address this circumstance depending on the form of contract delivery and the legal limitations of the owner. In public contracts, the owner may budget a percentage of the contract value as a "contingency" for addressing claims for unforeseen conditions. Private clients may be able to establish provisional sums to address these circumstances, sometimes soliciting prices for those contingency amounts using a schedule of provisional sums. For example, in a rock tunnel project where groundwater inflow is a major concern, the baselines may include the expected maximum flush (peak) inflow at the heading as well as a maximum sustained flow at the shaft or portal. If "x" is the baseline inflow, a provisional table could solicit pricing from the bidders that address the "what if " conditions if actual inflows are 1.5x or 2x or more. In this manner, the owner can forward-price the risks of encountering conditions more adverse than the baseline quantity. The provisional amounts are triggered only if the adverse conditions are encountered. If the conditions are not encountered, the owner does not pay.

In the instance of PPP delivery, one innovative approach used on the Port of Miami Tunnel in the United States utilized a "ladder" approach to sharing the costs for conditions beyond the baselines.

A risk analysis estimated that for an $800M contract amount, probable risks could approach $180M. The owner established a contingency fund in that amount. The first increment of costs above the baseline, $10M, was allocated to the contractor as a "deductible." The second increment of costs, $150M, was to be paid by the owner. A third increment of costs, $20M, was to be absorbed by the concessionaire. If the maximum contingency amount of $180 M was eclipsed, either party could request that the project be terminated, or both parties could negotiate a shared risk model going forward. The project is explained further in Chen (2001). This type of approach is a good example of how risks can be shared, even under PPP delivery.

Other permutations are possible with this ladder approach, including whether, at the end of the contract, unspent funds are allocated back to the parties. Under this arrangement, the contractor might be granted 50% or more of the unspent amount. This type of arrangement might incentivize cooperation between the parties to work together to mitigate the effects on known and unknown conditions on the project.

Summary

Underground construction is fundamentally different from surface-based construction and warrants different approaches to managing construction-related risks, primarily associated with the ground and groundwater conditions to be encountered.

Built on more than 40 years of lessons learned, a number of guidance publications offer recommendations for best practices associated with identifying and allocating construction-based risks that rely, fundamentally, on the contractor carrying those risks associated with the anticipated conditions, and the owner carrying the responsibility for conditions more onerous than the anticipated conditions.

The industry has also developed means of avoiding and expediently resolving disputes during the course of the project, so that focus in maintained on completing the project, not formulating claims.

How the contractor is compensated for the work can be configured in a number of ways, but desirably will include a balanced linkage between the baseline descriptions in the GBR and the payment terms. Provisional bid items can also be engineered that address conditions that exceed the baselines. In this manner, the contract will contain means for fairly compensating the contractor for the work performed, whether within or beyond the baselines.

Finally, the above philosophies pertain to all underground construction projects, irrespective of the form of contract delivery. Whether DBB, DB, or PPP delivery, there are proven ways to identify and fairly allocate the construction-related risks, and for sharing the risks of unforeseen conditions, should any be encountered.

Randall J. Essex, P.E.
Executive Vice President
Mott MacDonald,
The United States

Bibliography

A Code of Practice for Risk Management of Tunnel Works (2006). The International Tunneling Insurance Group.

Avoiding and Resolving Disputes During Construction (1991). *Technical Committee on Contracting Practices of the Underground Technology Research Council.* American Society of Civil Engineers.

Avoiding and Resolving Disputes in Underground Construction (1989). *Technical Committee on Contracting Practices of the Underground Technology Research Council.* American Society of Civil Engineers.

Better Contracting for Underground Construction (1974). *U.S. National Committee on Tunneling Technology.* National Academy of Sciences.

Chen, W.-P. (2009). Port of Miami Tunnel Update – a view from design builder's engineer. Rapid Excavation and Tunneling Conference, Las Vegas.

Dispute Resolution Board Foundation (2007). *Dispute Review Board Practice and Procedures Manual*.
Essex, R. (1997). Geotechnical baseline reports for underground construction. Technical Committee on Contracting Practices of the Underground Technology Research Council. American Society of Civil Engineers.
Essex, R. (2007). Geotechnical baseline reports for construction. Technical Committee on Contracting Practices of the Underground Technology Research Council. American Society of Civil Engineers.
Matyas, R.M., Mathews, A.A., Smith, R.J. and Sperry, P.E. (1995). *Construction Dispute Review Board Manual*. McGraw Hill Construction Series.
NRC (1984). *Geotechnical Site Investigations for Underground Projects*. Vols. I and II. National Academy of Sciences.
O'Carroll, J. and Goodfellow, R. (2015). *Guidelines for Improved Risk Management on Tunnel and Underground Construction Projects in the United States of America*. Underground Construction Association of SME.
Robinson, R.A., Kucker, M.S. and Gildner, J.P. (2001). Levels of geotechnical input for DB contracts for tunnel construction. Rapid Excavation and Tunneling Conference, June, San Diego, CA, USA.
The British Tunnelling Society (2003). The Joint Code of Practice for Risk Management of Tunnel Works in the UK.

Geotechnical baseline used in contractor's bid by Michal Uhrin (the Czech Republic)

This case does not deal with a geotechnical baseline report per se. It, however, presents a geotechnical baseline employed to address risks associated with feasibility of complicated underground construction works arising from potential variability of ground conditions. By rational and measurable definition of what is expected and designed for and what is beyond expectation, based on the level of information available at tender stage, it served similar purpose to that of a baseline report or at least followed the same philosophy. What makes this particular case interesting is the clarity of the geotechnical baseline, which was expressed in terms of only ten key parameters summarized in a simple table. Brief background to the case is as follows:

An international contractor was preparing a bid for a project comprising major underground works located in a post-Soviet country. The ultimate scope of the underground works was to excavate two major caverns enabling adjustments to the alignment and replacement of tunnel lining of existing metro lines. The proposed works were located in difficult ground conditions under and close to existing urban infrastructure.

The contract was planned to be set up under design and build conditions similar to that of the FIDIC Yellow Book. Prior to launching tender for construction works the client undertook geotechnical site investigation, carried out condition survey of assets that could be affected by the proposed works and hired an engineering consultant to prepare employer's requirements and a reference design. The reference design was denoted basic design and was meant to represent one of many possible design solutions satisfying the employer's requirements. The employer's requirements set out the geometrical and performance specifications for the works. The most important of those were, understandably, limited impact of the works on existing adjacent infrastructure and minimum disruption to standard operation of the metro network. These conditions were also the most difficult to meet. The client hired an engineer to manage the contract. The winning contractor was expected to carry out supplementary ground investigation and other surveys as necessary for their proposed approach, undertake detailed design, prepare workshop drawings, and method statements and carry out the construction works.

The approach of the subject contractor was based on sophisticated underground construction techniques including ground freezing, underground jacking of large diameter pipes, tunneling with sprayed concrete lining in clay under shallow cover and excavation with slurry shield. The feasibility or rather efficiency of these techniques largely depends on the ground conditions. For example, ground freezing becomes increasingly difficult if the groundwater is too warm, if there is too much groundwater flow or, on the other hand, in case of insufficient water saturation. Pipe jacking becomes difficult if the ground is far too hard whereas sprayed concrete lined tunnelling is complicated if the ground is far too soft. The impact of unexpected unfavorable ground conditions on construction cost and especially program may be very severe, beyond linear proportionality.

The contractor analysed the available ground investigation data, based their design and construction methodology on the expected conditions and proposed supplementary surveys where the existing investigation was not clear or dense enough. In order to define the range of ground condition within which their design and proposal was valid and to protect themselves from the risk of encountering different conditions they developed a geotechnical baseline and linked it with the proposed supplementary survey works. All these documents formed part of the contractor's proposal.

In the geotechnical baseline the contractor identified ten key parameters with the most impact on their proposal and presented them in tabular format (Table 15.1). They described each parameter, outlined its impact or consequence of exceeding the threshold and defined the threshold value and its method of measurement including location and number of repetitions. With such a clear definition of the baseline there is little room for misunderstanding and dispute. Prior to awarding the contract the client also has the opportunity to seek independent advice to verify whether the baseline fairly represents the ground conditions on site as per the information available at tender stage.

The bid of this particular contractor was eventually evaluated as the winning offer. However, the project as such is unfortunately on hold due to financing issues.

Michal Uhrin
Geotechnical Engineer
Czech Republic

15. Risk in Underground Construction

28 May - Geotechnical Baseline Elements

Issue	Parameter	Threshold	Consequences/impact	Method of measurement	Locations	Repetitions (minimum)	Significant values/criteria to be considered
Dimensioning of the technical solution and/or methods							
No excessive artesianism in silty sand	Groundwater head above surface	< 3m	Ground instability (lower galleries & pipes), soil treatment methods, program	Water level in stand-pipe piezometers (natural conditions)	> 5 stand-pipe piezometers	Water level not stabilized under ground-level after 5 days (2 readings per day)	all
Upper adits excavation - traditional							
Silty clay - undrained	Silty clay Permeability	< 10^{-7} m/s Except in case of sandy lenses	Construction methods, program	In-situ tests on the full scale thickness of the layer in natural conditions (e.g. slug test ASTM D4044-96-2008)	> 5 piezometers (minimum 2m slotted)	10 tests	av. +/− $1\sigma^{(*)}$
Silty clay - stiff enough	Silty clay Cohesion C_u	> 90 kPa	Face stabilisation (bolting) / grouting	In-situ and/or lab test on undisturbed samples	> 5 boreholes (vertical and/or horizontal)	10 samples	av. +/− 1σ
Within the silty clay unit, absence of continuous sandy layers hydraulically feeded leading to foresee methods other than localised drainage and localised grouting	Stratigraphy	Presence/absence	Construction method	CPTu testing and sampling	adequate number of CPTu and sampling to be agreed between the Contractor and the Engineer	to be defined during the Works	continuity

(continued)

28 May - Geotechnical Baseline Elements

Issue	Parameter	Threshold	Consequences/impact	Method of measurement	Locations	Repetitions (minimum)	Significant values/criteria to be considered
Pipe jacking							
Lateral friction on pipes	CPT tip resistance q_c	< 15 MPa for silty sand < 6 MPa for sandy clay	Construction methods, program (ex. vibrating system)	CPTu (undisturbed initial conditions)	> 5 CPTu	>20 m continuous readings (4 m/CPTu)	av. +/− 1σ
Soil treatment							
Ground freezing feasibility							
Ground water content (Sandy Silt & Silty Clay) sufficient	Ground water content	> 20%	Construction methods	Lab test on undisturbed samples	> 5 boreholes (vertical and/or horizontal)	10 samples	av. +/− 1σ
Low ground water circulation speed (<1 m/day)	Permeability in sandy silt	$< 5.10^{-6}$ m/s	Construction methods	In-situ tests on the full scale thickness of the layer in natural conditions (e.g. slug test ASTM D4044-96-2008)	> 5 piezometers (minimum 2m shielded)	10 tests	av. +/− 1σ
Ground water temperature	Ground water temperature	< 21°C	Program & cost of ground freezing	Water temperature in piezometers	In 5 piezometers	>20 readings (2 readings/day/piezometer)	av. +/− 1σ
Ground water chemistry	Ground water freezing point	> −3°C	Program & cost of ground freezing	Laboratory test on samples	> 5 boreholes (vertical and/or horizontal)	10 samples	av. +/− 1σ

Soil treatment *Ground freezing extension*				
Ground freezing extension with respect to the position of the lower pipe-jacking tubes (current geometry)	Stratigraphy	At least 10% of the interface between Sandy Silt Unit & Silty Clay Unit at or below the elevation of −47m (absolute elevation)	Program & cost of ground freezing	
	parameters CPTu (non treated soils)	> 10 CPTu	>40 m continuous readings (4 m/CPTu) interpolation with Kriging algorithm	av. +/− 1σ
Ground freezing extension with respect to the position of the vertical pipe-jacking tubes (walls of the caverns)	Stratigraphy	Right Separation: interface between Sandy Silt Unit & Silty Clay Unit not higher than −44.00 m (absolute elevation) Left Separation: interface between Sandy Silt Unit & Silty Clay Unit not higher than −43.00 m (absolute elevation)	Program & cost of ground freezing	
	parameters CPTu (non treated soils)	> 3 CPTu	>12 m continuous readings (4 m/CPTu)	av. +/− 1σ

¹NOTE: The values outside of the range of "significant values to consider" could be further examined through additional and more localised investigations/tests. The Contractor shall preagree on the number of tests/boreholes and perform these additional tests/boreholes in the close vicinity of the initial one for obtaining a new set of values to compare to the baseline thresholds.

15.4 Unforeseeability

It is always difficult to accurately evaluate the nature of ground conditions. In fact, nature of itself is never completely predictable nor are natural events completely foreseeable. This, in itself can give rise to disputes.

The following should be taken into account whenever the foreseeability (or lack of) is to be assessed:

- information generally available at the "before invitation to bid" stage;
- information provided by the employer (such as geotechnical surveys);
- results of the contractor's own surveys at the bid preparation phase;
- subjective factors, that is, what a well-experienced "reasonable" contractor should and could foresee, based on the above information, sources and site investigation.

When an issue as to what was, or was not foreseeable is to be decided, the most significant argument, however, is what the contractor had allowed or enabled through their own on-site actions and how they had responded to the resulting situation. In respect of early warning principles, the rule is, therefore, to notify the employer of any unforeseeable conditions at once, whenever they appear, and to coordinate the steps to be taken to eliminate the related risk of non-compliance with the contract.

Another useful tool for analysing what is, and what is not, foreseeable may be a requirement placed upon the bidder to submit (along with their bids) all information and data used during bid preparation. This information will then become available to the other bidders. For example, subsequent surveys performed by the individual bidders and details of expenses incurred in connection with them. Should an unsuccessful bidder (at the preparation phase) assess a particular hazard as foreseeable, the successful bidder cannot claim the same hazard as being unforeseeable. These pieces of information can be considered when variations are to be assessed and the validity of the contractor's claims evaluated. On the employer's side, however, it is always necessary to take all appropriate measures to prevent abuse of any sensitive commercial information.

The regulation of unforeseeability differs between particular jurisdictions. In international construction projects, FIDIC has laid down a standard for dealing with unforeseeability in contracts. Regarding the clear specifics of underground construction projects, FIDIC came to an agreement with the ITA on the preparation of a new sample form of contract to cover tunneling projects (read the details in the section below). Currently, sources are being prepared for assignment and a workgroup is being put together to prepare the model. The FIDIC approach to unforeseeability is described below.

15.5 "Unforeseeability" according to FIDIC forms

In the CONS/1999 Red Book at Sub-Clause 1.1.6.8, the term "unforeseeable" is defined as "not reasonably foreseeable by an experienced Contractor by the date for submission of the Tender." As such, the definition is left general while it is assumed that it will be necessary to evaluate every particular situation on a case-by-case basis. FIDIC fails to define the term "unforeseen." This term evokes a kind of subjective negligence, omission and/or phenomenon that has already been encountered. This raises the question: where are the limits of what can be foreseen subject to the reasonable costs incurred and within the span of time for preparing the bid by an experienced contractor? Situations do of course appear that are absolutely unforeseeable or that could have been foreseen by chance only, by an exceptional expert, and so on.

One of the key differences between the P&DB/1999 Yellow Book and the EPC/1999 Silver Book is in the risk allocation of unforeseeable physical conditions.

P&DB defines the term "unforeseeable" in the same way as CONS. EPC does not define the term at all, assuming the definition to be redundant, as unforeseeable risks are commonly allocated to the contractor. Whereas, with reference to its foreword the EPC standard form of contract shall only be used if there is some certainty that the likelihood that unforeseeable risks eventuate is rather low.

Given a particular situation, unforeseeability must be evaluated in respect of time for completion and the statistical frequency of event occurrences according to historical records. The following example is quoted in *The FIDIC Contracts Guide* (2000) at Section 274. If the contract completion period is three years, then an experienced contractor should have foreseen an event that tends to appear once in six years, but an event appearing once every ten years is deemed unforeseeable. For details, see the charts in Appendix E.

Underground construction is a fast-growing market sector, on account of the growing demand for utilization of underground space for infrastructure. Underground construction is highly dependent on the geological, hydrogeological, and geotechnical ground mass characteristics, which have a defining influence on the means and methods required for the successful implementation of the works. In addition the difficulty in predicting ground behavior and foreseeable conditions implies an inherent uncertainty in underground construction, which gives rise to unique risks regarding construction practicability, time and cost. Recognizing these unique characteristics of underground construction projects, which demand special contractual provisions for their successful completion, FIDIC and ITA-AITES (the International Tunneling and Underground Space Association) have formed a joint task group (TG 10) to propose a new form of contract for tunneling and underground works. TG10 is composed by six technicians and one lawyer, and totals over 200 years experience in procurement, contracting, design, engineering, construction, and dispute resolution in underground works.

In order to allow for maximum flexibility of employers and contractors alike in the choice of their contract management process, and for ease of understanding by users, the task group decided to develop the new form based on the 2017 edition, with particular guidance notes for the preparation of tender documents by the employer. The draft of the new form is currently under review.

Generally in underground construction projects the following is recommended (Concepts presented by FIDIC-ITA Task Group 10 at the FIDIC International Contract Users' Conference, London, 2015):

1. **Allocation of risk**. The ground and groundwater-related risks should be assigned to the employer, as the party who will most benefit from the completed project and as the party that can best control these risks. The performance related risk arising from expected ground conditions should be assigned to the contractor.
2. **Disclosure of all available geological and geotechnical information**. All available information should be transmitted to prequalified tenderers, avoiding the use of exculpatory language.
3. **Inclusion of a contractual geotechnical baseline**. A geotechnical contractual baseline should be included that sets out the contractual limits of the conditions anticipated to be encountered during construction, thus providing clear distinctions in the contract documents between expected and unexpected underground conditions.
4. **Inclusion of an "Unforeseeable Physical Conditions" clause**. For the case that actual ground conditions encountered differ from the predicted ones, an "unforeseeable physical conditions" clause should be incorporated in the contract documents to allow relief from the unforeseeable conditions and allow the contractual flexibility to compensate for them.
5. **Implementation of a ground classification system and of supporting particular conditions that properly reflect the effort of excavation and stabilization**. The contractual classification of ground conditions should be based on the measures the contractor has to take in order to excavate and support the ground, so as to minimize claims and disputes.
6. **Time for completion is largely influenced by ground conditions**. For this reason, time adjustment according to actually encountered ground conditions should be regulated in the contract documents.
7. **Provision of a flexible mechanism for remuneration according to ground conditions, foreseen and unforeseen**. A unit price contract payment system for items that are affected by ground and groundwater conditions should be used. The unit price structure should be organized to facilitate the distinction between fixed costs, time-related costs, value-related costs, and quantity-related costs.

15.6 Site data

Another vital aspect of the foreseeability issue is site data provided to the contractor as required by the Sub-Clause 4.10 of CONS and P&DB. Under this Sub-Clause, it applies that the employer shall, before the base date (28 days prior to the latest date for submission of the tender), provide the contractor with information and all relevant data available to them dealing with the sub-surface, on-site hydrological and geological conditions and environmental aspects. On this basis, the employer shall also make available to the contractor all such data that they acquire after the base date. Responsibility for interpretation of all this data rests with the contractor. To the extent practicable (taking into account cost and time), the contractor shall be deemed to have obtained all necessary information as to risks, contingencies and other circumstances which may influence or affect the tender or works. To the same extent, the contractor shall be deemed (prior to submitting the tender) to have inspected and examined the site, its surroundings, the above data, and other available information and to have satisfied themselves with all relevant matters, including (without limitation):

- the form and nature of the site, including sub-surface conditions;
- the hydrological and climatic conditions;
- the extent and nature of the work and goods necessary for the execution and completion of the works and the remedying of any defects;
- the laws, procedures and labor practices of the country;
- the contractor's requirements for access, accommodation, facilities, personnel, power, transport, water, and other services.

Risk is allocated to the contractor only to the extent that is reasonable and proportionate to the cost of the bid (e.g., site investigation, surveys) and time available for preparation of the bid.

Conversely, Sub-Clause 4.10 of EPC/1999 Silver Book transfers risk fully to the contractor. EPC stipulates that the employer must, before the base date, provide the contractor with all information and significant data available to them (relating to on-site hydrological and geological conditions) and environmental aspects. Likewise, the employer shall also make available to the contractor all such data acquired after the base date. Responsibility for verification and interpretation of all data rests with the contractor. In other words, the wording in the Silver Book contains the contractor's obligation to verify the data. Furthermore, the employer bears no responsibility for the accuracy, adequacy or completeness of such data except for the data and information provided by the employer as per Sub-Clause 5.1 of the Silver Book:

- portions, data, and information that are stated in the contract as being fixed or the responsibility of the employer;
- definitions of intended purposes of the works or any parts thereof;
- criteria for the testing and performance of the completed works; and
- portions, data, and information which cannot be verified by the contractor, except as otherwise stated in the contract.

It is common practice for employers, for various reasons, to carry out site inspections and investigations (including geological surveys) at the tender stage. This is to accommodate for budget contingencies, to prepare the tender design, to assess the criteria for risk evaluation, and so on. There may also be a requirement upon the lender to conduct a respective risk analysis, feasibility study, and so on. At the tender stage, bidders need all such information gained by the employer to enable them to foresee (as much as possible) the work conditions and physical conditions that might affect implementation.

Site data are vital for the selection of technical solutions and methods of construction in case of the design-build (DB) projects. It may therefore be impractical for the employer to provide such particulars when they do not yet know the particular technical details. In *Metcalf Construction Co. v. the United States*, (U.S. Ct. of Appeals for the Federal Circuit, Case No. 2013-5041, Feb. 11, 2014) the U.S. Court of Appeals for the Federal Circuit dealt with the issue of the responsibility for errors in site data in a design-build contract and reversed a decision of the U.S. Court of Federal Claims.

The U.S. Court of Federal Claims said Metcalf was entitled to rely on the government soils report only "for bidding purposes," but not in performing the project. In rejecting the trial court reasoning, the Federal Circuit stated that the government cannot avoid contractor reliance on data and reports provided by the government merely by including broad disclaimers of liability for differing site conditions in the contract. That is not acceptable to the court. With regard to government's legal responsibility for pre-bid information, the court stated that "We do not think that the language can fairly be taken to shift that risk to Metcalf, especially when read together with the other government pronouncements, much less when read against the longstanding background presumption against finding broad disclaimers of liability for changed conditions in *United Contractors v. the United States*, 368 F.2d, 585, 598 (Ct.Cl. 1966)." (For more information see http://www.constructionrisk.com).

Some DB projects have lower levels of risks associated with physical conditions and their impact on implementation conditions. Typically these are projects covering technology contracting with the use of EPC contracts where all bidders need very detailed site data. Obviously, the risk of the above physical conditions lies fully with the contractor who needs to know, for the assessment and selection of a technical solution, how the above conditions will influence their design and what are the procedures and methods the contractor should select while realizing the project in the given conditions.

In the case of underground projects, it is in the interests of the employer to allocate these risks to themselves and to use, typically, P&DB/1999 Yellow Book rather than EPC/1999 Silver Book if the risks associated with the physical conditions and their influence on the implementation conditions are significant.

The employer should provide the bidders with as much site information about sub-surface and hydrological conditions as possible and it is in the best interests of both contracting parties (and to the construction project as a whole) to be familiar with all relevant, available data.

Such data, however, exclude any irrelevant data, incorrect data, expert opinions and interpretations and further information not related to sub-surface or hydrological conditions (sub-surface conditions are the conditions underneath the ground surface, including those inside a water mass and those underneath riverbeds or sea beds; hydrological conditions are water flows, including those in rivers and seas; environmental aspects include, for example pollutants and contamination occurrences) (FIDIC, 2010).

The employer must, therefore, make the contractor familiar with the relevant data (above), both at the stage of tender preparation and during realization. Deliberately or negligently concealing such information may have responsibility-related consequences in tort or even criminal law, for example, breach of contract, damages, and fraud.

The contractor must receive such relevant information in time to reflect its influence in the bid price and technical solution. The FIDIC forms, therefore, require the employer to provide this information no later than 28 days before the bid submission date.

It is very important to realize that the first FIDIC DB forms (i.e., P&DB), contain the same risk allocation of the unforeseeable physical conditions as CONS. CONS and P&DB require the contractor to interpret the information provided and to acquire all other necessary information as is reasonably possible. "Reasonable possibility" will depend on timing, costs and other aspects such as the possibility of inspecting the site, access to site, and so on.

This requirement is tempered by the provision "To the extent which was practicable (taking account of cost and time) ... " In other words, bearing in mind that only one tenderer will be awarded the contract and be in position to recover their tendering costs, it is not reasonable (either time-wise or cost-wise), to expect all tenderers to undertake major and expensive site and other investigations, even if such were physically possible (FIDIC, 2011a).

EPC/1999 Silver Book then requires of the contractor to further verify the site data provided by the employer.

Water-related construction projects by Robert Werth (Germany)

When it comes to standard forms of international infrastructure construction projects there is rarely an alternative other than to use the FIDIC model contract forms, especially when funding is required. And there are good reasons for it.

The FIDIC rainbow suite (Red/Yellow/Silver Books in 1999 and 2017 editions) supplemented by the harmonized version of the Red Book (Pink Book) and the new Gold Book provide excellent tools for almost any kind of infrastructure projects. This is valid also for the broad range of water-related infrastructure construction projects.

The Red Book (or CONS as this form is officially called) is still the most popular standard form for measured construction contracts that fit water-related projects such as dams, harbors, dredging works, ports, and so on. The main reason is the unforeseeable nature of those projects mainly in respect to hydrological and geological ground conditions. It is typical of the Red Book (or re-measurement in general) that such risks are allocated to the employer and the actual necessity of the works is measured based on prices and rates proposed by the contractor.

But the use of the Red Book is not an absolute rule. More and more we can see that the Yellow Book (or P&DB as this form is officially called) is being used. One of the most interesting examples is the $5.25 billion Panama Canal Expansion, the 80-kilometer (49-mile) canal, which currently handles about 5% of world trade. The project involves the construction of a third set of locks and is intended to double the capacity of the canal by enabling larger vessels to use the waterway. The Panama Canal Authority has awarded a dry-excavation contract to the Group United for the Canal, a consortium led by Spanish contractor Sacyr under design-build delivery method using the (highly amended) Yellow Book. Three consortiums competed with their proposals and a stipend of $15 million was divided equally between the unsuccessful tenderers. Selection criteria were split between 55% technical and 45% price. The winning proposal had three water-saving basins per lock, while another proposal had double the amount of water-saving basins, which obviously increased the size and price of the work, so it was not possible to compete on the basis of lowest price.

At the beginning of 2014, a dispute arose about unexpected cost overruns estimated at US$1.6 billion. The contractor claimed that the employer provided poor geological surveys for the ground beneath the locks, leading to greater than anticipated cost.

The employer argued that the contractor has failed to support or validate the claims for cost overruns but that they were willing to consider the claims made by the contractor, provided that the contractor supported and presented these claims within the mechanisms established in the contract. The employer had already paid the contractor about $160 million in additional costs in areas that are subject to price escalations such as structural steel, rebar, diesel, cement and labour.

A classic dispute scenario was encountered where the contractor threatened to slow down and stop work on the canal expansion project if the employer continued to withhold payment and the employer threatened to issue a termination letter that would come into effect after 14 days and hire a construction manager that would finish the 28% of the unfinished works with the local subcontractors.

The Red Book is also frequently used for networks (either potable water or sewage systems). Technically any plant, such as water plants or wastewater-treatment plants, needs to be connected via networks with the households in the respective area. When it comes to contractual views the most regular scenario is to use the Red Book for the networks and the Yellow Book for the plant. Whether it will be via two different contracts or a division in sections within only one contract depends on the situation. Both cases are quite common.

On the other hand, water treatment; wastewater treatment plants or any plants related to the handling of waste will most probably work better with the Yellow Book.

The idea that the employer could make use of contractor's experience in the design stage is widely accepted and a rising number of Yellow Book contracts in such projects is good proof of market acceptance. There is a long list of Yellow Book projects available, such as the wastewater treatment plants for Vilnius in Lithuania, completed in 2010, at a cost of €45 million; Kotla Järve in Estonia, in 2009, at a cost of €26 million; Warsaw in Poland, in 2012, at a cost of €550 million; Nicosia in Cyprus, in 2012, at a cost of €25 million; Kielce in Poland, in 2012, at a cost of €58 million.

A good example of a plant typically executed under Yellow Book is the wastewater treatment plant. The experience of the contractor with design and/or construction under such specific circumstances may generate an advantage to the employer also for the whole operation phase. Employers do not want to refuse such an advantage by providing a detailed design with no contractor intervention. Another advantage for employers may be to include the operation period in the contract. That requires the contractor to train the employer's personnel and prove that it is possible to run the plant and secure all required performance parameters for a longer period (in contrast to only passing the test on completion under standard design-build delivery method). If the employer prefers such an arrangement, the main contract is the Yellow Book in combination with another part of the contract for operation of the work (as a part of the original tender already). It is not recommended setting up the operation period for longer than two years and it is also recommended having a clear distinction between the contractor's obligations under the design-build phase and the operation phase. Otherwise, it may create a scenario in which the operation phase would be part of the time for completion and the defect notification period would only start after the operation phase.

If the contractor is to operate the plant for a longer period and if they also bring their own personnel for the operation, then the so-called Gold Book might be the best option. The Gold Book (or DBO as this form is officially called) was invented for the design and build of a plant with minimum of 10 years of operations under the responsibility of the Contractor.

The Silver Book (or EPC as this form is officially called) is not widely used in water-related projects as under the EPC arrangement, the employers complain about the lack of control over technical solutions once the contract is signed and the contractors most likely do not want to accept the broad risk allocation on their side. However, there are some particular cases where the Silver Book perfectly suits, even in water-related projects.

This is the case in the construction of seawater desalination plants, where the Silver Book suits perfectly. The site is usually small so the ground conditions risk is reduced and easier to control and evaluate. There are no heavy loads to be considered, the foundations are simpler and the total risk remains small. The performance requirements for effluent are easily defined, there are clear measurements available and there is always a separate neutral authority supervising the results. On the other hand, there are no enormous amounts of by-products, which may have a significant impact on the price of the product in future (like sludge or other residues that originate within the sludge treatment in wastewater treatments plants, for example).

The site can be handed over to the contractor and when production starts, of course with all the relevant tests certified, the repayment can be agreed as a lump sum or by measurement of the water produced within a certain period.

For both Silver and Gold Book forms, the financing provided by contractor can be added for the whole or a defined part of the project. The repayment may be done within the monthly fee for operation cost. FIDIC does not provide a standard form for a DBFO delivery method, that is, where the contractor provides financing. However, financing may be included in the DBO contract within the particular conditions. Securities to be provided by the contractors are then as important as with any other loan agreement and they have to be tailored to the specific circumstances.

Robert Werth
FIDIC international Trainer
Adjudicator at FIDIC President's List
Germany

15.7 Sufficiency of the accepted contract amount

In Sub-Clause 4.11, CONS/1999 Red Book and P&DB/1999 Yellow Book stipulate that the contractor shall be deemed to have satisfied themselves as to the correctness and sufficiency of the accepted contract amount, and have based the accepted contract amount on the data, interpretations, necessary information, inspections, examinations, and satisfaction as to all relevant matters referred to in Sub-Clause 4.10 (and any further data) relevant to the contractor's design. Unless otherwise stated in the contract, the accepted contract amount covers all the contractor's obligations under the contract and all things necessary for the proper design, execution, and completion of the works and the remedying of any defects. EPC/1999 Silver Book allocates the risk of the unforeseeable physical conditions to the contractor and does not assume any significant modifications in price for the work that might result in connection with unforeseeable physical conditions.

15.8 Unforeseeable physical conditions

CONS/1999 Red Book and P&DB/1999 Yellow Book define (in Sub-Clause 4.12) "physical conditions" to mean "natural physical conditions and manmade and other physical obstructions and pollutants, which the contractor encounters on the site when executing works, including sub-surface and hydrological conditions." Climatic conditions are excluded.

These conditions are encountered on any construction site, that is, where the project is realized (permanent works) and where the technologies and materials are to be supplied, as well as any other places that might be specified in the contract as parts of the site. Adverse impacts of climatic conditions on sites are not, therefore, regulated by this sub-clause. Hydrological conditions also include water flows caused by off-site climatic phenomena. On-site physical conditions exclude on-site climatic conditions, and, therefore, the hydrological consequences of these on-site climatic conditions (FIDIC, 2000).

Adverse climatic conditions are covered separately as a shared risk pursuant to Sub-Clause 8.4 where the contractor may only claim extensions of time for completion but not additional payment. Occurrences of extremely adverse natural forces and their impacts are then covered as an employer risk and *force majeure*, see Section 15.10.

If the contractor encounters adverse physical conditions that they consider unforeseeable, they must notify them to the engineer as soon as practicable. This notice shall describe the physical conditions so they can be inspected by the engineer. The notice shall set out the reasons why the contractor considers them to be unforeseeable. The contractor shall continue executing the works, using such proper and reasonable measures as are appropriate for the physical conditions and shall comply with any instructions which the engineer may give. Where an instruction implies a variation, further work shall follow the variation procedures outlined in the contract, that is, mainly the price increase in connection with the variation shall be paid to the contractor.

Should the encountered physical conditions not be deemed a *force majeure*, the contractor must continue to realize the project without waiting for the engineer's instructions.

It is further stipulated by Sub-Clause 4.12 that:

> If and to the extent that the contractor encounters physical conditions which are unforeseeable, gives such a notice, suffers delay and/or incurs cost due to these conditions, the contractor shall be entitled to an extension of time for any such delay, if completion is or will be delayed and payment of any such cost shall be included in the contract price.

In other words, the contractor cannot add their profit markup to the additional costs due to these unforeseeable physical conditions. Here, it is again a shared risk, whereas the costs pursuant to the FIDIC forms mean all expenditure reasonably incurred (or to be incurred) by the contractor, whether on or off the site, including overhead and similar charges, but not profit.

Having received notice of the physical conditions and their inspection, the engineer shall decide if, and to what extent, these conditions are unforeseeable and decide on the contractor's claims. The engineer may reduce the claim for additional payment if, during the implementation of similar works, more favorable conditions appear than those that could have been reasonably foreseen when the contractor submitted their bid. The total sum, however, may not result in a reduced price for the work. The engineer must not delay payment of a contractor's claim beyond the point in time when they verify the "favorability" of the conditions during implementation of similar works.

Concerning risk allocation, a substantial shift is encountered in Sub-Clause 4.12 of the FIDIC EPC/1999 Silver Book, which has an updated title "*Unforeseeable Difficulties.*" Sub-Clause 4.12 stipulates that: "except as otherwise stated in the Contract, the Contractor shall be deemed to have obtained all necessary information as to risks, contingencies and other circumstances which may influence or affect the Works." It is further stipulated that the contractor—by signing the contract—accepts total responsibility for having foreseen all difficulties and costs of successfully completing the works and the contract price shall not be adjusted to take account of any unforeseen difficulties or costs.

This provision clearly stipulates that risk is allocated to the contractor except in situations defined by the contract (such as *force majeure*). *Force majeure* and its relationship with foreseeability are discussed below.

It is highly probable that this sub-clause and some of the other sub-clauses of the EPC/1999 Silver Book might be—depending on the circumstances—considered void by courts in some jurisdictions (see the Section 13.10).

Ground conditions risk in an EPC contract for a gas treatment plant by Cristina Della Moretta (Italy)

As an in-house construction lawyer, I have had the chance to work on many complex EPC projects in Mediterranean regions, such as Algeria, Tunisia, and the Middle East, as well as in Asiatic regions, such as Korea, Japan, and Thailand. Recently, I worked on a project as a contract manager, where latent and hidden site conditions were encountered in subsoil during the execution.

The project scope of work was the EPC for a gas treatment plant of approximately 235 mil. USD value, negotiated privately among the parties. The duration was estimated in twenty-five (25) months, but due to disruptions caused by both the employer and a neutral third party authority, hired by the client in charge of the inspections of site conditions, the execution and completion of the project was delayed and postponed for more than twelve (12) months. The third party authority was hired for geotechnical, geohazards investigation, and geotechnical engineering providing assistance on foundations and ground reinforcement.

The employer, a state oil company, provided the bidders of the tender regulated by international private law rules with its internal bespoke standard general and special terms and conditions of the contract and the related documentation. The law applicable to the contract was that of England and Wales.

The contract provided a specific duty on the contractor side to be acquainted of works and site conditions as follows:

> *"Contractor hereby represents and warrants that prior to entering into the Contract he has visited site and has fully acquainted himself as to all Site conditions which could affect the performance of the work and/or his obligations under the Contract including: i) the atmospheric (presence of air-born dust), meteorological (including but not limited to sand storms or lifting sand), topographic, geological and subsurface conditions; ii) all and any other general and local difficulties and conditions to be encountered and/or other conditions of the site that affect or may affect Contractor's performance of the work and contract obligations."*

Moreover, since the contractor accepted responsibilities of the performance of the work in case of a failure of a proper evaluation on the above-mentioned site conditions he would have not been entitled to claim employer for costs reimbursement and to an extension of time with exception of *"latent and hidden defects on site condition"* unforeseeable at that moment and discovered only at a later stage during the excavation.

As a consequence, contractor carried out an in-depth geotechnical and geological study on subsoil site conditions. According to these studies and analysis, the site was suitable for the following construction activities to be performed during the execution of the project. These results were aligned with information provided by the employer during the bidding phase to all the participants to the bid.

According to the said information, the employer requested the contractor to supply foundations based on piling of a certain type, therefore, contractor developed the foundation design and immediately started the excavations as soon such design was approved by the employer and the third party authority.

But at a certain point the contractor discovered five unexpected small cavities in a circumscribed area. The contractor immediately notified the employer of the above-mentioned discovery.

As a consequence, the employer and the third party authority immediately withdrew the approval of the foundation drawings previously released, forcing the contractor to stop the excavations. With no explanation and without providing evidence, employer, and third party authority requested contractor to perform additional geotechnical soil investigations throughout the gas treatment plant site ensuring that no critical situation was present prior to the prosecution of the excavations.

The contractor took immediate action, mobilizing the third party authority as well as contractor's geotechnical consultant in order to evaluate the situation. The results of such new investigations confirmed that no abnormal soil conditions were present, but that the latent and hidden site conditions were related only to that specific area of the site. Consistent results have been obtained, all geotechnical and chemical parameters were in line and congruent with the investigations performed before the beginning of the project execution, confirming that contractor's original foundations were correct and that subsoil was suitable to go ahead with the excavations and to execute the works.

Notwithstanding that, the employer requested the contractor to comply with a list of rigid inclusions, which consisted in reinforcing and improving soil conditions of a wide site area of the plant throughout a series of piles and activities. This instruction had direct consequences also to the design engineer of the plant changing the original scope of work.

The employer's and third party authority's decision was only due with the scope to further reduce their own risk profile beyond any contractual provision or international standards. In fact, neither employer nor the third party authority had been able to demonstrate the necessity of a soil improvement.

This instruction had direct consequences also to the design engineer of the plant changing the scope of work.

The contractor asked for employer's authorization to resume works, but unfortunately, the employer rejected such request preventing the contractor to carry out the project activities on time as per the project schedule.

Therefore, the contractor immediately noticed employer that such instruction would entitle him to time extension and costs compensation for the additional costs occurred, and changes in the design engineer since the employer had prevented contractor to execute the construction works and caused the contractor to incur additional costs, which he would not otherwise have incurred.

In accordance to *"Prevention principle,"* which is a long-established common law doctrine and which is applicable to this case, a party to a contract may not enforce a contractual obligation against the other party where it has prevented that party from performing that obligation. This ensures that a party is not entitled to take advantage of its own default.

In the present case, as described above, the employer prevented the contractor from completing work by the contractual completion date causing disruptions to contractor. Moreover, the contract did not provide the required additional time (*"Act of prevention"*) and consequently the contractor must only be required to complete the work on a *"reasonable time"* and in addition was entitled to costs compensation.

In fact although the contract provided an extension of time clause for the specific case of latent and hidden defects at site: *"Contractors shall be entitled to request a change order for an extension in completion date of any part of work, with the corresponding modification to the work time schedule, for that part of the work so affected, if the extension is required because of any of the following reasons:*

latent and hidden site conditions which Contractor could by no means have determined or anticipated even in the course of diligent sight surveys to be carried out by Contractor and assessments as required under Article 12.1, provided that such site conditions have a direct effect on the work time schedule and Contractor could not have avoided or mitigated this effect," the contract also provided that in case of concurrent delay of the contractor in performing its activities, such as happened in the present case, no time extension could be recognized:

> *"Furthermore, no time extension shall be allowed under the present Article for any period overlapping with delays due to any cause for which Contractor is not entitled to request a time extension".*

The employer strongly disagreed with the contractor position saying that the cause of such cavities would have been known elements for contractor, such as agriculture, climatic conditions, and ground water. The susceptibility of gypsum to dissolution when exposed to these elements would have been well known. The contractor was well aware of agricultural use of the site prior to execution of the contract.

Latent and hidden site conditions which contractor by no means determined and other eventual latent and hidden defect must be attributable to the employer's bid documents, since the presence of gypsum in the soil was well known to all parties, but neither employer nor geotechnical reports performed before and after the contract signature highlighted any risk of cavities formation due to presence of gypsum. Since the contractor had always complied with its contractual obligations supporting the employer instructions and following the international standards according to the *"Prevention Principle"* after a long period of discussions and negotiations the parties signed a settlement the principles of which were a balance of both contractor's and employer's rights.

In fact, considering that according to the *"prevention principle"* the contractor requested:

(i) the postponement of the completion date;
(ii) LDs to be declared unenforceable;
(iii) duty to complete the work on a "reasonable time" (i.e., time is set *"at large"*);
(iv) a proper compensation for its additional costs incurred as a result of the Act of Prevention (including prolongation costs, disruption costs, and additional financial costs) the employer replied that these requests could not been accepted since the contractor was responsible of a concurrent delay.

At the end, the settlement established that all the claims had been settled and extinguished and an adjustment to the completion date and contract price was agreed with loss on both parties.

The events changed the original contract price in fact with these adjustments, the contract price for all purposes under the contract including the calculation of liquidated damages was therefore agreed to be 314,120,650 US $.

In conclusion, it is strongly suggested both for employers and contractors to draft specific clauses, which protect themselves from risks related to underground unknown or unforeseen site conditions:

on employers side, clauses, which provide (i) time bar for contractor's notice; (ii) limit to compensation for direct job site costs incurred by contractor; on contractor side, clauses, which: (i) avoid that a concurrent delay between the parties could exclude the contractor's right to an extension of time or to a costs compensation; (ii) limit the disclaimer of the accuracy of site information reflected in the bid documents; (iii) carry out an in-depth site inspection making photographs and written reports;

As a general rule prior to bid the contractor must investigate the law applicable to the contract and what it provides with respect to allocation of site condition risks and in particular those related to unforeseeable and unforeseen site conditions.

Cristina Della Moretta, LL.M.
Lawyer – Contract Manager
Maire Tecnimont (Milan – Italy)

15.9 Unforeseeable operation of the forces of nature

The FIDIC CONS/1999 Red Book and P&DB/1999 Yellow Book define as employer's risk: "all operation of the forces of nature which are unforeseeable or against which an experienced contractor could not reasonably have been expected to have taken adequate preventative precautions" (as per Sub-Clause 17.3 h). EPC/1999 Silver Book allocates this risk to the contractor—with exception of the situation when the consequences of such unforeseeable natural forces would be so adverse that they would acquire the nature of *force majeure* (Clause 19 of the FIDIC forms).

If, and to what extent, natural, unforeseeable processes lead to losses or damaged construction work, the contractor must promptly give notice to the engineer and shall rectify this loss or damage to the extent required by the engineer.

Should the contractor suffer a delay or costs due to remedying this loss or damage, the contractor shall submit to the engineer an additional notice and will have the right to claim an extension of time due to such delay. If the completion is (or will be) delayed, a claim for payment and any associated costs will be included in the contract price.

Thus, the contractor can claim compensation for losses, damage, expenses for remedy, and the costs caused by extensions of time for completion due to a loss, damage or remedy, or even expenditures due to late instructions of the engineer during the remedying of losses and damages.

Under the FIDIC forms, insurance for works and contractor's equipment under Sub-Clause 18.2 shall also cover loss or damage to a part of the works which is attributable to the use or occupation by the employer of another part of the works, and loss or damage from the risks listed in sub-paragraphs (c), (g), and (h) of Sub-Clause 17.3, excluding (in each case) risks which are not insurable on commercially reasonable terms. This means that unforeseeable events caused by the forces of nature must be insured by the contractor.

Clairvoyance: A contractor's duty? by Gustavo Paredes and Katherine Waidhofer (Peru)

If clairvoyance were an exact science, then the wizard Merlin, Nostradamus, St. Malachy, and others would be contractors. However, that extrasensory perception without the help of technical means goes beyond earthly contractual agreements. But while this may seem to be clear, it is not so clear in the field of construction claims and disputes, because sometimes the contractor must assume obligations that go beyond their extrasensory perceptions.

One of the most frequent complaints by contractors at the worksite concerns unexpected soil conditions. It often happens that during the execution of the work, the contractor finds that the characteristics of the soil or subsoil on which he has to build differ from those physical or mechanical characteristics referred to in soil and/or subsoil studies carried out as part of the tender design.

This situation (unforeseen soil conditions) is known as the "great risk" in the construction industry. This was the term used by the Supreme Court of New Jersey in the case *PT & L Construction Co. Inc. v. the State of New Jersey* (1987). But this great risk had been recognized even earlier in *Foster Construction v. the United States* (1970).

Certainly, to complete the construction work, which is the purpose of the work contract, higher costs will be incurred to overcome unforeseen soil condition issues and complete the construction work. So, the question the psychic asks herself is: who should bear the higher costs for the execution of the work in unforeseen circumstances, the owner, or the contractor?

Also, dealing with unforeseen soil conditions to bring them closer to the conditions detailed in the project information may also affect the critical path and require additional time. Then another question arises: is the contractor entitled to an extension of the contract term to cover the extra overheads, or does the employer have the right to impose penalties for the work delay?

Now, to predict the future it is essential to know who assumed the risk for the unforeseen soil and/or subsoil conditions: the employer or the contractor?

Like almost all answers in matters of law, "It depends." Determining which party in a construction contract has assumed the "great risk" basically depends on the type of construction contract being executed and the obligations assumed by the parties. Then we can foresee how the great risk is assumed in two of the most commonly used forms of work contract: a construction contract designed by the employer and a turnkey contract.

In a construction contract designed by the employer, the main obligation of the contractor consists of the construction of the work, according to the requirements and engineering provided by the employer. In this type of contract, the contractor receives the design and carries out the construction process with the obligation to deliver the completed works in full accordance with the terms and instructions received from the employer.

In this case, the preparation of the exploration and soil mechanics study is not one of the contractor's obligations; neither is the contractor responsible for developing the design or its technical suitability. Therefore, under this type of contract, the contractor does not assume the risk for unforeseen soil conditions.

This is accepted practice in the construction industry. For example, Sub-Clause 4.12 of the Conditions of Contract for Construction for Building and Engineering Works designed by the Employer (the Red Book) of the International Federation of Consulting Engineers (FIDIC), states that if the contractor encounters adverse physical conditions considered unforeseeable, he should notify the Engineer as soon as possible.

In this case, it is understood that the contractor has the right to an extension of time or payment of additional costs, provided that it has been ascertained that the conditions were unforeseeable, that the contractor had duly notified the situation and had suffered some delay or incurred additional costs resulting from these conditions.

However, in this type of contract there is often a clause (drafted by the employer, not covered by the FIDIC Red Book), usually in a section called "contractor's statements," to which not much attention is usually paid. However, during the claim stage or in an arbitration itself, this clause can become one of the main defence weapons available to the employer when facing claims from the contractor.

We refer to that clause in which the contractor declares his awareness, for the purposes of executing the works, of the physical and mechanical soil and subsoil conditions of the area where the work is to be executed, and is satisfied with them. It is even customary for the contactor to visit and inspect the area, and this action is also included in his declaration.

With this clause has the cautious—or astute—employer transferred the "great risk" of unforeseen soil conditions to the contractor? Usually, under this type of contract it is the responsibility of the employer. In other words, is it the contractor's duty to be clairvoyant as well? The answer is no.

This declaration of awareness does not in itself transfer the "great risk" from the principal or owner to the contractor. This declaration must be understood as having limits of responsibility based on information received from the employer; or based on any information regarding the soil characteristics and properties that can be obtained by the contractor from an inspection of the area prior to construction, but does not make the contractor responsible for those unforeseen conditions.

For example, in *Spearin v. the United States* (1918), which is considered a leading case in construction law, the U.S. Supreme Court determined that if the contractor is obliged to build according to the plans and specifications prepared by the employer, the contractor will not be liable for the consequences of the defects in the plans and specifications. The court said that the owner's liability for the specifications is not affected by the usual clauses requiring contractors to visit the site, review plans, and to inform themselves of the requirements of the work. Therefore, for the "great risk" to be transferred to the contractor, there must be a clear and express agreement that leaves no doubt regarding the assumption of this risk by the contractor. This, in itself, further includes the contractor's right to factor this risk into his price.

A diligent contractor, when accepting this risk, will perform a "validation" of that information provided by the employer, and will even carry out further studies himself. Consequently, this risk will be reflected in the contract price.

Notwithstanding this, in most Latin American civil codes, the contractor's obligation is to immediately report to the principal any soil defects or the poor quality of any materials supplied by the employer, if discovered prior to or during the execution of the works and that may compromise their normal execution. In Peru, both the civil code and the public procurement law clearly make the contractor responsible for the immediate reporting of soil defects once identified. Many arbitral awards have been made on the application of this aspect of the law.

Interpretation of this obligation must depend on a consideration of the particular contractor concerned. If the contractor is experienced, he would be expected to give warning of the poor quality of the soil or unforeseen conditions as soon as possible, and not when the works are at an advanced stage.

The prompt reporting of such problems by the contractor could mean the difference between his receiving the full amount of the costs incurred to overcome these issues or only receiving partial payment if failing to act in accordance with the standards expected of an experienced contractor by allowing the works to advance (despite being aware or when he should have been aware), of the soil conditions.

However, the situation regarding "turnkey" contracts is different. There is no specific definition of this kind of contract in the Peruvian legislation; nevertheless, both nationally and internationally, it is understood and accepted as one in which the contractor is responsible for the design, procurement, construction, and operation of the works.

In this type of contract, the contractor assumes responsibility for unforeseen soil conditions. For example, Sub-Clause 4.12 of the General Conditions of Contract for EPC/Turnkey projects of the FIDIC Silver Book provides, in general terms, that unless otherwise stated in the contract, it will be assumed that the contractor has obtained all necessary information about the risks that may influence or affect the works; accepts full responsibility for foreseeing any difficulty and cost in the proper completion of the works, and that the contract price will not be adjusted due to unforeseen difficulties or costs. This is reasonable, given that the contractor, operating as a specialist and expert, should have made adequate provision for the reasonable scope of such risk in the price offered and contracted. Under Peruvian Public Procurement law, a similar design of contract is used, known in Spanish as "*concurso oferta,*" which follows the same rationale in economic terms and scope of liability.

However, it is important to point out that in certain cases such as where the project mainly involves underground works and tunnels and where subsoil conditions make it extremely difficult for the contractor to carry out inspections at the bidding stage, FIDIC does not recommend the use of the Silver Book. In these circumstances, the transfer of the risk to the contractor would disproportionately affect the contractual balance between the parties.

In conclusion, the answers to the questions posed at the beginning of this case study should be found in the specific obligations assumed by the parties in the work contract. However, in the absence of any express agreement in the contract, we can identify the type of contract being executed and use that as the starting point to determine who has taken the "great risk," and from there, determine the rights of the parties to guide efficient claims handling on site.

As can be seen, then, it is not necessary to resort to occult sciences or withdraw from reality to predict what will happen to a claim and/or charging of the duty of clairvoyance. The magic formula is knowing your customer's business.

Gustavo Paredes
Partner in NPG Abogados
Founder member of Construlegal and the Peruvian Society of Construction Law
Lecturer in Construction Law
Universidad Peruana de Ciencias Aplicadas Graduate School
Peru

Katherine Waidhofer
Lawyer
Member of the NPG Abogados Dispute Team
Specialist in construction law and arbitration
Peru

15.10 Force majeure

An unforeseeable physical phenomenon can become a *force majeure* event. FIDIC defines *force majeure* in Sub-Clause 19.1 as:

> an exceptional event or circumstance which is beyond a party's control, which such party could not reasonably have provided against before entering into the contract, which, having arisen, such party could not reasonably have avoided or overcome and which is not substantially attributable to the other party.

Force majeure must, therefore, be an exceptional event whether foreseeable or not. Under *force majeure* the contractor can claim an extension of the time for completion as well as additional payment. In Sub-Clause 19.1 (v) of EPC, a demonstrative enumeration of natural catastrophes such as earthquakes, hurricanes, typhoons, or volcanic activity is specified as being subject to a contactor's claims for an extension of time for completion only. Exclusively man-made *force majeure* events are subject to contractor's claims for additional payment. If a *force majeure* impedes execution of the unfinished construction work as a whole, for (1) a continuous period of 84 days, or (2) repeating spans of time adding up to more than 140 days altogether (for the same reason of the reported *force majeure*), then one of the contracting parties can give notice to the other of its termination of the contract.

It is interesting to note that FIDIC has moved away from using the term *force majeure* because of its unclear nature, diversity and definition in individual jurisdictions. FIDIC now refers to the respective issues as "exceptional risks."

15.11 Release from performance under law

In its extreme form, an unforeseeable physical phenomenon may lead to release from performance according to the governing law of contract. Under the FIDIC forms (Sub-Clause 19.6), it is stipulated that:

> If any event or circumstance outside the control of the Parties (including, but not limited to, Force Majeure) arises which makes it impossible or unlawful for either or both Parties to fulfil its or their contractual obligations or which, under the law governing the contract, entitles the parties to be released from further performance of the contract, then upon notice by either party to the other party of such event or circumstance the parties shall be discharged from further performance, without prejudice to the rights of either party in respect of any previous breach of the contract.

References

FIDIC (2000). *The FIDIC Contracts Guide* (1st Edition). FIDIC, Lausanne.
FIDIC (2010). *Conditions of Contract for Construction*. MDB Harmonised Edition. FIDIC, Lausanne.
FIDIC (2011). *FIDIC DBO Contract Guide* (1st Edition). FIDIC, Lausanne.

Further reading

Členové Pracovní Skupiny Čtuk Pro Konvenční Tunelování (2006). *Zásady a principy NRTM jako převažující metody konvenčního tunelování v. ČR*. Český tunelářský komitét ITA/AITES pro vlastní potřebu, Prague.
FIDIC (1999a). *Conditions of Contract for Construction* (1st Edition). FIDIC, Lausanne.
FIDIC (1999b). *Conditions of Contract for Plant and Design-Build*. (1st Edition). FIDIC, Lausanne.
FIDIC (1999c). *Conditions of Contract for EPC/Turnkey Projects* (1st Edition). FIDIC, Lausanne.
FIDIC (2008). *Conditions of Contract for Design, Build and Operate Projects*. (1st Edition). FIDIC, Lausanne.

FIDIC (2011b). *FIDIC Procurement Procedures Guide.* (1st Edition). FIDIC, Lausanne.

Kinlan, D. and Roukema, D. (2010). Adverse physical conditions and the Experienced Contractor Test. *Terra et Aqua*, 119, 3–13.

Klee, L. and Hruška, D. (2013) How to efficiently allocate the risk of unforeseeable physical conditions in underground construction? *Tunel* 3/2013.

Schneider, E. and Spiegl, M. (2012). *Contract Models for TBM Drives in Hard Rock: Codes in Austria and Switzerland and their Practical Implementation.* Berlin: Ernst & Sohn Verlag für Architektur und technische Wissenschaften GmbH & Co. KG.

The Association of British Insurers and British Tunnelling Society (2003). *The Joint Code of Practice for Risk Management of Tunnel Works in the UK.* British Tunnelling Society, London.

Walton, J.G. (2007). Unforeseen ground conditions and allocation of risks before the roof caved in. In *Society of Construction Law*, Auckland, New Zealand.

Working Group 19 Conventional Tunneling (2012). *Guidelines on Contractual Aspects of Conventional Tunnelling.* 4th draft. ITA/AITES 2012.

Website

http://www.constructionrisk.com.

16 Securities

16.1 Securities in construction

Numerous risks burden construction projects. These risks should ideally be allocated to the project participants (mainly to the contractor and the employer) based on their respective abilities to control them. The parties should insure themselves against individual risks but this is not always possible because some risks are non-insurable. In general, non-insurable risks include the risk that the contractor will fail to perform in accordance with the contract (executing the works and remedying the defects within the defects notification period) and the risk that the employer will fail to pay. An exception to the former is the so-called *Subcontractor Default Insurance* used in the United States. If participants cannot insure risks by way of an insurance policy, they may secure them by contractual means or further specific instruments. Examples of the former include contractual penalties and retention money. Examples of the latter include bank documents such as letters of credit, standby letters of credit, and bank guarantees.

The bank guarantee has become so popular during recent decades that it now appears in most standard forms of contracts in large construction projects. The principle of bank guarantees is that the bank will pay to the contractor or employer (at their request) a pre-agreed sum that will compensate adverse implications of the failure to act or of defective performance by either of the parties should the contractor or the employer fail to meet their obligations.

The requirement to issue such guarantees may sometimes come not only from the contract itself but directly by law. This is the case in the event of a guarantee for payment for the works in accordance with *Umowy o roboty budowlane* (contract for works) in Poland or where the public contracts are to be secured; for example, in Germany or the United States.

16.2 Bank guarantees

A bank guarantee is a versatile financial instrument that allows both financial and the non-financial obligations to be secured in national and international contracts entered into by legal (corporate) persons or natural persons as contractors or employers.

The most frequent types of guarantees in practice secure the duty to sign the contract by the contractor, contractor performance, employer advance payment, contractor duty to repair defects in the defects notification period and the guarantee that is used in place of retention money. Contractor guarantees are mainly for non-payment obligations to secure their performance. On the employer's side, there are payment guarantees securing the employer's duty to pay for the works, goods, or services received. Note: the above guarantees may be known by other names, depending on the jurisdiction.

The building construction and civil engineering industry rank themselves among the largest "users" of bank guarantees in terms of their amounts and frequency of use. The most common types of guarantees used in construction are tender guarantees (bid bonds), that is, security of the contractor's duty to sign the contract.

Regarding bank guarantees, a new party (the guarantor) with well-controlled and declared credit stands between the contractor and the employer. The guarantor secures the contractual duties of the parties in case of breach of contract. Should one of the parties fail to perform, the guarantor shall pay an agreed amount to the other party. The force of security is further enhanced by the abstract nature of such a bank guarantee and by the bank's duty to perform on the first demand without any objections. It implies, in practice, that the bank does not inquire into whether or not the breach of the contract really occurred and, further, is not even entitled to raise objections that the parties might otherwise raise between themselves.

16.3 Functions and parameters of bank guarantees

16.3.1 Vadium/tender guarantee/bid bond

- Beneficiary: The employer
- Ordering party: The contractor
- Amount: 1% to 5% of the future contract price
- Purpose: To secure the contractor's duty to sign the contract
- Substantial validity: Expiry of tendering period/validity of tender.

A tender guarantee will protect the employer against the risk that a contractor (the participant of the tender) becomes disinterested for any reason whatsoever, withdraws their bid prematurely, fails to sign the contract or to observe the parameters of their bid. The employer is thus compensated for the cost arising from the postponement of execution of the works, re-tendering, and so on. Submission of such a guarantee is often a precondition for admission to a particular public procurement.

16.3.2 Advance payment guarantee/down payment guarantee/advance payment bond

- Beneficiary: The employer
- Ordering party: The contractor
- Amount: 5% to 30% of contract price
- Purpose: To secure return of the advance payment should the contractor fail to perform
- Effectiveness clause: Effectiveness of guarantee is usually subject to payment of an advance payment to the contractor's particular account kept by an issuing bank
- Substantial validity: Foreseeable time for completion of delivery (+30 days).

This guarantee will find its application in construction projects with the contractor being funded by means of advance payments. The guarantee will secure to the employer return of the advance payment for the unaccomplished part of the obligation for which the advance payment had been given.

16.3.3 Performance guarantee/final guarantee/performance bond

- Beneficiary: The employer
- Ordering party: The contractor
- Amount: 5% to 10% of the contract price
- Purpose: To secure fulfilment of the contractor's contractual obligations
- Substantial validity: Until completion of the contract works (signing of the Taking-Over Certificate +30 days).

This guarantee secures the risk that the contractor may, for any reason whatsoever, breach their duty to complete the works. The guarantee is to cover, for example, the cost incurred in connection with such non-completion. The employer will usually require the security once the contract is signed or shortly after.

16.3.4 Warranty guarantee/maintenance guarantee/maintenance bond

- Beneficiary: The employer
- Ordering party: The contractor
- Amount: 5% to 10% of the contract price
- Purpose: To secure the contractor's contractual duty to repair all defects within the defects notification period and protect the employer against the contractor's unwillingness or inability to remedy the defects
- Substantial validity: Duration of the defects notification period.

This type of guarantee is required by the employer for works, plant, and so on for which a defects notification period has been agreed. If the contractor fails to remedy the defects within this period, the employer will use the guarantee to acquire funds to remedy the defects using the services of another contractor, if any.

16.3.5 Retention guarantee/retention bond

- Beneficiary: The employer
- Ordering party: The contractor
- Amount: 5% to 10% of the contract price
- Purpose: To secure the contractor's contractual duty to repair all defects within the defects notification period
- Effectiveness clause: Effectiveness of the guarantee is usually subject to payment of retention money to a particular account (usually at the issuing bank)
- Substantial validity: Completion of a certain stage of the project, expiry of defects notification period.

This guarantee is applied where the employer withholds, during the course of a construction project, a certain amount (retention) from payments to the contractor. If, however, the contractor wants to get the retention earlier, they may submit the bank guarantee at the level of the pre-agreed retention with the employer's consent.

16.3.6 Payment guarantee/payment bond

- Beneficiary: The contractor
- Ordering party: The employer
- Amount: As per contract (e.g., the full contract price, its portion, and so on)
- Purpose: To secure the employer's duty to pay
- Reduction clause: Each time after a partial payment is effected
- Substantial validity: 30 days after maturity of the final payment obligation.

This guarantee will secure the contractor against the employer's insolvency. The validity of such a guarantee is always limited by a fixed date. The term of validity expresses exactly when the rights of the guarantee beneficiary will expire and the timeframe for which the bank remains obliged to this beneficiary.

16.4 Specifics of retention guarantee

Retention guarantees are commonly used in construction projects. Retention, or the money withheld, is perceived as a portion of the contract price the employer will "retain" and pay to the contractor once the works/goods/services are taken over or in response to an interim invoice. This will be at some later date set out in the contract (such as after completion of a certain stage of the project, once a milestone is fulfilled or defect notification period expires). The retention is usually determined as a percentage and forms part of the agreed payment conditions.

The reason behind "withholding" a portion of the contract sum (usually at the level of 5% to 10%) is the employer's endeavor to secure fulfilment of the conditions of contract on the side of the contractor and to protect themselves against the contractor's unwillingness, lack of will, or impossibility of remedying the defects within the defects notification period.

The parties can agree on earlier payment of this retention—usually upon taking over of the works or once a certain milestone is achieved but provided that the contractor submits to the employer a bank guarantee in place of retention at the level agreed in the contract. This will favor the contractor; allowing them to improve their cash-flow because they will receive the retention earlier than they would be entitled to in accordance with the contract. This helps to protect the contractor against the employer's lack of will or impossibility of paying that could emerge after the defects notification period expires. Because of the significant length of the defects notification periods used in construction projects, the contractor is partly protected against inflationary impacts as well. The advantage for the employer is that they have the option to request payment should the contractor fail to meet their obligations because of bankruptcy.

In respect of the fact that the beneficiary can use the guarantee in the event of lacking, improper or untimely performance of the contractor's obligations under the contract, the retention guarantee serves, therefore, a similar purpose as the performance guarantee or the maintenance guarantee.

The retention guarantee is usually required when the taking over certificate is signed, unlike the performance guarantee, which is usually required by the employer shortly before the contract is signed and which generally secures performance in accordance with the conditions of contract, that is, to deliver on time and at the required quality.

The different nature of the retention guarantee versus the maintenance guarantee can be seen by the absence of any cash flow between the contracting parties through the maintenance guarantee. Substantially, both guarantees secure identical obligations, that is, fulfilment of the contractor's duties as they arise from the agreed defects notification period.

As a rule, retention and advance payment guarantees include a clause on their postponed effect from the moment when the retention is actually credited to the contractor's bank account. For example:

> Claims from this bank guarantee issued under reference of ...... can be raised only provided that the retention at the level of ...... will be credited in full to our client's account no. ...... kept by our bank ....

A less frequently used (and more problematic) alternative may be crediting the retention to an account kept by a bank other than the bank providing the guarantee. A problem will arise if an amount other than the one determined by the guarantee is credited, even though the difference may only be marginal. The circumstances under which the "other" amount (which is not expected by the parties) can be credited may relate to, for example, subtraction of the bank fees, rounding errors, inclusion of mutual debts and liabilities, and so on. Whenever the conditions upon which a bank guarantee is to be effective are agreed upon, it is usually in the best interests of the beneficiary that the issue is taken into account so they can be sure about the effectiveness of the bank guarantee.

Performance security and termination payment security in hydropower projects by Alex Blomfield (UK)

Given the complexity of hydropower project execution and weak balance sheets of some contractors and consultants, international hydropower construction contracts usually contain a wide range of performance security and payment structure mechanisms to protect the interests of the parties. Employers and project finance lenders tend to place great store in having on-demand bank guarantees backing performance (with a step-down in value following taking over) and any advance payments. Contractors often try to avoid providing on-demand bank guarantees and almost always try to limit their size, not least due to difficulty of finding willing issuing banks that meet minimum rating requirements throughout the life of the contract in the current uncertain international banking environment.

Retention offers an alternative mechanism for performance security, according to which the employer deducts or retains an agreed percentage of the amount of each payment certificate (usually 50%–10%) instead of paying each payment certificate in full. According to FIDIC, the employer pays the first half of the retention money to the contractor after the issuance of the taking over certificate for the works, and the outstanding balance of the retention money promptly after the latest of the expiry dates of the defects notification periods. However, if any work remains to be executed pursuant to provisions on defects liability and tests on completion, the engineer shall have the right to withhold certification of the estimated cost of this work until the contractor has executed the relevant work (in the case of the 1999 FIDIC Red Book or the FIDIC Yellow Book contracts or other contracts requiring engineer certification), or the employer shall have the right to withhold payment of the retention money until the contractor has executed such work. Of course, parties to international hydropower construction projects often choose to modify these standard FIDIC provisions on retention and often even delete the retention provisions altogether. In this way the parties avoid the adverse effects of retention on the liquidity of the contractor and the incentive for the contractor to front load its payment schedule. Instead, the parties often seek to negotiate a payment schedule with a neutral cash flow and performance securities with larger face value.

Employers seeking the most robust security of performance and payment insist upon parent company guarantees, collateral warranty agreements with major subcontractors and lien releases on taking over from all contractors and subcontractors. A parent company guarantee enables an employer to demand that a parent company remedy the breach of a contractor. It is particularly useful in giving an employer recourse against a strong balance sheet in the event of such employer needing to claim the maximum termination payments due under the main construction contract.

Collateral warranty agreements work as follows: Major subcontractors make warranties in relation to their works directly to the employer. The employer then has direct recourse against major subcontractors. A collateral warranty agreement therefore protects the employer in situations where the contractor becomes insolvent. Contractors tend to resist asking their subcontractors to sign such agreements.

In some jurisdictions, contractors and subcontractors have the right to claim a lien in the works if they have not been paid. Such liens can prevent taking over by the employer with clear title to the generation facility meaning that the employer could have difficulty operating the plant and earning revenue. In this way a contractor's non-payment of its subcontractors becomes an issue for the employer and its lenders. Requiring each contractor and major subcontractor to execute, and deliver, a waiver and release of liens as a condition to taking over is a way of mitigating this risk by employers. This forces each contractor to pay its major subcontractors in full and protects the employer against third party claims related to the works.

Alex Blomfield
Special Counsel
K&L Gates LLP
London
UK

16.5 Governing law

By agreement of the parties, bank guarantees can be made subject to any governing law. Selection of law must always be considered carefully, as not all legal systems define the guarantee in such an abstract form and only know the concept of suretyship. Therefore, major misunderstandings and disputes may arise in preparing the draft wordings if the works are executed abroad. Of course, it is then necessary to also take into account the legal expenses that might, where a dispute breaks out, influence the cost and the problems that the confusion between the guarantee and the suretyship may bring about in relation to the validity of the financial obligation and its level. As a unilateral act, the bank guarantee is usually subject to the law of the country of the issuing bank unless otherwise determined in the securing document.

If a bank guarantee is to be governed by a foreign law not usually used by the issuing bank, then such a bank will require of the ordering party an indemnification statement applicable to any damages caused to the bank by applying such a law. The bank will also require such indemnity in the event of high risk beneficiaries who have a history of non-standard conduct in their transactions in the past. A situation may appear in practice where the construction project participants (mostly employers) will ask for payment from the bank without due reason, giving rise to complicated litigation and injunction tactics. For the above reasons, insurance companies also provide policy cover against withdrawals from bank guarantees.

So-called "counter-guarantees" are also widely used in international transactions. In this case, the employer will usually appoint (mostly in public tendering) a bank which will issue the bank guarantee to secure the contractor. It is almost without exception a local bank with which the contractor obviously has no open credit link for the bank products to be provided.

The contractor's bank will then issue a "counter-guarantee" in favor of the above local bank at the employer's location. With this counter-guarantee in hand, the local bank will then issue the final guarantee where the beneficiary is already stated as the employer.

Different forms of securities may also be required or enabled by governing law. Take, for example, the provisions that regulate guarantees for payment of the contract price in Poland. These provisions have been in effect since amendments were made to the *Polish Civil Code* in 2010. These new provisions set out the contractor's right to require the issue of a security for the payment of the contract price on the basis of *Umowy o roboty budowlane* (contract for works). They are strict mandatory provisions and contractual deviations from them are ineffective. The provisions prescribe exhaustive enumeration of potential forms of guarantees. The contractor may require the guarantee to be issued at any time while the works under contract are executed. If the contractor does not receive any required security within a certain period of time (not less than 45 days), then the contractor will have the right to terminate the contract.

The differences between the Anglo-American and European jurisdictions must also be borne in mind whenever contracts for securing large construction projects are entered into. For example, specific formal demands are imposed on securities where English law is practiced. Special forms of "deeds" play a role in the event of a performance guarantee to be paid out on the first request. Such a guarantee is usually issued unilaterally by a bank or a financial institution in favor of the parties with which the bank shall not have any direct contractual relationship and receive nothing from them in return. "Consideration" (necessary for establishing a binding contract under common law) will usually be missing here. Given such circumstances, the security will have to be made in the form of a deed for it to be enforceable. On-demand performance security under English law was considered recently in *Doosan Babcock Ltd v. Comercializadora De Equipos Y Materiales Mabe Limitada* [2013] EWHC 3010 (TCC).

There is another typical form of security available in some jurisdictions protecting smaller contractors and subcontractors without any direct contractual relationships with the employer. In the United States, there are "mechanics liens," which actually create a right of lien, for example, to a fleet of machines or to work being constructed. Its variant rests with "direct payments" to subcontractors, guaranteed in certain, predefined situations—usually when the contractor fails to pay to a subcontractor as required by law, as is the case in Poland, for example.

Common law specifics related to securities by Rupert Choat and Aidan Steensma (UK)

Deeds play a central role in construction and engineering projects. Many construction and engineering contracts, and similar contracts such as collateral warranties, are entered into as deeds. The primary advantage of doing so is to secure the benefit of a longer limitation period than if the contract were not a deed (12 years instead of 6).

Deeds can also perform a special role when it comes to on-demand performance bonds. Such bonds are usually issued unilaterally by a bank or financial institution in favour of parties with whom it will have no direct commercial relationship and from whom it will receive nothing in return (known as "consideration" under English law). Ordinarily an agreement made without consideration will not be effective under English law unless executed as a deed.

The first reported English case on this issue dates from 1875 (*Morgan and Gooch v. Larivière*), where the House of Lords (England's highest court) in relation to a banker's letter of credit considered there to be "*great doubt whether there would have been held to be a sufficient consideration to support a promise at law*". Subsequent cases dealing with letters of credit have been more accommodating. They have held that consideration arises either by the beneficiary relying upon the letter to proceed with the project in question (*Urquhart Lindsay v. Eastern Bank* and *Dexters Ltd v. Schenker & Co*) or by the presentation of a compliant demand under the letter (*Elder Dempster Lines v. Ionic Shipping Agency*). A recent application of this approach is *RZB v. China Marine* decided in 2006. This case concerned an "irrevocable payment undertaking" given by a commercial party (China Marine) to a bank without any explicit consideration. The found sufficient consideration on both of the grounds noted above.

Other letter of credit cases have simply stated that such credits give rise to a contract between the bank and the beneficiary without analysing the difficulties of consideration mentioned above (e.g. *Hamzeh Malas & Sons v. British Imex Industries*). These cases emphasise the widespread usage and importance of letters of credit and might be said to support a specific exception to the doctrine of consideration based on mercantile usage.

A recent affirmation of this line of cases comes from a UK Supreme Court decision in *Taurus Petroleum Limited v. State Oil Marketing Company of the Ministry of Oil, Republic of Iraq*. That case involved a letter of credit which, unusually, set out promises both in favour of the beneficiary and the local confirming bank. It was said that no consideration had been given by the confirming bank. This was rejected by the court, with one judge noting:

> "*There is not, and could not consistently with important and well-established principles governing letters of credit be, any suggestion that these arrangements were not supported by consideration or that they are not binding according to their terms, as between all these three parties.*"

The above cases mostly concern contracts for the supply of goods where a letter of credit is given to support payment for the supply. Arguments might be made to distinguish this position from that which applies to on-demand bonds given in support of construction contracts. On the other hand, statements exist in English cases to the effect that letters of credit and on-demand bonds are to be treated in the same way.

Ultimately, therefore, whilst the law in this area may be moving toward a position where execution as a deed is unnecessary to avoid no consideration arguments, challenges to on-demand bonds may persist until an authoritative determination of the issue by an English court. Until that point, parties are best advised to ensure that on-demand bonds are executed as a deed to avoid unnecessary argument.

An example from Australia illustrates the risk well. In *Segboer v. AJ Richardson Properties* an on-demand bond was issued by a bank to secure performance of a building contract. In response to a call on the bond, the contractor contended that the bond had not been properly executed as a deed. The argument was ultimately determined against the contractor in court proceedings, but it is notable that once the contractor had raised its objection, the bank refused to pay. To do otherwise would have exposed the bank under its counter-indemnity with the contractor. Technical points like this are often therefore not ones which banks will waive without the assistance of a court (and the consequential delay to payment).

Rupert Choat
Barrister, Arbitrator & Mediator, Atkin Chambers
London, UK

Aidan Steensma
Of Counsel, CMS Cameron McKenna Nabarro Olswang LLP
London, UK

16.6 ICC rules related to securities

To overcome differences in interpretation, unify practices and exclude costly negotiations, the International Chamber of Commerce in Paris has prepared rules for various fields of business, transport, insurance, arbitration, banking, and so on. Guarantees are governed by the Uniform Rules for Demand Guarantees (URDG 758).

The URDG 758 consists of a set of contractual rules designed to regulate demand guarantees and counter-guarantees. The rules apply where they have been expressly incorporated by reference in a guarantee or counter-guarantee. Where this is the case, URDG 758 applies entirely unless specific articles are explicitly ruled out or amended. The URDG 758 may also apply even if not expressly incorporated by reference to the text of a guarantee or counter-guarantee in the event of (1) indirect, asymmetrical guarantees; and (2) as a result of trade usage or a consistent course of dealing.

URDG 758 aims to ensure fair practice and clear guarantees and counter-guarantees that should result in a shorter negotiating process while allowing the applicant greater opportunity to secure the beneficiary's acceptance.

16.7 Suretyship

Besides bank guarantees, contractual duties may be secured by suretyship. The main difference between these forms of security relates to the respective contract (for works between the employer and the contractor, for example). While a bank guarantee is an abstract instrument independent of this relationship, suretyship is the very opposite and fully reflects the main obligation. In the case of an abstract guarantee, the bank cannot raise objections to the main contract for works (for example). On the other hand, the bank is obliged to apply these objections to the very essence of matter where the suretyship is used even when the securing document does not contain any such provisions or when it contains contrary provisions.

In some countries, guarantees are issued in the form of suretyship (surety bond, *Bürgschaft* or *cautionnement*) even by the banks (as in Germany and France). The French wording of guarantees differs depending on their particular type (there are five types altogether) which is why French banks require a copy of the contract from the contractor so that the type of guarantee matches the respective contract.

A similar form of security is defined by the rules issued by the *Uniform Rules for Contract Bonds* (ICC publication No. 524; abbreviated "URCB" or "the Rules"). These rules have been drawn up by an ICC Working Party of Members representing the Commission on Insurance and the building and engineering industry for worldwide application in relation to contract bonds, that is, those bonds creating obligations of an accessory nature, where the liability of the guarantor is conditional upon an established default on the part of a contractor under the contract, which is the subject matter of the relevant bond. These rules are often used by insurance companies. The guarantor has to pay from their guarantee only when the ordering party has breached the contract. The guarantor does, however, have the right to apply any objections available to them by the contract against the ordering party.

A particularity of the "contract bond" is that the guarantor has an "option right." On finding that the contractual obligations have actually been breached on the ordering party's side (and that the beneficiary is entitled to payment), the guarantor may either pay out the guarantee or complete the contract. Such security will not enable the beneficiary to receive payment immediately. The beneficiary is, therefore, in a less advantageous position than with a guarantee payable on the first demand and without any objections.

Should a payment from a guarantee be made, a certificate of an (independent) third party or a guarantor's certificate must be submitted along with the relevant claim. Another option is submission of a final court award. Whenever a guarantee is to be issued in accordance with these rules, it has to be considered what option is to be selected by the parties should the guarantee be used and formulate the conditions upon which the guarantee can be applied accordingly. No matter which certificate the contracting parties prefer, they can refer any potential dispute to a court, if necessary.

These rules are intended for insurance companies. In some countries, the banks cannot provide them because they cannot accept, for example, completing the works in place of the contractor because the governing law restricts them to providing the financial guarantee only. Furthermore, it would be impractical for the bank to examine if contractual obligations have really been breached.

In the United States, large construction projects are frequently secured by means of a suretyship in the form of a "surety bond." These securities are issued by companies specializing in this field. Owing to the traditional restrictions on bank guarantees, a *stand-by letter of credit* is preferred in the United States and functions the same way as a bank guarantee payable on first demand.

16.8 Stand-by letter of credit

Stand-by letters of credit are essentially the same instrument as the bank guarantee with some small differences. These are discussed below. Both are payable on demand with the former originating in the United States. There, the volume of stand-by letters of credit issued significantly exceeds the amount of foreign transactions. Southeast Asia and South America also are other areas where the stand-by letters of credit are used to a significant extent.

What's the difference between guarantees and a stand-by letter of credit? The latter requires substantially the same obligation as an abstract guarantee—being irrevocable, independent of the contract to be secured, abstract and payable against the beneficiary's statement on "default"—a "negative document" certifying, for example, in the form of a statement, that the contractor has not fulfilled their obligations under the contract. The differences therefore relate to the format, terminology used, rules they are subject to and some of the techniques linked to the letters of credit.

There are standard rules for stand-by letters of credit such as the Uniform Customs and Practice for Documentary Credits provided by the International Chamber of Commerce (UCP 600) or the International Stand-by Practices (ISP98).

16.9 Securities under FIDIC forms

FIDIC forms include a number of sample forms of securities, attached as an appendix. From among the individual FIDIC forms, the largest spectrum of activities is covered by the Design, Build, and Operate form (2008; the "Gold Book") and EPC/1999 Silver Book. Thanks to standardization resulting from FIDIC's cooperation with the International Chamber of Commerce (ICC), the guarantees used in these forms come from the Uniform Rules for Demand Guarantees provided by the ICC.

The Tender Security is the first guarantee (normally included in the FIDIC forms), corresponding to the tender guarantee, as specified above. This guarantee is used to make the contractor (as a participant in the tendering process) comply with the tendering rules. This forces them to cooperate with the employer during the course of the tender, to timely enter into the contract for execution of the works, and to submit a performance security, discussed below.

In the case of an advance payment guarantee the employer will provide the contractor with a down payment for project mobilization requiring a security of the down payment. The guarantee takes effect once the contractor receives the advance payments— the level of which is gradually reduced on the basis of the parts of the works completed and already paid.

Performance security is provided in different versions under FIDIC forms. The first option is to issue the performance security as a demand guarantee, that is, the guarantee payable on first demand in accordance with the URDG rules. The employer/beneficiary is authorized to draw from this guarantee whenever the contractor breaches their obligations under the contract. The employer only has to specify such a breach in compliance with the relevant rules but does not need to prove it. Alternatively, issue of the performance security as a surety bond in the form of suretyship may be made by the bank in the role of guarantor. The surety bond is governed by the Uniform Rules for Contract Bonds. Performance security is governed by Sub-Clause 4.2 of the FIDIC forms where it is stipulated, for example, that the contractor shall obtain (at their cost) a performance security for proper performance, in the amount and currencies stated in the appendix to tender. The contractor shall deliver the performance security to the employer within 28 days after receiving the letter of acceptance and shall send a copy to the engineer. The performance security shall be issued by an entity from within a country (or other jurisdiction) approved by the employer, and shall be in the form annexed to the particular conditions or in another form approved by the employer. The contractor shall ensure that the performance security is valid and enforceable until the contractor has executed and completed the works and remedied any defects. If the terms of the performance security specify its expiry date, and the contractor has not become entitled to receive the performance certificate by the date 28 days prior to the expiry date, the contractor shall extend the validity of the performance security until the works have been completed and any defects have been remedied. The employer shall return the performance security to the contractor within 21 days after receiving a copy of the performance certificate.

Under Sub-Clause 4.2:

Employer shall not make a claim under the performance security, except for amounts to which the employer is entitled under the contract in the event of:

(a) failure by the contractor to extend the validity of the performance security as described in the preceding paragraph, in which event the employer may claim the full amount of the performance security,
(b) failure by the contractor to pay the employer an amount due, as either agreed by the contractor or determined under Sub-Clause 2.5 [Employer's Claims] or Clause 20 [Claims, Disputes and Arbitration], within 42 days after this agreement or determination,
(c) failure by the contractor to remedy a default within 42 days after receiving the employer's notice requiring the default to be remedied, or
(d) circumstances which entitle the employer to termination under Sub-Clause 15.2 [Termination by Employer], irrespective of whether notice of termination has been given.

The Retention Money Guarantee and the Maintenance Retention Guarantee are also dealt with by the FIDIC forms. The latter is used in the Gold Book to cover events where the contractor does not properly meet their duties to remedy defects and maintain the works. In their application for payment, if any, the employer must note that the contractor has breached their obligation and also in what way, that is, what is the nature of the defect. This guarantee reflects Sub-Clause 14.19 of the conditions of contract under which 5% of the payments are retained in favor of the maintenance fund.

The payment guarantee by the employer is to secure the employer's payment in case of a delay.

The parent company guarantee is a statement of a mother company (or another company within the ownership structure) as guarantor. This company guarantees that the contractor will duly perform. Should the contractor fail, the mother company will act as the contractor's guarantor. Issue of this parent company guarantee tends to be a precondition upon which the contract between the employer and the contractor can be entered into.

Further reading

Barru, D.J. (2005). How to guarantee contractor performance on international construction projects: comparing surety bonds with bank guarantees and standby letters of credit. *The George Washington International Law Review*, 37, 1.

Choat, R. and Peckett, V. (2012). *English Construction Law Developments 2012*. CMS Cameron McKenna's free online information service, London.

Fight, A. (2005). *Introduction to Project Finance*. Butterworth-Heinemann, Oxford.

Foz, X. and García, J. The ICC's new uniform rules for demand guarantees: URDG 758 more than just an update of URDG 458. Online. Available at: http://terralex.org/publication/dd96fc982f (accessed 3 May 2013).

Klee, L., Rollová, Z., Ručka, O. and Staněk, T. (2014). Bankovní záruky a další formy zajištění velkých výstavbových projektů. Stavebnictví [Civil Engineering] 3/2014.

Venoit, W.K. (2009). *International Construction Law: A Guide for Cross-Border Transactions and Legal Disputes*. ABA Publishing, Chicago.

17 Civil Engineering Works: Infrastructure Construction Projects

17.1 Investments in developing countries

In recent years, a number of post-communist countries have joined the European Union (EU) or are seeking to do so. The new member states are mainly from the Central and East European (CEE) region and many have experienced a surge in large investments in infrastructure projects co-financed by the EU, the European Investment Bank (EIB), and the World Bank. According to the procurement guidelines of the international and European financing institutions, tenders financed by them are, by definition, open to international competition for projects.

Interestingly, there is a remarkable difference between the tenders financed by international financial institutions and tenders financed by the European institutions, that is, the EU and EIB. Both seem to be at the root of contractual problems in many CEE countries. Whereas the World Bank and other international financial institutions that provide co-financing for infrastructure construction projects require well-established sample forms of contract for works to be used, the European institutions impose this condition only with respect to their financial support for "third countries" (i.e., outside of the EU). Within the EU, lawmakers—until recently—did not take any precautions. The underlying reason for such an approach is that well-established local standard forms already existed in Western Europe, for example, the ÖNORM B 2110 (Austria), the VOB/B (Germany), the AB 92 and ABT 93 (Denmark), the CCAG (France and Belgium), the DPR 207/2010 (Italy) and the UAV 1989 and 2012 (the Netherlands). Hence EU lawmakers assumed that sample forms were only needed in developing countries.

FIDIC standard forms were introduced to the CEE region in late 1990s, given the massive amount of international and European financing of construction projects. A lack of adequate local sample forms also played a role in their rapid introduction to the CEE. Under the Phare, Tacis, and ISPA programs, EU and EIB financiers scrutinized ex-ante that the FIDIC standard forms (generally the Red and Yellow Books) were being used in the proper way. FIDIC forms are international

---

International Construction Contract Law, Second Edition. Lukas Klee.
© 2018 John Wiley & Sons Ltd. Published 2018 by John Wiley & Sons Ltd.

benchmarks for their efficient risk allocation, tradition, respect, fairness, and a balanced approach to business.

The authors of the FIDIC forms have intentionally set the risk allocation in most of the standardized conditions to be balanced, efficient and appropriate. The balanced approach, as incorporated in the FIDIC standard forms for Construction and Plant and Design-Build (the 1999 Red and Yellow Books) is deemed appropriate in developed countries as giving the best results and providing the lowest transport infrastructure project costs in the long term.

However, employers in CEE region tend to modify the standardized FIDIC risk allocation to the disadvantage of contractors. Such modification of standard risk allocation usually causes the types of problems described in the *Check List for One Sided Contracts* (JICA, 2011), that is:

- bid failure and disruption of project implementation;
- non-participation in the bid of conscientious and capable contractors;
- contract award to a bidder who fails or is incapable of estimating the risks properly;
- poor construction quality and delay of the work due to lack of risk contingency;
- undermining the relationship of mutual trust and respect between the parties;
- unsubstantiated claims from the contractor;
- frequent disputes between the employer and the contractor;
- higher bid prices and/or large discrepancies between the bid and the final price;
- in extreme cases, the eventual termination of the contract.

Four factors are mentioned in the above list that could serve as motives for making a contract one-sided when preparing the contract documents: (1) the employer has not prepared sufficient budget; (2) lack of employer understanding of the terms and conditions, including appropriate allocation of rights and obligations, the capability of contract management and sense of ownership; (3) lack of time and calculation of costs required to create the contract documents; and (4) slavish adherence to domestic laws, regulations and domestic procedures (JICA, 2011).

Lessons learned in developed countries can help avoid or solve similar problems in developing countries lacking sufficient infrastructure or where large infrastructure projects are planned for the future.

The following text will compare the traditional treatment of construction project risks in developed countries such as the United States of America and the United Kingdom against the practices encountered in the CEE. Examples will illustrate what kind of consequences a distorted standard form of risk allocation may have.

17.2 The approach to the risk allocation in the United States

According to the U.S. Department of Transportation (http://international.fhwa.dot.gov):

The goal of an optimal allocation of risk is to minimize the total cost of risk on a project, not necessarily the costs to each party separately. Thus, it might sometimes seem as if one party is bearing more of the risk costs than the other party. However, if both owners and contractors take a long-term view and take into consideration the benefit of consistently applying an optimal method to themselves and to the rest of their industry, they will realize that over time optimizing risk allocation reduces everyone's cost and increases the competitiveness of all parties involved.

Poor risk allocation is one of the most frequent reasons for construction project litigation in the United States.

In the United States, individual transport infrastructure employers compile their contracts according to standard risk allocation manuals. For example, the *AASHTO Guide Specifications for Highway Construction* is widely used in general contracting as a delivery method. Numerous precedents and well-established adjudication practices of the courts confirm the advantages of efficient risk allocation. While proven to be effective, standard risk allocations are not standardized procedures with completely universal application. There is no standardized procedure that would eliminate the need to systematically identify the hazards and analyse the risks inherent to every particular construction project. No standardized procedure will replace a prudent employer's ability to determine priorities (such as speed, price, standard, minimization of environmental impacts, and so on) when preparing a project.

The U.S. Department of Transportation instructs that risk allocation should always be based on the following principles:

- Risk should be allocated to the party best able to control it. The employer, for example, will not burden the project with a risk surcharge in the contractor's contract price when retaining the risk of unforeseeable ground conditions. This is also confirmed by the recent award in *Metcalf Construction Co. v. the United States* (U.S Ct. of Appeals for the Federal Circuit, Case No. 2013-5041, February 11, 2014) where the U.S. Court of Appeals for the Federal Circuit reversed a decision of the U.S. Court of Federal Claims that had permitted the government to shift risk of unforseeable ground conditions to the contractor via contractual disclaimer in a design-build contract. The aim of the disclaimer was to deny any chance of contractor relief on a differing site condition claim. It is a clear signal to public employers that it is not acceptable to shift unforeseeable and uncontrollable risk to the contractor. It is also a confirmation of the necessity of balanced efficient risk allocation even in design-build contracts. This key decision comes at a critical time as the government (perhaps due to economic recession), seems to have adopted aggressive strategies to avoid paying reasonable contractor claims (for more information see http://www.constructionrisk.com).
- Risk should be allocated in accordance with project priorities. Take, for example, the situation where short completion time is a priority. The employer may then allocate some other risks beyond the standard to the contractor, but always in a transparent, appropriate and efficient way.

- To share a risk where it is convenient. Take, as a good example, extremely adverse climatic conditions where an "extremely bad weather risk" is to be shared between the parties.

Some (or all) of the risks beyond standard can be more conveniently allocated to the contractor where there are no major risks that would jeopardize a particular project and where a detailed risk analysis has been done. Of course, these risks have to be identified, or it must be at least possible to assess these risks independently. Any indeterminate requirement or general, illogical, risk shift will result in a non-assessment of the risk. In such cases, the setting of a contract price comes down to a mere guess. Such an initial condition cannot then lead to a successful construction project as it also complicates the tender process. Tendering may then take an intolerably long time because of a large number of requests by tenderers following the terms of reference in public procurement projects. Sometimes, a tender will have to be cancelled and announced anew in such situations. The resulting damages and impossibility of using, for example, a newly built road will ultimately burden the taxpayer.

17.3 The approach to the risk allocation in the United Kingdom

For many years, substantial efforts have been made in the UK to find a suitable model for transport infrastructure tendering. This was in response to projects inherently suffering from prolongation and price increases and long-term industry-wide concern. Many strategic steps have since been taken to make changes and provide solutions to these problems within the construction industry.

One of the key points was the development of a new form of contract called the new engineering contract (NEC) in the 1980s. Prepared by engineers, this contract is widely regarded as providing solid support for good project management. This form is commonly used in most large construction projects commissioned by public employers in the UK. The Crossrail project in London and the London 2012 Olympic Games are two recent examples. There are several, optional, NEC sample forms. The target price form is used most frequently because it has proven itself to save money (actual price below the level of the agreed target price) and minimize losses (price increases in excess of the agreed target price). This form is based on the pain/gain mechanism where the benefits and losses are shared between the employer and the contractor. NEC sample forms motivate and encourage cooperation between the participants. Moreover, these sample forms are a proven measure against employer-contractor "wars," which, in every case, have adverse impacts on projects.

With an NEC sample form, the program (time schedule) is used as a key project management tool and mutual compensation events are presented and defined in a clear, straightforward manner.

In the UK, there is also a unique standard used to manage delay and disruption-related issues during construction project realisation known as the SCL Protocol (the delay and disruption protocol, published by the United Kingdom Society of Construction Law; free to download at http://www.scl.org.uk/resources), which can be made a part of contract via a reference.

Additional instruments are available, for example, early contractor involvement (ECI), that is, an effort to make use of the contractor's experience and capabilities as early as at the public contract pre-awarding phase. Use of expert systems such as building information modeling (BIM), that is, the use of software modelling of a construction process as a whole, providing an ultimate overview of the works being executed and allowing the utmost cooperation between all participants.

Several strategic resolutions have taken place at the government level, including a special Act regulating construction in the UK. For example, *The Housing Grants, Construction and Regeneration Act* (1996) ("the Act"). At Section 108, the Act compels all parties who are parties to a construction contract to refer any dispute to adjudication as a first step. This is a mandatory provision by operation of law that cannot be changed by contract. During the dispute process, parties must adhere to short (and strict) time limits. For example, a dispute must be adjudicated within 28 days of notification of the dispute. If a party fails to comply with the adjudicator's resolution, the other party can compel performance through a streamlined litigation process at the Technology and Construction Court—a court dedicated to resolving disputes related to construction contracts. This court, in most instances, quickly confirms the previous adjudication award.

Construction of airports by Patrick Kain (South Africa)

Airports provide the infrastructure for landing and taking off of aircraft and for processing of passengers and cargo before loading or unloading onto aircraft. They can vary in size and scope from small gravel strips with basic facilities for passengers, which are typically for domestic flights in remote areas to large international airports that accommodate the Boeing 787 Dreamliner and the Airbus A380 aircraft.

Nationally, civil aviation authorities control aviation including airports. These authorities refer to International Civil Aviation Organization (ICAO) and/or the United States' Federal Aviation Authority (FAA) rules and regulations for guidance. While with the exception of the United States (where FAA compliance with regulations is mandatory), in other countries, these FAA and ICAO provide recommendations to national regulatory authorities; however, compliance with ICAO and the FAA regulations and standards is generally accepted as being mandatory.

Airports are complex infrastructure systems that include runways, taxiways, parking aprons, airfield lighting, refueling facilities, passenger terminal buildings, cargo terminals, hangars, control tower building, car parks, and other facilities. Larger airports also provide air-bridges to facilitate embarkation and disembarkation procedures for large aircraft. These are supported by communications, information, security, and safety systems, at various levels and to different groups of airport operatives and passengers.

Interdependency of systems is complex and requires good coordination to ensure that, for instance, in the case of passenger terminals, passengers and baggage are processed and managed in such a manner to ensure that from the time of check-in through departure and arrival at their destinations, passengers and baggage are handled efficiently and that passengers and baggage arrive without unnecessary problems.

The development of a new airport requires detailed planning and inputs from a wide variety of expertise including environmentalists, geologists, meteorologists, pavement specialists, architects, structural engineers, electrical engineers, mechanical engineers, electronics specialists, safety and security experts, and communications specialists among others. It also requires good coordination and consultation with relevant stakeholders from the planning process through design and construction right through to final commissioning.

While terminal buildings are the most visible facility at airports and terminals receive the most attention from the press and public, it is significant that terminal buildings represent only 20%–30% of the total infrastructure cost at most airports.

Slopes and obstructions on runways are severely restricted. Large areas of flat ground are required in order to conform to these stringent requirements. This is a problem and in many cases airports are built on poor ground with high water tables or even in swamplands, which can lead to high development costs, for example, where runways are built on poor ground, special techniques are needed, such as replacement of poor soil or placement of an interlocking pioneer layer over soft soils and provision of subsoil drainage. This coupled with high wheel loading and a severe limitation on time available for future maintenance means that airport pavement design is often complex and requires expert treatment. A major risk here is unforeseen soil conditions that could lead to major claims from paving contractors and on foundation works for terminal buildings. Therefore, detailed geotechnical investigations must be undertaken prior to design works if cost and schedule overruns due to unforeseen site conditions are to be avoided.

Depending on the size of the airport, and the need for multidisciplinary expertise, the project may be awarded to a single contractor or split into a number of discrete packages. When the project is split into a number of separate packages, a project manager coordinates work on the various contracts while a construction manager manages each work package. The overall project is managed by a project manager who is responsible for procurement of the various contract packages, monitoring the works and ensuring that cost and schedule are maintained and for other aspects of the development such as land acquisition, co-ordination with airlines, service providers, concessionaires (shops, restaurants, lounges, etc.) and reporting to the airport owners.

The construction managers are responsible for their individual construction packages and delivery to the project manager. The other option for a large airport is to award as a design and build project.

The different FIDIC contract documents are ideal for dealing with the different delivery methods mentioned above. The 1999 Red Book along with the sub-contract form would be appropriate for smaller airports and possibly even medium-sized airports; The 1999 Yellow Book would be appropriate for design and build on larger airports alternatively, the Red Book or a combination of the Red and Yellow Books would be appropriate if the development is done under a series of separate contracts under the direction of a dedicated project manager. Because of the nature of airports, it would be unusual to use the 1999 Silver Book except perhaps for fuel storage facilities that are generally not provided directly by airport authorities but by fueling companies under license or on a concession basis.

Airports are subject to change over time in order to accommodate either larger aircraft or increase in traffic volumes or to be upgraded to facilitate night operations. A number of measures would be required to accommodate these changes:

- strengthening of runway pavements;
- lengthening and widening of runways;
- provision of additional taxiways;

- extensions to aircraft parking areas;
- provision of airfield lighting;
- provision of additional fueling facilities;
- extensions to terminal buildings.

While extensions to terminal buildings can be carried out with some inconvenience to passengers, other extensions and major repair works to runways, taxiways, and aprons can involve disruption to air traffic and ground movements. For this reason, much of this work is scheduled at night when those areas are closed to traffic.

Moreover, work on runway pavements, particularly on airports with only one runway, must be carried out in such a manner that the runway is available for use the following day after a safety check of the works to ensure that the runway is safe for aircraft. Contracts must also include clearance of equipment, materials and workers from work areas in cases of emergency so work is planned in small sections to facilitate rapid clearance of the site and restoration to an operational state.

For these reasons, it is necessary to include special conditions to cover these provisions. This is easily done in FIDIC by making use of the "conditions of particular application"; however, it is found that such provisions are sometimes included (wrongly) in the "preliminary and general" section of the specifications.

For all airport works, but particularly refurbishment or extension works, it may be desirable to include a staged completion requirement in the contract. This is easily achieved with FIDIC as Sub-Clause 10.1 provides for taking over of the works in sections and for different defects notification periods for works taken over in sections.

Patrick Kain
International construction expert
South Africa

17.4 The approach to the risk allocation in Central and Eastern Europe

Established, experienced lenders respect and promote in their guidelines where projects financed by them abide by the principles of fairness and appropriately allocate risk. For example, the EIB requires that "the contractual conditions are fair and reasonable," the EBRD states:

> Contract conditions shall be drafted so as to allocate the risks associated with the contract fairly, with the primary aim of achieving the most economic price and efficient performance of the contract … Wherever appropriate, standard forms of contract incorporating generally accepted international conditions must be used

The World Bank states, "The conditions of contract shall provide a balanced allocation of risks and liabilities."

Government attempts at risk aversion are explicable as its agencies are liable and responsible to other authorities (such as regulators) for any expenditure arising under such contract. This often results in attempts to minimize the risks by shifting them to the contractor. This risk aversion may be the specific reason for recent issues which plague public procurement such as delays, cost overruns and lack of technical-executive contractual know-how in monitoring project implementation (Banica, 2013).

Some employers in the CEE procure public projects to be financed from EU funds with modified FIDIC contract forms. These sample forms tend to disadvantage the contractor through onerous provisions that dramatically skew the standard risk allocation.

The main trend was to replace the provisions of the FIDIC CONS/1999 Red Book or FIDIC P&DB/1999 Yellow Book with the provisions of the FIDIC EPC/1999 Silver Book. In this way, employers could deliberately avoid and shift the standard risk allocation to their advantage. Employers often did so on the advice of inexperienced lawyers or, in some cases, deliberately. Concerning legal advisors, understanding the legal and practical aspects of construction is essential to drafting a good document. The goal, after all, is to construct the project with as few problems as possible. The secondary goal is to protect the client (Sabo, 2013).

In many cases, employers were not aware of the long-term, negative consequences on particular projects and the construction industry as a whole. For example, the FIDIC EPC/1999 Silver Book, due its risk allocation concepts designed for EPC, is inherently unsuitable for use in large transport infrastructure projects. Furthermore Sub-Clauses in Silver Book such 4.12 or 5.1 are invalid in some jurisdictions (Kus, Markus, and Steding, 1999).

The following is a summary of some typical interventions/modifications of risk allocations witnessed in the CEE countries and worldwide.

17.4.1 Restricted competencies of the Engineer

Execution of the engineer's rights and duties consists concurrently of two agendas. The first is to act on the employer's behalf. The contractor may thus perceive the engineer's conduct as an action or inaction of the employer (such as the engineer's instruction regarding a variation). The second is that the engineer is a neutral third party who is professionally required to keep a fair balance between the contractor and the employer (such as during resolution of disputes, certifications, and so on).

In practice, employers try to restrict the engineer's powers, for example, by making the engineer's decisions subject to employer approval, or they withdraw disobedient engineers and replace them with obedient ones. This process starts at the contract phase between the employer and the engineer. Terms are agreed upon which imply the engineer is in fact the employer's representative. These steps often result in a paralysed system of project administration and management. As such, the engineer will become the one acting on the employer's behalf and the project will lose the advantages that come from the execution and purpose of the engineer's position. Whether the contract administration exercised by such a person is efficient or inefficient depends on the capabilities and good faith of the individuals in their positions.

The practice went so far and cases were encountered where the engineer was used as a tool for bad faith behavior by the employer. In such situations, variations are typically instructed by the engineer to be later declared invalid by the employer for lack of empowerment of the engineer (or conflict with public procurement law). Payments previously made for those variations were retrospectively offset by the employer against future payments for works done, with the effect being a loss on the contract or, in some cases, bankruptcy of the contractor.

However, different conditions were agreed in the main contract for works between the employer and the contractor (where the engineer had to be fair) and in the professional service agreement between the employer and the engineer (where the engineer was under threat of contractual penalties to avoid contractor claims). This further led to claims and lawsuits for damages by contractors against engineers.

17.4.2 Inefficient risk allocation

FIDIC EPC/1999 Silver Book risk allocation is used in transport infrastructure construction projects despite the fact that the use of general contracting (FIDIC CONS/1999 Red Book) or DB (FIDIC P&DB/1999 Yellow Book) is more efficient.

There are, for example, risks of errors in setting-out (Sub-Clause 4.7), wrong site data (Sub-Clause 4.10), unforeseeable physical conditions (Sub-Clause 4.12), and errors in the employer's requirements (Sub-Clauses 1.9 and 5.1) that are allocated to the employer under CONS/1999 Red Book and P&DB/1999 Yellow Book. Employers change these clauses and allocate risks caused by their own bad project preparation or negligence to the contractor by not allowing the contractor to claim any additional payments or extensions of time for completion in cases of risk realization. In doing so, the employer insures against their own inability to prepare the contract properly and on a timely basis by allocating the risk of defective contract preparation (and its consequences) to the contractor.

Sometimes, employers need to commence projects at any cost and without sufficient preparation. Reasons may be financial (conditions given by the lenders or subsidies providers), political (complete the project before the next elections), economic (the urgent need of a road, tunnel or bridge), dishonesty (corruption), international obligations (a treaty on infrastructure development), fear (lack of responsibility), or intentional avoidance of responsibility.

Another problem is that public employer had to choose consultants and designers on the basis of lowest price. Such procurement leads again to errors in tender designs and bad project preparation.

The employer may see a shift in risk allocation as an appropriate way to solve the problem of lack of preparation and the best way how to avoid responsibility. In practice, the employer will not achieve its goals in this way and projects affected by defective risk allocation will almost certainly end in trouble and dispute. Without efficient and fair contractual remedies, the contractor who accepted the onerous contract with inefficient risk allocations will defend potential claims under general principles of law. In civil law countries, for example, the principles of unjust enrichment and good faith protection will very likely be argued against the employer. Translated into the language of law, the absurd risk allocation may then be called unreasonable limitation of responsibility. Another (even worse) scenario may await the employer:

the contractor will terminate the contract and abandon the project after a risk is realized that could not have been controlled or accounted for in their bid price. The final, common scenario is one where the contractor goes into bankruptcy because of risk realization. The employer is then left to "clean up the mess" of conducting a new tender, resolving difficulties with warranties, and so on.

Take, as an example, the approach of a Romanian employer for a transport infrastructure public contract who went so far as to allocate the risk of unforeseeable physical conditions to the contractor even when there was not enough time to do the site inspections and explorations during tender preparations. This employer is exclusively assigning the liability for defects in their own design documents by making the strict wording of the FIDIC EPC/1999 Silver Book even more rigorous against the contractor. In this case, the employer removed exemptions of contractor liability (Sub-Clause 5.1) from the tender requirements. As such, the contract becomes impossible to price and evaluate and lacks transparency from the outset. The project is almost certainly doomed to failure—either ending in dispute or premature termination.

17.4.3 Limitation of contractors' claims

Limitation of the contractors' claims for additional payments and extensions of time take the form of either complete elimination or modifications in their parameters. Here, the matter in question is nothing more than a shift in risk allocation. For example, the employer will try to compensate their failure to meet basic obligations (such as to properly and timely provide the contractor with access to the site) by assigning the adverse implications to the contractor. In this way, they relieve the contractor of the possibility of claiming an additional payment or confining the claim to payment of direct costs regardless of additional lost profit and/or overhead surcharges.

17.4.4 Contractual determination of a maximum total contract price

Another extreme is in defining the upper limit of the total contract price as, for example, 110% of the tender price (except for adjustments or changes in legislation and cost). Guaranteed like this, such a maximum price (inherent in CM at-Risk projects) is obviously unreasonable in risky transport infrastructure projects. Again, it is likely that such provisions would be deemed void by a court in a dispute and that the contractor would finally succeed with their claims. Furthermore, such a provision presents a great risk in terms of the possibility of efficiently managing the project and bringing it to a successful conclusion—particularly in connection with the lowest bid price being the only criterion for success in the respective tender.

The Romanian experience by Claudia Teodorescu (Romania)

FIDIC forms are also used as contract conditions in Romania, in public procurement projects for roads and bridges, by the National Company for Road Infrastructure Administration, which is part of the Romanian Ministry of Transport (CNAIR), usually referred to as "the employer."

Between 2000 and 2010, Romanian authorities worked mainly with the Red Book (first edition, 1999) because Romanian legislation (related to design, quality in construction and finance) required the completed works to be measured, using unit and item prices that could not be varied.

However, the employer has constantly faced several problems in implementing its projects because of:

- slow procedures to ensure site access according to Sub-Clause 2.1 [*Right of Access to the Site*];
- errors in the initial setting-out data under Sub-Clause 4.7 [*Setting Out*];
- mistakes in site data under Sub-Clause 4.10 [*Site Data*];
- the design needing adjustment(s) to become applicable to the actual site conditions under Sub-Clause 17.3 (g) [*Employer's Risks*]; and
- slow procedures in obtaining permits under Sub-Clause 2.2 [*Permits, Licences or Approvals*].

One other constant impediment has been utilities' companies interfering with the works. As utilities are privately owned, utilities' owners have to be involved directly in the design and relocation of their networks (water, gas, oil, and, mainly, electricity). These third parties are mostly foreign companies, with their head offices outside Romania. Approval procedures usually go on for months or years. There are no clear, uniform procedures to be followed by contractors and utility owners change requirements as they please, sometimes even imposing on the employer and contractors conditions which cannot be implemented within the legal framework.

Preliminary archaeological investigations and site clearances should be carried out by the employer. If, following these preliminary investigations, information about important archaeological remains is revealed, the employer should not embark on ordinary site clearance.

Sub-Clause 4.24 (*Fossils*) should only apply to unexpected findings in the area of the works, about which no prior data was available. Passing responsibility for archaeological investigations and site clearance to the contractor usually leads to claims, which cannot be easily and strictly quantified, since they depend upon specialized third parties in this field, for example, archaeologists and museums.

Contractors have also been facing delayed payments for executed works, due to bureaucracy and legislative restrictions. Up to six months' delay in payment for works certified by the engineer, as overdue contractual time, is not exceptional. For executed and certified works, the employer has actually increased the period in which they are allowed to pay, from the date of approving the interim payment certificate.

Furthermore, cases occur when this period is extended by unofficial requests to the contractor not to invoice the amount due or by the employer withholding payment for supplementary verification, on various formal grounds. This also applies to payment for the engineer's services.

These practices often lead to even the most diligent of contractors hiring specialized companies for claims' support and reducing productivity (including demobilization of resources), in an attempt to overcome delay in payments. Such difficulties faced by contractors mean that they become more concerned with claims management and less concerned with the progress of the works.

These issues have resulted in a series of claims referred to dispute adjudication board (DAB) and, eventually, to arbitration. However, under the arbitration rules of the International Chamber of Commerce, these procedures are slow and costly. This consumes the resources of both the contractor and employer and it does not guarantee success or satisfactory compensation.

In addition, the Romanian government considered necessary to introduce the FIDIC conditions as internal legislation, so they will be accepted and generally applied both by national and local authorities, for major infrastructure projects. Decree No. 1405/2010 which introduced the general contract condition (GCC) of FIDIC Red Book (Appendix no. 2) and the GCC of FIDIC Yellow Book (Appendix no.1) was meant to ensure a more uniform approach to construction projects. By Clause 3 of Decree No. 1405/2010 it was stated that the particular contract conditions (PCC) would be approved by order of the Minister of Transports. Order no. 146/201, modified and appended by Order 2011/2012, presented the PCC for FIDIC Red Book and FIDIC Yellow Book. The FIDIC Yellow Book PCC have been recently modified by the Order of the Minister of Transport no. 600/2017. In recent years, employers (in an attempt to minimize errors and gaps in their tender documentation, caused by insufficient time for bid preparation) thought of the solution offered by the FIDIC Yellow Book (first edition, 1999). In this form, the design and all related risks are allocated to the contractor. These conditions have been chosen by employers as it takes less time to prepare the tender documentation and because of the imperative demand to start some projects before the cut-off dates of the financing memoranda. The employer has also included a number of specific clauses in these contracts, which have further altered the usual distribution of risks between the two parties.

Such contracts do not follow the principles of the FIDIC Yellow Book, as the employer is trying to limit:

- its risk for delayed expropriations under Sub-Clause 2.1 [*Right of Access to the Site*];
- its responsibility for errors in the setting-out data under Sub-Clause 4.7 [*Setting Out*];
- its responsibility for errors in site data under Sub-Clause 4.10 [*Site Data*];
- price increases for unforeseen physical conditions under Sub-Clause 4.12 [*Unforeseeable Physical Conditions*]. Furthermore, this Sub-Clause has been completely modified so that it does not allow any claims for time and costs for unforeseen circumstances or events.

With this shift in risks, the employer has changed a balanced Yellow Book risk allocation to a Silver Book risk allocation that is unsuitable for road and bridge (or underground) construction.

In terms of contract price determination, the employer is not allowed (under Romanian legislation), to stipulate payment as a lump sum or percentage of the contract price, according to the executed works. The employer has to demand accurate quantities' measurement. There is no proper measurement method for the correct valuation of the executed works. Romanian legislation states that there must be a bill of quantities and that contractors are fully responsible for the unit prices (Order 863/2008 of July 2, 2008, Instructions for the Application of Certain Provisions of Government Decision No. 28/2008 regarding the Frame-Content Approval of Public Investments Technical-Economic Documentation, as well as the Structure and Methodology of the General Estimate for Investment Objectives and Intervention Works). This leads to the conclusion that it might be difficult to adapt a lump-sum contract to the Romanian legislation and particularly to the common working practice. Thus, the employer is forced to alter the General Conditions of the FIDIC Yellow Book through particular conditions, in order to correlate it with the local legislation, by introducing restrictions specific to the FIDIC Red Book. For example, Sub-Clause 14.1 [*The Contract Price*] has been modified to include the submission by the contractor of a detailed, precise, complete bill of quantities and price breakdown for all items of works:

(a) Within 14 days from the approval of the Technical Design (produced in accordance with the Technical Specifications) by the Technical Economic Committee of the employer, the contractor will issue to the engineer, the Bill of Quantities detailed per work categories, containing the Unit Price per each Item of works. The summarised amount of all Items (Quantity * Unit Price) in the Bill of Quantities for each category of works must be (at most) equal to the Value included in the Cash Flow for that works category. The change introduced by Order 600/217 allows the updating of the Contractor's Cash Flow in accordance with the Bill of Quantities, under condition that the Contract Price and work' categories' values remain the same.

(b) Also, the contractor will submit a detailed Breakdown for each Unit Price within the Bill of Quantities. The Breakdown must include the costs for labour, materials, equipment, transport and percentages for indirect costs and profit. The engineer shall use this Breakdown to evaluate Modifications of Unit Prices and New Prices according to cl. 13.3, but its use will not be limited to that.

If the contractor refuses to provide this, the engineer will usually be unable to perform its duties and it will be prevented from carrying out the verifications, evaluations and analysis required by the contract.

Furthermore, employers introduced a provision in Sub-Clause 2.1 [*Access to Site*], which allows them to grant access:

- 28 days after the commencement date;
- by sections, gradually.

The contractor will not be entitled to any claims on the grounds of access to site being granted by sections; not only have the provisions concerning entitlement to claim been deleted, but there is a clear amendment stating the contrary: "The Contractor will not issue any Claim on the premise that access to site is to be assured gradually, by sections."

When faced with these restrictive particular conditions of contract—that is, the modified FIDIC Yellow Book—and also with site problems such as incomplete expropriations, lengthy procedures for clearance of forest areas, hydrological and geological reports that do not contain accurate data about the structure of soil or physical and climatic conditions in the region of the project, contractors gradually decrease resources used and productivity, in an attempt to reduce extra costs and to maintain production to match the employer's financial capability.

Therefore, the project implementation management is often replaced by claims' management, in disputing concurrent delays caused by employer and contractor and delays in the completion of the projects. In addition, the engineer's role in these contracts has been drastically reduced, both through particular conditions in the construction contracts and also through specifications and supervision contracts imposed by the employer. The engineer's actions regarding approvals and determinations are depending upon the employer's final approval. Payment procedures, methods of calculation and certifications, acceptance of supporting documents are frequently a "face-off" area for the employer and contractor, with the engineer caught in the middle.

Order 600/2017 has introduced new restrictions to Sub-Clause 3.1 [*Engineer's Duties and Authority*], employer's prior and formal approval being compulsory for changes in personnel (Sub-Clause 6.1), value engineering (Sub-Clause 13.2) and variation procedure (Sub-Clause 13.3).

The Sub-Clause 3.5 [*Determinations*] of the FIDIC Yellow Book has been radically adjusted by the PCC in Order 600/2017. This clause is meant to deal with both employer's (Sub-Clause 2.5) and contractor's (Sub-Clause 20.1) claims. Unless an agreement between the contractual parties is reached within 70 days from the submission date of the claim's particulars, within 84 days from the same moment the engineer shall issue a fair determination. If no agreement between the parties has been reached and the engineer has not issued his determination or either party is unhappy with the engineer's determination, each party can submit a notice of dissatisfaction, within 30 days. After 42 days from the notice of dissatisfaction issued in accordance with Sub-Clause 3.5, the unhappy party can address the matter to a court of law. Unless such a first court appeal has been submitted, the liable party shall no longer be held responsible and the claimant shall lose all related rights. In that moment, the annulment of the claim will become final, irrevocable, and binding for both parties. There are numerous changes to the PCC, operated through Order 600/2017, some of them being described below; the clauses and contract issues presented do not form an exhaustive analysis of all modifications to the PCC.

One modification concerns Sub-Clause 4.17 [*Contractor's Equipment*]. This establishes the strict control of the engineer over the mobilization by the contractor of its declared equipment, according to the program of execution. It empowers the engineer in observing the correspondence between program of works resources and actual resources on site, trying to deal with the situations of contractors' under-mobilization. Sometimes, contractors hide their own disruptions and delays, caused by under mobilization, inside alleged delays and disruptions purportedly caused by employer's risk events. By the amendments to Sub-Clause 4.17, the employer takes control over the compliance with the program of works resources, as guaranteed through tender procedure.

The Sub-Clause 8.1 [*Commencement Date*] is modified so that the employer will not issue the commencement date notice before the contractor completes the technical design.

Further on, the Sub-Clause 8.4 [*Extension of Time for Completion*] has been changed to reflect that no claims can rise from additional expropriations, reviewing the environmental agreement, modification of the technical-economic data due to changes in the design by the contractor. Also, no claims can be made in connection to design errors or additional operations, approvals, disruptions caused by design errors. On the other hand, it restates the recognition of contractor's right to claim for disruptions caused by utilities, archeological sites, additional expropriations, environmental protection requirements, other necessary approvals and permits, other events outside contractor's control.

Also Sub-Clause 8.6 [*Rate of Progress*] has been modified to highlight employer's control over the staged execution of the project, including division of the project into site sections.

The employer shall be entitled, based on Sub-Clause 14.2 [*Advance Payment*] of the PCC to charge penalties for non-reimbursement of the advance.

The employer is also entitled to deduct undue amounts from the interim payment certificate (IPC), according to the findings of authorized control entities or others (Sub-Clause 14.3 [*Application for Interim Payment Certificates*]).

The Sub-Clause 20.1 [*Contractor's Claims*], which stipulates that the claim is time bared by the 28 days' period notice, introduces additional requirements with regard to the records that are issued in supporting a claim, as well as concerning the periods in which the contractor can do so without losing its right to claim. After the particulars of the claim are issued, the engineer must give its motivated approval/disapproval within 84 days.

The Sub-Clauses 20.2, 20.3, and 20.4 concerning the DAB and Sub-Clause 20.6 concerning arbitration have been deleted from the contract. Instead, any unsolved dispute shall be brought in front of a Romanian court of law, for settlement, according to newly introduced Sub-Clauses 20.2, 20.3, 20.4, 20.5, 20.6, 20.7, and 20.8.

Other modifications to the PCC concern Sub-Clauses: 1.1.6.13 – 1.1.6.15, 1.7, 3.4, 4.2, 4.4, 4.24, 5.2, and 5.3 [*Contractor's Undertaking*], which underlines the contractor's complete liability for the design and related matters, 6.1, 13.1, and 13.3, which offers examples of possible modifications accepted, without being limitative, 14.1, 14.7.

Situations have occurred where the employer simply produced a notice under Sub-Clause 15.1 [*Notice to Correct*] and officially instructed the engineer to sign and deliver it to the contractor, without the right to correct, modify, or state its point of view. This kind of approach leads to numerous misunderstandings and misguided actions, with unpredictable effect on the contract management. This clause has also been appended by Order 600/2017 PCC, introducing new reasons for issuing notice to correct, such as: the penalties for contractor's under-mobilization are over 5% of the contract price, failure to replace personnel within 6 months from notice, repeated and serious breach of the contract by the contractor.

Contractors, sometimes, consider certain contractual documents as being approved simply by their submission to the engineer. For example, according to Sub-Clause 8.3:

> "If, at any time, the engineer gives notice to the contractor that a programme fails (to the extent stated) to comply with the contract or to be consistent with actual progress and the contractor's stated intentions, the contractor shall submit a revised programme to the engineer in accordance with this Sub-Clause, within 7 days."

The contractors never correct, complete or, in any way, revise the program of works in accordance with the engineer's comments and observations, but simply issue a program, which further includes mistakes of a technical, economic, or contractual nature. This approach is meant to make it impossible for the engineer to conduct a thorough analysis of the progress of works.

The amendments brought by Order 600/30.05.2017, published in 13.06.2017, to the PCC for FIDIC Yellow Book, reveal the intention of offering to the employer the possibility to supervise the contractor's mobilization and works' progress, at an early stage. It is also intended to balance the risks' allocation between employer and contractor and to separately address the effects of such risks, in terms of claims. It completely lacks flexibility in relation to amicable settlement, by the negation of dispute alternative resolution methods and by the introduction of court of law solutions, as unique option.

Claudia Teodorescu
Claims and dispute resolution expert
Romania

17.5 The Polish experience

Here are two examples of the Polish experience.

FIDIC Forms and contractual relationships in Poland by Aleksandra Marzec (Poland)

FIDIC forms of contract are widely used in Poland, especially in large, public investments co-financed by the EU. Consequently, the "FIDIC employer" is very often a public government authority. The main public employer in the field of large motorway and road construction projects is the General Directorate of Roads and Motorways (GDDKiA), which is a procurement agency of the Ministry of Infrastructure (currently the Ministry of Infrastructure and Development). The "FIDIC contractor" is a privately owned foreign or local construction company.

GDDKiA is a central government administration authority, established by virtue of the relevant legal act and exercising the state's authority by realizing the statutory administrative tasks that have been given to it. While performing its administrative tasks, GDDKiA enters into relationships under administrative law with both citizens and other legal entities. Such relationships are characterized by the superiority of one party (the government body) and the inferiority of the other party (citizen, other legal entity). When organizing public procurement for roads and motorways, GDDKiA enters into civil law contracts and therefore becomes a "party of the relationship" under civil law. As opposed to the relationships under administrative law, such a relationship under civil law is characterized by the equality of all parties. Therefore, all parties to the civil law contract, whether public or private entities, government bodies or citizens, have the same rights under civil law.

The rule of equality of the parties under civil law is closely related to the rule of autonomy of will of the parties and the freedom of contracting. Freedom of contracting means, among other things, the right to decide whether to enter into a contract or not, the right to freely choose the other party to the contract and the right to create, amend and terminate the contract. In practice, the rule of equality and the rule of freedom of contracting may be limited by other statutory acts, such as, for example, consumer protection acts or public procurement law.

Public procurement law is a *lex specialis* to the civil code. This basically means that where it is not otherwise specified in public procurement law, the provisions and rules of civil law should be applied. This principle is expressed clearly in Article 14 and Article 139 s.1 of the public procurement law, which states that: "the contract tendered according to public procurement law is a contract under civil law regulations." Therefore, the tendering procedures as described in the public procurement law are in fact specified procedures of concluding civil law contracts where one of the parties is a government authority or other public entity spending public funds.

As a result of applying public procurement law, the rule of freedom of contracting is in many ways limited. On the employer's side, the freedom of decision making regarding whether to enter into the contract or not is limited by the budget constraints. According to Article 44 of the *Public Finances Act*, public expenses can be disbursed in the amount and for the purposes described in the *Budget Act* or in the appropriate financial plan of the department of finance. Moreover, public finances should be spent purposefully and economically, with a view to achieving best value for money through appropriate and optimal means and methods. Therefore the employer will tender the contract only when there are sufficient funds to perform it according to public finance procedures.

The employer's freedom to choose the other party to the contract is limited by public procurement law. Thus the employer has no choice but to conclude a contract with a contractor who fulfills all conditions and wins the tender. A certain risk to the employer emerges because the winning bidder, even though they fulfil all tender conditions may turn out to be unreliable or have a bad reputation. This is sometimes impossible to verify in the procurement proceedings and may cause serious difficulties later on. On the other hand, the bidder's/contractor's freedom of contracting is, in practice, limited to the freedom to decide whether or not to participate in the particular public tender and what bid to submit. Otherwise they are wholly dependent on the procurement proceedings and the result of the tender. When the contractor's bid has been chosen, they cannot, in reality, withdraw from signing the contract.

The contractor's right to create and to negotiate the content of the contract is practically non-existent because the employer is obliged by public procurement law to introduce the essential terms and conditions of the contract in the terms of reference. In practice, employers very often attach a ready-made draft of the contract to the terms of reference and the contractor may only accept it and make an offer in the tender or step away. The contractor may only "negotiate" by asking questions under the terms of reference. However, it is solely at the employer's discretion whether to accept the contractor's suggestions.

After the contract has been tendered, both parties are again limited by public procurement law in their freedom to change and amend the contract as it is forbidden to introduce any significant changes unless those changes were anticipated in the terms of reference. This limitation is justified as "protecting the equality of the bidders"—the rationale being that significant changes to the contracts might influence the content of the bid of other bidders and the result of the procurement might be different (see below).

The *Public Procurement Act* contains provisions that modify the contractual rights of the party in favour of the public employer. It is justified by the need to protect the public employer who acts in the public's general interest; they are bearing more risk than usually taken by private entrepreneurs and therefore require increased protection. Such a statutory provision strengthening the position of the public employer in the contract is, for example, the statutory unilateral right of the employer to terminate the contract if the circumstances have changed significantly or in such a way that performance of the contract is not in the public interest any more. Otherwise unknown to other civil law contracts, public procurement contracts can be made void by a third party to the contract, such as the President of the Public Procurement Office, in circumstances outlined in the *Public Procurement Act*.

Under the freedom of contracting, parties can freely decide the content and purpose of the contract as long as it is not contrary to the "spirit" of the legal relationship, to the law (such as, for example, public procurement law, as described above) or to the principles of "community life." It seems acceptable under the rules of freedom of contracting to conclude a contract where the situation of the parties is not balanced and objectively much more advantageous to one over the other. The parties can enter into such a contract provided that they are fully aware of its consequences and neither of them has abused their dominant position before entering into such a contract. The principles of community life that should be abided by include equitable principles, commercial honesty, equal position of the parties of the contract, and treating the other party of the contract with loyalty and trust.

The question arises whether GDDKiA as the public employer and the party to the contract abuses its dominant position granted by the public procurement provisions or whether it really adheres to the equitable principles of contracting described above.

The latest examples (2014) of provisions of public procurement contracts in the recent public procurement procedures contain, for example, an unrealistically short period of time to perform the contract. This shifts excessively large risk and imposes numerous potential penalties on the contractor, including indemnity for possible loss of EU funding by the employer. This often requires the contractor to price the obligations of the employer, without documents, specifications and information which the employer should have provided. Polish public procurement law (*Public Procurement Act* and related ordinances) has been organized in such way that the procuring body (employer) shall define precisely the "public need" and seek the most economically advantageous way of satisfying that need. In practice, the scope has to be precisely specified and shall be deemed non-adjustable, that is, the most economically advantageous means the lowest price. There are various explanations for this *modus operandi*, one of the most popular being past experiences with corruption. In fact, limiting the right to negotiate the terms of the contract in the procurement process eliminates any possibility of offering favorable conditions for the preselected bidder. Similarly, limiting the selection criteria to price (with liberal participation conditions) should lead to transparent competition. However, such an approach usually facilitates the imposition of restrictive terms and conditions that cannot be influenced by the contractor. This "take it or leave it" approach offers only limited possibility to appeal the content under the terms of reference to the *Krajowa Izba Odwoławcza* (National Chamber of Appeals) (KIO). The KIO deals exclusively with *Public Procurement Act* violations (Art. 179). *The Civil Code* embraces the principle of freedom of contracts, that is, employers are free to create the terms of reference, including modifications to FIDIC forms. The only limitation would be a lack of bidders willing to participate in a tender. It is very difficult to prove that certain provisions of a contract breach the provisions of the *Public Procurement Act*. The bias in risks themselves is not illegal. It only becomes illegal if the risks are described in such way that they hinder the preparation of an offer. Even then the burden of proof is with the party that files the appeal (Article 29 and others). Typical modifications of FIDIC forms are then legal from the point of view of the KIO. There is no other court or body that would take into account the long-term effect of one-sided modifications and limit that practice. After EU accession the control over the rules of the public procurement system were transferred entirely to Poland as a member state. Due to unlimited employer powers of introducing specific conditions, FIDIC contracts (since 2004) started to gradually lose their original sense and balance. Nowadays, in such circumstances, contractors may often only choose between accepting these highly disadvantageous conditions or withdrawing from the market completely.

Aleksandra Marzec
Lawyer
District Chamber of Advocates in Katowice
Poland

Market environment prior to and after 2008: The need for change in procurement by Michał Skorupski (Poland)

The tendency to strengthen the bargaining position of the employer resulted from the situation as it existed in the 2004 to 2007. After joining the EU, Poland was promised significant subsidies for the development of its infrastructure and some argued that the supply side was not prepared to cope with the tasks in hand. The pre-accession projects were about to be completed and new financing perspectives negotiated. The years 2004 to 2007 in general were prosperous for the construction industry in Poland. In 2006 and at the beginning of 2007, a strong increase in construction prices was observed. The procurement law in those years offered a three-step appeal system, which was used by the contractors to block the commencement of some construction projects. In a well-known example, the tender procedure for the A4 construction contracts in the section Zgorzelec-Krzyżowa (western border) had to be cancelled and re-announced three times. The participation conditions were strict, and well-established companies were promoting themselves. This in turn resulted in quite a strong negotiating position of contractors who relied on balanced contract samples inherited from pre-accession programs without major adjustments in particular conditions. Moreover many of the infrastructure projects foresaw a dispute procedure in arbitration courts independent of the state, where arbitrators were often civil engineering professionals. Furthermore, Polish legislation in the area of construction law (the *Building Code*) and environmental law did not offer easy-to-follow solutions for timely initiation of projects.

In such conditions the government seemed to be seriously worried about the possibility of losing the subsidies negotiated from the EU for the years 2007 to 2013. The authorities started to work on new conditions for managing the projects in several different aspects. For example:

- New legislation in environmental law, building code, and public procurement law was introduced. While the construction and environmental obstacles in theory were minimized, the procurement law changes were clearly introduced to erode the contractors' power in the tender process; for example, instead of a three-stage appeal process now there was only one step available. The application fee to the court was also raised significantly making it almost prohibitively expensive to seek review. To speed up the project as a whole, authorities started to experiment with new procurement models, like design-build, which previously had been rarely used in Poland.
- The qualification criteria were drastically reduced; moreover, the government made specific efforts to invite companies from abroad to Poland (including Chinese companies).
- The contract forms were gradually amended to shift the powers on site to the employer. In this context it has to be recalled that, contrary to the practices under the Phare, Tacis, and ISPA programmes, the EU and EIB financiers no longer scrutinized ex-ante to ensure that the FIDIC standard forms, (generally the Red and Yellow Books), were used in a proper way.

The above measures were adopted not only in the construction contracts, but also to service contracts (engineering and design services).

The government concentrated on absorbing as much EU funding as possible, with little attention paid to the market position or economic signals. In the meantime the construction operators started to suffer from the collapse of the private construction market; offices, housing, and retail investments came to a grinding halt in 2008 with little finance available.

Since late 2008 more and more entities have participated in the public infrastructure market, with significant downward pressure put on prices and ambitious portfolios of projects executed by the government. So for next six years the market was much more competitive, with increasing bargaining power of the project owners. They had natural motivation to alter the FIDIC specific contract conditions increasing measures to command and control the contractor. Contracts became restrictive, liquidated damages unlimited, risks allocated almost entirely to the contractor.

Such circumstances led to some spectacular bankruptcies and project collapses in the public works sector. It seemed obvious, that the problem was not just on the contractors' side, but ultimately the project owners had their projects late with supply chain suffering from disputes and cash-flow limitations. The peak took place at the Euro 2012 contest, when the major projects were supposed to be open for public. A paradox was visible—with billions pumped in the infrastructure sector contractors were suffering, projects were late. Lot of people in the industry suffered personally. It all started to add to the political tensions and ultimately—let me suggest—contributed to change in power in Poland in 2015.

The now ruling Law and Justice party as one of their election promises offered to resolve the construction contracts problem. In fact in May 2016 a Council of Experts at the Ministry of Infrastructure and Construction have been created. The idea is that this will be a first step to create a body similar to Dutch CROW or British JCT, that will in long-term develop best practices in procurement and contracting. The council has agreed on basic risk allocation matrix for the two most used forms of contracts. Also in February 2017 some interim alterations to the previously used specific contract conditions were introduced. I had a pleasure to participate in negotiating those temporary measures. It is now difficult to predict whether the momentum will continue. Some key decisions are yet to be made in the area of change management or dispute resolution.

Michał Skorupski
Contract Manager
Member of SIDiR
Association of Consulting Engineers and Experts in Poland
Poland

17.5.1 Abnormally low price

A large part of the problems encountered in Poland originate from low contractor bid prices. In Poland, the only criterion taken into account in bid evaluation by employers was the lowest price. When planning expenditures to be financed by EU grants, the GDDKiA removed barriers of entry to the market by lowering the requirements for tender applicants. As a result, the number of contractors to whom contracts were awarded grew significantly. Contracts were even available to contractors from China and India. These contractors offered unrealistically low bid prices through price dumping. Faced with such a situation, established companies had to propose exceptionally low prices to stay competitive. The employer rarely rejects a tender if it contains an abnormally low price but is authorized to do so under the *Public Procurement Act* (Article 81, Section 1, item 4). Moreover, the notion of "abnormally low price" has not been precisely determined and the burden of proof requirement still remains a hurdle in the Polish legal system. For example, if a competitor A offers a very low price and competitor B wishes to appeal against the selection of the tender A, then competitor B has to prove that price A is abnormally low. In other words competitor B has to prove that competitor A will not be able to perform the contract for price A without a loss. In practice, this is difficult without full access to competitor A's books and records. In fact, the track record of KIO demonstrates that it is virtually impossible to convince judges of the fact that a competitor has offered an abnormally low price.

The price offered by the Chinese consortium COVEC (which built the A2 motorway) was 71% lower than the price anticipated by the employer. Despite this, the price was not considered to be exceptionally low by the proper authority (in this case the KIO) when applying Polish public procurement law. COVEC won the tender and, subsequently, abandoned the building site in 2011 and left huge debts to their subcontractors. The re-awarded contracts were 53% and 65% more expensive than the COVEC price, as well as 17% and 24% more expensive than the second-ranking company that had originally lost to COVEC. Contractors are forced to offer prices that are only marginally profitable. In such circumstances, any unforeseen problems in the contract or increase in material prices causes additional costs and put the contractor in peril of losing financial liquidity or falling into bankruptcy. This has already happened to a number of Polish and foreign construction companies participating in Polish construction projects.

Facing insolvency, the general contractors were relentlessly pressing their losses down by not paying their subcontractors, suppliers and service providers. This not only affects direct project participants but also small and medium-sized enterprises who are part of the overall supply chain.

Moreover, Polish construction contracts hardly ever provide for any adjustment or indexation of the contract price. As a result, the contract prices of large infrastructural projects (where time for completion extends over several years), are frozen and all risks of inflation or changes in the market burden the contractor. In the period 2010 to 2012, construction material prices in Poland increased significantly due to projects related to the European football championship. At the same time, the contract price could not be amended as in the vast majority of contracts Sub-Clause 13.8 had been deleted. Lately, the Polish courts have in some cases after several years of legal battles partly accepted the contractors claims for additional payments because of unforeseeable changes in cost.

17.5.2 Inefficient risk allocation

Against the constant and express advice of FIDIC itself, the FIDIC books continue to be significantly deformed by the public employers in Poland via the particular conditions. As a starting point it has to be kept in mind that in the FIDIC CONS/1999 Red Book, there are only few clauses where particular conditions are necessary, that is for example, Sub-Clause 1.1.3.6—tests after completion, Sub-Clause 1.6—form of contract agreement, and Sub-Clause 18.2—details of employer's insurances.

In Poland, the contractual practice has been reversed. As an example of a typical shift in risk allocation, take a 500 million euro design-build project of a railway station and subway construction co-financed by the EU (started in 2010). The following contractor's rights to file claims (FIDIC P&DB/1999 Yellow Book) were deleted via the 120 pages of particular conditions. In Sub-Clauses 1.9 (Errors in the Employer's Requirements), 10.3 (Interference with Tests on Completion), 11.8 (Contractor to Search), 12.2 (Delayed Tests), 12.4 (Failure to Pass Tests after Completion), 17.4 (Consequences of Employer's Risks), and 19.4 (Consequences of *Force Majeure*), both extension of time and additional payment claims were removed. Such intervention in an underground contract must of course cause negative consequences in project management and contract administration.

Furthermore, in Sub-Clauses 2.1 (Right of Access to the Site), 4.7 (Setting Out), 4.12 (Unforeseeable Physical Conditions), 4.24 (Fossils), 7.4 (Testing), 8.9 (Consequences of Suspension), 10.2 (Taking Over of Parts of the Works), 12.2 (Delayed Tests), 12.4 (Failure to Pass Tests after Completion), and 16.1 (Contractor's Entitlement to Suspend Work) the additional payment claims were deleted.

The Sub-Clause 8.4 EOT claims at (c) Exceptionally adverse climatic conditions and at (d) Unforeseeable shortages in the availability of personnel or Goods caused by epidemic or governmental actions were removed by employers as were Sub-Clauses 13.7 (Adjustments for Changes in Legislation), and 13.8 (Adjustments for Changes in Cost). This caused procurement processes to come to a grinding halt with thousands of questions from bidders and other participants about the changed conditions delaying projects for months.

These are only a few examples of the change in risk allocation. In reality, the contract has nothing in common with the original FIDIC forms. Such interventions confuse the contract and the parties must then rely on insufficient Polish governing law and unsettled precedents of Polish courts.

In another contract, a 200 million euro design-build project (started in 2013) of inner city transport infrastructure re-construction projects (co-financed by the EU), the FIDIC P&DB/1999 Yellow Book is deformed via 70 pages of particular conditions. Typical modifications are, for example, that Sub-Clause 8.7 contains dozens of contractual penalties (including milestones penalties) for the contractor but there are no penalties for the employer. The contractor also has the duty to submit daily progress reports (stipulated in the modified Sub-Clause 4.21) or face contractual penalty. High daily contractual penalties are established for the late submission of design, time schedule (Sub-Clause 8.3, Programme), quality assurance system (Sub-Clause 4.9), and so on. The engineer can comment on those documents and ask for modifications to be made. If these modifications are not incorporated by the contractor in seven days, the engineer/employer can file for a penalty. Those provisions are commonly abused by the employer and the engineer to gain a better bargaining position during realization and to impose penalties.

A typical example is a situation where the engineer has, for example, 14 days to approve the contractor's design or time program and waits until the last day of this period, causing critical delay. This in turn allows the employer to impose contractual penalties/delay damages.

Sub-Clauses such as 4.9, 4.21, and 8.3 are extended via particular conditions in an extreme way. For example, there are such onerous requirements in the content of the program, progress report and quality assurance plan that it is difficult to fulfil them. Short terms for submission of these documents (with contractual penalties for delay) are stipulated in the contract. These are almost impossible to submit on time because the contractor is not fully mobilized at this stage. Moreover, it is common practice that these documents are rejected many times without reason. Once again, this is an abuse of power and position by the engineer (employer) to gain greater control, strengthen their bargaining position, and seek contractual penalties.

Sub-Clause 8.3 contains, for example, a provision that the engineer will not accept the programme or its updates in which the time for completion will be extended based on pending or rejected claims by the engineer or the employer in accordance with Sub-Clause 20.1. In reality, all contractor claims are pending or rejected.

Furthermore, the contract contains a modification of Sub-Clause 10.2. The contractor must submit "complete documents" to have the taking over right to work. If the work is not taken over in the stated time, contractual penalties are triggered. Another typical example of conduct done "in bad faith" is where the employer creates artificial reasons to refuse taking over the works to impose contractual penalties/delay damages. This is done, for example, by demanding further documents stating that the submitted documents are not "complete." In this way contractual penalties increase—and the employer's bargaining position with them. Contractor claims and contractual penalties are usually off-set against the contractor's last invoice—often resulting in a loss on the project for the contractor.

Furthermore, the employer can terminate the contract for numerous reasons (named in the modified Sub-Clause 15.2 or for other reasons "caused" by the contractor). The contractor will pay a 15% contractual penalty, if the employer terminates the contract. The reasons for contractor termination are narrowed to late payments by the employer and there is no contractual penalty.

17.5.3 Consortiums

Problems also arise in connection with public procurement law where the contractor forms a consortium. Joint and several liability of such a "plural" contractor is mentioned both in the *Public Procurement Act* (Art. 141) and in the contract (1.14 c). As a result of this, it is in fact impossible to withdraw from a consortium contract. If withdrawal does take place, the remaining member of the consortium will always be liable to the employer for financing and realization of the contract. There are also no coherent regulations concerning the issue of a consortium partner falling into bankruptcy. In such circumstances, the remaining consortium partners bear responsibility for the insolvent partner's debt. All subcontractors of the bankrupt contractor as well as the employer will claim all outstanding payments from the solvent partners, instead of lodging a claim against the bankrupt estate. This combination of regulations effectively defeats (to some extent) the purpose of the insolvency proceedings as the other, remaining party is made responsible (to a large extent) for the insolvent party's debts. Consequently, one party's insolvency may very quickly lead to another party facing financial difficulties. Negative consequences for the particular construction project as a whole may also follow.

17.5.4 Contract administration: the Engineer

The position of the contract administrator is of key importance. A contract administrator (the engineer) hired by the employer on a professional service agreement basis coordinates, monitors, supervises the compliance with standards, certifies the works done, tests, taking over, participates in variation, price and time management, claim evaluation, contract interpretation, and dispute avoidance. They should help to perform a successful project in a fair way and in accordance with the contract achieving the demanded standard by the agreed time and for agreed price. According to FIDIC forms (both the CONS/1999 Red Book and P&DB/1999 Yellow Book), the engineer's role is to mediate solutions for numerous problems and disputes occurring between the employer and the contractor. The engineer is part of the employer's personnel but still acts as a third party and neutral mediator who settles disputes between the employer and the contractor quickly and effectively. In the original FIDIC forms, the role of the engineer had been as expert who had to provide determinations based on all relevant circumstances, after duly consulting the given problem with both parties (Sub-Clause 3.5 of the FIDIC forms). In Polish practice, the role of the engineer has been limited to the employer's representative who is wholly dependent on the employer's instructions. Such limitation of the engineer's role infringes upon the contractual equilibrium and leads to the paradox of the Polish construction contract where the court becomes the third party to the contract. If every dispute between the employer and the contractor must be solved by a court, effective and timely realization of the project becomes almost impossible.

The main reason why such a situation occurs is that there is no compatibility between the engineer's contract and the main contract. There is a conflict issue between those two contracts and the question arises: which contract should the engineer abide by in the first place? The engineer's contract provides an exhaustive catalogue of their duties—all of which are secured by rigid contractual penalties. Thanks to these, the engineer is effectively controlled by the employer. Also, according to the engineer's contract, one of the main goals of the engineer is to make sure that the contract does not exceed the employer's budget. Such a goal is often difficult to reconcile with the goal of performing the works in an "efficient, timely, proper and safe manner." According to Sub-Clause 3.1 "the employer undertakes not to impose further constraints on the engineer's authority, except as agreed with the contractor." At the same time, the engineer's contract states that "the engineer shall abide by the instructions given by the employer's project coordinator." There seems to be an obvious contradiction between these requirements and it is impossible for the engineer to fulfil the requirements of both contracts.

Contractors now are demanding that the engineers (companies performing this role as well as individuals) perform their duties under the contract with due diligence, that is, to take due regard of all relevant circumstances, including those circumstances which are advantageous to the contractor. It is quite typical in retrospect to prepare claims based purely on the inadequate performance of the engineer.

Negligence of the engineer is the contractual responsibility of the employer (Article 474 of the *Polish Civil Code*). However, the engineer may be personally liable for their actions if they exceed their proxy (Articles 103 and 104 of the *Polish Civil Code*). In all cases the engineer can even be held responsible for the contractor's loss occurring as result of unlawful conduct of the contractor (Articles 361, 415, and 430 of the *Polish Civil Code*). This serves as a timely reminder of the engineer's duties and potential individual responsibility.

During any construction process unexpected problems can arise. For example, unforeseeable ground conditions on site. Such problems require a prompt decision and clear instructions from the engineer (employer). However, the decision-making process of the Polish Public Employer tends to be rather ineffective and extremely prolonged. For example, when notified by the contractor about the discovery of a minor fossil (Sub-Clause 4.24), it took the employer a couple of months to make a decision on the issue. When notified by the contractor about the discrepancy between the documentation provided by the employer and the geological condition on the site (Sub-Clauses 4.1; 13.1), it took the employer over a year and a half to first acknowledge the problem and then give the contractor the required instructions as to the new technology of works. This obviously delays the works and makes it extremely difficult for the contractor to schedule properly.

Claims considerations by Aleksandra Marzec (Poland)

In 2004, employers began to abandon the idea of using dispute adjudication boards or arbitration tribunals. In fact, in the majority of transportation projects claim resolution is now limited only to the determination of the engineer (who is subject to employer pressure) and the courts. The movement away from ADR was meant to limit the influx of claims. The result has been the opposite—more and more cases are not solved on site but left to a future court outcome. The response of contractors was to strengthen their claims policy in order to gain a better bargaining position in court.

This is a great example of a broken will to resolve naturally encountered problems on site with common sense. Despite the culturally negative meaning of the word "claim," more and more claims are created and courts are flooded with cases that otherwise would have been resolved on site in due time.

The general claims consideration process concerning Polish large road or motorway construction investments is protracted and ineffective. A very short time to notify and quantify claims is often given (shorter than in original FIDIC form, for example, 14 days instead of 28 days for the notice according to the Sub-Clause 20.1). After the initial hurry, claims are considered and "sat on" for an excessively long period. Most of the claims are classified as interim and, as a result, the contractor does not receive any payment for the costs incurred until the final claim is considered. There is also no transparency in the justification of the engineer's and employer's decisions concerning claims.

It is also very often the case that the employer repeatedly extends the time for completion by short periods, even though the claims justify longer extensions and both parties know that it will be impossible to complete the project within the extended time. As a result, contractors are sometimes working on construction sites for several months without a granted extension of time. The "time at large" approach is not perceived in Poland in the same way as in common law countries and it is usual for participants of construction projects to assume the project as "officially" extended only in cases where a signed annex is attached to the contract. The contractor's situation becomes uncertain and, further, it makes it extremely difficult to prepare a reasonable and efficient schedule of the works complying with the contractual conditions. At the same time, the contractor is still required to deliver bank performance guarantees and insurance. These requirements are, in fact, almost impossible to satisfy because banks and insurers are often unwilling to issue such guarantees on the basis of an annex. It is an abnormal "vicious circle" type situation in which the contractor is in deadlock.

The ineffectiveness of the claim consideration process can be illustrated with the following example. A design was prepared without soil investigations and discrepancies between the design and actual conditions arose on site. Regardless of the fact that such discrepancies were the result of mistakes made during the design of works or changes in the environment, the problem needed immediate decisions to be made and reasonable technical solutions to be found in order to prevent suspensions or delays of works. In subsequent geological surveys and expert opinions, the errors of the design were revealed. However, for a considerable period of time, (over a year) the employer ignored the problem and only instructed the contractor to proceed according to the tender design and other documentation. This was despite an independent expert's opinion obtained by the contractor which was also approved by the engineer. When the engineer gave instruction of variation on the basis of this expert opinion, the employer demanded the engineer replace their staff and he was held personally responsible for these decisions. When the problem could no longer be ignored and the instructions of variation were eventually approved by the employer, the cost of a technical solution was several times higher than it should have been if the appropriate remedy had been applied immediately after discovering the problem. It was further necessary to extend the time for completion by over 300 days.

According to data obtained in February 2013, of 4,200 claims filed by contractors, 2,000 have been rejected, 2,000 were being still examined, and only 75 have been accepted. A further 53 claims were withdrawn by contractors. These numbers clearly illustrate the problem. It seems that the employer introduced a policy of not accepting claims in general based on a short-term (and often short-sighted) approach in an attempt: (1) to save public money; and (2) to strictly adhere to contract conditions under public procurement law. In 2018, the amount of disputed contractor claims solved by Polish courts is said to be around US$4 billion.

Any deductions from the payments due to the contractor (such as contractual penalties imposed by the employer) can prevent the contractor from continuing with the works. For example, the employer may make an arbitrary decision to withdraw a bank performance guarantee or impose contractual penalties by deducting them from payment. The contractor may then file a lawsuit in court but this is expensive and time-consuming. In the meantime, it is the contractor who bears the significant and additional financial burden of litigation. Moreover, as it was confirmed in the recent court practice, the courts tend to adjudicate that a bank guarantee (issued to the benefit of the employer as a performance bond) is an abstract legal act and the guarantor is not obliged or entitled to examine whether a demand of an employer for withdrawal of bank guarantee was substantially justified or not. Therefore, in the event of any dispute, concerning for example the justification of contractual penalties of either party, the contractor's position in such a possible dispute is much more difficult from the very beginning.

An example is the case (I CSK 748/12) where the Polish Supreme Court (the last instance court in Poland) confirmed that contractual penalties imposed on the contractor after a delay caused by GDDKiA are not acceptable as they are in conflict with the principle that a debtor cannot be in delay if the creditor is in delay. What is worth mentioning is that the respective project commenced in 2002.

Aleksandra Marzec
Lawyer
District Chamber of Advocates in Katowice
Poland

17.5.5 Specific legislation for subcontractors

In recent years, it has been the tendency of the Polish legislator to better protect the interests of the subcontractors. This move was in response to the large number of bad debts and bankruptcies among small- and medium-sized entrepreneurs involved in the construction business. As a first step, Article 647 was added to the *Polish Civil Code* in 2003. Article 647 stipulates that the employer and contractor are jointly and severally liable for the payment to the subcontractor and subsequent subcontractor. An employer is responsible for the payment to subcontractors and further subcontractors only if certain conditions are fulfilled (i.e., if they accept the basic terms and conditions of the subcontractor's contract in the prescribed period of time). However, if an employer was informed about the subcontractor's contract in writing but did not respond to it within 14 days, then according to the *Polish Civil Code,* they gave their implicit acceptance. Obviously, if an employer makes a payment directly to the subcontractor based on this provision, they will have a retrospective claim against the contractor (and such claim will usually be off-set by the contractor's payment). The same rules apply also to the contractor who is responsible for payment to further subcontractors. The rule of implied acceptance described above may lead to a risk of double payment for the same works. If the contractor (or employer) is unaware that they gave implicit acceptance for certain, further subcontractors or that they have not been paid properly, the employer may be forced to pay them for the work that has already been paid for to the subcontractor. If they pursue a retrospective claim against the subcontractor who was obliged to pay in the first place, this may not always be effective, for example, if the subcontractor became insolvent. These provisions are incorporated into all Polish FIDIC-based contracts in Sub-Clause 4.4.

A new, "special purpose act" named *"The Repayment of Some Unpaid Due Amount of the Entrepreneurs, which Resulted from the Realization of the Public Procurement Act"* (Dz.U. z 2012 r. poz. 891) came into effect in 2012 ("the Act"). This Act stipulates that any micro, small, or medium entrepreneur who performs some works, provides supplies or services connected with the public procurement granted by the GDDKiA, and who cannot avail themselves of Article 647 of the *Polish Civil Code* can be paid directly by the GDDKiA from the special national roads fund. The GDDKiA has a claim against the contractor to return the amount paid on the basis of this act. The procedure of confirming such amounts due is not transparent and it causes many practical problems. Moreover, the act applies only to the public procurements granted or initiated before the enactment of the act. Therefore, it is in fact only a temporary and short-term solution. Its retroactive application is also questionable from a legal point of view. While small subcontractors' and suppliers' interests are secured and their situation has improved, the question of whether the main contractor's rights and interests have been significantly infringed remains.

17.5.6 Courts and litigation

Arbitration clauses and dispute adjudication boards have been progressively removed from most of the Polish roads contracts based on FIDIC. Public employers (such as GDDKiA) have been instructed to do so by the General Attorney of the Treasury—the body which represents government departments in the courts. Sub-Clauses 20.2 to 20.8 are often replaced with only one sentence: "All disputes will be settled by the common court of the Employer's jurisdiction." As a result, all disputes resulting from large road and motorway projects are dealt with by the district court in Warsaw because it is the only court with the jurisdiction to do so. Court proceedings are lengthy and tend to distance themselves from facilitating current realization of the contract. A first instance decision can be appealed a further two times up the court hierarchy in Poland (including the cassation appeal before the Supreme Court). This means that litigation usually comes to an end long after the project is completed and contractual responsibilities discharged. Therefore, court proceedings do not really influence the actual realization of the project.

Recently in Poland there has not been many motorway, highway, or bypass construction project that has not experienced claims being notified during the execution of related works. These claims turn into litigation in the majority of cases. Current trends reveal that in 2010 the Polish courts handled 10 construction cases, in 2011 around 40 and in 2012 almost 100.

All the cases against GDDKiA reach the aforementioned District Court of Warsaw. This court, until recently, had dealt with some 1,500 cases a year, mainly in the field of family law, protection of personal property and accident indemnities.

To reduce this tendency, the *Public Procurement Act* was amended so that contractors are now automatically disqualified from participating in Polish tenders for three years if a Polish court confirms a penalty of 5% or more of the contract amount (Amendment of October 12, 2012, which came into force on 20 February 2013 (Dz.U. z 2012 r. poz. 1271)).

The use of alternative dispute resolution procedures in Poland is very limited. The benchmark is, of course, FIDIC's dispute adjudication board (DAB) comprising of suitably qualified adjudicators. If such an adjudication procedure were followed, it could prevent the parties from breaching the contract and many disputes could be settled without a court, while the contract is still "live" on site—provided of course that both parties respect the DAB's decision. However, the clauses stipulating DABs are usually removed from the contract. In fact only a few transportation projects have Sub-Clauses 20.3 and 20.4 remaining in force. The vast majority escalate disputes from the level of the engineer to the court directly.

According to data obtained on September 19, 2013, the value of court litigation involving GDDKiA and the contractors has reached approximately 6 billion PLN (US$2 billion), not including current claims worth 3.8 to 5 billion PLN. Therefore, total contractor claims amount to nearly 10 to 11 billion PLN (US$3.3 to 3.6 billion). In 2016 it was confirmed by the ministry of infrastructure and construction that the total value of litigations issued by the contractors against GDDKiA amounted to approximately 10 billion PLN (http://www.bankier.pl/wiadomosc/Wiceminister-infrastruktury-Roszczenia-wykonawcow-wobec-GDDKiA-to-okolo-10-mld-zl-3511079.html). The amount and value of claims indicate that there are some serious problems in the Polish approach to large infrastructure projects. In 2018, the amount of disputed contractor claims solved by Polish courts is said to be around US$4 billion.

At this stage GDDKiA seems to appreciate the problem and it officially declares to be ready to talk about amicable settlements with contractors where appropriate.

What is interesting, the legal dispute between Chinese COVEC and GDDKiA resulting from A2 motorway project, found its end in such an amicable settlement concluded between the parties in July 2017. The details of the settlement have not been made public but GDDKiA officially stated that the settlement covered mutual claims of both parties concerning A2 motorway project and it terminated the prolonged (over 6 years) litigation between the parties (https://www.gddkia.gov.pl/pl/a/26149/Ugoda-pomiedzy-GDDKiA-a-firma-COVEC-zawarta).

This case demonstrates how costly and time-consuming the litigations concerning large road construction projects can be and how ineffective and useless they are for either party, not to mention the public interest. Even more if they are terminated by an amicable settlement which, as it is often said, in fact means a failure of each party. The result of this case also proves how extremely difficult it is for either party of a dispute to evidence their claims and win the case before the public court, especially as so much time passes from the actual events on site. Therefore, it seems that the appropriate measures should be undertaken in the future to prevent arising such disputes in the first place, ADR development being one of them.

The number, extent, and complexity of matters being filed in connection with construction of roads are so huge that litigation often spreads over several months and the expected time for resolution can be given in years (and this is only in the first instance). Moreover, it cannot be foreseen when the relevant litigation will be definitely concluded once all avenues of appeal are exhausted. This brings further uncertainty because of the lack of settled precedents.

The uncertainty of the decisions of the Polish courts can be demonstrated by the outcomes concerning conditions precedent for claiming. One opinion is that the *Polish Civil Code* at Article 118 determines the limitation period for construction claims to be three years from the event or circumstance, and the freedom of contracts cannot take priority over this statutory rule because of Article 119 of the *Polish Civil Code* that reads that "limitation periods cannot be shortened or extended by legal action." Time limits for claims under the Sub-Clause 20.1 can be seen as shortening the limitation period. This opinion was confirmed in the judgment of the district court in Warsaw on July 13, 2011 (file: XXV C-701/10) and also on June 11, 2012 (file: XXV C-567/11), including the confirmation by the Court of Appeals (on the March 20, 2013 year; file No. VI ACa-1315/12), which ruled that the respective part of the Sub-Clause 20.1 is invalid under Polish law. The argument being that:

> there is no reason to assume that the scope of freedom of contract goes so far as to allow for free creation of contractual deadlines causing the extinction of claims related to property, in particular, where such claims are subject to statutory regulation on limitation.

On the other hand, there are several awards of the same court stating the opposite. For example in judgments on 6 June 2012 (file: XXV C-1215/10), on 7 March 2012 (file: XXV C-249/11) and on 30 April 2013 (file: XXV C-355/10). In the last case it was argued that:

in accordance with the general principle of freedom of contract stated in the art. 353 [1] of the Civil Code it is possible to contractually agree a period of time after which the creditor's claim expires. This is not contrary to the art. 119 of the Civil Code. The effects and functions of time bars and periods of limitation are different.

Until some Supreme Court precedent is in place, the uncertainty created by such contradictory awards will remain. Therefore, it is highly recommended to strictly observe the notification periods provided in the contract.

Contractor defense measures by Michał Skorupski (Poland)

Needless to say, the legal and market environment for years was far from favorable to private operators in the public construction sector (i.e., contractors, service engineering companies, design companies). This then lead to the setting up of intensified defence mechanisms and counter-claims emerging in the industry.

The role of claim management was elevated to an important part of any contract with a Polish public employer. The rule of limited trust and gathering evidence for any potential default or negligence on the employer's side generally prevailed. A typical large contract began with an assumption of bad faith and distrust of the other party. Meetings were recorded and letters analyzed to discover hidden meaning.

In this aggressive environment, contractors learned to use and misuse their rights and opportunities. Put simply, it was a matter of survival for them.

The increase of aggressive methods on the contractors' side have "stirred the hornet's nest" on the employers' side. Claim management departments, long-term advisory contracts, teams of lawyers dedicated to contract management are all commonplace in road or railway procurement projects. In the absence of any country-wide, commonly respected body for dialogue, it seemed legal language and discussions through lawyers were there to stay for the foreseeable future.

However in 2016, after introduction of the Council of Experts at the Ministry, some dialogue started to take place. It is too soon to decide whether the traditionally adversarial approach in infrastructure contracts will change. During past years contractors have learnt some techniques to defend their financial position in the contract, for example:

- financing through late payments or refusal to pay to the subcontractors; because the employer is legally responsible for the payments to the subcontractor, if the general contractor does not pay, the subcontractor can directly seek payment from the employer; so if the employer refuses to pay the last invoice of the general contractor (e.g., compensating liquidated damages), the general contractor does not pay the subcontractors
- copying ultra-restrictive contract conditions into the subcontracts; note however, that now the employers restrict such possibility (sic) and the general contractor has to take the risk!
- "optimization": this concept has a lot to do with misunderstanding of the principles of a design and build project; contractors now feel entitled to make changes in specification

(supplied in the DB project often by the employer as additional requirement), as long as the general functionality is satisfied
- provoking project owners mistakes in management to get a claim possibility

Let me be clear—the astute ways of escaping contractual liabilities have been invented and developed as response to the state approach. So it is now for the state to demonstrate some trust can be built in future.

Michał Skorupski
Contract Manager
Member of SIDiR
Association of Consulting Engineers and Experts in Poland
Poland

17.5.7 Consequences of inefficient risk allocation

In January 2014, FIDIC, EFCA, and SIDIR (a member of FIDIC and EFCA—representing the interests of consulting engineering firms in Poland) published a joint common press release entitled "*Engineering Consultants Concerned with Public Procurement Practices in Poland.*"

According to this document, FIDIC is particularly concerned with the imposition of particular conditions in contracts that drastically shift the fair balance of risk and responsibility and distort the FIDIC approach to best practice. The result has been low efficiency of national construction investment programs. This in turn has directly (or indirectly) led to massive litigation, bankruptcies, and loss of jobs in the Polish construction sector. FIDIC, EFCA, and SIDIR urged the Polish government and contracting authorities: (1) to award public contracts on the criterion of the most economically advantageous tender, as published in the new EU Procurement Directives; and (2) to re-introduce internationally accepted construction contracts, with any specific modifications to be agreed by all parties, but retaining the core features of balanced risk and responsibility.

At the beginning of 2014, another three large motorway and road projects were terminated in Poland simultaneously before completion. In these cases the consortium demanded from the GDDKiA the guarantee for payment of the residual amount of remuneration for each of the contracts. This was the contractor's statutory right under *the Civil Code*. The GDDKiA provided the consortium with a document, which, in the contractor's opinion, did not fulfill the conditions of the bank guarantee and gave no real security to the contractor because it could be revoked at any time by GDDKiA. As a consequence, the consortium notified the employer of termination of the contracts based on civil law provisions. In return, GDDKiA notified the consortium of termination of the same contracts based on breach of contract provisions the very next day.

Both parties claim that the other party's withdrawal was unfounded or unlawful and accordingly each party tried to penalize the other for terminating the contract. The consortium claims that GDDKiA had not provided the acceptable guarantee for payment and that GDDKiA's termination was late and therefore void. The GDDKiA in response claimed that the guarantee provided was sufficient and that the consortium was in delay and termination was justified. Also these cases resulted in prolonged litigations before Polish public courts, starting in 2014 and in 2017 still with any substantial judgement in the first instance. Needless to say, the disputes require significant amount of time, effort, and money from both parties, including specialized legal representation, costly experts' opinions and huge amount of documents. The mutual claims and allegations are not obvious or easy to prove for either party, especially as more and more time passes from the actual events on sites. And the public Polish courts must find such cases difficult to judge, especially bearing in mind that in the first instance such cases are being considered by a single judge, who is a lawyer and not an engineer. In this view, the role of dispute adjudication board as it was anticipated in original FIDIC seems even more significant and needed in the Polish construction practice.

In February 2014, the head of the GDDKiA was dismissed from office by the prime minister. This decision was a result of an overall evaluation of the work of the existing management. The official reasons were that the existing management team had been working together for six years and "fresh blood" was needed to ensure transport infrastructure investments financed from the new EU budget for the years 2014 to 2020 would continue. The following were mentioned as "serious problems" in Poland: delays in realization and poor relationships and cooperation with contractors and the greater construction industry. The new head will try to avoid repeating the "dark days" between 2007 to 2013, which will go down in history as a period of bankruptcies of many construction companies.

Poland is often referred to as the "largest construction site in Europe" but is an atypical beneficiary of European subsidies. Over the last seven years alone the length of motorways in Poland has tripled despite the financial crisis. However, any strong, viable companies that could export their services and expertise abroad have failed to develop in Poland despite the completion of a number of major road programs. This is in contrast to Spain, for example, where strong construction companies were brought to life thanks to EU subsidies. As a result of this, Spanish companies now own a 40% market share of the contractor tenders for GDDKiA.

To improve the current situation in the long term, it is crucial to revert to the application of a fair and balanced standard form of contract. If Poland and other CEE countries cannot achieve this goal by themselves, then it is the responsibility of the international and European funders to insist on this issue as a prerequisite for disbursing the funds. It is hardly comprehensible that the World Bank, the EBRD, and the EIB require developing countries to have contractual conditions that are fair and reasonable and provide a balanced allocation of risks and liabilities but refrain from requiring any contractual standards when spending European taxpayers' money in Europe.

One of the key questions is the position of the EU on these matters. In this context it is encouraging to note that the EU legislator adopted Regulation No 1316/2013 of the European Parliament and of the Council, establishing the *Connecting Europe Facility*, which states in Recital 65:

> In order to ensure broad and fair competition for projects benefitting from CEF funds, the form of the contract should be consistent with the objectives and circumstances of the project. Contract conditions should

be drafted in such a way as to fairly allocate the risks associated with the contract, in order to maximise cost-effectiveness and enable the contract to be performed with the optimum efficiency. This principle should apply irrespective of whether a national or international contract model is used.

Whereas before, the EU Commission could only act if the general principles of procurement were violated (such as transparency, fairness, and non-discrimination), the CEF Regulation can now provide the European Commission with a specific powers to investigate alleged shortcomings, even though the principle has only been addressed in a recital and not in an article in a regulation.

There still is an obvious regulation gap in EU law when compared with the leverage applied by the multilateral development banks vis-à-vis their borrowers, which prevents the EU commission from becoming legally engaged in case of misuse of contractual conditions by a state authority. A remedy to this inefficiency would help to put the CEE EU member states (particularly Poland), on a par with their Western European counterparts and would promote the further sound development and competitiveness of the European construction industry.

17.6 The Czech experience

In the Czech Republic, the development of managerial and legal aspects of large infrastructure projects was heavily influenced by the period of a centrally planned economy. The rules and principles used during the communist era would not have been appropriate in open market conditions. In fact, after the Velvet Revolution, there were two possible ways of moving forward. The first was to revert to the advanced, pre-World War II laws and traditions of the First Czechoslovak Republic or, second, to start a new tradition. The latter option was chosen. A new tradition meant that new standard contracts or some established foreign documents could be readily adopted. Thanks to the conditions for EU funding (ISPA, Phare) demanding the use of such time-proven forms of contract, FIDIC forms started to be used as a recognized standard in projects financed by the EU all over the CEE. Because of the lack of a traditional form of contract in the Czech Republic, FIDIC forms became a part of the public procurement system in the Czech Republic, as they have in Poland, Romania, Slovakia, and many other countries.

From the 1990s, the Czech Directory of Roads and Highways (DRH) has used the FIDIC CONS/1999 Red Book translated into Czech and, from 2002, in the form of a document called the *Commercial Conditions for Roads and Highways Construction* (*Obchodní podmínky staveb pozemních komunikací*). In the early years, participants of construction projects did not obey the rules stated in FIDIC forms and actually followed practices they were used to. Step by step, they started to understand and use the FIDIC contractual procedures.

General contracting remains the project delivery method of choice used for almost all construction projects in transportation infrastructure public procurement. DRH is responsible for the design and provides detailed drawings, specifications and a bill of quantities for the tender documentation. Rates and prices priced in the contractor's bid at their risk are re-measured according to the actual need and paid on the basis of monthly statements of works done. Contract administration is done by the engineer.

Right up until the tenders were received for the reconstruction of the D1 Highway in 2013, FIDIC forms were used without major adjustments per particular conditions, that is, a balanced risk allocation and the overall meaning of the contract stayed preserved.

However, at the eleventh hour of the tender process, DRH released 100 pages of new conditions that changed the balanced risk allocation in the FIDIC forms. The main factors causing this were political pressure and lack of knowledge of DRH legal counsels, in this case attorneys that later profited out of it because they were hired to solve the following questions and disputes. Numerous questions from bidders and other participants about the new conditions delayed the procurement process extensively. After this experience, DRH changed the particular conditions to become more balanced but this did not stop the claims that must have been noticed by the contractors because of confusing contractual conditions. The money spent for attorneys were later strongly criticised by the Supreme Audit Office, which lead to a reform and a new strategy being prepared.

In 2015, new translations of 1999 FIDIC forms were introduced and implemented step by step in large construction projects financed by the Czech Infrastructure Funding Agency. New balanced particular conditions for highway projects were prepared and FIDIC Rainbow Suite experience a "re-implementation". Further public clients such Railway Agency, Waterways Agency, City of Prague, Universities and Ministries now follow this path. Examples are to be seen for example here http://www.pjpk.cz/obchodni-podminky.

This strategy is accompanied by implementation of particular sector methodologies such as the:

- Methodology for Public Procurement of Design and Build Projects under FIDIC Forms (see it here http://www.sfdi.cz/soubory/obrazky-clanky/metodiky/2015_metodika_db_zaverecna_prezentace.pdf),
- Methodology for Variations Administration under FIDIC Forms for Public Procurement Projects under Czech/EU Public Procurement Law (see it here http://www.sfdi.cz/soubory/obrazky-clanky/metodiky/2018_metodika_variaci_1_vydani.pdf),
- Methodology for Construction Projects Time Management under FIDIC Forms (see it here http://www.sfdi.cz/soubory/obrazky-clanky/metodiky/2018_metodika_casove_rizeni_fidic.pdf),
- Methodology for Quantification of Financial Claims under FIDIC Forms (see it here http://www.sfdi.cz/soubory/obrazky-clanky/metodiky/2018_metodika_naroku.pdf),
- Methodology for Re-measurement under FIDIC Forms,
- Methodology for Most Economically Advantageous Tenders Procurement,
- Methodology for Abnormally Low Tenders Treatment,
- Methodology for Value Engineering under FIDIC Forms (all to be seen here http://www.sfdi.cz/pravidla-metodiky-a-ceniky/metodiky/).

The complete strategy goes with the motivation to improve the relationships in infrastructure construction and make the whole industry more efficient and attractive.

Local limits for development: An interview with Shy Jackson (UK) by Lukas Klee (the Czech Republic)

In the following discussion, the author interviews Shy Jackson—an experienced British construction lawyer. The questions examine the issue of how to recognize the local limits for construction law and management development in particular countries.

Q: *Does the target price system and ECI approach comply with EU legislation?*

A: It is important to remember that the UK is part of the EU, and, therefore, any tenders have to comply with the same regulations. The UK has different legal systems for its parts and, for example, the law in Scotland is not the same as the law in England, but EU procurement law applies everywhere. In that regard, there is nothing in EU procurement law that prohibits the use of target costs contracts or early contractor involvement. These methods can still be used as long as there is a fair and transparent process.

In that respect, it is important to understand how the price is built up and this was the issue in the decision on framework agreements by the High Court of Northern Ireland in the Henry Brothers case (*Henry Brothers (Magherafelt) Ltd v. Department of Education for Northern Ireland* [2009] Vol. 1 B.L.R 118). In that case, the department of education (DOE) had launched a procurement process for the award of a multi-supplier framework agreement for major construction works for the Northern Ireland Schools Modernization Program. The framework was to consist of a maximum of eight contractors and last for four years, with an estimated value of £550 to £650 million. The DOE stated that appointment to the framework would be on the basis of the most economically advantageous tenders (MEAT).

The claimant contractor (Henry Brothers) was unsuccessful and sought details of how the DOE had evaluated tenders and reached its decision in appointing contractors to the framework. The court considered the question, whether it was legitimate to use fee percentages for the purpose of determining the MEAT at the primary competition stage to establish price after the completion of the secondary (mini) competition stage. The court looked at how the pricing was determined (and because discussions would occur after the completion of the competitive stages of the procurement process), it was held that the process did not comply with the requirements of the *Public Contract Regulations* (2006) and was not consistent with the requirement for transparency, equal treatment of tenderers and the development of effective competition.

The court did not conclude that it is always necessary to require tenderers to provide detailed costings at the primary competition stage nor did it rule out the possibility of fee percentages being used as a legitimate pricing mechanism. The court followed the earlier decision in *McLaughlin & Harvey Ltd v. Department of Finance & Personnel* and set aside the framework agreement. Appeals against these two decisions were dismissed by the Court of Appeal in 2011 in *McLaughlin & Harvey v. Department of Finance & Personnel* and *Henry Brothers (Magherafelt) & Ors v. Department of Education for Northern Ireland*.

In conclusion, it is possible to use these methods, as is done in the UK, but they do raise various issues that need to be considered in order to ensure there is no breach of EU procurement rules. The EU is looking to modernize its procurement systems and on May 30, 2012, the Competitiveness Council held an orientation debate on the European Commission's proposals for modernization of EU public procurement policy. This followed with the European Parliament, in plenary session, adopting a resolution on modernization of public procurement on October

25, 2011 and the Green Paper published on January 27, 2011 by the European Commission to consult on the modernization of EU public procurement policy.

The new legislation, already agreed with council in June 2013, overhauls the current EU public procurement rules and for the first time sets common EU standards on concession contracts to boost fair competition and ensure best value for money by introducing new award criteria that place more emphasis on environmental considerations, social aspects, and innovation.

Thanks to the new criterion of the "most economically advantageous tender" (MEAT) in the award procedure, public authorities will be able to put more emphasis on quality, environmental considerations, social aspects, or innovation while still taking into account the price and life-cycle-costs of what is procured.

To fight social dumping and ensure that workers' rights are respected, the new laws will include rules on subcontracting and tougher provisions on "abnormally low bids."

Q: *Do public employers in the UK use the DB delivery method?*

With the DB delivery method, the particular bidders submit different technical solutions in their proposals. In using DB, how does the employer evaluate the proposals (with the help of committees or independent experts)? Do participants who do not win the tender question the proposals of other competitors through administrative procedures, and so on?

A: Public authorities do use DB forms of contract. It is a decision for each project as to whether that is a suitable form of contract. A road project may have less scope for different design proposals than the design of a train station.

By way of example, DB is the proposed form of contract for the Northern Line extension works and the recently completed East London Line project but is not used in the Crossrail project. It is common for the public authority to produce the initial designs which the contractor will then develop.

When using that form of contract, the public authority would normally appoint consultant engineers who will help to evaluate any proposals and will provide the approvals needed during the works. This also helps to ensure that there is a proper assessment of any proposals.

Although challenges to tender decisions are becoming more common, they are not usually on the basis of what design was used. Such a challenge will probably be quite difficult and less easy to decide than challenges based on pricing.

Q: *Do public employers in the UK use the obligatory lowest bid price approach in public procurement? Does setting a target price work?*

A: There is no obligatory lowest bid price approach in the UK. Indeed, choosing on the basis of the lowest price is sometimes seen as a risk since it makes it more likely that the cost and the risks have not been properly considered, leading to cost overruns at a later stage. Since a target cost is supposed to represent the price for the project, there is no problem in using it when assessing tenders.

Q: *Is there free international competition in construction of large infrastructure projects in the UK? Is there a market protection?*

A: The UK market is very open to international companies. This is helped by the use of English but it also represents a UK view that it is better for the market to be open to competition. There is no protection for local companies and international contractors such as Ferrovial, Strabag, Sisk, Vinci, Dragados, Hochtief, and Alstom are involved with the Crossrail project. It is, however, worth noting that they usually, but not always, operate in joint ventures with local companies.

Q: Does the ECI and cooperation approach work with international contractors?

A: As noted, international contractors tend to act in joint ventures with UK contractors and that helps them to understand how procurement works in the UK. They do sometimes need to invest some time in understanding how the contracts are intended to operate but that is not seen as a hurdle.

Q: In the UK, there is obviously a long-term strategy in infrastructure construction. What is the key factor that has led to the development, respect, and fulfillment of such a strategy? What are the key factors needed for the global construction industry to join forces and align interests as a whole?

A: What drove the development of a construction strategy in the UK was the recognition by government that construction is a large and important part of the economy and that infrastructure is crucial for economic growth. This, together with the need to cut costs in view of the economic situation, is driving the current effort to find better ways of managing construction. In addition, there are strong construction industry bodies in the UK that have always lobbied government and have been able to influence its thinking to some extent.

These reasons also apply outside the UK. Governments and bodies such as the World Bank and the EBRD are also recognizing that developing infrastructure is important to support the economy. These bodies also need to consider what is the best way to procure such works. But another key issue is the whole life cost and investing in structures and buildings that will last longer and would be easier to maintain. There is still a tendency to focus on the capital cost of a structure and not on the long-term maintenance cost. In addition, it is necessary to consider how to motivate the parties that take part in construction projects, so that there is less of a reason to invest in disputes and more of a reason to ensure projects are successful.

Q: Who exactly created the NEC Contract (people from public or private sector)? Is it created by all construction project participants (contractors, employers, consulting engineers, and so on)? Is it an industry compromise (in risk allocation, in claim setting, in taking over procedure, in contract administration)?

A: The NEC was created by the Institution of Civil Engineers (ICE) following an internal recommendation to review alternative contract strategies with the aim of identifying the needs for good practice. It took a very different approach from the ICE conditions of contract—the standard form then published by the ICE. The first edition was published in 1993, with a second edition in 1995, and a third edition in 2005. A revised third edition was published in April 2013. The ICE stopped publishing the ICE conditions of contract in 2011 and will only be publishing the NEC form of contract.

In contrast, the Joint Contracts Tribunal (JCT) is a standard form of contract used in the UK, which does try to represent all parts of the industry. The JCT form of contract, however, is traditionally used for building works and not for civil engineering works. The NEC does not present itself as representing all parties but it puts forward what it believes are good principles for project management that are based on collaboration.

Q: Are there specialized employees working for state authorities that are able to cooperate with the contractor, to make quick decisions and to be active? Are the public clients in the UK "intelligent?"

A: Some large public bodies, such as the Highways Agency, Transport for London, and Network Rail are very experienced and are happy to have dialogues with the industry to find out what is the best way to manage a project. Such bodies employ people from the construction industry who understand the issues and who are better at managing such projects.

However, when smaller bodies such as local authorities or hospitals manage construction projects, they do not always have the people with the right skills and experience. That sometimes gives rise to difficulties.

Q: *Do public employers in the UK hire traditional independent consulting engineers, that is, does government hire the private sector to administer public contracts? Is there free international competition for engineers?*

A: Contracts under English law usually require a party which is appointed to act independently and neutrally as the certifier—the person who, for example, decides what is the correct payment. That can be done by the employer but often an external consultant will be appointed for that role. It is usual for international consultancies to bid for such a role.

A good example is the case of *Costain Ltd v. Bechtel Ltd*, which concerned the role of the contract administrator on one of the Channel Tunnel contracts. It was held by the court that there was a duty on the contract administrator to act impartially in matters of assessment and certification.

Q: *Has BIM been implemented in the UK legal system as a norm?*

A: BIM is not yet implemented as a matter of norm, but it is becoming more common and is now also being seen in private projects. It is important to recognize that BIM is a very wide term that covers many things. There are different levels of BIM that can be used and it depends on how much an employer is willing to commit to. The level of encouragement to use BIM is clear from the publication of the protocol by the Construction Industry Council (http://staging.cic.org.uk/publications/) for the use of BIM, which provides a best practice guide and an outline scope of services for the role of information management and the British Standards Institution publishing an updated technical standard, PAS1192:2, which covers collaborative production of construction information.

Q: *Do you think it is practicable to have the detailed design be prepared by the client?*

A: The principle of having a complete design as part of the tender is a good one. It helps to give certainty on what is being built and allows more accurate pricing. It is, however, important to (1) ensure that the design is as accurate as possible, for example, by doing full ground investigation tests and (2) agree on who bears the risk in the event that the design has to change.

It is common in the UK for the employer to provide a full design or a preliminary design, which the contractor develops under a DB contract. The contracts will make it clear what happens if the design needs to change and that will usually depend on the reasons. For example, who bears the risk of ground conditions or issue in legislation.

Q: *FIDIC Red Book is a re-measured contract that includes claims, variations, and value engineering. EU procurement law that was implemented defines limited possibilities for additional works with a price limit of 50%. Some people interpret public procurement law in following way:*

1. *What is remeasured beyond bid price evaluations is considered as additional work.*
2. *What is subject to variation is considered as additional work.*
3. *Value engineering clauses cannot be used.*

Some projects encounter a higher number of additional works before all the works are completed and the participants fear to proceed with other variations even if they are necessary or inevitable. Project management lacks functional variation procedures and the project is often paralysed.

In past, re-measurement, variations, and claims were seen to be subject to the negotiated procedure without publication according to the Public Procurement Act. It is hard to imagine having to process a number of these procedures for every variation and change in tender estimates on a daily basis. Do you think it is practicable and efficient?

A: A re-measurement contract is a way to agree on payment where the actual quantities of works are not known. It is a good way because the employer is only paying for actual work done at agreed rates instead of paying a risk element in a lump-sum price contract. If the actual cost exceeds the tender estimate, that is not additional work but it suggests that the original estimate was not very good. This makes it clear why getting the right estimate is very important in order to avoid a higher cost than originally anticipated.

Establishing a price-cap seems arbitrary and something that ignores the nature of the re-measurement contracts. If the authority wants certainty then it should use a lump sum contract with a fixed price. A cap on genuine additional works could be good because it makes it clear that the employer cannot issue too many variations and it is such employer variations that often lead to more cost and delay.

I do not think that where there are additional works or variations that they need to go to public tender again (unless they are a very substantial change to the works). Additional works or variations are not a real change to the contract because the contract allows for that.

Q: Do you have some particular recommendations for the participants of infrastructure construction projects?

A: In my experience I find that it helps to be very clear on what the basis for the project is and what the employer is seeking to achieve. The parties should have open discussions about what they are trying to achieve and what are the issues and risks that can affect the project. The parties must then understand what the contract requires from them and ensure that they are in a position to deliver.

Many problems come out of people not reading or not understanding what the contract requires and it is always a good investment for the site team to spend some time in understanding what the contract requires in terms of management of the works. This helps to avoid legal issues such as whether a notice was served on time and who is responsible for certain risks. If there is a problem, it is best to deal with it openly and find a way to resolve it, rather than keep quiet and wait until the end of the project.

References

Banica, C. (2013). Standard forms of construction contracts in Romania. *Urbanism. Arhitectură. Construcții*, 4, 4.

JICA (2011). *Check List for One Sided Contracts for Use with 'Sample Bidding Documents under Japanese ODA Loans – Procurement of Works'*. Available at: http://www.jica.go.jp/activities/schemes/finance_co/procedure/guideline/pdf/check_e.pdf (accessed 1 March 2014).

Sabo, W. (2013). *The Definitive Guide to the American Institute of Architects (AIA) Construction Contract Documents. Legal Guide to AIA Documents* (5th Edition). Aspen Publisher, Chicago.

Further reading

Arcata Partners (April 2013). *Evolution of the Asphalt Prices in Poland and the Vulnerability of Road and Bridges Construction Companies to the Prices of Materials.* All-Polish Commerce Chamber for Roads, Warsaw.

EBRD (2010). *Procurement Policies and Rules.* http://www.ebrd.com/downloads/research/policies/ppr10.pdf.

EIB (2011). *Guide to Procurement for Projects Financed by the EIB.* Available at: http://www.eib.org/attachments/.

FIDIC (1999a). *Conditions of Contract for Construction.* (1st Edition). FIDIC, Lausanne.

FIDIC (1999b). *Conditions of Contract for Plant and Design-Build.* (1st Edition). FIDIC, Lausanne.

FIDIC (1999c). *Conditions of Contract for EPC/Turnkey Projects.* (1st Edition). FIDIC, Lausanne.

FIDIC (2000). *The FIDIC Contracts Guide.* (1st Edition). FIDIC, Lausanne.

Gazeta Prawna. Available at: http://serwisy.gazetaprawna.pl/transport/artykuly/731922,polska-budowlanka-moze-sporo-zyskac-na-bankructwie-zachodnich-wykonawcow-wszystko-w-rekach-gddkia.html (accessed 21 October 2013).

Gillion, F. *United Kingdom: Use and Misuse of FIDIC Forms of Contract in Central and Eastern Europe: The Worrying Trend of Silver Book Provisions in Public Works Contracts.* Online. Available at: http://fidic.org/sites/default/files/Frederickgil.pdf (accessed 12 July 2013).

Hartlev, K. and Liljenbøl, M.W. (2013). Changes to existing contracts under the EU public procurement rules and the drafting of review clauses to avoid the need for a new tender. *Public Procurement Law Review.* Issue 2 2013. Sweet & Maxwell.

Klee, L. and Teodorescu, C.A. (2013). Romanian experience with FIDIC forms in roads and bridges construction, *International Construction Law Review*, Informa, London.

Klee, L., Marzec, A. and Skorupski, M. (2014). The Use and Misuse of FIDIC Forms in Poland, *International Construction Law Review*, Informa, London.

Kus, A., Markus, J. and Steding, R. (1999). FIDIC's New Silver Book under the German Standard Form Contract Act. *International Construction Law Review*, Informa, London.

Smith, A. (2013) *RAPORT Polskie drogi – dlaczego Polska nie radzi sobie z inwestycjami infrastrukturalnymi?* Opracowany przez Centrum, Warsaw.

Winch G. (2010). *Managing Construction Projects.* Wiley-Blackwell, Oxford.

World Bank (2011). *Guidelines Procurement of Goods, Works, and Non-consulting Services.* http://siteresources.worldbank.org/INTPROCUREMENT/Resources/278019-1308067833011/Procurement_GLs_English_Final_Jan2011.pdf.

Websites

http://www.constructionrisk.com
http://international.fhwa.dot.gov
http://thematic/procurement_en.pdf
http://www.europarl.europa.eu
http://www.eic-federation.eu

18 Building Construction: Health Care Facilities

18.1 Health care facility construction project

Health care facility construction projects are one of the most demanding of all construction projects. Every such facility consists of areas and a variety of functional units where a spectrum of services is provided. For example, a health care facility may accommodate: hospitalized patients, specialized outpatient surgeries, diagnostic facilities (laboratories, x-ray examination rooms), and other spaces that support catering, accommodation and cleaning.

This diversity is naturally reflected in the broad range of legislative regulations and standards that must be borne in mind whenever a health care facility is constructed or run. Each of the extensive and ever developing functions of such a facility—including the extremely complicated equipment and telecommunications—requires dedicated knowledge and experience. No one individual can have such comprehensive knowledge which is why a large number of specialists are involved in the construction of such a health care facility. Particular functional units within the facility may also have competing needs and priorities that can only be realized subject to compliance with rigorous mandatory requirements, actual functional needs (such as those regarding operational linkage and inter-departmental relationships), financial limitations on the employer's side, and so on.

18.2 Pre-design planning phase

The phase of planning prior to commencement of design preparation is frequently required at the preliminary stage but is often neglected. This is an intermediate stage between strategic decision making and designing and is an ideal platform for managers and other staff involved in such a health care facility to express their visions, influence design (such as floor space), locations, and financing of the

---

International Construction Contract Law, Second Edition. Lukas Klee.
© 2018 John Wiley & Sons Ltd. Published 2018 by John Wiley & Sons Ltd.

project. This phase can also have an impact on the cost and efficiency of the facility as a whole for many decades of its expected useful life. The people involved in the pre-design planning phase must sometimes make difficult and unpopular decisions. These may include stoppages of planning and postponement of the commencement date so that the priorities and other factors can be reassessed in the meantime. The following, for example, will have to be taken into account in this phase:

- Inpatient to outpatient ratio-related trends. Despite pressure to restrict the length of hospitalization, expenses, and new equipment and services that facilitate broader outpatient care are ever growing. This is due to an aging population and better diagnostic techniques and equipment that result in more hospitalized patients.
- Use of intensive care. In the United States, for example, there is a "safety net" for 45 million uninsured patients for whom health care is not available elsewhere.
- Personnel shortages. Outflow of those in charge for better conditions, power of trade unions, legal minimum number of personnel required to be present depending on numbers of patients, and so on.
- Trends in development and technological innovation. Better technology leads to longer life expectancy of patients, better quality of life, productivity increases, reduced costs, and so on.
- Increasing expenses. Not only for labor, but also for insurance premiums, better contingency planning (e.g., against terrorism and natural disasters), research and development costs, adjustments for changes in costs over time.

This prior-to-design planning can be defined as a process that pre-determines proper selection of:

- *services* that will be in compliance with the facility's strategic purposes, business plan and forecast market development trends;
- *size* as based on demand expectations, available personnel, and equipment and level of comfort;
- *locality* as based on access routes, operational efficiency, and suitability of building(s);
- *structure of financing* such as from own funds, credit, leasing, shared private and public resources.

18.3 Design phase

Cooperation with a designer should commence as soon as possible. However, it is mainly the employer who will have to thoroughly consider all priorities at the planning phase. With respect to priorities and limits on the employer's side, the level of detail into which the tender design should go into must also be considered. Sometimes it is up to the designer to come up with alternative solutions while respecting the limitations imposed by the employer. Usually, the employer and their consultants should offer alternatives in respect of their intentions, strategies, and objectives.

Apart from the wide range of services to be provided, a health care facility must serve many diverse users and other concerned parties. Ideally, the owner's or user's key employees or representatives should take part in the design preparation phase. The designer, however, must also guarantee efficiency gains and benefits from the standpoint of patients, visitors, auxiliary personnel, volunteers, and service providers who do not usually take part in these design preparation efforts.

A well-designed health care facility, such as a hospital, will have to efficiently harmonize the functional requirements with the needs of its various users. The following sections will focus on the most significant health care facilities, that is, hospitals.

18.4 Basic structure of a hospital

The basic structure of a hospital tends to be as follows:

- Inpatient section/hospitalized patients
- Outpatient section
- Diagnostics department (complementary)
- Customer care facility
- Office areas
- Areas for support services and maintenance
- Areas for research, education, and training
- Relaxation and entertainment areas
- Parking, traffic, and access routes.

The individual parts are functionally interconnected to form various configurations. This allows for efficient logistics and for effective movement and communication to take place there. Possible configurations then depend on limitations due to on-site and climatic conditions, neighboring buildings, budget constraints, and so on.

Regardless of location, size, or budget, all hospitals have some common characteristics. In particular, those dealing with efficiency and cost effectiveness, flexibility, expandability, therapeutic requirements, cleanliness and hygiene, access requirements, internal circulation and logistics, aesthetics, safety, and use of information technologies.

18.5 Efficiency and cost effectiveness

Efficient configuration of a hospital should:

- allow efficient work of employees by minimizing distances between frequented areas;
- allow easy monitoring of patients, given the limited number of health care personnel;
- include all necessary areas, but avoid unnecessary ones. Making use of adjacent areas and multipurpose areas;

- provide an efficient system of logistics;
- consolidate outpatient functions on the ground floor for immediate access;
- put together groups or combinations of active areas meeting similar requirements due to their functional neighborhood (such as placing the intensive surgical care unit next to the operating theatres).

18.6 Flexibility and expandability

Health care will face ever-growing demands on facilities and treatment methods. In order to sustain steady development, hospitals should:

- follow a modular concept of planning and spatial layout;
- use standard sizes of rooms as often as possible;
- be equipped with easily available and modifiable electro-mechanical systems;
- be ready for future expansion and reconstruction (plugged fresh and wastewater piping connections, hidden portals in the event of underground logistics).

Reconstructions are usually carried out on an existing facility that brings with it huge risks. A hospital, for example, is interwoven with a multitude of networks such as medical gas or oxygen systems. Failure of the latter may threaten human life and must, therefore, be kept operable during reconstruction. A robotic rail transport network is another example of an internal system in a hospital used to transport ready-made meals, newly washed laundry and so on. Piping and fast transfer pneumatic-tube systems are used to move waste to an incineration plant and laundry to a dry-cleaning plant. All such systems feature sophisticated record keeping of their use.

18.7 Therapeutic environment

Inpatients are often scared and embarrassed by hospitals and these feelings may hinder their therapy. This is why great effort has to be made in making their stay as comfortable as possible. An interior design architect plays a key role in creating an environment enabling maximum therapeutic effect. Interior design should be based on an understanding of the facility as a whole, its purpose and on typical patient profile. Characteristics of patient profile will determine the parameters to which the interior ought to be adapted, for example, to the needs of older patients, those suffering loss of sensual perception, and the like. Therapeutic benefits are influenced by the following interior aesthetics.

18.8 Cleaning and maintenance

Hospital areas must be cleaned and the facilities within operational areas maintained. The following will facilitate these tasks:

- suitable and durable finishes of individual functional areas;
- meticulous workmanship of doorframe detail and joint areas to prevent layers of dirt building up in hard to reach places;
- sufficient and suitably placed basement areas for cleaning services;
- special materials, durable finishes and instructions for the sterile areas;
- design and durable finishes of interior parts and compatibility with disinfection systems;
- accessibility of ceiling ducts, skylight spaces, and partition walls.

18.9 Controlled circulation and accessibility

A hospital is an intricate system of mutually interrelated functions that require a steady movement of people and things. This circulation must be coordinated. Safe access must also be provided for wheelchairs and blind people. Moreover:

- When visiting diagnostic and other treatment areas, outpatients should not be able to access inpatient areas or come into contact with seriously ill or suffering patients.
- Typical routes frequented by outpatients must be simple and clearly sign posted.
- Visitors must have simple and direct routes to every patient-bed unit without intruding into other functional areas.
- Patient and visitor areas must be isolated from operational, logistic, storage, and other similar areas.
- Handling of waste, recyclables, and contaminated materials must be separated from areas where food is prepared and fresh supplies handled. Both of these routes must be separate from the routes for patients and visitors.
- Transfer of the deceased to post-mortem rooms and morgues must be out of patient and visitor sight.
- Dedicated lifts for supplies, food, and maintenance must be available.

18.10 Aesthetics

The aesthetics of an area closely relates to the therapeutic environment to be set up. Outer surroundings are also vital for improving the overall image of a hospital and are, in themselves, an important marketing tool. A better living environment will also help improve employee morale and patient care. For example, through:

- greater use of natural daylight, natural materials, and aesthetic surface finishes;
- use of visual stimuli such as works of art;
- attention paid to dimensions, colors, scaling. and details;
- clear, open and spacious public areas;
- homely, intimate atmosphere in patient rooms, common rooms, meeting rooms, and offices;
- exterior design compatibility with surrounding environment.

18.11 Health and safety

Hospitals have to comply with health and safety requirements in connection with:

- protection of property—including hazardous substances and drugs;
- protection of patients and employees;
- keeping violent or unstable patients under control;
- anti-terrorist measures.

Alarms and evacuation functions must have manual override capabilities to minimize the consequences of potential evacuations. For example, an evacuation due to a false alarm may have fatal consequences for seriously ill patients. Therefore, fire and alarm procedures have to be properly considered.

Drug preservation systems rank among other specifics. Monitoring and maintaining the temperature at which the drugs are kept is essential—even in the event of power failures. Alternative/back up emergency radio frequencies are another necessity. A wi-fi signal, for example, can jam other networks. Therefore, it is up to construction contractors to test what problems frequency interference may cause. Communication and control signals may affect sensitive electronic equipment and can interfere with things like window blind control or pacemakers. All technologies must, therefore, be tested for electromagnetic compatibility.

18.12 Use of information technology

Information technologies and methods of their use affect the efficiency of a hospital. Their applications are mainly as follows:

- *Informing patients and their relatives.* A hospital's web site is becoming increasingly important for this purpose. This is a portal where people can communicate with the hospital and find out important information. For example, registration processes, planning of examinations and treatments, informing future patients what to expect in hospital, fostering research, education and so on.
- *Facilitating communications between physicians.* Such as in the fields of personnel ratings, education, clinical research, record keeping, consultancy, and diagnostics.
- *Facilitating communication between employees.* Such as for recruiting new personnel, rating employee benefits, continuing professional education, discussing routine practice and so on.
- *Payments.* Invoicing, claims, contracts, communication with contractors, and the like can be carried out by means of the information systems.

18.13 Relevant regulations and standards

Hospitals rank themselves among the most regulated types of buildings worldwide. Individual countries usually have mandatory regulations specifying the requirements for material and technical equipment of their health care facilities. Regulations are typically also in place for outpatient care, single-day inpatient care, hospital care, pharmacy care, medical supply haulage, and ambulances.

These specific regulations are complemented by general ones such as:

- land-use planning, zoning and construction permit procedures;
- technical requirements of construction, buildings and plants;
- general technical requirements that ensure barrier-free and disabled access to buildings;
- fire safety and cooperation with state fire fighting bodies;
- occupational health and safely;
- drugs handling;
- radiation protection;
- infectious disease escalation contingency plans and hygienic requirements;
- waste management.

18.14 Health care facility construction project: Suitable delivery method

The following can be used as a guide when a suitable method of delivery is to be selected:

- extent of the employer's involvement in the project;
- employer's right to instruct variations;
- employer's position in claiming design defects;
- speed; and
- probability that the bid price will be kept.

18.14.1 Extent of employer's involvement in the project

Under general contracting (GC)/DBB, the engineer administers the project on behalf of the employer who is broadly engaged in the project this way. The employer engagement can be decreased by the use of design-build (DB) method that leads to lower level of contract administration. Close cooperation between the employer and construction manager is expected within a construction management (CM) project. This close cooperation begins at the preparation phase—that is, before project commencement. This makes CM in some cases problematic for public projects. However, for the construction of health care facilities in general, the CM could be a viable solution in respect of the extent to which the employer can get involved because, as mentioned, the employer's or user's key employees and representatives should take part in the design preparation phase and to jointly develop the basic and detailed design.

18.14.2 Employer's right to instruct variations

The lowest number of variation instructions is expected to appear in DB projects because it should mainly be up to the contractor as to how to carry out the works. Interventions with the contractor's methods, processes, and sequencing could result in major claims on the contractor's side (increasing the contract price or extending time for completion).

Variations are relatively frequent in GC. Here, the employer's basic design is being developed by the contractor into the detailed design that evokes variations. In the case of CM, the employer's variations then tend to appear on a regular basis—typically in residential complex projects.

Concerning the construction of health care facilities, the quality of project preparation, degree to which the user's visions and needs have been discussed in time, the employer's wish to intervene with medical technology deliveries and the like will obviously be vital for the employer's need for variations. It is then very likely that unique needs will develop and variations become necessary.

18.14.3 Employer's position in claiming design defects

The contractor will carry out the project according to the employer's design under GC. Responsibility for the design (scope of work correctness, feasibility, defects) rests with the employer and its designer. The contractor will develop the design to reflect the reality encountered during realization. This may lead to uncertainty in terms of responsibility for particular errors in the design and can give rise to disputes. As such, the employer's position may become complicated in pursuing the claims for design errors against the contractor. The employer's designer will typically be in conflict with the contractor's designer around professional issues if problems arise. Within a DB project, the contractor is, for most part, responsible for both the design and construction works (single point responsibility). Disputes about the design should, therefore, largely disappear and strengthen the employer's position whenever pursuing claims for design errors.

The employer's direct links to individual contractors is an advantage in the case of a CM project. However, responsibility for management, construction and design still remains divided because the designer, contractor, and construction manager are different entities.

18.14.4 Speed

GC is the slowest delivery method because there is no overlap of the design and construction phases. In DB on the other hand (where both of these phases overlap each other), the overall time tends to be shorter. A CM project presumes cooperation between the construction manager and the employer from the design preparation phase to ensure quickest possible completion.

Before the construction of a health care facility commences, the employer must determine if earliest possible completion time is the main priority.

18.14.5 Certainty of the bid price

Theoretically, the lowest probability that the stated bid price will be kept is under the CM method, followed by GC and, finally, by DB projects (highest probability). In any event, the employer must determine what weight to give the contract price criterion even here, and take into account other priories and options.

18.14.6 Final evaluation of the suitable delivery method

Construction contracts are awarded via tender. Thus, selection of delivery method is closely related to the method of tendering. The purpose of the tender is to select—within a certain period of time—an appropriate contractor based on their bid.

As discussed, a construction project (in general) and a health care facility project (in particular) is a very unique setup of processes. This kind of temporary multi-organization process and the successful management of it will depend on realized hazards, particular setup of relationships between construction project participants and expressly stated employer priorities such as time and cost.

It should, however, be stressed here that there is a substantial difference between public and private contracts for the construction of a health care facility. In the case of public projects it is common for the employer, that is, the state or one of its agencies to have their hands tied by rigid public procurement legislation.

When lowest bid price is the only criterion, tendering will often narrow the choice of delivery method to GC. In the case of public contracts, any effective use of the CM system is often excluded. This is despite the fact that this system would otherwise be a suitable option in terms of management and organization of a health care facility construction project. One and the same designer and construction manager can, within a CM project, contribute to the preparation, design and construction phases.

A contract funded by private entities may provide more freedom to the employer in determining the priorities. This will be reflected in more efficient methods of planning, project preparation, procurement, management, and coordination of the construction project.

Without doubt, preparation of the project by the employer constitutes the most important phase for successful completion of a health care facility construction project. With a public project, the employer will again be limited when investing in preparations, regardless of whether by lack of human resources, necessity to select consultants based on the lowest price criterion, hesitations in investing sufficient funding, inexperience, and the like.

Further reading

Cushman, R.F. (2011). *Proving and Pricing Construction Claims*. Wolters Kluwer, New York.

Hayward, C. (2006). *Healthcare Facility Planning: Thinking Strategically*. Health Administration Press, Chicago.

Klee, L. (2012a). *Smluvní vztahy výstavbových projektů*. Wolters Kluwer, Prague.

Klee, L. (2012b). *Příprava, řízení a organizace výstavbového projektu zdravotnického zařízení. Zdravotnické fórum [Healthcare Forum]*, May 2012.

Leibrock, C.A. (2011). *Design Details for Health: Making the Most of Interior Design's Healing Potential*. John Wiley & Sons, Inc., NewYork.

Murdoch, J.R. and Hughes, W. (2008). *Construction Contracts: Law and Management*. Taylor & Francis. New York.

Appendix A: Interactive Exercises

A.1 Interactive exercise 1: Delivery method selection

Assisted by the instructor, participants will divide themselves into two teams: Team A and Team B. Each team must nominate a speaker who will present arguments on their behalf to the group.

Project: Construction of hydroelectric power plant (with 70% of the contract volume being a civil engineering section with a high proportion of unforeseeable ground risks and the remaining 30% composed of plants).

Team A: Evaluate the scenario from the employer's point of view. Prepare a list of arguments for your nominated speaker who will propose a solution, that is, the appropriate delivery method. The solution must include a recommendation of an appropriate FIDIC form and its modifications. Team A also has to take into account contract price determination, design responsibility, risk allocation, employer's interest to get engaged in contract administration, and speed of completion.

Team B: Evaluate the scenario from the contractor's point of view. Prepare a list of arguments for your nominated speaker who will propose a solution, that is, the appropriate delivery method. The solution must include a recommendation of an appropriate FIDIC form and its modifications. Team B also has to take into account contract price determination, design responsibility, risk allocation, employer's interest to get engaged in contract administration, and speed of completion.

A.1.1 Task

Teams have 20 minutes to prepare their list of arguments with supporting reasons.
Team A's nominated speaker will have 5 minutes to present their team's argument.
Once Team A has finished, Team B may raise objections or suggestions.
Team B's nominated speaker will have 5 minutes to present their team's argument.
Once Team B has finished, Team A may raise objections or suggestions.
The instructor will then evaluate the presentations.

International Construction Contract Law, Second Edition. Lukas Klee.
© 2018 John Wiley & Sons Ltd. Published 2018 by John Wiley & Sons Ltd.

A.2 Interactive exercise 2: Claim for delayed site handover

Assisted by the instructor, participants will divide themselves into two teams: Team A and Team B. Each team must nominate a speaker who will present arguments on the team's behalf to the group.

Project: Construction of a highway in Eastern European country for the local highway authority. The employer awards the contract to a contractor composed of a consortium of international companies.

Conditions of contract: FIDIC CONS 1999 (Red Book).

The employer is responsible for obtaining the construction permit and land expropriation for the temporary and permanent site.

Facts: Handover of the complete site by the employer to the contractor should have taken place in 1/2012 in accordance with the contractor's tender (section "Time Schedule") where the completion terms of the works are stipulated as particular dates. The employer was supposed to hand over the site to the contractor as a whole. However, the site was handed over gradually (part by part). Some parts were missing because they had not been handed over. The employer also failed to obtain the construction permit in time and negotiations with the owner of one section of land became unexpectedly complicated. Construction should have been completed by October 2013.

Following the employer's failure to hand over the complete site, the contractor notified its claim for an extension of time for completion and for additional payment in compliance with the contract.

All sites were gradually handed over to the contractor (the last being in June 2012). A new time for completion was submitted for May 2014 by the contractor.

The employer appeared in urgent need to complete the project at a faster pace and instructed the contractor to accelerate and complete the work within the original timeframe (by October 2013).

A.2.1 Task

Team A: Evaluate the scenario from the employer's point of view. Prepare a list of arguments for your nominated speaker who will propose a procedure (negotiating position) while resolving the claims and acceleration in respect of the employer's interests.

Team B: Evaluate the scenario from the contractor's point of view. Prepare a list of arguments for your nominated speaker who will propose a procedure (negotiating position) while resolving the claims and acceleration in respect of the contractor's interests.

Teams have 30 minutes to prepare their list of arguments and for specifying a procedure in cooperation with the instructor.

Team A's nominated speaker will have 5 minutes to present their team's argument.
Once Team A has finished, Team B may raise objections or suggestions.
Team B's nominated speaker will have 5 minutes to present their team's argument.
Once Team B has finished, Team A may raise objections or suggestions.

The instructor will then evaluate the presentations.

The following issues must be taken into account when presenting your team's argument:

A.2.2 Time schedule (program)

Does the contractor's tender program allow for floats?

A.2.3 Site handover procedure

Was it clearly communicated/known (over the course of the construction project) when the individual sites were to be handed over? Did the gradual hand-over of the site have an influence on progress of works and/or on manufacture and delivery of the plants?

A.2.4 Mobilization

Were contractor capacities fully mobilized over the course of execution of works, as foreseen by the updated time schedules (programs)?

Was it efficient to demobilize/remobilize capacities in respect of the gradual hand-over of the site?

A.2.5 Acceleration

Is the instruction to accelerate legitimate?

How will the contractor's project team members respond to a delayed handover of the site and to the employer's instructions to accelerate? What will the contractor do if the engineer/employer refuses to accept their entitlement for additional payment due to acceleration?

A.2.6 Claims

How to prepare/defend the contractor's claim for increased site overheads?

How to prepare/defend the contractor's claim for increased headquarters' overheads?

How to prepare/defend the contractor's claim for additional payment due to a more complicated execution of works (loss of productivity) in respect of a gradual handover of the site?

How to prepare/defend the contractor's claim for additional payment due to acceleration?

What will the contractor's claim for additional payment and extension of time for completion consist of?

How will the claim be proved, documented, and quantified? How will the claim be defended by the employer?

A.3 Interactive exercise 3: Claim due to suspension of work

Assisted by the instructor, participants will divide themselves into two teams: Team A and Team B. Each team must nominate a speaker who will present arguments on their behalf to the group.

Project: Construction of a power plant for a global corporation (the employer) who will award the contract to a consortium of international companies (contractor).

Conditions of contract: FIDIC EPC 1999 (Silver Book).

Facts: The employer decided to stop project realization in the second year of construction. The contractor's personnel and equipment were fully mobilized. Manufacture of plants had reached an advanced stage.

A.3.1 Task

Team A: Evaluate the scenario from the employer's point of view. Prepare a list of arguments for your nominated speaker who will propose a procedure (negotiating position) for resolving the claims.

Team B: Evaluate the scenario from the contractor's point of view. Prepare a list of arguments for your nominated speaker who will propose a procedure (negotiating position) for resolving the claims.

Teams have 30 minutes to prepare their list of arguments and for specifying a procedure in cooperation with the instructor.

Team A's nominated speaker will have 5 minutes to present their team's argument.
Once Team A has finished, Team B may raise objections or suggestions.
Team B's nominated speaker will have 5 minutes to present their team's argument.
Once Team B has finished, Team A may raise objections or suggestions.
The instructor will then evaluate the presentations.
The following issues must be taken into account when presenting your team's argument:

A.3.2 Suspension

Does the employer have the right to suspend the works?
What are the consequences the suspension may have from the viewpoint of the contract?

A.3.3 Mobilization

Were contractor capacities fully mobilized over the course of execution of the works as foreseen by updated time schedules (programs)?
Was it efficient to demobilize/remobilize capacities due to suspension?
How will the contractor's project team members respond to instructions to suspend work once given?

How will the contractor proceed if the employer refuses to recognize their claims for additional payment and an extension of time for completion due to suspension?

A.3.4 Claims

How to prepare/defend the contractor's claim for increased site overheads due to suspension?

How to prepare/defend the contractor's claim for increased headquarters' overheads due to suspension?

How to prepare/defend the contractor's claim for additional payment due to a more complicated execution of works (loss of productivity) in respect of the suspension?

What will the contractor's claim for additional payment and suspension for completion consist of?

How will the claim be proved, documented and quantified?

How will the claim be defended by the employer?

A.4 Interactive exercise 4: Subcontractor claim for contractor delay (lack of cooperation, inadequate on-site coordination and improper, unclear, and delayed instructions)

Assisted by the instructor, participants will divide themselves into two teams: Team A and Team B. Each team must nominate a speaker who will present arguments on their behalf.

Project: Construction of a coal-fired power plant for a private employer, based on a DB contract in the EPC mode. The contractor will assign part of their contract (boiler area background plants, fan, and boiler fume extracting filter without desulfurization plant) to a subcontractor.

Facts: Conditions of contract: Contractor's bespoke form of contract in the EPC mode (i.e., maximum risk allocation to the contractor).

A.4.1 Task

Team A: Evaluate the scenario from the contractor's point of view. Prepare a list of arguments for your nominated speaker who will propose a procedure (negotiating position) while resolving the claims.

Team B: Evaluate the scenario from the subcontractor's point of view. Prepare a list for your nominated speaker who will propose a procedure (negotiating position) while resolving the claims.

Teams have 30 minutes to prepare their list of arguments and for specifying a procedure in cooperation with the instructor.

Team A's nominated speaker will have 5 minutes to present their team's argument.

Once Team A has finished, Team B may raise objections or suggestions.

Team B's nominated speaker will have 5 minutes for presenting their position.

Once Team B has finished, Team A may raise objections or suggestions.
The instructor will then evaluate the presentations.
The following additional facts must be considered:

A.4.2 Fact 1—Lack of cooperation

According to the contract, taking over of the works by the contractor from the subcontractor is subject to the execution of a demanding test on completion in the presence of electricity, contaminated gas from the boiler, and so on. Such a test is, therefore, dependent on the full completion of plants. The subcontractor will timely perform its works, including an individual test. The remaining parts of the plants (boiler, fume stack) are not yet finished by subcontractors of other contractors. As such, any test on completion cannot take place during takeover. The subcontractor wants to hand over its work and receive payment for it.

A.4.3 Fact 2—Inadequate on-site coordination

A different site than required and anticipated in the contractor's (subcontractor's) tender documents had been handed over by the employer. The contractor handed over to the subcontractor a site, which was 3 km away from the coal-fired power plant. Additional cost and risks accrue to the subcontractor in connection with transport (such as unloading, loading operations, additional transportation of bulk freight).

Access and on-site roads provided to the subcontractor are used otherwise than anticipated in the contractor's (subcontractor's) requirements and tender documents because of delay of a building section (concrete slab) by the contractor. Several subcontractors use the access roads meaning that the subcontractor had to construct a corridor. Additional cost and risks accrue to the subcontractor.

A.4.4 Fact 3—Improper, unclear, and delayed instructions

The subcontractor notified the contractor that performance parameters of the plant would not be fulfilled because of defective work of one of the other subcontractors. The subcontractor proposed a solution in its design and the contractor is under pressure to provide further instructions for variation including additional payment. Given that no consultation with the employer had taken place, the contractor hesitates in giving such instructions. Meanwhile, additional cost and risks accrue to the subcontractor.

Appendix B: Sample Letters (Examples of Formal Notices)

International Construction Contract Law, Second Edition. Lukas Klee.
© 2018 John Wiley & Sons Ltd. Published 2018 by John Wiley & Sons Ltd.

B.1 Contractor's sample letters: Notice of probable future event

Contract identification:

Letter identification:

Connected to:

Related correspondence:

Related Sub-Clauses:

Addressed to the Engineer (according to Sub-Clauses 1.1.2.4 and 1.3):

Date:

NOTICE OF PROBABLE FUTURE EVENT
In accordance with Sub-Clause 8.3

Dear .... ,

We give you notice of specific probable future event(s) or circumstance(s) as follows:

....

....

....

If the above described event(s) or circumstance(s) occur it (they) may:

(a) adversely affect the Work, namely

....

....

(b) increase the Contract Price

....

(c) delay the execution of Works

....

Yours sincerely

....

Contractor (according to Sub-Clauses 1.1.2.3 and 4.3)

Copies to:

Attachments:

B.2 Contractor's sample letters: Notice of contractor's claims

Contract identification:

Letter identification:

Connected to:

Related correspondence:

Related Sub-Clauses:

Addressed to the Engineer (according to Sub-Clause 1.1.2.4 and 1.3):

Date:

NOTICE OF CONTRACTOR'S CLAIM
In accordance with Sub-Clause 20.1

Dear .... ,

The Contractor notifies the following events or circumstances as reasons for a claim:

....

....

We therefore give you notice of claim for

(a) an Extension of Time for Completion according to Sub-Clause 8.4

....

(b) additional payment

....

The Contractor considers itself to be entitled referring to the following Clauses of the Conditions:

Example:

(a) *Error in Employer's Requirements 1.9 (P&DB), Delayed Drawings and Instructions 1.9 (CONS)*
(b) *Right of Access to the Site 2.1*
(c) *Setting Out 4.7*
(d) *Unforeseeable Physical Conditions 4.12*
(e) *Fossils 4.24*
(f) *Testing 7.4*
(g) *Extension of Time for Completion 8.4*
(h) *Consequences of Suspension 8.9*
(i) *Taking-Over of Parts of the Works 10.2*
(j) *Interferences with Tests on Completion 10.3*
(k) *Delayed Test 9.2*
(l) *Payment in Applicable Currencies 13.4*
(m) *Adjustments in Legislation 13.7*

Or otherwise in connection with the Contract:

....

Yours sincerely

....

Contractor (according to Sub-Clauses 1.1.2.3 and 4.3)

Copies to:

Attachments:

B.3 Contractor's sample letters: Contractor's claim No._____ submission (quantification)

Contract identification:

Letter identification:

Connected to:

Related correspondence:

Related Sub-Clauses:

Addressed to the Engineer (according to Sub-Clause 1.1.2.4 and 1.3):

Date:

CONTRACTOR'S CLAIM NO. _____SUBMISSIONS (QUANTIFICATION)
In accordance with Sub-Clause 20.1

Dear .... ,

With Reference to the Contractor's Claim issued on ....submitted to the Engineer we send you:

(a) *fully detailed claim,*
(b) *fully detailed claim, stating that the event or circumstance giving rise to the claim has a continuing effect. This fully detailed claim shall be considered as interim; we shall send further interim claims at monthly intervals, giving the accumulated delay and/or amount claimed.*

Therefore under this claim the Contractor requests:

1. .... days of Extension of Time for Completion.
2. To adjust the contract amount by an additional payment of ....

Yours sincerely

....

Contractor (according to Sub-Clauses 1.1.2.3 and 4.3)

Copies to:

Attachments:

B.4 Contractor's sample letters: Request for evidences of financial arrangements

Contract identification:

Letter identification:

Connected to:

Related correspondence:

Related Sub-Clauses:

Addressed to the Employer (according to Sub-Clauses 1.1.2.2 and 1.3):

Date:

REQUEST FOR EVIDENCES OF FINANCIAL ARRANGEMENTS
In accordance with Sub-Clause 2.4

Dear .... ,

The Contractor requests from the Employer to submit reasonable evidence that financial arrangements have been made and are being maintained which enable the Employer to pay the Contract Price in accordance with Sub-Clause 14. Any adjustments to the Accepted Contract Amount will be considered.

Yours sincerely

....

Contractor (according to Sub-Clauses 1.1.2.3 and 4.3)

Copies to:

Attachments:

B.5 Contractor's sample letters: Written confirmation of oral instruction

Contract identification:

Letter identification:

Connected to:

Related correspondence:

Related Sub-Clauses:

Addressed to the Engineer (according to Sub-Clauses 1.1.2.4 and 1.3):

Date:

WRITTEN CONFIRMATION OF ORAL INSTRUCTION
In accordance with Sub-Clause 3.3

Dear .... ,

On .... (date) the Engineer gave an Instruction to the Contractor which was understood as

....

....

.....

Due to the fact that this instruction was made orally, the Contractor confirms this instruction and will comply immediately.

As far as a possible Extension of Time for Completion (according Sub-Clause 8.4) is concerned, the Contractor will give notice within 28 days after issuing this confirmation.

Further remarks:

....

....

Yours sincerely

....

Contractor (according to Sub-Clauses 1.1.2.3 and 4.3)

Copies to:

Attachments:

B.6 Contractor's sample letters: Notice of dissatisfaction with a determination of the engineer

Contract identification:

Letter identification:

Connected to:

Related correspondence:

Related Sub-Clauses:

Addressed to the other Party with a copy to the Engineer (according to Sub-Clauses 1.1.2.4 and 1.3):

Date:

NOTICE OF DISSATISFACTION WITH A DETERMINATION OF THE ENGINEER

Dear .... ,

We give you notice of dissatisfaction with the Engineer's determination dated *(insert date)* with reference to Claim notice no. *(insert number)*.

We give notice that the Engineer failed to render its determination within due time after receiving the claim notice no. *(insert number)* and supporting particulars on ....

We consider that failure to render a determination in due time constitutes a dispute under Sub-Clause 20.4.

Yours sincerely

....

Contractor (according to Sub-Clauses 1.1.2.3 and 4.3)

Copies to:

Attachments:

B.7 Contractor's sample letters: Notice of contractor's entitlement to suspend work

Contract identification:

Letter identification:

Connected to:

Related correspondence:

Related Sub-Clauses:

Addressed to the Employer (according to Sub-Clauses 1.1.2.2 and 1.3):

Date:

NOTICE OF CONTRACTOR'S ENTITLEMENT TO SUSPEND WORK
In accordance with Sub-Clause 16.1

Dear .... ,

The Engineer failed to certify in accordance with Sub-Clause 14.6 *(or the Employer failed to comply with Sub-Clause 2.4 or Sub-Clause 14.7)* in the following manner

....

We give you notice that on the ... of .... 201 X we will suspend work *(or reduce the rate of work)* unless and until we receive the Payment Certificate *(reasonable evidence or payment, as the case may be and as described in the notice)*

....

....

....

Yours sincerely

....

Contractor (according to Sub-Clauses 1.1.2.3 and 4.3)

Copies to:

Attachments:

B.8 Contractor's sample letters: Notice of contractor's claim under the sub-clause 16.1

Contract identification:

Letter identification:

Connected to:

Related correspondence:

Related Sub-Clauses:

Addressed to the Engineer (according to Sub-Clauses 1.1.2.4 and 1.3):

Date:

NOTICE OF CONTRACTOR'S CLAIM UNDER THE SUB-CLAUSE 16.1
In accordance with Sub-Clauses 20.1 and 16.1

Dear .... ,

The Contractor notifies the following events or circumstances as reasons for a

Claim:

The Engineer failed to certify in accordance with Sub-Clause 14.6 *(or the Employer failed to comply with Sub-Clause 2.4 or Sub-Clause 14.7)* in the following manner

....

......

The Contractor, after giving not less than 21 days' notice to the Employer, suspended work.

Following our letter Nr/Ref .... we therefore give you notice of claim for

(a) an Extension of Time for Completion according to Sub-Clause 8.4

....

(b) additional payment

....

The Contractor considers itself to be entitled referring to the Sub-Clause 16.1.

Yours sincerely

....

Contractor (according to Sub-Clauses 1.1.2.3 and 4.3)

Copies to:

Attachments:

B.9 Contractor's sample letters: Application for taking over certificate

Contract identification:

Letter identification:

Connected to:

Related correspondence:

Related Sub-Clauses:

Addressed to the Engineer (according to Sub-Clauses 1.1.2.4 and 1.3):

Date:

APPLICATION FOR TAKING-OVER CERTIFICATE
In accordance with Sub-Clause 10.1

Dear .... ,

We hereby apply for a Taking Over Certificate for the following works:

....

Yours sincerely

....

Contractor (according to Sub-Clauses 1.1.2.3 and 4.3)

Copies to:

Attachments:

B.10 Employer's sample letters: Notice of employer's claim

Contract identification:

Letter identification:

Connected to:

Related correspondence:

Related Sub-Clauses:

Addressed to the Contractor (according to Sub-Clauses 1.1.2.3 and 4.3) and the Engineer (according to Sub-Clauses 1.1.2.4 and 1.3):

Date:

NOTICE OF EMPLOYER'S CLAIM
In accordance with Sub-Clause 2.5

Dear .... ,

The Employer notifies the following events or circumstances as reasons for a claim:

....

....

We therefore give you notice of claim for:

(a) *the below described payment under the Contract Conditions or otherwise in connection with the Contract.*

....

(b) *delay damages according to Sub-Clause 8.7 for:*

....

(c) *extension of Defects Notification Period of* .... *The expiry of the Defect Notification Period is........................, therefore this claim notice is made in time.*

The Engineer is requested to proceed in accordance with Sub-Clause 3.5.

Yours sincerely

....

Employer (according to Sub-Clauses 1.1.2.2 and 1.3)

Copies to:

Attachments:

B.11 Employer's sample letters: Answer to request for evidence of financial arrangements

Contract identification:

Letter identification:

Connected to:

Related correspondence:

Related Sub-Clauses:

Addressed to the Contractor (according to Sub-Clauses 1.1.2.3 and 4.3) and the Engineer (according to Sub-Clauses 1.1.2.4 and 1.3):

Date:

ANSWER TO REQUEST FOR EVIDENCE OF FINANCIAL ARRANGEMENTS
In accordance with Sub-Clause 2.4

Dear .... ,

(a) *With the attached documents the Employer gives evidence of its financial arrangements at the request of the Contractor.*
(b) *The Employer informs the Contractor of material changes in the financial arrangements. The attached documents are the detailed particulars.*

Yours sincerely

....

Employer

Copies to:

Attachments:

B.12 Engineer's sample letters: Engineer's determination

Contract identification:

Letter identification:

Connected to:

Related correspondence:

Related Sub-Clauses:

Addressed to the Parties

Date:

ENGINEER'S DETERMINATION
In accordance with Sub-Clause 3.5

Dear .... ,

We give you notice of my determination as to claim no. *(insert number)*. With regard to all relevant facts and circumstances, we determine that the Contractor is entitled to ..... days Extension of Time for Completion.

We have given approval/disapproval with comments on

....

We have consulted with the parties who have submitted the following statements:

....

....

....

The Contractor has submitted

(a) particulars
(b) supported by evidence
(c) including contemporary records
(d) which we have monitored

The Contractor has given notice of.......... on *(insert date)*:

(a) *This was in time because the Contractor became aware of the relevant facts on*
....

(b) *This was out of time because the Contractor became aware of the relevant facts on*
....

In accordance with Sub-Clause........ the Contractor is entitled to an extension of Time for Completion. In accordance with Sub-Clause 8.4 the relevant event must have an impact on an activity which lies on the critical path. Both requirements are met.

Yours sincerely

....

Engineer (according to Sub-Clauses 1.1.2.4 and 1.3)

Copies to:

Attachments:

B.13 Engineer's sample letters: Engineer's instruction

Contract identification:

Letter identification:

Connected to:

Related correspondence:

Related Sub-Clauses:

Addressed to the Contractor (according to Sub-Clauses 1.1.2.3 and 4.3)

Instruction no. *(insert number)*

Date:

ENGINEER'S INSTRUCTION
In accordance with Sub-Clause 3.3

Dear .... ,

We formally instruct you according to Sub-Clause 7.6:

(a) *To remove from the Site and replace any Plant or materials which is/are not in accordance with the Contract.*
(b) *To remove and re-execute any other work which is not in accordance with the Contract.*
(c) *To execute any work which is urgently required for safety of the Works.*

In particular we instruct you (choose the appropriate remedy) to remove, to re-execute and/or to execute (describe the Plant, material, work).

Yours sincerely

....

Engineer (according to Sub-Clauses 1.1.2.4 and 1.3)

Copies to:

Attachments:

B.14 Engineer's sample letters: Engineer's notice to correct

Contract identification:

Letter identification:

Connected to:

Related correspondence:

Related Sub-Clauses:

Addressed to the Contractor (according to Sub-Clauses 1.1.2.3 and 4.3)

Instruction no. *(insert number)*

Date:

ENGINEER'S NOTICE TO CORRECT
In accordance with Sub-Clause 15.1

Dear .... ,

The Contractor failed to carry out the following obligation under the Contract:

....

We give you a notice to make good the failure and to remedy it within ... days.

Yours sincerely

....

Engineer (according to Sub-Clauses 1.1.2.4 and 1.3)

Copies to:

Attachments:

B.15 Engineer's sample letters: Engineer's instruction to remove a person employed on the site

Contract identification:

Letter identification:

Connected to:

Related correspondence:

Related Sub-Clauses:

Addressed to the Contractor (according to Sub-Clauses 1.1.2.3 and 4.3)

Instruction no. *(insert number)*

Date:

ENGINEER'S INSTRUCTION TO REMOVE A PERSON EMPLOYED ON THE SITE

In accordance with Sub-Clause 6.9

Dear .... ,

We hereby require the Contractor to immediately remove the following person ....who:

(a) persists and engages in misconduct or lack of care;

(b) carries out duties incompetently or negligently;

(c) fails to conform with the provisions of the Contract; or

(d) persists and engages in conduct which is prejudicial to safety, health, or the protection of the environment.

Yours sincerely

....

Engineer (according to Sub-Clauses 1.1.2.4 and 1.3)

Copies to:

Attachments:

B.16 Engineer's sample letters: Engineer's instruction—lack of mobilization

Contract identification:

Letter identification:

Connected to:

Related correspondence:

Related Sub-Clauses:

Addressed to the Contractor (according to Sub-Clauses 1.1.2.3 and 4.3)

Instruction no. *(insert number)*

Date:

ENGINEER'S INSTRUCTION – LACK OF MOBILIZATION
In accordance with Sub-Clauses 4.21, 6.10, 8.3, 8.6

Dear .... ,

The Contractor submitted the following number of each class of Contractor's Personnel and of each type of Contractor's Equipment on the Site:................ The actual state on the Site does not correspond with the planned mobilization and actual progress is too slow to complete within the Time for Completion*(and/or (b) progress has fallen (or will fall) behind the current program under Sub-Clause 8.3)*.

We hereby instruct you to submit, under Sub-Clause 8.3, a revised program and supporting report describing the revised methods which the Contractor proposes to adopt in order to expedite progress and complete within the Time for Completion.

Yours sincerely

....

Engineer (according to Sub-Clauses 1.1.2.4 and 1.3)

Copies to:

Attachments:

Appendix C: Dictionary of Construction Terms: English, German, French, Hungarian, Czech, Russian, Polish, Spanish, Portuguese and Chinese

C.1 Dictionary—General part

ENGLISH	GERMAN	FRENCH	HUNGARIAN	CZECH
Employer	Besteller	Maître de l'ouvrage	Megrendelő	Objednatel
Contractor	Unternehmer	Entrepreneur	Vállalkozó	Zhotovitel
Engineer	Ingenieur	Maître d'œuvre	Mérnök	Správce stavby
Claim	Anspruch	Réclamation	Követelés	Claim
Notice of the claim	Anzeige des Anspruches	Avis de la réclamation	Követelés bejelentése	Oznámení claimu
Claim for extension of the time for completion	Anspruch an die Verlängerung der Baufertigstellungszeit	Réclamation à la prolongation du délai d'achèvement	A megvalósítás időtartamának meghosszabbítására irányuló követelésiranyulo koveteles	Claim na prodloužení doby pro dokončení
Claim for additional payment	Anspruch an die Zusatzvergütung	Réclamation au paiement supplémentaire	Többletkifizetés követelése	Claim na dodatečnou platbu
General conditions	Allgemeine Bedingungen	Conditions générales	Általános feltételek	Obecné podmínky
Particular conditions	Besondere Bedingungen	Conditions particulières	Különös feltételek	Zvláštní podmínky
Contract	Vertrag	Marché	Szerződés	Smlouva
Contract agreement	Vertragsdokument	L'acte d'engagement	Szerződéses feltételek összefoglalása (a szerződéses megállapodás)	Smlouva o dílo
Letter of acceptance	Annahmeschreiben	Lettre d'acceptation	Elfogadó levél	Dopis o přijetí nabídky
Letter of tender	Angebotsschreiben	Lettre d'offre	Ajánlati nyilatkozat	Dopis nabídky
Specifications	Leistungsbeschreibung	Spécifications	Részletes előírások (műszaki leírások)	Technická specifikace
Drawings	Zeichnungen	Dessins	Tervrajzok	Výkresy
Schedules	Listen	Echéanciers	Jegyzékek	Formuláře
Tender	Angebot	Offre	Ajánlat	Nabídka

Appendix C: Dictionary of Construction Terms

RUSSIAN	POLISH	SPANISH	PORTUGUESE	CHINESE
Заказчик	Zamawiający	Contratante/Empleador	Contratante	业主
Подрядчик	Wykonawca	Contratista	Contratado (empreiteiro)	承包商
Инженер	Inżynier	Ingeniero	Engenheiro	工程师
Претензия (требование)	Roszczenie	Reclamación	Demanda (reivindicação)	索赔
Уведомление о претензии	Powiadomienie o roszczeniu	Notificación de la reclamación	Aviso de demanda (notificação de reivindicação)	索赔通知
Требование о продлении срока завершения работ	Roszczenie do przedłużenie czasu na ukończenie	Reclamación para prórroga del plazo de terminación	Demanda (reivindicação) para prorrogação do prazo para conclusão	竣工时间延期索赔
Требование одополнительной оплате	Roszczenie o dodatkową płatność	Reclamación para pago adicional	Demanda (reivindicação) para pagamento complementar (adicional)	追加费用索赔
Общие условия	Warunki ogólne	Condiciones generales	Condições gerais	通用条件
Особые условия	Warunki szczególne	Condiciones especiales	Condições especiais (particulares)	专用条件
Контракт	Umowa	Contrato	Contrato	合同
Договор подряда	Akt umowy	Convenio/Acuerdo Contractual	Acordo contratual	合同协议书
Извещение об акцепте	List akceptujący	Carta de aceptación	Carta de aceitação (de aceite da proposta)	中标函
Оферта	Oferta	Carta de la oferta	Carta de proposta	投标函
Спецификация (Технические условия)	Specyfikacja	Especificaciones (técnicas)	Especificações (descrições técnicas)	技术规程
Чертежи	Rysunki	Planos	Desenhos	图纸
Приложения	Wykazy	Formulários/Anexos	Cronogramas (outros anexos)	数据表
Тендерное предложение	Dokumenty	Oferta	Proposta	投标书

Appendix C: Dictionary of Construction Terms

ENGLISH	GERMAN	FRENCH	HUNGARIAN	CZECH
Appendix to tender	Anhang zum Angebot	Appendice de l'offre	Ajánlati nyilatkozat függeléke	Příloha k nabídce
Bill of quantities	Leistungsverzeichnis	Devis quantitatif (cahier de charges)	Mennyiségkimutatás	Výkaz výměr
Dispute adjudication board	Streitbeilegungsstelle	Bureau de conciliation	Döntőbizottság	Rada pro rozhodování sporů
Commencement date	Tag des Baubeginns	Date de commencement	Kezdési időpont	Datum zahájení prací
Time for completion	Baufertigstellungszeit	Délai d'achèvement	Megvalósítás időtartama	Doba pro dokončení
Tests on completion	Fertigstellungstests	Tests d'achèvement	Átvételt megelőző Üzempróbák	Přejímací zkoušky
Taking-over certificate	Abnahmebescheinigung	Certificat de réception	Átadás-átvételi igazolás	Potvrzení o převzetí díla
Tests after completion	Tests nach Fertigstellung	Tests après achèvement	Átvétel utáni Üzempróbák	Zkoušky po dokončení
Defects notification period	Mängelanzeigefrist	Délai de notification des vices	Jótállási időszak	Záruční doba
Completion of outstanding work and remedying defects	Fertigstellung ausstehender Arbeiten und Behebung von Mängeln	Achèvement des travaux inachevés et suppression des vices	El nem végzett munkák befejezése és hiányok pótlása potlasa	Dokončení nedokončených prací na díle a odstranění vad
Extension of defects notification period	Verlängerung der Mängelanzeigefrist	Prolongation du délai de notification des vices	Jótállási időszak kiterjesztése	Prodloužení záruční doby
Performance certificate	Erfüllungsbescheinigung	Certificat d'exécution	Teljesítési igazolás	Potvrzení o splnění smlouvy
Taking over of the works and sections	Abnahme der Arbeiten und Abschnitte der Arbeiten	Réception des travaux et des tranches	A létesítmény és szakaszok átvétele	Převzetí díla a sekcí
Accepted contract amount	Vereinbarte Auftragssumme	Montant contractuel accepté	Elfogadott ajánlati ár	Přijatá smluvní částka
Contract price	Vertragspreis	Prix contractuel	Szerződéses Ár	Smluvní cena
Cost	Kosten	Coûts	Költségek	Náklady
Final payment certificate	Schlusszahlungsbescheinigung	Certificat de paiement final	Végszámla fizetési igazolás	Potvrzení závěrečné platby

Appendix C: Dictionary of Construction Terms 795

RUSSIAN	POLISH	SPANISH	PORTUGUESE	CHINESE
Приложение к оферте	Zdącznik do oferty	Apéndice de la oferta	Anexo à proposta	投标函附录
Сметный расчет	Przedmiar robót	Lista de cantidades	Relação (planilha) de quantidades	工程量表
Совет по урегулированию споров	Komisja rozjemstwa w sporach	Comisión para la resolución de controversias/Mesa de resolución de conflictos	Conselho de conciliação (Junta de conflitos)	争端裁網会
Дата начала работ (строительства объектов)	Data rozpoczęcia	Fecha de inicio	Data de início (dos trabalhos)	开工日期
Срок завершения работ (строительства объектов)	Czas na ukończenie	Plazo de terminación (ejecución)	Prazo para término (conclusão)	竣工时间
Контрольные испытания по завершении строительства	Próby końcowe	Praebas a la terminación	Testes finais (na conclusão)	竣工检验
Сертификат сдачи-приемки	Świadectwo przejęcia	Certificado de recepción de obra	Certificado de recepção da obra (de ocupação)	接收证书
Контрольные испытания после завершения строительства	Próby eksploatacyjne	Pruebas posteriores a la terminación	Testes depois do término (após a conclusão)	竣工后的检验
Гарантийный срок (период)	Okres zgłaszania wad	Período para la notificación de defectos	Período de notificação de falhas (prazo de garantia)	缺陷通知期
Завершение незаконченных работ и устранение недостатков	Ukończenie zalegjej pracy i usunięcie wad	Terminación de trabajos tendientes y reparación de defectos	Finalização dos trabalhos restantes na obra e eliminação de defeitos (condusão de obras pendentes e reparo de falhas)	完成扫尾工作和修补缺陷
Продление гарантийного срока (периода)	Przedłużenie okresu znaszania wad	Prórroga del plazo para la notificación de defectos	Prolongamento do prazo de garantia (prorrogação do período de notificação de falhas)	缺陷通知期的延长
Сертификат об исполнении контракта (свидетельство о выполнении условий контракта)	Świadectwo wykonania	Certificado de cumplimiento	Certificado de execução da obra (certificado de desempenho)	履约证书
Приемка объектов и их частей	Przejęcie robót i odcinków	Recepción de las obras y secciones	Recepção da obra e de seções (ocupação das obras e seções)	工程或区段的接收
Акцептованная сумма контракта	Zaakceptowana kwota kontraktowa	Monto contractual aceptado	Preço contratual aceito (valor aceito do contrato)	中标合同款额
Цена контракта	Cena kontraktowa	Precio del contrato	Preço da obra (preço do contrato)	合同价格
Расходы	Koszt	Costo	Despesas (custo)	费用
Окончательный (итоговый) платежный сертификат	Ostateczne świadectwo płatności	Certificado de pago final	Certificado de pagamento final	最终支付证书

ENGLISH	GERMAN	FRENCH	HUNGARIAN	CZECH
Final statement	Schlussrechnung	Décompte final	Készre jelentési nyilatkozat	Závěrečné vyúčtování
Application for final payment certificate	Beantragung der Schlusszahlungs bescheinigung	Demande de certificat de paiement final	Végszámla fizetési Igazolás igénylése	Žádost o potvrzení závěrečného vyúčtování
Foreign currency	Ausländische Währung	Devise étrangère	Valuta	Cizí měna
Interim payment certificate	Zwischenzahlungs-bescheinigung	Certificat de paiement provisoire	Közbenső fizetési Igazolás	Potvrzení průběžné platby
Local currency	Lokale Währung	Devise locale	Helyi valuta	Místní měna
Payment certificate	Zahlungsbescheinigung	Certificat de paiement	Fizetési igazolás	Potvrzení platby
Application for interim payment certificate	Beantragung einer Zwischenzahlungs-bescheinigung	Demande de certificats de paiement provisoire	Közbenső fizetési Igazolás igénylése	Žádost o potvrzení průběžné platby
Provisional sum	Behelfsbetrag	Somme provisionelle	Feltételes összeg	Podmíněný obnos
Retention money	Einbehalte	Retenue de garantie	Visszatartott összeg	Zadržné
Statement	Rechnung	Décompte	Kimutatás	Vyúčtování
Contractor's equipment	Ausrüstung des Unternehmers	Équipement de l'entrepreneur	Vállalkozó eszközei	Vybavení zhotovitele
Goods	Gütern	Biens	Áruk	Věci určené pro dílo
Materials	Materialien	Matériaux	Anyagok	Materiály
Plant	Anlagen	Installations industrielles	Berendezések	Technologické zařízení
Section	Abschnitt	Section	Szakasz	Sekce
Permanent works	Baumassnahmen	Ouvrages définitif	Végleges létesítmények	Stavba
Temporary works	Behelfsmassnahmen	Ouvrages provisoires	Ideiglenes létesítmények	Dočasné dílo
Works mean the permanent works and the temporary works, or either of them as appropriate.	Arbeiten werden sowohl die Baumassnahmen als auch die Behelfsmassnahmen verstanden, gegebenenfalls auch beide.	Travaux designe les travaux définitifs et les travaux provisoires, ou le cas échéant un seul des deux.	A létesítmény a végleges létesítményeket és az Ideiglenes létesítményeket is jelenti, vagy bármelyiket szükség szerint.	Dílo je stavba a dočasné dílo nebo kterékoli z uvedených tak, jak je to vhodné.

RUSSIAN	POLISH	SPANISH	PORTUGUESE	CHINESE
Окончательный комплект исполнительных записей (Заключительный отчет)	Rozliczenie ostateczne	Declaración final (relación valorada final de las obras ejecutadas)	Relação final dos trabalhos executados (demonstração final)	最终报表
Обращение за окончательным (итоговым) платежным сертификатом	Wystąpienie o ostateczne świadectwo płatności	Solicitud de certificado de pago final	Pedido de certificado do pagamento final	最终支付证书的申请
Иностранная валюта	Waluta obca	Moneda extranjera	Moeda estrangeira	外币
Промежуточный платежный сертификат	Przejściowe świadectwo płatności	Certificado de pago provisional	Certificado de pagamento provisório	期中支付证书
Местная валюта	Waluta miejscowa	Moneda Local	Moeda local	当地币
Платежный сертификат	Świadectwo płatności	Certificado de pago	Certificado de pagamento	支付证书
Обращение за промежуточным платежным сертификатом	Występowanie o przejściowe świadectwa płatności	Solicitud de certificados de pago provisionales	Requisição (pedido) de certificado de pagamento provisório	期中支付证书的申请
Резервная сумма	Kwota warunkowa	Monto provisional (valor estimado/cantidad provisional)	Valor provisório (quantia provisória)	暂定金额
Сумма удержания	Kwota zatrzymana	Monto retenido	Retenção de garantia (dinheiro retido)	保留金
Комплект исполнительных записей	Rozliczenie	Declaración (relación valorada de las obras ejecutadas)	Relação de trabalhos executados (demonstração)	报表
Оборудование подрядчика	Sprzęt wykonawcy	Equipos del Contratista	Equipamento do contratante (empreiteiro)	承包商的设备
Товары	Dobra	Bienes	Mercadorias (bens)	货物
Материалы	Materiały	Materiales	Materiais	材料
Механизация	Urządzenia	Equipos/Instalaciones	Instalações (tecnológicas)	永久设备
Часть	Odcinek	Sección	Seção	区段
Постоянные объекты	Roboty stałe	Obras permanentes	Obra definitiva (permanentes)	永久工程
Временные объекты	Roboty tymczasowe	Obras temporales	Obras temporárias	临时工程
Объекты обозначают как постоянные объекты, так и временные объекты или любые из них, в зависимости от контекста.	Roboty oznaczają roboty stałe i roboty tymczasowe lub jedne z nich, zależnie co jest odpowiednie.	Obras son las obras permanentes y las obras temporales, o cualquiera de ellas según corresponda.	Obras significam as obras permanentes e as obras temporárias, ou qualquer uma das duas, conforme apropriado.	工程指永久工程和临时工程, 或视情况指其中之一。

ENGLISH	GERMAN	FRENCH	HUNGARIAN	CZECH
Contractor's documents	Dokumente des Unternehmers	Documents de l'entrepreneur	Vállalkozó dokumentumai	Dokumenty zhotovitele
Employer's equipment	Ausrüstung des Bestellers	Equipement du maître de l'ouvrage	Megrendelő eszközei	Vybavení objednatele
Performance security	Erfüllungssicherheit	Garantie d'exécution	Teljesítési biztosíték	Zajištění splnění smlouvy
Site	Baustelle	Chantier	Helyszín	Staveniště
Unforeseeable means not reasonably foreseeable by an experienced contractor by the date for the submission of the tender.	Unvorhersehbar heisst, dass es auch einem erfahrenen Unternehmer zum Zeitpunkt der Vorlage des Angebots vernünftigerweise nicht möglich gewesen wäre, das Ereignis vorherzusehen.	Imprévisible signifie non raisonnablement prévisible pour un entrepreneur expérimenté à la date de la soumission de l'offre.	Előre nem látható egy tapasztalt vállalkozó által az ajánlat benyújtásáig ésszerűen előre nem látható dolgot jelent.	Nepředvídatelné je to, co není rozumně předvídatelné zkušeným zhotovitelem do data pro předložení nabídky.
Variation means any change to the works, which is instructed or approved as a variation.	Leistungsänderung ist jede Änderung der Arbeiten, die als eine Leistungsänderung angewiesen oder genehmigt ist.	Modifications designe tout changement dans les travaux, qui est ordonné ou approuvé comme une modification.	Változtatás a létesítmény bármely megváltoztatását jelenti, amelyet mint változtatást rendelnek el, vagy hagynak jóvá.	Variace je jakákoli změna díla nařízená nebo schválená jako variace.

RUSSIAN	POLISH	SPANISH	PORTUGUESE	CHINESE
Документация подрядчика	Dokumenty wykonawcy	Documentos del contratista	Documentação do contratado (empreiteiro)	承包商的文件
Оборудование Заказчика	Sprzęt zamawiającego	Equipos del contratante	Equipamento do contratante	业主的设备
Обеспечение исполнения Контракта	Zabezpieczenie wykonania	Garantía de cumplimiento	Garantia de execução (da obra)	履约保证
Строительная площадка	Plac budowy	Lugar de las obras / Emplazamiento	Canteiro de obra (Local)	现场
Непредвиденное обстоятельство обозначает то, что не мог разумно предвидеть опытный подрядчик на дату представления оферты.	Nieprzewidywalne oznacza racjonalnie niemożliwe do przewidzenia przez doświadczonego wykonawcę do daty składania dokumentów ofertowych.	Imprevisible significa lo que no es razonablemente previsible por un contratista con experiencia en la fecha de presentación de la oferta.	Imprevisível significa um evento não razoavelmente previsível por um contratante (empreiteiro) experiente até a data-base.	不可预见指一个有经验的承包商在提交投标文件那天还不能合理预见的。
Изменение обозначает любое изменение в работах, внесение которого поручено или согласовано как изменение.	Zmiana oznacza każdą zmianę w robotach, poleconą lub zatwierdzoną jako zmiana.	Variación significa cualquier cambio en las obras que es requerido o aprobado como una variación.	Variação significa qualquer mudança nas obras instmída ou aprovada como variação.	变更指按照指令或批准作为变更的对工程的任何变动。

C.2 Dictionary—Contractor's claims

ENGLISH	GERMAN	FRENCH	HUNGARIAN	CZECH
Contractor's claims	Ansprüche des Unternehmers	Réclamations de l'entrepreneur	A vállalkozó követelései	Claimy zhotovitele
1.9 - Delayed drawings or instructions	Verspätete Zeichnungen und Anorderungen	Dessins ou instructions retardés	Tervek vagy utasítások késedelme	Zpožděné výkresy a pokyny
2.1 - Right of access to the site	Recht auf Zugang zur Baustelle	Droit à l'accés au chantier	A helyszínre való bejutás joga	Právo přístupu na staveniště
4.7 - Setting out	Absteckungen	Implantation des ouvrages	Kitűzés	Vytyčování
4.12 - Unforeseeable physical conditions	Unvorhersehbare natürliche Bedingungen	Conditions physiques imprévisibles	Előre nem látható helyszíni körülmények Előre nem látható helyszíni körülmények	Nepředvídatelné fyzické podmínky
4.24 - Fossils	Funde	Fossiles	Régészeti leletek	Archeologické a další nálezy na staveništi
7.4 - Testing	Testläufe	Essais	Üzempróbák	Zkoušení
8.4 - Extension of time for completion	Verlängerung der Baufertigstellungszeit	Prolongation du délai d' achèvement	A megvalósítás időtartamának meghosszabbítása	Prodloužení doby pro dokončení
8.5 - Delays caused by authorities	Durch Behörden verursachte Verzögerungen	Retardes causés par les autorités	Hatóságok által okozott késedelmek	Zpoždění způsobená úřady
8.9 - Consequences of suspension	Folgen der Suspendierung	Conséquences de la suspension	Felfüggesztés következményei	Následky přerušení
10.2 - Taking over of parts of the works	Teilabnahme	Réception des parties des ouvrages	A létesítmény részeinek átvétele atvetele	Převzetí části díla
10.3 - Interference with tests on completion	Behinderung des Fertigstellungstests	Interférences avec les essais préalables à la réception	Beavatkozás az átvételt megelőző üzempróbákba	Překážky při přejímacích zkouškách
11.8 - Contractor to search	Nachforschungen des Unternehmers	Investigations de l'entrepreneur	Vállalkozó feladata a hibák feltárásában	Zjišťovaní příčiny vady zhotovitelem
12 - Measurement and evaluation	Aufmass und Bewertung	Métrés et valorisation	Felmérés és elszámolási értékmegállapítás	Měření a oceňování

Appendix C: Dictionary of Construction Terms 801

RUSSIAN	POLISH	SPANISH	PORTUGUESE	CHINESE
Претензии подрядчика	Roszczenia wykonawcy	Reclamaciones del contratista	Demandas do contratado (reivindicações do empreiteiro)	承包商的索赔
Задержка в предоставлении чертежей или даче указаний	Opóźnienie rysunków lub instrukcji	Demoras de los planos o instrucciones	Desenhos ou instruções atrasodos	拖延的图纸或指示
Право доступа на строительную площадку	Prawo dostępu do placu budowy	Derecho de acceso al lugar de la obra / Emplazamiento	Direito de entrar no canteiro de obra (de acesso ao local)	进入现场的权利
Разметка объектов	Wytyczenie	Trazado / Replanteo	Implantação (posicionamento)	放线
Непредвиденные геологические условия	Nieprzewidywalne warunki fizyczne	Condiciones físicas imprevisibles	Condições físicas imprevisíveis	不可预见的外界条件
Ископаемые	Wykopaliska	Fósiles	Achados arqueológicos (fósseis)	化石
Испытания	Dokonywanie prób	Pruebas	Testes	检验
Продление срока завершения работ (строительства объектов)	Przedłużenie czasu na ukończenie	Prórroga del plazo de terminación	Prolongamento do prazo para terminar (conclusão)	竣工时间的延长
Задержки, вызванные органами власти	Opóźnienia spowodowane przez władze	Retrasos / Demoras ocasionadas por las autoridades	Atrasos causados por autoridades	由公共当局引起的延误
Последствия приостановки работ	Konsekwencje zawieszenia	Consecuencias de la suspensión	Consequências da interrupção (suspensão)	暂停引起的后果
Приемка части объектов	Przejęcie części robót	Recepción de partes de las obras	Recepção (ocupação) de parte da obra	对部分工程的接收
Препятствие проведению контрольных испытаний по завершении строительства объектов	Przeszkoda w próbach końcowych	Interferencia con las pruebas a la terminación	Obstáculos à execução de testes finais (interferének nos testes iw conclusão)	对竣工检验的干扰
Выяснение причин недостатков подрядчиком	Obowiązek poszukiwania przez wykonawcę	Investigación / Búsqueda por parte del contratista (búsqueda de las causas de defectos por parte del contratista)	Verificação de defeitos pelo contratado (busca pelo empreiteiro)	承包商的调查
Измерение и оценка	Obmiary i wycena	Medición y evaluación	Medição e avaliação	计量和估价

ENGLISH	GERMAN	FRENCH	HUNGARIAN	CZECH
12.4 - Omissions	Nichtdurchführung von Arbeiten	Supressions	Mulasztások	Vypuštění práce
13.2 - Value engineering	Technische Rationalisierung	Plus-value d'ingénierie	Értékelemzés	Zlepšení
13.3 - Variation procedure	Durchführung der Leistungsänderung	Procédure de modification	Változtatási eljárás	Postup při variacích
13.7 - Adjustments for changes in legislation	Anpassungen aufgrund von Gesetzes änderungen	Ajustements pour changements dans la legislation	Jogszabályi módosulások miatti kiigazítások	Úpravy v důsledku změn legislativy
14.4 - Schedule of payments	Zahlungsplan	Echéancier de paiement	Fizetési ütemterv	Harmonogram plateb
14.8 - Delayed payment	Verspätete Zahlung	Retard de paiement	Késedelmes kifizetés	Zpožděná platba
16.1 - Contractor's entitlement to suspend work	Anspruch des Unternehmers auf Suspendierung der Arbeiten	Droit de l'entrepreneur à suspendre les travaux	Vállalkozó joga a munka felfüggesztésére	Oprávnění zhotovitele přerušit práci
16.4 - Payment on termination	Zahlung nach Kündigung	Paiement à la résiliation	Kifizetés felmondáskor	Platba při odstoupení
17.1 - Indemnities	Haftungsfreistellung	Indemnités	Kártérítés	Odškodnění
17.4 - Consequences of employer's risk	Folgen des Risikos des Bestellers	Conséquences des risques du maître de l'ouvrage	A Megrendelő kockázataival járó következmények	Důsledky rizik objednatele
18.1 - General requirements for insurances	Allgemeine Anforderungen an Versicherung	Exigences générales pour les assurances	A biztosításokkal szembeni általános követelmények	Obecné požadavky na pojištění
19.4 - Consequences of force majeure	Folgen der höheren Gewalt	Conséquences de la force majeure	A Vis Maior következményei	Důsledky vyšší moci
19.6 - Optional termination, payment and release	Freies Kündigungsrecht, Bezahlung und Befreiung	Résiliation optionnelle, paiement et exonération	Felmondás lehetősége, kifizetés és felmentés felmentes	Dobrovolné odstoupení, platba a osvobození z plnění

RUSSIAN	POLISH	SPANISH	PORTUGUESE	CHINESE
Отмена работ	Pominięcia	Omisiones	Omissões (de trabalho na obra)	省略
Функционально-стоимостной анализ	Inżynieria wartości	Ingeniería de Valor	Engenharia de valor (proposta de melhoria)	价值工程
Порядок внесения изменений	Procedura zmiany	Procedimiento de variación	Procedimento de variação	变更程序
Корректировка в связи с изменениями в законодательстве	Korekty wynikające ze zmian stanu prawnego	Ajustes por cambios en la legislación	Ajustes por mudanças na legislação	法规变化引起的调整
График платежей	Wykaz płatności	Calendario de pagos	Cronograma de Pagamentos	支付计划表
Задержка оплаты	Opóźniona płatność	Retraso en los pagos / Pagos atrasados	Pagamento atrasado	拖延的支付
Право подрядчика приостановить выполнение работ	Uprawnienie wykonawcy do zawieszenia pracy	Derecho del contratista a suspender los trabajos	Direito do empreiteiro (contratado) de suspender os trabalhos (obras)	承包商有权暂停工作
Оплата по расторжении контракта	Płatność przy odstąpieniu	Pago a la terminación / resolución	Pagamento na rescisão	终止时的支付
Гарантии освобождения от ответственности	Odszkodowania	Indemnizaciones (Exoneración de responsabilidades)	Indenização (liberação de responsabilidade)	保障
Последствия рисков Заказчика	Skutki zagrożeń stanowiących ryzyko zamawiającego	Consecuencias de los riesgos del contratante	Consequências dos riscos do contratante	业主的风险造成的后果
Общие требования к страхованию	Ogólne wymagania w odniesieniu do ubezpieczeń	Requisitos generales en materia de seguros	Requisitos gerais para seguros	有关保险的总体要求
Последствия обстоятельств непреодолимой силы (форс-мажор)	Następstwa siły wyższej	Consecuencias de la fuerza mayor	Consequências da força maior	不可抗力引起的后果
Расторжение контракта по усмотрению, оплата и освобождение от обязательств	Odstąpienie według uznania, płatność i zwolnienie	Terminación / Resolución opcional, pago y finiquito	Rescisão opcional, pagamento e quitação	可选择的终止、支付和解除履约

C.3 Dictionary—Employer's claims

ENGLISH	GERMAN	FRENCH	HUNGARIAN	CZECH
Employer's claims	Ansprüche des Bestellers	Réclamations du maître de l'ouvrage	A megrendelő követelései	Claimy objednatele
4.19 - Electricity, water and gas	Elektrizität, Wasser und Gas	Electricité, eau et gaz	Villamosenergia-, víz- és gázellátás	Elektřina, voda a plyn
4.20 - Employer's equipment and free-issue material	Ausrüstung des Bestellers und kostenlos beigestelltes Material	Equipement du maître de l'ouvrage et matériaux gracieusement mis à disposition	A megrendelő eszközei és a térítésmentesen rendelkezésre bocsátott anyag	Vybavení objednatele a objednatelem volně poskytovaný materiál
7.5 - Rejection	Zurückweisung	Rejet	Elutasítás	Odmítnutí
7.6 - Remedial work	Nachbesserung	Travaux de réparation	Helyreállítási munka	Nápravné práce
8.6 - Rate of progress	Baufortschrittrate	Cadences d'avancement	Előrehaladás üteme	Míra postupu prací
8.7 - Delay damages	Verzögerungsschadenersatz	Dommages de retard	Kötbér	Náhrada škody za zpoždění
9.4 - Failure to pass tests on completion	Fehlschlagen der Fertigstellungstests	Echec des essais préalables à la réception	Átvételt megelőző üzempróbák eredménytelensége	Neúspěšné přejímací zkoušky
10.2 - Taking over of parts of the works	Teilabnahme	Réception de parties des ouvrages	A létesítmény részeinek átvétele	Převzetí části díla
11.3 - Extension of defects notification period	Verlängerung der Mängelanzeigefrist	Prolongation de la période de garantie	A jótállási időszak meghosszabbítása	Prodloužení záruční doby
11.4 - Failure to remedy defects	Versäumnis der Mängelbeseitigung	Echec à la réparation des désordres	Hiányok pótlásának elmulasztása	Neúspěšné odstraňování vady
13.7 - Adjustments for changes in legislation	Anpassungen aufgrund von Gesetzesänderungen	Ajustements pour changements dans la legislation	Jogszabályok módosulása miatti kiigazítások	Úpravy v důsledku změn legislativy
15.3 - Valuation at date of termination	Bewertung zum Zeitpunkt der Kündigung	Valorisation à la date de résiliation	Felmondás napjára történő értékbecslés	Ocenění k datu odstoupení
15.4 - Payment after termination	Zahlung nach der Kündigung	Paiement après résiliation	Kifizetés felmondást követően	Platba po odstoupení
17.1 - Indemnities	Haftungsfreistellung	Indemnités	Kártérítés	Odškodnění

RUSSIAN	POLISH	SPANISH	PORTUGUESE	CHINESE
Претензии Заказчика	Roszczenia zamawiającego	Reclamaciones del contratante / empleador	Demandas (reivindicações) do contratante	业主的索赔
Электричество, вода и газ	Elektryczność, woda i gaz	Electricidad, agua y gas	Eletricidade, água e gás	电、水、气
Оборудование и материалы, предоставляемые Заказчиком	Sprzęt zamawiającego i materiał do wydania bezpłatnie	Equipos del contratante / Empleador y materiales de libre disposidón	Equipamento do contratante e material oferecido livremente pelo contratante (materiais fornecidos)	业主的设备和免费提供的材料
Отказ	Odrzucenie	Rechazo	Recusa (Rejeição)	拒收
Устранение недостатков	Prace zabezpieczające	Medidas correctivas (trabajos de reparación)	Trabalhos de reparação (reparos)	补救工作
Ход работ	Szybkość postępu pracy	Avance / ritmo de avance	Grau de evolução (ritmo de progresso)	进展速度
Возмещение заранее оцененных убытков, вызванных задержкой	Odszkodowanie umowne za opóźnienie	Indemnización por demora	Reembolso de prejuízo por atraso (danos por atraso)	误期损害赔偿费
Неудачный результат Контрольных испытаний по завершении строительства объектов	Niepowodzenie prób końcowych	Fracaso de las pruebas a la terminación	Fracasso nos testes finais (reprovação nos testes na conclusão)	未能通过竣工检验
Приемка части объектов	Przejęcie części robót	Recepción de partes de las obras	Recepção (ocupação) de parte dos trabalhos (obras)	对部分工程的接收
Продление гарантийного периода	Przedłużenie okresu znaszania wad	Prórroga del plazo para la notificación de defectos	Prolongamento do prazo de garantia (prorrogação do período de notificação de falhas)	缺陷通知期的延长
Неустранение недостатков	Zaniedbanie usunięcia wad	Incumplimiento en cuanto a la reparación de defectos	Não eliminação dos defeitos (falta de reparo das falhas)	未能补救缺陷
Корректировка в связи с изменениями в законодательстве	Korekty wynikające ze zmian stanu prawnego	Ajustes por cambios en la legislación	Ajustes por mudanças na legislação	法规变化引起的调整
Оценка на дату расторжения контракта	Wycena na datę odstąpienia	Valoración en la fecha de terminación	Avaliação (valoração) na data da rescisão	终止日期时的估价
Оплата после расторжения контракта	Płatność po odstąpieniu	Pagos después de la terminación	Pagamento após rescisão	终止后的支付
Гарантии освобождения от ответственности	Odszkodowania	Indemnizaciones (exoneración de responsabilidades)	Indenização (liberação de responsabilidade)	保障

ENGLISH	GERMAN	FRENCH	HUNGARIAN	CZECH
18.1 – General requirements for insurances	Allgemeine Anforderungen an Versicherung	Exigences générales pour les assurances	A biztosításokkal szembeni általános követelmények	Obecné požadavky na pojištění
18.2 – Insurance for works and contractor's equipment	Versicherungen der Arbeiten und der Ausrüstung des Unternehmers	Assurance des ouvrages et du matériel de l'entrepreneur	A létesítmény és a vállalkozó eszközeinek biztosítása	Pojištění díla a vybavení zhotovitele

RUSSIAN	POLISH	SPANISH	PORTUGUESE	CHINESE
Общие требования к страхованию	Ogólne wymagania w odniesieniu do ubezpieczeń	Requisitos generales en materia de seguros	Requisitos gerais dos seguros	有关保险的总体要求
Страхование объектов и оборудования подрядчика	Ubezpieczenie robót i sprzętu wykonawcy	Seguro de las obras y los equipos del contratista	Seguro das obras e equipamento do empreiteiro	工程和承包商的设备的保险

Appendix D: Claim Management System Under FIDIC Forms

D.1 Claim management team responsibilities

Comment: This is an example of an arrangement of a contractor's claim management system that can also be used by employers and/or engineers with necessary adjustments. Every project is different in terms of its size, price, time, country, and risk, so the number of employees must be adjusted accordingly. There should be one individual employee (or a team) dealing with the particular categories such as, for example, claim administration and quantification, design, time schedule (program), contract interpretation, monthly statements, invoicing, insurance, subcontractors, employer's claims, and mutual claims in a joint venture. Daily coordination meetings may be necessary in large projects where numerous site managers and claim managers need to share information as openly and efficiently as possible. Legal support may also be necessary in particular situations.

$$E = Employee$$

D.1.1 E1—Project manager

Examples of responsibilities:

E1 is a team manager and coordinator primarily responsible for identifying all factors that have an impact on time and price during the project.

E1 is responsible for claim management as a whole, that is, mainly for claim identification, keeping contemporary records, coordination of the team, early warnings, analysis of claims, decisions regarding the claim notice, consultation with the engineer or the employer, notification, and submission (quantification) of claims.

E1 is responsible for documentation, quantification and calculation of the value of claims for an extension of time for completion and additional payment (for the claim submission and enforcement).

E1 is responsible for deadlines (i.e., mainly for notification and submission of claims).

E1 is responsible for proper and efficient claim management organization and delegates responsibility for the purpose of efficient claim management.

E1 is responsible for coordination and consultation within the consortium (joint-venture).

E1 is responsible for the time schedule (program), progress reports and monthly statements and updating as per the contract.

E1 is responsible for proper and formal correspondence (i.e., mainly for notification and submission of claims).

D.1.2 E2—Design and time schedule (program)

Examples of responsibilities:

E2 is responsible for identifying all factors that have an impact on time and price related to the design and time schedule, that is, mainly for claim identification and keeping of contemporary records.

E2 is responsible for monitoring and analyzing the design works—mainly with regard to possible defects and respective claims.

E2 is responsible for the identification of the defects in the terms of reference (mainly the tender design, drawings, specifications, bill of quantities, and employer requirements).

E2 is responsible for time schedule updating due to EOT claim notifications and submissions (quantification).

E2 is responsible for the preparation and coordination of inputs for the updated time schedule.

Based on these inputs, the site manager prepares and updates the time schedule and adjusts it according to the engineer's requirements.

D.1.3 E3—Site manager

Examples of responsibilities:

E3 is responsible for identifying all factors that have impact on time and price during the project. Everything must be documented and contemporary evidence kept.

E3 prepares necessary materials and documents for E1 to enable proper coordination of the team, early warnings, analysis of the claims, decision of the claim notice, consultation with the engineer or employer, notification, and submission (quantification) of claims.

E3 is responsible for preparation of the documents and records for claim quantification and EOT evaluation/quantification (in cooperation with E2).

E3 is responsible for timely claim notification.

E3 is responsible for preparation of the documents and records for progress reports.

D.1.4 E4—Contract interpretation, monthly statements, invoicing, insurance, subcontractors, employer's claims, mutual claims in a joint venture

Examples of responsibilities:

E4 is responsible for identifying all factors that have an impact on time and price related to monthly statements, invoicing, insurance and subcontractors.

E4 is responsible for claim quantification (in cooperation with E3 for E1), that is, mainly claims for additional payment including mutual damages compensation, cost of suspension, delay, disruption, termination, and the effects of variation (such as acceleration and prolongation).

E4 is responsible for contract interpretation.

E4 is responsible for claim management in terms of cost control and payments (monthly statements, invoicing, and so on).

E4 is responsible for insurance claim management.

E4 is responsible for subcontractor claim management.

E4 is responsible for employer claim management defense.

E4 is responsible for mutual claims in a joint venture.

D.1.5 E5—Administrative support

Examples of responsibilities:

E5 is responsible for the evidence of claims and administrative support for the team.

E5 is responsible for systematic and clear evidence of letters and contemporary records.

810 Appendix D: Claim Management System Under FIDIC Forms

D.2 Claim management processes

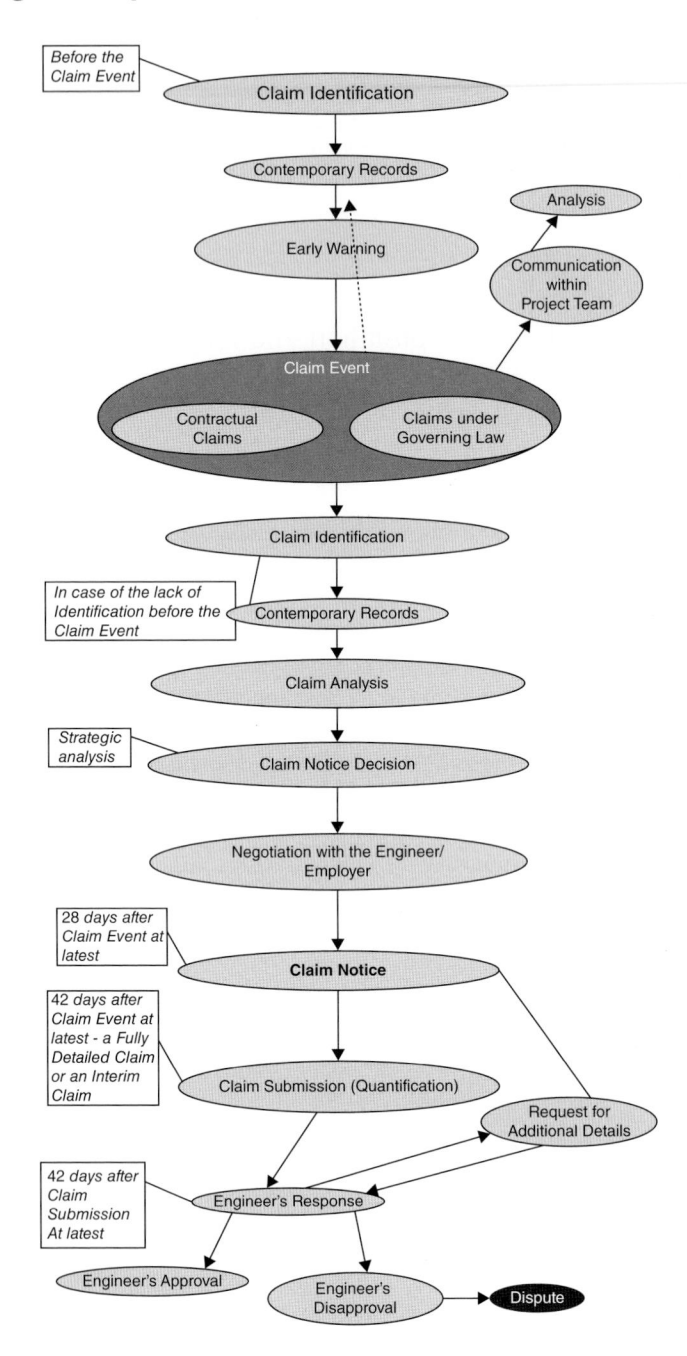

D.3 Table of contractor's claims under FIDIC CONS

Clause in FIDIC CONS 20.1	Contractor's claims
1.9	Delayed drawings or instructions
2.1	Right of access to the site
4.7	Setting out
4.12	Unforeseeable physical conditions
4.24	Fossils
7.4	Testing
8.4	Extension of time for completion
8.5	Delays caused by authorities
8.9	Consequences of suspension
10.2	Taking over of parts of the works
10.3	Interference with tests on completion
11.8	Contractor to search
12	Measurement and evaluation
12.4	Omissions
13.2	Value engineering
13.3	Variation procedure
13.7	Adjustments for changes in legislation
14.4	Schedule of payments
14.8	Delayed payment
16.1	Contractor's entitlement to suspend work
16.4	Payment on termination
17.1	Indemnities
17.4	Consequences of employer's risk
18.1	General requirements for insurances
19.4	Consequences of force majeure
19.6	Optional termination, payment and release

D.4 Table of employer's claims under FIDIC CONS

Clause in FIDIC CONS 2.5	Employer's claims
4.19	Electricity, water and gas
4.20	Employer's equipment and free-issue material
7.5	Rejection
7.6	Remedial work
8.6	Rate of progress
8.7	Delay damages
9.4	Failure to pass tests on completion
10.2	Taking over of parts of the works

Clause in FIDIC CONS 2.5	Employer's claims
11.3	Extension of defects notification period
11.4	Failure to remedy defects
13.7	Adjustments for changes in legislation
15.3	Valuation at date of termination
15.4	Payment after termination
17.1	Indemnities
18.1	General requirements for insurance
18.2	Insurance for works and contractor's equipment

Appendix E: FIDIC Forms Risk Allocation Charts

E.1 Chart No.1: Basic risk allocation alternatives in connection with unforeseeable physical conditions

Alternative	Risk allocation	Contractor's costs	Contractor's overhead	Contractor's profit
A.	Employer	Employer's risk	Employer's risk	Employer's risk
B.	Shared	Employer's risk	Employer's risk	Contractor's risk
C.	Contractor	Contractor's risk	Contractor's risk	Contractor's risk

E.2 Chart No. 2: Basic comparison of risk allocation (claims options) in FIDIC CONS/1999 red book, P&DB/1999 yellow book, and EPC/1999 silver book

E = Employer's risk; **C** = Contractor's risk; **S** = Shared risk

Clause	Identification of risk	Red Book	Yellow Book	Silver Book
1.9 Red Book	Delayed Drawings or Instructions (by the Employer)	E	–	–
1.9 Yellow Book	Errors in the Employer's Requirements	–	E	C
2.1	Right of Access to the Site	E	E	E
4.7	Setting Out (of original points, lines and levels of reference)	E	E	C

International Construction Contract Law, Second Edition. Lukas Klee.
© 2018 John Wiley & Sons Ltd. Published 2018 by John Wiley & Sons Ltd.

Appendix E: FIDIC Forms Risk Allocation Charts

Clause	Identification of risk	Red Book	Yellow Book	Silver Book
4.12	Unforeseeable Physical Conditions	S Time = E Costs = E Overhead = E Profit = C	S Time = E Costs = E Overhead = E Profit = C	C
4.24	Fossils	S Time = E Costs = E Overhead = E Profit = C	S Time = E Costs = E Overhead = E Profit = C	S Time = E Costs = E Overhead = E Profit = C
7.4	Employer's Delay in Performing Tests	E	E	E
7.5	Rejection of Plant, Material, or Workmanship	C	C	C
7.6	Remedial Work	C	C	C
8.4	Extension of Time for Completion	S Time = E Costs = C Overhead = C Profit = C	S Time = E Costs = C Overhead = C Profit = C	S Time = E Costs = C Overhead = C Profit = C
8.4	Exceptionally Adverse Climatic Conditions	S Time = E Costs = C Overhead = C Profit = C	S Time = E Costs = C Overhead = C Profit = C	C
8.5	Delays Caused by Authorities	S Time = E Costs = C Overhead = C Profit = C	S Time = E Costs = C Overhead = C Profit = C	S Time = E Costs = C Overhead = C Profit = C
8.6	Insufficient Rate of Progress	C	C	C
8.9	Consequences of Suspension	S Time = E Costs = E Overhead = E Profit = C	S Time = E Costs = E Overhead = E Profit = C	S Time = E Costs = E Overhead = E Profit = C
9.4	Failure to Pass Tests on Completion	C	C	C
10.2	Taking Over of Parts of the Works	E	E	E
10.3	Interference with Tests on Completion	E	E	E

Clause	Identification of risk	Red Book	Yellow Book	Silver Book
11.4	Failure to Remedy Defects	C	C	C
11.8	Contractor to Search for the Cause of any Defect	S Time = C Costs = E Overhead = E Profit = E	S Time = C Costs = E Overhead = E Profit = E	S Time = C Costs = E Overhead = E Profit = E
12.3	Evaluation	**E or C**	-	-
12.4 *Red Book*	Omission of any Work According to Variation	S Time = C Costs = E Overhead = E Profit = C	-	-
12.4 *Yellow & Silver Book*	Failure to Pass Tests After Completion	-	C	C
13.3	Variation Procedure	S Time = C Costs = E Overhead = E Profit = C	S Time = C Costs = E Overhead = E Profit = E	S Time = C Costs = E Overhead = E Profit = E
13.7	Adjustments for Changes in Legislation	S Time = E Costs = E Overhead = E Profit = C	S Time = E Costs = E Overhead = E Profit = C	S Time = E Costs = E Overhead = E Profit = C
13.8	Adjustments for Changes in Costs (Indexation)	**E or C**	**E or C**	C
14.8	Delayed Payment	E	E	E
15.4	Payment after Employer's Termination	C	C	C
16.1	Contractor's Entitlement to Suspend Work	E	E	E
16.4	Payment after Contractor's Termination	E	E	E
17.1	Indemnities	**E or C**	**E or C**	**E or C**

Clause	Identification of risk	Red Book	Yellow Book	Silver Book
17.4	Consequences of Employer's Risks	E	E	E
19.4	Consequences of *Force Majeure*	S Time = E Costs = E Overhead = E Profit = C	S Time = E Costs = E Overhead = E Profit = C	S Time = E Costs = E Overhead = E Profit = C

Index

ABN 2011 655, 656
abnormally low
    price 142, 735, 736
    tender 264, 265, 278
abnormally low tender (ALT) 264, 265, 278
ABU 2011 655, 656
acceleration
    constructive 94, 96, 233, 320, 329–332, 336–340, 509
    directed 329
    voluntary 340
adjudication 34, 78, 79, 96, 100, 208, 242, 261, 265, 303, 308, 321, 340, 349, 359–361, 386, 435, 444, 453, 454, 457, 459, 465, 466, 468, 469, 471–485, 489, 507, 509, 512, 528, 531, 532, 535, 537, 538, 541, 542, 545, 552, 566, 581, 582, 587, 591, 593, 596, 618, 620, 621, 674, 718, 727, 740, 742, 743, 747
    awards 56, 78, 720
    contractual 454
    statutory 58, 79, 454, 466, 471–473, 475, 476, 481, 618, 620, 621
ADR see alternative dispute resolution (ADR)
advance payment bond 705
advance payment guarantee 460, 705, 707, 714
Africa 17, 56, 128, 186, 187, 189, 195, 211, 213, 309, 332, 488, 489, 501, 505, 506, 553
AIA see American Institute of Architects (AIA)
alliancing 103, 140, 171, 362
ALT see abnormally low tender (ALT)
alternative dispute resolution (ADR) 15, 445, 483, 507, 552, 612, 618, 633, 743
American Institute of Architects (AIA) 424, 603, 606, 621, 754
analysis, managerial 20

anti-risk measures 21, 22
Arbeitsgemeinschaft (ARGE) 53
Australia 57, 58, 60, 67, 83, 92, 100, 140, 148, 171, 198, 230, 232, 339, 382, 385, 386, 388, 389, 425, 433, 445, 454, 475–477, 480, 481, 483, 485, 491, 516, 547, 564, 567, 615–617, 619, 645, 674, 711

bank guarantee 24, 131, 234, 248, 364, 474, 623, 703, 704, 706–709, 712, 713, 715, 741, 746
bid bond 704
bid pricing methods 247
bill of quantities 90, 94, 102–106, 169, 228, 247–250, 254, 255, 262, 320, 326, 400, 401, 403, 462, 523, 530, 539, 578, 584, 585, 727, 728, 749, 753
BIM see building information modeling (BIM)
BIMS see building information management systems (BIMS)
BOT see build-operate-transfer (BOT)
building construction 131, 168, 341, 436, 493, 615, 704, 756
building information management systems (BIMS) 155
building information modeling (BIM) 156–170, 240, 245, 246, 361, 590, 720, 753
build-operate-transfer (BOT) 143, 144, 146, 147, 149, 151, 152, 563
business custom 223, 229, 230

Central and Eastern Europe (CEE) 56, 220, 222, 436, 716, 722, 755
change
    substantial 274, 342, 368, 397, 455, 510, 513, 544, 643, 754
China 10, 13, 53, 60, 68, 146, 206, 301, 347, 453, 465, 491, 499, 557–561, 666, 735

International Construction Contract Law, Second Edition. Lukas Klee.
© 2018 John Wiley & Sons Ltd. Published 2018 by John Wiley & Sons Ltd.

Index

civil engineering works 1, 10, 188, 332, 656, 657, 716, 752
civil law 34, 36, 53, 55, 56, 59, 66, 68, 73, 76, 79–82, 84, 87, 88, 90, 91, 96, 97, 100, 231, 233, 239, 299–301, 303, 309, 312, 379, 380, 398, 404, 427, 434, 438, 439, 454, 491, 494, 503, 509, 511, 515, 516, 518, 534, 535, 538, 550, 563, 576, 577, 586, 652, 724, 731, 732, 746
claim
　additional payment 309, 367, 395, 430, 613, 614, 737
　contractor's 77, 175, 234, 290, 302, 304, 320, 356, 357, 359, 368, 370, 372, 383, 398, 401, 405–407, 429, 431, 435, 438, 535, 542, 546, 561, 562, 684, 693, 701, 730
　delay 93, 298, 303, 306, 381
　disruption 303, 309, 331, 408, 409, 427
　employer's 309, 311, 366, 369, 370, 372, 381, 399, 431, 432, 546, 715
　extension of time 14, 331, 332, 616
　global 94, 95, 99, 233, 234, 396, 404, 425–429, 440
　headquarters overhead 94, 233, 396, 402
　increased cost 84
　interest 400, 406
　lapse of 56, 79, 96, 273, 377, 379, 383, 610
　lost profit 406
　as part of contract price 273
　preparation cost 175, 400, 407, 466
　quantification 247, 262, 430, 432, 455, 539, 595, 809
　site overhead 400
　subcontractor 405, 770, 809
　time-barred 80, 377, 383
　from variations 354, 398, 399
claim management
　contractor's 429
　employer's 336, 431
　implementation 436
CM-at-risk 132, 378
common law 34, 36, 39, 55–59, 66, 76, 77, 79, 80, 82, 84, 86–89, 93, 94, 96, 99, 100, 174, 223, 230–233, 243, 257, 259, 290, 298–301, 303, 307, 312, 339–341, 343, 366, 370, 379–382, 406, 427, 434, 439, 454, 468, 486, 491, 503, 506, 509, 515–517, 522, 538, 549, 576, 594, 617–621, 647–649, 695, 710, 740

compatibility 177, 194, 635, 652, 654, 655, 739, 760, 761
condition precedent 96, 290, 366, 380–384, 386–389, 391, 486, 535, 566, 570, 652
CONS *see* Conditions of Contract for Construction
consortium 18, 19, 23–26, 31, 51–53, 143, 144, 163, 164, 264, 309, 549, 577, 606, 689, 736, 738, 746, 747
construction
　disputes 34, 35, 59, 208, 225, 231, 303, 425, 442, 444, 445, 451, 456, 460, 471, 472, 474, 483, 511, 618–620, 671
　management 102, 131, 171, 172, 192, 194, 198, 326, 503, 527, 601, 604, 605, 639, 676
construction project
　infrastructure 445, 493, 636, 689, 716, 724, 754
　phases 12
construction subcontract 49, 50, 524, 538, 539, 583
contract
　administration 3–5, 56, 90, 102, 103, 175, 189, 191, 222, 252, 282, 349, 350, 373, 442, 516, 523, 524, 557, 596, 602, 606, 670, 723, 737, 739, 749, 752
　bespoke 39, 46, 177, 204, 224, 230, 257, 387, 554
　construction 136
　contractor 629
　EPC 13, 15, 24, 25, 33, 44, 114, 133, 145, 146, 162, 164, 172–175, 177–186, 188–191, 196, 197, 201, 202, 205, 214, 339, 449, 516, 538, 563, 688, 693
　EPCM 192–201, 553
　price 5, 11, 13, 60, 61, 76–78, 80, 84, 87, 89, 103, 108, 123, 143, 173, 175, 176, 188, 207, 225, 227, 232, 233, 235, 237, 238, 244, 245, 247–251, 253, 255, 256, 261, 262, 273, 275, 277, 289, 304, 305, 308, 321–324, 326–328, 354, 357, 359, 369, 370, 372, 401, 432, 460, 505, 510, 511, 524, 531, 533, 538, 539, 556, 558, 561, 562, 569, 610, 611, 614, 626, 629, 637, 692, 693, 696, 697, 699, 704–706, 709, 710, 718, 719, 725, 727, 728, 730, 736, 763, 764
　risks 26, 642
contractual penalty 56, 59, 60, 73, 75, 76, 233, 280, 285, 304, 396, 737, 738

cost
    overruns 4, 14, 132, 190, 245, 263, 264, 314, 635–637, 690, 723, 751
    plus 103, 108, 131, 164, 193, 201, 248, 249, 251–253, 262, 273, 308, 354, 357–359, 545, 594, 607, 610
Czech Republic 166–170, 427, 436–438, 490, 655, 679, 680, 748, 749, 753

DAB *see* dispute adjudication board (DAB)
DB *see* design-build (DB)
DBO *see* Design, Build and Operate (DBO)
decision
    interim-binding 465
defects liability, statutory, 56, 95, 225, 511. 531, 534, 611, 708
delay
    claim 285, 286, 333, 399
    concurrent 59, 94, 300, 301, 308, 309, 396, 412, 413, 422, 695, 696, 728
    damages 56, 59, 62, 63, 77, 83, 93, 280, 281, 290, 298, 300, 303, 304, 306, 330, 352, 364, 370–373, 381, 382, 396, 399, 528, 546, 554, 737, 738
    and disruption protocol 100, 282, 291, 312, 363, 440, 441, 719
    delivery methods 2, 24, 38, 102, 103, 105, 142, 143, 153, 172, 192, 377, 602, 606, 633, 721
        extended 143
design-build (DB) 105, 172, 262, 523, 675, 688, 762
Design, Build and Operate (DBO) 100, 468, 524, 540, 579, 701, 714
designer 2, 3, 6, 9, 11, 12, 51, 83, 90, 95, 96, 103, 107, 114, 131, 138, 139, 153, 155, 157, 159, 160, 166, 170, 173, 174, 188, 191, 227, 234, 247, 425, 437, 442, 443, 445, 461, 504, 523, 546, 574, 577, 612, 624, 627, 640, 647–649, 674, 675, 724, 757, 758, 763, 764
design responsibility 38, 41, 102, 103, 108, 130, 131, 197, 557, 567, 583, 648
developing countries 5, 187, 199, 222, 244, 364, 506, 532, 553, 716, 717, 747
    investments 716
dispute adjudication board (DAB) 78, 208, 265, 308, 349, 359–361, 435, 444, 453, 459, 468, 469, 474, 475, 489, 509, 512, 528, 531, 537, 538, 541, 542, 566, 727, 740, 742, 743, 747

dispute board 129, 187, 228, 229, 442–445, 453, 454, 465, 466, 483, 484, 566, 593, 616, 671
    adjudication 78, 208, 265, 308, 349, 359–361, 435, 444, 453, 459, 468, 469, 474, 475, 489, 509, 512, 528, 531, 537, 538, 541, 542, 566, 727, 740, 742, 743, 747
dispute resolution board (DRB) 146, 242, 451, 452, 483, 671, 678
disruption 5, 21, 23, 41, 93, 100, 207, 230, 233–235, 239, 246, 247, 261, 280–284, 291, 301–303, 309, 312, 314, 319, 331, 332, 341, 363–365, 379, 386, 393, 396, 398, 399, 404–406, 408–410, 423, 426, 427, 436, 439–441, 444, 567, 586, 627, 629, 680, 693, 695, 696, 717, 719, 722, 729
    claim 303, 309, 331, 408, 409, 427
down payment guarantee 705
drawings 3, 7, 102–104, 108, 166, 169, 175, 176, 227, 228, 235, 276, 302, 314, 321, 322, 325, 326, 384, 397, 406, 408, 412, 462, 495, 496, 523, 530–532, 539, 559, 561, 569–572, 574–578, 604, 613, 614, 680, 694, 749
DRB *see* dispute resolution board (DRB)

early contractor involvement (ECI) 125, 154, 162, 254, 590, 720, 750
EBRD *see* European Bank for Reconstruction and Development (EBRD)
EIB *see* European Investment Bank (EIB)
employer's
    requirements 95, 102, 105, 107–111, 116, 117, 119–121, 126, 157, 164, 165, 171, 173–176, 188, 198, 227, 522–524, 528, 529, 536–538, 541, 546, 563, 568, 569, 573, 578, 625, 633, 647, 680, 724, 737
    risks 119, 120, 290, 296, 379, 397, 406, 555, 556, 561, 624, 625, 697, 726, 729, 737
ENAA forms of contract 597
engineer
    certification 8, 708
    neutrality 56, 90
    restricted competencies of 723
engineer procure construct (EPC) 15, 102, 172, 192, 562, 573

engineer procure construct (EPC) (*cont'd*)
   bespoke 177
   FIDIC 84, 107, 109, 172, 176, 177, 186, 562, 595, 596, 693, 723, 724
   turnkey 133, 185, 195
engineer procure construction management (EPCM) 102, 109, 172, 188, 192–202, 213, 214, 378, 553
EOT *see* extension of time (EOT)
EPC *see* engineer procure construct (EPC)
EPCM *see* engineer procure construction management (EPCM)
European Bank for Reconstruction and Development (EBRD) 171, 221, 243, 459, 460, 463, 464, 722, 747, 752, 755
European Investment Bank (EIB) 220, 221, 243, 362, 437, 464, 499, 515, 716, 722, 734, 747, 755
European Union Funds 220
extension of time (EOT) 5, 14, 40, 41, 79, 93, 94, 108, 123, 164, 175, 178, 180, 203, 208, 233, 234, 248, 258, 280–282, 285, 287, 290, 294, 298, 299, 301–303, 305–309, 315, š19 329–333, 335, 336, 339, 340, 343, 352, 359, 364–368, 371, 372, 375, 377, 382, 383, 386–388, 390–392, 396, 397, 399, 407, 408, 430, 431, 439, 478, 482, 502, 506, 530, 535, 558, 560–562, 582, 595, 610, 611, 616, 628, 630, 692, 694–698, 701, 729, 737, 740

fast track projects 153
FEED *see* front end engineering design (FEED)
FIDIC
   dispute 469, 474, 483, 749
   expansion 485
   influence 489
   membership 488
FIDIC forms
   in Brazil 493
   design responsibility 567
   in Russia 492
   in Southeast Asia 491
final guarantee 705, 709
fitness for purpose 56, 95, 96, 103, 106, 173, 193, 197, 550, 551, 576, 577, 640, 647–650
float ownership 285–287

force majeure 17, 34, 80, 86, 87, 95–97, 100, 148, 175, 203, 207–209, 235–237, 309, 311, 390, 397, 412, 498, 519, 531, 539, 541, 545, 555, 556, 558, 560–562, 571, 625, 628, 634, 635, 692, 693, 697, 700, 701, 737
forms of contract 36, 39, 85, 206, 208, 222, 230, 233, 257, 282, 326, 362, 442, 443, 459, 461–464, 490, 499, 513, 518, 524, 538, 548, 562, 581, 585, 587, 598, 609, 618, 645, 647, 670, 672, 675, 677, 678, 684, 685, 719, 736, 747, 748, 751, 752
front end engineering design (FEED) 188
frustration of purpose 80, 87, 88

general contracting 102, 104–106, 131, 175, 261, 378, 523, 607, 647, 718, 724, 749, 762
Gold Book FIDIC 349, 463, 468, 470, 524, 540, 543, 545, 547, 549, 672, 689, 691, 714, 715
good faith 4, 5, 56, 60, 69, 73, 80–84, 92–94, 96, 121, 134, 232–234, 237, 239, 240, 299, 349, 361, 379, 382, 383, 390–393, 450, 460, 549, 581, 586, 596, 597, 650, 652, 654, 723, 724
Green Book 524, 538, 599
guaranteed maximum price 253, 601, 607

hardship 80, 87, 100, 476
hazard 2, 4, 5, 21–23, 39, 102, 132, 143, 202, 208, 250, 253, 314, 315, 367, 383, 395, 398, 456, 555, 567, 573, 624, 626, 632, 633, 635, 646, 664, 684, 693, 718, 761, 764
   typical 23
health care facilities 1, 3, 756, 758, 762, 763
hospital 82, 139, 156, 369, 486, 498, 500, 501, 638, 676, 752, 756–762
Hungary 474, 475, 483, 490, 542, 547, 548
hydropower 136, 137, 189–192, 255, 256, 651, 708

ICC *see* International Chamber of Commerce (ICC)
IchemE forms of contract 598
impossibility 80, 87–89, 94, 403, 706, 707, 719
impracticability 80, 87, 89
imprévision 80, 84, 85

Index   **821**

INCOTERMS *see* International Commercial Terms (INCOTERMS)
insurance 1, 2, 12, 20, 21, 23, 24, 32, 37, 51, 53, 95, 107, 118, 132, 146, 158, 175, 192, 196, 234, 244, 248, 253, 364, 369, 371, 395, 400, 405, 406, 413, 528, 531, 539, 542, 545, 547, 550, 551, 555, 556, 576, 577, 581, 591, 623–625, 627, 630–633, 635, 640–663, 665, 666, 674, 678, 697, 703, 709, 712, 713, 736, 740, 757, 807, 809, 811, 812
  CAR 118, 657–662
  for contractor's personnel 641, 642
  EAR 657
  against injury of persons and damage to property 641
  negotiating 652
  standards 655
  for works and contractor's equipment 641, 697
intercultural aspects 432
international business 15, 31, 51, 57, 73, 221, 223
International Chamber of Commerce (ICC) 6, 208, 217, 225, 456, 462, 507, 517, 597, 712–714, 727
  case 6, 77, 174, 281, 302, 332, 340, 364, 367, 370, 371, 380, 407, 456, 468–471
  forms of contract 597
  rules related to securities 712
International Commercial Terms (INCOTERMS) 217
interpretation 5, 8, 10, 13, 56, 67, 69, 75, 83, 146, 162–164, 176, 225, 226, 239, 240, 255, 261, 276, 295, 300, 301, 319, 326, 347, 380, 390, 391, 399, 411, 466, 503, 509, 515, 519, 527, 531, 544, 549, 560, 577, 612, 655, 668, 670, 687, 688, 691, 699, 712, 739, 749, 807, 809
invalid clauses 224, 613

joint venture 2, 12, 15, 23, 51–54, 114, 147, 152, 172, 179, 180, 185, 186, 188, 332, 437, 445, 491, 548, 549, 751, 807–809

lex
  causae 224
  constructionis 217, 230, 232, 234, 240, 243

liability
  defects 56, 95, 225, 511, 531, 534, 539, 609, 611, 708
  limitation of 56, 79, 233, 410, 552, 555, 625, 644, 651
liquidated damages 14, 35, 41, 47, 56, 59–73, 75, 178–181, 194, 198, 207, 209, 233, 241, 284, 299, 301, 302, 306, 307, 309, 331, 334–337, 340, 376, 387, 388, 390, 392, 399, 412, 439, 477, 496, 498, 603, 608, 616, 627, 676, 696, 735, 745
lump sum 36, 39, 59, 102, 103, 105, 129–131, 173, 174, 176, 189, 206, 227, 249, 251, 252, 255, 262, 273, 277, 321–328, 333, 334, 349, 354, 419, 438, 439, 459, 462, 495, 496, 515, 517, 519, 521, 524, 528, 536, 538, 553, 561, 594, 598, 599, 607, 614, 629, 638, 691, 727, 754

maintenance bond 705
maintenance guarantee 705, 707
managerial analysis 20
milestone payments 254, 255, 629
mining 1, 172, 173, 195, 199, 438, 440, 548, 553, 554
multiple-prime contracts 103, 138

New Engineering Contract (NEC) 95, 205, 217, 491, 580, 719

options 60, 71, 103, 110, 111, 117, 147, 162, 173, 194, 219, 250–253, 273, 303, 314, 324, 332, 342, 345, 352, 354, 362, 377, 378, 425, 446, 468, 511, 529, 552, 571, 582, 584, 587, 589–593, 764
orgalime forms of contract 599

P&DB 108, 226, 262, 304, 310, 315, 366, 383, 488, 490, 523, 524, 528, 529, 531, 536–538, 541, 542, 548, 554, 555, 561, 567–569, 640, 642, 643, 685, 686, 688, 689, 691, 692, 697, 723, 724, 736, 737, 739
particular conditions 40, 44, 46, 107, 161, 174, 177, 187–189, 205, 225, 227, 230, 259, 260, 262, 289, 300, 303, 324, 406, 427, 461–463, 486, 487, 503, 504, 506, 507, 511, 512, 515, 519–522, 528, 531,

822 Index

particular conditions (*cont'd*)
  536–541, 547, 558, 564, 566–569, 573, 575, 641, 643, 644, 646, 664, 686, 691, 714, 727, 728, 734, 736, 737, 746, 749
partnering 103, 138–140, 171, 453, 585, 588
payment
  bond 705, 706
  guarantee 460, 704–707, 714, 715
PCSA *see* preconstruction services agreement (PCSA)
performance
  bond 178, 179, 181, 183, 499, 705, 710, 711, 741
  guarantee 131, 199, 309, 406, 705, 707, 710, 740, 741
  release from 701
  responsibility 56, 95
Poland 53, 168, 225, 275–279, 300, 383, 385, 434–436, 445, 490, 690, 703, 709, 710, 731, 733–737, 740, 741, 743, 745–748, 755
PPP *see* public and private partnership (PPP)
preconstruction services agreement (PCSA) 154
proactivity 233, 234
progress payments 254, 475–478, 480
project finance 25, 26, 136, 190, 245, 278, 515, 627, 636, 639, 651, 652, 708, 715
provisional sum 250, 251, 262, 528, 677
public and private partnership (PPP) 143
public procurement law 97, 104, 111, 222, 273, 274, 276, 278, 313, 342, 362, 436, 494, 504, 505, 513, 514, 699, 700, 724, 731–734, 736, 738, 741, 749, 753, 755

reasonable skill 56, 95, 162, 550–552, 591, 647, 649, 650
Red Book FIDIC 43, 44, 191, 226, 258, 259, 261, 301, 324, 349, 369, 381, 410, 411, 455, 456, 461, 487, 500, 515, 517, 520, 532–536, 542, 545, 553, 698, 708, 727, 728, 753
regulators 2, 3, 723
re-measurement 6, 13, 103–105, 248–250, 254, 255, 261, 262, 273, 352, 354, 530, 594, 614, 689, 749, 753, 754
representative office 50, 463

retention bond 706
retention guarantee 706, 707, 715
risk
  allocation 4, 12, 14, 26, 31, 35–38, 40–42, 45, 46, 55, 80, 84, 88, 103–106, 113–115, 117–119, 121, 125, 126, 129, 131–133, 135, 144, 148–152, 165, 172, 174, 175, 187, 189, 216, 222, 223, 229, 230, 250, 252, 253, 273, 349, 353, 358, 359, 366, 367, 377, 378, 383, 445, 523, 531, 539, 542, 543, 549, 554, 555, 557–562, 594, 595, 607, 611, 624, 631, 632, 644, 666, 667, 674, 676, 685, 687, 689, 691, 693, 717–719, 722–725, 727, 735–737, 746, 749, 752
  analysis 20–22, 41, 438, 677, 687, 719
  design 148, 150, 175, 206, 378, 516, 543, 561, 569, 633, 640, 642, 645, 650
  execution 634
  management 2, 22, 29, 31, 32, 35, 50, 54, 112, 115, 117, 127, 141, 266–268, 489, 561, 623, 624, 630–632, 639, 663, 665, 668, 675, 676, 679, 702
  post-construction 635
  project preparation 633
  site 148, 150–152, 634
  uncontrollable 56, 80, 718
  in underground 4, 664
  unforeseeable 117, 130, 667, 685
Romania 54, 225, 436, 490, 725–727, 730, 748, 754, 755
Russia 15, 347, 373, 374, 376, 377, 457, 458, 490, 492, 493, 501, 519, 521, 522, 791

sanctions, contractual 466, 595
scheme for construction projects 473
SCL Protocol 94, 247, 282–285, 292, 298, 301–304, 319, 329, 330, 396, 402, 404, 409, 425, 719
Serbia 234, 240, 437, 490, 547
sharia 56, 96, 393, 506
short form of contract 524, 538
Silver Book FIDIC 636
site data 187, 372, 379, 557, 560, 686, 688, 689, 724, 726, 727
South Africa 57, 77, 226, 229, 259, 261, 332, 398, 442, 444, 453, 467, 491, 553, 554, 585, 674, 720, 722
Southeast Asia 433, 434, 491, 713
specifications 3, 16, 71, 90, 102–105, 107, 108, 110, 111, 129, 144, 146, 157, 167,

173, 177, 198, 206, 227–229, 268, 270, 276, 277, 314, 319, 355, 384, 442, 447, 494–498, 523, 529–533, 567–571, 574–576, 578, 604, 608, 613, 614, 635, 647, 661, 662, 680, 699, 718, 722, 728, 733, 749
standard form of contract 39, 85, 222, 257, 362, 499, 518, 548, 563, 685, 747, 752
standard sample forms 224
stand-by letter of credit 713
subsidiary foreign 50
substantial completion 41, 56, 76, 223, 386, 509, 606
sufficiency of the accepted contract amount 227, 691
suretyship 24, 709, 712–714
suspension 45, 57, 149, 150, 258–261, 306, 308–311, 314, 361, 375, 379, 402, 405, 406, 415, 422, 423, 437, 468, 482, 499, 500, 520, 522, 531, 539, 549, 552, 559, 610, 614, 628, 629, 658, 737, 741
  contractor 308
  employer 308
  under FIDIC 306

taking-over 77, 78, 315, 431, 511, 534, 611, 614, 658, 705
target price 140–142, 154, 193, 201, 249, 252–254, 354, 359, 594, 719, 750, 751
taxation 23, 199, 255, 509
tender guarantee 704, 714
termination 5, 7, 8, 18, 26, 28–30, 32, 34, 40, 48, 53, 56, 57, 59, 74, 82, 84, 86, 90–92, 103, 104, 131, 140, 180, 181, 208, 218, 225, 245, 248, 249, 256, 257, 259–261, 265, 273, 277, 286, 287, 290, 306, 308–311, 327, 332, 336, 345, 352, 359, 370–372, 379, 397, 412, 425, 435, 461, 466–468, 472, 476, 477, 479, 480, 497–499, 504, 509, 531, 533–535, 539, 541, 542, 545–547, 549, 552, 565, 594, 608, 611, 616, 628, 667, 671, 690, 701, 708, 715, 725, 727–729, 738–740, 746, 747
  contractor 310, 311, 738
  in convenience 56, 90, 91, 311
  employer 310
  under FIDIC 309
  force majeure 311

time
  bar 56, 79, 80, 233, 307, 366, 367, 377, 379–386, 388–393, 399, 545–547, 566, 595, 617, 696, 730, 745
  for completion 7, 21, 40, 41, 56, 93, 94, 102, 108, 123, 153, 172, 175, 193, 208, 233, 234, 237, 238, 248, 263, 275, 277, 280, 282, 283, 285, 287, 288, 290, 293–295, 297–299, 303–305, 314–316, 319, 320, 329–331, 340, 352, 359, 365–368, 372, 375–378, 380–382, 395–397, 399–401, 408, 428, 429, 431, 506, 519, 528–530, 537, 539, 541, 551, 556, 561, 562, 569, 571, 573, 575, 610, 614, 628, 630, 633, 653, 685, 686, 690, 692, 697, 701, 705, 724, 729, 736, 738, 740, 741, 763
  extension of 5, 14, 40, 41, 79, 93, 94, 108, 123, 164, 175, 178,180, 203, 208, 233, 234, 248, 258, 280–282, 285, 287, 290, 298, 299, 301–303, 305–309, 315, 319, 329–333, 335, 336, 339, 340, 343, 352, 359, 364–368, 371, 375, 377, 382, 383, 386–388, 390–392, 396, 397, 399, 407, 408, 430, 431, 439, 478, 482, 502, 506, 530, 535, 561, 562, 582, 595, 610, 611, 616, 628, 630, 692, 694–698, 701, 729, 737, 740
  under FIDIC forms 9, 90, 251, 261, 303, 304, 306, 308, 309, 312, 315, 348, 355, 358, 368, 369, 394, 398, 429, 431, 454, 456, 466, 518, 527, 552, 554, 567, 595, 611, 714
  at large 93, 94, 100, 233, 290, 298–300, 312, 332, 509, 740
  related issues 56, 93, 299, 300, 303
trade usage 226, 229, 230, 712
tunnel works 665, 679, 702

UAE see United Arab Emirates (UAE)
underground 4, 122, 123, 130, 176, 232, 378, 524, 554, 572, 612, 633, 634, 653, 664, 666–669, 671, 672, 674, 678–680, 684–686, 688, 696, 700, 702, 727, 737, 759
unforeseeability 656, 684, 685
unforeseeable
  forces of nature 379, 808
  physical conditions 123, 225, 232, 236, 364, 379, 397, 546, 556, 561, 666, 667,

unforeseeable (cont'd)
   685, 686, 689, 692, 693, 702, 724, 725, 737
unification 97, 215–217, 220, 630
United Arab Emirates (UAE) 69, 85, 96, 98, 99, 212, 245, 247, 259–261, 321, 322, 324, 328, 382, 532–536, 674

vadium 704
variation
   clause 12, 176, 207, 234, 274, 275, 313, 323, 324, 326, 343
   constructive 319–321, 399
   directed 232, 234, 251, 274, 319, 320, 399
   under FIDIC Forms 315
   management 12, 245, 283, 313
   voluntary 319, 321, 399

VOB 100, 491, 580, 608–610, 612, 621, 622, 656, 716

warranty guarantee 705
World Bank (WB) 29, 144, 220, 221, 444, 459, 463, 464, 485, 488, 491, 499, 502, 508, 515, 549–552, 598, 716, 722, 752, 755

Yellow Book 101, 108, 110, 118–123, 129, 161, 164, 187, 191, 226, 227, 238, 239, 262, 285–287, 293, 295, 297, 304, 315, 349, 366, 371–373, 383, 462, 464, 469, 499, 500, 509, 511, 516, 523, 536, 542–544, 546, 548, 553, 562, 563, 565, 599, 628, 640, 642, 643, 645, 646, 650, 679, 685, 688–692, 708, 716, 717, 721, 724, 727–730, 736, 737